Cybersecurity Hyperglossary

Precise and consistent communication is vital in the complex and ever-expanding field of cybersecurity and its related domains. This hyperglossary offers more than just plain English definitions of 5,555 terms and abbreviations; it's a meticulously crafted resource designed to foster a shared understanding across a diverse audience, from seasoned professionals to newcomers. By providing clear definitions and an innovative network of hyperlinked references, it enhances communication in critical areas, reduces misunderstandings, and facilitates a more engaging and interconnected learning experience across the broad landscape of information risk and security, privacy, governance, compliance, business continuity, ethics, and more.

Beyond basic definitions, this book delves into the nuances and origins of cybersecurity language, promoting vocabulary standardisation and reducing misinterpretations in various professional contexts. Furthermore, it bridges the communication gap between technical experts and non-technical stakeholders, empowering effective collaboration and informed decision-making. This book is a key tool for education and professional development, supported by a vibrant online community where experts collaborate to refine and evolve our terms of art. Ultimately, this comprehensive hyperglossary, coupled with community insights, offers an unparalleled advantage in navigating and shaping the future of cybersecurity understanding.

Gary Hinson, PhD, MBA, is an information security specialist with a particular interest in the human and business aspects of both protecting and exploiting information. His career stretches back to the mid-1980s as a practitioner, manager, and consultant in the fields of IT system administration, information security, and IT auditing for multinationals in several industries. For more than a decade until COVID, Gary created monthly packages of security awareness materials for subscribers. These days, Gary consults and teaches on the ISO/IEC 27000-series "ISO27k" information security management standards and information security metrics.

Cybersecurity Hyperglossary

Dr. Gary Hinson, MBA

CRC Press
Taylor & Francis Group
Boca Raton London New York

CRC Press is an imprint of the
Taylor & Francis Group, an **informa** business

Designed cover image: Shutterstock Image ID 2007809843

First edition published 2026
by CRC Press
2385 NW Executive Center Drive, Suite 320, Boca Raton FL 33431

and by CRC Press
4 Park Square, Milton Park, Abingdon, Oxon, OX14 4RN

CRC Press is an imprint of Taylor & Francis Group, LLC

ISBN: 978-1-041-09552-1 (hbk)
ISBN: 978-1-041-09553-8 (pbk)
ISBN: 978-1-003-65067-6 (ebk)

DOI: 10.1201/9781003650676

Typeset in Calibri
by codeMantra

Contents

Foreword

Language, usually meant to communicate, often leads to misunderstandings. Even in the same country speaking the same language, different disciplines, trades, and professions often use different words to mean more or less the same thing often rendering clear communication the victim. This issue becomes even more pronounced in technology, where rapid innovation collides with deep specialisation. Within a single domain – take security, for example – terminology between, say, risk management and incident response can vary dramatically. Between civilian activity and the military, the differences in terms can be even more stark. What's referred to as a *data breach* in the civilian sector is called *spillage* by the U.S. Department of Defense. While one group will talk about *vulnerabilities*, others will discuss *attack surface*. What IT professionals might say is *data normalisation*; an epidemiologist will call *harmonisation*. This plethora of terms often creates confusion, slows collaboration, and makes interdisciplinary efforts more complex than they need to be.

This extraordinary glossary was created to meet that challenge head-on. With over 5,000 clearly defined tech terms and over 700 acronyms decoded, it offers a unified language for professionals working across IT management and operations, cybersecurity, risk management, artificial intelligence, and related fields. More than just definitions, it provides rich explanations and real-world context – clarifying not just what a term means, but *how* and *where* it's used. The goal is not only to reduce ambiguity but also to foster better understanding between technologists, managers, policymakers, and users.

What makes this work truly exceptional, and what sets it apart from typical glossaries, is its completeness. Thanks to the years of meticulous research and dedication by Dr. Gary Hinson, this volume captures virtually every significant term in the modern digital ecosystem. But it goes further still – unlike many reference tools, this glossary often includes full descriptions, nuanced usage notes, and, where relevant, quick links to external resources for deeper exploration.

This monumental tome will prove invaluable for anyone navigating today's tech landscape. For managers encountering unfamiliar jargon, for editors striving for clarity and consistency, and for professionals and students alike who need a trustworthy source of meaning, this glossary will become the go-to standard when clear, concise terminology is important. Whether in textbooks or RFPs, work orders or product or engineering specifications, or legal documents, the right words are paramount. Quite literally, this monumental work gets everyone on the same page.

Kudos to Dr. Hinson for this major contribution to just about anyone dealing with the digital universe – which these days, is pretty much all of us.

Krag Brotby
CISM, CGEIT, GRC guru

Language shapes how we think. In security, it shapes how we act, how we collaborate, and how we fail.

Cybersecurity, as a field, has suffered for years from a fragmented vocabulary. We borrow terms from engineering, risk management, military doctrine, academia, and marketing. We invent new ones at a breakneck pace, often without checking if they already exist elsewhere. Worse, we use the same words to mean different things depending on our background, our role, or our latest framework of choice.

And people get very protective over those words. Some of the biggest arguments I've seen are over whether or not cybersecurity should have a space or not. Really. I've had hate mail and harassment over it.

The result is confusion, chaos, and a lack of holistic thinking.

This matters. Cybersecurity is not a standalone discipline. It is a domain of security, sitting alongside physical, personnel, and technical domains. It intersects with safety, governance, operations, and culture. If we're going to respond to the complex, dynamic threats we face, we have to be able to work together.

That requires a shared language.

This hyperglossary is a starting point. Not a definitive guide, and not an attempt to impose a single top-down doctrine. Instead, it's an effort to bring some coherence to the words we use every day. To make it possible to understand one another, spot patterns and align our work. It won't be exhaustive or final. Language evolves, and so must this.

I've lost count of the meetings I've sat in where people thought they disagreed, but were speaking different security dialects. Where decisions got delayed because two teams were using different definitions for "threat" or "control." These moments add friction. At scale, they cause real harm.

More fundamentally, we need this clarity to make progress. It's hard to build shared models, improve resilience, or even teach effectively if we can't agree on what basic terms mean. Whether you're writing policy, engineering a system, running an incident, or trying to explain a risk to a boardroom, having a consistent, plain-language vocabulary makes life easier.

This isn't about dumbing things down. It's about raising the standard of thinking. Clear language doesn't just improve communication. It forces us to be precise. It makes hidden assumptions visible. It helps identify gaps in understanding and practice. And it makes space for genuine collaboration across disciplines.

We're at a point where the complexity of our systems, the capabilities of our threats, and the interconnectedness of everything demand better cooperation. That can't happen if we're all talking past each other.

Take this glossary as a tool. Use it, challenge it, add to it. Let it be something we build together, rather than something we argue over. Because the sooner we can speak the same language, the sooner we can get on with solving the problems that matter.

James Bore
Chartered Security Professional

Preface

This hyperglossary is the result of a personal quest to make sense of the rich language of cybersecurity. This book's size is a testament to the breadth and complexity of the subject, coupled with an extraordinary rate of change. I started this writing project back for my own benefit in the 1990s, at about the time that a group coordinated by the UK Department of Trade and Industry adopted a corporate security manual, becoming BS 7799 "Code of Practice for Information Security Management" in 1995.

Cybersecurity: in common use, this primarily refers to technological/IT security controls protecting computer systems, networks, and the associated data against attacks from the Internet. There's more to it, though.

Information security was a novelty back then, one that intrigued me with its focus on protecting and exploiting information. Since then, we've seen the rise of IT security and lately **cybersecurity** as computing and the Internet have become integral parts of modern life. Nevertheless, I appreciate that original focus on protecting and exploiting the valuable information content: to me, the computer systems and technologies are merely tools for data processing (now *there's* an historic term!).

Hyperglossary: contraction of **hyper**-linked **glossary**, an intuitive reference combining the best features of a glossary, dictionary, wiki, thesaurus, and encyclopaedia with specialist inputs, plain English definitions, and extensive cross-referencing.

The field can appear fragmented and scattered, with experts in various areas naturally developing their own jargon and specialised meanings. To address the challenge, I developed the **hyperglossary** format in 2001, making a reference resource even more valuable. I find the combination of clear plain-English definitions with embedded links to further information a powerful and intuitive way to capture and utilise the details. What's more, it's *fun* to release my inner geek, following my nose from term-to-term, rediscovering and reconnecting with concepts I'd almost forgotten much as I enjoyed browsing Roget's Thesaurus and encyclopaedias when I was a teen.

In recent years, I've incorporated terms relating to the risk and security aspects of **I**nternet **o**f **T**hings and **A**rtificial **I**ntelligence, with quantum computing just around the corner. While the pace of change in technology and cybersecurity keeps us professionals on our toes, it makes things tricky for business people and others struggling to keep up. Being left behind presents significant information risks in its own right; for example, unpatched IT systems are more vulnerable to ransomware, and mis- or dis-information is threatening democracy and personal freedoms, both real and present dangers as we see from the news headlines.

By publishing this book, I hope to foster greater consistency in our language, not only for those immersed in the field but also for technology and other professionals, business leaders, regulatory authorities, standards bodies, and others. Given that English is a foreign language for some of you, I have tried hard to create reasonably simple and accessible definitions, although the technical complexities and conceptual aspects sometimes frustrate that aim. I tried, honestly I tried.

Beyond simply a curated collection of terms and definitions, this book supports a vibrant online community through which cybersecurity professionals, from students to seasoned experts, share their knowledge and collectively enhance our understanding of the field. Ultimately, the hyperglossary *plus* the global community of readers makes an unbeatable combination. Read on for opportunities to play your part in moving things forward.

PURPOSE

The primary purpose of this hyperglossary is to provide a comprehensive, user-friendly reference for anyone seeking to understand and use the terminology of cybersecurity and related domains.

Specifically, it aims to:

- Provide reasonably clear and concise definitions of about 5,000 key terms-of-art plus expansions of about 700 abbreviations, acronyms, and initialisms. Pragmatic explanations complement the formal definitions. Clearer communication improves understanding, enabling us to engage more productively in daily work, debate, research, policy-making, and decision-making.
- Acknowledge the origins of the concepts and terms we use today, while appreciating the subtleties of different meanings, emphases, and interpretations as the field matures.
- Standardise our vocabulary where appropriate, encouraging consistency and reducing misinterpretation across laws, regulations, standards, policies, procedures, guidelines, advertisements, job descriptions, management and audit reports, emails, presentations, articles, conversations, and more. Language issues present information risks in this area, worth avoiding or mitigating I feel. Greater linguistic alignment should reduce unnecessary fragmentation and divergence within the field, presenting a more unified front.
- Bridge the communication gaps between technical experts and non-technical individuals such as business leaders and industry regulators – a common problem arising from limited familiarity and fluency in each other's languages, perspectives, and worlds.
- Facilitate teaching, training, knowledge sharing, learning, and personal development within the cybersecurity profession, reducing barriers to entry and progression.
- Enable and support transnational discussion, collaboration, innovation, and technical development. Cybersecurity is most certainly a *global* concern.
- Lead the way in aligning terminology, especially concerning core terms such as 'threat,' 'vulnerability,' 'impact,' and 'risk.' If we wish to be taken seriously as professional experts, we really ought to agree on the fundamentals and be consistent in how we put things across.

SCOPE

This hyperglossary encompasses a broad spectrum of cybersecurity-related areas, including the following:

- Risk, particularly the proactive management of information risk as a business imperative.
- Information security, protecting all forms of information (not just digital data).
- Risk and security aspects of **I**nformation, **O**perational, **C**ommunications, **V**irtual, and **S**mart **T**echnologies (**IT**, **OT**, **CT**, **VT**, and **ST**) – and perhaps others.
- Privacy and data protection.
- Governance, accountability, rôles, and responsibilities.
- Compliance and conformity – similar but distinct concerns.
- Ethics and morality, navigating conflicts in ways that demonstrate integrity and foster trust.

- Business continuity, including resilience, **D**isaster **R**ecovery, and contingency planning.
- Various forms of assurance such as testing, reviewing, assessing, and auditing, including supply chain assurance, a substantial issue with cloud computing and globalisation.
- The intersection of technological areas such as **A**rtificial **I**ntelligence and **I**nternet **o**f **T**hings, plus other concerns such as environmental sustainability and climate change, with cybersecurity.

While striving for comprehensive coverage, the field continues to expand rapidly. Therefore, ever since its inception decades ago, the hyperglossary has been and remains a dynamic product, evolving and maturing with ongoing research and input from the global community as the language itself changes. The book you are reading is merely a snapshot in time.

Language can be misused or misunderstood and, despite writing this hyperglossary, I am not immune. While I have made every effort to research and define terms carefully, they often have 'flexible' meanings in practice and my interpretations may not always align with or capture the original authors' intentions. Context is crucial.

Many definitions include quoted text from authoritative sources such as international standards, but the quotes may not always be complete or perfectly up-to-date. *Please* refer to the original sources using the provided 'More info' links if it matters to you, especially if you plan to develop and share variant definitions.

Finally, to be absolutely clear, I am *not* a lawyer. This hyperglossary does not constitute legal advice. In some jurisdictions and circumstances, certain terms may have specific legal interpretations that differ significantly from those presented here. Do not rely on this glossary for anything critical or vital: it is intended solely for educational purposes. Always seek advice from competent, trustworthy, qualified, and experienced professional advisors and carefully evaluate their guidance.

AUTHOR PERSPECTIVE

With a career spanning several decades in the information risk and security domain, I have come to appreciate the value of global alignment and coordination within the field, particularly concerning the language we share.

My journey began after transitioning from a microbiology/genetics post-doc in the early 1980s to an initial role as a DEC system/network administrator at a UK pharmaceuticals R&D division. For two decades, primarily in the UK and Europe, I gained extensive, multi-faceted experience in information risk management, technology audit, and information security management within major power generation, defence and financial services companies, providing me with a broad understanding of the challenges and nuances across diverse sectors.

Throughout my career, I have not only witnessed but also contributed, in a small way, to the evolution and maturity of this critical field. Long-term involvement with the committee behind the ISO/IEC 27000 standards has instilled in me a strong preference for pragmatic, real-world solutions in cybersecurity.

Since completing an MBA in 2000 and emigrating to NZ, my focus shifted more towards the governance, management, and strategic aspects, consulting for **S**mall and **M**edium-sized **B**usinesses and running my own micro-business. The challenges of applying security principles in resource-constrained environments have become increasingly evident. Coupled with ever-changing information risks, cybersecurity requires frequent realignment with both overarching business objectives and technology capabilities.

METHODS AND SOURCES

The definitions provided in the hyperglossary represent a synthesis of my professional experience since the 80s, with authoritative sources such as:

- Industry standards and publications (*e.g.* ISO27k and the NIST Cybersecurity Framework).
- Assorted conceptual models and approaches (*e.g.* COBIT and DVMS).
- A bulging home office library with getting on for 200 cybersecurity books to hand and a dozen more in the 'read me' pile for this bookworm.
- Academic research and scholarly articles, plus pieces by professionals in the industry journals.
- Reputable vendor documentation plus marketing materials and market analyst reports.
- Insightful and sometimes provocative contributions from fellow experts through various professional social media platforms (*e.g.* LinkedIn, ISACA Engage, the ISO27k Forum, various blogs plus the SANS, RISKS and CRYPTO-GRAM newsletters).
- Relevant laws and regulations (*e.g.* GDPR and SOC2).
- Practical experience gained through decades of real-world application.

Despite my high ideals and grand expectations, I consider myself a realist and pragmatist. As you will soon see, I favour commonsense explanations reflecting commonplace usage within the field, while also acknowledging the context of more formal definitions where relevant. My aim is to provide definitions that are both accurate and readily understandable for a diverse audience. Please accept my apologies in advance for any misinterpretations: I am entirely human.

STRUCTURE AND USE

By convention, the glossary is organised alphabetically from A to Z, with a few numeric entries (such as 2FA) appearing at the beginning. A typical entry consists of the following:

- Term:
  - The singular cybersecurity-related word, phrase, abbreviation, acronym, or initialism being defined, along with common variants and abbreviations (picked out in **bold**).
  - For the sake of brevity, different word forms of essentially the same term are normally combined under a single entry rather than being listed separately.
- Definition:
  - A reasonably clear and concise plain-English explanation of the term, with links to the definitions of words and phrases elsewhere within the hyperglossary (these are functional hyperlinks in the eBook version). Alternative definitions are provided for terms with distinct meanings, depending on the context in which they are used.
  - Pragmatic guidance, examples, and notes covering various nuances.
  - In *italics*, cited content quoted from definitive references (such as standards) with minor editorial changes in some cases. Rather than citing every term from every reference, I have selected the most appropriate, well-phrased, or definitive ones, sometimes incorporating different interpretations to emphasise other perspectives.
  - 'See also' links to related or similar terms.
  - *'Cf.'* links to distinct, complementary, contrasting, or often-confused terms.
  - 'More info' links to more information on the web.

Check the hyperglossary whenever you encounter unfamiliar cybersecurity terminology. The hyperglossary format is designed for easy browsing with ~39,000 hyperlinks, 99% of which are internal cross-references while the remaining 1% are external/Internet URLs. At times, you will find yourself exploring related concepts at length, flowing intuitively between terms and definitions in the eBook. You may prefer the printed book for ready reference, quiet reflection/self-study, and note-taking.

The uncited definitions and explanations in this hyperglossary (*i.e.* my inputs) are generally valid and applicable within the context of information risk, information security, and related areas. Having *tried* to define terms generically and straightforwardly, based on my knowledge and experience as well as any cited references, I would be flattered if you find my definitions useful enough to share or circulate further. However, if you do, ***please* cite this cybersecurity hyperglossary** (with a hyperlink to hyperglossary.com if appropriate), just as I have openly acknowledged my sources.

> It is evident from the reference sources that some definitions have been doing the rounds for years, with successive authors adding their spin and occasionally taking off at tangents. With this book, I hope to guide us all gently back in line.

YOUR PART IN THIS UNDERTAKING

To foster a dynamic and collaborative approach to cybersecurity terminology, I have established an online hub for the global community of reader. Our discussion forum (a Google group) is specifically intended to debate the terms and definitions, suggest additions or clarifications, point out errors that ought to be corrected, and offer alternative interpretations. We are keen to share insights into the terminology and its practical application. Connect with your peers and contribute to the collective understanding of cybersecurity language.

> Please join us at Hyperglossary.com We are a diverse global group of information risk and security professionals, students, academics, technologists and language experts, standardisers, and others. Participation is free: this is your opportunity to participate and contribute your wisdom to the *next* edition of the hyperglossary.

Future updates to both the print and eBook versions will be informed by the active participation of this community. Working together, I believe we can clarify the jargon, bridge communication gaps, reduce ambiguity (risk!), and foster a more consistent lexicon.

CONCLUDING REMARKS

I invite you to explore this Cybersecurity hyperglossary, engage with the online community, and contribute to its ongoing development. Working together, we can achieve greater clarity and understanding in this vital field. Browse around, think, learn, and join in the debate.

OK, that's more than enough preamble from me.

Go!

Acknowledgements

I am very grateful to the following:

- Everyone who has coined, defined, used, discussed, and refined the *thousands* of terms of art in this book.
- The academics, gurus, practitioners, innovators, and creatives who built and continue driving the field forward.
- My long-suffering wife, family, and friends patiently looking on as I became utterly immersed in this project.
- Colleagues and acquaintances who encouraged me to keep going when the task seemed endless.
- The editorial and production teams from Taylor & Francis who made the dream a reality.
- You, dear reader, in the hope that you will provide constructive feedback via Hyperglossary.com, putting me straight where I got things wrong, suggesting terms and alternative definitions and most of all *using* these terms as defined in your work, edging us ever closer to consensus, productive communications, and genuine understanding.

Thank you one and all.

Dr. Gary Hinson, MBA

The beginning of wisdom
is the definition of terms.

Socrates

Define your terms,
you will permit me again to say,
or we shall never understand one another.

Voltaire

Author Biography

Dr. Gary Hinson, MBA is an information security specialist with a particular interest in the human and business aspects of both protecting and exploiting information.

Following an honours degree in genetics at the University of York in 1983, then a PhD and postdoctoral research in molecular biology/microbial genetics at the University of Leicester, I transitioned into my first proper job in 1987. Thanks to some IT experience in connection with the development of DNA fingerprinting, I became a DEC VAX systems and network administrator ('sysmgr') for the research and development arm of Beecham Pharmaceuticals. The commercial value of research information was very evident with heavy investment to develop and protect intellectual property, primarily by legal means (drug patents). At the time, however, the vulnerabilities associated with 'knowledge workers' and the early networks were barely understood and not fully appreciated by management. Management concerns regarding protection of medical, personal and business data were not obvious, at least not to me. As a privileged user deep in the bowels of IT, I had ready access to the databases, applications, drug designs plus medical safety and efficacy studies, even executive emails, with essentially no auditing or oversight. Looking back, we were quite naïve and trusting.

By 1990, I had developed a professional interest in the information risk and security field when it was more commonly known as computer or IT security (pre-dating 'cyber'!). It seemed odd to me that systems and network security was such a low strategic priority with no obvious intent to improve. The research staff and managers had been physically threatened by animal liberation/anti-vivisection activists, indicating (to me) an increased threat elevating the information risks. Management, however, were mostly thinking in terms of perimeter fences and security guards and there were problems there too!

When Beecham was taken over by SmithKline – a much larger US-based pharmaceutical company – we were instructed by senior management simply to join and merge the two sprawling DECnet networks without regard to the information risks that I believed were substantial. Network node *addressing* was a concern but information security was barely an afterthought.

Time to move on.

For more than a decade I learned the ropes in corporate security and audit positions, mostly in the UK and Europe. My work for an electricity company, initially in IT security, was an opportunity to implement BS 7799 protecting both **I**nformation **T**echnology and **O**perational **T**echnology (real-time process control systems, then known as SCADA/ICS) in a critical infrastructure context. I was shoulder-tapped for a move into Internal Audit and an excellent grounding in assurance, governance, strategy and senior management, with an 'executive' (part-time) MBA from the University of Bath in 2000. Leading the UK/European technology audit functions for BAE SYSTEMS and Siemens exposed me to defence, aeroospace and high-tech industries facing their own unique risk, security, governance, compliance and cultural challenges.

Since 2000, I have been consulting, writing and selling *gigabytes* of information risk and security awareness and training content, policies *etc.,* supporting clients implementing the ISO/IEC 27000 standards and nurturing from scratch the vibrant 5,500-strong "ISO27k Forum". I emigrated to New Zealand in 2005.

As a member of ISO/IEC JTC 1/SC 27, I enjoy contributing to the information security management standards and interacting with hundreds of professional peers. It's good to give something back to the community and stay in touch with innovative approaches.

Now living on a rural farm block near Napier in New Zealand, I have ample opportunity to cogitate on infosec and AI while repairing fences, installing a backup generator, tending to our animals or trout fishing. I love the natural beauty of the NZ countryside, spoilt only by the roar of heavy machinery and chainsaws as the surrounding pine forest is being harvested. Oh and the occasional earthquake or flood - harsh lessons in resilience and the perils of underinvestment in infrastructure being all too evident down here on the Far Side!

Disclaimer

The information provided within this cybersecurity hyperglossary is intended for general knowledge and informational purposes only. While every effort has been made to ensure accuracy and completeness, the dynamic nature of the cybersecurity field and the potential for differing interpretations mean that errors and omissions are inevitable. The content of this book should not be considered professional advice. You are *strongly* encouraged to verify critical information with authoritative sources and consult with qualified professionals for specific guidance related to your particular circumstances. The author and publisher disclaim any liability for errors or omissions in the content of this hyperglossary or for any actions taken based on the information provided herein.

#

DOI: 10.1201/9781003650676-1

TERM	MEANING
0-day	*Abbrev:* zero-day.
2FA	*Abbrev:* **two**-**F**actor **A**uthentication.
2G/GSM, 3G/UMTS, 3½G/HSDPA, 4G/LTE, 5G, 6G,...	Second and successive **G**enerations of the cellular digital networks used by devices such as cellphones/smartphones, SMS/TXT messaging, and data communications including mobile Internet access. Defined by the ITU under IMT-2000 and later standards. The 5G standards were introduced in 2017. The 6G standards are under development, with 6G products expected to emerge in 2030–2032. **H**igh-**S**peed **D**ownlink **P**acket **A**ccess (3½G) and earlier services are deprecated with limited use. See also **G**lobal **S**ystem for **M**obile communications, **U**niversal **M**obile **T**elecommunications **S**ystem, **L**ong **T**erm **E**volution.
3DES	*Abbrev:* **triple** **D**ata **E**ncryption **S**tandard.
3-D Secure	Datacommunications security protocol developed for VISA to protect online transactions involving credit cards. Covers three domains (hence "3-D"): (1) acquirer (bank or credit card company), (2) card issuer, and (3) interoperability (infrastructure). Supersedes **S**ecure **E**lectronic **T**ransaction.
419	Section number of the Nigerian penal code criminalising advance fee frauds. May refer to other social engineering scams as well; hence, email scammers are known colloquially as 419ers.

A

TERM	MEANING
AAA	*Abbrev:* **A**uthentication, **A**uthorisation, and **A**ccounting.
AAL	*Abbrev:* **A**uthenticator **A**ssurance **L**evel.
A/B testing	Systematic comparison. "A statistical way of comparing two (or more) techniques, typically an incumbent against a new rival. A/B testing aims to determine not only which technique performs better but also whether the difference is statistically significant. A/B testing usually considers only two techniques using one measurement but can be applied to any finite number of techniques and measures" *(ISACA glossary).*
ABAC	*Abbrev:* **A**ttribute-**B**ased **A**ccess **C**ontrol.
***Abbrev*:**	Abbreviation of 'Abbreviation of.' Click any underlined definitions for their entries. Strictly speaking, some are acronyms (such as infosec) or initialisms (such as IT and USB) but for simplicity, *Abbrev:* covers them all.
Abend (abnormal end)	See crash.
Absolute assurance	*Total* certainty, *utter* confidence – a practically unattainable objective. "A level of assurance that is impossible to achieve" (*OCEG GRC Glossary*).
ABUEA	*Abbrev:* **A**ttribute-**B**ased **U**nlinkable **E**ntity **A**uthentication.
Abuse case	Description of unwelcome, inappropriate and potentially malicious computer user interactions with an application, developed to explore the risks and controls. "Describes the intentional and unintentional misuses of the software. Abuse cases should challenge the assumptions of the system design" *(SCP QRG).*
Acceptable **[**or **A**llowable**] I**nterruption **W**indow **(AIW)**	Organisation-defined term, *e.g.* this could be the daily time slot during which management accepts the need to suspend locally provided (non-cloud) information services for essential administrative activities such as backups and patching. "The maximum period of time that a system can be unavailable before compromising the achievement of the enterprise's business objectives" *(ISACA glossary).* See also **M**aximum **T**olerable **O**utage.
Acceptable **U**se **P**olicy **(AUP)**	Policy or guideline laying out and contrasting acceptable against unacceptable use of information, **I**nformation **T**echnology services, systems, networks, *etc.* in plain English for a general audience. "A policy that establishes an agreement between users and the enterprise that defines, for all parties, the ranges of use that are approved before gaining access to a network or the Internet" *(ISACA glossary).*

TERM	MEANING
Acceptance criteria	Stakeholders' requirements or conditions for taking delivery of and starting to use something, such as a new or modified computer system or information services. Suggests formally specified functional and/or nonfunctional requirements and some form of acceptance test to gain assurance. "Criteria that a solution must satisfy to be accepted by customers" *(ISACA glossary)*.
Acceptance statement	"Formal management declaration to assume responsibility for risk ownership, risk treatment and residual risk" *(ISO/IEC 29134:2024)*.
Acceptance test	Category/class of tests towards the end of the development phase of the **S**oftware **D**evelopment **L**ife**C**ycle, marking the critical control point as products are handed over from the design and development team to operations and the users or customers. Primarily applies to computer systems, bespoke applications and cloud services, plus other important/valuable products, devices, equipment, facilities, *etc*. Intended to provide assurance to customers, users, or other stakeholders that their requirements, specifications, and expectations have been and will be adequately satisfied or exceeded; hence, the products can be accepted, whether conditionally (*e.g.* subject to any remaining issues being resolved) or unconditionally. "Test of a system or functional unit usually performed by the purchaser on his premises after installation with the participation of the vendor to ensure that the contractual requirements are met" *(ISO/IEC 2382)*. "Testing performed to determine whether a customer, acquirer, user, or their designee should accept a solution" *(ISACA glossary)*. See also **U**ser **A**cceptance **T**est, **P**roduction **A**cceptance **T**est, **S**ecurity **A**cceptance **T**est.
Accept design option	See risk acceptance. "An intentional design decision to embrace, or concede to the current level of risk, reward, and compliance" *(OCEG GRC Glossary)*.
Access, accessible	Capability of a person, computer program, agent, organisation, *etc.* to enter, interact with, and so use (if not misuse and abuse!) a controlled asset such as information, data, a site, building, facility, room, person, system, network, **D**ata**B**ase, file, filing cabinet, folder, disk, other device, or storage media. "Obtain the use of a resource" *(ISO/IEC 2382)*. "Ability of the rights holders to use or benefit from a certain service or product. Note: Restrictions can be caused by distance to the source (*e.g.* water supply network does not reach a certain neighbourhood) or unaffordability (*e.g.* service is too costly for a certain household or group of people), among other reasons" *(ISO 22300)*. See also accessibility.

TERM	MEANING
Access authority	Organisation, department, person, system, program, or function that determines whether to grant (permit) or deny (refuse) access to one or more controlled information assets such as personal information. "An entity responsible for monitoring and granting access privileges for other authorized entities" *(CNSSI 4009)*.
Access card, proximity card, pass card, access badge, staff pass, ID card, RFID (Radio Frequency IDentification) tag, …	Authentication device that (normally) communicates wirelessly with a card reader (normally) located at an access-controlled door or gate to determine whether the expected cardholder is authorised to proceed. Vulnerable to being lost, stolen, or handed to someone else, and perhaps cloned or hacked. Often carries the authorised holder's photograph as well, giving vigilant and diligent security guards, receptionists, and other workers the chance to determine at a glance whether the person presenting, wearing, or using the card resembles the mugshot (assuming they have not simply replaced the photo or faked the entire pass).
Access control, access-control	Control designed to mitigate unacceptable risks by restricting access to one or more assets, permitting authorised and appropriate access whilst preventing unauthorised or inappropriate access. May be physical (such as a lock), electronic/digital (such as encryption), or procedural (such as a nightclub bouncer checking the VIP guest list). Often critically or vitally important, implying the need for strong assurance that the control is correctly specified, designed, implemented, configured, operating, managed, maintained, and governed. "Means of ensuring that the resources of a data processing system can be accessed only by authorized entities in authorized ways" *(ISO/IEC 2382)*. "Means to ensure that physical and logical access to assets is authorized and restricted based on business and information security requirements" *(ISO/IEC 27002)*. "The processes, rules and deployment mechanisms that control access to information systems, resources and physical access to premises" *(ISACA glossary)*. "The process of granting or denying requests for access to systems, applications and information. It can also refer to the process of granting or denying requests for access to facilities" *(NZISM)*. "Ensures that resources are only granted to those users who are entitled to them" *(SANS glossary)*.
Access **C**ontrol **F**acility № 2 **(ACF2)**	Mainframe user authentication, access control, and auditing application for IBM z/OS and z/VM **O**perating **S**ystems. See also RACF.

TERM	MEANING
Access **C**ontrol **L**ist **(ACL), access control table**	Security metadata associated with a computer file, folder, disk, port, *etc.* typically specifying which users may or may not access or change the object's security settings, in what manner, under what conditions, and whether successful and/or unsuccessful attempts to do so are logged. ACL capabilities and functions vary between **O**perating **S**ystems. "An internal computerized table of access rules regarding the levels of computer access permitted to logon IDs and computer terminals" *(ISACA glossary)*. "A mechanism that implements access control for a system resource by listing the identities of the system entities that are permitted to access the resource" *(SANS glossary)*. See also access list.
Access **C**ross **D**omain **S**olution **(ACDS)**	"A system permitting access to multiple security domains from a single client device" *(AusISM)*.
Access gateway	"An architectural construct that provides the system user access to multiple security domains from a single device, typically a workstation" *(NZISM)*.
Accessibility	Ease of use, particularly for people coping with disabilities. Physical and mental issues (such as poor or no vision or hearing, dyslexia, illiteracy, Parkinsonism, cerebral palsy, weakness, loss or inability to control limbs, dementia, colour blindness, and epilepsy) can make interacting with, controlling and using computer systems more challenging than for able bodied people.
Access list	In conjunction with access controls, specifies who or what can or cannot access a controlled resource, possibly with additional criteria such as time and type of access permitted or denied, *e.g.* the nightclub doorman's VIP guest list. "List of entities, together with their access rights, that are authorized to access a resource" *(ISO/IEC 2382)*. See also **A**ccess **C**ontrol **L**ist, access policy.
Access management	Directing, planning, organising, leading, and controlling activities involved in determining who is permitted or forbidden specified modes and means of access to information, systems, facilities, *etc.* May include defining and/or applying access rules and control requirements, dealing with conflicts and changes, analysing logs, monitoring and responding to issues, alarms or alerts, testing and maintaining the controls. "Maintenance of access information which consists of four tasks: account administration, maintenance, monitoring, and revocation" *(SANS glossary)*.

TERM	MEANING
Access matrix	Table relating individual computer users or rôles (on one axis) to the computer systems, application functions, and/or classes of data (on the other axis), showing the types of access permitted and/or denied (within the body of the table). "Uses rows to represent subjects and columns to represent objects with privileges listed in each cell" *(SANS glossary)*.
Access method	How access to a controlled resource is obtained, *e.g.* physical, online, illicit, official. "The technique used for selecting records in a file, one at a time, for processing, retrieval or storage. The access method is related to, but distinct from, the file organization, which determines how the records are stored" *(ISACA glossary)*.
Access path	"The logical route that an end user takes to access computerized information. Note: Typically includes a route through the operating system, telecommunications software, selected application software and the access control system" *(ISACA glossary)*.
Access permission	"All of a subject's access rights with respect to some object" *(ISO/IEC 2382)*. See also access right.
Access **P**oint **(AP), W**ireless **A**ccess **P**oint, **Wi-Fi A**ccess **P**oint **(WAP)**	Network router providing Wi-Fi services. "A device that logically connects wireless client devices operating in infrastructure to one another and provides access to a distribution system, if connected, which is typically an organization's enterprise wired network" *(NIST SP 800-48 and SP 800-121)*. "Device or piece of equipment that allows wireless devices to connect to a wired network. Note: The connection uses a wireless local area network (WLAN) or related standard" *(ISO/IEC 27033-6)*. "A point that accesses the network" *(ISACA glossary) (!)*.
Access **P**oint **N**ame **(APN)**	Gateway linking a mobile network to the Internet or another network. Malware may surreptitiously alter the APN on mobile devices, redirecting users to access points monitored and controlled by hackers.
Access policy, access control policy	Security policy or a set of defined rules determining authorised and controlled access to information assets such as functions, tables, or records in a **D**ata**B**ase, or programs, files, and folders on a computer system on a network, or the facilities housing such assets. Typically used to develop an access list and configure access controls to achieve appropriate access rights (*e.g.* read, write, delete, and/or control) for user rôles which are then assigned to individual users authorised to perform those rôles. See also **R**ôle-**B**ased **A**ccess **C**ontrol, access matrix.

TERM	MEANING
Access right	Individual people, systems, programs, organisations, *etc.* may be granted or denied access to controlled assets such as data, transactions/functions, or physical locations according to whether the access is authorised, *i.e.* their logical access rights, permissions, or attributes match the access rules or criteria associated with those assets according to the access policy. May be documented in the form of an access matrix or permit. "Permission for a subject to access a particular object for a specific type of operation. Example: Permission for a process to read a file but not write to it" *(ISO/IEC 2382)*. "The permission or privileges granted to users, programs or workstations to create, change, delete or view data and files within a system, as defined by rules established by data owners and the information security policy" *(ISACA glossary)*. See also right, access permission.
Access risk	Uncertain possibility and consequences of access to information assets, particularly unauthorised or inappropriate access. "The risk that information may be divulged or made available to recipients without authorized access from the information owner, reflecting a loss of confidentiality" *(ISACA glossary)*.
Access to personal information	Access to personal information. "The ability to view personal information held by an organization. This ability may be complemented by an ability to update or correct the information. Access defines the intersection of identity and data, that is, who can do what to which data. Access is one of the fair information practice principles. Individuals need to be able to find out what personal information an entity has on file about them and how the information is being used. Individuals need to be able to correct erroneous information in such records" *(Trust Services Criteria)*.
Accident	While information security incidents may result from deliberate acts by hackers, malware, fraudsters, spies, *etc.*, the greater proportion by number are in fact the result of inadvertent or unintentional acts, natural or chance events, or errors. Physical accidents (health and safety failures) and illnesses that befall workers may qualify as information security incidents since people are information assets.
Accommodation address	Mail drop postal address used for convenience and sometimes to conceal the true location/identity of a fraudster by giving the appearance of belonging to a legitimate business or an innocuous member of the public.

TERM	MEANING
Account	a. *[Noun]* Computer user profile or userID. b. *[Noun]* Financial ledger. c. *[Noun]* Descriptive report or story (as in 'an account of the proceedings'). d. *[Noun]* Something to be considered or borne in mind (as in 'taken into account'). e. *[Verb]* To explain, justify or excuse something (as in 'call to account' in accountability). f. *[Verb]* To record something in the books (as in 'account for' in accounting).
Account harvesting	"Process of collecting all the legitimate account names on a system" *(SANS glossary)*.
Account hijack, account takeover	Taking control of a target's bank, credit card, email, computer, or other account by means of hacking, social engineering, malware, or coercion, typically as part of identity fraud or some other attack.
Account number	See **P**rimary **A**ccount **N**umber.
Accountability	Being accountable. In contrast to responsibility and authority, this sticky property cannot be unilaterally delegated or passed by the accountable person or organisation to another; in other words, **the buck stops here**. "Property that ensures that the actions of an entity may be traced uniquely to that entity" *(ISO/IEC 2382)*. "State of being accountable. Notes: Accountability relates to an allocated responsibility. The responsibility can be based on regulation or agreement or through assignment as part of delegation. For systems, accountability is a property that ensures that actions of an entity can be traced uniquely to the entity. In a governance context, accountability is the obligation of an individual or organization to account for its activities, for completion of a deliverable or task, accept the responsibility for those activities, deliverables or tasks, and to disclose the results in a transparent manner" *(ISO/IEC TS 5723)*. "State of being accountable. Notes: Accountability relates to an allocated responsibility. The responsibility can be based on regulation or agreement or through assignment as part of delegation. Accountability involves a person or entity being accountable for something to another person or entity, through particular means and according to particular criteria" *(ISO/IEC 22989)*. "The ability to map a given activity or event back to the responsible party" *(ISACA glossary)*.

TERM	MEANING
Accountability of governance	"The ability of governance to ensure that enterprise objectives are achieved by evaluating stakeholder needs, conditions and options; setting direction through prioritization and decision making; and monitoring performance, compliance and progress against plans. In most enterprises, governance is the responsibility of the board of directors under the leadership of the chairperson" *(ISACA glossary)*.
Accountable	Someone (a person or organisation) who is held/called to account by an authority for a failure (such as a privacy breach or some other incident) is formally required to explain their part in the failure. They may be sanctioned or penalised in some way (disciplinary action, dismissal, prosecution, fine, restriction or withdrawal of privileges, additional oversight, *etc.*), if the authority determines that they did not adequately fulfil their obligations. "Required or expected to justify actions or decisions; being answerable and responsible for those actions & decisions" *(NZISM)*. "Answerable for actions, decisions and performance" *(ISO/IEC 22989)*.
Accountable material	"Requires the strictest control over its access and movement. Includes TOP SECRET data, some types of caveated data and any data designated as accountable material by its originator" *(AusISM)*.
Accountable party	The person or organisation held to account. "The individual, group or entity that is ultimately responsible for a subject matter, process or scope" *(ISACA glossary)*.
Accounting	Principles and practices of systematically, formally, and thoroughly recording and cross-checking various details such that relevant parties can be held to account for their activities. Most Information Technology systems, for instance, can automatically record information about user logons, use of privileges and overrides, alerts, alarms and other potentially significant events in their logs or accounting files, with utilities to search and report on them, even if these days the details are no longer needed to recharge users for their use of the computers (common practice prior to the 1990s).
Accreditation	Process of verifying that an organisation or individual is competent to check/audit and certify others, to a level of assurance required by a trusted authority acting on behalf of stakeholders. "A procedure by which an authoritative body gives formal recognition, approval and acceptance of the associated residual security risk with the operation of a system and issues a formal approval to operate the system" *(NZISM)*. *Cf.* certification.

TERM	MEANING
Accreditation authority	"The authoritative body or individual responsible for systems accreditation" *(NZISM)*.
Accuracy, accurate	Truthful and valid, faithfully representing factual objective reality. An integrity property. "Measure of closeness of results of observations, computations, or estimates to the true values or the values accepted as being true" *(ISO 17572-1)*. "Quality of that which is free of error [and/or] qualitative assessment of freedom from error, a high assessment corresponding to a small error [and/or] quantative measure of the magnitude of error, preferably expressed as a function of the relative error, a high value of this measure corresponding to a small error" *(ISO/IEC 2382)*. "The fraction of predictions that a classification model predicted correctly. In multiclass classification, accuracy is defined as correct predictions divided by total number of examples. In binary classification, accuracy is defined as true positives plus true negatives divided by total number of examples" *(ISACA glossary)*. "Ability to get the true result. For quantitative tests, the accuracy expresses the closeness of agreement between the true value and the value obtained by applying the test procedure a number of times" *(FSRCoP)*. *Cf.* precision.
ACD	*Abbrev:* **A**ctive **C**yber **D**efence.
ACF2	*Abbrev:* **A**ccess **C**ontrol **F**acility № **2**.
ACKnowledgement **(ACK)**	Positively recognise and accept/agree that something is valid, true, legitimate, authentic, *etc.* "Affirmative response, by a receiver, to a sender, indicating that transmitted data have been received" *(ISO/IEC 2382)*. "A flag set in a packet to indicate to the sender that the previously sent packet was accepted correctly by the receiver without error or that the receiver is now ready to accept a transmission" *(ISACA glossary)*.
ACL	*Abbrev:* **A**ccess **C**ontrol **L**ist.
ACME	*Abbrev:* **A**utomated **C**ertificate **M**anagement **E**nvironment.
ACPO guidelines	Influential ACPO Good Practice Guide for Digital Evidence offered succinct, pragmatic guidance for UK police gathering digital forensic evidence, last updated by the **A**ssociation of **C**hief **P**olice **O**fficers in 2011. Built on four basic principles: "(1) No action taken by law enforcement agencies, persons employed within those agencies or their agents should change data which may subsequently be relied upon in court; (2) In circumstances where a person finds it necessary to access original data, that person must be competent to do so and be able to give evidence explaining the relevance and the implications of their actions; (3) An audit trail or

TERM	MEANING
	other record of all processes applied to digital evidence should be created and preserved. An independent third party should be able to examine those processes and achieve the same result; (4) The person in charge of the investigation has overall responsibility for ensuring that the law and these principles are adhered to." Superseded by the **F**orensic **S**cience **R**egulator's **C**ode **o**f **P**ractice. See also ISO/IEC 27050 standards.
Acquirer	Person or organisation that purchases, obtains, receives, or is given something. "Stakeholder that procures a product or service from another party. Note: Procurement may or may not involve the exchange of monetary funds" *(ISO/IEC 27036-1)*. "The stakeholder who obtains a solution from a supplier" *(ISACA glossary)*.
Acquisition	Initial phase or activity in the process of gathering, analysing, and presenting forensic evidence, or the act of acquiring something. "Process of creating a copy of data within a defined set. Note: The product of an acquisition is a potential digital evidence copy" *(ISO/IEC 27037)*. "A process by which digital evidence is duplicated, copied, or imaged" *(NIST SP 800-101)*. "Process for obtaining a product or service" *(ISO/IEC 27036-1)*. "The process of obtaining solutions by establishing and executing supplier agreements" *(ISACA glossary)*.
ACS	*Abbrev:* **A**utomation and **C**ontrol **S**ystem.
ACSC	*Abbrev:* **A**ustralian **C**yber **S**ecurity **C**entre.
Action	Activity, act, movement, reactions, response, *etc.* "The mechanism by which the agent transitions between states of the environment in reinforcement learning. The agent chooses the action by using a policy" *(ISACA glossary)*. "An act taken against an Asset by a Threat Agent. Requires first that contact occurs between the Asset and Threat Agent" (*O-RT*).
Actions & control	"A specific way, usually used in combination, that an organization addresses risk, reward, and compliance" *(OCEG GRC Glossary)*.
Activation function	"Function applied to the weighted combination of all inputs to a neuron. Note: Activation functions allow neural networks to learn complicated features in the data. They are typically non-linear" *(ISO/IEC 22989)*.
Active code	"Program code embedded in the contents of a web page. When the page is accessed by a web browser, the embedded code is automatically downloaded and executed on the user's workstation. Ex. Java, ActiveX (MS)" *(SANS glossary)*.

TERM	MEANING
Active Cyber Defence (ACD)	Adaptive mechanisms defending against network security threats. "Synchronized, real-time capability to discover, detect, analyze, and mitigate threats and vulnerabilities" *(CNSSI 4009)*. "Helps organisations to find and fix vulnerabilities, manage incidents or automate disruption of cyber-attacks. Some services are designed primarily for the public sector, whereas others are made available more broadly to private sector or citizens, depending on their applicability and viability" *(UK National Cyber Security Strategy 2022)*.
Active Directory (AD)	Microsoft's architecture to administer and control network resources (computers, user IDentities, groups, *etc.*) through a hierarchical directory structure. Resource collections are organised into domains under Domain Controllers. Domains can be associated into trees, and large organisations may have forests of trees. AD authenticates and authorises access to resources in the directory, using several protocols and sets of rules called Group Policy Objects. See also AD Domain Services, AD Lightweight Directory Services, AD Federation Services, AD Certificate Services, Microsoft Entra ID.
Active Directory Certificate Services (AD CS)	Digital certificate management services provided by a Windows server for Active Directory.
Active Directory Domain Services (AD DS)	Directory services associated with a Microsoft Active Directory network, used to locate resources within the local domain and other domains through the global catalogue. Automatically replicated across Domain Controllers for resilience. Critically important domain-related data (such as passwords) are stored in a Directory Information Tree file called, by default, %SystemRoot%\NTDS\ntds.dit. This is obviously enough a bullseye triple-word-score lottery-win diamond-studded flag for hackers actively targeting an organisation's Microsoft network, with hacking and administrative tools available to facilitate compromise.
Active Directory Federation Services (AD FS)	Proprietary Microsoft technology blending Lightweight Directory Access Protocol with Security Assertion Markup Language for Identification & Authentication, authorisation, and access control purposes including Single Sign On within Active Directory. See also Microsoft Entra ID.
Active Directory Lightweight Directory Services (AD LDS)	Described by Microsoft as an 'independent mode of Active Directory' providing directory services for networked applications, based on Lightweight Directory Access Protocol.
Actively exploited vulnerability	"A vulnerability for which there is reliable evidence that a malicious actor has exploited it in a system without permission of the system owner" *(EU CRA)*.

TERM	MEANING
Active **M**anagement **T**echnology **(AMT)**	Hardware subsystem incorporated into some Intel **C**entral **P**rocessing **U**nit chips to facilitate low-level system management. In 2017, Intel disclosed a design flaw in AMT with severe vulnerability allowing hackers to gain privileged access to systems using the "Q series" chipset, either locally or through the network. Begs questions about the wisdom of allowing low-level privileged system management in this way, through hardware that bypasses normal **U**nified **E**xtensible **F**irmware **I**nterface and **O**perating **S**ystem security (a backdoor), and why this design was ever approved.
Active recovery site (mirrored)	"A recovery strategy that involves two active sites, each capable of taking over the other's workload in the event of a disaster. Note: Each site will have enough idle processing power to restore data from the other site and to accommodate the excess workload in the event of a disaster" *(ISACA glossary)*.
Active response	"A response in which the system either automatically, or in concert with the user, blocks or otherwise affects the progress of a detected attack. Note: Takes one of three forms: amending the environment, collecting more information or striking back against the user" *(ISACA glossary)*.
Active shooter, active killer	Well-armed suicidal terrorist or brutally unhinged nutcase who indiscriminately and violently attacks innocent people with intent to injure or kill as many as possible before being arrested, disarmed, disabled, or killed. An extreme safety threat (danger) to everyone in the vicinity.
ActiveX	Deprecated Microsoft technology for interactive web pages. Malicious ActiveX controls (a form of malware) may potentially compromise the users' systems, *e.g.* if the browser security settings allow, even unauthenticated ('unsigned') ActiveX controls may access files on the user's hard drive. Microsoft dropped Active X support from its browsers in 2016.
Activist	Relatively mild extremist.
Activity monitor	"Aims to prevent virus infection by monitoring for malicious activity on a system, and blocking that activity when possible" *(SANS glossary)*.
Actor	a. Performer in stage plays, films, and TV shows, *e.g.* Arnold Schwarzenegger, Anthony Hopkins, Greta Garbo, ... b. "Entity that fills a thematic role in a script. Examples: An agent, a co-agent, a beneficiary, a patient" *(ISO/IEC 2382)*. "Organization or individual that fulfils a role" *(ISO 23234)*. See also bad actor.

TERM	MEANING
Actuary	Insurance professional who uses probability theory and advanced mathematical/statistical techniques to analyse data and so quantify, and hence manage risk with scientific rigour.
Actuating function	Functional part of an application, system, or organisation which can command an actuator.
Actuator	Mechanical device that acts (moves, applies force) when commanded, such as a solenoid, stepper motor, or motorised arm that opens or closes a valve. "A device component responsible for enacting physical changes within an environment, *e.g.*, relays, solenoids, switches" *(ISACA glossary)*.
Acunetix	Commercial penetration testing/hacking tool. An example of dual-use technology, popular with black, grey, and white hats. More info: https://www.acunetix.com/
Acute risk	"Time-bound, discrete events, for example a major fire or a terrorist attack. Contrast with chronic risks" *(UK Resilience Lessons Digest 2023)*. *Cf.* chronic risk.
AD	*Abbrev:* **A**ctive **D**irectory.
Adaptive **Grad**ient **(AdaGrad)**	**A**rtificial **I**ntelligence/**M**achine **L**earning algorithm that dynamically adjusts the learning rate for each parameter. "A sophisticated gradient descent algorithm that rescales the gradients of each parameter, effectively giving each parameter an independent learning rate" *(ISACA glossary)*.
Adaptive authentication	"This varies the level or degree of authentication required where unusual login requests occur. For example, out of normal hours, from an unusual geolocation, from an unknown device and so on. When an unusual authentication request is received, Adaptive Authentication may request additional credentials such as a one-time code provided to a known mobile phone number" *(NZISM)*.
ADCON	Military term meaning the combination of manual control with management control. *Cf.* administrative control.
AD CS	*Abbrev:* **A**ctive **D**irectory **C**ertificate **S**ervices.

TERM	MEANING
Address	a. *[Verb]* To take account of, work on, deal appropriately with, tackle, fix, *etc.* b. *[Noun]* Identifies the source and destination of datacommunications messages (see network address) or the physical place on Earth where a person lives or a premises is located (postal address), allowing messages, letters, and parcels to be routed accordingly and delivered. c. *[Noun]* Specified location in computer memory, a specific cell in a spreadsheet, *etc.* d. *[Noun]* Speech, monologue, soliloquy, lecture, or sermon.
Addressing	a. Assigning/allocating or using an address. "The method used to identify the location of a participant in a network. Note: Ideally, specifies where the participant is located rather than who they are (name) or how to get there (routing)" *(ISACA glossary)*. b. The act of taking account of, working on, dealing appropriately with, tackling, fixing, *etc.*
Addressing exception	Addressing exception. "An exception that occurs when a program calculates an address that is outside the bounds of the storage that is available to the program" *(ISACA glossary)*.
Address Resolution Protocol **(ARP)**	"A protocol for mapping an Internet Protocol address to a physical machine address that is recognized in the local network. A table, usually called the ARP cache, is used to maintain a correlation between each MAC address and its corresponding IP address. ARP provides the protocol rules for making this correlation and providing address conversion in both directions" *(SANS glossary)*.
Address space	The maximum number of addresses that can be uniquely identified with a given addressing protocol, *e.g.* an 8-bit computer processor with an 8-bit addressing bus can natively address just 2^8 (*i.e.* 256) memory locations, each containing an 8-bit byte, without special technical arrangements to extend or concatenate registers and thus address additional memory locations. "The number of distinct locations that may be referred to with the machine address. Note: For most binary machines, it is equal to 2^n, where n is the number of bits in the machine address" *(ISACA glossary)*.

TERM	MEANING
Address **S**pace **L**ayout **R**andomisation **(ASLR)**	Security technique that pseudorandomises memory addressing for processes, function calls, *etc.,* frustrating hacking attempts to invoke or replace privileged functions occupying fixed and hence predictable addresses through buffer overflows and similar exploits. See also **K**ernel **A**ddress **S**pace **L**ayout **R**andomisation.
AD DS	*Abbrev:* **A**ctive **D**irectory **D**omain **S**ervices.
Adequate security	Control arrangements deemed or believed sufficient to achieve and maintain an acceptable level of risk. May yet turn out to be inadequate or excessive under various circumstances. "Security protections commensurate with the risk resulting from the unauthorized access, use, disclosure, disruption, modification, or destruction of information. This includes ensuring that information hosted on behalf of an agency and information systems and applications used by the agency operate effectively and provide appropriate confidentiality, integrity, and availability protections through the application of cost-effective security controls" *(OMB Circular A-130).*
AD FS	*Abbrev:* **A**ctive **D**irectory **F**ederation **S**ervices.
Ad hoc test	See unstructured test.
Ad injection	Browser malware that displays advertisements and (in some cases) steals personal information from infected systems. See also adware, Cross-Site Scripting, HTML injection.
AD LDS	*Abbrev:* **A**ctive **D**irectory **L**ightweight **D**irectory **S**ervices.
Administration **(admin), administrator, administrative, administer**	The operational donkey-work of management involving network, systems, security, project, team, group, department, and other technology and business administration. Keeping things in good order, running smoothly, is an essential yet often undervalued and thankless rôle, without which entropy rules, routine processes soon fall apart and chaos reigns.
Administrative access	Privileged account or access right allowing administrators to perform administrative activities. "Elevated or increased privileges granted to an account for that account to manage systems, networks and/or applications. Administrative access can be assigned to an individual's account or a built-in system account" *(ISACA glossary).*

TERM	MEANING
Administrative account	Administrative userID, usually a privileged user account, sometimes a privileged non-interactive ID to perform autonomous activities such as routine backups. "A user account with full privileges on a computer. Such an account is intended to be used only when performing personal computer (PC) management tasks, such as installing updates and application software, managing user accounts, and modifying operating system (OS) and application settings" *(NIST SP 800-114)*. "Dedicated accounts with escalated privileges and used for managing aspects of a computer, domain, or the whole enterprise information technology infrastructure. Common administrator account subtypes include root accounts, local administrator and domain administrator accounts, and network or security appliance administrator accounts" *(CIS Controls)*.
Administrative control	Control associated with, involving or integral to administrative activities such as computer system, network, or application management, *e.g.* the account administration processes for authorising and assigning applicable access rights to rôles, then allocating relevant rôles to the users. "The rules, procedures and practices dealing with operational effectiveness, efficiency and adherence to regulations and management policies" *(ISACA glossary)*. *Cf.* ADCON.
Admissible	Forensic evidence including analytical findings and expert witness testimony *must* be trustworthy if it is to be presented in court. Dubious evidence (*e.g.* if there is good reason to suspect or believe that it was *not* in fact properly collected, stored, and analysed in full accordance with applicable laws/regulations and standards of good forensic practice) may be ruled inadmissible by the judge, in which case it cannot be used in court to support or refute a case.
ADP	*Abbrev:* **A**dvanced **D**ata **P**rotection.
ADS	*Abbrev:* **A**lternate **D**ata **S**tream.
Advanced **D**ata **P**rotection **(ADP)**	Apple's proprietary end-to-end encryption scheme.
Advanced **E**ncryption **S**tandard **(AES), AES-128, AES-256**	**N**ational **S**ecurity **A**gency-approved cryptographic algorithm replaced **D**ata **E**ncryption **S**tandard. Specified in the standard FIPS 197 with 128- or 256-bit keys. A symmetric cryptography block cipher strong enough for TOP SECRET classified information, although widespread distrust of the NSA following Ed Snowden's revelations casts doubt on that assertion/belief, and there are even stronger algorithms for US military/governmental use. "A public algorithm that supports keys from 128 bits to 256 bits in size" *(ISACA glossary)*.

TERM	MEANING
Advanced Key Processor **(AKP)**	"A cryptographic device that performs all cryptographic functions for a management client node and contains the interfaces to 1) exchange information with a client platform, 2) interact with fill devices, and 3) connect a client platform securely to the primary services node (PRSN)" (*CNSSI 4009*).
Advanced Persistent Threat **(APT)**	Highly sophisticated, sustained, and ultimately damaging cyberattack, or a campaign involving a series of attacks, by a very resourceful, determined, and capable adversary, typically cyber-spooks. Generally involves a combination of methods and tools, such as custom malware, social engineering, hacking (including hacked hardware, software, or firmware, including *things*), and/or physical intrusion. Aside from the extreme technical challenges of characterising and understanding APTs, tracing and attributing their sources and even consistently naming the variants and the associated originators is tricky (something a crowdsourced APT spreadsheet addresses). "An adversary that possesses sophisticated levels of expertise and significant resources which allow it to create opportunities to achieve its objectives by using multiple attack vectors (*e.g.*, cyber, physical, and deception). These objectives typically include establishing and extending footholds within the information technology infrastructure of the targeted organizations for purposes of exfiltrating information, undermining or impeding critical aspects of a mission, program, or organization; or positioning itself to carry out these objectives in the future. The advanced persistent threat: (i) pursues its objectives repeatedly over an extended period of time; (ii) adapts to defenders' efforts to resist it; and (iii) is determined to maintain the level of interaction needed to execute its objectives" *(NIST SP 800-39)*. See also APT#.
Advance fee fraud	Type of fraud/social engineering in which the fraudster fools a naïve and vulnerable victim into sending money as 'advance fees' supposedly in order to secure a substantial pay-out (such as an inheritance or lottery win) or other benefit (such as an immigration visa) which, strangely enough, gets tantalizingly close but never quite materialises. Commonly known as a 419 scam. Originally perpetrated by letter, Telex, and FAX, latterly by email, SMS/TXT messaging, social media, *etc.*
Adversarial Example **(AE)**	Image constructed specifically to mislead or deceive an Artificial Intelligence machine vision system into misclassifying the subject (such as mis-identifying a camouflaged enemy tank as a bush).

TERM	MEANING
Adversary, adversarial, enemy, malicious actor	Deliberate threat agent, *i.e.* a malicious organisation, people, or person (such as hackers, cybercriminal gangs, competitors, workers, fraudsters, VXers, lobbyists, rumour-mongers, saboteurs/cyberteurs, pressure groups, snoops, spooks, or terrorists) intent on attacking, compromising, exploiting, and perhaps harming the target in some way. "A threat agent" *(ISACA glossary)*.
Advisory service, consulting service	Provision of advice and guidance to clients by specialists. "Services through which internal auditors provide advice to an organization's stakeholders without providing assurance or taking on management responsibilities. The nature and scope of advisory services are subject to agreement with relevant stakeholders. Examples include advising on the design and implementation of new policies, processes, systems, and products; providing forensic services; providing training; and facilitating discussions about risks and controls" *(IIA GIAS)*.
Adware	Annoying, distracting software that displays advertisements, *etc.* Considered by some to be malware since it is often covert, seldom knowingly authorised, consumes storage and processing capabilities, and may have undesirable side-effects. "A software package that automatically plays, displays or downloads advertising material to a computer after the software is installed on it or while the application is being used. Note: In most cases, this is done without any notification to the user or without the user's consent. The term adware may also refer to software that displays advertisements, whether or not it does so with the user's consent; such programs display advertisements as an alternative to shareware registration fees. These are classified as adware in the sense of advertising supported software but not as spyware. Adware in this form does not operate surreptitiously or mislead the user, and it provides the user with a specific service" *(ISACA glossary)*. See also ad injection, ransomware, crimeware, scareware, spouseware, stalkerware, spyware.
Adwind, AlienSpy, Frutas, Unrecom, Sockrat, JSocket, jRat	Heavily obfuscated species of **R**emote **A**ccess **T**rojan malware available to rent on the black market (**M**alware-**as**-**a**-**S**ervice). Java-based, hence capable of executing on many **I**nformation **T**echnology platforms. Frutas emerged in 2012 and variants were still in the wild 6 years later.
AE	*Abbrev:* **A**dversarial **E**xample.
AES	*Abbrev:* **A**dvanced **E**ncryption **S**tandard.

TERM	MEANING
Affirmation	Formal attestation, statement, or claim confirming something. "A written or oral statement confirming implementation, or lack of implementation, of processes that meet the intent and value of one or more model practices. Affirmations must be provided: By people who have a process role that involves implementing, following, or supporting processes; In an interactive forum where the appraisal team has control over the interaction Examples of affirmations: Oral affirmations include: interview responses, presentations, and demonstrations, and can include responses to questions on white boards, Skype/Instant Message chat boards, *etc*. Written affirmations include: emails, instant messages, and data contained in systems, documents" *(ISACA glossary)*.
Affirmative cyber risk	Cyber incidents *explicitly* covered in cyberinsurance or other forms of insurance. *Cf.* non-affirmative cyber risk.
After-action report, final exercise report	"Document that records, describes and analyses the actual disruption or exercise, drawing on debriefs and reports from observers, and derives lessons from it. Note: The after-action report documents the results from the after-action review" *(ISO 22300)*.
After **F**irst **U**nlock **(AFU)**	State of a mobile phone after the user has authenticated and unlocked it at least once by entering a PIN code, pattern, or biometric. In this state, the device **O**perating **S**ystem dynamically decrypts files and enables functions and features (such as the camera) that were automatically disabled **B**efore **F**irst **U**nlock, facilitating extensive data access by the user ... and potentially by forensic analysts or hackers.
Agency	a. *[Adjective]* Self-determination, the capability of a person or organisation to act independently in their own interest, controlling their own activities, decisions, and environment, free of undue influence or constraint. *Cf.* agent. b. *[Noun]* Part of government. "Any executive agency or department, military department, Federal Government corporation, Federal Government-controlled corporation, or other establishment in the Executive Branch of the Federal Government, or any independent regulatory agency" *(NIST SP 800-171)*. "New Zealand Government departments, authorities, agencies or other bodies established in relation to public purposes, including departments and authorities staffed under the Public Service Act" *(NZISM)*.
Agency control	Agency control. "This description applies where an Agency has direct control of agency information systems and data. It follows that Non-Agency Control occurs where direct control is impaired or does not or cannot exist" *(NZISM)*. *Cf.* non-agency control.
Agency head	"The government employee with ultimate responsibility for the secure operation of agency functions, whether performed inhouse or outsourced" *(NZISM)*.

TERM	MEANING
Agent	a. Person who somehow (usually covertly, hence 'secret agent') obtains legitimate access to confidential proprietary or personal information but betrays their position of trust by disclosing or permitting access to the information by an unauthorised third party, typically through a collector. See also spy. b. Benign or malicious program, person or organisation acting on behalf of or representing another, *e.g.* gathering and passing on data from one system or network for collation and analysis centrally in conjunction with data fed by agents elsewhere, a custodian or steward holding and protecting information assets, or a 'go-between' facilitating recruitment, property sales, or business deals. "In artificial intelligence (AI), an autonomous program or system designed to perceive and interact with its environment to make decisions and take actions to achieve specific goals. Also referred to as an intelligent agent" *(ISACA glossary)*. *Cf.* agency.
Agentic Artificial **I**ntelligence **(Agentic AI), intelligent agent**	**A**rtificial **I**ntelligence architecture involving distributed intelligent semi- or fully autonomous, self-learning agents, taking rational decisions and acting on behalf and in the interests of their owners/controllers according to their local circumstances.
Agent provocateur	French term literally translated as 'agent who provokes,' such as a secret agent (spy, mole) who infiltrates an organisation and incites or causes them to act illegally or inappropriately in such a way that they are likely to be caught in the act. A cyberteur.
AGI	*Abbrev:* **A**rtificial **G**eneral **I**ntelligence.
Agile, agile development	Software engineering approach involving making frequent small/incremental/evolutionary changes (iterations or sprints) to a production system, with rapid user/customer feedback after each release directing the next round. "A development methodology that uses an iterative approach to deliver solutions incrementally through close collaboration and frequent reassessment" *(OMB Circular A-130)*. "A methodology of adopting flexible, adaptable and iterative processes" *(ISACA glossary)*. "Evidence that the organization can respond quickly and positively to changes and stress" (*OCEG GRC Glossary*). See also **R**apid **A**pplication **D**evelopment, **C**ontinuous **D**evelopment, DevOps.
Aggregation	Collection and collation of information from disparate sources. Due to explicit and/or inferred relationships between aggregated items, analysis can reveal structures and new knowledge; hence, **D**ata**B**ases are usually more valuable than the data items they contain: the whole is greater than the sum of the parts. "Acquisition of sensitive information by collecting and correlating information of lesser sensitivity" *(ISO/IEC 2382)*. "A term used to describe compilations of data that may require a higher level of protection than their component parts" *(AusISM)*.

TERM	MEANING
Agreement	Joint commitment of two or more parties to a common objective. "Mutual acknowledgement of terms and conditions under which a working relationship is conducted" *(ISO/IEC 27036-1)*.
AgriTech, AgroTech, AgTech	Contractions of **agri**cultural **tech**nology, particularly the development and exploitation of innovative **I**nformation **T**echnology within farming and the agricultural industry/sector. See also Biotech, EdTech, FinTech, FoodTech, GovTech, EcoTech/GreenTech, HealthTech, LegalTech, RegTech, RetailTech, and other tech neologisms.
AH	*Abbrev:* **A**uthentication **H**eader.
AI	*Abbrev:* **A**rtificial **I**ntelligence.
AI agent	**A**rtificial **I**ntelligence agent. "Automated entity that senses and responds to its environment and takes actions to achieve its goals" *(ISO/IEC 22989)*.
AI Auditor	ISACA's qualification for **I**nformation **T**echnology auditors, risk and compliance analysts auditing **A**rtificial **I**ntelligence systems. More info: https://www.isaca.org/credentialing/aaia
AI component	Component of an **A**rtificial **I**ntelligence system. "Functional element that constructs an AI system" *(ISO/IEC 22989)*.
AICPA	*Abbrev:* **A**merican **I**nstitute of **C**ertified **P**ublic **A**ccountants.
AIGP	*Abbrev:* **A**rtificial **I**ntelligence **G**overnance **P**rofessional.
Aircrack ng	Wi-Fi network hacking and penetration testing tool, capable of cracking WEP, WPA, and WPA2/PSK.
AirCyber	Initiative from BoostAeroSpace SAS spreading security awareness and good practices through the aerospace and defence industry, with conformity assessments and certification aimed at small to medium-sized suppliers for Airbus and its European partners. More info: https://boostaerospace.com/aircyber/
Air gap	Complete physical and logical separation between entities, *e.g.* isolating highly secure networks from less-secure ones by prohibiting any connections or information transfers between them. Tends to fail-insecure; in other words, if the air gap is somehow breached, the construct may be highly vulnerable if excessive trust (faith) or reliance was placed on the air gap. See also data diode.
Air lock, air-lock, airlock	See man-trap.
AI system impact assessment	Analysis of the potential effects, consequences, or value of an **A**rtificial **I**ntelligence system. "Formal, documented process by which the impacts on individuals, groups of individuals, or both, and societies are identified, evaluated and addressed by an organization developing, providing or using products or services utilizing artificial intelligence" *(ISO/IEC 42001)*.

TERM	MEANING
AKP	*Abbrev:* **A**dvanced **K**ey **P**rocessor.
Alarm	Audio/visual warning of the occurrence of a critical security and/or vital safety condition or incident requiring an urgent, high-priority response (*e.g.* fire/smoke, intruder, flood, or a gross system integrity, brake or control failure). See also alert.
Alarm system	System comprising one or more types of alarms/alerts, *e.g.* intruder/security alarms, fire/smoke alarms, industrial process alarms, electrical alarms. May interface with building management or other systems for coordinated/consolidated monitoring and control, particularly in complex safety-critical environments such as factories and prisons.
Alert	a. *[Noun]* Warning indication that a security event (*e.g.* audit or security log file full, system shutdown initiated, user authentication failure, access-controlled door held open) has occurred. While definitions vary, alerts *generally* signal important warnings but not necessarily critical or vital conditions requiring less urgent responses than alarms. They are usually logged for analysis and follow-up action when convenient. However, a particular flurry, sequence or cascade of alerts may itself be cause for alarm. "Part of public warning that captures attention of first responders and people at risk in a developing emergency situation" *(ISO 22300)*. "'Instant' indication that an information system and network may be under attack, or in danger because of accident, failure or human error" *(ISO/IEC 27033-1)*. b. *[Adjective]* Security aware, vigilant, and primed to react quickly and appropriately to threats, events, and incidents as they unfold. Think: meercats and other prey species.
Alerting system	a. System for alerting. May refer specifically to the computer element, whereas the overall system potentially includes the definition of various alert and alarm criteria and situations, design and implementation, testing, monitoring, maintenance, response plans, escalation, *etc.*, as part of the process and safety engineering. "Provides real-time information about security issues, including vulnerabilities and exploits that are currently happening" *(ISACA glossary)*. b. Whichever computer system raised an alert – not always immediately obvious in, say, a busy process control room.
Alert situation	The particular circumstances or conditions intended to trigger an alert, *e.g.* if a chemical manufacturing process exceeds a temperature or pressure warning setpoint, alerting the human or automated controllers to a potential concern. "The point in an emergency procedure when the elapsed time passes a threshold and the interruption is not resolved. The enterprise entering into an alert situation initiates a series of escalation steps" *(ISACA glossary)*.

TERM	MEANING
Algorithm, cipher, cypher	Logical function, process, and/or protocol at the heart of an information system such as a cryptosystem or **A**rtificial **I**ntelligence system, *e.g.* determines the calculations, actions, or operations necessary to encrypt plaintext and decrypt ciphertext, or to make real-time decisions when controlling a robotic machine tool. "Finite ordered set of well-defined rules for the solution of a problem" *(ISO/IEC 2382)*. "A finite set of well-defined, unambiguous rules for the solution of a problem in a finite number of steps. It is a sequence of operational actions that lead to a desired goal and is the basic building block of a program" *(ISACA glossary)*. "A finite set of step-by-step instructions for a problem-solving or computation procedure, especially one that can be implemented by a computer [and] An algorithm that employs the science of cryptography, including encryption algorithms, cryptographic hash algorithms, digital signature algorithms, and key agreement algorithms" *(SANS glossary)*.
Algorithm analysis	Algorithm analysis. "A software verification and validation (V&V) task to ensure that the algorithms selected are correct, appropriate and stable, and meet all accuracy, timing and sizing requirements" *(ISACA glossary)*.
Algorithmic justice	"Actively identifying and dismantling harmful biases within algorithms, promoting fairer development and deployment, and promoting accountability and transparency" *(ISACA glossary)*.
All-hazards	Risk management objective to identify and address a wide variety of potential events, incidents, disasters, emergencies, *etc.* "Naturally occurring event, human induced event (both intentional and unintentional) and technology caused event with potential impact on an organization, community or society and the environment on which it depends" *(ISO 22300)*.
Allocated requirement	"Requirement that results from levying all or part of a higher-level requirement on a solution's lower-level design component. Requirements can be assigned to logical or physical components, including people, consumables, delivery increments and architecture" *(ISACA glossary)*.
All-of-government	"Refers to the entire New Zealand state sector" *(NZISM)*.
Allocated space	"Area on digital media, including primary memory, which is in use for the storage of data, including metadata" *(ISO/IEC 27037)*.
Allow list	Politically correct form of whitelist. "A list that confirms items being analysed are acceptable … the opposite of a deny or block list" *(NZISM)*.

TERM	MEANING
Alpha test	Software self-assessment performed by its developer, a peer, or the development team, the first phase of testing by humans as opposed to, say, automated source code syntax/typo checks by the compiler. Being so closely involved in the process, developers *may* fail to recognise inherent logical errors and misinterpreted functional or nonfunctional requirements that beta testers *may* spot. Or not.
Alternate **D**ata **S**tream **(ADS)**	For interoperability with the Macintosh **H**ierarchical **F**ile **S**ystem, Windows **N**ew **T**echnology **F**ile **S**ystem can associate additional 'streams' of information with files (other than the details normally shown in folder listings), each of which can contain additional data, even executable programs with malware implications. A legitimate use for ADS is the zone.identifier "**M**ark **O**f [The] **W**eb" metadata stream indicating if the file arrived from trusted or untrusted local or remote (Internet) sources, optionally including the source **U**niform **R**esource **L**ocator.
Alternate facilities, alternate site	"Alternate operating location selected to be used by an organization when normal business operations cannot be carried out using the normal location after a disruption has occurred" *(ISO/IEC 27031)*. "Locations and infrastructures from which emergency or backup processes are executed when the main premises are unavailable or destroyed. Note: Includes other buildings, offices or data processing centers" *(ISACA glossary)*.
Alternate process	Different approach or way of doing things. "An automatic or manual process designed and established to continue critical business processes from point-of-failure to return-to-normal" *(ISACA glossary)*.
Alternative routing	"A service that allows the option of having an alternate route to complete a call when the marked destination is not available. Note: In signaling, alternate routing is the process of allocating substitute routes for a given signaling traffic stream in case of failure(s) affecting the normal signaling links or routes of that traffic stream" *(ISACA glossary)*.
Amazon **W**eb **S**ervices **(AWS)**	Brand name for Amazon's global cloud infrastructure. See also Azure, **G**oogle **C**loud **P**latform.
American **I**nstitute of **C**ertified **P**ublic **A**ccountants **(AICPA)**	US trade body for **C**ertified **P**ublic **A**ccountants, merged in 2017 with the **C**hartered **I**nstitute of **M**anagement **A**ccountants. More info: https://www.aicpa-cima.com/home

TERM	MEANING
American **N**ational **S**tandards **I**nstitute **(ANSI)**	Private non-profit organisation promoting voluntary standards and conformity assessment in the US. Mission: "To enhance both the global competitiveness of U.S. business and the U.S. quality of life by promoting and facilitating voluntary consensus standards and conformity assessment systems, and safeguarding their integrity." See also **N**ational **I**nstitute of **S**cience and **T**echnology. More info: https://www.ansi.org/
Ambiguous	Uncertain/unclear and potentially risky situation, definition, or meaning increasing the possibility of misinterpretation and misunderstanding. "A property that refers to the presence of multiple, unclear, or conflicting interpretations of conditions, events, or behaviors in a system" *(OCEG GRC Glossary)*.
Amplification attack, reflection attack	Type of attack in which servers are tricked into transmitting a large volume of network traffic to a target system, potentially overloading it, causing a **D**enial-**o**f-**S**ervice. **N**etwork **T**ime **P**rotocol, **D**omain **N**ame **S**ystem, or other request packets with spoofed source **I**nternet **P**rotocol addresses matching the target are sent to one or more servers which then forward their responses to the target instead of the originator. See also **D**istributed **R**eflective **D**enial-**o**f-**S**ervice.
AMT	*Abbrev:* **A**ctive **M**anagement **T**echnology.
Analogue	a. *[Adjective]* Continuously variable as opposed to a step function such as digital. b. *[Noun]* Artificial model representing and simulating something real, such as a virtual assistant.
Analysis, analytics	Process of systematically exploring, examining, investigating, and evaluating information relating to risks, incidents, forensic evidence, *etc*. in some depth. "Evaluation of potential digital evidence in order to assess its relevance to the investigation. Note: Potential digital evidence, which is determined to be relevant, becomes digital evidence" *(ISO/IEC 27042-2)*. "The examination of acquired data for its significance and probative value to the case" *(NIST SP 800-101)*. "1. To separate into elemental parts or basic principles to determine the nature of the whole. 2. A course of reasoning showing that a certain result is a consequence of assumed premises. 3. The methodical investigation of a problem and the separation of that problem into smaller related units for further detailed study (Source: ANSI)" *(ISACA glossary)*. "Any form of test, comparison or analytical method performed on an item/exhibit or relevant material recovered from an item/exhibit" *(FSRCoP)*.

TERM	MEANING
Analysis criteria	Analysis criteria. "The criteria used to analyze, quantify and select ways to address risk, reward, and compliance" *(OCEG GRC Glossary)*.
Analytical model	Mathematical formula for generating metrics (such as a trend in a relevant security parameter) from measurements (normally a time series of values of the parameter), giving meaning to the numbers ("See, I told you things *are* getting better!"). "Algorithm or calculation combining one or more base measures and/or derived measures with associated decision criteria" *(ISO/IEC 27000)*.
Analytical technique	Systematic method or approach for analysis, *e.g.* a classic 'scientific' technique is to study current knowledge and generate a credible theoretical hypothesis, then test it against reality using experimental data and so advance the state of knowledge. "The examination of ratios, trends and changes in balances and other values between periods to obtain a broad understanding of the enterprise's financial or operational position and to identify areas that may require further or closer investigation. Note: Often used when planning the assurance assignment" *(ISACA glossary)*.
Anarchy, anarchism, anarchist	For ideological or other reasons, anarchists typically seek to overthrow the government and disrupt civil society by (among other things) sabotaging vulnerable parts of the **C**ritical **N**ational **I**nfrastructure.
Angler	Modular crimeware kit, in the wild in 2016, used for phishing.
Angry IP Scanner, ipscan	Network security administration/penetration testing tool like nmap. It scans (queries) **I**nternet **P**rotocol address and port ranges to identify nodes.
Annotate, annotation	Prepare pertinent 'margin' notes to accompany a particular document, topic, or activity, *e.g.* explaining the content in more detail, commenting on and critiquing it, raising queries and concerns, elaborating or suggesting alternative interpretations and conclusions. "The process of labeling or tagging data to provide examples from which a machine learning (ML) algorithm can develop a model" *(ISACA glossary)*.
Annual audit, statutory audit	Financial audit conducted by external auditors to confirm that the information in the organisation's annual report and accounts is accurate and truthful. This involves checking the integrity of any financial or other systems on which the accounts are based, and testing the organisation's compliance with applicable laws and regulations, *e.g.* concerning accounting practices and tax treatments.

TERM	MEANING
Anomaly, anomalous	Something markedly different, unusual, abnormal, unexpected, or exceptional, hence intriguing and perhaps of concern. While large data anomalies (such as numerous data values completely missing for a significant period) may be easily spotted by eye (provided someone is looking!), small anomalies in large data sets or **DataBases** can be identified much more easily and reliably by systematic statistical analysis, *e.g.* applying Benford's law. Such anomalies are inherently interesting, hinting at the possibility of unexpected relationships, biases, or events, perhaps even information security incidents such as bugs, flaws, frauds, malware, or hacks in progress. Anomalous data communications (*e.g.* an unusual surge or dip in network traffic volume, or unusual senders and recipients) and activities (*e.g.* unusual out-of-hours working) may indicate issues worthy of investigation (*e.g.* 'technical issues,' misconfiguration, fraud, information theft/spying, malware). "Unusual or statistically rare" *(ISACA glossary)*.
Anomaly detection	The process of identifying anomalous conditions, outliers or spurious items, *etc.* in a data set or sequence. Naturally implies the ability to distinguish anomalous from normal if extreme values, potentially indicating a genuine discontinuity or flaw in the model, a subjective or arbitrary determination based on an accurate understanding of the data variability and (often) statistical analysis of objective evidence. "Detection on the basis of whether the system activity matches that defined as abnormal" *(ISACA glossary)*.
Anonymity	Someone's right to go about their life and business without unnecessarily revealing their identity, *e.g.* whistleblowers or for privacy reasons. Typically achieved through discretion, sometimes through a trusted third party or using techniques such as anonymisation, tokenisation, or redaction. With careful design, the systematic process of identifying and authenticating messages, instructions, data, *etc.* can be logically and practically separated from identifying and authenticating the originating people, organisations, systems, *etc.* May conflict with law enforcement and other sociological or ethical expectations, objectives, requirements, or obligations such as personal accountability. "Characteristic of information that does not permit a personally identifiable information principal to be identified directly or indirectly" *(ISO/IEC 29100)*. "The quality or state of not being named or identified" *(ISACA glossary)*.

TERM	MEANING
Anonymisation	Permanent and complete removal of the personal information necessary to identify specific individuals in a **D**ata**B**ase, document, *etc.,* normally for privacy reasons. "Process by which personally identifiable information (PII) is irreversibly altered in such a way that a PII principal can no longer be identified directly or indirectly, either by the PII controller alone or in collaboration with any other party" *(ISO/IEC 29100)*. "Irreversible severance of a data set from the identity of the data contributor to prevent any future reidentification, even by the organization collecting the data under any condition" *(ISACA glossary)*. *Cf.* pseudonymisation.
Anonymous	a. Information of unstated origin that is not and cannot be linked unambiguously to a specific, identifiable person, subject, originator, or source. b. Name of a 'hacker collective' – a loosely organised and indistinct group of pranksters, hackers, digital vigilantes, and subversive hacktivists active for two decades from about 2004. Their proclamations famously included the line "We are legion" spoken in a synthetic voice emanating from a stylised mask. See also LulzSec.
ANSI	*Abbrev:* **A**merican **N**ational **S**tandards **I**nstitute.
Anti-pass-back	Physical security access control arrangement such as a man trap designed to prevent someone presenting their access card to open a one-person-at-a-time controlled entrance for themselves, then handing their card back to someone else (typically an unauthorised visitor) permitting them also to access the controlled area. Electronic access control systems may keep track of individuals, preventing them from re-accessing an area unless they have previously exited it, requiring them to present their access cards at *both* entry *and* exit points. "A security mechanism preventing an access card or similar device from being used to enter an area a second time without first leaving it (so that the card cannot be passed back to a second person who wants to enter)" *(PCI Card Production and Provisioning Physical Security Requirements)*.
Antiphishing, anti-phishing	Cluster of information risk and security management techniques and controls to mitigate the risks associated with phishing. "Software that identifies phishing content and attempts to block the content or warn the user about the suspicious nature of the content" *(ISACA glossary)*.

TERM	MEANING
Antivirus, antimalware	Software application/program/package/system and associated services and controls to mitigate the risk of malware by avoiding, detecting, preventing, and/or removing infections with viruses, worms, Trojans, spyware, ransomware, rootkits, *etc*. "A widely used technology to prevent, detect and remove many categories of malware, including computer viruses, worms, Trojans, keyloggers, malicious browser plug-ins, adware and spyware [and] An application software deployed at multiple points in an IT architecture. It is designed to detect and potentially eliminate virus code before damage is done and repair or quarantine files that have already been infected" *(ISACA glossary)*.
AP	*Abbrev:* **A**ccess **P**oint.
API	*Abbrev:* **A**pplication **P**rogramming **I**nterface.
APN	*Abbrev:* **A**ccess **P**oint **N**ame.
app	*Abbrev:* **app**lication.
Appearance	How or what something *appears* to be – a subjective impression. "The act of giving the idea or impression of being or doing something" *(ISACA glossary)*.
Appearance of independence	For an auditor, scientist, judge or similar professional rôle, the *appearance* of being independent is almost as important as the actuality. It affects the nature and quality of interactions with stakeholders, including aspects such as access to sensitive information, tolerance, influence, and mutual respect (trust). "The behavior that is appropriate of an IS auditor to meet the situations occurring during audit work (interviews, meetings, reporting, *etc*.). Note: An IS auditor should be aware that appearance of independence depends on the perceptions of others and can be influenced by improper actions or associations" *(ISACA glossary)*.
Appetite	Hunger or desire, *e.g.* risk appetite. "A range for the value of an indicator that defines a preferred or expected level of variation around a target" *(OCEG GRC Glossary)*. *Cf.* tolerance.
Applet	A cute little application program. "A program written in a portable, platform-independent computer language, such as Java, JavaScript, or Visual Basic. Notes: An applet is usually embedded in an HyperText Markup Language (HTML) page downloaded from web servers. Applets can only perform a restricted set of operations, thus preventing, or at least minimizing, the possible security compromise of the host computers. However, applets expose the user's machine to risk if not properly controlled by the browser, which should not allow an applet to access a machine's information without prior authorization of the user" *(ISACA glossary)*.

TERM	MEANING
Appliance	Computer system or device dedicated to a specific purpose, ready to use straight out of the box ('plug and play'), requiring little if any configuration or management. Home networking and entertainment devices and smart 'white goods' (washing machines, refrigerators, *etc.*) are appliances with embedded systems. See also **Internet of *Things***.
Application (app), application program, application software	a. Computer program or suite of programs providing useful functions. Applications on smartphones, tablet and portable PCs, social media or (supposed) security apps downloaded from the web and installed by naïve users, may be Trojans, spyware, or other malware, especially on jailbroken devices. "A program, or group of programs, hosted on enterprise assets and designed for end-users. Applications are considered a software asset in this document. Examples include web, database, cloud-based, and mobile applications" *(CIS Controls)*. "The use of information resources (information and information technology) to satisfy a specific set of user requirements" *(OMB Circular A-130 Appendix III)*. "A computer program or set of programs that performs the processing of records for a specific function. Notes: Applications contrast with systems programs, such as an operating system or network control program, and with utility programs, such as copy or sort. [and] A program that processes business data through activities such as data entry, update or query. Notes: Contrasts with systems programs, such as an operating system or network control program, and with utility programs, such as copy or sort. [and] A software designed to fill the specific needs of a user; for example, software for navigation, payroll or process control. Contrasts with support software and system software" *(ISACA glossary)*. b. Situation in which something might be usefully and gainfully employed or utilised (applied). c. Process and form for applying for a job, grant, loan, permission, network access, *etc*.
Application acquisition review	"An evaluation of an application system being acquired or evaluated, that considers matters such as: appropriate controls being designed into the system, the processing of information in a complete, accurate and reliable manner; the application will function as intended; the application will application functionality in compliance with any applicable statutory provisions and compliance with the established system acquisition process" *(ISACA glossary)*. See also system development audit.
Application architecture	Architecture and design of an application program or system. "A description of the logical grouping of capabilities that manage the objects necessary to process information and support the enterprise's objectives" *(ISACA glossary)*.

TERM	MEANING
Application benchmarking	Application benchmark. "The process of establishing the design and operation of automated controls within an application" *(ISACA glossary)*.
Application component	Component part of an application such as a function or subroutine.
Application containerisation	"A mechanism that is used to isolate applications from each other within the context of a running operating system instance. In much the same way that a logical partition (LPAR) provides segmentation of system resources in mainframes, a computing environment — employing containers — segments and isolates the underlying system services so that they are logically sequestered from each other" *(ISACA glossary)*.
Application control, application security	Security control over, or within, an application, such as access controls, backups, **D**ata**B**ase security, and the associated administrative controls, *e.g.* change control. "The policies, procedures and activities designed to provide reasonable assurance that objectives relevant to a given automated solution (application) are achieved" *(ISACA glossary)*. "An approach in which only an explicitly defined set of trusted applications are allowed to execute on systems" *(AusISM)*.
Application development, software development, systems development, development, application programming	Process, method, approach, phase, or stage within which new or updated software is coded (*i.e.* source code is written). Sometimes broadened to include the preceding specification and architecture/design phases, and perhaps the subsequent software testing, version control, change and configuration management, and implementation activities. "The act or function of developing and maintaining application programs in production" *(ISACA glossary)*.
Application development review	"An evaluation of an application system under development that considers matters such as: appropriate controls are designed into the system; the application will process information in a complete, accurate and reliable manner; the application will function as intended; the application will function in compliance with any applicable statutory provisions and in compliance with the established system development life cycle process" *(ISACA glossary)*. See also system development audit.
Application development sandbox	See development environment. "A standalone computer, virtual machine or virtual environment used to conduct software development removed from production infrastructure" *(ISACA glossary)*.
Application implementation review	"An evaluation of any part of an implementation project. Note: Examples include project management, test plans and user acceptance testing (UAT) procedures" *(ISACA glossary)*. See also system development audit, testing, implementation.
Application maintenance review	"An evaluation of any part of a project to perform maintenance on an application system. Note: Examples include project management, test plans and user acceptance testing (UAT) procedures" *(ISACA glossary)*. See also system development audit.

TERM	MEANING
Application **P**rogramming **I**nterface **(API)**	In a **S**ervice-**O**riented **A**rchitecture, complete applications can be assembled Lego-style from building blocks – essentially subroutines, subsystems, or functions providing discrete information services accessed through APIs. While individual services or microservices and APIs may be securely specified, designed, and implemented, ensuring overall system security can be challenging due to numerous interfaces and issues such as scope, context, dynamics, and complexity, plus the almost inevitable flaws and bugs. "Set of functions, protocols, parameters, and objects of different formats, used to create software that interfaces with the features or data of an external system or service" *(ISO/IEC/IEEE 26531)*. "A set of routines, protocols and tools referred to as building blocks used in business application software development" *(ISACA glossary)*.
Application proxy	Network service mediating the data flowing to and from applications running on a server. "A service that connects programs running on internal networks to services on exterior networks by creating two connections, one from the requesting client and another to the destination service" *(ISACA glossary)*.
Application security	See application control. "The security aspects supported by the application, primarily with regard to the roles or responsibilities and audit trails within the applications" *(ISACA glossary)*.
Application **S**ervice **P**rovider **(ASP)**	Organisation offering applications via the Internet, *i.e.* **S**oftware-**a**s-**a**-**S**ervice. "A managed service provider (MSP) that deploys, hosts and manages access to a packaged application to multiple parties from a centrally managed facility. Note: The applications are delivered over networks on a subscription basis" *(ISACA glossary)*. See also **C**loud **S**ervice **P**rovider.
Application software tracing and mapping	"A specialized tool that can be used to analyze the flow of data through the processing logic of the application software and document the logic, paths, control conditions and processing sequences. Notes: Both the command language or job control statements and programming language can be analyzed. This technique includes program/system: mapping, tracing, snapshots, parallel simulations and code comparisons" *(ISACA glossary)*.
Application-**S**pecific **I**ntegrated **C**ircuit **(ASIC)**	**I**ntegrated **C**ircuit designed, preprogrammed, and dedicated to perform a particular function with high efficiency/performance and reliability such as **R**ead-**O**nly **M**emory chips storing firmware and **F**ield-**P**rogrammable **G**ate **A**rrays used for **D**igital **S**ignal **P**rocessing, industrial automation, **A**rtificial **I**ntelligence/**D**eep **L**earning, cryptography, *etc.* "Integrated circuit customized for a particular use" *(ISO/IEC 22989)*. "A solid-state device designed to perform a single or small group of functions" *(ISACA glossary)*.

TERM	MEANING
Application system	Either just an application program itself, or the broader system potentially including the computer server; the **O**perating **S**ystem and middleware (*e.g.* a **D**ata**B**ase **M**anagement **S**ystem); the network, administrative, and business services; the data; and various groups of people or organisations involved in designing, developing, providing, using, supporting, maintaining, managing, and benefiting from the app. "An integrated set of computer programs designed to serve a particular function that has specific input, processing and output activities. Note: Examples include general ledger, manufacturing resource planning and human resource (HR) management" *(ISACA glossary).*
Application whitelist	Application of whitelisting to applications. "An approach in which all executables and applications are prevented from executing by default, with an explicitly defined set of allowed executables" *(NZISM).*
Appraisal	Formal or official assessment. "An examination of one or more processes by a trained team using an appraisal reference model as the basis for determining, at a minimum, strengths and weaknesses" *(ISACA glossary).*
Appropriate evidence	"The measure of the quality of the evidence" *(ISACA glossary).*
Approval	See authorisation.
Approved Destruction Facility	"The status of 'approved facility' for the destruction of media and equipment, applies to a specific installation/site, and is granted by the Director-General GCSB under the NZISM [if deemed] capable of securely destroying IT equipment, devices and media to the standard required under the NZISM and related policies and that procedural security meets the required standards" *(NZISM).*
APT	*Abbrev:* **A**dvanced **P**ersistent **T**hreat.
APT#	Identifier for a state-sponsored (spooky) hacker group such as the North Korean APT38 (also known as Lazarus Group) using **A**dvanced **P**ersistent **T**hreat malware. Identification is difficult due to the groups evolving, actively evading detection and misleading analysts working independently. Likewise, attribution to specific countries is problematic due to false flag operations, disinformation, and global politics.
Arbitrary	Subjective, according to someone's preference. Vulnerabilities that reportedly allow 'arbitrary commands' are a cybersecurity red flag since adversaries who exploit them can effectively take full control of a compromised system.

TERM	MEANING
Architecture	Overall grand design or blueprint for an organisation's information systems, networks, and business processes, linking even higher-level objectives from various strategies to lower-level designs for individual systems, subsystems, domains, and processes. May incorporate the information security architecture. In the physical security context, the architectural design of a facility can help or hinder security and safety. "Fundamental organisation of a system embodied in its components, their relationships to each other, and to the environment, and the principles guiding its design and evolution" *(ISO/IEC 27033-1)*. "The design of the structure of a system, including logical components, and the logical interrelationships of a computer, its operating system, a network, or other elements" *(**T**rust **S**ervices Criteria)*. "Description of the fundamental underlying design of the components of the business system, or of one element of the business system (*e.g.*, technology), the relationships among them and the manner in which they support enterprise objectives" *(ISACA glossary)*.
Archive, archival	Secure long-term storage of valuable information, designed to ensure its integrity, availability, and often (but not necessarily) its confidentiality and so maintain its value. May be required for compliance reasons, *e.g.* organisations are obliged by applicable laws/regulations to provide certain types of business record several years after they were created. In a few cases, the retention period is indefinite. Since only valuable information is archived, assurance that it can in fact be restored when needed is a non-negotiable requirement, so prove it! "Store backup files and any associated journals, usually for a given period of time" *(ISO/IEC 2382)*. "A lasting collection of computer system data or other records that are in long-term storage" *(ISACA glossary)*.
Area	a. Region, place, location, site, facility, domain, zone, concept, *etc.*, within some sort of physical or notional boundary, not necessarily sharply or explicitly declared. b. Two-dimensional measure of the extent of a surface, plane, or layer.
Armour	Strong protective plates, typically comprising layers of leather, steel, Kevlar/carbon-fibre/composite materials and ceramics that absorb and spread the energy, resisting penetration by weapons such as swords, daggers/knives, shrapnel, and bullets. The physical security version of hardening.

TERM	MEANING
Arms-length	Indicates a notional separation between parties, giving a degree of independence and plausible deniability of their collusion or involvement in nefarious activities such as **O**ffensive **C**yberspace **O**perations, anti-competitive behaviours such as price fixing, cabal, or *coup d'etat.*
ARP	*Abbrev:* **A**ddress **R**esolution **P**rotocol.
ARPANET (Advanced Research Projects Agency Network)	"A pioneer packet-switched network that was built in the early 1970s under contract to the US Government, led to the development of today's Internet, and was decommissioned in June 1990" *(SANS glossary).*
Arson	Deliberately setting fire to or burning something without its owner's permission, or with intent to defraud another (such as an insurance company). A form of sabotage. A threat to many tangible assets.
Artefact, artifact	a. Glitch, interruption, error, problem, unnatural occurrence. "A form of objective evidence that is an output of the work being performed and the process being followed. It must demonstrate the extent of implementing, performing or supporting the organizational or project processes that can be mapped to one or more model practices. Artifacts must be provided by people with a process role to implement, perform, follow or support processes" *(ISACA glossary).* "Something observed in an examination or analysis that was not originally present but occurs as a result of the procedures employed for examination or analysis" *(FSRCoP).* b. Object such as an item of evidence or a record.
Artificial **G**eneral **I**ntelligence **(AGI), General AI, strong AI, full AI, superintelligence**	Generic/adaptable form of **A**rtificial **I**ntelligence, far closer to human intelligence and sentience than today's limited AI approaches such as generative AI. "Type of AI system that addresses a broad range of tasks with a satisfactory level of performance. Notes: Compared to narrow AI; AGI is often used in a stronger sense, meaning systems that not only can perform a wide variety of tasks, but all tasks that a human can perform" *(ISO/IEC 22989).* "Systems that demonstrate broad capabilities of intelligence, including reasoning, planning, and the ability to learn from experience, and with these capabilities at or above human-level" (Microsoft researchers, cited by Ada Lovelace Institute). *Cf.* **Gen**erative **A**rtificial **I**ntelligence.
Artificial **I**ntelligence **(AI), cognitive system**	**I**nformation **T**echnology system based on neural networks employing **D**eep **L**earning, **M**achine **L**earning, **L**arge **L**anguage **M**odels, and/or **N**atural **L**anguage **P**rocessing techniques, having been trained on big data sets to simulate or emulate the rational reasoning, cognitive, and decision-making capabilities of intelligent humans. AI-related terms, concepts, and practices are emerging from a rapidly evolving cluster of complex and

TERM	MEANING
	disruptive technologies with significant information risk, information security, privacy, compliance, business, and societal implications. While the information risks and ethical concerns associated with AI are challenging and potentially disturbing, AI systems show promise in the cybersecurity field, *e.g.* automated network/system intrusion, phishing, malware and fraud detection, prevention and response, and the intelligent design of business processes and systems. "Interdisciplinary field, usually regarded as a branch of computer science, dealing with models and systems for the performance of functions generally associated with human intelligence, such as reasoning and learning" *(ISO/IEC 2382)*. "Research and development of mechanisms and applications of AI systems. Note: Research and development can take place across any number of fields such as computer science, data science, humanities, mathematics and natural sciences" *(ISO/IEC 22989)*. "Discipline concerned with the building of computer systems that perform tasks requiring intelligence when performed by humans" *(ISO/IEC 39794-16)*. "An advanced computer system that can simulate human capabilities, such as analysis, based on a predetermined set of rules" *(ISACA glossary)*. "A technology in which a computing system is coded to 'think for itself', adapting and operating autonomously. AI is increasingly used in more complex tasks, such as medical diagnosis, drug discovery, and predictive maintenance" *(UK National Cyber Security Strategy 2022)*.
Artificial **I**ntelligence **G**overnance **P**rofessional **(AIGP)**	IAPP's professional qualification concerning technological foundations and the **A**rtificial **I**ntelligence **S**oftware **D**evelopment **L**ife**C**ycle, AI's effects on people and principles, applicability of laws, responsible AI governance and risk management, and ongoing issues and concerns. More info: https://store.iapp.org/ai-governance-professional-aigp-online-training/
Artificial **I**ntelligence **(AI) system**	Information Technology system (hardware and software) plus the associated data, network infrastructure, people, *etc.* involved in providing **A**rtificial **I**ntelligence services. "Engineered system that generates outputs such as content, forecasts, recommendations or decisions for a given set of human-defined objectives. Notes: The engineered system can use various techniques and approaches related to artificial intelligence to develop a model to represent data, knowledge, processes, *etc.* which can be used to conduct tasks; AI systems are designed to operate with varying levels of automation" *(ISO/IEC 22989)*.

TERM	MEANING
Artificial SuperIntelligence (ASI)	Concept of an **A**rtificial **I**ntelligence system that substantially exceeds human levels of intelligence, reasoning, *etc.* in general, rather than just in specific areas (narrow AI).
ASI	*Abbrev:* **A**rtificial **S**uper**I**ntelligence.
ASIC	*Abbrev:* **A**pplication-**S**pecific **I**ntegrated **C**ircuit.
ASLR	*Abbrev:* **A**ddress **S**pace **L**ayout **R**andomisation.
ASP	*Abbrev:* **A**pplication **S**ervice **P**rovider.
Assembler	Program that translates assembly language into machine code instructions appropriate for the particular **C**entral **P**rocessing **U**nit on which the code is to execute.
Assembly language	Any low-level programming language using symbolic representations of machine code – similar to shorthand.
Assert, assertion	Unilaterally state or claim something to be true, without *necessarily* having or providing the evidence to prove it, *e.g.* trust centre. "Any formal declaration, or set of declarations, about a subject matter made by management. Note: Assertions should usually be made in writing and commonly contain a list of specific attributes about the subject matter or about a process involving the subject matter" *(ISACA glossary)*.
Assertive	Dominant, coercive, overbearing, or authoritarian, able to exert strong influence on another without resorting to overt aggression or violence. A powerful technique in many social engineering attacks as well as legitimate controlling activities ("Hands up! You're nicked!" for instance).
Assessment, assess	Process of analysing, reviewing, testing, examining, and/or evaluating something to reach an opinion, decision, or judgement. "A broad review of the different aspects of a company or function that includes elements not covered by a structured assurance initiative. Note: May include opportunities for reducing the costs of poor quality, employee perceptions of quality aspects, proposals to senior management on policy, goals, *etc.*" *(ISACA glossary)*. "The action of evaluating, estimating, or judging against defined criteria. Different types of assessment (*i.e.*, qualitative, quantitative, and semi-quantitative) are used to assess risk. Some types of assessment yield measures [or results]" *(NIST SP 800-55v1)*. "The application of expert judgement to devise an examination strategy (see Examination strategy) based upon a framework of circumstances in the form of written submission details, photographs, 'preview' examinations of items, discussions with submitting officers *etc.*, that addresses in an effective way the identified key issues in the case" *(FSRCoP)*.

TERM	MEANING
Assessment result	"The output or outcome of an assessment" *(SP 800-55v1)*.
Assessor	Competent person who conducts an assessment, evaluation, or examination. "Person who leads and conducts a privacy impact assessment. Notes: The assessor may be supported by one or more other internal and/or external experts as part of their team; The assessor may be an expert internal or external to the organization" *(ISO/IEC 29134)*. See also evaluator.
Asset	Something of value to its owner, a resource. May be tangible (*e.g.* a building, hardware, executed contract or licence/approval, person – possibly an agent, cash, or padlock), intangible (*e.g.* knowledge, experience, know-how, skill, capability, competence, tradecraft, information, software, creative idea, concept, relationship, virtual organisation, brand, reputation, trust, loyalty, goodwill, bank credit, application or service, right or permission, understanding, verbal contract, obligation), or indeterminate (*e.g.* trademark, patent, firmware, data, **D**ata**B**ase, system, security). "Legal right or organisational resource which is controllable by an entity and has the capacity to generate economic benefits" *(ISO 10668)*. "Anything that has value to the organization" *(ISO/IEC 27002)*. "Anything of value to an agency, such as IT equipment and software, information, personnel, documentation, reputation and public confidence" *(NZISM)*. "Anything of value, such as ICT equipment, software or data" *(AusISM)*. "Something of either tangible or intangible value that is worth protecting, including people, information, infrastructure, finances and reputation" *(ISACA glossary)*. "The information, information system, or information system component that is breached or impaired by the Threat Agent in a manner whereby its value is diminished or the act introduces liability to the Primary Stakeholder" *(O-RT)*. "Things that have value to anyone involved in the processing of personally identifiable information (PII). Note: In the context of a privacy risk management process, an asset is either PII or a supporting asset" *(ISO/IEC 29134)*. "Item, thing or entity that has potential or actual value to an organization. Notes: Value can be tangible or intangible, financial, or non-financial, and includes consideration of risks and liabilities. It can be positive or negative at different stages of the asset life. Physical assets usually refer to equipment, inventory and properties owned by the organization. Physical assets are the opposite of intangible assets, which are non-physical assets such as leases, brands, digital assets, use rights, licences, intellectual property rights, reputation, or agreements. A grouping of assets referred to as an asset system could also be considered as an asset. Life, health and welfare of humans and other living beings can also be an asset" *(ISO 23234)*. See also information asset. *Cf.* liability.

TERM	MEANING
Asset management	Systematic, professional management of one or more types/classes of assets (such as buildings/properties, financial, computing hardware and software, or information) to achieve objectives specified by their owners, custodians, and other stakeholders.
Asset operator	Person or organisation operating (using, controlling) an asset such as a computer system. *Cf.* asset owner.
Asset owner, liability owner	Organisation, rôle, or person who literally/legally or notionally owns an asset or liability, along with any associated property rights and obligations, responsibilities, or social expectations. May be a custodian, steward, or agent acting on behalf of the legal owner. May be accountable for its protection/security and legitimate exploitation to optimise its value. See also information owner, data owner, file owner, network owner, domain owner, process owner, product owner, risk owner, service owner, system owner.
Asset value	A measure of the worth of an asset to someone, usually its legal owner or possessor. "The value of an asset to both the business and to competitors" *(ISACA glossary)*.
Assignment	Allocation or appointment of someone (usually an employee) to a particular task, rôle, position, project, *etc.*, or the engagement itself – the work package.
Assurance	Provision of a certain level of trust, confidence, confirmation, or proof of something, normally as a result of competently reviewing, checking, testing, or auditing it against relevant specifications, expectations, or objectives, *e.g.* a 'security-assured' program has *presumably* been tested to confirm that it satisfies information security requirements. "The act of objectively and competently evaluating subject matter to provide conclusions and confidence that statements and beliefs about the subject matter are justified and true" *(OCEG GRC Glossary)*. "Statement intended to increase the level of stakeholders' confidence about an organization's governance, risk management, and control processes over an issue, condition, subject matter, or activity under review when compared to established criteria" *(IIA GIAS)*. "An IT audit and assurance professional is engaged to issue a written communication expressing a conclusion about the subject matters for which the accountable party is responsible. Assurance refers to a number of related activities designed to provide the reader or user of the report with a level of assurance or comfort regarding the subject matter. Note: Assurance engagements could include support for audited financial statements, reviews of controls, compliance with required standards and practices, and compliance with agreements, licenses, legislation and regulation" *(ISACA glossary)*.
Assurance actions & controls	"Actions & controls that primarily serve assurance activities" *(OCEG GRC Glossary)*.

TERM	MEANING
Assurance control	Control designed to mitigate unacceptable assurance risks. While assurance is itself a form of detective control (*e.g.* examinations identifying and disclosing issues to management), various controls can strengthen assurance processes, *e.g.* recruitment, training, and oversight to ensure that technology auditors are sufficiently competent, diligent, trustworthy, experienced, *etc.* for their audit engagements.
Assurance engagement, assurance initiative	Assurance engagement. "An objective examination of evidence for the purpose of providing an assessment on risk management, control or governance processes for the enterprise. Note: Examples may include financial, performance, compliance and system security engagements" *(ISACA glossary)*.
Assurance provider	"Someone who conducts assurance activities" *(OCEG GRC Glossary)*.
Assurance risk	Uncertainty relating to the assurance required and provided, *e.g.* whether the particular sampling approach proposed for an audit will or will not discover issues, what kinds of issues it might or might not reveal, and hence whether the approach is appropriate or needs to be reconsidered in a particular situation.
Assurance service	Service providing or relating to some form of assurance, *e.g.* testing, reviewing, inspecting, assessing, auditing. "Services through which internal auditors perform objective assessments to provide assurance. Examples of assurance services include compliance, financial, operational/performance, and technology engagements. Internal auditors may provide limited or reasonable assurance, depending on the nature, timing, and extent of procedures performed" *(IIA GIAS)*.
Asymmetric cryptography, asymmetric encryption/ decryption, public key cryptography	Type of cryptosystem that uses pairs of mathematically related but quite different public and private keys to either encrypt or decrypt. Although the pairs of keys are relatively simple and quick to generate on a computer, it is infeasible to guess or calculate either key from the other without additional information due to the complex mathematics and long key lengths involved. "Cryptography in which a public key and a corresponding private key are used for encryption and decryption. Note: If a public key is used for encryption, the corresponding private key must be used for decryption, and vice versa" *(ISO/IEC 2382)*. See also **P**ublic **K**ey **I**nfrastructure. *Cf.* symmetric cryptography.
Asymmetric cryptography algorithm, asymmetric cipher	Cryptographic algorithm for asymmetric cryptography. "A type of cipher that combines a widely distributed public key and a closely held, protected private key. A message that is encrypted by the public key can only be decrypted by its mathematically related counterpart" *(ISACA glossary)*.

TERM	MEANING
Asynchronous **T**ransfer **M**ode **(ATM)**	"A high-bandwidth, low-delay switching and multiplexing technology that allows integration of real-time voice, video and data. It is a data-link layer protocol. Note: ATM is a protocol-independent transport mechanism. It allows high-speed data transfer rates of up to 155 Mbit/s." *(ISACA glossary)* *Cf.* **A**utomated **T**eller **M**achine.
Asynchronous transmission	Type of digital datacommunications protocol or modulation method in which each character of a message is preceded by a start bit and followed by one or two stop bits (and, often, a parity bit) to distinguish it from the unmodulated carrier. "A transmission method where characters are sent one at a time" *(ISACA glossary)*. *Cf.* synchronous transmission.
ATM	*Abbrev:* **A**synchronous **T**ransfer **M**ode or **A**utomated **T**eller **M**achine or **At** **T**he **M**oment, depending on context.
AtomBombing	Code injection exploit that alters the atom tables used internally by Windows to store and communicate strings during program execution.
Atomic	"A condition of smart contracts where one or more conditions defined by the smart contract must be met for the transaction to execute in its entirety" *(ISACA glossary)*. See also smart contract.
Atomic swap	"A peer-to-peer exchange of assets across separate blockchains triggered by predetermined rules, without the use of a third-party service and through the use of self-enforced smart contracts. It requires an exchange of assets on both sides or the transaction will not occur" *(ISACA glossary)*. See also smart contract.
ATT&CK (Adversarial Tactics, Techniques, & Common Knowledge)	MITRE's taxonomy/**D**ata**B**ase of cyber-attack tactics and techniques, first published in 2015. Contrived name complements D3FEND. "ATT&CK is a knowledge base of cyber adversary behavior and taxonomy for adversarial actions across their lifecycle. ATT&CK has two parts: ATT&CK for Enterprise, which covers behavior against enterprise IT networks and cloud, and ATT&CK for Mobile, which focuses on behavior against mobile devices" *(MITRE ATT&CK FAQ)*. More info: https://attack.mitre.org/
Attack	Type of information security incident actively and deliberately perpetrated by someone (the attacker or adversary) on one or more victims (people and/or organisations) without their permission. *Cf.* accident or natural event. Taking control of more than half the mining power of a cryptocurrency blockchain network may be called a "51% attack." "Attempt to violate computer security. Examples: Malicious logic, wiretapping" *(ISO/IEC 2382)*. "Attempt to destroy, expose, alter, disable, steal or gain unauthorized access to or make unauthorized use of an asset" *(ISO/IEC 27000)*. "Successful or unsuccessful unauthorized attempt to destroy, alter, disable, gain access to an asset or any attempt to expose, steal, or make unauthorized use of an asset" *(ISO/IEC 27002)*. "An actual occurrence of an adverse event" *(ISACA glossary)*.

TERM	MEANING
Attacker	Adversary who deliberately mounts an attack. "Person deliberately exploiting vulnerabilities in technical and non-technical security controls in order to steal or compromise information systems and networks, or to compromise availability to legitimate users of information system and network resources" *(ISO/IEC 27033-1)*.
Attack mechanism	The method and means by which an attack is perpetrated. "A method used to deliver the exploit. Unless the attacker is personally performing the attack, an attack mechanism may involve a payload, or container, that delivers the exploit to the target" *(ISACA glossary)*.
Attack surface	Notional 3-dimensional representation of the organisation's information assets, risks, *etc.* where one axis in some way represents vulnerabilities and/or their exposure by various parts of the organisation, forming a complex and dynamic 'surface' that might be actively attacked or exploited by hackers, malware, *etc.* to the corresponding extent. Implies that improving the protection of information assets and/or reducing the exposure or extent of vulnerabilities will somehow improve the organisation's information security and reduce the area … without necessarily stating how that might be achieved. A security metric. "The IT equipment and software used in a system. The greater the attack surface the greater the chances are of an attacker finding an exploitable vulnerability" *(NZISM)*. "The amount of ICT equipment and software used in a system. The greater the attack surface the greater the chances of an adversary finding an exploitable security vulnerability" *(AusISM)*. See also security landscape, risk universe, risk profile, heatmap.
Attack toolkit	See crimeware.
Attack vector	Path, process, or mechanism by which a vulnerable network, system, device, application, organisation, building, site, model, *etc.* might be actively compromised and exploited by an adversary. "Path or means by which an attacker can gain access to a computer or network server in order to deliver a malicious outcome [such as] IoT devices [and] smart phones" *(ISO/IEC 27032)*. "A path or route used by the adversary to gain access to the target (asset). Note: There are two types of attack vectors: ingress and egress (also known as data exfiltration)" *(ISACA glossary)*.
Attagging	Use of **Q**uick **R**esponse codes (perhaps stuck on top of legitimate QR codes) containing malicious JavaScript or **U**niform **R**esource **L**ocators linking to infectious or phishing websites. Exploits victims' naïveté regarding the threat and inability to interpret the codes by eye.

TERM	MEANING
Attention mechanism	Facility for an **A**rtificial **I**ntelligence system to focus on (pay extra attention to) heavily weighted parts of the content during the training process. "In artificial intelligence (AI), a powerful feature used in machine learning (ML) and deep learning (DL) that weights the importance of different inputs, thus enhancing the model's ability to process and interpret complex data patterns, leading to more accurate and relevant outcomes" *(ISACA glossary)*.
Attest, attestation	Formally documented assertion by a duly authorised and accountable person that the organisation complies with (fulfils the requirements of) particular laws/regulations or professional practices such as relevant governance, accounting, and audit standards. Although highly stylised and carefully worded to exclude other liabilities, the signatories are personally accountable for the veracity of such statements; hence, attestation is usually taken very seriously, making it a surprisingly powerful administrative control, akin to taking an oath. "An engagement in which an IT auditor is engaged to either examine management's assertion regarding a particular subject matter or the subject matter directly" *(ISACA glossary)*.
Attribute	a. *[Noun]* Measurable or observable characteristic, quality, or parameter. "Property or characteristic of an object that can be distinguished quantitatively or qualitatively by human or automated means" *(ISO/IEC 27000)*. b. *[Verb]* To ascribe the source, origin, or ownership of something. See also provenance.
Attribute-**B**ased **A**ccess **C**ontrol **(ABAC)**	"An access control method where subject requests to perform operations on objects are granted or denied based on assigned attributes of the subject, assigned attributes of the object, environment conditions, and a set of policies that are specified in terms of those attributes and conditions" *(NIST SP 800-162)*. *Cf.* **R**ule-**B**ased **A**ccess **C**ontrol, **R**ôle-**B**ased **A**ccess **C**ontrol, **R**ealm-**B**ased **A**ccess **C**ontrol.
Attribute-**B**ased **U**nlinkable **E**ntity **A**uthentication **(ABUEA)**	Means for people to authenticate themselves anonymously, without revealing so much personal information that their identity can be 'linked' (inferred or determined) from other information, thereby compromising their privacy. See ISO/IEC 27551.

TERM	MEANING
Attribute sample	Quality Control/audit sampling method that compares the rate of occurrence of item characteristics (*e.g.* visible defects in goods on a production line, inaccurate or dubious financial figures in a ledger, suspicious entries in a log or evidence of noncompliance) to determine whether a response is justified (*e.g.* reject the entire batch or investigate further). Can also be used for Quality Assurance and process improvement, *e.g.* to identify adverse trends worthy of management attention, hopefully forestalling the occurrence of quality failures or other incidents. "A method to select a portion of a population based on the presence or absence of a certain characteristic" *(ISACA glossary)*. See also stratified sample, random sample, systematic stratified sample, time series analysis, convenience sample, discovery sample.
Attribute value	"Specific occurrence of an attribute. Example: 'Blue' is an attribute value for the attribute 'color'" *(ISO/IEC 2382)*.
Attribution	a. Acknowledgement referencing or citing the attributed source, originator, and/or owner of Intellectual Property being reproduced elsewhere in order to thank them and (hopefully) reduce the risk of being accused of plagiarism or copyright abuse. Although legally speaking attribution *may* be irrelevant to copyright infringement, it is generally considered ethical, polite, helpful, and valuable. Be nice! b. Cybersecurity incidents are often blamed on (attributed to) certain perpetrators according to someone's evaluation of evidence in the malware or hacking tools used, or other clues such as the demands and claims made. However, perpetrators of illegal acts are (for obvious reasons) keen to remain undercover and may deliberately mislead analysts (false-flags). Furthermore, attacks often involve a blend of code, tools, and techniques from disparate sources, obtained through the hacking underground scene. "Process of attempting to assign a device to an individual and may be progressed through a number of different methods, each method having different risks. Cell site analysis may be one method by which patterns of usage may be assessed against what would be expected if a given device was used by a specific person, as opposed to if it was not used by that person" *(FSRCoP)*.
Audience	People who are the *intended* recipients of one or more communicated messages, as distinct from those who actually receive them (*e.g.* by interception or surveillance). "The person or group that is intended to receive a message" *(OCEG GRC Glossary)*.

TERM	MEANING
Audit	Structured, formal, and disciplined assurance process of systematic examination, review, assessment, testing, consideration, evaluation, and reporting by one or more competent and trusted people who – crucially – are independent of the subject area or matters being audited. In many organisations, 'audit' also refers to the business department or function (usually Internal Audit, Quality Audit, *etc.*) and/or third party organisation (External Audit) responsible for auditing. Derived from the Latin *audio* (to listen). "Systematic, independent and documented process for obtaining audit evidence and evaluating it objectively to determine the extent to which the audit criteria are fulfilled. Notes: An audit can be an internal audit (first party) or an external audit (second party or third party), and it can be a combined audit (combining two or more disciplines). 'Audit evidence' and 'audit criteria' are defined in ISO 19011" *(ISO/IEC 27000)*. [Additional note] "An internal audit is conducted by the organization itself, or by an external party on its behalf" *(ISO/IEC 42001)*. "A formal inspection and verification to check whether a standard or set of guidelines is being followed, records are accurate or efficiency and effectiveness targets are being met. Note: May be carried out by internal or external groups" *(ISACA glossary)*. "A structured process of examination, review, assessment, testing and reporting against defined requirements or objectives. Auditors should be independent of any IT system, business process, agency, function, site, supplier or other subject area being audited" *(NZISM)*. "Information gathering and analysis of assets to ensure such things as policy compliance and security from vulnerabilities" *(SANS glossary)*. "A systematic, independent and documented process for obtaining evidence and evaluating it objectively to determine the extent to which specified criteria are fulfilled. In forensic science an audit usually involves determining whether the forensic unit's quality procedures have been complied with" *(FSRCoP)*.
Auditability	Measure of the capability of being audited. This assurance objective for important systems, processes, business relationships, *etc.* implies the need to generate and retain high-integrity records of relevant events and activities (*e.g.* security logs) that can be independently reviewed if and when required, along with transparency and trustworthiness. A significant challenge for **A**rtificial **I**ntelligence systems. "The level to which transactions can be traced and audited through a system" *(ISACA glossary)*.

TERM	MEANING
Auditable unit	See audit universe. "The subjects, units or systems that are capable of being defined and evaluated. Notes: Auditable units may include: Policies, procedures and practices; Cost centers, profit centers and investment centers; General ledger account balances; Information systems (manual and computerized); Major contracts and programs; Organizational units, such as product or service lines; Functions, such as information technology (IT), purchasing, marketing, production, finance, accounting and human resources (HR); Transaction systems for activities, such as sales, collection, purchasing, disbursement, inventory and cost accounting, production, treasury, payroll, and capital assets; Financial statements; Laws and regulations" *(ISACA glossary)*.
Audit accountability	The audit function and individual auditors can be held to account by an authority (typically the Board of Directors or Audit Committee) for failing to achieve specified objectives and expectations, as can every other business function or person. "A performance measurement of service delivery including cost, timeliness and quality against agreed service levels" *(ISACA glossary)*.
Audit authority	Authority formally assigned to an audit function, team, or individual through applicable statutes, policies, and contracts by stakeholders such as senior management, permitting their access to relevant information necessary to perform their duties. "A statement of an employee's position within the enterprise, including lines of reporting and the rights of access" *(ISACA glossary)*.
Audit charter	High-level scope and purpose or mission statement for the audit function. "A document approved by those charged with governance that defines the purpose, authority and responsibility of the internal audit activity. Notes: The charter should: Establish the internal audit function's position within the enterprise; Authorize access to records, personnel and physical properties relevant to the performance of IS audit and assurance engagements; Define the scope of audit function's activities" *(ISACA glossary)*. See also internal audit charter.
Audit checklist	Aspects of concern or items of evidence that an auditor intends to gather, investigate, and evaluate during an audit engagement. The document format reflects the auditor's personal preferences and style, *e.g.* **I**nternal **C**ontrols **Q**uestionnaire, mind map, or 'shopping list.'
Auditee	Person, function, department, or organisation being audited.

TERM	MEANING
Audit engagement	A specific audit with its authorised scope and purpose or objectives (*e.g.* plan and resources, and in due course the findings, evidence, analysis, and report arising). "A specific audit assignment, task or review activity, such as an audit, control self-assessment review, fraud examination or consultancy. An audit engagement may include multiple tasks or activities designed to accomplish a specific set of related objectives" *(ISACA glossary)*.
Audit evidence	The evidence gathered and analysed in the course of an audit engagement, typically consisting of copies of pertinent documentation, the auditors' contemporaneous notes or transcripts from interviews, meetings and observations, and digital content retrieved from computer systems. "The information used to support the audit opinion" *(ISACA glossary)*.
Audit expert system	"The expert or decision support systems that can be used to assist IS auditors in the decision-making process by automating the knowledge of experts in the field. Note: This technique includes automated risk analysis, systems software and control objectives software packages" *(ISACA glossary)*.
Audit file	a. Hardcopy and/or digital file/s containing information relating to an audit engagement, such as the scope and objectives, plan, working papers (*e.g.* audit checklist), audit evidence, findings, analysis, and report. Constitutes the formal, definitive record of a completed audit. Generally valuable and confidential; hence must be adequately secured. b. Audit log.
Audit independence, auditor independence	Capability, opportunity, and resolute determination of an auditor to gather evidence and analyse information dispassionately, deciding, acting, and reporting independently, free of undue influence, interference, constraint, or pressure from auditees. Implies or involves detached impartiality and objectivity without bias and prejudice, acting with absolute integrity, fairness, neutrality, balance, even-handedness, *etc*. An *essential* factor and unique driver of value in auditing, particularly a competent, diligent, and trustworthy auditor's state of mind and attitudes, regardless of their employment status or reporting line. "1. Self-governance. 2. The freedom from conditions that threaten objectivity or the appearance of objectivity. Such threats to objectivity must be managed at the individual auditor, engagement, functional and organizational levels. Independence includes Independence of mind and Independence in appearance" *(ITAF)*. "The state of being free from structural or functional conditions that threaten the ability of the assurance provider to perform assurance activities with objectivity and without any undue influence. It includes the independence of the assurance provider from those who own, manage, operate,

TERM	MEANING
	or support the activity being assured" *(OCEG GRC Glossary)*. "The freedom from conditions that may impair the ability of the internal audit function to carry out internal audit responsibilities in an unbiased manner" *(IIA GIAS)*. See also agency.
Audit log	Formally documented historical sequence (a data file) of significant security events such as logons, authorisations, bypasses/overrides, alerts, and security/audit configuration changes, defined according to system configuration parameters, securely recorded in real time primarily for subsequent audit and forensic purposes. "A chronological record of system activities, including records of system accesses and operations performed in a given period" *(NIST SP 800-171)*. *Cf.* audit trail.
Audit logging	Privileged process/act of generating and appending audit records to an audit log. "Recording of data on information security events for the purpose of review and analysis, and ongoing monitoring" *(ISO/IEC 27033-1)*.
Audit objective	Objective, purpose, or goal/s of an audit engagement – what it was expected or required to achieve. "The specific goal(s) of an audit. Note: These often center on substantiating the existence of internal controls to minimize business risk" *(ISACA glossary)*.
Auditor	Person performing an audit. An independent specialist with a challenging vocation. "Person who conducts an audit" *(ISO/IEC 17021-1)*
Auditor's opinion	"A formal statement expressed by the IS audit or assurance professional that describes the scope of the audit, the procedures used to produce the report and whether or not the findings support that the audit criteria have been met. Notes: The types of opinions are: Unqualified opinion—Notes no exceptions or none of the exceptions noted aggregate to a significant deficiency; Qualified opinion—Notes exceptions aggregated to a significant deficiency (but not a material weakness); Adverse opinion—Notes one or more significant deficiencies aggregating to a material weakness" *(ISACA glossary)*.
Audit plan	Given finite resources (*e.g.* auditors, auditees, time, money, management support), audit engagements are prioritised, scoped, and scheduled to optimise the value generated by satisfying audit objectives, *e.g.* providing assurance regarding the organisation's management of significant risks or compliance. "1. A plan containing the nature, timing and extent of audit procedures to be performed by engagement team members in order to obtain sufficient appropriate audit evidence to form an opinion. Notes: Includes the areas to be audited, the type of work planned, the high-level objectives and scope of the work, and topics such as budget, resource allocation, schedule dates, type of report and its intended audience and other general aspects of the work. 2. A high-level description of the audit work to be performed in a certain period of time" *(ISACA glossary)*.

TERM	MEANING
Audit program	Plan for an individual audit engagement. "A step-by-step set of audit procedures and instructions that should be performed to complete an audit" *(ISACA glossary)*.
Audit record	Record in an audit log or trail, or pertinent evidence obtained by auditors during the course of an audit engagement. "An individual entry in an audit log related to an audited event" *(NIST SP 800-171)*.
Audit responsibility	Responsibility associated with auditing, such as considering the evidence dispassionately, without bias, prejudice, fear, or favour. "The roles, scope and objectives documented in the service level agreement (SLA) between management and audit" *(ISACA glossary)*.
Audit risk	Risk affecting or arising from audit engagements such as misinformation, disinformation, deception, collusion, coercion, social engineering, bribery, fraud, false or misleading accusations; management interference, pressure, diversion or misdirection, inappropriate restriction or exploitation of privileged access; accidental damage to the information security of information systems, data or information; noncompliance, nonconformity; inappropriate/undue reliance on ineffective, inaccurate, or unreliable information, controls, people, organisations, systems, processes, reports, plans, promises, *etc.*; scope, budget or timescale blowouts, inordinate delays, untimely reporting; incompetent, inept or plain lazy auditing, poor planning, inadequate resourcing, failing to identify, correctly diagnose or disclose relevant matters, inadequate, inaccurate, incomplete or misleading assurance; undue stress, intimidation, threats, physical violence, *etc*. "The risk of reaching an incorrect conclusion based upon audit findings. Notes: The three components of audit risk are: Control risk; Detection risk; Inherent risk" *(ISACA glossary)*. See also audit subject matter risk.
Audit sampling	It unusual to be able to analyse *all* data points in depth during an audit engagement, so most audits involve a representative subset of the data selected by the auditor/s using an appropriate sampling method. "The application of audit procedures to less than 100 percent of the items within a population to obtain evidence about a particular characteristic of the population" *(ISACA glossary)*. See also data sample, random sample, stratified sample, systematic stratified sample, time series analysis, attribute sample, discovery sample.
Audit scope	Scope (intended and authorised coverage, less any explicit exclusions) of an individual audit or of the audit function as a whole. "Extent and boundaries of an audit. Notes: The audit scope generally includes a description of the physical and virtual-locations, functions, organizational units, activities and processes, as well as the time period covered; A virtual location is where an organization performs work or provides a service using an on-line environment allowing individuals irrespective of physical locations to execute processes" *(ISO 19011)*.

TERM	MEANING
Audit subject matter risk	Risk associated with whatever is being audited. "The risk relevant to the area under review: Business risk (customer capability to pay, credit worthiness, market factors, *etc.*); Contract risk (liability, price, type, penalties, *etc.*); Country risk (political, environment, security, *etc.*); Project risk (resources, skill set, methodology, product stability, *etc.*); Technology risk (solution, architecture, hardware and software infrastructure network, delivery channels, *etc.*)" *(ISACA glossary)*.
Audit time	The allotted hour, day, week, period or eternity in which audits take place. Strangely, the clock runs slower for auditees than for auditors, a phenomenon known as audit relativity. "Time needed to plan and accomplish a complete and effective audit of the client organization's management system" *(ISO/IEC 17021-1)*.
Audit tools	"Automated tools to aid the analysis of the contents of audit logs" *(ISO/IEC 27033-1)*.
Audit trail	Chronological records of important transactions or stages in a business or computer process, which may be used to reconstruct the exact sequence of events, *e.g.* an **I**nformation **T**echnology system security log is typically configured to record important information such as successful and failed system logons, and security alarms and alerts with timestamps. "A logical path linking a sequence of events, in the form of data, used to trace the transactions that have affected the contents of a record" *(ISACA glossary)*. "Data collected for the potential use in a security audit" *(ISO/IEC 2382)*. *Cf.* audit log.
Audit universe	Expansive view of all the in-scope areas or aspects (auditable units) that might potentially be audited at some point. "An inventory of audit areas that is compiled and maintained to identify areas for audit during the audit planning process. Notes: Traditionally, the list includes all financial and key operational systems and other units that would be audited as part of the overall cycle of planned work. The audit universe serves as the source from which the annual audit schedule is prepared. The universe will be periodically revised to reflect changes in the overall risk profile" *(ISACA glossary)*. See also audit plan.
Augmented intelligence	Combination or supplementation of natural human intelligence with **A**rtificial **I**ntelligence.

TERM	MEANING
Augmented reality	Real-time computer analysis of a scene to provide supplementary information, *e.g.* a 'head-up display' with a computer-generated visual overlay superimposed on the real scene, or 'force feedback' giving a pilot or driver physical cues through the vehicle controls about potentially dangerous operating conditions. "A computer-generated simulation that adds enhancements to existing reality enabling a user to interact with reality in a more meaningful way. It is often accessed through mobile applications that blend digital enhancements with the real world while ensuring that the user can easily distinguish between the two" *(ISACA glossary)*.
AUP	*Abbrev:* **A**cceptable **U**se **P**olicy.
Australia **I**nformation **S**ecurity **M**anual **(AusISM)**	"A cybersecurity framework that an organisation can apply, using their risk management framework, to protect their information technology and operational technology systems, applications and data from cyberthreats. The ISM is intended for chief information security officers, chief information officers, cybersecurity professionals and information technology managers." More info: https://www.cyber.gov.au/business-and-government/cyber-security-frameworks/ism
Australian **C**yber **S**ecurity **C**entre **(ACSC)**	Australian government's cybersecurity agency. Part of the **A**ustralian **S**ignals **D**irectorate, based at the **A**ustralian **S**ignals **I**ntelligence **O**rganisation in Canberra. Spooky. More info: https://www.cyber.gov.au/about-us
Authentic, authenticity	Verifiably genuine, not counterfeit or fake. "Property that an entity is what it claims to be" *(ISO/IEC 27002)*. "The property of being genuine and being able to be verified and trusted; confidence in the validity of a transmission, a message, or message originator" *(NIST SP 800-39)*.
Authentication, authentication control, authenticate	Control process or mechanism in which a specific individual user, system, message, block of data, *etc.* is positively identified and confirmed authentic, typically on the basis of something they know (*e.g.* a secret password) and sometimes something they have (credentials), something they are (meaning biometrics), and/or where they are (their virtual/network or physical location). Usually involves cryptography. Authentication is a critical and hence inherently risky control: if the process fails, is bypassed, undermined, spoofed, or disabled, dependent security controls (such as access controls, audit trails, logging, and alerting) are also rendered ineffective, often with no indication initially of anything amiss. "Act of verifying the claimed identity of an entity" *(ISO/IEC 2382)*. "Provision of assurance that a claimed characteristic of an entity is correct" *(ISO/IEC 27002)*. "1. The act of verifying identity, *i.e.*, user, system. Note: Can also refer to the verification of the correctness of a piece of data. [or] 2. The act of verifying the identity of a user or the user's eligibility to access computerized information.

TERM	MEANING
	Note: Authentication is designed to protect against fraudulent logon activity. It can also refer to the verification of the correctness of a piece of data" *(ISACA glossary)*. "The process of identifying an individual, device or system before granting access to system resources or data. Usually based on a set of credentials such as an identifier (such as a user or device name) and an authenticator (such as a password or some other authentication factor). Authentication is distinct from Authorisation" *(NZISM)*. "Verifying the identity of a user, process or device as a prerequisite to allowing access to resources in a system" *(AusISM)*. "Process of confirming the correctness of the claimed identity" *(SANS glossary)*. "A set of controls that are used to verify the identity of a user, or other entity, interacting with the software" *(SCP QRG)*. "The process of verifying the identity or other attributes claimed by or assumed of an entity (user, process, or device) or to verify the source and integrity of data" *(**T**rust **S**ervices **C**riteria)*. "The process of verifying the identity, or other attributes of a user, process or device" *(UK National Cyber Security Strategy 2022)*. "Verifying the identity of a user, process, or device, often as a prerequisite to allowing access to resources in a system" *(NIST SP 800-171)*. See also authorisation, validation, verification.
Authentication, **A**uthorisation, and **A**ccounting **(AAA)**	Important computer security controls associated with the logon process, *i.e.* authentication to verify the user's claimed identity, authorisation or allocation of the user's defined access rights and permissions, and logging relevant details concerning the user's logon and subsequent activities for accounting, accountability, and auditing purposes. See also **I**dentification **&** **A**uthentication.
Authentication **H**eader **(AH)**	"The protocol used to provide connectionless integrity and data-origin authentication for Internet Protocol (IP) datagrams and to provide protection against replays (RFC 4302). Notes: AH ensures data integrity with a checksum that a message authentication code, such as MD5, generates. To ensure data-origin authentication, AH includes a secret shared key in the algorithm that it uses for authentication. To ensure replay protection, AH uses a sequence number field within the IP authentication header" *(ISACA glossary)*. "Part of the protocol used for authentication within IPSec, it provides authentication, integrity and anti-replay for the entire packet (both the header and data payload)" *(NZISM)*. "A protocol used in Internet Protocol Security (IPsec) that provides data integrity and data origin authenticity but not confidentiality" *(AusISM)*.
Authentication mechanism	Means of authenticating something or someone's asserted identity, validity, *etc.* "Hardware or software-based mechanisms that force users to prove their identity before accessing data on a device" *(NIST SP 800-101)*.

TERM	MEANING
Authentication system	"A system or mechanism used to identify a user through associating an incoming request with a set of identifying credentials. The credentials provided are compared to those on a file in a database of the authorized user's information on a local operating system, user directory service, or within an authentication server. Examples of authentication systems can include active directory, MultiFactor Authentication (MFA), biometrics, and tokens" *(CIS Controls)*.
Authenticator	See token. "Something the claimant possesses and controls (typically a cryptographic module or password) that is used to authenticate the claimant's identity. This was previously referred to as a token" *(NIST SP 800-63-4)*.
Authenticator Assurance Level **(AAL)**	"A category describing the strength of the authentication process" *(NIST SP 800-63-3)*.
Authenticity	Measure of truth, authenticity, and veracity. "Property that an entity is what it claims to be" *(ISO/IEC 27000)*. "The concept of undisputed authorship" *(ISACA glossary)*. "Validity and conformance of the original information" *(SANS glossary)*.
Authorisation, authorise, approval	Permitted, accepted, and/or agreed by management or some other authority as being in the best interests of the organisation, the workforce, the stakeholders, or society at large. "Granting of rights, which includes the granting of access based on access rights" *(ISO/IEC 2382)*. "The process of determining if the end user is permitted to have access to an information asset or the information system containing the asset" *(ISACA glossary)*. "The process of granting (or revoking) access privileges to an individual, device or system" *(NZISM)*. "Approval, permission, or empowerment for someone or something to do something" *(SANS glossary)*. "The official management decision given by a senior organizational official to authorize operation of an information system and to explicitly accept the risk to organizational operations (including mission, functions, image, or reputation), organizational assets, individuals, other organizations, and the Nation based on the implementation of an agreed-upon set of security controls" *(NIST SP 800-39)*. "A set of controls that grant or deny a user, or other entity, access to a system resource. This is usually based on hierarchical roles and individual privileges within a role, but also includes system to system interactions" *(SCP QRG)*. "The process of granting access privileges to a user, program, or process by a person that has the authority to grant such access" *(**Trust Services Criteria**)*. *Cf.* unauthorised.

TERM	MEANING
Authorisation system	"A system or mechanism used to determine access levels or user/client privileges related to system resources including files, services, computer programs, data, and application features. An authorization system grants or denies access to a resource based on the user's identity. Examples of authorization systems can include active directory, access control lists, and role-based access control lists" *(CIS Controls)*.
Authorised representative	"A natural or legal person established within the Union who has received a written mandate from a manufacturer to act on its behalf in relation to specified tasks" *(EU CRA)*.
Authorising officer	"An executive with the authority to formally accept the security risks associated with the operation of a system and to authorise it to operate" *(AusISM)*.
Authority	a. Person, rôle, organisation, *etc.* of high status or seniority (such as a manager, regulator, government agency, tribal elder, or significant other) or a stakeholder that commands respect, compliance, and/or obedience, thus exerting influence or control over subordinates by the threat or action of calling them to account. b. Power to make decisions, allocate resources, determine priorities, *etc.*
Autodiscovery	Some servers advertise their information services (such as multimedia or printing) by routinely broadcasting network messages, allowing them to be 'discovered' (contacted, used) by other nodes on the network.
Automated application control	Application control that operates automatically, without contemporaneous human intervention. "The controls that have been programmed and embedded within an application" *(ISACA glossary)*.
Automated **C**ertificate **M**anagement **E**nvironment **(ACME)**	Protocol for administering digital certificates, defined in RFC 8555. More info: https://www.rfc-editor.org/info/rfc8555
Automated control	Control embedded in an electronic or mechanical system, capable of operating automatically or autonomously, without contemporaneous human intervention, *e.g.* the governor on a steam engine. See also automated application control. *Cf.* manual control.
Automated decision-making	"Process of making a decision by automated means without any human involvement" *(ISO/IEC 27562)*.

TERM	MEANING
Automated testing	Many forms of testing can be partially if not fully automated, ranging from simply recording and replaying manual tests (*e.g.* for regression testing and multiple-choice tests for professional qualifications) to systematically applying varying loads in stress testing or checking the quality and security of complex source code. Testing tools or suites can help by: generating and managing test data and environments (*e.g.* virtual systems); planning, orchestrating, and executing tests; dynamically modifying, curtailing, or extending tests depending on findings; measuring and recording, analysing, evaluating, and reporting test results.
Automatic, automation, automated	Works independently and mechanistically, without contemporaneous and deliberate human involvement or action. "Pertaining to a process or system that, under specified conditions, functions without human intervention" *(ISO/IEC 22989)*. See also autonomous.
Automatic summarisation	"Task of shortening a portion of natural language content or text while retaining important semantic information" *(ISO/IEC 22989)*.
Automation and control solution	Product allegedly able to satisfy customer requirements for automation and control, thereby 'solving' their problems.
Automation and Control System **(ACS), automation system**	Operational Technology system.
Autonomous, autonomy	Self-determined and self-controlled, capable of operating independently, receiving and analysing sensory inputs, making smart decisions and taking appropriate actions without contemporaneous human intervention, *e.g.* self-driving/driverless cars, drones, and robots. "Characteristic of a system that is capable of modifying its intended domain of use or goal without external intervention, control or oversight" *(ISO/IEC 22989)*. See also automatic.
Autonomous system	Autonomous system. "One network or series of networks that are all under one administrative control. An autonomous system is also sometimes referred to as a routing domain. An autonomous system is assigned a globally unique number, sometimes called an Autonomous System Number (ASN)" *(SANS glossary)*. "A collection of IP networks for which the routing is under the control of a specific entity or domain" *(UK National Cyber Security Strategy 2022)*.
Autonomous weapon	'Fire-and-forget' cyberweapon capable of acting autonomously using Artificial Intelligence to complete complex reconnaissance, surveillance, and/or combat missions with little if any direct involvement and real-time control by human operators, in contrast to remote-controlled or dumb weapons. May be a physical device or malware.
Autorooter	Software tool (malware) that gives hackers or script kiddies highly privileged 'root' access to vulnerable systems.

TERM	MEANING
Availability	Core objective of information security, along with confidentiality and integrity comprising the CIA triad. Availability primarily concerns the requirement for information, systems, people, and processes to be operational and accessible when needed, implying the use of resilience and/or recovery controls to guard against unacceptable disruption or interruption of necessary services. "Ability of a functional unit to be in a state to perform a required function under given conditions at a given instant of time or over a given time interval, assuming that the required external resources are provided. Note: The availability defined here is an intrinsic availability where external resources other than maintenance resources do not affect the availability of the functional unit. Operational availability, on the other hand, requires that the external resources be provided. [and] property of data or of resources being accessible and usable on demand by an authorized entity" *(ISO/IEC 2382)*. "Property of being accessible and usable upon demand by an authorized entity" *(ISO/IEC 27000)*. "The ability to ensure timely and reliable access to, and use of, information" *(ISACA glossary)*. "The assurance that systems and data are accessible and useable by authorised entities when required" *(AusISM)*. "The need to ensure that the business purpose of the system can be met and that it is accessible to those who need to use it" *(SANS glossary)*. "A measure of a system's accessibility and usability" *(SCP QRG)*. "Ensuring timely and reliable access to and use of information" *(NIST SP 800-171)*.
Availability control	Control designed to mitigate unacceptable availability risks. Its main purpose is to maintain availability of information and information services at a desired or necessary level (resilience and performance), or to regain availability following an incident or outage (recovery). See also integrity control, confidentiality control.
Availability risk	Risk involving or affecting the availability of information, such as uncertainty as to whether it will or will not be accessible when actually required for some purpose, leading to unclear consequences. "The risk that service may be lost or data are not accessible when needed" *(ISACA glossary)*. See also information risk, information security risk, confidentiality risk, integrity risk.
Avalanche	Global cybercriminal botnet infrastructure used for phishing, malware distribution, and money mule recruitment.
Average precision	Measurement function used to improve the quality of **A**rtificial **I**ntelligence models. "A metric for summarizing the performance of a ranked sequence of results. Average precision is calculated by taking the average of the precision values for each relevant result in a ranked list (each result in the ranked list where the recall increases relative to the previous result)" *(ISACA glossary)*.

TERM	MEANING
Avoid design option	See risk avoidance. "A design option to cease all activity or terminate sources that give rise to the opportunity, obstacle, or obligation" *(OCEG GRC Glossary)*.
Aware, awareness	Vigilant and alert, with a heightened capability to recognise, appreciate, and respond appropriately and promptly to changing circumstances. "The idea of being acquainted with, mindful of, conscious of and well informed on a specific subject, which implies knowing and understanding a subject and acting accordingly" *(ISACA glossary)*. See also security awareness.
AWS	*Abbrev:* **A**mazon **W**eb **S**ervices.
Axiom	Fundamental information security policy requirement, architectural principle, or rule. Axioms may be derived from first principles, and/or from sources such as the control objectives originally defined in BS 7799 to justify and underpin the organisation's information security policy statements, standards, procedures, guidelines, and controls.
Azure	Brand name for Microsoft's global cloud infrastructure. See also **A**mazon **W**eb **S**ervices, **G**oogle **C**loud **P**latform.
Azure Active Directory	See Microsoft Entra ID.

B

TERM	MEANING
B2B	*Abbrev:* **B**usiness-**to**-**B**usiness.
B2C	*Abbrev:* **B**usiness-**to**-**C**onsumer.
BabyShark	Malware species used by the Kimsuky hacker group. Script written in **V**isual **B**asic.
Backbone	High-capacity infrastructural 'trunk route' digital network typically linking data centres, cities, and countries. "The main communication channel of a digital network. It is the part of a network that handles major traffic. Notes: Employs the highest-speed transmission paths in the network and may also run the longest distances. Smaller networks are attached to the backbone, and networks that connect directly to the end-user or customer are called 'access networks.' A backbone can span a geographic area of any size, from a single building to an office complex to an entire country. Or, it can be as small as a backplane in a single cabinet" *(ISACA glossary)*.
Back channel	See covert channel.
Backdoor	Cryptic control bypass function in a program allowing users to access the system or decrypt content without proper authorisation. Sometimes coded in for legitimate software development, testing, or support purposes (*e.g.* 'cheat codes' used to bypass/shortcut past the early stages in an electronic game), occasionally for dubious, unethical, nefarious, or malicious purposes (*e.g.* hacking, coercion, embezzlement, fraud or covert licence compliance checks, or introduced by malware), or for intelligence purposes (*e.g.* Skipjack, Dual_EC_DRBG). "A means of regaining access to a compromised system by installing software or configuring existing software to enable remote access under attacker-defined conditions" *(ISACA glossary)*. "A tool installed after a compromise to give an attacker easier access to the compromised system around any security mechanisms that are in place" *(SANS glossary)*. *Cf.* trapdoor, bug.
Background check	Preemployment screening process that evaluates a candidate or new starter's social and family situation, identity, employment record, qualifications, immigration status, criminal record, credit status, *etc.* to identify possible security and trustworthiness issues. A service often provided by specialist suppliers. The nature, extent, and thoroughness of the checks varies widely in practice due to legal and time constraints, privacy concerns, policy, costs and practicalities, the requirements of the rôle, *etc.* See also security clearance, positive vetting.
Backpropagation	"An algorithm for iteratively adjusting the weights used in a neural network system. Backpropagation is often used to implement gradient descent" *(ISACA glossary)*.

TERM	MEANING
Backup	Snapshot copy of data, programs, configurations, *etc.* from a computer system at a given point in time. In theory, backups enable recovery to a known state after an incident (such as a ransomware infection or data centre fire) but in practice things don't always go to plan. Integrity and availability are critical concerns for backups, plus confidentiality if the information content is sensitive; hence, backups should be risk-assessed and appropriately secured, normally by means of documented policies and procedures, redundancy (multiple backup copies, stored diversely), firesafes, offline and off-site storage, encryption, oversight/monitoring, *etc.* Most importantly of all, restoration and recovery must be tested, safely, *before* an incident happens for real because if it fails then, it is too late: an incident may have become a disaster. That's Murphy's law. "The files, equipment, data and procedures available for use in the event of a failure or loss, if the originals are destroyed or out of service" *(ISACA glossary)*. "Pertaining to a procedure, technique, or hardware used to help recover lost or destroyed data or to keep a system operating" *(ISO 2382-12)*. *Cf.* archive.
Backup centre	See hot site. "An alternate facility used to continue IT/IS operations when the primary data processing (DP) center is unavailable" *(ISACA glossary)*.
Backward **P**ass **D**ifferentiable **A**pproximation **(BPDA)**	Adversarial attack technique intended to compromise the security of an **A**rtificial **I**ntelligence system by exploiting flawed controls involving obfuscated gradients.
BAD	*Abbrev:* **B**roken **A**s **D**esigned. *Cf.* WAD.
Bad actor	Euphemism for an adversary such as a malicious hacker, insider, spy/enemy agent/cyber-spook, criminal, or fraudster intent on exploiting vulnerable networks, systems, people, organisations, nations, *etc.*, typically by undermining, bypassing, evading, or negating/disabling the security controls meant to stop them. Nothing to do with appalling performances on stage and screen, after all. "A term for a cybercriminal or hacker [and] An individual, group, country or entity who intentionally causes harm" *(ISACA glossary)*.
Badge	Handheld physical token used in person to identify the holder and/or denote their authority and status as, say, an employee or a police officer. A simple business card offers very little assurance of the holder's legitimacy, whereas an embossed or cast metal badge is a little harder to duplicate or steal. A photo ID such as a driver's licence or corporate access card helps link the holder to the photo and name on the card, *provided* someone diligently checks the laminated image against the person and appreciates the risk of forgery, hinting at a common concern for all types of badge. "A card or other device that is presented or displayed to obtain access to an otherwise restricted facility as a symbol of authority (*e.g.*, the police) or a simple means of identification. Note: Also used in advertising and publicity" *(ISACA glossary)*.

TERM	MEANING
Badge access	See access card.
Bailey	Courtyard in a Mediaeval castle.
Baiting	Social engineering method of [figuratively] dangling something attractive in front of victims, such as a 419 or phishing email, an infectious USB memory stick that has *apparently* been dropped/ lost, or a **Q**uick **R**esponse code linking to a malicious website.
Bait-and-switch	Ancient social engineering trick (fraud) in which a victim is enticed to purchase an attractive display item (the bait) that is then surreptitiously substituted (switched) after purchase for an item of much lesser value. In cybersecurity, phishing involves using what *appears* to be a legitimate request by a trusted organisation to trick victims into disclosing sensitive information (normally their logon credentials) which may then be passed through to that organisation to complete an apparently normal logon process, leaving both the individuals and organisations unaware that they have been scammed. An example of a **T**ime **O**f **C**heck/**T**ime **O**f **U**se issue.
Balancing control	Control that involves reconciling complementary (equal and opposite) values, as in double-entry bookkeeping, *etc.*
Bank **I**dentification **N**umber **(BIN)**, **I**ssuer **I**dentification **N**umber **(IIN)**	First six digits of a payment card number identifying the card issuer. This part is neither confidential nor sufficient to identify an individual credit/debit card or account. Analogous to the *make* of a car as opposed to the **V**ehicle **I**dentification **N**umber. See also **P**rimary **A**ccount **N**umber.
Bank Trojan, banking Trojan, online banking Trojan, banker Trojan	Trojan (such as Zeus) that captures user authentication credentials (typically by keylogging) and/or hijacks web sessions (**M**an-**I**n-**T**he-**M**iddle attacks) to steal funds from online bank accounts.
Barbed wire	Fencing wire with numerous sharp barbs to snag the clothing and prick the skin of any intruders foolish enough to climb over. A physical security control with some deterrent effect, though less extreme than razor wire, spikes, and armed guards with attitude.
Bare metal	Refers to the tangible computer hardware platform on which host **O**perating **S**ystems, including hypervisors, run, as distinct from the emulated hardware on which guest OSs run in a virtual system.
Base case	Default, lowest common denominator or baseline. "A standardized body of data created for testing purposes. Notes: Users normally establish the data. Base cases validate production application systems and test the ongoing accurate operation of the system" *(ISACA glossary)*.

TERM	MEANING
Base measure	"Measure defined in terms of an attribute and the method for quantifying it. Note: a base measure is functionally independent of other measures" *(ISO/IEC/IEEE 15939)*. "A measure that is functionally independent of other measures and cannot be expressed in other terms. A base measure is defined in terms of an attribute and the method for quantifying it" *(ISACA glossary)*.
Baseline	Lowest level, layer, or part of something, the foundation or basis on which to build. "A specification or product that has been formally reviewed and agreed on, serves as the basis for further development and can only be changed through formal change control procedures" *(ISACA glossary)*. "Information and controls that are used as a minimum implementation or starting point to provide a consistent minimum standard of systems security and information assurance" *(NZISM)*.
Baseline configuration	See baseline security. "A documented set of specifications for a system or a configuration item within a system that has been formally reviewed and agreed upon at a given point in time, and that can only be changed through change control procedures" *(NIST SP 800-171)*.
Baseline control	Information security control that (in accordance with a corporate baseline security standard or policy) is required in all circumstances unless superseded by a stronger, approved control or formally declared exempt. For example, a baseline security requirement for passwords might specify "at least 8 characters," giving a basic or minimal level of user authentication for low-risk systems, whereas more stringent criteria for password length, complexity, reuse, storage, *etc.* would be appropriate for medium-risk systems, with **M**ulti**F**actor **A**uthentication and custom controls for high-risk systems.
Baseline security	Baseline for information, physical, cyber, or other forms of security in a given situation (such as a particular organisation, physical security zone or data classification level, or a genuine security culture). Forms a sound, stable, dependable, and trustworthy platform on which additional security can be implemented where appropriate. May be documented in a baseline security standard.
Baseline security standard	Corporate information security standard defining the organisation's baseline controls
Base station, wireless base station	"Equipment that provides the connection between mobile or cellular phones and the core communication network" *(ISO/IEC 27033-6)*.

TERM	MEANING
Bashdoor	See shellshock.
Basic authentication	"The simplest web-based authentication scheme that works by sending the username and password with each request" *(SANS glossary)*.
Basic collection	**C**entral **I**ntelligence **A**gency term for **O**pen-**S**ource **Int**elligence including information 'voluntarily disclosed' by individuals. It is not clear what techniques are or are not permitted to 'encourage' individuals to 'volunteer' information, but at least the CIA acknowledges their use of both standard collection and special collection.
Basic Input/Output System (BIOS)	Low-level PC motherboard firmware that interacts with peripherals such as disks, keyboards, and mice, completes self-checks, and initiates the **O**perating **S**ystem boot sequence. Normally stored on a ROM, EPROM or EEPROM potentially capable of being electronically updated or physically replaced, hence vulnerable. Introduced in 1975 and deprecated in favour of **U**nified **E**xtensible **F**irmware **I**nterface from 2005.
Bastion	See bastion host. "A system heavily fortified against attacks" *(ISACA glossary)*.
Bastion host	Server proactively hardened and securely maintained to minimise vulnerabilities. "[Server that] has been hardened in anticipation of vulnerabilities that have not been discovered yet" *(SANS glossary)*.
Batch control	a. Set of process controls applied to the manufacture of a batch of materials or goods, ensuring product consistency, quality, safety, *etc*. b. Integrity control to prevent the unauthorised addition, duplication, modification, or removal of transactions in the queue awaiting batch processing. "The correctness checks built into data processing systems for batches of input data, particularly in the data preparation stage. Notes: There are two main forms of batch controls: sequence control, which involves numbering the records in a batch consecutively so that the presence of each record can be confirmed, and control total, which is a total of the values in selected fields within the transactions" *(ISACA glossary)*. **See also** run-to-run.
Batch processing [environment]	Production of *multiple* identical or minimally customised products in one go, collectively, as opposed to producing each one separately, piecemeal. "Operating environment in which input data are collected and processed in groups, rather than being processed as each input arrives" *(ISO/IEC 2382)*. "The processing of a group of transactions at the same time. Note: Transactions are collected and processed against the master files at a specified time" *(ISACA glossary)*.

TERM	MEANING
Battery backup	Electronic devices need electricity to operate normally, making them dependent on the power supply and vulnerable to power interruptions. For devices that are at all important, power interruptions constitute a substantial risk; hence, batteries are an important form of control to maintain services as long as necessary to restore the primary or standby supply. Unfortunately, batteries bring their own risks (such as finite capacities and lifetimes, leakage of corrosive chemicals, fires, and explosions) which must also be addressed. See also **U**ninterruptible **P**ower **S**upply.
Battlement	High walkway topping Medieval castle walls, usually crenelated, from which defenders could fire arrows, spears, and stones, and pour boiling oil on attackers below.
Bayesian analysis	Heuristic technique based on Bayes' theorem, sometimes used to identify potential threats (such as spam and malware). "A mathematical model that uses probability to aid in answering theoretical questions about unidentified parameters" *(ISACA glossary)*.
Bayesian methodology	Method or technique based on Bayes' theorem. "Statistical approach to data analysis based on Bayes' theorem where uncertainty is quantified by combining existing information with new information to create forecast models" *(NIST SP 800-55v1)*.
Bayesian network	"Probabilistic model that uses Bayesian inference for probability computations using a directed acyclic graph" *(ISO/IEC 22989)*. "Graphs that compactly represent the relationship between random variables for a given problem. These graphs aid in reasoning or decision-making in the face of uncertainty. These networks are usually represented as graphs in which the link between any two nodes is assigned a value representing the probabilistic relationship between those nodes" *(ISACA glossary)*.
Bayes' theorem	Probability function, originally developed by Thomas Bayes. "An equation for calculating the probability that something is true if something potentially related to it is true. If $P(A)$ means 'the probability that A is true' and $P(A\|B)$ means 'the probability that A is true if B is true,' then Bayes' Theorem tells us that $P(A\|B) = (P(B\|A) P(A))/P(B)$" *(ISACA glossary)*.
BCM	*Abbrev:* **B**usiness **C**ontinuity **M**anagement.
BCMS	*Abbrev:* **B**usiness **C**ontinuity **M**anagement **S**ystem.
BCP	*Abbrev:* **B**usiness **C**ontinuity **P**lan or **B**est **C**urrent **P**ractice, depending on context.
BCR	*Abbrev:* **B**inding **C**orporate **R**ules.

TERM	MEANING
BDA	*Abbrev:* **B**usiness **D**ependency **A**nalysis.
BEC	*Abbrev:* **B**usiness **E**mail **C**ompromise.
BDS	*Abbrev:* **B**ei**D**ou Navigation **S**atellite System.
Before **F**irst **U**nlock **(BFU)**	State of a mobile phone that has just been powered on or booted, before the user has authenticated and unlocked it with a PIN code, pattern, or biometric. Similar to a BIOS password. The device **O**perating **S**ystem automatically disables certain functions and features until **A**fter **F**irst **U**nlock. Modern phones with encrypting file systems are more resistant (but not immune) to forensic tools and hackers in this state, unless the encryption can be overcome.
Behaviour	Human activity. "Observable actions of a person or group of people, informed by beliefs and values" *(OCEG GRC Glossary)*.
Bei**D**ou **N**avigation **S**atellite **S**ystem **(BDS)**	Chinese-owned **G**lobal **N**avigation **S**atellite **S**ystem.
Belief	Inherent or innate understanding. "Unobservable ideas and assumptions of a person or group, often caused by experience, perception, and personality" *(OCEG GRC Glossary)*.
Bell–LaPadula model	Formal model or architecture developed by David Elliott Bell and Leonard J. LaPadula in 1973 applies strict (mandatory) access control rules (usually expressed as 'no read up, no write down') and other constraints (such as the tranquillity principle) to maintain data confidentiality. Subjects (generally programs or systems) can neither read objects (generally data) at a higher level of classification nor write to or share data with objects or subjects at lower classification levels in the hierarchy. *Cf.* Biba model.
Benchmark	Measurement relative to a specified comparator, standard or objective, such as the security maturity level achieved by other similar organisations or the performance of another system. "A standard against which measurements or comparisons can be made" *(ISACA glossary)*.
Benchmark appraisal	Benchmark appraisal. Often a number of parameters are quantified and compared in the same assessment, leading to a complex and generally subjective overall assessment, indicating areas of potential improvement. "A consistent and reliable assessment method that results in a rating. This includes clear and repeatable process steps, which are capable of achieving high accuracy and reliable appraisal results through the collection of objective evidence from multiple sources. A maturity level profile or capability level profile must be produced as part of this appraisal process and allows Appraisal Sponsors to compare an organization's or project's process implementation with others. Like other appraisal methods, benchmark appraisals identify opportunities for improving both process implementation and business performance" *(ISACA glossary)*.

TERM	MEANING
Benchmarking	Conducting a benchmark assessment. "A systematic approach to comparing enterprise performance against peers and competitors in an effort to learn the best ways of conducting business. Notes: Examples include benchmarking of quality, logistic efficiency and various other metrics" *(ISACA glossary)*.
Benefit	Something worthwhile, valuable, advantageous. "A measure of the positive impact that an event has on the organization" *(OCEG GRC Glossary)*. "An outcome whose nature and value (expressed in various ways) are considered advantageous by an enterprise" *(ISACA glossary)*.
Benford's law	Physicist Frank Benford realised that the digits in a set of numbers (such as the $values of corporate expense claims) tend to be unevenly distributed: high-value digits such as 9 normally occur less often than low values such as 1, especially for the most significant digits. Statistical analyses and tools use Benford's law to identify data subsets with anomalous distributions, such as expense or tax claims by a particular worker that might have been systematically and fraudulently manipulated or falsified. One of several techniques for identifying patterns, correlations, anomalies, and exceptions in **D**ata**B**ases according to the nature and distribution of the data (metadata).
Benign	Having harmless, negligible, neutral, or beneficial intent or consequences. *Cf.* malicious.
BER	*Abbrev:* **B**it **E**rror **R**ate (or **R**atio).
Best **C**urrent **P**ractice **(BCP)**	**I**nternet **E**ngineering **T**ask **F**orce's description of a *de facto* level of performance, security, *etc.* Serially numbered and occasionally updated BCPs are used to document evolving or dynamically changing practices for which static standards are impracticable or inappropriate. *Cf.* **B**usiness **C**ontinuity **P**lan.
Best evidence	Forensic evidence originally gathered or seized from the scene of a crime and destined to be produced (presented) in court (*e.g.* the defendant's actual computer disk) rather than forensic copies made for forensic analysis (*e.g.* bit-copies of the hard drive). Evidence is considered 'best' if there is none better. Although forensic copies may sometimes be presented in court for various reasons (*e.g.* if the best evidence has unfortunately gone missing or degraded in storage), they carry slightly less weight than best evidence and beg questions about the capabilities and competence of whoever failed to protect and produce the best evidence.
Best possible value	"A value of an indicator that is likely to be achieved under the best possible assumptions and best possible execution" *(OCEG GRC Glossary)*.

TERM	MEANING
Best practice	By convention or common impression, the *ultimate* approach. However, since practices are often highly context-dependent, so-called best practices may be inappropriate, inadequate, ineffective, or even detrimental in particular situations; hence, related terms such as good practice are preferred. "A proven activity or process that has been successfully used by multiple enterprises" *(ISACA glossary)*. *Cf.* **B**est **C**urrent **Pr**actice.
Beta test	Software test performed by a select group of tame users with the dubious privilege of gaining advance access to new program releases in return for bug reports. *Cf.* alpha test.
BFT	*Abbrev:* **B**yzantine **F**ault **T**olerance.
BFU	*Abbrev:* **B**efore **F**irst **U**nlock.
BGP	*Abbrev:* **B**order **G**ateway **P**rotocol.
BGP hijack	Network hack in which the perpetrator deliberately circulates incorrect **B**order **G**ateway **P**rotocol routing information to misdirect, intercept, or block Internet traffic. Security controls such as **R**esource **P**ublic **K**ey **I**nfrastructure mitigate the risks.
BHO	*Abbrev:* **B**rowser **H**elper **O**bject.
BIA	*Abbrev:* **B**usiness **I**mpact **A**nalysis.
BianLian	Species of ransomware in the wild in 2023.
Bias, cognitive bias, biased	Presence of systematic or systemic errors or inaccuracies in information, processes, systems, analysis, or decision-making due to issues such as flawed algorithms, incomplete or skewed data sets, or human cognitive failings and prejudices. Can lead to incorrect or inappropriate outcomes such as failure to identify, understand, evaluate, and treat information risks appropriately, or unfair (inequitable, unbalanced) treatment of people. A troublesome problem in **A**rtificial **I**ntelligence, especially if the internal models are not sufficiently transparent or are so complex that biases remain unrecognised. "Systematic deviation of a value from a reference value" *(ISO/IEC 2382)*. "Systematic difference in treatment of certain objects, people or groups in comparison to others. Note: Treatment is any kind of action, including perception, observation, representation, prediction or decision" *(ISO/IEC 22989)*. "In machine learning (ML), systemic errors or distortions either in algorithms, data, or models that lead to prejudiced results" *(ISACA glossary)*. "A pattern of deviation in judgement whereby inferences about other people and situations may be drawn in an illogical fashion. These include expectation, confirmation, contextual and motivational biases, anchoring effects or focalism (related to expectation and confirmation biases), role effects (*e.g.* adversarial roles) and reconstructive effects (rely on memory rather than contemporaneous notes)" *(FSRCoP)*. *Cf.* unbiased.

TERM	MEANING
Biba model	Formal model or architecture developed by Kenneth J. Biba in 1975 applies strict (mandatory) access control rules (usually expressed as 'no read down, no write up') to maintain data integrity. Subjects (generally programs or systems) can neither corrupt higher-level objects (generally data) nor be corrupted by lower-level objects or subjects in the hierarchy. *Cf.* Bell–LaPadula model.
Bidirectional traceability	Capability to track, trace, or follow a process or activity sequentially from start-to-finish *or* in the reverse direction, *e.g.* using the 'Trace Precedents' feature in MS Excel to identify any spreadsheet cells that were used in a formula in the selected cell (looking upstream), and 'Trace Dependents' to identify any other (downstream) cells using the selected cell. "An association that enables the ability to trace in either direction between logical entities, *e.g.*, from requirements to design to code to test to the end solution, or from customer requirements to product component requirements" *(ISACA glossary)*.
Big data	*Huge* (multi-exabyte), rapidly changing, highly complex data sets that cannot be processed adequately with conventional **D**ata**B**ase **M**anagement **S**ystems or applications, requiring radically different approaches. Security-related logs in large organisations *may* approach this scale, where conventional data analyses intended to predict impending security threats can take so long to complete that the incidents may have already happened by the time the predictions are processed and reported. Term often misused by advertisers with a penchant for hyperbole. "Huge and diverse sets of information, encompassing structured and unstructured data, generated at high volume, velocity, and variety (the three Vs)" *(ISACA glossary)*. See also **U**ser **B**ehaviour **A**nalytics, **S**ecurity **I**nformation and **E**vent **M**anagement, **I**ntrusion **D**etection **S**ystem/**I**ntrusion **P**revention **S**ystem, **N**etwork **T**raffic **A**nalysis.
Big Brother	Name of the overbearing authoritarian establishment in George Orwell's dystopian novel "Nineteen eighty-four." Euphemism for mass surveillance.
BIN	*Abbrev:* **B**ank **I**dentification **N**umber.
Binary	Number system with precisely two values (*e.g.* zero or one, true or false, on or off, up or down, red or blue, …). Today's computers are mostly binary, comprised of electronic switches and logic gates implementing Boolean functions. "Characterized by a selection, choice or condition that has two possible different values or states" *(ISO/IEC 2382)*. "The base 2 number system (2^n). Permissible digits are 0 and 1" *(ISACA glossary)*.

TERM	MEANING
Binary classification	Binary classification with precisely two categories or levels. "A type of machine learning (ML) task that categorizes observations into two groups (*e.g.*, positive review/negative review, spam email/non-spam email, healthy patient/diseased patient)" *(ISACA glossary)*.
Binary code	Binary code. "A code whose representation is limited to 0 and 1" *(ISACA glossary)*.
Binary scheme	Conformity approach that applies explicit pass/fail criteria, *e.g.* to decide whether to award a certificate. "Labelling schemes which has a list of cybersecurity features which must be included for the device to pass and obtain a label" *(ISO/IEC 27404 DRAFT)*.
Binder	Hacker term for a program combining multiple executables within one, or a compiled dossier of information about a target.
Binding **C**orporate **R**ules **(BCR)**	"Personal data protection policies which are adhered to by a controller or processor established on the territory of a Member State for transfers or a set of transfers of personal data to a controller or processor in one or more third countries within a group of undertakings, or group of enterprises engaged in a joint economic activity" ***(G**eneral **D**ata **P**rotection **R**egulation)*. "A set of rules that allow multinational organizations to transfer personal data from the EU to their affiliates outside of the EU" *(ISACA glossary)*.
Biometric (biological metric)	Measurable biological characteristic of a person, such as their fingerprint, iris or retinal image, palmprint, ear shape, facial shape, voice or veinous pattern, signature, cursive writing and typing dynamics, gait or DNA profile, that can be used as a credential to identify and/or authenticate them. "Pertaining to the use of specific attributes that reflect unique personal characteristics, such as a fingerprint, an eye blood-vessel print, or a voice print, to validate the identity of a person" *(ISO/IEC 2382)*. "Measurable physical characteristic used to identify or verify an individual" *(AusISM)*. "Uses physical characteristics of the user to determine access [and] A security technique that verifies an individual's identity by analyzing a unique physical attribute, such as a handprint" *(SANS glossary)*.
Biometric data	Biometric information about individuals. Personal information. "Personal data resulting from specific technical processing relating to the physical, physiological or behavioural characteristics of a natural person, which allow or confirm the unique identification of that natural person, such as facial images or dactyloscopic data" ***(G**eneral **D**ata **P**rotection **R**egulation)*. "Personal data resulting from specific technical processing relating to the physical, physiological or behavioral characteristics of a natural person, which allow or confirm the unique identification of that natural person, such as facial images or dactyloscopic data" *(ISACA glossary)*.

TERM	MEANING
Biometric lock	Physical access control device that uses a fingerprint or some other biometric to authenticate people and (in low-end locks or consumer-grade *things* lacking a PIN pad) identify them as well. "Door and entry locks that are activated by biometric features, such as voice, retina, fingerprint or signature" *(ISACA glossary)*.
BIOS	*Abbrev:* **B**asic **I**nput/**O**utput **S**ystem.
BIOS password	Some BIOS firmware incorporates a function to require the user to enter a password to complete the boot sequence and use a device. Although this prevents casual access to files, *etc.*, the control is weak and easily defeated or bypassed by a competent hacker or forensics specialist with physical access to the device.
Biotech	Contraction of **bio**logical **tech**nology, particularly the development and exploitation of innovative technologies within the biological products industry, *e.g.* molecular modelling of pharmaceuticals and vaccines. See also AgriTech, EcoTech/GreenTech, EdTech, FinTech, FoodTech, GovTech, HealthTech, LegalTech, RegTech, RetailTech, and other tech neologisms.
Birthday paradox	Counterintuitive statistical fact that, in a random group of at least 23 people, it is 'likely' (*i.e.* the probability is greater than 50%) that two of them celebrate their birthdays on the same day of the year. Has been used as the basis for a cryptanalytic attack that exploits relationships between two sets of data (*e.g.* passwords and the corresponding hash values) where a match between *any* value from one set against *any* value from the other set is considered significant (*i.e.* discovering any valid password in an entire password file). This is far more likely than finding a match to a given value (*e.g.* finding the password for a particular userID). A valid concern if *all* entries in a fingerprint **D**ata**B**ase are scanned for *any* matches as opposed to, say, scanning a particular set of prints/DNA samples from a crime scene or suspect against the database, especially given the small but finite probability of false matches.
Bit (binary digit)	A single binary value, either one or zero, on or off, up or down, heads or tails, blue or red, ... "The smallest unit of information storage; a contraction of the term 'binary digit'; one of two symbols – '0' (zero) and '1' (one) – that are used to represent binary numbers" *(SANS glossary)*. "A contraction of the term binary digit, and the most basic and smallest unit of computing information. A bit may be in one of two states, logic 1 or logic 0. It can be thought of as a switch that is either on or off. Bits are usually combined into computer words of various sizes, called 'bytes'" *(ISACA glossary)*.

TERM	MEANING
BITB	*Abbrev:* Browser In The Browser.
Bit-bucket, sinkhole	Notional device or network address to which unwanted data/traffic can be sent. Antivirus analysts sometimes hijack the command and control features of malware to send stolen data down a sinkhole instead of going to the criminals behind the scams. See also blackhole.
Bit Error Rate (or Ratio) (BER)	Measure of the rate of occurrence of erroneous bits in a digital data stream. "Number of erroneous bits divided by the total number of bits transmitted, received, or processed over some stipulated period of time" *(ISO/IEC 2382)*.
BitPaymer	Species of ransomware in the wild in 2019. Targeted medium to large organisations, demanding ransoms between ~$50 k and ~$1 m.
Bit-stream image	See bitwise image. "Bit-stream backups, also referred to as mirror image backups, involve the backup of all areas of a computer hard disk drive or other type of storage media. Notes: Such backups exactly replicate all sectors on a given storage device, including all files and ambient data storage areas" *(ISACA glossary)*.
Bitwise image, bit-copy	Bit-by-bit identical image copy of all readable information on a storage medium that includes not only conventional data content but also metadata, **A**lternate **D**ata **S**treams, and the unallocated spaces *between* data files, past the end-of-file markers. Normally used for forensic purposes. May include remnants of data left behind after files have been incompletely deleted or moved, and perhaps (using special forensic techniques and/or hardware) data from disk sectors marked unreadable by the firmware.
Black bag operations (black bag ops)	Covert activities to penetrate, infiltrate, or otherwise physically compromise a target's premises in order to capture useful intelligence, filling the notional swag bag. See also black ops.
Black box testing, basic testing	Assurance approach where the testers are given no information about the internal architecture of an application, system, device, or whatever under test, other than what they can discern by testing. Emulates attempted compromise or misuse by outsiders or by ordinary users. "A test methodology that assumes no knowledge of the internal structure and implementation detail of the assessment object" *(NIST SP 800-53A)*. "A method of software testing that examines the functionality of an application without peering into its internal structures of workings. This method of test can be applied to virtually every level of software testing: unit, integration, system, and acceptance" *(NIST SP 800-192)*. "A testing approach that focuses on the functionality of the application or product and does not require knowledge of the code intervals" *(ISACA glossary)*. See also zero-knowledge attack. *Cf.* white box testing, grey box testing.

TERM	MEANING
BlackCat, ALPHV	Species of ransomware in the wild in 2024. Used by Scattered Spider.
Black hat	Malicious, self-serving, unethical hacker or cracker. *Cf.* grey hat, white hat.
Blackhole	List of email servers believed to be pumping out spam, used as a crude form of spam filtering ('crude' in that it tars all users of those servers with the same broad brush).
Blacklist, blocklist, deny list	List of email addresses, mail servers (see blackhole), **U**niform **R**esource **L**ocators (see bit-bucket), people, applications, *etc.* that management deems unacceptable, banned, or barred. Since the default action for unlisted items is usually to permit their access or use, this control can fail insecure. "A list of email senders who have previously sent spam to a user" *(NIST SP 800-114)*. *Cf.* whitelist.
Blackmail	Form of coercion or extortion used to force someone into doing something inappropriate, illegal, or simply against their will, *e.g.* by threatening to reveal some embarrassing corporate or personal secret (perhaps a previous criminal act or sexual proclivity) if they do not go along with the blackmailer's instructions. See also sextortion.
Black market, criminal underground	Unofficial, covert, unregulated, and untaxed commercial market for stolen property (both physical and intellectual) plus the knowledge, tools, processes (such as money laundering), and other resources of the criminal fraternity. See also hacker underground, Darknet, Silk Road.
Black operations (black ops)	Covert ('blacked-out') activities normally run by government-sponsored or state security services to infiltrate, undermine, or otherwise compromise an adversary, in a manner that permits them plausibly to deny the existence, knowledge, or sponsorship of the operation, typically because it is unethical or illegal. See also black bag ops.
Blackout, power cut	Extended interruption to the power feed. Computers and other electronic systems without alternative power sources such as battery backup, **U**ninterruptible **P**ower **S**upply, or standby generators, will of course fail in a blackout, potentially corrupting critical system or data files in the process as well as interrupting services. "Widespread electrical power outage" *(ISO/IEC 27019)*. See also dip, brownout, surge, spike.
BlackPOS	Species of POS memory-scraping malware in the wild in 2014. Compromised the US retailer Target.

TERM	MEANING
Blackshades	Species of malware deceptively marketed as an antivirus and anti-spyware package until the cybercriminal operation behind it was shut down by the **F**ederal **B**ureau of **I**nvestigation in 2014.
Black start	"Start-up of an electric power system from a total or partial black-out through internal or external energy resources" *(ISO/IEC 27019)*.
Black swan event	Outlier/extreme/rare event which is *so* unusual that it could not reasonably have been predicted using risk analysis processes and models. Metaphorical term coined by Nassim Nicholas Taleb, originally in connection with financial management but later applied across other fields. We humans find it difficult to even contemplate, let alone deal rationally with black swans. Many of us struggle even to take credible worst-case scenarios seriously enough to prepare/plan accordingly.
Black team	Stealthier variant of the red team, *i.e.* a penetration test team tasked with evading, disabling, or bypassing security controls in order to compromise an organisation, but covertly, discreetly, or secretly, *e.g.* without prior warning. The name vaguely alludes to blackout screens. May employ deception and other techniques typically employed by genuine hackers and unethical adversaries. See also blue, purple, and white teams.
Blaster	Infamous network worm from 2003.
Blast-RADIUS	Vulnerability in the RADIUS protocol allows an attacker to gain unauthorised access to controlled network services.
Bleichenbacher	Swiss cryptanalyst who invented a clever brute force attack on PKCS #1 v1.5, used by **S**ecure **S**ockets **L**ayer. Millions of automated challenges and responses concerning the validity of the message padding are used to determine the key. Partly responsible for the deprecation of SSL.
Blended attack	Form of attack that combines methods, for instance using social engineering to dupe a target into unwittingly infecting their system with malware. "Attack that seeks to maximize the severity of damage and speed of contagion by combining multiple attack vectors" *(ISO/IEC 27032)*.

TERM | **MEANING**

Bletchley Park

For decades until 1987, this manor house and grounds North of London housed a TOP SECRET UK government communications, cryptography, and training unit. During the second World War, Alan Turing, Tommy Flowers, Max Newman, Harry Hinsley, and team designed and built the Colossus computer here to decrypt German and Japanese traffic including Enigma. Now an outstanding museum, well worth a virtual or in-person visit. More info: https://bletchleypark.org.uk/

Bloatware

Software that has become 'bloated' through the incremental addition of marginally useful functions and features, making it more complex and less secure (more vulnerable) as a consequence.

Block

a. *[Verb]* To prevent something from taking place.

b. *[Noun]* Unit of data, either of a fixed size (so many bits, bytes, or characters) or delineated by specific marker sequences, control characters, *etc.*

c. *[Noun]* "Unit in which data is stored and retrieved on disk and tape devices" *(ISO/IEC 27040)*.

Blockchain

Distributed data architecture used to establish an auditable, high-integrity record of changes to data by linking each change in a ledger to predecessors in the logical sequence using digital signatures. Does not rely on a trusted authority. Commonly applied in cryptocurrencies such as Bitcoin. "A distributed, protected journaling and ledger system. Use of blockchain technologies can enable anything from digital currency (*e.g.*, Bitcoin) to any other value-bearing transaction" *(ISACA glossary)*.

Blockchain explorer

"Front-end applications or user interfaces that allow a user to view individual records on a blockchain" *(ISACA glossary)*.

Blockchain technology

Information Technology supporting/enabling blockchain. "A particular way of storing data. A blockchain is an example of a distributed ledger – a type of append-only, tamper-proof storage technology" *(UK National Cyber Security Strategy 2022)*.

Block cypher

Symmetric cryptography algorithm that encrypts a block consisting of a defined number of sequential plaintext characters at a time. "Encrypts one block of data at a time" (*SANS glossary*). "A public algorithm that operates on plaintext in blocks (strings or groups) of bits" *(ISACA glossary)*. *Cf.* stream cypher.

TERM	MEANING
Block height	"The number of blocks preceding a specific block in a blockchain ledger. It is typically used to identify a specific block (*e.g.*, block ID)" *(ISACA glossary)*.
Blocklist, block-list	Politically correct version of blacklist.
Block producer, miner, validator	Function that creates valid transaction blocks from transaction data for incorporation into a blockchain. "An entity used for proof-of-stake on a blockchain network" (*ISACA glossary*).
Blooper	Embarrassing and often humorous human error. Variously known as a bailout, balls-up, bloomer, blunder, boner, booboo, boob, botch, bungle, bust-up, clanger, corpsing, gaffe, foul-up, fumble, *faux pas*, goof-up, howler, mistake, screwup, SNAFU, Spoonerism, wipeout, *etc.* An accidental integrity failure.
BLP	*Abbrev:* **B**ypass **L**abel **P**rocessing.
Blue	Prefix in a few terms that follow, implying the exploitation of Bluetooth connections, with or without the device owner's authorisation and/or knowledge.
BlueBorne	Cluster of Bluetooth driver spoofing vulnerabilities, disclosed in 2017, affecting over five billion Android, Linux, and Apple devices.
Bluebugging	Covert exploitation of security vulnerabilities in someone's Bluetooth equipment to bug them, *e.g.* by surreptitiously causing a compromised Bluetooth cellphone to call another number and so transmit private conversations in the vicinity of the compromised device.
Bluejacking	Sending unsolicited text, audio, or video messages (*e.g.* spam) to a Bluetooth device. While that may be annoying, it is essentially harmless but Bluejacking may also encompass more sinister Bluesnarfing, Bluespying, or Bluebugging attacks that involve hijacking the victim's device.
BlueKeep	**R**emote **D**esktop **P**rotocol vulnerability affecting legacy systems running deprecated Windows versions that are no longer supported by Microsoft. Exploited since 2019 by cryptominer malware and potentially vulnerable to network worms. See also EternalBlue.
Bluesnarfing	Hacking a Bluetooth device, violating the user's privacy, and potentially compromising confidential personal and/or proprietary data such as email or SMS/TXT messages, contact details, diaries, and photos/videos stored on the device.
Bluespying	Type of hacker attack that exploits security vulnerabilities on Bluetooth equipment to spy on the user, *e.g.* accessing stored **G**lobal **P**ositioning **S**ystem data to determine where they have been.

TERM	MEANING
Blue team	Defenders tasked with protecting some part of the enterprise (or at least its flags) against mock attacks by outsmarting the red team and other penetration testers. Nothing to do with Bluetooth, unless that provides a viable attack vector (which it often does). "A team of cybersecurity staff (including incident response consultants) charged with defending the enterprise during scheduled assessments called 'red team' exercises" *(ISACA glossary)*. "The people who perform defensive cybersecurity tasks, including placing and configuring firewalls, implementing patching programs, enforcing strong authentication, ensuring physical security measures are adequate and a long list of similar undertakings" *(SANS glossary)*. See also purple, black, and white teams.
Bluetooth Classic	2.4 GHz 79-channel frequency-hopping spread spectrum low power (~100 mW) radio **P**ersonal **A**rea **N**etwork protocol used by wireless speakers, portable printers, *etc.* "Wireless technology standard for exchanging data over short distances. Note: 'Bluetooth' is a trademark owned by the Bluetooth SIG" *(ISO/IEC 27033-6)*. "A wireless protocol that allows two similarly equipped devices to communicate with each other within a short distance (*e.g.*, 30 ft.)" *(NIST SP 800 101)*. *Cf.* Bluetooth **L**ow **E**nergy, ZigBee. More info: https://www.bluetooth.com/
Bluetooth Low Energy (BluetoothLE), Wibree	Nokia developed this 2.4 GHz 40-channel frequency-hopping spread spectrum low-power (~100 mW) energy-efficient wireless variant of Bluetooth Classic, originally branded Wibree. Typically used for short-range digital communications between *things* such as laptops, smartphones, smart TVs, wireless headphones, hearing aids, and fitness monitors, plus mesh networking and device location. The flexible protocol suite offers various cybersecurity options including **A**dvanced **E**ncryption **S**tandard for encryption, hashing, and Diffie–Hellman key exchange. Various device-pairing and data communications methods offer different levels of protection against eavesdropping, **M**an-**I**n-**T**he-**M**iddle, and other attacks, as well as RF noise immunity. The limited computational and battery power typical of *things*, plus architectural flaws, bugs, implementation issues, and insecure user behaviours (such as accepting inappropriate pairing requests), increase the probability of vulnerabilities and hence compromises. See also ZigBee. More info: https://www.bluetooth.com/
Bluff ransomware, bluffware	Malware that gives the *appearance* of having encrypted or otherwise blocked access to the users' data in order to extort a ransom payment out of naïve victims, but in reality is simply displaying the message (which typically warns against further checks by threatening to destroy the data). A form of scareware using social engineering.

TERM	MEANING
BMIS	*Abbrev:* **B**usiness **M**odel for **I**nformation **S**ecurity.
BMS	*Abbrev:* **B**uilding **M**anagement **S**ystem.
Board of Directors, the Board	Most senior level of (usually nonexecutive) management within the organisation with overarching accountability for protecting and legitimately exploiting the organisation's assets on behalf of its owners or other stakeholders. The Board typically delegates responsibility for corporate governance including information risk and security management to the executive officers while retaining a strategic oversight rôle – a delicate balance of power. "Individuals with responsibility for overseeing the strategic direction of the entity and the obligations related to the accountability of the entity. Depending on the nature of the entity, such responsibilities may be held by a board of directors or supervisory board for a corporation, a board of trustees for a not-for-profit entity, a board of governors or commissioners for a government entity, general partners for a partnership, or an owner for a small business" ***(T**rust **S**ervices **C**riteria).*
Body camera **(bodycam)**	Portable **C**losed **C**ircuit **T**ele**V**ision camera worn on or about a person, records the activities of people around or interacting with the wearer. The police are increasingly using body cameras both to record valuable evidence from scenes of crime and to exonerate themselves if accused of excessive violence, *etc.* Miniature cameras can be used for covert surveillance (*i.e.* spying) as well as for more mundane activities such as recording extreme sports. See also dashcam.
Body language	See nonverbal communication.
Bogus boss	Fraud/social engineering attack involving techniques such as **B**usiness **E**mail **C**ompromise and caller ID spoofing to fool vulnerable victims into believing they are interacting with a 'boss' – an assertive manager or a similar authority figure (such as an executive, auditor, investigator, or security professional). Posing as the boss, the fraudsters coerce victims into initiating inappropriate and unauthorised transactions such as wire transfers, changing the payee bank account details for scheduled payments, or making refunds to a nominated account. Alternatively the fraudsters might extract valuable/sensitive information, gain access rights, authority or privilege, or have security controls disabled/bypassed allowing them to engineer further compromises.
Bogus email	See **B**usiness **E**mail **C**ompromise.

TERM	MEANING
Boiler room	Fraud/social engineering attack involving heavy promotion of over-valued or non-existent stocks and shares by bogus stockbrokers promising big investment returns to naïve investors.
Bollard	Strong post mounted firmly in the ground, intended to reduce the risk of vehicular attacks on a facility. A physical security control.
Bomb	The classic kinetic weapon containing a high-explosive charge with a detonator triggered by some sort of timer or controller. An extreme physical security threat presented by terrorists and mortal enemies. "A Trojan horse that attacks a computer system when a specific logical event occurs (logic bomb) or when a specific time-related logical event occurs (time bomb). It can also be hidden in electronic mail or data and triggers a computer system attack when read in a certain way (letter bomb). Similar to: Trojan horse, virus and worm" *(ISACA glossary)*.
Boosting	"A machine learning technique that iteratively combines a set of simple and not very accurate classifiers (referred to as 'weak' classifiers) into a classifier with high accuracy (a 'strong' classifier) by upweighting the examples the model is currently misclassifying" *(ISACA glossary)*.
Boot, bootstrap, boot sequence, boot-up	Initial sequence of activities shortly after a typical Information Technology device is powered up or initialised and completes its Power-On Self-Test. Derived from the curious notion of 'picking yourself up by your own boot straps,' sometimes represented literally in cartoons where the laws of physics can be flagrantly disregarded. "Initialize a computer by loading the operating system and possibly clearing memory" *(ISO/IEC 2382)*. "1. To initialize a computer system by clearing memory and reloading the operating system. 2. To cause a computer system to reach a known beginning state. A boot program, in firmware, typically performs the boot function, which includes loading basic instructions that tell the computer how to load programs into memory and how to begin executing those programs. A distinction can be made between a warm boot and a cold boot. A cold boot starts the system from a powered-down state. A warm boot restarts the computer while it is powered up. Important differences between the two procedures are: a power-up self-test, in which various portions of the hardware, *e.g.*, memory, are tested for proper operation, is performed during a cold boot, while a warm boot does not normally perform such self-tests; a warm boot does not clear all memory" *(ISACA glossary)*.

TERM	MEANING
Boot sector virus	Form of malware that infects the boot sector (the **M**aster **B**oot **R**ecord) on a disk, *i.e.* that part of the disk which is accessed first by the bootloader in order to load the **O**perating **S**ystem and so start up the system.
Booter	See stresser.
Bootkit	Type of malware that subverts supposedly secure boot features, compromising the system early in the boot sequence, even before the **O**perating **S**ystem, drivers, and applications such as antivirus load. See also rootkit.
Bootloader, boot loader, bootstrap	Software function/utility, normally stored in firmware, that completes the **I**nitial **P**rogram **L**oad when a computer system is booted. It locates on the disk or network, validates, loads into main memory, and initiates execution of the **O**perating **S**ystem on a computer device such as a PC or *thing* when it boots-up. "A short computer program that is permanently resident or easily loaded into a computer, and whose execution brings a larger program, such as an operating system or its loader, into memory" *(ISACA glossary)*. See also **U**nified **E**xtensible **F**irmware **I**nterface, secure boot.
Border **G**ateway **P**rotocol **(BGP)**	Protocol to exchange routing information for Internet traffic between autonomous systems (groups of connected networks such as those belonging to an **I**nternet **S**ervice **P**rovider's customers). Vulnerable to BGP hijacking in which false routes are propagated accidentally or maliciously, potentially disrupting datacommunications. Specified across about 30 current **R**equest **F**or **C**omment standards. "An inter-autonomous system routing protocol. BGP is used to exchange routing information for the Internet and is the protocol used between Internet service providers" *(SANS glossary)*.
Border router	See external router.
Bot (robot), zombie	a. Networked computer under the remote control of hackers, often compromised using Trojans. The owner of the computer usually remains oblivious to the compromise. Often corralled together in botnets. Also known as a zombie, as in the 'living dead' of Hammer horror fame. b. Any autonomous piece of software capable of roaming systems and/or networks, whether for benign (*e.g.* indexing web pages for search engines) or malicious (*e.g.* spyware) purposes. "Automated software program used to carry out specific tasks. Notes: This word is often used to describe programs, usually run on a server, that automate tasks such as forwarding or sorting e-mail. A bot is also described as a program that operates as an agent for a user or another program or simulates a human activity. On the Internet, the most ubiquitous bots are the programs, also called spiders or crawlers, which access websites and gather their content for search engine indexes" *(ISO/IEC 27032)*. See also agent.

TERM	MEANING
Bot master, botmaster	Hacker or cracker who commands and controls a botnet.
Botnet	Network of bots used for hacking/cybercriminal activities such as spamming, identity fraud, carrying out **D**istributed **D**enial-**of**-**S**ervice attacks, or as launch pads for attacking other systems. Botnets comprising hundreds or thousands of compromised machines are rented out to hackers on the black market. "A large number of compromised computers that are used to create and send spam or viruses or flood a network with messages as a denial of service attack" *(SANS glossary)*. "Collection of remotely controlled malicious bots that run autonomously or automatically on compromised computers [such as] Distributed denial-of-service (DDoS) nodes, where the botnet controller can direct the user's computer to generate traffic to a third-party site as part of a coordinated DDoS attack" *(ISO/IEC 27032)*. "A term derived from a robot network; a large automated and distributed network of previously compromised computers that can be simultaneously controlled to launch large-scale attacks, such as a denial-of-service attack, on targeted victims" *(ISACA glossary)*.
Botware	Malware used to command and control a bot, allowing the bot master to download, install, and run a code module for a particular type of network attack, *etc*.
Bounced	Emails that are undeliverable for some reason (*e.g.* addressee unknown) may be returned with an explanatory note ("bounced") or silently deleted – the former approach helps senders but gives spammers clues about the status of email addresses. The latter consumes negligible resources.
Bouncer	See security guard.
Boundary	Demarcation between zones, typically where private property abuts public land or someone else's private property, or private networks abut public networks, or the edge of someone's personal space, or the edge of the playing zone for a cricket match. "Logical and physical controls used to define a perimeter between the organization and the outside world" *(ISACA glossary)*. See also perimeter, boundary conditions.
Boundary condition, boundary value	Data values, ranges, or other characteristics (such as number of bytes) that distinguish or separate valid from invalid data, implying different processing and perhaps triggering security controls in well-designed software. These make insightful edge and corner cases for software testing. "1. A data value that corresponds to a minimum or maximum input, internal or output value specified for a system or component. 2. A value that lies just inside or just outside of a specified range of valid input and output values" *(ISACA glossary)*. See also fuzzing.

TERM	MEANING
Boundary test, boundary value analysis	Testing technique exploring an application system's handling of boundary conditions (edge and corner cases). "A selection technique in which test data are chosen to lie along boundaries of the input domain or output range classes, data structures, procedure parameters, *etc.* Choices often include maximum, minimum and trivial values or parameters. This technique is often called stress testing. [and] A testing technique using input values just below and just above the defined limits of an input domain, and with input values causing outputs to be just below and just above the defined limits of an output domain" *(ISACA glossary)*.
BPDA	*Abbrev:* **B**ackward **P**ass **D**ifferentiable **A**pproximation.
BPR	*Abbrev:* **B**usiness **P**rocess **R**eengineering.
BRAIN.A	Widely held to have been the first personal computer virus, created in 1986 as a proof-of-concept by two Pakistani geeks who subsequently set up an **I**nternet **S**ervice **P**rovider called Brain Communications. Spread on floppy disks. Strictly speaking, it was not a true virus since it did not attach itself to executable programs, and it was predated by viruses on other platforms such as Creeper (DEC PDP-10, 1971), ANIMAL/PERVADE (Univac, 1974), and Elk Cloner (Apple II, 1981).
Branch analysis	"A test case identification technique that produces enough test cases so that each decision has a true and a false outcome at least once" *(ISACA glossary)*.
Branch coverage	"A test coverage criterion that requires that for each decision point, each possible branch is executed at least once. Branch coverage is synonymous with decision coverage and contrasts with condition coverage, multiple condition coverage, path coverage and statement coverage" *(ISACA glossary)*.
Brand	Set of commonly held perceptions, values, and beliefs in the minds of prospects and customers about an organisation and/or its products, *e.g.* "They are trustworthy and high quality." Whereas logos and phrases may be trademarked, inventions patented, designs registered, and written/spoken words copyrighted, the intangible emotional aspect of brands makes them difficult to describe, let alone protect, yet brands can be *extremely* valuable, yet vulnerable, corporate information assets. "Marketing-related intangible asset including, but not limited to, names, terms, signs, symbols, logos and designs, or a combination of these, intended to identify goods, services or entities, or a combination of these, creating distinctive images and associations in the minds of stakeholders, thereby generating economic benefits/values" *(ISO 10668)*. See also reputation.

TERM	MEANING
Brand value	"Economic value of the brand in transferable monetary units. Note: The result obtained can be either a single economic value or a range of values" *(ISO 10668)*.
Breach	Form of information security incident normally involving deliberate action by someone, as opposed to those with purely accidental causes, *e.g.* penetrating a defensive barrier such as a wall or firewall, or actively compromising security in general. "Circumvention or disablement of some element of computer security, with or without detection, which could result in a penetration of the data processing system" *(ISO/IEC 2382)*.
Break-glass	Alludes to fire alarms physically protected by thin glass panels, designed to be broken and triggered during an emergency. May apply to fully privileged administrative userID reserved solely for emergency use by pre-authorised **I**nformation **T**echnology professionals (*e.g.* if they are locked out of their regular accounts), with appropriate controls preventing and detecting unauthorised use.
Breakpoint, code breakpoint, control breakpoint, program breakpoint	a. Debugging capability to interrupt a program's execution deliberately in order to examine and perhaps change its internal parameters, registers, *etc.* "Point in a program, module, or statement where execution may be suspended depending on a specific condition or event. Notes: A breakpoint is set to permit manual or automatic monitoring of program performance or results. There may be more than one breakpoint" *(ISO/IEC 2382)*. See also checkpoint. b. Point at which something or someone under severe stress fails or snaps.
Bribe, bribery	Offered, promised, or actual provision and acceptance of illicit financial or other inducements with the expectation of favours in return, such as the opportunity to bid favourably for or win a contract, or lenience ('turning a blind eye') following a compliance failure. A form of corruption and malfeasance that, despite being both unethical and illegal, is an integral part of business life in some cultures and industries.
Bricking, Permanent **D**enial-**o**f-**S**ervice **(PDoS)**	Damaging a device, taking it out-of-service (no longer operational) in such a way that it is impossible or uneconomic to recover it, making it 'as useful as a brick.' May result from an accident (such as a bug or error when updating flash BIOS, or mechanical damage such as dropping the device in the sea), a deliberate attack, or, exceptionally, a vendor advising its customers to junk a critically vulnerable firewall that cannot be patched.

TERM	MEANING
BrickerBot	Malware that infects *things* and, if they fail a simple security test, irreparably damages their file systems, thus bricking them. A vigilante worm.
[Network] Bridge	Device connecting network segments at the OSI data link layer. Uses MAC addresses to forward traffic between segments. Typically used to connect different types of networks (*e.g.* Ethernet and token ring) or to segment a network. "A product that connects a local area network (LAN) to another local area network that uses the same protocol (for example, Ethernet or token ring)" *(SANS glossary)*. "A data link layer device developed in the early 1980s to connect local area networks (LANs) or create two separate LAN or wide area network (WAN) segments from a single segment to reduce collision domains. Notes: A bridge acts as a store-and-forward device by moving frames toward their destination. This is achieved by analyzing a data packet's MAC header, which represents the hardware address of an NIC" *(ISACA glossary)*.
Bring Your Own Cloud (BYOC)	Corporate scheme and policy allowing workers to use certain cloud computing services for business purposes, *provided* suitable information security controls (such as those protecting classified information, *e.g.* strong user authentication, data encryption, and other access controls) are employed. Unless blocked by network security controls, cloud applications (such as Google Docs or Office365) and cloud storage (such as Google Drive or Dropbox) may be used by workers to exfiltrate valuable information from the organisation. See also **B**ring **Y**our **O**wn **D**evice.
Bring Your Own Device (BYOD)	Corporate scheme and policy allowing workers to use their **P**ersonally **O**wned **D**evices for business purposes, *provided* suitable information security controls are employed (*e.g.* a BYOD or **A**cceptable **U**se **P**olicy mandating management authorisation and the use of **M**obile **D**evice **M**anagement, encryption, and antivirus software on PODs). Blurs the distinction between work and personal life, and can lead to questions around ownership and control of the respective data. "An enterprise policy used to permit partial or full integration of user-owned mobile devices for business purposes" *(ISACA glossary)*. See also **B**ring **Y**our **O**wn **T**hing.
Bring Your Own Key/s (BYOK)	Cloud computing security architecture in which customers manage and protect their cryptographic keys themselves, rather than depending on the **C**loud **S**ervice **P**roviders to do so.
Bring Your Own Thing (BYOT)	Corporate scheme and policy allowing workers to use their *things* for business purposes, *provided* suitable information security controls are employed (*e.g.* policies, **M**obile **D**evice **M**anagement, encryption, and antivirus software). A variant or part of **B**ring **Y**our **O**wn **D**evice.

TERM	MEANING
Brownout	Reduction in power supply voltage lasting more than just a few micro- or milliseconds, enough to dim incandescent lights (hence the name) and cause the failure of electronic systems having inadequate voltage regulation. See also dip, surge, spike, blackout.
Browser **H**elper **O**bject **(BHO)**	Program that loads and runs automatically when Internet Explorer is launched. Some BHOs are malicious, *i.e.* malware.
Browser hijack	Malware attack that changes the user's normal browser home page or new tab selection to access an inappropriate and perhaps malicious website.
Browser **I**n **T**he **B**rowser **(BITB)**	Phishing technique involving the use of custom HTML and JavaScript to trick users into believing they are authenticating to a legitimate website through a pop-up window, whereas in fact they are sending their logon credentials to the phisher.
Brute force [attack], exhaustive attack	a. Form of cryptanalytic attack in which multiple passwords, PIN codes, or encryption keys are entered in an attempt to guess the correct one by chance, having exhausted the key space. Often involves automated tools such as rainbow tables but may be performed manually against low-entropy PINs and weak passwords. "A cryptanalysis technique or other kind of attack method involving an exhaustive procedure that tries all possibilities, one-by-one [and] An attack that involves methodically trying all possible combinations of passwords or encryption keys until the correct one is found" *(SANS glossary)*. "A class of algorithms that methodically try all possible combinations until a solution is found" *(ISACA glossary)*. "When an automated continuous attack is conducted against a system or file to decrypt or discover passwords and data. Often used as an entry point for privilege escalation" *(NZISM)*. b. Straightforward, direct, noisy/obvious, crude, unsubtle, full-frontal attack on physical security using violent force such as ram-raiding, chain-sawing through fences and walls, and threatening/assaulting security guards or receptionists with guns and explosives.
Brute-force password attack, password crack	Crude attack on passwords by generating and trying potential passwords, either repeatedly presenting the guesses for authentication or hashing them and searching a password file for the corresponding hash values. "A method of accessing an obstructed device by attempting multiple combinations of numeric/alphanumeric passwords" *(NIST SP 800-101)*.
Brute Ratel	Powerful hacking/red-teaming tool from Dark Vortex. An example of dual-use technology used by black, grey, and white hats. More info: https://bruteratel.com/

TERM	MEANING
BS7858:2012	British Standard code of practice for preemployment security screening (background checks and security clearance).
B-to-B, B2B	*Abbrev:* **B**usiness-**to**-**B**usiness.
Buffer overflow	Software bug or design flaw that allows – or fails to prevent – a buffer space in memory being over-filled with excessive amounts of data, such that it overwrites adjacent memory locations. While this normally results in the program simply crashing, hackers are adept at crafting malicious data in such a way that the overspill is directly executed or points to another memory location where exploit code has also been inserted. Buffers are used internally to hold interim values for calculations and text operations, plus data input through the keyboard or arriving through the network: these may also be vulnerable to overflows if unchecked. "An anomaly that occurs when a program or process tries to store more data in a buffer (temporary data storage area) than it was intended to hold. Notes: Because buffers contain a finite amount of data, excess data can overflow into adjacent buffers, corrupting or overwriting their valid data. Although it may occur accidentally through programming error, buffer overflow is also an increasingly common type of security attack on data integrity. In buffer overflow attacks, the extra data may contain codes designed to trigger specific actions, which in effect, send new instructions to the attacked computer that can damage user files, change data or disclose confidential information" *(ISACA glossary)*. "Occurs when a program or process tries to store more data in a buffer (temporary data storage area) than it was intended to hold. Since buffers are created to contain a finite amount of data, the extra information – which has to go somewhere – can overflow into adjacent buffers, corrupting or overwriting the valid data held in them" *(SANS glossary)*.
Buffer overflow attack	Attack attempting to exploit a buffer overflow vulnerability. "A method of overloading a predefined amount of memory storage in a buffer, which can potentially overwrite and corrupt memory beyond the buffer's boundaries" *(NIST SP 800-101)*.
Bug	a. *[Noun]* Programming fault or defect accidentally inserted into a program by a software developer or – literally – an insect causing an electrical fault in a computer system. Most bugs are trivial and benign but some create vulnerabilities that may lead to security incidents such as a crash or compromise. "A fault in a program that causes it to perform in an unintended or unanticipated manner" *(ISACA glossary)*. See also web bug, flaw, error. b. *[Noun]* Covert surveillance device used to monitor, track, or snoop surreptitiously on the online activities, conversations, *etc.* of individual targets, potentially compromising trade secrets or personal information.

TERM	MEANING
	c. *[Verb]* To conduct covert surveillance, *e.g.* by placing monitoring devices and location trackers in/on a target. d. *[Verb]* To annoy or pester someone, usually inadvertently or casually but potentially a deliberate distraction technique.
Bugbear	Malware species in the wild in 2002.
Bug bounty	Corporate scheme to encourage and reward the ethical reporting of software bugs and flaws, particularly those creating security vulnerabilities, by third parties (generally). "A monetary reward to researchers for the discovery and reporting of software and other information system vulnerabilities" *(NZISM)*. See also responsible disclosure.
Building **M**anagement **S**ystem **(BMS)**	**O**perational **T**echnology coordinating, supervising/monitoring, and controlling various computer systems in a building, such as the electricity supply, **H**eating **V**entilating and **A**ir **C**onditioning, lighting, security alarm, and card access control systems.
Bulk data transfer	Datacommunications technique typically involving the physical carriage of high-density data storage media such as portable hard drives and backup tapes between facilities, organisations, archives, *etc.*, avoiding various issues associated with networking. "A data recovery strategy that includes recovery from complete backups that are physically shipped offsite once a week. Notes: Specifically, logs are batched electronically several times daily and then loaded into a tape library located at the same facility as the planned recovery" *(ISACA glossary)*.
BULLRUN	TOP SECRET **N**ational **S**ecurity **A**gency 'decryption program' disclosed by whistleblower Ed Snowden. Part of a global surveillance/SIGINT framework systematically snooping on encrypted traffic including **S**ecure **S**ockets **L**ayer and (some) **V**irtual **P**rivate **N**etworks using cryptanalysis on [deliberately weakened] cryptographic protocols. See also Edgehill.
Burglary	Trespass with intent to steal.
Burp [suite]	Penetration testing/hacking tool for attacking web applications. Free and commercial versions. An example of dual-use technology, popular with black, grey, and white hats. More info: https://portswigger.net/burp
Business	a. Organisation, whether commercial/profit-driven or not. b. Activities of an organisation, particularly those relating to its main products and strategic objectives (its 'core business') but also its support and administrative activities, including commercial/financial management. c. Industry, trade, or profession, *e.g.* the entertainment business.

TERM	MEANING
Business continuity	Continuity of an organisation's core business activities by means of resilience, recovery, and contingency arrangements and plans to mitigate the effects of incidents and disasters that might disrupt production, computer systems, networks, and other essential business processes, supply chains, *etc.* "Capability of an organization to continue the delivery of products and services within acceptable time frames at predefined capacity during a disruption" *(ISO 22300)*. "A term for preventing, mitigating and recovering from disruption. Notes: The terms 'business resumption planning,' 'disaster recovery planning' and 'contingency planning' may also be used in this context as they focus on recovery aspects of continuity. For that reason, the 'resilience' aspect should also be taken into account" *(ISACA glossary)*.
Business **C**ontinuity **M**anagement **(BCM)**	Process of directing, controlling and overseeing the organisation's approach to business continuity, such as **B**usiness **I**mpact **A**ssessment to characterise business-critical processes and identify the supporting systems and resources, plus the creation, exercising, maintenance, and assurance of **B**usiness **C**ontinuity **P**lans, *etc.* "Process of implementing and maintaining business continuity" *(ISO 22300)*. "Holistic management process that identifies potential threats to an organization and the impacts to business operations whose threats, if realized, might cause, and which provides a framework for building organizational resilience with the capability for an effective response that safeguards the interests of its key stakeholders, reputation, brand and value-creating activities" *(ISO/IEC 27031)*.
Business **C**ontinuity **M**anagement **S**ystem **(BCMS)**	**M**anagement **S**ystem for business continuity, emphasising the associated governance arrangements. "Part of the overall management system that establishes, implements, operates, monitors, reviews, maintains and improves business continuity. Note: The management system includes organizational structure, policies, planning activities, responsibilities, procedures, processes and resources" *(ISO 22300)*.
Business **C**ontinuity **P**lan [or **P**rogram] **(BCP)**	Preconsidered preparative planning approach intended to ensure the continued operation of essential business processes (including essential supporting systems, resources, and so forth), despite serious incidents or disasters that might occur, through a suitable combination of controls such as resilience, **D**isaster **R**ecovery, and contingency arrangements that will minimise the extent and duration of adverse impacts. "Documented information that guides an organization to respond to a disruption and resume, recover and restore the delivery of products and services consistent with its business continuity objectives" *(ISO 22300)*. "Documented procedures that guide organizations to respond, recover, resume, and restore to a pre-defined level of operation following disruption. Note: Typically this covers resources, services and activities required to ensure the continuity of critical business functions"

TERM	MEANING
	(ISO/IEC 27031). "A plan used by an enterprise to respond to the disruption of critical business processes (depends on the contingency plan for the restoration of critical systems)" *(ISACA glossary)*. "The plan for emergency response, backup operations, and post-disaster recovery steps that will ensure the availability of critical resources and facilitate the continuity of operations in an emergency situation" *(SANS glossary)*. "A plan that focuses on sustaining an organization's mission or business processes during and after a disruption, and may be written for mission or business processes within a single business unit or may address the entire organization's processes" *(OMB Circular A-130)*. *Cf.* **B**est **C**urrent **P**ractice.
Business control	Control designed to mitigate unacceptable business risks. "The policies, procedures, practices and organizational structures designed to provide reasonable assurance that business objectives will be achieved and undesired events will be prevented or detected" *(ISACA glossary)*.
Business-critical	Class of information asset, business function, process, *etc.* that is critical to the organisation's core purposes, strategic objectives, or mission. The potential severity of information security incidents affecting such assets, the scale and nature of the impacts, implies that realistic threats acting on known vulnerabilities almost certainly qualify as high risks. See also Tier 1, 2, or 3, safety-critical.
Business **D**ependency **A**nalysis **(BDA)**	"A process of identifying resources critical to the operation of a business process" *(ISACA glossary)*.
Business directory fraud	Through social engineering, fraudsters manipulate victims into over-paying for entries in business directories, listings, or **D**ata**B**ases that are largely worthless and may not even exist. Common techniques include persistent cold-calling and spamming, misrepresenting the directories, misleading websites, submitting invoices to 'renew' non-existent subscriptions directly to lowly procurement or accounts clerks or personal assistants, innocuous-looking forms using the word 'insertions' (meaning paid advertisements) in the small print, inducements such as 'free offers' and entries in business awards, and baseless coercive threats from self-styled 'debt collection agencies.'
Business **E**mail **C**ompromise **(BEC),** Email **A**ccount **C**ompromise **(EAC),** **M**an-**I**n-**T**he-**E**mail **(MITE)**	Lucrative type of social engineering attack involving misuse or falsification of email **ID**entities/addresses/accounts or systems (*e.g.* through hacking, spyware, or simply faking email sender addresses) to defraud victims. There are many variants, *e.g.* masquerading as a boss or supplying a false invoice in order to trick an accounts clerk to change the payee's bank account and so divert funds into the fraudster's money laundering process. See also **V**endor **E**mail **C**ompromise.

TERM	MEANING
Business function	Business function. "An activity that an enterprise does, or needs to do, to achieve its objectives" *(ISACA glossary)*.
Business impact	Adverse effects of incidents on the business, potentially those involving lost production, disruption of commercial activities, devaluation of brands and loss of reputation, customer and employee defection, reduction of stock value, increased costs, increased regulatory oversight, prosecution, *etc*. In comparison to the immediate or short-term effects, it is difficult to identify or ascribe and quantify impacts over the longer term. "The net effect, positive or negative, on the achievement of business objectives" *(ISACA glossary)*.
Business Impact Analysis **[or** Assessment**] (BIA)**	That part of risk analysis which involves investigating the potential business impacts of various events, incidents, and disasters on critical business processes. "Process of analysing the impact over time of a disruption on the organization. Note: The outcome is a statement and justification of business continuity requirements" *(ISO 22300)*. "Process of analysing operational functions and the effect that a disruption might have upon them" *(ISO/IEC 27031)*. "The process of evaluating the criticality and sensitivity of information assets by determining the impact of losing the support of any resource to an enterprise. This establishes the escalation of a loss over time, identifies the minimum resources needed to recover and prioritizes the recovery of processes and the supporting system. Note: This process captures income loss, unexpected expense, legal issues (regulatory compliance or contractual), interdependent processes and loss of public reputation or public confidence" *(ISACA glossary)*. "Determines what levels of impact to a system are tolerable" *(SANS glossary)*. "The identification of critical business processes, and the potential damage or loss that may be caused to the organization resulting from a disruption to those processes. Business impact analysis identifies: the form the loss or damage will take; how that degree of damage or loss is likely to escalate with time following an incident; the minimum staffing, facilities and services needed to enable business processes to continue to operate at a minimum acceptable level; the time for full recovery of the business processes" *(ENISA RM glossary)*.
Business interruption	Incident that halts production. "Any event, whether anticipated (*i.e.*, public service strike) or unanticipated (*i.e.*, blackout), that disrupts the normal course of business operations at an enterprise" *(ISACA glossary)*.
Business model	Coherent suite of corporate objectives, sometimes expressed as a strategy, mission statement, set of values, governance structure, organogram, *etc*. "A model that describes how a company creates, delivers, and captures value for its stakeholders. It defines the fundamental aspects of a company's operations, such as its target customers, value proposition, revenue streams, cost structure, and key resources and activities" *(OCEG GRC Glossary)*.

TERM	MEANING
Business **M**odel **f**or **I**nformation **S**ecurity **(BMIS)**	"A holistic and business-oriented model that supports enterprise governance and management information security and provides a common language for information security professionals and business management" *(ISACA glossary)*.
Business objective	Business objective – something management and other stakeholders expect or require the organisation to do or achieve. "A further development of business goals into tactical targets and desired results and outcomes" *(ISACA glossary)*.
Business partner	"An individual or business (and its employees), other than a vendor, that has some degree of involvement with the entity's business dealings or agrees to cooperate, to any degree, with the entity (for example, a computer manufacturer who works with another company who supplies it with parts)" *(**T**rust **S**ervices **C**riteria)*.
Business process	Process performed by workers within the organisation for business reasons. "An interrelated set of cross-functional activities or events that result in the delivery of a specific product or service to a customer" *(ISACA glossary)*.
Business process control	Process control applied to business processes, *e.g.* production **Q**uality **C**ontrol designed to prevent low-quality products being delivered, or various integrity controls embedded within financial processes.
Business process integrity	Integrity (completeness, timeliness, reliability, *etc.*) of a business process. "Controls over business processes that are supported by the enterprise resource planning system (ERP)" *(ISACA glossary)*.
Business process owner	Notional owner of a business process, generally a manager in charge/control of and responsible for it. "The individual responsible for identifying process requirements, approving process design and managing process performance. Note: Must be at an appropriately high level in the enterprise and have the authority to commit resources to process-specific risk management activities" *(ISACA glossary)*.
Business **P**rocess **R**eengineering **(BPR)**	Systematic redesign of an existing business process, *e.g.* to improve its reliability, quality, security, or cost-effectiveness, often through greater automation. "The thorough analysis and significant redesign of business processes and management systems to establish a better-performing structure that is more responsive to the customer base and market conditions while yielding material cost savings" *(ISACA glossary)*.
Business **R**esumption [or **R**ecovery] **P**lan **(BRP)**	Preparations to recover or restore and so resume essential business activities following a disaster that has disrupted them, typically by providing business-critical information services temporarily from a secondary facility, possibly a mobile site.

TERM	MEANING
Business risk	Risk involving or affecting the business. "The probability that a situation with uncertain frequency and magnitude of loss (or gain) could prevent the enterprise from meeting its business objectives" *(ISACA glossary)*.
Business sponsor	"The individual accountable for delivering the benefits and value of an IT-enabled business investment program to the enterprise" *(ISACA glossary)*.
Business system	System, application, service, *etc.* supporting an organisation's business activities.
Business-**to**-**B**usiness **(B2B, B-to-B)**	Production and sale of commercial products (goods and/or services) by one business organisation to another, *i.e.* between trading partners, as opposed to **B**usiness-**to**-**C**onsumer (retailing, *i.e.* all but the final link in a supply chain). "Transactions in which the acquirer is an enterprise or individual operating in the scope of their professional activity. In this case, laws and regulations related to consumer protection are not applicable. Notes: A contract's general terms should be communicated to the other party and approved. Some companies require the other party to fill out a check-box with a description such as, 'I specifically approve the clauses.' This is not convincing; the best solution is adopting a digital signature scheme, which allows the approval of clauses and terms with a nonrepudiation condition" *(ISACA glossary)*.
Business-**to**-**C**onsumer **(B2C, B-to-C)**	Essentially, commercial retailing of products (goods and/or services) to individual customers rather than to other organisations (**B**usiness-**to**-**B**usiness). May be direct-to-market sales by primary producers (*e.g.* at the farm gate) but usually involves a supply chain connecting primary producers to consumers via B2B intermediaries, each (allegedly!) adding value in some way. "Selling processes in which the involved parties are an enterprise, which offers goods or services, and a consumer. In this case, there is comprehensive legislation that protects the consumer. Notes: Comprehensive legislation can include: Contracts established outside the merchant's property (such as the right to end a contract for a full refund or a return policy for goods); Distance contracts (such as rules that establish how a contract should be written, specific clauses or how a contract should be transmitted to the consumer and approved); An electronic form of contract (such as an Internet contract or the option for the consumer to exit a procedure without having their data recorded)" *(ISACA glossary)*.
Business-to-Consumer eCommerce	"The processes by which enterprises conduct business electronically with their customers and/or the public at large using the Internet as the enabling technology" *(ISACA glossary)*.

TERM	MEANING
Business unit	Business unit, *i.e.* a substantial part of an enterprise, generally quite self-contained although it may utilise or provide products (goods and/or services) to the remainder. "An organizational unit that is subordinate to the enterprise and often responsible for specific products, customers, or geography" *(OCEG GRC Glossary)*.
BYOC	*Abbrev:* **B**ring **Y**our **O**wn **C**loud.
BYOD	*Abbrev:* **B**ring **Y**our **O**wn **D**evice.
BYOK	*Abbrev:* **B**ring **Y**our **O**wn **K**ey.
BYOT	*Abbrev:* **B**ring **Y**our **O**wn *Thing*.
Bypass **L**abel **P**rocessing **(BLP)**	"A technique that involves reading a computer file while bypassing the internal file/data set label. This process can result in the bypassing of the security access control system" *(ISACA glossary)*.
Byte	Smallest addressable unit of computer data, usually but not necessarily eight bits (an octet). "A sequence of adjacent bits, often an octet, operated on as a unit" *(ISACA glossary)*. "A fundamental unit of computer storage; the smallest addressable unit in a computer's architecture. Usually holds one character of information and usually means eight bits" *(SANS glossary)*. See also word.
Byzantine fault	Class of obscure system flaws with symptoms or characteristics that depend on the observer's perspective or context. Of particular concern when engineering critical or vital systems. Faulty or compromised hardware or software may generate data that differ and perhaps *appear* normal to some other systems, frustrating the use of simple consensus to spot and react to exceptions.
Byzantine **F**ault **T**olerance **(BFT)**	Fault-tolerant system architecture designed to avoid or at least identify and respond appropriately to Byzantine faults. "The property of a system that allows it to withstand failures and continue to function even if some of the nodes fail or act maliciously" *(ISACA glossary)*.

C

TERM	MEANING
C², C2, C&C	See Command and Control.
CA	*Abbrev:* Certification Authority or Contract Account, depending on context.
CAB	*Abbrev:* Conformity Assessment Body – see Certification Body.
Cabinet Office Briefing Rooms (COBR)	"The UK central government response to emergencies is underpinned through use of COBR; the physical location, usually in Westminster, from which the central response is activated, monitored and co-ordinated and which provides a focal point for the government's response and an authoritative source of advice for local responders" *(UK National Cyber Security Strategy 2022)*.
CAE	*Abbrev:* Chief Audit Executive.
Caesar's cipher	Cryptographic algorithm originally used by Julius Caesar to encrypt secret messages for soldiers in the Roman colonies. A simple monoalphabetic substitution cipher, easy to break today but evidently adequate to meet Caesar's data confidentiality requirements back then. See also Vigenére's cipher.
CAF	*Abbrev:* Cyber Assessment Framework.
Cain and Able, Cain	Password recovery and hacking tool capable of brute force and dictionary attacks on a wide variety of password hashes and cryptographic keys, on Windows systems.
CAIQ	*Abbrev:* Consensus Assessment Initiative Questionnaire.
Calibrate, calibration	Process to check and align a measurement function, instrument, or process with a reference standard (usually indirectly via secondary standards, themselves calibrated against a definitive primary standard stored under specified conditions with strong physical security and environmental control, and strictly limited access) ensuring sufficient accuracy and repeatability of measured values for the required purposes, reducing the need for tolerance. An important information integrity control. "The set of operations that establish, under specified conditions, the relationship between values indicated by a measuring instrument or measuring system, or values represented by a material measure, and the corresponding known values of a measurand" *(FSRCoP)*.

TERM	MEANING
California Consumer Protection Act of 2018 (CCPA)	European-style privacy law imposing obligations on medium to large commercial organisations to 'implement and maintain reasonable security procedures and practices' in order to protect personal data (as defined in the Act) and give Californians the right to opt out of companies selling or exchanging (giving away) their personal data.
Caller ID (identity)	Technological function to display and store a phone caller's phone number on the called phone, enabling the recipient to identify the caller, call them back, *etc.* Unfortunately, the technology is not sufficiently secure to prevent social engineers spoofing their numbers (*e.g.* so fraudsters appear to be calling from a trusted bank's number).
Camaro Dragon	One of several groups of elite hackers/cyber-spooks apparently of Chinese origin, targeting European foreign affairs workers with **A**dvanced **P**ersistent **T**hreat remote control malware spread via infected USB memory sticks in 2023.
Camouflage (camo)	Concealing one's presence by mimicking and thus blending into the background using natural colours, shapes, and textures. An ancient physical security technique used by many prey and predator species, including humans (*e.g.* hunters, soldiers).
Canadian Security Intelligence Service (CSIS)	Canada's national intelligence agency. Vision: "A safe, secure and prosperous Canada, through trusted intelligence and advice." More info: https://www.canada.ca/en/security-intelligence-service.html
CANbus (Controller Area Network bus)	Communications standards for microcontrollers (**E**lectronic **C**ontrol **U**nits) and other electronic devices in vehicles, developed by Bosch. The primary security requirements in such environments are to ensure data and system integrity and availability.
Canonical	Orthodox, conventional, conforming to a generally accepted rule or format.
Canonicalize	"To reduce various encodings and representations of data to a single simple form" *(SCP QRG)*.
CANVAS	Commercial network security/penetration test tool. Automates *hundreds* of exploits against known vulnerabilities.

TERM	MEANING
Capability, capable	Ability, competence, suitability, capacity, and willingness to do something successfully, *i.e.* capably. "Ability to perform a specified activity" *(ISO 19440)*. "An aptitude, competency or resource that an enterprise may possess or require at an enterprise, business function or individual level that has the potential, or is required, to contribute to a business outcome and to create value" *(ISACA glossary)*.
Capability **M**aturity **M**odel **(CMM)**	Conceptual approach promoting systematic structuring and gradual development of business capabilities from informal, *ad hoc*, unreliable beginnings to more formal, consistent, and productive 'levels,' primarily by increasing management and process controls. "1. A model that contains the essential elements of effective processes for one or more disciplines. It also describes an evolutionary improvement path from ad hoc, immature processes to disciplined, mature processes with improved quality and effectiveness. 2. A model, from the Software Engineering Institute (SEI), used by many enterprises to identify best practices useful in helping them assess and increase the maturity of their software development processes. Notes: CMM ranks software development enterprises according to a hierarchy of five process maturity levels. Each level ranks the development environment according to its capability of producing quality software. A set of standards is associated with each of the five levels. The standards for level one describe the most immature or chaotic processes, and the standards for level five describe the most mature or quality processes. This maturity model indicates the degree of reliability or dependency a business can place on a process to achieve its desired goals or objectives. It is also a collection of instructions that an enterprise can follow to gain better control over its software development process" *(ISACA glossary)*.
Capacity	Capability of a computer system, server, device, **D**ata**B**ase, network, generator, *etc.* to deliver the required services, process the requisite number of transactions, store sufficient data, *etc.* Related to availability and performance. "Combination of all the strengths and resources available within an organization, community or society that can reduce the level of risk or the effects of a crisis. Note: Capacity can include physical, institutional, social, or economic means as well as skilled personnel or attributes such as leadership and management" *(ISO 22300)*. "A range for an indicator that defines the maximum level of variation around a target that the organization is unwilling, unable and incapable to address; and may result in jeopardy or ruin" *(OCEG GRC Glossary)*. See also capacity management.
Capacity management	Dynamically aligning the provision of computer systems and services with changing demands, in order to maintain service levels (availability and performance) within acceptable bounds.

TERM	MEANING
Capacity test, capacity stress test, volume test	Testing a system, network, device, function, service, control, *etc.* under substantial loading to determine its ability to withstand stress as it approaches its maximum capacity. Involves monitoring and measuring its capabilities (*e.g.* performance, responsiveness, throughput, integrity, resilience, recovery, security) as the stressor level changes. "A test for testing an application with large quantities of data to evaluate its performance during peak periods" *(ISACA glossary)*. See also stress test.
CAPEC (Common Attack Pattern Enumeration and Classification)	MITRE's catalogue of cyber-attack techniques, methods, and mechanisms – "a comprehensive dictionary of known patterns of attack employed by adversaries to exploit known weaknesses in cyber-enabled capabilities. It can be used by analysts, developers, testers, and educators to advance community understanding and enhance defenses" (MITRE). See also **C**ommon **W**eakness **E**numeration. More info: https://capec.mitre.org/
Capstone	Generic codename for the culmination of a lengthy intelligence operation.
CAPTCHA (Completely Automated Public Turing test to tell Computers and Humans Apart)	Visual online puzzle that is easy for a human to solve but tougher for a bot. "A type of challenge-response test used in computing to ensure that a response was not generated by a computer. An example is the site request given to website users to recognize and type a phrase posted using various challenging-to-read fonts" *(ISACA glossary)*.
Capture **T**he **F**lag **(CTF)**	Emulation of an attack, or a planned campaign consisting of multiple attacks, on an organisation or its sites, networks, **I**nformation **T**echnology systems, or parts thereof, in which the side on the offensive (commonly called the red team) attempt to place markers (such as fake bombs) and/or retrieve predesignated Information (the flags) to prove that they largely or completely defeated the defenders (the blue team). See also purple team.
Carbanak	Bank Trojan in-the-wild built with Carberp.
Carberp	Crimeware kit for building Trojans. As with Zeus, the source code for Carberp was released onto the Internet.
Card access control, card swipe	Physical security system uses personal RFID cards to identify individual workers on site and either permit or deny them access through security doors, turnstiles, mantraps, or other barriers according to zoning rules. Security may be increased with PIN pads and biometric readers for **M**ulti**F**actor **A**uthentication, CCTV coverage, and security guards at manned checkpoints. "A physical control technique that uses a secured card or ID to gain access to a highly sensitive location. Notes: If built correctly, card swipes act as a preventive control over physical access to sensitive locations. After a card has been swiped, the application attached to

TERM	MEANING
	the physical card swipe device logs all card users who try to access the secured location. In this way, the card swipe device prevents unauthorized access and logs all attempts to enter the secured location" *(ISACA glossary)*.
Carder	Criminal who steals, counterfeits, trades, and/or validates credit card data.
Carding	Stealing, counterfeiting, trading, or validating credit card data.
Careless	Without due care, failing to act sufficiently cautiously under the circumstances. Less severe than negligent or reckless.
Carnivore	Early Internet surveillance system implemented around the turn of the millennium by the **F**ederal **B**ureau of **I**nvestigation as PC software, capable of selectively monitoring Internet traffic to/from specified users by 'packet sniffing' (tapping) particular network cables. Based on even earlier surveillance systems such as Omnivore. Renamed DCS1000 to *appear* less threatening. Superseded by ever more sophisticated and capable surveillance systems.
CARTA	*Abbrev:* **C**ontinuous **A**daptive **R**isk and **T**rust **A**ssessment.
CASB	*Abbrev:* **C**loud **A**ccess **S**ecurity **B**roker.
Cascade, cascading failure	Information security incidents adversely affecting something (such as electricity generation) on which something else depends (most electrical and electronic devices in that case) are likely to cause widespread, rolling, and longer-lasting disruption as the effects spread, with additional impacts further down the line. At a more general level, any significant incident creates stress and may divert attention and resources from other matters, perhaps leading to or failing to address further incidents. Such dependencies are commonplace in any complex situation or system.
Cascaded connections	"Links to other systems that occur when connected systems are themselves connected to other systems [which] may result in multiple indirect (cascaded) connections to systems with differing security implementations, data, equipment and other aspects important for the security and assurance of systems" *(NZISM)*. "Occur when one network is connected to another, which is then connected to another, and so on" *(AusISM)*.
Cascading risk	"The knock-on impacts of a risk that cause further physical, social or economic disruption. For example, severe weather could cause flooding, which then causes damage to electricity infrastructure, resulting in a power outage which then disrupts communications service providers (and so on)" *(UK Resilience Lessons Digest 2023)*.

TERM	MEANING
Case and Incident Management (CIM)	System supporting a busy **security operations** function dealing with a mix of routine cases (such as security configuration changes) and incidents (such as network intrusions). *Cf.* **Coordinated Incident Management**, **Common Information Management**, **Comprehensive Incident Management**.
Cashing out	Hacker phrase for the process of converting 'hot' (stolen) information assets into untraceable cash through various black market trades and money laundering schemes. See also monetise.
CASP+	See SecurityX (a rebranded qualification).
Catastrophic interference, catastrophic forgetting	While Artificial Intelligence systems are being taught new knowledge and capabilities, they may abruptly lose those acquired previously unless appropriate steps are taken to ensure retention.
Catastrophic risk	Risk that may lead to *extremely* damaging, even existential impacts. "Those risks with the potential to cause extreme, widespread and/ or prolonged impacts, including significant loss of life, and/or severe damage to the UK's economy, security, infrastructure systems, services and/or the environment. Risks of this scale would require coordination and support from the UK government" *(UK Resilience Lessons Digest 2023)*.
Catfishing	Fraud perpetrated through social media involving the use of sockpuppets to mislead, hook, and then compromise targets.
CATNAP (Cheapest Available Technology/ Technique Narrowly Avoiding Prosecution)	Spending the least amount necessary to satisfy the letter of the law, where there is no apparent business advantage in going any further. A drawback of setting low hurdles in compliance-driven cultures
Cause	"The trigger or potential trigger of events that lead to a consequence including agents or forces that are responsible for bringing something into existence or changing it" *(OCEG GRC Glossary)*.
Caveat	Warning, alert, cautionary statement, qualification, or proviso, derived from the Latin *cavere* (beware), *e.g. caveat emptor* (buyer beware), *caveat lector* (reader beware). "A marking that indicates that the information has special requirements in addition to those indicated by the classification and any prescribed endorsement. The term covers codewords, source codewords, releasability indicators and special-handling caveats" *(NZISM)*.
CB	*Abbrev:* **C**ertification **B**ody.
CBEST	*Abbrev:* **C**ritical National Infrastructure **B**anking Supervision and **E**valuation **T**esting.

TERM	MEANING
CBRN	*Abbrev:* **C**hemical, **B**iological, **R**adiological, and **N**uclear.
CC	*Abbrev:* **C**ommon **C**riteria, **C**reative **C**ommons, or **C**ertified in **C**ybersecurity, depending on context.
CCH	*Abbrev:* **C**ommon **C**ontrols **H**ub.
CCI	*Abbrev:* **C**ritical **C**orporate **I**nfrastructure. See Critical Infrastructure.
C|CISO	*Abbrev:* **C**ertified **C**hief **I**nformation **S**ecurity **O**fficer.
CCM	*Abbrev:* **C**loud **C**ontrols **M**atrix.
CCOA	*Abbrev:* **C**ertified **C**ybersecurity **O**perations **A**nalyst.
CCP	*Abbrev:* **C**ritical **C**ontrol **P**oint.
CCPA	*Abbrev:* **C**alifornia **C**onsumer **P**rotection **A**ct.
CCRA	*Abbrev:* **C**ommon **C**riteria **R**ecognition **A**rrangement.
CCSP	*Abbrev:* **C**ertified **C**loud **S**ecurity **P**rofessional.
CCSS	*Abbrev:* **C**rypto**C**urrency **S**ecurity **S**tandards.
CCTV	*Abbrev:* **C**losed **C**ircuit **T**ele**V**ision.
CDN	*Abbrev:* **C**ontent **D**elivery **N**etwork.
CDPSE	*Abbrev:* **C**ertified **D**ata **P**rivacy **S**olutions **E**ngineer.
CDS	*Abbrev:* **C**ross-**D**omain **S**olution.
Cease and desist letter, demand letter, infringement notification	Lawyer's letter formally requiring someone permanently to stop doing something, generally reinforced with an explicit or implicit threat to take legal action against them if they persist.
CEH, C|EH	*Abbrev:* **C**ertified **E**thical **H**acker.
CEI	*Abbrev:* **C**ritical **E**nterprise **I**nfrastructure. See Critical Infrastructure.
Cell	Smallest semi-autonomous functional unit in a commercial, military, terrorist, or other organisation, network, manufacturing production line, *etc.*, generally one of many similar cells all supplied, supported by, serving and thereby forming important parts of a common infrastructure.

TERM	MEANING
Cellular **N**etwork **I**solation **C**ard **(CNIC), SIM clone**	Special **S**ubscriber **I**dentity **M**odule card used in forensic analysis of a cellphone enabling the examination of stored data without it connecting to the cellular network and perhaps receiving a remote wipe command. Emulates a SIM from the original cellular provider. "A SIM card that isolates the device from cell tower connectivity" *(NIST SP 800-101)*.
CE mark	**E**uropean **U**nion product labelling/branding scheme and mark intended to designate products that conform with applicable EU standards or regulations covering health and safety, radio frequency emissions, *etc.* Subverted by Chinese and other far Eastern manufacturers and importers, allegedly denoting "**C**hinese **E**xport" on shoddy substandard and often counterfeit products.
CE marking	"A marking by which a manufacturer indicates that a product with digital elements and the processes put in place by the manufacturer are in conformity with the essential cybersecurity requirements set out in Annex I and other applicable Union harmonisation legislation providing for its affixing" *(EU CRA)*.
Center for **I**nternet **S**ecurity **(CIS)**	US not-for-profit organisation promoting good cybersecurity practices, such as the CIS Critical Security Controls plus security benchmarking and vulnerability scanning tools, hardened **O**perating **S**ystem images, and a community of practice. More info: https://www.cisecurity.org/
Central **I**ntelligence **A**gency **(CIA)**	Spooky US government agency responsible for overseas intelligence and intelligence on foreigners, relating to illegal drugs, arms trafficking, terrorism, *etc.* See also **F**ederal **B**ureau of **I**nvestigation, **D**epartment of **H**omeland **S**ecurity. More info: https://www.cia.gov/
Centre for the **P**rotection of **N**ational **I**nfrastructure **(CPNI)**	UK government security services body formerly responsible for guidance and advice concerning physical, personnel, and information security arrangements (including cybersecurity) protecting critical national infrastructure. Replaced by the **N**ational **P**rotective **S**ecurity **A**uthority.
CEO	*Abbrev:* **C**hief **E**xecutive **O**fficer.
CER	*Abbrev:* **C**rossover **E**rror **R**ate.
Cerber	Species of ransomware. Evidently does not run on Russian-language computers, hinting at its possible origin. Available to rent via **R**ansomware-**a**s-**a**-**S**ervice. Flawed cryptosystem in the initial version was presumably replaced in Cerber 2.
CERT	*Abbrev:* **C**omputer **E**mergency **R**esponse **T**eam.

TERM	MEANING
Certificate	a. Statement formally claiming/asserting or confirming a system's conformity with a defined specification or standard. b. Statement (a credential) formally claiming/asserting or confirming a professional's education, competence, and hence qualification to work in a particular area of expertise. See digital certificate.
Certificate **R**evocation **L**ist **(CRL)**	Published list of digital certificates that have been revoked by the **C**ertification **A**uthority and are therefore invalid. **P**ublic **K**ey **I**nfrastructure systems are *supposed* to check for, and handle, certificates that have been revoked, for instance if the CA has been compromised meaning that fake certificates are or might be in circulation. "An instrument for checking the continued validity of the certificates for which the certification authority (CA) has responsibility. Notes: The CRL details digital certificates that are no longer valid. The time gap between two updates is critical and poses a risk in digital certificate verification" *(ISACA glossary)*. *Cf.* **O**nline **C**ertificate **S**tatus **P**rotocol.
Certificate **T**ransparency **(CT)**	Digital certificate authentication mechanism using a distributed ledger (a Merkle tree) containing details of certificates issued by **C**ertification **A**uthorities.
Certification	Process by which something is formally evaluated against a set of predefined criteria and, if appropriate, confirmed compliant or in conformity through the issue of a paper or digital certificate. "Procedure by which a third party gives assurance that all or part of a data processing system conforms to security requirements" *(ISO/IEC 2382)*. "The process by which the controls and management of an information system is formally evaluated against any specific risks identified and the requirements of the NZISM. A key output is a formal assurance statement that the system conforms to the requirements of the NZISM" *(NZISM)*.
Certification audit	External audit conducted for certification purposes, generally a formal compliance audit by an accredited auditor providing assurance that the organisation is in conformity with and fully satisfies the requirements of a standard such as ISO/IEC 27001. "Audit carried out by an auditing organization independent of the client and the parties that rely on certification, for the purpose of certifying the client's management system. Notes: In the definitions which follow, the term 'audit' has been used for simplicity to refer to third-party certification audit. Certification audits include initial, surveillance, re-certification audits, and can also include special audits. Certification audits are typically conducted by audit teams of those bodies providing certification

TERM	MEANING
	of conformity to the requirements of management system standards. A joint audit is when two or more auditing organizations cooperate to audit a single client. A combined audit is when a client is being audited against the requirements of two or more management systems standards together. An integrated audit is when a client has integrated the application of requirements of two or more management systems standards into a single management system and is being audited against more than one standard" *(ISO/IEC 17021-1)*.
Certification [or **C**ertificate] **A**uthority **(CA)**	Trusted body that digitally signs and issues digital certificates to authenticated users or systems in a **P**ublic **K**ey **I**nfrastructure. "Authority trusted by one or more users to create and assign public-key certificates. Notes: Optionally, the certification authority can create the users' keys. The role of the certification authority in this process is to guarantee that the individual granted the unique certificate is, in fact, who he or she claims to be. Usually, this means that the CA has an arrangement with an institution which provides it with information to confirm an individual's claimed identity. CAs are a critical component in information security and electronic commerce because they guarantee that the two parties exchanging information are really who they claim to be" *(ISO/IEC 27033-1)*. "A trusted third party that serves authentication infrastructures or enterprises, registers entities and issues entities certificates" *(ISACA glossary)*. "An official with the authority to assert that a system complies with prescribed controls within a standard" *(NZISM)*. *Cf.* **C**ertification **B**ody, **C**ontract **A**ccount.
Certification **B**ody **(CB), registrar, C**onformity **A**ssessment **B**ody **(CAB)**	Accredited assurance organisation deemed sufficiently independent, competent, diligent, and trustworthy to review and certify other organisations' conformity with specifications or requirements formally defined in applicable standards or regulations such as ISO/IEC 27001. *Cf.* **C**ertification **A**uthority.
Certification document	Certification document. "Document indicating that a client's information security management system (ISMS) conforms to specified ISMS standards and any supplementary documentation required under the system. Note: This definition does not limit the number of documents collectively known as certification documents" *(ISO/IEC 27006-1)*.
Certification **P**ractice **S**tatement **(CPS)**	Policy document formally and explicitly defining a given **P**ublic **K**ey **I**nfrastructure. "A detailed set of rules governing the certificate authority's (CA) operations. It provides an understanding of the value and trustworthiness of certificates issued by a given CA. Note: In terms of the controls an enterprise observes, this is the method used to validate the authenticity of certificate applicants and the CA's expectations of how its certificates may be used" *(ISACA glossary)*.

TERM	MEANING
Certification report	"A report generated by a certification body of a Common Criteria scheme that provides a summary of the findings of an evaluation" *(NZISM)*. "An artefact of Common Criteria evaluations that outlines the outcomes of a product's evaluation" (AusISM).
Certified **C**hief **I**nformation **S**ecurity **O**fficer **(C|CISO)**	EC Council's senior-level qualification for **C**hief **I**nformation **S**ecurity **O**fficers. Covers: information security management principles, controls, compliance and audit management, governance, and risk management; business acumen; general technical knowledge; strategic security portfolio management; and financial management. More info: https://www.eccouncil.org/train-certify/certified-chief-information-security-officer-cciso/
Certified **C**loud **S**ecurity **P**rofessional **(CCSP)**	ISC2's qualification for cloud security specialists with at least five years' experience. Covers: cloud concepts, architecture, and design; cloud data security; cloud platform and infrastructure security; cloud application security; cloud security operations; and legal, risk, and compliance. More info: https://www.isc2.org/certifications/ccsp
Certified **C**ybersecurity **O**perations **A**nalyst **(CCOA)**	ISACA's qualification for cyber risk managers with a few years' experience. Covers: technology essentials; incident detection and response; cybersecurity principles and risks; securing assets; and adversarial tactics, techniques, and procedures. More info: https://www.isaca.org/credentialing/ccoa
Certified **D**ata **P**rivacy **S**olutions **E**ngineer **(CDPSE)**	ISACA's qualification for privacy professionals. Covers: privacy governance, privacy architecture, and data lifecycle. More info: https://www.isaca.org/credentialing/cdpse
Certified **E**thical **H**acker **(CEH, C|EH, CEH Master)**	EC Council's flagship qualification for penetration testers, cyber incident responders and the like, addressing the trust and competence issues that arise naturally when an organisation employs or commissions hackers to probe and investigate their information security controls. More info: https://www.eccouncil.org/train-certify/certified-ethical-hacker-ceh
Certified in **C**ybersecurity **(CC)**	ISC2's entry-level cybersecurity qualification for newcomers with no **I**nformation **T**echnology work experience. Covers: security principles; business continuity, disaster recovery and incident response; access control and network security; and security operations. More info: https://www.isc2.org/certifications/cc
Certified in **E**merging **T**echnology **(CET)**	ISACA's entry-level qualification encompasses the foundations of cloud, blockchain, **I**nternet **o**f *Things*, and **A**rtificial **I**ntelligence. More info: https://www.isaca.org/credentialing/cet

TERM	MEANING
Certified Information Privacy Manager **(CIPM)**	IAPP's qualification for privacy managers. Covers: privacy operational lifecycle, data governance, privacy framework development and implementation, creating a vision and forming the privacy team, assessing **A**rtificial **I**ntelligence, supply chain risk management, and performance measurement. See also CIPP. More info: https://store.iapp.org/cipm-exam/
Certified Information Privacy Professional **(CIPP)**	IAPP's suite of qualifications for privacy professionals, covering a principles-based framework plus laws and practices specific to Asia (CIPP/A), Canada (CIPP/C), China (CIPP/CN), Europe (CIPP/E) or the US (CIPP/U). See also CIPM. More info: https://iapp.org/certify/cipp/
Certified Information Privacy Technologist **(CIPT)**	IAPP's qualification for privacy technicians. Covers: privacy engineering and risk analysis, encryption and nonrepudiation, identifiability and anonymity, interfaces, tracking and surveillance, interference and other privacy harms, privacy risks due to **A**rtificial **I**ntelligence and **M**achine **L**earning, integration of security with privacy, and privacy governance. More info: https://iapp.org/certify/cipt/
Certified Information Security Manager **(CISM)**	ISACA's qualification for information risk and security management professionals. Covers: information security governance, information security risk management, information security program, and incident management. More info: https://www.isaca.org/credentialing/cism
Certified Information Systems Auditor **(CISA)**	ISACA's preeminent qualification for **I**nformation **T**echnology auditors worldwide. Covers: information systems auditing process; governance and management of IT; information systems acquisition, development, and implementation; information systems operations and business resilience; and protection of information assets. *Cf.* **C**ybersecurity and **I**nfrastructure **S**ecurity **A**gency, **C**ybersecurity **I**nformation **S**haring **A**ct. More info: https://www.isaca.org/credentialing/cisa
Certified Information Systems Security Professional **(CISSP)**	ISC2's qualification for cybersecurity practitioners and managers with at least 5 years' experience. Covers: security and risk management, asset security, security architecture and engineering, communications and network security, identity and access management, security assessment and testing, security operations, and software development security. More info: https://www.isc2.org/certifications/cissp
Certified in Risk and Information Systems Control **(CRISC)**	ISACA's qualification for information risk and security management professionals. Covers: corporate **I**nformation **T**echnology governance, IT risk assessment, risk response and reporting, and IT and security. More info: https://www.isaca.org/credentialing/crisc

TERM	MEANING
Certified **I**nternal **A**uditor (CIA®)	The **I**nstitute of **I**nternal **A**uditors, Inc. qualification for internal auditors. Syllabus covers foundations of internal auditing; ethics and professionalism; governance, risk management, and control; fraud risks; engagement planning; information gathering, analysis and evaluation; engagement supervision and communication; internal audit operations; internal audit plan; quality of the internal audit function; and engagement results and monitoring. More info: https://www.theiia.org/en/certifications/cia/
Certified in the **G**overnance of **E**nterprise **IT** (CGEIT)	ISACA's qualification for **I**nformation **T**echnology governance professionals. Covers: governance of enterprise IT, IT resources, benefits realisation, and risk optimisation. More info: https://www.isaca.org/credentialing/cgeit
Certifi-Gate	Vulnerability in digital certificate handling by some privileged remote access/systems administration tools on Android, exploited by malware in 2015.
CET	*Abbrev:* **C**ertified in **E**merging **T**echnology.
Cf.	*Abbrev:* **c**on**f**er – Latin for 'compare or contrast against,' also indicates 'as opposed to' or 'do not confuse with.'
CFD	*Abbrev:* **C**ontrol **F**low **D**iagram or **C**ontract **F**or **D**ifferences, depending on context.
CFG	*Abbrev:* **C**ontrol **F**low **G**uard.
CFO	*Abbrev:* **C**hief **F**inancial **O**fficer.
CGEIT	*Abbrev:* **C**ertified in the **G**overnance of **E**nterprise **IT**.
CGI	*Abbrev:* **C**ommon **G**ateway **I**nterface or **C**omputer-**G**enerated **I**magery, depending on context.
ChaCha20	Family of stream ciphers.
Chaff	Thin metallic strips released *en masse* by a warplane or ship to confuse, distract, and so misdirect enemy radar systems – a physical countermeasure. See also flare.
Chain letter	Item or piece of correspondence (*e.g.* letter, postcard, email) urging the recipient to pass it on to others. The content of chain letters varies and, although some are legitimate, most are fraudulently using social engineering techniques to part fools from their valuables (*e.g.* pyramid schemes). Apart from consuming network bandwidth, data storage capacity, wasting users' time, and fooling victims, chain letters sometimes gain false respectability as a result of being passed on, and effectively endorsed, by trusted but foolish intermediaries.

TERM	MEANING
Chainmail	Flexible but heavy body armour constructed from interlocking steel rings, guarding against glancing blows from weapons such as swords and spears. Supplemented by armour plates, shields, and helmets protecting the most vulnerable areas of the body against direct hits and penetration.
Chain of custody, chain of evidence	Maintenance of a complete, accurate, and trustworthy record of the physical custody, protection, and treatment of forensic evidence at every point between its original collection and eventual presentation in court, such that there is no reasonable doubt as to its origin, authenticity, and integrity. "Demonstrable possession, movement, handling and location of material from one point in time until another. Note: Material includes information and other associated assets in the context of ISO/IEC 27002" *(ISO/IEC 27002)*. "The process of evidence handling (from collection to presentation) that is necessary to maintain the validity and integrity of evidence. Notes: Includes documentation of who had access to the evidence and when and the ability to identify that the evidence is the exact item that was recovered or tested. Lack of control over evidence can lead to it being discredited. Chain of custody depends on verifying that evidence could not have been tampered with. This is accomplished by sealing off the evidence so it cannot be changed and providing a documentary record of custody to prove that the evidence was, at all times, under strict control and not subject to tampering" *(ISACA glossary)*. "A process that tracks the movement of evidence through its collection, safeguarding, and analysis lifecycle by documenting each person who handled the evidence, the date/time it was collected or transferred, and the purpose for any transfers" *(NIST SP 800-101)*.
Challenge	a. *[Verb]* To pose a question intended to raise or dispel doubt or concern, or to elicit a strong reaction, *e.g.* a lawyer cross-examining a witness in court, or a sentry calling "Halt! Who goes there?," anticipating a specific response from a friendly. b. *[Noun]* Something difficult to overcome or complete successfully.
Challenge-response	Protocol or process in which the respondent must provide the correct, anticipated response or credential when challenged, otherwise the challenger knows something is amiss. Mediaeval gatekeepers demanded "Who goes there?" in anticipation of a visitor revealing the secret pass word to authenticate themselves and so be allowed to pass through a gateway. Nowadays used to establish network communications by confirming that a counterparty holds the correct private key without actually disclosing the key over the network, typically by having them encrypt and return a nonce supplied by the challenger who can then decrypt the response with the respondent's public key to verify that the respondent does in fact hold the corresponding private key (a zero knowledge approach).

TERM	MEANING
Challenge-response token	Challenge-response token. "A method of user authentication carried out through use of the Challenge Handshake Authentication Protocol (CHAP). Notes: When a user tries to log into the server using CHAP, the server sends the user a 'challenge,' which is a random value. The user enters a password, which is used as an encryption key to encrypt the 'challenge' and return it to the server. The server is aware of the password. It, therefore, encrypts the 'challenge' value and compares it with the value received from the user. If the values match, the user is authenticated. The challenge/response activity continues throughout the session, protecting it from password-sniffing attacks. In addition, CHAP is not vulnerable to 'man-in-the-middle' attacks because the challenge value is a random value that changes on each access attempt" *(ISACA glossary)*.
CHAMP (Counter-electronics High-powered microwave Advanced Missile Project)	Boeing's **ElectroMagnetic Pulse** cyberweapon which directs intense bursts of electromagnetic energy at selected target buildings (and perhaps vehicles and other cyberweapons) from a passing aircraft or drone in order to destroy/disable the electronics of computer systems, devices, and network infrastructure within. A form of cybertage.
Chance	See probability.
Change	Difference, alteration. "A holistic and proactive approach to managing the transition from a current to a desired organizational state, focusing specifically on the critical human, or 'soft' elements of change. Note: Includes activities such as culture change (values, beliefs and attitudes), development of reward systems (measures and appropriate incentives), organizational design, stakeholder management, human resources policies and procedures, executive coaching, change leadership training, team building and communication planning and execution" *(ISACA glossary)*.
Change control	Control designed to mitigate unacceptable change risks through a management process for proposing, reviewing, and accepting or rejecting changes to a process, system, and/or the associated documentation. Part of change management. "The processes, authorities and procedures used for all changes made to a computerized system and/or the system data. Change control is a vital subset of the quality assurance program in an enterprise and should be clearly described in the enterprise standard operating procedures" *(ISACA glossary)*.
Change enablement	"A holistic and systemic process of ensuring that relevant stakeholders are prepared and committed to the changes involved in moving from a current state to a desired future state" *(ISACA glossary)*.
Change key	Physical key that can only open a single master-keyed lock. See also sub-master key.

TERM	MEANING
Change management, management of change	Totality of management activities used to plan, risk-assess, authorise, control, direct, and document various changes to the organisation, such as its computer systems, business processes, products, corporate structure, workers, policies, strategies, plans, priorities, algorithms, keys, controls, *etc*. "A holistic and proactive approach to managing the transition from a current to a desired organizational state, focusing specifically on the critical human, or 'soft,' elements of change. Note: Includes activities such as culture change (values, beliefs and attitudes), development of reward systems (measures and appropriate incentives), organizational design, stakeholder management, human resources policies and procedures, executive coaching, change leadership training, team building and communication planning and execution" *(ISACA glossary)*.
Change risk, change-related risk	Risk related to, associated with or caused by change, or conversely the risk of stasis – failing to respond appropriately and promptly to change. "A change in technology, regulation, business process, functionality, architecture, users or other variables that affect the enterprise business and technical environments and the level of risk associated with systems in operation" *(ISACA glossary)*.
Channel	Conduit/pipe, electromagnetic frequency, time-slot, mechanism/method, *etc.* used for communication. "The medium used to get the message from the communicator to the audience" *(OCEG GRC Glossary)*.
Channel coding	See **F**orward **E**rror **C**orrection.
Chaos engineering	Techniques to design and build resilient, robust systems capable of withstanding complex and challenging situations. *Deliberately* creating or simulating fault conditions in cloud-based systems is one (albeit risky) way to gain assurance that the protective arrangements are both sufficient and effective.
Chaos Gorilla	Simian Army tool that emulates outages of entire **A**mazon **W**eb **S**ervices zones to test the effectiveness of the resilience arrangements. See also chaos engineering, Chaos Monkey.
Chaos Monkey	Simian Army tool that randomly terminates **V**irtual **M**achines in the cloud to test the effectiveness of the resilience arrangements. See also chaos engineering, Chaos Gorilla.
Characterisation	"Synonym for 'unique identifier' … an operating system, programme, library or other programmatic element in the form of a checksum which can be calculated from a 'known good' component and stored for comparison should there be any concern that components have been damaged or compromised. Forensic methods may also provide characterisation indicators but are likely to require additional levels of expertise" *(NZISM)*.

TERM	MEANING
Chatham House rule	Informal, trust-based arrangement (an ethical gentleman's agreement) to show discretion and protect the anonymity of the sources of sensitive information disclosed confidentially. "When a meeting, or part thereof, is held under the Chatham House Rule, participants are free to use the information received, but neither the identity nor the affiliation of the speaker(s), nor that of any other participant, may be revealed" *(Chatham House)*.
Cheat	Dishonest, unethical, untrustworthy person who deliberately bends or breaks the rules for personal gain. A fairly minor form of fraud.
Cheat code	See key chord.
Check	Review, analyse, inspect, examine, test, or verify that (to an appropriate degree of confidence, depending on the context and tolerance) something is as required, specified, or expected, thereby confirming or gaining assurance and perhaps releasing it if so, or else retaining it, holding it back or rejecting it. A ubiquitous control. See also check-in, check-out, checklist, check digit, checkpoint, checksum, desk check, fact-check, error check, transcription check.
Check digit	Single digit initially calculated systematically from the digits in a numeric **ID**entifier (*e.g.* a bank account number), then attached to it, such that subsequent changes in any of the digits (*e.g.* due to data entry errors, a noisy datacommunications channel, or malicious interference) will *probably* invalidate the recalculation and comparative check, flagging the change. "A numeric value, calculated mathematically, added to data to ensure that original data have not been altered or that an incorrect but valid match has not occurred. Notes: Check digit control is effective in detecting transposition and transcription errors" *(ISACA glossary)*. See also parity, checksum.
Check digit verification (self-checking digit)	Process of digitally recalculating and verifying the check digit. "A programmed edit or routine that detects transposition and transcription errors by calculating and checking the check digit" *(ISACA glossary)*.
Check-in, check in, sign in	a. Identify and perhaps authenticate as part of a security process, such as when passengers arrive at a port, a worker comes on duty at the start of their shift, a visitor signs the visitor book at reception, or a user logs on to the network. b. Introduce a new or changed resource to an asset management system that will track and protect it.

TERM	MEANING
Checklist	Succinct list of things to do (a skeletal procedure) or items to check and perhaps check-off (click, tick/cross/mark, or strike out) as they are completed. A useful prompt/reminder, particularly for unfamiliar yet important issues. "A list of items used to verify the completeness of a task or goal. Notes: Used in quality assurance (and, in general, in information systems audits) to check process compliance, code standardization, error prevention and other items for which consistency processes or standards have been defined" *(ISACA glossary)*.
Check-out, checkout, check out, sign out	a. Activity concluding a controlled process or session, such as when a user logs off the network, a visitor returns their pass on leaving the building, or a shopper checks and completes a purchase. b. Remove a (copy of) a controlled resource from an asset management system in order to check, change or use it. c. Cursory review.
Checkpoint, checkpoint restart, checkpoint restart process	a. Static record or snapshot of the state of a computer system, application program, **D**ata**B**ase, *etc.* at one point in time to which the system may be rolled back if necessary. "A point in a routine where sufficient information can be stored to allow the restart of computation from that point" *(ISACA glossary)*. "Point in a program, suitable for interrupting the execution of this program, at which a sequence of instructions is inserted to record the status and the results, to inspect them, and to restart" *(ISO/IEC 2382)*. See also breakpoint, backup. b. Physical guard house or similar place manned by security guards through which people and vehicles must pass some sort of inspection (*e.g.* checking ID cards, metal detectors).
Checkpoint and **R**estore **I**n **U**serspace **(CRIU)**	Linux tool to checkpoint (freeze and take a static snapshot of) an application, then later (*e.g.* after performing a higher priority task) restore it to continue executing where it left off, without needing access to the heavily protected **O**perating **S**ystem kernel.
Checkpointing	Process of introducing checkpoints. "The process of storing a block in the history of a blockchain at intervals and refusing to accept divergent blockchain without these blocks" *(ISACA glossary)*.
Checks and balances	Checking and reconciliation of accounts or data files compiled separately but supposed to match item-for-item. In double-entry bookkeeping, for instance, every credit in one ledger should correspond to an equal and opposite debit in another; hence, the total value of a debit account should balance (precisely equal) the total value of the matching credit account. Any discrepancy should be investigated.

TERM	MEANING
Checksum, check value	Basic error-detection technique that involves calculating a characteristic value from some digital data which is transmitted or stored with the data, and can be checked to verify integrity of the data transmission or storage. "A value generated by an algorithm and associated with an input value and/or whole input file. The checksum value can be used to assess its corresponding input data or file later and verify that the input has not been maliciously altered. If a subsequent checksum value no longer matches the initial value, the input may have been altered or corrupted" *(ISACA glossary)*. "A value that is computed by a function that is dependent on the contents of a data object and is stored or transmitted together with the object, for the purpose of detecting changes in the data" (*SANS glossary*). "Verifies or checks the integrity of data. A good checksum algorithm: is easily to compute; will usually output a significantly different value, even for small changes made to the input; and can detect many types of data corruptions ... often used to verify the integrity of operating system, programme, library or other programmatic elements, images and firmware updates ... check digits and parity bits are special uses of checksums" *(NZISM)*. See also hash, parity.
Chemical, **B**iological, **R**adiological, and **N**uclear **(CBRN)**	Refers to the risk of *extreme* terrorist or military attacks potentially involving 'dirty bombs' spreading radioactive material, genetically engineered microbes, Sarin-type poisonous chemical incidents, or nuclear weapons. See also **N**uclear, **B**iological and **C**hemical.
ChewBacca	Species of memory-scraping malware.
C|HFI	*Abbrev:* Computer **H**acking **F**orensic **I**nvestigator.
Chief **A**udit [or **A**ssurance] **E**xecutive **(CAE), Head of [Internal] Audit**	Director or senior/executive manager with overall responsibility for internal audit and perhaps other assurance activities or functions. See also Chief **E**xecutive **O**fficer, Chief **F**inancial **O**fficer, Chief **I**nformation **O**fficer, Chief **I**nformation **S**ecurity **O**fficer, Chief **O**perating **O**fficer, Chief **R**isk **O**fficer, Chief **S**ecurity **O**fficer, Chief **T**echnology **O**fficer. At home in the C-suite. "The leadership role responsible for effectively managing all aspects of the internal audit function and ensuring the quality performance of internal audit services in accordance with Global Internal Audit Standards®. The specific job title and/or responsibilities may vary across organizations" *(IIA GIAS)*.
Chief **E**xecutive **O**fficer **(CEO)**	Director or senior/executive manager with overall responsibility for the organisation as a whole – the most senior executive. "The highest ranking individual in an enterprise" *(ISACA glossary)*. See also Chief **A**udit **E**xecutive, Chief **F**inancial **O**fficer, Chief **I**nformation **O**fficer, Chief **I**nformation **S**ecurity **O**fficer, Chief **O**perating **O**fficer, Chief **R**isk **O**fficer, Chief **S**ecurity **O**fficer, Chief **T**echnology **O**fficer. At home in the C-suite.

TERM	MEANING
Chief **F**inancial **O**fficer **(CFO)**	Director or senior/executive manager with overall responsibility for financial management and reporting, investment, *etc.* "The individual primarily responsible for managing the financial risk of an enterprise" *(ISACA glossary)*. See also **C**hief **A**udit **E**xecutive, **C**hief **E**xecutive **O**fficer, **C**hief **I**nformation **O**fficer, **C**hief **I**nformation **S**ecurity **O**fficer, **C**hief **O**perating **O**fficer, **C**hief **R**isk **O**fficer, **C**hief **S**ecurity **O**fficer, **C**hief **T**echnology **O**fficer. At home in the C-suite.
Chief **I**nformation **O**fficer **(CIO)**	Director or senior/executive manager with overall responsibility for Information Technology. "The most senior enterprise official who is accountable for IT advocacy, aligning IT and business strategies, and planning, resourcing and managing the delivery of IT services, information and the deployment of associated human resources. Notes: In some cases, the CIO role has been expanded to become the chief knowledge officer (CKO). The CKO deals in knowledge, not just information" *(ISACA glossary)*. See also **C**hief **A**udit **E**xecutive, **C**hief **E**xecutive **O**fficer, **C**hief **F**inancial **O**fficer, **C**hief **I**nformation **S**ecurity **O**fficer, **C**hief **O**perating **O**fficer, **C**hief **R**isk **O**fficer, **C**hief **S**ecurity **O**fficer, **C**hief **T**echnology **O**fficer. At home in the C-suite.
Chief **I**nformation **S**ecurity **O**fficer **(CISO)**	Executive manager, typically having overall responsibility for facilitating the governance and management of information risks, information security, *etc.* "The individual in charge of information security in an enterprise" *(ISACA glossary)*. "A senior executive with overall responsibility for the governance and management of information risks within an agency. This may include coordination between security, ICT and business functions to ensure risks are properly identified and managed" *(NZISM)*. "A senior executive who is responsible for coordinating communication between security and business functions as well as overseeing the application of controls and associated security risk management processes" *(AusISM)*. See also **I**nformation **S**ecurity **M**anager, **C**hief **A**udit **E**xecutive, **C**hief **E**xecutive **O**fficer, **C**hief **F**inancial **O**fficer, **C**hief **I**nformation **O**fficer, **C**hief **O**perating **O**fficer, **C**hief **R**isk **O**fficer, **C**hief **S**ecurity **O**fficer, **C**hief **T**echnology **O**fficer. At home in the C-suite.
Chief **O**perating **O**fficer **(COO)**	Director or senior/executive manager with overall responsibility for facilitating day-to-day operations and production. See also **C**hief **A**udit **E**xecutive, **C**hief **E**xecutive **O**fficer, **C**hief **F**inancial **O**fficer, **C**hief **I**nformation **O**fficer, **C**hief **I**nformation **S**ecurity **O**fficer, **C**hief **R**isk **O**fficer, **C**hief **S**ecurity **O**fficer, **C**hief **T**echnology **O**fficer. At home in the C-suite.

TERM	MEANING
Chief Risk Officer (CRO)	Director or senior/executive manager with overall responsibility for facilitating the management of all types of risk. "An executive tasked with assessing and responding to risk to an enterprise's assets" *(ISACA glossary)*. See also **C**hief **A**udit **E**xecutive, **C**hief **E**xecutive **O**fficer, **C**hief **F**inancial **O**fficer, **C**hief **I**nformation **O**fficer, **C**hief **I**nformation **S**ecurity **O**fficer, **C**hief **O**perating **O**fficer, **C**hief **S**ecurity **O**fficer, **C**hief **T**echnology **O**fficer. At home in the C-suite.
Chief Security Officer (CSO)	Director or senior/executive manager with overall responsibility for facilitating security, including physical security and perhaps information security. Typically chairs a Security Committee and reports to executive management. "The individual typically responsible for all physical and digital security matters in an enterprise" *(ISACA glossary)*. See also **C**hief **A**udit **E**xecutive, **C**hief **E**xecutive **O**fficer, **C**hief **F**inancial **O**fficer, **C**hief **I**nformation **O**fficer, **C**hief **I**nformation **S**ecurity **O**fficer, **C**hief **O**perating **O**fficer, **C**hief **R**isk **O**fficer, **C**hief **T**echnology **O**fficer. At home in the C-suite.
Chief Technology Officer (CTO)	See **C**hief **I**nformation **O**fficer. "The individual who focuses on technical issues in an enterprise. Notes: Often viewed as synonymous with chief information officer (CIO)" *(ISACA glossary)*. See also **C**hief **A**udit **E**xecutive, **C**hief **E**xecutive **O**fficer, **C**hief **F**inancial **O**fficer, **C**hief **I**nformation **O**fficer, **C**hief **I**nformation **S**ecurity **O**fficer, **C**hief **O**perating **O**fficer, **C**hief **R**isk **O**fficer, **C**hief **S**ecurity **O**fficer. At home in the C-suite.
Chinese wall, paper wall	*Notional* separation between workers, business functions/departments/units/teams, organisations, networks, systems, *etc.* intended to reduce the probability of inappropriate passage of confidential information between them, avoid conflicts of interest, and/or maintain divisions of responsibility. Depends largely on processes, trust, competence, diligence, and conformity; hence, policies, procedures, guidelines, training, security awareness, and oversight are all relevant, increasing the costs of control. Nevertheless, being paper-thin, this is a weak control that fails-insecure.
Chip	*Abbrev:* micro**chip**. See **I**ntegrated **C**ircuit.
Chip-n-PIN, chip and PIN, chip card	Physically secure payment, charge, store, bank, credit, or debit, card containing an embedded cryptographic module – in practice, a small **I**ntegrated **C**ircuit chip laminated within the card. Compared to magnetic stripe cards, it is extremely difficult for forgers to duplicate well-designed and implemented cryptographic modules due to their physical and logical security controls. Normally, the user must enter their correct PIN code into the chip-n-PIN card reader to authenticate themselves and 'unlock' the card (**M**ulti**F**actor **A**uthentication), further controlling against loss or theft of the card, provided neither the card reader nor the PIN code has been compromised (two known modes of attack).
Chipzilla	See Spectre.

TERM	MEANING
Chosen plaintext attack	Cryptanalytic technique in which the analyst can obtain the ciphertext corresponding to some plaintext of his choosing, which acts as a crib. "Analytical attack in which a cryptanalyst can submit an unlimited number of plaintext messages and examine the corresponding ciphertext" *(ISO/IEC 2382)*. See also known plaintext.
Christmas tree	One of the earliest network worms, released in 1987. Less damaging than The Internet Worm.
Chronic risk	"Continuous challenges which gradually erode our economy, community, way of life and/or national security (*e.g.* money laundering, antimicrobial resistance). Contrast with acute risks" *(UK Resilience Lessons Digest 2023)*.
CI	*Abbrev:* **C**onfiguration **I**tem, **C**ritical **I**nfrastructure, **C**ompetitive **I**ntelligence, **C**ounter-**I**ntelligence, or **C**onfidential **I**nformant, depending on context.
CIA	*Abbrev:* **C**entral **I**ntelligence **A**gency, **C**ertified **I**nternal **A**uditor or **C**onfidentiality, **I**ntegrity and **A**vailability, depending on context.
CIA triad	Primary objective of information security to protect information assets against the compromise of their **C**onfidentiality, **I**ntegrity, and **A**vailability. Note: in addition to those three, other objectives may also be relevant under various circumstances, *e.g.* assurance, auditability, accountability, non-repudiation, and compliance, although most are covered by a broad interpretation of 'integrity.' *Cf.* Parkerian hexad.
CIFS	*Abbrev:* **C**ommon **I**nternet **F**ile **S**ystem.
CIM	*Abbrev:* **C**oordinated **I**ncident **M**anagement, **C**ommon **I**nformation **M**anagement, **C**omprehensive **I**ncident **M**anagement, **C**ase and **I**ncident **M**anagement, or **C**omputer-**I**ntegrated **M**anufacturing, depending on context.
CIO	*Abbrev:* **C**hief **I**nformation **O**fficer.
Cipher	Cryptographic algorithm used to generate/code (encrypt) and decode (decrypt) ciphertext. "An algorithm that performs encryption" *(ISACA glossary)*.
Ciphertext, cyphertext, cryptogram	Bit string or sequence of characters that makes no sense as-is but which can be transformed into the corresponding plaintext using the correct cryptographic algorithm/s and decryption key/s. "Data produced through the use of encryption, the semantic content of which is not available without the use of cryptographic techniques" *(ISO/IEC 2382)*. "Information generated by an encryption algorithm to protect the plaintext that is unintelligible to the unauthorized reader" *(ISACA glossary)*. "The encrypted form of the message being sent" *(SANS glossary)*.

TERM	MEANING
CIPM	*Abbrev:* **C**ertified **I**nformation **P**rivacy **M**anager.
CIPP	*Abbrev:* **C**ertified **I**nformation **P**rivacy **P**rofessional.
CIPT	*Abbrev:* **C**ertified **I**nformation **P**rivacy **T**echnologist.
Circumstantial evidence	Forensic evidence that is peripheral, implicated, or related in some indirect way with an incident, requiring inference to make the association. *Cf.* direct evidence.
CIRT	*Abbrev:* **C**omputer (or **C**yber) **I**ncident **R**esponse **T**eam. See Computer **E**mergency **R**esponse **T**eam.
CIS	*Abbrev:* **C**enter for **I**nternet **S**ecurity.
CISA	*Abbrev:* **C**ertified **I**nformation **S**ystems **A**uditor, **C**ybersecurity **I**nformation **S**haring **A**ct, or **C**ybersecurity and **I**nfrastructure **S**ecurity **A**gency, depending on context.
CISA KEV	*Abbrev:* **C**ybersecurity and **I**nfrastructure **S**ecurity **A**gency's **K**nown **E**xploited **V**ulnerability **D**ata**B**ase.
CIS Critical Security Controls, CIS controls	Simplified set of 18 critical cybersecurity controls recommended by CIS and mapped to NIST's Cybersecurity Framework and SP 800-53, ISO27k, PCI DSS, HIPAA, NERC CIP, and FISMA. First released in 2008, reaching version 8.1 as of 2024. "A prescriptive, prioritized, and simplified set of best practices that you can use to strengthen your cybersecurity posture. Today, thousands of cybersecurity practitioners from around the world use the CIS Controls and/or contribute to their development via a community consensus process." More info: https://www.cisecurity.org/controls
CISM	*Abbrev:* **C**ertified **I**nformation **S**ecurity **M**anager.
CISO	*Abbrev:* **C**hief **I**nformation **S**ecurity **O**fficer.
CISSP	*Abbrev:* **C**ertified **I**nformation **S**ystems **S**ecurity **P**rofessional.
Citadel	**R**emote **A**ccess **T**rojan generated using the Zeus crimeware kit installs a remotely configurable botnet to mount various attacks.
Citizen programmer	Self-taught amateur software developer who writes spreadsheet macros, utilities, **D**ata**B**ases, custom reports, and/or other programs and scripts more as a hobby interest than a profession. Despite their obvious keenness and aptitude, their competence is uncertain due to limited awareness and training in software engineering, policies, methods, *etc.* including cybersecurity and assurance. See also **E**nd-**U**ser **C**omputing.
Civil contingencies risks	"Any event that poses a serious threat to safety and security of livelihoods either locally or nationally. They include, among others, threats to lives, health, critical infrastructure, economy, and sovereignty" *(UK Resilience Lessons Digest 2023)*.

TERM	MEANING
CK	*Abbrev:* **C**rypt-**K**ey.
Claim	Assertion or verifiable statement of fact, *e.g.* a patent claim defines possible applications of an invention protected by the patent; an insurance claim is a request by an insured party for compensation under the policy as a result of an insured event; manufacturers' claims regarding their products may include information security, privacy, and other features and strengths.
Clarifying **L**awful **O**verseas **U**se of **D**ata **(CLOUD) Act of 2018**	US law with a contrived name concerning requests to the US by foreign organisations for intercepted data. Provisions in the law are *intended* to authorise and facilitate appropriate requests for legitimate law enforcement purposes but block inappropriate disclosures.
Clark–Wilson model	Formal model or architecture developed by David D. Clark and David R. Wilson in 1987 elaborates on the Biba model to protect the integrity of all forms of information, not just computer data.
Class, classify, classification, category	Pragmatic grouping-together and labelling of similar or related information assets that are believed to share similar risks and hence control requirements. While classification is a quick process that reduces the need individually to risk-assess and identify security controls needed to protect every single asset in each class, the appropriate generic controls still need to be applied. Furthermore, generic controls may not be ideal for a specific situation; hence, higher classes may require more intense risk analysis and bespoke controls. Classification typically involves confidentiality or privacy criteria but more complex schemes may also take account of integrity and availability requirements. Unfortunately, there is no universal agreement on classification labels and their meanings; hence, in addition to the conformity issues within any organisation there are additional risks of misinterpretation leading to inadequate or inappropriate security when classified materials are shared between organisations or business units with different understandings. "The identification of two or more categories in which an item belongs" *(ISACA glossary)*. "The categorisation of systems and data according to the expected impact if it was to be compromised" *(AusISM)*.
Classical data analysis	"A data analysis technique where data collection is followed by the imposition of a model, and the analysis, estimation, and testing that follow focus on the parameters of that model" *(NIST SP 800-55v1)*. *Cf.* **E**xploratory **D**ata **A**nalysis.
Classification scheme	Formal description of an organisation's classification processes; applicability, authority, rôles, responsibilities, and accountability; criteria/rules to be applied; levels, tags, or labels; and the associated controls. May cover upgrading/downgrading and relabelling arrangements, assurance controls, enforcement, and more.

TERM	MEANING
Classified data	"Data that would cause damage, serious damage or exceptionally grave damage to the national interest, an organisation or an individual if compromised (*i.e.* data assessed as PROTECTED, SECRET or TOP SECRET)" *(AusISM)*.
Classified information	Information with a designated class or level. In the government/military context, the designations usually concern confidentiality requirements such as SECRET. "Government information that requires protection from unauthorised disclosure" *(NZISM)*.
Classified system	"Systems that process, store or communicate classified information" *(NZISM)*.
Clear, wipe	Basic low-assurance form of sanitisation or plain deletion of data. Typically leaves residues that may be recovered trivially or with concerted effort and maybe forensic tools and techniques. "Cause one or more storage locations to be set in a prescribed state, usually that corresponding to zero or that corresponding to the space character" *(ISO/IEC 2382)*. "Sanitize using logical techniques on data in all user-addressable storage locations for protection against simple non-invasive data recovery techniques using the same interface available to the user" *(ISO/IEC 27040)*.
Clearing	"Overwriting classified data on a data medium that has a particular security classification and security category, so that this data medium may be reused for writing at the same security classification and security category" *(ISO/IEC 2382)*. *Cf.* clear/wipe.
Cleartext	See plaintext. "Data that is not encrypted" *(ISACA glossary)*.
Clickbait, click-bait, click bait	Something attractive or intriguing (such as fake news, kittens, and scantily clad people) that lures unsuspecting computer users to click a link, open an attachment, install or run a program or whatever, leading typically to their devices being infected with malware and/or their being defrauded or otherwise compromised. A form of social engineering. The thriving underground market in clickbait pays a premium for clickbait pages with tens or hundreds of thousands of affluent and/or naïve visitors.
Click fraud	Fraud techniques targeting click-through affiliate marketing schemes that pay a bounty for visitors' clicks. In one form, malware surreptitiously swaps genuine affiliate codes embedded in **U**niform **R**esource **L**ocators and cookies for codes linked to the fraudsters' own accounts. In another, malware racks up large pay-per-click charges and/or artificially inflates website reputational ratings (and hence commercial value) by 'clicking' online advertisements.
Clickjacking	Hacking technique that surreptitiously an unexpectedly diverts visitors' browsers to a different website, typically then launching malware attacks against visitors' devices. See also click fraud.

TERM	MEANING
Click-regret	That sinking feeling that follows an unwise click on a dubious link, app, attachment, or security warning message.
Client	Customer, recipient, or beneficiary of a service. "Functional unit that receives shared services from a server" *(ISO/IEC 2382)*.
Client-server	Technical architecture or design typically involving dedicated and powerful **I**nformation **T**echnology systems (servers) providing shared information services via networks to individual distributed/remote systems (clients), *e.g.* a web server providing website content to browser applications running on various user devices. "Pertaining to a method of distributed processing in which a client obtains services from a server" *(ISO/IEC 2382)*. "A term used to broadly describe the relationship between the receiver and provider of a service. Generally, the client-server describes a networked system where front-end applications, like the client, make service requests to another networked system. Client-server relationships are defined primarily by software. In a local area network (LAN), the workstation is the client, and the file server is the server. However, client-server systems are inherently more complex than file-server systems. Two disparate programs must work in tandem, and there are many more decisions to make about separating data and processing between the client workstations and the database server. The database server encapsulates database files and indexes, restricts access, enforces security and provides applications with a consistent interface to data via a data dictionary" *(ISACA glossary)*.
Climate	General or local conditions of weather, ecology, economy, business, market, *etc.* "The collective perception about self, surroundings, and others – including perceptions about culture, some aspect of culture, or some topical area" *(OCEG GRC Glossary)*.
Climate change	Long-term global temperature increases leading to potentially existential risks for organisms (including humans!) that cannot survive sustained mean temperatures a few degrees warmer or the associated environmental impacts such as rising sea levels, melting ice caps, droughts, food shortages, and more extreme weather incidents.
Clipper chip	Failed US government initiative in the mid-1990s to introduce a cryptographic subsystem on a proprietary computer chip using Skipjack with cryptographic keys recoverable by the authorities, allowing them to decrypt data at will. Aside from flaws in the cryptographic design, introducing additional security vulnerabilities, and the obvious trust, privacy, and oversight issues relating to key escrow and surveillance, black hats would simply avoid Clipper, thus negating its alleged purpose. The project's incredible naïveté hints at ulterior motives: the real goal *might* have been to raise awareness of the social issues arising from the use of strong encryption, particularly by criminals and terrorists. Side-effects included stimulating the dissemination and use of other strong encryption systems, and a backlash against invasions of privacy by the authorities.

TERM	MEANING
Clipping	Removing the extremes of a signal or data set, *i.e.* values that are likely to cause processing issues or dubious outliers that would otherwise skew the analysis. "A technique for handling outliers. Specifically, clipping includes reducing feature values that are greater than a set maximum value down to that maximum value. It also involves increasing feature values that are less than a specific minimum value up to that minimum value" *(ISACA glossary)*.
Clone, cloning	Controlled security devices such as authentication tokens and passes, keys, virtual systems, **D**ata**B**ases, and programs are vulnerable to being duplicated/copied illicitly unless there are adequate preventive and/or detective controls. They may also be cloned for legitimate reasons such as backups, **B**usiness **C**ontinuity **M**anagement, **D**isaster **R**ecovery, hardware replacement, testing or forensic purposes.
ClOp	Cybercriminal gang, active in 2023, responsible for the MOVEit Transfer incident.
Closed **C**ircuit **T**ele**V**ision **(CCTV)**	Private audio-visual surveillance system typically used by security guards to monitor premises, safes, vaults, card access-controlled doors/gates, security checkpoints, *etc.* Record evidence of legitimate access plus any intruders, thieves, and saboteurs; by local councils, public bodies, prisons, and the police to oversee public places for disorder, crimes, and safety issues; and by industrial plant operators to monitor production operations and machinery. Modern CCTV systems use networked high-definition digital IP cameras. Some use **A**rtificial **I**ntelligence-enabled machine vision to monitor/track individual assets, *e.g.* automatically disabling manufacturing robots or dangerous machinery if workers enter safety-critical zones.
Close call	See near miss.
Cloud	See cloud computing.
CLOUD	*Abbrev:* **C**larifying **L**awful **O**verseas **U**se of **D**ata Act.
Cloud **A**ccess **S**ecurity **B**roker **(CASB)**	Similar to a firewall, acts as a trusted go-between, linking cloud computing users with their **C**loud **S**ervice **P**roviders and cloud systems/services, applying security rules (policies) to the commands and data *in transit*. CASB services may include access control, encryption, **D**ata **L**oss **P**revention, malware protection, *etc.* "Software or appliances that are positioned between an enterprise technology infrastructure and a cloud service provider (CSP)" *(ISACA glossary)*.
Cloud bursting	Capacity management technique whereby private cloud services temporarily utilise public cloud services to handle peaks in demand – assuming the business benefits and security controls offset the associated costs and information risks.

TERM	MEANING
Cloud computing, cloud [computing] **services,** [the] **cloud**	Provision of distributed, network-based information processing services within a **S**ervice-**O**riented **A**rchitecture typically giving access from anywhere (meaning users typically only need a compatible browser and network connection) and scalability, with performance and resilience advantages if well-engineered. However, cloud computing can also raise governance, ownership, compliance, and other information security and privacy issues. "Convenient, scalable on-demand network access to a shared pool of resources that can be provisioned rapidly and released with minimal management effort or service provider interaction" *(ISACA glossary)*. "Uses a network of external servers accessed over the internet, rather than a local server or a personal computer, to store or transfer data. This could be used, for example, to host a website or corporate email accounts, or for storing or transferring data files" *(UK Cyber Security Breaches Survey 2023)*. "Utilization of remote servers in the data-center of a cloud provider to store, manage, and process your data instead of using local computer systems" *(SANS glossary)*. "Just someone else's computer" (Internet meme).
Cloud **C**ontrols **M**atrix **(CCM)**	Generic suite of information security controls applicable to various types of cloud computing services, as defined by the **C**loud **S**ecurity **A**lliance. Addresses both the **C**loud **S**ervice **P**roviders' and consumers' perspectives. More info: https://cloudsecurityalliance.org/research/working-groups/cloud-controls-matrix/
CloudCracker	Cloud-based commercial service offered to crack by brute force attack on the NT hash values used as part of the **P**oint-to-**P**oint **T**unnelling **P**rotocol and MS-CHAP cryptographic processes.
Cloud environment	Cloud computing environment. "A virtualized environment that provides convenient, on-demand network access to a shared pool of configurable resources such as network, computing, storage, applications, and services. There are five essential characteristics to a cloud environment: on-demand self-service, broad network access, resource pooling, rapid elasticity, and measured service. Some services offered through cloud environments include Software as a Service (SaaS), Platform as a Service (PaaS), and Infrastructure as a Service (IaaS)" *(CIS Controls)*.
Cloud **S**ecurity **A**lliance **(CSA)**	Industry body for **C**loud **S**ervice **P**roviders and their customers, promoting good practices in the information security, privacy, and risk aspects of cloud computing. *Cf.* **C**ontrol **S**elf-**A**ssessment.
Cloud **S**ervice **P**rovider **(CSP)**	Organisation offering cloud computing services, usually on a commercial basis. See also **A**pplication **S**ervice **P**rovider. *Cf.* **C**ontent **S**ecurity **P**olicy.

TERM	MEANING
Cloud Smart	Common name of a US government federal strategy on cloud computing, including the commercial, information security and other aspects. A 2018 update to Cloud First, the original 2010 strategy.
Cloud storage, Web storage, online storage	Service allowing remote access to stored data through the Internet. As with cloud computing, the geographical storage location may be unknown to the user which can raise governance, ownership, compliance, and other information security and privacy issues, while the involvement of external organisations and network communications may expose proprietary data to various risks including unauthorised access, corruption, and Denial-of-Service.
Cluster	Two or more closely coupled computer servers configured to appear as a single operating unit, sharing the processing load and (usually) disks. Can provide higher availability/resilience and performance than a single computer, albeit with additional costs, complexity, and associated constraints. The architectural principle extends to cloud servers with virtualisation, potentially across regions sharing fast (low-latency) network connections.
Cluster controller	"A communication terminal control hardware unit that controls a number of computer terminals. Note: All messages are buffered by the controller and then transmitted to the receiver" *(ISACA glossary)*.
Clustering	Process of defining, forming, and maintaining a cluster. "An algorithm for dividing data instances into groups—not a predetermined set of groups, but groups identified by the execution of the algorithm because of similarities found among the instances. The center of each cluster is known as the 'centroid'" *(ISACA glossary)*.
Cluster of PII	"Personally identifiable information which is processed for a consistent functional purpose. Note: Clusters of PII are described independently of the technical representation of data objects. On a regular basis, the clusters of PII also include PII which is not stored electronically" *(ISO/IEC 27555)*.
CM	*Abbrev:* **C**onfiguration **M**anagement.
CMA	*Abbrev:* **C**omputer **M**isuse **A**ct.
CME	*Abbrev:* **C**ommon **M**alware **E**numeration.
CMM	*Abbrev:* **C**apability **M**aturity **M**odel.
CMMC	*Abbrev:* **C**ybersecurity **M**aturity **M**odel **C**ertificate.
CNA	*Abbrev:* **C**omputer **N**etwork **A**ttack.
CNCI	*Abbrev:* **C**omprehensive **N**ational **C**ybersecurity **I**nitiative.

TERM	MEANING
CND	*Abbrev:* **C**omputer **N**etwork **D**efense.
CNE	*Abbrev:* **C**omputer **N**etwork **E**xploitation.
CNI	*Abbrev:* **C**ritical **N**ational **I**nfrastructure. See **C**ritical **I**nfrastructure.
CNIC	*Abbrev:* **C**ellular **N**etwork **I**solation **C**ard.
CNN	*Abbrev:* **C**onvolutional **N**eural **N**etwork or **C**able **N**ews **N**etwork, depending on context.
CNO	*Abbrev:* **C**omputer **N**etwork **O**perations.
CNSS	*Abbrev:* **C**ommittee on **N**ational **S**ecurity **S**ystems.
CNSSI 4009	US "Committee on National Security Systems Instruction № 4009: Glossary" (2022). A 252-page glossary of information assurance-related terms used by the US government and defence industry. Identifies ~200 authoritative (original) sources for the definitions, mostly NIST standards. [Online access now requires a DoD Root Certificate.]
Co-adaptation	"A process by which neurons predict patterns in training data by relying almost exclusively on outputs of other specific neurons instead of the network's behavior as a whole" *(ISACA glossary)*.
Cobalt Strike	Powerful red team penetration testing/hacking tool, described by its vendor as 'threat emulation software.' 'Beacon' is the name of the multifunctional payload. An example of dual-use technology, popular with black, grey, and white hats. More info: https://www.cobaltstrike.com/
COBIT	ISACA's conceptual framework for corporate technology governance, management, risk, and control. "The current [2019] iteration of COBIT, which builds on and integrates more than 25 years of developments in the field of enterprise governance of information and technology (I&T). It not only incorporates new insights from science but also operationalizes these insights as practices. COBIT is a broad and comprehensive I&T governance and management framework that continues to establish itself as a generally accepted framework for I&T governance. Notes: Earlier versions of COBIT focused on information and technology (IT), whereas COBIT 2019 focuses on information **and** technology aimed at the whole enterprise, recognizing that I&T has become crucial in the support, sustainability and growth of enterprises" *(ISACA glossary)*. More info: https://www.isaca.org/resources/cobit
COBR	*Abbrev:* **C**abinet **O**ffice **B**riefing **R**ooms.

TERM	MEANING
Code, coding scheme, codify, codification	a. Use of words, symbols, strings, phrases, sounds, or images to represent and communicate messages via an encoding process. A crude form of substitution, potentially made more secure through the use of multiple code books, **O**ne-**T**ime **P**ads, steganography, *etc.* "Collection of rules that maps the elements of a first set onto the elements of a second set. Notes: The elements of either set may be characters or character strings. The first set is called coded set and the second set is called code set. Each element of the code set may be related to more than one element of the coded set but the reverse is not true" *(ISO/IEC 2382)*. See also coding, PIN code. b. Explicit 'codified' behavioural framework or structure, or an implicit understanding, appreciation, and acknowledgement of the principles and rules of appropriate/inappropriate behaviour, such as a code of ethics, code of conduct, code of practice, or **A**cceptable **U**se **P**olicy.
Code audit	Audit of source code to gain assurance regarding aspects such as code quality, security, appropriateness, maintainability, and **I**ntellectual **P**roperty **R**ights (*e.g.* conformity with policies and other requirements; well documented with no backdoors or dubious functions). "An independent review of source code by a person, team or tool to verify compliance with software design documentation and programming standards. Correctness and efficiency may also be evaluated. This contrasts with code inspections, code reviews and code walkthroughs" *(ISACA glossary)*.
Code book, codebook	If a list of code words is too long to remember and communicate reliably to those who need to code or decode messages, it may be necessary to prepare and distribute one or more lists from which to lookup codes and their plaintext equivalents. The security issues are similar to those associated with the generation and distribution of encryption keys, *e.g.* ensuring that code books do not fall into enemy hands and cannot simply be reconstructed by the enemy through educated guesswork, known plaintext attacks, or other forms of cryptanalysis.
Code injection	Hacking techniques to insert malicious content into programs during their execution, exploiting various **O**perating **S**ystem and application flaws and bugs, specifically injection flaws. Used by some malware. See also AtomBombing, Cross-Site Scripting, HTML injection.
Codename, codeword	Private monicker or tag for an initiative, tactic, project, planned attack, *etc.* enabling insiders to talk discreetly about the subject, hopefully without tipping off outsiders. An example of security by obscurity. "A short (usually a single word) description of a project, operation or activity, typically assigned used for reasons of reliability, clarity, brevity, or secrecy. Each code word is assembled in accordance with the specific rules of the code and assigned a unique meaning" *(NZISM)*.

TERM	MEANING
Code of conduct	Set of corporate rules for acceptable/unacceptable worker behaviours, typically expressed as a policy, guideline, agreement, rulebook, *etc*. "Sets out the principles, values, standards, or rules of behavior that guide the organization's decisions, procedures, and systems. The Code of Conduct is, in effect, a set of the most important core policies" *(OCEG GRC Glossary)*. See also code, code of ethics, code of practice.
Code of ethics	Comprehensive set of rules, ideals, objectives, principles, practices, and/or values deemed ethical by the organisation, culture, or society. Given that a written code cannot realistically cover all possible ethical issues, a substantial part inevitably remains unstated: however, workers are expected to interpret and apply the guidance sensibly when facing novel situations and dilemmas, acting in the best interests of the organisation, culture, or society. "A document designed to influence employees' individual and organizational behavior by defining organizational values and the rules to be applied in certain situations. Note: A code of ethics is adopted to assist those in the enterprise called upon to make decisions in understanding the difference between 'right' and 'wrong' and to apply this understanding to their decisions" *(ISACA glossary)*. See also code of conduct, code of practice.
Code of practice	Codification of flexible, pragmatic guidelines or principles indicating how organisations should behave in situations or contexts. Intended to supplement and achieve or improve compliance or conformity with laws/regulations and standards. See also code of conduct, code of ethics, **A**cceptable **U**se **P**olicy.
Code Red	Network worm that infected unpatched vulnerable web servers running Microsoft IIS software in 2001. Compromised websites were defaced with "HELLO! Welcome to http://www.worm.com! Hacked By Chinese!"
Code repository **(code repo)**	Online archival facility or library for storing, managing, controlling access to, and sharing software source code (applications, utilities, functions, libraries) plus the associated documentation, test data, testing scripts, metadata, *etc*. within a development team. With strong version control, code changes are tracked and can be reverted if necessary, *e.g.* if conflicts arise when parallel changes are merged. Checking out the specific materials needed to build a particular software release can automatically generate the **S**oftware **B**ill **of M**aterials. A key part of a structured change management process for software companies.

TERM	MEANING
Coding	a. Writing source code for software or firmware. "1. In software engineering, the process of expressing a computer program in a programming language. 2. The transforming of logic and data from design specifications (design descriptions) into a programming language" *(ISACA glossary)*. b. Translating or transliterating messages or other information content into code. See also encode. c. Tagging financial transactions with accounting codes or classifying them into relevant classes or categories for further processing (or similar activities for other types of data).
Coercion	Assertively or aggressively forcing someone to do something against their wishes (*e.g.* pay a ransom to recover their data), typically through physically intimidating, threatening, or blackmailing them, putting them under duress.
Coercivity	Magnetic force that will completely demagnetise a ferromagnetic material such when wiping the data stored on hard disk or mag-stripe bank card. Measured in Teslas. "A measure of the resistance of a magnetic material to changes in magnetisation, equivalent to the field intensity necessary to demagnetise any magnetised material. The amount of coercive force required to reduce any residual magnetic induction to zero. Normally used in describing the characteristics of degaussing magnetic media" *(NZISM)*. "A property of magnetic material, used as a measure of the amount of coercive force required to reduce the magnetic induction to zero from its remnant state" *(AusISM)*.
Cognitive computing	"Category of AI systems that enables people and machines to interact more naturally. Note: Cognitive computing tasks are associated with machine learning, speech processing, natural language processing, computer vision and human-machine interfaces" *(ISO/IEC 22989)*.
Cognitive hacking	See social engineering.
Coinhive	Species of cryptominer malware in the wild in 2018. Infected systems mined Monero cryptocurrency.
CoinVault	Species of ransomware that used 256-bit **A**dvanced **E**ncryption **S**tandard.

TERM	MEANING
Cold site, shell site	Secondary facility with a minimalist **I**nformation **T**echnology setup – little more than a vacant office/suite provided with electrical power and air conditioning. It may take days, perhaps weeks to bring the site fully into operation as a data centre if a disaster befalls the primary site, assuming sufficient IT equipment, data backups, people, *etc.* are available or can be obtained in that timescale. This minimalist approach to IT **D**isaster **R**ecovery *may* be somewhat faster and less risky than buying or renting suitable accommodation on the open market and *may* be appropriate for low-availability IT services that are not business-critical but is far from best practice. "Facility with at least the equipment necessary to support the installation and operation of an alternative data processing system" *(ISO/IEC 2382)*. "An IS backup facility that has the necessary electrical and physical components of a computer facility but does not have the computer equipment in place. Notes: The site is ready to receive the necessary replacement computer equipment in the event that the users have to move from the main computing location to the alternative computer facility" *(ISACA glossary)*. See also warm, hot, and mirror site.
Collaborative **R**esearch **I**nto **T**hreats **(CRITS)**	MITRE project and open-source Unix-based web-based platform/tool for specialists to share artefacts and collaborate with trusted colleagues to analyse malware and other cyber threats, systematically archiving valuable information for future analyses. See also ATT&CK, TAXII. More info: https://www.mitre.org/our-impact/intellectual-property/collaborative-research-threats-crits
Collateral	a. Associated, related, proximal (as in 'collateral damage'). b. Asset offered as a guarantee to a lender, that may be forfeited if the borrower defaults on the loan.
Collection, collect	a. *[Noun]* Set or group of related or associated items collated (systematically gathered together), such as data in a **D**ata**B**ase or postage stamps in an album. b. *[Verb]* To locate and retrieve or gather and amass valuable materials such as forensic evidence, intelligence, or personal information. "Process of gathering the physical items that contain potential digital evidence" *(ISO/IEC 27037)*. "The process of obtaining personal information from the individual directly (for example, through the individual's submission of an internet form or a registration form) or from another party such as a business partner" *(**T**rust **S**ervices **C**riteria)*.

TERM	MEANING
Collector, handler	Someone who gathers intelligence on/about or from certain targets, potentially using OSINT, HUMINT, SIGINT, TECHINT, COMINT, IMINT, ELINT, black bag ops, agents, and other sources plus techniques such as deception, surveillance, and subterfuge. See also agent, spy, spook.
Collision	When two or more things (*e.g.* vehicles, network packets, **D**ata**B**ase data changes, or hash values) coincide, arriving at the same place at the same time. "Condition that results from concurrent transmissions on the transmission medium" *(ISO/IEC 2382)*. "When multiple systems transmit simultaneously on the same wire" *(SANS glossary)*.
Collusion	Conspiracy and nefarious collaboration between individuals or organisations to negate the division of responsibilities, breach Chinese walls, commit fraud, *etc.*
Co-location	Shared use of commercial data centre facilities by multiple customers. "Installation of telecommunications facilities on the premises of other telecommunications carriers" *(ISO/IEC 27011)*.
Colossus	World's first digital programmable computer, designed by Alan Turing, Max Newman, Tommy Flowers, and colleagues at the UK Government Code and Cypher School at Bletchley Park North of London in 1943 during the second World War. Although it was programmed mechanically using patch cables and switches, its sole purpose was to break encrypted teleprinter messages by brute force attack on the keys used on the German Lorenz cryptography machines; hence, arguably it was not a *general-purpose* computer (*Cf.* ENIAC) but was the first cyberweapon.
Combination [code, number]	See PIN code.
Combination lock	Physical lock that can be unlocked with the correct numeric sequence (a PIN code).
Comfort zone	Domain within which we feel safe and secure, and beyond which we feel uncomfortable – possibly threatened and vulnerable, in other words at risk.
COMINT (Communications Intelligence)	Spying on the content (data) and nature (metadata) of communications to gather useful intelligence information. Part of SIGINT. See also HUMINT, TECHINT, OSINT, COMINT, IMINT, ELINT.
Command	a. *[Noun]* Direct order or mandatory instruction. b. *[Verb]* To exert control, be in charge of, or have authority over something or someone. c. *[Verb]* To engender, as in command respect.

TERM	MEANING
Command and Control (C², C2, C&C)	Generally, systems and processes for directing and monitoring diverse operations. In the hacking context, C² normally refers to the covert remote direction and management of malware botnets through the Internet by a bot master. In the military context, C2 or C&C refers to the command structure, lines of communication, *etc.*
Commercially confidential, commercial-in-confidence	Class of business information whose value to its owner relies at least in part on it being withheld from unauthorised parties such as competitors and customers. See also trade secret.
Commercial **O**ff-**T**he-**S**helf **(COTS)**	Generic, commodity, mass-market software package, as opposed to bespoke software developed or customised specifically for individual customers. "Items that can be purchased from a commercial supplier and used without tailoring" *(ISACA glossary)*.
Commit	a. To make a commitment, *e.g.* "We commit to deliver on time." b. To carry out, perpetrate, or perform an act, *e.g.* commit new data to a **D**ata**B**ase, commit fraud.
Commitment	Promise, pledge, declared intention or agreement. "Declarations made by management to customers regarding the performance of one or more systems that provide services or products. Commitments can be communicated in written individualized agreements, standardized contracts, service level agreements, or published statements (for example, a security practices statement). A commitment may relate to one or more trust services categories. Commitments may be made on many different aspects of the service being provided or the product, production, manufacturing, or distribution specifications" *(Trust Services Criteria)*.
Commit point	Timepoint at which new, altered or deleted data records are committed to (recorded in) a **D**ata**B**ase. Well-designed database systems incorporate controls such as locks and control totals to detect and prevent some types of data integrity incident occurring before the commit point, plus journaling and checkpoints to recover from some subsequent incidents.
Committed value	"A value of an indicator that is likely to be achieved given current assumptions and planned execution" *(OCEG GRC Glossary)*.
Committee on **N**ational **S**ecurity **S**ystems **(CNSS)**	US government body responsible for defining policy on information security, cybersecurity, information assurance, and related matters for US government and defence systems, formed from the **N**ational **S**ecurity **T**elecommunications and **I**nformation **S**ystems **S**ecurity **C**ommittee in 2001.

TERM	MEANING
Committee **O**f the **S**ponsoring **O**rganizations of the **T**readway commission **(COSO)**	Primarily known for its "Internal Control – Integrated Framework" first published in 1992 and updated in 2013, comprising the control environment, risk management, control activities, information and communication, and monitoring processes. "A joint initiative of five private-sector organizations and is dedicated to providing thought leadership through the development of frameworks and guidance on enterprise risk management, internal control, and fraud deterrence" *(Trust Services Criteria)*. More info: https://www.coso.org/
Common control, general control	Commonplace, popular, and widespread information security control. a. Information security control shared between multiple organisations, departments, people, applications, networks, systems, *etc.* "A security or privacy control that is inherited by multiple information systems or programs. Note: a control is inherited by an information system when the control is selected for the system but the control is developed, implemented, assessed, authorized, and monitored by entities other than those responsible for the system" *(OMB Circular A-130)*. b. Multi-purpose control to mitigate multiple unacceptable risks, *e.g.* well-designed incident management, response, and recovery approaches help the organisation deal appropriately and flexibly with various types, scales, and severities of incident.
Common **C**ontrols **H**ub **(CCH)**	Commercial service from the **U**nified **C**ompliance **F**ramework providing detailed information on compliance obligations and other information security, privacy, information risk management, and governance-related practices (known as 'controls' within CCH) recommended or required by about a thousand standards, laws, and regulations ('authority documents'). By systematically and painstakingly analysing the sources, they identify common/shared requirements. CCH clients may potentially save money by implementing common controls as part of a suite (a security baseline) rather than individually and perhaps repeatedly to satisfy each compliance obligation separately. See also **S**ecure **C**ontrols **F**ramework.
Common **C**riteria **(CC)**	Formal, internationally recognised scheme defined in the ISO 15408 standards to specify, design, develop, test, evaluate, and certify secure **I**nformation **T**echnology systems for government and defence customers, where 'secure' is explicitly and formally defined through the **T**arget **O**f **E**valuation, **P**rotection **P**rofile, **S**ecurity **T**arget, **S**ecurity **F**unctional **R**equirements, **S**ecurity **A**ssurance **R**equirements, and **E**valuation **A**ssurance **L**evel. The **I**nformation **T**echnology **Sec**urity Evaluation scheme distributes the substantial costs across participating organisations (product vendors and customers) while also improving quality, reducing duplication, and facilitating use of common assurance mechanisms by various nations, agencies, *etc.*

TERM	MEANING
	"A formal, internationally-recognised scheme, defined in the ISO 15408 standard [which] describes process to specify, design, develop, test, evaluate and certify as secure IT systems, where 'secure' is explicitly and formally defined" *(NZISM)*. "An international standard for product evaluations" *(AusISM)*. *Cf.* **C**reative **C**ommons, **C**ertified in **C**ybersecurity. More info: https://www.commoncriteriaportal.org
Common **C**riteria **R**ecognition **A**rrangement **(CCRA)**	"An international agreement which facilitates the mutual recognition of Common Criteria evaluations by certificate producing schemes, including the Australian and New Zealand certification scheme" *(NZISM)*.
Common **G**ateway **I**nterface **(CGI)**	Script or program that executes on a web server in response to a request and perhaps parameters from a web browser. Used to generate dynamic/interactive web pages. "Mechanism is used by HTTP servers (web servers) to pass parameters to executable scripts in order to generate responses dynamically" *(SANS glossary)*.
Common **I**nformation **M**anagement **(CIM)**	Information management framework to normalise and protect stored information using authentication and authorisation for access, and to secure datacommunications with integrity and confidentiality controls. Used for **S**ecurity **I**nformation and **E**vent **M**anagement systems such as Splunk. *Cf.* **C**oordinated **I**ncident **M**anagement, **C**omprehensive **I**ncident **M**anagement, **C**ase and **I**ncident **M**anagement.
Common **I**nternet **F**ile **S**ystem **(CIFS)**	Networking protocol developed by Microsoft in the 1990s to replace **S**erver **M**essage **B**lock v1, although parallel improvements in SMB rendered CIFS unnecessary.
Common **M**alware **E**numeration **(CME)**	Coordination process run by MITRE to assign a common identifier to newly detected malware that may otherwise be identified/named independently by several antivirus companies or malware analysts, causing confusion. Replaced by **M**alware **A**ttribute **E**numeration and **C**haracterization.
Common secure configuration	"Recognized, standardized, and established benchmarks that stipulate secure configuration settings for specific information technology platforms/products and instructions for configuring those system components to meet operational requirements. These benchmarks are also referred to as security configuration checklists, lockdown and hardening guides, security reference guides, and security technical implementation guides" *(NIST SP 800-171)*.
Common **V**ulnerabilities and **E**xposures **(CVE)**	MITRE's original reference **D**ata**B**ase of known software security vulnerabilities. See **C**ommon **W**eakness **E**numeration, **E**xploit **P**rediction **S**coring **S**ystem, **M**alware **A**ttribute **E**numeration and **C**haracterization.

TERM	MEANING
Common **V**ulnerability **S**coring **S**ystem **(CVSS)**	Free and open system for determining the severity of disclosed **I**nformation **T**echnology system vulnerabilities by a generic, supplier-agnostic assessment and numeric approach, crudely generating severity scores between 0 and 10 to help prioritise responses where appropriate. Feeds into corporate risk assessments covering other aspects of information risk such as the exposure, business impacts, and controls. Operated by FIRST. *Cf.* **S**takeholder-**S**pecific **V**ulnerability **C**ategorisation. More info: https://www.first.org/cvss/
Common **W**eakness **E**numeration **(CWE)**	MITRE's community-developed dictionary of commonplace types or classes of hardware and software vulnerabilities. Grew out of the **C**ommon **V**ulnerabilities and **E**xposures. See also CAPEC. More info: https://cwe.mitre.org/
Communication	Process of passing information between people, organisations, systems, devices, *things*, nodes, networks, functions, subunits, *etc.*
Communication centre	"Building where facilities for providing telecommunications business are sited" *(ISO/IEC 27011)*.
Communication path, communication route, communication channel	Linkage, conduit, cable, line, frequency, *etc.* taken by messages or packets being communicated through a network connecting endpoints (sender or transmitter and recipient or receiver), possibly traversing intermediate nodes.
Communications **Sec**urity **(COMSEC)**	Arrangements to protect the information content of communications, and possibly associated metadata (*e.g.* who is communicating, when, by what communication paths/mechanisms, and how much information is exchanged), and to maintain routes and services on networks and point-to-point links. Concerns confidentiality, integrity, and availability of information content and services. "Computer security applied to data communication" *(ISO/IEC 2382)*. "Controls applied taken to deny unauthorised access to information derived from information and communication systems and to ensure the authenticity of related communications and data" *(NZISM)*. "The controls applied to protect telecommunications from unauthorised interception and exploitation, as well as ensure the authenticity of such telecommunications" *(AusISM)*.
Communications **S**ecurity **E**stablishment **(CSE)**	Canada's national cryptologic agency (cyber-spooks) responsible for foreign SIGINT, cyber operations, and government cyber security. More info: https://www.cse-cst.gc.ca/en
Communications **T**echnology **(CT)**	Technology providing datacommunications capabilities, *e.g.* networking, radio, fibre optics, cellular systems, satellites. See also **I**nformation **T**echnology, **O**perational **T**echnology, **M**obile **T**echnology, **V**irtual **T**echnology, **S**mart **T**echnology.

TERM	MEANING
Communications system	System for communicating.
Communicator	a. "The person or group that sends or signals a message" *(OCEG GRC Glossary)*. b. Communications device remarkably reminiscent of a modern-day flip-phone, used by Captain Kirk to request urgent transportation from many a hostile situation to the safety of the Star Trek vessel USS Enterprise.
Community risk register	Ranked list of risks of concern to a group. "A register communicating the assessment of risks within a local resilience area which is developed and published as a basis for informing local communities and directing civil protection workstreams" *(UK Resilience Lessons Digest 2023)*.
Companion virus	Virus that takes advantage of the **O**perating **S**ystem's prioritisation of file names with certain extensions, *e.g.* a virus executable named *game.com* may be executed in preference to *game.exe,* the program the user intended to run. Companion viruses typically execute covertly, then launch the intended program, hoping that the user remains blissfully unaware of the subterfuge.
Compartmentalisation	Separating things between compartments, zones, categories, *etc.* according to particular characteristics, such as classification levels, and restricting communication/passage between them in order to isolate them and mitigate risks. "Division of data into isolated blocks with separate security controls for the purpose of reducing risk. Example: The division of data relative to a major project into blocks corresponding to subprojects, each with its own security protection, in order to limit exposure of the overall project" *(ISO/IEC 2382)*. "A process for protecting very high-value assets or environments where trust is an issue. Access to an asset requires two or more processes, controls or individuals" *(ISACA glossary)*.
Compensating control, compensating security measure	Control that is suboptimal but sufficient to mitigate a risk to some extent and/or achieve compliance with a security obligation, requirement, or expectation where, in practice, the *ideal* control (such as patching or replacing an insecure application or system) is not presently feasible, *e.g.* due to strict change controls for compliance, business, or safety reasons. A temporary, pragmatic workaround, substitute or compromise control that to some extent compensates for control gaps, vulnerabilities, practical or resource constraints, issues, *etc.* "An internal control that reduces the risk of an existing or potential control weakness resulting in errors and omissions" *(ISACA glossary)*.

TERM	MEANING
Competence, competent, competency	Capability of doing something properly, skilfully, expertly. "Ability to apply knowledge and skills to achieve intended results" *(ISO/IEC 27000)*. "The ability to perform a specific task, action or function successfully [and] The strengths of an enterprise or what it does well. Note: Can refer to the knowledge, skills and abilities of the assurance team or individuals conducting the work" *(ISACA glossary)*. "The degree to which an Assurance Provider can use sophisticated, professional, and structured techniques to evaluate subject matter" *(OCEG GRC Glossary)*. "Knowledge, skills, and abilities" *(IIA GIAS)*. "The skills, knowledge and understanding required to carry out a role, evidenced consistently over time through performance in the workplace. The ability to apply knowledge and skills to achieve intended results" *(FSRCoP)*. *Cf.* incompetent.
Competent authority	Competent authority. "Regulatory bodies as described in the Network and Information Systems (NIS) Regulations 2018. There are multiple competent authorities responsible for different sectors covered by NIS" *(UK National Cyber Security Strategy 2022)*.
Competitive [or **C**ompetitor] **I**ntelligence **(CI)**	May be explicitly defined to distinguish authentic and ethical means of gathering information on competitors (such as collating details from their websites and social media) from more illicit ones (such as hacking, social engineering, physical site penetration, and other industrial espionage techniques). However, the term is usually undefined, referring implicitly to licit and/or illicit approaches, *e.g.* "Espionage using legal, or at least not obviously illegal, means" *(SANS glossary)*. *Cf.* **C**onfiguration **I**tem, **C**ritical **I**nfrastructure, **C**ounter-**I**ntelligence, **C**onfidential **I**nformant.
Compile, compilation	a. Systematically collect or accumulate items into a curated, structured, or ordered set, such as the terms and definitions in this hyperglossary. b. "Translate all or part of a program expressed in a high-level language into a program expressed in an intermediate language, an assembly language, or a machine language" *(ISO/IEC 2382)*. "The process of translating a program expressed in a problem-oriented or procedure-oriented language into object code. Compilation contrasts with assembling and interpret" *(ISACA glossary)*.
Compiler	Person, organisation, or function that compiles. "1. A computer program that translates programs expressed in a high-level language into their machine-language equivalents. 2. A computer program that takes the finished source-code listing as input and outputs the machine-code instructions that the computer must have to execute the program" *(ISACA glossary)*.
Complainant	Person or organisation making an 'official' complaint. "A person who makes a complaint or allegation that a criminal offence has, or may have, occurred" *(FSRCoP)*.

TERM	MEANING
Completeness check	Automated preprocessing test for missing or invalid data, *e.g.* in mandatory fields of an online form, or the manual equivalent on paper. "A procedure designed to ensure that no fields are missing from a record" *(ISACA glossary)*.
Complex	Multifactorial, complicated, involved, tortuous, obscure, poorly understood, difficult, not simple or straightforward … "A property that refers to the interconnected, interdependent, and interrelated nature of the parts of a system that often gives rise to nonlinear dynamics, emergent properties and unpredictable outcomes" *(OCEG GRC Glossary)*.
Complexity	Risks relating to or arising from the sophistication and fragility of complex technologies, systems, processes, relationships, *etc.* that generally constrains the level of information security achieved in practice, although paradoxically complexity is beneficial for security in the case passwords, cryptographic keys, and ciphertext. "Condition of an organizational system with many diverse and autonomous but interrelated and interdependent components or parts where those parts interact with each other and with external elements in multiple end non-linear ways. Note: Complexity is the characteristic of a system where behaviour cannot be determined only as the sum of individual variables behaviours" *(ISO 22300)*.
Compliance	Fulfilment of obligations or mandatory requirements formally imposed on the organisation or individuals by third-parties or authorities through legislation (laws), industry regulations or contracts, for which they can be held accountable. There are costs, benefits, and uncertainties (risks) associated with both compliance and noncompliance, making this a business and personal matter with strong ethical overtones. "A term that refers to the adherence to, and the ability to demonstrate adherence to, mandated requirements defined by laws and regulations, as well as voluntary requirements resulting from contractual obligations and internal policies" *(ISACA glossary)*. "A measure of the degree to which obligations are proven to be addressed" *(OCEG GRC Glossary)*. "Adherence to laws, regulations, contracts, policies, procedures, and other requirements" *(IIA GIAS)*. *Cf.* conformity.
Compliance audit	Competent, independent determination of the extent to which the organisation complies with and fulfils its obligations or expectations under applicable laws/regulations, standards, contracts, *etc.*

TERM	MEANING
Compliance control	Control designed to mitigate unacceptable compliance risks, ideally achieving compliance and being able to demonstrate or prove it if required. Implies the need for compliance obligations to be clearly identified and mandated, *e.g.* in applicable laws, regulations, or executed and enforceable contracts. Alternative strategies or tactics (such as seeking to deny, avoid, or evade compliance checks; fabricating evidence or concealing/destroying evidence of noncompliance; coercing compliance checkers; restricting, frustrating, and delaying their checks; or callously accepting the possibility of compliance penalties as a cost of doing business) are considered unethical and may be illegal, making them risky, particularly for those deemed accountable. See for example dieselgate. *Cf.* conformity control.
Compliance document	Compliance document. "Policies, standards and procedures that document actions that are required or prohibited. Violations may be subject to disciplinary actions" *(ISACA glossary)*. See also **C**ommon **C**ompliance **H**ub.
Compliance management	"The act of managing processes and resources to achieve the desired level of compliance" *(OCEG GRC Glossary)*.
Compliance monitoring	Techniques for evaluating compliance more-or-less continuously (as opposed to periodically or sporadically), *e.g.* with suitable checking and reporting built-in routinely to systems and business processes, raising alarms for identified exceptions and alerts for risky situations.
Compliance risk	Business or individual risk associated with or arising from compliance or noncompliance, *e.g.* the possibility of a fine or other sanction/penalty if caught in contravention of an applicable law or regulation, hinting at the uncertainties of being both caught in contravention and found accountable. "The probability and consequences of an enterprise failing to comply with laws, regulations or the ethical standards and codes of conduct applicable to the enterprise's industry" *(ISACA glossary)*. *Cf.* conformity risk.
Compliance test	Compliance test. "Control tests designed to obtain evidence on both the effectiveness of the controls and their operation during the audit period" *(ISACA glossary)*.
Component	Constituent part such as a resistor or some other electronic part, a function or subroutine within an application system, or an operating or business unit within an organisation or model. "One of five elements of internal control, including the control environment, risk assessment, control activities, information and communication, and monitoring activities" *(Trust **S**ervices **C**riteria)*. "Software or hardware intended for integration into an electronic information system" *(EU CRA)*. A general term used to mean one

TERM	MEANING
	part of something more complex. Notes: For example, a computer system may be a component of an IT service, or an application may be a component of a release unit. Components are cooperating packages of executable software that make their services available through defined interfaces. Components used in developing systems may be commercial off-the-shelf software (COTS) or purposely built. However, the goal of component-based development is to ultimately use as many predeveloped, pretested components as possible" *(ISACA glossary)*.
Compound/Accelerate Actions & Controls	"Actions & controls that compound, accelerate, and increase the impact of favorable events to maximize benefit and promote future occurrence" *(OCEG GRC Glossary)*.
Comprehensive audit	Audit that covers all areas of scope thoroughly, in depth. "An audit designed to determine the accuracy of financial records and evaluate the internal controls of a function or department" *(ISACA glossary)*.
Comprehensive **I**ncident **M**anagement **(CIM)**	System supporting efficient and effective [crisis and] incident management, *e.g.* a repository making relevant procedures and other information (such as contact details and location maps) readily accessible to those in particular crisis or incident management rôles. *Cf.* **C**oordinated **I**ncident **M**anagement, **C**ommon **I**nformation **M**anagement, **C**ase and **I**ncident **M**anagement.
Comprehensive **N**ational **C**ybersecurity **I**nitiative **(CNCI)**	US strategic program to improve the cybersecurity capabilities of government agencies and critical [national] infrastructure, initiated by President George W. Bush in 2008. See also NIST **C**yber**S**ecurity **F**ramework.
Compromise	a. *[Verb]* To attack intending to cause an event or incident, in fact any failure of confidentiality, integrity, or availability, or any situation that bypasses or disables security controls, or that threatens or merely has the *potential* to harm or weaken an organisation or individual in some way. "Violation of computer security whereby programs or data may have been modified, destroyed, or made available to unauthorized entities" *(ISO/IEC 2382)*. Refers to a loss of confidentiality, integrity, or availability of information, including any resultant impairment of (1) processing integrity or availability of systems or (2) the integrity or availability of system inputs or outputs" *(Trust **S**ervices Criteria)*. *Cf.* exploit. b. *[Noun]* Negotiated resolution, agreement, or settlement where each party makes (or *appears* to make) concessions to the other.

TERM	MEANING
Compromising emanation	Military term for emanation from classified systems that may inadvertently disclose sensitive information, *i.e.* data and metadata. "Signals that are unintentionally emitted and that, if intercepted and analyzed, may reveal sensitive information being processed or transmitted. Examples: Acoustic emanation, electromagnetic emanation" *(ISO/IEC 2382)*. "Unintentional signal that, if intercepted and analyzed, would disclose the information transferred, received, handled, or otherwise processed by any telecommunications or automated information systems equipment" *(Air Force Air Intelligence, Surveillance and Reconnaissance Agency instruction 33-203)*. See also emanation security, TEMPEST.
CompTIA	*Abbrev:* **Comp**uting **T**echnology **I**ndustry **A**ssociation.
Computationally infeasible, computationally intensive	Refers to the likely inability to solve extremely tough mathematical challenges using current or anticipated computer technologies, algorithms, or approaches, within a stated timeframe. A risky determination given imperfect knowledge of current cryptanalytical methods, vulnerabilities in cryptosystems, *etc.*, while predicting future technological advances in areas such as **A**rtificial **I**ntelligence and quantum computing is notoriously difficult.
Compute	Rationally calculate, analyse, determine, or decide.
Computer, computer system, computer device, computing	System, device, equipment, or apparatus that computes, ranging from an abacus and slide rule to a supercomputer and everything in between. Deliberately vague, all-inclusive term covers a wide variety of digital and analogue **I**nformation, **O**perational, **S**mart, **V**irtual and **C**ommunications **T**echnologies. Prior to the 1940s, the original 'computers' were people diligently performing mental arithmetic. "Functional unit that can perform substantial computations, including numerous arithmetic operations and logic operations without human intervention. Notes: A computer may consist of a stand-alone unit or several interconnected units. In English, in information processing, the term computer usually refers to a digital computer" *(ISO/IEC 2382)*. "[Computer] 1. A functional unit that can perform substantial computations, including numerous arithmetic operations (or logic operations), without human intervention during a run. 2. A functional programmable unit that consists of one or more associated processing units and peripheral equipment, is controlled by internally stored programs and can perform substantial computations, including numerous arithmetic operations, or logic operations, without human intervention. [and] [Computer system] A functional unit consisting of one or more computers and associated peripheral input and output devices and software that uses common storage for all or part of a program and all or part of the data necessary for the execution of the program. A computer system executes user-written or user-designated programs; performs user-designated data manipulation,

TERM	MEANING
	including arithmetic and logic operations; and can execute programs that modify themselves during their execution. A computer system may be a stand-alone unit or may consist of several interconnected units" *(ISACA glossary)*.
Computer abuse	a. "Willful or negligent unauthorized activity that affects or involves the computer security of a data processing system" *(ISO/IEC 2382)*. b. Stress-relief mechanism for angry and frustrated computer users. Trust me, shouting helps, kicking not so much.
Computer-**A**ided **A**udit **T**echnique [or **T**ool] **(CAAT)**	"Any automated audit technique, such as generalized audit software (GAS), test data generators, computerized audit programs and specialized audit utilities" *(ISACA glossary)*.
Computer audit	Audit involving one or more computers. See technology audit.
Computer crime	Computer crime. "Crime committed through the use, modification, or destruction of hardware, software, or data [and] crime committed with the aid of, or directly involving, a data processing system or computer network" *(ISO/IEC 2382)*.
Computer **E**mergency **R**esponse **T**eam **(CERT),** **C**yber **E**mergency **R**esponse **T**eam**,** **C**omputer **I**ncident **R**esponse **T**eam **(CIRT),** **C**yber **I**ncident **R**esponse **T**eam**,** **C**omputer **S**ecurity **I**ncident **R**esponse **T**eam **(CSIRT)**	**I**ncident **R**esponse **T**eam that specifically handles **I**nformation **T**echnology-related (cyber) incidents. Many countries have national CERTs, globally supported and coordinated (*e.g.* for vulnerability assessment) through the CERT **C**oordination **C**enter (CERT/CC) in **C**arnegie **M**ellon **U**niversity's renowned **S**oftware **E**ngineering **I**nstitute based in Pittsburgh, PA. "Team of security experts to support the handling of information security incidents" *(ISO/IEC 27019)*. "CERT – A group of people integrated at the enterprise with clear lines of reporting and responsibilities for standby support in case of an information systems emergency. This group acts as an efficient corrective control and should also be the single point of contact for all incidents and issues related to information systems. [and] CSIRT – The technical team responsible for addressing security incidents" *(ISACA glossary)*.
Computer forensics	See digital forensics. "The application of the scientific method to digital media to establish factual information for judicial review. Notes: This process often involves investigating computer systems to determine whether they have been used for illegal or unauthorized activities. As a discipline, it combines elements of law and computer science to collect and analyze data from information systems (*e.g.*, personal computers, networks, wireless communication and digital storage devices) in a way that makes it admissible as evidence in a court of law" *(ISACA glossary)*.
Computer fraud	Computer fraud. "Fraud committed with the aid of, or directly involving, a data processing system or computer network" *(ISO/IEC 2382)*.

TERM	MEANING
Computer Hacking Forensic Investigator **(C|HFI)**	EC-Council's qualification for digital forensics investigators or analysts. Covers practical, methodical techniques for forensic investigation of various systems and devices, cloud services, malware incidents, *etc*. More info: https://www.eccouncil.org/train-certify/computer-hacking-forensic-investigator-chfi/
Computer Misuse Act **(CMA)**	UK law criminalises unauthorised access to a computer, unauthorised computer access with intent to commit further crime, and unauthorised modification of data – in other words hacking and cracking. The law was enacted in 1990 after Prince Phillip's mailbox on the Prestel system had been hacked but the authorities were unable to convict the hackers responsible under extant legislation (on appeal, they were acquitted of fraud since it was not proven that they profited from the hack).
Computer network	Computer network. "Network whose nodes consist of computers and data communication equipment, and whose branches are data links [and] network of data processing nodes that are interconnected for the purpose of data communication" *(ISO/IEC 2382)*.
Computer Network Attack **(CNA)**	US military term for offensive cyberwar capability.
Computer Network Defense **(CND)**	US military term for defensive cyberwar capability. [In other contexts, CND may be the **C**ampaign for **N**uclear **D**isarmament.]
Computer Network Exploitation **(CNE)**	US military term for cyberwar reconnaissance/espionage function.
Computer Network Operations **(CNO)**	US military term for cyberwar capability comprising **C**omputer **N**etwork **E**xploitation, **C**omputer **N**etwork **A**ttack, and **C**omputer **N**etwork **D**efense, all within **I**nformation **O**perations.
Computer security	See cybersecurity. "Protection of data and resources from accidental or malicious acts, usually by taking appropriate actions. Note: These acts may be modification, destruction, access, disclosure, or acquisition, if not authorized" *(ISO/IEC 2382)*.
Computer system audit	Audit involving one or more computers. See technology audit. "Examination of the procedures used in a data processing system to evaluate their effectiveness and correctness, and to recommend improvements" *(ISO/IEC 2382)*.
Computer vision, machine vision	"Capability of a functional unit to acquire, process and interpret data representing images or video. Note: Computer vision involves the use of sensors to create a digital image of a visual scene. This can include images, such as images that capture wavelengths beyond those of visible light such as infrared imaging" *(ISO/IEC 22989)*. "A subfield of artificial intelligence (AI) concerned with enabling computers to interpret and understand visual information such as images and videos" *(ISACA glossary)*.

TERM	MEANING
Computing **T**echnology **I**ndustry **A**ssociation **(CompTIA)**	US-based trade association for **I**nformation **T**echnology professionals. Offers the CompTIA Security+, PenTest+, CySA+, and SecurityX qualifications, among others. More info: https://www.comptia.org/en/certifications/
COMSEC	*Abbrev:* **Com**munications **Sec**urity.
Confidence trick (con)	A form of social engineering in which the target is fooled into inappropriately trusting a confidence trickster. See fraud.
Concept	a. Abstract idea or mental model. b. One of the first macro viruses dating back to 1995.
Concept of **Op**eration **(ConOp)**	Describes the principles or mechanisms of operation of a system, control, process, *etc*. "A document describing the characteristics of an information systems and its intended use. It is used to communicate the intent and system characteristics to all stakeholders" *(NZISM)*.
Concurrency control	**D**ata**B**ase integrity control to coordinate linked or dependent transactions such that they can be committed simultaneously and consistently. "A class of controls used in a database management system (DBMS) to ensure that transactions are processed in an atomic, consistent, isolated and durable manner (ACID). This class of controls implies that only serial and recoverable schedules are permitted and that committed transactions are not discarded when undoing aborted transactions" *(ISACA glossary)*.
Concurrent access	"A failover process, in which all nodes run the same resource group and access the external storage concurrently. There can be no Internet Protocol (IP) or mandatory access control (MAC) address in a concurrent resource group" *(ISACA glossary)*.
Condition	a. Status, situation, *e.g.* healthy/sick/dead, red/amber/green. "A state of reality" *(OCEG GRC Glossary)*. b. Requirement, obligation, expectation, demand.
Conduit	a. Tube or duct physically enclosing and protecting data or power cabling against mechanical damage, vandalism, fire, fluid ingress, *etc*. "A tube, duct or pipe used to protect cables" *(NZISM)*. b. Specific path, route, or mechanism for communications, *e.g.* a 'speaking tube,' railway line, and the ocean are mechanical conduits capable of carrying sounds.
Confabulation	Neural defect, disorder, disease, or injury resulting in false 'memories', *i.e.* stored data integrity failures. Affects some humans and, it seems, many **A**rtificial **I**ntelligence/**L**arge **L**anguage **M**odel systems.
Conficker	Prolific network worm, released in 2008 and remained in the wild for at least 8 years.

TERM **MEANING**

Confide Disclose sensitive or delicate information to a trusted person, with the implicit expectation or explicit requirement that they will keep it confidential.

Confidence

a. Strongly held belief implying a willingness to proceed on the basis it is true, even if others perceive the action to be risky.

b. Confidential (in confidence).

c. Probability of being correct (confidence level or limit).

Confidence interval, confidence limit Range of possible values between lower and upper limits with a statistically determined probability of containing the actual value. Narrower intervals indicate less-variable data and more accurate or confident predictions at the same probability level, *e.g.* 95%. "A range specified for an estimate to indicate margin of error, combined with a probability that a value will fall in that range" *(ISACA glossary)*.

Confidence trickster, con-man, con-artist Confident person who uses social engineering techniques such as pretexting and masquerading to establish false confidence in themselves in order to con, fool, cheat, scam, or defraud victims.

Confident Bold, assertive, self-assured, or convinced, *i.e.* having confidence.

Confidential, in confidence Class, category, type, or item of information that is sensitive or delicate and must therefore be adequately protected against unauthorised or inappropriate access or disclosure. See also confidentiality, highly confidential.

CONFIDENTIAL Commonplace classification label for confidential information intended for limited distribution within the organisation or to designated and trustworthy third parties, on a default deny basis. While the intention is reasonably self-evident, the label, definition, and associated controls are organisation- and context-specific. "Information, the unauthorized disclosure of which reasonably could be expected to cause damage to the national security that the original classification authority is able to identify or describe" *(Executive Order 13526)*. *Cf.* SECRET, TOP SECRET, ULTRA.

Confidential **I**nformant **(CI)** Law enforcement term for a spy or mole, either trained and placed within a target organisation as an undercover agent or recruited from within, possibly through coercion or social engineering. *Cf.* **C**onfiguration **I**tem, **C**ritical **I**nfrastructure, **C**ompetitive **I**ntelligence, or **C**ounter-**I**ntelligence.

Confidential information Confidential information. "Information that is not intended to be made available or disclosed to unauthorized individuals, entities or processes" *(ISO/IEC 27002)*. "It's in a diary" (Dire Straits, Private Investigations).

TERM	MEANING
Confidentiality, sensitivity, secrecy	Preventing inappropriate or unauthorised access to, or disclosure of, valuable, sensitive or private information. A core objective of information security, along with availability and integrity (the CIA triad). "Property of data that indicates the extent to which these data have not been made available or disclosed to unauthorized individuals, processes, or other entities" *(ISO/IEC 2382)*. "Property that information is not made available or disclosed to unauthorized individuals, entities, or processes" *(ISO/IEC 27000)*. "Preserving authorized restrictions on access and disclosure, including means for protecting privacy and proprietary information" *(ISACA glossary)*. "The assurance that data is disclosed only to authorised entities" *(AusISM)*. "To ensure that information is disclosed only to authorized parties" *(SCP QRG)*. "Preserving authorized restrictions on information access and disclosure, including means for protecting personal privacy and proprietary information" *(NIST SP 800-171)*.
Confidentiality control	Control designed to mitigate unacceptable confidentiality risks. Its primary purpose is to prevent unauthorised or inappropriate recipients from accessing, obtaining, or receiving confidential information. See also integrity control, availability control.
Confidentiality risk	Risk involving or affecting confidentiality, *e.g.* the possibility of inappropriate disclosure of sensitive information, someone's refusal to divulge vital personal information 'for privacy reasons,' or the ability of an encryption algorithm to withstand cryptanalysis. See also information risk, information security risk, integrity risk, availability risk.
Configurable control	Control with adjustable rather than fixed parameters, *e.g.* a system's security setting for minimum password length can typically be modified by a privileged administrator. "Typically, an automated control that is based on, and therefore dependent on, the configuration of parameters within the application system" *(ISACA glossary)*.
Configuration, **config**ure **(config)**	Particular arrangement of items and parameter settings determining the operation and security of a system.
Configuration **I**tem **(CI)**	Piece of technology (such as a particular item of hardware, source code or compiled program, hardware device/equipment, *etc.*) plus related technical information (such as parameters or set-points) being managed through the organisation's **C**onfiguration **M**anagement **S**ystem. "Component of an infrastructure—or an item, such as a request for change, associated with an infrastructure—that is (or is to be) under the control of configuration management. Note: May vary widely in complexity, size and type, from an entire system (including all hardware, software and documentation) to a single module or a minor hardware component" *(ISACA glossary)*. *Cf.* **C**ritical **I**nfrastructure, **C**ompetitive **I**ntelligence, **C**ounter-**I**ntelligence, **C**onfidential **I**nformant.

TERM	MEANING
Configuration **M**anagement **(CM)**	Subset of change management activities involving the configuration of computer systems and infrastructure, including the parameters or settings and relationships (*e.g.* a certain combination of specific versions of the hardware, firmware, **O**perating **S**ystem, and layered software might be tested thoroughly as a complete system, those tests potentially being invalidated if changes such as patches or updates are made to any part). An invaluable integrity control for critical or vital systems. "The control of changes to a set of configuration items over a system life cycle" *(ISACA glossary)*. "Establish a known baseline condition and manage it" *(SANS glossary)*. "A collection of activities focused on establishing and maintaining the integrity of information technology products and systems through the control of processes for initializing, changing, and monitoring the configurations of those products and systems throughout the system development life cycle" *(NIST SP 800-171)*.
Configuration **M**anagement **S**ystem **(CMS)**	**I**nformation **T**echnology system plus related engineering processes for administering and using data relating to **C**onfiguration **I**tems in support of **C**onfiguration **M**anagement.
Configuration settings	"The set of parameters that can be changed in hardware, software, or firmware that affect the security posture and/or functionality of the system" *(NIST SP 800-171)*.
Conflict of interest	Situation in which a person or organisation's loyalty is (potentially or actually) divided between mutually exclusive responsibilities, *e.g.* where their obligations to a third party (*e.g.* to report a security incident) conflict with their self-interest (*e.g.* if disclosure would trigger an investigation and perhaps enforcement for noncompliance). "A situation, activity, or relationship that may influence, or appear to influence, an internal auditor's ability to make objective professional judgments or perform responsibilities objectively" *(IIA GIAS)*.
Confirmability	Capability of being tested, checked, verified, validated, or audited in some way, in order to provide adequate assurance. Purely faith-based statements, claims, or assertions are inherently untestable. "Measure of the extent to which a program is designed and structured in such a manner that all of its parts can be readily tested" *(ISO/IEC 2382)*.
Confirmation	Positive, supportive, or agreeable assurance. "The number of blocks added to the blockchain after the network accepts that a particular transaction has been executed" *(ISACA glossary)*.
Conformity, conformance	Discretionary acceptance and adoption/implementation of a standard, policy, contractual term, *etc.* or, more generally, fulfilment of a requirement or expectation. There are costs, benefits, and uncertainties (risks) associated with both conformity and nonconformity, making this a business and personal matter with strong ethical overtones. "Fulfilment of a requirement. Note: the term 'conformance' is synonymous but deprecated" *(ISO/IEC 27000)*. *Cf.* compliance.

TERM	MEANING
Conformity assessment	Process of generating assurance that specified and applicable conformity requirements, obligations, or expectations are satisfied. "Demonstration that specified requirements are fulfilled" *(ISO/IEC 17000)*. "The process of verifying whether the essential cybersecurity requirements set out in Annex I have been fulfilled" *(EU CRA)*.
Conformity **A**ssessment **B**ody **(CAB)**	See **C**ertification **B**ody. "Body that performs conformity assessment activities, excluding accreditation" *(ISO/IEC 17000)*.
Conformity assessment scheme, conformity assessment program	"Set of rules and procedures that describes the objects of conformity assessment, identifies the specified requirements and provides the methodology for performing conformity assessment. Notes: A conformity assessment scheme can be managed within a conformity assessment system. A conformity assessment scheme can be operated at an international, regional, national sub-national, or industry sector level. A scheme can cover all or part of the conformity assessment functions" *(ISO/IEC 17000)*.
Conformity assessment system	Recognised assurance approach to assessing (and generally certifying) conformity. "Set of rules and procedures for the management of similar or related conformity assessment schemes. Note: A conformity assessment system can be operated at an international, regional, national, sub-national, or industry sector level" *(ISO/IEC 17000)*.
Conformity control	Control intended to mitigate conformity risks, ideally achieving conformity by fulfilling the requirements and expectations, and being able to demonstrate or prove it if required. Implies the need for those requirements and expectations to be clearly identified and accepted, *e.g.* in the terms and conditions of a formal policy, agreement, or understanding between the parties. Alternative strategies or tactics (such as seeking to deny, avoid, or evade conformity checks; fabricating evidence or concealing/destroying evidence of nonconformity; coercing conformity checkers; restricting, frustrating, and delaying their checks; or callously accepting the possibility of penalties and other adverse consequences) are considered unethical, making them risky, particularly for those deemed accountable. *Cf.* compliance control.
Conformity Monkey	Simian Army tool that checks the configuration of cloud servers against good practices, shutting down non-conformant systems. See also Security Monkey.
Conformity risk	Business or individual risk associated with or arising from conformity or nonconformity, *e.g.* the possibility of some sort of sanction such as distrust and perhaps termination of a productive business or employment relationship if nonconformity is identified or strongly suspected, hinting at the uncertainties of being both caught in contravention and penalised.

TERM	MEANING
Conformity [or conformance] tester	Person assessing conformity. "Individual assigned to perform test activities in accordance with a given conformance testing standard and associated testing methodology. An example of such a standard is ISO/IEC 19790 and the testing methodology specified in ISO/IEC 24759" *(ISO/IEC 19896-1)*.
Congestion	Capacity constraint, *e.g.* where the volume of traffic entering a network path exceeds the available bandwidth. Typically reduces performance and **Q**uality **o**f **S**ervice, increases latency, and may lead to timeouts or dropouts (availability events, issues, or incidents). Whereas congestion is normally unintentional, hackers may *deliberately* inject/generate spurious network traffic in order to conceal their nefarious activities or cause computer systems to delay/drop critical security event/alert/alarm messages or fail-insecure.
Connected places	"A community that integrates information and communication technologies and IoT devices to collect and analyse data to deliver new services to the built environment, and enhance the quality of living for citizens" *(UK National Cyber Security Strategy 2022)*.
Connection forwarding	"The use of network address translation to allow a port on a network node inside a local area network to be accessed from outside the network. Alternatively, using a Secure Shell server to forward a Transmission Control Protocol connection to an arbitrary port on the local host" *(NZISM)*.
Connectionism, connectionist paradigm, connectionist model, connectionist approach	"Form of cognitive modelling that uses a network of interconnected units that generally are simple computational units" *(ISO/IEC 22989)*.
ConOp	*Abbrev:* **Con**cept of **Op**eration.
Consensus **A**ssessment **I**nitiative **Q**uestionnaire **(CAIQ)**	Crude cloud computing security checklist from the **C**loud **S**ecurity **A**lliance concerning compliance with the **C**loud **C**ontrols **M**atrix, provided as "a set of questions a cloud consumer and cloud auditor may wish to ask of a cloud provider … a simplified distillation of the issues, best practices, and control specifications from [the CSA's] Guidance and CCM, intended to help organisations build the necessary assessment processes for engaging with cloud providers." Anticipates simple binary yes/no answers to complex issues; hence (being cynical), respondents are likely to offer the most flattering responses (a systematic bias). *Cf.* **I**nternal **C**ontrols **Q**uestionnaire**.**
Consensus mechanism	"A fault-tolerant mechanism used in blockchain/distributed ledger systems to achieve the necessary agreement on data values or the state of the network among distributed processes or multiagent systems" *(ISACA glossary)*.

TERM	MEANING
Consent	Permission granted freely (without coercion) and explicitly by an adequately informed person. "Personally identifiable information (PII) principal's freely given, specific and informed agreement to the processing of their PII" *(ISO/IEC 29100)*. "Any freely given, specific, informed and unambiguous indication of the data subject's wishes by which he or she, by a statement or by a clear affirmative action, signifies agreement to the processing of personal data relating to him or her" *(**G**eneral **D**ata **P**rotection **R**egulation)*. "Any freely given, specific, informed and unambiguous indication of the data subject's wishes by which he or she, by a statement or by a clear affirmative action, signifies agreement to the processing of personal data relating to him or her" *(ISACA glossary)*. "This privacy requirement is one of the fair information practice objectives. Individuals must be able to prevent the collection of their personal data, unless legally required. If an individual has a choice about the use or disclosure of his or her information, consent is the individual's way of giving permission for the use or disclosure. Consent may be affirmative (for example, opting in) or implied (for example, not opting out). There are two types of consent: explicit consent – a requirement that an individual "signifies" his or her agreement with a data controller by some active communication between the parties; [and] implied consent – when consent may reasonably be inferred from the action or inaction of the individual" *(**T**rust **S**ervices **C**riteria)*. See also informed consent.
Consequence, consequential	Material effect, net result, harmful outcome, or impact of a causal relationship when the cause of an event materialises, such as when a threat acts on a vulnerability leading to a harmful incident. The immediate impacts may lead to further issues for other organisations or individuals, spreading but gradually dissipating over time and distance like ripples on a pond. "Outcome of an event affecting objectives. Notes: A consequence can be certain or uncertain and can have positive or negative direct or indirect effects on objectives; Consequences can be expressed qualitatively or quantitatively; Any consequence can escalate through cascading and cumulative effects" *(ISO 31000)*. "<loss> loss of life, damage to property or economic disruption, including disruption to transport systems, that can reasonably be expected as a result of an attack on an organization in the supply chain or by the use of the supply chain as a weapon" *(ISO 22300)*. "The result of a realized risk. A consequence can be certain or uncertain and can have positive or negative, direct or indirect effects on objectives. Consequences can be expressed qualitatively or quantitatively" *(ISACA glossary)*. "The outcome or potential outcome of an event or series of events" *(OCEG GRC Glossary)*.

TERM	MEANING
Consistent, consistency	Reliable, dependable, staying essentially the same over time with only minor and explainable deviations, if any. An information integrity property, important when communicating messages, metrics, *etc.* as an indication that important matters are in fact sufficiently well understood and controlled. "The degree of uniformity, standardization and freedom from contradiction among the documents or parts of a system or component" *(ISACA glossary)*.
Consistency checker	Person, function, device, or tool intended to identify inconsistency (howsoever defined). "A software tool used to test requirements in design specifications for consistency and completeness" *(ISACA glossary)*.
Console	Specially designated terminal device or port on a system intended for system management/administrative purposes such as displaying security events, alerts, and alarms, and configuring the system. Due to its privileged nature, the console should be physically secured, *e.g.* adjacent to the server, PABX in a secure access-controlled area. On some systems, users who have been automatically locked out of other terminals/ports (*e.g.* as a result of someone repeatedly trying and failing to enter their passwords) are still able to logon at the console, a control against that particular form of **D**enial-**o**f-**S**ervice.
Console log	Log of privileged console activities and messages. "An automated detail report of computer system activity" *(ISACA glossary)*.
Conspicuous consumption	Without a credible explanation for their wealth, successful fraudsters, and other criminals living the high life on their ill-gotten gains risk being noticed, reported to, and investigated by the authorities.
Conspire	To collude nefariously/secretly with the intention of jointly committing something unethical, inappropriate, deceptive, harmful, and/or illegal (such as fraud).
Conspiracy	Nefarious/secret plan to conspire.
Consumer	Customer who buys a retail product, typically for their own or their family's consumption and benefit. "Natural person who is acting for purposes that are outside their trade, business, craft or profession. Note: Person who is a potential buyer of a labelled product" *(ISO/IEC 27404 DRAFT)*. "One who utilizes goods" *(ISACA glossary)*. "A natural person who acts for purposes which are outside that person's trade, business, craft or profession" *(EU CRA)*.
Consumer guide	"Product specific advice concerning evaluated products can consist of findings from mutually recognised information security evaluations. This may include the Common Criteria, findings from GCSB internal evaluations, any recommendations for use and references to relevant policy and other standards" *(NZISM)*.

TERM	MEANING
Contact event	"Occurs when a Threat Agent establishes a physical or virtual (*e.g.*, network) connection to an Asset" *(O-RT)*.
Contact frequency	"The probable frequency, within a given timeframe, that a Threat Agent will come into contact with an Asset" *(O-RT)*.
Container	Physical or virtual vessel to contain something, such as a portable software package including the associated library functions, capable of executing under various **O**perating **S**ystems. "A packaged environment that includes all necessary dependencies, executables and code for particular applications to run separately from the host computing device" *(ISACA glossary)*.
Containment	Time-critical process to restrict the spread of something, such as a network worm, infectious disease, or disinformation. "Actions taken to limit exposure after an incident has been identified and confirmed" *(ISACA glossary)*.
Contaminate	Taint or discredit forensic evidence, *e.g.* through gaps in the chain of custody or unexplained physical or logical changes.
Contamination	"Introduction of data of one security classification or security category into data of a lower security classification or different security category" *(ISO/IEC 2382)*.
Content **D**elivery **N**etwork **(CDN)**	Essentially a geographically dispersed commercial web content caching service that, where possible, delivers popular content from copies held on web servers near to the user rather than from the original sources. Reduces latency, increases download speeds, and can help mitigate the effect of **D**enial-**o**f-**S**ervice attacks and other incidents.
Content filter, content filtering	"A filter that examines content to assess conformance against a security policy" *(AusISM)*. "The process of monitoring communications such as email and web pages, analysing them for suspicious content, and preventing the delivery of suspicious content to users" *(NIST SP 800-114)*. "The process of monitoring communications, including email and web pages, analysing them for any suspicious or unwanted content, and preventing the delivery of suspicious or unwanted content" *(NZISM)*. "Controlling access to a network by analyzing the contents of the incoming and outgoing packets, and either letting them pass or denying them, based on a list of rules. Note: Differs from packet filtering in that content filtering analyzes the data in the packet and packet filtering analyzes the attributes of the packet itself, *e.g.*, source/target IP address and transmission control protocol (TCP) flags" *(ISACA glossary)*.

TERM	MEANING
Content Security Policy (CSP)	Instructions in the HTML header concerning what the browser should or should not do with content from an appropriately coded web page, *e.g.* not loading or interpreting third party files containing JavaScript, ActiveX, fonts, *etc* that might be used for cross-site scripting or other code injection attacks on the browser. An exception allows browser plug-ins to override the CSP, though, creating a vulnerability. However, the presence of malicious plug-ins on a system suggests even more significant issues. *Cf.* **C**loud **S**ervice **P**rovider.
Context	Surrounding environments or situation within which things have purpose and meaning. "External and internal factors to be taken into account when undertaking a capability assessment. Notes: External context includes the following: the cultural, social, political, legal, regulatory, financial, technological, economic, natural and competitive environment, whether international, national, regional or local; key drivers and trends having an impact on the objectives of the organization; relationships with, and perceptions and values of, external interested parties. Internal context includes: the organization's mandate; business sensitivity; governance, organizational structure, roles and accountabilities; resources and knowledge [*e.g.* capital, time, people, processes, systems and technologies]; organizational culture" *(ISO 22300)*. "The overall set of internal and external factors that might influence or determine how an enterprise, entity, process or individual acts. Note: Context includes: Technology context (technological factors that affect the ability of an enterprise to extract value from data); Data context (data accuracy, availability, currency and quality); Skills and knowledge (general experience and analytical, technical, and business skills); Organizational and cultural context (political factors and whether the enterprise prefers data over intuition); Strategic context (strategic objectives of the enterprise)" *(ISACA glossary)*.
Contextual information [or data]	Metadata that may provide additional context or supporting information enabling the nature of the associated data or information content to be guessed or interpreted more readily.
Conti	Species of ransomware in the wild in 2022. The Conti group dismantled its infrastructure and disbanded in mid-2022, its members dispersing among other hacker groups such as Hive.
Contingency	Unanticipated and often inherently unpredictable situation, incident or disaster (*e.g.* a bomb, plane crash, flood, or fire), logical/technical disaster (*e.g.* malware outbreak, equipment breakdown, software flaw/bug, hack or similar attack on a major business system or network), and business disaster (*e.g.* a serious fraud or hostile takeover attempt). The appropriate responses are contingent (dependent) on the exact nature, scale and severity of the incident, the context (*e.g.* timepoint) in which it occurs, and the resources available. "Possible future event, condition or eventuality" *(ISO 22300)*.

TERM	MEANING
Contingency plan, contingency management, contingency thinking	Forward-thinking, flexible planning approach for preparing, motivating, and marshalling the organisation's people and other resources to cope as effectively as possible in a contingency situation such as a major incident or disaster. Involves preparing and exercising general-purpose plans or preparations (such as forming a crisis management team from competent, capable people still available), stocking up on tools and resources (such as duct tape, walkie-talkies, and white boards), and building capabilities (such as resourcefulness, adaptability, and a willingness to 'go the extra mile' and 'do whatever it takes') ahead of time. Incidents that are expected or predictable should be covered by conventional risk management activities such as mitigating controls, resilience, and **D**isaster **R**ecovery plans. "Plan for backup procedures, emergency response, and post-disaster recovery" *(ISO/IEC 2382)*. "Process of developing advance arrangements and procedures that enable an enterprise to respond to an event that might occur by chance or unforeseen circumstances [and] Plan used by an enterprise or business unit to respond to a specific systems failure or disruption" *(ISACA glossary)*. "A plan for emergency response, backup operations, and post-disaster recovery in a system, as part of a security program, to ensure availability of critical system resources and facilitate continuity of operations in a crisis" *(ENISA RM glossary)*.
Continual improvement	Determined, conscious effort to mature or get better at doing something (or at least not to get any worse!) in a systematic and often gradual (if not literally continuous) manner. "Recurring activity to enhance performance" *(ISO/IEC 27000)*.
Continuing [or **C**ontinued] **P**rofessional **E**ducation **(CPE)**	Many professional qualifications formally require holders to continue their education beyond any initial training courses or certification examination preparation classes, in order to maintain their knowledge and competence. CPE 'credits' can typically be claimed for a wide range of activities that any professional actively engaged in the field is likely to be doing routinely. For details, consult the organisations issuing qualifications for their CPE requirements (if any).
Continuity	Continuing without significant interruption or change. "Strategic and tactical capability, pre-approved by management, of an organization to plan for and respond to conditions, situations and events in order to continue operations at an acceptable predefined level. Note: Continuity is the more general term for operational and business continuity to ensure an organization's ability to continue operating outside of normal operating conditions. It applies not only to for-profit companies, but to organizations of all types, such as non-governmental, public interest and governmental" *(ISO 22300)*. "Preventing, mitigating and recovering from disruption. Note: The terms business resumption planning, disaster recovery planning and contingency planning also may be used in this context; they all concentrate on the recovery aspects of continuity" *(ISACA glossary)*.

TERM	MEANING
Continuous **A**daptive **R**isk and **T**rust **A**ssessment **(CARTA)**	Assurance approach involving automated security monitoring that is continuous as opposed to periodic/sporadic (*e.g.* penetration testing), integrated from the hardware platform to the application layers, contextual and adaptive, responding to risks in real time (*e.g.* using Security Orchestration, Analysis and Response).
Continuous auditing approach	"Allows IS auditors to monitor system reliability on a continuous basis and to gather selective audit evidence through the computer" *(ISACA glossary)*.
Continuous availability	Absolute requirement for systems providing critical or vital services, where the impacts of disruptive incidents are untenable, the associated risks are extreme, and effective mitigating controls (such as high-availability fault-tolerant architectures) are therefore essential. More generally, a reasonable objective for most other systems although the risks may be lower. "Nonstop service, with no lapse in service; the highest level of service in which no downtime is allowed" *(ISACA glossary)*.
Continuous improvement, Kaizen	**Q**uality **A**ssurance philosophy and risk management processes involved in identifying and addressing production issues or potential concerns routinely and systematically in order to minimise **Q**uality **C**ontrol failures without compromising other business objectives (such as cost management and resilience). "The goals of continuous improvement (Kaizen) include elimination of waste (activities that add cost, but do not add value); just-in-time (JIT) delivery; production load leveling of amounts and types; standardized work; paced moving lines; and right-sized equipment. Notes: A closer definition of the Japanese usage of Kaizen is to take it apart and put it back together in a better way. What is taken apart is usually a process, system, product or service. Kaizen is a daily activity whose purpose goes beyond improvement. It is also a process that, when done correctly, humanizes the workplace, eliminates hard work (both mental and physical), and teaches people how to do rapid experiments using the scientific method and how to learn to see and eliminate waste in business processes" *(ISACA glossary)*.
Continuous [or continual] learning, lifelong learning	Concept or approach to incremental education, ongoing as opposed to being limited to the formative stages of a system or a person's lifetime. "Incremental training of an AI system that takes place on an ongoing basis during the operation phase of the AI system life cycle" *(ISO/IEC 22989)*.

TERM	MEANING
Continuous monitoring plan	"A document that describes the plan for the continuous monitoring and assurance in the effectiveness of controls for a system" *(AusISM)*.
Continuous risk and control monitoring	"A process that includes: Developing a strategy to regularly evaluate selected information and technology (I&T)-related controls/metrics; Recording and evaluating I&T-related events and the effectiveness of the enterprise in dealing with those events; Recording changes to I&T-related controls or changes that affect I&T-related risk; Communicating the current risk and control status to enable information-sharing decisions involving the enterprise" *(ISACA glossary)*.
Continuous **T**hreat **E**xposure **M**anagement **(CTEM)**	Misleading marketing buzzword for cybersecurity activities intended to identify, prioritise, and mitigate topical risks involving networked systems. It actually involves automated monitoring of attack surfaces, meaning exposed known vulnerabilities, as opposed to threats.
Contract	Binding agreement between two or more parties, for various strengths of 'binding.' Formal contracts prepared by qualified lawyers and signed ('executed') by duly authorised representatives are normally legally binding on the parties but may be unenforceable (especially any terms deemed 'unfair' by the courts or overridden by laws such as the fair use provisions of copyright law). Verbal, informal, presumed, or social contracts *may* also be legally binding, although naturally they are harder to prove and hence enforce. If someone breaks the seal on shrink-wrapped software, for instance, they *may* be deemed to have accepted the licence terms and conditions visible through the clear plastic film, implying a contractual commitment. Generally speaking, contracts may not be unilaterally imposed by one party on the other (*e.g.* email disclaimers); hence, a signature and/or a 'consideration' (normally a payment) may be necessary to demonstrate someone's willingness to commit. "An agreement between two or more persons or entities, which is intended to be enforceable at law and includes a contract made by deed or in writing" *(NZISM)*.
Contract Account (CA)	Blockchain wallet managed automatically by a smart contract. "The account (or address) created when a smart contract is deployed by the smart contract owner. Contract account contains the runtime virtual machine bytecode for a contract" *(ISACA glossary)*. *Cf.* **C**ertification **A**uthority.
Control, safeguard, countermeasure, measure, protective measure, protection mechanism …	a. *[Noun]* Something which mitigates risk, *i.e.* it prevents or at least reduces the probability of an information security incident, reduces uncertainty (*e.g.* determining whether controls are effective or incidents have occurred), and/or reduces or limits the impacts, damage, harm, costs, or other adverse consequences caused or triggered by or simply arising from an incident. Some controls mitigate threats

TERM	MEANING
	(*e.g.* deterrents) or impacts (*e.g.* backups), although most mitigate vulnerabilities. "Measure that is modifying risk. Notes: controls include any process, policy, device, practice, or other actions which modify risk. It is possible that controls [do] not always exert the intended or assumed modifying effect" *(ISO/IEC 27000)*. "Measure that maintains and/or modifies risk. Notes: Controls include, but are not limited to, any process, policy, device, practice or other conditions and/or actions which maintain and/or modify risk. Controls may not always exert the intended or assumed modifying effect" *(ISO/IEC 31000)*. "The means of managing risk, including policies, procedures, guidelines, practices or organizational structures, which can be of an administrative, technical, management or legal nature" *(ISACA glossary)*. "Any person, policy, process, or technology that has the potential to reduce the Loss Event Frequency (LEF) – Loss Prevention Controls – and/or Loss Magnitude (LM) – Loss Mitigation Controls" *(O-RT)*. "Policies and procedures that are part of the entity's system of internal control. The objective of an entity's system of internal control is to provide reasonable assurance that principal system objectives are achieved" *(**T**rust **S**ervices **C**riteria)*. "Any action taken by management, the board, and other parties to manage risk and increase the likelihood that established objectives and goals will be achieved" *(IIA GIAS)*. b. *[Verb]* To exert influence over, dominate, coerce, or attempt to direct and constrain something such as a system, machine, person, organisation, perception, process, market, and price Types of control include ABAC, access, administrative, application, assurance, authentication, automated, availability, baseline, batch, business, change, common, compensating, compliance, concurrency, confidentiality, configurable, conformity, corrective, covert, cryptographic, cybersecurity, detective, deterrent, discretionary access, environmental, governance, hybrid, information flow, infrastructure, input, integrity, key, logical access, management, mandatory access, manual, media access, network, organisational, output, people, physical/mechanical, preventive, privacy, process, processing, quality, RBAC, remote, security, system-specific, technological, validation, verification, and version control.
Controllability, controllable	Extent to which something (such as a system, machine, process, organisation, or person) is capable of being actively controlled or governed, *e.g.* kept within acceptable legal, ethical, or policy bounds (tolerance limits), enabled or disabled, brought into compliance or conformity. However, a controllable item is not necessarily under control. "Property of an AI system that allows a human or another external agent to intervene in the system's functioning" *(ISO/IEC 22989)*. "Property of a system that allows a human or another external agent to intervene in the system's functioning. Note: Such a system is heteronomous" *(ISO/IEC TS 5723)*.

TERM	MEANING
Control activity	"An action established through policies and procedures that help ensure that management's directives to mitigate risks to the achievement of objectives are carried out" *(Trust Services Criteria)*.
Control centre, control room, control hub	Centralised and dedicated industrial facility, room, area, or hub housing and bringing together numerous indicating and control devices, systems, *etc.* for the plant and site/s, plus the professionals overseeing and operating them. "Hosts the recovery meetings that manage disaster recovery operations" *(ISACA glossary)*.
Control design option	"A design option to implement actions and controls that govern and manage the opportunity, obstacle, or obligation according to its nature" *(OCEG GRC Glossary)*.
Control **F**low **D**iagram **(CFD)**	Visual representation of the flow of control through a process, application, system, or organisation, including alternative routes depending on logic, decision points, and criteria. "A diagram that depicts the set of all possible sequences in which operations may be performed during the execution of a system or program. Types include box diagram, flowchart, input-process-output chart and state diagram. Contrasts with data flow diagram" *(ISACA glossary)*. *Cf.* **C**ontract **F**or **D**ifferences.
Control **F**low **G**uard **(CFG)**	Windows internal security feature intended to prevent memory corruption leading to security vulnerabilities by summarily terminating potentially malicious processes that call invalid callback addresses. Extends basic buffer overflow protection, **D**ata **E**xecution **P**revention, and **A**ddress **S**pace **L**ayout **R**andomisation.
Control framework	Control framework. "A set of fundamental controls that facilitates the discharge of business process owner responsibilities to prevent financial or information loss in an enterprise" *(ISACA glossary)*.
Controlled area	Information asset-containing area to some extent under control, *e.g.* a corporate facility, an executive's plush home office, or an itinerant manager's shabby hotel room/car. "Any area or space for which the organization has confidence that the physical and procedural protections provided are sufficient to meet the requirements established for protecting the information or system" *(NIST SP 800-171)*. See also zone.
Controlled **T**echnical **I**nformation **(CTI)**	US government term for unclassified technical information that nevertheless deserves protection. A subset of **C**ontrolled **U**nclassified **I**nformation.
Controlled **U**nclassified **I**nformation **(CUI)**	US government term for unclassified information that nevertheless deserves protection, typically for compliance reasons (*e.g.* privacy). Structured into categories such as critical infrastructure, defence, export control, and financial. Covers various types of

TERM	MEANING
	information such as **C**ontrolled **T**echnical **I**nformation. Intended to replace myriad similar terms (such as **S**ensitive **B**ut **U**nclassified and **F**or **O**fficial **U**se **O**nly) now officially deprecated. "Information the Government creates or possesses, or that an entity creates or possesses for or on behalf of the Government, that a law, regulation, or Government-wide policy requires or permits an agency to handle using safeguarding or dissemination controls" *(32 CFR 2002)*. "Information that law, regulation, or governmentwide policy requires to have safeguarding or disseminating controls, excluding information that is classified under Executive Order 13526, Classified National Security Information, December 29, 2009, or any predecessor or successor order, or the Atomic Energy Act of 1954, as amended" *(NIST SP 800-171)*. See also Executive Order 13526.
Controller	Authority, regulator, person, device, *thing*, organisation, *etc.* that commands, directs, regulates, or supervises another, similar to a manager. "The natural or legal person, public authority, agency or other body which, alone or jointly with others, determines the purposes and means of the processing of personal data; where the purposes and means of such processing are determined by Union or Member State law, the controller or the specific criteria for its nomination may be provided for by Union or Member State law" *(**G**eneral **D**ata **P**rotection **R**egulation)*. "The natural or legal person, public authority, agency or other body which, alone or jointly with others, determines the purposes and means of the processing of personal data" *(ISACA glossary)*.
Control objective	Explicit definition of the business objective/s, risk mitigation purpose/s, or rationale for a control, *i.e.* what it is primarily intended to achieve for the organisation, individual, or society. "Statement describing what is to be achieved as the result of implementing controls" *(ISO/IEC 27000)*. "A statement of the desired result or purpose to be achieved by implementing control procedures in a particular process" *(ISACA glossary)*. See also information security objective.
Control owner	Rôle or person who is accountable to management or other stakeholders and authorities for the effective design and operation of an important control, *e.g.* the Chairman of the Board or **C**hief **E**xecutive **O**fficer typically 'owns' the organisation's governance arrangements as a whole. "A person to whom the enterprise has assigned the authority and accountability for making control-related decisions and who is responsible for ensuring that the control is implemented and is operating effectively and efficiently" *(ISACA glossary)*. See also risk owner, asset owner, information owner, process owner.

TERM	MEANING
Control perimeter	The notional area, domain, or zone (such as the physical boundary of a secure facility, or the logical extent of a system or network) within which a control operates, hopefully achieving the desired risk mitigation effect. "The boundary defining the scope of control authority for an entity. Notes: For example, if a system is within the control perimeter, the right and ability exist to control it in response to an attack" *(ISACA glossary)*.
Control plane	Network function determining *how* packets are forwarded, *e.g.* routing and load balancing. "The administrative interface that allows for the management and orchestration of a system's infrastructure" *(AusISM)*.
Control practice	"Key control mechanism that supports the achievement of control objectives through responsible use of resources, appropriate management of risk and alignment of IT with business" *(ISACA glossary)*.
Control process	Set of activities intended to detect, restrict/contain, resolve, or prevent the occurrence/recurrence of incidents. "The policies, procedures, and activities designed and operated to manage risks to be within the level of an organization's risk tolerance" *(IIA GIAS)*.
Control risk	Uncertainties relating to a control, such as its design, suitability, sufficiency, strength, quality, value, reliability, trustworthiness, and effectiveness in practice. Mitigated by systems security engineering, competent analysis and explicit specification of the security requirements, control testing, and other assurance measures. "Risk that assets are lost/compromised or that financial statements are materially misstated, due to lack of, or ineffective, design and/or implementation of internal controls" *(ISACA glossary)*. "The risk that a material error exists that would not be prevented or detected on a timely basis by the system of internal controls" *(ITAF)*.
Control **S**elf-**A**ssessment **(CSA), control risk self-assessment**	Typically, a regular management review process to self-assess the status of governance across the organisation, including information security and other forms of risk management and control. May simply involve managers completing checklists, surveys, or **I**nternal **C**ontrols **Q**uestionnaires of some form, hinting at integrity concerns due to self-interest and incompetence without additional assurance. "A method/process by which management and staff at all levels collectively identify and evaluate risk and controls within their business areas. This assessment may be under the guidance of a facilitator, such as an auditor or risk manager" *(ISACA glossary)*. *Cf.* **C**loud **S**ecurity **A**lliance.

TERM	MEANING
Control **S**trength **(CS)**	One of the factors (parameters) in the FAIR method, CS estimates the ability for controls to mitigate risks (or rather to 'reduce vulnerabilities' in FAIR terms) to information assets under analysis. Strong controls are well designed, fully implemented, highly effective, robust/resilient, unlikely to be bypassed/disabled, used, managed, maintained, *etc.* See also **P**robable **L**oss **M**agnitude, **L**oss **E**vent **F**requency, **T**hreat **Cap**ability, **T**hreat **E**vent **F**requency. *Cf.* control weakness.
Control system	System providing governance and control-related capabilities and functions.
Control total	Value (such as a grand total or count of the number of items) that can be used as a simple cross-check for integrity failures on a data set or process, *e.g.* used to confirm that all records transmitted through an interface were duly received and processed by a **D**ata**B**ase, before committing the changes.
Control unit, control section	Low-level functional subunit within a **C**entral **P**rocessing **U**nit that governs (coordinates, directs, and controls) data processing activities, interrupts, *etc.* "The area of the central processing unit (CPU) that executes software, allocates internal memory and transfers operations between the arithmetic-logic, internal storage and output sections of the computer" *(ISACA glossary)*.
Control weakness	"A deficiency in the design or operation of a control procedure. Control weaknesses can result in risk not being reduced to an acceptable level in the relevant activity area (relevant risk threatens achievement of the objectives that are relevant to the activity area being examined). Control weaknesses can be material when the design or operation of one or more control procedures does not reduce to a relatively low level the risk that misstatements, caused by illegal acts or irregularities, may occur and not be detected by the related control procedures" *(ISACA glossary)*.
Convenience sample	Survey of public toilets? Alternatively, in audit sampling: "The use of a dataset that is not gathered scientifically in order to run quick experiments. Later on, it is essential to switch to a scientifically gathered dataset" *(ISACA glossary)*. *Cf.* stratified sample, random sample, systematic stratified sample, time series analysis, attribute sample, discovery sample.
Convergent thinking	Refining and narrowing down possibilities to focus on finding the 'ideal' solution to a complex problem. "Focused on high-likelihood possibilities, most favorable/unfavorable conditions and events, current and most relevant circumstances, and most rewarding/riskiest outcomes" *(OCEG GRC Glossary)*. *Cf.* divergent thinking.
Convince	Strongly persuade someone of something by demonstrating or proving it, providing assurance.

TERM	MEANING
Convolution	Technique to analyse data, *e.g.* to identify 'edges' separating areas of an image. "Mathematical operation involving a sliding dot product or cross-correlation of the input data" *(ISO/IEC 22989)*.
Convolutional **N**eural **N**etwork **(CNN),** **D**eep **C**onvolutional **N**eural **N**etwork **(DCNN)**	"Feed forward neural network using convolution in at least one of its layers" *(ISO/IEC 22989)*.
COO	*Abbrev:* **C**hief **O**perating **O**fficer.
Cookie	Small text file sent by a web server to the browser and later retrieved, normally to track web browsing habits or to continue or resume previous sessions. If browser and website settings permit, different websites or JavaScript may access and reuse the information in cookies, raising privacy and other information security issues. "A web browser message used for the purpose of identifying users and possibly preparing customized web pages for them. Notes: The first time a cookie is set, a user may be required to go through a registration process. Subsequent to this, whenever the cookie's message is sent to the server, a customized view based on that user's preferences can be produced. The browser's implementation of cookies has, however, brought several security concerns, allowing breaches of security and the theft of personal information (*e.g.*, user passwords that validate the user identity and enable restricted web services)" *(ISACA glossary)*.
Coordinated **I**ncident **M**anagement **(CIM)**	System and approach to help coordinate, command and control those responding to incidents, *e.g.* emergency services dealing with a serious accident or civil emergency, or cyber incident responders from supply chain partners and authorities jointly tackling a ransomware attack. "Process for IRTs from multiple organizations to work together to handle information security incidents" *(ISO/IEC 27035-4)*. *Cf.* **C**ommon **I**nformation **M**anagement, **C**omprehensive **I**ncident **M**anagement, **C**ase and **I**ncident **M**anagement
Copyleft	Movement using copyright law, in stark contrast to its normal application, to *permit* rather than *prevent* free access to and collaborative or community development of **I**ntellectual **P**roperty with the express requirement that derivative works are covered by the same permissive conditions. Denoted by an inverted copyright symbol. See also **C**reative **C**ommons, GNU General Public License.
Copy protection, copy prevention	Technical controls typically involving encryption and dongles, intended to prevent or restrict the ability of users to copy or use software and other **I**ntellectual **P**roperty except on the original authentic storage media used for legitimate distribution. "Use of special techniques to detect or prevent the unauthorized copying of data, software, or firmware" *(ISO/IEC 2382)*.

TERM	MEANING
Copyright	Legal and moral protection giving the creators of original materials **I**ntellectual **P**roperty **R**ights over the copying, use and dissemination of the information by others with the ability to permit or prohibit various activities through licences, contracts, or agreements, for decades (typically 70 years). Aside from being unethical and often illegal, the wanton or casual abuse of copyright (piracy and plagiarism) is a strong disincentive for creative originators (like me) to continue investing in, creating and releasing **I**ntellectual **P**roperty. "The protection of writings, recordings or other ways of expressing an idea. The idea itself may be common, but the way it was expressed is unique, such as a song or book" *(ISACA glossary)*. See also copyleft.
Core competency	"Set of skills and know how present within a management system, directly aligned with the objectives of the management system supporting the achievement of the objectives and not elsewhere present within the organization at a competitive level" *(ISO/IEC 27022)*.
CORE IMPACT	Commercial network security and penetration test tool. Automates *hundreds* of exploits against known vulnerabilities. More info: https://www.coresecurity.com/
Core network	"Part of a mobile telecommunication network that connects the access network to the wider communication network. The Internet and other public networks are examples of wider communication networks" *(ISO/IEC 27033-6)*.
Core process	"[Process that] delivers apparent and direct customer value and is derived from the core competencies of the management systems" *(ISO/IEC 27022)*. See also management process, support process.
Corner case	Unanticipated and potentially harmful situations (including cybersecurity incidents) can occur when multiple parameters, factors or conditions simultaneously approach their limits, putting software and systems under stress. Testing can simulate this by deliberately driving data values, volumes, loading, temperatures, *etc.* towards boundary conditions, figuratively 'pushing things into a dark corner' to check whether controls intended to rate-limit, avoid unsafe modes, generate warnings, trigger alerts and alarms, gracefully degrade performance, initiate failover responses, *etc.* function correctly in practice. See also edge case.
Corporate fraud	Fraud committed by workers or agents of an organisation or body corporate with the direct involvement, or knowledge and tacit acceptance, of senior management (although of course, being fraud, that can be tough to determine, demonstrate, and prove in court) as opposed to a single fraudster or a small group of perpetrators.

TERM	MEANING
Corporate governance	Overall governance of the enterprise as a whole. "The system by which enterprises are directed and controlled. The board of directors is responsible for the governance of their enterprise. Corporate governance consists of the leadership and organizational structures and processes that ensure the enterprise sustains and extends strategies and objectives" *(ISACA glossary)*.
Corporate information security policy	Highest-level policy statement in which executive management formally lays out and commits the organisation to an overall position on information security and related matters, *e.g.* information risk, cybersecurity, safety, privacy, ethics, governance, compliance, assurance. Typically states generic principles and/or axioms that are amplified through topic-specific policies plus supporting procedures, guidelines, security awareness, training, management direction and oversight, *etc.* "Document that describes management direction and support for information security in accordance with business requirements and relevant laws and regulations. Note: The document describes the high-level information security requirements that have to be followed throughout the organisation" *(ISO/IEC 27033-1)*.
Corporate **S**ocial **R**esponsibility **(CSR), corporate sustainability, conscience or citizenship, sustainable or responsible business, conscious capitalism**	Emerging form of self-regulation for organisations to be *seen* to achieve wider social and ethical objectives, in addition to conventional (capitalist, competitive, profit-driven) business objectives. In the information security context, CSR typically concerns privacy and integrity, *e.g.* not intrusively capturing and exploiting personal information about workers and third parties, and overtly supporting the care and maintenance of shared community resources such as the Internet and the environment rather than merely using them.
Correct/recover actions & controls	"Actions & controls that slow down or decrease the impact of unfavorable events, and return the organization to its original state, stable state, or superior state after harm has occurred to minimize harm and prevent future occurrences" *(OCEG GRC Glossary)*.
Correction	Resolution of an error. "Action to eliminate a detected nonconformity" *(ISO/IEC 27000)*.
Corrective action	"Action to eliminate the cause of a nonconformity and to prevent recurrence" *(ISO/IEC 27000)*.
Corrective control	Form of control intended to minimise, contain, or reverse the damage caused by a security incident, *e.g.* restoring damaged or lost data from backups or extinguishing a fire. "A control designed to correct errors, omissions, unauthorized uses and intrusions, once they are detected" *(ISACA glossary)*. *Cf.* preventive control, detective control.

TERM	MEANING
Corroborating evidence	Evidence supporting other evidence. May not be directly related to the case, *e.g.* an alibi supporting someone's assertion that they were otherwise engaged elsewhere when a crime was committed.
Corruption, corrupt	Common form of integrity failure, *e.g.* data corruption caused by malware, bugs, and user errors, and human corruption involving coercion, bribery, and dubious ethics. "A threat action that undesirably alters system operation by adversely modifying system functions or data" *(SANS glossary)*.
CORS	*Abbrev:* **C**ross-**O**rigin **R**esource **S**haring.
COSMICENERGY	Species of malware identified in 2023 by researchers (although probably not actually in the wild), targeting **I**ndustrial **C**ontrol **S**ystems/**O**perational **T**echnology in the energy supply industry. Exploits vulnerable SQL Server software, with malicious Python and C++ components that can command **R**emote **T**erminal **U**nits to shut down equipment.
COSO	*Abbrev:* **C**ommittee **O**f the **S**ponsoring **O**rganizations of the Treadway commission.
Cost–benefit analysis	Evaluation of the net value anticipated, promised, or achieved by an investment. "A net result analysis that relies on the addition of positive factors and the subtraction of negative factors to build a business case supporting a risk response" *(ISACA glossary)*. "Compares the cost of implementing countermeasures with the value of the reduced risk" *(SANS glossary)*.
COTS	*Abbrev:* **C**ommercial **O**ff-**T**he-**S**helf.
Counter-countermeasure	Control intended to counteract, evade or negate a countermeasure, *e.g.* advanced missile guidance systems that are less vulnerable to misdirection by chaff, flare, or unauthorised commands.
Counterfeit	a. *[Noun]* Pirated, fake, fabricated copy misrepresented as an original, authentic asset, thereby infringing the true owner's **I**ntellectual **P**roperty **R**ights and defrauding the purchaser. Numerous mass-produced counterfeit products and bank notes are in circulation, some of which are not merely passable but so authentic that even experts struggle to distinguish them from the genuine articles … although bargain-basement pricing may be a clue. b. *[Verb]* "[To] simulate, reproduce or modify a material good or its packaging without authorization" *(ISO 22300)*.
Counterfeiter	Fraudster who counterfeits.
Counter-**I**ntelligence, counter**i**ntelligence **(CI)**	Intelligence activities and methods to protect sensitive and valuable information, counteracting intelligence gathering (spying). *Cf.* **C**onfiguration **I**tem, **C**ritical **I**nfrastructure, **C**ompetitive **I**ntelligence, **C**onfidential **I**nformant.

TERM	MEANING
Countermeasure	Generally synonymous with control. May refer more specifically to a reactive or corrective control in some contexts. "Action, device, procedure, technique, or other measure that is designed to minimize vulnerability" *(ISO/IEC 2382)*. "Action taken to lower the likelihood of a security threat scenario succeeding in its objectives, or to reduce the likely consequences of a security threat scenario" *(ISO 22300)*. "The reduction of threats or vulnerabilities through any direct process" *(ISACA glossary)*. "Actions, devices, procedures, or techniques that meet or oppose (*i.e.*, counters) a threat, a vulnerability, or an attack by eliminating or preventing it, by minimizing the harm it can cause, or by discovering and reporting it so that corrective action can be taken" *(CNSSI 4009)*. "Reactive methods used to prevent an exploit from successfully occurring once a threat has been detected. Intrusion Prevention Systems (IPS) commonly employ countermeasures to prevent intruders form gaining further access to a computer network. Other counter measures are patches, access control lists and malware filters" *(SANS glossary)*.
Counterstrike, counter-hack	Retaliatory attack directed against the *alleged* or *apparent* perpetrator of a prior attack. Aside from escalating tensions and perhaps being illegal, a counterstrike may be misdirected, for instance if the perpetrator was incorrectly identified, perhaps because the original attack involved spoofing or other covert, coercive, or deceptive false-flag techniques. A highly risky approach.
Counterterrorism	Government-sponsored activities such as propaganda, intelligence, surveillance, and cybertage, intended to counteract, undermine, prevent, or otherwise mitigate terrorism.
Cover, coverage	Scope, type, or nature of insurance provided, normally defined in the policy in terms of events, perils, or hazards, assets, *etc.* included or excluded, plus the limits of liability and specified terms and conditions. "The proportion of known attacks detected by an intrusion detection system (IDS)" *(ISACA glossary)*.
Coverage analysis	"The determination and assessment of measures associated with the invocation of program structural elements to determine the adequacy of a test run. Coverage analysis is useful when attempting to execute each statement, branch, path or iterative structure in a program. Tools that capture this data and provide reports summarizing relevant information have this feature" *(ISACA glossary)*.
Covert	Covered. Refers to secretive, hidden, surreptitious, undercover, quiet, or silent activities or devices, often unauthorised and malicious in nature, such as bugs used for surveillance or spying. See also covert control, cryptic.

TERM	MEANING
Covert channel, back channel	Covert or cryptic mechanism allowing confidential information to be discreetly communicated and extracted from a supposedly secure system, network, or location (such as a **S**ensitive **C**omparted **I**nformation **F**acility) bypassing confidentiality controls. Examples include steganography and out-of-band communications, *e.g.* manipulating a circuit's current demand using specific operating sequences in order to pass information to a compromised or illicitly attached current-monitoring device, micro-manipulating the timing of network packets to convey information that would normally be dismissed as jitter, or using wideband spread-spectrum radio transmissions that resemble noise. "Transmission channel that may be used to transfer data in a manner that violates security policy" *(ISO/IEC 2382)*. "The means by which information can be communicated between two parties in a covert fashion using normal system operations. For example by changing the amount of hard drive space that is available on a file server can be used to communicate information" *(SANS glossary)*. See also backdoor. *Cf.* side channel.
Covert control	Control designed to be covert such as a 'silent alarm' that summons a response without audibly alerting intruders on-site, various forms of monitoring and logging that discreetly record evidence of incidents for later analysis, and surveillance in general.
Coveware	Niche US company offering support services to organisations hit by ransomware, such as negotiating ransoms.
Cowrie	Open-source honeypot application that logs brute force attacks and shell interactions on UNIX-based servers, for analysis. More info: https://www.cowrie.org/
CPE	*Abbrev:* **C**ontinuing [or **C**ontinuous] **P**rofessional **E**ducation.
CPNI	*Abbrev:* **C**entre for the **P**rotection of **N**ational **I**nfrastructure.
CPS	*Abbrev:* **C**ertification **P**ractice **S**tatement.
CPTED	*Abbrev:* **C**rime **P**revention **T**hrough **E**nvironmental **D**esign.
CPU	*Abbrev:* **C**entral **P**rocessing **U**nit – see processor.
Crack, cracker, cracking	Malicious hack or cybercriminal act, generally motivated by the prospect of personal gain. Passwords, cryptosystems, and safes may be cracked, *e.g.* by brute force attacks. "To 'break into' or 'get around' the security of a software program. Notes: For example, certain newsgroups post serial numbers for pirated versions of software. A cracker may download this information in an attempt to crack the program so he/she can use it. Crack is commonly used in the case of cracking (unencrypting) a password or other sensitive data" *(ISACA glossary)*.

TERM	MEANING
Crambus	Iranian-backed group of cyber-spooks, also known variously as APT34, Cobalt Gypsy, OilRig, and Helix Kitten. Active since 2014. Allegedly used PowerShell-based and other malware to compromise a middle-Eastern government's target networks and systems in 2023.
Crash, abend	a. Unplanned sudden computer system, application, process, or device failure resulting from an unhandled exception/error condition triggered accidentally, *e.g.* by a bug, flaw, or power glitch, or deliberately by a hack, malware, or cybertage. "The sudden and complete failure of a computer system or component" *(ISACA glossary)*. b. Sudden, energetic, unplanned, and hazardous impact between physical objects, perhaps resulting from catastrophic failure of the collision-avoidance capabilities of an autonomous vehicle. c. Drastic reduction of stock values on the stock markets, causing instability and perhaps collapse of the global financial industry.
Crash dump	File containing a snapshot of the contents of main memory at the time of a crash. Used by software developers to analyse the status of the stack, heap, registers, buffers, pointers, *etc.* to discover what caused the crash. Used by hackers to find confidential information such as passwords and encryption keys that had been held temporarily in memory. Used by malware analysts to identify cryptic malware.
CRC	*Abbrev:* **C**yclic **R**edundancy **C**heck.
Creative **C**ommons **(CC)**	Not-for-profit organisation promoting free access to and use of **I**ntellectual **P**roperty as in copyleft. Their standardised licences cater for various situations ranging from placing information unencumbered into the public domain, through requiring attribution of the owner, to restrictions on commercial use and modification. *Cf.* **C**ommon **C**riteria, **C**ertified in **C**ybersecurity.
Credential	Something a person, system, *etc.* presents to confirm (authenticate) their asserted identity (*e.g.* a passport, password, biometric, security token, or digital certificate) or professional capabilities (*e.g. résumé* or *curriculum vitae* plus the original, authentic qualification or competence certificates). "Data that are transferred to establish the claimed identity of an entity" *(ISO/IEC 2382)*.
Credentialed analysis	"In vulnerability analysis, passive monitoring approaches in which passwords or other access credentials are required. Note: Usually involves accessing a system data object" *(ISACA glossary)*.
Credential stuffing	Automated brute force attack involving attempting to logon to multiple websites using lists of usernames, passwords, and other credentials accumulated from other sources, such as previous hacks. If a logon succeeds (proving the credentials valid), further information may be obtained from the compromised userID, perhaps leading to direct exploitation and further compromises (identity fraud).

TERM	MEANING
Credible	Believable. Social engineers and fraudsters work hard to make their pretexts credible to fool their targets into trusting them inappropriately.
Credit card number	See **P**rimary **A**ccount **N**umber.
Credit risk	Uncertainty relating to credit, *e.g.* the possibility of a borrower defaulting on a mortgage, and the debtor foreclosing on the property. "The potential that a borrower or creditor will fail to meet financial obligations in accordance with agreed terms" *(ISACA glossary)*.
Crenelated	Classic ⊓-⊓-⊓-⊓-⊓ shaped tops to the battlements of Mediaeval castles. Archers cowered behind the uprights of the parapet for protection while raining down arrows upon the attackers below through the crenels (notches). An ancient physical security control.
CREST (International)	UK-based government-supported not-for-profit organisation and scheme to test and accredit penetration testers. Given the trusted, privileged nature of the work, pentesters must be competent in order for their clients to place any reliance on their assurance efforts, and must be trustworthy since they are likely to gain access to valuable and/or confidential information assets if (when!) tested security controls fail. Offers CREST Practitioner, CREST Registered, and CREST Certified qualifications. See also CBEST. More info: https://www.crest-approved.org/
Crib	Useful hint for a cryptanalyst, often consisting of some known plaintext that might reveal if the correct decryption key has been found by a brute force attack on the ciphertext. Standard or routine parts of a message (such as a date/timestamp, predictable sequence number, message type or protocol identifier, greeting or signature) may be useful cribs.
Crime	Act prohibited by law that can be punished by government authorities under the criminal justice system. Can range from minor offenses such as traffic violations, to serious offenses such as violent assault and murder. See also cybercrime. *Cf.* tort.
Crime **P**revention **T**hrough **E**nvironmental **D**esign **(CPTED)**	Physical architectural design philosophy that seeks to deter attacks by criminals against people innocently using shopping malls, railway stations, walkways between parking lots and buildings, *etc.* or against the properties. Even lighting and landscaped areas free of hidey-holes permit more effective surveillance monitoring and escape routes for potential victims, while barriers and visual cues help distinguish private from public property. Thorny bushes near windows and walls, and razor wire deter casual if not professional intruders. "Process for analysing and assessing crime and security risks to guide development, urban design, site management and the use of the built environment in order to prevent and reduce crime and the fear of crime, and to promote and improve

TERM	MEANING
	public health, quality of life and sustainability. Note: Environmental design refers to the applied arts and sciences dealing with creating the human-designed environment" *(ISO 22341)*.
Crimeware, crimeware kit, attack toolkit, exploit kit	Software package used to generate and/or distribute malware using libraries of technical exploits, plus the infection and remote-control elements including functions to report statistics on the status of the exploitation process. A few crimeware kits (such as Carberp and Zeus) have been released onto the Internet. Some are traded commercially on the black market or hacker underground. Most are jealously guarded by the hackers who created and maintain them and/or the cybercriminals who pay for and exploit them. "A type of malware used by cyber criminals. The malware is designed to enable the cyber criminal to make money off of the infected system (such as harvesting key strokes, using the infected systems to launch Denial of Service Attacks, etc.)" *(SANS glossary)*. See also malware, ransomware, adware, scareware, spouseware, stalkerware, spyware.
Criminal	a. *[Noun]* Person who commits crime. b. *[Adjective]* Relating to crime.
Criminality	Illegal acts, punishable under criminal law.
Criminal underground	See black market and hacker underground.
CRISC	*Abbrev:* **C**ertified in **R**isk and **I**nformation **S**ystems **C**ontrol.
Crisis	Chaotic situation associated with a serious incident or emergency, characterised by some disorder and instinctive behaviours or panic. Literal survival of the affected people, organisation, group, team, political party, nation, *etc.* is generally the overriding priority in a crisis; hence, other considerations (including security) *may* be downplayed or disregarded at least until the crisis subsides. "Unstable condition involving an impending abrupt or significant change that requires urgent attention and action to protect life, assets, property or the environment" *(ISO 22300)*.
Crisis management	Management activities during a crisis such as evacuating buildings, calling the emergency services, triage, and initiating incident management activities as order is gradually restored. "Holistic management process that identifies potential impacts that threaten an organization and provides a framework for building resilience, with the capability for an effective response that safeguards the interests of the organization's key interested parties, reputation, brand and value-creating activities, as well as effectively restoring operational capabilities. Note: Crisis management also involves the management of preparedness, mitigation response, and continuity or recovery in the event of an incident, as well as management of the overall programme through training, rehearsals and reviews to ensure the preparedness, response and continuity plans stay current and up to date" *(ISO 22300)*.

TERM	MEANING
Crisis management team	Workers responsible for crisis management. "Group of individuals functionally responsible for directing the development and execution of the response and operational continuity plan, declaring an operational disruption or emergency/crisis situation, and providing direction during the recovery process, both pre- and post-disruptive incident. Note: The crisis management team can include individuals from the organization as well as immediate and first responders and interested parties" *(ISO 22300)*.
Criteria	Plural of criterion. Conditions, specification, parameters, or demands that are expected or required to be satisfied. Used for direction, evaluation, assurance, measurement, and other purposes. "The benchmarks used to measure or evaluate the subject matter" *(Trust Services Criteria)*. "The standards and benchmarks used to measure and present the subject matter and against which an IS auditor evaluates the subject matter. Notes: Criteria should be: Objective—free from bias; Measurable—provide for consistent measurement; Complete—include all relevant factors to reach a conclusion; Relevant—relate to the subject matter. In an attestation engagement, benchmarks against which management's written assertion on the subject matter can be evaluated. The practitioner forms a conclusion concerning subject matter by referring to suitable criteria" *(ISACA glossary)*.
Critical, criticality	a. Crucial, essential, extremely valuable, or utterly indispensable. An imprecise overused emotionally charged context-dependent adjective. "Qualitative description used to emphasize the importance of a resource, process or function that must be available and operational constantly or available and operational at the earliest possible time after an incident, emergency or disaster has occurred" *(ISO/IEC 27031)*. "The importance of a particular asset or function to the enterprise, and the impact if that asset or function is not available" *(ISACA glossary)*. b. Particularly serious or grave situation or highly risky event capable of causing, precipitating, or developing into a crisis. c. Involving painstaking and perhaps biased or prejudiced criticism or critique. d. Particularly negative, demeaning, or damning. *Cf.* vital.
Critical asset	Critical asset. "Asset which can have a direct impact on production or generation, transmission, storage and distribution of electric power, gas, oil and heat" *(ISO/IEC 27019)*.
Critical Control Point (CCP)	"Point, step or process at which controls can be applied and a threat or hazard can be prevented, eliminated or reduced to acceptable levels" *(ISO 22300)*. "(QA) A function or an area in a manufacturing process or procedure, the failure of which, or loss of control over, may have an adverse effect on the quality of the finished product and may result in an unacceptable health risk" *(ISACA glossary)*.

TERM	MEANING
Critical customer	a. Customer who complains, bitterly, about crappy products, such as a dead parrot. b. "Entity, the loss of whose business would threaten the survival of an organization" *(ISO 22300)*.
Critical data, critical information	Data or information that, for some objective or subjective reason, is considered crucial, particularly valuable, absolutely indispensable, necessary, or vital to something important. Its corruption or loss is thought likely to prove devastating – a show-stopper. "Data that are identified during the risk assessment process as crucial to the method and/or finding, particularly in terms of the accuracy or traceability, therefore protection steps should be in place to reduce the risk of irretrievable loss or data corruption" *(FSRCoP)*.
Critical design review	Unusually important or utterly indispensable design review. "A review to verify that the detailed design of one or more configuration items satisfies specified requirements; to establish the compatibility among the configuration items and other items of equipment, facilities, software and personnel; to assess risk areas for each configuration item; and, as applicable, to assess the results of producibility analyses, review preliminary hardware product specifications, evaluate preliminary test planning and evaluate the adequacy of preliminary operation and support documents" *(ISACA glossary)*.
Critical discipline	"The background disciplines that comprise the interdisciplinary approach to GRC, including: Governance & Oversight, Strategy & Performance, Risk & Decision Support, Compliance & Ethics, Security & Continuity, and Audit & Assurance" *(OCEG GRC Glossary)*.
Critical facility	Critical facility. "Physical structure, network or other asset that provide services that are essential to the social and economic functioning of a community or society" *(ISO 22300)*.
Critical finding	Critical finding. "Findings or results that meet one or more of the following criteria: (a) Have a significant impact on the opinion provided. (b) Cannot be repeated or checked in the absence of the item/exhibit or sample, or after completion or conclusion of the examination of an incident, fire, collision or explosion scene. (c) Could be interpreted differently by a suitably qualified practitioner in the [forensic science activity] in question" *(FSRCoP)*.
Critical findings check	Competent assessment and evaluation of critical findings for assurance reasons, *e.g.* to determine whether they qualify as admissible evidence. "A check on any critical finding to ensure they are acceptable" *(FSRCoP)*.
Critical function	Critical function. "Business activities or information that cannot be interrupted or unavailable for several business days without significantly jeopardizing operation of the enterprise" *(ISACA glossary)*.

TERM	MEANING
Critical indicator	Critical indicator. "Quantitative, qualitative or descriptive measure used to assess the hazard being monitored to identify the potential for the development of an incident, accident or emergency. Note: Critical indicators provide information about the most important integral characteristics of the structural state of a facility" *(ISO 22300)*.
Critical **I**nfrastructure **(CI), C**ritical **C**orporate **I**nfrastructure **(CCI), C**ritical **E**nterprise **I**nfrastructure **(CEI), C**ritical **N**ational **I**nfrastructure **(CNI)**	Shared infrastructure services and supplies, such as electricity, water, fuel, food, telecommunications, government, law enforcement, armed services, and the security services (CI), that are considered critical for a nation (CNI) or organisation (CCI, CEI). Significant failure of any of these, perhaps as a result of a physical or electronic attack on the computer equipment, networks, *things*, or people monitoring and controlling them, is likely to cause immediate disruption and substantial economic damage as well as perhaps causing injuries, deaths, environmental incidents, *etc.*, making these attractive targets in cyberwar and for ransomware attacks. "Systems and assets, whether physical or virtual, so vital to the United States that the incapacity or destruction of such systems and assets would have a debilitating impact on cybersecurity, national economic security, national public health or safety, or any combination of those matters" *(NIST **C**yber **S**ecurity **F**ramework)*. "Those critical elements of infrastructure (namely assets, facilities, systems, networks or processes and the essential workers that operate and facilitate them), the loss or compromise of which could result in: (a) major detrimental impact on the availability, integrity or delivery of essential services – including those services whose integrity, if compromised, could result in significant loss of life or casualties – taking into account significant economic or social impacts; and/or (b) significant impact on national security, national defence, or the functioning of the state" *(UK National Cyber Security Strategy 2022)*. "Set of organizations and facilities that are essential for the functioning of society and the economy as a whole. Note: A failure or malfunction of such organizations and facilities can result in sustained supply shortfalls, make a significant impact on public security and have other wide-ranging impacts" *(ISO/IEC 27019)*. "Systems whose incapacity or destruction will have a debilitating effect on the economic security of an enterprise, community or nation" *(ISACA glossary)*. See also cyberinfrastructure. *Cf.* **C**onfiguration **I**tem, **C**ompetitive **I**ntelligence, **C**ounter-**I**ntelligence, **C**onfidential **I**nformant.
Critical **N**ational **I**nfrastructure **B**anking **S**upervision and **E**valuation **T**esting **(CBEST)**	UK financial services industry voluntary scheme initiated by the Bank of England and based on CREST, to accredit and guide penetration testers in testing banking and other **C**ritical **N**ational **I**nfrastructure systems. Uses threat intelligence to adapt pentest techniques to topical attack methods. More info: https://www.bankofengland.co.uk/financial-stability/operational-resilience-of-the-financial-sector/cbest-threat-intelligence-led-assessments-implementation-guide

TERM	MEANING
Critical or important function	Critical function. "A function, the disruption of which would materially impair the financial performance of a financial entity, or the soundness or continuity of its services and activities, or the discontinued, defective or failed performance of that function would materially impair the continuing compliance of a financial entity with the conditions and obligations of its authorisation, or with its other obligations under applicable financial services law" *(DORA)*.
Critical product and service	Critical product. "Resource obtained from a supplier, which, if unavailable, would disrupt an organization's critical activities and threaten its survival. Note: Critical products or services are essential resources to support an organization's high priority activities and processes identified in its business impact analysis" *(ISO 22300)*.
Critical server	Critical server. "A server that provides critical network or security services. For example, a Microsoft Active Directory Domain Services domain controller or an authentication server" *(AusISM)*.
Critical **S**uccess **F**actor **(CSF)**	Factor deemed critical to the success of a project, initiative, mission, organisation, investment, *etc.* "The most important issue or action for management to achieve control over and within its IT processes" *(ISACA glossary)*. *Cf.* **C**yber**S**ecurity **F**ramework.
Critical supplier	Critical supplier. "Provider of critical products or services. Note: This includes an 'internal supplier', who is part of the same organization as its customer" *(ISO 22300)*.
Critical thinking	Ability to consider, discern, and take account of the credibility and veracity of information, while ignoring, discounting, or challenging dubious, biased, or malicious sources in order to develop informed, sound, objective understandings and valid opinions. An increasingly valuable skill, given the rising volume of poor-quality information (noise, misinformation) and ever more sophisticated deliberate attempts to mislead us through disinformation.
Criticality analysis	"Process designed to systematically identify and evaluate an organization's assets based on the importance of its mission or function, the group of people at risk, or the significance of an undesirable event or disruption on its ability to meet expectations" *(ISO 22300)*. "Evaluation of resources or business functions to identify their importance to the enterprise, and the impact if a function cannot be completed or a resource is not available" *(ISACA glossary)*.

TERM	MEANING
Critically	"Of essential importance with respect to objectives and/or outcomes" *(ISO 22300)*.
CRITS	*Abbrev:* **C**ollaborative **R**esearch **I**nto **T**hreats.
CRIU	*Abbrev:* **C**heckpoint and **R**estore **I**n **U**serspace.
CRL	*Abbrev:* **C**ertificate **R**evocation **L**ist.
CRO	*Abbrev:* **C**hief **R**isk **O**fficer.
Cron	Commonplace UNIX/Linux scheduling application. Sometimes used to launch malware, possibly conventional scripts or utilities that have been altered to exploit their privileges.
Cross-border data transfer	"The transfer of personal data to recipients outside of the territory in which the data originate" *(ISACA glossary)*.
Cross-border processing	"Either (a) processing of personal data which takes place in the context of the activities of establishments in more than one Member State of a controller or processor in the Union where the controller or processor is established in more than one Member State; or (b) processing of personal data which takes place in the context of the activities of a single establishment of a controller or processor in the Union but which substantially affects or is likely to substantially affect data subjects in more than one Member State" *(**G**eneral **D**ata **P**rotection **R**egulation)*. "Processing of personal data in the context of the activities of establishments in more than one country of a controller or processor, where the controller or processor is established in more than one country; or processing of personal data in the context of the activities of a single establishment of a controller or processor union but which substantially affects or is likely to substantially affect data subjects in more than one country" *(ISACA glossary)*.
Cross certification, cross certificate, cross signature	Mutual recognition process in which a **C**ertification **A**uthority signs and issues a digital certificate that can be used to authenticate the public key of another trusted CA, and *vice versa*. "A certificate issued by one certificate authority (CA) to a second CA that allows users of the first certification authority to obtain the public key of the second CA and verify the certificates that the second CA created. Note: Often refers to certificates issued to each other by two CAs at the same level in a hierarchy" *(ISACA glossary)*.
Cross-**D**omain **S**olution **(CDS)**	"A controlled interface that enables secure manual and/or automatic access and/or information transfer between different security domains while protecting the confidentiality, integrity and availability of each domain. There are several types of CDS including access, multi-level and transfer gateways" *(NZISM)*. "A system capable of implementing comprehensive data flow security policies with a high level of trust between two or more differing security domains" *(AusISM)*.

TERM	MEANING
Cross-**O**rigin **R**esource **S**haring **(CORS)**	HTTP header and browser security mechanism controlling scripted access to resources (information content or services) provided from other domains.
Cross signature	See cross certification.
Cross-**S**ite **R**equest **F**orgery **(CSRF, XSRF)**	"A type of malicious exploit of a website whereby unauthorized commands are transmitted from a user that the website trusts (also known as a one-click attack or session riding). CSRF is pronounced sea-surf" *(ISACA glossary)*. "An external website or application forces a client to make an unintended request to another application that the client has an active session with. Applications are vulnerable when they use known, or predictable, URLs and parameters; and when the browser automatically transmits all required session information with each request to the vulnerable application" *(SCP QRG)*.
Cross-Site **S**cripting **(XSS)**	Web hacking technique in which badly designed websites (*e.g.* some bulletin-board systems) with inadequate data entry validation are made to return malicious **U**niform **R**esource **L**ocators, HTML, JavaScript, or other executable code (malware) to the user's browser for execution (*e.g.* to manipulate or disclose their supposedly private cookies or other local data). [Usually abbreviated to "XSS" to avoid confusion with **C**ascading **S**tyle **S**heets.] A form of code injection. "Injection of malicious scripts into otherwise benign and trusted websites. Notes: Cross-site scripting (XSS) attacks occur when an attacker uses a web application to send malicious code, generally in the form of a browser-side script, to a different end user. Flaws that allow these attacks to succeed are widespread and occur anywhere a web application uses input from a user within the output that it generates without validating or encoding it" *(ISACA glossary, citing OWASP)*. See also **X**ml e**X**ternal **E**ntities.
Crossover **E**rror **R**ate **(CER)**	In authentication systems, the tolerance or sensitivity configuration setpoint at which false rejections and false acceptances are equally likely to occur.
CrowdStrike incident, CrowdStrike glitch	CrowdStrike is a US-based cybersecurity company. On Friday July 19th 2024, a faulty update to its Falcon e**X**tended **D**etection and **R**esponse software was released with inadequate pre-release testing. Following rapid automatic deployment to thousands of corporate customers, more than 8 million systems crashed worldwide, causing widespread business disruption for days and US$5 billion in estimated losses.
CRUD (**C**reate, **R**ead, **U**pdate, **D**elete)	Fundamental operations or activities on stored data in a **D**ata**B**ase, *i.e.* **C**reate (generate a new record), **R**ead (retrieve stored data), **U**pdate (modify stored data), and **D**elete (erase a record or else flag it as such if it needs to be retained due to still being referenced elsewhere).

TERM	MEANING
Cryptanalysis, cryptanalyst, cryptanalytic, crypto	Study and practice of breaking cryptosystems by any means, normally through a combination of mathematics, language analysis, brilliant intuition, lots of time, powerful computers, and sheer hard work. The cryptanalyst may attempt to find and exploit mathematical or technical weaknesses in the algorithm (perhaps inserted deliberately, *i.e.* backdoors) and/or the system and processes that implement it, guess the keys by brute force, or somehow disentangle the relationships between known plaintext such as a crib and the corresponding ciphertext. "Analysis of a cryptographic system, its inputs or outputs, or both, to derive sensitive information, such as plaintext" *(ISO/IEC 2382)*. "The mathematical science that deals with analysis of a cryptographic system in order to gain knowledge needed to break or circumvent the protection that the system is designed to provide. In other words, convert the cipher text to plaintext without knowing the key" *(SANS glossary)*. *Cf.* cryptography.
Cryptic	Surreptitious, deliberately hidden, secretive, concealed or non-obvious, such as a fiendishly difficult crossword puzzle. Not necessarily unauthorised or malicious. See also covert.
Crypt-**K**ey **(CK)**	"The term used to describe the UK's use of cryptography to protect the critical information and services on which the UK government, military and national security community rely, including from attack by our most capable adversaries" *(UK National Cyber Security Strategy 2022)*.
Crypto	Ambiguous contraction of **crypto**graphy (usually), otherwise **crypto**logy, **crypto**currency, *etc.* depending on context.
Crypto AG	Swiss-based high-grade commercial/national security cryptographic equipment supplier covertly owned by the US (**C**entral **I**ntelligence **A**gency) and German (**B**undes**N**achrichten**D**ienst) intelligence agencies until 2018. "Operation Rubicon" was a scandalous supply chain compromise of a type the spooky intelligence community warns and worries about.
Cryptocurrency, crypto, cybercurrency	Tradeable, decentralised, and largely anonymous digital money such as Bitcoin, Monero, Zcash, and Litecoin. Protected against counterfeiting by cryptographic means including blockchain. Generated by cryptomining. "A digital currency and payment system, *e.g.* Bitcoin" *(UK National Cyber Security Strategy 2022)*.
Crypto**C**urrency **S**ecurity **S**tandard **(CCSS)**	Crypto**C**urrency **C**ertification **C**onsortium (C4)'s cybersecurity framework comprising specified objectives (framed as cybersecurity requirements) for cryptocurrency systems such as exchanges, applications, and storage, plus a system certification scheme involving conformity assessments and accompanying competence certificates for practitioners and auditors. More info: https://cryptoconsortium.org/

TERM	MEANING
Cryptogram	See ciphertext.
Crypto-Gram	Bruce Schneier's long-running monthly newsletter/digest of his recent cryptography articles and commentaries. More info: https://www.schneier.com/crypto-gram/
Cryptographic algorithm	Algorithm used for cryptography. "An algorithm used to perform cryptographic functions, such as encryption, integrity, authentication, digital signatures or key establishment" *(AusISM)*.
Cryptographic equipment	"A generic term for commercial cryptographic equipment and High Assurance Cryptographic Equipment" *(AusISM)*.
Cryptographic erase	With various important provisos concerning the level of risk, overall process, technology, algorithm, key length and complexity, *etc.* encrypting data or overwriting it with ciphertext, and then destroying the key, *may* render confidential information permanently irretrievable. "Method of sanitization in which the encryption key for the encrypted target data is sanitized, making recovery of the decrypted target data infeasible" *(ISO/IEC 27040)*.
Cryptographic hash	See hash.
Cryptographic key, cryptovariable	Value used to transform data in a cryptographic operation by controlling the algorithm in a particular manner, *e.g.* to decrypt a message previously encrypted with the same key in symmetric cryptography. *Note:* 'cryptovariable' may be the correct technical term but almost nobody except über-crypto-geeks use it: 'key' is simpler and more widely understood. "Bit string that controls the operations of encryption or decryption" *(ISO/IEC 2382)*. *Cf.* physical (non-cryptographic) key.
Cryptographic module	Tamper-resistant computer subsystem consisting of data processing, storage, and communications hardware and firmware, designed to perform cryptographic operations such as receiving, encrypting, and returning a nonce using a private key in a challenge-response authentication scenario.
Cryptographic protocol	Specified algorithm/s, parameters (*e.g.* key length), and associated processes for cryptographic authentication, encryption, *etc.* "Specified cryptographic algorithms, parameters (such as key length) and processes for managing, establishing and using encrypted communications" *(NZISM)*. "An agreed standard for secure communication between two or more entities to provide confidentiality, integrity, authentication and non-repudiation of data" *(AusISM)*.
Cryptographic software	Cryptographic application. "Software designed to perform cryptographic functions" *(AusISM)*.

TERM	MEANING
Cryptographic system, ciphersystem, cryptosystem	Cryptographic system – computer system or device that employs cryptography. Generally taken to include the cryptographic algorithm, the key management processes, external interfaces, software supporting operations, and sometimes even the entire **P**ublic **K**ey **I**nfrastructure. "Documents, devices, equipment, and associated techniques that are used together to provide a means of encryption or decryption" *(ISO/IEC 2382)*. "Set of cryptographic primitives that are used to provide information security services. Most often, the term is used in conjunction with primitives providing confidentiality, *i.e.*, encryption" *(ISACA glossary)*. "A related set of hardware or software used for cryptographic communication, processing or storage, and the administrative framework in which it operates" *(NZISM)*.
Cryptographic system material	"Material that includes, cryptographic key, equipment, devices, documents, firmware or software that contains or describes cryptographic logic" *(NZISM)*.
Cryptography, cryptographic, cryptographer, crypto	From Ancient Greek (*κρυπτός* or *kryptós* meaning hidden and *γράφειν* or *graphein* meaning writing), the science, study, and practice of creating systems to hide information and to find and retrieve it when needed. Involves the use of mathematical algorithms for encryption, hashing, authentication, *etc.* "Discipline that embodies the principles, means, and methods for the transformation of data in order to hide their semantic content, prevent their unauthorized use, or prevent their undetected modification" *(ISO/IEC 2382)*. "The study of mathematical techniques related to aspects of information security, such as confidentiality, data integrity, entity authentication and data origin authentication" (*ISACA glossary*). "The study of secure communications techniques that allow only the sender and intended recipient of a message to view its contents" *(NZISM)*. "The science or study of analysing and deciphering codes and ciphers; cryptanalysis" *(UK National Cyber Security Strategy 2022)*. *Cf.* cryptanalysis, cryptology.
Cryptojacking	Neologism for incidents involving surreptitious cryptomining on compromised systems, stealing and misusing finite system resources such as its processing and memory capacity.
CryptoLocker	Species of ransomware.
Cryptology	Literally, the study of 'hidden writing' which encompasses *both* cryptography *and* cryptanalysis. Sometimes shortened to 'crypto,' although usually that means **crypto**graphy.
Cryptominer, cryptomining	Application that attempts to generate and/or validate new cryptocurrency, consuming significant computer resources (particularly the graphics processor) and power in the process. Along with spyware, identity fraud, **I**ntellectual **P**roperty theft, and coercion (ransomware), cryptomining is a way for cybercriminals to make money from malware-infected systems without their owners' knowledge and consent. See also cryptojacking.

TERM	MEANING
Cryptonym	Innocuous codename assigned to a project, assignment, system, individual, organisation, incident, *etc.* to reduce the possibility of disclosing sensitive information.
Cryptoperiod	"The useful life of the cryptographic key" *(NZISM)*.
Cryptoprimitive (cryptographic primitive)	See primitive.
Cryptorbit	Species of ransomware in the wild in 2016.
Crypto security	a. Cryptographic security (cryptography), *e.g.* encryption. b. Cryptocurrency security, *e.g.* blockchain.
Cryptosystem	Contraction of **crypto**graphic **system**.
Cryptovariable	See cryptographic key.
Cryptowall	Species of cryptographic ransomware.
CryptXXX	Species of cryptographic ransomware. Flaws in the cryptosystem implementation substantially weakened this malware.
Cryzip	One of the earliest species of cryptographic ransomware, in the wild in 2006.
CS	*Abbrev:* **C**ontrol **S**trength.
CSA	*Abbrev:* **C**loud **S**ecurity **A**lliance, **C**ontrol **S**elf-**A**ssessment, or **C**yber**S**ecurity **A**dvisory, depending on context.
CSE	*Abbrev:* **C**ommunications **S**ecurity **E**stablishment.
CSET	*Abbrev:* **C**yber **S**ecurity **E**valuation **T**ool.
CSF	*Abbrev:* **C**yber **S**ecurity **F**ramework or **C**ritical **S**uccess **F**actor, depending on context.
CSIS	*Abbrev:* **C**anadian **S**ecurity **I**ntelligence **S**ervice.
CSO	*Abbrev:* **C**hief **S**ecurity **O**fficer.
CSP	*Abbrev:* **C**loud **S**ervice **P**rovider, **C**ontent **S**ecurity **P**olicy, **C**loud **S**ecurity **P**olicy, **C**yber **S**ecurity **P**olicy, or [NIST] **C**yber **S**ecurity **P**rofessional, depending on context.
CSR	*Abbrev:* **C**orporate **S**ocial **R**esponsibility.
CSRF	*Abbrev:* **C**ross-**S**ite **R**equest **F**orgery.
C-suite	An organisation's executive managers (the 'chiefs') such as the **C**hief **E**xecutive **O**fficer, **C**hief **F**inancial **O**fficer, **C**hief **I**nformation **O**fficer, **C**hief **I**nformation **S**ecurity **O**fficer, **C**hief **O**perating **O**fficer, **C**hief **R**isk **O**fficer, **C**hief **S**ecurity **O**fficer, **C**hief **A**udit **E**xecutive, and **C**hief **T**echnology **O**fficer (titles and responsibilities vary).

TERM	MEANING
CT	*Abbrev:* **C**ertificate **T**ransparency.
CTB-locker	Species of ransomware.
CTEM	*Abbrev:* **C**ontinuous **T**hreat **E**xposure **M**anagement.
CTF	*Abbrev:* **C**apture **T**he **F**lag.
CTI	*Abbrev:* **C**ontrolled **T**echnical **I**nformation.
CTO	*Abbrev:* **C**hief **T**echnology **O**fficer.
CUI	*Abbrev:* **C**ontrolled **U**nclassified **I**nformation.
Culture	Behaviours, beliefs, ethical values, *etc.* commonly held and espoused by members of a social group such as an organisation, business unit, department, team, industry, group, club, profession, sect, or nation. "A pattern of behaviors, beliefs, assumptions, attitudes and ways of doing things" *(ISACA glossary)*. "An emergent property of a group of people caused by the interaction of individual beliefs, values, mindsets, and behaviors and demonstrated by observable norms and articulated opinions that shape beliefs, values, mindsets, and behaviors in wide-ranging and durable ways" *(OCEG GRC Glossary)*. See also security culture.
Current residual risk	"The level of residual risk under currently operating actions & controls" *(OCEG GRC Glossary)*.
Current risk	"The risk state that exists in the moment, taking into account those actions that have already been taken but not actions that are anticipated or have been proposed" *(ISACA glossary)*.
Current skill level	"Existing level of skill a person, or 'typical' person in a group, possesses" *(OCEG GRC Glossary)*.
Custodian	Temporary/surrogate owner or steward who takes possession of, and is reasonably expected to look after, care for and protect, an asset such as an information asset, acting on behalf and in the best interests of its true owner. "Person or entity that has custody, ownership, control or possession of Electronically Stored Information" *(ISO/IEC 27050-1)*. See also data custodian.
Customer	Procurer/purchaser of commercial products in return for a consideration (generally money). Internal customers work for the same organisation as the suppliers. "The party responsible for buying or accepting a solution or for authorizing payment for a solution. Customers may also be end users" *(ISACA glossary)*. "An individual or entity that purchases products or services" *(OCEG GRC Glossary)*.

TERM	MEANING
Customer requirement	Requirement of a customer, or the consolidated and rationalised set of requirements expressed by multiple customers and prospective customers, or somebody's interpretation and synthesis of what they believe might be the customers' requirements, or something. "The result of eliciting and consolidating needs, and resolving conflicts among those needs, expectations, constraints, and interfaces that clarifies and defines the solutions with affected stakeholders in a way that is acceptable to them" *(ISACA glossary)*.
CVE	*Abbrev:* **C**ommon **V**ulnerabilities and **E**xposures.
CVSS	*Abbrev:* **C**ommon **V**ulnerability **S**coring **S**ystem.
CVV (Card Verification Value), CVV2 (2nd-generation CVV), CSC (Card Security Code), CAV (Card Authentication Value), CAV2 (2nd-generation CAV), CVC (Card Validation Code), CVC2 (2nd-generation CVC), CID (Card Identification number)	Value encoded on the magnetic stripe or a 3- or 4-digit decimal number normally printed rather than embossed on a credit/debit/bank card, that can be used only to verify the card number. According to PCI-DSS, the CVV *must not* be stored by a merchant: after it has been used to validate the card number, it should be erased from memory so that if the merchant's systems are ever compromised by crackers, they will not gain the fullz ... provided they haven't installed their own data monitoring/logging software to capture the data *in transit* or during processing.
CWE	*Abbrev:* **C**ommon **W**eakness **E**numeration.
Cyber	*Abbrev:* **Cyber**netics.
Cyber **A**ssessment **F**ramework **(CAF)**	Guidance from the UK **N**ational **C**yber **S**ecurity **C**entre to "organisations responsible for vitally important services and activities ... with a particular focus on essential functions which if compromised could potentially cause significant damage to the economy, society, the environment, and individuals' welfare, including loss of life." Aimed primarily at cybersecurity professionals working in the public sector and large organisations classed as part of the **C**ritical **N**ational **I**nfrastructure or covered by the UK **N**etwork and **I**nformation **S**ecurity regulations, derived from the **E**uropean **U**nion equivalent. Specifies a set of 14 principles to be interpreted and applied in delivering 'anticipated outcomes' for cybersecurity, resilience, and safety, as opposed to, say, a prescriptive checklist. Covers **I**nformation **T**echnology and **O**perational **T**echnology. "Provides a systematic and comprehensive approach to assessing the extent to which cyber risks to essential functions are being managed by the organisation responsible" *(UK National Cyber Security Strategy 2022)*. More info: https://www.ncsc.gov.uk/collection/cyber-assessment-framework

TERM	MEANING
Cybergeddon, cyber-Armageddon	Full-blown unrestrained cyberwar between highly capable and well-resourced nations or groups would undoubtedly inflict devastating economic damage with horrendous social consequences on a global scale, analogous to the nuclear weapons posturing and threats of **M**utually **A**ssured **D**estruction during the Cold War.
Cyberattack, cyber attack, cyber-attack	Attack staged primarily through electronic means, particularly through the Internet. "An attack, via cyberspace, targeting an enterprise's use of cyberspace for the purpose of disrupting, disabling, destroying, or maliciously controlling a computing environment/infrastructure; or destroying the integrity of the data or stealing controlled information" *(CNSSI 4009)*. "Malicious attempts to exploit vulnerabilities in information systems or physical systems in cyberspace and to damage, disrupt or gain unauthorized access to these systems" *(ISO/IEC TS 27100)* … [additional note: "Common cyber attacks to consumer IoT are basic attacks that could be carried out by script kiddies and amateur hackers" *(ISO/IEC 27404 DRAFT)*. "A malicious and deliberate attempt by an individual or organisation to breach the information system of another individual or organisation" *(UK Cyber Security Breaches Survey 2023)*. "Deliberate exploitation of computer systems, digitally-dependent enterprises and networks to cause harm" *(UK National Cyber Security Strategy 2022)*. "A malicious ICT-related incident caused by means of an attempt perpetrated by any threat actor to destroy, expose, alter, disable, steal or gain unauthorised access to, or make unauthorised use of, an asset" *(DORA)*.
Cyberbully	Someone who uses social media, email, *etc.* to harass, embarrass, intimidate, threaten, coerce, and/or traumatise victims.
Cyber command	Military command centre for cyber operations, such as the US Cyber Command reportedly based at Fort Meade, Maryland.
Cybercop	"An investigator of activities related to computer crime" *(ISACA glossary)*.
Cybercrime	Crime in cyberspace. Colloquially, the use or exploitation of **I**nformation **T**echnology and/or the Internet by cybercriminals to plan, coordinate, commit/perpetrate, or profit from crime. "Category of crime involving technology that may or may not involve the Internet" *(ISACA glossary)*. "Involves gaining unauthorised access, or causing damage, to computers, networks, data or other digital devices, or the information held on those devices. Examples of cyber crime include hacking or unauthorised access into online accounts (*e.g.* banking, email or social media accounts), denial of service attacks, or devices being infected by a virus or other malicious software (including ransomware)" *(UK Cyber Security Breaches Survey 2023)*. "Cyber-dependent crime

TERM	MEANING
	(crimes that can only be committed through the use of ICT devices, where the devices are both the tool for committing the crime and the target of the crime); or cyber-enabled crime (crimes that may be committed without ICT devices, like financial fraud, but are changed significantly by use of ICT in terms of scale and reach)" *(UK National Cyber Security Strategy 2022)*.
Cybercriminal, cybercrook	Criminal who uses **I**nformation **T**echnology systems and networks (particularly the Internet) to commit crime. "An individual or entity that uses technology with malicious intent" *(ISACA glossary)*.
Cybercurrency	See cryptocurrency.
Cyber-dependencies	Technology has penetrated so deeply and extensively into modern society that we have become highly reliant (dependent) on it, particularly in relation to critical infrastructure providing power, water, food, telecommunications, *etc*.
Cyber ecosystem	"The totality of interconnected infrastructure, persons, processes, data, information and communications technologies, along with the environment and conditions that influence those interactions" *(UK National Cyber Security Strategy 2022)*.
Cyberespionage, cyberspying	Spooky use of computer systems and networks (particularly the Internet) to spy on targets. "Activities conducted for the reason of security, business, politics or technology to find information that ought to remain secret. It is not inherently military" *(ISACA glossary)*.
Cyber Essentials, Cyber Essentials Plus	Government-backed basic (minimalist) organisational cybersecurity certification scheme from the UK National Cyber Security Centre, revolving around just five key controls: firewalls, secure configurations, patching, user access controls, and malware prevention. The 'Plus' version increases assurance with stronger conformity assessments. "The NCSC recommends Cyber Essentials as the minimum standard of cyber security for all organisations." Sets the very lowest of low hurdles, too low even for a supple Caribbean island limbo dancer. More info: https://www.ncsc.gov.uk/cyberessentials/overview
Cyber-extortion	Cybercriminal exploitation of illegitimate access to and control over sensitive and/or valuable information in order to coerce victims out of money, *etc*. Attacks typically involve the use of hacking, malware (*e.g.* ransomware), and social engineering to steal or leverage the value of data, **I**ntellectual **P**roperty, storage media, or **I**nformation **T**echnology devices. See also extortion.

TERM	MEANING
Cyber-facilitated fraud	"Deception to make a gain, or cause a loss, in relation to money, services, property or goods, which uses data or access obtained through one or more of the following: ransomware; viruses, spyware or malware; denial of service attacks; hacking – unauthorised access to devices (including, computers, smartphones and other internet-connected devices), as well as online takeovers; phishing attacks" *(UK Cyber Security Breaches Survey 2023)*.
Cyber harassment	Harassment or coercion conducted through the Internet, generally, such as revenge porn and spam bombing.
Cyber incident	Information security incident involving technology. "Actions taken through the use of computer networks that result in an actual or potentially adverse effect on an information system and/or the information residing therein. See incident" *(CNSSI 4009)*. "An occurrence that actually or potentially poses a threat to a computer, internet-connected device, or network – or data processed, stored, or transmitted on those systems – which may require a response action to mitigate the consequences" *(UK National Cyber Security Strategy 2022)*.
Cyberinfrastructure	Computing elements of global, national, or corporate infrastructures, especially automated systems interconnected through networks such as the Internet.
Cyberinsurance, cyber insurance, cyber-insurance, cyber risk insurance	Insurance against specified cyber-risks, a form of risk sharing.
Cybernetics (cyber, cyber-)	Study of governance and control mechanisms such as feedback loops, robotics, and latterly **I**nformation **T**echnology, particularly anything involving the Internet. Derived from the Greek words kubernao (κυβερνάω) meaning to steer, direct, and control, and kubernetes (κυβερνήτης) meaning helmsman. A jargon prefix/buzz-word, much abused by marketers, journalists, politicians, *etc.* and widely misinterpreted. Prefixed with 'cyber' or 'cyber-,' many terms appear hi-tech and sexy whereas in fact most are old hat.
Cyber persona	"Digital representation of an individual or organisation necessary to interact in cyberspace" *(ISO/IEC 27110)*.
Cyber-physical system	Digital system that interfaces with, monitors, directs, and controls mechanical machinery (*e.g.* robotics, automated numerically controlled machine tools, actuators for electrically operated valves, switches, contactors, relays, actuators, motors, *etc.*, sensors on industrial plant or in vehicles and buildings) and electronics in general (*e.g.* networkable scientific measuring or analytical devices, power quality monitoring, battery energy storage systems). "Interacting digital, analog, physical, and human components engineered for function through integrated physics and logic" *(NIST SP 800-171)*. See also **O**perational **T**echnology.

TERM	MEANING
Cyber-prepping	Preparing to survive cyberwar or extreme cyber incidents including post-apocalyptic social disorder and infrastructural collapse.
Cyberpunk	a. Science fiction genre characterised by classic futuristic works such as William Gibson's book *Neuromancer.* b. Proudly nonconformist anti-establishment youth with a deep fascination for the cyber world and hacking plus (as usually lamely depicted by conventional media) piercings, tattoos, and a curious obsession with dark hoodies and stylised, sinister facemasks.
Cyber resilience	Resilience, robustness, stability, and hence dependability of the cyberinfrastructure. "The ability of an organisation to continue to carry out its mission by anticipating and adapting to cyber threats and other relevant changes in the environment and by withstanding, containing and rapidly recovering from cyber incidents" *(Financial Stability Board's Cyber Lexicon, 2018).* "The ability to adapt to disruptions caused by cyber security incidents while maintaining continuous business operations. This includes the ability to detect, manage and recover from cyber security incidents" *(AusISM).* "The overall ability of systems, organisations and citizens to withstand cyber events and, where harm is caused, recover from them" *(UK National Cyber Security Strategy 2022).*
Cyber **R**esilience **A**ct ([EU] **CRA)**	"REGULATION OF THE EUROPEAN PARLIAMENT AND OF THE COUNCIL on horizontal cybersecurity requirements for products with digital elements and amending Regulations (EU) No 168/2013 and (EU) 2019/1020 and Directive (EU) 2020/1828." **E**uropean **U**nion regulation specifies cybersecurity standards for Information Technology devices (products with digital elements) in the EU. Low-risk products can be documented and self-assessed by their suppliers, whereas medium- and high-risk products require stronger assurance. Became law in October 2024 despite concerns from the open-source movement. More info: https://data.consilium.europa.eu/doc/document/PE-100-2023-INIT/en/pdf
Cyber risk, cyber-risk, cyberrisk, cybersecurity risk	Potentially damaging or harmful situation involving technology such as deliberate attacks via the Internet by hackers, extortionists, criminals, social engineers, fraudsters, terrorists, cyber-spooks, or other competent adversaries. "The potential that a given cyber threat will exploit the vulnerabilities of an information system and cause harm" *(UK National Cyber Security Strategy 2022).* "The potential for loss or disruption caused by an incident and is to be expressed as a combination of the magnitude of such loss or disruption and the likelihood of occurrence of the incident" *(EU CRA).*
Cyber risk insurance	See cyberinsurance.

TERM	MEANING
Cybersecurity, cyber-security, cyber security	Primarily refers to technological/**I**nformation **T**echnology security controls protecting computer systems, networks, and the associated data against attacks from the Internet. However, the definition is sometimes widened to include information security as a whole, while some refer specifically to defensive countermeasures within cyberwar, Internet security, **C**ritical **N**ational **I**nfrastructure security, or even securing virtual worlds. *Caveat lector.* "Safeguarding of people, society, organizations and nations from cyber risks. Note: Safeguarding means to keep cyber risk at a tolerable level" *(ISO/IEC TS 27100)*. "The activities necessary to protect network and information systems, the users of such systems, and other persons affected by cyber threats" *(EU Cybersecurity Act)*. "The protection of information assets by addressing threats to information processed, stored and transported by internetworked information systems" *(ISACA glossary)*. "Prevention of damage to, protection of, and restoration of computers, electronic communications systems, electronic communications services, wire communication, and electronic communication, including information contained therein, to ensure its availability, integrity, authentication, confidentiality, and nonrepudiation" *(DoD dictionary)*. "The ability to protect or defend the use of cyberspace from cyber attacks" *(CNSSI 4009)*. "The process of protecting information by preventing, detecting, and responding to attacks" *(NIST CSF)*. "Includes any processes, practices or technologies that organisations have in place to secure their networks, computers, programs or the data they hold from damage, attack or unauthorised access" *(UK Cyber Security Breaches Survey 2023)*. "Measures used to protect the confidentiality, integrity and availability of systems and data" *(AusISM)*. "The protection of internet-connected systems (to include hardware, software and associated infrastructure), the data on them, and the services they provide, from unauthorised access, harm or misuse. This includes harm caused intentionally by the operator of the system, or accidentally, as a result of failing to follow security procedures or being manipulated into doing so" *(UK National Cyber Security Strategy 2022)*.
Cyber**S**ecurity **A**ct **(2019) ([EU] CSA)**	"REGULATION (EU) 2019/881 OF THE EUROPEAN PARLIAMENT AND OF THE COUNCIL of 17 April 2019 on ENISA (the European Union Agency for Cybersecurity) and on information and communications technology cybersecurity certification and repealing Regulation (EU) No 526/2013." More info: https://eur-lex.europa.eu/legal-content/EN/TXT/?uri=CELEX:32019R0881
Cybersecurity and **I**nfrastructure **S**ecurity **A**gency **(CISA)**	Agency of the US **D**epartment of **H**omeland **S**ecurity, founded in 2018. Leads a network of business partners strengthening federal cybersecurity and protecting the **N**ational **C**ritical **F**unctions forming the critical [national] infrastructure. *Cf.* **C**ertified **I**nformation **S**ystems **A**uditor, **C**ybersecurity **I**nformation **S**haring **A**ct. More info: https://www.cisa.gov/

TERM	MEANING
Cybersecurity architecture	Cybersecurity architecture. "Description of the structure, components and topology (connections and layout) of security controls within the IT infrastructure of an enterprise. Note: The security architecture shows how defense-in-depth is implemented and how layers of control are linked, and is essential to designing and implementing security controls in any complex environment" *(ISACA glossary)*.
Cybersecurity **B**ody **O**f **K**nowledge **(CyBOK)**	"A unique resource, providing for the first time an underpinning body of knowledge encompassing the breadth and depth of cyber security, showing that cyber security encompasses a wide range of disciplines" *(UK National Cyber Security Strategy 2022)*.
Cyber security breach	Cybersecurity breach. "Any incident that results in unauthorised access of data, applications, services, networks and/or devices by bypassing their underlying security mechanisms" *(UK Cyber Security Breaches Survey 2023)*.
Cyber **S**ecurity **E**valuation **T**ool **(CSET)**	Questionnaire-style self-assessment application from the **C**ybersecurity and **I**nfrastructure **S**ecurity **A**gency concerning a variety of cyber security controls drawn from several frameworks/standards such as NIST's **C**yber**S**ecurity **F**ramework and **C**ybersecurity **M**aturity **M**odel **C**ertification. See also **I**nternal **C**ontrols **Q**uestionnaire. More info: https://github.com/cisagov/cset/releases
Cyber security event	Cybersecurity event. "An occurrence of a system, service or network state indicating a possible breach of security policy, failure of safeguards or a previously unknown situation that may be relevant to security" *(AusISM)*. *Cf.* cyber security incident.
Cyber **S**ecurity **F**ramework **(CSF), cybersecurity framework**	a. NIST's "Framework for Improving Critical Infrastructure Cybersecurity" reflects the timeline of an incident and the need for appropriate information security controls that precede, accompany, or follow an incident through the identify, protect, detect, respond, and recover phases (called 'functions' within CSF). The US Cybersecurity Enhancement Act 2014 required NIST to develop "a prioritised, flexible, repeatable, performance based, and cost-effective approach, including information security measures and controls that may be voluntarily adopted by owners and operators of critical infrastructure to help them identify, assess, and manage cyber risks." It is essentially a simple risk and incident management structure to help protect the US **C**ritical **N**ational **I**nfrastructure against cyber risks (called 'cybersecurity risks' within CSF), drawing on several other standards and methods for the controls. *Cf.* **C**ritical **S**uccess **F**actor. More info: https://www.nist.gov/cyberframework b. "Basic set of concepts used to organise and communicate cybersecurity activities" *(ISO/IEC 27110)*.

TERM	MEANING
Cyber security incident	Security incident involving cybersecurity/technology. "An unwanted or unexpected cyber security event, or a series of such events, that has either compromised business operations or has a significant probability of compromising business operations" (*AusISM*). *Cf.* cyber security event.
Cybersecurity Information Sharing Act **2015** **(CISA)**	US law to encourage the sharing of cyberthreat indicators between US corporations and the US government by limiting their liabilities in so doing. *Cf.* **C**ertified **I**nformation **S**ystems **A**uditor, **C**ybersecurity and **I**nfrastructure **S**ecurity **A**gency.
Cybersecurity **M**aturity **M**odel **C**ertificate **(CMMC)**	NIST/US **D**epartment **o**f **D**efense cybersecurity assurance scheme for assessing/auditing and rating defence suppliers between 'Basic Cybersecurity Hygiene' and 'Advanced' levels according to the nature and quality of the cybersecurity controls they operate, in order to protect **C**ontrolled **U**nclassified **I**nformation as it traverses supply chains. More info: https://dodcio.defense.gov/cmmc/About/
Cybersecurity objectives	Cybersecurity objectives. "Objectives that address the cybersecurity risks that could affect the achievement of the entity's overall business objectives (including compliance, reporting, and operational objectives)" *(Trust Services Criteria)*.
Cybersecurity risk	See cyber risk.
Cyberspace	Vague term, inconsistently defined, used, and understood, typically referring vaguely to **I**nformation **T**echnology, particularly the Internet, and sometimes Internet culture, virtual systems, virtual worlds, collaborative working, social media, *etc.* "A global domain within the information environment consisting of the interdependent network of information systems infrastructures including the Internet, telecommunications networks, computer systems, and embedded processors and controllers" *(CNSSI 4009)*.
Cyber-spook	Elite state/government-employed, backed, or tolerated group using advanced malware, hacking, and social engineering methods for spying, cybertage, or political reasons. See also spook.
Cybersquatting	Illicit exploitation and misappropriation of commercial trademarks in the cyber/**I**nformation **T**echnology context, *e.g.* using copycat or lookalike domain names or **U**niform **R**esource **L**ocators for phishing, fraud, or other attacks. See also typosquatting.
Cyber stalking	Grooming or snooping on victims through the Internet, generally, typically continuing to contact and coerce them after being asked or told to desist.

TERM	MEANING
Cyberstrike	Attack in, on or through cyberspace. See also cyber-tactic.
Cyber-tactic	Offensive security attack mounted through or against cyberspace, using techniques such as phishing or hacking. See also cyberstrike.
Cybertage	Sabotage in cyberspace that compromises computer systems/devices, **D**ata**B**ases, networks, data, or information, *e.g.* destroys or damages them, interrupts or delays business activities, or leads to the loss of valuable business or the inappropriate disclosure of confidential information. Whereas sabotage *usually* implies inflicting physical damage (such as arson), cybertage often affects intangible information assets, *e.g.* using malware, hacking, disinformation, or propaganda.
Cyberterrorism	Commission of terrorist acts in cyberspace. More informally, the use or exploitation of **I**nformation **T**echnology and the Internet to create terror.
Cyberteur	Person who commits cybertage, such as a mole or cyber-spook.
Cyberthreat, cyber threat	Threat or threat agent active in the cybersecurity domain – particularly substantial, highly capable ones backed by governments and other resourceful and determined adversaries. "Any potential circumstance, event or action that could damage, disrupt or otherwise adversely impact network and information systems, the users of such systems and other persons" *(EU CSA)*. "Any circumstance or event with the potential to harm systems or data" *(AusISM)*. "Anything capable of compromising the security of, or causing harm to, information systems and internet connected devices (to include hardware, software and associated infrastructure), the data on them and the services they provide, primarily by cyber means" *(UK National Cyber Security Strategy 2022)*.
Cyber Trust Mark	US consumer product voluntary labelling scheme to assess and certify conformity of **I**nformation **T**echnology equipment with NIST cybersecurity standards. Administered by the **F**ederal **C**ommunications **C**ommission. More info: https://www.fcc.gov/CyberTrustMark
Cyber-vandalism	Computer-enabled wanton damage, or wanton damage of computers.
Cyber-vigilante	Person who uses hacking, malware, social engineering, *etc.* to further a malicious personal agenda or obsession.
Cyberwar, cyber-war, cyber war, cyberwarfare, **E**lectronic **W**arfare **(EW), offensive cyber effects operations**	Deliberate exploitation of vulnerabilities in an adversary's computing and telecommunications capabilities, networks, *etc.* by a nation state as an act of war intended to disrupt vital parts or the entirety of their **C**ritical **N**ational **I**nfrastructure, disable their national defences and offensive capabilities, inflict crippling economic damage, *etc.* Due to exclusions in the small print for 'acts of war,' incidents classed as cyberwar attacks *may* not be covered by cyberinsurance. "Activities supported by military organizations with the purpose of threatening the survival and well-being of society/ foreign entity" *(ISACA glossary)*. See also cyber-Armageddon.

TERM	MEANING
Cyberweapon	Tool or technique (such as a computer, malware, hacking, social engineering, cybertage, spying, coercion, or EMP weapon) capable of being used offensively to attack an adversary's **C**ritical **N**ational **I**nfrastructure as part of cyberwar or a similar military mission, and/or to defend against such attacks.
CYBEX (Cybersecurity information Exchange framework), X.1500 (2011)	**I**nternational **T**elecommunication **U**nion – **T**elecommunication standardization sector (ITU-T) recommendation (standard) X.1500 defines structured mechanisms for CERTs, incident responders, *etc.* to document and share information derived by analysis of cybersecurity incidents, vulnerabilities, *etc.*
CyBOK	See **Cy**bersecurity **B**ody **O**f **K**nowledge.
CybOX (Cyber Observable eXpression)	Schema for specifying, capturing, characterising, and communicating or sharing **I**nformation **T**echnology system and network events and properties for event management and logging, malware characterisation, intrusion detection/prevention, incident response, and digital forensics. See also STIX, TAXII, ATT&CK, CRITS.
Cyclic Redundancy Check (CRC)	Basic error-detection technique for datacommunications and storage in which the checksum (essentially a simple, non-cryptographic hash) is calculated and transmitted with the payload and verified on receipt to detect bit errors (integrity failures resulting from noise, packet collisions, *etc.*) *in transit* or in storage. "A type of checksum algorithm that is not a cryptographic hash but is used to implement data integrity service where accidental changes to data are expected" *(SANS glossary)*. Cf. parity.
Cylinder lock	Most common form of physical lock, used on many front doors. When someone inserts the correct key into the keyway, internal pins are lifted to exactly the right positions to allow the plug to be rotated in the hull, thereby retracting the latch so the door can be opened.
Cynefin framework	Framework or conceptual model concerning situations or systems that are described as **simple** (stable and predictable), **complicated** (largely predictable through cause-and-effect relationships), **complex** (largely unpredictable, linkages rationalised only after the fact), **chaotic** (inherently unstable and unpredictable), or **disordered** (of unknown status). Different modes of thinking, controlling or directing, planning, and responding are appropriate in each case.
Cypher-	Archaic British spelling of cipher that, paradoxically, is used in some modern compound words concerning cryptography.
Cyphertext	See ciphertext.
CySA+ (Cybersecurity Analyst)	CompTIA's qualification for cybersecurity analysts. Covers: security operations, vulnerability management, incident response and management, and reporting and communication. *Cf.* **C**ertified **I**nformation **S**ystems **A**uditor. More info: https://www.comptia.org/certifications/cybersecurity-analyst

D

TERM	MEANING
D3FEND (Detection, Denial, and Disruption Framework Empowering Network Defense)	MITRE's taxonomy/DataBase of cybersecurity controls, first published in 2025. Contrived name complements ATT&CK. "D3FEND is a knowledge base, but more specifically a knowledge graph, of cybersecurity countermeasure techniques … a catalog of defensive cybersecurity techniques and their relationships to offensive/adversary techniques." More info: https://d3fend.mitre.org/
DA	*Abbrev:* **D**ata **A**nalytics.
DAC	*Abbrev:* **D**iscretionary **A**ccess **C**ontrol.
Dactyloscopic	Relating to fingerprints or palmprints, *i.e.* the characteristic patterns of ridges on the skin that can be used to identify individuals – a biometric.
Dark	Refers to attempting to become invisible by literally turning off the lights, or by stopping or avoiding the use of radio transmissions or emanations and electronic communications that are liable to be intercepted.
DarkSide	**R**ansomware-**as**-**a**-**S**ervice used to attack Colonial Pipeline in 2021, compromising about 100 Gb of data and production **I**nformation **T**echnology and **O**perational **T**echnology services, thereby interrupting nearly half the fuel normally supplied to the Eastern US, sparking a regional emergency.
Darknet, darkweb, dark web, invisible web, hidden web	Covert part of the deep web offering criminal/black market illicit and illegal products such as hacking, **R**ansomware-**as**-**a**-**S**ervice, money laundering, and drugs. Aside from blocking or evading search engine spiders, Darkweb sites and applications may exploit novel protocols making them inaccessible to users who lack the requisite access authority, knowledge, keys, and/or tools. "Network of secret websites within the Internet that can only be accessed with specific software" *(ISO/IEC 27032)*.
Dashcam (dashboard camera)	**C**losed **C**ircuit **T**ele**V**ision camera mounted in or on a vehicle (not necessarily literally on the dashboard) to record traffic incidents, bad driving, road rage, accidents, *etc.* A form of surveillance. See also body cam.
DAST	*Abbrev:* **D**ynamic **A**pplication **S**ecurity **T**esting.
Data	Electronic representations of information within a computer system or network. In digital computers, data (and indeed software) is parcelled into bytes. Strictly speaking, "data" is the plural of "datum" but it is widely used in the singular. "Reinterpretable representation of information in a formalized manner suitable

TERM	MEANING
	for communication, interpretation, or processing" *(ISO/IEC 2382)*. "Collection of values assigned to base measures, derived measures and/or indicators" *(ISO/IEC 27004)*. "Representations of facts, concepts or instructions in a manner suitable for communication, interpretation or processing by humans or by automated means. In the simplest terms, data are pieces of information" *(ISACA glossary)*. *Cf.* software, hardware, firmware, application.
Data accuracy	Data accuracy. "A component of data quality that indicates whether the data values stored for an object are the correct values and are represented in a consistent and unambiguous form" *(ISACA glossary)*.
Data analysis	Data analysis. "Systematic investigation of relevant, evidence-based information obtained in monitoring the process and its flow in a real or planned system" *(ISO 22300)*. "Obtaining an understanding of data by considering samples, measurement and visualization. Data analysis can be particularly useful when a data set is first received, before the first model is built, and is crucial for understanding experiments and debugging problems with the system" *(ISACA glossary)*.
Data **A**nalytics **(DA)**	Fancy marketing term for the common-or-garden study and analysis of data. Typically involves the use of statistics to examine and glean useful information from large, complex data sets, also known as big data.
Data annotation	Adding relevant metadata (*e.g.* notes about ownership, provenance/origin, and type) to data items or collections. "Process of attaching a set of descriptive information to data without any change to that data. Note: The descriptive information can take the form of metadata, labels and anchors" *(ISO/IEC 22989)*.
Data at rest	Digital bits-n-bytes taking a well-earned break from the daily grind? Alternatively, "Data stored on stable non-volatile storage" *(ISO/IEC 27040)*. "Information residing on media storage facility or a system that is not in use" *(NZISM)*. "Data that resides on media or a system" *(AusISM)*. *Cf.* data in motion.
Data augmentation	Creative approach to paucity of data ... or fraud? "Process of creating synthetic samples by modifying or utilizing the existing data" *(ISO/IEC 22989)*.
Data availability	Data availability. "The fact that data is accessible and services are operational" *(ENISA RM glossary)*.

TERM	MEANING
Data**B**ase **(DB** or **db),** **database system**	Structured and managed collection of data and information. The structuring, accumulation, and collation of data, plus the relationships between items, along with the software functions to manage, manipulate, and report them, can make DBs far more valuable than plain, unmanaged 'flat files' or simple lists and tables. The most important computer systems often are DBs, making DB cybersecurity controls such as those protecting data integrity or controlling access an extremely important facet of information security. "Collection of data organized according to a conceptual structure describing the characteristics of these data and the relationships among their corresponding entities, supporting one or more application areas" *(ISO/IEC 2382)*. "A collection of data, often with controlled redundancy, organized according to a schema to serve one or more applications. The data are stored so that they can be used by different programs without considering the data structure or organization. A common approach is used to add new data and modify and retrieve existing data" *(ISACA glossary)*. "Organized collection of data, generally stored and accessed electronically from a computer system. Databases can reside remotely or on-site. Database Management Systems (DMSs) are used to administer databases, and are not considered part of a database for this document" *(CIS Controls)*. "A collection of information (often but not exclusively electronic) in a structured format allowing searching which may be used for purposes of interpretation" *(FSRCoP)*.
Data**B**ase **A**dministrator **(DBA)**	Privileged user who administers **D**ata**B**ases. Normally responsible for running the **D**ata**B**ase **M**anagement **S**ystem, configuring, maintaining, and tuning DBs, *e.g.* setting up user rôles and defining their access rights to tables and cells, monitoring DB security logs, and managing backups. "Person or group of persons who is responsible for database administration" *(ISO/IEC 2382)*. "An individual or department responsible for the security and information classification of the shared data stored on a database system. This responsibility includes the design, definition and maintenance of the database" *(ISACA glossary)*.
Database analysis	Analysis, review, investigation, evaluation, test, or audit of some aspect of a **D**ata**B**ase meaning the data content, application, and/or system, *e.g.* the architecture and design, logical structure, conformity and compliance, information risks (including threats, vulnerabilities, and impacts), information security arrangements (including confidentiality, integrity and availability controls), performance and capacity, documentation, administration and management, monitoring, maintenance, support, *etc.* "A software verification and validation (V&V) task to ensure that the database structure and access methods are compatible with the logical design" *(ISACA glossary)*.

TERM	MEANING
DataBase Management System (DBMS)	Specialised software system supporting DataBase applications. Provides management functions to organise data (usually in the form of tables, matrices, lists, or sets) and data security (*e.g.* enforcing referential integrity). Provides a standardised interface or abstraction layer between the application and the underlying Operating System and hardware. Optimised for performance and throughput, *e.g.* caching frequently accessed data to reduce disk reads. "System, based on hardware and software, for defining, creating, manipulating, controlling, managing, and using databases. Note: The software for using a database may be part of the database management system or may be stand-alone" *(ISO/IEC 2382)*. "A software system that controls the organization, storage and retrieval of data in a database" *(ISACA glossary)*. *Cf.* Management System.
Database security	Protection of DataBases against unacceptable risks. "A set of controls that ensure that software interacts with a database in a secure manner and that the database is configured securely" *(SCP QRG)*. "The degree to which a database is protected from exposure to accidental or malicious alteration or destruction" *(ISACA glossary)*.
Data breach	Breach of security, policy, law, trust, *etc.* involving data. "Compromise of security that leads to the accidental or unlawful destruction, loss, alteration, unauthorized disclosure of, or access to protected data transmitted, stored or otherwise processed" *(ISO/IEC 27040)*. "The unauthorised movement or disclosure of information on a network to a party who is not authorised to have access to, or see, the information" *(UK National Cyber Security Strategy 2022)*. *Cf.* privacy breach.
Data classification	Classification of data and/or other forms of information according to criteria or rules formally defined in a classification scheme. "The assignment of a level of sensitivity to data (or information) that results in the specification of controls for each level of classification. Levels of sensitivity of data are assigned according to predefined categories as data are created, amended, enhanced, stored or transmitted. Classification level is an indication of the value or importance of the data to the enterprise" *(ISACA glossary)*.
Data classification scheme	See classification scheme. "An enterprise scheme for classifying data by factors such as criticality, sensitivity and ownership" *(ISACA glossary)*.
Data Collection Unit, pod	Network device or *thing* that gathers data from other *things* such as distributed sensors, smart meters, *etc.* and forwards it to a central/control system, passing commands in the opposite direction. Used in Industrial Control Systems, SCADA, Operational Technology, Industrial Internet of *Things*, and Internet of *Things*.

TERM	MEANING
Datacommunications, data communications, datacomms, datacoms	Communication (transmission and reception) of digital data by some means. "Transfer of data among functional units according to sets of rules governing data transmission and the coordination of the exchange" *(ISO/IEC 2382)*. "The transfer of data between separate computer processing sites/devices using telephone lines, microwave and/or satellite links" *(ISACA glossary)*. *Cf.* telecommunications.
Data concerning health	"Personal data related to the physical or mental health of a natural person, including the provision of health care services, which reveal information about his or her health status" *(**G**eneral **D**ata **P**rotection **R**egulation)*. See also **P**rotected **H**ealth **I**nformation.
Data confidentiality	Data confidentiality. "The protection of communications or stored data against interception and reading by unauthorized persons" *(ENISA RM glossary)*.
Data controller	Organisation or person gathering, holding, and using personal information, responsible for ensuring it is adequately secured in order to protect the data subjects' privacy. Accountable for securing the information, even if it is actually processed by a separate organisation (a data processor). See also controller.
Data corruption	Data corruption. "Accidental or intentional violation of data integrity" *(ISO/IEC 2382)*.
Data custodian	Organisation, rôle, or person formally responsible for custodianship (protection) of data placed in their care by its owner/s. "Individual(s) and department(s) responsible for the storage and safeguarding of computerized data" *(ISACA glossary)*.
Data dictionary	Formal description of the data fields of records in a **D**ata**B**ase, ideally including their information security characteristics. "Database that contains metadata" *(ISO/IEC 2382)*. "Repository that stores all the details that correspond to the data flow diagram (DFD) stores, processes and flows. It may be called a database that contains the name, type, range of values, source and authorization for access for each data element in a system. It also indicates which application programs use those data so that when a data structure is contemplated, a list of the affected programs can be generated" *(ISACA glossary)*.
Data diddling	"Changing data with malicious intent before or during input into the system" *(ISACA glossary)*.
Data diode	"A device that allows data to flow in only one direction" *(NZISM)*.
Data **E**ncryption **A**lgorithm **(DEA)**	Symmetric cryptography algorithm specified for the **D**ata **E**ncryption **S**tandard in FIPS PUB 46 (withdrawn in 2005).

TERM	MEANING
Data Encryption Standard **(DES)**	Standard specifying a cryptographic algorithm (**D**ata **E**ncryption **A**lgorithm) for US government use, published in FIPS PUB 46 in 1977. Still used by legacy IT systems, albeit normally in the somewhat more secure form of triple-DES. Vulnerable to brute force attacks with a key length constrained by the standard to 56 bits rather than the maximum of 64; hence, DES is deprecated. "A legacy algorithm for encoding binary data that was deprecated in 2006. DES and its variants were replaced by the Advanced Encryption Standard (AES)" *(ISACA glossary)*. *Cf.* **D**igital **E**vidence **S**pecialist.
Data entry validation	See input validation.
Data exception	Data exception. "Exception that occurs when a program attempts to use or access data incorrectly" *(ISO/IEC 2382)*.
Data Execution Prevention **(DEP)**	**O**perating **S**ystem security feature intended to prevent the execution of data-only pages in memory that happen to contain executable code/processing instructions (*e.g.* as a result of a buffer overflow having been exploited by malware).
Data exfiltration	Data exfiltration. "Unauthorized acquisition of data from any network or endpoint" *(ISACA glossary)*.
Data flow	Movement, communication, or transfer of data/information from sender to recipient along a path. "Movement of data through the active parts of a data processing system in the course of the performance of specific work" *(ISO/IEC 2382)*. "The flow of data from the input (in Internet banking, ordinarily user input at his/her desktop) to the output (in Internet banking, ordinarily data in a bank's central database). Data flow includes travel through communication lines, routers, switches and firewalls, and processing through various applications on servers that process the data" *(ISACA glossary)*.
Data flow control function	Function controlling data flow, typically determining the rate and direction or routing of data.
Data Flow Diagram **(DFD)**	"A diagram that depicts data sources, data sinks, data storage, processes performed on data (represented as nodes) and logical flow of data (represented as links between the nodes)" *(ISACA glossary)*.
Data governance	Governance of digital data or, more broadly, of information.
Data Governance Act **2022 ([EU] DGA)**	**E**uropean **U**nion regulation to facilitate and encourage trustworthy sharing of data concerning health, mobility (traffic), environment, agriculture, public administration, *etc.* within the EU, for research and other purposes. Established mechanisms (such as trusted data intermediaries and altruistic disclosure), rules, and a regulatory framework, plus technological security/privacy controls such as anonymisation and pseudonymisation. More info: https://digital-strategy.ec.europa.eu/en/policies/data-governance-act

TERM	MEANING
Datagram	See packet. "A packet (encapsulated with a frame containing information) transmitted in a packet-switching network from source to destination" *(ISACA glossary)*.
Data in motion	Digital bits-n-bytes on the move, jiggling about with noisy Brownian motion, steadfastly refusing to stay still and be counted? Alternatively, "Data being transferred from one location to another. Note: These transfers typically involve interfaces that are accessible and do not include internal transfers (*i.e.,* never exposed to outside of an interface, chip, or device)" *(ISO/IEC 27040)*. See also data in transit. *Cf.* data at rest.
Data integrity	Data integrity. "Property of data whose accuracy and consistency are preserved regardless of changes made" *(ISO/IEC 2382)*. "The degree to which a collection of data is complete, consistent and accurate" *(ISACA glossary)*. "The confirmation that data which has been sent, received, or stored are complete and unchanged" *(ENISA RM glossary)*.
Data in transit	Digits piled in the back of a white van? Alternatively, "Information that is being conveyed across a communication medium" *(NZISM)*. See also data in motion.
Data in use	Data currently being processed. "Information that has been decrypted for processing by a system" *(NZISM)*.
Data **L**oss [or **L**eakage] **P**revention **(DLP)**	Security technology designed to monitor, identify, log/alert, and if appropriate, block the inappropriate transfer of confidential information through a network port or firewall, *e.g.* to prevent workers, malware, or hackers disclosing or passing personal information, credit card numbers, trade secrets, or other **I**ntellectual **P**roperty to third parties through the Internet, whether by accident or on purpose. Conceptually similar to **I**ntrusion **D**etection **S**ystem/**I**ntrusion **P**revention **S**ystem but concerns extrusion rather than intrusion. "Detecting and addressing data breaches, exfiltration or unwanted destruction of data" *(ISACA glossary)*.
Data masking	Security techniques to anonymise, pseudonymise, or conceal (*e.g.* redact, obfuscate) personal information in a data file, **D**ata**B**ase, *etc.* protecting the privacy of data subjects while also allowing legitimate data analysis and use.
Data miner	Form of malware that covertly collects information on web users, *e.g.* recording personal information submitted by them through online forms. *Cf.* data mining.

TERM	MEANING
Data minimisation	Policy and practice of not over-collecting or hoarding data unnecessarily for reasons such as privacy compliance, risk mitigation, focus, plausible deniability, and reserving data storage capacity for more valuable content. "Principle that requires data to be adequate, relevant and limited to what is necessary in relation to the purposes for which they are processed" *(ISACA glossary)*.
Data mining	"Computational process that extracts patterns by analysing quantitative data from different perspectives and dimensions, categorizing them, and summarizing potential relationships and impacts" *(ISO/IEC 22989)*. "The use of computers to analyze large data sets to look for patterns that assist people in making business decisions" *(ISACA glossary)*. *Cf.* data miner.
Data object	"Element which contains personally identifiable information (PII). Example: such elements are for instance files, documents, records or attributes. Concrete data objects can be, *e.g.* invoices, contracts, personal files, visitor lists, personnel planning sheets, user accounts, log entries, consent documents, *etc.* Note: In the context of this document data objects usually contain PII and can be combined with other data objects … in a cluster of PII … The individual data object … can be of varying complexity" *(ISO/IEC 27555)*.
Data owner	Organisation, rôle, or person who notionally or literally owns and is responsible and usually accountable to management or other authorities for the proper protection and legitimate exploitation of valuable data. "Individual(s) who has responsibility for the integrity, accurate reporting and use of computerized data" *(ISACA glossary)*. See also information owner, file owner, system owner.
Data poisoning attack	See poisoning attack.
Data Privacy Framework	Adopted by the **E**uropean **U**nion and **U**nited **S**tates of **A**merica in 2023 as a replacement for the failed Privacy Shield scheme, this agreement allows for personal data on EU citizens to be transferred to and processed by US organisations with privacy controls deemed adequate to satisfy the **G**eneral **D**ata **P**rotection **R**egulation.

TERM	MEANING
Data **P**rocessing **(DP), A**utomatic **D**ata **P**rocessing **(ADP)**	a. Largely archaic terms for what is now commonly known as the Information Technology function, department, unit, or team … or, more prosaically, just 'IT' or 'Technology.' b. Computing. 'Data processing' persists in laws and regulations. "Systematic performance of operations upon data. Example: Arithmetic or logic operations upon data, merging or sorting of data, assembling or compiling of programs, or operations on text, such as editing, sorting, merging, storing, retrieving, displaying, or printing. Note: The term data processing must not be used as a synonym for information processing" *(ISO/IEC 2382)*. "Any operation or set of operations that are performed on personal data or on sets of personal data, whether or not by automated means, such as collection, recording, organization, structuring, storage, adaptation or alteration, retrieval, consultation, use, disclosure by transmission, dissemination or otherwise making available, alignment or combination, restriction, erasure or destruction" *(ISACA glossary)*.
Data processor	Organisation that processes personal information on behalf of another (the data controller). Typically, an **I**nformation **T**echnology or cloud services company. "A natural or legal person, public authority, agency or other body that processes personal data on behalf of the controller" *(ISACA glossary)*.
Data protection	Protection of personal data. "Implementation of appropriate administrative, technical or physical means to guard against unauthorized intentional or accidental disclosure, modification, or destruction of data [and] implementation of administrative, technical, or physical measures to guard against the unauthorized access to data" *(ISO/IEC 2382)*.
Data **P**rotection **A**ct **(DPA)**	2018 UK privacy law that applies to all organisations processing personal data of individuals in the UK. Incorporates requirements and rights based on the OECD Privacy Principles, *e.g.* obtain informed consent from individuals before processing their personal data, and take reasonable steps to protect personal information from unauthorised access, use, disclosure, or modification. Overseen by the **I**nformation **C**ommissioner's **O**ffice.
Data protection authority	Governmental regulator officially responsible for promoting awareness, overseeing, and enforcing data protection laws and privacy regulations. "Independent authority that monitors and supervises the application of a data protection law" *(ISACA glossary)*.
Data Protection Directive	"Directive 95/46/EC of the European Parliament and of the Council on the protection of individuals with regard to the processing of personal data and on the free movement of such data" which sought to harmonise information protection or privacy laws across the **E**uropean **U**nion and further afield (*e.g.* Australia, Canada, and New Zealand). Deprecated and superseded by **G**eneral **D**ata **P**rotection **R**egulation.

TERM	MEANING
Data Protection Officer (DPO)	"Enterprise officer who is responsible for informing and advising the enterprise about its data protection obligations and monitoring its compliance with them. The General Data Protection Regulation (GDPR) requires some enterprises to appoint a data protection officer" *(ISACA glossary)*.
Data quality	Data integrity metric. "Characteristic of data that the data meet the organization's data requirements for a specific context" *(ISO/IEC 5259-1)*.
Data quality checking	Data (or information) integrity checking and assurance process, part of data security. "Process in which data is examined for completeness, bias and other factors which affect its usefulness for an AI system" *(ISO/IEC 22989)*.
Data remanence, data persistence	"Residual information remaining on a device or storage media after clearing or sanitising the device or media" *(NZISM)*. See also remanence.
Data sampling	Process of selecting data samples from a dataset for various purposes. "Process to select a subset of data samples intended to present patterns and trends similar to that of the larger dataset being analysed. Note: Ideally, the subset of data samples will be representative of the larger dataset" *(ISO/IEC 22989)*. See also audit sampling.
Data security	Cybersecurity protecting digital data, specifically, against unacceptable cyber risks or, more broadly, the protection and legitimate exploitation of information. "Computer security applied to data" *(ISO/IEC 2382)*. "The controls that seek to maintain confidentiality, integrity and availability of information" *(ISACA glossary)*. "Measures used to protect the confidentiality, integrity and availability of data" *(AusISM)*. *Cf.* information security.
Dataset, data set	Collection of digital data or information, organised to facilitate legitimate access, analysis, and use – typically in a Data**B**ase or expert system. "Collection of data with a shared format. Examples: Micro-blogging posts from June 2020 associated with hashtags #rugby and #football; Macro photographs of flowers in 256 × 256 pixels. Note: Datasets can be used for validating or testing an AI model. In a machine learning context, datasets can also be used to train a machine learning algorithm" *(ISO/IEC 22989)*. "A collection of related records" *(ISACA glossary)*.
Data spill	"An information security incident that occurs when information is transferred between two security domains by an unauthorised means. This can include from a classified network to a less classified network or between two areas with different need-to-know requirements" *(NZISM)*. "The accidental or deliberate exposure of data into an uncontrolled or unauthorised environment, or to people without a need-to-know" *(AusISM)*.

TERM	MEANING
Datasploit	Application supporting both offense using, and defences against, social engineering attacks. Mines open-source intelligence sources and correlates information on individuals, domains, email addresses, phone numbers, *etc*. An example of dual-use technology, popular with black, grey, and white hats. See also Burp suite, Maltego.
Data stealing/thieving/ theft malware	Malware that surreptitiously harvests and exfiltrates valuable proprietary information or personal information from infected systems and networks to be exploited directly or sold on the black market.
Data subject, Personally Identifiable Information (PII) principal	Person whose personal information it is. "The individual about whom personal information is collected" *(Trust Services Criteria)*. "A natural person whose personal data are collected, held or processed" *(ISACA glossary)*.
Data Subject Access Request (DSAR), Subject Access Request (SAR), Data Subject Request (DSR)	Formal request made of a data controller by a data subject to gain access to their own personal information under privacy laws such as the **G**eneral **D**ata **P**rotection **R**egulation or **C**alifornia **C**onsumer **P**rotection **A**ct, *e.g.* to check its accuracy, correct or delete it, or to confirm whether it is being held and used lawfully in accordance with the stated purposes. Note: the legal implications of such terms, and subjects' legal rights, vary: however, this hyperglossary is *not* legal advice.
Data validation	Data validation. "Process used to determine if data are accurate, complete, or meet specified criteria. Note: Data validation may include format checks, completeness checks, check key tests, reasonableness checks, and limit checks" *(ISO/IEC 2382)*. "The process of determining that data or a process for collecting data is acceptable according to a predefined set of tests and the results of those tests" *(NIST SP 800-55v1)*. "1. A process used to determine whether data are inaccurate, incomplete or unreasonable. The process may include format checks, completeness checks, check key tests, reasonableness checks and limit checks. 2. The checking of data for correctness or compliance with applicable standards, rules and conventions" *(ISACA glossary)*. "Verification that the properties of all input and output data match what is expected by the application and that any potentially harmful data is made safe through the use of data removal, replacement, encoding, or escaping" *(SCP QRG)*.
DB or db	*Abbrev:* **D**ata**B**ase. *Cf.* dB (decibel).
DBA	*Abbrev:* **D**ata**B**ase **A**dministrator.
DBMS	*Abbrev:* **D**ata**B**ase **M**anagement **S**ystem.
DC	*Abbrev:* **D**omain **C**ontroller.
DCNN	*Abbrev:* **D**eep **C**onvolutional **N**eural **N**etwork.

TERM	MEANING
DCS	*Abbrev:* **D**istributed [or **D**igital] **C**ontrol **S**ystem.
DCU	*Abbrev:* **D**ata **C**ollection **U**nit.
DDoS	*Abbrev:* **D**istributed **D**enial-**o**f-**S**ervice.
DEA	*Abbrev:* **D**ata **E**ncryption **A**lgorithm.
Dead drop	See drop.
Dead **L**etter **B**ox **(DLB)**	See drop.
Dead double	Identity thief who assumes the identity of a dead person.
Debug, debugging	Tracing and eliminating coding errors in software and firmware, or more generally finding and fixing issues, architectural flaws, and problems in virtually anything. Term coined by computing pioneer rear admiral Grace Hopper in the early days of electronic computing when creepy-crawlies (moths and other bugs) caused reliability issues with circuit boards and open frame relays. "Detect, locate, and eliminate errors in programs" *(ISO/IEC 2382)*. "Action of analysing malfunctions in computer systems" *(ISO/IEC 27019)*. "Determining the exact nature and location of a program error and fixing the error" *(ISACA glossary)*.
Debugger	"Software designed to assist debugging" *(ISO/IEC 2382)*.
Deception, deceit	Lying, lie, fabrication, or deliberate, manipulative concealment of the truth.
Deception technology	Advanced honeypot systems designed to lure, divert, contain, and gather information (intelligence) on hackers inside corporate networks, all the while deceiving them into believing they are genuinely gathering reconnaissance, exploiting vulnerabilities, and capturing flags. A potentially valuable approach in some circumstances, but potentially costly and risky too (*e.g.* distracting, diverting, and misleading cybersecurity resources while engendering a false sense of security).
Deceptive software	"Software which performs activities on a user's computer without first notifying the user as to exactly what the software will do on the computer, or asking the user for consent to these actions [such as] a program that hijacks user configurations, a program that causes endless popup advertisements which cannot be easily stopped by the user, [or] adware and spyware" *(ISO/IEC 27032)*.
Decision criteria	"Thresholds, targets, or patterns used to determine the need for action or further investigation, or to describe the level of confidence in a given result" *(ISO/IEC/IEEE 15939)*.

TERM	MEANING
Decision maker	Whoever or whatever chooses between multiple options, objectives, approaches, courses of action, strategies, responses, *etc.* May be a human, computer or information system, team, organisation, administration or society, mechanical machine or some combination thereof. Not necessarily entirely rational/sensible, objective, and consistent in practice. "Top management or a person designated by the top management, and given delegated authority to make decisions" *(ISO 23234)*.
Decision-making criteria	"The principles, values, rules, variables, conditions, targets, tolerances, and other thresholds used to select an option or make a decision" *(OCEG GRC Glossary)*.
Decision tree	"Model for which inference is encoded as paths from the root to a leaf node in a tree structure" *(ISO/IEC 22989)*.
Declarative	Elaborating on the desired output, goal, or objective to be achieved, as in strategy development. *Cf.* imperative.
Declarative knowledge	"Knowledge represented by facts, rules and theorems. Note: Usually, declarative knowledge cannot be processed without first being translated into procedural knowledge" *(ISO/IEC 22989)*.
Declassification	Authorised removal or downgrading of classification level on information for which the current class is no longer appropriate (*e.g.* outdated, irrelevant, or already disclosed), thereby increasing permitted access. "A process whereby information is reduced to an unclassified state. Subsequently an administrative decision can be made to formally authorise its release into the public domain" *(NZISM)*. "A process whereby requirements for the protection of data are removed and an administrative decision is made to formally authorise its release into the public domain" *(AusISM)*. See also redaction.
Decode	Convert encoded messages, words, characters, or bit sequences into their plaintext human-readable equivalents, making sense of them (hopefully!).
Decrypt, decryption, decipher, decipherment	Figuratively, if not literally, reversal of the encryption process requiring the relevant algorithm and key to recover the original content (generally plaintext) from the ciphertext. "Process of obtaining, from a ciphertext, the original corresponding data. Note: A ciphertext may be encrypted a second time, in which case a single decryption does not produce the original plaintext" *(ISO/IEC 2382)*. "A technique used to recover the original plaintext from the ciphertext so that it is intelligible to the reader. The decryption is a reverse process of the encryption" *(ISACA glossary)*. "The process of transforming an encrypted message into its original plaintext" *(SANS glossary)*.

TERM	MEANING
Decryptor	Application capable of decrypting data on systems infected with ransomware, whether provided by the criminals to victims following payment of the ransom, or created by white hats employed by antivirus companies or spooks to exploit cryptographic flaws or coding bugs in the ransomware.
Deduplication	Reduction or elimination of redundant information. "Method of reducing storage needs by eliminating redundant data, which is replaced with a pointer to the unique data copy. Note: Deduplication is sometimes considered a form of compression" *(ISO/IEC 27040).*
Deep cover	Infiltrating a target organisation so effectively that the infiltrator becomes highly trusted and may gain privileged access to its innermost secrets, albeit increasing the risk of the agent being turned or going native. See also mole, sleeper.
Deep fake, deepfake	Refers to disinformation generated by **D**eep **L**earning **A**rtificial **I**ntelligence systems. Advanced audio-visual techniques can 'put words into the mouths' of celebrities, politicians, activists, and adversaries, making them *appear* to express something they did not. Just as written materials can be edited or fabricated, small changes to genuine audio-visual content (such as deleting the word "not" or changing a frown into a smile) are easily made, yet can dramatically affect the meaning or interpretation of, say, a political speech or public statement. As the technology advances, wholescale changes are becoming even easier to make and yet harder to spot, leading to *de novo* fabrication of lengthy video clips in fake settings with fake audiences. There are serious implications for society through large-scale social engineering such as fake news, misinformation, misdirection, propaganda, coercion, blackmail, fraud, espionage, information warfare and cyberwar, threatening forensics, authority, accountability, trust, critical thinking, and society at large. "Media manipulated by deep learning and other AI techniques to generate and synthesize convincing yet false representations of faces and facial expressions, sounds, voices, and speech, to depict individuals or scenes falsely, typically to promote misinformation or other malicious reasons" *(ISACA glossary).*
Deep **L**earning **(DL), deep neural network learning**	Form of **M**achine **L**earning using artificial neural networks to discern patterns and other information from big data for image and speech recognition, **N**atural **L**anguage **P**rocessing, *etc.* "Approach to creating rich hierarchical representations through the training of neural networks with many hidden layers. Note: Deep learning is a subset of ML" *(ISO/IEC 22989).* "A multilevel algorithm that gradually identifies things at higher levels of abstraction, *e.g.*, image classification" *(ISACA glossary).* See also **A**rtificial **I**ntelligence.

TERM	MEANING
Deep packet inspection	Third-generation firewalls can examine the payloads (data content) of network packets, as well as the Internet Protocol addresses and protocol information in the packet headers, in order to apply more granular security rules. Their ability to access the content of network traffic raises privacy and confidentiality concerns: these are trusted devices. "A type of network packet filtering that evaluates the data and header of a packet transmitted through an inspection point" *(ISACA glossary)*.
Deep state	Allegedly the true seat of power, a sinister and covert conspiracy within supposedly democratic governments. Information, misinformation, or disinformation? You decide.
Deep web, Deepweb, Deep net, Deepnet	Internet sites and services that are not readily accessible and searchable using conventional search engines such as Google. Includes the Darknet, plus web pages, and servers protected behind corporate firewalls.
Defame, defamation, defamatory	Stating, suggesting, or implying something false that *unduly* harms the reputation of another person. A true (factually accurate and correct) statement is *not* defamatory, even though it may be distinctly uncomplimentary or harmful to someone's reputation, perhaps triggering a strong emotional or physical response. See also libel, slander.
Default	a. Preset/initial/zero-effort configuration. Straight out of the box, newly installed software and hardware typically has standardised and convenient but relatively weak/low-security settings, *e.g.* passwords that are widely known in the hacker and spook communities. "Pertaining to an attribute, data value, or option that is assumed when none is explicitly specified. Example: In Fortran, the default naming convention specifies that names beginning with one of the letters I through N denote variables of integer type" *(ISO/IEC 2382)*. "A computer software setting or preference that states what will automatically happen in the event that the user has not stated another preference. For example, a computer may have a default setting to launch or start Netscape whenever a GIF file is opened; however, if using Photoshop is the preference for viewing a GIF file, the default setting can be changed to Photoshop. Default accounts are provided by the operating system vendor (*e.g.*, root in UNIX)" *(ISACA glossary)*. b. Failure to repay a loan – a financial risk, often mitigated by having the legal right to seize collateral assets.
Default deny, need-to-know	Access control principle stating that information should only be released to authenticated individuals if they have a legitimate purpose or reason for using the information, and are authorised to do so. "A policy whereby access is denied unless it is specifically allowed or the inverse of default" *(ISACA glossary)*.

TERM	MEANING
Default password	Initial weak password for a privileged account enabled when a computer system, device, *thing*, application, or information service is first installed and configured. "The password used to gain access when a system is first installed on a computer or network device. Notes: A large list published on the Internet and maintained at several locations exists. Failure to change these after the installation leaves the system vulnerable" *(ISACA glossary)*.
Default permit, need-to-withhold	Access control principle stating that information should normally be released or disclosed unless such access needs to be explicitly denied for some specific, legitimate reason.
Defect	Identified bug, flaw, fault, or other inherent and apparent issue with a system, process, application, person, organisation, product, *etc.*
Defence-**i**n-**D**epth **(DiD)**	Particular military strategy to drain the enemy's resources and buy time by deceiving/misdirecting them into attacking a series of dummy targets, setting the scene for a spirited counterattack. "The practice of layering defenses to provide added protection. Defense in depth improves security by increasing the effort needed in an attack by placing multiple barriers between an attacker and enterprise computing and information resources" *(ISACA glossary)*. "A layered combination of complementary countermeasures" (*Official ISC2 Guide to the CISSP CBK, 2007*). "The approach of using multiple layers of security to guard against failure of a single security component" *(SANS glossary)*. *Cf.* layered defence.
Defence **s**cience and **t**echnology **l**aboratory **(Dstl)**	Part of the UK **M**inistry **O**f **D**efence responsible for the application of science and technology to national defence and security, including biosecurity and cybersecurity. Formed along with QinetiQ from the **D**efence **E**valuation **R**esearch **A**gency in 2001.
D3FEND	*Abbrev:* **D**etection, **D**enial, and **D**isruption **F**ramework **E**mpowering **N**etwork **D**efense.
Defend **T**rade **S**ecrets **A**ct 2016 **(DTSA)**	US federal law provides some legal protection for confidential proprietary information classed as trade secrets, supplementing state laws and harmonising the approach.
Definition of scope	"Process for the establishment of global parameters for the performance of Risk Management within an organization. Within the definition of scope for Risk Management internal and external factors have to be taken into account" *(ENISA RM glossary)*.
Defensive security, defence, passive security, reactive security	Security practices that deter, prevent, react, or respond to attacks and other incidents, generally by minimising vulnerabilities and/or impacts, for instance using silent alarms, tell-tales, or whistleblower's hotlines coupled with highly efficient incident response practices to react quickly and decisively to the very earliest signs of trouble. *Cf.* offensive security.

TERM	MEANING
DEFR	*Abbrev:* **D**igital **E**vidence **F**irst **R**esponder.
Defragmentation, defrag	Process of clearing free space on a magnetic disk containing fragmented files, then systematically moving and storing all the fragments of large files contiguously to speed up file retrieval by minimising disk head movements.
Defraud	To commit fraud – *not* the removal of fraud.
Degauss, degaussing	Secure erasure process that applies an *extremely* strong magnetic field to magnetic data storage media such as computer disks or tapes to destroy the stored data. In addition to concerns over the equipment and operating procedures, the extremely high density of modern magnetic storage methods, high coercivity of the materials, and use of disk mirroring and similar redundant storage/error correction techniques make degaussing less reliable in practice than it may appear, although subsequent physical destruction of degaussed media increases assurance. "Render data unreadable by applying a strong magnetic field to the media" *(ISO/IEC 27040)*. "The application of variable levels of alternating currents for the purpose of demagnetizing magnetic recording media. Notes: The process involves increasing the alternating current field gradually from zero to some maximum value and back to zero, leaving a minimal residue of magnetic induction on the media. Degauss generally means to erase" *(ISACA glossary)*. "A process for reducing the magnetisation of a magnetic storage device to zero by applying a reverse (coercive) magnetic force, rendering any previously stored data unreadable" *(AusISM)*.
Degausser	Device or person that degausses. "An electrical device or permanent magnet assembly which generates a coercive magnetic force to destroy magnetic storage patterns in order to sanitise magnetic media" *(NZISM)*. "An electrical device or permanent magnet assembly which generates a coercive magnetic force for the purpose of degaussing magnetic storage devices" *(AusISM)*.
Deidentification	Systematic process of removing, scrambling, obscuring, tokenising, aggregating, summarising, or otherwise preventing access to specific information capable of identifying individuals, organisations, sources, *etc.* for privacy, confidentiality, discretion, discrimination, commercial, national security, compliance, ethical or other reasons. "Information that cannot reasonably identify, relate to, describe, be associated with or linked, directly or indirectly, to a particular consumer" *(ISACA glossary)*. See also anonymisation, redaction.
De-identified dataset	Dataset containing deidentified or anonymised data. "Dataset resulting from the application of a de-identification process" *(ISO/IEC 27562)*.

TERM	MEANING
Delegate	a. *[Verb]* To pass a responsibility to a subordinate. b. *[Noun]* Subordinate to whom responsibility has been passed, *e.g.* the person officially representing an organisation at a meeting or event, possibly empowered to make decisions and vote on its behalf. "A person or group of personnel who may authorise noncompliance with requirements in this manual on the specific authority of the agency head" *(NZISM)*.
Delegated authority, delegation, delegator, delegate, delegatee	Refers to someone (the delegator) passing some of their authority (responsibility and power) to someone else (the delegate or delegatee, generally a subordinate) within specified parameters, *e.g.* giving them the ability to sign-off (authorise) expenses claims or procurement orders up to a certain dollar value, make decisions within a certain area, or represent (stand in for) them at a meeting. Implies the delegator's trust in the delegate and often involves additional controls such as oversight and mentoring. While the delegate is personally accountable for any incidents arising from their actions and inactions, the delegator generally shares the risk and remains personally accountable for their decision to delegate authority.
Deletion [of personal information]	"Process by which personally identifiable information (PII) is changed in a manner so that it is no longer present or recognizable and usable and can only be reconstructed with excessive effort. Notes: In this document the term deletion covers all such synonyms: disposition mechanism, erasure, destruction, destruction of data storage media [while] deletion refers to the elimination of the bit patterns or comparable practices, not simply marking or moving the data to be hidden. As a result, excessive effort for PII reconstruction will be required, considering all the means likely reasonably to be used, e.g. available state of the art of technology, human and technical resources, costs and time. For selecting the methods for deletion, a risk-based approach is to be taken into account, including sensitivity of PII and potential use of forensic tools. Required measures can change during time depending on the state of the art of technology and other factors. PII can be also changed by applying an irreversible de-identification technique. Such data often fall out of privacy legislation. Further guidance on a de-identification technique can be found in ISO/IEC 20889-11" *(ISO/IEC 27555)*.
Deletion class	"Combination of a standard deletion period ... and an abstract starting point for the period run" *(ISO/IEC 27555)*.
Deletion period	"Time period after which a specific cluster of personally identifiable information (PII) ... should be deleted. *(ISO/IEC 27555)*.
Deletion rule	"Combination of deletion period ... and specific conditions for the starting point of the period run" *(ISO/IEC 27555)*.
Demand letter	See cease and desist letter.

TERM	MEANING
De-Militarised Zone (DMZ), perimeter network, screened subnet, no man's land	Special network segment in between external networks (such as the Internet) and internal corporate networks, within which proxy servers and firewalls are intended to identify and restrict unauthorised traffic while passing legitimate traffic. Systems that need to connect to the Internet (such as web servers, **D**omain **N**ame **S**ystem servers, application servers or front-ends, and mail servers) are typically located in the DMZ, and are hardened. "Perimeter network (also known as a screened sub-net) inserted as a 'neutral zone' between networks" *(ISO/IEC 27033-1)*. "A small, isolated network that serves as a buffer zone between trusted and untrusted networks. Note: A demilitarized zone is typically used to house systems, such as web servers, that must be accessible from both internal networks and the Internet" *(ISACA glossary)*. "A small network with one or more servers that is kept separate from an agency's core network, either on the outside of the agency's firewall, or as a separate network protected by the agency's firewall. Demilitarised zones usually provide public domain information to less trusted networks, such as the Internet" *(NZISM)*. See also zone.
Demodulation	The converse of modulation, *i.e.* retrieving the original modulating information from a modulated signal, without the carrier. "The process of converting an analog telecommunications signal into a digital computer signal" *(ISACA glossary)*.
Denial-of-Service (DoS)	Type of information security event, incident, or attack that impacts information availability, *e.g.* by deliberately or accidentally overloading a system or network, thereby impeding or preventing its legitimate use. "Prevention of authorized access to resources or the delaying of time-critical operations" *(ISO/IEC 2382)*. "Prevention of authorized access to a system resource or the delaying of system operations and functions, with resultant loss of availability to authorized users" *(ISO/IEC 27033-1)*. "An assault on a service from a single source that floods it with so many requests that it becomes overwhelmed and either stops completely or operates at a significantly reduced rate" *(ISACA glossary)*. "The prevention of authorized access to a system resource or the delaying of system operations and functions" *(SANS glossary)*. "An attempt by an adversary to prevent legitimate access to online services (typically a website), for example, by consuming the amount of available bandwidth or the processing capacity of the server hosting the online service" *(AusISM)*. See also **D**istributed **D**enial-**o**f-**S**ervice, **D**istributed **R**eflective **D**enial-**o**f-**S**ervice.
Deny list	Politically correct form of blacklist. "A set of items to be excluded, blocked or prevented from execution … the opposite of an allow list which confirms that items are acceptable" *(NZISM)*.

TERM	MEANING
DEP	*Abbrev:* **D**ata **E**xecution **P**revention.
Department	Corporate or governmental unit, function, team, or group with a particular focus and purpose, such as Finance, **H**uman **R**esources, or **I**nformation **T**echnology. "Subordinate to the enterprise and often cuts across multiple business units providing shared services such as human resources, information technology (IT), compliance, risk management, and other services" *(OCEG GRC Glossary)*.
Department of **H**omeland **S**ecurity **(DHS)**	Spooky US government agency responsible for intelligence and surveillance in support of defence, counterterrorism, **C**ritical **N**ational **I**nfrastructure protection, *etc.* See also **F**ederal **B**ureau of **I**nvestigation, **C**entral **I**ntelligence **A**gency. More info: https://www.dhs.gov/
Dependable, dependability	Measure of the extent to which a system, network, person, team, organisation, *etc.* can be relied upon or trusted to perform as expected under all anticipated and ideally unanticipated circumstances. Implies a level of assurance as to the suitability and effectiveness of its resilience, recoverability and contingency preparations, and clarity of the requirements. "<Of an item> Ability to perform as and when required. Notes: Dependability includes availability, reliability, recoverability, maintainability, and maintenance support performance, and, in some cases, other characteristics such as durability, safety and security. Dependability is used as a collective term for the time-related quality characteristics of an item" *(IEC 60050-192)*.
Dependence, dependency	Reliance on the presence, assets/resources, products, support, permission, or actions of another. "Entity relationship or an attribute relationship that denotes that the existence of one entity or attribute is of interest only if another entity or attribute, respectively, exists" *(ISO/IEC 2382)*. *Cf.* independence.
Deposition	Legal process requiring someone in court under oath to provide immediate verbal answers to verbal questions. A form of discovery. *Cf.* interrogatory.
Deprecated	Withdrawn and no longer recommended for use. If significant flaws are discovered in cryptosystems, for instance, the corresponding standards, algorithms, protocols, *etc.* are, at some point, removed from service and superseded (hopefully) by better ones.
Derived measure	"Measure that is defined as a function of two or more values of base measures" *(ISO/IEC/IEEE 15939)*. "Measure defined as a function of two or more base measures often expressed as ratios, composite indices or other aggregate summary measures" *(ISACA glossary)*.

TERM	MEANING
Derived requirement	Additional system/application/service/product requirement or expectation reasonably inferred and specified by systems analysis, supplementing or elaborating on those actually specified by users, managers, customers, *etc*. Detailed nonfunctional requirements relating to compliance, application/system/network/data administration, support, maintenance, security, and assurance, for instance, are seldom specified in detail by nonspecialists, let alone detailed technical internals. Even functional requirements may be superficially, informally, and inadequately specified, *e.g.* "The replacement system must do everything the current system does, only better, faster, easier ..."! "Requirements not explicitly stated in customer requirements but inferred and developed from: Contextual requirements, e.g., applicable standards, laws, policies, common practices, management decisions; Requirements needed to specify a solution component. Derived requirements can also emerge during the analysis and design of solution components" *(ISACA glossary)*.
Derogation	Legal dispensation relating to relaxing/not applying some part of a law, for specific reasons, *e.g.* privacy laws may be partially disregarded to protect national security. A kind of exemption.
DES	*Abbrev:* **D**ata **E**ncryption **S**tandard or **D**igital **E**vidence **S**pecialist, depending on context.
Descramble	"Recover the original digital signal from a scrambled digital signal" *(ISO/IEC 2382)*. Does not apply to eggs.
Descriptive norms	Simply portraying certain current behaviours/activities as 'normal,' 'typical,' or 'conventional' passively encourages most people to conform and follow suit, while subtly discouraging nonconformity, *e.g.* management mentioning – in a positive manner – the number of incident reports recently received (as opposed to moaning about the problems) can increase reporting levels. "Observation of what others do, providing information about what is 'normal' in a particular culture" *(OCEG GRC Glossary)*. *Cf.* injunctive norms.
Design	a. *[Noun]* Distinctive physical expression, shape, or other characteristics of a product that is typically associated with a particular brand or trademark. b. *[Noun]* Structured and documented architecture, blueprint. "As used in the COSO definition of internal control, the internal control system design is intended to provide reasonable assurance of the achievement of an entity's objectives" *(**T**rust **S**ervices **C**riteria)*. c. *[Verb]* To analyse requirements systematically, then architect something (*e.g.* a system or 'solution') intended to satisfy those requirements. A critical part of the **S**oftware **D**evelopment **L**ife**C**ycle and product development in general. "The process of defining the architecture, components, interfaces and other characteristics of a system or component" *(ISACA glossary)*.

TERM	MEANING
Design criteria	Design specifications – the particular objectives, characteristics, functionality, *etc.* required of a new or modified system. "The criteria used to select actions & controls that address risk, reward, and compliance" *(OCEG GRC Glossary)*.
Design effectiveness	Suitability, appropriateness, relevance, and quality of the architecture. "Occurring when the enterprise's controls are operated as prescribed by persons possessing the necessary authority and competence to perform the control effectively, satisfy the enterprise's control objectives and effectively prevent or detect errors or fraud that could result in material misstatements in the financial statements" *(ISACA glossary)*. "Evidence of logically designed actions & controls relative to objectives, opportunities, obstacles, and obligations. This is accomplished by evaluating the design actions & controls against suitable criteria" *(OCEG GRC Glossary)*. "If the company's controls are operated as prescribed by persons possessing the necessary authority and competence to perform the control effectively, and if they satisfy the company's control objectives and can effectively prevent or detect errors or fraud that could result in material misstatements in the financial statements, they are considered to be designed effectively" *(ITAF)*.
Design factors	"Factors that can influence the design of an enterprise's governance system and position it for success in the use of information and technology (I&T). In COBIT® 2019, design factors include: enterprise strategy, enterprise goals, risk profile, I&T-related issues, threat landscape, compliance requirements, role of IT, sourcing model for IT, IT implantation methods, technology adoption strategy and enterprise size" *(ISACA glossary)*.
Design options	Architectural choices requiring decisions during the design and perhaps later during development of a system or other product. "Broad design decisions to address an opportunity, obstacle, or obligation" *(OCEG GRC Glossary)*.
Design phase	Critical early phase during the product lifecycle in which architects and engineers design the product to satisfy the consolidated and detailed requirements, making key decisions that will affect the rest of its life, *i.e.* the build/development, implementation, configuration, operation/use, support and maintenance, and retirement/replacement activities. "The period of time in the software life cycle during which the designs for architecture, software components, interfaces and data are created, documented and verified to satisfy requirements" *(ISACA glossary)*.

TERM	MEANING
Design review	Given the wide-ranging and long-term significance of a product's design, competent review and fine-tuning of the design is a key control prior to management authorisation to proceed. It is a concern for iterative software development methods where the design may remain somewhat fluid for some time ... but by the same token, that suggests numerous security improvement opportunities. The security design is fundamental to cybersecurity, so a security design review or vulnerability assessment is invaluable. "A formal, recorded, comprehensive and systematic examination of a solution or component design to determine whether the design meets applicable requirements, identifies problems and proposes solutions" *(ISACA glossary)*.
Desk check, desk-check	Paperwork/administrative check performed (literally or figuratively) at the desk, *e.g.* confirming that the organisation has a privacy policy or **B**usiness **C**ontinuity **P**lan that should, in theory at least, satisfy business objectives and any applicable third party obligations. "Static analysis technique, perhaps including manual simulation of program execution, in which source code, test results, or other documentation are visually examined, usually by the person who generated them, to identify faults, violations of development standards, or other problems [and] manual simulation of program execution to detect faults through step-by-step examination of the source program for errors in function or syntax" *(ISO/IEC 2382)*. See also tabletop exercise.
Destroy, destruct	Physically and/or logically obliterate information such that it is no longer recoverable in usable form, even using forensic techniques. In some circumstances, the process may further involve erasing any trace of its prior existence (*e.g.* deleting associated metadata). "Sanitize using physical techniques that make recovery infeasible using state of the art laboratory techniques and results in the subsequent inability to use the media for storage of data. Note: Disintegrate, incinerate, melt, pulverize, and shred are destruct forms of sanitization" *(ISO/IEC 27040)*. *Note*: "destroy" is the English verb form, whereas "destruct" is an Americanism, a contraction of "destruction." See also purge.
Destruction	Act or process of destroying. "Result of actions taken to ensure that media cannot be reused as originally intended and that information is virtually impossible or prohibitively expensive to recover" *(ISO/IEC 27040)*.
Detect	a. To identify, notice, reveal, or discover the occurrence of something untoward – an event or incident. A core function within the NIST **C**yber **S**ecurity **F**ramework along with identify, protect, respond, and recover. "Develop and implement appropriate activities to identify the occurrence of a cybersecurity event. The Detect Function enables timely discovery of cybersecurity events" *(NIST CSF)*. b. To extract information from a modulated radio transmission.

TERM	MEANING
Detectability	Extent to which something (such as an incident or a control failure) is expected to be reliably and promptly detected in good time if it occurs. One of several factors potentially relevant to risk analysis and control selection, and a particular challenge with complex, high-risk systems such as **A**rtificial **I**ntelligence, financial, safety-critical, and security systems.
Detection risk	Uncertainty around whether something inappropriate, illegal, unethical, *etc.* will or will not be identified in time to be addressed effectively, or indeed ever. "Risk that assets are lost or compromised or financial statements are materially misstated due to failure of an enterprise's internal controls to detect errors or fraud in a timely manner" *(ISACA glossary).* "The risk that the IS audit or assurance professional's substantive procedures will not detect an error that could be material, individually or in combination with other errors" *(ITAF).*
Detective actions & controls	"Actions & controls that detect the occurrence of favorable and unfavorable events" *(OCEG GRC Glossary).*
Detective control	Form of security control intended to detect an incident ideally while it is still in progress (*i.e.* timing is critical), log the details, and/or raise an alert or alarm, triggering the appropriate manual or automated response. "Controls designed to detect and report when errors, omissions and unauthorized uses or entries occur" *(ISACA glossary). Cf.* preventive control, corrective control.
Deterrent, deterrent control	Form of preventive control such as warnings and penalties intended to deter, *i.e.* put off and so reduce the likelihood or threat of attack, compromise, recklessness, *etc.*
Developer	Organisation or individual that creates a product. "Entity that creates an assembled final IoT device or IoT product. Notes: 'final' in this definition means the stage of delivery to the IoT service Developer in the assembly process. A Developer is usually the applicant for a cybersecurity label or the holder of the issued label, *i.e.* the party which is responsible for the security characteristics of a product" *(ISO/IEC 27404 DRAFT).* "A person or group that designs and/or builds, and/or documents and/or configures the hardware and/or software of computerized systems" *(ISACA glossary).* See also software developer.
Development, develop	a. Logically the next stage of the classic innovation lifecycle following research (*e.g.* elaboration and specification of requirements) and design (formulation of the architecture) in which a product is manufactured, built, or assembled, possibly in small quantities for proof-of-concept or pilot testing and refinement of the design and/or the manufacturing process. b. Maturation, growing up, accumulating experience, and perhaps wisdom. c. Application, software, or system development.

TERM	MEANING
Development environment	Set of computer systems, networks, devices, data, and supporting tools and processes used by software developers for application, software, or system development. *Cf.* production environment, test environment.
Development method, development methodology	Defines the overall approach to product development (*e.g.* sequential waterfall or iterative methods for software development) plus procedural details such as the mandatory and discretionary documentation, process controls, management reviews, and key control/authorisation steps. Every approach has its pros and cons, risks and opportunities, and costs and benefits. Choosing the best overall approach and detailed method in a given situation is a complex, multifactor, context-dependent, dynamic, and thus uncertain (risky) management decision.
Device	Discrete item of computing or networking equipment, a piece of hardware or electronic technology, or more generally a machine, construct, method, technique, or approach with a specific purpose (*e.g.* a hinge, a diplomatic strategy). Many electronic devices also qualify as things or systems. "Combination of hardware and software, or solely software, that allows a user to perform actions" *(ISO/IEC 29134)*. "A generic term for a computer subsystem, such as a printer, serial port or disk drive that frequently requires its own controlling software termed a device driver" *(ISACA glossary)*.
Device access control software	Security application controlling the use of datacommunications ports and peripheral devices (*e.g.* USB memory sticks) on a computer system. "Software that can be installed to restrict access to communications ports such as USB, Serial HDMI and Ethernet Ports. Device access control software can either block all access to a communications port or allow access using an allow listing approach based on device types, manufacturer's identification, or even unique device identifiers" *(NZISM)*. "Software that can be used on a system to restrict access to communications ports. Device access control software can block all access to a communications port or allow access based on device types, manufacturer's identification or even unique device identifiers" *(AusISM)*.
Device code flow, device code authentication	OAuth 2.0 authentication method/protocol for browser-less smart devices such as many *things*. Having contacted an online authentication server, an application running on the device generates and displays a one-time authentication code that the user forwards to the authentication server via a laptop, smartphone, *etc.* Provided the code is authenticated, the server supplies the device with an access token needed to use network services.

TERM	MEANING
Device IDentity (device ID)	Means of identifying the class, type, or generation of device (which determines how to interact with, configure, use, and control it) and/or an individual device (*e.g.* to locate, access, and account for it). Inconsistent, unidentified, hidden, anonymous, or compromised devices including those that deliberately misrepresent themselves (such as USB Rubber Ducky), can present security risks, hence the value of device authentication as well. "Uniquely identifies a specific device" *(ISACA glossary)*.
DevOps (Development – Operations integration)	Software engineering method that integrates application development and testing with **I**nformation **T**echnology operations functions/teams and automates processes to cut cycle times for software updates from months to hours. A practical extension of Agile, a form of **R**apid **A**pplication **D**evelopment, and other continuous development methods. "An enterprise software development phrase used to denote a type of agile relationship between development and Information Technology (IT) operations. The goal of DevOps is to change and improve the relationship between development and operations by advocating better communication and collaboration between these two business units" *(ISACA glossary)*. "A set of practices that combines software development (Dev) and IT operations (Ops) [that] aims to shorten the systems development life cycle and provide continuous delivery with high software quality" *(NZISM)*. See also DevSecOps.
DevSecOps (Development – Security – Operations integration)	Extension of DevOps to integrate software development, testing, and software/infrastructure security with security operations. Extensive process automation speeds things up, improves repeatability, and is well suited to cloud computing (*e.g.* automatically provisioning virtual systems, installing and configuring applications, and validating the installations including the security aspects).
Dexter	Species of memory-scraping Point-of-Sale system malware in the wild in 2012.
DFD	*Abbrev:* **D**ata **F**low **D**iagram.
DFIR	*Abbrev:* **D**igital **F**orensics and **I**ncident **R**esponse.
DGA	*Abbrev:* **D**ata **G**overnance **A**ct.
Dharma	Species of ransomware in the wild in 2019. Targeted small organisations, demanding ransoms of about $1k.
DHCP	*Abbrev:* **D**ynamic **H**ost **C**ontrol **P**rotocol.
DHS	*Abbrev:* **D**epartment of **H**omeland **S**ecurity.

TERM	MEANING
Dialler	Old-skool form of malware which silently calls a premium rate phone number on the victim's modem, committing toll fraud. See also war dialler.
Diagnostic	Supports determination of the nature and likely causes of problems, concerns, issues, diseases, *etc.* by identifying and analysing related symptoms, evidence, and contributory factors. "Pertaining to the detection, analysis, or description of faults, failures, or mistakes" *(ISO/IEC 2382)*. "Pertaining to the detection and isolation of faults or failures (*e.g.*, a diagnostic message and a diagnostic manual)" *(ISACA glossary)*.
Dial-back	Primitive **M**ulti**F**actor **A**uthentication control originally developed for telephone modems to respond to inbound callers who simply assert their identities, then drop the call, dialling them back on their pre-authorised phone numbers to logon and continue the session. "Used as a control over dial-up telecommunications lines. The telecommunications link established through dial-up into the computer from a remote location is interrupted so the computer can dial back to the caller. The link is permitted only if the call is coming from a valid phone number or telecommunications channel" *(ISACA glossary)*.
Dialogue management	"Task of choosing the appropriate next move in a dialogue based on user input, the dialogue history and other contextual knowledge, to meet a desired goal" *(ISO/IEC 22989)*.
Diavol	Hacker/malware/cybercriminal gang active in 2022.
Dictionary attack	Cryptanalytic attempt to guess or crack a password using words from the dictionary, in various combinations (*e.g.* forwards, backwards, with numbers prepended or appended, with punctuation and embedded spaces, foreign or lookalike characters). A more sophisticated form of brute force attack. "An attack that tries all of the phrases or words in a dictionary, trying to crack a password or key. A dictionary attack uses a predefined list of words compared to a brute force attack that tries all possible combinations" *(SANS glossary)*.
DiD	*Abbrev:* **D**efence-**i**n-**D**epth.
Dieselgate	Assurance and ethics scandal involving the manufacturer's deliberate programming of VW diesel cars to detect and respond to emissions testing in progress, cutting exhaust emissions to ace the test but increasing emissions under normal operating conditions. A sign of things to come, perhaps, as everyday objects are smartened-up, becoming *things* capable of evading dumb checks and controls.

TERM	MEANING
Differential backup	Backup of files created or changed since the most recent image backup. In contrast to incremental backups, a system can be recovered simply by restoring the most recent image and the latest differential backup. However, differentials contain more data; hence, they take longer to write, and use more storage, than most incrementals.
Differential privacy	Formal mathematical method enabling the disclosure of modified data relating to a dataset without identifying and potentially compromising the privacy of individuals whose personal or otherwise confidential data may be included in the dataset, while not materially affecting the statistical validity and utility of the information disclosed. "Achieved by adding randomly generated noise to obfuscate personal identifiability. Computations performed on altered data are only statistically/directionally correct (*i.e.*, not accurate)" *(ISACA glossary)*. See also obfuscation, tokenisation, redaction.
Diffie–Hellman groups	"A method used for specifying the modulus size used in the hashed message authentication code algorithms. Each DH group represents a specific modulus size. For example, group 2 represents a modulus size of 1024 bits" *(NZISM)*.
Diffie–Hellman key exchange	Brilliant cryptographic protocol based on modular exponentiation that enables two parties to generate and share a secret over an insecure communication path without exchanging sensitive information (not least, the secret itself) such that it is easy for both parties to compute the shared secret but *extremely* difficult for an eavesdropper to derive it from intercepted information. The shared secret is typically then used as a key for symmetric cryptography of data transmissions between the parties. The foundation for secure communications over **V**irtual **P**rivate **N**etworks and **T**ransport **L**ayer **S**ecurity. Published by Whitfield Diffie and Martin Hellman in 1976.
Digest	See hash.
Digisig	*Abbrev:* **Digi**tal **sig**nature.
Digit	a. Single unsigned numeric character/value, *e.g. '0' or* 'C' (not necessarily in base 10). "Character that represents a natural number. Examples: One of the characters 0 through 9 in the decimal system; these digits plus the characters A through F used in the hexadecimal system. Note: The mathematical term 'natural number' denotes all non-negative integers" *(ISO/IEC 2382)*. b. *Abbrev:* **Dig**ital b**it**. See bit. c. Finger.
Digital	Composed of, based on, or involving the use of, bits. "Pertaining to data that consist of digits as well as to processes and functional units that use those data" *(ISO/IEC 2382)*.

TERM	MEANING
Digital asset	The valuable bits. "Any token—whether created in a peer-to-peer and/or cryptographic environment—that exists in a digital format with the token holder having the ability and right to use or transfer the digital asset. All cryptocurrencies and cryptotokens are subsets of digital assets" *(ISACA glossary)*.
Digital certificate	Data file containing information about a person, organisation, or system along with their public key plus a digital signature from the **C**ertification **A**uthority authenticating the certificate itself and (to some extent, depending on the nature of the checking performed and thus assurance provided) the corresponding person, organisation, or system.
Digital certification	See **P**ublic **K**ey **I**nfrastructure. "A process to authenticate (or certify) a party's digital signature; carried out by trusted third parties" *(ISACA glossary)*.
Digital code signing	Process of generating and linking a digital signature with computer code (such as the source or executable code for an application program, library function, or device driver), such that its authenticity (origin) and integrity (absence of subsequent code changes or substitution) can be assured, *provided* the cryptographic and other controls are effective. "The process of digitally signing computer code to ensure its integrity" *(ISACA glossary)*.
Digital device	Digital/computer device. "Electronic equipment used to process or store digital data" *(ISO/IEC 27037)*.
Digital evidence	Forensic evidence in the form of digital/computer data (*e.g.* the contents of a hard drive, tablet, smartphone, or USB memory stick) gathered in connection with investigating, proving, or disproving a crime. "Information or data, stored or transmitted in binary form, that may be relied on as evidence" *(ISO/IEC 27037)*.
Digital evidence copy	See forensic copy. "Copy of the digital evidence that has been produced to maintain the reliability of the evidence by including both the digital evidence and verification means where the method of verifying it can be either embedded in or independent from the tools used in doing the verification" *(ISO/IEC 27037)*.
Digital **E**vidence **F**irst **R**esponder **(DEFR)**	First responder for an incident involving digital technology. "Individual who is authorized, trained and qualified to act first at an incident scene in performing digital evidence collection and acquisition with the responsibility for handling that evidence. Note: Authority, training and qualification are the expected requirements necessary to produce reliable digital evidence, but individual circumstances may result in an individual not adhering to all three requirements. In this case, the local law, organisational policy and individual circumstances should be considered" *(ISO/IEC 27037)*.

TERM	MEANING
Digital Evidence Specialist **(DES)**	Digital/computer forensics professional. "Individual who can carry out the tasks of a [Digital Evidence First Responder] and has specialized knowledge, skills and abilities to handle a wide range of technical issues. Note: A DES may have additional niche skills, for example, network acquisition, RAM acquisition, Linux or Mainframe knowledge" *(ISO/IEC 27037). Cf.* **D**ata **E**ncryption **S**tandard.
Digital forensics, cyber forensics, computer forensics	Forensic analysis of digital evidence obtained from various electronic devices and computer equipment, *things*, communications or network links and services, or storage media. "The process of identifying, preserving, analyzing and presenting digital evidence in a manner that is legally acceptable in any legal proceedings" *(ISACA glossary).*
Digital Forensics and Incident Response **(DFIR)**	Identification, investigation, and remediation of cybersecurity incidents, including the collection, preservation, and analysis of digital forensic evidence.
Digital investigation	Digital investigation. "Use of scientifically derived and proven methods towards the identification, collection, transportation, storage, analysis, interpretation, presentation, distribution, return, and/or destruction of digital evidence derived from digital sources, while obtaining proper authorizations for all activities, properly documenting all activities, interacting with the physical investigation, preserving digital evidence, and maintaining the chain of custody, for the purpose of facilitating or furthering the reconstruction of events found to be incidents requiring a digital investigation, whether of criminal nature or not" *(ISO/IEC 27043).* Wow! See also digital forensics.
Digital Millennium Copyright Act 1998 **(DMCA)**	US law prohibiting piracy technologies/devices that may be used to bypass or defeat software/hardware copy protection mechanisms.
Digital nomad	Free-ranging (nomadic) remote worker based on-the-road or in convenient locations such as hotels, using **M**obile **T**echnology with wireless communications and Internet connectivity.
Digital operational resilience	See cyber resilience. "The ability of a financial entity to build, assure and review its operational integrity and reliability by ensuring, either directly or indirectly through the use of services provided by ICT third-party service providers, the full range of ICT-related capabilities needed to address the security of the network and information systems which a financial entity uses, and which support the continued provision of financial services and their quality, including throughout disruptions" *(DORA).*

TERM	MEANING
Digital preservation	Archival of data. "The coordinated and ongoing set of processes and activities that ensure long-term, error-free storage of digital information, with means for retrieval and interpretation, for the entire time span the information is required" *(AusISM)*.
Digital **R**ights **M**anagement **(DRM)**	Cryptographic access controls used to permit or deny certain types of use of Intellectual Property according to the owner's wishes, potentially exceeding the constraints available under copyright law (*e.g.* fair use can be prevented through technological means).
Digital **S**ervice **P**rovider **(DSP)**	Commercial supplier of digital information services such as Information Technology hardware and software maintenance, cloud storage, network monitoring, threat intelligence, and training. "Manages a suite of IT services like an organisation's network, cloud computing and applications" *(UK Cyber Security Breaches Survey 2023)*.
Digital **sig**nature **(digisig)**	Cryptographic hash of a message or file, constructed with the sender's private key, used to 'seal' the message/file, thus enabling any subsequent changes to be detected, and so authenticate both the message (for data integrity) and the sender (giving non-repudiation and resistance to impersonation). "Data appended to a message, that allow the recipient of the message to verify the source of the message" *(ISO/IEC 2382)*. "An electronic identification of a person or entity using a public key algorithm that serves as a way for the recipient to verify the identity of the sender, integrity of the data and proof of transaction" *(ISACA glossary)*. "A cryptographic process that allows the proof of the source (with non-repudiation) and the verification of the integrity of that data" *(AusISM)*. "A hash of a message that uniquely identifies the sender of the message and proves the message hasn't changed since transmission" *(SANS glossary)*.
Digital **S**ignature **A**lgorithm **(DSA)**	Asymmetric cryptographic algorithm used to generate and validate digital signatures. "An asymmetric cryptographic algorithm that produces a digital signature in the form of a pair of large numbers. The signature is computed using rules and parameters such that the identity of the signer and the integrity of the signed data can be verified" *(SANS glossary)*.
Digital **S**ignature **S**tandard **(DSS)**	"The US Government standard that specifies the Digital Signature Algorithm (DSA), which involves asymmetric cryptography" *(SANS glossary)*.
Digital storage medium	"Device on which digital data may be recorded" *(ISO/IEC 27037, adapted from ISO/IEC 10027)*.

TERM	MEANING
Digital twin	Virtual and often real-time emulation of live **I**nformation **T**echnology or **O**perational **T**echnology systems, used for requirements analysis, planning, developing and testing changes, training, auditing, *etc*. "A virtual replica or representation of assets, processes, systems, or institutions in the built, societal, or natural environments that provides insight into how complex physical assets and citizens behave, helping organisations improve decision-making and optimise processes. Changes in the real world are reflected in the twin, and changes in the twin can be replicated automatically in the real world" *(UK National Cyber Security Strategy 2022)*. See also mimic panel, parallel simulation.
Digital **V**alue **M**anagement **S**ystem **(DVMS)**	Overarching governance/cybersecurity framework or model for generating, protecting, and enhancing the business value of data, based around NIST **C**yber **S**ecurity **F**ramework. Draws on good practices from ISO27k and other sources to manage digital risk, resilience, and strategic value. *Cf.* **M**anagement **S**ystem. More info: https://dvmsinstitute.com/
[Data] Diode	"A device that allows data to flow in only one direction" *(NZISM)*.
Dip	Momentary/transient reduction in supply voltage, lasting a few micro- or milliseconds. Most dips pass without incident but electronic systems with insufficient voltage regulation may fail. See also brownout, spike, surge, blackout.
Direct evidence	Forensic evidence that derives from or is closely related to an incident. *Cf.* circumstantial evidence.
Direct reporting engagement	Internal audit or consulting engagement providing assurance and/or advice directly to client management, rather than to third parties. "An engagement in which management does not make a written assertion about the effectiveness of their control procedures and an IS auditor provides an opinion about subject matter directly, such as the effectiveness of the control procedures" *(ISACA glossary)*.
Direction-setting criteria	"The criteria used to set the direction for the organization and its objectives based on external/internal context, culture, and stakeholder needs" *(OCEG GRC Glossary)*.
Disaster	Terrible, potentially existential incident such as a major fire, flood, earthquake, fraud, hack, or ransomware attack. Distinguished from ordinary events, incidents, or crises by its severity, scale, and lasting impact on the nations, organisations, and individuals directly or indirectly involved. "Situation where widespread human, material, economic or environmental losses have occurred that exceeded the ability of the affected organization, community or society to respond and recover using its own resources" *(ISO 22300)*. "An emergency event of such great magnitude that it overwhelms the capacity to respond and takes considerable time from which to recover" *(ISACA glossary)*.

TERM	MEANING
Disaster declaration	Formal invocation of an appropriate response (initiating the relevant parts of a **D**isaster **R**ecovery **P**lan) following rapid initial analysis/triage on a disaster. Typically signals a distinct change of business priorities and governance (*e.g.* greater local management discretion and spending power). "The communication to appropriate internal and external parties that the disaster recovery plan (DRP) is being put into operation" *(ISACA glossary)*.
Disaster **R**ecovery **(DR)**	Fallback arrangements to recover computer systems, data, and services supporting critical business functions from backups, perhaps at an alternative/secondary location using cloud-based or mobile **I**nformation **T**echnology facilities, following a major incident affecting the primary IT and datacommunications production facilities. "Ability of the ICT elements of an organization to support its critical business functions to an acceptable level within a predetermined period of time following a disruption" *(ISO/IEC 27031)*. "Activities and programs designed to return the enterprise to an acceptable condition. The ability to respond to an interruption in services by implementing a disaster recovery plan (DRP) to restore an enterprise's critical business functions" *(ISACA glossary)*. "The process of restoring a system to full operation after an interruption in service, including equipment repair/replacement, file recovery/restoration" *(ENISA RM glossary)*.
Disaster **R**ecovery **P**lan **(DRP)**	Documentation of an organisation's **D**isaster **R**ecovery arrangements, covering various aspects and scenarios. "A set of human, physical, technical and procedural resources to recover, within a defined time and cost, an activity interrupted by an emergency or disaster" *(ISACA glossary)*. "[ICT disaster recovery plan] Clearly defined and documented plan which recovers ICT capabilities when a disruption occurs. Note: It is called ICT continuity plan in some organizations" *(ISO/IEC 27031)*. "The process of recovery of IT systems in the event of a disruption or disaster" *(SANS glossary)*.
Disaster recovery plan desk check	"Typically a read-through of a disaster recovery plan (DRP) without any real actions taking place. Notes: Generally involves a reading of the plan, discussion of the action items and definition of any gaps that might be identified" *(ISACA glossary)*.
Disaster recovery plan walk-through	"Generally a robust test of the recovery plan requiring that some recovery activities take place and are tested. A disaster scenario is often given and the recovery teams talk through the steps that they would need to take to recover. As many aspects of the plan as possible should be tested" *(ISACA glossary)*.
Disaster risk reduction	"Policy aimed at preventing new and reducing existing disaster risk and managing residual risk, all of which contribute to strengthening resilience and therefore to the achievement of sustainable development" *(ISO 22300)*.

TERM	MEANING
Disaster tolerance	Composite measure, evaluation, estimation, or projection of an organisation, community, or nation's capability, capacity, and willingness to survive and recover from various disasters. Highly subjective and context-dependent. "The time gap during which the business can accept the non-availability of IT facilities" *(ISACA glossary)*. See also resilience.
Disclaimer	Attempt to share risk by explicitly and expressly denying responsibility for something, passing it to the counterparty. Often used to limit legal liabilities. See also notification.
Disclosure	Revelation of confidential information. May be deliberate and voluntary (*e.g.* tax disclosures), accidental or forced (*e.g.* by coercion, blackmail or social engineering), authorised and permitted, or unauthorised and forbidden. "Violation of computer security whereby data have been made available to unauthorized entities" *(ISO/IEC 2382)*. "The release, transfer, provision of access to, or divulging in any other manner of information outside the entity holding the information. Disclosure is often used interchangeably with the terms sharing and onward transfer" *(Trust Services Criteria)*. See also discovery.
Discovery	Forensics term for the enforced disclosure of evidence to the counterparty in an official investigation or court case. A strong reason to limit the collection and storage of information whose very existence might prove embarrassing or damaging to the organisation or individuals concerned (*e.g.* risk assessment results or audit recommendations that were not taken seriously). "Process by which each party obtains information held by another party or non-party concerning a matter. Note: Discovery is applicable more broadly than to parties in adversarial disputes. Discovery is also the disclosure of hardcopy documents, Electronically Stored Information and tangible objects by an adverse party. In some jurisdictions the term disclosure is used interchangeably with discovery" *(ISO/IEC 27050-1)*. See also disclosure, deposition, interrogatory, subpoena.
Discovery sample	Two-phase audit sampling method using a preliminary evaluation of initial samples to identify any dubious datasets worthy of additional analysis/testing, *e.g.* those whose sample reveals a higher-than-expected error count. "A form of attribute sampling that is used to determine a specified probability of finding at least one example of an occurrence (attribute) in a population" *(ISACA glossary)*. See also attribute sample, stratified sample, random sample, systematic stratified sample, time series analysis, convenience sample.

TERM	MEANING
Discretion, discreet	a. Avoiding unwelcome exposure or notoriety by actively evading publicity, remaining out-of-sight out-of-mind. A valuable if fragile control. b. Freedom, latitude, or permission to make important decisions and act independently, perhaps non-compliantly, given circumstances, genuine, credible rationales, and trustworthiness.
Discretionary, nonmandatory	Optional, voluntary, freely chosen, reflecting the use of discretion, *e.g.* management's selection and adoption, or rejection, of security controls that are not legislated or otherwise mandatory, generally for business, ethical or other reasons.
Discretionary **A**ccess **C**ontrol **(DAC)**	Decisions on whether and how to control access to data can be made by the users of a DAC system using their discretion, as opposed to being coded and incorporate irrevocably into a **M**andatory **A**ccess **C**ontrol system as an inherent part of its technical architecture. "Logical access control filters that may be configured or modified by the users or data owners" *(ISACA glossary)*. "Something the user can manage, such as a document password" *(SANS glossary)*.
Discussion forum, forum, discussion group, group, email reflector, mail exploder	Social networking capability for group members to circulate and discuss/debate matters of common interest. Messages (potentially including spam, misinformation, disinformation, or other inappropriate/unwelcome content) sent to the group by a member through email or the website are automatically 'reflected' back to all members by email and may be archived on a website allowing them to be searched. Messages containing sensitive content (*e.g.* intended for a specific group member or someone else entirely) may be exploited directly or forwarded/disclosed by members, perhaps used for profiling and social engineering (*e.g.* blackmail, coercion). "Functional unit that replicates a message as required and routes the resulting copies to various recipients indicated by a distribution list" *(ISO/IEC 2382)*.
Dishonest	Someone 'ethically challenged' who lies, deceives, cheats, or defrauds others for their own benefit. They cannot be relied upon, making them untrustworthy and probably unworthy of and unsuitable for various privileges and responsibilities.
Disinfect	Eliminate a malware infection from a system, normally by deleting the malicious software from wherever it is stored and (hopefully!) improving the security controls to prevent reinfection. "To remove malware from within a file" *(NIST SP 800-114)*.

TERM	MEANING
Disinformation	Information that is intended *deliberately* to mislead, deceive, coerce, or manipulate (such as propaganda or obfuscation). "[Information] deliberately created to mislead, harm, or manipulate a person, social group, organization, or country" *(Cybersecurity and Infrastructure Security Agency)*. "Information that is intentionally false or misleading, spread with the intent to cause harm or achieve a broader aim" *(NZSTE)*. *Cf.* misinformation.
Disintegrate	Fall to pieces or rip asunder. "Destruct by separating media into its component parts" *(ISO/IEC 27040)*.
Disk image	a. Copy of the digital data on a computer disk, typically created by an image backup. b. In digital forensics, a bit-copy of the entire contents of a disk or other storage medium using approved hardware, software, and processes. c. In virtualisation, a virtual disk made available to a guest **O**perating **S**ystem by the hypervisor.
Disk mirroring, RAID (Redundant Array of Inexpensive Disks)	Technique in which data are simultaneously written to and read from multiple disks, usually for resilience and/or performance reasons. Various technical configurations are possible with different advantages, disadvantages, capabilities, and information risks. "The practice of duplicating data in separate volumes on two hard disks to make storage more fault-tolerant. Mirroring provides data protection in the case of disk failure because data are constantly updated to both disks. [and] A storage configuration that uses hardware or software to write information to multiple disks to improve performance and fault-tolerant capabilities and/or save large files simultaneously" *(ISACA glossary)*.
Disk **O**perating **S**ystem **(DOS)**	**O**perating **S**ystem that loads from disk, such as the original **M**icro**S**oft or **P**ersonal **C**omputer-**DOS**, or today's FreeDOS.
Disposal	Act or process of discarding something. "A phase of the data life cycle that pertains to how an entity removes or destroys data or information" *(Trust Services Criteria)*.
Disposition	Eventual outcome or result of something – how things turned out and where they ended up. "Range of processes associated with implementing records retention, destruction or transfer decisions which are documented in disposition authorities or other instruments" *(ISO 30300)*.

TERM	MEANING
Disrupt, disruption, disruptive	Causing harmful and often somewhat chaotic interruption, discontinuity, or disarray, whether intentionally (an attack) or not (an accident). "Incident, whether anticipated or unanticipated, that causes an unplanned, negative deviation from the expected delivery of products and services according to an organization's objectives" *(ISO/IEC 27002)*. "Incident whether anticipated (*e.g.* hurricane) or unanticipated (*e.g.* power failure/outage, earthquake, or attack on ICT systems/infrastructure) which disrupts the normal course of operations at an organization location" *(ISO/IEC 27031)*. "A circumstance or event that interrupts or prevents the correct operation of system services and functions" *(SANS glossary)*.
Disruptive event	Disruptive event. "Occurrence or change that interrupts planned activities, operations or functions, whether anticipated or unanticipated" *(ISO 22300)*.
Distraction	Misdirection technique commonly used by social engineers, burglars, pick-pockets, and hackers to divert the victim's attention briefly while exploiting a physical or logical vulnerability.
Distress	An extreme, highly emotional and debilitating form of stress such as that experienced by people caught up in a serious accident, crisis, incident, or disaster, when coping mechanisms and mental reserves are exhausted. May result in floods of tears, wailing, and other obvious symptoms, or conversely withdrawal and silence.
Distributed **C**ontrol **S**ystem, **D**igital **C**ontrol **S**ystem **(DCS)**	Originally a term for a process control computer system that uses digital technology rather than analogue electromechanical controls. Latterly used to denote SCADA-like **I**ndustrial **C**ontrol **S**ystems/**O**perational **T**echnology distributed around industrial plant, usually fault-tolerant and semi- or fully autonomous.
Distributed **D**enial-**o**f-**S**ervice **(DDoS)**	Type of **D**enial-**o**f-**S**ervice attack using numerous systems (typically bots) to generate large volumes of network traffic, thereby flooding and possibly overloading the target systems or network, causing them to slow or stop providing **I**nformation **T**echnology services, becoming unresponsive. Can also occur by accident, *e.g.* when a website is swamped by an overwhelming number of users "A denial-of-service (DoS) assault from multiple sources" *(ISACA glossary)*. "A distributed form of denial-of-service attack" *(AusISM)*. See also **D**istributed **R**eflective **D**enial-**o**f-**S**ervice.
Distributed **R**eflective **D**enial-**o**f-**S**ervice **(DRDoS)**	Some **D**istributed **D**enial-**o**f-**S**ervice attacks use **U**ser **D**atagram **P**rotocol rather than **T**ransmission **C**ontrol **P**rotocol, taking advantage of UDP servers (such as **D**omain **N**ame **S**ystem servers) to amplify the volume of traffic, and **I**nternet **P**rotocol address spoofing to forward the amplified responses to a victim's system rather than back to the originator. No relation to DRDoS, an early **D**isk **O**perating **S**ystem from **D**igital **R**esearch. See also **D**enial-**o**f-**S**ervice.

TERM	MEANING
Distributed scan	"Scan that uses multiple source addresses to gather information" *(SANS glossary)*.
Distribution system	"Distribution grid for the transport of electrical energy using a high, medium or low voltage grid, or a local or regional distribution network for the transport of gas, oil or heat" *(ISO/IEC 27019)*.
Distributor	"A natural or legal person in the supply chain, other than the manufacturer or the importer, that makes a product with digital elements available on the Union market without affecting its properties" *(EU CRA)*.
Divergent thinking	Using creative problem-solving techniques such as brainstorming to develop, consider, and refine a broader range of possibilities, options, approaches, and potential solutions. "Considering all possibilities, conditions and events, circumstances, and outcomes" *(OCEG GRC Glossary)*. *Cf.* convergent thinking.
Diverse routing	Innate capability of a packet-switched network architecture whereby individual data packets may safely take various routes between source and destination nodes (*e.g.* dynamically re-routing around links with performance constraints) before being assembled to deliver the message content intact, in the correct sequence. The redundancy increases flexibility, availability, and resilience. "A method of routing traffic through split cable facilities or duplicate cable facilities. Notes: This can be accomplished with different or duplicate cable sheaths. If different cable sheaths are used, the cable may be in the same conduit and, therefore, subject to the same interruptions as the cable it is backing up. The communication service subscriber can duplicate the facilities by having alternate routes, although the entrance to and from the customer premises may be in the same conduit. The subscriber can obtain diverse routing and alternate routing, including dual entrance facilities, from the local carrier. However, acquiring this type of access is time-consuming and costly. Most carriers provide facilities for alternate and diverse routing, although the majority of services are transmitted over terrestrial media, which are usually located in the ground or basement. Ground-based facilities are at great risk due to the aging infrastructures of cities. In addition, cable-based facilities usually share space with mechanical and electrical systems that can pose great risk due to potential human error and disasters" *(ISACA glossary)*.
Diversify, diversification	Business continuity technique involves deliberately reducing dependence on individual products, suppliers, workers, communication paths, *etc.* by seeking alternatives – not just more of the same (redundancy) but something different. A resilience control.

TERM	MEANING
Diversity	a. The result of successful diversification. b. Equitability principle of including and valuing people with different backgrounds, races, ethnicity, genders, sexual orientations, ages, and capabilities.
Division of responsibilities, separation of duties, segregation of duties	Control requiring the involvement of more than one individual or organisation to complete a business process, *e.g.* a member of staff enters data but someone else, normally a supervisor or manager, must review and authorise it for processing. Normally reinforced by controlled access to the corresponding system functions. Reduces the possibility of fraud, barring collusion between the individuals or coercion, and data entry errors. "Practice of dividing steps in a function among different individuals so as to keep a single individual from being able to subvert the process" *(PCI Card Production and Provisioning Physical Security Requirements).*
DKIM	*Abbrev:* **D**omain**K**eys **I**dentified **M**ail.
DLL	*Abbrev:* **D**ynamic **L**ink **L**ibrary.
DLP	*Abbrev:* **D**ata **L**oss **P**revention.
DMARC	*Abbrev:* **D**omain-based **M**essage **A**uthentication, **R**eporting, and **C**onformance.
DMCA	*Abbrev:* **D**igital **M**illennium **C**opyright **A**ct.
DMZ	*Abbrev:* **D**e-**M**ilitarised **Z**one.
DNS	*Abbrev:* **D**omain **N**ame **S**ystem.
DNSSEC	*Abbrev:* **D**omain **N**ame **S**ystem **SEC**urity.
DNSpionage	Species of **R**emote **A**ccess **Tro**jan malware in the wild in 2019. Uses **D**omain **N**ame **S**ystem tunnelling to communicate with the attacker's **C**ommand and **C**ontrol systems.
Document, documented	a. *[Noun]* Information recorded in physical (paper) or digital (electronic) form such as strategies, plans, policies, procedures, reports, meeting agendas, or minutes. For a document to have lasting value rather than becoming shelfware, it should be readily accessible to its intended audience/s, clearly written, and, if necessary, protected from inappropriate or unauthorised access. Important documents may need ongoing maintenance, *e.g.* periodic reviews and updates to maintain their integrity (accuracy, relevance, and completeness), and reauthorisation by management. "Named, structured unit of text and possibly images that can be stored, edited, retrieved, and exchanged among systems or users as a separate unit" *(ISO/IEC 2382).* "A collection of information and data, regardless of the medium, that generally has permanence and can be read by humans or

TERM	MEANING
	can be read by humans or machines. Documents can be work products reflecting the implementation of processes that meet the intent and value of one or more model practices. Documents may be embedded within an automated, robotic or online system. Documents can be physical hard copies or soft copies that are accessible via hyperlinks in a web-based environment or application. Documents are used and kept updated" *(ISACA glossary)*. See also documentation. b. *[Verb]* To create, generate, capture, or record documents (see above).
Documentation	a. The act or process of capturing pertinent information about various business activities (*e.g.* strategies, plans, policies, processes, decisions, specifications, tests, analyses) in reference materials that can (where relevant) be read, studied/analysed, discussed, amended, reviewed, evaluated, approved by relevant stakeholders, circulated, shared, disclosed, published, stored, and ultimately discarded, lost, or destroyed. b. The output, product, or results of the documentation process, *i.e.* the documents produced.
Documented information	ISO's clumsy term conflating formal documents (such as policies and procedures) with records (*i.e.* evidence or artefacts generated by systems, activities, and processes such as completed change control forms), more generally known as 'documentation.' "Information required to be controlled and maintained by an organisation and the medium on which it is contained. Notes: documented information can be in any format and media and from any source. Documented information can refer to the management system, including related processes, information created in order for the organisation to operate (documentation), [and] evidence of results achieved (records)" *(ISO/IEC 27000)*.
DoD dictionary	US **D**epartment **o**f **D**efense "dictionary of military and associated terms" (2017). Nearly 400 pages of terms, definitions, abbreviations, acronyms, and initialisms. More info: https://apps.dtic.mil/sti/pdfs/AD1029823.pdf
Domain	Area, region, field of concern/interest/expertise, group of resources, *etc.* On the web, user-friendly domain names such as SecAware.com are associated with the numeric **I**nternet **P**rotocol addresses for the corresponding servers by the **D**omain **N**ame **S**ystem. Resources in a Microsoft network are grouped into domains through **A**ctive **D**irectory. "That part of a computer network in which the resources or addressing are under common control. Note: The domain scheme may be geographical or organizational [and] specific field of knowledge or expertise" *(ISO/IEC 2382)*. "A domain name locates an organisation or other entity

TERM	MEANING
	on the internet and corresponds to an Internet Protocol (IP) address" *(UK National Cyber Security Strategy 2022)*. "A sphere of knowledge, or a collection of facts about some program entities or a number of network points or addresses, identified by a name. On the Internet, a domain consists of a set of network addresses. In the Internet's domain name system, a domain is a name with which name server records are associated that describe sub-domains or host. In Windows NT and Windows 2000, a domain is a set of network resources (applications, printers, and so forth) for a group of users. The user need only to log in to the domain to gain access to the resources, which may be located on a number of different servers in the network" *(SANS glossary)*. See also security domain, zone.
Domain-based **M**essage **A**uthentication, **R**eporting, and **C**onformance **(DMARC)**	Standardised method for authenticating the originator of emails using **S**ender **P**olicy **F**ramework and/or **D**omain**K**eys **I**dentified **M**ail according to the domain's policy published as a **D**omain **N**ame **S**ystem record, optionally reporting the outcome by email. "A scalable mechanism by which a mail-originating organization can express domain-level policies and preferences for message validation, disposition, and reporting, that a mail-receiving organization can use to improve mail handling" *(NZISM)*.
Domain **C**ontroller **(DC)**	**A**ctive **D**irectory server in charge of a domain.
Domain hijack	Subversion of the system that directs user requests to particular web servers, *e.g.* by seizing ownership or administrative control of the domain or compromising the **D**omain **N**ame **S**ystem server to redirect users to a server under the hijackers' control. "An attack by which an attacker takes over a domain by first blocking access to the domain's DNS server and then putting his own server up in its place" *(SANS glossary)*.
Domain**K**eys **I**dentified **M**ail **(DKIM)**	Cryptographic email authentication protocol intended to prevent email spoofing or tampering and ensure message integrity. Domain owners publish their DKIM public keys as txt records through **D**omain **N**ame **S**ystem. "Defines a mechanism by which email messages can be cryptographically signed, permitting a signing domain to claim responsibility for the introduction of a message into the mail stream. Message recipients can verify the signature by querying the signer's domain directly to retrieve the appropriate public key, and thereby confirm that the message was attested to by a party in possession of the private key for the signing domain" *(NZISM)*. See also **S**ender **P**olicy **F**ramework, **D**omain-based **M**essage **A**uthentication, **R**eporting and **C**onformance.

TERM	MEANING
Domain name	"A domain name locates an organization or other entity on the Internet. For example, the domain name 'www.sans.org' locates an Internet address for 'sans.org' at Internet point 199.0.0.2 and a particular host server named 'www.' The 'org' part of the domain name reflects the purpose of the organization or entity (in this example, 'organization') and is called the top-level domain name. The 'sans' part of the domain name defines the organization or entity and together with the top-level is called the second-level domain name" *(SANS glossary)*.
Domain **N**ame **S**ystem **(DNS)**	Network protocols and systems let us refer to Internet nodes by memorable domain names (such as SecAware.com) rather than their numeric **I**nternet **P**rotocol addresses. "A hierarchical database distributed across the Internet, which allows names to be resolved into IP addresses (and vice versa) to locate services, such as web and email servers" *(ISACA glossary)*. "The way that Internet domain names are located and translated into Internet Protocol addresses. A domain name is a meaningful and easy-to-remember 'handle' for an Internet address" *(SANS glossary)*.
Domain **N**ame **S**ystem **poisoning (DNS poisoning), DNS cache poisoning, cache poisoning**	Attack that subverts **D**omain **N**ame **S**ystem servers or records to direct victims covertly to a malicious domain, phishing or infectious website, *etc.* instead of the benign one they anticipated, *e.g.* by 'poisoning' cached DNS data with false linkages or by exploiting the 'zone transfer' process used to share data among DNS servers. "Corrupts the table of an Internet server's DNS, replacing an Internet address with the address of a vagrant or scoundrel address. Notes: If a web user looks for the page with that address, the request is redirected by the scoundrel entry in the table to a different address. Cache poisoning differs from another form of DNS poisoning in which the attacker spoofs valid email accounts and floods the in-boxes of administrative and technical contacts. Cache poisoning is related to URL poisoning or location poisoning, in which an Internet user's behavior is tracked by adding an identification number to the location line of the browser that can be recorded as the user visits successive pages on the site" *(ISACA glossary)*. See also pharming.
Domain **N**ame **S**ystem **SEC**urity extensions **(DNSSEC)**	Additions to the **D**omain **N**ame **S**ystem protocols allow domain owners to digitally sign their DNS records, improving authentication.

TERM	MEANING
Domain owner	a. Person or organisation who formally owns an Internet domain such as hyperglossary.com, as officially registered with the registrar responsible for the **T**op-**L**evel **D**omain (all the .coms in this example). b. "A domain owner is responsible for the secure configuration of the security domain throughout its life-cycle, including all connections to/from the domain" *(NZISM).* See also asset owner, information owner, data owner, file owner, network owner, service owner, system owner.
Domain slamming	Unethical and barely legal social engineering scam to trick domain owners into transferring their registrations to a different fee-charging agent, believing they are merely renewing.
Domotics	Neologism derived from *domus* (Latin for home) and robotics or informatics, meaning home automation, **I**nternet **o**f ***T**hings*, and smart homes in particular.
Dongle	Copy protection hardware device used to 'unlock' (*i.e.* permit access to and use of) software on the particular computer into which it is physically plugged. Also, a hardware authentication token. Both forms normally use cryptography and tamper resistance to prevent the devices being illicitly duplicated or fabricated, but the corresponding applications may be vulnerable to hacking, bypassing, or negating the protection.
Door open alarm	Physical security arrangement that monitors an access-controlled door, triggering an alarm if it is opened (*e.g.* opening an emergency fire exit may sound the fire alarm to evacuate the building) or held open much longer than it would take even the slowest person to pass through (*e.g.* a card access-controlled office door propped open for some reason may sound an annoying local 'peeper' and/or a silent/remote alarm in the security guard house). Electronic door-open alarms may be manually overridden or silenced for authorised purposes such as office moves or refits, but such overrides should preferably trigger indicators (such as a flashing warning light), automated reminders, or cancellation/timeouts to prevent them being forgotten and left in effect beyond the allotted time.
DORA (**D**igital **O**perational **R**esilience **A**ct)	**E**uropean **U**nion regulation concerning digital operational resilience imposes strict cybersecurity obligations on **E**uropean **U**nion financial services organisations. Five focus areas: risk management, (ICT-related) incident management, assurance (*e.g.* penetration testing) for ICT resilience, ICT supply chain risk management, and information sharing/collaboration. Official title: "Regulation (EU) 2022/2554 of the European Parliament and of the Council of 14 December 2022 on digital operational resilience for the financial sector and amending Regulations (EC) No 1060/2009, (EU) No 648/2012, (EU) No 600/2014, (EU) No 909/2014 and (EU) 2016/1011." More info: https://eur-lex.europa.eu/legal-content/EN/TXT/?uri=CELEX:32022R2554

TERM	MEANING
Dorkbot	Windows malware in the wild from 2011 to 2016. **R**emote **A**ccess **T**rojan spread via infectious websites (including chef Jamie Oliver's), social networks, **I**nstant **M**essaging, and USB devices, delivering various payloads including bank Trojans, keyloggers, and **D**istributed **D**enial-**o**f-**S**ervice engines. The botnet's command-and-control structure was disrupted by the authorities with assistance from technology companies in 2016.
DoS, DOS	*Abbrev:* **D**enial-**o**f-**S**ervice or **D**isk **O**perating **S**ystem, respectively.
Double agent	Agent who surreptitiously remains loyal to and acts in the interests of one party while giving the *appearance* of loyalty towards another. A form of sabotage or cybertage.
Double extension	**O**perating **S**ystems and applications often determine a file's type according to the final extension on its name, preceded by a full-stop (*e.g.* files containing executable programs often end with *.exe*). Systems may not display the extension for known file types. Additional full-stops and characters preceding the final extension (such as *.txt* and *.exe*) may be treated as part of the file name. Some malware uses this and other social engineering techniques to fool victims, for instance an email might entreat the user to 'open the attached text file containing a disputed invoice,' whereas the attachment is actually a malicious program that executes when the victim opens it.
Double-extortion	Ransomware attacks increasingly involve disclosure of stolen data to add even more weight to the ransom demand.
Double-entry bookkeeping	Financial accounting process used since Roman times in which every transaction is recorded as a complementary pair of credits and debits (equal in value but opposite in sign) in the relevant accounts or ledgers. Any discrepancy between the running totals of the paired accounts when they are reconciled generally indicates a simple data entry or calculation error but *could* point to fraud, corruption, or theft.
Down for everyone or just me?	Useful website availability test service that simply checks whether websites are presently up (online, responding) or down (offline, dead). More info: https://downforeveryoneorjustme.com/
Downgrade attack	Networking protocols commonly allow the use of certain older, weaker, and perhaps deprecated cryptographic algorithms for backwards compatibility. Adversaries exploit these downgrade capabilities to weaken and then hijack the connections, inject malicious content, steal credentials, *etc.*
Downloader	Function or component of malware which downloads additional code (usually the payload) through the Internet. This arrangement allows criminals to change the malware dynamically, *e.g.* to evade antivirus software, attack specific new targets, or extend previous attacks. See also fileless malware.

TERM	MEANING
Downstream	Later activities in a time sequence, such as the delivery and use of a business's products by its customers, or subsequent stages in a lifecycle. "Handling processes and movements of products and services that occur after an entity in the supply chain takes custody of the products and responsibility for services" *(ISO/IEC 27036-1)*. *Cf.* upstream.
Dox, DoX, doxing, DoXing	Leet terms derived from 'docs' (documents), referring to the process of illicitly gathering and perhaps disclosing personal information on targets by researching their presence on social media and other sources such as hacked personnel DataBases. Has harassing, bullying, or threatening overtones of coercion, similar to stalking, grooming, snooping, spying, and other forms of social engineering.
DoXware, doxware	See leakware.
DP	*Abbrev:* **D**ata **P**rocessing.
DPA	*Abbrev:* **D**ata **P**rotection **A**ct.
DPO	*Abbrev:* **D**ata **P**rotection **O**fficer.
DR	*Abbrev:* **D**isaster **R**ecovery.
Dragonfly	See **S**imultaneous **A**uthentication of **E**quals.
Draining, infiltration, urban exploration	'Urban sport' involves exploring insecure drains, service ducts, and other voids to undermine physical perimeter controls in order to gain unauthorised internal access to sites or buildings. A risky, dangerous form of trespass and a significant if underappreciated risk for many otherwise secure industrial or urban facilities.
DRDoS	*Abbrev:* **D**istributed **R**eflective **D**enial-**o**f-**S**ervice.
Dridex, Bugat, Cridex	Multifunctional evolving antivirus-evading malware with botnet, bank Trojan, and ransomware capabilities. The **F**ederal **B**ureau **o**f **I**nvestigation tried to disrupt the Dridex infrastructure by blackholing C^2 traffic in 2016 but it remained active in 2019. Two alleged Russian members of Evil Corp (the cybercriminal gang behind Dridex) were indicted for their part in stealing ~$70 m from organisations around the globe.
Drive-by download, Web-inject malware	Mode of malware infection involving the user merely browsing to an infectious website where vulnerabilities in the browser software are silently exploited, usually without the user even being aware of the compromise.

TERM	MEANING
Driver	a. Software interface to the firmware associated with a hardware device (such as a disk drive, keyboard, or computer motherboard), providing data communications and functions for monitoring, controlling, and using the device. "A program that links a peripheral device or internal function to the operating system and provides for activation of all device functions" *(ISACA glossary)*. b. Motivational, determining, or decisive factor. "An event or other activity that results in the identification of an assurance/audit need" *(ISACA glossary)*.
Driver pins	In most physical locks, these standard-length metal cylinders are pushed back against springs into the hull by the variable-length key pins when a key is inserted into the keyway. Provided the key pins and driver pins meet along a straight shear line due to the correct key having been inserted (or with skilful use of a pick), the plug can be rotated at the shear line to open or close the lock.
DRM	*Abbrev:* **D**igital **R**ights **M**anagement.
Drone, Unmanned Autonomous Vehicle (UAV)	Unmanned aircraft, normally used for surveillance. Basic drones (toys) are remote-controlled by human operators nearby, while sophisticated military versions (UAVs) may operate autonomously using **G**lobal **P**ositioning **S**ystem and intelligent control systems to complete surveillance or attack missions across immense distances. Raises safety, privacy, security, and ethical concerns.
Drop, dead drop, Dead Letter Box (DLB)	Physical or electronic location where messages, parcels, files, *etc.* may be safely (anonymously, covertly, and asynchronously) delivered to a collector, competitor, spy/spook, or cybercriminal. Modern-day spies may use anonymous Internet services, encryption, steganography, and covert channels to pass information but still rely on dead drops to pass physical assets such as **O**ne-**T**ime **P**ads, goods purchased with stolen credit card numbers, fake passports or credentials, and good ol' fashioned cash. See also live drop.
Dropper	Malware which delivers/contains, unpacks, and installs other malware on an infected system. See also downloader.
DROWN (Decrypting RSA with Obsolete and Weakened eNcryption)	Contrived name for a hack that compromises **T**ransport **L**ayer **S**ecurity sessions by exploiting a vulnerability in the deprecated **S**ecure **S**ockets **L**ayer v2 protocol, exposing RSA private keys. See also POODLE, Heartbleed.
DRP	*Abbrev:* **D**isaster **R**ecovery **P**lan.

TERM	MEANING
Dry-pipe fire extinguisher system	Sprinkler system for a building in which the fire extinguishant (*e.g.* water) is rapidly injected into the pipework under pressure only when the system is triggered by an alarm or the fire brigade attends, rather than the whole system being full and pressured continuously (which increases the risk of leaks). "A sprinkler system that does not have water in the pipes during idle usage, unlike a fully charged fire extinguisher system that has water in the pipes at all times. Note: The dry-pipe system is activated at the time of the fire alarm and water is emitted to the pipes from a water reservoir for discharge to the location of the fire" *(ISACA glossary)*.
DSAR	*Abbrev:* **D**ata **S**ubject **A**ccess **R**equest.
DSP	*Abbrev:* **D**igital **S**ervice **P**rovider or **D**igital **S**ignal **P**rocessing, depending on context.
DSR	*Abbrev:* **D**ata **S**ubject **R**equest. See **D**ata **S**ubject **A**ccess **R**equest.
Dstl	*Abbrev:* **D**efence **s**cience and **t**echnology **l**aboratory.
DTSA	*Abbrev:* **D**efend **T**rade **S**ecrets **A**ct.
Dual-control	Form of control requiring the actions of more than one person, *e.g.* when two soldiers must insert and turn their keys at the same moment into locks placed several meters apart to launch a missile (as seen on TV). "A procedure in which two or more entities (usually persons) operate in concert to protect a system resource so that no single entity acting alone can access that resource" *(ISACA glossary)*.
Dual-stack [network] device	"A product that implements both IP version 4 and 6 protocol stacks" *(NZISM)*. "ICT equipment that implements both Internet Protocol version 4 and Internet Protocol version 6 protocol stacks" *(AusISM)*.
Dual-use technology	Technology that can be used for *both* offensive and defensive purposes, to wage war *and* to secure peace. Strong encryption, for instance, protects information and communications regardless of the nature of the information and the communicating parties: it is valued and used by criminals, terrorists, the authorities including governments, militia, and law enforcement, and the public alike.
Due care	Obligation or expectation that fiduciary officers/executives of an organisation duly protect its assets and act in its best interests, just as a prudent person would be expected to do. "The level of care expected from a reasonable person of similar competency under similar conditions" *(ISACA glossary)*. "The responsibility that managers and their organisations have a duty to provide for information security to ensure that the type of control, the cost of control, and the deployment of control are appropriate for the system being managed" *(NIST SP 800-30)*. "Ensures that a minimal level of protection is in place in accordance with the best practice in the industry" *(SANS glossary)*. See also negligence. *Cf.* due diligence, duty of care.

TERM	MEANING
Due diligence	Assurance activities in preparation for important corporate activities such as mergers, acquisitions, and the execution of major contracts. Also compliance, *e.g.* enforcing policies and ensuring that security controls are effectively protecting valuable information assets. "The performance of actions generally regarded as prudent, responsible and necessary to conduct a thorough and objective investigation, review or analysis" *(ISACA glossary)*. "The requirement that organizations must develop and deploy a protection plan to prevent fraud, abuse, and additional deploy a means to detect them if they occur" *(SANS glossary)*. *Cf.* due care, duty of care.
Due professional care	"The diligence that a person with a special skill would exercise under a given set of circumstances" *(ISACA glossary)*.
Dump	Data file containing authentication credentials such as usernames and passwords or credit/bank card numbers and related information such as the cardholder's name and the CVV, possibly fullz, stolen by a hacker or carder, then made available on the hacker underground.
DumpSec	Common name for a security audit utility that extracts ('dumps') security configuration parameters from a system into a file for analysis "A security tool that dumps a variety of information about a system's users, file system, registry, permissions, password policy, and services" *(SANS glossary)*.
Dumpster diving	Figuratively or literally jumping into and rummaging through the contents of commercial or domestic waste bins to retrieve discarded but valuable and often sensitive information for social engineering, hacking, coercion, *etc.* "Obtaining passwords and corporate directories by searching through discarded media" *(SANS glossary)*.
Dunning–Kruger effect	Cognitive bias leading people with limited competence to overestimate their own capabilities, or *vice versa*. First described by David Dunning and Justin Kruger.
Duqu	**A**dvanced **P**ersistent **T**hreat worm similar to, and perhaps derived from, Stuxnet.
Durable, durability	Long-lasting, hardy, strong, resilient, robust, able to endure harsh operating conditions and environs while remaining functional. "Ability of a functional unit to perform a required function under given conditions of use and maintenance, until a limiting state is reached. Note: A limiting state of a functional unit may be characterized by the end of the useful life, unsuitability for any economic or technological reasons, or other relevant factors" *(ISO/IEC 2382)*.

TERM	MEANING
Duration	Time-span during which something exists or takes place. "A measure that estimates how long an event or impact might last" *(OCEG GRC Glossary)*.
Duress alarm, duress button	Type of silent alarm that can be triggered by a worker to signal that they are experiencing some form of hardship (coercion, threat, hold-up, robbery, *etc*.), typically by hitting a concealed 'panic button,' releasing a dead-mans-handle or entering a particular combination of keys (such as their normal password or PIN code immediately preceded or followed by, say, the hash symbol) into a system that has been specifically designed and configured to incorporate this function (such as a bank teller's workstation or security guard station).
Duty of care	Responsibility, obligation, official duty, requirement, or expectation to ensure that others are not harmed by one's action or inaction. "Moral or legal obligation to ensure the safety, well-being or interests of others" *(ISO 22300). Cf.* due care, due diligence.
DVMS	*Abbrev:* **D**igital **V**alue **M**anagement **S**ystem.
DVMS CPD (**D**igital **V**alue **M**anagement **S**ystem **C**reate, **P**rotect and **D**eliver)	Overarching architectural perspective on the **D**igital **V**alue **M**anagement **S**ystem that positions cybersecurity as an essential part of management, integral to the business. Links governance arrangements with processes to develop and execute strategy, improve, gain assurance, and innovate.
Dynamic **A**pplication **S**ecurity **T**esting **(DAST)**	In effect, penetration testing of an application, checking (from the network perspective) whether its exposed ports and services have known vulnerabilities. See also **S**tatic **A**pplication **S**ecurity **T**esting, **I**nteractive **A**pplication **S**ecurity **T**esting.
Dynamic **H**ost **C**onfiguration **P**rotocol **(DHCP)**	"A protocol used by networked computers (clients) to obtain IP addresses from DHCP servers, and parameters such as default gateways, subnet masks, and domain name system (DNS) server IP addresses. Notes: The DHCP server ensures that all IP addresses are unique (*e.g.*, no IP address is assigned to a second client while the first client's assignment is valid [its lease has not expired]). Thus, IP address pool management is done by the server and not by a human network administrator" *(ISACA glossary)*.
Dynamic **L**ink **L**ibrary **(DLL)**	Library of executable code, data, icons, *etc*. that can be loaded and shared between Windows programs. If a malicious DLL is present in the same folder as a benign executable program, it may be loaded and executed in preference to the intended DLL stored elsewhere, compromising the system. "A collection of small programs, any of which can be called when needed by a larger program that is running in the computer. The small program that lets the larger program communicate with a specific device such as a printer or scanner is often packaged as a DLL program (usually referred to as a DLL file)" *(SANS glossary)*.

TERM	MEANING
Dynamic port	See ephemeral port.
Dynamic **R**andom-**A**ccess **M**emory **(DRAM)**	Volatile random-access computer memory, normally implemented as a set of **I**ntegrated **C**ircuits on a **P**rinted **C**ircuit **B**oard (a **D**ual **I**n-line **M**emory **M**odule).
Dyre	Bank Trojan capable of **M**an-**I**n-**T**he-**M**iddle attacks, monitoring online banking sessions to capture browser snapshots and logon credentials. Discovered in 2014.

E

TERM	MEANING
E2EE	*Abbrev:* **E**nd-**to**-**E**nd **E**ncryption.
EA	*Abbrev:* **E**nterprise **A**rchitecture.
EAC	*Abbrev:* **E**mail **A**ccount **C**ompromise. See **B**usiness **E**mail **C**ompromise.
EAL	*Abbrev:* **E**valuation **A**ssurance **L**evel.
EAM	*Abbrev:* **E**nterprise **A**sset **M**anagement or **E**mbedded **A**udit **M**odule, depending on context.
EAP	*Abbrev:* **E**xtensible **A**uthentication **P**rotocol or **E**mergency **A**ction **P**lan, depending on context.
Early warning	Predictive indication of a problem, event, incident, or disaster ahead. "Provision of information through local networks, allowing affected individuals to take action to avoid or reduce risks and to prepare responses" *(ISO 22300)*.
EASM	*Abbrev:* **E**xternal **A**ttack **S**urface **M**anagement.
Easter egg	Trojan horse function hidden within an otherwise legitimate program. Although normally benign (such as a simple computer game or shout-out for the developers), the fact that a covert function has been coded and passed through program testing hints at a possible governance issue with the **S**oftware **D**evelopment **L**ife**C**ycle, begging the question "What *else* might be going on in there?." "Hidden functionality within an application program, which becomes activated when an undocumented, and often convoluted, set of commands and keystrokes are entered. Easter eggs are typically used to display the credits for the development team and are intended to be nonthreatening" *(NIST SP 800-28)*.
Eavesdrop, eavesdropping, eavesdropper	To listen in or snoop on someone or something covertly. May involve literally listening and watching from nearby, or remotely using surveillance equipment such as binoculars, bugs, cameras, spyware, keyloggers and backdoors, network analysers, passive reflectors modulating infrared laser beams, and wiretaps, with obvious adverse implications for privacy and confidentiality. "Unauthorized interception of information-bearing emanations" *(ISO/IEC 2382)*. "Listening to a private communication without permission" *(ISACA glossary)*. "Simply listening to a private conversation which may reveal information which can provide access to a facility or network" *(SANS glossary)*.
EBIOS Risk Manager	**I**nformation **T**echnology risk management method developed by **A**gence **N**ationale de la **S**écurité des **S**ystèmes d'**I**nformation – France's national cybersecurity agency. More info: https://cyber.gouv.fr/en/publications/ebios-risk-manager-method

TERM	MEANING
ECC	*Abbrev:* **E**lliptic **C**urve **C**ryptography or **E**rror **C**orrection **C**ode, depending on context.
ECCM	*Abbrev:* **E**lectronic **C**ounter-**C**ounter**M**easures.
EC Council, EC-Council	International Council of E-Commerce Consultants, a US-based training body for cybersecurity-related rôles, formed in 2001. Provider of **C**ertified **E**thical **H**acker, **C**omputer **H**acking **F**orensics **I**nvestigator, **C**ertified **C**hief **I**nformation **S**ecurity **O**fficer, and **C**ertified **S**ecurity **A**nalyst qualifications. More info: https://www.eccouncil.org/
ECDH	*Abbrev:* **E**lliptic **C**urve **D**iffie–**H**ellman.
Echelon	**N**ational **S**ecurity **A**gency-led global mass surveillance program launched in the 1960s in conjunction with what became the Five Eyes. France has a similar program dubbed 'Frenchelon' with satellite ground stations ('spy stations') located in mainland France and some of its overseas territories.
ECI (Exceptionally **C**ompartmented **I**nformation)	Category or class (classification level) of hyper-sensitive US intelligence information.
ECM	*Abbrev:* **E**lectronic **C**ounter**M**easure.
eCommerce	*Abbrev:* **e**lectronic **Commerce**.
Economic coercion	"Any act by a state intended to influence the behaviour of another state by disrupting existing commercial relationships" *(NZSTE)*.
Economic espionage	Euphemism for state-sponsored industrial espionage (surveillance, spying) directed against foreign corporations and (usually) their intellectual assets. May also involve cybertage.
Economic operator	Commercial organisation, company. "The manufacturer, the authorised representative, the importer, the distributor, or other natural or legal person who is subject to obligations in relation to the manufacture of products with digital elements or to the making available of products with digital elements on the market in accordance with this Regulation" *(EU CRA)*.
EcoTech, GreenTech	Contraction of **eco**logical or **green tech**nology, particularly the development and exploitation of innovative techologies for sustainability and environmental protection. See also AgriTech, Biotech, EdTech, FinTech, FoodTech, GovTech, HealthTech, LegalTech, RegTech, RetailTech, and other tech neologisms.
Eco-warrior	Activist or extremist who may sabotage organisations they believe to be exploiting and wantonly harming the natural environment through their operations (*e.g.* mining and oil companies destroying the rain forests, or 'scientific' whaling).

TERM	MEANING
ECP	*Abbrev:* **E**le**c**tronic **P**rotective measures.
EDA	*Abbrev:* **E**xploratory **D**ata **A**nalysis.
EDGE	*Abbrev:* **E**nhanced **D**ata for **G**SM **E**volution.
Edge case	In software testing, boundary conditions may be analysed using test data values slightly below, directly on, and slightly above the boundary (the 'edge'). Such situations should ideally be covered by the program specifications, particularly if there are cybersecurity or safety implications, *i.e.* the potential to cause data/system confidentiality, integrity, or availability issues (such as enabling inappropriate access to protected memory, corrupting a **D**ata**B**ase, crashing the server, or losing control of a robot or weapon). See also corner case.
Edgehill	UK government intelligence program run by **G**overnment **C**ommunications **H**ead**Q**uarters, cryptanalysing online communications and data (SIGINT) in collaboration with **N**ational **S**ecurity **A**gency. Its existence was revealed in a TOP SECRET briefing disclosed by whistleblower Ed Snowden. See also BULLRUN, Tempora.
EDI	*Abbrev:* **E**lectronic **D**ata **I**nterchange or **E**quity, **D**iversity, and **I**nclusion, depending on context.
Edit control	"The manual or automated detection of errors in the input portion of information sent to the computer for processing, allowing the user to edit data errors before processing" *(ISACA glossary).*
Editing, edit	Process of changing documented information, particularly the manual correction of typographical errors in written or typed content. "The process of ensuring that data conform to predetermined criteria and enable early identification of potential errors" *(ISACA glossary).*
EDPR	*Abbrev:* **E**uropean **D**ata **P**rotection **B**oard.
EDR	*Abbrev:* **E**ndpoint **D**etection and **R**esponse.
EdTech	Contraction of **ed**ucational **tech**nology, particularly the development and exploitation of innovative **I**nformation **T**echnology within the educational industry/sector. See also AgriTech, Biotech, EcoTech/GreenTech, FinTech, FoodTech, GovTech, HealthTech, LegalTech, RegTech, RetailTech, and other tech neologisms.
[Information security] Education	General knowledge and expertise in relation to recognising and minimising information risks through appropriate security controls. Achieved initially through the school/education system, advice from parents and teachers, *etc.* and then extended through security awareness and training activities during employment, supplementing work and general life experience and self-development. "Process of receiving or giving systematic instruction, especially at a school or university" *(ISO/IEC 19896-1).*

TERM	MEANING
Effect	"A measure that estimates the likelihood and impact that an event has on objectives" *(OCEG GRC Glossary)*.
Effective, sound	Functional, productive, working as intended. "An aspect of Total Performance which demonstrates evidence of logically designed actions & controls that address appropriate objectives, opportunities, obstacles, and obligations; and evidence that these actions & controls are operating as designed" *(OCEG GRC Glossary)*.
Effectiveness	Measure of the quality or suitability of something for some purpose. "Extent to which planned activities are realized and planned results [are] achieved" *(ISO/IEC 27000)*. "Ability to apply knowledge and skills in a productive manner, characterized by attributes of behaviour such as aptitude, initiative, enthusiasm, willingness, communication skills, team participation, and leadership" *(ISO/IEC 19896-1)*. "[Of controls] Encompasses both the suitability of the design of controls and the operating effectiveness of controls to provide reasonable assurance that the entity's principal system objectives are achieved" *(**T**rust **S**ervices **C**riteria)*.
Efficiency	Comparative measure of the consumption of input resources by something (a machine, person, activity, function, or organisation) in relation to its outputs (products, achievements, progress, quality). "Relationship between the results achieved and resources used" *(ISO 9000)*.
Efficient, lean	Ability to do something well, achieving results without wasting resources. "An aspect of Total Performance which demonstrates evidence that the organization productively uses financial, human, and other capital resources without wasted effort or expense" *(OCEG GRC Glossary)*.
e.g.	*Abbrev:* ***e**xempli **g**ratia* – Latin for "for example" or "such as."
EGIT	*Abbrev:* **E**nterprise **G**overnance of **I**nformation and **T**echnology.
EGP	*Abbrev:* **E**xterior **G**ateway **P**rotocol.
Egress	Leaving a building, system, network, *etc.* "The exiting of network communications" *(ISACA glossary)*. *Cf.* ingress.
Egress filtering	Selective blocking of traffic as it exits a network or system, *e.g.* to prevent malware-infected or hacked computers on corporate networks from sending spam or attacking systems on external networks, or to block highly classified information from passing from a SECRET system onto an unclassified domain. "Filtering outbound traffic" *(SANS glossary)*. *Cf.* ingress filtering.

TERM	MEANING
EINSTEIN	Covert US government network security monitoring/intrusion detection capability originally developed by US-CERT and deployed in 2004. The current incarnation, EINSTEIN 3, is being developed by the **N**ational **S**ecurity **A**gency. It reportedly monitors traffic flowing through authorised gateways between the internal government network/s and the outside world, while a cloud-based distributed sensor version is (also) under consideration, presumably to counter threats arising from the **I**nternet **o**f ***T**hings* and proliferating Internet connectivity.
Elasticity	See scalability.
Electronic archive	Long-term data store (see archive). "Long-term repository of Electronically Stored Information. Notes: Electronic archives can be on-line, and therefore accessible, or off-line and not easily accessible. Backup systems (*e.g.*, tape, virtual tape) are not intended to be electronic archives, but rather data protection systems (*i.e.*, recovery mechanisms for disaster recovery and business continuity)" *(ISO/IEC 27050-1)*.
electronic **Commerce (eCommerce)**	Outdated, quaint, and largely forgotten term for online retail shopping and commercial procurement. "The processes by which enterprises conduct business electronically with their customers, suppliers and other external business partners, using the Internet as an enabling technology. Notes: E-commerce encompasses both business-to-business (B2B) and business-to-consumer (B2C) ecommerce models but does not include existing nonInternet ecommerce methods based on private networks such as the electronic data interchange (EDI) and the Society for Worldwide Interbank Financial Telecommunication (SWIFT)" *(ISACA glossary)*.
Electronic **C**ounter-**C**ounter**M**easure **(ECCM)**, **E**lectronic **P**rotective measure **(ECP)**	Defensive technique to avoid electronic communications or systems being compromised by an adversary or indeed by friendly forces, *e.g.* using spread-spectrum, burst, covert, and/or spoof transmissions, and TEMPEST.
Electronic **C**ounter**M**easure **(ECM)**	Offensive technique to disrupt an adversary's electronic communications or systems, for instance by jamming their radio links, transmitting false beacons, or misleading their automated target-acquisition systems. The electronic equivalent of chaff. See also **E**lectronic **C**ounter-**C**ounter**M**easures.
Electronic **D**ata **I**nterchange **(EDI)**	Business-to-business eCommerce architecture conceived a good decade before the Internet and Web were invented, still alive and kicking in industry niches today (*e.g.* healthcare) albeit integrating or migrating to Web-based **A**pplication **P**rogramming **I**nterfaces and cloud services. "The electronic transmission of transactions (information) between two enterprises, promoting a more efficient paperless environment and often replacing the use of standard documents, including invoices or purchase orders" *(ISACA glossary)*.

TERM	MEANING
electronic Discovery, eDiscovery	"Discovery that includes the identification, preservation, collection, processing, review, analysis, or production of Electronically Stored Information. Note: Although electronic discovery is often considered a legal process, its use is not limited to the legal domain" *(ISO/IEC 27050-1).*
Electronic document	Digital document. "An administrative document (a document with legal validity, such as a contract) in any graphical, photographic, electromagnetic (tape) or other electronic representation of the content. Notes: Almost all countries have developed legislation concerning the definition, use and legal validity of an electronic document. An electronic document in whatever media that contain the data or information used as evidence of a contract or transaction between parties is considered together with the software program capable of reading it. The definition of a legally valid document as any representation of legally relevant data, not only those printed on paper, was introduced into the legislation related to computer crime. In addition, many countries in defining and disciplining the use of such instruments have issued regulations defining specifics, such as the electronic signature and data interchange formats" *(ISACA glossary).*
Electronic **H**ealth **R**ecord **(EHR)**	Digital data containing sensitive personal information concerning a patient's health, status, conditions, diagnoses, illnesses, treatments, test results, scans, *etc.*
Electronic information system	Computer system. "System, including electrical or electronic equipment, capable of processing, storing or transmitting digital data" *(EU CRA).*
ELectronic **INT**elligence **(ELINT)**	Gleaning useful intelligence information from the characteristics of electronic signals, aside from any intended communications content. Spectrum analysis and direction-finding techniques, for instance, can be used to characterise and perhaps identify a specific source of radiated electronic signals (not necessarily a radio transmitter as such). Part of SIGINT.
Electronic **mail (email, e-mail, E mail, mail)**	Popular digital communications mechanism that originally used private commercial networks (such as AOL, CompuServe, and internal corporate networks) before largely transitioning to mail servers on the Internet in the 1990s. Similar to the postal mail system, emails are sent and received asynchronously, meaning they wait in the recipient's mailbox until being opened and read, as opposed to real-time and near-real-time online chat systems such as **I**nstant **M**essaging. Vulnerable to numerous information security threats and incidents such as malware, spam, 419s and other frauds, coercion, misinformation, disinformation and social engineering, unpredictable delays and occasional non-delivery or misdelivery of messages, interception or inappropriate and unauthorised disclosure of confidential information, hacking of

TERM	MEANING
	mail servers, spoofing of email headers and message content, cryptanalysis, **T**raffic **A**nalysis, *etc*. "Correspondence [in the form of messages] between user terminals over a computer network. Note: In English, spelling variations are: E mail, E-mail, Email, and email" *(ISO/IEC 2382)*.
Electro**M**agnetic **P**ulse **(EMP) weapon, e-bomb,** **H**igh-**E**nergy **R**adio **F**requency **(HERF) gun**	Most electrical and electronic devices are inherently highly vulnerable to extremely strong electromagnetic fields and high voltages (such as those produced by nearby lightning strikes, nuclear explosions, or, at close range, Taser-type devices), and/or to the accompanying power surges, unless they are sufficiently well designed, engineered, shielded, and protected to be resilient. EMP-based cyberweapons (missiles, bombs, hand-deployed devices, *etc.*) are intended for cybertage, cyberwar, or cyberterrorism, perhaps physically damaging critical parts of the enemy's cyberinfrastructure, *e.g.* CHAMP.
Electronic **S**erial **N**umber **(ESN)**	Digital identifier burned into a device by the manufacturer. "A unique 32-bit number programmed into CDMA phones when they are manufactured" *(NIST SP 800-101)*.
Electronic signature	Digital signature. "Any technique designed to provide the electronic equivalent of a handwritten signature to demonstrate the origin and integrity of specific data (*e.g.*, digital signatures)" *(ISACA glossary)*.
El Gamal	Homomorphic public key (asymmetric) cryptographic protocol used principally to calculate and add a valid digital signature to an encrypted message without having to decrypt it first, hence requiring no knowledge of the content other than its creator.
Elicitation	Extraction of valuable information from intelligence sources using techniques such as persuasion, deception, and coercion. Social engineering technique whereby, during an apparently innocuous conversation, someone is surreptitiously probed for additional details.
Electrically **E**rasable **P**rogrammable **R**ead-**O**nly **M**emory **(EEPROM)**	Type of **P**rogrammable **R**ead-**O**nly **M**emory **I**ntegrated **C**ircuit that can be erased/reset one byte at a time by a voltage pulse, then reprogrammed. See also **E**rasable **P**rogrammable **R**ead-**O**nly **M**emory and flash memory.
Electronically **S**tored **I**nformation **(ESI) analysis**	Forensic analysis of digital evidence. "Element of an electronic discovery process focused on evaluating Electronically Stored Information for content and context to identify facts, relationships, key patterns, and other features that can lead to improved understanding of an ESI corpus. Note: Content and context can include key patterns, topics, people and discussions" *(ISO/IEC 27050-1)*.

TERM	MEANING
Electronically Stored Information (ESI) collection	Seizure or collection of digital evidence, *e.g.* from a crime scene. "Element of an electronic discovery process focused on gathering Electronically Stored Information and other related material" *(ISO/IEC 27050-1).*
Electronically Stored Information (ESI) identification	"Element of an electronic discovery process focused on locating potential sources and the criteria for selecting potentially relevant Electronically Stored Information" *(ISO/IEC 27050-1).*
Electronically Stored Information (ESI) preservation	Safe and secure storage of digital evidence to protect its integrity and value as much as possible. "Element of an electronic discovery process focused on ensuring that Electronically Stored Information is protected against inappropriate alteration or destruction. Note: In some matters or jurisdictions, there can be requirements to prevent spoliation of Electronically Stored Information" *(ISO/IEC 27050-1).*
Electronically Stored Information (ESI) processing	Extraction/recovery of usable digital evidence from storage media, *etc.* "Element of an electronic discovery process focused on extracting Electronically Stored Information and converting it, if necessary, to forms more suitable for ESI review and ESI analysis" *(ISO/IEC 27050-1).*
Electronically Stored Information (ESI) production	Providing, disclosing, or presenting digital evidence in court. "Element of an electronic discovery process focused on delivering or making available Electronically Stored Information. Notes: ESI production can also include getting Electronically Stored Information in appropriate forms and using appropriate delivery mechanisms. ESI production can be to any person or organisation" *(ISO/IEC 27050-1).*
Electronically Stored Information (ESI) review	Review of available digital evidence. "Element of an electronic discovery process focused on screening Electronically Stored Information based on specific criteria. Note: In some matters or jurisdictions, Electronically Stored Information that is considered privileged can be excluded from production" *(ISO/IEC 27050-1).*
Electronic Warfare (EW)	See cyberwar.
Elevation or escalation of privilege	Multistage attack on a computer system or device, application, information service, person, organisation, *etc.* in which an outsider (*e.g.* an intruder, hacker, or malware) first gains entry or a foothold innocuously through an inadequately secured entry-point at a general user access level, then exploits internal vulnerabilities to gain further access to and compromise assets that are not directly accessible from outside. Hackers commonly gain unprivileged access to target systems first (*e.g.* by registering as a basic user with limited rights), then use commands (often scripted for convenience and speed) to exploit technical vulnerabilities and gain privileged or unrestricted access and hence pwn the systems.

TERM	MEANING
Elliptic **C**urve **C**ryptography **(ECC)**	Form of public key encryption that relies on the unique mathematical properties of elliptic curves to generate pairs of related keys that are extremely difficult (*i.e.* computationally intensive) to generate from either one alone (a trapdoor function). "An algorithm that combines plane geometry with algebra to achieve stronger authentication with smaller keys compared to traditional methods, such as RSA, which primarily use algebraic factoring. Note: Smaller keys are more suitable to mobile devices" *(ISACA glossary)*.
Elliptic **C**urve **D**iffie–**H**ellman **(ECDH)**	Algorithm for cryptographic key exchange based on elliptic curve cryptography.
Email	*Abbrev:* **Electronic mail**.
Email **A**ccount **C**ompromise **(EAC)**	See **B**usiness **E**mail **C**ompromise.
Email bomb, spam bomb	Attempt to fill or overload a victim's email system by sending huge quantities of spam to it, *e.g.* by deliberately disclosing their email address to known spammers and high-volume mailing lists, causing frustration, cyber harassment, and **D**enial-**o**f-**S**ervice.
Emanation	Stream of energy (*e.g.* electromagnetic fields, power line fluctuations, lights, or sounds) emitted or radiated by a source (*e.g.* electronic device), incidentally and unintentionally conveying information. See also compromising emanation, side channel.
Emanations analysis	Emanation analysis. "Gaining direct knowledge of communicated data by monitoring and resolving a signal that is emitted by a system and that contains the data but is not intended to communicate the data" *(SANS glossary)*.
Emanation security	"The counter-measures, techniques and processes employed to reduce classified emanations from a facility and its systems to an acceptable level. Emanations can be in the form of RF energy, sound waves or optical signals" *(NZISM)*. See also TEMPEST, **S**ensitive **C**ompartmented **I**nformation **F**acility, Faraday shield.
Embarrass, embarrassment, embarrassing	Inappropriate or untimely disclosure of something particularly private relating to an individual, or highly confidential relating to an organisation. Whereas the impacts of such incidents on mature adults or companies may be trivial and temporary (shame), under some circumstances acute embarrassment can trigger extreme emotional reactions and lead to adverse consequences such as suicide, resignation, and perhaps a change of administration (accountability in action).

TERM	MEANING
Embedded **A**udit **M**odule **(EAM)**	Functions integral to an application system, routinely generating and storing records of significant activities and events (an audit trail) for subsequent analysis. Any means of disabling, reconfiguring, or bypassing the EAM, or editing, deleting, substituting, or concealing the saved records, would clearly be of concern to auditors intending to rely on the data, emphasising the design, implementation, management, and assurance of integrity controls and other security measures. "An integral part of an application system designed to identify and report specific transactions or other information based on predetermined criteria. Identification of reportable items occurs as part of real-time processing. Reporting may be real-time online or use store and forward methods. It is also known as an integrated test facility or a continuous auditing module" *(ISACA glossary)*.
Embedded malware	Malware (such as **A**dvanced **P**ersistent **T**hreats) hidden so deeply within a computer system (possibly in the hardware, microcode, firmware, device drivers, or **O**perating **S**ystem kernel) that only competent forensic analysis (possibly involving access to the source code, compilers and specialist tools) may reveal its presence.
Embedded software	"Software part of a larger system that performs some of the requirements of that system, *e.g.*, software used in an aircraft or rapid transit system. Such software does not provide an interface with the user" *(ISACA glossary)*.
Embedded system	Usually a diminutive computer system, perhaps a *thing*, encased entirely within a piece of electrical, electronic, or mechanical equipment such as a computerised machine tool or industrial plant, multifunction device, or **I**ndustrial **C**ontrol **S**ystem, monitoring and controlling the equipment. Often based on a custom **O**perating **S**ystem, designed to perform specific functions very efficiently, as opposed to multipurpose computing. May interface to a SCADA system or the **I**nternet **of** ***Things***.
Embezzlement	Theft of assets entrusted to a fraudster by the victim, *e.g.* deposits stolen by a dishonest fund manager. See also malfeasance.
Emergency	Particularly serious and dangerous situation or crisis that erupts with little if any warning. "Sudden, urgent, usually unexpected occurrence or event requiring immediate action. Note: An emergency is usually a disruption or condition that can often be anticipated or prepared for, but seldom exactly foreseen" *(ISO 22300)*.

TERM	MEANING
Emergency access	Route in to an access-controlled site, facility, building, room, system, *etc.* for use under exceptional/urgent circumstances, *e.g.* to fight a fire or get to work when all key holders are unavailable, or when someone forgets their logon password. "The process of a system user accessing a system that they do not hold appropriate security clearances for due to an immediate and critical emergency requirement" *(NZISM)*. See also emergency intervention.
Emergency **A**ction **P**lan **(EAP)**	Plan to help people survive life-threatening emergency situations or crises such as active shooters, holdups, attacks by terrorists or criminal gangs, bomb threats or blasts, or natural disasters. Such events may occur suddenly without warning; hence, the EAP and associated exercises prepare people for the possibility, practicing their responses (*e.g.* evacuate, hide, or defend yourself).
Emergency intervention	High-risk situation in which a competent support professional is explicitly authorised by management to intervene directly, *e.g.* modify a system, typically using a privileged emergency userID, bypassing, overriding, or skipping the normal system access controls and code migration processes in order to diagnose and resolve an urgent production issue.
Emergency management	Plans and preparations to deal with emergencies. "Overall approach for preventing emergencies and managing those that occur. Note: In general, emergency management utilizes a risk management approach to prevention, preparedness, response and recovery before, during and after potentially destabilizing events and/or disruptions" *(ISO 22300)*.
Emergency management capability	"Overall ability to effectively manage prevention, preparedness, response and recovery before, during and after potentially destabilizing or disruptive events" *(ISO 22300)*.
Emergency **O**perations **C**entre **(EOC), war room**	Highly resilient facilities and function providing a focal point in which to manage the response to disruptive disasters, *e.g.* directing, supporting, coordinating, and monitoring various incident response and recovery activities. Calmly informing and liaising between internal and external stakeholders, providing reliable, timely, and trustworthy information, is an important part of the EOC's rôle.
Emergency services	Collective name for the (mostly) public bodies who respond to various civil emergencies and crises, such as the police, fire brigade, ambulance, and other "blue light" services.
Emergency situation	Serious incident in progress, or one appearing and believed to be so (a false alarm). "A situation requiring the evacuation of a site. Examples include fires and bomb threats" *(NZISM)*.

TERM	MEANING
Emerging risk	Risk or risk category that is projected to become more important, increasing markedly in probability and/or impact over a specified timescale (*e.g.* within the year ahead or over the next N years). The inherent uncertainties of any risk are compounded by limited historical and topical information concerning associated factors such as the threats, vulnerabilities, impacts, controls, incidents, dependencies, complexities, rate of change, and detectability, and by simple human fear of the unknown.
Emissions **Sec**urity **(EMSEC)**	Securing systems against compromising emanations, *e.g.* using TEMPEST equipment in Faraday cages. "The protection resulting from all measures taken to deny unauthorised persons information of value that might be derived from communications systems and cryptographic equipment intercepts and the interception and analysis of compromising emanations from cryptographic—equipment, information systems, and telecommunications systems" *(Air Force Air Intelligence, Surveillance and Reconnaissance Agency instruction 33-203).* See also TECHINT, HUMINT, SIGINT, OSINT, COMINT, IMINT, ELINT, SCIF.
Emotet	Multifunctional malware that evolved from a bank Trojan in 2014 to become a loader for various forms of malware. Still in the wild in 2022. Used the EternalBlue exploit against **S**erver **M**essage **B**lock.
Emotion recognition	"Task of computationally identifying and categorizing emotions expressed in a piece of text, speech, video or image or combination thereof. Note: Examples of emotions include happiness, sadness, anger and delight" *(ISO/IEC 22989).*
Empower, empowerment	Give someone (generally a subordinate) more discretion/latitude and authority, enabling them to decide, do, and achieve more. Requires and indicates that the superior trusts them. "Authority given to a person or group to perform a specific task" *(ISACA glossary).*
EMS	*Abbrev:* **E**nterprise **M**obile **S**ecurity or **E**nterprise **M**obility **S**uite (see **M**obile **D**evice **M**anagement) or **E**nhanced **M**essaging **S**ervice, depending on context.
EMSEC	*Abbrev:* **Em**issions **Sec**urity.
Emulate, emulation	Imitate or copy something, hoping to be better than the original in some way. "Use of a data processing system to imitate another data processing system, so that the imitating system accepts the same data, executes the same programs, and achieves the same results as the imitated system. Note: Emulation is usually achieved by means of hardware or firmware" *(ISO/IEC 2382).* See also virtualisation. *Cf.* simulate/simulation.

TERM	MEANING
Encapsulate, encapsulation	Nested or concatenated network message structure with one type of data (the payload) packaged within another (the carrier), generally for communications security or routing purposes. "The technique used by layered protocols in which a lower-layer protocol accepts a message from a higher-layer protocol and places it in the data portion of a frame in the lower layer. In software development, it is a technique that isolates a system function or a set of data and the operations on those data within a module and provides precise specifications for the module" *(ISACA glossary)*. "The inclusion of one data structure within another structure so that the first data structure is hidden for the time being" *(SANS glossary)*.
Encapsulating Security Payload (ESP)	Cryptographic protocol, part of the IPsec suite, providing confidentiality, data integrity, and authentication for networks. "A protocol used for encryption and authentication within IPSec" *(NZISM)*. "A protocol designed to provide a mix of security services in IPv4 and IPv6. ESP can be used to provide confidentiality, data origin authentication, connectionless integrity, an antireplay service (a form of partial sequence integrity) and (limited) traffic flow confidentiality. (RFC 4303). Note: The ESP header is inserted after the IP header and before the next-layer protocol header (transport mode) or before an encapsulated IP header (tunnel mode)" *(ISACA glossary)*.
EnCase, OpenText Forensic	Popular digital forensics support tool-suite, used to examine (acquire, analyse, assess, evaluate, and report) digital evidence. A commercial product from OpenText Corporation. More info: https://www.opentext.com/products/forensic
Enclave	"Collection of information systems connected by one or more internal networks under the control of a single authority and security policy. The systems may be structured by physical proximity or by function, independent of location" *(CNSSI 4009)*.
Enclave boundary	"Point at which an enclave's internal network service layer connects to an external network's service layer, *i.e.*, to another enclave or to a Wide Area Network (WAN)" *(CNSSI 4009)*.
Encode	Transform information into a different representational format, perhaps for communications integrity and efficiency reasons or to facilitate automation and carrier signal modulation, *e.g.* converting text characters into their ASCII, EBCDIC, Morse code, or **Q**uick **R**esponse code equivalents. *Cf.* decode, secret code, encryption.
Encoder	The function that, or person who, encodes. "In sequence-to-sequence models, the part of the architecture that processes the input sequence to provide the vectors that are leveraged by the decoder (*e.g.*, the component that processes English sentences in an English-to-Spanish machine translator)" *(ISACA glossary)*.

TERM	MEANING
Encryption, encrypt, encipher, encipherment	Application of cryptography to maintain data confidentiality by preventing anyone without the correct decryption key/s gaining access to, extracting or determining the original plaintext or semantic content (meaning). "Cryptographic transformation of data. Notes: The result of encryption is ciphertext. The reverse process is called decryption" *(ISO/IEC 2382)*. "The process of taking an unencrypted message (plaintext), applying a mathematical function to it (encryption algorithm with a key) and producing an encrypted message (ciphertext)" *(ISACA glossary)*. "The transformation of data from plaintext (recognisable/readable data) to ciphertext (encrypted and not readable) using a cryptographic key. Data is encrypted using an encryption key to produce ciphertext and decrypted to plaintext using a decryption key. These keys may be the same (symmetric encryption) or two different keys (asymmetric encryption). Encryption alone does not prevent interference or unauthorised access but denies the intelligible content to unauthorised individuals, organisations or other would-be interceptors" *(NZISM)*. "Any procedure used in cryptography to convert plain text into cipher text to prevent anyone but the intended recipient from reading that data" *(NIST SP 800-101)*. "Cryptographic transformation of data (called 'plaintext') into a form (called 'cipher text') that conceals the data's original meaning to prevent it from being known or used" *(SANS glossary)*.
Encryption algorithm	Encryption algorithm: mathematical function and/or process (defined sequence of operations) involved in encrypting plaintext and decrypting ciphertext, *e.g.* **A**dvanced **E**ncryption **S**tandard. "A mathematically based function or calculation that encrypts/decrypts data, including block or stream ciphers" *(ISACA glossary)*.
Encryption key	Encryption key. "A piece of information in a digitized form used by an encryption algorithm to convert the plaintext to the ciphertext" *(ISACA glossary)*.
Endorsement	a. Confirmation of extended authority, *e.g.* permission to drive **H**eavy **G**oods **V**ehicles or motorbikes, added to a regular car licence. "Certain information may bear an endorsement marking in addition to a security classification. Endorsement markings are not security classifications in their own right and must not appear without a security classification. Endorsement markings are warnings that the information has special requirements in addition to those indicated by the security classification and should only be used when there is a clear need for special care. Endorsement markings may indicate: the specific nature of information; temporary sensitivities; limitations on availability; or how recipients should handle or disclose information" *(NZISM)*. b. Reputation boost, *e.g.* a glowing job reference from a referee, or positive feedback on a product from a customer. May be faked (disinformation) or misleading (misinformation).

TERM	MEANING
Endpoint	See endpoint device. "Any device that is connected to a network and serves as an entry point to that network" *(EU CRA)*. "A device that can communicate with a connected network" *(ISACA glossary)*.
Endpoint [incident] **D**etection and **R**esponse **(EDR)**	Software agents monitor endpoint devices for suspicious activities signalling potential threats or incidents (such as malware infections, zero-day attacks, or hacks), passing information to a server for analysis, triggering automated responses (*e.g.* logging off users to contain incidents), and notifying security personnel. "Systems focused on detecting and investigating suspicious activities on end points" *(ISACA glossary)*. See also e**X**tended **D**etection and **R**esponse.
Endpoint device	Networked electronic computer, device, or *thing*. "Network connected ICT hardware device. Note: Endpoint device can refer to desktop computers, laptops, smart phones, tablets, thin clients, printers or other specialized hardware including smart meters and Internet of things (IoT) devices" *(ISO/IEC 27002)*.
End-to-End Encryption **(E2EE)**	Messages are encrypted at source, communicated through the network including all intermediate servers in encrypted form (often with additional cryptographic processing) and decrypted at the final destination – as opposed to being encrypted, decrypted, and re-encrypted perhaps several times along the way. The obvious advantage is that the plaintext is not available to third parties at intermediate points, provided the encryption is strong enough to resist cryptanalysis anyway.
End-user, end user	See user. Term sometimes used by snooty **I**nformation **T**echnology professionals to refer dismissively or disparagingly to those who merely *use* computer systems, networks, devices, services, *etc.* without really understanding them. "1. A person, device, program or computer system that uses an information system for the purpose of data processing in information exchange. 2. A person whose occupation requires the use of an information system but does not require any knowledge of computers or computer programming" *(ISACA glossary)*.
End-**U**ser **C**omputing **(EUC)**	Practice of software development, coding, scripting, and support by citizen programmers. "The ability of end users to design and implement their own information system using computer software products" *(ISACA glossary)*.
End-user devices	"Information technology (IT) assets used among members of an enterprise during work, off-hours, or any other purpose. End-user devices include mobile and portable devices such as laptops, smartphones and tablets, as well as desktops and workstations. For the purpose of this document, end-user devices are a subset of enterprise assets" *(CIS Controls)*.

TERM	MEANING
Energy management system	"Equipment or infrastructure used to monitor, measure and control the energy consumption in private households, residential buildings or industrial customer installations. Note: The term 'energy management system' is also commonly used to refer to a set of applications used by operators of a transmission power grid to monitor, control and optimize the performance of the generation and/or transmission system" *(ISO/IEC 27019)*.
Energy supply	Provision of energy, usually electricity. "Process of generation, production or storage of energy for delivery to customers and the operation of an energy supply network" *(ISO/IEC 27019)*.
Energy utility	Power company. "Legal body or a person that supplies energy in the form of electricity, gas, oil or heat to other parties, to an energy distribution network or to a storage complex" *(ISO/IEC 27019)*.
Enforce, enforcement	Use of sanctions to discourage and penalise noncompliance or non-fulfilment of obligations, expectations, *etc.* May include additional oversight and the imposition of charges and changes by an authority on the organisations or individuals concerned. Has distinctly negative, demotivational, punitive connotations, in contrast to reinforcement.
Engagement, gig	Specific, discrete activity for which someone (usually a contractor or consultant) is engaged, assigned, employed, or contracted, such as an audit or consulting assignment, project, or performance. "A specific internal audit assignment or project that includes multiple tasks or activities designed to accomplish a specific set of related objectives" *(IIA GIAS)*.
Engagement conclusion	End of an engagement, or a summary of its key findings. "Internal auditors' professional judgment about engagement findings when viewed collectively. The engagement conclusion should indicate satisfactory or unsatisfactory performance" *(IIA GIAS)*.
Engagement letter	Contract formally specifying the authority, scope, and objectives, expectations, or requirements of an engagement (such as the deliverables and timescales) plus the associated terms and conditions. "Formal document that defines an IS auditor's responsibility, authority and accountability for a specific assignment" *(ISACA glossary)*.
Engagement objective	Engagement objective. "Statements that articulate the purpose of an engagement and describe the specific goals to be achieved" *(IIA GIAS)*.
Engagement planning	Planning performed before and often during an engagement. "Process during which internal auditors gather information, assess and prioritize risks relevant to the activity under review, establish engagement objectives and scope, identify evaluation criteria, and create a work program for an engagement" *(IIA GIAS)*.

TERM	MEANING
Engagement result	Report or other deliverable/s produced by an engagement, or more importantly the business outcome and value ultimately achieved by the client. "The findings and conclusion of an engagement. Engagement results may also include recommendations and/or agreed upon action plans" *(IIA GIAS)*.
Engagement supervisor	Person who guides, directs, oversees, or manages an engagement. "An internal auditor responsible for supervising an internal audit engagement, which may include training and assisting internal auditors as well as reviewing and approving the engagement work program, workpapers, final communication, and performance. The chief audit executive may be the engagement supervisor or may delegate such responsibilities" *(IIA GIAS)*.
Engagement work program	Plans, methods, procedures, checklists, *etc.* to be used in the course of an engagement. "A document that identifies the tasks to be performed to achieve the engagement objectives, the methodology and tools necessary, and the internal auditors assigned to perform the tasks. The work program is based on information obtained during engagement planning" *(IIA GIAS)*.
Engineering	The systematic and rigorous application of fundamental scientific, mathematical, and physical principles to specify, design, build, manage, maintain, and improve machines and processes that work well together, forming reliable, effective, efficient, productive, safe, and secure systems. Applications and specialisms include mechanical engineering, structural engineering, civil engineering, chemical engineering, electrical engineering, systems engineering, software engineering, **B**usiness **P**rocess **R**eengineering, safety engineering, social engineering, security engineering, reverse engineering, genetic engineering, production engineering, automobile engineering, aerospace engineering, financial engineering, *etc.*
Enhanced **D**ata for **G**SM **E**volution **(EDGE)**	"An upgrade to GPRS to provide higher data rates by joining multiple time slots" *(NIST SP 800-101)*.
Enhanced **M**essaging **S**ervice **(EMS)**	"An improved message system for GSM mobile devices allowing picture, sound, animation and text elements to be conveyed through one or more concatenated SMS messages" *(NIST SP 800-101)*. See also **S**hort **M**essaging **S**ervice, **G**lobal **S**ystem for **M**obile communications.
Enhancement	Improvement, betterment, strengthening, enlargement, *etc.* (context-dependent). "The application of process(es) to reveal additional detail or make that which is already visible more readily distinguishable from the background" *(FSRCoP)*.

TERM	MEANING
ENIAC (Electronic Numerical Integrator And Calculator)	First Turing-complete (general-purpose) electronic computer. Designed at the University of Pennsylvania by Mauchly and Eckert, ENIAC was delivered to the US Army in 1946 to calculate ballistics tables. It used 17,500 electronic valves (vacuum tubes) and 1,500 relays, weighed 30 tons and consumed 150 kW. It was programmed mechanically over several days using patch cables and switches. 50 years later, ENIAC was replicated as a single **I**ntegrated **C**ircuit approximately 3½ cm square, comparable to a Pentium-class **C**entral **P**rocessing **U**nit chip. See also Colossus.
ENISA	**E**uropean **U**nion agency for cybersecurity, originally named the **E**uropean **N**etwork **I**nformation **S**ecurity **A**gency. More info: https://www.enisa.europa.eu/
ENISA risk management glossary	Glossary appendix I from "Risk Management: Implementation principles and Inventories for Risk Management/Risk Assessment methods and tools" (2006), ENISA. More info: https://www.enisa.europa.eu/sites/default/files/publications/D1_Inventory_of_Methods_Risk_Management_Final.pdf
Enrolment	Process whereby, for instance, the physical characteristics of people whose identities have been authenticated by some other means are measured by and registered on biometric security devices, thus associating biometric characteristics with userIDs.
Enterprise	a. Entire organisation meaning the business, corporation, group, or conglomerate as a whole. "A natural or legal person engaged in an economic activity, irrespective of its legal form, including partnerships or associations regularly engaged in an economic activity" *(**G**eneral **D**ata **P**rotection **R**egulation)*. "A group of individuals working together for a common purpose, typically within the context of an organizational form such as a corporation, public agency, charity or trust" *(ISACA glossary)*. "The most superior unit that encompasses the entirety of the organization" *(OCEG GRC Glossary)*. "One or more organizations sharing a definite mission, goals and objectives which provides an output such as product or service" *(IEC 61508-4)*. b. Substantial project, initiative or activity, generally commercial in nature, *e.g.* criminal enterprise. c. Fictional Constitution-class heavy cruiser starship named after a decidedly non-fictional US nuclear-powered aircraft carrier.
Enterprise **A**rchitecture **(EA)**	Enterprise architecture. "A description of the fundamental underlying design of the business system components or one element of the business system (*e.g.*, technology), the relationships among them and the manner in which they support the enterprise's objectives" *(ISACA glossary)*.

TERM	MEANING
Enterprise architecture for IT	Technology architecture. "A description of the fundamental underlying design of the IT components of the business, the relationships among them and the manner in which they support the enterprise's objectives" *(ISACA glossary)*.
Enterprise asset	Enterprise asset. "Assets with the potential to store or process data. For the purpose of this document, enterprise assets include end-user devices, network devices, non-computing/Internet of Things (IoT) devices, and servers, in virtual, cloud-based, and physical environments" *(CIS Controls)*.
Enterprise **A**sset **M**anagement **(EAM)**	Structured and often software-assisted asset management processes for corporate assets (particularly valuable tangible assets such as buildings, industrial plant, vehicles, and corporate infrastructure) from their acquisition through to disposal, including preventive maintenance and repair activities.
Enterprise governance	See governance. "A set of responsibilities and practices exercised by the board and executive management with the goal of providing strategic direction, ensuring that objectives are achieved, ascertaining that risk is managed appropriately and verifying that the enterprise's resources are used responsibly" *(ISACA glossary)*.
Enterprise **G**overnance of **I**nformation and **T**echnology **(EGIT)**	Information Technology governance. "A concern for the value delivery from digital transformation and the mitigation of business risk that results from digital transformation. Three main outcomes can be expected after successful adoption of EGIT: benefits realization, risk optimization and resource optimization" *(ISACA glossary)*.
Enterprise **R**isk **M**anagement **(ERM)**	Broad, holistic corporate governance activity involving systematically identifying, assessing, treating, and monitoring/tracking risks that are significant to, and at the scale of, the enterprise as a whole (sometimes known as 'bet the farm' risks). This wide brief encompasses business/commercial, strategic, tactical and operational, geopolitical, health and safety, financial, liquidity, currency, product, market, counterparty, supply chain, environmental, people, compliance, cyber/technological and, of course, information risks. "The discipline by which an enterprise in any industry assesses, controls, exploits, finances and monitors risk from all sources for the purpose of increasing the enterprise's short- and long-term value to its stakeholders" *(ISACA glossary)*.
Enticement	Inducing or permitting someone to commit a crime that they would have committed anyway (*e.g.* the police using closely monitored 'bait cars' to entice vehicle thieves), then prosecuting them for so doing. A form of social engineering. *Cf.* entrapment.

TERM	MEANING
Entity	Generic, deliberately vague all-inclusive term frequently used in standards to indicate something nondescript such as an organisation, body, or item. "Any concrete or abstract thing that exists, did exist, or might exist, including associations among these things. Examples: A person, an object, an event, an idea, a process, *etc.* Notes: An entity exists whether data about it are available or not [and] active element within a subsystem. Cooperation between entities in a layer is controlled by one or more protocols" *(ISO/IEC 2382)*. "Item relevant for the purpose of operation of a domain that has recognizably distinct existence. Note: An entity can have a physical or a logical embodiment. Example: A person, an organization, a device, a group of such items, a human subscriber to a telecom service, a SIM card, a passport, a network interface card, a software application, a service or a website" *(ISO/IEC 27002)*. "Something that has a separate and distinct existence and that can be identified within context" *(ISO 22300)*. "A legal entity or management operating model of any size established for a particular purpose. A legal entity may, for example, be a business enterprise, a not-for-profit organization, a government body, or an academic institution. The management operating model may follow product or service lines, divisions, or operating units, with geographic markets providing for further subdivisions or aggregations of performance" *(Trust Services Criteria)*.
Entity-wide	"Activities that apply across the entity — most commonly in relation to entity-wide controls" *(Trust Services Criteria)*.
Entrapment	Inducing someone to commit a crime they would *not* otherwise have committed. Prosecution may fail if this is a legitimate and credible defence. *Cf.* enticement. "Deliberate planting of apparent flaws in a data processing system for the purpose of detecting attempted penetrations or for confusing an intruder about which flaws to exploit" *(ISO/IEC 2382)*. "Deliberate planting of apparent flaws in an information system for the purpose of detecting attempted penetrations" *(CNSSI 4009)*.
Entropy	Measure of randomness or disorder. A high degree of entropy in encryption keys is critical to prevent cryptanalysts directly guessing the keys by brute force, while high entropy in the ciphertext reduces the possibility of revealing useful information about the encryption algorithm, key, or plaintext through discernible patterns. Keys generated pseudorandomly have marginally less entropy than those of the same length generated randomly, a small difference that weakens them.

TERM	MEANING
Environment	Literally, the biosphere. Figuratively, the local context or business situation. "1. Everything that supports a system or the performance of a function. 2. The conditions that affect the performance of a system or function" *(ISACA glossary)*.
Environmental	Relating to or concerning the environment. "Of or having to do with the matters that can damage the physical elements of information systems (for example, fire, flood, wind, earthquake, power surges, or power outages). An entity implements controls and other activities to detect, prevent, and manage the risk of casualty damage to the physical elements of the information system from environmental elements" ***(Trust Services Criteria)***.
Environmental control	Control designed to mitigate unacceptable environmental risks such as decreasing the likelihood of adverse environmental conditions by maintaining appropriate levels of various parameters, *e.g.* using suitable **H**eating, **V**entilating, and **A**ir-**C**onditioning systems for office and computer facilities, or actively avoiding or reducing the emission of 'greenhouse gases' by various means.
Environmental risk	Risk pertaining to the local environment or the global ecosphere, *e.g.* physical degradation of archived materials due to humidity, temperature, and lighting issues, or climate change. "Threats to natural resources, human health and wildlife" *(ISACA glossary)*.
Environmental, **S**ocial, and **G**overnance **(ESG)**	Approach to evaluating an organisation's posture, risks, and opportunities concerning environmental performance (*e.g.* its policies and practices on climate change), social factors (*e.g.* relationships with local and global communities), and governance (*e.g.* leadership, executive pay, and internal controls).
EOC	*Abbrev:* **E**mergency **O**perations **C**entre.
Ephemeral port, dynamic port, private port	High-numbered network port opened only temporarily for a specific purpose (*e.g.* to pass data between authenticated and connected client and server nodes), as opposed to those accessible persistently (*e.g.* port 80 for HTTP traffic).
EPIC (**E**lectronic **P**rivacy **I**nformation **C**enter)	Privacy advocacy and activist group, describing itself as a "public interest research center in Washington, DC." More info: https://epic.org/
EpicShelter	Secret US surveillance system allegedly developed by Ed Snowden according to Oliver Stone's 2016 biographical film Snowden.
EPSS	*Abbrev:* **E**xploit **P**rediction **S**coring **S**ystem.
Equation Group	Hacker group allegedly associated with the **N**ational **S**ecurity **A**gency.

TERM	MEANING
Equipment under control	Restrained devices behaving themselves, playing nicely together? "Equipment, machinery, apparatus, or plant used for manufacturing, process, transportation, medical, or other activities" *(IEC 61508-4).*
Eradicate, eradication	To eliminate or remove something completely and permanently. "The process of identifying and removing the root cause of an incident from the network when containment measures have been deployed after the incident occurs" *(ISACA glossary).*
Erasable **P**rogrammable **R**ead-**O**nly **M**emory **(EPROM)**	Type of **P**rogrammable **R**ead-**O**nly **M**emory **I**ntegrated **C**ircuit that can be erased/reset by exposure to ultraviolet light through a transparent window located above the silicon chip, then reprogrammed. See also **E**lectrically **E**rasable **P**rogrammable **R**ead-**O**nly **M**emory.
Erase, erasure	To wipe out, delete, or remove. "The data subject's ability to obtain the erasure of personal data from the controller; also known as the right to be forgotten" *(ISACA glossary).*
Error	Accidental wrongdoing – the act or the result. A breakdown or failure of integrity. Although errors cause a far greater number of information security incidents than deliberate attacks, the effects are *usually* relatively minor. Furthermore, many errors are noticed and corrected immediately by the people, systems, or devices that caused them, with next to no consequential impact. Rarely, however, unnoticed/uncorrected errors (such as software bugs, the inappropriate or inept use of statistics, or errors of judgement) can have extremely serious or grave consequences such as corrupting business- or safety-critical data or leading to bad decisions and strategies. "Discrepancy between a computed, observed or measured value or condition and the true, specified or theoretically correct value or condition" *(ISO/IEC 2382).* "A deviation between a computed, observed or measured value or condition and the true, specified or theoretically correct value or condition" *(ISACA glossary).* "Anything which affects the accuracy and/or precision of an observation" *(FSRCoP).* See also mistake, tolerance.
Error check	Check for certain types of error, *e.g.* by proofreading or reviewing information, comparing checksums, or validating digital signatures. See also error detection, error correction.
Error correction	Manual or automated process of identifying and responding to various types of data error, often resolving the errors although for various reasons this may not always be possible, and may even introduce additional errors making things worse. Error correction codes, protocols, algorithms, and mechanisms are valuable integrity controls for datacommunications, storage, and processing, in general, and can be vital where the risk of data corruption is high or extreme (*e.g.* passing financial values or cryptographic keys over a noisy communication path). "Method used to correct erroneous data produced during data transmission, transfer, or storage" *(ISO/IEC 2382).*

TERM	MEANING
Error Correction Code (ECC)	Mathematical encoding scheme to reduce the error rate for digital data by checking for, and ideally identifying and reversing, bit errors, *e.g.* using a checksum or parity bit.
Error detection	Process, function, or system for detecting/identifying errors. "Techniques used to identify errors in data transfers" *(ISACA glossary)*. See also error check, error correction.
Escape	In virtualisation, refers to making an unauthorised connection from a guest system into the hypervisor, host **O**perating **S**ystem, or another guest. Allows hacking and data leakage between virtual systems, or access from a sandbox to the host.
Escort	Someone who accompanies or goes with another. "An individual who supervises visitors to secure areas to ensure uncleared visitors are not exposed to classified information, conversations equipment and other classified materials. Such visitors may include maintenance staff, IT contractors and building inspectors" *(NZISM)*. "A person who ensures that when maintenance or repairs are undertaken to ICT equipment that uncleared personnel are not exposed to data they are not authorised to access" *(AusISM)*.
Escrow	Safekeeping or custodianship of an asset by an escrow agent, enabling its release to one or more third parties if certain conditions (usually specified formally in an escrow agreement) are met. Examples include key escrow and source code escrow. The control hinges on the trustworthiness and competence of the agent.
Escrow agent	Escrow agent, the person or organisation trusted to keep an asset safe on behalf of others. "A person, agency or enterprise authorized to act on behalf of another to create a legal relationship with a third party regarding an escrow agreement; also known as the custodian of an asset according to an escrow agreement. Note: As it relates to a cryptographic key, an escrow agent is the agency or enterprise charged with the responsibility for safeguarding the key components of the unique key" *(ISACA glossary)*.
Escrow agreement	Contract for the provision of escrow services specifying (in part) the terms and conditions under which the asset may be released or disclosed – why, how, when, and to whom. "A legal arrangement whereby an asset (often money but sometimes other property such as art, a deed of title, website, software source code or a cryptographic key) is delivered to a third party (named an escrow agent) to be held in trust or otherwise pending a contingency or the fulfillment of a condition(s) in a contract. Notes: Upon the occurrence of the escrow agreement, escrow agents will deliver the asset to the proper recipient; otherwise, the escrow agents are bound by their fiduciary duty to maintain the escrow account. Source code escrow signifies a deposit of the source code for the software into an account held by an escrow agent.

TERM	MEANING
	Escrow is typically requested by a party licensing software (*e.g.*, licensee or buyer) to ensure maintenance of the software. The software source code is released by the escrow agent to the licensee if the licensor (*e.g.*, seller or contractor) files for bankruptcy or otherwise fails to maintain and update the software as promised in the software license agreement" *(ISACA glossary)*.
Escrow fraud	Type of fraud in which an escrow agent betrays the trust placed in them by the owner of assets placed in their care, normally embezzling the assets.
Escrow password	See emergency access. "Passwords that are written down and stored in a secure location (like a safe) that are used by emergency personnel when privileged personnel are unavailable" *(SANS glossary)*.
ESG	*Abbrev:* **E**nvironmental, **S**ocial, and **G**overnance.
ESI	*Abbrev:* **E**lectronically **S**tored **I**nformation. See digital evidence. "Data or information of any kind and from any source, whose temporal existence is evidenced by being stored in or on any electronic medium. Notes: ESI includes traditional e-mail, memos, letters, spreadsheets, databases, office documents, presentations and other electronic formats commonly found on a computer. ESI also includes system, application and file-associated metadata such as timestamps, revision history, and file type. Electronic medium can take the form of, but is not limited to, storage devices and storage elements" *(ISO/IEC 27040)*.
ESN	*Abbrev:* **E**lectronic **S**erial **N**umber.
ESP	*Abbrev:* **E**ncapsulating **S**ecurity **P**ayload.
Espionage	See spying. "Various intelligence activities involving the clandestine collection of information or materials for the purpose of obtaining an advantage over a rival" *(NZSTE)*.
Essential	The very essence of something, being crucially, critically, or vitally important to it. Likely to cause serious, severe, or existential impacts if it fails.
Essential communications	Critical or vital communications involving significant information risks, therefore deserving strong information security, resilience, safety, *etc.* "Communications whose contents are necessary for the prevention of or relief from disasters and for the maintenance of public order in adverse conditions" *(ISO/IEC 27011)*.
Essential function	Critical or vital function involving significant information risks, therefore deserving strong information security, resilience, safety, *etc.*

TERM	MEANING
Establishing the context	Framing, setting boundaries/scope, and clarifying objectives for a planned activity, according to the context. "Defining the external and internal parameters to be taken into account when managing risk, and setting the scope and risk criteria for the risk management policy" *(ISO Guide 73)*.
EternalBlue	**N**ational **S**ecurity **A**gency hacking tool exploited a zero-day vulnerability in Windows **S**erver **M**essage **B**lock. A month prior to hacker group Shadow Brokers disclosing this and other tools in April 2017, the NSA notified Microsoft who issued a critical patch. Unpatched, unmaintained, or unsupported networked systems were vulnerable to the Petya, WannaCry, and other ransomware outbreaks.
Ethereal	See Wireshark.
Ethical, ethics	Behaviour broadly accepted as appropriate, right, and proper, at least within the culture or organisation in which it occurs. Ethical beliefs and standards vary culturally and individually, however: a practice considered ethical within the hacker underground, for instance, may be entirely unacceptable and inappropriate (unethical) to society at large including information security and law enforcement professionals.
Ethical dilemma	Situation in which ethical constraints, objectives, rules, laws, regulations, directives, *etc.* come into conflict, requiring a worker either to make a difficult personal decision regarding how to resolve the dilemma and achieve the most beneficial or least damaging net outcome, or to seek further guidance from management, trustworthy colleagues, *etc.*
Ethical hacking	Hacking or penetration testing of computer networks and systems, *etc.* by white hats that is explicitly sanctioned, authorised, permitted, or commissioned by their owners for the purposes of identifying known security vulnerabilities. Normally covered by an explicit contract defining the scope, nature of tests permitted and forbidden, ethical and technical constraints, confidentiality and protection of the findings, *etc.* plus various other controls such as competent oversight, realtime monitoring, and hefty professional indemnity insurance.
Ethics hotline	See whistleblower's hotline.
Ettercap	Hacking/penetration testing tool, capable of mounting **M**an-**I**n-**T**he-**M**iddle attacks on **L**ocal **A**rea **N**etwork traffic.
EUC	*Abbrev:* **E**nd-**U**ser **C**omputing.

TERM	MEANING
European **D**ata **P**rotection **B**oard **(EDPB)**	Independent **E**uropean **U**nion body tasked with supervising and coordinating data protection (privacy) arrangements under **G**eneral **D**ata **P**rotection **R**egulation across Europe, for instance liaising with and guiding national privacy ombudsmen or supervisory authorities. Based in Brussels. More info: https://www.edpb.europa.eu/edpb_en
EV (Extended Validation)	Certification authorities may conduct additional checks on applicants for their digital certificates, typically offering the resulting 'EV' certificates at a higher price reflecting the additional costs and trustworthiness. They typically confirm the identity and legal status of the applicant organisation with the relevant national authorities – a kind of corporate background check – as required by the CA/Browser Forum, an industry body. Several inappropriate certification incidents (mis-issuance) call into question the value of voluntary compliance with an industry code, leading to calls for stronger oversight, tighter regulation and accreditation.
Evacuation	Act or process of efficiently emptying out a building, vehicle, zone, *etc.* of people, generally due to a genuine or emulated emergency. "Organized, phased and supervised movement of people from dangerous or potentially dangerous areas to places of safety" *(ISO 22300)*.
Evacuation drill	Evacuation exercise. "Activity that practises a particular skill related to evacuation and often involves repeating the same thing several times. EXAMPLE: A drill to practise safely evacuating a neighbourhood or village from a landslide" *(ISO 22300)*.
Evaluate, evaluation	Judge, appraise, or assess the value, quality, or significance of something relative to applicable expectations, requirements, or criteria. "Systematic process that compares the result of measurement to recognised criteria to determine the discrepancies between intended and actual performance. Note: Gaps in performance are inputs into the continual improvement process" *(ISO 22300)*. "An examination of products, processes, services or environments to identify strengths and weaknesses" *(ISACA glossary)*. "The act of judging subject matter by comparing evidence against suitable criteria" *(OCEG GRC Glossary)*.
Evaluation appraisal	Evaluation appraisal. "A consistent and reliable assessment method typically used to identify improvement opportunities or business performance without a rating. This includes clear and repeatable process steps used to conduct an initial gap analysis, performance improvement progress monitoring or readiness for benchmark appraisals or sustainment appraisals" *(ISACA glossary)*.

TERM	MEANING
Evaluation Assurance Level (EAL)	Assurance metric indicating the depth and rigor to which secure Information Technology products are evaluated against the Common Criteria on an 8-point scale. EAL0 is the simplest, most basic level, and EAL7 the most advanced. "Set of assurance requirements that represent a point on the Common Criteria pre-defined assurance scale" *(CNSSI 4009)*. "A numeric representation of the security functionality of a product gained from undertaking a Common Criteria evaluation. Each EAL comprises a number of assurance components, covering aspects of a product's design, development and operation. The range covers EAL0 (lowest) to EAL7 (highest)" *(NZISM)*.
Evaluation metric	Evaluation metric. "A measure used to assess how well models perform their tasks like accuracy, precision, or recall" *(ISACA glossary)*.
Evaluator	Person who assesses the value of something relative to expectations, requirements, or other criteria. "Individual assigned to perform evaluations in accordance with a given evaluation standard and associated evaluation methodology. Note: An example of an evaluation standard is ISO/IEC 15408 with the associated evaluation methodology given in ISO/IEC 18045" *(ISO/IEC 19896-1)*. See also assessor.
Evasion attack	Evading or bypassing controls in order to compromise a target, *e.g.* a burglar exploiting an inadequately secured loading dock, fire exit, or window to slip inside a building, while security guards protect the main entrance. "Attack where the attacker is able to avoid correct behaviour of an AI system on specific input or classes of inputs" *(ISO/IEC 27090 DRAFT)*.
Event	Generally, a trivial or benign form of incident, possibly just a small part of a developing situation (perhaps a symptom, indicator, flag, or forewarning) or a minor accident, *e.g.* while a single logon failure may simply result from someone forgetting or mistyping their credentials, it *might* be the first indication of a someone trying to guess someone else's password, perhaps even a determined credential stuffing or brute force attack. "Occurrence or change of a particular set of circumstances. Notes: An event can be one or more occurrences, and can have several causes. An event can consist of something not happening. An event can sometimes be referred to as an 'incident' or 'accident'" *(ISO/IEC 27000). [Further note]* "An event without consequences can also be referred to as a 'near miss', 'incident', 'near hit' or 'close call'" *(ISO Guide 73)*. "Occurrence or change of a particular set of circumstances. Notes: An event can be one or more occurrences, and can have several causes and several consequences. An event can also be something that is expected which does not happen, or something that is not expected which does happen. An event can be a risk source" *(ISO 31000)*.

TERM	MEANING
	"Something that happens at a specific place and/or time" *(ISACA glossary)*. "Something that happens, including a change in condition or behavior" *(OCEG GRC Glossary)*. "In the context of system logs, an event constitutes an evident change to the normal behaviour of a network, system or user" *(AusISM)*. "An observable occurrence in a system or network" *(SANS glossary)*. See also information security event.
Event type	Organisation-defined category, class, label, or tag associated with an event, incident, request, *etc.* for statistical and event-handling purposes, *e.g.* when Help Desk staff record it in the ticketing system typically used for problem/call management, or when logged automatically by a computer. "One of three possible types of events for the purpose of IT risk management: threat event, loss event and vulnerability event. Notes: The ability to consistently and effectively discern the different types of events that contribute to risk is a critical element in developing good risk-related metrics and well-informed decisions. Unless these categorical differences are recognized and applied, any resulting metrics lose meaning and, as a result, decisions based on those metrics are far more likely to be flawed" *(ISACA glossary)*.
Evidence	Facts that are evident, relevant, and hopefully convincing. Information used to demonstrate, substantiate, support, prove, disprove, or refute an argument, hypothesis, claim, assertion, accusation, *etc.* "1. Information that proves or disproves a stated issue. 2. Information that an auditor gathers in the course of performing an IS audit; relevant if it pertains to the audit objectives and has a logical relationship to the findings and conclusions it is used to support" *(ISACA glossary)*. "Information that either by itself or when used in conjunction with other information is used to establish proof about an event or action. Evidence does not necessarily prove truth or existence of something but contributes to establish proof" *(ENISA RM glossary)*. "Directly measurable characteristics of an IoT product that represent objective and demonstrable proof that a specific activity satisfies a specified requirement. Note: Examples are test reports, handbooks, files, checklists, scripts or images" *(ISO/IEC 27404 DRAFT)*. "Anything which is (or may be) admissible in criminal proceedings to assist the court in making any decision. This includes physical items/exhibits and information" *(FSRCoP)*. See also digital evidence, forensic evidence.
Evidence preservation facility	Typically a safe, vault, evidence room or similar secure storage facility providing excellent physical protection for forensic evidence. "Secure environment or a location where collected or acquired evidence is stored. Note: An evidence preservation facility should not be exposed to magnetic fields, dust, vibration, moisture or any other environmental elements (such as extreme temperature or humidity) that may damage the potential digital evidence within the facility" *(ISO/IEC 27037)*.

TERM	MEANING
Evil twin	Network hack using a fake/spoofed public Wi-Fi hotspot that forwards traffic from connected devices to a genuine public Wi-Fi hotspot or otherwise to the Internet. Silently intercepts/monitors traffic and has full access to any unencrypted content. It may also perform **M**an-**I**n-**T**he-**M**iddle attacks, surreptitiously manipulating the traffic *en route*.
EW	*Abbrev:* **E**lectronic **W**arfare. See cyberwar.
e-waste (electronic **waste)**	Unless competently checked and sanitised, surplus, redundant, or broken electronic and electrical equipment such as computer devices, peripherals, *things*, storage devices, components, subsystems, modules, spare parts, and even consumables (such as used laser printer transfer belts) and paperwork (such as system administration manuals and configuration printouts) destined for recycling or disposal may contain storage media, **I**ntegrated **C**ircuits and **P**rinted **C**ircuit **B**oards, *etc.* containing sensitive information; hence, there is a risk of inappropriate disclosure, in addition to the environmental and health and safety hazards arising from noxious and toxic chemicals such as gallium arsenide and **P**oly**C**hlorinated **B**iphenyls.
Examination **(exam)**	a. Formal test or assessment to determine whether a student or candidate's knowledge and competence in a particular area of study and expertise reaches the level deemed necessary for a pass mark, generally leading to the award of a qualification with evidence in the form of a fancy certificate (a credential). b. Analysis, evaluation in general. "A technical review that makes the evidence visible and suitable for analysis; as well as tests performed on the evidence to determine the presence or absence of specific data" *(NIST SP 800-101)*.
Exception	Extraordinary occurrence such as an unusual event, an unanticipated (and therefore potentially unhandled) state, condition or data value, an unauthorised noncompliance or nonconformity (whether intentional or not), or a situation requiring an unconventional or unplanned response (such as a special audit or contingency). "Condition that may arise during execution of a program, that may cause a deviation from the normal execution sequence, and for which means exist to define, raise, recognize, ignore, or handle it. Examples: '(ON ERROR) condition' in PL/1; overflow; range error" *(ISO/IEC 2382)*. "An event that causes suspension of normal program execution. Types include addressing exception, data exception, operation exception, overflow exception, protection exception and underflow exception" *(ISACA glossary)*. "The formal acknowledgement that a requirement of the NZISM cannot be met and that a dispensation from the particular compliance requirement is granted by the Accreditation Authority. This exception is valid for the term of the Accreditation Certificate or some lesser time as determined by the Accreditation Authority" *(NZISM)*. *Cf.* exemption.

TERM	MEANING
Exceptions and waivers	"An exception is NOT the same as a waiver. An exception means that the requirement need not be followed. A waiver means that some alternative controls or conditions are implemented" *(NZISM)*.
Exception report	"Reports generated by a program that identifies transactions or data that appear to be incorrect. Note: Exception reports contain items that may be outside a predetermined range or may not conform to specified criteria" *(ISACA glossary)*.
Exculpatory evidence	Forensic evidence allegedly demonstrating that someone or something was *not* involved in an incident, potentially absolving them of blame. "Evidence that tends to decrease the likelihood of fault or guilt" *(NIST SP 800-101)*. *Cf.* inculpatory.
Executable code	See machine code. "The machine language code generally referred to as the object or load module" *(ISACA glossary)*.
Execution, execute	a. Perform, carry out, operate, run, or put into effect something such as a strategy, plan, procedure, computer code for a program/application, contract, or agreement. b. Terminate a life deliberately and summarily, with extreme prejudice, *e.g.* murder, capital punishment, or sacrifice.
Executive management, executives, executive team, the Execs, senior management, top management, mahogany row, *etc.*	Senior managers running the organisation routinely in conjunction with lower management tiers and staff. Ultimately accountable to corporate stakeholders for both protecting and exploiting the organisation's assets. On behalf of the organisation's legal owners and other external stakeholders, the governing body (normally the Board of Directors) gives executives both the obligation or responsibility and the authority or control over the organisation's resources, *e.g.* ensuring that information risks are identified, assessed, and treated in accordance with the organisation's business objectives, exercising diligence and due care. In short, **the buck stops here**. "Person or group of people who have delegated responsibility from the governing body for implementation of strategies and policies to accomplish the purpose of the organization. Note: executive management is sometimes called top management and can include Chief Executive Officers, Chief Information Officers, Chief Financial Officers, Chief Information Officers, and similar roles" *(ISO/IEC 27000)*. "A group of executives, often a group of the senior-most executives in an organization" *(OCEG GRC Glossary)*. See also C-suite.
Executive Order 13526	Edict issued by the US president in 2009 concerning "Classified National Security Information." Formally defines three specific classification labels: Confidential, Secret, and Top Secret. More info: https://www.archives.gov/isoo/policy-documents/cnsi-eo.html

TERM	MEANING
Exemption, waiver	Noncompliance explicitly authorised by the relevant authority after due consideration and consultation with information risk and security experts. Normally limited in duration as well as scope, and compensating controls may be mandated. The person requesting an exemption (normally the information owner or risk owner) remains personally accountable for the residual risk and any consequential incidents. See also derogation. *Cf.* exception.
Exercise, drill	a. *[Noun]* Planned, managed, and observed activity, emulating a realistic business scenario or emergency situation to rehearse or practice, refine/improve, and gain assurance concerning the responses. "Activity that practises a particular skill and often involves repeating the same thing several times. EXAMPLE: A fire drill to practise safely evacuating a building on fire" *(ISO 22300)*. "Process to train for, assess, practise, and improve performance in an organization. Notes: Exercises can be used for validating policies, plans, procedures, training, equipment, and inter-organizational agreements; clarifying and training personnel in roles and responsibilities; improving inter-organizational coordination and communications; identifying gaps in resources; improving individual performance and identifying opportunities for improvement; and a controlled opportunity to practise improvisation. An exercise does not need an expectation of pass or fail. See also test" *(ISO 22300)*. b. *[Verb]* To use or apply, *e.g.* "In deciding not to prosecute, she exercised her discretion."
Exercise coordinator	Exercise leader, manager, or organisational representative. "Person responsible for planning, conducting and evaluating exercise activities. Note: In larger exercises, this function can include several people/staff and can be called 'exercise control.' Some countries use a term such as 'exercise director' or similar instead of 'exercise coordinator.' The exercise coordinator role is also responsible for the cooperation among internal and external entities" *(ISO 22300)*.
Exercise plan	Schedule/timetable, scope, scenarios, objectives, resources, rôles, *etc.* concerning a planned exercise, *e.g.* rehearsing and refining emergency/incident responses for business continuity and safety purposes. "Document in which the exercise policy plan has been translated to exercise goals and exercises, and in which an exercise programme for a certain year is reflected" *(ISO 22300)*.
Exercise programme	"Series of exercise activities designed to meet an overall objective or goal" *(ISO 22300)*.
Exfiltration, exfiltrate, egress	Covert extraction (removal, theft) of sensitive/valuable information assets from a supposedly secure system, device, network, or organisation. Suggests that the information is being 'pushed out' or 'carried out' by an agent within (a person or malware), but it may also be 'pulled out' by someone on the outside (a social engineer, hacker, *etc.*). *Cf.* infiltration.

TERM	MEANING
Exhaustive attack	See brute force attack.
Existential	Literally a matter of existence and survival such as disastrous incidents involving key risks leading to organisational collapse and failure, or the threat of extinction to vulnerable species due to climate change.
Exit strategy, exit plan	Whereas normally we consider the risks when going into a new situation, there may also be substantial risks involved in staying there and/or in getting out. With cloud computing, for instance, a breakdown in the relationship with the **C**loud **S**ervice **P**rovider may lead to problems for the organisation in retrieving its information and transferring the service to another CSP or in-house. Preparing a strategy or plan for ending the relationship gracefully is a form of **B**usiness **C**ontinuity **M**anagement, part of risk management.
Experience	Intangible knowledge, wisdom, competence, and/or skill that accumulates as one does something repeatedly. A valuable information asset. "Involvement at a practical level with projects related to the field of competence" *(ISO/IEC 19896-1).*
Experimentation	Scientific process involving the generation and testing of hypotheses by gathering pertinent information under strictly controlled experimental conditions. "A systematic approach to the process of testing new ideas, methods, or activities that applies principles and techniques at the data collection stage to ensure the generation of valid, defensible, and supportable conclusions" *(NIST SP 800-55v1).*
Expert, Subject Matter Expert (SME), expertise	Specialist with technical expertise – an unusually deep and extensive knowledge plus special skills, competencies, and capabilities in a particular topic or subject area, typically acquired during their career. "A practitioner who is competent to provide evidence of opinion in the [criminal justice system] in relation to a [forensic science activity]" *(FSRCoP).*
Expert system	**A**rtificial **I**ntelligence system emulating an expert. "Knowledge-based system that provides for solving problems in a particular domain or application area by drawing inferences from a knowledge base developed from human expertise. Notes: The term 'expert system' is sometimes used synonymously with 'knowledge-based system', but should be taken to emphasize expert knowledge. Some expert systems are able to improve their knowledge base and develop new inference rules based on their experience with previous problems" *(ISO/IEC 2382).* "AI system that accumulates, combines and encapsulates knowledge provided by a human expert or experts in a specific domain to infer solutions to problems" *(ISO/IEC 22989).*

TERM	MEANING
Expert witness	Expert with extensive experience and undeniable skill in specialised subjects such as cybersecurity, capable of analysing, presenting, and interpreting facts objectively for the court. Offers an informed, factual, dispassionate, and independent opinion on forensic evidence, free of bias towards the prosecution and the defence.
Explainability	Extent to which something can be rationally explained, understood, or justified. "Property of an AI system to express important factors influencing the AI system results in a way that humans can understand. Note: It is intended to answer the question 'Why?' without actually attempting to argue that the course of action that was taken was necessarily optimal" *(ISO/IEC 22989)*.
Exploding gradient	"Phenomenon of backpropagation training in a neural network where large error gradients accumulate and result in very large updates to the weights, making the model unstable" *(ISO/IEC 22989)*.
Exploit, sploit, exploitation	a. *[Verb]* To take advantage of or use. Although in the information security domain the term usually implies a negative, unethical, unwelcome, inappropriate, unauthorised, illegitimate, or harmful activity, it can also be positive (*e.g.* an organisation legitimately exploits its assets and capabilities to achieve its business objectives). "To take advantage of a vulnerability. Typically this is an intentional action designed to compromise the software's security controls by leveraging a vulnerability" *(SCP QRG)*. b. *[Noun]* Hacking program, malware payload, script, tool, technique, trick, and/or process used by a threat agent to take advantage of a security vulnerability. 'Sploit' is a leet form. "A method used to take advantage of a vulnerability" *(ISACA glossary)*. *Cf.* compromise.
Exploitable vulnerability	Vulnerability that is exposed to viable threats. "A vulnerability that has the potential to be effectively used by an adversary under practical operational conditions" *(EU CRA)*.
Exploit kit	See crimeware.
Exploit **P**rediction **S**coring **S**ystem **(EPSS)**	FIRST-led community project developing a model to estimate the threat, *i.e.* the probability that a given software vulnerability will actually be exploited in practice. Drew on threat intelligence from **C**ommon **V**ulnerabilities and **E**xposures and expert analysis. More info: https://www.first.org/epss/
Exploratory **D**ata **A**nalysis **(EDA)**	"Initial examination of data to determine its salient characteristics and assess its quality. Note: EDA can include identification of missing values, outliers, representativeness for the task at hand – see data quality checking" *(ISO/IEC 22989)*. "A data analysis technique where data collection is immediately followed by analysis with the goal of inferring what model would be appropriate" *(NIST SP 800-55v1)*. *Cf.* classical data analysis.

TERM	MEANING
Exposure	Relative, subjective measure of the degree to which a vulnerability could be exploited by a threat, *e.g.* although DMZ servers are generally more exposed to Internet hackers than corporate systems within its internal networks, they are less exposed to insider threats. A prominent organisation with strong brands, or a celebrity, is more exposed than their discreet and lesser-known peers – an example of security by obscurity. "Possibility that a particular attack will exploit a particular vulnerability of a data processing system" *(ISO/IEC 2382)*. "Extent to which an organization and/or interested party is subject to an event" *(ISO 31073)*. "The potential loss to an area due to the occurrence of an adverse event" *(ISACA glossary)*. "A threat action whereby sensitive data is directly released to an unauthorized entity" *(SANS glossary)*.
e**X**tended **D**etection and **R**esponse **(XDR)**	Whereas **E**ndpoint **D**etection and **R**esponse monitors and attempts to secure endpoints (networked **I**nformation **T**echnology systems or devices) individually, XDR collates, analyses, prioritises, and responds to security information (such as alarms and alerts) from *multiple* devices in the wider context of an organisation's entire network.
e**X**tensible **A**ccess **C**ontrol **M**arkup **L**anguage **(XACML)**	e**X**tensible **M**arkup **L**anguage function to specify authorisation policies, rôles, and access controls for **A**ttribute-**B**ased **A**ccess **C**ontrol. "A declarative online software application user access control policy language implemented in eXtensible Markup Language (XML)" *(ISACA glossary)*.
Extensible **A**uthentication **P**rotocol **(EAP)**	Flexible network framework capable of supporting multiple authentication methods and protocols, *e.g.* EAP-TLS (EAP-**T**ransport **L**ayer **S**ecurity), EAP-PSK (EAP-**P**re-**S**hared **K**ey), LEAP (**L**ightweight EAP). "A framework that supports multiple, optional authentication mechanisms for PPP, including clear-text passwords, challenge-response, and arbitrary dialog sequences" *(SANS glossary)*. *Cf.* **E**mergency **A**ction **P**lan.
Exterior **G**ateway **P**rotocol **(EGP)**	"A protocol which distributes routing information to the routers which connect autonomous systems" *(SANS glossary)*.
External	Outside, beyond the outer physical or notional perimeter or boundary of a person, system, network, organisation, site/property/facility, *etc. Cf.* internal.
External **A**ttack **S**urface **M**anagement **(EASM)**	That part of cybersecurity concerned with attacks perpetrated via external networks, particularly the Internet. Automation allows mapping and continuous monitoring of all externally exposed network systems, services, *etc.* (not just those managed by IT Department!) for known attack vectors.

TERM	MEANING
External audit	Audit conducted by or on behalf of some external party such as a regulatory authority, **C**ertification **B**ody, customer, or other stakeholder. "External audit includes what are generally termed a 'second-' or 'third-party' audit. Second-party audits are conducted by parties having an interest in the organisation, such as commissioning parties, or by other persons on their behalf. Third-party audits are conducted by external independent organisations. Such organisations provide certification or registration of conformity with requirements such as those of ISO 9001" *(FSRCoP)*. *Cf.* internal audit.
External context, external factors	Broad business, political, and social environment or situation within which the organisation exists and operates. "External environment in which the organisation seeks to achieve its objectives. Notes: External context can include the following: the social, cultural, political, legal, regulatory, financial, technological, economic, geological environment, whether international, national, regional or local; key drivers and trends affecting the objectives of the organisation; external interested parties relationships, perceptions, values, needs and expectations; contractual relationships and commitments; the complexity of networks and dependencies" *(ISO/IEC 27005)*. "External environment in which the organization seeks to achieve its objectives. Note: External context can include: the cultural, social, political, legal, regulatory, financial, technological, economic, natural and competitive environment, whether international, national, regional or local; key drivers and trends having impact on the objectives of the organization; and relationships with, and perceptions and values of external stakeholders" *(ISO Guide 73)*. "Categories of sources and forces that originate outside of the organization including: industry factors, market factors, economic, technology, societal, legal, political, environmental, demographic factors" *(OCEG GRC Glossary)*. *Cf.* internal context.
Externally exposed enterprise assets	"Refers to enterprise assets that are public facing and discoverable through domain name system reconnaissance and network scanning from the public internet outside of the enterprise's network" *(CIS Controls)*.
External network	External/third party network. "A network not controlled by the organization" *(NIST SP 800-171)*.
External party	Term used in the ISO27k standards as a synonym for third party. External implies *either* a totally distinct organisation *or* a part of the same organisation that falls outside the scope of its **I**nformation **S**ecurity **M**anagement **S**ystem.
External router, border router	"A router at the extreme edge of the network under control, usually connected to an Internet service provider (ISP) or other service provider" *(ISACA glossary)*.

TERM	MEANING
External stakeholder	External stakeholder. "An individual, institution, or entity outside of the organization that is affected by, or has an interest in, the company's decisions and activities" *(OCEG GRC Glossary)*.
External storage	"The location that contains backup copies to be used in case recovery or restoration is required in the event of a disaster" *(ISACA glossary)*.
External system, external component	External system or component. "A system or component of a system that is outside of the authorization boundary established by the organization and for which the organization typically has no direct control over the application of required security controls or the assessment of security control effectiveness" *(NIST SP 800-171)*.
External system service	Information service provided by an external system. "A system service that is implemented outside of the authorization boundary of the organizational system (*i.e.*, a service that is used by but not a part of the organizational system) and for which the organization typically has no direct control over the application of required security controls or the assessment of security control effectiveness" *(NIST SP 800-171)*.
External system service provider	Information service provider of an external system. "A provider of external system services to an organization through a variety of consumer producer relationships, including joint ventures, business partnerships, outsourcing arrangements (*i.e.*, through contracts, interagency agreements, lines of business arrangements), licensing agreements, and/or supply chain exchanges" *(NIST SP 800-171)*.
External user	Third party user. "Users, other than entity personnel, who are authorized by entity management, customers, or other authorized persons to interact with the entity's information system" *(**T**rust **S**ervices **C**riteria)*.
Extinguisher	Manual or automated device for putting out fires using an extinguishant gas (such as carbon dioxide, nitrogen, or FM-200), liquid (such as water), foam, powder, or cloth (fire blanket). May be portable/handheld, mounted to a vehicle, or permanently installed within a facility. A corrective control.
Extortion	Use of coercion (typically involving threats of cybertage, disclosure of confidential information or **D**enial-**of**-**S**ervice through ransomware, or physical harm) to obtain assets (generally money) from a target individual or organisation.

TERM	MEANING
Extranet	"Extension of an organisation's Intranet, especially over the public network infrastructure, enabling resource sharing between the organisation and other organisations and individuals that it deals with by providing limited access to its Intranet. Note: For example, an organisation's customers can be provided access to some part of its Intranet, creating an extranet, but the customers cannot be considered 'trusted' from a security standpoint" *(ISO/IEC 27033-1)*. "A private network that resides on the Internet and allows a company to securely share business information with customers, suppliers or other businesses as well as to execute electronic transactions. Notes: Different from an Intranet in that it is located beyond the company's firewall. Therefore, an extranet relies on the use of securely issued digital certificates (or alternative methods of user authentication) and encryption of messages. A virtual private network (VPN) and tunneling are often used to implement extranets, to ensure security and privacy" *(ISACA glossary)*.
Extraterritoriality	Legal principle that potentially gives the authorities powers over foreigners beyond their normal jurisdiction, *e.g.* European courts prosecuting and penalising non-European organisations for failing to comply with **G**eneral **D**ata **P**rotection **R**egulation by protecting the privacy rights of **E**uropean **U**nion citizens whose personal information they obtain.
Extremist, extremism	Someone whose views or ideology are way out of line with the general population. Between activist and terrorist on a notional threat scale.
Extrusion	Unauthorised transfer of information from the internal to external environments, typically using network connections and/or various covert channels or methods such as a drop. *Cf.* intrusion.

F

TERM	MEANING
Face recognition, facial recognition	Biometric derived from automated visual analysis of the characteristic size, shape, and layout of a human's facial features. "Automatic pattern recognition comparing stored images of human faces with the image of an actual face, indicating any matching, if it exists, and any data, if they exist, identifying the person to whom the face belongs" *(ISO/IEC 22989)*.
Facilitate	Enable, allow, remove barriers to smooth the way and provide the conditions, permissions, and resources necessary for something to proceed easily.
Facility	a. Place, site, installation, building, room, *etc.* "Plant, machinery, property, building, transportation units at sea/land/airport, and other items of infrastructure or plant and related systems that have a distinct and quantifiable business function of service. Note: A facility can have formal boundaries as defined by, for example, legislation" *(ISO 22300)*. "An area that facilitates government business. For example, a facility can be a building, a floor of a building or a designated area on the floor of a building" *(NZISM)*. "A physical space where business is performed. For example, a facility can be a building, a floor of a building or a designated space on the floor of a building" *(AusISM)*. "One or more physical locations containing systems or system components that process, store, or transmit information" *(NIST SP 800-171)*. See also **S**ensitive **C**ompartmented **I**nformation **F**acility. b. Function or capability to do something easily.
Fact, factual	Objective, proven or provable truth, supported by credible evidence, free of subjective interpretation, conjecture, and bias. "A truth known by actual experience or observation; something known to be true" *(FSRCoP)*.
Fact-check, fact check	Process of investigating and testing (critically evaluating) claims or assertions portrayed as facts in order to establish (confirm or refute) their veracity, accuracy, and credibility, to a level of confidence, proof, or rigour appropriate to the context, situation, audience, and implications.
Factor	a. Integer that divides another integer exactly, leaving no fractional residue (*e.g.* 2, 3, 4, and 6 are all factors of 12). Factorisation is the determination of factors for a given integer – a non-trivial mathematical and computing challenge for *very* large integers. b. Relevant variable, parameter, or characteristic that can account for or predict an outcome (*e.g.* voter fraud may be a factor in a disputed election). "A category of forces in the internal or external context" *(OCEG GRC Glossary)*. c. Company that lends money to businesses based on the anticipated value of their debtors (accounts receivable).

TERM	MEANING
Factor **A**nalysis of **I**nformation **R**isk **(FAIR)**	Open Group's structured risk analysis method examines various parameters (factors) in order to estimate the probable frequency (probability of occurrence) and probable magnitude of future loss events or scenarios (incidents) over a given period (*e.g.* a year). The probable frequency relates to the threats and vulnerabilities (susceptibilities). More info: https://www.fairinstitute.org/what-is-fair
Failover, fail-over	Manual or automated process for transferring the provision of resilient information services between redundant equipment, campuses, and/or communication paths following a failure, increasing service availability and hopefully avoiding unplanned interruptions, thereby averting more serious incidents. "The capability to switch over automatically (typically without human intervention or warning) to a redundant or standby information system upon the failure or abnormal termination of the previously active system" *(CNSSI 4009)*. "The transfer of service from an incapacitated primary component to its backup component" *(ISACA glossary)*.
Failsafe, fail-safe, fail-secure, fail-closed	Engineering principle/approach used heavily in safety-critical (vital) and other high security system and process architectures whereby a control failure or some adverse situation leaves the system/process in an inherently safe or secure – albeit perhaps only partially functional – state or condition. "Pertaining to avoidance of compromise in the event of a failure" *(ISO/IEC 2382)*. "A system or component that automatically places itself in a safe operational mode in the event of a failure" *(IEEE)*. See also secure-by-default, secure-by-design, **P**ower-**O**n **S**elf-**T**est.
Fail-soft, failsoft, fail-gracefully, fail-gently	Resilience arrangement that identifies impending performance/capacity constraints or other operational issues and responds dynamically by, for instance, de-prioritising relatively unimportant activities, shedding non-critical loads, or requesting additional resources in the hope of avoiding incidents. "Pertaining to a functional unit continuing to function in a degraded mode despite faults or manual out-of-limits operations. Note: Fault tolerance is a means for achieving failsoft operations" *(ISO/IEC 2382)*. "Selective termination of affected nonessential processing when hardware or software failure is determined to be imminent" *(CNSSI 4009)*. See also fault tolerance.
Fail-unsafe, fail-unsecure, fail-insecure, fail-open	Undesirable state for systems and processes that have not been *explicitly* designed to be safe and secure (*i.e.* failsafe) under all conditions, and hence are 'fragile', *e.g.* an access control that fails spontaneously or is actively disabled or bypassed in an attack, may permit inappropriate access that it was supposed to have prevented or at least detected. In the absence of compensating controls, security by obscurity can fail spectacularly if details of a supposedly obscure vulnerability are widely disclosed.

TERM	MEANING
Failure	Unplanned, unintended, unwelcome, and generally problematic situation, occurrence, event, or incident. "The inability of a system or component to perform its functions within specified performance requirements" *(IEEE).*
Failure analysis	Analysis of evidence relating to a failure in order to diagnose and determine the cause/s or factors that caused it … or that failed to prevent it (a different class of failure). "Determining the exact nature and location of a program error to fix the error, to identify and fix other similar errors and to initiate corrective action to prevent future occurrences of this type of error. Contrasts with debugging" *(ISACA glossary).*
Failure mode	Circumstances, conditions, or situations responsible for a failure, potentially precipitating an incident. "Manner by which a failure is observed. Note: It generally describes the way failure occurs and its impact on the operation of the system" *(ISO/IEC 27031).*
Failure Modes and Effects Analysis (FMEA)	Structured bottom-up engineering problem-solving method, pioneered by NASA, to analyse potential reliability, health and safety or security risks, or issues early in the **S**oftware **D**evelopment **L**ife**C**ycle, identifying how the system might possibly fail (*e.g.* due to **S**ingle **P**oints **o**f **F**ailure) and the consequences of those failures. Used to design more resilient, reliable, robust, secure, and safe systems.
FAIR	*Abbrev:* **F**actor **A**nalysis of **I**nformation **R**isk.
Fair use	Copyright laws generally permit *limited* use of copyright materials without the **I**ntellectual **P**roperty owner's explicit permission. The exemptions typically allow reproduction (such as quoting and summarising) of non-substantial or inconsequential parts of copyright materials for limited research and educational purposes, or to create backup/archive copies.
Faith	Sometimes described as 'blind trust' or 'wishful thinking,' faithful people believe in something without requiring hard evidence of its validity and veracity, sometimes to the point of ignoring or flatly and irrationally denying credible evidence to the contrary. Faith is not a control but a potentially harmful form of delusion, manipulation, coercion, or social engineering.
Fake	Spoofed or fabricated item that misrepresents the genuine article. See also counterfeit, deepfake.
Fake news	Propaganda in the form of fabricated 'news' stories circulated online through websites and social media, with the specific aim of misleading and influencing (coercing) the general public or specific target groups. Fake news stories may also be used as clickbait to drive traffic to a website, or for phishing.

TERM	MEANING
Fallback, fallback procedure	Use of robustness, resilience, redundancy, and/or failover features in a system or process to continue to deliver limited critical services under emergency conditions when the primary mechanisms have been compromised in an incident. A form of contingency planning. "A plan of action or set of procedures to be performed if a system implementation, upgrade or modification does not work as intended. Notes: May involve restoring the system to its state prior to the implementation or change. Fallback procedures are needed to ensure that normal business processes continue in the event of failure and should always be considered in system migration or implementation" *(ISACA glossary)*. See also failover.
False acceptance, type I error	Authentication failure in which an impostor is incorrectly associated with someone else's identity. "Occurs when an unauthorized person is identified as an authorized person by the biometric system" *(ISACA glossary)*. *Cf.* false rejection.
False **A**cceptance **R**ate **(FAR)**	Commonplace metric for a biometric system, measuring the proportion of authentications that exhibit type 1 errors. "The measure of the likelihood that the biometric security system will incorrectly accept an access attempt by an unauthorized user. A system's false acceptance rate typically is stated as the ratio of the number of false acceptances divided by the number of identification attempts" *(CNSSI 4009)*. See also **F**alse **R**ejection **R**ate.
False alarm	Normally refers to an unreliable alarm being triggered inappropriately, without the anticipated alarm condition having occurred. May also refer to an alarm *not* being triggered or being suppressed despite the alarm condition occurring. Whether intentional or accidental, both situations are control failures that may constitute security events or incidents.
False authorisation	See false acceptance.
False flag	Attempt to get an attack attributed to an innocent party, deflecting blame from and buying time for the true perpetrator while denigrating the falsely accused, tying up their resources with strenuous denial and outrage.
False negative	A positive finding falsely reported as a negative. "An example in which the model mistakenly predicted the negative class" *(ISACA glossary)*.
False positive	A negative finding falsely reported as a positive. "An erroneous acceptance of the hypothesis that a statistically significant event has been observed" *(NIST SP 800-55v1)*. "An example in which the model mistakenly predicted the positive class" *(ISACA glossary)*.

TERM	MEANING
False rejection, type II error	Authentication failure in which the system denies or fails to confirm a person's true identity. "When an authentication system fails to recognize a valid user" *(SANS glossary)*. *Cf.* false acceptance.
False **R**ejection **R**ate **(FRR)**	Commonplace metric for a biometric system, measuring the proportion of authentications that exhibit type II errors. "The measure of the likelihood that the biometric security system will incorrectly reject an access attempt by an authorized user. A system's false rejection rate typically is stated as the ratio of the number of false rejections divided by the number of identification attempts" *(CNSSI 4009)*. See also **F**alse **A**cceptance **R**ate.
False sense of security	Vulnerability involving an unwarranted and inappropriate faith in the security/control arrangements stemming from inadequate assurance and naïveté, *e.g.* believing that antivirus software totally prevents malware incidents.
Faraday shield or cage	Conductive metal foil or fine mesh enclosure designed to prevent the passage of radio waves, whether incoming or outgoing from the protected zone, for information security or safety reasons or to prevent RF interference. See also compromising emanation, **S**ecure **C**ompartmented **I**nformation **F**acility.
Fast-flux, fast-flux botnet	Black hat high-availability and concealment technique to change addresses of their command and control servers (single flux) and the **D**omain **N**ame **S**ystem servers (double flux) every few minutes to redirect botnet traffic (commands and/or data) dynamically to any of a set of distributed servers (perhaps a botnet) so that, even if individual servers in the set are shut down by the authorities, others remain reachable. "Protection method used by botnets consisting of a continuous and fast change of the DNS records for a domain name through different IP addresses" *(SANS glossary)*.
Fast **H**ealthcare **I**nteroperability **R**esources **(FHIR)**	Standard specification for secure exchange of medical data among healthcare information systems. Through REST APIs, systems communicate CRUD over HTTPS using XML, JSON, or RDF data formats, apparently. Managed by **H**ealth **L**evel **7** International. More info: https://www.hl7.org/index.cfm
Fault	a. Problem with a computer system, network, or device such as a security incident, complete or partial system failure (outage), program error/bug, virus, power cut, or some other generally unanticipated and/or undesirable mode of operation. "Abnormal condition that may cause a reduction in, or loss of, the capability of a functional unit to perform a required function" *(ISO/IEC 2382)*. b. Discontinuity in the Earth's crust caused by tectonic movements that can trigger earthquakes or volcanic eruptions, either of which can *really* spoil your day.

TERM	MEANING
Fault tolerance, fault-tolerant	High-availability architectural/design goal that systems should survive hardware faults and other incidents that would otherwise cause failures or unplanned outages. A strong but specific and costly form of resilience. "Ability of a functional unit to continue to perform a required function in the presence of faults or errors" *(ISO/IEC 2382)*. "A system's level of resilience to seamlessly react to hardware and/or software failure" *(ISACA glossary)*.
Fault tree analysis	"A top-down, deductive failure analysis in which an undesired state of a system (top event) is analyzed using Boolean logic to combine a series of lower-level events. An analytical approach whereby an undesired state of a system is specified and the system is then analyzed in the context of its environment of operation to find all realistic ways in which the undesired event (top event) can occur" *(NIST SP 800-30)*.
Fax [machine], facsimile, telefax, telecopy	"Transmission over a telecommunication system of images of pages and the creation of copies of those images at the receiving location" (ISO/IEC 2382). "A device that allows copies of documents to be sent over a telephone network" *(NZISM)*.
FBI	*Abbrev:* **F**ederal **B**ureau of **I**nvestigation.
FEC	*Abbrev:* **F**orward **E**rror **C**orrection.
Federal **B**ureau of **I**nvestigation **(FBI)**	Spooky US government agency responsible for *domestic* intelligence and surveillance targeting US citizens. Formed/renamed from the Bureau of Investigation by J Edgar Hoover in 1935. See also **C**entral **I**ntelligence **A**gency, **D**epartment of **H**omeland **S**ecurity. More info: https://www.fbi.gov/
Federal **I**nformation **S**ecurity **M**anagement **A**ct 2002 **(FISMA)**	US law imposing information risk-based security and privacy obligations on government agencies and, to some extent, their suppliers. "A statute (Title III, P.L.107-347) that requires agencies to assess risk to information systems and provide information security protections commensurate with the risk. FISMA also requires that agencies integrate information security into their capital planning and enterprise architecture processes, conduct annual information systems security reviews of all programs and systems, and report the results of those reviews to OMB" *(CNSSI 4009)*.
FedRAMP (Federal **R**isk and **A**uthorization **M**anagement **P**rogram**)**	US program imposing good practice security standards (principally NIST SP 800-53) on the suppliers of cloud computing services for government use.
Feedback	Information relating to the output or arising from/created by an activity, returned to the input of the same activity. Potentially a control mechanism: positive feedback drives the activity harder in the same direction, whereas negative feedback tends to moderate/slow, stop, or reverse it. "The reaction from the audience to a message" *(OCEG GRC Glossary)*.

TERM	MEANING
Feed **F**orward **N**eural **N**etwork **(FFNN)**	"Neural network where information is fed from the input layer to the output layer in one direction only" *(ISO/IEC 22989)*.
Femto cell, home cell, small cell	Cellphone signal repeater or base station providing cellular services in a limited local area, typically within a building, where the conventional cellular coverage is inadequate. "Small, low-power cellular base station. Note: A femto cell is typically designed for use in a home or small businesses" *(ISO/IEC 27033-6)*.
FFNN	*Abbrev:* **F**eed **F**orward **N**eural **N**etwork.
FHIR	*Abbrev:* **F**ast **H**ealthcare **I**nteroperability **R**esources.
Fibre channel, fiber channel	"Serial I/O interconnect capable of supporting multiple protocols, including access to open system storage, access to mainframe storage, and networking. Note: Fibre Channel supports point to point, arbitrated loop, and switched topologies with a variety of copper and optical links running at speeds from 1 gigabit per second to over 10 gigabits per second" *(ISO/IEC 27040)*.
Fibre channel interconnect	"Serial Small Computer System Interface (SCSI) transport protocol used on Fibre Channel interconnects" *(ISO/IEC 27040)*.
Fidelity insurance, fidelity bond	Insurance against the costs and losses to an organisation arising from incidents involving deliberate acts of disloyalty or dishonesty by its workers or agents (*e.g.* advisors and other service providers).
FIDO Alliance, Fast IDentity Online	Trade association aiming to standardise authentication through a suite of open and free specifications, *e.g.* FIDO **U**niversal **2**nd **F**actor (FIDO U2F), FIDO **U**niversal **A**uthentication **F**ramework (FIDO UAF), and FIDO2 combining **Web Auth**entication (WebAuthn) with FIDO **C**lient **T**o **A**uthenticator **P**rotocol (CTAP). See also passkey. More info: https://fidoalliance.org/
Fiduciary	Responsibility based on trust and ethics, *e.g.* officers of an organisation are legally and morally required, obliged, or bound to act in the best interests of the organisation's owners and other stakeholders, even if doing so conflicts with their personal interests. See also malfeasance, due care, fidelity insurance.
Fifth line [of accountability]	"The Governing Authority (Board) is ultimately accountable and responsible for the governance, management, and assurance of performance, risk, and compliance. While the governing authority may choose to delegate, this plenary accountability means that the governing authority must use due care to ensure that the right information systems are in place to learn about and address important performance, risk, and compliance issues – especially those that present 'red flags'" *(OCEG GRC Glossary)*. See three lines of defence model, first line, second line, third line, and fourth line.

TERM	MEANING
File	Assemblage of related information in physical (paper) or digital (data) form, such as an executable file, source code file, parameter file, log file, data file, customer file, personnel file, patient file, report file, or case file. "1. A set of related records treated as a unit, *e.g.*, in stock control, a file can consist of a set of invoices. 2. The largest unit of storage structure that consists of a named collection of all occurrences in a database of records of a particular record type" *(ISACA glossary)*.
File integrity monitoring	Administrative control function/process to monitor files for loss of integrity caused by corruption, degradation, interference/noise, bit errors, hardware or software issues, malware infection, replacement, or other unauthorised changes. Indicators or symptoms of integrity failures can include changes in file dates or sizes, parity or checksum errors, invalidation of digital signatures, unreliability, inability to access, read or execute the file, or (for paper files) disarray, tamper-evident marking such as a broken seal or signs of an office break-in. "Detecting changes to files and configurations to determine any changes to a baseline" *(ISACA glossary)*.
Fileless malware	Cloud-based malware that executes from dynamic memory, exploiting applications and utilities such as web browsers, PowerShell, and **W**indows **M**anagement **I**nstrumentation supposedly without leaving behind distinctive files on an infected system's disks. Powersploit's obfuscated PowerShell scripts, for instance, may not be detected reliably by antivirus packages and, even if they remain on the disk, may escape forensic analysis, perhaps concealed inside other files or in obscure folders.
File management	"A set of controls that cover the interaction between the code and other system files" *(SCP QRG)*.
File owner	Organisation, rôle, or person who literally/legally or notionally owns a computer or paper file, along with any associated property rights and obligations, responsibilities, or social expectations. May be a custodian, steward, or agent acting on behalf of the legal owner. May be accountable for its protection/security and legitimate exploitation to optimise its value. See also asset owner, data owner, information owner, system owner, network owner, infrastructure owner.
File system, filesystem	Structured, systematic, organised, indexed, or catalogued arrangement for digital data storage, search, retrieval, and referencing. "A software mechanism that defines the way that files are named, stored, organized, and accessed on logical volumes of partitioned memory" *(NIST SP 800-101)*.

TERM	MEANING
Filing system	Structured, systematic, organised, and usually indexed or catalogued physical (paper-based) arrangement for information storage, search, retrieval, and referencing. "Any structured set of personal data which are accessible according to specific criteria, whether centralised, decentralised or dispersed on a functional or geographical basis" *(**G**eneral **D**ata **P**rotection **R**egulation)*. "Structured set of personal data which are accessible according to specific criteria, whether centralized, decentralized or dispersed on a functional or geographical basis" *(ISACA glossary)*.
Filter	Means of controlling the flow of something according to its characteristics, such as security rules for a firewall or email service to pass, block, reject, redirect, copy, or delay particular types of traffic. "A device that controls the flow of data in accordance with a security policy" *(NZISM)*.
Filtering	"Process of accepting or rejecting data flows through a network, according to specified criteria" *(ISO/IEC 27033-1)*.
Financial action & controls	"Insurance, captives, hedging, reserves, or other financial instruments used to address risk, reward, and compliance" *(OCEG GRC Glossary)*.
Financial capital	"Liquidity, budgets, and other economic resources" *(OCEG GRC Glossary)*.
Finder	"An individual or organisation that reports a vulnerability under an agency's VDP [**V**ulnerability **D**isclosure **P**olicy?]" *(NZISM)*.
Finding	Conclusion resulting from competent analysis and evaluation of factual evidence. "The results of the examination and analyses carried out according to the documented examination strategy" *(FSRCoP)*. "In an engagement, the determination that a gap exists between the evaluation criteria and the condition of the activity under review. Other terms, such as 'observations,' may be used" *(IIA GIAS)*.
Fingerprint	Literally, the print mark left behind on a surface by a finger, a biometric. Often used figuratively to indicate characteristics that uniquely identify a person (*e.g.* using DNA profiling), system, or data. Despite theoretical claims as to their uniqueness, gathering and analysing any kind of fingerprint create practical constraints on the achievable accuracy; hence, there is a small but finite possibility that fingerprints from different individuals, systems, or data may not be distinguished in practice. Furthermore, being biometrics, confidentiality is a challenge for the owner, especially as they cannot be changed if compromised, at least not without surgery. "Sending strange packets to a system in order to gauge how it responds to determine the operating system" *(SANS glossary)*. See also hash.

TERM	MEANING
FinTech	Contraction of **fin**ancial **tech**nology, particularly the development and exploitation of innovative **I**nformation and **C**ommunications **T**echnology within the financial services industry. "Digital innovations and technology-enabled business model innovations in the financial sector" *(ISO/IEC 27562)*. See also AgriTech, Biotech, EcoTech/GreenTech, EdTech, FoodTech, GovTech, HealthTech, LegalTech, RegTech, RetailTech, and other tech neologisms.
FIPS 197 (**F**ederal **I**nformation **P**rocessing **S**tandard № **197)**	Standard published by NIST in 2001 specifying **A**dvanced **E**ncryption **S**tandard. More info: https://csrc.nist.gov/files/pubs/fips/197/final/docs/fips-197.pdf
FIPS-validated cryptography	"A cryptographic module validated by the Cryptographic Module Validation Program (CMVP) to meet the requirements specified in FIPS Publication 140-3 (as amended). As a prerequisite to CMVP validation, the cryptographic module is required to employ a cryptographic algorithm implementation that has successfully passed validation testing by the Cryptographic Algorithm Validation Program (CAVP)" *(NIST SP 800-171)*.
Fire	a. Along with smoke, one of many physical security threats, whether caused by accident or intentionally (arson). See also flood, intruder, malicious damage. b. "Initiate the action specified by a rule when the condition stated by the rule is satisfied" *(ISO/IEC 2382)*.
Fireball	Species of malware in the wild in 2018. A browser hijacker and downloader.
Firesafe	Safe or vault engineered, constructed, and installed to protect flammable contents (such as valuable backup/archival storage media) against the high temperatures of a building fire, as well as theft. Conformity of a given model to a particular fire resistance standard (*e.g.* **U**nderwriters **L**aboratories) may be tested and certified, requiring the firesafe contents to remain below a specified temperature (*e.g.* 65°C) for a specified period (*e.g.* an hour), while the entire firesafe is baked in an oven at a specified temperature (*e.g.* 927°C).
Firewall	Specialised network router or security application specifically configured as a security gateway monitoring, controlling, and filtering traffic between network segments, nodes, and devices according to a set of access control rules. "Type of security barrier placed between network environments – consisting of a dedicated device or a composite of several components and techniques – through which all traffic from one network environment traverses to another, and vice versa, and only authorized traffic, as defined by the local security policy, is allowed to pass" *(ISO/IEC 27033-1)*. "A system or combination of systems that enforces a boundary between two or more networks, typically forming a

TERM	MEANING
	barrier between a secure and an open environment such as the Internet" *(ISACA glossary)*. "A network protection device that filters incoming and outgoing network data, based on a series of rules" *(NZISM)*. "A logical or physical discontinuity in a network to prevent unauthorized access to data or resources" *(SANS glossary)*. See also packet filter, stateful firewall, deep packet inspection.
Firmware	Software loaded into a non-volatile memory chip or similar hardware device, normally embedded in hardware interfaces to control and communicate with specialist devices such as plant controllers, disk drives, or network cards. "Ordered set of instructions and associated data stored in a way that is functionally independent of main storage, usually in a ROM" *(ISO/IEC 2382)*. "The combination of a hardware device, *e.g.*, an IC, and computer instructions and data that reside as read only software on that device. Such software cannot be modified by the computer during processing" *(ISACA Glossary)*. "Software embedded in a hardware device" *(NZISM)*. "Computer programs and data stored in hardware – typically in read-only memory (ROM) or programmable read-only memory (PROM) – such that the programs and data cannot be dynamically written or modified during execution of the programs" *(NIST SP 800-171)*. *Cf.* hardware, middleware, wetware, malware, ransomware, adware, crimeware, scareware, shelfware, spouseware, stalkerware, spyware.
FIRST (Forum of Incident Response and Security Teams)	Global community, established in 1990, linking and supporting diverse cybersecurity and incident response teams. Runs CVSS and other projects, systems, and **S**pecial **I**nterest **G**roups. Collaborates with ISO, IEC, and other standards bodies. More info: https://www.first.org/
First line [of defence or accountability]	Managers primarily responsible for managing risks in the organisation as an integral part of their routine functions. "Individuals and teams that own and manage performance, risk, and compliance associated with day-to-day operational activities" *(OCEG GRC Glossary)*. See also second line, third line, fourth line, fifth line.
First responder	Someone 'first on scene' to assist at a serious physical, safety, or cyber crisis or emergency. Generally, a worker specifically tasked, trained, and prepared for the rôle, with the cool temperament, specialist knowledge, skills, and tools to offer immediate assistance (such as first aid and triage), take charge, liaise with colleagues, assess and secure the scene, pass status information to the incident management function, arrange evacuation, *etc.*
First responder interface	"Systems used to document and communicate information about a breach or other security incident by those first responding to the breach or incident" *(ISACA glossary)*.

TERM	MEANING
FISA	*Abbrev:* **F**oreign **I**ntelligence **S**urveillance **A**ct.
FISMA	*Abbrev:* **F**ederal **I**nformation **S**ecurity **M**anagement **A**ct.
Five Eyes	Strategic alliance/collaboration between the governments of the USA, Canada, UK, Australia, and New Zealand to share intelligence capabilities and information. Evolved from the UKUSA bilateral 'special arrangement' that had in effect been in place since the second World War or before. Whereas a nation's security services are not supposed to snoop on their own citizens, they can do so via their Five Eyes partners – a convenient means of bypassing the governance control. "The name of the intelligence alliance between the USA, UK, Canada, Australia and New Zealand which helps share information to keep its citizens as safe as possible from threats" *(UK National Cyber Security Strategy 2022)*.
Flare	Fireworks released *en masse* by a warplane to confuse and so misdirect heat-seeking missiles – a countermeasure. See also chaff.
Flash memory [media, chip, Integrated Circuit]	Type of **P**rogrammable **R**ead-**O**nly **M**emory **I**ntegrated **C**ircuit that can be erased/reset block-by-block, then reprogrammed. Commonly packaged as USB memory sticks, solid-state disks, and SD or compact flash memory cards. "A specific type of EEPROM" *(NZISM)*. See also **E**rasable **P**rogrammable **R**ead-**O**nly **M**emory and **E**lectrically **E**rasable **P**rogrammable **R**ead-**O**nly **M**emory.
Flash Read-**O**nly **M**emory **(ROM)**	Misleadingly named digital storage medium for firmware that can, in fact, be written and perhaps rewritten using a special 'flash' mode, although it normally can only be read. "Non-volatile memory that is writable" *(NIST SP 800-101)*.
Flaw, loophole	Fundamental and inherent vulnerability, weakness, or failing. In the context of software security, flaws are generally interpreted as fundamental defects or errors in the system architectural design that create or expose information security vulnerabilities. More formally in software engineering terms, they are situations that result in undefined states. Likewise, flaws in corporate governance, risk management, information security management, **B**usiness **C**ontinuity **M**anagement, *etc.* can result in an organisation's abject failure to characterise and appropriately treat foreseeable risks. "Error of commission, an omission, or an oversight that allows protection mechanisms to be bypassed or disabled" *(ISO/IEC 2382)*.
Flood	a. Surprisingly common physical security threat. Due to climate change, the number of natural disasters involving flooding and tsunamis has increased markedly in recent years, while leaking pipes, blocked sewers, and sprinkler systems remain as prevalent as ever. See also fire, intruder, malicious damage.

TERM	MEANING
	b. *Accidentally* overwhelm a computer system or network with a high volume of traffic, *e.g.* an abnormally high peak load on a heavily promoted website or a tsunami of spurious packets generated by a hardware error or anomalous situation on a node. c. *Deliberately* overwhelm a computer system or network with large volumes of generated traffic in an attempt to cause a **D**enial-**o**f-**S**ervice or to slip a covert attack past security controls that fail-unsafe. "Accidental or intentional insertion of a large volume of data resulting in denial of service" *(ISO/IEC 2382)*. "An attack that attempts to cause a failure in (especially, in the security of) a computer system or other data processing entity by providing more input than the entity can process properly" *(SANS glossary)*. See also **D**istributed **D**enial-**o**f-**S**ervice.
Fly lead	Tiny collar or weight to ground your pet insect? "A lead that connects IT equipment to the fixed infrastructure of the facility. For example, the lead that connects a workstation to a network wall socket" *(NZISM)*.
FM-200	Fire suppressant or extinguishant chemical from DuPont popular in automated fire control systems.
FMEA	*Abbrev:* **F**ailure **M**odes and **E**ffects **A**nalysis.
FNV (Fowler-**N**oll-**V**o)	Fast and efficient algorithm typically generates 32-, 64-, or 128-bit hash values. Used for various purposes in Linux, MySQL, OpenSSL, and gzip.
Folkways	Behavioural conventions that are generally acceptable/expected or unacceptable/frowned upon within a given social context or situation, *e.g.* hand-shaking, bowing, showing deference to authority. "Informal norms that govern everyday behaviors and social etiquette that are not strictly enforced, but where violations may lead to mild disapproval or social awkwardness (*e.g.*, table manners, punctuality, and appropriate dressing)" *(OCEG GRC Glossary)*.
Follow-up activity	"Activity that determines whether management has taken appropriate corrective actions to resolve deficiencies" *(ISACA glossary)*.
FoodTech	Contraction of **food tech**nology, particularly the development and exploitation of innovative computing technologies within the food industry. See also AgriTech, Biotech, EcoTech/GreenTech, EdTech, FinTech, GovTech, HealthTech, LegalTech, RegTech, RetailTech, and other tech neologisms.
Foothold, launch pad stepping stone	Computer system initially compromised on a hacked network, from which further probes and attacks may be launched. May be any vulnerable networked system, including *things*, multifunction devices, desktops, portables, servers, *etc.*

TERM	MEANING
Forbid	Explicitly prohibit, *i.e.* withhold consent, authorisation, or permission for someone to do something, go somewhere, *etc.* or face the consequences.
Force	a. Pressure to change the direction or speed of something, either physically or metaphorically. "A cause that is an emergent property of volatility, uncertainty, complexity, or ambiguity in the internal or external context" *(OCEG GRC Glossary)*. b. Powerful organisation, unit, team, or group of people, *e.g.* the police or armed forces, the workforce, a 'force to be reckoned with.'
Foreign **I**ntelligence **S**urveillance **A**ct 1978 **(FISA)**	US law unilaterally permitting the US government to snoop on foreigners' information for US intelligence, counterterrorism and (presumably) cyberwar, economic, political, or other purposes. Established the **F**oreign **I**ntelligence **S**urveillance **C**ourt as a SECRET oversight body to mediate official access requests by the **N**ational **S**ecurity **A**gency, **C**entral **I**ntelligence **A**gency, **F**ederal **B**ureau of **I**nvestigation, or other agencies/authorities.
Foreign interference	"An act by a foreign state, often acting through a proxy, which is intended to influence, disrupt or subvert New Zealand's national interests by deceptive, corruptive or coercive means. Normal diplomatic activity, lobbying and other genuine, overt efforts to gain influence are not considered interference" *(NZSTE)*.
Foreign national	"A person who is not an Australian citizen" *(AusISM)*.
Foreign system	"A system that is not managed by, or on behalf of, the Australian Government" *(AusISM)*.
Forensic, forensics	Relating to the law courts, *e.g.* forensic evidence. 'Forensic' is the adjective form. 'Forensics' is the noun. "Related to, or used in, courts of law. Note: This applies to video-surveillance used to produce legal evidence" *(ISO 22300)*. "The practice of gathering, retaining, and analyzing computer-related data for investigative purposes in a manner that maintains the integrity of the data" *(CNSSI 4009)*. See also digital forensics.
Forensic audit	See special audit.
Forensic copy	In order to guarantee the integrity of digital evidence, forensic analysis is performed on evidential copies that have been produced by appropriate methods and can be verified correct, while retaining the pristine best evidence to be presented in court. More than merely a duplication of an item of forensic evidence, a forensic copy is produced using a specified, forensically sound method that gives an extremely high level of assurance that the copy is an authentic and complete duplicate of the original, *e.g.* a bitwise image of a computer disk, created using proven and trustworthy forensic tools, with a cryptographic hash value identical to the original.

TERM	MEANING
	"A bit-for-bit reproduction of the information contained on an electronic device or associated media, whose validity and integrity has been verified using an accepted algorithm" *(NIST SP 800-101)*.
Forensic evidence	Evidence destined to be used in court. The legal system imposes strict integrity requirements on evidence, requiring strong assurance controls such as provision of the best evidence supported by a valid and unbroken chain of custody in order for it to be admissible.
Forensic examination	Formal, systematic, painstaking analysis and evaluation of forensic evidence by a forensic specialist. "The process of collecting, assessing, classifying and documenting digital evidence to assist in the identification of an offender and the method of compromise" *(ISACA glossary)*.
Forensic **S**cience Regulator **C**ode **o**f **P**ractice **(FSRCoP)**	Published under Crown Copyright by the UK Forensic Science Regulator in 2023, the code requires organisations providing forensic services in criminal cases to have **Q**uality **M**anagement **S**ystems and be accredited to standards such as ISO/IEC 17020 and 17025. A second version is expected to come into force towards the end of 2025. More info: https://www.gov.uk/government/publications/statutory-code-of-practice-for-forensic-science-activities
Forensic specialist, forensic analyst	Professional expert, trained, competent, diligent, trustworthy, and qualified in forensic techniques. "Locates, identifies, collects, analyzes, and examines data, while preserving the integrity and maintaining a strict chain of custody of information discovered" *(NIST SP 800-101)*.
Forger	a. Fraudster who commits forgery. b. Blacksmith.
Forgery	Fraudulent counterfeiting of items such as negotiable instruments (*e.g.* banknotes) and credentials.
Fork bomb, wabbit	Malware that spawns one or more copies of itself and starts those copies running, thus exponentially increasing in number until it exhausts finite computer system resources and thus, generally, brings the entire system crashing to a halt (a **D**enial-**o**f-**S**ervice attack). "Works by using the fork() call to create a new process which is a copy of the original. By doing this repeatedly, all available processes on the machine can be taken up" *(SANS glossary)*.
Formal, formalised, formality	Serious, structured, and documented process with strong controls to ensure strict conformity.
Form grabber, grabber, form jacking	Malware that captures data entered by the victim into online forms, particularly credentials used for authentication.

TERM	MEANING
For **O**fficial **U**se **O**nly **(FOUO)**	Deprecated US government label applied to unclassified information containing content that may have been exempt from mandatory disclosure under the **F**reedom **of** **I**nformation **A**ct. Replaced by **C**ontrolled **U**nclassified **I**nformation.
Forward **E**rror **C**orrection **(FEC), channel coding**	Digital datacommunications technique/protocol using an **E**rror-**C**orrection **C**ode algorithm to incorporate redundancy within the data stream, allowing a receiving system to detect and, if possible, reverse some data errors, reconstructing uncorrupted content ideally without the need for retransmissions. Has application in computer memory and disk communications, as well as networking, satellite and radio communications. "Error controlling mechanism for channels with a large amount of interference" *(ISACA glossary).*
FOSS	*Abbrev:* **F**ree **O**pen-**S**ource **S**oftware.
FOUO	*Abbrev:* **F**or **O**fficial **U**se **O**nly.
Fourth line [of accountability]	"The Executive team is accountable and responsible for the portfolio of organization-wide performance, risk, and compliance. The Fourth Line gains information from the First Line and the Second Line and assurance from the Third Line to make decisions about managing performance, risk, and compliance" *(OCEG GRC Glossary).* See three lines of defence model, first line, second line, third line, and fifth line.
Fragmentation, frag	Splitting something (*e.g.* network packets or files) into pieces for some reason (*e.g.* to limit the maximum size) while allowing them to be reassembled correctly later on. "The process of storing a data file in several 'chunks' or fragments rather than in a single contiguous sequence of bits in one place on the storage medium" *(SANS glossary).* See also defrag.
Fragment Overlap Attack	"A TCP/IP Fragmentation Attack that is possible because IP allows packets to be broken down into fragments for more efficient transport across various media. The TCP packet (and its header) are carried in the IP packet. In this attack the second fragment contains incorrect offset. When packet is reconstructed, the port number will be overwritten" *(SANS glossary).*
Frame	a. Falsely yet credibly accuse someone of something untoward, such as a crime, or deflect the blame their way in such a way that they *appear* guilty whereas the guilty party *appears* innocent. An integrity failure involving social engineering. b. Permanent physical structure into which a door or window is attached. Its inherent strength plus that of its fixture to the surrounding support and any hinges, catches, or locks, are critical to the ability to resist brute force attacks, fires, accidents, *etc.* c. Conceptual boundary, scope, or context ('frame of reference').

TERM	MEANING
	d. Network structure enveloping a packet fore-and-aft with addressing/routing and protocol information. "Data that is transmitted between network points as a unit complete with addressing and necessary protocol control information. A frame is usually transmitted serial bit by bit and contains a header field and a trailer field that 'frame' the data. (Some control frames contain no data.)" *(SANS glossary)*.
Framework	Conceptual model, physical structure, or skeleton linking related items together, providing a logical basis or structural foundation for construction, understanding, and use. Expressed in the form of blueprints, architecture, and design specifications, wire-frame diagrams showing nodes with linkages, systems (including **M**anagement **S**ystems), methods, approaches, protocols, standards, policies, guidelines, *etc.* May be theoretical or practical, rigid and formal, or flexible and customisable. Information security frameworks typically concern governance, information risk, compliance, privacy, and related matters, in whole or in part. "A basic conceptual structure used to solve or address complex issues. An enabler of governance. A set of concepts, assumptions and practices that define how something can be approached or understood, the relationships among the entities involved, the roles of those involved and the boundaries (what is and is not included in the governance system)" *(ISACA glossary)*.
Fraud, con	Theft, misappropriation, or similar crime involving deliberate deception or misrepresentation of the target/victim by a fraudster, usually for unfair advantage or gain. *Many* forms of fraud are known, *e.g.* assuming someone else's name and masquerading as them (identity fraud), promising a large payout on receipt of an advance fee, causing people unwittingly to call a premium-rate phone number and so rack up a large bill (toll fraud), tricking people into downloading malware or visiting unsavoury/undesirable websites (clickbait and phishing), falsifying or inflating expenses claimed (expenses fraud), falsifying financial records (accounting or tax fraud), substituting bank account numbers (payment fraud). "Any act involving the use of deception to obtain illegal advantage" *(ISACA glossary)*. "Any intentional act characterized by deceit, concealment, dishonesty, misappropriation of assets or information, forgery, or violation of trust perpetrated by individuals or organizations to secure unjust or illegal personal or business advantage" *(IIA GIAS)*. See also scam.
Fraud detection system	**I**nformation **T**echnology system and associated policies, procedures, *etc.* to detect, report, and perhaps investigate and resolve fraud – essentially a fraud **M**anagement **S**ystem. "Software as an application that supports monitoring, detection, and management of fraud or other misuse across users (*e.g.* customers), accounts,

TERM	MEANING
	channels, products and other entities (*e.g.* kiosks). Note: To deploy the fraud detection system, enterprise applications can integrate with a fraud detection engine that assesses the fraud risk of a transaction, from user navigation and application access, to any type of activity, such as a change of address, payment or retrieval of sensitive information" *(ITU-T X.1157).*
Fraud recovery fraud	Follow-on fraud in which fraudsters typically claiming to be lawyers, barristers, police officers, *etc.* promise to help victims of prior frauds recover their losses, prosecute the original fraudsters, *etc.* Fraud victims have, in effect, already demonstrated their naïveté, gullibility, and susceptibility in earlier incidents and may still be ignorant or in a psychological state of denial, hence being relatively vulnerable to subsequent frauds by selfish heartless exploitative nasty low-life pond scum totally devoid of compassion or morals.
Fraudster, con artist	Deceitful, deceptive person who commits fraud. Sometimes incorrectly called 'the fraud' which, strictly speaking, is the incident itself, not the perpetrator.
FREAK (Factoring RSA Export Keys)	Vulnerability in OpenSSL, disclosed in 2015, whereby a Man-In-The-Middle agent can request from an unpatched and insecurely configured server an 'export grade' (512-bit) RSA session key that is *much* more easily factored (broken) than the usual 1024-bit key, enabling HTTPS communications with the client to be decrypted. See also POODLE.
Freedom **O**f **I**nformation **A**ct **(FOIA), Official Information Act, Privacy Act**	Laws in many jurisdictions require public bodies to disclose potentially sensitive information under certain conditions, typically for public interest reasons, on request by a member of the public following the prescribed procedures. When entire documents or data sets are to be disclosed under FOIA, it may be necessary to redact parts, *e.g.* to safeguard ongoing covert operations and operatives (typically informers, moles, and spies) or to protect privacy or national security.
Free **O**pen-**S**ource **S**oftware **(FOSS)**	Software source code that its owner deliberately publishes and permits or encourages others to use, change, and ideally improve as a collaborative public/community effort. 'Free' refers to liberty, not necessarily price: some FOSS suppliers, for instance, provide additional chargeable services such as professional support and patching. "Software the source code of which is openly shared and which is made available under a free and open-source licence which provides for all rights to make it freely accessible, usable, modifiable and redistributable" *(EU CRA).*
Freeware	Software that is legitimately and legally free of usage restrictions, typically having been released intentionally into the public domain by its owner. "A type of software available free of charge" *(ISACA glossary).*

TERM	MEANING
Freezer spray	Hardware hacking or digital forensics tool. Deep-freezing RAM **I**ntegrated **C**ircuits using a freezer spray makes them retain their contents for longer when the system is powered off, perhaps long enough to enable the data to be recovered using specialist equipment.
Frequency	Number of occurrences within a defined time. "Number of events or outcomes per defined unit of time. Note: Frequency can be applied to past events or to potential future events, where it can be used as a measure of likelihood/probability" *(ISO 31073)*. "A measure that estimates how often the same event might occur" *(OCEG GRC Glossary)*.
Frequency analysis	Basic cryptanalytic technique using the distribution of individual characters, character sequences, or words in typical plaintext to guess at possible substitutions in ciphertext or code, *e.g. e* and *i* are the most frequent letters in most English texts, while *an, in, on, to,* and *of* are very common two-, three-, or four-character sequences (allowing for the usual leading and trailing spaces).
Frequency-hopping	Transmissions on a radio that automatically follows a rapidly changing cryptographically determined sequence of spot frequencies, making it harder or impossible for unauthorised listeners using basic radio receivers to reconstruct the complete transmission as opposed to authorised listeners using receivers programmed to follow the same frequency sequence. "Repeated switching of frequencies during radio transmission according to a specified algorithm, to minimize unauthorized interception or jamming of telecommunications" *(CNSSI 4009)*.
Frontier model	Advanced/cutting-edge **Ar**tificial **I**ntelligence system.
FSB (**F**ederal'naya **S**luzhba **B**ezopasnosti)	Russian intelligence service equivalent to the US **F**ederal **B**ureau **o**f **I**nvestigation, succeeded the Soviet KGB. Responsible for domestic state and border security, 'economic security' (industrial espionage), and for countering spying, organised crime, and terrorism.
FSRCoP	*Abbrev:* **F**orensic **S**cience **R**egulator's **C**ode **o**f **P**ractice.
FUD (**F**ear, **U**ncertainty, and **D**oubt)	Social engineering technique involving an emotional appeal based around disinformation, *i.e.* the deliberate dissemination of rumours, negative comments, exaggerated/false claims, and bare lies to hoodwink (mislead) targets into believing an 'alternative reality' or at least undermine their acceptance of the truth. Used in unethical marketing, propaganda, and lobbying. Taken to extreme, this may constitute fraud.

TERM	MEANING
Full-scale exercise	Business continuity exercise with a wide scope, emulating a serious and widespread incident that needs coordination between multiple responding organisations. "Exercise that involves multiple organizations or functions and includes actual activities" *(ISO 22300)*.
Fullz	Leet term for dumps containing full payment card details including the card numbers, CVV, cardholder's name and expiry date, and perhaps other personal information.
Function, functional, functionality	a. Operational purpose, intent, method, activity, process, algorithm, and subroutine, *e.g.* mathematical, application, system, or cryptographic functions. "1. A mathematical entity whose value (the value of the dependent variable) depends on the values of one or more independent variables, with not more than one value of the dependent variable corresponding to each permissible combination of values from the respective ranges of the independent variables. 2. A specific purpose of an entity, or its characteristic action. 3. In data communication, a machine action, such as carriage return or line feed" *(ISACA glossary)*. b. Department, team, business unit, agency, or some other part of an organisation, *e.g.* **I**nformation **T**echnology and **A**ccounts **P**ayable functions.
Functional analysis	Functional analysis. "A type of analysis that verifies whether or not each safety-critical software requirement is covered and that an appropriate criticality level is assigned to each software element" *(ISACA glossary)*.
Functional exercise	"Exercise to train for, assess, practise and improve the performance of single functions designed to respond to and recover from an unwanted event. Note: Functions can include an emergency operations centre (EOC) team, a crisis management team or fire-fighters decontaminating mock victims" *(ISO 22300)*.
Functional requirement	Requirement concerning the intended and unintended functions of a computer application, *i.e.* what it is and is not supposed to do or achieve for the users. "A requirement that specifies the function(s) that a system or system component must be able to perform" *(ISACA glossary)*. *Cf.* nonfunctional requirement.
Functional safety	"The detection of a potentially dangerous condition resulting in the activation of a protective or corrective solution to prevent hazardous events from arising, or the act of providing mitigation to reduce the consequence of the hazardous event. The aspect of the overall safety of a solution, solution component or piece of equipment that depends on the automatic protection mechanisms operating correctly in response to its inputs or failure in a predictable manner (fail-safe). An automatic protection system may be designed to properly handle likely human errors, hardware, solution or solution component failures and operational/environmental stress" *(ISACA glossary)*.

TERM	MEANING
Functional segregation	"Segregation based on the device function or intended function" *(NZISM)*.
Functional test	Category/type of test concerning the functionality required of a computer system, device, *thing*, product, cloud service, control, *etc.* "1. Testing that ignores the internal mechanism or structure of a system or component and focuses on the outputs generated in response to selected inputs and execution conditions. 2. Testing conducted to evaluate the compliance of a system or component with specified functional requirements and corresponding predicted results Synonymous with black-box testing and input/output driven testing. Contrasts with testing, structural" *(ISACA glossary)*. See also load test.
Fuzzing, fuzz testing	Software security assurance method (a form of black box testing) typically using large volumes of generated data to verify processing and application controls around boundary conditions, perhaps identifying vulnerabilities or other inappropriate system behaviours such as undefined internal states or conditions. "A method used to discover errors or potential security vulnerabilities in software" *(AusISM)*. "Similar to fault injection in that invalid data is input into the application via the environment, or input by one process into another process. Fuzz testing is implemented by tools called fuzzers, which are programs or script that submit some combination of inputs to the test target to reveal how it responds" *(NIST SP 800-95)*. "The use of special regression testing tools to generate out-of-spec input for an application in order to find security vulnerabilities" *(SANS glossary)*.

G

TERM	MEANING
GA	*Abbrev:* **G**enetic **A**lgorithm.
Galileo	EU-owned **G**lobal **N**avigation **S**atellite **S**ystem.
GameOver Zeus	Malware species in the wild in 2011. A variant of the Zeus family using a botnet with a distributed (peer-to-peer) rather than centralised command and control structure.
Gaming the system	Rule-driven systems and processes may be deliberately manipulated by those involved to gain advantage, just as game players may 'bend the rules' or 'push the boundaries.' Surrogation is one example. Potentially unethical and, taken to extreme, may constitute fraud.
GAN	*Abbrev:* **G**enerative **A**dversarial **N**etwork.
GandCrab	Ransomware species, offered as an online service (**M**alware-**as**-**a**-**S**ervice) with regular updates and technical support to help victims pay the ransom and decrypt their data.
Gap analysis	Examination of the differences or discrepancies between two states, such as the current or as-is state *versus* the desired or to-be state (part of change management), or the gap between expectations, requirements, or obligations imposed or suggested by laws, standards, policies, contracts, *etc.* and the actual situation in reality (part of compliance management). "A comparison that identifies the difference between the actual and the expected/specified system status" *(ENISA RM glossary)*.
Gardening leave	Workers in the course of leaving an organisation's employment or engagement/assignment may be explicitly excluded by management from the premises and its networks/systems, *etc*. This enforced paid leave mitigates unacceptable insider risks, particularly if they were in privileged/trusted positions with extensive access to information and other valuable corporate assets and/or if their competence, loyalty, or trustworthiness is in doubt (*e.g.* dismissals). 'Sending them home to do the gardening' may be deemed less risky/costly than allowing them to work normally during their notice periods.
GARP	*Abbrev:* **G**lobal **A**ssociation of **R**isk **P**rofessionals.
GASF	*Abbrev:* **G**IAC **A**dvanced **S**martphone **F**orensics.
Gate	Physical access control intended to limit access to a controlled area or zone only to those with permission to enter. The physical nature, strength, and integrity of a gate and any locks (along with the associated usage, guarding, monitoring, key management, and maintenance activities) govern the ability of intruders to slip or break through, while the nature, strength, and integrity of the associated fences, walls, and other physical barriers determine whether intruders can simply bypass it.

TERM	MEANING
Gateway	Logical security analogue of a gate, restricting access to a controlled network zone or device. See firewall. "Functional unit that connects two computer networks having different network architectures. Examples: LAN gateway, mail gateway. Note: The computer networks may be either local area networks, wide area networks, or other types of networks" *(ISO/IEC 2382)*. "Device that converts a protocol to another protocol" *(ISO/IEC 27040)*. "A physical or logical device on a network that serves as an entrance to another network (*e.g.*, router, firewall or software)" *(ISACA glossary)*. "Interface providing compatibility between networks by converting transmission speeds, protocols, codes, or security measures" *(CNSSI 4009)*. "Connections between two or more systems from different security domains to allow access to or transfer of information according to defined security policies. Some gateways can be automated through a combination of physical or software mechanisms. Gateways are typically grouped into three categories: access gateways, multilevel gateways and transfer gateways" *(NZISM)*. "[Device which] securely manages data flows between connected networks from different security domains" *(AusISM)*.
GAWN	*Abbrev:* **G**IAC **A**ssessing and **A**uditing **W**ireless **N**etworks.
GBFA	*Abbrev:* **G**IAC **B**attlefield **F**orensics and **A**cquisition.
GCAD	*Abbrev:* **G**IAC **C**loud Security **A**rchitecture and **D**esign.
GCCC	*Abbrev:* **G**IAC **C**ritical **C**ontrols **C**ertification.
GCDA	*Abbrev:* **G**IAC **C**ertified **D**etection **A**nalyst.
GCED	*Abbrev:* **G**IAC **C**ertified **E**nterprise **D**efender.
GCFA	*Abbrev:* **G**IAC **C**ertified **F**orensic **A**nalyst.
GCFE	*Abbrev:* **G**IAC **C**ertified **F**orensic **E**xaminer.
GCFR	*Abbrev:* **G**IAC **C**loud **F**orensics **R**esponder.
GCHQ	*Abbrev:* **G**overnment **C**ommunications **H**ead**Q**uarters.
GCIA	*Abbrev:* **G**IAC **C**ertified **I**ntrusion **A**nalyst.
GCIH	*Abbrev:* **G**IAC **C**ertified **I**ncident **H**andler.
GCIL	*Abbrev:* **G**IAC **C**yber **I**ncident **L**eader.
GCIP	*Abbrev:* **G**IAC **C**ritical **I**nfrastructure **P**rotection.
GCLD	*Abbrev:* **G**IAC **CL**ou**D** Security Essentials.
GCP	*Abbrev:* **G**oogle **C**loud **P**latform.

TERM	MEANING
GCPN	*Abbrev:* GIAC Cloud PenetratioN Tester.
GCSA	*Abbrev:* GIAC Cloud Security Automation.
GCTD	*Abbrev:* GIAC Cloud Threat Detection.
GCTI	*Abbrev:* GIAC Cyber Threat Intelligence.
GCWN	*Abbrev:* GIAC Certified WiNdows Security Administrator.
GDPR	*Abbrev:* General Data Protection Regulation.
GCPM	*Abbrev:* GIAC Certified Project Manager.
GDAT	*Abbrev:* GIAC Defending Advanced Threats.
GDSA	*Abbrev:* GIAC Defensible Security Architect.
GEIR	*Abbrev:* GIAC Enterprise Incident Response.
GenAI	*Abbrev:* Generative Artificial Intelligence or (rarely) **Gen**eral **A**rtificial **I**ntelligence (see Artificial General Intelligence).
General coding practices	"A set of controls that cover coding practices that do not fit easily into other categories" *(SCP QRG)*.
General computer control	"A control, other than an application control, that relates to the environment in which computer-based application systems are developed, maintained and operated and is therefore applicable to all applications. The objectives of general controls are to ensure the proper development and implementation of applications and the integrity of program and data files and computer operations. Like application controls, general controls may be either manual or programmed. Examples of general controls include the development and implementation of an IS strategy and security policy, the organization of IS staff to separate conflicting duties and the development of a disaster prevention and recovery plan" *(ISACA glossary)*.
General control	See common control.
General **D**ata **P**rotection **R**egulation **(GDPR)**	Virtually *identical* privacy laws were adopted across the **E**uropean **U**nion in 2018. GDPR introduced the right to be forgotten and other new requirements plus potentially *massive* ($billions) fines for non-compliance. However, this hyperglossary is *not* legal advice. IANAL.
General **P**acket **R**adio **S**ervice **(GPRS)**	Second-generation cellular network datacommunications protocol. Part of **G**lobal **S**ystem for **M**obile communications. "A packet switching enhancement to GSM and TDMA wireless networks to increase data transmission speeds" *(NIST SP 800-101)*.

TERM	MEANING
General user	"A system user who can, with their normal privileges, make only limited changes to a system and generally cannot bypass system security" *(NZISM)*.
Generative **A**dversarial **N**etwork **(GAN)**	Machine Learning algorithm that creates fake examples using a 'generator' neural network, feeding them along with genuine examples to a second 'discriminator' neural network. The generator is fine-tuned to increase the proportion of plausible but fake examples accepted by the discriminator, while the discriminator is fine-tuned to spot the fakes more consistently, improving both networks. "An architecture consisting of two neural networks, the generator and the discriminator, competing as adversaries in a zero-sum game, with the generator creating new data and the discriminator iteratively refining its ability to distinguish real data from generated data" *(ISACA glossary)*.
Generative **A**rtificial **I**ntelligence **(GenAI)**	Application of Artificial Intelligence to generate contextually appropriate written, verbal, or visual content in response to user prompts. "A branch of artificial intelligence (AI) that, by using models to learn underlying patterns and relationships within data, addresses the creation of new and diverse content, such as images, text, audio, or code" *(ISACA glossary)*. *Cf.* **Gen**eral **AI** (see Artificial General Intelligence).
Generative **P**retrained **T**ransformer **(GPT)**	Large Language Model trained with a substantial volume of data such as information freely published on the Internet (*e.g.* ChatGPT and Bard), internal corporate information (in-house GPTs), or specialist inputs (expert systems).
Genericide	Process in which dominant trademarks/brand names such as Aspirin, Coke, Kleenex, Hoover, WD-40, Band-Aid, Google, and ChatGPT gradually become associated with an entire category or type of generic products from various suppliers, all similar or equivalent at least in consumers' minds.
Generic process control	"A control that applies to all processes of the enterprise" *(ISACA glossary)*.
[Electrical] **Generator, generating set, emergency generator**	Alternator turned by an engine, motor, windmill, *etc.* to generate electricity. Typically used to restore electrical power to essential equipment during a grid blackout for business continuity purposes. Whereas small portable petrol-powered generators for home use generate about a kilowatt, large permanently installed diesel-powered industrial generators (including those used by black-start generating stations) typically generate hundreds of kilowatts, sometimes tens of megawatts.

TERM	MEANING
Genesis [marketplace/store]	Underground/illicit online cybercrime service offering stolen credentials, cookies, and system fingerprints, accessed by a persistent botnet. Active since 2017.
Genetic **A**lgorithm **(GA)**	Algorithm or approach that emulates the natural process whereby populations (of potential solutions to computing problems) evolve and adapt gradually through genetic inheritance and recombination, mutation and survival of the fittest. "Algorithm which simulates natural selection by creating and evolving a population of individuals (solutions) for optimization problems" *(ISO/IEC 22989)*.
Genetic data	Personal information (biometric data) relating to an individual's genetic makeup, such as their DNA sequence, DNA fingerprint, and genetic markers for characteristics and diseases. "Personal data relating to the inherited or acquired genetic characteristics of a natural person which give unique information about the physiology or the health of that natural person and which result, in particular, from an analysis of a biological sample from the natural person in question" *(**G**eneral **D**ata **P**rotection **R**egulation)*.
GENIE	SECRET US intelligence programs systematically compromising **I**nformation **T**echnology devices (endpoints) with spyware, extending the interception performed on communications links and **I**nternet **S**ervice **P**roviders (midpoints).
Gentleman's agreement	An 'understanding' – an informal arrangement or weak form of contract between individuals who trust each other. Based on the principle that 'a gentleman's word is his bond,' which of course hinges on the meaning of both 'gentleman' and 'bond.'
GEVA	*Abbrev:* **G**IAC **E**nterprise **V**ulnerability **A**ssessor.
Geolocation	Some portable computer devices and *things* use **G**lobal **P**ositioning **S**ystem, cell-sites, Wi-Fi services, or other means to identify their locations, and by implication the whereabouts of the corresponding users. Locational information can be sensitive, for instance allowing high-worth individuals/marks (such as executives, politicians, and celebrities) to be targeted. It can also be very valuable, *e.g.* to track a lost/stolen smartphone or vehicle, or a pet, child, Alzheimer's sufferer, or convict on day-release.
GFACT	*Abbrev:* **G**IAC **F**ound**A**tional **C**ybersecurity **T**echnologies.
Ghost	Chinese ransomware gang using **R**emote **A**ccess **Tro**jan since 2021. Its malware variants have been named Ghost, Cring, Crypt3r, Phantom, Strike, Hello, and Rapture.

TERM	MEANING
GIAC	US-based cybersecurity web examination and professional qualification company founded in 1999 by The Escal Institute of Advanced Technologies (trading as SANS Institute) under the name **G**lobal **I**nformation **A**ssurance **C**ertification. Offers more than fifty (!) qualifications (see below). More info: https://www.giac.org/
GIAC **A**dvanced **S**martphone **F**orensics **(GASF)**	GIAC's qualification for experienced digital forensics professionals. Covers: fundamentals of **M**obile **T**echnology forensics and forensic examination, device file system analysis and mobile application behaviour, event artefact analysis, and identification and analysis of mobile device malware. More info: https://www.giac.org/certifications/advanced-smartphone-forensics-gasf/
GIAC **A**ssessing and **A**uditing **W**ireless **N**etworks **(GAWN)**	GIAC's qualification for professionals securing wireless networks. Covers: weak encryption, IEEE 802.11 fuzzing, and Bluetooth; bridging the air gap, **D**enial-**o**f-**S**ervice, RFID attacks, and applications; hotspots, **N**ear **F**ield **C**ommunication, **S**oftware-**D**efined **R**adio attacks, and rogue networks; and wireless sniffing and client attacks, WPA, and ZigBee. More info: https://www.giac.org/certifications/assessing-auditing-wireless-networks-gawn/
GIAC **B**attlefield **F**orensics and **A**cquisition **(GBFA)**	GIAC's qualification for spooks and **I**ntelligence **C**ommunity (military/defense) professionals. Covers: efficient data acquisition from a wide range of (captured) devices, rapidly producing actionable intelligence, and manually identifying and acquiring data. More info: https://www.giac.org/certifications/battlefield-forensics-acquisition-gbfa/
GIAC **C**ertified **D**etection **A**nalyst **(GCDA)**	GIAC's qualification for security analysts. Covers: **S**ecurity **I**nformation and **E**vent **M**anagement architecture and SOF-ELK big data analytics platform; service profiling, advanced endpoint analytics, baselining, and user behaviour monitoring; and tactical SIEM detection and post-mortem analysis. More info: https://www.giac.org/certifications/certified-detection-analyst-gcda/
GIAC **C**ertified **E**nterprise **D**efender **(GCED)**	GIAC's qualification for experienced cybersecurity professionals. Builds on GIAC Security Essentials. Covers: network and cloud-based defensive infrastructure; penetration testing; digital forensics; incident response; network monitoring, forensics, and logging; and packet, intrusion, and malware analysis. More info: https://www.giac.org/certifications/certified-enterprise-defender-gced/
GIAC **C**ertified **F**orensic **A**nalyst **(GCFA)**	GIAC's qualification for forensic analysts formally investigating security incidents involving Windows and Linux systems. More info: https://www.giac.org/certifications/certified-forensic-analyst-gcfa/

TERM	MEANING
GIAC **C**ertified **F**orensic **E**xaminer **(GCFE)**	GIAC's qualification for digital forensics professionals. Covers: Windows forensics and data triage; registry, USB device, shell, and email forensics plus log analysis; and advanced web browser forensics. More info: https://www.giac.org/certifications/certified-forensic-examiner-gcfe/
GIAC **C**ertified **I**ncident **H**andler **(GCIH)**	GIAC's qualification for practitioners dealing with cybersecurity incidents. Covers: incident handling, computer crime investigation and common hacker tools, techniques, and exploits. More info: https://www.giac.org/certifications/certified-incident-handler-gcih/
GIAC **C**ertified **I**ntrusion **A**nalyst **(GCIA)**	GIAC's qualification for intrusion analysts. Covers network and server monitoring, **T**raffic **A**nalysis, intrusion detection, configuring and monitoring **I**ntrusion **D**etection **S**ystems, plus reading, interpreting, and analysing network traffic and related logs. More info: https://www.giac.org/certifications/certified-intrusion-analyst-gcia/
GIAC **C**ertified **P**roject **M**anager **(GCPM)**	GIAC's qualification for technology project managers. Covers: project governance (management structure and framework); time and cost management, communications, and **H**uman **R**esources; and quality and risk management, procurement, stakeholder management, and project integration. More info: https://www.giac.org/certifications/certified-project-manager-gcpm/
GIAC **C**ertified **Web** Application Defender **(GWEB)**	GIAC's qualification for web application security professionals. Covers: access control, AJAX security testing and authentication; **C**ross-**O**rigin **R**esource **S**haring, **C**ross-**S**ite **R**equest **F**orgery; encryption; file upload, response readiness, proactive defence, input flaws and validation; app framework issues and serialisation, session security and business logic, basics, architecture, configuration, and security. More info: https://www.giac.org/certifications/certified-web-application-defender-gweb/
GIAC **C**ertified **W**i**N**dows Security Administrator **(GCWN)**	GIAC's qualification for Windows security administrators. Covers: securing PowerShell, zero trust **M**ulti**F**actor **A**uthentication, endpoint protection, **O**perating **S**ystem and application hardening, **P**ublic **K**ey **I**nfrastructure management, and restricting administrative compromise. More info: https://www.giac.org/certifications/certified-windows-security-administrator-gcwn/
GIAC **C**loud **F**orensics **R**esponder **(GCFR)**	GIAC's qualification for incident response and digital forensics professionals. Covers: tracking and responding to incidents affecting Amazon, Google, and Microsoft cloud services, including logging, anomaly identification, and data extraction. More info: https://www.giac.org/certifications/cloud-forensics-responder-gcfr/

TERM	MEANING
GIAC **C**loud **P**enetratio**N** Tester **(GCPN)**	GIAC's qualification for penetration testers. Covers: cloud fundamentals, environment mapping, and service discovery; **A**mazon **W**eb **S**ervices and Azure cloud services and attacks, and cloud-native applications with containers and **C**ontinuous **I**ntegration/**C**ontinuous **D**elivery. More info: https://www.giac.org/certifications/cloud-penetration-tester-gcpn/
GIAC **C**loud Security **A**rchitecture and **D**esign **(GCAD)**	GIAC's qualification for cloud security architects. Covers: **I**dentity and **A**ccess **M**anagement, zero trust, network architecture and design, data protection, and centralised monitoring. More info: https://www.giac.org/certifications/cloud-security-architecture-design-gcad/
GIAC **C**loud **S**ecurity **A**utomation **(GCSA)**	GIAC's qualification for DevSecOps/cloud security professionals. Covers: DevOps and DevSecOps fundamentals, secure infrastructure, and configuration management; securing cloud architecture and continuous security monitoring; data and secrets protection, compliance; and secure automation of deployment, runtime, and content delivery. More info: https://www.giac.org/certifications/cloud-security-automation-gcsa/
GIAC **Cl**ou**d** Security Essentials **(GCLD)**	GIAC's qualification for inexperienced cloud security professionals. Covers: evaluation of **C**loud **S**ervice **P**roviders; planning, deploying, hardening, and securing single and multi-cloud environments; and basic cloud resource auditing, security assessment, and incident response. More info: https://www.giac.org/certifications/cloud-security-essentials-gcld/
GIAC **C**loud **T**hreat **D**etection **(GCTD)**	GIAC's qualification for cloud security incident response professionals. Covers: detecting attacks in the cloud, investigations and cyber threat intelligence, and assessments and automation in **A**mazon **W**eb **S**ervices and Azure. More info: https://www.giac.org/certifications/cloud-threat-detection-gctd/
GIAC Continuous **Mon**itoring **(GMON)**	GIAC's qualification for network security architects and security operations professionals. Covers: security architecture and **S**ecurity **O**perations **C**entres; network security architecture and monitoring; and endpoint security architecture, automation, and continuous monitoring. More info: https://www.giac.org/certifications/continuous-monitoring-certification-gmon/
GIAC **C**ritical **C**ontrols **C**ertification **(GCCC)**	GIAC's qualification for cybersecurity professionals using the CIS Critical Security Controls. Covers: background, purpose, implementation, and auditing of the 18 controls; and defences, implementation groups, control sensors, policies, cloud guidance, tools, automation, control measures, and standards mapping. More info: https://www.giac.org/certifications/critical-controls-certification-gccc/

TERM	MEANING
GIAC **C**ritical **I**nfrastructure **P**rotection **(GCIP)**	GIAC's qualification for critical infrastructure security professionals. Covers: **B**ulk **E**lectric **S**ystems cyber system identification and strategies to reduce impact ratings, NERC **C**ritical **I**nfrastructure **P**rotection terms and standards, strategic approaches for supporting technologies, and recurring tasks and strategies for CIP program maintenance. More info: https://www.giac.org/certifications/critical-infrastructure-protection-gcip/
GIAC **C**yber **I**ncident **L**eader **(GCIL)**	GIAC's qualification for incident managers. Covers: preparing for assessing, remediating, and closing incidents; developing, managing, and improving the team and process; identifying threats, vulnerabilities, and common attacks, and handling each incident type; and managing incident tasks and facilitating communications. More info: https://www.giac.org/certifications/cyber-incident-leader-gcil/
GIAC **C**yber **T**hreat **I**ntelligence **(GCTI)**	GIAC's qualification for incident response professionals. Covers: cyber threat intelligence; **O**pen-**S**ource **INT**elligence, campaigns, uses, and intrusion analysis; attribution, collecting and storing data sets; kill chain, diamond model, and courses of action matrix; and malware as a collection source, pivoting and sharing intelligence. More info: https://www.giac.org/certifications/cyber-threat-intelligence-gcti/
GIAC **D**efending **A**dvanced **T**hreats **(GDAT)**	GIAC's qualification for penetration testers. Covers: **A**dvanced **P**ersistent **T**hreats; detecting and preventing payload deliveries, exploitation, and post-exploitation activities; using cyber deception to gain intelligence for threat hunting and incident response; and adversary emulation. More info: https://www.giac.org/certifications/defending-advanced-threats-gdat/
GIAC **D**efensible **S**ecurity **A**rchitect **(GDSA)**	GIAC's qualification for security architects. Covers: network- and data-centric security strategies to architect a layered defence; assessing existing technology implementations to improve prevention, detection, and response; and understanding and applying zero trust principles. More info: https://www.giac.org/certifications/defensible-security-architecture-gdsa/
GIAC **E**nterprise **I**ncident **R**esponse **(GEIR)**	GIAC's qualification for incident response professionals. Covers: **I**ncident **R**esponse **T**eam management and coordination, enterprise incident detection and threat hunting, large-scale event correlation and timeline analysis, and multi-platform artefact analysis in various environments. More info: https://www.giac.org/certifications/enterprise-incident-responder-geir/
GIAC **E**nterprise **V**ulnerability **A**ssessor **(GEVA)**	GIAC's qualification for professional vulnerability assessors. Covers: vulnerability assessment framework planning and methodology; discovery and validation using network scanning, PowerShell scripting, *etc.* and remediation and reporting techniques. More info: https://www.giac.org/certifications/enterprise-vulnerability-assessor-geva/

TERM	MEANING
GIAC e**X**perienced **C**yber **S**ecurity **(GX-CS)**	GIAC's qualification for experienced cybersecurity professionals. Covers: network and **O**perating **S**ystem security, overall cybersecurity, tools and techniques, and common attacks and defences. More info: https://www.giac.org/certifications/experienced-cyber-security-gxcs/
GIAC e**X**perienced **F**orensics **A**nalyst **(GX-FA)**	GIAC's qualification for experienced digital forensics professionals. Covers: Windows host file system artefacts, system triage, volatile evidence, and log analysis; enterprise threat hunting identification and detection; and malicious threat actor activity in enterprise environments. More info: https://www.giac.org/certifications/experienced-forensics-analyst-gxfa/
GIAC e**X**perienced Forensics **E**xaminer **(GX-FE)**	GIAC's qualification for experienced digital forensics professionals. Covers: application execution, proving existence and recovering deleted artefacts, cloud storage artefact analysis, profiling configurations, investigating network activity and tracking physical devices, investigating file and folder interactions and browser activity, profiling userID usage, and investigating external device and USB activity. More info: https://www.giac.org/certifications/experienced-forensics-examiner-gxfe/
GIAC e**X**perienced Incident **H**andler **(GX-IH)**	GIAC's qualification for experienced cybersecurity incident handlers and analysts. Covers: incident handling and computer crime investigation, and computer and network hacker exploits. More info: https://www.giac.org/certifications/experienced-incident-handler-gxih/
GIAC e**X**perienced Intrusion **A**nalyst **(GX-IA)**	GIAC's qualification for intrusion analysts. Covers: protocol, network, and intrusion analysis. More info: https://www.giac.org/certifications/experienced-intrusion-analyst-gxia/
GIAC e**X**perienced **P**enetration **T**ester **(GX-PT)**	GIAC's qualification for experienced penetration testers (red/purple teamers). Covers: reconnaissance, network and vulnerability scanning, password attacks, exploitation, elevation of privilege, command and control, **A**ctive **D**irectory attacks, and Linux and Windows pentesting tools. More info: https://www.giac.org/certifications/experienced-penetration-tester-gxpt/
GIAC e**X**ploit Researcher and Advanced **P**enetratio**N** Tester **(GXPN)**	GIAC's qualification for penetration testers. Covers: network and cryptographic attacks; elevation of privilege and client-side attacks; restricted environments; Scapy, fuzzing, and source code analysis; shellcode and memory basics; and stack overflows and defeating advanced stack protections on Windows and Linux. More info: https://www.giac.org/certifications/exploit-researcher-advanced-penetration-tester-gxpn/

TERM	MEANING
GIAC **F**ound**A**tional **C**ybersecurity **T**echnologies **(GFACT)**	GIAC's entry-level qualification for cybersecurity professionals. Covers: hardware and virtualisation, networking, **O**perating **S**ystems, web, cloud, and data storage; **I**nformation **T**echnology fundamentals – logic and programming, Windows, Linux; and security foundations and threat landscape: concepts, exploitation and mitigation, forensics, and post-exploitation. More info: https://www.giac.org/certifications/foundational-cybersecurity-technologies-gfact/
GIAC **I**nformation **S**ecurity **F**undamentals **(GISF)**	GIAC's entry-level qualification for information security professionals. Covers: cybersecurity terminology, network basics, security policies, incident response, passwords, and introduction to cryptographic principles. More info: https://www.giac.org/certifications/information-security-fundamentals-gisf/
GIAC **I**nformation **S**ecurity **P**rofessional **(GISP)**	GIAC's qualification for information security professionals. Covers all eight domains of the ISC2 CISSP: asset security, communications and network security, **I**dentity and **A**ccess **M**anagement, security assessment and testing, security engineering, security operation, security and risk management, and software development security. More info: https://www.giac.org/certifications/information-security-professional-gisp/
GIAC **i**OS and **m**acOS **E**xaminer **(GIME)**	GIAC's qualification for digital forensics professionals. Covers: Apple Mac and iOS file systems, triage, application data, incident response, malware, intrusion analysis, user data and timeline analysis. More info: https://www.giac.org/certifications/ios-macos-examiner-gime/
GIAC Law of Data Security & Investigations [**leg**al] **(GLEG)**	GIAC's qualification for information security professionals involved in legal/compliance. Covers: business policies, conformity; contracts, agreements; data retention, eDiscovery; fraud, misuse; cybersecurity, investigations; and **I**ntellectual **P**roperty, privacy, **P**ersonally **I**dentifiable **I**nformation. More info: https://www.giac.org/certifications/law-data-security-investigations-gleg/
GIAC **M**achine **L**earning **E**ngineer **(GMLE)**	GIAC's qualification for cybersecurity professionals on **A**rtificial **I**ntelligence/**M**achine **L**earning. Covers: anomaly detection and optimisation; convolutional and deep learning neural networks; data acquisition, exploration, visualisation, manipulation, and analysis; inferential statistics and probability; loss functions; Python; and supervised and unsupervised learning. More info: https://www.giac.org/certifications/machine-learning-engineer-gmle/

TERM	MEANING
GIAC Mobile Device Security Analyst **(GMOB)**	GIAC's qualification for professionals securing **M**obile **T**echnology. Covers: managing Android and iOS devices and applications, jailbreaking and rooting mobile devices, mitigating mobile malware and theft, analysing and reverse-engineering applications, manipulating application behaviour, security assessing applications, and manipulating and intercepting encrypted network traffic. More info: https://www.giac.org/certifications/mobile-device-security-analyst-gmob/
GIAC **N**etwork **F**orensic **A**nalyst **(GNFA)**	GIAC's qualification for network forensics professionals. Covers: network architecture, protocols, and protocol reverse engineering; encryption, encoding, NetFlow analysis, attack visualisation, security event, and incident logging; and network analysis tools and proxies. More info: https://www.giac.org/certifications/network-forensic-analyst-gnfa/
GIAC **O**pen **S**ource **I**ntelligence **(GOSI)**	GIAC's qualification for **O**pen-**S**ource **INT**elligence professionals. Covers: OSINT methods, data collection, analysis, and reporting; harvesting data from the dark web; and operational security. More info: https://www.giac.org/certifications/open-source-intelligence-gosi/
GIAC **Pen**etration Tester **(GPEN)**	GIAC's qualification for penetration testers. Covers: test planning, scoping, and reconnaissance; in-depth network and host scanning and exploitation, post-exploitation, and infiltrating; Azure overview, integration, and attacks; and in-depth password attacks. More info: https://www.giac.org/certifications/penetration-tester-gpen/
GIAC **P**ublic **C**loud **S**ecurity **(GPCS)**	GIAC's qualification for cloud security professionals. Covers: evaluation and comparison of public **C**loud **S**ervice **P**roviders; auditing, hardening, and securing public cloud environments; and introduction to multi-cloud compliance and integration. More info: https://www.giac.org/certifications/public-cloud-security-gpcs/
GIAC **Py**thon **C**oder **(GPYC)**	GIAC's qualification for Python developers. Covers: Python language essentials, packet and data analysis, website and **D**ata**B**ase interaction, regular expressions, and exception handling and debugging. More info: https://www.giac.org/certifications/python-coder-gpyc/

TERM	MEANING
GIAC Red Team Professional **(GRTP)**	GIAC's qualification for professional penetration testers and red teamers. Covers: building adversary emulation using threat intelligence, attack infrastructure, target reconnaissance, gaining initial access, enumeration, network propagation, Active Directory attacks, bypassing defences (exploitation), collecting and exfiltrating sensitive data, and assignment reporting. More info: https://www.giac.org/certifications/red-team-professional-grtp/
GIAC Response and Industrial Defense **(GRID)**	GIAC's qualification for Operational Technology cybersecurity professionals. Covers: active defence, detection, and analysis in Industrial Control Systems; discovery and monitoring; digital forensics and incident response; malware analysis; and threat analysis and intelligence. More info: https://www.giac.org/certifications/response-industrial-defense-grid/
GIAC Reverse Engineering Malware **(GREM)**	GIAC's qualification for malware specialists. Covers: malware analysis using malware code and behavioural analysis fundamentals; Windows assembly code concepts and characteristics; in-depth analysis of malicious executables and self-defending malware; and analysis of malicious document files, .NET programs, and protected executables. More info: https://www.giac.org/certifications/reverse-engineering-malware-grem/
GIAC Security Essentials **(GSEC)**	GIAC's entry-level qualification for information security practitioners with some knowledge of Information Technology systems and networks. More info: https://www.giac.org/certifications/security-essentials-gsec/
GIAC Security Leadership Certification **(GSLC)**	GIAC's qualification for leaders and managers of the information security function. Covers: building a security program that meets business needs; managing security operations, teams, and projects; and the program lifecycle. More info: https://www.giac.org/certifications/security-leadership-gslc/
GIAC Security Operations Certified **(GSOC)**	GIAC's qualification for blue teamers, incident investigators, Security Operations Centre managers, *etc.* Covers: SOC monitoring, incident response, incident management systems, Threat Intelligence Platforms and Security Information and Event Management; analysis and defence; and designing, automating, and enriching security operations. More info: https://www.giac.org/certifications/security-operations-certified-gsoc/
GIAC Security Operations Manager **(GSOM)**	GIAC's qualification for Security Operations Centre managers and leaders. Covers: designing, planning, and managing the SOC; prioritising and collecting logs; developing alert use cases and incident response playbooks; and SOC metrics, analytics, and strategies. More info: https://www.giac.org/certifications/security-operations-manager-gsom/

TERM	MEANING
GIAC **Str**a**t**egic Planning, Policy, and Leadership **(GSTRT)**	GIAC's qualification for **C**hief **I**nformation **S**ecurity **O**fficers. Covers: business and threat analysis, security programs and security policy, and effective leadership and communications. More info: https://www.giac.org/certifications/strategic-planning-policy-leadership-gstrt/
GIAC **S**ystems and **N**etwork **A**uditor **(GSNA)**	GIAC's qualification for **I**nformation **T**echnology auditors. Covers: auditing, risk assessments, and reporting; network and perimeter auditing and monitoring; web application auditing; and auditing and monitoring in Windows and Unix environments. More info: https://www.giac.org/certifications/systems-network-auditor-gsna/
GIAC **W**eb **A**pplication **P**enetration **T**ester **(GWAPT)**	GIAC's qualification for penetration testers and web application developers. Covers: overview, authentication attacks, and configuration testing; web app session management, SQL injection, testing tools; and **C**ross-**S**ite **R**equest **F**orgery and cross-site scripting, client injection attack, reconnaissance, and mapping. More info: https://www.giac.org/certifications/web-application-penetration-tester-gwapt/
GIAS	*Abbrev:* **G**lobal **I**nternal **A**udit **S**tandards®.
GICSP	*Abbrev:* **G**lobal **I**ndustrial **C**yber **S**ecurity **P**rofessional.
GIG	*Abbrev:* **G**lobal **I**nformation **G**rid.
Gig	See engagement.
GII	*Abbrev:* **G**lobal **I**nformation **I**nfrastructure.
GIME	*Abbrev:* **G**IAC **i**OS and **m**acOS **E**xaminer.
GISF	*Abbrev:* **G**IAC **I**nformation **S**ecurity **F**undamentals.
GISP	*Abbrev:* **G**IAC **I**nformation **S**ecurity **P**rofessional.
GLEG	*Abbrev:* **G**IAC **leg**al (Law of Data Security & Investigations).
Global **A**ssociation of **R**isk **P**rofessionals **(GARP)**	US-based professional association for risk managers, founded in 1996. Originally focused on financial risk, then extended to cover sustainability and climate risk and latterly **A**rtificial **I**ntelligence risk.
Global **I**ndustrial **C**yber **S**ecurity **P**rofessional **(GICSP)**	GIAC's qualification for **O**perational **T**echnology cybersecurity professionals. Covers: **I**ndustrial **C**ontrol **S**ystem components, purposes, deployments, drivers, and constraints; attack surfaces, methods, and tools; system and network security architectures and techniques; incident response; and governance. More info: https://www.giac.org/certifications/global-industrial-cyber-security-professional-gicsp/

TERM	MEANING
Global **I**nformation **G**rid **(GIG)**	"The globally interconnected, end-to-end set of information capabilities for collecting, processing, storing, disseminating, and managing information on demand to warfighters, policy makers, and support personnel. The GIG includes owned and leased communications and computing systems and services, software (including applications), data, security services, other associated services, and National Security Systems. Non-GIG IT includes stand-alone, self-contained, or embedded IT that is not, and will not be, connected to the enterprise network" *(CNSSI 4009)*.
Global **I**nformation **I**nfrastructure **(GII)**	"Worldwide interconnections of the information systems of all countries, international and multinational organisations, and international commercial communications" *(CNSSI 4009)*. In practice, this includes but extends beyond the Internet.
Global **I**nternal **A**udit **S**tandards® **(GIAS)**	The **I**nstitute of **I**nternal **A**uditors' standards covering the practice of internal auditing. Built on 15 guiding principles. Excerpts of the Standards are used by permission of the IIA. ©2024 The Institute of Internal Auditors, Inc. All rights reserved. More info: https://www.theiia.org/en/standards/
Global **N**avigation **S**atellite **S**ystem **(GNSS)**	Geolocation service using a network of orbiting radio satellites running extremely accurate atomic clocks, allowing a receiver to calculate its three-dimensional position (latitude, longitude, and altitude) to within a few meters by simultaneous reference to several satellite signals. A GNSS receiver unit in a vehicle, for instance, can track the vehicle's position and report it remotely if coupled with a radio transmitter such as a cellphone, creating surveillance capabilities and raising privacy implications. Vulnerable to interference caused by physical obstructions, electrical noise, solar flares, *etc.*, or to deliberate spoofing or jamming. A useful way of tracking valuable portable information assets such as backup tape carriers, missiles, executives, politicians, celebrities, wilderness hikers, spooks, high-worth/vulnerable individuals, *things*, criminals, terrorists, and assets in general. "A constellation of Earth-orbiting satellites that provide positioning, navigation, and timing (PNT) services worldwide. The primary function of a GNSS is to determine the precise location of receivers on Earth's surface or in near-Earth space. The system allows electronic receivers to determine their location within a few meters" *(International Telecommunications **U**nion)*. See also **G**lobal **P**ositioning **S**ystem, **B**ei**D**ou Navigation **S**atellite System, **Glo**balnaya **Na**vigazionnaya **S**putnikovaya **S**istema, Galileo.
Globalnaya **Na**vigazionnaya **S**putnikovaya **S**istema **(GLONASS)**	Russian-owned **G**lobal **N**avigation **S**atellite **S**ystem.

TERM	MEANING
Global **P**ositioning **S**ystem **(GPS)**	US-owned global geolocation service – a **G**lobal **N**avigation **S**atellite **S**ystem.
Global **S**ystem for **M**obile Communications **(GSM)**	"A set of standards for second generation, cellular networks currently maintained by the 3rd Generation Partnership Project (3GPP)" *(NIST SP 800-101)*.
GLONASS	*Abbrev:* **Glo**balnaya **Na**vigazionnaya **S**putnikovaya **S**istema.
GMLE	*Abbrev:* **G**IAC **M**achine **L**earning **E**ngineer.
GMOB	*Abbrev:* **G**IAC **Mob**ile Device Security Analyst.
GMON	*Abbrev:* **G**IAC Continuous **MON**itoring.
GNFA	*Abbrev:* **G**IAC **N**etwork **F**orensic **A**nalyst.
GNSS	*Abbrev:* **G**lobal **N**avigation **S**atellite **S**ystem.
GNU General Public License	Copyleft style of permissive licence adopted by the GNU Project to encourage collaborative sharing by the community. More info: https://www.gnu.org/licenses/gpl-3.0.en.html
Goal, **Q**uestion, **M**etric **(GQM)**	Straightforward method or process for systematically determining the goals, objectives, or expected outcomes of some business activity, posing rhetorical questions concerning their efficacy, efficiency, suitability, *etc.* (the kinds of things that management might like to know), and finally designing or selecting suitable metrics to address those questions.
Going native, being turned	Deep cover agents, moles, or sleepers may become so tightly ensconced into the targetorganisation that they build a strong affinity to it and to their work colleagues/associates, ultimately supplanting their loyalty towards the agency that originally placed them, perhaps even becoming double agents.
GoldenEye	Species of ransomware in the wild in 2017. A variant of Petya. Used to target German HR departments, arriving in the guise of a spreadsheet with malicious macros, attached to a job application email.
Good practice	Framework, process, control, *etc.* broadly acknowledged as generally adequate, suitable, valuable, or recommended, in a generic and subjective manner. "A proven activity or process that has been successfully used by multiple enterprises and shown to produce reliable results" *(ISACA glossary)*. See also best practice.
Google **C**loud **P**latform **(GCP)**	Brand name for Google's global cloud infrastructure. See also Azure, **A**mazon **W**eb **S**ervices.
GOSI	*Abbrev:* **G**IAC **O**pen-**S**ource **I**ntelligence.

TERM	MEANING
Governance	Coherent, overarching system or framework of management/administrative controls (structures and reporting relationships, accountability, oversight, metrics, monitoring, feedback and assurance mechanisms, *etc.*) and rules (principles, policies, processes, *etc.*) to determine business objectives, formulate strategies, and execute them efficiently and effectively. Involves informing, guiding, directing, and controlling corporate decision-making and activities, while leaving enough room for creativity, innovation, and self-determination/autonomy (implying a degree of tolerance and trust in the management structures and managers). Includes enterprise-wide corporate governance and subsidiary aspects such as project governance and information security governance. A broad, high-level integrity control that flexes with the business, adapting dynamically to keep things heading the right way. "Human-based system comprising directing, overseeing and accountability" *(ISO/IEC 38500).* "The method by which an enterprise evaluates stakeholder needs, conditions and options to determine balanced, agreed-upon enterprise objectives to be achieved. It involves setting direction through prioritization, decision making and monitoring performance and compliance against the agreed-upon direction and objectives" *(ISACA glossary).* "The process of determining enterprise objectives, setting direction to achieve those objectives, and monitoring performance to adjust strategy as necessary" *(NIST IR 8286C).* "The act of indirectly guiding, controlling, and evaluating an entity by constraining and conscribing resources" *(OCEG GRC Glossary).* "The combination of processes and structures implemented by the board to inform, direct, manage, and monitor the activities of the organization toward the achievement of its objectives" *(IIA GIAS).* See also **G**overnance, **R**isk, and **C**ompliance.
Governance actions & controls	"Actions & controls that primarily serve governance activities to constrain and conscribe the organization or some aspect of it" *(OCEG GRC Glossary).*
Governance component	Governance component. "Factors that, individually and collectively, contribute to the successful operation of the enterprise's governance system over information and technology (I&T). Components interact with each other resulting in a holistic governance system for I&T. Components include processes; organizational structures; principles, policies and procedures; information; culture, ethics and behavior; people, skills and competencies; and services, infrastructure and applications" *(ISACA glossary).*
Governance enabler	Something that enables, facilitates, supports, or encourages effective governance, or removes blockers. "Something (tangible or intangible) that assists in the realization of effective governance" *(ISACA glossary).*

TERM	MEANING
Governance framework	Governance framework. "A basic conceptual structure used to solve or address complex issues. In the governance context, a framework is used to build a governance system for the enterprise. In COBIT 2019, a governance framework should: 1. be based on a conceptual model, identifying the key components and relationships among components to maximize consistency and allow automation. 2. be open and flexible, allowing for the addition of new content and the ability to address new issues in the most flexible way while maintaining integrity and consistency. 3. align to relevant major standards, frameworks and regulations" *(ISACA glossary)*.
Governance of information security, information security governance	Strategic direction, structure, guidance, and oversight of information security. "System by which an organisation's information security activities are directed and controlled" *(ISO/IEC 27000)*.
Governance, **Risk** [management] [and] **A**ssurance **(GRA)**	Overall concept or framework encompassing governance, risk management, and assurance. A slightly more focused variant of **G**overnance, **R**isk, and **C**ompliance with less emphasis on compliance, or perhaps just a rebadging of it for marketing reasons.
Governance, **Risk** [management] [and] **C**ompliance **(GRC)**	Overall concept or framework encompassing governance, risk management, and compliance. "A business term used to group the three closely related disciplines responsible for operations and the protection of assets" *(ISACA glossary)*. "A collection of integrated capabilities that enable an organization to reliably achieve objectives, address uncertainty, and act with integrity … An interdisciplinary approach of integrated capabilities, interconnected relationships, and interlinked shared values, which enable Principled Performance" *(OCEG GRC Glossary)*. See also **G**overnance, **R**isk, and **A**ssurance.
Governance system	Systematic approach to specify, design, implement, and maintain governance arrangements comprising organisational management structures, processes, controls, information flows, accountabilities, escalation paths, *etc.* An effective system is woven deeply into the fabric of the organisation, providing a balance of direction and latitude, both guiding and responding to changes. "The core requirements that underlie the governance over enterprise information and technology. In COBIT 2019, the six principles for a governance system are: 1. Providing stakeholder value. 2. Holistic approach. 3. Dynamic governance system. 4. Governance distinct from management. 5. Tailored to enterprise needs. 6. End-to-end governance system" *(ISACA glossary)*.
Governing authority, board [of directors]	"The most superior level of accountability and authority" *(OCEG GRC Glossary)*.

TERM	MEANING
Governing body	Most senior body which governs (*i.e.* guides and oversees at a strategic level) an organisation, as distinct from its management. "Person or group of people who are accountable for the performance and conformance of the organization. Note: Governing body can in some jurisdictions be a board of directors" *(ISO/IEC 27000)*. "Person or group of people who are accountable for the performance and conformance of the organization. Notes: Not all organizations, particularly small organizations, will have a governing body separate from top management. A governing body can include, but is not limited to, board of directors, committees of the board, supervisory board, trustees or overseers" *(ISO/IEC 42001)*.
Government **C**ommunications **H**ead**Q**uarters **(GCHQ)**	UK cyber-spooks, responsible for SIGINT and other intelligence, surveillance, and governmental technical support activities. Evolved from the Government Code and Cypher School, established during the first World War. "The centre for the government's signals intelligence activities and Cyber National Technical Authority (NTA)" *(UK National Cyber Security Strategy 2022)*.
Government **C**yber **C**oordination **C**entre **(GCCC)**	"Proposed joint venture between GSG, CDDO and NCSC bringing together their respective functions and areas of expertise to better coordinate operational cyber security efforts across government, transform how cyber security data and threat intelligence is used across government and truly enhance government's ability to 'defend as one'" *(UK National Cyber Security Strategy 2022)*.
Government **S**ecure **I**nternet **(GSI)**	Relatively secure UK government internal/private network, implemented in 1997.
GovTech	Contraction of **gov**ernment **tech**nology, particularly the development and exploitation of innovative **I**nformation and **C**ommunications **T**echnology within central and local government. See also AgriTech, Biotech, EcoTech/GreenTech, EdTech, FinTech, FoodTech, HealthTech, LegalTech, RegTech, RetailTech, and other tech neologisms.
GPCS	*Abbrev:* **G**IAC **P**ublic **C**loud **S**ecurity.
Gpcode	One of the earliest species of ransomware, in the wild in 2006.
GPEN	*Abbrev:* **G**IAC **Pen**etration Tester.
GPG, GNUPG (GNU Privacy Guard)	OpenPGP-compliant cryptographic email application developed by the GNU Project. More info: https://gnupg.org/
GPRS	*Abbrev:* **G**eneral **P**acket **R**adio **S**ervice.
GPS	*Abbrev:* **G**lobal **P**ositioning **S**ystem.
GPYC	*Abbrev:* **G**IAC **Py**thon **C**oder.

TERM	MEANING
GQM	*Abbrev:* **G**oal, **Q**uestion, **M**etric.
GRA	*Abbrev:* **G**overnance, **R**isk, and **A**ssurance.
Graphite	a. Smartphone spyware used for surveillance. Sold by Israeli firm Paragon Solutions. See also Pegasus. b. **F**ree **O**pen-**S**ource **S**oftware utility to graph values, *e.g.* for network and system performance monitoring. c. Uncompressed diamond, a form of carbon found in pencils.
GRC	*Abbrev:* **G**overnance, **R**isk, and **C**ompliance.
GRCA	*Abbrev:* **G**overnance **R**isk **C**ontrol **A**uditor.
GRC Assessment Framework 'Burgundy Book'	OCEG guidance on reviewing and auditing to gain assurance on the organisation's **G**overnance, **R**isk, and **C**ompliance activities. Provides models, methods, and tools. More info: https://www.oceg.org/grc-assessment-tools-burgundy-book/
GRC Auditor **(GRCA)**	OCEG's qualification for **I**nformation **T**echnology audit professionals. Covers: assurance aspects of the GRC Capability Model 'Red Book' and GRC Assessment Framework 'Burgundy Book' including **G**overnance, **R**isk, and **C**ompliance, strategy, performance management, ethics, internal control, security, and privacy. More info: https://www.oceg.org/certifications/grc-audit-certification/
GRCP	*Abbrev:* **G**overnance **R**isk **C**ompliance **P**rofessional.
GRC Professional **(GRCP)**	OCEG's qualification for **G**overnance, **R**isk, and **C**ompliance professionals. Covers the GRC Capability Model and key concepts. More info: https://www.oceg.org/certifications/grc-professional-certification/
GreenTech	See EcoTech.
GREM	*Abbrev:* **G**IAC **R**everse **E**ngineering **M**alware.
Grey box testing, focused testing	Assurance approach where the testers are given *limited* information about the internal structure of an application, system, device, or whatever under test – such as details of particular middleware or application controls that need to be evaluated. "A test methodology that assumes some knowledge of the internal structure and implementation detail of the assessment object" *(CNSSI 4009). Cf.* white box testing, black box testing.
Grey hat	Hacker having characteristics of both white and black hats, or indeterminate. Black hats seldom openly acknowledge their true motivations, dubious ethics, and self-serving nature, normally *claiming* to be legitimate white hats (*e.g.* 'security researchers' and 'penetration testers') while concealing or denying their black hat tendencies and nefarious activities. With obsessive personality type, *some* white hats 'take their work home with them,' working independently under their own initiative within self-determined guardrails.

TERM	MEANING
Greyware	See Potentially Unwanted Program.
GRID	*Abbrev:* GIAC Response and Industrial Defense.
Grieving curve	Psychiatrist Elisabeth Kübler-Ross described five emotional states that people suffering deep personal loss (such as death of a close friend or relative) typically experience in sequence, namely, denial, anger, bargaining, depression, and finally acceptance. Although seldom literally life-changing, individual workers, organisations, and even entire nations or cultures may experience broadly similar 'roller-coaster rides' when faced with major challenges, changes, incidents, or shocks.
Ground truth	Powdered facts, available by the jar, ideal for sprinkling liberally over misinformation and disinformation to increase credibility. "Value of the target variable for a particular item of labelled input data. Note: The term ground truth does not imply that the labelled input data consistently corresponds to the real-world value of the target variables" *(ISO/IEC 22989)*.
Group	Most Information Technology systems allow security administrators to configure and manage common permissions for entire groups of users performing similar rôles (*e.g.* staff, managers, or administrators), rather than having to configure and manage the rights and privileges individually for each person (although this is also possible, *e.g.* through ACLs). Aside from users, other resources (such as servers and devices) may also be grouped together in various ways to ease administration, rule-setting, monitoring, *etc.* See also discussion forum, social network, classification.
Group affirmation	See social proofing.
Group of undertakings	"A controlling undertaking and its controlled undertakings" *(General Data Protection Regulation)*.
Group **P**olicy **O**bject **(GPO)**	Access control ruleset within Active Directory. The object is a container for groups of access control policies (settings and permissions).
Group-think	See social proofing.
GRTP	*Abbrev:* GIAC Red Team Professional.
GSEC	*Abbrev:* GIAC Security Essentials.
GSI	*Abbrev:* Government Secure Internet.
GSLC	*Abbrev:* GIAC Security Leadership Certification.
GSM	*Abbrev:* Global System for Mobile communications.
GSNA	*Abbrev:* GIAC Systems and Network Auditor.
GSOC	*Abbrev:* GIAC Security Operations Certified.

TERM	MEANING
GSOM	*Abbrev:* **G**IAC **S**ecurity **O**perations **M**anager.
GSTRT	*Abbrev:* **G**IAC **Strat**egic Planning, Policy, and Leadership.
Guard	a. *[Noun]* Security guard. b. *[Noun]* "Functional unit that provides a security filter between two data processing systems operating at different security levels or between a user terminal and a database to filter out data that the user is not authorized to access" *(ISO/IEC 2382)*. c. *[Verb]* To oversee and/or protect something.
Guardrail	a. Preventive control analogous to the crash-barriers on dangerous sections of road, intended to keep traffic safely on the highway in its lane, protected from adjacent hazards such as sharp drops or opposing traffic. b. Commercial security product supporting DevSecOps.
Guard tour, site security patrol system	Physical security arrangement that tags/logs/records and perhaps tracks in real time the security guards, as they patrol the facilities routinely, especially lone guards working out-of-hours (nightshifts and weekends), in order to identify and perhaps raise the alarm and trigger a suitable response if a guard fails to complete the round (*e.g.* absent, asleep, lost/taking shortcuts, injured, kidnapped, or killed *en route*). Typically involves guards authenticating themselves ('checking-in' or 'tagging') at strategically positioned points on a planned tour using mechanical time-stampers, access cards, keys, barcode readers, **G**lobal **P**ositioning **S**ystem, **C**losed **C**ircuit **Tele**Vision cameras, radios, biometric scanners, *etc.* that record the dates and times of check-ins. May be combined with duress alarms.
Guest system, guest operating system	**O**perating **S**ystem for a single **V**irtual **M**achine provided, managed, and substantially if not perfectly secured by the hypervisor.
Guide	a. *[Verb]* To aid, assist, or direct in a general way, offering guidance. b. *[Noun]* Person who assists or directs, an aide. "Person appointed by the client to assist the audit team" *(ISO/IEC 17021-1)*.
Guideline, guidance	Explanation of how information security controls, processes, and systems operate, with supplementary information and advice to help and encourage workers to utilise them properly. Usually documented, sometimes supported by security awareness, training, oversight, and compliance/conformity activities since, despite being a discretionary term, many of the controls covered by guidelines concern mandatory obligations, requirements, and rules defined in laws, regulations, policies, *etc.* "Description that clarifies what should be done and how, to achieve the objectives set out in policies" *(ISO/IEC 27000)*. "A description of a particular way of accomplishing something that is less prescriptive than a procedure" *(ISACA glossary)*.

TERM	MEANING
GWAPT	*Abbrev:* **G**IAC **W**eb **A**pplication **P**enetration **T**ester.
GWEB	*Abbrev:* **G**IAC Certified **Web** Application Defender.
GX-CS	*Abbrev:* **G**IAC e**X**perienced **C**yber **S**ecurity.
GX-FA	*Abbrev:* **G**IAC e**X**perienced **F**orensics **A**nalyst.
GX-FE	*Abbrev:* **G**IAC e**X**perienced **F**orensics **E**xaminer.
GX-IH	*Abbrev:* **G**IAC e**X**perienced **I**ncident **H**andler.
GX-IA	*Abbrev:* **G**IAC e**X**perienced **I**ntrusion **A**nalyst.
GX-PT	*Abbrev:* **G**IAC e**X**perienced **P**enetration **T**ester.
GXPN	*Abbrev:* **G**IAC e**X**ploit Researcher and Advanced **P**enetratio**N** Tester.

H

TERM	MEANING
H&S	*Abbrev:* **H**ealth and **S**afety.
Habitual behaviours	"Semi-automatic human actions informed by beliefs and values and governed by free will and discipline" *(OCEG GRC Glossary).*
HACE	*Abbrev:* **H**igh **A**ssurance **C**ryptographic **E**quipment.
Hack, hacking	At MIT in the late 1950's, a 'hack' was an ingenious, quick, inelegant, and superficial modification to a system that accomplished the desired goal without fundamentally changing its architecture. Later came to mean a benign and obsessive fascination with technology. Now refers to accessing, exploring, and often exploiting vulnerable computer systems, networks, and *things* without the owners' authorisation, knowledge, and/or permission; hence, unethical and often both malicious and illegal, although cracking is more specific. "Intentionally accessing a computer system without the authorization of the user or the owner" *(ISO/IEC 27032).*
Hacker, haxxor, h4xx0r …	Someone who hacks. 'Haxxor,' plus variants such as 'h4xx0r,' are Leet versions. "Technically sophisticated computer enthusiast who uses his or her knowledge and means to gain unauthorized access to protected resources" *(ISO/IEC 2382).* "An individual who attempts to gain unauthorized access to a computer system" *(ISACA glossary).* "Unauthorized user who attempts to or gains access to an information system" *(CNSSI 4009).* See also cracker.
Hacker underground	Somewhat covert social network or community of individuals and groups of hackers, crackers, malware authors (VXers), script kiddies, bot masters, *etc.* linked through Internet websites, chat rooms, bulletin boards, conferences and club meetings, *etc.* Increasingly linked to criminal gangs, cybercriminal activities (*e.g.* the use of crimeware), and the black market.
Hacktivism, hacktivist, hactivism, hactivist	Use of hacking/cracking techniques to further the aims of ideological activist/extremist groups promoting human rights, anarchy, and religious/national bigotry,. *e.g.* through website defacement. May be a part of, or provide a cover for, more sinister attacks such as terrorism, sabotage, cybertage, industrial espionage, spying, or information warfare. "Hacking for a politically or socially motivated purpose" *(ISO/IEC 27032).*
HAEP	*Abbrev:* **H**igh **A**ssurance **E**valuation **P**rogram.
Hajime	Worm similar to Mirai in that it infects *things* through their Telnet ports using default userIDs and passwords, recruiting them to a botnet. In the wild in 2017.

TERM	MEANING
Hallucination	a. False human perceptions involving strange dream-like sights, sounds, smells/tastes, or feelings. b. Inaccurate albeit credibly and confidently presented response from an **A**rtificial **I**ntelligence/**L**arge **L**anguage **M**odel. An unfortunate drawback to the **M**achine **L**earning approach of systematically analysing natural language samples to derive and apply linguistic rules mechanistically, despite limited comprehension or appreciation of often complex subject matter. To be fair to the robots, we humans are also prone to 'reading between the lines', 'jumping to conclusions' and 'faking it', taking us 'away with the fairies.' "In generative artificial intelligence (AI), the generation of false or misleading information presented as fact" *(ISACA glossary)*.
Ham	a. Email which the recipient considers legitimate and welcome, *i.e.* not spam. b. Radio amateur, amateur actor, or pig meat.
HAN	*Abbrev:* **H**ome **A**rea **N**etwork.
Handler	See collector.
Handprint scanner	Biometric reader based on the unique geometry of the human hand. "A biometric device used to authenticate a user through palm scans" *(ISACA glossary)*.
Hanlon's razor	Robert J. Hanlon wrote "Never attribute to malice that which can be adequately explained by stupidity." Naturally risk-averse information security professionals tend to assume that most incidents are caused intentionally by malicious adversaries, whereas many are simple accidents, coincidences, and 'misfortune'/'bad luck' (meaning random factors). Stupidity may involve ignorance and/or incompetence.
Harass, harassment	Relatively minor form of bullying, intimidation, pestering, or coercion, generally bothersome and annoying rather than hurtful or violent but it's a matter of degree and perception by the victim.
Hardening, harden	Process of making something more robust or secure by proactively reducing its vulnerabilities, *e.g.* by configuring a server according to applicable security standards, removing unnecessary software, and applying relevant security patches. "Process of securing a system by reducing its surface of vulnerability. Note: Hardening typically includes the removal of unnecessary software, unnecessary usernames or logins and the disabling or removal of unnecessary services" *(ISO/IEC 27033-6)*. "The process of configuring a computer or other network device to resist attacks" *(ISACA glossary)*. "The process of identifying and fixing vulnerabilities on a system" *(SANS glossary)*.

TERM	MEANING
Hardware	Tangible technology asset such as a computer system or device. *Cf.* software, firmware, wetware, data, and information. "All or part of the physical components of an information processing system. Example: Computers, peripheral devices" *(ISO/IEC 2382)*. "A generic term for any physical component of information and communication technology, including peripheral equipment and media used to process information" *(NZISM)*. "A generic term for ICT equipment" *(AusISM)*. "Physical equipment, as opposed to programs, procedures, rules and associated documentation; contrasts with software" *(ISACA glossary)*. "A physical electronic information system, or parts thereof capable of processing, storing or transmitting digital data" *(EU CRA)*. "The material physical components of a system" *(NIST SP 800-171)*. *Cf.* software, firmware, middleware, wetware, malware, ransomware, adware, crimeware, scareware, shelfware, spouseware, stalkerware, spyware.
Hardware driver	Hardware driver. "Applications responsible for establishing communication between hardware and software programs" *(NIST SP 800-101)*.
Hardware hack	Deliberate manipulation of hardware to compromise, defeat/disable, or bypass physical or electronic/digital security controls built in to devices, such as access-controlled functions and data.
Hardware **S**ecurity **M**odule **(HSM)**	Physically secure cryptographic subsystem comprising a trusted environment within which private keys can safely be stored and cryptographic operations can safely be performed. "A device, card or appliance usually installed inside of a PC or server to provide cryptographic functions. HSM's are usually physically and electronically hardened to reduce the possibility of tampering or other interference" *(NZISM)*. See also **T**rusted **P**latform **M**odule. *Cf.* **H**ierarchical **S**torage **M**anagement.
Harm, damage	*[In the context of information risk and security]* Adverse effects resulting from incidents that materially reduce the confidentiality, integrity, or availability of information, which in turn cause secondary impacts such as increased costs, losses, injury/death, and inability to operate normally. "Injury or damage to the health of people, or damage to property or the environment" *(ISO/IEC Guide 51)*. "A measure of the negative impact that an event has on the organization" *(OCEG GRC Glossary)*.
Harvesting	Systematic collection of personal information such as names and email addresses, from **D**ata**B**ases, websites, forums, contact lists, *etc.* typically for the purpose of sending spam.

TERM	MEANING
Hash, hash value, hash code, digest, message digest, cryptographic hash, hash function, hashing, trapdoor function, irreversible encryption, irreversible encipherment, one-way encryption	Characteristic output value produced by passing a string or file (the 'message') through a so-called 'one-way encryption' or 'trapdoor' cryptographic hashing function such as SHA-2. Although the original content may not be reliably recreated from the hash value, its validity and integrity can be verified by recalculating and comparing the hash against one calculated previously, stored, and communicated securely. Used to validate passwords, digital certificates, digital evidence, plus electronic files, messages, functions, and transactions, and for pseudorandom bit generation. "Encryption that produces ciphertext from which the original data cannot be reproduced. Note: Irreversible encryption is useful in authentication. For example, a password might be irreversibly encrypted and the resulting ciphertext stored. A password presented later would be irreversibly encrypted identically and the two strings of ciphertext compared. If they are identical, the presented password is correct" *(ISO/IEC 2382)*. "[Hashing] 1. A technique involving using a hash function (algorithm) to create hash valued or checksums that validate message integrity. 2. In data processing and machine learning, a mechanism for bucketing categorical data, particularly when the number of categories is large, but the number of categories actually appearing in the dataset is comparatively small. [and] [Hash] A cryptographic function takes an input of an arbitrary length and produces an output (also known as a message digest) that is a standard-sized binary string. The output is unique to the input in such a way that even a minor change to the input results in a completely different output. Modern cryptographic hash functions are also resistant to collisions (situations in which different inputs produce identical output); a collision, while possible, is statistically improbable. Cryptographic hash functions are developed so that input cannot be determined readily from the output. [and] [Hash function] 1. An algorithm that maps or translates one set of bits into another (generally smaller) so that a message yields the same result every time the algorithm is executed using the same message as input. 2. Fixed values derived mathematically from a text message" *(ISACA glossary)*. "The result of a one-way, cryptographic function that converts a data string of any length into a unique fixed-length bit string. Typically applied to passwords and messages to protect against loss and/or add resistance to attacks. Hashing algorithms or functions are often are designed as a one-way cryptographic transformation so that it's impossible to reverse the hash process and reconstitute the original string. The values returned by a hash function are variously described as hash values, hash codes, digests, or simply hashes. One common use of a hash is a data structure called a hash table, widely used in computer software for indexing and rapid retrieval of database elements. Note that a hash is not the same as data encryption although it does

TERM	MEANING
	utilise cryptographic functions" *(NZISM)*. "An algorithm (the hash function) which takes as input a string of any length (the message) and generates a fixed length string (the message digest or fingerprint) as output. The algorithm is designed to make it computationally infeasible to find any input which maps to a given digest, or to find two different messages that map to the same digest" *(AusISM)*. "The process of using a mathematical algorithm against data to produce a numeric value that is representative of that data" *(NIST SP 800-101)*. "An algorithm that computes a value based on a data object thereby mapping the data object to a smaller data object. (Cryptographic) hash functions are used to generate a one way 'check sum' for a larger text, which is not trivially reversed. The result of this hash function can be used to validate if a larger file has been altered, without having to compare the larger files to each other. Frequently used hash functions are MD5 and SHA1" *(SANS glossary)*.
Hash-based Message Authentication Code (HMAC) algorithm	"A cryptographic construction that can be used to compute Message Authentication Codes using a hash function and a secret key" *(AusISM)*. "In cryptography, a keyed-hash message authentication code (HMAC) is a specific type of message authentication code (MAC) using a cryptographic hash function and a cryptographic key" *(NZISM)*.
Hash collision	It is possible, although unlikely, for two different input strings or files to produce the same hash due to the finite number of possible hash values that hashing algorithms generate (the hash-space). Relatively weak hashing algorithms such as MD5 with small hash-spaces are more likely to suffer collisions and are deprecated in favour of stronger algorithms with much larger hash-spaces such as the SHA-2 or SHA-3 families. "Occurrence of the same hash value for two or more different keys" *(ISO/IEC 2382)*.
Hash total	See hash. "The total of any numeric data field in a document or computer file. This total is checked against a control total of the same field to facilitate the accuracy of processing" *(ISACA glossary)*.
Hash value	See hash. "String of bits which is the output of a hash-function" *(ISO/IEC 10118-1)*.
Hazard	Health and safety or insurance term equivalent to danger, threat, threat agent, risk, risk source, *etc.* depending on context and specified definitions. "Source of potential harm. Note: Hazard can be a risk source" *(ISO 22300)*. "A condition or event that poses a risk to safety. Hazards can be internal or external" *(ISACA glossary)*. "A cause that has the potential to eventually result in harm" *(OCEG GRC Glossary)*. "Non-malicious risks such as extreme weather events, accidents or the natural outbreak of disease. Contrast with threat" *(UK Resilience Lessons Digest 2023)*.

TERM	MEANING
Hazard monitoring function	"Activities to obtain evidence-based information on hazards in a defined area used to make decisions about the need for public warning" *(ISO 22300)*.
Health and **S**afety **(H&S)**	Risk management techniques, approaches, and safety controls designed to reduce the risk of personal injury or death of workers or other people facing hazardous conditions, such as operating a smartphone while driving or crossing a road, or using/maintaining industrial plant inappropriately. This qualifies as an information risk and security issue if you accept that people are information assets with valuable knowledge and expertise worth protecting.
Health **I**nsurance **P**ortability and **A**ccountability **A**ct 1996 **(HIPAA)**	US law concerning privacy and security of Protected **H**ealth **I**nformation, principally **E**lectronic **H**ealth **R**ecords associated with health insurance: "An Act To amend the Internal Revenue Code of 1986 to improve portability and continuity of health insurance coverage in the group and individual markets, to combat waste, fraud, and abuse in health insurance and health care delivery, to promote the use of medical savings accounts, to improve access to long-term care services and coverage, to simplify the administration of health insurance, and for other purpose." More info: https://aspe.hhs.gov/reports/health-insurance-portability-accountability-act-1996
HealthTech	Contraction of **health tech**nology, particularly the development and exploitation of innovative computing technologies within the healthcare industry. See also AgriTech, Biotech, EcoTech/GreenTech, EdTech, FinTech, FoodTech, GovTech, LegalTech, RegTech, RetailTech, and other tech neologisms.
Heap	Extensive area of memory in which the data values of program variables are stored (pile up) while an application executes. Each heap must be actively managed by the program, *e.g.* releasing space after use to avoid the heap growing and perhaps overflowing. See also stack.
Heap overflow memory leak	Class of software vulnerability similar to buffer overflow in which conditions such as inadequate type or bounds checking and exception handling in programs lead to variable values exceeding their allocated space on the heap and issues such as program or computer systems crashes, and unauthorised disclosure of confidential data such as passwords and cryptographic keys. See also stack overflow.
Hearsay	Rumours, *e.g.* unsubstantiated statements, claims, or assertions by a third party about someone involved in a court case. Normally inadmissible as forensic evidence unless it satisfies specific court rules. A form of circumstantial (indirect) evidence.

TERM	MEANING
Heartbleed	Cryptographic hacking attack that exploits vulnerable OpenSSL implementations, compromising X.509 digital certificates to steal confidential data (such as passwords) passed over **S**ecure **S**ockets **L**ayer. Thanks in part to Heartbleed, SSL is deprecated in favour of **T**ransport **L**ayer **S**ecurity.
Heatmap, heat-map, heat map	Notional two-dimensional graphical representation of the business with coloured overlay indicating trouble-spots, concerns, issues, or problems (normally in red), areas of lesser concern (amber) or of strength (green). The map may represent physical locations or facilities, business units, departments, processes, systems, network domains, *etc.* A security metric. See also **P**robability-**I**mpact **G**raphic, attack surface, risk profile, risk matrix, risk universe, security landscape.
Hellcat	Ransomware gang active in 2025.
Help desk, helpdesk, help-desk, helpline, service desk …	Corporate support function offering guidance and advice to workers and/or customers, *etc.* Also a funnel for support and change requests, incident reports, *etc.* typically invoking the incident response process then tracking and coordinating activities, communicating effectively throughout to brief and keep all those who need to be in-the-loop updated. “A service offered via telephone/Internet by an enterprise to its clients or employees that provides information, assistance and troubleshooting advice regarding software, hardware or networks. Notes: A help desk is staffed by people who can either resolve the problem on their own or escalate the problem to specialized personnel. A help desk is often equipped with dedicated customer relationship management (CRM) software that logs the problems and tracks them until they are solved” *(ISACA glossary)*. “A live or on-demand channel for individuals to ask questions before or while they are engaged in a task” *(OCEG GRC Glossary)*.
Heteronomy, heteronomous	“Characteristic of a system operating under the constraint of external intervention, control or oversight” *(ISO/IEC 22989)*. *Cf.* autonomous.
Heuristic	Method involving learning from experience – a rule-of-thumb. Some antivirus software uses heuristic techniques to identify possible malware by its unusual patterns of behaviour, while Bayesian anti-spam methods learn from user selections to differentiate spam from ham. “A quick solution to a problem, which may or may not be the best solution” *(ISACA glossary)*.
Hiddad	One of several nasty species of malware that infects Android mobiles, in the wild in 2018. Bundled legitimate applications with malware.
HIDS	*Abbrev:* **H**ost-based **I**ntrusion **D**etection **S**ystem.

TERM	MEANING
Hierarchical **S**torage **M**anagement **(HSM)**	Data are saved to different storage devices and media according to the frequency of access, *e.g.* primary storage (typically solid state) is the fastest but most costly and hence limited form reserved for data accessed frequently, such as caches; secondary storage (*e.g.* magnetic hard drives) is somewhat slower but less expensive; tertiary storage may involve mounting and retrieving data from offline media optimised for stable medium- to long-term storage (*e.g.* backups and archives). HSM technology can automate the associated data classification and management (*e.g.* monitoring access and moving data between tiers), and the policies can get quite sophisticated, with various information risk and security implications.
High Assurance	"A generic term encompassing Common Criteria Evaluation Assurance Levels (EAL) 5, 6 and 7. Alternatively refers to the independent (unrelated) ASD High Assurance Evaluation Scheme" *(NZISM)*.
High Assurance Cryptography	"The U.S. ranks cryptographic products and algorithms through a certification programme and categorising the products and algorithms into product types. Product types are defined in the US National Information Assurance Glossary" *(CNSSI 4009)*. which defines Type 1 and 2 products, and Type 3 and 4 algorithms. Type 1 products are used to protect systems requiring the most stringent protection mechanisms" *(NZISM)*.
High **A**ssurance **C**ryptographic **E**quipment **(HACE)**	"The equivalent to United States Type 1 cryptographic products & equipment. Previously described as High Grade Cryptographic Products & Equipment, the term HACE includes classified CCI, and other GCSB Specific devices" *(NZISM)*. "Cryptographic equipment that has been authorised by ASD for the protection of SECRET and TOP SECRET data" *(AusISM)*.
High **A**ssurance **E**valuation **P**rogram **(HAEP)**	"The rigorous investigation, analysis, verification and validation of products by ASD to protect SECRET and TOP SECRET data" *(AusISM)*.
High assurance ICT equipment	"ICT equipment that has been designed and authorised for the protection of SECRET and TOP SECRET data" *(AusISM)*.
High-grade cryptographic equipment	"The equivalent to United States Type 1 cryptographic equipment" *(NZISM)*.
Highly confidential	Very sensitive information, more than merely confidential. See also secret.
High-**S**peed **D**ownlink **P**acket **A**ccess **(HSDPA), 3.5G, 3½G**	Mobile phone protocol introduced as a stopgap before 4G was ready, hence also known as 3.5G or 3½G. Provided faster data services than **U**niversal **M**obile **T**elecommunications **S**ystem (3G).

TERM	MEANING
High-value server	See server. "A server that provide important network services or contains important data repositories. For example, a Domain Name System server, database server, email server, file server or web server" *(AusISM)*.
Hijack	Deliberately and maliciously seize control of something (such as a computer system, enterprise network, communications link, session, or conversation) or someone (typically a high-value target) away from its owner or custodian.
Hijacking, hijack attack	Hijack attack. "An exploitation of a valid network session for unauthorized purposes" *(ISACA glossary)*. "A form of active wiretapping in which the attacker seizes control of a previously established communication association" *(SANS glossary)*.
HIPAA	*Abbrev:* **H**ealth **I**nsurance **P**ortability and **A**ccountability **A**ct.
HIPPA	See **H**ealth **I**nsurance **P**ortability and **A**ccountability **A**ct … and typo.
HMI	*Abbrev:* **H**uman–**M**achine **I**nterface.
Hoax	Deliberate false alarm. Triggering the fire alarm may, for instance, allow an intruder to access a controlled facility if the fire exits unlock automatically. See also virus hoax.
Hold file, suspense file	Transactions or data items that fail integrity or other checks are commonly flagged or placed in this special holding area pending manual inspection and cancellation or release, instead of being processed.
Home **A**rea **N**etwork **(HAN)**	**L**ocal **A**rea **N**etwork in a residential property, using various networking protocols such as Wi-Fi, Bluetooth, ZigBee, and/or wired Ethernet, often linking *things* to each other and the Internet. See also **P**ersonal **A**rea **N**etwork.
Homomorphic encryption	Cryptographic technique/algorithm that allows encrypted data to be transformed mathematically without having to decrypt it first, thus preserving the confidentiality of the plaintext during processing, *e.g.* El Gamal. "A type of encryption that supports two primitive operations in the ciphertext/encrypted space—multiplication and addition of two homomorphically encrypted values—wherein the decrypted product or sum provides a meaningful (*i.e.*, when decrypted, the result would be the same as if performed on unencrypted values) value (only category of encryption wherein operations of encrypted yield meaningful result[s])" *(ISACA glossary)*.
Honest	Does not (knowingly) lie or deceive. An honest person has personal integrity and is straightforward, ethical, open, and trustworthy.

TERM	MEANING
Honeymonkey, honey client	"Automated system simulating a user browsing websites. The system is typically configured to detect web sites which exploit vulnerabilities in the browser" *(SANS glossary)*.
Honeypot, honeynet	Networked computers deliberately configured as decoys to lure hackers or malware for forensic investigation, or more simply as a security alerting/early-warning mechanism. "A specially configured server, also known as a decoy server, designed to attract and monitor intruders in a manner so that their actions do not affect production systems" *(ISACA glossary)*. "Programs that simulate one or more network services that you designate on your computer's ports. An attacker assumes you're running vulnerable services that can be used to break into the machine. A honey pot can be used to log access attempts to those ports including the attacker's keystrokes. This could give you advanced warning of a more concerted attack" *(SANS glossary)*.
Honeytoken	File, object, or token in a networked **I**nformation **T**echnology system intended as a decoy to lure, or canary to reveal, hackers, fraudsters, and insider threats at work, *e.g.* a fake entry in a customer **D**ata**B**ase with a PO Box, email address, telephone number, or file access alert monitored by the **I**nformation **S**ecurity **M**anager to check for unauthorised disclosure or inappropriate use of the DB.
Honour, honour system, code of honour	Social factors constrain ethical people to behave in accordance with the expectations of their peer groups. Along with trust, this weak control is decreasingly effective overall due to declining social values and an evident lack of social responsibility by some members of many groups, societies, and cultures. Cheating and selfishness is a way of life for some, to the detriment of society as a whole.
Horizon scanning	"A systematic examination of information to identify potential threats, risks, emerging issues and opportunities allowing for better preparedness and the incorporation of mitigation and exploitation into the policy-making process" *(UK National Cyber Security Strategy 2022)*.
Host [machine]	a. Synonym for computer system, server or node. "Computer on which a program or file is installed" *(ISO/IEC 2382)*. "Any computer that has full two-way access to other computers on the Internet. Or a computer with a web server that serves the pages for one or more Web sites" *(SANS glossary)*. b. Person, group, organisation, *etc.* that welcome another to join in a shared activity or event, such as jointly delivering a podcast or having a meal. c. "Entity that receives feedback from a reviewer as part of a peer review. Note: The entity can be an organization, partnership, community, city, region, country or other body" *(ISO 22300)*.

TERM	MEANING
Host-based Intrusion Detection System (HIDS)	Intrusion Detection System involving software running on systems (servers or nodes) and monitoring the network traffic as it arrives at and/or departs from those systems, as opposed to directly monitoring traffic flowing on the network (see Network Intrusion Detection System). "Software, resident on a system, which monitors system activities for malicious or unwanted behaviour" *(AusISM)*. "[HIDS] use information from the operating system audit records to watch all operations occurring on the host that the intrusion detection software has been installed upon. These operations are then compared with a pre-defined security policy. This analysis of the audit trail imposes potentially significant overhead requirements on the system because of the increased amount of processing power which must be utilized by the intrusion detection system. Depending on the size of the audit trail and the processing ability of the system, the review of audit data could result in the loss of a real-time analysis capability" *(SANS glossary)*.
Host-based intrusion prevention system	See Intrusion Prevention System. "A security device, resident on a specific host, which monitors system activities for malicious or unwanted behaviour and can react in real-time to block or prevent those activities" *(NZISM)*. "Software, resident on a system, which monitors system activities for malicious or unwanted behaviour and can react in real-time to block or prevent those activities" *(AusISM)*.
Host operating system	Operating System running on bare metal on which the hypervisor runs guest systems for each of the virtual systems. An integral part of some hypervisor software.
Hot site	Secondary, fallback location with an Information Technology facility that, following a disaster affecting the primary/main (production) location, can be made fully operational within a short period (typically just a few hours at most), due to having been pre-fitted with all essential hardware, power supplies, air conditioners, network connections, and physical access controls, and having ready access to data backups from the main site. "Fully equipped computer center that provides an immediate alternative data processing capability" *(ISO/IEC 2382)*. "A fully operational offsite data processing facility equipped with both hardware and system software to be used in the event of a disaster" *(ISACA glossary)*. "Backup site that includes phone systems with the phone lines already connected. Networks will also be in place, with any necessary routers and switches plugged in and turned on. Desks will have desktop PCs installed and waiting, and server areas will be replete with the necessary hardware to support business-critical functions. Within a few hours, a hot site can become a fully functioning element of an organisation" *(CNSSI 4009)*. See also cold, warm, and mirror site.

TERM	MEANING
Hot standby	Redundant computer system, server, device, facility, supplier, person, *etc.* capable of continuing operations if the normal service provider fails, with minimal delay or reduction in service – ideally seamlessly, without the change even being noticed (except by the Information Technology operations team anyway!). "Configuration in which a redundant functional unit can be immediately brought into service should the primary functional unit fail" *(ISO/IEC 2382)*.
HPKP	*Abbrev:* **H**TTP **P**ublic **K**ey **P**inning.
HSDPA	*Abbrev:* **H**igh-**S**peed **D**ownlink **P**acket **A**ccess.
HSM	*Abbrev:* **H**ardware **S**ecurity **M**odule or **H**ierarchical **S**torage **M**anagement, depending on context.
HSTS (**H**TTP **S**trict **T**ransport **S**ecurity)	In its HTTP headers, a website can request that clients only use HTTPS, not plain HTTP, reducing the risk of site spoofing, **M**an-**I**n-**T**he-**M**iddle attacks, *etc.*
HTML	*Abbrev:* **H**yper**T**ext **M**arkup **L**anguage.
HTML entity encode	"The process of replacing certain ASCII characters with their HTML entity equivalents. For example, encoding would replace the less than character '<' with the HTML equivalent '<.' HTML entities are 'inert' in most interpreters, especially browsers, which can mitigate certain client side attacks" *(SCP QRG)*.
HTML injection	Web hacking technique exploiting inadequate data validation to manipulate HTML code sent between a web browser and web server, *e.g.* to reveal or spoof cookies or send a user's logon credentials to the hacker. An example of code injection. See also Cross-Site Scripting.
HTTP **P**ublic **K**ey **P**inning **(HPKP)**	Obsolete method for digital certificate authentication involving a field in HTTP headers. By checking a website's cryptographic hashes of the public keys of its **C**ertification **A**uthorities, a client can reduce the risk of HTTPS **S**ecure **S**ockets **L**ayer/**T**ransport **L**ayer **S**ecurity certificate spoofing, **M**an-**I**n-**T**he-**M**iddle attacks, *etc.* Deprecated in favour of **C**ertificate **T**ransparency.
Hub	a. Literal or notional focal point such as a community hall or marae, a social centre, and meeting place potentially capable of serving as an emergency liaison and local coordination point in a natural disaster situation such as a major storm or earthquake. b. Basic **L**ocal **A**rea **N**etwork device working at layer 1 (physical) of the OSI stack. Effectively a junction box for LAN cables. "A common connection point for devices in a network, hubs are used to connect segments of a local area network (LAN). Notes: A hub contains multiple ports.

TERM	MEANING
	When a packet arrives at one port, it is copied to the other ports so that all segments of the LAN can see all packets" *(ISACA glossary)*. "Network device that functions at layer 1 of the OSI reference model. Note: There is no real intelligence in network hubs; they only provide physical attachment points for networked systems or resources" *(ISO/IEC 27033-1)*. "A network device that operates by repeating data that it receives on one port to all the other ports. As a result, data transmitted by one host is retransmitted to all other hosts on the hub" *(SANS glossary)*. *Cf.* switch.
Hull	Body of a mechanical lock or padlock housing, to some extent concealing and physically protecting the internal lock mechanism.
Human capital	"The collective knowledge, skills, abilities, and experiences of an organization's workforce, along with the relationships, attitudes, and values that enable them to work together to achieve the organization's objectives" *(OCEG GRC Glossary)*.
Human factors	All aspects of information security depend to some extent on the actions or inactions of human beings; hence, behavioural, sociological, and psychological factors influence the level or quality of information security achieved in practice, *e.g.* we struggle to recall and accurately type random strings of characters, limiting the achievable strength of memorised passwords.
Human firewall	Effective security awareness, training, and education, combined with motivational leadership and a supportive corporate culture, improve workers' capability to spot and deal with a wide variety of information risks, supplementing the technological or cybersecurity controls such as firewalls. Alert humans are a particularly important 'layer 8' defence against scams, frauds, and other social engineering attacks attempting to exploit human vulnerabilities while evading or neutralising technical controls. "A person prepared to act as a network layer of defense through education and awareness" *(ISACA glossary)*.
Human–**M**achine **I**nterface **(HMI)**	Display screen, annunciator/mimic panel, *etc.* presenting industrial plant operators with information from the SCADA/**I**ndustrial **C**ontrol **S**ystems and a keyboard, switch panel, or some other way for them to interact with the distributed systems. "User interface for operating and monitoring a process control system or a plant" *(ISO/IEC 27019)*.
Human–machine teaming	See augmented intelligence. "Integration of human interaction with machine intelligence capabilities" *(ISO/IEC 22989)*.
HUMINT (Human Intelligence)	Military practice of gathering intelligence primarily from or using people (sources and agents). See also TECHINT, SIGINT, OSINT, COMINT, IMINT, ELINT.

TERM	MEANING
Hybrid analysis	Free online malware analysis service uses CrowdStrike Falcon Sandbox to subject uploaded samples to both runtime and memory dump analysis. See also VirusTotal.
Hybrid application control	"A combination of manual and automated activities, all of which must operate for the control to be effective. Note: Sometimes referred to as computer-dependent application controls" *(ISACA glossary)*.
Hybrid attack	"Builds on the dictionary attack method by adding numerals and symbols to dictionary words" *(SANS glossary)*.
Hybrid cloud	Provision of cloud services through the Internet on equipment belonging partly to a **C**loud **S**ervice **P**rovider and partly to the user of those services. See also public, private cloud.
Hybrid control	Control that combines various approaches, systems, elements, participants, or protocols (*e.g.* identification and authentication, technology plus process) or perhaps one that can be categorised in different ways (*e.g.* a door lock is both a physical control and an access control). "A security or privacy control that is implemented for an information system in part as a common control and in part as a system-specific control" *(OMB Circular A-130)*.
Hybrid encryption	"An application of cryptography that combines two or more encryption algorithms, particularly a combination of symmetric and asymmetric encryption" *(SANS glossary)*.
Hybrid hard drive	"Non-volatile magnetic media that use a cache to increase read and write speeds and reduce boot time. The cache is normally flash memory media or battery backed RAM" *(NZISM)*.
Hydra	See THC Hydra.
Hype	Intensive, exaggerated, and biased promotional, political, publicity, or advertising messaging, a commonplace form of social engineering verging on unethical disinformation. See also fake news.
Hypercall	**V**irtual **T**echnology function emulating a system call, mediating guest **O**perating **S**ystem access via the hypervisor to the host OS and thence to the bare metal resources, *e.g.* memory and disk. "A stopgap between a hypervisor and the host to filter and control privileged operations" *(ISACA glossary)*.
Hyperglossary	Contraction of **hyper**linked **glossary**, an intuitive reference resource combining the best features of a glossary, dictionary, wiki, thesaurus, and encyclopaedia with specialist inputs, plain English definitions, and *extensive* cross-referencing between related terms. Hopefully not overhyped but what do you think? More info: https://www.hyperglossary.com/

TERM	MEANING
Hyper-online	Variously termed a cult, subculture, or global community, these are people who use social media obsessively, a compulsion that can cause stress, anxiety, and other mental health or social issues.
HyperText Markup Language (HTML)	Instructions (code) for web browsers on how to display and handle web content.
Hypervisor, Virtual Machine Monitor (VMM)	Virtual Technology program that emulates a conventional Operating System, providing virtual systems with shared processing services and access to the underlying hardware platform (bare metal) resources. Security vulnerabilities in the hypervisor may result in inappropriate interactions such as escape. "A type of software that allows multiple virtual machines to be run on a host machine or group of host machines" *(ISACA glossary)*. See also hypercall.
Hysteresis [loop]	Feature of controls designed to keep a measured parameter (such as pressure) within a defined tolerance range rather than attempting to maintain a setpoint precisely. The parameter cycles between upper and lower limits, giving the control (such as running a pump or opening a relief valve) more time to act. Plotting the controlled parameter against time gives two sigmoid curves that separate between the increasing and decreasing phases, forming a loop with some lag or slack in the control action. Helps prevent the control oscillating too rapidly about the start/stop setpoint, stressing, and perhaps prematurely wearing out mechanical switches, relays, motors, *etc.* at the cost of reduced precision.

[redacted]

TERM	MEANING
IA	*Abbrev:* **I**nformation **A**ssurance or **I**nternal **A**udit, depending on context.
IAAP	*Abbrev:* **I**ntegrated **A**udit & **A**ssurance **P**rofessional.
IaaS	*Abbrev:* **I**nfrastructure-**a**s-**a**-**S**ervice.
IAB	*Abbrev:* **I**nitial **A**ccess **B**roker.
IACS	*Abbrev:* **I**ndustrial **A**utomation and **C**ontrol **S**ystem.
IAD	*Abbrev:* **I**nternal **A**udit **D**epartment.
IANAL (I Am Not A Lawyer)	… and therefore none of this is, or should be construed as, legal advice. Don't take my word for it.
IAPP	US-based trade body supporting privacy professionals and the like. Offers AIGP, CIPM, CIPP, and other qualifications. More info: https://iapp.org/about/
IAST	*Abbrev:* **I**nteractive **A**pplication **S**ecurity **T**esting.
IC	*Abbrev:* **I**ntelligence **C**ommunity or **I**ntegrated **C**ircuit or **I**n **C**ommand (*e.g.* "2IC" means second-in-command), depending on context.
IcedID	Multifunctional malware, primarily a bank Trojan, sharing the same distribution mechanism as Emotet. Can intercept (proxy) **V**irtual **P**rivate **N**etwork traffic and perform HTML injection and **U**niform **R**esource **L**ocator redirection attacks. In the wild in 2019.
ICEP	*Abbrev:* **I**ntegrated **C**ompliance & **E**thics **P**rofessional.
ICS	*Abbrev:* **I**ndustrial **C**ontrol **S**ystems.
ICMP	*Abbrev:* **I**nternet **C**ontrol **M**essage **P**rotocol.
ICQ	*Abbrev:* **I**nternal **C**ontrols **Q**uestionnaire or "I Seek You" Instant Messaging application, depending on context.
ICT	*Abbrev:* **I**nformation and **C**ommunications **T**echnology.
ICT asset	**I**nformation and **C**ommunications **T**echnology asset. "A software or hardware asset in the network and information systems used by the financial entity" *(DORA)*.
ICT concentration risk	"An exposure to individual or multiple related critical ICT third-party service providers creating a degree of dependency on such providers so that the unavailability, failure or other type of shortfall of such provider may potentially endanger the ability of a financial entity to deliver critical or important functions, or cause it to suffer other types of adverse effects, including large losses, or endanger the financial stability of the Union as a whole" *(DORA)*.

TERM	MEANING
ICT equipment	Information and Communications Technology device such as a computer, network hub, or smartphone. "Any device that can process, store or communicate data, such as computers, multifunction devices, network devices, smartphones, digital cameras, electronic storage media, smart devices and other radio devices" *(AusISM).*
ICT Readiness for Business Continuity **(IRBC)**	"Capability of an organization to support its business operations by prevention, detection and response to disruption and recovery of ICT services" *(ISO/IEC 27031).*
ICT-related incident	Incident involving or affecting Information and Communications Technology, *e.g.* malware infection, hack, computer theft, or data centre flood. "A single event or a series of linked events unplanned by the financial entity that compromises the security of the network and information systems, and have an adverse impact on the availability, authenticity, integrity or confidentiality of data, or on the services provided by the financial entity" *(DORA).* See also major ICT-related incident.
ICT risk	Cyber risk. "Any reasonably identifiable circumstance in relation to the use of network and information systems which, if materialised, may compromise the security of the network and information systems, of any technology dependent tool or process, of operations and processes, or of the provision of services by producing adverse effects in the digital or physical environment" *(DORA).*
ICT service	Information and Communications Technology service. "Digital and data services provided through ICT systems to one or more internal or external users on an ongoing basis, including hardware as a service and hardware services which includes the provision of technical support via software or firmware updates by the hardware provider, excluding traditional analogue telephone services" *(DORA).*
ICT third-party risk	"An ICT risk that may arise for a financial entity in relation to its use of ICT services provided by ICT third-party service providers or by subcontractors of the latter, including through outsourcing arrangements" *(DORA).*
ID	*Abbrev:* **ID**entity, **ID**entifier, **ID**entify, **ID**entification, or **I**ntrusion/Intruder **D**etection, depending on context.
IDEA	*Abbrev:* **I**nternational **D**ata **E**ncryption **A**lgorithm.
Identifiability	Capability to uniquely identify and thus distinguish something or someone from others. "Condition which results in a personally identifiable information (PII) principal being identified, directly or indirectly, on the basis of a given set of PII" *(ISO/IEC 29100).* "A condition that results in a personally identifiable information (PII) principal being identified, directly or indirectly, on the basis of a given set of PII" *(ISACA glossary).*

TERM	MEANING
IDentification **(ID)**	a. Assertion by a person, computer system, organisation, *etc.* or recognition, of their identity, usually (but not necessarily) verified by subsequent authentication. "Process involving the search for, recognition, and documentation of potential digital evidence" *(ISO/IEC 27037).* "Process of recognizing the attributes that identify an entity" *(ISO 22300).* b. Recognition, labelling/naming, or characterisation of something, such as a threat, vulnerability, incident, impact, risk, opportunity, change, issue/concern, requirement, or obligation.
Identification and **A**uthentication **(I&A)**	Process of verifying whether a person, *etc.* legitimately holds the identity they claim, in order to reduce the risk of masquerading, identity fraud, unauthorised access, *etc.* See also **A**uthentication, **A**uthorisation, and **A**ccounting.
Identification criteria	"The criteria used to identify opportunities, obstacles, and obligations that stand in front of the organization and its objectives" *(OCEG GRC Glossary).*
IDentifier **(ID)**	Name, code, tag, or label for someone or something in particular, such as a computer user (UserID), worker or customer, or a device (*e.g.* serial number, **I**nternet **P**rotocol, or **M**edia **A**ccess **C**ontrol address).
IDentify **(ID)**	a. To determine, with sufficient assurance for the purpose, precisely who a person is (their individual identity), or what something is (such as a particular network device). A core function within NIST **C**yber **S**ecurity **F**ramework along with protect, detect, respond, and recover. "Develop an organisational understanding to manage cybersecurity risk to systems, people, assets, data, and capabilities. The activities in the Identify Function are foundational for effective use of the Framework. Understanding the business context, the resources that support critical functions, and the related cybersecurity risks enables an organisation to focus and prioritize its efforts, consistent with its risk management strategy and business needs" *(NIST CSF).* b. To discover or reveal – see detect. c. To claim or purport to be, or associate with, *e.g.* "I identify as *Homo sapiens*."

TERM	MEANING
IDentity **(ID)**	Label used to denote an individual person (*e.g.* their name), computer device/*thing*/system (*e.g.* MAC address, **I**nternet **P**rotocol address), account holder (*e.g.* **P**rimary **A**ccount **N**umber), cellphone (IMEI), cellphone subscriber (IMSI), radio operator (callsign), *etc.* May be used to control, direct, monitor, tag, or log their associated activities. "One or more characters used to identify or name a data element and possibly to indicate certain properties of that data element" *(ISO/IEC 2382)*. "A set of attribute values that unambiguously distinguishes one entity from another. The total list of an entity's attribute values allows it to be unambiguously distinguished from all other entities within a given context and also recognized as a single identity in that context" *(ISACA glossary)*. "Unique data used to represent a person's identity and associated attributes. A name or a card number are examples of identifiers. A unique label used by a system to indicate a specific entity, object, or group" *(NIST SP 800-171)*. "Whom someone or what something is, for example, the name by which something is known" *(SANS glossary)*.
Identity and **A**ccess **M**anagement **(IAM)**	"A framework that encapsulates people, processes and products to identify and manage the data used in an information system, authenticate users and grant or deny access rights to data and system resources. The goal of IAM is to provide appropriate access to enterprise resources" *(ISACA glossary)*. "A framework of business processes, policies and technologies that enable and support the management of electronic or digital identities, authorisation, privileges and access to organisational resources. Identity management deals with attributes related to a user (including people, machines, devices and systems). Access Management applies organisation processes, policies and security to enable and manage access. The two aspects are highly interdependent and are most effectively managed conjointly. An IAM framework is a key element in Privileged Access Management (PAM) and Zero Trust architectures" *(NZISM)*.
Identity fraud, identity theft	Type of fraud in which the fraudster masquerades as, impersonates, or falsely assumes the victim's identity, typically as a prelude to stealing or misappropriating financial or other assets such as confidential information. Often involves theft (*e.g.* using infostealer malware), falsification (counterfeiting or faking), or guessing of credentials used to authenticate the holder's claimed identity, exploiting **I**dentification & **A**uthentication vulnerabilities, and misrepresentation.

TERM	MEANING
Identity theft	See identity fraud. Strictly speaking, the theft of personal information is just the first step and sometimes it is not even stolen but willingly provided or disclosed by data subjects for some reason (*e.g.* on a typical LinkedIn profile or **C**urriculum **V**itae).
Idle standby	"A fail-over process in which the primary node owns the resource group and the backup node runs idle, only supervising the primary node. Notes: In case of a primary node outage, the backup node takes over. The nodes are prioritized, which means that the surviving node with the highest priority will acquire the resource group. A higher priority node joining the cluster will thus cause a short service interruption" *(ISACA glossary)*.
IDPP	*Abbrev:* **I**ntegrated **D**ata **P**rivacy **P**rofessional.
IDS/IPS	*Abbrev:* **I**ntrusion **D**etection **S**ystem and/or **I**ntrusion **P**revention **S**ystem.
i.e.	*Abbrev: **id est*** – Latin for "that is."
IEC	*Abbrev:* **I**nternational **E**lectrotechnical **C**ommission – a Geneva-based global standards body focused on harmonising electrical and electronic technologies, safety, compatibility, interoperability, *etc.* More info: https://iec.ch/homepage
IEC 62443	Multipart IEC standard concerning the security of industrial automation and control (**O**perational **T**echnology) systems. Supersedes the ISA 99 series from the **I**nternational **S**ociety of **A**utomation. Builds on the ISO27k information risk-based approach. Defines five **S**ecurity **L**evels from SL0 (no special requirement) up to SL4 (requires 'protection against intentional misuse using sophisticated means with extensive resources'). More info: https://www.iec.ch/blog/understanding-iec-62443
IECQ (International Electrotechnical Commission Quality assessment system for electronic components)	Global certification system covering the supply of electronic components plus the associated materials, assemblies/modules, and processes. Uses quality assessment specifications based on IEC standards. More info: https://www.iecq.org/
IEEE 802.11	"A family of specifications developed by the Institute of Electrical and Electronics Engineers (IEEE) for wireless local area network (WLAN) technology. 802.11 specifies an over-the-air interface between a wireless client and a base station or between two wireless clients" *(ISACA glossary)*.

TERM	MEANING
IETF	*Abbrev:* Internet Engineering Task Force.
IGOP	*Abbrev:* Integrated Governance & Oversight Professional.
IIA®	*Abbrev:* The Institute of Internal Auditors, Inc.
IIN	*Abbrev:* Issuer Identification Number. See Bank Identification Number.
IIoT	*Abbrev:* Industrial IoT.
IKE	*Abbrev:* Internet Key Exchange.
Illegitimate	Literally, not legitimate with connotations of inappropriateness, unethicality, *etc.*
ILOVEU, Love letter	Network worm in 2000 spread to Outlook contacts via email, fooling victims into believing they had received a love letter from a friend (social engineering).
Image	a. Visual/graphical record, facsimile, or representation of a scene or subject (*e.g.* a photograph, video, or sketch). b. Intangible profile, appearance, or brand, *e.g.* a competent, knowledgeable worker may present a 'professional image' to peers and managers. c. See image copy. "Graphical content intended to be presented visually. Note: This includes graphics that are encoded in any electronic format, including, but not limited to, formats that are comprised of individual pixels (*e.g.* those produced by paint programs or by photographic means) and formats that comprised of formulas (*e.g.* those produced as scalable vector drawings)" *(ISO/IEC 22989)*. "An exact bit-stream copy of all electronic data on a device, performed in a manner that ensures the information is not altered" *(NIST SP 800-101)*.
[Mirror] Image copy, image backup	Backup replicating all the data files from a device, disk, volume, or partition, normally stored separately on a different device and/or storage medium for resilience and recovery reasons. See also incremental backup, differential backup, forensic copy, bitwise image, archive.
Image enhancement	Image enhancement. "A transformation of a pictorial image that seeks to increase the value of the information of interest that potentially diminishes other information. Enhancement may actually reduce the information content of the imagery but can aid its interpretation" *(FSRCoP)*.

TERM	MEANING
Image persistence, image retention, screen burn	Static images displayed on a computer screen over a long period can 'burn in' as the phosphor or liquid crystals are damaged, leaving permanent marks that may be visible when the display is showing some other image or when powered off. "LCD/LED/OLED and plasma technologies can be susceptible to persistence or retention of an image or 'ghost' image on the screen. This can also led to screen burn-in, as can occur in traditional CRT monitors" *(NZISM)*.
Image recognition	"Image classification process that classifies object(s), pattern(s) or concept(s) in an image" *(ISO/IEC 22989)*. See also **O**ptical **C**haracter **R**ecognition.
Imaging	a. Creating an image copy. "Process of creating a bitwise copy of digital storage media. Note: The bitwise copy is also called a physical copy. Example: When imaging a hard drive, the DEFR would also copy data that has been deleted" *(ISO/IEC 27037)*. "A process that allows one to obtain a bit-for-bit copy of data to avoid damaging the original data or information when multiple analyses are performed. Notes: The imaging process helps in obtaining residual data, such as deleted files, fragments of deleted files and other information present, from the disk for analysis. This is possible because imaging duplicates the disk surface, sector by sector" *(ISACA glossary)*. b. Visual recording, *e.g.* X-ray imaging.
IMAP (**I**nternet **M**essage **A**ccess **P**rotocol)	Protocol for synchronising one or more email clients with a mail server. In contrast to POP3, a user's emails normally remain on the mail server with IMAP, while the email client has a 'view' of them; hence, the user sees the same emails and folder structure from any logged-on device; also IMAP connections between email client and mail server (*including* the user's mail server logon credentials) can be encrypted. See also SMTP.
IMEI	*Abbrev:* **I**nternational **M**obile **E**quipment **I**dentity.
IMINT (**Im**age **Int**elligence)	Intelligence information collected from images such as still photographs and videos, used to identify objects and activities, *e.g.* to determine the size and composition of military forces. See also HUMINT, TECHINT, SIGINT, OSINT.

TERM	MEANING
Immutable storage	Data storage mechanism designed to prevent the data being changed or deleted having been stored, *e.g.* a WORM drive or cloud storage with suitable security controls. Should prevent ransomware or other incidents damaging backups and archives, provided it functions as designed. "[Immutable] A term that describes something that is unable to be modified after creation" *(ISACA glossary)*.
Impact	Adverse outcome, harm, or consequences caused by or arising from an information security incident, leading to direct and/or indirect (consequential) losses/costs to the organisation/s and/or individual/s concerned. "Adverse change to the level of business objectives achieved" *(ISO/IEC 27000)*. "Outcome of a disruption affecting objectives" *(ISO 22300)*. "A magnitude of loss resulting from a threat exploiting a vulnerability" *(ISACA glossary)*. "A measure that estimates the consequence of an event" *(OCEG GRC Glossary)*. "A measure of the negative effect to the business resulting from the occurrence of an undesired event; what would be the result of a vulnerability being exploited" *(SCP QRG)*. "The result or effect of an event. The event may have a positive or negative effect on the entity's strategy or business objectives" *(IIA GIAS)*. "With respect to security, the effect on organizational operations, organizational assets, individuals, other organizations, or the Nation (including the national security interests of the United States) of a loss of confidentiality, integrity, or availability of information or a system. With respect to privacy, the adverse effects that individuals could experience when an information system processes their PII" *(NIST SP 800-171)*.
Impact analysis, consequence analysis	Systematic, structured exploration and consideration of the potential, likely, or actual consequences of various incidents on the organisation, workers, or other affected parties. "Process of analysing all operational functions and the effect that an operational interruption can have upon them. Note: Impact analysis is part of the risk assessment process and includes business impact analysis. Impact analysis identifies how the loss or damage will manifest itself; the degree for potential escalation of damage or loss with time following an incident; the minimum services and resources (human, physical, and financial) needed to enable business processes to continue to operate at a minimum acceptable level; and the timeframe and extent within which activities, functions and services of the organization should be recovered" *(ISO 22300)*. "A study to prioritize the criticality of information resources for the enterprise based on the costs (or consequences) of adverse events. In an impact analysis, threats to assets are identified and potential business losses are determined for different time periods. This assessment is used to justify the safeguards required and recovery time frames. This analysis is the basis for establishing the recovery strategy" *(ISACA glossary)*.

TERM	MEANING
Impact assessment	Impact assessment – see impact analysis. "A review of the possible consequences of a risk" *(ISACA glossary)*.
Impact value	"The assessed worst-case potential impact that could result from a compromise of the confidentiality, integrity, or availability of information expressed as a value of low, moderate, or high" *(NIST SP 800-171)*.
Impairment	"A condition that causes a weakness or diminished ability to execute audit objectives. Notes: Impairment to organizational independence and individual objectivity may include personal conflict of interest; scope limitations; restrictions on access to records, personnel, equipment, or facilities; and resource limitations (such as funding or staffing)" *(ISACA glossary)*.
Impartial, impartiality	Capability and intention to be and remain neutral, objective, and substantially free of bias and prejudice in a given situation. "Actual or perceived presence of objectivity. Notes: Objectivity means that conflicts of interest do not exist or are resolved so as not to adversely influence subsequent activities. Other terms commonly used to convey the element of impartiality are objectivity, independence, freedom from conflict of interests, freedom from bias, lack of prejudice, neutrality, fairness, open-mindedness, even-handedness, detachment and balance" *(ISO 22300)*.
Imperative	Elaboration on the process, resources, and decisions leading to an objective, as in planning *Cf.* declarative.
Impersonation	Masquerading as another person (identity fraud), computer system, organisation, authority, manager, contact, partner, counterparty, *etc.* for social engineering purposes. "An entity that mimics a system, process or person in an attempt to manipulate the user into an action that can cause an unexpected or unwanted event to a system" *(ISACA glossary)*.
Implant	"Electronic device or electronic equipment modification designed to gain unauthorized interception of information-bearing emanations" *(CNSSI 4009)*. See also bug, mole.
Implementation, implement	a. Process of putting something into practice or production, such as configuring and releasing a newly installed computer system or application. "The process of translating a design into hardware components, software components or both" *(ISACA glossary)*. See implementation phase. b. End result of implementing something. "In business, the full economic life cycle of an investment program through retirement (*i.e.*, when the full expected value of the investment is realized, as much value as is deemed possible has been realized or it is determined that the expected value cannot be realized and the program is terminated)" *(ISACA glossary)*.

TERM	MEANING
Implementation phase, release	Implementation and change management activities that occur between constructing/delivering and starting to use and hopefully gain the benefit of a computer system, information service, strategy, plan, project, policy, procedure, *etc.* Arguably the most risky and stressful phase in the software development lifecycle (crunch time!) with the distinct possibility of 'teething problems' or abject failure, especially if a new, unfamiliar, and as-yet-unproven system is replacing or substantially modifying an existing one, or if it is innovative, critical/vital, complex, inadequately tested, poorly specified, under-resourced, rushed, *etc.* "The period of time in the software life cycle during which a software product is created from design documentation and debugged" *(ISACA glossary).*
Importer	"A natural or legal person established in the Union who places on the market a product with digital elements that bears the name or trademark of a natural or legal person established outside the Union" *(EU CRA).*
Imputation	Process of filling-in and smoothing-over knowledge gaps with information of dubious value, just as I am doing right now in attempting to define this obscure term. "Procedure where missing data are replaced by estimated or modelled data" *(ISO/IEC 22989).* "The replacement of unknown, unmeasured, or missing data with a particular value. The simplest form of imputation is to replace all missing values with the average of that variable" *(NIST SP 800-55v).*
IMSI	*Abbrev:* **I**nternational **M**obile **S**ubscriber **I**dentity.
IMSI-catcher	Device to capture **I**nternational **M**obile **S**ubscriber **I**dentities from nearby phones by masquerading as a cellular base station and spoofing the authentication. See also Stingray.
IMT	*Abbrev:* **I**ncident **M**anagement **T**eam.
In-band	"Communication or transmission that occurs within a previously established communication method or channel. Note: The communications or transmissions often take the form of a separate protocol, such as a management protocol over the same medium as the primary data protocol" *(ISO/IEC 27040). Cf.* out-of-band.
Incentive	Inducement, promised or anticipated benefit or gain. "Financial and non-financial things that encourage favorable conduct" *(OCEG GRC Glossary).*
Incident	Situation in which an information risk materialises, *i.e.* one or more threats exploit one or more vulnerabilities (typically exposed or inadequately protected by inadequate, weak/ineffective, failed, or absent information security controls) causing material impacts on the organisation and stakeholders. Includes the result of deliberate breaches plus serious accidents and natural events. Provided adequate detective controls are in place, incidents

TERM	MEANING
	typically generate alarms or alerts and log entries, ideally early in the process allowing the organisation to respond promptly, thus minimising the impacts. *"*Single or a series of unwanted or unexpected information security events that have a significant probability of compromising business operations and threatening information security" *(ISO/IEC 27005)*. "Single or a series of unwanted or unexpected information security breaches or events, whether of criminal nature or not, that have a significant probability of compromising business operations or threatening information security" *(ISO/IEC 27043)*. "Event that can be, or could lead to, a disruption, loss, emergency or crisis" *(ISO 22300)*. "A violation or imminent threat of violation of computer security policies, acceptable use policies, guidelines or standard security practices" *(ISACA glossary)*. "An event that has been assessed as having an actual or potentially adverse effect on the security or performance of a system" *(ENISA RM glossary)*. "An occurrence that actually or imminently jeopardizes, without lawful authority, the confidentiality, integrity, or availability of information or an information system; or constitutes a violation or imminent threat of violation of law, security policies, security procedures, or acceptable use policies" *(NIST SP 800-171)*. "An adverse network event in an information system or network or the threat of the occurrence of such an event" *(SANS glossary)*. See also near-miss, event, crisis, emergency.
Incident command	See incident management. "Process that is conducted as part of an incident management system, and which evolves during the management of an incident" *(ISO 22300)*.
Incident coordinator	"Person responsible for leading all incident response activities and coordinating the incident response team. Note: an organization can decide to use another term for the incident coordinator" *(ISO/IEC 27035-1)*. The professionals who "manage and coordinate cross-government response to significant incidents and engage with victims" *(UK NCSC)*.
Incident detection	Until an information security incident has been noticed by the affected parties, it cannot be analysed and no specific response can be triggered. This is a critical first step in the incident management process with implications for detective controls, alarms, alerts, logging, *etc.* and, of course, information risks.
Incident handlers	The professionals who "manage and respond to incidents, engage with victims and where necessary support coordinators on significant incidents" *(UK NCSC)*.

TERM	MEANING
Incident handling	Actions undertaken by incident handlers and other experts to address incidents. "Actions of detecting, reporting, assessing, responding to, dealing with, and learning from information security incidents" *(ISO/IEC 27035-1)*. "An action plan for dealing with intrusions, cyber-theft, denial of service, fire, floods, and other security-related events. It is comprised of a six step process: Preparation, Identification, Containment, Eradication, Recovery, and Lessons Learned" *(SANS glossary)*.
Incident management	Rational direction of activities to bring an incident under control, assess the situation, and respond accordingly. Follows on from crisis management and leads into contingency management. "The management and coordination of activities to investigate, and remediate, an actual or potential occurrence of an adverse cyber event that may compromise or cause harm to a system or network" *(UK National Cyber Security Strategy 2022)*.
Incident **M**anagement **S**ystem **(IMS)**	Management system for various types of incident, or at least some sort of system supporting incident management. "System that defines the roles and responsibilities of personnel and the operating procedures to be used in the management of incidents" *(ISO 22300)*.
Incident **M**anagement **T**eam **(IMT)**	"Team consisting of appropriately skilled and trusted members of an organization responsible for leading all information security incident management activities, in coordination with other parties both internal and external throughout incident lifecycle. Note: The head of this team can be called the incident manager who has been appointed by top management to adequately respond to all types of incidents" *(ISO/IEC 27035-1)*. See also Incident **R**esponse **T**eam.
Incident preparedness	Readiness to deal with incidents. "Activities taken to prepare for incident response" *(ISO 22300)*.
Incident recovery	Final clear-up phase following an incident which achieves a return to (near) normality.
Incident reporters	The professionals who "produce professional products on incidents to ensure all relevant government partners and agencies are updated on developments" *(UK NCSC)*.
Incident response	What the Incident **R**esponse **T**eam does, *i.e.* investigate, assess, react appropriately to, and in time resolve and help the organisation learn from, incidents. "Actions taken to mitigate or resolve an information security incident, including those taken to protect and restore the normal operational conditions of an information system and the information stored in it" *(ISO/IEC 27035-1)*.

TERM	MEANING
	"Actions taken in order to stop the causes of an imminent hazard and/or mitigate the consequences of potentially destabilizing events or disruptions, and to recover to a normal situation. Note: Incident response is part of the emergency management process" *(ISO 22300)*. "The response of an enterprise to a disaster or other significant event that may significantly affect the enterprise, its people or its ability to function productively. Incident response may include evacuation of a facility, initiating a disaster recovery plan (DRP), performing a damage assessment or any other measures necessary to bring an enterprise to a more stable status" *(ISACA glossary)*. "The activities that address the short-term, direct effects of an incident, and may also support short-term recovery" *(UK National Cyber Security Strategy 2022)*. "The structured process of identifying, managing, and mitigating the effects of cybersecurity incidents to minimize damage, recover operations, and prevent future occurrences" *(SANS glossary)*.
Incident **R**esponse **P**lan **(IRP)**	Planned procedure enabling the organisation to deal promptly, efficiently and effectively with one or more information security incidents. "The operational component of incident management (also called IRP). Note: The plan includes documented procedures and guidelines for defining the criticality of incidents, reporting and escalation processes and recovery procedures" *(ISACA glossary)*. "The documentation of a predetermined set of instructions or procedures to detect, respond to, and limit consequences of an incident against an organisation's IT system(s)" *(CNSSI 4009)*. "A plan for responding to information security incidents as defined by the individual agency" *(NZISM)*. "A document that describes the plan for responding to cyber security incidents" *(AusISM)*.
Incident **R**esponse **T**eam **(IRT)**	People readied (trained, motivated, primed, and prepared) to respond promptly, efficiently, and effectively to various security incidents. "Team of appropriately skilled and trusted members of an organization that respond to and resolved incident in a coordinated way. Notes: there can be several IRTs, one for each aspect of the incident. Computer Emergency Response Team (CERT) and Computer Security Incident Response Team (CSIRT) are specific examples of IRTs in organizations and sectorial, regional, and national entities wanting to coordinate their response to large scale ICT and cybersecurity incidents" *(ISO/IEC 27035-1)*. See also CERT.
Incinerate	Destroy by burning, a technique used to prevent further disclosure of information on storage media. "Destruct by burning media completely to ashes" *(ISO/IEC 27040)*.
Incompetent, incompetence	Literally, not sufficiently competent, skilled, experienced, and capable to perform an activity, duty, task, or rôle to the required level. Often used pejoratively as a personal criticism, implying idiocy, carelessness, *etc*.

TERM	MEANING
Inconsistent, inconsistently	Lacking in consistency and therefore unreliable, untrustworthy, and of dubious value. Particularly significant for anything important, significant, serious, critical, or vital.
Incremental backup	Backup of files that have been created or changed since the previous incremental or image backup. To restore a computer system fully, it is generally necessary to restore the entire sequence of incremental backups subsequent to the most recent image backup. "Incremental backups only backup the files that have been modified since the last backup. If dump levels are used, incremental backups only backup files changed since last backup of a lower dump level" *(SANS glossary)*. See also differential backup.
Incremental development	Software development approach (such as iterative or **R**apid **A**pplication **D**evelopment) involving sequential delivery of relatively minor evolutionary program and functional changes rather than fewer but more significant step-changes (the waterfall method). "A software development technique in which requirements definition, design, implementation and testing occur in an overlapping, iterative (rather than sequential) manner, resulting in incremental completion of the overall software product. Contrasts with rapid prototyping, the spiral model and the waterfall model" *(ISACA glossary)*.
Incremental test	Assurance process focused on testing changes made since the previous test, rather than retesting previously tested aspect every time. Presumes full knowledge of the changes made, and a high degree of independence between changes not often found in systems, hence is normally complemented by regression tests and others. "The deliberate testing of only the value added functionality of a software component" *(ISACA glossary)*. See also integration test, system test, penetration test, load test, stress test, security test, acceptance test.
Incriminate, incriminating, incrimination	Provision of information indicating someone's guilt or involvement in an illegal or otherwise inappropriate, unauthorised, or forbidden activity.
Inculpatory evidence	Forensic evidence allegedly proving that someone or something *was* involved in an incident, and hence, they may be culpable (guilty of some offence). "Evidence that tends to increase the likelihood of fault or guilt" *(NIST SP 800-101)*. *Cf.* exculpatory.
Independent	Not dependent, reliant, linked, or associated but free of external influence, control or constraint, objective, unbiased, and dispassionate. Along with personal integrity, a fundamental requirement for science, forensics, and auditing (see audit independence), and important for other forms of assurance such as testing and product evaluation.

TERM	MEANING
Independent attitude	"An attitude with an impartial point of view. This attitude allows an IS auditor to act objectively and with fairness" *(ISACA glossary)*.
Independent Test Laboratory (ITL)	Independent, competent, and trustworthy commercial scientific testing facility. "Third-party security testing body that conducts security evaluations for products" *(ISO/IEC 27404 DRAFT)*.
Independent Verification and Validation (IV&V)	"A comprehensive review, analysis, and testing (software and/or hardware) performed by an objective third party to confirm (*i.e.*, verify) that the requirements are correctly defined, and to confirm (*i.e.*, validate) that the system correctly implements the required functionality and security requirements" *(CNSSI 4009)*.
Indicator	Something that gives 'an indication' – often an indirect, approximate, vague, and/or imprecise measure or symptom of something, as opposed to a metric. "Measure that provides an estimate or evaluation of something" *(ISO/IEC 27000)*. "A measure of progress toward or status of an objective" *(OCEG GRC Glossary)*.
Indicator Of Attack (IOA)	Incident response or threat intelligence term for the characteristic evidence indicating that computer systems are currently in the process of being compromised by hackers or malware, *e.g.* malicious network probes used to enumerate devices, map the network, and search for exploitable vulnerabilities. See also Indicator Of Compromise.
Indicator Of Compromise (IOC)	Incident response or threat intelligence term for the characteristic evidence indicating that computer systems have been compromised by hackers or malware. Artefacts such as log entries, executable files, scripts, running processes, network services, and open ports may provide useful clues about the existence and nature of even covert incidents (*e.g.* spyware and rootkits). See also Indicator Of Attack.
Indirect connection	"A connection to a device or network, which does not take place directly but rather as part of a larger system that is directly connectable to such device or network" *(EU CRA)*.
Induction, responsibility induction, orientation, sheep-dip	Process of introducing new workers to the organisation, its business, history, mission, objectives, governance and management, culture, rules, rôles, responsibilities, *etc.* Informing and motivating them have to be balanced against the possibility of eroding the very qualities that led to their being employed, and overloading them at the start. In practice, the process extends well beyond the typical Human Resources-led training session as newcomers interact with their new managers, peers, and other colleagues, gradually becoming assimilated into the team and corporate culture and hopefully security-aware.

TERM	MEANING
Industrial **A**utomation and **C**ontrol **S**ystem **(IACS)**	**O**perational **T**echnology system monitoring and controlling industrial plant, geographically dispersed utility equipment (remote valves, switches, temperature/pressure gauges), *etc.* See also **A**utomation and **C**ontrol **S**ystem, **S**upervisory **C**ontrol **A**nd **D**ata **A**cquisition, **I**ndustrial **C**ontrol **S**ystem.
Industrial complex	Alludes to a sinister and oppressive widespread conspiracy between large, powerful commercial organisations and the state (more specifically, the deep state), not unlike Big Brother. Trigger term linked to misinformation and disinformation, or to information depending on one's perspective. See also narrative.
Industrial **C**ontrol **S**ystems **(ICS)**	Low-level embedded systems and related **O**perational **T**echnology equipment (**I**ndustrial **I**nternet **o**f *Things* smart *things*, actuators, relays, and sensors) controlling industrial plant (valves, pumps, motors, machine tools, ovens, robots, *etc.*). "An information system used to control industrial processes such as manufacturing, product handling, production, and distribution. Industrial control systems include supervisory control and data acquisition systems used to control geographically dispersed assets, as well as distributed control systems and smaller control systems using programmable logic controllers to control localized processes" *(NIST SP 800-39)*. "An information system used to control industrial processes, such as manufacturing, product handling, production and distribution, or to control infrastructure assets" *(UK National Cyber Security Strategy 2022)*. See also **S**upervisory **C**ontrol **A**nd **D**ata **A**cquisition, **I**ndustrial **A**utomation and **C**ontrol **S**ystem, **P**rocess **C**ontrol **S**ystem.
Industrial espionage	Use of unethical, illicit, surreptitious, and often illegal surveillance, spying, and similar techniques to gather sensitive and valuable information from competitors, either directly (*e.g.* by physical site penetration or coercing insiders) or via common business partners or other third parties such as private detectives or information brokers.
Industrial **I**nternet **o**f **T**hings **(IIoT)**	**I**nternet **o**f *Things* applied to industrial (*e.g.* manufacturing shop floor automation) and commercial contexts (*e.g.* reading and controlling electricity, gas, or water meters), as opposed to consumer/home/personal purposes. Industrial *things* include robotic plant, most **S**upervisory **C**ontrol **A**nd **D**ata **A**cquisition/ **I**ndustrial **C**ontrol **S**ystem devices, modern smart vehicles, and machine tools. See also mesh network.
Infect, infection, infectious	By analogy to the biological process, malware is said to 'infect' vulnerable computer systems when it spreads to, executes on, and thus compromises them.

TERM	MEANING
Inference	Logically surmising, presuming, or deducing something from available information. "Reasoning by which conclusions are derived from known premises. Notes: In AI, a premise is either a fact, a rule, a model, a feature or raw data; The term 'inference' refers both to the process and its result" *(ISO/IEC 22989)*.
Inference attack	a. Type of cryptanalytic attack that relies on inferring certain properties or values to break the cryptosystem. b. Type of **D**ata**B**ase or **A**rtificial **I**ntelligence system attack in which certain combinations of queries, perhaps in conjunction with information obtained separately, can be used to infer additional, often sensitive information that is not directly available (*e.g.* queries that report results quickly are probably working with smaller datasets or samples than equivalent queries of similar complexity that take much longer to execute). c. Some other kind of attack involving logical analysis. "Inference attacks rely on the user to make logical connections between seemingly unrelated pieces of information" *(SANS glossary)*.
Infiltrator, infiltration, ingress	Outsider who somehow manages to work their way into a privileged position of trust within the organisation or penetrate its computer systems and networks, gaining internal/insider access to corporate assets typically with the intent of stealing proprietary information (industrial espionage), sabotaging critical business processes, committing cybertage, and/or recruiting insiders. Long-term physical infiltration by moles and sleepers is popular in spy novels but uncommon in the commercial world due to the high costs and risks compared to, say, employing, bribing or coercing insiders, social engineering, short-term physical site penetration (*e.g.* trespass, draining), deploying malware, hacking, *etc. Cf.* exfiltration.
INFOCON (INFormation Operations CONdition)	US military indicator of cyberwar status, ranging from 5 (normal) up to 1 (maximum readiness).
Information	Expression of knowledge that has meaning and hence value. Knowledge itself is intangible information, although it may be represented, stored, expressed, communicated, and processed in the form of writing, diagrams, speech, expressions, mime, sign language, Morse code, semaphore, smoke signals, computer data, *etc.* "Knowledge concerning objects, such as facts, events, things, processes, or ideas, including concepts, that within a certain context has a particular meaning" *(ISO/IEC 2382)*. "Data processed, organized and correlated to produce meaning" *(ISO 22300)*. "An asset that, like other important business assets, is essential to an enterprise's business. It can exist in many forms. It can be printed or written on paper, stored electronically, transmitted by post or by using electronic means, shown on films, or spoken in conversation"

TERM	MEANING
	(ISACA glossary). "Any communication or representation of knowledge such as facts, data, and opinions in any medium or form, electronic as well as physical. Information includes any text, numerical, graphic, cartographic, narrative, or any audio or visual representation" *(NZISM)*. "Any communication or representation of knowledge such as facts, data, or opinions in any medium or form, including textual, numerical, graphic, cartographic, narrative, electronic, or audiovisual forms" *(OMB Circular A-130)*.
Information actions & controls	"Communications and reports up, down, and across the organization used to address risk, reward, and compliance" *(OCEG GRC Glossary)*.
Information and Communications Technology (ICT)	*Explicit* extension of **I**nformation **T**echnology to include **C**ommunications **T**echnology. Note: plain "IT" almost always implies both aspects. "Includes: information management; technology infrastructure; and technology-enabled business processes and services" *(NZISM)*. "Technology for gathering, storing, retrieving, processing, analyzing and transmitting information" *(ISO 9241)*. *Cf.* **O**perational **T**echnology, **M**obile **T**echnology, **V**irtual **T**echnology, **S**mart **T**echnology.
Information and communication technology disaster recovery	See **D**isaster **R**ecovery. "Ability of the information and communication technology elements of an organization to support its critical processes and activities to an acceptable level within a predetermined period of time following a disruption" *(ISO/IEC 27031)*.
Information and communication technology disaster readiness	See **D**isaster **R**ecovery. "State of an information and communication technology (ICT) function in which it has the knowledge, skills, processes, architecture, infrastructure and the related technologies in preparation for a potential event that would lead to either an intolerable disruption of ICT or an intolerable data loss" *(ISO/IEC 27031)*.
Information and systems	"Refers to information in electronic form (electronic information) during its use, processing, transmission, and storage and systems that use, process, transmit or transfer, and store information or that produce, manufacture, or distribute products" *(**T**rust **S**ervices **C**riteria)*.
Information architecture	High-level design perspective on the sources, flows, stores, processing and legitimate exploitation of information or data within the enterprise, and perhaps beyond (*e.g.* information content and services provided to or by third parties). "One component of IT architecture (together with applications and technology)" *(ISACA glossary)*.

TERM	MEANING
Information asset	Valuable information and, in some interpretations, the computer systems, storage media, or people that store/hold and/or process it. Vulnerable to various information risks. Depending partly on the jurisdiction and situation, an information asset held by the organisation may legally belong to the organisation, to an individual (*e.g.* personal information), to a third party who revealed or entrusted it to another (thereby creating a custodial responsibility, whether explicit or implicit), or may be a part of the common wealth or public property or of unknown origin and provenance. "Any information or related equipment has value to an organisation. This includes equipment, facilities, patents, intellectual property, software and hardware. Information Assets also include services, information, and people, and characteristics such as reputation, brand, image, skills, capability and knowledge" *(NZISM)*. "Data and the associated software and infrastructure used to process, transmit, and store information or to produce, manufacture, or distribute products" *(Trust Services Criteria)*. "A collection of information, either tangible or intangible, that is worth protecting" *(DORA)*.
Information asset owner	See information owner.
Information **A**ssurance **(IA)**	Act of assessing and evaluating the suitability and adequacy of arrangements protecting valuable information. "Measures that protect and defend information and information systems by ensuring their availability, integrity, authentication, confidentiality, and non-repudiation. These measures include providing for restoration of information systems by incorporating protection, detection, and reaction capabilities" *(CNSSI 4009)*.
Information broker	Someone who trades commercially in information. While the consulting, publishing, news, and other industries trade legitimately in information, unethical brokers trade in information that has been obtained illegally (stolen), compromised, or disclosed inappropriately, *e.g.* obtained under false pretences through social engineering or coercion.
Information capital	"Data, communications, and intelligence" *(OCEG GRC Glossary)*.
Information consumer, information user	"An individual, group, or any entity that receives information" *(OCEG GRC Glossary)*.
Information flow control	Control over the passage or movement of information between endpoints, *e.g.* permitting bidirectional or unidirectional flow. "Procedure to ensure that information transfers within a system do not violate the security policy" *(NIST SP 800-171)*.
Information **M**anagement **(IM)**	Systematic, professional management of one or more types/classes of information to achieve objectives specified by its owners, custodians, and other stakeholders.

TERM	MEANING
Information need	Strong desire, requirement, or desperate demand for information. "Insight necessary to manage objectives, goals, risks and problems" *(ISO/IEC/IEEE 15939).*
Information Operations (IO)	Information operations. "The integrated employment of the core capabilities of electronic warfare, computer network operations, psychological operations, military deception, and operations security, in concert with specified supporting and related capabilities, to influence, disrupt, corrupt, or usurp adversarial human and automated decision-making process, information, and information systems while protecting our own" *(CNSSI 4009).*
Information overload	Subjective human impression or experience that new information is arriving faster than it can be processed, potentially leading to stress, exhaustion, and withdrawal (dysfunction, zoning-out, depression). See also overload.
Information owner	Organisation, rôle, or person who notionally or literally owns and is responsible and usually accountable to management or other authorities for the proper protection and legitimate exploitation of valuable information. May be a custodian, steward, or agent acting on behalf of the legal owner. May be required or expected to: commission and sponsor information risk analyses, approve risk evaluations and fund the corresponding risk treatments including controls, define access policies and authorise access, and review and monitor the effectiveness of the controls and own the residual risks. See also asset owner, control owner, data owner, infrastructure owner, network owner, process owner, risk owner, system owner, service owner, problem owner.
Information processing	Archaic term for Information Technology. "Systematic performance of operations upon information, that includes data processing and may include operations such as data communication and office automation. Note: The term information processing must not be used as a synonym for data processing" *(ISO/IEC 2382).*
Information processing facility	Archaic term for data centre, computer suite/room, *etc*. "Any information processing system, service or infrastructure, or the physical location housing it" *(ISO/IEC 27002).*
Information producer	"An individual, group, or any entity that produces data/information to send to another individual, group, or entity" *(OCEG GRC Glossary).*
Information protection, data protection	Whereas privacy is the primary concern of information/data protection laws, they may also require accuracy, informed consent, usage only for stated purposes and destruction once the purpose is achieved, extending the remit beyond confidentiality and control or ownership.

TERM	MEANING
Information resource	See information asset. "Information and related resources, such as personnel, equipment, funds, and information technology" *(NIST SP 800-171)*.
Information **R**etrieval **(IR)**	Recalling or remembering previously stored information. "Task of retrieving relevant documents or parts of documents from a dataset, typically based on keyword or natural language queries" *(ISO/IEC 22989)*.
Information risk	Risk involving or affecting information, normally involving the deliberate, incidental, or accidental action of [one or more] threats on [one or more] exposed vulnerabilities relating to [one or more] information assets, causing [one or more] impacts. See also information security risk.
Information **R**isk **A**ssessment **M**ethodology № **2 (IRAM2)**	Second version of the **I**nformation **S**ecurity **F**orum's systematic information risk management process involving scoping, **B**usiness **I**mpact **A**ssessment, threat profiling, vulnerability assessment, risk evaluation, and risk treatment.
Information **R**isk **M**anagement **(IRM),** **I**nformation **R**isk and **S**ecurity **M**anagement **(IRSM)**	Activities involved in identifying, evaluating, and treating risks pertaining to information, particularly the use of information security controls to mitigate unacceptable information risks. Includes the governance arrangements and management activities such as preparing and executing strategies, policies, plans, *etc.*; monitoring performance and other metrics; managing incidents; and integrating these with other business activities (such as risk management, **B**usiness **C**ontinuity **M**anagement**,** compliance management, and **I**nternal **A**udit) in support of the organisation's mission and objectives.
Information **R**isk **M**anagement **S**ystem **(IRMS)**	**M**anagement **S**ystem by which the organisation's information risks are systematically identified, assessed, evaluated, treated, and monitored, supporting the achievement of business objectives. See also **I**nformation **S**ecurity **M**anagement **S**ystem.
Information **sec**urity **(infosec)**	Act of securing, guarding, or protecting information without unduly restricting its legitimate exploitation. In more detail, the risk management and assurance activities involving the specification, design, implementation, operation, measurement, management, monitoring and maintenance of controls, and other risk treatments in order to satisfy requirements for confidentiality, integrity, and availability of information by constraining the number and/or severity of incidents. Broader in scope than **I**nformation **T**echnology security or cybersecurity since it encompasses other technologies (such as **O**perational **T**echnology) and information of all forms (including knowledge and **I**ntellectual **P**roperty), not just digital data and computer systems. "Preservation of confidentiality, integrity and availability of information. Note: in addition,

TERM	MEANING
	other properties, such as authenticity, accountability, non-repudiation, and reliability can also be involved" *(ISO/IEC 27000)*. "The assurance that information is protected against disclosure to unauthorized users (confidentiality), improper modification (integrity) and nonaccess when required (availability). Information security deals with all formats of information—paper documents, digital assets, intellectual property in people's minds and verbal and visual communications" *(ISACA glossary)*. "The protection of information and systems from unauthorized access, use, disclosure, disruption, modification, or destruction to provide confidentiality, integrity, and availability. Note: the term 'cybersecurity' can be used interchangeably with 'information security'" *(NIST SP 800-55v1)*. "Measures relating to the confidentiality, availability and integrity of information that is processed, stored and communicated by electronic or any other means" *(NZISM)*. "Refers to the practice of protecting information from unauthorized access, disclosure, alteration, destruction, or disruption" *(SANS glossary)*.
Information security architecture	High-level architectural blueprint or design for the organisation's information security arrangements, linking even higher-level information security, Information, risk, compliance, and business strategies through to security designs for individual computer systems, business processes, technologies, applications, *etc*. "An embedded, integral part of the enterprise architecture that describes the structure and behavior for an enterprise's security processes, information security systems, personnel and organizational sub-units, showing their alignment with the enterprise's mission and strategic plans" *(NIST SP 800-39)*.
Information **S**ecurity **A**ssessment **(ISA)**	a. Assurance process to quantify residual information risks by reviewing the effectiveness of information security controls. b. Excel spreadsheet detailing information security control requirements for automotive companies, derived from ISO/IEC 27001:2013 Annex A under the TISAX scheme by **V**erband **D**er **A**utomobilindustrie, an automotive industry trade body. "An information security requirements catalogue based on key aspects of the international standard ISO/IEC 27001. It is used by companies both for internal purposes as well as assessments by suppliers and service providers who process sensitive information from their respective companies" *(ENX.com)*. More info: https://www.vda.de/dam/jcr:80a83325-3287-456f-a4f1-01afb2cc063f/ISA6_EN_FINAL.xlsx
Information security breach	Incident that compromises information. "Compromise of information security that leads to the undesired destruction, loss, alteration, disclosure of, or access to, protected information transmitted, stored or otherwise processed" *(ISO/IEC 27002)*.

TERM	MEANING
Information security continuity	Business continuity arrangements for any business-critical parts or functions of the information security department. "Processes and procedures for ensuring continued information security operations" *(ISO/IEC 27000)*.
Information security control	Control designed to mitigate unacceptable information security risks, *e.g.* by achieving and maintaining adequate levels of information confidentiality, integrity, and availability (the CIA triad).
Information security design	Architecture for the controls addressing information security risks and control objectives or other requirements of a system or process. May comprise explicit security design documents, be distributed among various design, development and operations documents, policies, procedures, change records, *etc.* or be undocumented, merely implicit.
Information security event	Event involving the compromise of information security. "Identified occurrence of a system, service or network state indicating a possible breach of information security policy or failure of controls, or a previously unknown situation that may be security relevant" *(ISO/IEC 27000)*. "Occurrence indicating a possible information security breach or failure of controls" *(ISO/IEC 27002)*. "Occurrence indicating a possible breach of information security or failure of controls" *(ISO/IEC 27035-1)*. See also security event.
Information **S**ecurity **F**orum **(ISF)**	Professional/trade body that conducts original research and develops information security standards, guidelines, methods, tools, and services (such as security benchmarking) for its corporate members. Its conferences are highly regarded and free for members. Was originally the **E**uropean **S**ecurity **F**orum. More info: https://www.securityforum.org/
Information security governance	Governance of the information security function and activities. "The set of responsibilities and practices exercised by the board and executive management with the goal of providing strategic direction, ensuring that objectives are achieved, ascertaining that risk is managed appropriately and verifying that the enterprise's information security resources are used responsibly" *(ISACA glossary)*.
Information security incident	See incident. "One or multiple related and identified information security events that can harm an organization's assets or compromise its operations" *(ISO/IEC 27002)*. "Single or a series of unwanted or unexpected information security events that have a significant probability of compromising business operations and threatening information security" *(ISO/IEC 27035-1)*. "Related and identified information security events that can harm an organization's assets or compromise its operations" *(ISO/IEC 27035-1)*. "An occurrence or activity that may threaten the confidentiality, integrity or availability of a system or the information stored, processed or communicated by it or by any other process or system and processes" *(NZISM)*.

TERM	MEANING
Information security incident management	See incident management. "Exercise of a consistent and effective approach to the handling of information security incidents" *(ISO/IEC 27002)*. "Processes for detecting, reporting, assessing, responding to, dealing with, and learning from information security incidents" *(ISO/IEC 27000)*. "Collaborative activities to handle information security incidents in a consistent and effective way" *(ISO/IEC 27035-1)*.
Information security investigation	"Application of examinations, analysis and interpretation to aid understanding of an information security incident. [SOURCE: ISO/IEC 27042, modified]" *(ISO/IEC 27035-1)*.
Information **S**ecurity **M**anagement **(ISM)**	Corporate function responsible for day-to-day management of information security, managing technical, procedural, and physical controls, systems, processes, standards, *etc.* Led by the **I**nformation **S**ecurity **M**anager.
Information **S**ecurity **M**anagement **S**ystem **(ISMS)**	**M**anagement **S**ystem by which information security strategies are defined and executed, and security operations are designed, directed, monitored, overseen, and controlled in order to mitigate unacceptable information risks. "The policies, procedures, guidelines, and associated resources and activities, collectively managed by an organisation, in the pursuit of protecting its information assets ... a systematic approach for establishing, implementing, operating, monitoring, reviewing, maintaining and improving an organisation's information security to achieve business objectives ... based upon a risk assessment and the organisation's risk acceptance levels designed to effectively treat and manage risks ... analysing requirements for the protection of information assets and applying appropriate controls to ensure the protection of these information assets, as required, contributes to the successful implementation of an ISMS ..." *(ISO/IEC 27000)*. *Note*: although 'information security management system' is not formally defined as such in the glossary section of ISO/IEC 27000, both 'information security' and 'management system' are separately defined, the abbreviation 'ISMS' is expanded in Section 0.1 'Overview' and an ISMS is described in Section 3.2 "What is an ISMS?." See also **I**nformation **R**isk **M**anagement **S**ystem, **P**rivacy **I**nformation **M**anagement **S**ystem.
Information **S**ecurity **M**anagement **S**ystem **(ISMS) professional**	"Person who establishes, implements, maintains and continuously improves one or more information security management system processes" *(ISO/IEC 27000)*.
Information **S**ecurity **M**anagement **S**ystem **(ISMS) scope**	Formally documented description of the boundary of an organisation's **I**nformation **S**ecurity **M**anagement **S**ystem, defined in terms that make sense in the business context, *e.g.* the ISMS may apply to the entire enterprise (potentially with exceptions) or a specified part (*e.g.* one or more business units, departments, functions, sites/locations, countries, *etc.*). The scope could also be defined

TERM	MEANING
	in relation to the organisation's information risks (*e.g.* 'The ISMS is used to manage information risks classed as high or above') or information assets (*e.g.* 'The ISMS protects digital data, computer systems and networks') or some combination of factors. "The organization shall determine the boundaries and applicability of the information security management system to establish its scope. When determining this scope, the organization shall consider: a) the external and internal issues referred to in 4.1; b) the requirements referred to in 4.2; c) interfaces and dependencies between activities performed by the organization, and those that are performed by other organizations. The scope shall be available as documented information" *(ISO/IEC 27001 clause 4.3).*
Information Security Manager (ISM)	Manager (leader) of the **I**nformation **S**ecurity **M**anagement function. Typically reports to a **C**hief **I**nformation **S**ecurity **O**fficer.
Information security objective	Requirement or expectation relating to information security. An obvious objective is to ensure the confidentiality, integrity, and availability of information but there are other possibilities, such as facilitating the legitimate exploitation of information, providing assurance, competently managing information risks, or cost-effectively managing information security. Can be framed in technology, process, risk, business, strategic, operational, or other terms according to the context. Can declare desired goals and/or unwanted anti-goals (such as reducing the number and severity of incidents). Can be broad or specific. Usually phrased in terms of anticipated outcomes but may specify methods, approaches or techniques to achieve intended outcomes. See also control objective.
Information security policy	Policy concerning, or relating in some way to, the security and protection of information. "A high-level document that describes how an agency protects its systems. The CSP [**C**yber **S**ecurity **P**olicy?] is normally developed to cover all systems and can exist as a single document or as a set of related documents" *(NZISM).*
Information security policy manual or suite	Organisation's collection of policies relating to information risk and information security. May incorporate or reference policies in related areas such as physical security, privacy, governance, compliance, cybersecurity, incident management, and **B**usiness **C**ontinuity **M**anagement.
Information security program	a. The organisation's current and/or planned activities, projects, investments, initiatives, *etc.* concerning information security and related areas, in whole or in part. "The combination of technical, operational and procedural measures and management structures implemented to provide for the confidentiality, integrity and availability of information based on business requirements and risk analysis" *(ISACA glossary).* b. Software application providing information security functions.

TERM	MEANING
Information security risk	Uncertain possibility of incidents involving or affecting information security, in particular the loss of information confidentiality, integrity, and/or availability (the CIA triad). "Potential that a threat will exploit a vulnerability of an asset or group of assets and thereby cause harm to an organisation" *(ISO/IEC 27000)*. "The risk to organizational operations (including mission, functions, image, reputation), organizational assets, individuals, other organizations, and the Nation due to the potential for unauthorized access, use, disclosure, disruption, modification, or destruction of information and/or information systems" *(NIST SP 800-39)*. See also information risk, confidentiality risk, integrity risk, availability risk.
Information service	Service revolving around the generation, processing, and provision of information, such as electronic publishing, email, or espionage. Usually but not necessarily automated using technology.
Information sharing community	"Group of organisations that agree to share information. Note: an organisation can be an individual" *(ISO/IEC 27000)*.
Information superiority	Given the strategic importance of obtaining an adversary's information and its value, spooks generally aim to be *even better* than their peers and opponents at gathering, interpreting, and making use of foreign intelligence while, at the same time, protecting domestic intelligence from disclosure, interception, surveillance, spying, *etc.*
I**nformation S**ystem **(IS)**	System, computer, *thing*, host, node, device, client, server, application, process, service, technology, *etc.* involved in generating, storing, processing, manipulating, using/exploiting, and communicating information. Often ambiguously shortened to 'system': is that just the computer itself or the whole structure? "Information processing system, together with associated organizational resources such as human, technical, and financial resources, that provides and distributes information [and] system consisting of a conceptual schema, information base, and information processor, forming together a system for keeping and manipulating information" *(ISO/IEC 2382)*. "Set of applications, services, information technology assets, or other information-handling components" *(ISO/IEC 27002)*. "The combination of strategic, managerial and operational activities involved in gathering, processing, storing, distributing and using information and its related technologies. Note: Information systems are distinct from information technology (IT) in that an information system has an IT component that interacts with the process components" *(ISACA glossary)*. "A discrete set of information resources organized for the collection, processing, maintenance, use, sharing, dissemination, or disposition of information" *(NIST SP 800-171)*.

TERM	MEANING
Information system-related security risks	"Risks that arise through the loss of confidentiality, integrity, or availability of information or information systems and consider impacts to the organization (including assets, mission, functions, image, or reputation), individuals, other organizations, and the Nation. See Risk" *(NIST SP 800-39)*.
Information system resilience	Information system resilience. "The ability of an information system to continue to: (i) operate under adverse conditions or stress, even if in a degraded or debilitated state, while maintaining essential operational capabilities; and (ii) recover to an effective operational posture in a time frame consistent with mission needs" *(NIST SP 800-39)*. "The ability of an information system to operate under adverse conditions or stress, even if in a degraded or debilitated state, while maintaining essential operational capabilities, and to recover to an effective operational posture in a time frame consistent with mission needs" *(OMB Circular A-130)*.
Information **S**ystem **S**ecurity **O**fficer **(ISSO)**	**I**nformation **A**sset **O**wner or **R**isk **O**wner in the US government **I**nformation **T**echnology context. "Individual assigned responsibility by the senior agency information security officer, authorizing official, management official, or information system owner for maintaining the appropriate operational security posture for an information system or program" *(NIST SP 800-39)*. See also **S**ystem **S**ecurity **O**fficer.
Information **T**echnology **(IT), technology**	Encompasses all aspects of technology and tools used to create, store, process, exploit, manage, and communicate/share information, including hardware, software, firmware, **C**ommunications **T**echnology, **O**perational **T**echnology, **M**obile **T**echnology, **V**irtual **T**echnology, **S**mart **T**echnology plus the professionals who specialise in this expansive field. "The hardware, software, communication and other facilities used to input, store, process, transmit and output data in whatever form" *(ISACA glossary)*. "Any services, equipment, or interconnected system(s) or subsystem(s) of equipment, that are used in the automatic acquisition, storage, analysis, evaluation, manipulation, management, movement, control, display, switching, interchange, transmission, or reception of data or information by the agency. For purposes of this definition, such services or equipment if used by the agency directly or is used by a contractor under a contract with the agency that requires its use; or to a significant extent, its use in the performance of a service or the furnishing of a product. Information technology includes computers, ancillary equipment (including imaging peripherals, input, output, and storage devices necessary for security and surveillance), peripheral equipment designed to be controlled by the central processing unit of a computer, software, firmware and similar procedures, services (including cloud computing and help-desk

TERM	MEANING
	services or other professional services which support any point of the life cycle of the equipment or service), and related resources. Information technology does not include any equipment that is acquired by a contractor incidental to a contract which does not require its use" *(NIST SP 800-171)*. See also **I**nformation **T**echnology **D**epartment, plus AgriTech, Biotech, EdTech, FinTech, FoodTech, GovTech, HealthTech, LegalTech, RegTech, RetailTech, and other tech neologisms.
Information Technology application	See application. "Electronic functionality that constitutes parts of business processes undertaken by, or with the assistance of, IT" *(ISACA glossary)*.
Information Technology architecture	See technology architecture. "A description of the fundamental underlying design of the IT components of the business, the relationships among them and the manner in which they support the enterprise's objectives" *(ISACA glossary)*.
Information **T**echnology **C**ertified **A**ssociate **(ITCA)**	ISACA's entry-level qualification covers foundations of computing, networks, infrastructure, cybersecurity, software development, and data science. More info: https://www.isaca.org/credentialing/itca
Information **T**echnology **D**epartment **(IT, IT Department or ITD)**	Name of the corporate function typically responsible for providing **I**nformation and **C**ommunications **T**echnology services to the organisation through a shared infrastructure. Alternatives include Technology, [**A**utomated] **D**ata **P**rocessing, Computing, or Computer Department.
Information **T**echnology **D**isaster **R**ecovery **(IT DR)**	See **D**isaster **R**ecovery.
Information Technology governance	Governance of technology, including **I**nformation **T**echnology. "The responsibility of executives and the board of directors; consists of the leadership, organizational structures and processes that ensure that the enterprise's IT sustains and extends the enterprise's strategies and objectives" *(ISACA glossary)*.
Information Technology governance framework	**I**nformation **T**echnology governance framework. "A model that integrates a set of guidelines, policies and methods that represent the organizational approach to IT governance" *(ISACA glossary)*.
Information Technology incident	Technology incident. "Any event not part of the ordinary operation of a service that causes, or may cause, an interruption to or a reduction in the quality of that service" *(ISACA glossary)*.

TERM	MEANING
Information Technology infrastructure	Technology infrastructure. "The set of hardware, software and facilities that integrate an enterprise's IT assets. Notes: Specifically, the equipment (including servers, routers, switches and cabling), software, services and products used in storing, processing, transmitting and displaying all forms of information for the enterprise's users" *(ISACA glossary)*.
Information **T**echnology **I**nfrastructure **L**ibrary **(ITIL)**	Governance framework/management structure designed to align **I**nformation **T**echnology services with, and hence support/enable achievement of, the organisation's business objectives, including risk management. Developed originally for the UK government in the 1980's as a set of about thirty books, later rationalised and condensed to five. "The UK Office of Government Commerce (OGC) IT Infrastructure Library, which is a set of guides on the management and provision of operational IT services" *(ISACA glossary)*.
Information Technology-related incident	Incident involving or affecting **I**nformation **T**echnology or other technology. "An IT-related event that causes an operational, developmental and/or strategic business impact" *(ISACA glossary)*.
Information Technology risk	Information risk involving technology. "The business risk associated with the use, ownership, operation, involvement, influence and adoption of IT within an enterprise" *(ISACA glossary)*.
Information Technology risk register	Risk register for **I**nformation **T**echnology risks, technology risks, and/or information risks. "A repository of the key attributes of potential and known IT risk issues. Attributes may include name, description, owner, expected/actual frequency, potential/actual magnitude, potential/actual business impact and disposition" *(ISACA glossary)*.
Information Technology risk scenario	Credible technology-related scenario to analyse the associated risks. "The description of an IT-related event that can lead to a business impact" *(ISACA glossary)*.
Information **T**echnology **S**ecurity **M**anager **(ITSM)**	See **I**nformation **S**ecurity **M**anager. "Executive within an agency that acts as a conduit between the strategic directions provided by the CISO and the technical efforts of systems administrators. The main responsibility of ITSMs is the administrative controls relating to information security within the agency" *(NZISM)*.
Information Technology service	Technology-based information service. "The day-to-day provision to customers of information and technology infrastructure and applications and support for their use—*e.g.*, service desk, equipment supply and moves, and security authorizations" *(ISACA glossary)*.
Information Technology user	See user. "A person who uses IT to support or achieve a business objective" *(ISACA glossary)*.

TERM	MEANING
Information Warfare (IW), infowar	Unethical and often illegal activities to obtain trade secrets or other proprietary or confidential information from a competitor or other adversary, or to mislead and manipulate them through social engineering, *e.g.* using fake news and propaganda. "The competition between offensive and defensive players over information resources" *(SANS glossary)*. See also cyberwar.
Informed consent	Just as patients are required to consent to (permit) surgical procedures after having been informed of the associated risks and benefits, data subjects (under most circumstances) are required to be informed about how their personal information will be used and protected at the time it is collected from them, giving them the choice to opt-out.
Infosec	*Abbrev:* **info**rmation **sec**urity.
Infosec Registered Assessors Program	"An initiative of the Australian Cyber Security Centre designed to register suitably qualified individuals to carry out security assessments for systems" *(AusISM)*.
Infostealer	Contraction of **info**rmation **stealer**, a prevalent and sinister type of malware intended to exfiltrate valuable information surreptitiously from a compromised system, device, network, organisation, or even individual. The stolen info may be exploited in many non-exclusive ways, *e.g.* offered for sale on the black market via information brokers, sold to clients who commissioned the attack, used to coerce payments from the victim by threatening disclosure and hinting at deeper infiltration, and/or used directly to make money by any means, ethical and legal or not (identity fraud, for instance).
Infrared device	"Devices such as mice, keyboards and pointing devices that have an infrared communications capability" *(AusISM)*.
Infrastructure	Framework providing basic services essential for the survival and well-being of the world as a whole, or of a country, state, city, organisation, home, person, *etc.* May include physical structures such as foundations, columns, and beams. Usually involves the provision of food and water, safety and security, housing, healthcare, wealthcare, power, and more. In the **I**nformation **T**echnology context, it is mostly computing and networking hardware platforms and cables, plus shared services that integrate the systems, providing monitoring, management, and access. "The collection of physical or virtual resources that supports an overall IT environment, including the server, storage, and network elements" *(Trust Services Criteria)*. See also cyberinfrastructure, **C**ritical **I**nfrastructure, **P**ublic **K**ey **I**nfrastructure.

TERM	MEANING
Infrastructure-as-a-Service (IaaS)	Cloud computing services model providing customers with access to Internet-based virtual systems on which they can load guest systems, middleware, and applications. The service provider's responsibilities, including the information security aspects, are limited to the bare metal, hypervisor, and network access. "A form of cloud computing that offers the capability to provision processing, storage, networks and other fundamental computing resources, enabling the customer to deploy and run arbitrary software, including operating systems and applications" *(ISACA glossary)*. "Where the cloud service provider offers access to a variety of capabilities and technologies on demand. Service is provided either over the public Internet or through dedicated connections" *(NZISM)*. See also **P**latform-**as-a-S**ervice, **S**oftware-**as-a-S**ervice.
Infrastructure control, infrastructural control	a. Control designed to mitigate unacceptable risks **to** an infrastructure service, *e.g.* laws, regulations, contractual terms, and standards concerning the security (resilience, reliability, …) of electrical power supplied by generators to the grid. Includes various controls within/integral to the infrastructure, *e.g.* grid status monitoring, performance management, and proactive maintenance. b. Control designed to mitigate unacceptable risks **from** an infrastructure service to customers/users, *e.g.* generator-backed **U**ninterruptible **P**ower **S**upplies for critical servers and vital equipment.
Infrastructure owner	Organisation, rôle, or person who literally/legally or notionally owns an infrastructure (as a whole or just a part, *e.g.* the electrical distribution grid in a given region) along with any associated property rights and obligations, responsibilities, or social expectations. May be a custodian, steward, or agent acting on behalf of the legal owner. May be accountable for its protection/security and legitimate exploitation to optimise its value. See also asset owner, information owner, network owner, system owner, service owner.
Infrastructure resilience	Techniques to ensure the availability and continuity of corporate and national infrastructures delivering essential services such as datacommunications, power, and water, despite potentially disruptive events, incidents, and disasters (infrastructure risks). "The timely and efficient prevention, absorption, recovery, adaptation and transformation of national infrastructure's essential structures and functions, which have been exposed to current and potential future hazards. Implementing resilience across all disruption phases should be done through collaborative risk and uncertainty management, multi-hazard assessment, and methods that embrace the systemic nature of national infrastructure" *(Principles for Resilient Infrastructure, UN Office for Disaster Risk Reduction, 2022)*.

TERM	MEANING
Infrastructure risk	Uncertain possibility of incidents involving or affecting an infrastructure. "The risk that information and technology (I&T) infrastructure and systems may be unable to effectively support the current and future needs of the business in an efficient, cost-effective and well-controlled fashion" *(ISACA glossary)*.
Infringement notification, infringement letter	See cease and desist letter.
Inherent effect	"The effect of uncertainty in the absence of actions & controls" *(OCEG GRC Glossary)*.
Inherent risk, raw risk, untreated risk, baseline risk	Amount of risk that is believed to exist in a situation regardless of any risk treatments intended to mitigate it – essentially the starting point for risk management activities, and potentially the current or actual risk level if treatments are ineffective. "The level of risk or exposure that does not account for the actions management has taken or might take (*e.g.*, implementing controls)" *(ISACA glossary)*. "The level of risk in the absence of actions & controls" *(OCEG GRC Glossary)*. "The combination of internal and external risk factors that exists in the absence of any management actions" *(IIA GIAS)*.
Initial Access Broker	Someone specialising in breaking in to a network by phishing, hacking, or malware, who then sells that illicit access or foothold to cybercriminals.
Initialisation **V**ector **(IV)**	Random or pseudorandom number used in conjunction with a private key to encrypt data. Must have sufficient entropy to resist brute force attacks ... unlike **W**ired **E**quivalent **P**rotocol. "A vector used in defining the starting point of an encryption process within a cryptographic algorithm" *(FIPS 140-2)*. See also seed.
Initial **P**rogram **L**oad **(IPL)**	Boot process for a mainframe or other computer. "The initialization procedure that causes an operating system to be loaded into storage at the beginning of a workday or after a system malfunction" *(ISACA glossary)*.
Injection, inject	"A general term for attack types that inject code that is then interpreted/executed by the application" (*OWASP*). "Scripted piece of information inserted into an exercise that is designed to elicit a response or decision and facilitate the flow of the exercise. Note: Injects can be written, oral, televised and/or transmitted via any means (*e.g.* phone, email, fax, voice, radio or sign)" *(ISO 22300)*.
Injection flaw	Category of software design flaws that allow attackers to manipulate input data in such a way that vulnerable applications mistakenly interpret and act upon malicious commands within user-supplied data. Normally mitigated by validation routines that explicitly check input data for invalid/inappropriate content

TERM	MEANING
	(such as escape characters signalling embedded commands and end-of-string markers) *prior* to passing them to the application: clearly, the validation routines must themselves be resistant to injection attacks. See also code injection, HTML injection, Cross-Site Scripting.
Injunctive norm	Prematurely describing or implying that *intended* behaviours are 'normal,' 'typical,' or 'conventional' actively encourages most people to change their ways and conform with expectations. For instance, discussing the few incident notifications recently received as if they were commonplace can increase incident reporting. "Perceived behavior of what most people approve of, providing information on what one 'should' do" *(OCEG GRC Glossary). Cf.* descriptive norms.
Ingress	Moving into a building, system, network, *etc.* "Traffic that comes into a network" *(ISACA glossary). Cf.* egress.
Ingress filtering	Selective blocking of traffic on its arrival onto a network, *e.g.* to prevent recognised inbound hacking attacks or spam reaching their destinations. "Filtering inbound traffic" *(SANS glossary). Cf.* egress filtering.
Input control	a. Control designed to mitigate unacceptable input risks, such as data entry validation by a computer system or fact-checking by a critical thinker. "Techniques and procedures used to verify, validate and edit data to ensure that only correct data are entered into the computer" *(ISACA glossary)*. b. More generally, control relevant to inputs to a process, business unit, or organisation, such as **Q**uality **C**ontrol and invoicing integrity checks for raw materials and products received by a manufacturer.
Input data	Digital data or information fed into a system or process "Data for which an AI system calculates a predicted output or inference" *(ISO/IEC 22989)*.
Input risk	Uncertain possibility of issues with inputs to a system, process, and decision, *e.g.* invalid, incomplete/missing, inaccurate, out-dated/late, unauthorised, inappropriate, or malicious information (data or commands) entered into a computer, causing incidents. See also processing risk, output risk.
Input validation, data entry validation	Validation of data entered manually or fed automatically to an application, system, function, *etc.* applying various predefined rules to block invalid data types, values, ranges, *etc.* while passing valid data. Can be quite sophisticated, dynamically applying business logic and explicit security tests relevant to the business and processing context, *e.g.* to detect and respond appropriately to both casual typos and determined SQL injection attacks.

TERM	MEANING
Input validation attack	Input validation attack. "Where an attacker intentionally sends unusual input in the hopes of confusing an application" *(SANS glossary)*.
Insecure	Lacking in self-confidence, nervous, and prone to self-doubt, an emotional condition. In the information security context, unsecure is generally a more appropriate term.
Insecurity	a. Lack of, or inadequate, security. See unsecure. b. The state of being insecure.
Insider	Member of a closed group, team, club, organisation, *etc.* See also worker. *Cf.* outsider.
Insider threat	Information security threat arising from or relating to insiders, who typically are more trusted, have greater access to protected information assets, and are monitored less assiduously, than outsiders. "Threats to an enterprise that come from individuals within the enterprise, such as employees or contractors" *(ISACA glossary)*. "The threat that an insider will use her/his authorized access, wittingly or unwittingly, to do harm to the security of the United States. This threat can include damage to the United States through espionage, terrorism, unauthorized disclosure, or through the loss or degradation of departmental resources or capabilities" *(NIST SP 800-171)*.
Insider trading	Illegally trading a company's stocks and shares, or manipulating the markets, with the benefit of confidential internal information, *e.g.* a company director or advisor who pre-emptively sells the company's stock (either in person or through a friend, family member, broker, or another intermediary/agent) in anticipation of a corporate announcement or disclosure of an adverse incident or unexpectedly poor performance.
Inspect, inspection, inspector	Check, look at, or into something, closely, in order to evaluate it, typically against an applicable standard, requirement, or specification.
Installation	a. Process of installing something such as computer, device, network, peripheral, program, driver, change/update/upgrade, patch, fix, server, service, machine tool, door, monarch, or piece of artwork. "The phase in the system life cycle that includes assembly and testing of the hardware and software of a computerized system. Installation includes installing a new computer system, software or hardware or otherwise modifying the current system" *(ISACA glossary)*. See also implementation. b. Something that has been installed.

TERM	MEANING
Installation test	a. Verification that a recently installed computer, device, network, peripheral, program, driver, change/update/upgrade, patch, fix, server, service, machine tool, door, monarch, piece of artwork, *etc.* is functional, operating correctly (meaning as specified, as designed, or satisfying whatever other criteria might be of concern to the testers). b. Test, assessment, review, or audit of an entire operating facility, or a significant part thereof such as a computer installation (*i.e.* a number of servers housed within a computer suite including the essential supporting services such as power, air conditioning, and networking plus the staff).
Instance	Single occurrence of something, such as a **D**ata**B**ase system, process, or **V**irtual **M**achine currently executing on a server.
Instant Messaging (IM)	Form of real-time person-to-person communications originally using typed messages like SMS/TXT, but gradually expanded to include audio and video modes. Used for online chatting, such as conversations between customers and technical support functions. Vulnerable to malware, disclosure of confidential information, social engineering, SPIM, and other threats. "A facility for exchanging messages in real-time with other people over the Internet and tracking the progress of a given conversation" *(NIST SP 800-101)*. "An online mechanism or a form of real-time communication between two or more people based on typed text and multimedia data. Note: Text is conveyed via computers or another electronic device (*e.g.*, cellular phone or handheld device) and connected over a network, such as the Internet" *(ISACA glossary)*.
Instruction, statement	Direction to do something from management (*e.g.* an edict/policy or system/network management command) or for other reasons (*e.g.* a low-level **D**ata **P**rocessing statement in the machine code being executed by the **C**entral **P**rocessing **U**nit). "1. A program statement that causes a computer to perform a particular operation or set of operations. 2. In a programming language, a meaningful expression that specifies one operation and identifies its operands, if any" *(ISACA glossary)*.
Instructor	Person who instructs, trains, or teaches, informing/imparting knowledge and hopefully inspiring and motivating students. "Individual who teaches" *(OCEG GRC Glossary)*.
Insurance	Risk-sharing financial service whereby insurers guarantee to compensate customers to a specified extent for certain losses caused by 'insured events,' as defined by reams of small-print, arcane legal interpretations and practices, in return for regular payments (premiums).
Intangible	Literally untouchable, *i.e.* having no physical presence or substance, such as an emotion, concept, or most **I**ntellectual **P**roperty (valuable information content, thoughts, and ideas). *Cf.* tangible.

TERM	MEANING
Intangible asset	Valuable information content, knowledge, data, capabilities, and concepts such as Intellectual Property, brands, trade secrets personal information, privacy, competence, experience, assurance, integrity, trust, friendship, love, and security. "Identifiable non-financial asset with no physical substance" *(ISO 10668)*. "An asset that is not physical in nature. Note: Examples include intellectual property (patents, trademarks, copyrights and processes), goodwill and brand recognition" *(ISACA glossary)*.
Intangible resource	See intangible asset. "Resources that refer to non-physical assets, such as knowledge, brand equity, and organizational culture" *(OCEG GRC Glossary)*.
Integer underflow, wraparound, wrap	By deliberate manipulation (*e.g.* malware) or through errors (*e.g.* noise), the value of an integer variable in a program may be reduced from a positive to a negative value, causing problems such as buffer overflows or sidestepping data validation checks in software that presumes only positive (unsigned) integer values.
Integrated **A**ction & **C**ontrol **M**odel **(IACM)**	"A structure that considers the purpose and types of actions & controls used for the governance, management, and assurance of performance, risk, and compliance" *(OCEG GRC Glossary)*.
Integrated **A**udit & **A**ssurance **P**rofessional **(IAAP)**	OCEG's qualification for audit and assurance professionals. Covers: who can perform integrated audit and assurance and how it gives confidence to stakeholders, how to do it, tools and techniques, planning and coordinating, and design optimisation. More info: https://www.oceg.org/certifications/iaap-integrated-audit-assurance-professional/
Integrated **C**ircuit **(IC), microchip, chip**	Assemblage of micro-miniature electronic components forming complex circuits on a semiconducting substrate such as silicon. "Small piece of semiconductive material that contains interconnected electronic elements" *(ISO/IEC 2382)*. "An electronic circuit comprised of capacitors, transistors and resistors that is the building block of most electronic devices and equipment" *(ISACA glossary)*. *Cf.* **I**ntelligence **C**ommunity.
Integrated **C**ircuit **C**ard **Id**entifier **(ICCID)**	"The unique serial number assigned to, maintained within, and usually imprinted on the (U)SIM" *(NIST SP 800-101)*.
Integrated **C**ompliance & **E**thics **P**rofessional **(ICEP)**	OCEG's qualification for compliance professionals. Covers: using **G**overnance, **R**isk, and **C**ompliance for compliance and ethics; the compliance and ethics model; key risk areas; internal controls; business conduct; and regulatory compliance. More info: https://www.oceg.org/certifications/new-icep-integrated-compliance-ethics-professional/
Integrated **D**ata **P**rivacy **P**rofessional **(IDPP)**	OCEG's qualification for privacy professionals. Covers OCEG's Data Privacy Capability Model. More info: https://www.oceg.org/certifications/idpp-integrated-data-privacy-professional/

TERM	MEANING
Integrated **G**overnance & **O**versight **P**rofessional **(IGOP)**	OCEG's qualification for governance professionals. Covers: principles and practices for Boards of Directors and executive teams and committees, and skills to provide governance and oversight. More info: https://www.oceg.org/certifications/igop-integrated-governance-oversight-professional/
Integrated **M**anagement **S**ystem **(IMS)**	"Management system that integrates all of an organization's systems – like information security management and business continuity management – and processes in to one complete framework, enabling an organization to work as a single unit with unified objectives" *(ISO/IEC 27022)*.
Integrated performance support	"A function that provides the exact information needed to solve a learner's question at the moment of need. The goal is to increase performance by empowering individuals with self-help resources in the flow of work rather than interrupting work with periodic and episodic learning" *(OCEG GRC Glossary)*.
Integrated plan	"Details processes and resources allocated to reliably achieve objectives, address uncertainty, and act with integrity" *(OCEG GRC Glossary)*.
Integrated **P**olicy **M**anagement **P**rofessional **(IPMP)**	OCEG's qualification for those managing policies. Covers: terms and definitions, principles, and drivers; integrating policy management with the business; structure of the OCEG Policy Management Capability Model; management actions and controls; and design and implementation. More info: https://www.oceg.org/certifications/ipmp-integrated-policy-management-professional/
Integrated **R**isk **M**anagement **(IRM)**	Alignment with, or incorporation of, an organisation's risk management activities and goals within other routine business activities and goals, such as financial, personnel, product, and strategic management, rather than being discrete, special, and sporadic.
Integrated **R**isk **M**anagement **P**rofessional **(IRMP)**	OCEG's qualification for risk managers. Covers: quantitative and qualitative risk management, risk financing, operational risk management, and decision theory and support. More info: https://www.oceg.org/certifications/irmp-integrated-risk-management-professional/
Integrated **S**ecurity & **C**ontinuity **P**rofessional **(ISCP)**	OCEG's qualification for information security professionals. Covers principles and practices from: information security, information privacy, business continuity, and emergency response. More info: https://www.oceg.org/certifications/iscp-integrated-security-continuity-professional/
Integrated **S**trategy & **P**erformance **P**rofessional **(ISPP)**	OCEG's qualification for strategy and performance professionals. Covers: business strategy, strategic finance, strategy formulation, and performance management. More info: https://www.oceg.org/certifications/ispp-integrated-strategy-performance-professional/

TERM	MEANING
Integrated **T**est **F**acility **(ITF)**	a. Self-assessment function built in to a computer system or application. "A testing methodology in which test data are processed in production systems. Notes: The data usually represent a set of fictitious entities such as departments, customers or products. Output reports are verified to confirm the correctness of the processing" *(ISACA glossary)*. Cf. integration test. b. Laboratory setup using automation to conduct multiple product tests in parallel or in the same session, such as checking vehicle emissions, power, range, and noise. See also dieselgate.
Integration test	Testing phase in conventional software development methods where, having been tested individually (unit tests), functional modules, subsystems, *etc.* are brought together and interoperate as a partial or complete system. "Progressive linking and testing of programs or modules in order to ensure their proper functioning in the complete system" *(ISO/IEC 2382)*. "An orderly progression of testing in which software elements, hardware elements or both are combined and tested to evaluate their interactions, until the entire system has been integrated" *(ISACA glossary)*. See also system test, regression test, **P**roduction **A**cceptance **T**est.
Integrity	Cluster of information properties or characteristics such as completeness, currency, authenticity, quality, accuracy, and trustworthiness of information, data, systems, people, organisations, *etc.* One of the core information protection objectives of information security alongside confidentiality and availability (the CIA triad). "Property of accuracy and completeness" *(ISO/IEC 27000)*. "Property of safeguarding the accuracy and completeness of assets" *(ISO 22300)*. "Property whereby data have not been altered in an unauthorized manner since they were created, transmitted, or stored" *(ISO/IEC 29167-19)*. "The guarding against improper information modification or destruction, and includes ensuring information non-repudiation and authenticity" *(ISACA glossary)*. "The state of being whole and complete by fulfilling obligations, honoring promises, and cleaning up the mess if a promise is broken" *(OCEG GRC Glossary)*. "The assurance that data has been created, amended or deleted only by authorised individuals" *(AusISM)*. "The assurance that information is accurate, complete and valid, and has not been altered by an unauthorized action" *(SCP QRG)*. "In information security, integrity means that information has not been changed accidentally, or deliberately, and is accurate and complete" *(UK National Cyber Security Strategy 2022)*. "Behavior characterized by adherence to moral and ethical principles, including demonstrating honesty and the professional courage to act based on relevant facts" *(IIA GIAS)*. "Guarding against improper information modification or destruction and includes ensuring information non-repudiation and authenticity" *(NIST SP 800-171)*. "The need to ensure that information has not been changed accidentally or deliberately, and that it is accurate and complete" *(SANS glossary)*.

TERM	MEANING
Integrity control	Control designed to mitigate unacceptable integrity risks. Its primary purpose is to keep information, information systems and services reasonably complete, accurate, functional, valuable, current, trustworthy, reliable, *etc.* using cryptographic hashes, referential integrity, data entry/input validation, assurance, transparency, honesty and ethics, policies and procedures, *etc.* See also confidentiality control, availability control.
Integrity risk	Risk involving or affecting integrity, such as the uncertain possibility of unauthorised changes to a computer system or data, or the possible loss of trust following an incident. "The risk that data may be unavailable due to incompleteness or inaccuracy" *(ISACA glossary)*. See also information risk, information security risk, confidentiality risk, availability risk.
Intellectual asset, intellectual capital	Largely undocumented yet potentially highly valuable intangible information assets such as knowledge, experience, creative ideas, and mental/conceptual models within workers' heads and **A**rtificial **I**ntelligence models, that accompany, support, and enable understanding, intellect, intelligence, skills, abilities, expertise, innovation, and so forth.
Intellectual **P**roperty **(IP)**	Valuable information that formally belongs to someone and is protected by **I**ntellectual **P**roperty **R**ights. "Intangible assets that belong to an enterprise for its exclusive use. Examples include patents, copyrights, trademarks, ideas and trade secrets" *(ISACA glossary)*. *Cf.* **I**nternet **P**rotocol.
Intellectual **P**roperty **R**ights **(IPR)**	Morally and potentially legally enforceable rights of the legal owner of **I**ntellectual **P**roperty to determine how the information is used and/or copied or disseminated by others, *e.g.* through software licensing/copyright, patent, trademark, **P**lant **V**ariety **R**ight or contract laws, and non-disclosure agreements.
Intelligence, INTEL	a. Information gathered and exploited by the spooky intelligence community. Not all intelligence is necessarily confidential since published or open-source information, such as that obtained by profiling targets using social media may be just as useful as information obtained from covert sources by spying, hacking, and surveillance. "Information that has been deliberately organised to give someone an advantage when making decisions under conditions of uncertainty. Intelligence may be obtained from secret or open sources, but is usually classified to protect the advantage it confers" *(NZSTE)*. See also security intelligence. b. Cleverness, smartness, intellectual capabilities in general – a cluster of characteristics and abilities relating to performance, capacity, and integrity of information processing. See also sentience.

TERM	MEANING
Intelligence **C**ommunity **(IC)**	Spies, analysts, collectors, managers, strategists, cryptographers and cryptanalysts, hackers, language and cultural specialists, politicians, diplomats, couriers, *etc.* collectively engaged in law enforcement, counterterrorism, national security (defensive and offensive), cyberwar, *etc. Cf.* **I**ntegrated **C**ircuit.
Intended purpose	Desired, required, or demanded purpose. "The use for which a product with digital elements is intended by the manufacturer, including the specific context and conditions of use, as specified in the information supplied by the manufacturer in the instructions for use, promotional or sales materials and statements, as well as in the technical documentation" *(EU CRA)*.
Intention, call to action	Something planned and deliberate. "What the communicator wants the audience to believe, value, or do as a consequence of the message" *(OCEG GRC Glossary)*.
Interactive **A**pplication **S**ecurity **T**esting **(IAST)**	Combines **D**ynamic **A**pplication **S**ecurity **T**esting with **R**untime **A**pplication **S**elf-**P**rotection – in other words, penetration testing of an application combined with security monitoring and reporting functions embedded within the application. Through automation and regression testing, supports **R**apid **A**pplication **D**evelopment and DevOps. See also **S**tatic **A**pplication **S**ecurity **T**esting.
Interactive authentication	"Authentication that involves the interaction of a person with a system" *(AusISM)*.
Intercept	Item of intelligence in its raw (as originally intercepted) or processed (*e.g.* decrypted) state. Mostly data or other forms of information, including metadata.
Interception [of communications]	Laws and regulations in several jurisdictions concern the authorised and unauthorised monitoring/capturing of communications for various purposes by various parties using various means. The basic principles were established way back when commercial and military secrets were passed by couriers and letters, and have been updated to cover computer data and telecommunications.
Interdiction	Physical security threat that compromises electronic products at some point in the supply chains linking their designers and manufacturers to the consumers, *e.g.* by substituting firmware or inserting tiny surveillance chips on **P**rinted **C**ircuit **B**oards.
Interested party	Person or organisation that is materially involved with or directly affected by something, as opposed to merely having a casual interest in it. "Person or organization that can affect, be affected by, or perceive itself to be affected by a decision or activity" *(ISO/IEC 27002)*. "Person or organization that can affect, be affected by, or

TERM	MEANING
	perceive itself to be affected by a decision or activity" (*ISO/IEC 27002*). "Person or organization that can affect, be affected by, or perceive itself to be affected by a decision or activity. EXAMPLE: Customers, owners, personnel, providers, bankers, regulators, unions, partners or society that can include competitors or opposing pressure groups. Notes: A decision maker can be an interested party. Impacted communities and local populations are considered to be interested parties. This constitutes one of the common terms and core definitions of the high level structure for ISO management system standards. The original definition has been modified by adding the example and the notes to entry" *(ISO 22300)*. See also third party, stakeholder.
Interface	Functional, logical, or physical junction between two or more parts, across which information flows, such as an **A**pplication **P**rogramming **I**nterface or a network interface. "1. A shared boundary between two functional units, defined by functional characteristics, common physical interconnection characteristics, signal characteristics and other characteristics, as appropriate. The concept involves the specification of the connection of two devices having different functions. 2. A point of communication between two or more processes, persons or other physical entities. 3. A peripheral device that permits two or more devices to communicate. [and] A shared boundary across components, humans, services, hardware or software that needs or exchanges information or data. Either the term 'interface' or 'connection' may be used to describe this boundary" *(ISACA glossary)*.
Interference	a. Contemporaneous transmissions on the same frequencies preventing or degrading reception of wanted electromagnetic signals, whether intentionally (*e.g.* jamming) or accidentally transmitted (*e.g.* intermodulation, spurii, static, solar flare). b. More generally, impeding, delaying, or preventing something, *e.g.* someone participating reluctantly ('passive-aggressively') in an investigation or audit, producing information slowly and only that explicitly requested or conversely accompanied by a large volume of extraneous material.
Interim audit	See surveillance audit.
Interlock	Vital (safety-critical) mechanical, electromechanical, or electronic control device or linkage, *e.g.* a relay that removes power to the air conditioning fans if the fire system enters an alarm condition upon detecting heat or smoke, in order not to fan the flames (literally!).

TERM	MEANING
Internal	Within the outer physical or notional perimeter or boundary of a person, system, network, organisation, site/property, *etc.* *Cf.* external.
Internal attack	See insider threat. "Attack perpetrated by people or entities directly or indirectly linked with the legitimate manufacturer, originator of the goods or rights holder (staff of the rights holder, subcontractor, supplier, *etc.*)" *(ISO 22300).*
Internal audit, internal auditing	Audit conducted on behalf of the organisation by **I**nternal **A**udit Department, or by suitably independent and competent workers or consultants. Generally scoped and approved by, and reported to, senior management and maybe other stakeholders. "Audit conducted by, or on behalf of, an organization itself for management review and other internal purposes, and which can form the basis for an organization's self-declaration of conformity. Note: In many cases, particularly in smaller organizations, independence can be demonstrated by the freedom from responsibility for the activity being audited" *(ISO 22300).* "An independent, objective assurance and advisory service designed to add value and improve an organization's operations. It helps an organization accomplish its objectives by bringing a systematic, disciplined approach to evaluate and improve the effectiveness of governance, risk management, and control processes" *(IIA GIAS).* "Sometimes called a first-party audit, conducted by, or on behalf of, the organisation itself for internal purposes" *(FSRCoP). Cf.* external audit.
Internal audit charter	High-level scope and purpose or mission statement for an internal audit function. "A formal document that includes the internal audit function's mandate, organizational position, reporting relationships, scope of work, types of services, and other specifications" *(IIA GIAS).* See also audit charter.
Internal **A**udit **D**epartment **(IAD or IA)**	Corporate assurance function responsible for performing internal audits. "A professional individual or group responsible for providing an organization with assurance and advisory services" *(IIA GIAS).*
Internal audit mandate	Senior management's overall rationale, requirements, and information access permission for Internal Audit. "The internal audit function's authority, role, and responsibilities, which may be granted by the board and/or laws and regulations" *(IIA GIAS).*
Internal audit manual	Suite of policies and procedures used by internal auditors. "The chief audit executive's documentation of the methodologies (policies, processes, and procedures) to guide and direct internal auditors within the internal audit function" *(IIA GIAS).*

TERM	MEANING
Internal context, internal factors	Internal context, the situation, circumstances, and factors within an organisation, business unit, industry, nation, culture, system, *etc.* "Internal environment in which the organization seeks to achieve its objectives. Notes: Internal context can include: vision, mission and values; governance, organizational structure, roles and accountabilities; strategy, objectives and policies; the organization's culture; standards, guidelines and models adopted by the organization; capabilities, understood in terms of resources and knowledge (*e.g.* capital, time, people, processes, systems and technologies); data, information systems and information flows; relationships with internal interested parties, taking into account their perceptions and values; contractual relationships and commitments; internal interdependencies and interconnections" *(ISO/IEC 27005)*. "Internal environment in which the organization seeks to achieve its objectives. Note: Internal context can include: governance, organizational structure, roles and accountabilities; policies, objectives, and the strategies that are in place to achieve them; the capabilities, understood in terms of resources and knowledge (*e.g.* capital, time, people, processes, systems and technologies); information systems, information flows and decision-making processes (both formal and informal); relationships with, and perceptions and values of internal stakeholders; the organization's culture; standards, guidelines and models adopted by the organization; and form and extent of contractual relationships" *(ISO Guide 73)*. "Categories of sources and forces that originate inside of the organization" *(OCEG GRC Glossary)*. *Cf.* external context.
Internal control	Discretionary control voluntarily adopted by the organisation, as opposed to one mandated or imposed upon it by some authority. Various types are used, often in combination, *e.g.* technological, process, administrative, and physical controls. Collectively, internal controls form the enterprise-wide system of governance and management activities intended to ensure that the organisation achieves its objectives in a controlled manner, overcoming risks by design and intent (deliberately and systematically reducing uncertainties) rather than by sheer good fortune. "The policies, procedures, practices and organizational structures designed to provide reasonable assurance that business objectives will be achieved and undesired events will be prevented or detected and corrected" *(ISACA glossary)*. "A process, effected by an entity's board of directors, management, and other personnel, designed to provide reasonable assurance regarding the achievement of objectives relating to operations, reporting, and compliance" *(Trust Services Criteria)*.
Internal control environment	The corporate, business or technological context, culture, situation, or scope within which internal controls operate, *e.g.* workers may appreciate, accept, resent, ignore, or actively oppose and evade various controls. "The relevant environment on which the controls have an effect" *(ISACA glossary)*.

TERM	MEANING
Internal control structure	"The dynamic, integrated processes—effected by the governing body, management and all other staff—that are designed to provide reasonable assurance regarding the achievement of the following general objectives: Effectiveness, efficiency and economy of operations; Reliability of management; Compliance with applicable laws, regulations and internal policies. Management's strategies for achieving these general objectives are affected by the design and operation of the following components: Control environment; Information system; Control procedures" *(ISACA glossary)*.
Internal **C**ontrols **Q**uestionnaire **(ICQ)**	Structured audit checklist or working paper concerning the internal controls to be investigated and evaluated during an audit engagement, typically phrased in the form of a set of rhetorical open-ended questions and prompts for the auditor with spaces to reference evidence received and record the initial findings, preliminary analysis, and any concerns or issues arising.
Internal enterprise assets	"Refers to non-public facing enterprise assets that can only be identified through network scans and reconnaissance from within an enterprise's network through authorized authenticated or unauthenticated access" *(CIS Controls)*.
Internal network	Internal network. "A network in which the establishment, maintenance, and provisioning of security controls are under the direct control of organizational employees or contractors or in which the cryptographic encapsulation or similar security technology implemented between organization-controlled endpoints provides the same effect (with regard to confidentiality and integrity). An internal network is typically organization-owned yet may be organization-controlled while not being organization-owned" *(NIST SP 800-171)*.
Internal penetrator	"An authorized user of a computer system who oversteps his/her legitimate access rights. Notes: This category is divided into masqueraders and clandestine users" *(ISACA glossary)*.
Internal stakeholder	Internal stakeholder. "Stakeholders with an internal influence from within the organization; Personnel (and unions that represent the workforce), Managers, Executives, Board members, and Owners (who are involved in the organization)" *(OCEG GRC Glossary)*.
INTERNAL USE	Class of information that is intended for general use by workers and, if necessary and appropriate, by selected third parties such as clients, suppliers, or contractors.
International **D**ata **E**ncryption **A**lgorithm **(IDEA)**	Symmetric block cipher with 128-bit keys used, for instance, in PGP.

TERM	MEANING
International Mobile Equipment Identity (IMEI)	15-digit identifier for a cellphone. "A unique identification number programmed into GSM and UMTS mobile devices" *(NIST SP 800-101)*. See also **G**lobal **S**ystem for **M**obile communications, **U**niversal **M**obile **T**elecommunications **S**ervice.
International Mobile Subscriber Identity (IMSI)	64-bit unique identification number for a cellphone service *subscriber*'s country (the first 3 digits) and supplier (the next 2 or 3 digits) plus the individual subscriber (the remainder, usually 10 digits). "A unique number associated with every GSM mobile phone subscriber, which is maintained on a (U)SIM" *(NIST SP 800-101)*. See also **G**lobal **S**ystem for **M**obile communications, **U**niversal **M**obile **T**elecommunications **S**ervice.
International organisation	"An organisation and its subordinate bodies governed by public international law, or any other body which is set up by, or on the basis of, an agreement between two or more countries" *(General Data Protection Regulation)*.
International Telecommunications Union, Telecommunication Standardization Sector (ITU-T)	"International Telecommunications Union, Telecommunication Standardization Sector (formerly 'CCITT'), a United Nations treaty organization that is composed mainly of postal, telephone, and telegraph authorities of the member countries and that publishes standards called 'Recommendations'" *(SANS glossary)*.
[An] **internet [lower case i]**	Generic network-of-networks such as (but not necessarily) the Internet as we know it, plus interconnections between private networks in some industries, *e.g.* Interpol. "Collection of interconnected networks called an internetwork or just an internet" *(ISO/IEC 27033-1)*. "Two or more networks connected by a router" *(ISACA glossary)*. "A term to describe connecting multiple separate networks together" *(SANS glossary)*.
[The] **Internet [capital i]**	Global public network-of-networks. Despite the presence of substantial threats, vulnerabilities, and impacts making the Internet an *extraordinarily* risky environment in information security terms, human society has become substantially dependent on it. "Global system of inter-connected networks in the public domain" *(ISO/IEC 27033-1)*. "The world's largest network using Transmission Control Protocol/Internet Protocol (TCP/IP) to link government, university and commercial institutions" *(ISACA glossary)*. "A global computer network, providing a variety of information and communication facilities, consisting of interconnected networks using standardised communication protocols" *(UK National Cyber Security Strategy 2022)*.

TERM	MEANING
Internet Control Message Protocol **(ICMP)**	Part of the Internet Protocol suite, a network-layer messaging protocol for basic monitoring and administration of IP networks using messages, such as ICMP echo request and echo reply (see ping). "A set of protocols that allow systems to communicate information about the state of services on other systems. Notes: For example, ICMP is used in determining whether systems are up, maximum packet sizes on links and whether a destination host/network/port is available. Hackers typically use (abuse) ICMP to determine information about the remote site" *(ISACA glossary).* "An Internet Standard protocol that is used to report error conditions during IP datagram processing and to exchange other information concerning the state of the IP network" *(SANS glossary). Cf.* Simple Network Management Protocol.
Internet Crime Complaint Center **(IC3)**	Federal Bureau of Investigation's "central hub for reporting cyber-enabled crime." Handles Intellectual Property Rights matters, hacking, economic espionage, online extortion, international money laundering, identity fraud, and other Internet-facilitated crimes. More info: https://www.ic3.gov/
Internet Engineering Task Force **(IETF)**	"An organization with international affiliates as network industry representatives that sets Internet standards. This includes all network industry developers and researchers concerned with the evolution and planned growth of the Internet" *(ISACA glossary).* "The body that defines standard Internet operating protocols such as TCP/IP. The IETF is supervised by the Internet Society Internet Architecture Board (IAB). IETF members are drawn from the Internet Society's individual and organization membership" *(SANS glossary).* More info: https://www.ietf.org/
Internet Key Exchange **(IKE)**	IPsec cryptographic protocol for establishing a security association, using Diffie–Hellman key exchange to share a secret key. Version 2 was specified 2005 in RFC 4306. More info: https://datatracker.ietf.org/doc/html/rfc4306
Internet Key Exchange Extended Authentication **(IKE-EA)**	"Used to provide an additional level of authentication by allowing IPSec gateways to request additional authentication information from remote users. As a result, users are forced to respond with credentials before being allowed access to the connection" *(NZISM).*
Internet Message Access Protocol **(IMAP)**	Communications protocol used to read email stored on mail servers from email client applications on PCs, laptops, cellphones, *etc.* via the Internet. Specified by RFC 9051. "A method of communication used to read electronic messages stored in a remote server" *(NIST SP 800-101).* "A protocol that defines how a client should fetch mail from and return mail to a mail server. IMAP is intended as a replacement for or extension to the Post Office Protocol (POP). It is defined in RFC 1203 (v3) and RFC 2060 (v4)" *(SANS glossary).*

TERM	MEANING
Internet **o**f **T**hings **(IoT), Internet of everything, pervasive computing, ubi**quitous **comp**uting **(ubicomp), ambient intelligence, ambient media, everyware, Insecurity of Things, Internet of Threats, *etc.***	Rapidly expanding universe of mostly small, portable electronic devices (‘*things*’), typically used for remote monitoring and control through wireless networks and (often) Internet connections. Some *things* communicate directly with each other. Associated with significant information risks, especially in the case of cheap consumer goods designed to appeal to the naïve mass market in the short term. At the current stage of technology, product, and market development, information security is barely considered, let alone being an explicit architectural objective for many IoT *things*. “Infrastructure of interconnected entities, people, systems and information resources together with services that process and react to information from the physical world and virtual world” *(ISO/IEC 22989)*. “A collection of sensors, actuators and computing capabilities that work together to solve a problem or provide a service over the Internet” *(ISACA glossary)*. “The totality of devices, vehicles, buildings and other items embedded with electronics, software and sensors that communicate and exchange data over the internet” *(UK National Cyber Security Strategy 2022)*. See also **I**ndustrial **I**nternet **o**f *T***hings**, **M**obile **T**echnology, mesh network.
Internet **o**f **T**hings **(IoT) device**	See *thing*. “Entity of an IoT system that interacts and communicates with the physical world through sensing or actuating. Note: An IoT device can be a sensor or an actuator” *(ISO/IEC 22989)*. *[Alternative note]* “In this document, an IoT device is usually a physical product, which can be bought off-the-shelf by a consumer, *e.g.* a router, bulb or toy” *(ISO/IEC 27404 DRAFT)*.
Internet **o**f **T**hings **(IoT) system**	“System providing functionalities of IoT. Note: An IoT system can include, but not be limited to, IoT devices, IoT gateways, sensors and actuators” *(ISO/IEC 22989)*.
Internet **P**rotocol **(IP)**	Suite of networking protocols for datacommunications between devices over networks, providing basic functions such as addressing, routing, packet management, and error handling. Part of the TCP/IP suite. The original name ‘**I**nternetworking **P**rotocol’ has fallen into disuse. “The method or protocol by which data is sent from one computer to another on the Internet” *(SANS glossary)*. “Specifies the format of packets and the addressing scheme” *(ISACA glossary)*. *Cf.* **I**ntellectual **P**roperty.
Internet **P**rotocol **address (IP address)**	Network address (identifier) for a node on a TCP/IP network, consisting of 32 bits (IP version 4) or 128 bits (IPv6), conveniently communicated for humans as small groups of decimal or hexadecimal numbers separated by dots or colons, respectively, or using the associated domain name. “A unique binary number used to identify devices on a TCP/IP network. May be IP version 4 or 6” *(ISACA glossary)*. “A computer’s inter-network address that is assigned for use by the Internet Protocol and other protocols. An IP version 4 address is written as a series of four 8-bit numbers separated by periods” *(SANS glossary)*.

TERM	MEANING
Internet Protocol **flood** **(IP flood)**	"A denial of service attack that sends a host more echo request ('ping') packets than the protocol implementation can handle" *(SANS glossary)*.
Internet Protocol **forwarding** **(IP forwarding)**	"An Operating System option that allows a host to act as a router. A system that has more than 1 network interface card must have IP forwarding turned on in order for the system to be able to act as a router" *(SANS glossary)*.
Internet Protocol **sec**urity **(IPsec)**	Suite of cryptographic datacommunications protocols providing confidentiality and integrity for IP traffic. Commonly used for **V**irtual **P**rivate **N**etworks, securing data over untrusted networks such as the Internet. Includes **E**ncapsulating **S**ecurity **P**ayload and **A**uthentication **H**eader protocols, Security Associations, ISAKMP or IKE for key management, and transport mode or tunnel mode. "A set of protocols developed by the Internet Engineering Task Force (IETF) to support the secure exchange of packets" *(ISACA glossary)*. "A suite of protocols for secure communications through authentication or encryption of Internet Protocol (IP) packets as well as including protocols for cryptographic key establishment" *(AusISM)*. "A developing standard for security at the network or packet processing layer of network communication" *(SANS glossary)*.
Internet Protocol **[packet] spoofing** **(IP spoofing)**	"An attack using packets with spoofed source Internet packet (IP) addresses. Notes: This technique exploits applications that use authentication based on IP addresses. This technique may enable an unauthorized user to gain root access to the target system" *(ISACA glossary)*. "The technique of supplying a false IP address" *(SANS glossary)*.
Internet Protocol **telephony** **(IP telephony)**	See **V**oice **O**ver **I**nternet **P**rotocol. "The transport of telephone calls over IP networks" *(AusISM)*.
Internet proxy system	See proxy server.
Internet security	"Preservation of confidentiality, integrity and availability of information over the Internet" *(ISO/IEC 27032)*.
Internet **S**ervice **P**rovider **(ISP)**	Commercial organisation providing access to the Internet and information services such as email or VoIP. "Organization that provides Internet services to a user and enables its customers access to the Internet. Note: Also, sometimes referred to as an Internet access provider (IAP)" *(ISO/IEC 27032)*. "A third party that provides individuals and enterprises access to the Internet and a variety of other Internet-related services" *(ISACA glossary)*.
Internet standard	"A specification, approved by the IESG and published as an RFC, that is stable and well-understood, is technically competent, has multiple, independent, and interoperable implementations with substantial operational experience, enjoys significant public support, and is recognizably useful in some or all parts of the Internet" *(SANS glossary)*. *Cf.* ISO **I**nternational **S**tandard.

TERM	MEANING
Interpretation	Attempt to make sense of, understand, or explain information. "Synthesis of an explanation, within agreed limits, for the factual information about evidence resulting from the set of examinations and analysis making up the investigation" *(ISO/IEC 27042)*. "The consideration of the findings from the work implementing the examination strategy. Interpretation may be investigative, evaluative or, in certain circumstances, categorical" *(FSRCoP)*.
Interrogatory	Legal process requiring someone to provide sworn written answers to written questions. A form of discovery. *Cf.* deposition.
Interrupt	a. *[Verb]* To break the flow of communications or activities with a higher-priority/urgent message or instruction. b. *[Noun]* The message or instruction that interrupts. "A hardware or software signal stemming from an event that requires immediate attention" *(ISACA glossary)*. "A signal that informs the OS that something has occurred" *(SANS glossary)*.
Interruption window	See **M**aximum **T**olerable **O**utage. "The time that the company can wait from the point of failure to the restoration of the minimum critical services or applications. After this time, the progressive losses caused by the interruption are excessive for the enterprise" *(ISACA glossary)*.
Interval scale	"From the Stevens Scale of Measurement, a quantitative measurement scale using variables with equal values and no true zero, such as time and temperature" *(NIST SP 800-55v1)*.
In the wild	Malware or other forms of exploit that are 'at large,' circulating and causing real-world impacts, as opposed to those which have only ever been seen in laboratories or in the fertile imaginations of malware analysts.
Intranet	"Private computer network that uses Internet protocols and network connectivity to securely share part of an organisation's information or operations with its employees" *(ISO/IEC 27033-1)*. "A computer network, especially one based on Internet technology, that an organization uses for its own internal, and usually private, purposes and that is closed to outsiders" *(SANS glossary)*.
Intruder	Person lacking the requisite authority and permission who gains unauthorised physical access to a controlled area, or logical access to a computer network, system, device, *etc.* May also be vermin, *e.g.* rats or termites. "An individual or group that gains access to the network and its resources without permission" *(ISACA glossary)*.

TERM	MEANING
Intrusion, penetration	a. Hacking attack on a network or system originating externally. "Unauthorized access to a network or a network-connected system, *i.e.* deliberate or accidental unauthorized access to an information system, to include malicious activity against an information system, or unauthorized use of resources within an information system" *(ISO/IEC 27033-1)*. "Any event during which unauthorized access occurs" *(ISACA glossary)*. "Gaining unauthorized logical access to sensitive data by circumventing a system's protections" *(SANS glossary)*. *Cf.* extrusion. b. Unauthorised physical access to, or infiltration of, a site/location/facility, *e.g.* by an industrial spy, saboteur, burglar, or other outsider, or indeed by an insider. c. Form of attack on communications systems involving the injection of modified or fabricated messages intended to confuse and deceive.
Intrusion detection	Process to identify and log the presence of unauthorised visitors or users on a computer system, network device, or physical location and (normally) raise an intrusion alert or alarm, triggering the appropriate incident response. A particular form of incident detection. "Formal process of detecting intrusions, generally characterized by gathering knowledge about abnormal usage patterns as well as what, how, and which vulnerability has been exploited so as to include how and when it occurred" *(ISO/IEC 27039)*. "The process of monitoring the events occurring in a computer system or network to detect signs of unauthorized access or attack" *(ISACA glossary)*.
Intrusion **D**etection **S**ystem **(IDS)**	Electronic (*e.g.* **H**ost-based **I**ntrusion **D**etection **S**ystem or **N**etwork **I**ntrusion **D**etection **S**ystem) or physical controls (*e.g.* infrared detectors, microswitches or vibration detectors on doors and windows, and pressure pads under access routes) to detect intruders as part of intrusion detection. IDS typically works either generically by detecting anomalies (such as movement within an office in the dead of night – prone to false positives), or specifically by detecting the signatures or characteristics of known types of attack (such as the distinctive sound of breaking glass – prone to false negatives). A form of defensive security. "Technical system that is used to identify that an intrusion has been attempted, is occurring, or has occurred and possibly respond to intrusions in information systems and networks" *(ISO/IEC 27039)*. "A system that inspects network and host security activity to identify suspicious patterns that may indicate a network or system attack" *(ISACA glossary)*.

TERM	MEANING
	"An automated system used to identify an infringement of security policy from an internal or external source" *(NZISM)*. "An automated system used to identify an infringement of security policy. IDS can be host-based or network-base" *(AusISM)*. "A security management system for computers and networks. An IDS gathers and analyzes information from various areas within a computer or a network to identify possible security breaches, which include both intrusions (attacks from outside the organization) and misuse (attacks from within the organization)" *(SANS glossary)*. See also **I**ntrusion **P**revention **S**ystem, **S**ecurity **I**nformation and **E**vent **M**anagement, **N**etwork **T**raffic **A**nalysis **U**ser **B**ehaviour **A**nalytics.
Intrusion prevention	Process to identify the presence of unauthorised visitors or users, and, where appropriate, automatically take the necessary action to deny them further access (*e.g.* blocking or diverting suspicious network traffic emanating from presumably compromised systems or networks). "Formal process of actively responding to prevent intrusions" *(ISO/IEC 27033-1)*. "A preemptive approach to network security used to identify potential threats and respond to them to stop, or at least limit, damage or disruption" *(ISACA glossary)*. See also **I**ntrusion **P**revention **S**ystem.
Intrusion **P**revention **S**ystem **(IPS)**	Computer system to automate or support intrusion prevention by responding appropriately to detected intrusions – an obvious yet fiendishly difficult extension of **I**ntrusion **D**etection **S**ystems. "Variant on intrusion detection systems that are specifically designed to provide an active response capability" *(ISO/IEC 27039)*. "A system designed to not only detect attacks but also prevent the intended victim hosts from being affected by the attacks" *(ISACA glossary)*. "A security device, resident on a specific host, which monitors system activities for malicious or unwanted behaviour and can react in real-time to block or prevent those activities" *(NZISM)*. See also **S**ecurity **I**nformation and **E**vent **M**anagement, **U**ser **B**ehaviour **A**nalytics, **N**etwork **T**raffic **A**nalysis.
Intrusive monitoring	See surveillance. "In vulnerability analysis, the process of gaining information by performing checks that affect the normal operation of a system or by crashing the system" *(ISACA glossary)*.
Intumescent strip	Special material affixed to gaps around doors that swells in the heat of a fire, thereby sealing the gaps and so limiting both the exit of heat and smoke and the entry of fresh oxygenated air. A physical security control.
Invalid	a. Not valid. b. Physically weak or disabled person.

TERM	MEANING
Inverse split tunnelling	"A particular configuration of split tunnelling where only specifically authorised and trusted systems are able to be simultaneously communicated with via the external network connection" *(NZISM)*. *Cf.* split tunnelling.
Investigation	Act or systematic process of gathering information on and analysing a situation, occurrence or non-occurrence, event, or incident. "Systematic or formal process of inquiring into or researching, and examining facts or materials associated with a matter. Note: Materials can take the form of hardcopy documents or ES" *(ISO/IEC 27050-1)*. "Application of examinations, analysis, and interpretation to aid understanding of an incident" *(ISO/IEC 27042)*. "The collection and analysis of evidence with the goal to identify the perpetrator of an attack or unauthorized use or access" *(ISACA glossary)*.
Investigatory **P**owers **A**ct **(IPA), snoopers' charter**	2016 UK law gave spooks, the police, Inland Revenue and other authorities (snoops) powerful rights to gather evidence (including both data and metadata) of serious crime through surveillance. The right to intercept communications sent by or to individuals overseas, in bulk (mass surveillance), raised substantial concerns over civil liberties and privacy, leading to the Data Retention and Acquisition Regulations 2018 which aligned the Act with European laws.
Invicti	Vendor of a commercial application security testing tool that uses both **D**ynamic **A**pplication **S**ecurity **T**esting and **I**nteractive **A**pplication **S**ecurity **T**esting scanning. An example of dual-use technology, popular with black, grey, and white hats. More info: https://www.invicti.com/
Invocation	"Act of declaring that an organization's business continuity arrangements need to be put into effect in order to continue delivery of key products or services" *(ISO 22300)*.
Involuntary behaviours	"Automatic, often instinctual human actions informed by beliefs and values and governed by nature" *(OCEG GRC Glossary)*.
Invulnerable	Literally, not vulnerable. Paradoxically, the supreme confidence stemming from the belief that one is invulnerable to something itself constitutes a vulnerability to unanticipated modes of attack or compromise, as well as control failures and mistaken risk analysis. Absolute security is literally unattainable, an oxymoron.
IOA	*Abbrev:* **I**ndicator **Of** **A**ttack.
IOC	*Abbrev:* **I**ndicator **Of** **C**ompromise.
IoT	*Abbrev:* **I**nternet **o**f ***T**hings*.

TERM	MEANING
IoT product	Internet of *Things* thing, or service. "Any Internet of Things good or service. Notes: Good in this context can take the form of an IoT device, IoT solution, or IoT system along with bundled software. Services can include connectivity, cloud computing resources, maintenance, technical support, *etc.*" *(ISO/IEC 27404 DRAFT).*
IoT service	Internet of *Things* service. "Service that provides an outcome to its users via Internet of Things technology. Note: In this document, an IoT service usually means a software or application providing a non-physical product for a consumer, such as an e-mail or cloud service. Services are usually stand-alone products, which can be bought and used by a consumer" *(ISO/IEC 27404 DRAFT).*
IoT solution	Result of dissolving the Internet of *Things* in a solvent? Or the commercially offered means of addressing perceived problems, issues, or requirements by means of the Internet of *Things*. "Seamlessly integrated bundle of technologies, potentially including sensors, gateways and actuators. Notes: These can solve a specific problem or need, or they can be used to build additional functionality in other non-IoT solutions. Within the scope of the present document a solution typically combines hardware components (physical devices like a router, bulb, toy or sensors/actuators) and associated IoT services (*e.g.* an application for remote control or cloud space) and can be bought *e.g.* off-the-shelf by a consumer" *(ISO/IEC 27400).*
IoT system	Internet of *Things* system. "System providing functionalities of IoT. Notes: IoT system is inclusive of IoT devices, IoT solutions, IoT gateways, sensors and actuators. In the context of this document, this also includes applications and backend that support IoT solutions" *(ISO/IEC 27400).*
IP	*Abbrev:* Internet Protocol or Intellectual Property, depending on context.
IP camera, network camera	Digital Closed Circuit TeleVision camera that transmits streaming video across a TCP/IP network (usually) rather than through a dedicated point-to-point connection. Networked video traffic may be passed to local and/or remote monitoring stations. Unencrypted data and metadata may be viewed and modified by hackers and snoops, while network capacity constraints, Denial-of-Service attacks, hacks, and physical damage to the cabling or equipment may interrupt or compromise the service (*e.g.* replaying previously recorded footage in place of the real-time live video stream to conceal an intrusion in progress).
IPA	*Abbrev:* Investigatory Powers Act.

TERM	MEANING
IPMP	*Abbrev:* **I**ntegrated **P**olicy **M**anagement **P**rofessional.
IPR	*Abbrev:* **I**ntellectual **P**roperty **R**ights.
IPS	*Abbrev:* **I**ntrusion **P**revention **S**ystem.
IPsec	*Abbrev:* **I**nternet **P**rotocol **sec**urity.
IP telephony	See **V**oice **O**ver **I**nternet **P**rotocol. "The management and transport of voice communications over IP networks" *(NZISM).*
IR	*Abbrev:* **I**nformation **R**etrieval or **I**nfra-**R**ed, depending on context.
IRAM2	*Abbrev:* **I**nformation **R**isk **A**ssessment **M**ethodology № **2**.
IRBC	*Abbrev:* ICT **R**eadiness for **B**usiness **C**ontinuity.
IrDA	*Abbrev:* **I**nfrared **D**ata **A**ssociation, the trade body that defined a short-range (literally line-of-sight) datacommunications standard using near-infrared light. Superseded by Bluetooth and other RF network technologies, plus Li-Fi.
IRM	*Abbrev:* **I**nformation **R**isk **M**anagement, **I**ntegrated **R**isk **M**anagement or even **I**nsider **R**isk **M**anagement, depending on context.
IRMP	*Abbrev:* **I**ntegrated **R**isk **M**anagement **P**rofessional.
IRMS	*Abbrev:* Information Risk Management System.
IRSM	*Abbrev:* **I**nformation **R**isk and **S**ecurity **M**anagement.
IRP	*Abbrev:* **I**ncident **R**esponse **P**lan.
Irregularity	a. Something out of the ordinary, out of sequence, unpredictable, or random, *e.g.* irregular heartbeat. b. Euphemism for breach, nonconformity, or noncompliance. "Violation of an established management policy or regulatory requirement. It may consist of deliberate misstatements or omission of information concerning the area under audit or the enterprise as a whole, gross negligence or unintentional illegal acts" *(ISACA glossary).*
IRT	*Abbrev:* **I**ncident **R**esponse **T**eam.
ISA	*Abbrev:* **I**ndustrial **S**ociety of **A**utomation or **I**nformation **S**ecurity **A**ssessment depending on context.
ISA/IEC 62443-1-1	International standard from the **I**nternational **S**ociety of **A**utomation and **I**nternational **E**lectrotechnical **C**ommission: "Security for automation and control systems – Overview and Guidance for the ISA 62443 Series" (2007). Update immintent. More info: https://www.isa.org/standards-and-publications/isa-standards/isa-iec-62443-series-ofstandards

TERM	MEANING
ISACA	Well-respected global professional/trade body, originally (in 1969) named the **I**nformation **S**ecurity **A**nd **C**ontrol **A**ssociation, with ~180,000 members (as of 2025). ISACA's remit expanded from assurance and **I**nformation **T**echnology auditing to encompass information/cyber risk and security management, operations, and governance. Issuer of qualifications such as CISA, CISM, CCOA, CDPSE, CGEIT, and CRISC. More info: https://www.isaca.org/
ISACA glossary	Defines over 2,000 terms of art relevant to technology auditing. More info: https://www.isaca.org/resources/glossary
ISAE 3402	International equivalent of deprecated US standard SAS 70.
ISAKMP (Internet Security Association and Key Management Protocol)	Secure key exchange and management protocol within IPsec.
ISAKMP aggressive mode	"An IPSec protocol that uses half the exchanges of main mode to establish an IPSec connection" *(NZISM)*.
ISAKMP main mode	"An IPSec protocol that offers optimal security using six packets to establish an IPSec connection" *(NZISM)*.
ISAKMP quick mode	"An IPSec protocol that is used for refreshing security association information" *(NZISM)*.
IS audit, IS auditor	ISACA's terms for technology audit and technology auditor, in which 'IS' is evidently an abbreviation of **I**nformation **S**ystem/s, despite being undefined in the ISACA glossary.
ISC2	Professional association/trade body with ~675,000 members in cybersecurity. Previously named the **I**nternational **I**nformation **S**ystems **S**ecurity **C**ertification **C**onsortium and abbreviated as $(ISC)^2$. Issues qualifications such as CISSP and SSCP. More info: https://www.isc2.org/
ISCP	*Abbrev:* **I**ntegrated **S**ecurity & **C**ontinuity **P**rofessional.
ISF	*Abbrev:* **I**nformation **S**ecurity **F**orum.
ISIRT (Information Security Incident Response Team)	One or more information security professionals trained, competent, and ready to deal with information security incidents.
ISM	*Abbrev:* **I**nformation **S**ecurity **M**anager.
ISMS	*Abbrev:* **I**nformation **S**ecurity **M**anagement **S**ystem.
ISMS project	"Structured activities undertaken by an organisation to implement an ISMS" *(ISO/IEC 27000)*.

TERM	MEANING
ISO	International Organization for Standardization – a global, independent (non-governmental) standards body based in Geneva. 'ISO' is not an abbreviation but a contraction of the Greek *isos* meaning equal. "International Organization for Standardization, a voluntary, non-treaty, non-government organization, established in 1947, with voting members that are designated standards bodies of participating nations and non-voting observer organizations" *(SANS glossary)*. More info: https://www.iso.org/
ISO27k	*Abbrev:* ISO/IEC 27000 standards.
ISO 9000:2015	International standard "Quality management systems – Fundamentals and vocabulary" defines terms relating to the management of product quality. More info: https://www.iso.org/standard/45481.html
ISO/IEC 17000:2020	International standard "Conformity assessment – Vocabulary and general principles" defines terms relating to conformity assessment and accreditation of certification bodies. More info: https://www.iso.org/standard/73029.html
ISO/IEC 17021-1:2015	International standard "Conformity assessment — Requirements for bodies providing audit and certification of management systems. Part 1: Requirements" formally specifies principles and requirements for competence, consistency, and impartiality of management systems auditors. More info: https://www.iso.org/standard/61651.html
ISO/IEC TS 17027:2014	**T**echnical **S**pecification/international standard "Conformity assessment — Vocabulary related to competence of persons used for certification of persons" defines terms relating to the certification of individuals' competence. More info: https://www.iso.org/standard/62024.html
ISO 19011:2018	International standard "Guidelines for auditing management systems" tells ISO **M**anagement **S**ystem conformity certification auditors how to do it. New version imminent. More info: https://www.iso.org/standard/70017.html
ISO 22300:2021	International standard "Security and resilience — Vocabulary" defines specialist terms used in various ISO standards. New version imminent. More info: https://www.iso.org/standard/77008.html
ISO 22301:2019	International standard "Security and resilience — Business continuity management systems — Requirements" formally specifies a **B**usiness **C**ontinuity **M**anagement **S**ystem against which organisations may be certified. See also ISO 22313. More info: https://www.iso.org/standard/75106.html

TERM	MEANING
ISO 22313:2020	International standard "Security and resilience — Business continuity management systems — Guidance on the use of ISO 22301" accompanies and expands on ISO 22301, providing additional guidance on the practice of **B**usiness **C**ontinuity **M**anagement. Replaced British Standard BS 25999-1. More info: https://www.iso.org/standard/75107.html
ISO 22341:2021	International standard "Security and resilience — Protective security — Guidelines for crime prevention through environmental design" offers guidance on designing physical security controls to deter criminal attacks on people and property. More info: https://www.iso.org/standard/50078.html
ISO/IEC 22989:2022	International standard "Information technology – Artificial intelligence – Artificial intelligence concepts and terminology" provides a glossary of **A**rtificial **I**ntelligence terms. More info: https://www.iso.org/standard/74296.html
ISO 23234:2021	International standard "Buildings and civil engineering works — Security — Planning of security measures in the built environment" concerns physical security for construction projects. More info: https://www.iso.org/standard/75004.html
ISO/IEC 2382:2015	International standard "Information technology – Vocabulary" is the latest revision of one of the earliest Information Technology glossaries. First published as ISO 2382:1974 before '**D**ata **P**rocessing' morphed into 'computing,' then '**I**nformation **T**echnology,' and latterly 'technology.' "ISO 2382 was initially based mainly on the usage to be found in the Vocabulary of Information Processing which was established and published by the International Federation for Information Processing and the International Computation Centre, and in the American National Dictionary for Information Processing Systems and its earlier editions published by the American National Standards Institute (formerly known as the American Standards Association)." More info: https://www.iso.org/standard/63598.html
ISO/IEC 27000 standards, (ISO27k)	Set of information security standards produced by an international committee of experts representing their national standards bodies mostly **ISO/IEC J**oint **T**echnical **C**ommittee **1**, **S**ub-**C**ommittee **27**. More info: https://committee.iso.org/home/jtc1sc27
ISO/IEC 27000:2018	International standard "Information security management systems — Overview and vocabulary" introduces ISO27k plus a glossary of information security terms used in the standards. See also ISO 31073, ISO Guide 73, SD6, ISO 31000. More info: https://www.iso.org/standard/73906.html

TERM	MEANING
ISO/IEC 27001:2022 (ISO 27001)	International <u>standard</u> "Information Security Management Systems – Requirements" <u>formally</u> <u>specifies</u> an <u>**I**nformation **S**ecurity **M**anagement **S**ystem</u> against which <u>organisations</u> may opt to be <u>certified</u> <u>conformant</u>, ideally by duly <u>accredited</u> <u>certification bodies</u>. Evolved from BS 7799 in the 1990s. <u>More info</u>: https://www.iso.org/standard/27001
ISO/IEC 27002:2022	International <u>standard</u> on "Information security controls" lays out a structured catalogue of generic, commonplace, <u>good practice</u> <u>information security</u> <u>controls</u>, categorised into four major themes (<u>organisational</u>, people, physical, and <u>technological</u>) and tagged with five <u>attributes</u> (*e.g.* the 'control type' can be <u>preventive</u>, <u>detective</u>, and/or <u>corrective</u>). Evolved from BS 7799 in the 1990s. Initially numbered ISO/IEC 17799 when released in 2005. <u>More info</u>: https://www.iso.org/standard/75652.html
ISO/IEC 27003:2017	International <u>standard</u> "Information security management systems – Guidance" advice on <u>implementing</u> the <u>ISO27k</u> standards. <u>More info</u>: https://www.iso.org/standard/63417.html
ISO/IEC 27004:2016	International <u>standard</u> "Information security management — Monitoring, measurement, analysis and evaluation" describes how to <u>design</u> a <u>metrics</u> <u>system</u> for <u>measuring</u> and hence <u>systematically</u> improving the <u>**I**nformation **S**ecurity **M**anagement **S**ystem</u>. <u>More info</u>: https://www.iso.org/standard/64120.html
ISO/IEC 27005:2022	International <u>standard</u> "Guidance on managing information security risks" describes <u>risk analysis</u>, <u>risk assessment</u>, and other <u>risk management</u> practices in general terms, advising <u>organisations</u> to choose <u>methods</u> that suit their <u>purposes</u>. <u>More info</u>: https://www.iso.org/standard/80585.html
ISO/IEC 27006-1:2024	International <u>standard</u> "Requirements for bodies providing audit and certification of information security management systems – Part 1: General" directs <u>accredited</u> <u>certification bodies</u> on the <u>formal</u> <u>processes</u> for auditing <u>conformity</u> and <u>certifying</u> <u>**I**nformation **S**ecurity **M**anagement **S**ystems</u>. <u>More info</u>: https://www.iso.org/standard/82908.html
ISO/IEC TS 27006-2:2021	<u>**T**echnical **S**pecification</u>/international <u>standard</u> "Requirements for bodies providing audit and certification of information security management systems — Part 2: Privacy information management systems" is used to <u>accredit</u> <u>**C**ertification **B**odies</u> offering <u>**P**rivacy **I**nformation **M**anagement **S**ystems</u> <u>conformity</u> <u>certificates</u>. <u>More info</u>: https://www.iso.org/standard/71676.html

TERM	MEANING
ISO/IEC 27007:2020	International standard "Guidelines for information security management systems auditing" advises on auditing the **M**anagement **S**ystem aspects of an ISO/IEC 27001 **I**nformation **S**ecurity **M**anagement **S**ystem, *i.e.* the main body clauses as opposed to Annex A's information security controls. More info: https://www.iso.org/standard/77802.html
ISO/IEC TS 27008:2019	**T**echnical **S**pecification/international standard "Guidelines for the assessment of information security controls" concerns **I**nformation **T**echnology audits against ISO/IEC 27002. More info: https://www.iso.org/standard/67397.html
ISO/IEC 27010:2015	International standard "Information security management for inter-sector and inter-organizational communications" offers guidance on sharing information about information security risks, controls, events, and/or incidents that span the boundaries between organisations, industry sectors, and/or nations, particularly those affecting **C**ritical **N**ational **I**nfrastructure or involving crime, terrorism, money laundering, drug trafficking, *etc.* More info: https://www.iso.org/standard/68427.html
ISO/IEC 27011:2024, ITU-T X.1051	International standard "Code of practice for Information security controls based on ISO/IEC 27002 for telecommunications organizations" gives implementation advice tailored to the telecoms industry. The identical standard was published by ISO/IEC as ISO/IEC 27011 and by the ITU-T as X.1051. More info: https://www.iso.org/standard/80584.html
ISO/IEC 27013:2021	International standard "Guidance on the integrated implementation of ISO/IEC 27001 and ISO/IEC 20000-1" concerns the joint implementation of **M**anagement **S**ystems for both information security and **I**nformation **T**echnology services. More info: https://www.iso.org/standard/78752.html
ISO/IEC 27014:2020, ITU-T X.1054	International standard "Governance of information security" concerns (... cue drum roll ...) the governance of information security. The identical standard was published by ISO/IEC as ISO/IEC 27014 and by the ITU-T as X.1054 (free download). More info: https://www.itu.int/rec/T-REC-X.1054-202104-I/en
ISO/IEC TR 27016:2014	**T**echnical **R**eport/international standard "Information security management – Organizational economics" concerns the application of economic theory to information security. More info: https://www.iso.org/standard/43756.html
ISO/IEC 27017:2015, ITU-T X.1631	International standard "Code of practice for information security controls based on ISO/IEC 27002 for cloud services" offers information security advice to the providers and acquirers of cloud computing services. New version imminent. More info: https://www.iso.org/standard/43757.html

TERM	MEANING
ISO/IEC 27018:2025	International standard "Guidelines for protection of Personally Identifiable Information (PII) in public clouds acting as PII processors" concerns privacy in the context of cloud computing. More info: https://www.iso.org/standard/27018
ISO/IEC 27019:2024	International standard "Information security controls for the energy utility industry" is more widely applicable than its title suggests, covering information security for **O**perational **T**echnology including **S**upervisory **C**ontrol **A**nd **D**ata **Ac**quisition and **I**ndustrial **C**ontrol **S**ystems. The standard's scope explicitly excludes nuclear power. It should be read and applied in conjunction with ISO/IEC 27002 and other ISO27k standards. More info: https://www.iso.org/standard/85056.html
ISO/IEC 27021:2017	International standard "Competence requirements for information security management professionals" is, in effect, a standardised core syllabus for ISO27k training courses. More info: https://www.iso.org/standard/61003.html
ISO/IEC TS 27022:2021	**T**echnical **S**pecification/international standard "Guidance on information security management system processes" describes an **I**nformation **S**ecurity **M**anagement **S**ystem as a suite of processes. More info: https://www.iso.org/standard/61004.html
ISO/IEC TR 27024	**Draft** **T**echnical **R**eport/international standard "Use of ISO/IEC 27110 family of standards in governmental/regulatory requirements" is intended to assist organisations to determine which ISO27k standards are recommended or required of them for national legal/regulatory compliance reasons. More info: https://www.iso27001security.com/html/27024
ISO/IEC TS 27028	**Draft** **T**echnical **S**pecification/international standard "Guidance on ISO/IEC 27002 attributes" will offer advice on extending and using the control attributes for various purposes. More info: https://www.iso27001security.com/html/27028
ISO/IEC 27031:2011	International standard "Guidelines for information and communications technology readiness for business continuity" covering the **I**nformation **T**echnology aspects of business continuity and **D**isaster **R**ecovery management. See also ISO 22301. More info: https://www.iso.org/standard/27031
ISO/IEC 27032:2023	International standard "Guidelines for Internet security" advises on securing networks against deliberate attacks such as hacking and malware, committed through the Internet. More info: https://www.iso.org/standard/76070.html

TERM	MEANING
ISO/IEC 27033-1:2015	International standard "Network security — Overview and concepts" gives a general introduction to the remaining parts of this network security standard. More info: https://www.iso.org/standard/63461.html
ISO/IEC 27033-2:2012	International standard "Guidelines for the design and implementation of network security" offers generic guidance on network security architectural design and implementation. More info: https://www.iso.org/standard/51581.html
ISO/IEC 27033-3:2010	International standard "Reference networking scenarios — threats, design techniques and control issues" provides examples demonstrating how the ISO/IEC 27033 standards are intended to address a range of network security threats. More info: https://www.iso.org/standard/51582.html
ISO/IEC 27033-4:2014	International standard "Securing communications between networks using security gateways" is about network and application firewalls and Intrusion Protection System *(sic)*. More info: https://www.iso.org/standard/51583.html
ISO/IEC 27033-5:2013	International standard "Securing communications across networks using Virtual Private Networks (VPNs)" concerns **V**irtual **P**rivate **N**etworks. More info: https://www.iso.org/standard/51584.html
ISO/IEC 27033-6:2016	International standard "Securing wireless IP network access" addresses information security for Wi-Fi and 3G/4G cellular networks. More info: https://www.iso.org/standard/51585.html
ISO/IEC 27033-7:2023	International standard "Guidelines for network virtualization security" offers guidance on securing virtual networks. More info: https://www.iso.org/standard/80972.html
ISO/IEC 27034-1:2011	International standard "Application security — Overview and concepts" introduces a multipart standard concerning the information security aspects of application software. More info: https://www.iso.org/standard/44378.html
ISO/IEC 27034-2:2015	International standard "Application security — Organization normative framework." Explains the structure and relationships between policies, procedures, rôles, tools, and techniques for application security. More info: https://www.iso.org/standard/55582.html
ISO/IEC 27034-3:2018	International standard "Application security management process" describes the overall process for managing application security. More info: https://www.iso.org/standard/55583.html

TERM	MEANING
ISO/IEC 27034-5:2017 ISO/IEC 27034-5-1:2018	International standard "Protocols and application security controls data structure" explains how organisations can define a library of security controls for use by multiple applications, perhaps share them with other organisations. The dash-1 part contains the XML schemas. More info: https://www.iso.org/standard/55585.html
ISO/IEC 27034-6:2016	International standard "Application security — case studies" provides generic examples illustrating the use of application security controls during software development. More info: https://www.iso.org/standard/60804.html
ISO/IEC 27034-7:2018	International standard "Application security — Assurance prediction framework" establishes a framework allowing programs to trust each other under defined conditions. More info: https://www.iso.org/standard/66229.html
ISO/IEC 27035-1:2023	International standard "Information security incident management — Principles and process" lays out the concepts, principles, and activities involved in incident management, introducing the remaining parts of ISO/IEC 27035. More info: https://www.iso.org/standard/78973.html
ISO/IEC 27035-2:2023	International standard "Information security incident management — Guidelines to plan and prepare for incident response" concerns assurance that the organisation is in fact ready to respond appropriately to information security incidents that may yet occur. More info: https://www.iso.org/standard/78974.html
ISO/IEC 27035-3:2020	International standard "Information security incident management — Guidelines for ICT incident response operations" concerns the organisation and processes necessary for the information security function to prepare for and respond to deliberate attacks against Information Technology systems and networks. More info: https://www.iso.org/standard/74033.html
ISO/IEC 27035-4:2024	International standard "Information security incident management — Coordination" concerns the coordination of information security incident responses among multiple organisations affected or involved. More info: https://www.iso.org/standard/80973.html
ISO/IEC 27036-1:2021	International standard "Cybersecurity — Supplier relationships — Overview and concepts" explains the concepts and introduces the other parts of ISO/IEC 27036. More info: https://www.iso.org/standard/82905.html

TERM	MEANING
ISO/IEC 27036-2:2022	International standard "Cybersecurity — Supplier relationships — Part 2: Requirements" specifies fundamental information security requirements pertaining to business relationships to help suppliers and acquirers understand and treat the associated information risks. More info: https://www.iso.org/standard/82060.html
ISO/IEC 27036-3:2023	International standard "Guidelines for hardware, software, and services supply chain security" guides providers and acquirers of **I**nformation **T**echnology products on the management of supply chain information risks such as malware and counterfeit products, and the integration of information risk management into the **S**oftware **D**evelopment **L**ife**C**ycle. Identifies controls from ISO/IEC 27002. More info: https://www.iso.org/standard/82890.html
ISO/IEC 27036-4:2016	International standard "Guidelines for security of cloud services" addresses specified information risks associated with the use of cloud services, for **C**loud **S**ervice **P**roviders and consumers. More info: https://www.iso.org/standard/59689.html
ISO/IEC 27037:2012	International standard "Guidelines for identification, collection, acquisition and preservation of digital evidence" covers the early stages of digital forensics work. More info: https://www.iso.org/standard/44381.html
ISO/IEC 27038:2014	International standard "Specification for digital redaction" covers *some* of the information risks relating to the redaction of sensitive content from documents that have to be disclosed for some reason (such as under the Freedom of Information Act or a court order). More info: https://www.iso.org/standard/44382.html
ISO/IEC 27039:2015	International standard "Selection, deployment and operations of intrusion detection and prevention systems (IDPS)" covers just that. More info: https://www.iso.org/standard/56889.html
ISO/IEC 27040:2024	International standard "Storage security" concerns the **I**nformation **T**echnology security aspects of data storage. More info: https://www.iso.org/standard/80194.html
ISO/IEC 27041:2015	International standard "Guidance on assuring suitability and adequacy of incident investigative method" is a digital forensics standard. More info: https://www.iso.org/standard/44405.html
ISO/IEC 27042:2015	International standard "Guidelines for the analysis and interpretation of digital evidence" is also a digital forensics standard. More info: https://www.iso.org/standard/44406.html
ISO/IEC 27043:2015	International standard "Incident investigation principles and processes" is yet another digital forensics standard. More info: https://www.iso.org/standard/44407.html

TERM	MEANING
ISO/IEC 27045	**Draft** international standard "Big data security and privacy — Guidelines for managing big data risks" will improve organisations' capabilities for security and privacy around big data. More info: https://www.iso27001security.com/html/27045
ISO/IEC 27046	**Draft** international standard "Big data security and privacy — Implementation guidelines" will advise how to go about implementing the processes described in ISO/IEC 27045. More info: https://www.iso27001security.com/html/27046
ISO/IEC 27050-1:2019	International standard "Electronic discovery — Overview and concepts" explains the concepts and introduces the remaining ISO/IEC 27050 standards on electronic discovery and digital forensics. More info: https://www.iso.org/standard/78647.html
ISO/IEC 27050-2:2018	International standard "Electronic discovery — Guidance for governance and management of electronic discovery" provides guidance on identifying and treating the information risks associated with the eDiscovery and forensics processes. More info: https://www.iso.org/standard/66230.html
ISO/IEC 27050-3:2020	International standard "Electronic discovery — Code of practice for electronic discovery" is a basic, generic, how-to-do-it guide to eDiscovery. More info: https://www.iso.org/standard/78648.html
ISO/IEC 27050-4:2021	International standard "Electronic discovery — Technical readiness" offers guidance on the technology/tools and systems supporting eDiscovery and forensics. More info: https://www.iso.org/standard/74034.html
ISO/IEC 27070:2021	International standard "Requirements for establishing virtualized roots of trust" concerns the provision of critical cryptographic functions from the cloud. More info: https://www.iso.org/standard/56571.html
ISO/IEC 27071:2023	International standard "Security recommendations for establishing trusted connections between devices and services" concerns mutual authentication between devices and services using **P**ublic **K**ey **I**nfrastructure and **H**ardware **S**ecurity **M**odules. More info: https://www.iso.org/standard/56572.html
ISO/IEC 27090	**Draft** international standard "Guidance for addressing security threats and compromises to artificial intelligence systems" will help organisations address cybersecurity risks relating to **A**rtificial **I**ntelligence. More info: https://www.iso27001security.com/html/27090
ISO/IEC 27091	**Draft** international standard "Artificial Intelligence – Privacy protection" will address **A**rtificial **I**ntelligence privacy risks. More info: https://www.iso27001security.com/html/27091

TERM	MEANING
ISO/IEC 27099:2022	International standard "Public key infrastructure – Practices and policy framework" concerns information security management requirements for **P**ublic **K**ey **I**nfrastructure **T**rust **S**ervice **P**roviders (essentially, **C**ertification **A**uthorities). More info: https://www.iso.org/standard/56590.html
ISO/IEC TS 27100:2020	**T**echnical **S**pecification/international standard "Cybersecurity — Overview and concepts" attempts (unsuccessfully!) to distinguish cybersecurity from information security. More info: https://www.iso.org/standard/72434.html
ISO/IEC 27102:2019	International standard "Guidelines for cyber-insurance" is a useful guide to what cyberinsurance is and how it works. More info: https://www.iso.org/standard/72436.html
ISO/IEC TR 27103:2018	**T**echnical **R**eport/international standard on "Cybersecurity and ISO and IEC standards" provides background on the concepts and practices involved in proactively managing cyber risks using ISO27k. More info: https://www.iso.org/standard/72437.html
ISO/IEC TR 27109	**Draft** **T**echnical **R**eport/international standard "Cybersecurity education and training" *may* identify national guidelines relating to cybersecurity professionals (intent uncertain at this early stage). More info: https://www.iso27001security.com/html/27109
ISO/IEC TS 27110:2021	**T**echnical **S**pecification/international standard "Cybersecurity framework development guidelines" offers guidance to organisations developing cybersecurity frameworks. See also ISO/IEC 27103, NIST **C**yber **S**ecurity **F**ramework. More info: https://www.iso.org/standard/72435.html
ISO/IEC 27400:2022	International standard "IoT security and privacy — Guidelines" offers guidance on the principles, information, and privacy risks, and the controls applicable to **I**nternet **o**f *Things*. More info: https://www.iso.org/standard/44373.html
ISO/IEC 27402:2023	International standard **"**IoT security and privacy — Device baseline requirements" describes basic security and privacy controls for *things*. More info: https://www.iso.org/standard/80136.html
ISO/IEC 27403:2024	International standard "IoT security and privacy – Guidelines for IoT-domotics" covers security and privacy for domotics. More info: https://www.iso.org/standard/78702.html
ISO/IEC 27404	**Draft** international standard "Cybersecurity labelling framework for consumer IoT" hopes to standardise IoT security/privacy labelling. More info: https://www.iso27001security.com/html/27404

TERM	MEANING
ISO/IEC TR 27550:2019	Technical Report/international standard "Privacy engineering for system life cycle processes" offers guidance on engineering privacy in to Information Technology systems and business processes. More info: https://www.iso.org/standard/72024.html
ISO/IEC 27551:2021	International standard "Requirements for attribute-based unlinkable entity authentication" specifies how to authenticate people anonymously without compromising their privacy using ABUEA. More info: https://www.iso.org/standard/72018.html
ISO/IEC 27553-1:2022	International standard "Security and privacy requirements for authentication using biometrics on mobile devices – Local modes" concerns biometric user authentication on mobile devices, where biometric data remain on the device. More info: https://www.iso.org/standard/71671.html
ISO/IEC 27553-2	**Draft** international standard "Security and privacy requirements for authentication using biometrics on mobile devices – Remote modes" will concern biometric user authentication on mobile devices, where biometric data are sent over networks. More info: https://www.iso27001security.com/html/27553
ISO/IEC 27554:2024	International standard "Application of ISO 31000 for assessment of identity-related risk" advises on using the ISO 31000 approach to risk management for identity management. More info: https://www.iso.org/standard/71672.html
ISO/IEC 27555:2021	International standard "Guidelines on personally identifiable information deletion" suggests a systematic approach to delete personal information with adequate assurance. More info: https://www.iso.org/standard/71673.html
ISO/IEC 27556:2022	International standard "User-centric privacy preferences management framework" lays out an architecture to handle personal information in a controlled manner in accordance with privacy-by-design and other requirements. More info: https://www.iso.org/standard/71674.html
ISO/IEC 27557:2022	International standard "Application of ISO 31000:2018 for organizational privacy risk management" guides organisations on managing privacy risks within overall risk management. More info: https://www.iso.org/standard/71675.html
ISO/IEC 27559:2022	International standard "Privacy-enhancing data de-identification framework" provides a framework for mitigating the privacy risks associated with anonymisation of personal information. More info: https://www.iso.org/standard/71677.html

TERM	MEANING
ISO/IEC TS 27560:2023	International standard "Consent record information structure" specifies how to record data subjects' consent to **D**ata **P**rocessing. More info: https://www.iso.org/standard/80392.html
ISO/IEC 27561:2024	International standard "Privacy operationalisation model and method for engineering (POMME)" contrives to elaborate on a systematic approach for engineering system for privacy. More info: https://www.iso.org/standard/80394.html
ISO/IEC 27562:2024	International standard "Privacy guidelines for fintech services" advises on privacy architectures for fintech. More info: https://www.iso.org/standard/80395.html
ISO/IEC TR 27563:2023	Technical **R**eport/international standard "Security and privacy in artificial intelligence use cases – Best practices" elaborates on information security and privacy of 136 **A**rtificial **I**ntelligence use cases. More info: https://www.iso.org/standard/80396.html
ISO/IEC TS 27564	**Draft** Technical **S**pecification/international standard "Guidance on the use of models for privacy engineering" will explain how to use various types of models in privacy engineering. More info: https://www.iso27001security.com/html/27564
ISO/IEC 27565	**Draft** international standard "Guidelines on privacy preservation based on zero knowledge proofs" will explain how someone can demonstrate, cryptographically, that they know a secret (such as a biometric or other personal information) without disclosing the secret, using a zero-knowledge protocol. More info: https://www.iso27001security.com/html/27565
ISO/IEC 27566-1	**Draft** international standard "Age assurance systems — Framework" will lay out the core principles and a framework for determining someone's age or age range independently of their identity, for use in age-related eligibility decisions. More info: https://www.iso27001security.com/html/27566
ISO/IEC 27566-2	**Draft** international standard "Age assurance systems — Technical approaches and guidance for implementation" will presumably delve into smart ways of using technology to determine a person's age or age range (early days for this standard). More info: https://www.iso27001security.com/html/27566
ISO/IEC 27566-3	**Draft** international standard "Age assurance systems — Benchmarks for benchmark analysis" will cover ways to compare and contrast various age assurance systems using metrics. More info: https://www.iso27001security.com/html/27566
ISO/IEC TS 27570:2021	Technical **S**pecification/international standard "Privacy guidelines for smart cities" addresses privacy concerns relating to smart cities, *e.g.* through surveillance and tracking of individuals. More info: https://www.iso.org/standard/71678.html

TERM	MEANING
ISO/IEC 27701:2019	International standard "Extension to ISO/IEC 27001 and to ISO/IEC 27002 for privacy information management — Requirements and guidelines" formally specifies a **P**rivacy **I**nformation **M**anagement **S**ystem that builds on an ISO27k **I**nformation **S**ecurity **M**anagement **S**ystem to cater for privacy. See also ISO/IEC TS 27006-2. The ISMS and PIMS are both certifiable. New version imminent. More info: https://www.iso.org/standard/71670.html
ISO 27799:2016	International standard "Information security management in health using ISO/IEC 27002" advises on the implementation of ISO/IEC 27002:2013 in the healthcare/medical industry. New version imminent. More info: https://www.iso.org/standard/62777.html
ISO/IEC 29100: 2024	International standard "Privacy framework" describes a systematic approach to managing privacy risks and controls. More info: https://www.iso.org/standard/85938.html
ISO/IEC 29134:2023	International standard "Guidelines for privacy impact assessment" explains the process for evaluating the potential impacts of privacy breaches and determining how to mitigate unacceptable privacy risks. More info: https://www.iso.org/standard/86012.html
ISO 31000:2018	International standard "Risk management – Guidelines" explains the principles underlying a framework and process for managing all manner of risks, not just information risks. More info: https://www.iso.org/standard/65694.html
ISO 31073:2022	International standard "Risk management – Vocabulary" defines terms and concepts for risk and risk management. More info: https://www.iso.org/standard/79637.html
ISO/IEC 42001:2023	International standard "Artificial intelligence – Management system" formally specifies requirements for an **A**rtificial **I**ntelligence **M**anagement **S**ystem. More info: https://www.iso.org/standard/81230.html
ISO/IEC TS 5723:2022	**T**echnical **S**pecification/International standard "Trustworthiness – Vocabulary" defines trust-related terms. More info: https://www.iso.org/standard/81608.html
ISO Guide 73:2009	ISO guideline "Risk management – Vocabulary – Guidelines for use in standards" was originally intended for internal use by ISO/IEC committees developing various standards. Became a *de facto* set of risk-related definitions. Withdrawn but still available. More info: https://www.iso.org/obp/ui/#iso:std:iso:guide:73:ed-1:v1:en
ISO/IEC JTC 1/SC 27 **S**tanding **D**ocument **6** **(SD6)**	ISO/IEC working document "Glossary of IT Security Terminology," an Excel spreadsheet containing a detailed glossary of information security terms used by JTC 1/SC 27, the committee developing ISO27k and other information security standards. Freely available. More info: https://tinyurl.com/SC27SD6

TERM	MEANING
Isogeny-based cryptography	Promising post-quantum derivative of elliptic curve cryptography, designed to be resistant to attacks using conventional *and* quantum computing technologies, yet practical for encryption (and perhaps digital signatures, *etc.*).
Isolate	Disconnect or shield from threats, *e.g.* when systems are taken offline to prevent or interrupt remote network exploitation by hackers or malware, severing their remote command and control capabilities, or circuit breakers are tripped and locked out to permit safe facilities or equipment maintenance. "Includes disconnection from other systems and any external connections. In some cases system isolation may not be possible for architectural or operational reasons. Isolation may also include the quarantine of suspected or known malware and unwanted content" *(NZISM)*.
ISPP	*Abbrev:* **I**ntegrated **S**trategy & **P**erformance **P**rofessional.
ISSO	*Abbrev:* **I**nformation **S**ystem **S**ecurity **O**fficer.
Issue-specific policy	Topic-specific policy. "An Issue-Specific Policy is intended to address specific needs within an organization, such as a password policy" *(SANS glossary)*.
IT	*Abbrev:* **I**nformation **T**echnology.
ITAF	*Abbrev:* **I**nformation **T**echnology **A**udit **F**ramework.
IT audit	**I**nformation **T**echnology audit. See technology audit.
IT Audit **F**ramework **(ITAF)**	ISACA's standards and best practices for technology audit and assurance engagements, succinctly summarised in this ~100-page free document. More info: https://tinyurl.com/ISACAITAF
ITCA	*Abbrev:* **I**nformation **T**echnology **C**ertified **A**ssociate.
Item	Thing, object, piece, possibly one of a set. "Anything that is submitted, recovered, collected, sampled or derived as part of the forensic process" *(FSRCoP)*.
Iterative [or incremental] software development	Group of software development methods that repeatedly cycle through a core process that may involve analysis prompting clarification and elaboration of the requirements, refinement of the design, incremental development and modification of the software, regression and other testing, and early release into production … with feedback from users, administrators, and other stakeholders feeding in to the next cycle. *Cf.* waterfall development.
ITIL	*Abbrev:* **I**nformation **T**echnology **I**nfrastructure **L**ibrary.
ITL	*Abbrev:* **I**ndependent **T**est **L**aboratory.

TERM	MEANING
IT [or ICT] security, data security, computer security, technology security	Strictly speaking, that part of information security concerned with protecting information stored, processed, and communicated as digital data by computer systems, devices, equipment, and networks. Often in practice liberally interpreted to mean any/all of information risk and security management. See also cybersecurity.
ITU-T	*Abbrev:* **I**nternational **T**elecommunications **U**nion, **T**elecommunications Standardization Sector.
IV	*Abbrev:* **I**nitialisation **V**ector.
IV&V	*Abbrev:* **I**ndependent **V**erification **&** **V**alidation.
IW	*Abbrev:* **I**nformation **W**arfare.

J

TERM	MEANING
Jackpotting	Attack on a bank **A**utomated **T**eller **M**achine that causes it to spew out cash like hitting the jackpot on a Las Vegas fruit machine. Various techniques are used, mostly by overcoming the physical security controls to manipulate the cash dispenser mechanism directly and/or to compromise its control circuits and software.
Jail	See sandbox.
Jailbreak	Overcome or bypass **O**perating **S**ystem security functions intended to restrict applications to a sandbox, thereby limiting privileged access to **I**nformation **T**echnology devices, primarily for information security or commercial reasons (*e.g.* to prevent the installation of apps not authorised and sold through the official app store). Can be (partially) overridden by users, hackers, spyware, or other malware.
Jamming	Deliberately using a powerful transmitter or RF noise source to block the reception of radio signals, *e.g.* interfering with and so preventing legitimate use of a wireless network, **G**lobal **P**ositioning **S**ystem, satellite or microwave communications, radar, broadcasting, cellphone, wireless **C**losed **C**ircuit **T**ele**V**ision camera, or a security guard's walkie-talkie. "An attack in which a device is used to emit electromagnetic energy on a wireless network's frequency to make it unusable" *(NIST SP 800-48)*.
Java	Popular programming language for mobile code.
JavaScript **(JS)**	Programming language widely used on the Web to code user interactivity into web pages, *e.g.* menus that slide open to reveal the site structure when moused over. *Cf.* Java.
Jerusalem, Black Box	One of the earliest computer viruses, first discovered in Jerusalem in 1987. This **D**isk **O**perating **S**ystem virus repeatedly inserted itself into DOS programs when they were executed but since it was only ~1800 bytes, the infection often remained unnoticed unless it broke those programs or, on Friday 13th, it displayed a black box while deleting files.
Jigsaw	Species of ransomware.
Jitter	Precise timing of packets and transmission elements over a communications path varies slightly due to differences in the transmissions and random factors such as noise. Datacommunications protocols therefore incorporate sufficient tolerance. Potentially constitutes a covert channel. "Short-term noncumulative variations of the significant instants of a digital signal from their ideal positions in time" (*ISO/IEC 2382*). "The modification of fields in a database while preserving the aggregate characteristics of that make the database useful in the first place" *(SANS glossary)*.

TERM	MEANING
John the Ripper, "John"	Hacking/penetration testing tool used to perform brute force attacks against inadequately secured hashed password files.
Joint PII controller	"Personally identifiable information (PII) controller that determines the purposes and means of the processing of PII jointly with one or more other PII controllers" *(ISO/IEC 27701)*.
Joint **T**errorism **A**nalysis **C**entre **(JTAC)**	UK intelligence unit responsible for coordinating activities and sharing information pertaining to terrorism. Based within MI5 but collaborates with **G**overnment **C**ommunications **H**ead**Q**uarters, **S**ecret **I**ntelligence **S**ervice, and other British and foreign intelligence agencies.
Joint **T**est **A**ction **G**roup **(JTAG)**	Hardware interface standard/serial port allowing very low-level testing of chips on **P**rinted **C**ircuit **B**oards, intended for **Q**uality **C**ontrol at the end of PCB production, firmware debugging, *etc.* using physically connected or networked diagnostic equipment. Potentially vulnerable to sophisticated attacks undermining the **R**oot **o**f **T**rust, *e.g.* by replacing trusted firmware with a hacked version containing a backdoor.
Journal, journaling	**D**ata**B**ase security/control method in which steps leading up to a commit point are saved temporarily (cached) until the commit successfully completes, enabling the sequence to be reversed or reapplied if interrupted by an incident, for instance a power, system, or network failure, bug, or data collision (simultaneous but conflicting changes to the same data item).
JTAC	*Abbrev:* **J**oint **T**errorism **A**nalysis **C**entre.
JTAG	*Abbrev:* **J**oint **T**est **A**ction **G**roup.
Jump server, jump host, jump box	Hardened security device that controls access and traffic flows between two network zones/domains, *e.g.* system administrators using dedicated and secure internal systems to manage servers located in the DMZ. "A computer which is used to manage important or critical resources in a separate security domain. Also known as a jump host or jump box" *(AusISM)*.
Jurisdiction	Physical or logical domain within which a person, court, or other body has the (legal) authority to act.

K

TERM	MEANING
Kaizen	See continuous improvement.
KAISER	See **K**ernel **P**age **T**able **I**solation.
Kali Linux, BackTrack	Debian-based Linux distribution popular with penetration testers, digital forensics and network security analysts, hackers, and the like. Includes numerous tools such as Metasploit, nmap, Wireshark, and Aircrack ng. Originally named BackTrack.
KASLR	*Abbrev:* **K**ernel **A**ddress **S**pace **L**ayout **R**andomisation.
KCI	*Abbrev:* **K**ey **C**ompliance **I**ndicator or **K**ey **C**ontrol **I**ndicator, depending on context.
Kedi	Species of **R**emote **A**ccess **T**rojan malware, in the wild in 2017. Exploits vulnerabilities in the Citrix remote access system.
Keep	Strong, well-protected building of last resort within a castle, in which the owners lived and secured their most valuable assets, not least themselves. The Mediaeval equivalent of a panic or safe room, only without a petrified Jodie Foster.
Kerberos	Cryptographic **I**dentification & **A**uthentication protocol or architecture developed by MIT. "A means of verifying the identities of principals on an open network. It accomplishes this without relying on the authentication, trustworthiness, or physical security of hosts while assuming all packets can be read, modified and inserted at will. It uses a trust broker model and symmetric cryptography to provide authentication and authorization of users and systems on the network" *(NIST SP 800-95)*. "A system developed at the Massachusetts Institute of Technology that depends on passwords and symmetric cryptography (DES) to implement ticket-based, peer entity authentication service and access control service distributed in a client-server network environment" *(SANS glossary)*.
Kerckhoffs' principle	In ~1883, Auguste Kerchchoffs wrote "The design of a system should not require secrecy and compromise of the system should not inconvenience the correspondents"; in other words it should be irrelevant whether a cryptographic algorithm or cryptosystem (as distinct from the key) is disclosed or published. Inspired Claude Shannon's maxim "The enemy knows the system." Note: competent professional scrutiny of a cryptosystem (which implies its disclosure) is an important assurance control since "Anyone can invent a security system that he himself cannot break" (Schneier's law, an example of the Dunning–Kruger effect).

TERM	MEANING
Kernel	Tasty core protected by the hard outer shell of a nut. **O**perating **S**ystem kernels handle critical functions, including many low-level privileged security functions such as mediating access to memory pages, storage, and peripheral devices, plus security logging and alerting. If the kernel protection is compromised (*e.g.* by malware or hackers), system security is largely if not totally negated. "The essential center of a computer operating system, the core that provides basic services for all other parts of the operating system. A synonym is nucleus. A kernel can be contrasted with a shell, the outermost part of an operating system that interacts with user commands. Kernel and shell are terms used more frequently in Unix and some other operating systems than in IBM mainframe systems" *(SANS glossary)*.
Kernel **A**ddress **S**pace **L**ayout **R**andomisation **(KASLR)**	Security control that pseudorandomises the memory addresses of privileged **O**perating **S**ystem kernel functions, making it harder for malware and hackers to call or manipulate them. See also **A**ddress **S**pace **L**ayout **R**andomisation, **K**ernel **P**age **T**able **I**solation.
Kernel mode	A privileged and hence relatively risky processing context for administrative applications and functions. "Used for execution of privileged instructions for the internal operation of the operating system. In kernel mode, there are no protections from errors or malicious activity, and all parts of the system and memory are accessible" *(ISACA glossary)*. *Cf.* user mode.
Kernel **P**age **T**able **I**solation **(KPTI), KAISER**	Low-level **O**perating **S**ystem or **C**entral **P**rocessing **U**nit firmware microcode security technique to keep kernel memory isolated and entirely separate from user processes, rather than (for performance reasons) sharing the same memory areas, which increases the possibility of malicious exploitation (such as by Spectre).
KEV	*Abbrev:* **K**nown **E**xploited **V**ulnerabilities.
Key	a. Cryptographic key. b. In physical security, the mechanical device or electronic code that unlocks a mechanical or electromechanical lock. c. Switch on a keyboard or keypad used to detect someone typing a character into a device. d. Indexed data field in a **D**ata**B**ase, used to cross-link tables. May be a primary, foreign, or candidate key. e. Something considered important, valuable, critical, or vital, such as a **K**ey **P**erformance **I**ndicator or key control.

TERM	MEANING
Key chord, cheat code	Particular combination of keys or buttons pressed simultaneously or in sequence to trigger a special device function, such as the <Ctrl-Alt-Del> "Vulcan mind-meld" secure interrupt sequence on a Windows PC. Key chords are commonly used to enter advanced configuration, bypass or reset functions, such as cheat codes advancing the player several levels or becoming invincible in computer games (a time-saver for the games' developers!). "Specific hardware keys pressed in a particular sequence on a mobile device" *(NIST SP 800-101)*.
Key Compliance Indicator (KCI)	Particularly significant, notable, or valuable indicator of compliance/conformity. "Indicators that help govern, manage, and provide assurance about compliance related to an objective" *(OCEG GRC Glossary)*. See also **Key Performance Indicator**, **Key Risk Indicator**, **Key Milestone Indicator**, **Key Goal Indicator**, **Key Control Indicator**.
Key control	a. Control designed to mitigate one or more key risks, bringing them within management's risk appetite. b. Control relating to physical or cryptographic keys, *e.g.* safekeeping, authorisation, issue and return, generation, duplication, record-keeping.
Key Control Indicator (KCI)	Indicator of parameters such as cost-effectiveness, strength, or reliability for key controls. "A measure of the effectiveness of controls to indicate a failure or weakness which may result in the increased likelihood or impact of risk events" *(ISACA glossary)*. See also **Key Performance Indicator**, **Key Risk Indicator**, **Key Milestone Indicator**, **Key Goal Indicator**, **Key Compliance Indicator**.
Key escrow	Secure safekeeping of cryptographic keys by an escrow agent in case there is a legitimate need to decrypt encrypted material later despite, for instance, the keys being lost or corrupted, or the holder forgetting or refusing to disclose them. If the escrow agent is untrustworthy, incompetent or careless, or coerced (*e.g.* by the government, criminals, or terrorists), there is obviously a risk of key disclosure or loss.
Key exchange	Process for passing cryptographic keys between two parties, *e.g.* prior to establishing an encrypted HTTPS connection. "Process of exchanging public keys (and other information) in order to establish secure communications" *(CNSSI 4009)*.
Key Goal Indicator (KGI)	Particularly significant, notable, or valuable indicator of the (rate of) achievement of particular goals or objectives. "Indicator that is an ex-post measure for the achievement of a goal/objective" *(ISO/IEC 27022)*. "A measure that tells management after the fact whether an IT process has achieved its business requirements; usually expressed in terms of information criteria" *(ISACA glossary)*. *Cf.* **Key Performance Indicator**, **Key Risk Indicator**, **Key Compliance Indicator**, **Key Control Indicator**, **Key Milestone Indicator**.

TERM	MEANING
Key holder, keyholder	Trusted person or rôle designated to hold the physical keys needed to unlock and access a secure area, site, or facility, particularly out-of-hours. They are of course expected or required to protect the keys and authenticate access requests by third parties.
Keying material	See key. "Cryptographic keys generated or used by cryptographic equipment or software" *(AusISM).*
Key length	Number of bits in a cryptographic key. Affects the amount of effort involved in brute force attacks, each extra bit doubling the average time if they are all used in the algorithm. "The size of an encryption key measured in bits" *(ISACA glossary).*
Key loader, key injector	Physically secure, tamper-resistant key management hardware device used to transport and install cryptographic keys to cryptosystems in the field. "A self-contained unit that is capable of storing at least one plaintext or encrypted cryptographic key or a component of a key that can be transferred, upon request, into a cryptographic module" *(CNSSI 4009).*
Keylogger	Malware that covertly records a computer user's keystrokes. Hardware keyloggers may be devices inserted into the keyboard cable or connector where they may appear to be ferrite RF interference suppressors, or fitted within the keyboard, PC, or wireless keyboard receiver. Software keyloggers are typically Trojans. "Software used to record all keystrokes on a computer" *(ISACA glossary).*
Key management	a. Controlled processes and the associated computer hardware, datacommunications services, key loaders, *etc.* for securely distributing cryptographic keys to authorised users and systems, handling activities such as revocation and replacement of lapsed or compromised keys, key escrow, *etc.* "The generation, exchange, storage, use, destruction and replacement of keys in a cryptosystem" *(ISACA glossary).* "The management of cryptographic keys and associated hardware and software … includes their generation, registration, distribution, installation, usage, protection, storage, access, recovery and destruction" *(NZISM).* "The use and management of cryptographic keys and associated hardware and software. It includes their generation, registration, distribution, installation, usage, protection, storage, access, recovery and destruction" *(AusISM).* b. Processes for handling and controlling the fabrication, circulation/distribution, secure storage, and use of physical keys, especially master keys.
Key management plan	Plan determining how keys are to be managed. "Describes how cryptographic services are securely deployed within an agency [and] documents critical key management controls to protect keys and associated material during their life cycle, along with other controls to provide confidentiality, integrity and availability of keys" *(NZISM).*

TERM	MEANING
Key Milestone Indicator (KMI)	Particularly significant, notable, or valuable indicator relating to milestones. "A Boolean value (yes/no) or a percentage value (% complete) that measures the degree to which a milestone is met" *(OCEG GRC Glossary)*. See also **Key Performance Indicator**, **Key Risk Indicator**, **Key Compliance Indicator**, **Key Goal Indicator**, **Key Control Indicator**.
Key Performance Indicator (KPI)	Particularly significant, notable, or valuable performance indicator. "Indicator that is an ex-ante measure, which allow a prediction if a goal/objective will be achieved in the future" *(NIST SP 800-55v1)*. "A type of performance measurement" *(ISACA glossary)*. "A metric of progress toward intended results" *(SP 800-55v1)*. "Quantifiable measure that an organization uses to gauge or compare performance in terms of meeting its strategic and operational objectives" *(ISO 22300)*. "Indicators that help govern, manage, and provide assurance about performance related to an objective" *(OCEG GRC Glossary)*. See also **Key Risk Indicator**, **Key Compliance Indicator**, **Key Milestone Indicator**, **Key Goal Indicator**, **Key Control Indicator**.
Key pin	Inside most physical locks, a series of variable-length key pins are displaced by the cut edge of the key when it is inserted into the keyway, pressing the concentric driver pins up into the hull against their springs. Provided the correctly shaped key is inserted, the junctions between the key pins and driver pins align along a shear line, allowing the plug to be rotated to open or close the lock.
Key risk	Particularly significant source or cause of uncertainty, a subjective and context-dependent determination. Whereas any risk may be considered key within the narrow scope of, say, a specific process or system, and at any point in time some risks are much more important than others, 'key risk' generally refers to 'bet the farm' business risks that are significant (material) or existential to the enterprise as a whole, threatening its mission.
Key Risk Indicator (KRI)	a. Metric concerning one or more key risks. "A metric used to measure risk" *(NIST SP 800-55v1)*. "Indicators that help govern, manage, and provide assurance about risk related to an objective" *(OCEG GRC Glossary)*. b. Particularly significant, notable, or valuable indicator concerning risk. "A subset of risk indicators that are highly relevant and possess a high probability of predicting or indicating important risk" *(ISACA glossary)*. See also **Key Performance Indicator**, **Key Compliance Indicator**, **Key Milestone Indicator**, **Key Goal Indicator**, **Key Control Indicator**.
Key space	Essentially the maximum total number of possible key values. Strong modern cryptosystems have such large key spaces that brute force attacks are very unlikely to succeed using currently available technology (they are 'computationally infeasible').

TERM **MEANING**

Key stretching "A defence against brute force and similar system attacks by increasing the time required to complete hashing and making an attack more time-consuming" *(NZISM)*.

Keyway Slot in a cylinder lock into which the key can be inserted. In addition to its overall dimensions, wards in the keyway prevent the insertion of grossly misfitting keys (*e.g.* from other manufacturers) and thick/crude lock picks or screwdrivers, levers, or wrenches that might otherwise be used to force the lock open.

[Cyber] Kill chain Military-style term for the sequence of an attack from reconnaissance and identification of targets through to exploitation and escape, a concept now applied in the cybersecurity context to hacks and malware infections, *etc.*

Kill switch

a. Alludes to a covert capability for a spooky adversary to interrupt (temporarily or permanently) critical technologies, impacting the services they provide.

b. Emergency stop switch on a dangerous electromechanical machine such as a lathe or robot.

c. Trigger on a gun or similar ballistic weapon.

Kimsuky Hacker group associated with the North Korean government, targeting governmental/military information concerning the Korean peninsula using social engineering (principally spear phishing), **A**dvanced **P**ersistent **T**hreats, and BabyShark malware.

Kismet Wireless networking analytical tool (**N**etwork-based **I**ntrusion **D**etection **S**ystem, used for both defensive and offensive purposes (a dual-use technology).

Kleptography Cryptanalytic technique inserts a 'subliminal' backdoor into a cryptographic system, using cryptography to conceal the compromise and control its use.

Klez Species of malware in the wild in 2002.

KMI *Abbrev:* **K**ey **M**ilestone **I**ndicator.

Knowledge Something known, *i.e.* an intangible form of information that has meaning and value. "Collection of facts, events, beliefs, and rules, organized for systematic use" *(ISO/IEC 2382)*. "Facts, information, truths, principles or understanding acquired through experience or education. Note: An example of knowledge is the ability to describe the various parts of an information assurance standard" *(ISO/IEC TS 17027)*. "<artificial intelligence> Abstracted information about objects, events, concepts or rules, their relationships and properties, organized for goal-oriented systematic use. Notes: Knowledge in the AI domain does not imply a cognitive capability, contrary to usage of the term in some other domains. In particular, knowledge

TERM	MEANING
	does not imply the cognitive act of understanding; Information can exist in numeric or symbolic form; Information is data that has been contextualized, so that it is interpretable. Data is created through abstraction or measurement from the world" *(ISO/IEC 22989)*. See also intellectual asset.
Known Exploited Vulnerabilities (KEV)	Cybersecurity & Infrastructure Security Agency maintains this catalogue detailing software vulnerabilities actively exploited in the wild, encouraging organisations to prioritise these in their vulnerability management processes. More info: https://www.cisa.gov/known-exploited-vulnerabilities-catalog
Known plaintext [attack]	Cryptanalysts often stand a better chance of breaking a cryptosystem if they can examine both the ciphertext and the corresponding plaintext, possibly just a part such as a standard preamble, title, and salutation/greeting. "Analytical attack in which a cryptanalyst possesses a substantial quantity of corresponding plaintext and ciphertext" *(ISO/IEC 2382)*. See also crib.
Know Your Customer (KYC)	"Process to verify the identity of a customer in order to prevent financial crime, money laundering and terrorism financing" *(ISO 12812-1)*.
Kompromat	Sensitive and potentially compromising information on an individual, the threatened disclosure of which is used to blackmail them. The Russian-style word reflects the popularity of this technique with the Russian intelligence services … but it is in fact a commonplace technique globally, not limited to spooks.
Kovter	Family of malware in the wild in 2019. Originally scareware, morphed into click fraud code injection malware, then fileless malware.
KPI	*Abbrev:* **K**ey **P**erformance **I**ndicator.
KPTI	*Abbrev:* **K**ernel **P**age **T**able **I**solation.
Krack (Key reinstallation attack)	Family of exploits against flawed cryptographic protocols and implementations in which encrypted nonces are captured during the key exchange and replayed to generate valid session keys. A proof-of-concept allowed wireless hackers to eavesdrop on WPA2-encrypted Wi-Fi connections and perhaps modify or inject malicious packets. Other key exchanges *may* be similarly vulnerable to replay attacks.
KRI	*Abbrev:* **K**ey **R**isk **I**ndicator.
Krotten	One of the earliest species of data-encrypting ransomware dating back to 2006.
KYC	*Abbrev:* **K**now **Y**our **C**ustomer.

L

TERM	MEANING
L2TP	*Abbrev:* **L**ayer **2** **T**unnelling **P**rotocol.
Label, labelling	Descriptive marker or tag literally or figuratively attached to or associated with something, such as data. "Target variable assigned to a sample" *(ISO/IEC 22989)*. See also classification, protective marking.
Labelling scheme	"Application or instantiation of the conformity assessment scheme or programme for the labelling of consumer IoT, taking into account the additional administrative or regulatory requirements of each nation or region. Note: A labelling scheme is a type of conformity assessment scheme from ISO/IEC 17000" *(ISO/IEC 27404 DRAFT)*.
Laboratory, lab	Purpose-built facility in which research is performed, typically by conducting scientific experiments under controlled conditions. "Organisation with a management system providing evaluation and or testing work in accordance with a defined set of policies and procedures and utilizing a defined methodology for testing or evaluating the security functionality of IT products. Note: These organisations are often given alternative names by various approval authorities. For example, IT Security Evaluation Facility (ITSEF), Common Criteria Testing Laboratory (CCTL), Commercial Evaluation Facility (CLEF)" *(ISO/IEC 19896-1)*.
Lag time	'Pregnant pause,' *e.g.* the delay between the release of security patches and their installation on vulnerable systems, or hysteresis.
Lagging [or lag] indicator	Indicator giving a delayed rather than real time indication of changes in whatever is being monitored or measured. "A metric that tracks the outcome of events or trends" *(NIST SP 800-55v1)*. "Indicators that provide information about past events or conditions" *(OCEG GRC Glossary)*. "A metric for the achievement of a goal; an indicator relating to the outcome or result of an enabler. Notes: This indicator is available only after the fact or event" *(ISACA glossary)*. *Cf.* leading indicator.
LAN	*Abbrev:* **L**ocal **A**rea **N**etwork.
Large **L**anguage **M**odel **(LLM)**	Type of **A**rtificial **I**ntelligence neural network system using **D**eep **L**earning techniques trained on big data to produce well-phrased and *seemingly* well-researched textual, audio-visual, or other outputs. Potentially vulnerable to numerous threats, both intentional (*e.g.* someone deliberately manipulating the training data in order to bias a model) and accidental (*e.g.* unrecognised biases, errors, and omissions in the training data). "A language model trained on massive amounts of text data to generate human-like text, analyze information, translate languages, and output code, among other types of content" *(ISACA glossary)*. See also **M**achine **L**earning, **N**atural **L**anguage **P**rocessing.

TERM	MEANING
Latency, dwell time	Delay, *e.g.* the pregnant pause between a message (a data packet) being sent from one system onto a network connection and its delivery to the destination system – a combination of the time taken for physical transit between the ends at something approaching the speed of light, and the processing involved in message transmission and reception. In some contexts (*e.g.* disk drives and **C**entral **P**rocessing **U**nits), latency *may* include the time taken to acknowledge, process, and respond to messages, commands, transactions, *etc.* In networking, latency generally excludes the time taken to establish or tear down a semi-persistent link, only measuring message transit times. Latency constrains the achievable speed/performance and responsiveness and relates to the capacity/throughput of the mechanisms used (*e.g.* parallel *vs.* serial data, fibre-optic *vs.* satellite links). "The time it takes a system or network to respond. Notes: More specifically, system latency is the time a system takes to retrieve data. Network latency is the time it takes for a packet to travel from source to destination" *(ISACA glossary)*. *Cf.* lag time.
Latency Monkey	Simian Army tool that introduces artificial delays in network traffic to test how cloud servers respond to network congestion, beyond the normal latency.
Latent	Inherent, subtle, or trace remaining.
Latent print/mark	Latent fingerprint. "Transferred impression of friction ridge detail not readily visible" *(FSRCoP)*.
Lateral movement	Gradual infiltration of a victim's network by hackers following the initial penetration as further vulnerable systems are compromised and exploited.
Launch pad	See foothold.
Layer **2** **F**orwarding Protocol **(L2FP)**	"An Internet protocol (originally developed by Cisco Corporation) that uses tunneling of PPP over IP to create a virtual extension of a dial-up link across a network, initiated by the dial-up server and transparent to the dial-up user" *(SANS glossary)*.
Layer 2 switch	See switch. "Data link layer devices that can divide and interconnect network segments and help to reduce collision domains in Ethernet-based networks" *(ISACA glossary)*.
Layer **2** **T**unnelling Protocol **(L2TP)**	Protocol at data link layer 2 of the OSI stack for tunnelling data through networks, providing **V**irtual **P**rivate **N**etworking. L2TP implementations are normally supplemented with IPsec since L2TP itself does not encrypt traffic. "An extension of the Point-to-Point Tunneling Protocol used by an Internet service provider to enable the operation of a virtual private network over the Internet" *(SANS glossary)*.

TERM	MEANING
Layer 8+	Sardonic reference to the existence of one or more layers notionally *above* layer 7 (application) at the top of the OSI stack. These upper levels leave the networking technology behind, concerning the influence of individual users, organisations, and governments for aspects such as funding, policies, and politics.
Layered defence	Control principle whereby multiple overlapping or complementary 'layers' of protection are applied, all of which would have to be breached, overcome, disabled, or bypassed in order to impact or compromise the protected information assets. This is a structured, systematic approach, more than simply increasing the number of controls. *Cf.* defence-in-depth. See also Swiss cheese model.
Lazarus Group, APT38	North Korean state-sponsored hacker group, allegedly responsible for the Sony hack, WannaCry ransomware incident, an audacious and partially successful cyber-heist on the Bangladeshi central bank, a $1.5 billion theft of Ethereum cryptocurrency and others.
LDAP	*Abbrev:* **L**ightweight **D**irectory **A**ccess **P**rotocol.
Lead auditor	a. Qualification awarded on completion of a training course for conformity/compliance auditors, *e.g.* ISO/IEC 27001 certification or **I**nformation **S**ecurity **M**anagement **S**ystem internal auditors. Its credibility and value depend largely on the quality of the training course and company, plus the trainer. *Cf.* lead implementer. b. Person responsible for verifying heavy metal stock-takes.
Leader, leadership	Person who inspires, encourages, motivates, and guides others towards specified and hopefully shared objectives. "Individuals at any level of the organization who have the de facto attention and respect of the workforce regardless of their title or position" *(OCEG GRC Glossary)*.
Lead implementer	Qualification awarded on completion of a training course for those leading management system implementations, *e.g.* an ISO/IEC 27001 **I**nformation **S**ecurity **M**anagement **S**ystem. Its credibility and value depend largely on the quality of the training course and company, plus the trainer. *Cf.* lead auditor.
Leading [or lead] indicator	Indicator that changes ahead of whatever is being monitored or measured, giving advance warning. "A metric for the application of good practices; an indicator relating to the functioning of an enabler. Notes: This indicator will provide an indication of the possible outcome of the enabler" *(*ISACA glossary*)*. "A predictive metric that tracks events or behaviors that precede incidents" (*NIST SP 800-55*). "Indicators that provide information about future events or conditions" *(OCEG GRC Glossary)*. *Cf.* lagging indicator.

TERM	MEANING
Lead risk indicator	"A forward-looking metric that provides an early warning that risk may soon be realized before an event has occurred" *(ISACA glossary)*.
Leak site	Website through which ransomed/stolen data are disclosed and sold.
Leakware, DoXware, doxware	Strains of ransomware that threaten to disclose the victim's confidential information as a means of extortion.
Learning activity, educational activity	"A directed collection of learning content that helps students achieve learning objectives by enhancing student ability from current skill level to target skill level" *(OCEG GRC Glossary)*.
Learning content	Teaching material and educational collateral, or more precisely the intangible information imparted by means of teaching to students. "The content in a learning activity includes text, image, audio, and video and takes the form of lecture, discussion, debate, and demonstration" *(OCEG GRC Glossary)*.
Learning objective	"Statements that define an educational activity's expected goal(s). Learning objectives can be used to structure the content of educational activities" *(OCEG GRC Glossary)*. *Cf.* learning outcome.
Learning outcome	Result achieved by learning, training, or other educational activities. "A statement that reflects what the learner will be able to do as a result of participating in the educational activity" *(OCEG GRC Glossary)*. *Cf.* learning objective.
Least privilege, minimum privilege	Information security principle involving restricting the privileges or rights assigned to an individual person, function, or system, consistent with their authorised and intended purpose. "Restriction of the access rights of a subject to only those rights that are necessary for the execution of authorized tasks" *(ISO/IEC 2382)*. "The principle that a security architecture should be designed so that each entity is granted the minimum system resources and authorizations that the entity needs to perform its function" *(CNSSI 4009)*. "The minimisation of access rights and permissions for users, accounts, applications, systems, devices and computing processes to the absolute minimum necessary in order to perform routine, authorised activities and maintain the safe and secure operation of agency or organisational systems" *(NZISM)*. "The principle that a security architecture is designed so that each entity is granted the minimum system authorizations and resources needed to perform its function" *(NIST SP 800-171)*. "The principle of allowing users or applications the least amount of permissions necessary to perform their intended function" *(SANS glossary)*.

TERM	MEANING
Least trust	"The principle that a security architecture should be designed in a way that minimizes 1) the number of components that require trust, and 2) the extent to which each component is trusted" *(CNSSI 4009)*.
Leet, 1337	Adolescent hacker slang like pig-Latin, in which letters or syllables are replaced by phonetically or visually similar letters, numbers, or punctuation characters. Effectively a low-integrity substitution coding algorithm. 'Leet' (normally written as '1337') is a contraction and deliberate misspelling of 'elite,' referring to the inflated egos and arrogance of hackers who perceive themselves as higher life forms with a deep understanding of complex technologies that are way beyond most mere mortals. See also pwn, n00b, warez, pr0n.
LEF	*Abbrev:* **L**oss **E**vent **F**requency.
Legacy Information **T**echnology **(legacy IT)**	Computing devices, systems, applications, *etc.* that are considered obsolescent, no longer supported or maintained by the vendors and therefore increasingly insecure as discovered vulnerabilities accumulate and are exploited. "Refers to systems and their component software and hardware that are outside of vendor support, on extended support and/or on bespoke support arrangements" *(UK National Cyber Security Strategy 2022)*. See also technical debt.
Legacy Information **T**echnology **system (legacy IT system)**	Legacy computer system. Regardless of **I**nformation **T**echnology in the term, there are legacy issues with all forms of technology. For instance, the practical difficulties of patching, maintaining, and recertifying vital (safety-critical) and embedded **O**perational **T**echnology systems, coupled with lengthy lifecycles, can leave them *years* or *decades* behind, especially if they are no longer supported by the original suppliers. "An ICT system that has reached the end of its lifecycle (end-of-life), that is not suitable for upgrades or fixes, for technological or commercial reasons, or is no longer supported by its supplier or by an ICT third-party service provider, but that is still in use and supports the functions of the financial entity" *(DORA)*. "An outdated computer system" *(ISACA glossary)*.
Legacy stash	Arrangement to disclose one's passwords, PIN codes, financial and other important information to one's survivors or executors of one's will in the event of one's death. **Don't take your passwords to the grave!**
Legal hold, hold, hold order [or notice], preservation order, suspension order, freeze notice	Court order prohibiting further processing/use, modification, or destruction of information. "Process of suspending the normal disposition or processing of records and Electronically Stored Information as a result of current or anticipated litigation, audit, government investigation or other such matters" *(ISO/IEC 27050-1)*.

TERM	MEANING
Legal retention period	"Time period within which the data objects ... of a cluster of personally identifiable information (PII) ... are available in the PII controller's organization as required by legal provisions" *(ISO/IEC 27555)*.
LegalTech	Contraction of **legal tech**nology, particularly the development and exploitation of innovative **I**nformation **T**echnology within the legal industry. See also AgriTech, Biotech, EcoTech/GreenTech, EdTech, FinTech, FoodTech, GovTech, HealthTech, RegTech, RetailTech, and other tech neologisms.
Legion	"Software to detect unprotected shares" *(SANS glossary)*.
Legion of Doom	Hacker group named after a cartoon series, that achieved notoriety in the 1980s. Members socialised and planned activities through an invitation-only bulletin board system.
Legitimate	Right and proper, genuine, appropriate, authorised, sanctioned, legal, *etc. Cf.* illegitimate.
Legitimate interest	"The basis for lawful processing of data" *(ISACA glossary)*.
Level of assurance	Relative measure of the credibility, quality, and hence value of an assurance activity. "The degree to which the subject matter has been examined or reviewed" *(ISACA glossary)*. "A measure of the degree of confidence that an assurance provider can deliver to an information consumer about statements an information provider makes about the subject matter" *(OCEG GRC Glossary)*.
Level of control	Relative measure of the effectiveness, reliability, and hence trustworthiness and value of a control.
Level of risk	Qualitative measure of the perceived importance or significance of a risk. "Significance of a risk, expressed in terms of the combination of consequences and their likelihood" *(ISO/IEC 27005)*.
Lewin change model	Way back in the 1940s, psychologist Kurt Lewin developed a theoretical 3-stage model of changes, *i.e.* unfreeze (thaw), change, then (re-)freeze. This simplistic approach remains widely used today, *e.g.* when a 'change freeze' is imposed by the business on **I**nformation **T**echnology systems during critical periods to avoid [some of] the associated risks.
LFI	*Abbrev:* **L**ocal **F**ile **I**nclusion.
Liability	Resource of dubious or negative value to its owner. *Cf.* asset, reliability.
Libel, libellous	Defaming or falsely accusing someone of something in a written or otherwise permanently recorded form such as a published article, web page, letter, email, **I**nstant **M**essaging, or SMS/TXT message. *Cf.* slander.

TERM	MEANING
Libgen	Contraction of **Lib**rary **Gen**esis, a large illicit online **D**ata**B**ase of pirated **I**ntellectual **P**roperty.
Library	Structured collection or **D**ata**B**ase of valuable reference information such as books; source code or executable code for common software functions, utilities, and programs; security controls; algorithms; metrics; and policies, procedures, standards, specifications, reports, and other documentation. Proactively curated, administered, and maintained, *e.g.* indexed/catalogued to facilitate study and reuse. "Pre-written code, classes, procedures, scripts, configuration data, and more, used to develop software programs and applications. It is designed to assist both the programmer and the programming language compiler in building and executing software" *(CIS Controls)*.
Licence, licensing agreement	Permission optionally granted by the legal owner of copyright materials (including software, data, and other information assets), patented inventions, or trademarks for someone to copy, use, and exploit them within certain constraints, often on payment of a royalty. A type of permit. "A contract that establishes the terms and conditions under which a piece of software is being licensed (*i.e.,* made legally available for use) from the software developer (owner) to the user" *(ISACA glossary)*.
Licensee	Person or organisation granted certain permissions to copy, use, or exploit **I**ntellectual **P**roperty by the licensor through a licence, agreement, or contract.
Licensor	Owner of **I**ntellectual **P**roperty that grants one or more licensees certain permissions to copy, use, or exploit their IP through licences, agreements, or contracts.
Lifecycle, life cycle, life-cycle	Chronological sequence of activities from start to finish, 'cradle to grave' as it were. Applies to almost everything, from people and organisations to jobs, careers, relationships, concepts, systems, applications, and products, ranging in timescale from practically instantaneous atomic decay to the life of the universe. "Mutual acknowledgement of terms and conditions under which a working relationship is conducted" *(ISO/IEC 27036-1)*. "Evolution of a system, product, service, project or other human-made entity, from conception through retirement" (*ISO/IEC 22989*). "A series of stages that characterize the course of existence of an organizational investment (*e.g.,* product, project, program)" *(ISACA glossary)*. See also **S**oftware **D**evelopment **L**ife**C**ycle.
Lifelong learning	See continuous learning.

TERM	MEANING
Lifespan	Total elapsed time of a lifecycle. Even after fixes (generally patches) have been released for zero-day vulnerabilities, it inevitably takes a while to implement them – years in some cases. Although strictly speaking they no longer qualify, the zero-day tag and associated vulnerabilities often linger like a bad smell long after they have been identified and fixes released.
Li-Fi (Light-Fidelity)	Short-range high-speed wireless (near-infrared) networking technology based on the IEEE 802.11bb standard. See also IrDA.
Lightning	Electrical storms and strikes can cause electrical surges, spikes, blackouts, fires, *etc.*, damaging sensitive electronics due to the powerful discharge of static electricity and occasionally wiping magnetic storage media due to the intense magnetic fields.
Lightweight Directory Access Protocol **(LDAP)**	Standard X.500-based protocol for accessing and managing distributed directory services in a TCP/IP network. "A software protocol for enabling anyone to locate organizations, individuals, and other resources such as files and devices in a network, whether on the public Internet or on a corporate Intranet" *(SANS glossary)*.
Likejacking	Hack that substitutes malware in place of legitimate JavaScript or other code that runs in the browser when someone clicks a 'like' button on social media.
Likelihood	Probability, possibility, chance, propensity, or potential. "The probability of something happening" *(ISACA glossary)*. "Chance of something happening. Notes: In risk management terminology, the word 'likelihood' is used to refer to the chance of something happening, whether defined, measured or determined objectively or subjectively, qualitatively or quantitatively, and described using general terms or mathematically [such as a probability or a frequency over a given time period]; The English term 'likelihood' does not have a direct equivalent in some languages; instead, the equivalent of the term 'probability' is often used. However, in English, 'probability' is often narrowly interpreted as a mathematical term. Therefore, in risk management terminology, 'likelihood' is used with the intent that it should have the same broad interpretation as the term 'probability' has in many languages other than English" *(ISO Guide 73)*. "A measure that estimates the occurrence of an event" (*OCEG GRC Glossary*). "The possibility that a given event will occur" *(IIA GIAS)*.
Limited assurance	"A level of assurance resulting from reviews, compilations, and other activities performed by competent personnel who are sufficiently objective about the subject matter" *(OCEG GRC Glossary)*.
Limit check	"A test that measures specified amount fields against stipulated high or low limits of acceptability. Notes: When both high and low values are used, the test may be called a range check" *(ISACA glossary)*. See also tolerance.

TERM	MEANING
Limited higher access	"The process of granting a system user access to a system that they do not hold appropriate security clearances for, for a limited period of time" *(NZISM)*.
Lines of Accountability (LoA) model	Governance model distributes accountability to various functions or hierarchical layers within an organisation. "A model that helps organizations govern, manage and provide assurance over performance, risk, and compliance by allocating specific responsibilities to different individuals or groups within the organization and creating a layered approach to produce and preserve value" *(OCEG GRC Glossary)*.
Linting	a. Automated testing of digital certificates for technical integrity issues, errors, nonconformities with the formal requirements for each type of certificate, and inconsistencies potentially indicative of tampering, prior to digital signing and issuance by the Certificate Authority and at other critical stages. An important assurance control, given the need for trustworthiness. b. Static Application Security Testing on source code to identify various errors. The term alludes to the process of removing little fragments of fluff from newly manufactured garments.
Live CD	Bootable disk image on CD-ROM, DVD, USB memory stick, or other portable storage medium, containing an Operating System and other software such as forensics tools. Used illegitimately to explore and exploit stored data, the network, and other resources on an Information Technology system without leaving traces on the computer's hard drives, or legitimately for live forensics analysis, hardware hacking, or data recovery purposes.
Live drop	Covert arrangement for a spy to meet his/her collector in person to exchange assets such as information and cash. See also dead drop.
Live forensics	Forensic analysis on a running computer system, typically to capture volatile evidence that would be lost if the system was shut down. See also live CD.
Living off the Land (LotL)	Hacker tactic involves exploiting resources already available on compromised systems, such as administrative tools and functions.
LLM	*Abbrev:* Large Language Model.
LM	*Abbrev:* Loss Magnitude.

TERM	MEANING
Load-shedding	Fail-soft resilience arrangement whereby a heavily loaded and highly stressed system (such as a busy network router operating as a firewall) selectively sheds or de-prioritises less important activities, services, functions, or capabilities as it approaches its capacity and performance limits in order to continue providing essential or higher-priority ones for as long as possible. De-prioritising security relative to business functions (fail-insecure) can have serious consequences if the loading/stressing can be caused deliberately, or simply exploited serendipitously, by hackers.
Load test	Test of the capability, performance, and capacity of a computer system, device, network, application, *etc.* to handle heavy loads by simulating multiple simultaneous users, large volumes of traffic or complex transactions, *etc.*, up to and perhaps beyond the required, specified, and designed levels, possibly under arduous conditions. See also smoke test, stress test, unit test, integration test, system test, security test, acceptance test.
Local **A**rea **N**etwork **(LAN)**	Digital datacommunications network connecting devices within a limited area such as a building, by cables or wirelessly. "A communication network that serves several users within a specified limited geographic area" *(ISACA glossary)*. See also **W**ide **A**rea **N**etwork, **P**ersonal **A**rea **N**etwork, **H**ome **A**rea **N**etwork, **M**etropolitan **A**rea **N**etwork, **S**torage **A**rea **N**etwork.
Local **F**ile **I**nclusion **(LFI)**	Type of application hack that exploits the capability to 'include' (call and execute) files on the server, similar to subroutines. If an application's file inclusion function does not properly validate and sanitise user input, hackers may call known vulnerable scripts or files containing sensitive information, then exploit them. See also **R**emote **F**ile **I**nclusion, SQL injection.
Local **S**ecurity **C**ommittee **(LSC)**	Committee responsible for directing and coordinating physical and information security within an individual business unit, site, or location.
Location **I**nformation **(LOCI)**	"The Location Area Identifier (LAI) of the phone's current location, continuously maintained on the (C/U)SIM when the phone is active and saved whenever the phone is turned off" *(NIST SP 800-101)*.
Lock	a. Physical security device typically requiring the correct physical key, access card, or combination (PIN code) to open a locked door, safe, *etc.* "A mechanism for keeping something secure or restricting access to functionality or data" *(ISACA glossary)*. b. **D**ata**B**ase integrity control which temporarily grants exclusive write/update/delete access to one computer process or user, preventing potentially conflicting data changes being made simultaneously on the same records or data items by others.

TERM	MEANING
Lockable commercial cabinet	"A cabinet that is commercially available, of robust construction and is fitted with a commercial lock" *(NZISM)*.
LockBit	Species of ransomware in the wild – the most prolific form of **R**ansomware-**as**-**a**-**S**ervice in 2022–2023. Since 2020, LockBit affiliates (customers) have attacked organisations of varying sizes across **C**ritical **I**nfrastructure sectors such as financial services, food and agriculture, education, energy, government and emergency services, healthcare, manufacturing, and transportation.
LockerGoga	Species of ransomware in the wild in 2019. Caused serious incidents at several industrial firms.
Lock Out Tag Out (LOTO)	Type of health and safety control in which, for instance, maintenance workers attach their personal padlocks/tags to safety shrouds on the main power switch or circuit breaker, physically preventing out-of-service electrical equipment being re-energised until *everybody* has completed the work and removed *all* their locks/tags. A failsafe physical control.
Locky	Family of ransomware in the wild in 2016 with *dozens* of variants.
Lockpick, lock pick	Person attempting, or the tool often used, to open a physical lock without the correct key, often without access authority and permission to enter unless the owner has simply lost their key and called a locksmith.
Log, log file	a. *[Noun]* Historical record of events, errors, alarms, conditions, activities, transactions, changes, visitors, *etc.*, recorded in a (preferably well-controlled, tamper-resistant) data file, logbook, **D**ata**B**ase, *etc.* for subsequent review and analysis (for accounting or security reasons). "An electronic record of activity (*e.g.,* authentication, authorization and accounting) [and] Files created specifically to record various actions occurring on a system being monitored, such as failed login attempts, full disk drives and email delivery failures" *(ISACA glossary)*. b. *[Verb]* To record information that is – or might turn out to be – significant. "To record details of information or events in an organized record-keeping system, usually sequenced in the order in which they occurred" *(ISACA glossary)*. See also security log, audit trail.
Log4Shell	Vulnerability in Apache Log4j, a popular open-source Java-based library of log analysis and management functions that allowed attackers to execute arbitrary code by manipulating the logs on vulnerable systems.
Log analyst, log analyser	Person performing log analysis or the computer tool/system automating the process. "A tool used to track and analyze logs" *(ISACA glossary)*.

TERM	MEANING
Logging facility, logger	Function, application, system, or service potentially supporting log management, *e.g. configuration, collation, consolidation, centralisation,* storage, analysis, anomaly detection, and security. "Functional unit that records events and physical conditions, usually with respect to time" *(ISO/IEC 2382)*. "A facility that includes the software component which records system events and associated details, the transmission (if necessary) of these records (logs) and how they are stored and secured" *(NZISM)*. "A facility that includes software which generates events and their associated details, the transmission (if necessary) of event logs, and how they are stored" *(AusISM)*.
Logic bomb	Form of malware designed to lay dormant but self-activate at some point, *e.g.* at a certain time (*i.e.* a time bomb), when a certain user logs on, or when a particular situation or combination of events occurs on the system (*e.g.* the developer is removed from the payroll), leading to some malicious action (*e.g.* shutdown the system, modify or delete data, disable security controls, make a fraudulent payment to the developer's Swiss bank account). A form of cybertage. "Malicious logic that causes damage to a data processing system when triggered by some specific system condition" *(ISO/IEC 2382)*. "Programs or snippets of code that execute when a certain predefined event occurs. Logic bombs may also be set to go off on a certain date or when a specified set of circumstances occurs" *(SANS glossary)*. See also wiper.
Logical access	Access to computer data or other resources, functions, *etc.* by a defined mechanism or route. "The ability to interact with computer resources granted using identification, authentication and authorization" *(ISACA glossary)*.
Logical access control	Automated information security control protecting electronic information assets (data/software, folders, disks, tapes, *etc.*) against access by unauthorised users, programs, or systems. "Use of mechanisms related to data or information to provide access control. Example: The use of a password" *(ISO/IEC 2382)*. "The policies, procedures, organizational structure and electronic access controls designed to restrict access to computer software and data files" *(ISACA glossary)*.
Logical connection	"A virtual representation of a data connection implemented through a software interface" *(EU CRA)*.
Logical security	Computerised/automated security, as opposed to physical, manual, or other aspects. See also cybersecurity.
LogoFAIL	Cluster of vulnerabilities in some systems that display a manufacturer's logo early in the boot sequence while loading drivers. Flaws and bugs in the UEFI code that read and render the logo file present opportunities for mischief.

TERM	MEANING
Logoff, log off, logout, log out, sign-off, sign-out ...	Process whereby a user signs off, normally by pressing keys or clicking buttons to end an active session on a computer system or network, relinquishing their access rights until they next logon. A logged-on computer left unlocked and unattended may be exploited by a passer-by, taking advantage of the logged-on user's permissions, with consequences that may range from nil (*e.g.* a kind person simply logs them off) through pranks and mischief (*e.g.* sending a spoof email inviting colleagues to a night on the town at the logged-on user's expense) to serious (*e.g.* cybertage, information theft, or fraud). "End a session" *(ISO/IEC 2382)*. "The act of disconnecting from a network or system" *(ISACA glossary)*.
Logon, log on, login, log in, sign-on, sign-in, ...	Process whereby a user identifies and authenticates to a computer system or network in order to pick up the permissions associated with their userIDs. During the sessions (*i.e.* until they logoff), activities, rights and permissions, and security events are associated with their userID, may trigger alarms and alerts, and may be recorded in audit trails and security logs for accountability and auditing purposes. "Initiate a session" *(ISO/IEC 2382)*. "The act of connecting to a network or system, which typically requires entry of a user ID and password" *(ISACA glossary)*.
LOIC	*Abbrev:* **L**ow **O**rbit **I**on **C**annon.
Lokibot	Species of Android malware in the wild in 2018. Multifunctional with bank Trojan, spyware, and ransomware capabilities.
Long **S**hort-**T**erm **M**emory **(LSTM)**	"Type of recurrent neural network that processes sequential data with a satisfactory performance for both long and short span dependencies" *(ISO/IEC 22989)*.
Long **T**erm **E**volution **(LTE), 4G**	Fourth-**G**eneration cellular phone/mobile network services, released in 2008.
LoRa (Long Range)	Wireless networking standard with a range of about 10 miles, used for **I**nternet **o**f *Things*, **I**ndustrial **I**nternet **o**f *Things*, and other purposes. "A proprietary member of the family of low-power wide area network (LPWAN) protocols designed for low-bandwidth, battery-powered devices requiring extended range" *(ISACA glossary)*.
LoRA (Low Rank Adaptive)	Technique to fine-tune (customise) the most relevant parts of a **L**arge **L**anguage **M**odel without the overhead of updating it all.
Loss event	"Occurs when a Threat Agent's action (Threat Event) is successful in breaching or impairing an Asset" *(O-RT)*.
Loss **E**vent **F**requency **(LEF)**	One of the risk factors (parameters) in the FAIR method, an estimate of the probability of harmful incidents. "The probable frequency, within a given timeframe, that a Threat Agent will inflict harm upon an Asset" *(O-RT)."* See also **C**ontrol **S**trength, **P**robable **L**oss **M**agnitude, **T**hreat **Cap**ability, **T**hreat **E**vent **F**requency.

TERM	MEANING
Loss flow	"The probable frequency, within a given timeframe, that a Threat Agent will inflict harm upon an Asset" *(O-RT)*.
Loss **M**agnitude **(LM)**	"The probable magnitude of loss resulting from a Loss Event" *(O-RT)*.
Loss scenario	Potential cyber incident. "The story of loss that forms a sentence from the perspective of the Primary Stakeholder" *(O-RT)*.
LotL	*Abbrev:* Living **o**ff **t**he **L**and.
LOTO	*Abbrev:* **L**ock **O**ut **T**ag **O**ut.
LOVEINT	Contraction of **love**r **int**elligence, *i.e.* using national security capabilities to gather intelligence on suitors, lovers, and partners, potentially for blackmail purposes or for background checks.
Love letter	See ILOVEU.
Lower assurance	"A more limited level of assurance resulting from activities such as self-assessments and benchmarking performed by the personnel responsible for the subject matter" *(OCEG GRC Glossary)*. *Cf.* high assurance.
Low **O**rbit **I**on **C**annon **(LOIC)**	Cyberweapon that 'fires' multiple TCP or UDP requests at a web server in order to consume its resources, causing it to slow down and perhaps crash or expose exploitable vulnerabilities, *i.e.* a **D**enial-**o**f-**S**ervice attack. A simple JavaScript version can execute in a web browser, while more sophisticated standalone variants can participate in botnets for coordinated **D**istributed **D**enial-**o**f-**S**ervice attacks.
LSC	*Abbrev:* **L**ocal **S**ecurity **C**ommittee.
LSTM	*Abbrev:* **L**ong **S**hort-**T**erm **M**emory.
Luck	Misfortune is often ascribed to 'bad luck' just as good fortune is ascribed to 'good luck,' whereas the outcome is often wholly or largely a matter of probability, risk, and randomness.
Ludd, Luddite	Ned Ludd used sabotage to frustrate the progress of mechanisation and industrialisation. In 1779 in central England, Ludd smashed two knitting machines in a 'fit of passion,' leading to him being blamed jokingly for similar incidents subsequently. Activists and saboteurs with a grudge against the machines and their owners are still called Luddites, more than two centuries on.
Lulz, lolz	Leet form of 'laughs,' derived from **L**augh **O**ut **L**oud (LOL), an abbreviation common in SMS/TXT messaging.
LulzSec (Lulz Security)	Hacker group, related to Anonymous, which achieved global notoriety in 2011 through hacks on Sony and other high-profile targets.

M

TERM	MEANING
MaaS	*Abbrev:* **M**alware-**a**s-**a**-**S**ervice.
MAC	*Abbrev:* **M**edia **A**ccess **C**ontrol, **M**andatory **A**ccess **C**ontrol, or **M**essage **A**uthentication **C**ode, depending on context.
Machine code, machine language, object code	Binary code (low-level instructions and data) that can be understood and executed directly by a digital computer's **C**entral **P**rocessing **U**nit, as opposed to, say, human-readable source code for a program that first needs to be compiled or translated. "Computer instructions and definitions expressed in a form (binary code) that can be recognized by the CPU of a computer. All source code, regardless of programming language, is eventually converted to machine code. [and] The logical language a computer understands" *(ISACA glossary).*
Machine ethics	Academic field of study into the controls that are appropriate and necessary to direct, control, or constrain machines (such as robots, autonomous vehicles, and cyberweapons) that utilise advanced **A**rtificial **I**ntelligence, hopefully without negating the potential advantages they bring to humankind.
Machine language	See machine code.
Machine **L**earning **(ML)**	Form of **A**rtificial **I**ntelligence system designed to extract and retain useful knowledge from training data. "Process of optimizing model parameters through computational techniques, such that the model's behaviour reflects the data or experience" *(ISO/IEC 22989).* "A program or system that builds (*i.e.,* trains) a predictive model from input data" *(ISACA glossary).* "The development and use of computer systems that adapt and learn from data with the goal of improving accuracy" *(NIST SP 800-55v1).* "Process using computational techniques to enable systems to learn from data or experience" *(ISO 12812-1).* See also **A**rtificial **I**ntelligence, **D**eep **L**earning, **L**arge **L**anguage **M**odel, **N**atural **L**anguage **P**rocessing.
Machine **L**earning **(ML) algorithm**	Algorithm for **M**achine **L**earning. "Algorithm to determine parameters of a machine learning model from data according to given criteria" *(ISO/IEC 22989).*
Machine **L**earning **(ML) model**	"Mathematical construct that generates an inference or prediction based on input data or information. Note: A machine learning model results from training based on a machine learning algorithm" *(ISO/IEC 22989).* "The model artifact created by the machine learning training process. The process of training a machine learning model involves providing a machine learning model algorithm (that is, the learning algorithm) with training data" *(ISACA glossary).*
Machine to **M**achine **(M2M)**	"Technologies that allow both wireless and wired systems to communicate with other devices of the same type" *(ISO/IEC 27033-6).*

TERM	MEANING
Machine **T**ranslation **(MT)**	"Task of automated translation of text or speech from one natural language to another using a computer system" *(ISO/IEC 22989)*.
Macro	a. Source code for a computer function or a relatively simple program. See also script, macro virus. b. Large in size and scope, *e.g.* macro metric.
Macro metric	High-level broad-scope overview metric supporting big-picture thinking and strategic decisions. *Cf.* micro-metric.
Macro virus	Form of malware that infects data files used by word processing, spreadsheet, and other programs with insecure built-in scripting/command languages such as **V**isual **B**asic for **A**pplications.
MAD	*Abbrev:* **M**aximum **A**cceptable **D**owntime, **M**utually **A**ssured **D**estruction, or **M**arketing and **Ad**vertising, depending on context.
MAEC	*Abbrev:* **M**alware **A**ttribute **E**numeration and **C**haracterization.
Magerit	Open method for Information Technology risk analysis and management, developed by **C**onsejo **S**uperior de **A**dministración **E**lectrónica, Spain's Higher Council for Electronic Government. Published in 1997, updated in 2005 and 2014.
Magic link	Unique, lengthy, complex, and hence difficult-to-guess URL that temporarily permits a single access to a system (in effect, a **O**ne-**T**ime **P**assword). It may be sent to a user's registered email address or to their cellphone via SMS/TXT messages enabling them to reset a forgotten password, perhaps with some other form of authentication such as their device's network address.
Magic packet	Specially crafted (possibly malformed) network message capable of triggering a specific – and perhaps unauthorised and inappropriate – activity/response in a network device, *e.g.* waking a computer from standby ('wake-on-LAN'), entering a diagnostic mode or activating malware such as opening a backdoor in a previously installed or built-in Trojan.
Magnetic remanence	See remanence.
Magstripe (magnetic stripe)	Magnetic storage strip once common on bank cards, credit/debit cards, *etc.* prior to the introduction of chip-n-pin. Machine-readable tracks on the strip contain standing data relating to the card number, expiry date, *etc.* along with integrity check values. A relatively basic and cheap security control, highly vulnerable to duplication and forgery using readily available card readers/writers, hence deprecated ... but still used for some low-security applications.

TERM	MEANING
Main establishment	Headquarters. "(a) As regards a controller with establishments in more than one Member State, the place of its central administration in the Union, unless the decisions on the purposes and means of the processing of personal data are taken in another establishment of the controller in the Union and the latter establishment has the power to have such decisions implemented, in which case the establishment having taken such decisions is to be considered to be the main establishment; (b) as regards a processor with establishments in more than one Member State, the place of its central administration in the Union, or, if the processor has no central administration in the Union, the establishment of the processor in the Union where the main processing activities in the context of the activities of an establishment of the processor take place to the extent that the processor is subject to specific obligations under this Regulation" ***General Data Protection Regulation***).
Maintainability	Capability of being maintained. Well-engineered equipment is not only designed for a long productive life, but to facilitate periodic and economic servicing (*e.g.* testing, adjusting, repairing, or replacing worn parts *before* they fail). "Ability of a functional unit, under given conditions of use, to be retained in, or restored to, a state in which it can perform a required function when maintenance is performed under given conditions and using stated procedures and resources" *(ISO/IEC 2382)*. "The ease with which a software system or component can be modified to correct faults, improve performance or other attributes, or adapt to a changed environment; synonymous with modifiability" *(ISACA glossary)*.
Maintenance, maintain	Process of, or people responsible for, monitoring and ideally proactively preventing or at least minimising the rate and addressing any deterioration, decay or obsolescence of plant, equipment, hardware, software, firmware, facilities, systems, networks, **D**ata**B**ases, strategies, plans, controls, policies, *etc.* in order to continue delivering acceptable operations, functionality, performance, security, reliability, *etc.* "Set of activities intended to keep a functional unit in, or to restore it to, a state in which it can perform a required function. Note: Maintenance includes activities such as monitoring, tests, measurements, replacements, adjustments, repairs, and in some cases administrative actions" *(ISO/IEC 2382)*. "Measures used in the field of energy supply that are normally related to inspection, fault clearance and improvement" *(ISO/IEC 27019)*. "Quality assurance (QA) activities, such as adjusting, cleaning, modifying and overhauling equipment to assure performance in accordance with requirements. Maintenance of a software system includes correcting software errors, adapting software to a new environment and making enhancements to software" *(ISACA glossary)*. See also preventive maintenance.

TERM	MEANING
Major ICT-related incident	Particularly serious or significant ICT-related incident. "An ICT-related incident that has a high adverse impact on the network and information systems that support critical or important functions of the financial entity" *(DORA)*.
Major nonconformity	Particularly serious or significant nonconformity, taking account of the context or situation in which it occurs. In the case of certification audits, indicates a finding that blocks the issue of a conformity certificate until/unless satisfactorily resolved – a show-stopper. "Nonconformity that affects the capability of the management system to achieve the intended results. Note: Nonconformities could be classified as major in the following circumstances: — if there is a significant doubt that effective process control is in place, or that products or services will meet specified requirements; — a number of minor nonconformities associated with the same requirement or issue could demonstrate a systemic failure and thus constitute a major nonconformity" *(ISO/IEC 17021-1)*. *Cf.* minor nonconformity, observation.
Malfeasance, misfeasance, nonfeasance	Deliberate commission of inappropriate, unethical, or illegal acts, such as failing in fiduciary duties, embezzlement, bribery, or extortion, particularly by public officials or officers of an organisation ('corporate malfeasance').
Malicious	With malice, mean, and nasty, intending to cause or knowingly and deliberately causing harm to another. *Cf.* benign.
Malicious actor	Malicious actor. See also adversary, bad actor.
Malicious code, malicious logic	See malware. "Program implemented in hardware, firmware, or software, and whose purpose is to perform some unauthorized or harmful action. Examples: A logic bomb, a Trojan horse, a virus, a worm" *(ISO/IEC 2382)*. "Any software that attempts to subvert the confidentiality, integrity or availability of a system. Types of malicious code include logic bombs, trapdoors, Trojans, viruses and worms" *(NZISM)*. "Software or firmware intended to perform an unauthorized process that will have an adverse impact on the confidentiality, integrity, or availability of a system. Examples of malicious code include viruses, worms, Trojan horses, spyware, some forms of adware, or other code-based entities that infect a host" *(NIST SP 800-171)*. "Software (*e.g.,* Trojan horse) that appears to perform a useful or desirable function, but actually gains unauthorized access to system resources or tricks a user into executing other malicious logic" *(SANS glossary)*.
Malicious code infection	"An information security incident that occurs when malicious code is used to infect a system. Example methods of malicious code infection [include] viruses, worms and Trojans" *(NZISM)*. "The occurrence of malicious code infecting a system" *(AusISM)*.

TERM	MEANING
Malicious content	"Applications, documents, files, data or other resources that have malicious features or capabilities embedded, disguised or hidden in them" *(ISO/IEC 27032).*
Malicious damage	Deliberate or wilful damage to (usually) physical assets, such as arson, vandalism, or sabotage. One of many physical security threats. See also fire, flood, intruder, cybertage.
Malinformation (malicious information)	See disinformation. "[Information] based on fact, but used out of context to mislead, harm, or manipulate" *(Cybersecurity and Infrastructure Security Agency). Cf.* misinformation.
Malspam (malicious spam)	Whereas most spam is merely annoying (junk email) and relatively benign, fraudsters and hackers use spam to circulate nasty emails with malicious intent, such as phishing, malware, or **B**usiness **E**mail **C**ompromise.
Maltego	Application supporting both offense using, and defences against, social engineering attacks. Identifies and displays relationships (social networks) between people, organisations, websites, email addresses, technologies, *etc.* using open-source intelligence sources such as social media and search engines. An example of dual-use technology, popular with black, grey, and white hats. See also Datasploit.
Malvertising	Online advertising that attempts to exploit vulnerabilities in visitors' browsers to infect their systems with malware. Often placed on otherwise benign and normally trustworthy websites without the website owner even being aware of the threat, but sometimes on blatantly malicious sites using various deceptive tricks to lure victims.
Malware (malicious software)	Software programs designed, developed, and released with malicious intent or purposes (such as damaging, deleting, corrupting or preventing legitimate access to computer systems, data, networks, *etc.* and/or harming the users' or owners' interests) including computer viruses, network worms, Trojan horses, rootkits, logic bombs, time bombs, ransomware, spyware, scareware, *etc.* "Software designed with malicious intent containing features or capabilities that can potentially cause harm directly or indirectly to the user and/or the user's computer system [such as] Viruses, worms and trojans" *(ISO/IEC 27032).* "Malicious software designed specifically to damage or disrupt a system, attacking confidentiality, integrity, or availability. Note: Viruses and Trojan horses are examples of malware" *(ISO/IEC 27033-1).* "Malicious software designed to infiltrate or damage a computer system or obtain information from it without the owner's consent. Examples of

TERM | **MEANING**

malware include computer viruses, worms, Trojan horses, spyware and adware" *(ISACA glossary)*. "A computer program that is covertly placed onto a computer with the intent of compromising the privacy, accuracy, or reliability of the computer's data, applications, or OS" *(NIST SP 800-114)*. "A generic term for a number of different types of malicious code" *(SANS glossary)*. *Cf.* hardware, middleware, firmware, wetware, ransomware, adware, crimeware, scareware, shelfware, spouseware, stalkerware, spyware.

Malware-as-a-Service (MaaS)
Illicit black market sellers offer various forms of malware to rent, along with associated services such as botnets and money laundering.

Malware Attribute Enumeration and Characterization (MAEC)
MITRE's structured language used to share technical information about newly discovered malware among the white hat professional antivirus community.

MAM
Abbrev: **M**obile **A**pplication **M**anagement. See **M**obile **D**ata **M**anagement.

MAN
Abbrev: **M**etropolitan **A**rea **N**etwork.

Managed Service Provider (MSP)
Commercial contractor/supplier of services such as technology management, provisioning, configuration, and support. "Third parties that provide a set of defined services to a customer and assume the responsibility of running, maintaining, and securing those services" *(UK National Cyber Security Strategy 2022)*.

Manage, management, management team

a. The act of managing, *i.e.* directing, guiding, overseeing, supervising, motivating, aligning, monitoring, and controlling one or more parts of the organisation, particularly its workers. Revolves around the use of information, *e.g.* defining and implementing policies, making key decisions, formulating and executing strategies and plans to achieve the organisation's mission and business objectives, reacting appropriately to risks and opportunities, all within the corporate governance structures and arrangements determined by senior management. "Coordinated activities to direct and control an organization" *(ISO 9000)*. "The planning, building, running and monitoring of activities in alignment with the direction set by the governance body to achieve the enterprise objectives" *(ISACA glossary)*. "The act of directly guiding, controlling, and evaluating an entity by arranging and operating resources" *(OCEG GRC Glossary)*.

b. Collective noun for an organisation's managers.

TERM	MEANING
Management actions & controls	"Actions & controls that primarily serve management activities to address opportunities, obstacles, and obligations" *(OCEG GRC Glossary).*
Management control, supervisory control	a. Control designed to mitigate unacceptable management risks, *e.g.* structured and systematic strategy formulation, policy-making and planning activities, plus the associated monitoring and compliance activities within appropriate corporate governance arrangements. b. Internal control performed by a manager, supervisor, team leader, or a similar person such as reviews, inspections, and other forms of oversight, authorisation, and attestation.
Management Engine (ME)	Intel x86 **C**entral **P**rocessing **U**nits have an additional CPU management subsystem embedded in the Northbridge, apparently intended to support big enterprise deployments. Since it interacts with the CPU at such a low level, vulnerabilities in the ME could, if exploited, compromise the CPU in much the same way as a rootkit. The ME cannot be disabled, making this a concern in risky, high-security situations (*e.g.* **C**ritical **N**ational **I**nfrastructure).
Management information	Internal information used to manage the organisation, its business, systems, resources, processes, capabilities, risks, performance, *etc.* Directives, policies, commands/instructions, decisions, and guidance generally cascade from the top (senior management) down, while operational information flows from the bottom up. In both directions, intermediate management levels add value (hopefully!) by consolidating, validating, and summarising the information for the intended audiences. Management information also flows laterally between corporate functions, allowing coordination, alignment, learning, prioritisation, and adaptation.
Management process	Systematic planning, organising, directing, leading, and controlling activities performed manually by managers or automatically by computer systems, in order to manage various resources and business, core and support processes, *e.g.* the recruitment process. "Process that defines the objectives of the management system to achieve the strategic objectives set by the organization's governing body" *(ISO/IEC 27022).*
Management risk	Uncertain possibility relating to management, particularly strategic decisions and governance matters affecting the organisation's mission and key business objectives.

TERM	MEANING
Management **S**ystem **(MS)**	Coherent governance framework comprising a structured suite of management activities and management controls such as policies, procedures, rôles and responsibilities, monitoring, and assurance arrangements. May be formalised (as in various ISO **M**anagement **S**ystems) or not. "Set of interrelated or interacting elements of an organisation to establish policies and objectives and processes to achieve those objectives. Notes: a management system can address a single discipline or several disciplines. The system elements include the organisation's structure, roles and responsibilities, planning, operation; the scope of a management system may include the whole of the organisation, specific and identified functions of the organisation, specific and identified sections of the organisation, or one or more functions across a group of organisations" *(ISO/IEC 27000)*. See also **I**nformation **S**ecurity **M**anagement **S**ystem, **I**ntegrated **M**anagement **S**ystem, **C**onfiguration **M**anagement **S**ystem.
Management traffic	"Communications generated by system administrators and processes over a network in order to manage and control a device" *(NZISM)*.
Manager	Superior, leader, or supervisor for one or more members of staff. The executives delegate responsibility for implementation of the organisation's information security principles, axioms, and the Policy Manual via the Security Committee and **C**hief **S**ecurity **O**fficer, through Information Security Management and the **I**nformation **S**ecurity **M**anager, to managers, and through them, to their subordinates. In this manner, information security is everyone's responsibility – a fundamental security principle. "Personnel who manage others" *(OCEG GRC Glossary)*.
Manchester Mark I	One of the very first digital computers to use programs stored on magnetic drums and cathode ray tubes. Constructed at Manchester University in 1949, it used 4,200 thermionic valves (vacuum tubes) as digital switches in racks that filled a sizeable room. Modern-day electronic handheld calculators and digital watches contain a similar number of transistor switches on a piece of silicon just a few square millimetres in size.

TERM	MEANING
Mandatory	Systems and workers *must* (*i.e.* they are obliged or compelled to) comply with applicable laws, regulations, and contractual terms, or conform with applicable corporate policies, agreements, directions, commands/instructions, or other requirements, unless they have been granted a legitimate exemption by the relevant authority, or if compliance/conformity would conflict with some higher obligation or principle (such as health and safety). See also **M**andatory **A**ccess **C**ontrol. *Cf.* discretionary, **D**iscretionary **A**ccess **C**ontrol.
Mandatory **A**ccess **C**ontrol **(MAC)**	Whether access is or is not permitted to information, and if so the type of access according to the type of information, is strictly determined by the architecture, coding, and controls built in to a well-designed MAC system, as opposed to a **D**iscretionary **A**ccess **C**ontrol system where the users and administrators have discretion. Typically involves the use of cryptographic authentication and encryption and other strong security controls implementing the Bell–LaPadula model. Used by governments and the military to enforce (*i.e.* mandate) restrictions reflecting the classification of data. "Logical access control filters used to validate access credentials that cannot be controlled or modified by normal users or data owners" *(ISACA glossary)*. "A means of restricting access to objects based on the sensitivity (as represented by a security label) of the information contained in the objects and the formal authorization (*i.e.,* clearance, formal access approvals, and need-to-know) of subjects to access information of such sensitivity" *(CNSSI 4009)*. "Where the system controls access to resources based on classification levels assigned to both the objects and the users. These controls cannot be changed by anyone" *(SANS glossary)*. *Cf.* **M**edia **A**ccess **C**ontrol, **M**essage **A**uthentication **C**ode.
Mandatory boundary	"Obligations that an organization must address because of some legitimate authority (*e.g.,* laws, rules, regulations)" *(OCEG GRC Glossary)*.
Mandatory leave, enforced vacation	As a matter of policy, workers in trusted or privileged rôles may be required to take leave in blocks of a defined minimum length (*e.g.* a week or two) as a control against fraud and impropriety. The hope is that whoever fills in for the person on vacation has the chance to identify/reveal and investigate tell-tale discrepancies or indicators that the fraudster would normally have concealed. Proactively preparing and training them for this tricky task *should* make the control more effective, but such foresight is vanishingly rare in practice.
Man **I**n **T**he **B**rowser **(MITB)**	Man-In-The-Middle attack involving a keylogger that hijacks the user's privileged online session, intercepting and manipulating their keystrokes through the browser, typically injecting/altering transactions and tricking them into unknowingly authenticating fraudulent transactions despite security control mechanisms such as passwords, security tokens, or SMS messages. See also bank Trojan.

TERM	MEANING
Man In The Email **(MITE)**	See **B**usiness **E**mail **C**ompromise.
Man-In-The-Middle **(MITM), A**dversary **i**n **T**he **M**iddle **(AiTM), malware in the middle, session hijack**	Class/type of attacks in which an adversary/attacker/red team/agent/unknown enemy (not necessarily a man!) intercepts and compromises authentication and other messages passing between two parties/systems, generally using masquerading to fool each party into believing that they are the legitimate counterparty. May involve stolen, faked, or genuine digital certificates obtained under false pretences (social engineering/fraud), malware, hacking the processes and systems, and evading/bypassing or negating various controls. Exploits the trust placed in connections that communicating parties believe to be direct and secure. "A strategy in which the attacker intercepts the communication stream between two components of the target system and then replaces the traffic with the intruder's own, eventually assuming control of the communication" *(ISACA glossary)*. "A man-in-the-middle attack is a type of cyber attack in which the attacker secretly intercepts and relays messages between two parties who believe they are communicating directly with each other. The attack is a type of eavesdropping in which the attacker intercepts and then controls the entire conversation" *(SANS glossary)*. See also proxy, POODLE, bogus boss.
Manipulation detection, modification detection	Detective control designed to identify unauthorised or inappropriate changes to a controlled information asset such as an important system, program, **D**ata**B**ase, dataset, control, parameter, configuration setting, document, and negotiable instrument. Such an event may result in an entry in a log and triggers an alert or alarm, initiating a manual or automated response such as entering a failsafe or more secure condition. "Procedure that is used to detect whether data have been modified, either accidentally or intentionally" *(ISO/IEC 2382)*.
Man-trap, man trap, mantrap, airlock, air-lock, air lock	Secure cubicle in which a person is physically detained pending their **I**dentification **&** **A**uthentication to proceed. A physical access control. Sophisticated versions may include **C**losed **C**ircuit **T**ele**V**ision monitoring, body scanners (for concealed weapons, recording devices, *etc.*), weighing scales to prevent multiple occupancy, plus anti-pass-back controls. "The secured space between doors operating on an electronic interlocking basis that may be accessed by a card-reader access system or a remote-control device, provided that all movement and activity is monitored" *(PCI Card Production and Provisioning Physical Security Requirements)*.
Manual control, administrative control, procedural control	Control that involves workers performing activities or processes, *e.g.* administering technological controls, responding to alarms or checking and authorising transactions. *Cf.* automated control and physical security. See also management control.

TERM	MEANING
Manufacturer	Commercial organisation that makes products (particularly physical goods) in volume, generally on factory production lines. "A natural or legal person who develops or manufactures products with digital elements or has products with digital elements designed, developed or manufactured, and markets them under its name or trademark, whether for payment, monetisation or free of charge" *(EU CRA)*.
MAO	*Abbrev:* **M**aximum **A**cceptable **O**utage.
Margin for error	See tolerance.
Mark	"Legally registered trade mark or otherwise protected symbol which is issued under the rules of an accreditation body or of a certification body, indicating that adequate confidence in the systems operated by a body has been demonstrated or that relevant products or individuals conform to the requirements of a specified standard" *(ISO/IEC 27006)*. See also trademark and target.
Mark of the Web (MotW), Zone.Identifier	Metadata associated with files (stored in an **A**lternate **D**ata **S**tream on Windows systems), indicating the zones from which the files originated (*i.e.* local computer, local intranet, trusted sites, Internet or restricted [untrusted] sites). Used by the **O**perating **S**ystem and applications for security purposes, *e.g.* warning the user and requiring their explicit acceptance before executing programs from the Internet.
Markov chain	"An algorithm for working with a series of events (for example, a system being in particular states) to predict the possibility of a certain event based on which other events have occurred and to identify probabilistic relationships between the different events" *(ISACA glossary)*.
Masking	"A computerized technique of blocking out the display of sensitive information, such as passwords, on a computer terminal or report" *(ISACA glossary)*.
Masque attack	Family of security vulnerabilities and exploits on Apple iOS.
Masquerade	Form of attack in which the attacker impersonates (pretends to be) someone or something else. Normally foiled by authentication mechanisms such as a challenge-response to determine whether they have the correct credentials. May involve spoofing or social engineering. "Pretense by an entity to be a different entity in order to gain unauthorized access" *(ISO/IEC 2382)*. "Attackers that penetrate systems by using the identities and logon credentials of legitimate users" *(ISACA glossary)*. "A type of threat action whereby an unauthorized entity gains access to a system or performs a malicious act by illegitimately posing as an authorized entity" *(CNSSI 4009)*. "A type of attack in which one system entity illegitimately poses as (assumes the identity of) another entity" *(SANS glossary)*.

TERM	MEANING
Mass surveillance	Dark, foreboding term with strongly Orwellian overtones concerning the widespread, systematic, intrusive, and largely indiscriminate surveillance of the public by government agencies, ostensibly for the purposes of crime and threat detection, counterterrorism, *etc.* From the authorities' perspective, a legitimate and necessary public safety/security mechanism. From other perspectives, potentially a substantial threat to privacy, human rights, liberty, and democracy, made worse by the resources and sheer power of the authorities operating under a cloak of secrecy with dubious regulatory oversight and accountability ...
Master key	Whereas a conventional physical lock can only be opened by keys of the pattern matching that lock, locks can be designed as a set that can be opened using *either* master keys with special patterns that work across the entire set *or* with the correct sub-master or change keys. Janitors and security guards may use sub-master keys to clean, check, and lock particular offices, stores, buildings, cell-blocks, *etc.,* while the Chief Security Guard, Facilities Manager, or Warden holds the master key, the physical security equivalent of the ROOT password on a computer server giving full access. If the master key is ever lost or compromised (*e.g.* stolen or copied), *all* the master-keyed locks may have to be changed to restore security.
Matanbuchus	Species of fileless **M**alware-**a**s-**a**-**S**ervice in the wild in 2021. Delivered through the network as a **D**ynamic **L**ink **L**ibrary. Can execute PowerShell commands or call applications with malicious payloads and functions, such as Cobalt Strike or Qakbot. Uses scheduled tasks to persist on infected systems.
Material	a. *[Noun]* Information content, data, intelligence. b. *[Adjective]* Substantial, serious, significant, impactful, meaningful, *etc.*
Materiality	Significance in management, business, professional, or societal terms. "An auditing concept regarding the importance of an item of information with regard to its impact or effect on the functioning of the entity being audited. An expression of the relative significance or importance of a particular matter in the context of the enterprise as a whole" *(ISACA glossary).*

TERM	MEANING
Material misstatement	"An untrue statement, whether accidental or intentional, that affects the results of an audit to a measurable extent" *(ISACA glossary).* "A significant error or omission in financial statements that could potentially influence the decisions of information consumers of those statements. It can be caused by an error, fraud, or the misapplication of accounting principles. Material misstatements can affect the accuracy and reliability of financial information and may cause financial statements to be misleading or incomplete. Materiality is determined based on the size and nature of the misstatement, as well as its potential impact on the financial statements and the decisions of users of those statements" *(OCEG GRC Glossary).*
Material weakness	"A deficiency or a combination of deficiencies in internal control, such that there is a reasonable possibility that a material misstatement will not be prevented or detected on a timely basis. Weakness in control is considered 'material' if the absence of the control results in failure to provide reasonable assurance that the control objective will be met. A weakness classified as material implies that: Controls are not in place and/or controls are not in use and/or controls are inadequate; Escalation is warranted. There is an inverse relationship between materiality and the level of audit risk acceptable to the IS audit or assurance professional, *i.e.,* the higher the materiality level, the lower the acceptability of the audit risk, and vice versa" *(ISACA glossary).*
Maturity	Literally, the development stage of a process, organisation, person, *etc.,* reflecting its age. Figuratively, an indicator of its integrity, quality, breadth, reliability, *etc.* regardless of age. "The degree of reliability or dependency a business can place on a process to achieve desired goals or objectives" *(ISACA glossary).* "The level of development, progress, or sophistication of a particular process, function, or organization" *(OCEG GRC Glossary).*
Maturity level	Maturity metric. "A rating that describes the degree to which organizational unit processes meet the intentions and values articulated in a predefined set of practice areas. The rating is based on the achievement of a specified set of practice group levels within the predefined set of practice areas" *(ISACA glossary).*
Maturity model	"A structured framework that is used to assess and measure an organization's maturity or level of development in a particular area" *(OCEG GRC Glossary).*
Maximum **A**cceptable **D**owntime **(MAD)**	See **M**aximum **T**olerable **O**utage.
Maximum **A**cceptable **O**utage **(MAO)**	See **M**aximum **T**olerable **O**utage.

TERM	MEANING
Maximum **T**olerable **D**owntime **(MTD)**	See **M**aximum **T**olerable **O**utage.
Maximum **T**olerable **O**utage **(MTO)**	The longest of time that a system, computer, service, network, function, business unit, supply chain, *etc.* can be substantially or completely out of action (regardless of cause) before it causes *severe* harm (possibly irreparable and existential damage) to the enterprise and stakeholders including dependent supply chains. An important back-stop requirement, risk management, and **B**usiness **C**ontinuity **M**anagement parameter, albeit subjective, dynamic, and context-dependent, with significant strategic implications for the resilience, **D**isaster **R**ecovery, and contingency arrangements needed. Note: other terms of art typically involve some organisation-defined permutation of the following: **maximum, allowable, tolerable, acceptable, period of, downtime, interruption, window**, and **outage**. Such terms are vaguely similar to MTO with refinements such as scope (*e.g.* some may apply to particular information systems and services, others to all) and extremity (*e.g.* planned brief outage windows for routine backups *vs.* unplanned indeterminate outages cause by disastrous incidents such as ransomware). "Maximum time an enterprise can support processing in alternate mode" *(ISACA glossary)*.
Maximum **T**olerable **P**eriod of **D**isruption **(MTPD)**	See **M**aximum **T**olerable **O**utage. "Time it would take for adverse impacts, which can arise as a result of not providing a product/service or performing an activity, to become unacceptable" *(ISO 22300)*.
Mazo	Hacker/malware/cybercriminal gang, active in 2022.
MBCO	*Abbrev:* **M**inimum **B**usiness **C**ontinuity **O**bjective.
MBSA (Microsoft **B**aseline **S**ecurity **A**nalyzer**)**	Deprecated Microsoft tool to scan Windows 8.1 and older systems for missing security patches, *etc.* Superseded by Windows Update.
MD5 (Message **D**igest № **5)**	Hash algorithm developed by Ron Rivest of RSA fame. Generates a 128-bit hash. Due to cryptographic vulnerabilities known since 2009, MD5 is deprecated in favour of the SHA-2 family of algorithms. *"A one way cryptographic hash function" (SANS glossary)*.
MDM	*Abbrev:* **M**obile **D**evice **M**anagement.
ME	*Abbrev:* **M**anagement **E**ngine.
Meaconing	Interception and rebroadcast or fabrication of navigation signals to mislead, misdirect, or confuse the enemy or an inbound missile through inaccurate or missing bearings. Cryptographically signing and authenticating beacon signals can mitigate but not eliminate the risks.

TERM	MEANING
Meaconing, Intrusion, Jamming and Interference **(MIJI)**	US military communications security term for meaconing, intrusion, jamming, and interference.
Media [or Medium] **A**ccess **C**ontrol **(MAC)**	Part of layer 2 in the network stack providing functions/services such as flow-control and the framing (encapsulation) of packets. *Cf.* Mandatory Access Control.
Media **A**ccess **C**ontrol **(MAC) address**	48-bit unique address/identity for a **N**etwork **I**nterface **C**ontroller on a computer, typically written as 6 hexadecimal pairs. Initially allocated by the NIC manufacturer and hardcoded into its firmware as a default, although on some devices it can be reconfigured in the device driver or networking software.
Media **A**ccess **C**ontrol **(MAC) header, Ethernet header**	Layer 2 data fields in the header of a network packet specifying information such as the source (transmitter) and destination addresses, and message type.
Mean	a. Average. "The sum of the data points divided by the number of data points. Commonly referred to as the average" *(SP 800-55v1)*. b. Tight-fisted, stingy, unwilling to spend (even if justified). c. Nasty, grumpy, sour, caffeine-deprived (mean-spirited).
Meaningful misunderstanding	"Occurs when an information producer makes statements that contain material errors or omissions that could affect the decisions of information users of those statements" *(OCEG GRC Glossary)*.
Mean **T**ime **B**etween **F**ailures **(MTBF)**	Indication of the anticipated reliability of a piece of equipment, system, control, service, *etc.* under specified operating conditions. Normally determined by engineering analysis, testing, simulation, and modelling, or by analysis of failure modes and rates in the field. Accelerated wear tests might subject, say, a braking system to higher-than-expected temperatures or loads to predict the MTBF and confirm what actually happens at – and past – the point of failure. A resilience metric. "Mean duration of operation between consecutive failures of a functional unit under given conditions. Note: Mean time between failures can be derived from a theoretical model or from observations" *(ISO/IEC 2382)*.
Mean **T**ime **T**o **D**etect **(MTTD)**	Security metric measuring the average time delay between incidents occurring or starting and being detected. Theoretically useful to reduce detection lag, but of limited value in practice since the timing start point is often unknown, uncertain, or arbitrary. The metric is easily gamed by manipulating the start point, perhaps also the detection point. "A metric that tracks the average amount of time that a problem exists before it is found" *(NIST SP 800-55v1)*.

TERM	MEANING
Mean **T**ime **T**o **R**espond **[or Resolve, Recover, Recovery, Restore ...], (MTTR)**	Security metric ostensibly measuring the duration of incidents. The start and endpoints should be determined consistently, typically using the help desk job ticketing system. In theory, MTTR can help speed up incident response and resolution, but in practice the metric is easily gamed by delaying incident reporting and prematurely declaring incidents resolved. "A metric that tracks the average amount of time that it takes to recover from a product or system failure" *(NIST SP 800-55v1).*
Measurability	Capability of being quantified. "Ability to assess an attribute of an entity against a metric" *(ISO/IEC TS 5723).*
Measure	a. *[Verb]* To quantify, count, size, or weigh something, determining the relevant parameter value/s by measurement. b. *[Noun]* Individual measurement value. "A standard used to evaluate and communicate performance against expected results. Notes: Measures are normally quantitative in nature capturing numbers, dollars, percentages, *etc.,* but they can also address qualitative information such as customer satisfaction. Reporting and monitoring measures help an enterprise gauge progress toward effective implementation of strategy" *(ISACA glossary).* c. *[Noun]* Contraction of measurement. "Variable to which a value is assigned as the result of measurement" *(ISO/IEC 15939).* "Quantifiable and objective values that result from measurement" *(SP 800-55v1).* d. *[Noun]* Contraction of countermeasure, meaning a control.
Measurement	a. Quantification process. "Process to determine a value" *(ISO/IEC 27000).* "The process of obtaining quantitative values using quantitative methods" *(NIST SP 800-55v1).* b. Value of a parameter, ideally expressed in defined, standardised units with an appropriate degree of precision according to the context and purpose, *e.g.* "The height of the door should be 2.22 metres ±5 millimetres."
Measurement function	Measurement function: calculation for a compound measure. "Algorithm or calculation performed to combine two or more base measures" *(ISO/IEC/IEEE 15939).*
Measurement method	Method of measuring something. "Logical sequence of operations, described generically, used in quantifying an attribute with respect to a specified scale. Note: the type of measurement method depends on the nature of the operations used to quantify an attribute. Two types can be distinguished as follows: subjective – quantification involving human judgment; [and] objective – quantification based on numerical rules" *(ISO/IEC/IEEE 15939).*

TERM	MEANING
Measures **O**f **E**ffectiveness **(MOE)**	"A probability model based on engineering concepts that allows one to approximate the impact a give action will have on an environment. In Information warfare it is the ability to attack or defend within an Internet environment" *(SANS glossary)*.
Media	Plural of medium, refers to storage media, news media ('the media,' *i.e.* journalists and broadcasting), social media, *etc.* depending on context. "A generic term for any type of hardware or material that is capable of storing or retaining data. The following examples, while not a definitive list, includes any type of 'floppy disk,' tapes, all types of optical disks, HDD, SSD, USB, RAM, Flash, ROM, EPROM, printer cartridges, printer drums and so on" *(NZISM)*. "A generic term for hardware, often portable in nature, which is used to store data" *(AusISM)*. "Physical devices or writing surfaces including, but not limited to, magnetic tapes, optical disks, magnetic disks, Large-Scale Integration (LSI) memory chips, and printouts (but not including display media) onto which information is recorded, stored, or printed within a system" *(NIST SP 800-171)*.
Media (or Medium) **A**ccess **C**ontrol **(MAC)**	Networking layer controlling the hardware that physically interfaces with the transmission medium, *e.g.* wired Ethernet or wireless WiFi transceivers. "Lower sublayer of the OSI Model Data Link layer" *(ISACA glossary)*. *Cf.* **M**andatory **A**ccess **C**ontrol.
Media **A**ccess **C**ontrol **address (MAC address), physical [device] address**	Unique identity assigned to a network device to identify it. Usually a 48-bit hexadecimal value generated by the device's manufacturer, permanently stored in firmware. Can be spoofed by manipulating the software that uses the MAC address. "A 48-bit unique identifier assigned to network interfaces for communications on the physical network segment" *(ISACA glossary)*. "A physical address; a numeric value that uniquely identifies that network device from every other device on the planet" *(SANS glossary)*.
Media destruction	"The process of physically damaging the media with the objective of making the data stored on it inaccessible. To destroy media effectively, only the actual material in which the data is stored needs to be destroyed" *(NZISM)*.
Media disposal	"The process of relinquishing control of media when no longer required, in a manner that ensures that no data can be recovered from the media" *(NZISM)*. "The process of relinquishing control of media when it is no longer required" *(AusISM)*.
Median	Value at the mid-point of a dataset arranged in order, normally smallest-to-biggest: half the data points are smaller than the median and half are bigger. "The value of the point that has half the data smaller than that point and half the data larger than that point" *(NIST SP 800-55v1)*. "The value in the middle of a sorted list of values or, if the number of values is even, the average of the two in the middle" *(ISACA glossary)*.

TERM	MEANING
Media oxidation	Degradation of data storage media. "The deterioration of the media on which data are digitally stored due to exposure to oxygen and moisture. Notes: Tapes deteriorating in a warm, humid environment are an example of media oxidation. Proper environmental controls should prevent, or significantly slow, this process" *(ISACA glossary).*
Media sanitisation	Sanitisation of storage media. "The process of securely erasing or overwriting data stored on media" *(NZISM).* "The process of erasing or overwriting data stored on media so that it cannot be retrieved or reconstructed" *(AusISM).*
MedusaLocker	Species of ransomware in the wild in 2022. Infects via vulnerable **R**emote **D**esktop **P**rotocol configurations, phishing, and spam, then spreads laterally through the **L**ocal **A**rea **N**etwork. Strongly encrypts victims' files with 256-bit **A**dvanced **E**ncryption **S**tandard.
MEHARI (Method for Harmonized Analysis of Risk)	Free open-source risk management method developed by CLUSIF (**Clu**b de la **S**écurité de l'**I**nformation **F**rançais) in 2010 with the following steps: context identification, risk identification, risk assessment, risk treatment, and monitoring. More info: https://clusif.fr/wp-content/uploads/2015/10/mehari-2010-overview.pdf
Melissa	Macro virus dating back to 1999, spread via email.
Melt	Fate of a bar of chocolate left on a sunny dashboard ... "Destruct by changing media from a solid to a liquid state generally by the application of heat" *(ISO/IEC 27040).*
Membership inference attack	Attempted compromise of an **A**rtificial **I**ntelligence/**M**achine **L**earning system to infer the composition of its training data. "Attack where the attacker is able to attribute training data membership" *(ISO/IEC 27090 DRAFT).*
Memory leak	See heap overflow.
Memory management	"A set of controls that address memory and buffer usage" *(SCP QRG).*
Memory-safe programming languages	Some programming languages can prevent developers inadvertently introducing bugs affecting memory usage, *e.g.* by attempting to read or write memory locations either side of a declared range ('out of bounds'), or within the declared range where data have been deleted ('use after free'). Such issues are common with memory-unsafe languages such as C and C++; therefore, short of systematically hunting down and fixing all such issues, moving to memory-safe languages such as Rust, C#, Swift, and Go can improve the quality and security of software. "Programming languages that prevent the introduction of security vulnerabilities related to memory use. Examples of memory-safe programming languages include C#, Go, Java, Ruby, Rust and Swift. Examples of non-memory-safe programming languages include Assembly and C/C++" *(AusISM).*

TERM	MEANING
Memory-scraping malware, RAM-scraper	Type of malware that monitors and captures confidential data in working memory in the course of processing. While such malware commonly infects point-of-sale systems implying a criminal motive, the technique has broader application for national and industrial espionage and other nefarious purposes such as stealing valuable intellectual assets such as cryptographic keys and passwords (*e.g.* keyloggers), for surveillance or cybertage. See also Spectre.
Merkle tree	Cryptographic architecture patented by Ralph Merkle in 1979 in which hash values for two or more data blocks are themselves hashed, and so on 'up the tree,' thus ensuring integrity of the entire data structure. "A data structure within which all nodes other than 'leaf nodes' (nodes to which no subnodes are attached) include the hash values of all subnodes. Use of a cryptographically strong hashing function (*i.e.,* a message digest) can allow rapid (logarithmic) verification of the integrity of all nodes on the tree" *(ISACA glossary).* See also blockchain.
Mesh network, mesh topology, completely connected configuration	*Ad hoc* networking architecture with which wireless **I**nformation **T**echnology devices communicate with others within range, passing on messages including commands and data using BluetoothLE or other protocols. Used in some **I**nternet **o**f *Things* applications such as smart metering and smart homes. "A network topology in which devices are connected with many redundant interconnections between network nodes (primarily used for backbone networks) [and] A fault-tolerant topology in which network nodes and endpoints are mostly, if not fully, interconnected" *(ISACA glossary).*
Message	a. Information being communicated, the content, or payload of datacommunications. "The content of what is communicated" *(OCEG GRC Glossary).* b. Text and/or graphics displayed on a screen, whiteboard, Post-it note, *etc.*
Message **A**uthentication **C**ode **(MAC)**	Application of hashing to network packets, guarding against changes to the payload *en route. Cf.* **M**andatory **A**ccess **C**ontrol, **M**edia **A**ccess **C**ontrol.
Message cadence	"The velocity and frequency of sending a message" *(OCEG GRC Glossary).*
Message digest	See hash. "The result of a cryptographic hash function taking an input of an arbitrary length and producing an output that is a standard-sized binary string. The output is unique to the input and even a minor change to the input results in a completely different output. Modern cryptographic hash functions are also resistant to collisions (situations in which different inputs produce identical outputs). A collision, while possible, is statistically improbable. Cryptographic hash functions are developed so that the input cannot be determined readily from the output" *(ISACA glossary).*

TERM	MEANING
Message Queue Telemetry Transport (MQTT)	Extremely lightweight messaging protocol designed for *things* and machine-to-machine datacommunications with limited processing capability and network bandwidth. Messages are sent ('published') to a stream for reception by devices that 'subscribe' to the stream. Messages may be relayed by 'brokers.' Version 5 of the standard was published by OASIS Open in 2017. "An ultra-lightweight communication protocol widely used in the Internet of Things" *(ISACA glossary)*.
Metadata	Information, data, or parameters about data (such as details of the senders and recipients of phone calls and emails or the dates and times or sizes of messages, and the PRAGMATIC characteristics of security metrics) that may be sensitive and/or valuable in its own right. "Data about data or data elements, possibly including their data descriptions, and data about data ownership, access paths, access rights and data volatility" *(ISO/IEC 2382)*. "Data that defines and describes other data" *(ISO/IEC 11179-1)*. "Descriptive data about the content and context used to identify data" *(AusISM)*. See also **Tr**affic **An**alysis.
Metal Oxide Varistor (MOV)	Cheap electronic component designed to absorb the energy and limit the maximum voltage caused by typical power line spikes but not necessarily surges or multiple/more extreme spikes. MOVs are physically degraded by each spike and, since under-rated or exhausted they may catch fire, should be replaced periodically.
Metasploit [Framework]	Hacking/penetration testing tool, originally open-source but now also commercial products with additional features. Automates *hundreds* of well-known exploits. An example of dual-use technology, popular with black, grey, and white hats. More info: https://www.metasploit.com/
Method, methodology	Specified means and/or process for doing something, such as performing a scientific or forensic investigation, developing application software, or managing information risks. "Definition of an operation which can be used to produce data or derive information as an output from specified inputs. Note: Ideally, a method should be atomic (*i.e.* it should not perform more than one function) in order to promote re-use of methods and the processes derived from them and to reduce the amount of work required to validate processes" *(ISO/IEC 27041)*. "A logical sequence of operations, described generically for analysis (*e.g.* for the identification and/or quantification of drugs or explosives, or the determination of a DNA profile) or for comparison of items to establish their origin or authenticity (*e.g.* fingerprint/footwear mark/toolmark examination; microscopic identifications)" *(FSRCoP)*. "Policies, processes, and procedures established by the chief audit executive to guide the internal audit function and enhance its effectiveness" *(IIA GIAS)*.

TERM	MEANING
Metric	Quantified parameter that is directly related and thereby characterises or describes something of interest or concern (such as a security control or risk) in order to assess or evaluate it and inform decisions concerning it (*e.g.* to determine whether the control adequately mitigates the risk or needs to be improved). The result of a formal measurement process providing pertinent, factual, timely data in a meaningful and useful form. "Defined measurement method and measurement scale" *(ISO/IEC 14102)*. "A quantifiable entity that allows the measurement of the achievement of a process goal. Notes: Metrics should be SMART—specific, measurable, actionable, relevant and timely. Complete metric guidance defines the unit used, measurement frequency, ideal target value (if appropriate), the procedure to carry out the measurement and the procedure to interpret the assessment" *(ISACA glossary)*. "Measures and assessment results designed to track progress, facilitate decision-making, and improve performance with respect to a set target" *(NIST SP 800-55v1)*. See also indicator, PRAGMATIC.
Metropolitan **A**rea **N**etwork **(MAN)**	Digital wireless network serving a metropolitan area such as a city, town, or campus. "Network for connecting local area networks located in the same urban area. Note: A MAN generally operates at a higher speed than the networks interconnected, crosses administrative boundaries, and supports several access methods" *(ISO/IEC 2382)*. "A data network intended to serve an area the size of a large city" *(ISACA glossary)*. See also **L**ocal **A**rea **N**etwork, **P**ersonal **A**rea **N**etwork, **W**ide **A**rea **N**etwork.
MFA	*Abbrev:* **M**ulti**F**actor **A**uthentication.
MI5 (Military Intelligence branch 5), Secret Service	UK national (domestic) intelligence service, dedicated to protecting the interests of British citizens, both within the UK and abroad. Originally the fifth branch of the Directorate for Military Intelligence, part of the War Office in the first World War. See also **S**ecret **I**ntelligence **S**ervice.
MI6	*Abbrev:* **M**ilitary **I**ntelligence branch **6**. See **S**ecret **I**ntelligence **S**ervice.
Michelangelo	Computer virus, widely hyped by the news media in 1992 but negligible in impact since most infected systems were successfully disinfected prior to the payload being triggered on Michelangelo's birthday, March 6th. Based on Stoned.
Microchip	See **I**ntegrated **C**ircuit.
Microcode	Very lowest-level software in a **C**entral **P**rocessing **U**nit, linking machine code instructions to the hardware that actually performs various arithmetic operations (*e.g.* add, subtract), the fundamental basis for a digital computer. In effect, microcode is the firmware within a CPU.

TERM	MEANING
Microcontroller	Single-purpose low power **S**ystem **on** **C**hip, typically powering embedded systems in home appliances, robotics, and industrial machines. In contrast to general purpose computers such as PCs, they are programmed to perform specific tasks efficiently.
Micro-fraud	Fully automated form of salami fraud in which the amounts stolen tend to be extremely small, possibly fractions of the smallest discrete unit of currency (*e.g.* tenths of a cent). Such fractional amounts are normally subject to rounding rules designed to avoid systematic bias but successful micro-fraudsters subvert the process and the associated checks and balances.
Micro-metric	Low-level fine-grained metric concerning a specific, detailed point of particular interest or concern for operational reasons. *Cf.* macro metric.
Microservice	Function providing a tightly defined narrow-scope single-purpose information service within a **S**ervice-**O**riented **A**rchitecture.
Microsoft Entra ID, Azure Active Directory	Microsoft's cloud-based **I**dentity and **A**ccess **M**anagement system, formerly called Azure Active Directory.
Middleware	Software layer between the **O**perating **S**ystem and applications, connecting the two with common services and capabilities. "Another term for an application programming interface (API). It refers to the interfaces that allow programmers to access lower- or higher-level services by providing an intermediary layer that includes function calls to the services" *(ISACA glossary)*. See also hardware, firmware, software.
MIJI	*Abbrev:* **M**eaconing, **I**ntrusion, **J**amming, and **I**nterference.
Milestone	Notional marker post between successive phases of a project. A key control point where important decisions and changes may be made concerning the future direction, as well as demonstrating progress achieved to date (perhaps triggering staged payments). "A terminal element that marks the completion of a work package or phase. Notes: A milestone is typically marked by a high-level event such as project completion, receipt, endorsement or signing of a previously defined deliverable, or a high-level review meeting at which the appropriate level of project completion is determined and agreed to. A milestone is associated with a decision that outlines the future of a project and, for an outsourced project, may have a payment to the contractor associated with it" *(ISACA glossary)*.
Mimic panel	**Su**pervisory **C**ontrol **A**nd **D**ata **Ac**quisition Human Machine Interface device that presents a graphical representation of industrial plant to the operators, like a wiring diagram embedded with lights and meters showing the status of important machinery, services, *etc.* with audio-visual alerts and alarms. See also digital twin.

TERM	MEANING
Mimicry	Truly ancient form of disinformation or social engineering typically involving the use of fakery to conceal an adversary's true identity and nature by *appearing* to be benign (*e.g.* foe acting as friend). May be visual (*e.g.* camouflage) or use olfactory and/or auditory cues (*e.g.* faking pheromones and mating calls to lure prey).
Mimikatz	Open-source hacking/penetration testing tool, developed in 2007, that exploits a vulnerability in Windows **l**ocal **s**ecurity **a**uthority **s**ubsystem **s**ervice to grab passwords and other digital credentials from memory in plaintext.
Miner	a. Block producer for a **P**roof **o**f **W**ork blockchain. b. Mine-worker, a person who digs coal, minerals, *etc.* from the ground. *Cf.* minor.
Minimum **B**usiness **C**ontinuity **O**bjective **(MBCO)**	"Minimum level of services and/or products that is acceptable to the organization to achieve its business objectives during a disruption" *(ISO/IEC 27031)*. "Minimum capacity or level of services and/or products that is acceptable to an organization to achieve its business objectives during a disruption" *(ISO 22300)*.
Minimum **V**iable **S**ecure **P**roduct **(MVSP)**	Generic, basic, minimalist controls checklist intended as a cybersecurity baseline for vendors of **B**usiness-**to**-**B**usiness software and business process outsourcing services. Public domain. More info: https://mvsp.dev/
Minor	a. Small, insignificant, trivial, of little if any consequence. b. Child as legally defined and protected in a given jurisdiction. *Cf.* miner.
Minor nonconformity	Nonconformity that is not considered major, *i.e.* relatively insignificant, not a failure to satisfy a specified mandatory requirement. Unlikely to block certification (unless numerous) but worth bringing to the attention of management – perhaps an early indication or symptom of a developing issue or risk that ought to be addressed. "Nonconformity that does not affect the capability of the management system to achieve the intended results" *(ISO/IEC 17021-1)*. *Cf.* observation.
Minting	Generation of cookies containing falsified authentication credentials, enabling hackers to commit identity fraud by purporting to be authenticated users of the corresponding websites.
Mindsets	"Individual perceptions about self, surroundings, and others – including perceptions about culture, some topical area, or how to approach work" *(OCEG GRC Glossary)*.

TERM	MEANING
Mirai	Species of malware in the wild in 2019. Used a list of default userIDs and passwords to infect insecure *things*, recruiting them to a botnet for **D**istributed **D**enial-**o**f-**S**ervice and possibly other attacks. The source code was published/disclosed in 2016, leading to a string of copycat variants.
Mirror site, dual-live site	Provision of **I**nformation **T**echnology services simultaneously from multiple facilities (typically data centres) at physically separated/ diverse locations, increasing resilience against certain classes of disaster affecting any individual site while paradoxically increasing some risks (primarily due to the added complexity and reliance on networks). Generally involves near-real-time replication of data and synchronisation of transaction commit points between sites, load balancing, *etc.* "An alternate site that contains the same information as the original. Notes: Mirrored sites are set up for backup and disaster recovery and to balance the traffic load for numerous download requests. Such download mirrors are often placed in different locations throughout the Internet" *(ISACA glossary)*. See also hot, warm, and cold site, disk mirroring.
Misappropriation	Fraud involving the misuse of assets belonging an organisation by workers, *e.g.* expenses fraud. See also embezzlement.
Miscarriage of justice	Incident involving an egregious failure of the legal system. "A term that covers the following: (a) An unsafe conviction. (b) A wrongful acquittal. (c) Inability to bring an offender to justice. (d) Delaying bringing an offender to justice. (e) Inability to clear the innocent. (f) Delaying the clearing of the innocent" *(FSRCoP)*.
Mischa	Species of ransomware, often distributed with Petya.
Misdirection	Use of distraction to trick someone by diverting their attention from the action, such as lookalike domain names containing visually similar foreign characters in place of what appear to be letters from the normal alphabet, sleight-of-hand magic tricks, or picking someone's pocket having apparently bumped into them or dropped something at their feet.
Misinformation, malinformation	Information that is inaccurate, incomplete, outdated, or otherwise misleading and of low integrity and value, generally generated and circulated accidentally or naïvely/unwittingly, as opposed to deliberately (disinformation). "False [information], but not created or shared with the intention of causing harm" ***(C**ybersecurity and **I**nfrastructure **S**ecurity **A**gency)*. "Information that is unintentionally false or misleading, usually spread out of ignorance" *(NZSTE)*.

TERM	MEANING
Misinterpretation	Risk of someone accidentally misunderstanding, drawing inaccurate or misleading inferences, or perhaps intentionally misreading, something such as an SMS/TXT message, email, instruction, permission, or prohibition.
Mis-issuance	Failure of the validation process leading to the inappropriate issue of a digital certificate, or indeed some other credential.
Mislead, misleading, misled	Deliberately or accidentally lead someone astray by providing inaccurate, biased, incomplete, out-of-context or plain wrong information.
Misrepresentation	Lying, exaggerating, or misleading, giving a false account of something, typically to trick or coerce the victim into doing something inappropriate. A commonplace fraud and social engineering technique.
Mission	Key, central, critical, vital, or core purpose, goal, or objective for an organisation, team, department, project, initiative, person, *etc.* – its main, overriding priority and prime focus, its raison d'être. "An objective that states who the organization serves, what it does, and what it hopes to achieve today and in the long term" *(OCEG GRC Glossary)*.
Mission-critical	Mission critical – anything that can materially affect achievement or satisfaction of the mission. By definition, such things are key.
Mission-critical application	Mission critical application. "An application that is vital to the operation of the enterprise. The term is very popular for describing the applications required to run day-to-day business operations" *(ISACA glossary)*.
Mistake	Human error. "Human action or inaction that can produce an unintended result" *(ISO/IEC 2382)*.
Misuse detection	Incident detection approach that seeks to differentiate normal, regular, benign activity from something different, abnormal, suspicious, and potentially malicious, worthy of further analysis. "Detection based on whether a system activity matches an activity defined as 'bad'" *(ISACA glossary)*.
MITE	*Abbrev:* **M**an-**I**n-**T**he-**E**mail. See **B**usiness **E**mail **C**ompromise.
Mitigate, mitigation	Reduce, limit, tackle, contain, or address. "Limitation of any negative consequence of a particular incident" *(ISO 22300)*. "Steps taken to reduce the severity of a vulnerability. These can include removing a vulnerability, making a vulnerability more difficult to exploit, or reducing the negative impact of a successful exploitation" *(SCP QRG)*. See also risk mitigation.
MITM	*Abbrev:* **M**an-**I**n-**T**he-**M**iddle.

TERM	MEANING
Mix network	Datacommunications method (architecture, system or protocol) designed to pool and transmit messages from multiple participants in an anonymous, untraceable fashion such as Tor.
ML	*Abbrev:* **M**achine **L**earning.
MMS	*Abbrev:* **M**ultimedia **M**essaging **S**ervice.
Moat	Deep ditch around a Mediaeval castle, sometimes filled with water, designed to make it difficult for attackers to scale or breach the castle walls, slowing them down and thereby increasing their exposure to counterattack (*e.g.* spears, arrows, and boiling oil). Today's equivalents include 'sterile areas' around important facilities and the DMZ.
Mobile code	Program capable of executing on different types of system, *e.g.* well-designed Java programs can be executed on *any* **O**perating **S**ystem which hosts a conformant Java virtual machine. While such portability can be tremendously convenient for software developers and users, malware such as network worms may exploit security vulnerabilities in the technical architecture (*e.g.* breaking out of the sandbox) to spread far and wide. "Software programs or parts of programs obtained from remote systems, transmitted across a network, and executed on a local system without explicit installation or execution by the recipient" *(NIST SP 800-171)*.
Mobile computing	Computers designed to be used on-the-go – typically small, self-contained, lightweight, rugged, battery-powered, and wirelessly networked portable or wearable devices. "A technology that extends wireless computing to small devices that run specifically designed applications and is capable of expanding an enterprise network to reach remote places under circumstances that would not permit connectivity by other means. Note: Mobile computing is comprised of smartphones, tablets and wearable devices. [and] portable electronic equipment that can connect to the Internet" *(ISACA glossary)*. See also thing.

TERM	MEANING
Mobile device, mobile end user device	Portable computing and telecommunications device such as a smartphone, portable or tablet PC. Thanks to innovative **M**obile **T**echnology, modern mobile devices are effective platforms but constraints such as miniaturisation, portability, wireless connections, battery power, and price limit the processing and memory capacity, which in turn makes them hard to secure against malware and hacks, plus simple theft, damage, or loss. On top of that, naïve users don't always appreciate and use security features/functions properly, sometimes ill-advisedly disabling important controls, *e.g.* jailbreaking. "A small mobile computer such as a smartphone or tablet" *(NIST SP 800-114)*. "Portable electronic equipment that can connect to the Internet" *(ISACA glossary)*. "A portable computing or communications device. For example, smartphones, tablets and laptops" *(AusISM)*. "Small, enterprise issued end-user devices with intrinsic wireless capability, such as smartphones and tablets. Mobile end-user devices are a subset of portable end-user devices, including laptops, which may require external hardware for connectivity" *(CIS Controls)*. "A small hand-held device that has a display screen with touch input and/or a QWERTY keyboard and may provide users with telephony capabilities" *(NIST SP 800-101)*. "A portable computing device that has a small form factor such that it can easily be carried by a single individual; is designed to operate without a physical connection (*e.g.,* wirelessly transmit or receive information); possesses local, non-removable, or removable data storage; and includes a self-contained power source. Mobile devices may also include voice communication capabilities, on-board sensors that allow the devices to capture information, or built-in features that synchronize local data with remote locations. Examples include smartphones, tablets, and e-readers" *(NIST SP 800-171)*.
Mobile **D**evice **M**anagement **(MDM), Enterprise Mobile Security, Enterprise Mobility Suite, Mobile Application Management**	Remote access software installed on corporate laptops and **P**ersonally **O**wned **D**evices used for **B**ring **Y**our **O**wn **D**evice, or on *things*, allowing privileged, trusted, authorised administrators to manage the mobile devices and applications remotely and securely, ensuring that the organisation's information and interests are protected. Typically has administrative, monitoring, and security capabilities. Information risks vary between products.
Mobile Disaster Recovery facility, mobile site	**D**isaster **R**ecovery facility in a trailer or container fitted out with computer servers, disks, networking equipment, *etc.*, driven to a suitable (secondary) location on demand. "A mobile/temporary facility that serves as a business resumption location. The facility is typically delivered to an alternative site and can house information technology and staff" *(ISACA glossary)*.

TERM	MEANING
Mobile **S**ubscriber **I**ntegrated **S**ervices **D**igital **N**etwork **(MSISDN)**	Full phone number, complete with country code, associated with a cellphone. "The international telephone number assigned to a cellular subscriber" *(NIST SP 800-101)*.
Mobile **T**echnology **(MT)**	Technology developed for and exploited by mostly small, light-weight, battery-powered portable or wearable systems using wireless communications (**I**nternet **o**f ***T**hings*) plus mobile systems such as those within and controlling vehicles (*e.g.* engine-, braking- or emissions-management systems, avionics, navigational, guidance and tracker systems, digital tachographs). See also **C**ommunications **T**echnology, **I**nformation **T**echnology, **O**perational **T**echnology, **V**irtual **T**echnology, **S**mart **T**echnology.
Mobistealth	Commercial surveillance software for smartphones including various iOS and Android devices. Ostensibly for 'parental control,' this powerful spyware allows someone secretly to compromise the device, access its stored data (*e.g.* contacts, photographs, videos, SMS/TXT messages, and emails) and metadata (*e.g.* details of phone calls made and websites visited), and surreptitiously monitor its user (*e.g.* location tracking, keylogging, and bugging/audio recording), regardless of their ethical and legal privacy rights.
Modbus	Commonplace **S**upervisory **C**ontrol **A**nd **D**ata **A**cquisition/**I**ndustrial **C**ontrol **S**ystem network communications protocol, used to pass readings and **O**perational **T**echnology control signals/commands between devices.
Mode	a. Mechanism, means, or transmission/modulation technology used to communicate (*e.g.* voice, email, SMS/TXT, **A**mplitude **M**odulation, **C**ontinuous **W**ave [Morse code], semaphore, smoke signals), to encrypt data (chain mode, block mode), to get somewhere (walk, car, bus, *etc.*), *etc.* b. Data value that occurs most often in a dataset. "The value of the random sample that occurs with the greatest frequency. This value is not necessarily unique" *(NIST SP 800-55v1)*. "The value that occurs most often in a sample of data. Like the median, the mode cannot be directly calculated" *(ISACA glossary)*.

TERM	MEANING
Model	a. Simplified, visual representation of a system, method, process, or approach developed for designing, understanding, documenting, and explaining its architecture, internal structure (*e.g.* functional subunits or steps), conceptual relationships, *etc.* "A method to describe a given set of components and how those components relate to each other to describe the main workings of an object, system, or concept" *(ISACA glossary)*. See also framework. b. Theoretical representation of a complex situation, based on fundamental scientific and logical principles. "Physical, mathematical or otherwise logical representation of a system, entity, phenomenon, process or data" *(ISO/IEC 22989)*. c. "In machine learning (ML), the outcome of a training process. A trained model can automatically process data that was not used for its training to perform a specific set of tasks" *(ISACA glossary)*. d. Someone's visualisation of an ideal or exemplary person (a rôle model), sometimes used to beguile naive and gullible customers into buying something in the hope of enhancing their self-image and perceived worth. e. Distinctive product line, *e.g.* Ford Model T.
Model exfiltration attack, model theft, model stealing attack, model extraction attack	Illicit copying (theft) of an **A**rtificial **I**ntelligence system's **I**ntellectual **P**roperty, attempting to emulate or reconstruct its model using information obtained by prompts and responses or by other means. "Attack where the attacker is able to copy the model (or sufficient parts thereof) either through direct access, or through (potentially repeated) use of attacker supplied inputs and observing corresponding outputs of the AI system" *(ISO/IEC 27090 DRAFT)*.
Model inversion attack	Attempt using carefully crafted queries to reveal sensitive data or other valuable information that was used to train an **A**rtificial **I**ntelligence system. "Attack where the attacker is able to retrieve the original data (or sufficient parts thereof) that was used to generate the model through (potentially repeated) use of attacker supplied inputs and observing corresponding outputs of the AI system" *(ISO/IEC 27090 DRAFT)*.
MOE	*Abbrev:* **M**easures **O**f **E**ffectiveness.
Mole	Agent who has discreetly infiltrated, been implanted, or been recruited from within an organisation by an adversary. A type of cyberteur.
Monetise	Generate financial value (profit) from something – by fair means or foul. See also cashing out.

TERM	MEANING
Money laundering	Criminal processes to convert stolen or fraudulently obtained and traceable assets into untraceable cash, typically by successively passing them through money mules, fences, and dubious financial transactions intended to 'wash them clean of,' and thereby obscure, their origin and nature. Thanks to proactive monitoring, mandatory reporting, and other relatively strong controls within the financial industry, cashing out is one of the highest-risk parts of any criminal or terrorist activity involving substantial amounts of money.
Money mule, mule	Person handling or laundering criminal proceeds. Often the unwitting and naïve victims of fraud or coercion, who nevertheless commit criminal acts rendering them liable to prosecution.
Money **T**ransfer **A**gent **(MTA)**	Financial services such as Western Union and MoneyGram that receive funds at one location and pay out, often in cash, at another. The anonymity offered by such services has often been used to launder money, attracting the attentions of both the criminal underground and regulatory authorities.
Monitor, monitoring	Observing, overseeing, or watching over something such as an organisation, system, network, or process, looking for and ideally acting appropriately on discovering anomalies, particularly indications of security incidents, errors/discrepancies, *etc.* May be authorised or unauthorised/illicit and discreet/secretive such as surveillance. "Determining the status of a system, a process or an activity. Note: to determine the status there may be a need to check, supervise or critically observe" *(ISO/IEC 27000)*. "Continual checking, supervising, critically observing or determining the status in order to identify change from the performance level required or expected. Note: Monitoring can be applied to a risk management framework, risk management process, risk or risk control" *(ISO 31073)*. "Ongoing and periodic activities that observe actions & controls, and the information generated by these controls, to gauge effectiveness, efficiency, responsiveness, and resilience" *(OCEG GRC Glossary)*.
Monitor and review	"A process for measuring the efficiency and effectiveness of the organization's Risk Management processes is the establishment of an ongoing monitor and review process. This process makes sure that the specified management action plans remain relevant and updated. This process also implements control activities including re-evaluation of the scope and compliance with decisions" *(ENISA RM glossary)*.
Monitoring process owner	Person, function, department, unit, organisation, *etc.* that notionally owns and is responsible for a monitoring process or activity. "Individual or legal entity responsible for the receipt, integration, generation, analysis, transfer and output of data. Note: A monitoring process or owner of a system within the monitoring process can be represented, *e.g.* by a sub-contractor" *(ISO 22300)*.

TERM	MEANING
Monkeywrenching	Sabotage. Alludes to the idea of a saboteur using a monkey wrench as an all-purpose hammer to damage industrial machinery. See also Luddite.
Monoalphabetic	Cryptographic substitution process (such as Caesar's cipher) that substitutes letters or characters in the plaintext with letters from a single alphabet or character set. *Cf.* polyalphabetic.
Monoculture	"The case where a large number of users run the same software, and are vulnerable to the same attacks" *(SANS glossary)*.
Monte Carlo method [or analysis]	Modelling technique involving multiple runs of a model with fuzzing of one or more input parameters within defined bounds, and statistical analysis to determine their influence on the outputs and hence the model's sensitivity to various factors. Term alludes to, say, a roulette table at the famous casino. "A probabilistic sensitivity analysis used to account for uncertainty" *(NIST SP 800-55v1)*. "The use of randomly generated numbers as part of an algorithm" *(ISACA glossary)*.
Moral hazard	Believing themselves adequately protected by controls such as insurance, people may accept more risk than otherwise – and why not? This can be taken into account by the insurer determining insurance premiums that reflect the anticipated risks *after* insurance is in effect, rather than before, and specifying various security controls the insured organisations are required to have in place.
MORAY	Obsolete and deprecated US **S**pecial **I**ntelligence **S**ervice term for COMINT. See also UMBRA, SPOKE.
Mores [pronounced 'morays']	"More formalized and serious norms that are deeply ingrained in a culture and have moral significance. Violating mores can lead to severe social disapproval, ostracism, or even legal consequences (*e.g.,* honesty, respect for elders, and adherence to religious practices)" *(OCEG GRC Glossary)*.
Morphing meerkat	Phishing kit in the wild in 2025. Uses email server details from **D**omain **N**ame **S**ystem MX lookups to add authenticity to bait web pages, tricking victims into providing their authentication credentials to the phishers, which may then be passed through to the genuine email providers, and subsequently exploited.
Morris worm, the Internet worm	The first network worm that spread widely across the early Internet in 1988. Written and released by Robert Tappan Morris ostensibly as an experiment to determine the size of the Internet. "A worm program written by Robert T. Morris, Jr. that flooded the ARPANET in November, 1988, causing problems for thousands of hosts" *(SANS glossary)*.

TERM	MEANING
Motion detector, shock detector, vibration detector	Physical security device monitoring an area or a valuable piece of equipment for movement, typically using passive infrared radiation, **C**losed **C**ircuit **T**ele**V**ision, or tremblers to detect movement and trigger an alarm.
Motte	Hill or mound of earth and rubble on which many Mediaeval castles were constructed, giving defenders a vantage point while forcing attackers into an uphill battle (literally).
MotW	*Abbrev:* **M**ark **o**f **t**he **W**eb.
MOV	*Abbrev:* **M**etal **O**xide **V**aristor.
MOVEit Transfer	File transfer application from Progress Software, widely compromised in 2023 by the Cl0p gang exploiting a zero-day vulnerability to commit cyber-extortion.
MPLS	*Abbrev:* **M**ulti-**P**rotocol **L**abel **S**witching.
MQTT	*Abbrev:* **M**essage **Q**ueue **T**elemetry **T**ransport.
MSP	*Abbrev:* **M**anaged **S**ervice **P**rovider.
MT	*Abbrev:* **M**achine **T**ranslation.
MTA	*Abbrev:* **M**oney **T**ransfer **A**gent.
MTBF	*Abbrev:* **M**ean **T**ime **B**etween **F**ailures.
MTD	*Abbrev:* **M**aximum **T**olerable **D**owntime.
MTO	*Abbrev:* **M**aximum **T**olerable **O**utage.
MTPD	*Abbrev:* **M**aximum **T**olerable **P**eriod of **D**isruption.
MTTD	*Abbrev:* **M**ean **T**ime **T**o **D**etect.
MTTR	*Abbrev:* **M**ean **T**ime **T**o **R**espond (or **R**esolve or **R**ecover).
Muieblackcat	Botnet in the wild in 2015, based on a PHP bot or vulnerability scanner.
Multicast	Networking technique to send data simultaneously to a group of recipient nodes. "Broadcasting from one host to a given set of hosts" *(SANS glossary)*.

TERM	MEANING
Multi**F**actor **A**uthentication **(MFA)**	Strengthened form of user authentication in which different *types* of credential are required (*e.g.* a secret password plus a security token or a biometric plus a device location determined by GPS). Multiples of a single credential type (*e.g.* two passwords) are not considered multifactor. "A combination of more than one authentication method, such as token and password (or personal identification number [PIN]) or token and biometric device" *(ISACA glossary)*. "An electronic authentication method in which a user is granted access to a network or application only after successfully presenting two or more pieces of evidence to an authentication mechanism (*e.g.* a password and a one-time passcode)" *(UK Cyber Security Breaches Survey 2023)*. "A security system that verifies a user's identity by requiring multiple credentials, which may be of the same factor or type. Initial authentication normally requires a username and password. MFA requires other—additional—credentials, for example as a code from the user's smartphone, the answer to a security question, a fingerprint, or facial recognition" *(NZISM)*. "Authentication using two or more different authentication factors. This may include something users know, something users have or something users are" *(AusISM)*. "Authentication using two or more different factors to achieve authentication. Factors include something you know (*e.g.,* PIN, password), something you have (*e.g.,* cryptographic identification device, token), or something you are (*e.g.,* biometric)" *(NIST SP 800-171)*.
Multifunction device	Networked device offering functions or services such as printing, scanning, and FAXing. May be vulnerable to hackers and malware on the network in addition to user and configuration errors, physical attacks/damage/accidents, software bugs, *etc.* Many contain significant data storage capacity, potentially exposing cached copies of printed/scanned/FAXed documents, *etc.* "The class of devices that combines printing, scanning, copying, faxing or voice messaging functionality within the one piece of equipment. These are often designed to connect to computer and communications networks simultaneously" *(NZISM)*. "ICT equipment that combines printing, scanning, copying, faxing or voice messaging functionality in the one device. These devices are often designed to connect to computer and telephone networks simultaneously" *(AusISM)*.
Multifunctional malware	Malware that has the capability for multiple functions or modes of operation (*e.g.* having the characteristics of, or being able to switch between, a network worm, Trojan, spyware, and ransomware), generally achieved by downloading modules, exploits, and parameters from the Internet over a command and control channel.

TERM	MEANING
Multi-homed	"You are 'multi-homed' if your network is directly connected to two or more ISP's" *(SANS glossary)*.
Multilevel device	"Functional unit that can simultaneously process data of two or more security levels without risking to compromise computer security" *(ISO/IEC 2382)*.
Multilevel gateway	"A gateway that enables access, based on authorisation, to data at many classification and releasability levels where each data unit is individually marked according to its domain" *(NZISM)*.
Multi-**L**evel **M**arketing **(MLM)**	Marketing strategy or compensation structure in which profits from sales are distributed among participants who join the scheme. Whereas genuine MLM schemes are generally legal, they can be indistinguishable from unethical, fraudulent, and potentially illegal pyramid/Ponzi schemes, even by the specialists, authorities, and courts, let alone naïve investors.
Multimedia **M**essaging **S**ervice **(MMS)**	"An accepted standard for messaging that lets users send and receive messages formatted with text, graphics, photographs, audio, and video clips" *(NIST SP 800-101)*.
Multiplexing	"To combine multiple signals from possibly disparate sources, in order to transmit them over a single path" *(SANS glossary)*.
Multi-**P**rotocol **L**abel **S**witching **(MPLS)**	"Technique, developed for use in inter-network routing, whereby labels are assigned to individual data paths or flows, and used to switch connections, underneath and in addition to normal routing protocol mechanisms. Note: Label switching can be used as one method of creating tunnels" *(ISO/IEC 27033-1)*.
Multi-**S**tate **I**nformation **S**haring and **A**nalysis **C**enter **(MS-ISAC)**	Collaborative **C**enter for **I**nternet **S**ecurity and **C**ybersecurity & **I**nfrastructure **S**ecurity **A**gency initiative providing threat intelligence and cybersecurity guidance to US state, local, territorial, and tribal governments. More info: https://www.cisecurity.org/ms-isac
Murphy's law	In short, "Anything that can go wrong, will." Many risk and audit professionals believe that the eponymous Edward A. Murphy Jr. was an optimist, and that even things that cannot go wrong sometimes do. And at the worst possible moment too (according to Finagle and Sod).
Mustang Panda	One of several groups of elite hackers/cyber-spooks apparently of Chinese origin, targeting European and Asia-Pacific political organisations with **R**emote-**A**ccess **T**rojans in 2023.

TERM	MEANING
Mutex	Contraction of **mut**ual **ex**clusion or **mut**ually **ex**clusive, a programming method that briefly 'locks' a shared resource (such as a record or field in a **D**ata**B**ase) while it is being accessed by a process, temporarily preventing other, conflicting processes from attempting to process it at the same instant causing data integrity issues. "A lock set by a smart contract code before access is permitted to a shared resource or function, and released after its use, to prevent multiple threads from simultaneously gaining access to the locked region of the code" *(ISACA glossary)*.
Mutual aid agreement	"Pre-arranged understanding between two or more entities to render assistance to each other" *(ISO 22300)*.
MVSP	*Abbrev:* **M**inimum **V**iable **S**ecurity **P**roduct.

N

TERM	MEANING
NaaS	*Abbrev:* **N**etwork-**a**s-**a**-**S**ervice.
Nagware	Neologism referring to software that repeatedly displays annoying reminders to do something (such as upgrade Windows), regardless of user preferences. Whether it qualifies as adware, malware, or a **P**otentially **U**nwanted **P**rogram is a moot point: nobody enjoys being nagged. For most it is an unwelcome diversion, and yet patching and maintaining software is an important security process.
Named **E**ntity **R**ecognition **(NER)**	"Task of recognizing and labelling the denotational names of entities and their categories for sequences of words in a stream of text or speech. Notes: Entity refers to concrete or abstract thing of interest, including associations among things; 'Named entity' refers to an entity with a denotational name where a specific or unique meaning exists; Denotational names include the specific names of persons, locations, organizations and other proper names based on the domain or application" *(ISO/IEC 22989)*.
Nanocore	Species of multifunctional **R**emote **A**ccess **T**rojan malware in the wild in 2019. Spread via spam as an infectious Excel spreadsheet.
Narrative	Story. Within cybersecurity, the term generally implies *false* narratives involving misinformation and disinformation deliberately generated and circulated via social media bots for manipulative reasons (social engineering).
Narrow Artificial **I**ntelligence **(Narrow AI)**	"Type of AI system that is focused on defined tasks to address a specific problem. Note: Compared to general AI" *(ISO/IEC 22989)*.
NAS	*Abbrev:* **N**etwork **A**ccess **S**erver or **N**etwork **A**ttached **S**torage, depending on context.
NAT	*Abbrev:* **N**etwork **A**ddress **T**ranslation.
National **C**ounterintelligence and **S**ecurity **C**enter **(NCSC)**	US government body under the Office of the **D**irector of **N**ational **I**ntelligence. Mission: "To lead and support the counterintelligence and security activities of the US Government, the US Intelligence Community, and US private sector entities who are at risk of intelligence collection, penetration or attack by foreign and other adversaries." *Cf.* NZ and UK **N**ational **C**yber **S**ecurity **C**entres. More info: https://www.dni.gov/index.php/ncsc-home
National **C**ritical **F**unctions **(NCF)**	US government functions and private sector organisations whose disruption, corruption, or dysfunction would devastate America. Grouped by **C**ybersecurity & **I**nfrastructure **S**ecurity **A**gency into four areas: connections (digital communications, networks, **G**lobal **P**ositioning **S**ystem, broadcasting); distribution of goods, people, and utilities (transport); management; and supplies of vital materials, goods, and services, across 16 sectors. *Cf.* **N**ational **C**yber **F**orce. More info: https://www.cisa.gov/topics/risk-management/national-critical-functions

TERM	MEANING
National Cybercrime Team, NPCC Cybercrime Team	Part of the UK nationwide **N**ational **P**olice **C**hiefs' **C**ouncil, led by the City of London Police Commissioner for the Home Office.
National **C**yber **F**orce **(NCF)**	UK cyber-spook unit established in 2020, drawing personnel from **G**overnment **C**ommunications **H**ead**Q**uarters, **M**inistry **O**f **D**efence and the **S**ecret **I**ntelligence **S**ervice. Their rôle is to disrupt terrorist command and control structures, support military/battlefield/cyber-war objectives, and generally disrupt adversaries' activities, *e.g.* by distributing propaganda, misinformation, and disinformation.
National **C**ybersecurity and **C**ommunications **I**ntegration **C**enter **(NCCIC)**	Part of the **D**epartment of **H**omeland **S**ecurity responsible for coordinating cybersecurity and communications protection efforts by the US government (*e.g.* US-CERT), plus commercial organisations and foreign governments. Information concerning active threats and exploits is analysed and shared with the community, and the incident response, mitigation, and recovery efforts are coordinated.
National **C**yber **S**ecurity **C**entre **(NCSC)**	a. New Zealand government body, part of the **G**overnment **C**ommunications **S**ecurity **B**ureau, whose mission is "to protect Aotearoa New Zealand's wellbeing and prosperity through trusted cyber security services." *Cf.* **N**ational **C**ounterintelligence and **S**ecurity **C**enter [US]. b. UK government body under **G**overnment **C**ommunications **H**ead**Q**uarters focused on national security threats in cyberspace as the UK's 'authority on cyber security' (whatever that means!), fostering liaison between the public and private sectors and dealing with state-level Incidents. Formed in 2016 from the **C**entre for **C**yber **A**ssessment, UK **C**omputer **E**mergency **R**esponse **T**eam, **C**ommunications **E**lectronics **S**ecurity **G**roup (GCHQ's information security arm), plus the 'cyber-related responsibilities' of the **C**entre for the **P**rotection of **N**ational **I**nfrastructure. "The UK's technical authority for cyber threats, providing a unified national response to cyber incidents to minimise harm, helping with recovery and learning lessons for the future" *(UK National Cyber Security Strategy 2022). Cf.* US **N**ational **C**ounterintelligence and **S**ecurity **C**enter.
National **I**nstitute of **S**tandards and **T**echnology **(NIST)**	Part of the US **D**epartment **o**f **C**ommerce providing standards (such as the SP 800-series and time standards) and scientific laboratory/measurement services. Mission: "To promote U.S. innovation and industrial competitiveness by advancing measurement science, standards, and technology in ways that enhance economic security and improve our quality of life." See also **A**merican **N**ational **S**tandards **I**nstitute. More info: https://www.nist.gov/

TERM	MEANING
National **S**ecurity **A**gency **(NSA)**	Powerful, spooky, and highly secretive arm of the US **D**epartment **o**f **D**efense responsible for various global SIGINT, counterterrorism, foreign intelligence, counterintelligence, national and commercial espionage and related surveillance activities, including massive bulk data collection programs and Stuxnet. Bradley Manning and Ed Snowden's disclosures of top secret information from the NSA indicating the sheer breadth and depth of the NSA's mass surveillance activities, penetration and coercion of powerful commercial and government organisations, and subsequent revelations concerning the lack of effective oversight and accountability, caused uproar among proponents of human rights, civil liberty, privacy, and democracy, as well as adverse social, political, and commercial repercussions for the US and its allies. There is a distinct possibility that, under cover of 'the war against [communism, drugs, terrorism or whatever],' the NSA has amassed sufficient information and power to manipulate, coerce, and control the US government that is supposedly its master, thereby ensuring its continued funding and at least partial immunity to the laws of the land, leaving both the NSA and the US government with the thorny problem of re-establishing their credibility and restoring public confidence. *Cf.* the US Navy's **N**aval **S**upport **A**ctivity.
National **S**ecurity **L**etter **(NSL)**	Official instruction from the **F**ederal **B**ureau **o**f **I**nvestigation about protecting America against spying, terrorism, or other threats to national security, *e.g.* mandating the disclosure of confidential information pertinent to an investigation by an organisation. May also impose a nondisclosure obligation under circumstances specified in law, forbidding recipients from even disclosing the fact that they are subject to an NSL. See also warrant canary.
NIST	*Abbrev:* **N**ational **I**nstitute of **S**tandards and **T**echnology.
National **P**rotective **S**ecurity **A**uthority **(NPSA)**	"The UK's National Technical Authority for physical and personnel protective security, working to make the UK less vulnerable and more resilient to national security threats." More info: https://www.npsa.gov.uk/
National **R**isk **R**egister **(NRR)**	Over 150 pages describing risks (mostly threats and hazards in fact) deemed significant to the UK, categorised as terrorism; cyber; state; geographic and diplomatic; accidents and systems failures; natural and environmental [plus] human, animal, and plant health; societal; or conflict and instability. "The National Risk Register is the external [published, unclassified] version of the National Security Risk Assessment which is the government's assessment of the most serious risks facing the UK" *(National Risk Register 2025)*.

TERM	MEANING
National security	Primarily military arrangements protecting an entire nation-state against adversaries such as other states and terrorists. Encompasses defence of the realm and protection of the populace and other national interests against actual or perceived foreign threats, plus diplomacy and offensive actions.
National **S**ecurity **R**isk **A**ssessment **(NSRA)**	Classified UK government process for identifying, analysing, and evaluating all manner of risks concerning national security. "Assesses, compares and prioritises the top national level risks facing the UK, focusing on both likelihood of the risk occurring and the impact it would have, were it to happen. It is the main tool for assessing the most serious civil contingencies risks facing the UK" *(UK Resilience Lessons Digest 2023)*.
Native file	File sporting a grass skirt with a bone through its nose? No! "Electronic document in a native format. Note: Native files are frequently proprietary" *(ISO/IEC 27050-1)*.
Native format	Raw information-rich data storage file format (such as .docx for MS Word documents, containing the printable text and image content plus markup, comments, and other metadata). "Organisation and representation of data and metadata that an operating system or application uses when data is stored. Notes: Native formats typically contain the most complete representation of the data. While it is often possible to convert this data to other formats, there can be a loss of information (*e.g.,* metadata is stripped) or modification of the information. In many circumstances or jurisdictions native format is that format in which a hardcopy document or ESI is stored or used in the normal course of its use/business" *(ISO/IEC 27050-1)*.
Natural disaster	Flood, wildfire, storm, tornado, volcanic eruption, earthquake, *etc.* "Any 'act of God' (*e.g.,* fire, flood, earthquake, lightning, or wind) that disables a system component" *(SANS glossary)*.
Natural language	Means by which human beings normally communicate with each other, such as English. "Language that is or was in active use in a community of people and whose rules are deduced from usage. Notes: Natural language is any human language, which can be expressed in text, speech, sign language, *etc.;* Natural language is any human language, such as English, Spanish, Arabic, Chinese or Japanese, to be distinguished from programming and formal languages, such as Java, Fortran, C++ or First-Order Logic" *(ISO/IEC 22989)*.
Natural **L**anguage **G**eneration **(NLG)**	"Task of converting data carrying semantics into natural language" *(ISO/IEC 22989)*.

TERM	MEANING
Natural Language Processing **(NLP)**	Field within Artificial Intelligence and Machine Learning concerning linguistics, *i.e.* the interpretation, processing, and generation of natural (human) language. "<System> Information processing based upon natural language understanding or natural language generation. <Discipline> Discipline concerned with the way systems acquire, process and interpret natural language" *(ISO/IEC 22989).* See also Deep Learning, Large Language Model. *Cf.* Neuro-Linguistic Programming.
Natural Language Understanding **(NLU), natural language comprehension**	"Extraction of information, by a functional unit, from text or speech communicated to it in a natural language, and the production of a description for both the given text or speech and what it represents" *(ISO/IEC 22989).*
Natural number	Generally, a positive integer or count, *i.e.* a whole/round number with no fraction. For *some* mathematical purposes, zero may be included.
NBC	*Abbrev:* Nuclear, Biological, and Chemical.
NCCIC	*Abbrev:* National Cybersecurity and Communications Integration Center.
NCCoE	*Abbrev:* National Cybersecurity Center of Excellence. Part of the Applied Cybersecurity Division of NIST. More info: https://www.nccoe.nist.gov/
NCF	*Abbrev:* National Critical Functions or National Cyber Force, depending on context.
NCP	*Abbrev:* Network Control Protocol.
NCSC	*Abbrev:* National Counterintelligence and Security Center [US] or National Cyber Security Centre [NZ] or National Cyber Security Centre [UK], depending on context.
NCSP	*Abbrev:* NIST Cyber Security Professional.
NDA	*Abbrev:* Non-Disclosure Agreement.
NDR	*Abbrev:* Network [incident] Detection and Response.
Near Field Communication **(NFC)**	Short-range wireless networking technologies such as Bluetooth designed to link nearby Information Technology devices over a few tens of meters at most. "A form of contactless, close proximity, radio communications based on radio-frequency identification (RFID) technology" *(NIST SP 800-101).*

TERM	MEANING
Near miss, near-miss, near hit, near-hit, close call, close shave	Term adapted from the aviation industry, referring to the close physical approach of aircraft that could easily have led to an accident. In information security, it means a situation or event that could easily have led to an incident if it weren't for sheer good fortune. Can present valuable learning and improvement opportunities *if* reported, analysed, evaluated, and responded to as if it was an actual security incident. "Negative example of a concept to be learned that is quite similar to a positive example of that concept and may help to isolate the significant features of the latter" *(ISO/IEC 2382).*
Need-to-know	See default deny. "Legitimate requirement of a prospective recipient of data to know, to access, or to possess any sensitive information represented by these data" *(ISO/IEC 2382)*. "Principled approach to controlling what individuals can see. Employees can access only the data, systems and spaces necessary to do their job" *(ISACA glossary).* "The principle of telling a person only the information that they require to fulfil their role" *(NZISM).* "The principle of restricting an individual's access to only the data they require to fulfil the duties of their role" *(AusISM).*. *Cf.* default permit.
Need-to-withhold	See default permit. *Cf.* default deny.
Negative feedback	a. Complaints and criticisms fed back to the originators of documents, training courses, systems, standards, products, *etc.* b. Connecting the *inverted* output of an amplifying component, unit, or system back to its input reduces the output and, with proportional control, can stabilise the level. *Cf.* positive feedback.
Negligence, negligent	Failing to exercise due care. Implies more than simply carelessness, *e.g.* incompetence, recklessness, perhaps even wilful sabotage, or cybertage.
NER	*Abbrev:* **N**amed **E**ntity **R**ecognition.
NERC CIP	*Abbrev:* **N**orth American **E**lectric **R**eliability **C**orporation **C**ritical **I**nfrastructure **P**rotection.
Nessus	Vulnerability scanning tool, now a commercial product while the original open-source version became OpenVAS.
NetBIOS	Deprecated network protocol. Highly vulnerable. Very insecure. Bad news. Avoid like the plague.
Netcat	Network security and hacking tool capable of listening for and transmitting packets.

TERM	MEANING
Netmask	"32-bit number indicating the range of IP addresses residing on a single IP network/subnet/supernet. This specification displays network masks as hexadecimal numbers. For example, the network mask for a class C IP network is displayed as 0xffffff00. Such a mask is often displayed elsewhere in the literature as 255.255.255.0" *(SANS glossary)*.
Network	a. Datacommunications connections linking various computers, *i.e.* the cables, wireless links and devices such as routers, switches, and hubs. "A system implemented with a collection of interconnected components. Such components may include routers, hubs, cabling, telecommunications controllers, key distribution centers, and technical control devices" *(NIST SP 800-171)*. "A system of interconnected computers and the communication equipment used to connect them" *(ISACA glossary)*. b. Community of people, organisations, *etc.* with common interests, connected by personal interactions and contacts, social media, messaging, email, *etc.* – see social network. c. Datacommunications infrastructure as a whole, *i.e.* the linkages *plus* the linked devices *plus* the network services and traffic, possibly also the associated users. Indistinct and dynamic, hence often portrayed as a cloud. "Arrangement of entities and their interconnections. Note: In network topology or in an abstract arrangement, the interconnected entities are points on a scheme, and the interconnections are lines on the scheme. In a computer network, the interconnected entities are computers or data communication equipment, and the interconnections are data links" *(ISO/IEC 2382)*.
Network access	Access to traffic on a network, or to a system via a network. "Access to a system by a user (or a process acting on behalf of a user) communicating through a network (*e.g.,* local area network, wide area network, the internet)" *(NIST SP 800-171)*.
Network **A**ccess **C**ontrol, **N**etwork **A**dmission **C**ontrol **(NAC)**	Approach for restricting devices from gaining access to a network and controlling what they can do once connected. Devices are typically identified and checked for security issues including nonconformity with security policies. "Policies and processes used to control access to a network and actions on a network, including authentication checks and authorisation controls" *(NZISM)*.
Network **A**ccess **S**erver **(NAS)**	Gateway device that secures point-to-point connections with remote devices, typically in conjunction with a RADIUS server.

TERM	MEANING
Network address	Similar to an email or postal address, identifies the source/origin and/or destination/target nodes, computer systems, or networks for datacommunications messages. Used for network routing, management, logging, tracing/tracking, broadcasting, *etc.* Specified in most network protocols. For obvious reasons, *should* be unambiguous for efficient delivery and unique within a given network to avoid conflict and confusion. For security reasons, may require authentication to mitigate the risk of spoofing. "An identifier for a node or host on a telecommunications network" *(ISACA glossary).*
Network **A**ddress **T**ranslation **(NAT)**	Basic firewall, router, or server function to spoof public **I**nternet **P**rotocol addresses externally on packets originating within a private internal network, without breaking various network protocols. Keeping internal IP addresses confidential makes it slightly harder for Internet hackers to discover and map the internal network architecture, and allows additional security, *e.g.* raising the alarm if packets with internal IP addresses appear on the public side of the NAT server, indicating a possible breach/incident or a firewall configuration failure. "A methodology for modifying network address information in IP datagram packet headers while they are in transit across a traffic routing device for the purpose of remapping one IP address space into another" *(ISACA glossary).* "[NAT] is used to share one or a small number of publicly routable IP addresses among a larger number of hosts. The hosts are assigned private IP addresses, which are then 'translated' into one of the publicly routed IP addresses. Typically home or small business networks use NAT to share a single DLS or Cable modem IP address. However, in some cases NAT is used for servers as an additional layer of protection. [and] The translation of an Internet Protocol address used within one network to a different IP address known within another network. One network is designated the inside network and the other is the outside" *(SANS glossary).*
Network Administration or Administrator (NetAdmin)	Corporate administrative function performing routine technical operations and management of computer networks. "Day-to-day operation and management of network processes, and assets using networks" *(ISO/IEC 27033-1).* "An individual who is responsible for planning, implementing and maintaining the telecommunications infrastructure; also may be responsible for voice networks. Note: For smaller enterprises, the network administrator may also maintain a local area network (LAN) and assist end users" *(ISACA glossary).*

TERM	MEANING
Network analyser	Network device that monitors, logs, analyses, and perhaps acts upon, passing traffic, *e.g.* raising security alerts. "Device or software used to observe and analyze information flowing in networks. Note: Prior to the information flow analysis, information should be gathered in a specific way such as by using a network sniffer" *(ISO/IEC 27033-1)*. "A tool that creates a signal and characterizes the devices that receive it to help diagnose problems with Internet connectivity, WiFi network setups and issues on remote servers" *(ISACA glossary)*. See also sniffer.
Network and **I**nformation **S**ecurity **(NIS) directives, NIS and NIS2**	The original "NIS" was **E**uropean **U**nion directive (EU 2016/1148) requiring certain critical infrastructure providers serving the EU to ensure resilience through appropriate **I**nformation **T**echnology/cyber and physical security controls. NIS applied regulatory oversight to the provision of critical energy, transport, health, and drinking water suppliers, plus cyberinfrastructure such as online marketplaces, search engines, and cloud computing services, and was implemented by national laws in member states. It was replaced in 2024 by EU directive 2022/2555 "NIS2," covering a wider range of organisations classified as either critical or important. The core aim remains to achieve adequate cyber risk management consistently for the EU's critical infrastructure, thereby improving resilience.
Network-**as**-**a**-**S**ervice **(NaaS)**	As if **P**latform-**as**-**a**-**S**ervice, **I**nfrastructure-**as**-**a**-**S**ervice, and **S**oftware-**as**-**a**-**S**ervice weren't enough already, Fujitsu coined this term for the provision of software-defined network services. In relation to cloud computing, it is taken to include virtual networks using **V**irtual **P**rivate **N**etworks, flexible network capacity, *etc.*
Network **A**ttached **S**torage **(NAS)**	Disk, tape, or similar data storage devices connected to the network. "Storage device or system that connects to a network and provide file access services to computer systems" *(ISO/IEC 27040)*.
Network-based **I**ntrusion **D**etection **S**ystem **(NIDS)**	**I**ntrusion **D**etection **S**ystem involving monitoring all the network traffic traversing the cables or wireless channels, as opposed to monitoring network traffic destined for or generated by a particular servers or nodes (see **H**ost-based **I**ntrusion **D**etection **S**ystem). "A network-based IDS system monitors the traffic on its network segment as a data source. This is generally accomplished by placing the network interface card in promiscuous mode to capture all network traffic that crosses its network segment. Network traffic on other segments, and traffic on other means of communication (like phone lines) can't be monitored. Network-based IDS involves looking at the packets on the network as they pass by some sensor. The sensor can only see the packets that happen to be carried on the network segment it's attached to. Packets are considered to be of interest if they match a signature. Network-based intrusion detection passively monitors network activity for indications of attacks.

TERM	MEANING
	Network monitoring offers several advantages over traditional host-based intrusion detection systems. Because many intrusions occur over networks at some point, and because networks are increasingly becoming the targets of attack, these techniques are an excellent method of detecting many attacks which may be missed by host-based intrusion detection mechanisms" *(SANS glossary)*.
Network control	Control designed to mitigate unacceptable network risks, *e.g.* firewall, datacommunications protocols with security functions, or group rules and norms for social networks.
Network **C**ontrol Protocol **(NCP)**	Deprecated networking protocol used for remote access, file transfer, email, *etc.* on ARPANET prior to the adoption of TCP/IP.
Network [incident] **D**etection and **R**esponse **(NDR)**	Automated network security monitoring, intended to identify and react appropriately to malicious or suspicious activities potentially indicative of an attack.
Network device	Device connected to and forming part of a network.
Network element	Network node, device, system, or component. "Information system that is connected to a network" *(ISO/IEC 27033-1)*.
Network [protocol] fuzzer	Testing tool for constructing and sending malformed network packets, duplicate packets, packets out-of-sequence, *etc.* to check whether network devices, services, and applications can handle such problems elegantly, without crashing or failing-unsafe/open.
Network infrastructure	Network infrastructure. "The infrastructure used to carry information between workstations and servers or other network devices. For example: cabling, junction boxes, patch panels, fibre distribution panels and structured wiring enclosures" *(NZISM)*. "Refers to all of the resources of a network that make network or internet connectivity, management, business operations, and communication possible. It consists of hardware and software, systems and devices, and it enables computing and communication between users, services, applications, and processes. Network infrastructure can be cloud, physical, or virtual" *(CIS Controls)*.
Network **I**nvestigative **T**echnique **(NIT)**	**F**ederal **B**ureau of **I**nvestigation term for a tool or method used to investigate and gather forensic evidence from computer networks and systems.
Network management	Network management – activities involved in specifying, designing, implementing, configuring, securing, monitoring, and maintaining datacommunications networks, either directly or in conjunction with network engineers, architects, and other specialists. "Process of planning, designing, implementing, operating, monitoring and maintaining a network" *(ISO/IEC 27033-1)*.

TERM	MEANING
Network management traffic	Traffic (instructions and data) involved in configuring, monitoring, and securing a network. "Network traffic generated by system administrators over a network in order to control workstations and servers. This includes standard management protocols and other network traffic that contains data relating to the management of the network" *(AusISM)*.
Network mapping	"To compile an electronic inventory of the systems and the services on your network" *(SANS glossary)*.
Network monitoring	Form of routine surveillance focused on data traffic, metadata, and (more broadly) activities occurring on a computer network, for purposes such as cybersecurity, performance and capacity management, anomaly detection, and general network and systems administration. "Process of continuously observing and reviewing data recorded on network activity and operations, including audit logs and alerts, and related analysis" *(ISO/IEC 27033-1)*.
Network Operations Centre (NOC)	Corporate function operating (monitoring and managing) multiple networks, including network security administration. *Cf.* **N**on-**O**fficial **C**over.
Network owner	Organisation, rôle, or person who literally/legally or notionally owns a network along with any associated property rights and obligations, responsibilities, or social expectations. May be a custodian, steward, or agent acting on behalf of the legal owner. May be accountable for its protection/security and legitimate exploitation to optimise its value. Social networks are assets that can be figuratively 'owned' by the organisations or people that originally established, nurtured/grew, and continue to influence them. See also asset owner, information owner, system owner, service owner, infrastructure owner.
Network perimeter	Network perimeter. "The secured boundary between the private and locally managed side of a network, often a company's intranet, and the public-facing side of a network, often the Internet" *(FSRCoP)*.
Network protection device	"A category of network device used specifically to protect a network. For example, a firewall session border controller *etc*" *(NZISM)*.

TERM	MEANING
Network protocol	a. Datacommunications network protocol for the formatting, meaning, and handling of various types of network message. Some protocols primarily concern data transportation, network management, routing or security, but most have mixed purposes, *e.g.* **I**nternet **P**rotocol, **T**ransmission **C**ontrol **P**rotocol, **U**ser **D**atagram **P**rotocol, **P**oint-to-**P**oint **P**rotocol, **A**ddress **R**esolution **P**rotocol, **B**order **G**ateway **P**rotocol, **D**omain **N**ame **S**ystem, **M**edia **A**ccess **C**ontrol, **D**ynamic **H**ost **C**onfiguration **P**rotocol, **N**etwork **T**ime **P**rotocol, **L**ightweight **D**irectory **A**ccess **P**rotocol, **H**yper**T**ext **T**ransfer **P**rotocol, **F**ile **T**ransfer **P**rotocol, **S**imple **M**ail **T**ransfer **P**rotocol, **S**hort **M**essaging **S**ervice, **I**nternet **C**ontrol **M**essage **P**rotocol, **S**imple **N**etwork **M**anagement **P**rotocol, SOAP, **P**assword **A**uthentication **P**rotocol, **R**emote **A**uthentication **D**ial-**I**n **U**ser **S**ervice, OAuth2, **S**ecure **SH**ell, **O**nline **C**ertificate **S**tatus **P**rotocol, **A**utomated **C**ertificate **M**anagement **E**nvironment, 3-D Secure, **S**ecurity **A**ssertion **M**arkup **L**anguage. b. Social networks also have their protocols, perhaps codified as a set of group rules and expectations but usually implicit in the language and nature of interactions between and reactions by members (social norms).
Network risk	Uncertain possibility of incidents involving various networks including datacommunications (*e.g.* unauthorised interception of traffic, interference) and social networks (*e.g.* coercion and other social engineering).
Network security administration	Administrative risk management tasks involved in securing/protecting a datacommunications network such as securely configuring and monitoring the devices/nodes, firewalls, connections, communication paths, protocols, traffic, users, applications, backups, logs, alarms, and alerts.
Network security policy	Policy concerning network security. "Set of statements, rules and practices that explain an organisation's approach to the use of its network resources, and specify how its network infrastructure and services should be protected" *(ISO/IEC 27033-1)*.

TERM	MEANING
Network service	Application running on a network node, host, or server providing information services or functions through the network, *e.g.* email, cloud storage, cloud computing, cellular phones, SMS/TXT messaging.
Network stack	Conceptual model comprising an integrated, modular set of interoperable layers providing network services and protocols, building up from the base physical layer (hardware converting digital bits to/from analogue modulation on a cable or wireless interface) through increasingly sophisticated mid-layers to the application layer at the top (where applications such as email and web browsers can communicate over networks without having to handle the entire process, *e.g.* the establishment of sessions and message routing). The OSI model has 7 layers whereas TCP/IP merges some, ending up with just 4. Security functions (such as authentication, encryption, and error correction) are provided by various layers, the entire stack working together to deliver effective network security. See also layer 8+.
Network tap	"Hardware devices that hook directly onto the network cable and send a copy of the traffic that passes through it to one or more other networked devices" *(SANS glossary)*.
Network topology	Design or architecture of a network, primarily in terms of the physical configuration – the structure created by connections between nodes (*e.g.* star, ring, bus, mesh, or hybrid networks) – or the logical security arrangements forming distinct layers or domains sharing a single network structure (*e.g.* to prioritise the communication of time-critical video content over email and web content that can wait its turn). Even social networks have topologies with clusters of close social connections, special interest groups, more distant or remote acquaintances, plus social influencers. "The basic configuration and architecture of a set of interconnected nodes" *(ISACA glossary)*.
Network **T**raffic **A**nalysis **(NTA)**	Network management techniques to identify meaningful events and incidents of concern in the flow of traffic on a datacommunications network. "A means of identifying patterns in network communications. Notes: Traffic analysis does not need to have the actual content of the communication but analyzes where traffic occurs, when and for how long communications take place, and the quantity of information transferred" *(ISACA glossary)*. See also **T**raffic **A**nalysis, **S**ecurity **I**nformation and **E**vent **M**anagement, **U**ser **B**ehaviour **A**nalytics, **I**ntrusion **D**etection **S**ystem/**I**ntrusion **P**revention **S**ystem.
Network weaving	"Penetration technique in which different communication networks are used to gain access to a data processing system to avoid detection and trace-back" *(ISO/IEC 2382)*.

TERM	MEANING
Neural **N**etwork **(NN), neural net, artificial neural network**	Machine learning model originally inspired by the structure of the brain with layers of interconnected nodes (mathematical functions representing neurons). The outputs of one layer are input to the next. Connections between nodes are weighted as the network learns from training data. Weights are trained by backpropagation, an algorithm that calculates the error of the network's output and adjusts the weights accordingly. "Network of primitive processing elements connected by weighted links with adjustable weights, in which each element produces a value by applying a nonlinear function to its input values, and transmits it to other elements or presents it as an output. Notes: Neural networks are modeled on the functioning of neurons in the nervous system. The nonlinear function is usually a threshold function" *(ISO/IEC 2382)*. "Network of one or more layers of neurons connected by weighted links with adjustable weights, which takes input data and produces an output. Notes: Neural networks are a prominent example of the connectionist approach; Although the design of neural networks was initially inspired by the functioning of biological neurons, most works on neural networks do not follow that inspiration anymore" *(ISO/IEC 22989)*. "Networks, inspired by the structure of the human brain, that learn by processing data through three layers (input, hidden, and output). They can be trained to match any input to various outputs, including binary ones, making them versatile tools in deep learning (DL) for tasks like image recognition" *(ISACA glossary)*.
Neuro-**L**inguistic **P**rogramming **(NLP)**	Unscientific and discredited theory touted by some social engineers concerning their supposed ability to exploit interactions between neurology and linguistics to 'program' behaviour. Pure snake oil, although NLP proponents who *believe* they have superpowers are likely to be highly self-confident and therefore persuasive – a kind of placebo effect or self-fulfilling prophecy. *Cf.* **N**atural **L**anguage **P**rocessing.
Neuron	Brain cell. "Primitive processing element which takes one or more input values and produces an output value by combining the input values and applying an activation function on the result. Note: Examples of nonlinear activation functions are a threshold function, a sigmoid function and a polynomial function" *(ISO/IEC 22989)*.
New **Z**ealand [government] **I**nformation **S**ecurity **M**anual **(NZISM)**	"The New Zealand Government's manual on information governance, assurance, and information systems security … Its role is to promote a consistent approach to information assurance and information security across all New Zealand Government agencies." More info: https://nzism.gcsb.govt.nz/

TERM	MEANING
New Zealand's Security Threat Environment **(NZSTE)**	"An assessment by the New Zealand Security Intelligence Service" published in 2023. More info: https://www.nzsis.govt.nz/assets/NZSIS-Documents/New-Zealands-Security-Threat-Environment-2023.pdf
NFC	*Abbrev:* **N**ear **F**ield **C**ommunication.
NFV (Network Function Virtualisation)	Virtualisation software/**V**irtual **T**echnology mediates between individual network functions or services (*e.g.* routing, content delivery, **N**etwork **A**ddress **T**ranslation, **V**irtual **P**rivate **N**etworks, load balancing, **I**ntrusion **D**etection **S**ystem/**I**ntrusion **P**revention **S**ystem, and firewalls) and real networks. Being virtual, the functions can be dynamically enabled/disabled (blackholed) and allocated different resources, *e.g.* to cope with the overload caused by a massive influx of requests to a popular website, perhaps a **D**istributed **D**enial-**o**f-**S**ervice attack.
NGFW (Next-Generation FireWall)	Supposedly (according to various marketing and sales departments) the *next* best thing in firewalls with the capability to understand high-level application protocols and so control application traffic. See also **S**ecure **W**eb **G**ateway, **S**ecure **A**ccess **S**ervice **E**dge.
Nibble	Small bite or half a byte, *i.e.* 4 digital bits. "An equivalent of four binary digits or half a byte. Nibble can be represented by one hexadecimal digit" *(ISACA glossary)*.
NIDS	See **N**etwork-based **I**ntrusion **D**etection **S**ystem.
Nikto	Open-source tool for penetration testing/hacker attacks on web servers.
Nimda	Network worm derived from Code Red in 2001. Used multiple modes of infection to spread widely and quickly. 'Nimda' is 'admin' spelt backwards, hinting at the VXer's geeky sense of humour.
NIPRnet	*Abbrev:* **N**onclassified **I**nternet **P**rotocol **R**outer **net**work. US **D**epartment **of D**efense data network for nonclassified but not for SECRET or higher classes of information. See also SIPRnet.
NIS	*Abbrev:* **N**etwork and **I**nformation **S**ystems regulations.
NIS2	*Abbrev:* second **N**etwork and **I**nformation **S**ystems regulation.
NIST	*Abbrev:* **N**ational **I**nstitute of **S**tandards and **T**echnology.
NIST CSF	*Abbrev:* **NIST C**yber **S**ecurity **F**ramework.
NIST **C**yber **S**ecurity **P**rofessional **(NCSP)**	Training and certification program based around the NIST **C**yber **S**ecurity **F**ramework, drawing also on good practices from other sources such as COSO, ISO/IEC 27005, ISO 31000, MEHARI, EBIOS, OCTAVE, FAIR, and DVMS CPD. More info: https://www.nistcybersecurityprofessional.website/

TERM	MEANING
NIST IR 7298 revision 3 (2019)	NIST's **I**nteragency **R**eport "Glossary of Key Information Security Terms," an extensive compilation of over 9,000 (!) terms and definitions collated from numerous SP 800 and FIPS standards, plus CNSSI 4009 and other cited references. Can be downloaded or browsed and searched online through the NIST Computer Security Division – **C**omputer **S**ecurity **R**esource **C**enter. More info: https://www.nist.gov/publications/glossary-key-information-security-terms-3
NIST IR 8286C-upd1	NIST's **I**nteragency **R**eport "Staging Cybersecurity Risks for Enterprise Risk Management and Governance Oversight." This supplement to NIST IR 8286 "describes how information, as recorded in cybersecurity risk registers (CSRRs), may be integrated as part of a holistic approach to ensuring that risks to information and technology are properly considered for the enterprise risk portfolio. This cohesive understanding supports an enterprise risk register (ERR) and enterprise risk profile (ERP) that, in turn, support the achievement of enterprise objectives." More info: https://doi.org/10.6028/NIST.IR.8286C-upd1
NIST SP (Special Publication) 800 series	NIST's highly regarded public domain standards promote a broad range of good practices in information security, **I**nformation **T**echnology security, cybersecurity, privacy, cryptography, secure software development, *etc*. There are over 600 current NIST standards plus about 100 drafts (revisions or new standards), of which over 200 are SP 800 standards. More info: https://csrc.nist.gov/publications/SP 800
NIST SP 800-30 revision 1	NIST standard "Guide for Conducting Risk Assessments" (2012) provides guidance on conducting risk assessments of federal information systems and organisations, expanding on SP 800-39. More info: https://csrc.nist.gov/pubs/sp/800/30/r1/final
NIST SP 800-37 revision 2	NIST standard "Risk Management Framework for Information Systems and Organizations" (2018) describes the **R**isk **M**anagement **F**ramework with guidance. The RMF process covers information security characterisation ('categorization'); control selection, implementation, assessment; control authorisations; and continuous risk and control monitoring/maintenance. More info: https://csrc.nist.gov/pubs/sp/800/37/r2/final
NIST SP 800-39	NIST standard "Managing Information Security Risk" (2011) explains a structured and tiered approach to manage 'information security risk' in support of FISMA at the organisation, mission/business process, and Information Technology system levels. More info: https://csrc.nist.gov/pubs/sp/800/39/final

TERM	MEANING
NIST SP 800-48 revision 1	NIST standard "Guide to Security Legacy IEEE 802.11 Wireless Networks" was withdrawn in 2018 in favour of 802.11i. More info: https://csrc.nist.gov/pubs/sp/800/48/r1/final
NIST SP 800-53 revision 5	NIST standard "Security and Privacy Controls for Information Systems and Organizations" (2020–2025) provides a substantial reference catalogue of security and privacy controls suitable for federal information systems *other* than those associated with US national security and defence, in several parts/volumes. More info: https://csrc.nist.gov/pubs/sp/800/53/r5/upd1/final
NIST SP 800-53A revision 5	NIST standard "Assessing Security and Privacy Controls in Information Systems and Organizations" (2022) lays out a methodical yet customisable process for gaining assurance regarding the effectiveness of SP 800-53-style security and privacy controls within a **R**isk **M**anagement **F**ramework. More info: https://csrc.nist.gov/pubs/sp/800/53/a/r5/final
NIST SP 800-55v1	NIST standard "Measurement Guide for Information Security: Volume 1 — Identifying and Selecting Measures" (2024) "provides guidance on how an organization can develop information security measures to identify the adequacy of in-place security policies, procedures, and controls. It explains the measures prioritization process and how to evaluate measures." More info: https://csrc.nist.gov/pubs/sp/800/55/v1/final
NIST SP 800-63-3	NIST standard "Digital Identity Guidelines" (2020) specifies technical requirements for digital services to identify and authenticate users of US federal agencies' networked systems. More info: https://csrc.nist.gov/pubs/sp/800/63/3/upd2/final
NIST SP 800-95	NIST standard "Guide to Secure Web Services" (2007) expands on Internet security for online services. More info: https://csrc.nist.gov/pubs/sp/800/95/final
NIST SP 800-101 revision 1	NIST standard "Guidelines on Mobile Device Forensics" (2014) concerns digital forensics practices for recovering digital evidence from cellphones, *things*, *etc*. More info: https://csrc.nist.gov/pubs/sp/800/101/r1/final
NIST SP 800-114 revision 1	NIST standard "User's Guide to Telework and Bring Your Own Device (BYOD) Security" (2016) covers the cybersecurity aspects of teleworking using corporate or personally owned PCs or portable **I**nformation **T**echnology devices under BYOD schemes. More info: https://csrc.nist.gov/pubs/sp/800/114/r1/final
NIST SP 800-121 revision 2	NIST standard "Guide to Bluetooth Security" (2022) explains the risks and security features associated with Bluetooth. More info: https://csrc.nist.gov/pubs/sp/800/121/r2/upd1/final

TERM	MEANING
NIST SP 800-162	NIST standard "Guide to Attribute Based Access Control (ABAC) Definition and Considerations" (2019) explains how to use subject attributes to authenticate, authorise, and control them. More info: https://csrc.nist.gov/pubs/sp/800/162/upd2/final
NIST SP 800-171 revision 3	NIST standard "Protecting Controlled Unclassified Information in Nonfederal Systems and Organisations" (2024) offers basic cybersecurity guidance for unclassified information. More info: https://csrc.nist.gov/pubs/sp/800/171/r3/final
NIST SP 800-192	NIST standard "Verification and Test Methods for Access Control Policies/Models" (2017) explains how to check implemented access controls rigorously and systematically against the corresponding policies and specifications/requirements. More info: https://csrc.nist.gov/pubs/sp/800/192/final
NIST SP 800-218	NIST standard "Secure Software Development Framework (SSDF): Recommendations for Mitigating the Risk of Software Vulnerabilities" (2022) identifies a core set of high-level secure software development practices that can be integrated into various **S**oftware **D**evelopment **L**ife**C**ycles to reduce system vulnerabilities, reduce the impacts of their exploitation/compromise, and address root causes to improve the associated processes. See also **S**ecure **S**oftware **D**evelopment **F**ramework. More info: https://csrc.nist.gov/pubs/sp/800/218/final
NIT	*Abbrev:* **N**etwork **I**nvestigative **T**echnique.
NLP	*Abbrev:* **N**atural **L**anguage **P**rocessing or **N**euro-**L**inguistic **P**rogramming, depending on context.
NLZ	*Abbrev:* **N**o **L**one **Z**one.
nmap	Network security administration/penetration testing/hacking tool originally developed by an old-school hacker called Fyodor. Capable of port scanning and *much* more. Uses custom IP packets to characterise network links and devices. An example of dual-use technology, popular with black, grey, and white hats. More info: https://nmap.org/
NN	*Abbrev:* **N**eural **N**etwork.
NOC	See **N**etwork **O**perations **C**entre or **N**on-**O**fficial **C**over, depending on context.
Node	Computing/networking equipment with one or more network connections, *e.g.* routers, firewalls, networked application systems, file servers, web servers, email servers, workstations, *things*, PCs, laptops, tablet PCs, and smartphones. "In a network, entity that

TERM **MEANING**

is connected to one or more other entities. Notes: In network topology or in an abstract arrangement, the nodes are points on a scheme. In a computer network, the nodes are computers or data communication equipment. A network may contain end nodes and intermediate nodes. [and] in a data network, point where one or more functional units interconnect transmission channels or data circuits" *(ISO/IEC 2382)*. "Any device designed to facilitate the communication of information destined for multiple system users. For example: cryptographic devices, firewalls, routers, switches and hubs" *(NZISM)*. "ICT equipment designed to facilitate the communication of data. For example, routers, switches and wireless access points" *(AusISM)*. "Electronic devices required for communication and interaction between devices on a computer network. Network devices include wireless access points, firewalls, physical/ virtual gateways, routers, and switches. These devices consist of physical hardware, as well as virtual and cloud-based devices. For the purpose of this document, network devices are a subset of enterprise assets" *(CIS Controls)*. "Point at which terminals are given access to a network [and] A neuron in a hidden layer" *(ISACA glossary)*.

Noise — Interference that degrades the integrity of a communications activity and, if serious, its availability. Usually but not necessarily random and natural. "Disturbance that affects a signal and that may distort the information carried by the signal" *(ISO/IEC 2382)*. "Data transmission or data set disturbances, such as static, that cause messages to be misinterpreted by the receiver" *(ISACA glossary)*. "Anything that causes difficulties during the communication process" *(OCEG GRC Glossary)*.

No Lone Zone (NLZ), no lone working — Physical security policy, procedure, and protocol that prohibits workers from unaccompanied/sole access to designated secure areas (zones). "Area, room, or space that, when staffed, must be occupied by two or more appropriately cleared individuals who remain within sight of each other" *(CNSSI 4009)*. "An area in which personnel are not permitted to be left alone such that all actions are witnessed by at least one other person" *(NZISM)*.

No man's land — Disputed buffer zone separating warring combatants on a battlefield. See **De-Militarised Zone**.

Nomenclator — Vulnerable but widely used and trusted form of encryption from the 16th until the early 20th Centuries, using a combination of codes and substitution.

Nominal scale — Sequence of qualitative indicators (category labels, ordinal values) such as green ⇨ yellow ⇨ red or nil ⇨ negligible ⇨ low ⇨ medium ⇨ high ⇨ extreme or for that matter 1 ⇨ 2 ⇨3. *Implies* a steady progression in the associated values without actually quantifying the values or the steps between them. "From the Stevens Scale of Measurement, a scale that labels named variables into classifications" *(NIST SP 800-55v1)*.

TERM	MEANING
Non-affirmative cyber risk, silent cyber risk	Potentially ambiguous insurance policies neither include nor exclude cyber incidents. The insurer and insured will probably differ in their interpretations of the small print, while their lawyers rejoice.
Non-agency control	"This description applies where an Agency does NOT have direct control of elements of agency information systems and data. This may occur, for example, where data centre operations are out-sourced" *(NZISM)*. *Cf.* agency control.
Nonce	Contraction of '**N**umber used **once**,' a pseudorandom number often used as part of the challenge in cryptographic challenge-response protocols with the intention of preventing replay attacks (but see Krack). "A limited or single-use value, typically small, used for initialization, seed generation or some other special purpose" *(ISACA glossary)*. "A random or non-repeating value that is included in data exchanged by a protocol, usually for the purpose of guaranteeing the transmittal of live data rather than replayed data, thus detecting and protecting against replay attacks" *(CNSSI 4009)*.
Noncompliance	Failure to comply with, achieve, fulfil, or uphold a mandatory obligation specified in a law, regulation, and executed contract, *i.e.* a compliance exception. If revealed or discovered, the responsible parties may be called to account, potentially leading to enforcement action such as penalties or other sanctions. *Cf.* nonconformity.
Non-computing/ Internet of Things (IoT) device	See *thing*. "Devices embedded with sensors, software, and other technologies for the purpose of connecting, storing, and exchanging data with other devices and systems over the internet. While these devices are not used for computational processes, they support an enterprise's ability to conduct business processes. Examples of these devices include printers, smart screens, physical security sensors, industrial control systems, and information technology sensors. For the purpose of this document, non-computing/IoT devices are a subset of enterprise assets" *(CIS Controls)*.
Nonconformity, non-conformity	Failure to satisfy, meet, achieve, or uphold a discretionary requirement (a rule) specified in a policy, procedure, guideline, directive, command/instruction, standard, agreement, *etc.* "Non-fulfilment of a requirement" *(ISO/IEC 27000)*. See also major nonconformity, minor nonconformity, observation. *Cf.* conformity, noncompliance.
Non-**D**isclosure **A**greement **(NDA)**	Understanding, perhaps contractual and legally binding, between two or more parties to share confidential information (**I**ntellectual **P**roperty that may be proprietary, personal, or official) between themselves but not to disclose it to third parties except by mutual authorisation, or unless legally obliged to do so. May not expressly

TERM	MEANING
	prohibit the recipient from exploiting the information themselves, although most Westerners would consider that unethical and inappropriate. "A legal contract between at least two parties that outlines confidential materials the parties wish to share with one another for certain purposes but wish to restrict from generalized use; a contract through which the parties agree not to disclose information covered by the agreement. Notes: Also called a confidential disclosure agreement (CDA), confidentiality agreement or secrecy agreement, an NDA creates a confidential relationship between the parties to protect any type of trade secret. As such, an NDA can protect non-public business information. In the case of certain governmental entities, the confidentiality of information other than trade secrets may be subject to applicable statutory requirements, and in some cases must be revealed to an outside party requesting the information. Generally, the governmental entity will include a provision in the contract to allow the seller to review a request for information that the seller identifies as confidential and the seller may appeal such a decision requiring disclosure. NDAs are commonly signed when two companies or individuals are considering doing business together and need to understand the processes used in one another's businesses solely for the purpose of evaluating the potential business relationship. NDAs can be 'mutual,' meaning that both parties are restricted in their use of the materials provided, or they can only restrict a single party. It is also possible for an employee to sign an NDA or NDA-like agreement with a company at the time of hiring; in fact, some employment agreements will include a clause restricting 'confidential information' in general" *(ISACA glossary)*.
Non-disclosure of communications	Keeping both data content and metadata relating to datacommunications confidential to the communicating parties. "Requirement not to disclose the existence, the content, the source, the destination and the date and time of communicated information" *(ISO/IEC 27011)*.
Non-Executive **D**irector **(NED), nonexec, independent director, external director**	Board member without executive responsibilities (not a member of the executive/senior management team) nor an employee or material owner of the organisation, providing independent oversight, objective guidance, and wisdom on significant governance and strategic matters such as senior management appointments, performance and compensation, enterprise risk and assurance. May be compensated like a consultant for their time and expenses, or purely voluntary (despite the duties and liabilities).
Nonfunctional requirement	Broad category of application requirements *other* than the business functions so eagerly anticipated and commonly specified as functional requirements by users, concerning aspects such as technology platforms, middleware, and networking; system installation, configuration, monitoring, and administration/management; cybersecurity; capacity and performance for efficient use of

TERM	MEANING
	resources; resilience; compliance and conformity; and support and maintenance – essentially everything that enables and supports the delivery of valuable, usable, cost-effective, and secure information processing, aside from the actual processing.
Non-interactive authentication	"Authentication between systems or services that does not involve the interaction of a person" *(AusISM)*.
Non-interactive user identity	Type of userID intended for automated system logons and file/resource ownership by computers and applications, rather than by people.
Non-**O**fficial **C**over **(NOC)**	Spooky term for a mole, a spy working undercover on behalf of an intelligence agency, posing as an ordinary, innocuous worker such as a journalist, academic, or consultant. *Cf.* **N**etwork **O**perations **C**entre.
Non-repudiation	Having sufficient evidence to prove that something (such as a business transaction or activity by a specific individual) did or did not take place as claimed. An integrity control. "Ability to prove the occurrence of a claimed event or action and its originating entities" *(ISO/IEC 27002)*. "The assurance that a party cannot later deny originating data; provision of proof of the integrity and origin of the data, verifiable by a third party. Note: A digital signature can provide nonrepudiation" *(ISACA glossary)*. "Providing proof that a user performed an action, and in doing so preventing a user from denying that they did so" *(AusISM)*. "The ability for a system to prove that a specific user and only that specific user sent a message and that it hasn't been modified" *(SANS glossary)*. *Cf.* repudiation, plausible deniability.
Nonstatistical sampling	Unscientific, informal, or casual sampling. "Method of selecting a portion of a population, based in professional judgment and experience, for the purpose of quickly confirming a proposition. This method does not allow drawing mathematical conclusions regarding the entire population" *(ISACA glossary)*. *Cf.* random sampling.
Nonverbal communication, non-vocal communication, body language	Animals, including humans, communicate in many ways besides spoken or written language – and even then, the way words are expressed usually conveys additional information beyond the literal meaning, *e.g.* through gestures, posture, intonation, volume, cadence, pace, and emphasis. Increases the possibility of information leakage or side-channel communications since we are often both unaware of, and less able to control, *how* we express things as opposed to *what* we say.
Non-volatile flash memory media	"A specific type of electrically erasable programmable read-only memory" *(AusISM)*.
Non-volatile storage, nonvolatile storage	Disk, tape, flash memory, or other information storage medium (*e.g.* stone tablet, DNA) that can passively store data for years without power. "Storage device whose contents are not lost when power is cut off" *(ISO/IEC 2382)*. "Storage that retains its contents even after power is removed" *(ISO/IEC 27040)*.

TERM	MEANING
Non-volatile medium	Permanent (technically, semi-permanent, *i.e.* medium to long-term) storage medium such as stone or wax tablet, paper, vinyl, CD, or USB memory stick. "A type of media which retains its information when power is removed" *(NZISM)*.
N00b, noob	Leet term for a 'newbie,' someone relatively new to hacking, implying a degree of naïveté, lack of knowledge, innocence, inexperience, and/or incompetence – a pert, not an expert.
Normalisation	Scientific process of scaling raw values in a sample to match the range of equivalent samples, negating any per-sample offset attributable to the measurement or analytical methods, ambient conditions, time of collection, *etc.* "The conversion of information into consistent representations and categorization" *(NIST SP 800-55v1)*. "1. The elimination of redundant data. 2. The process of converting an actual range of values into a standard range of values, typically −1 to +1 or 0 to 1" *(ISACA glossary)*.
Norms	"Customs, rules, or expectations that a group socially reinforces, usually through informal means" *(OCEG GRC Glossary)*.
North American **E**lectric **R**eliability **C**orporation **C**ritical **I**nfrastructure **P**rotection **(NERC CIP)**	Set of cybersecurity standards and guidelines for the American and Canadian electricity infrastructure, covering ten domains: asset identification and inventory, security assessment and authorisation, personnel security, physical security, operations security, communications security, information security, event management, security controls testing, and vulnerability management.
No Such Agency	See **N**ational **S**ecurity **A**gency.
Notification	Formal disclosure of an event or incident such as a privacy breach to stakeholders such as relevant authorities and the victims (data subjects), generally to satisfy legal compliance obligations (including those imposed by contracts with other organisations). "Part of public warning that provides essential information to people at risk regarding the decisions and actions necessary to cope with an emergency situation" *(ISO 22300)*.
Notifying authority	"The national authority responsible for setting up and carrying out the necessary procedures for the assessment, designation and notification of conformity assessment bodies and for their monitoring" *(EU CRA)*.
NotPetya	Species of ransomware in the wild in 2017. A broken variant of Petya with nonfunctional decryption keys. Tens of thousands of Maersk computers had to be rebuilt and restored from backups after a NotPetya outbreak.

TERM	MEANING
Not **S**afe **F**or **W**ork **(NSFW)**	Has inappropriate/indecent adult/pornographic content. Aside from its offensiveness, it may be illegal or conflict with corporate policies to access, create, or communicate such material while at work or via the organisation's networks and computer equipment.
NPSA	*Abbrev:* **N**ational **P**rotective **S**ecurity **A**uthority.
NRR	*Abbrev:* **N**ational **R**isk **R**egister.
NSA	*Abbrev:* **N**ational **S**ecurity **A**gency.
NSFW	*Abbrev:* **N**ot **S**afe **F**or **W**ork.
NTA	*Abbrev:* **N**etwork **T**raffic **A**nalysis or **N**ational **T**echnical **A**uthority, depending on context.
NTLM (Windows NT LAN Manager)	Old Microsoft suite of cryptographic protocols used for network user authentication and traffic encryption. Does not support modern algorithms and is vulnerable to brute force attacks, hence deprecated in favour of Kerberos.
Nuclear	Crimeware kit.
Nuclear, **B**iological and **C**hemical **(NBC)**	Refers to the risk of terrorist or military attacks potentially involving 'dirty bombs' spreading radioactive material, genetically engineered microbes, and Sarin-type poisonous chemical incidents, as opposed to nuclear bombs or kinetic (violent/explosive) and milder methods. See also **Ch**emical, **B**iological, **R**adiological, and **Nu**clear.
Null session, anonymous logon	"A way of letting an anonymous user retrieve information such as user names and shares over the network or connect without authentication. It is used by applications such as explorer.exe to enumerate shares on remote servers" *(SANS glossary)*.
NZ Eyes Only	"A caveat indicating that the information is not to be passed to or accessed by foreign nationals" *(NZISM)*. Similar designations are used as refinements modifying the usual national security classifications *e.g.* "SECRET: AUS, US and UK Eyes Only."
NZISM	See **N**ew **Z**ealand **I**nformation **S**ecurity **M**anual.
NZSTE	See **N**ew **Z**ealand **S**ecurity **T**hreat **E**nvironment.

O

TERM	MEANING
0-day, 'oh-day'	See zero-day.
OAuth2 (Open Authentication version 2.0), OAuth	User authentication standard (also termed a framework, *i.e.* a system and protocol) in which Resource Owners (Information Technology users) need to be authorised by trusted **A**uthorisation **S**ervers and granted a token in order for their Clients to gain access to their resources hosted by **R**esource **S**ervers over HTTP. Specified in RFC 6749. See also device code flow, OpenID Connect. More info: https://www.rfc-base.org/txt/rfc-6749.txt
Obfuscation	Deliberately hiding or concealing the true nature or extent of something, such as a person's identity, a hacker's location, the fact that an attack is taking or has taken place, malware code, or other confidential information. "The deliberate act of creating source or machine code that is difficult for humans to understand" *(ISACA glossary)*. See also steganography, redaction.
Object	a. *[Noun]* Something tangible. "Item characterized through the measurement of its attributes" *(ISO/IEC 27000)*. "Single and distinct entity that can be identified" *(ISO 22300)*. b. *[Noun]* Purpose, focus or aim of something. See also objective. c. *[Verb]* To resist, refuse, or complain about something.
Object code	See machine code. "Machine-readable instructions produced from a compiler or assembler program that has accepted and translated the source code" *(ISACA glossary)*.
Objective	a. *[Noun]* Intended purpose, direction or outcome from something, whether interim (milestone) or ultimate (goal), realistic or aspirational (stretch target, bullseye, aiming point). "A statement of a desired outcome" *(ISACA glossary)*. "Result to be achieved. Notes: an objective can be strategic, tactical, or operational; objectives can relate to different disciplines (such as financial, health and safety, and environmental goals) and can apply at different levels (such as strategic, organisation-wide, project, product and process). An objective can be expressed in other ways, *e.g.* as an intended outcome, a purpose, an operational criterion, as an information security objective or by the use of other words with similar meaning (*e.g.* aim, goal, or target). In the context of information security management systems, information security objectives are set by the organisation, consistent with the information security policy, to achieve specific results" *(ISO/IEC 27000)*. "A measurable outcome to achieve" *(OCEG GRC Glossary)*. b. *[Adjective]* Dispassionate, factual, evidence-based, rational, balanced, impartial, equitable, *etc. Cf.* subjective.

TERM	MEANING
Objective evidence	Objective evidence. Facts indicating, demonstrating, confirming, or proving something without subjectivity, bias, prejudice, *etc.* "Data supporting the existence or verity of something. Note: Objective evidence can be obtained through observation, measurement, test, or other means" *(ISO 9000)*. "Artifacts or affirmations used as indicators of the implementation or habit and persistence of processes to meet the intent and value of one or more model practices" *(ISACA glossary)*.
Objective in appearance	"The avoidance of facts and circumstances that are so significant that a reasonable and informed third party would be likely to conclude, weighing all the specific facts and circumstances, that a firm, audit function or a member of the audit team's integrity, objectivity or professional skepticism has been compromised" *(ISACA glossary)*.
Objective of mind	"The state of mind that permits the expression of a conclusion without being affected by influences that compromise professional judgment, thereby allowing an individual to act with integrity and exercise objectivity and professional skepticism" *(ISACA glossary)*.
Objective-setting criteria	"The criteria used to set objectives and results in accordance with the organization's direction" *(OCEG GRC Glossary)*.
Objectivity	Capabilities of being objective, independent, impartial, unbiased, *etc.* "The degree to which an Assurance Provider can be impartial, disinterested, independent, and free to conduct necessary activities and to form an opinion about the subject matter" *(OCEG GRC Glossary)*. "An unbiased mental attitude that allows internal auditors to make professional judgments, fulfill their responsibilities, and achieve the Purpose of Internal Auditing without compromise" *(IIA GIAS)*. "The ability to exercise judgment, express opinions and present recommendations with impartiality" *(ISACA glossary)*. *Cf.* subjectivity.
Object of labelling	Item being labelled. "IoT product seeking eligibility and currently being assessed for a particular cybersecurity label" *(ISO/IEC 27404 DRAFT)*.
Obligation	Something one is obliged/obligated, forced, mandated, compelled, or required to do or not to do, *e.g.* to comply with relevant laws, regulations, contracts, and policies. "A requirement that an organization must or should address because of a promise, whether mandatory or voluntary" *(OCEG GRC Glossary)*. See also responsibility, accountability.

TERM	MEANING
Obscure	a. *[Noun]* Unclear, uncertain, unknown, concealed, hidden, rare. b. *[Verb]* To hide or conceal something from view. "Block the user's view of part or all of a displayed object with another. Example: To partially block one window with another" *(ISO/IEC 2382)*. See also redaction.
Observation	a. Information that an observer observes, notes, perceives, and perhaps records and reports. "The receipt of messages through electronic, sensory or vibrational signals and the human senses" *(ISACA glossary)*. b. In the context of conformity certification, an audit finding that is not sufficiently significant or relevant to constitute a nonconformity, perhaps an improvement opportunity, issue/concern, or something peripheral/out of scope, reported for management's information and consideration.
Observational data	"Data captured through the observation of an activity or behavior without the direct involvement of the subject" *(NIST SP 800-55v1)*.
Observer	Person (ideally, someone suitably independent, competent, objective, diligent, authorised, *etc.*) who passively watches and listens to something, whether literally or figuratively, typically gathering and evaluating information, and providing feedback for one or more stakeholders. "Person who accompanies the audit team but does not audit" *(ISO/IEC 17021-1)*. "Participant who witnesses the exercise while remaining separate from exercise activities. Note: Observers can be part of the evaluation process" *(ISO 22300)*.
Obstacle	Something that blocks or impedes movement, whether physically or conceptually. "An uncertain future event that may, on balance, have a negative effect on objectives" *(OCEG GRC Glossary)*.
Occupational fraud	Fraud committed by a worker against the organisation for which they work. Strictly speaking the definition excludes fraud committed by workers against third parties by means of the organisation's facilities (*e.g.* its phone and email services, company letterhead), although that may constitute a failure to conform with corporate policies, codes of ethics, *etc.* could be corporate fraud, and may well be illegal.
OCEG	US-based nonprofit organisation and community of professionals specialising in **G**overnance, **R**isk, and **C**ompliance plus related areas such as ethics. Founded in 2002 as the **O**pen **C**ompliance and **E**thics **G**roup. More info: https://www.oceg.org/
OCEG GRC glossary	OCEG's glossary of about 350 **G**overnance, **R**isk, and **C**ompliance terms, available in several languages. More info: https://www.oceg.org/glossary/en/

TERM	MEANING
OCEG GRC Capability Model, 'Red Book'	OCEG's **G**overnance, **R**isk, and **C**ompliance capability model/ framework plus strategy, audit, ethics/culture and **I**nformation **T**echnology. Members (subscribers) can purchase an extended version covering tools and techniques. See also GRC Assessment Framework. More info: https://www.oceg.org/grc-capability-model-red-book/
OCO	*Abbrev:* **O**ffensive **C**yberspace **O**perations.
OCR	*Abbrev:* **O**ptical **C**haracter **R**ecognition.
OCSP	*Abbrev:* **O**nline **C**ertificate **S**tatus **P**rotocol.
OCTAVE (Operationally Critical Threat, Asset, and Vulnerability Evaluation)	Framework for systematically identifying and managing information security risks, developed by **C**arnegie **M**ellon **U**niversity's **S**oftware **E**ngineering **I**nstitute in 1999. The process involves identifying information assets that are important to the organisation's mission, plus the associated threats and the vulnerabilities that may expose those assets to the threats. More info: https://insights.sei.cmu.edu/library/operationally-critical-threat-asset-and-vulnerability-evaluation-octave-framework-version-10/
Octet	Block of eight bits, normally denoted a byte, which is sufficient to encode up to 256 characters and symbols. "A sequence of eight bits. An octet is an eight-bit byte" *(SANS glossary).*
Offensive cyber	a. Obnoxious overuse of the undefined and unclear term 'cyber.' b. Offensive security. "Adding, deleting or manipulating data on systems or networks to deliver a physical, virtual or cognitive effect. Offensive cyber operations often exploit technical vulnerabilities, use systems or networks in ways that their owners and operators would not intend or condone, and may rely on deception or misrepresentation" *(UK National Cyber Security Strategy 2022).*
Offensive **C**yberspace **O**perations **(OCO)**	Offensive security through the Internet, generally conducted by agents operating at arms-length from the instigator. "Cyberspace operations intended to project power by the application of force in or through cyberspace" *(DoD dictionary).*
Offensive security, proactive security	Whereas most information security controls are passive and/or reactive in nature, offensive or proactive security involves 'taking the fight to the attacker,' *e.g.* by disrupting criminal organisations or deliberately goading, provoking, or enticing hackers to attack honeypot systems. Focuses on the threat or threat agent components of risk. *Cf.* defensive security.

TERM	MEANING
Off-hook audio protection	"A method of mitigating the possibility of an active, but temporarily unattended handset inadvertently allowing discussions being undertaken in the vicinity of the handset to be heard by the remote party. This could be achieved through the use of a hold feature, mute feature, push-to-talk handset or equivalent. May not be effective on smart phones/cell phones" *(NZISM)*. "A method of mitigating the possibility of an active handset inadvertently allowing background discussions to be heard by a remote party. This can be achieved through the use of a hold feature, mute feature, push-to-talk handset or equivalent" *(AusISM)*.
Official information	Class/category of information typically relating to governmental administration, *etc.* "Any information held by a government department or agency. See the Official Information Act 1982 (as amended)" *(NZISM)*.
Offline, off-line	Disconnected from the network. Neither available nor accessible for usage and administration by electronic/digital means, whether by intention or due to an incident. Offline backups and archives, for instance, may be saved onto portable storage media such as magnetic tapes, DVDs, USB memory sticks, or magnetic disks, then physically unplugged and removed into secure storage such as a firesafe unless/until restoration is needed under carefully controlled conditions to minimise risks. "Pertaining to the operation of a functional unit that takes place either independently of, or in parallel with, the main operation of a computer" *(ISO/IEC 2382)*. *Cf.* off-network and online.
Off-network, off-net	Similar to offline but can refer to functional standalone systems, storage devices, *etc.* that are physically air-gapped or otherwise isolated from networks, particularly the Internet. *Cf.* online.
O-ISM3 (Open Group Information Security Management Maturity Model)	Open Group's free information risk and security management standard combines a business-driven perspective with a maturity model. Defines 45 information security processes and metrics comprising a **M**anagement **S**ystem. Version 2.0 was published in 2017. More info: https://www.opengroup.org/forum/security/infosecmanagement
OLA	*Abbrev:* **O**perational **L**evel **A**greement.
OMB Circular A-130	US government **O**ffice of **M**anagement and **B**udget circular "Managing Information as a Strategic Resource." More info: https://obamawhitehouse.archives.gov/sites/default/files/omb/assets/OMB/circulars/a130/a130revised.pdf

TERM	MEANING
One-**T**ime **P**ad **(OTP)**	*Theoretically* unbreakable cryptosystem which uses a randomly generated shared key at least as long as the plaintext. While the algorithm may be as simple and efficient as a bitwise exclusive-OR (XOR) operation (as in stream ciphers), achieving the full theoretical strength in practice means the encryption key *must* be truly random and *must* never be reused (other than for decryption!), creating key generation and distribution problems in addition to the need to restrict knowledge of the key to the authorised parties. Implementation flaws (such as those affecting **P**seudo**R**andom **N**umber **G**eneration) and process issues (such as users or systems disclosing or reusing the key) limit the security achievable in practice. See also **O**ne-**T**ime **P**assword, Vernam cipher.
One-**T**ime **P**assword **(OTP), single use password**	Password generated and used just once, using a pseudo-random method of generation that can be replicated by the authenticating system. Usually implemented in a dedicated hardware security token such as RSA's SecureID. Although *theoretically* strong, implementation flaws (such as **P**seudo**R**andom **N**umber **G**eneration and unlimited attempts to guess passwords) and procedural issues (such as **M**an-**I**n-**T**he-**M**iddle attacks) limit the security achievable in practice. See also **T**ime-based **O**ne-**T**ime **P**assword, **O**ne-**T**ime **P**ad, nonce.
One-way encryption	See hash. "Irreversible transformation of plaintext to cipher text, such that the plaintext cannot be recovered from the cipher text by other than exhaustive procedures even if the cryptographic key is known" *(SANS glossary)*.
One-way function	Hash function. "A (mathematical) function, f, which is easy to compute the output based on a given input. However given only the output value it is impossible (except for a brute force attack) to figure out what the input value is" *(SANS glossary)*. See also trapdoor function.
Online, on-line	State of a computer system, application, or service in which it is functional and available to users, particularly via networks such as the Internet. "Pertaining to the operation of a functional unit when under the control of a computer" *(ISO/IEC 2382)*. *Cf.* offline and off-network.
Online **C**ertificate **S**tatus **P**rotocol **(OCSP)**	Network protocol to determine whether an X.509 digital certificate has or has not been revoked by the applicable **C**ertification **A**uthority. "A protocol used for receiving the status of an X.509 certificate" *(ISACA glossary)*. *Cf.* **C**ertificate **R**evocation **L**ist.

TERM	MEANING
Online chat	Online electronic messaging services (such as **I**nstant **M**essaging, SMS/TXT, and email) and social media used for person-to-person communications through the Internet, cellular, or other networks. Vulnerable to malware, disclosure of confidential information, social engineering, spam/SPIM, misinformation, misinterpretation, and various other information security threats.
Online services	Online services. "Services such as social media, online collaboration tools, web browsing, instant messaging, IP telephony, video conferencing, file sharing websites and peer-to-peer applications" *(AusISM)*.
Online storage	See cloud storage.
Online **T**rust **A**lliance **(OTA)**	Industry body representing the commercial interests of a group of vendors of *things*. The name of the group is somewhat ironic given the sorry state of security in the **I**nternet **o**f ***T**hings* at present, and widespread distrust of the vendors responsible.
On-**T**he-**F**ly **E**ncryption **(OTFE), real-time encryption, transparent encryption, live encryption**	Digital data are automatically encrypted as they are stored to disk or into the cloud, and decrypted when retrieved for processing. *Provided* the cryptographic system and keys are sufficiently robust, this reduces the risk of unauthorised access to stored data. The decrypted plaintext remains vulnerable in RAM.
Open door policy	Notional if not literal term for someone (generally a manager) making the effort to be approachable, open, willing to listen to, and deal appropriately with, concerns expressed informally by workers, encouraging them to communicate or interact.
OpenDNS	Part of CISCO providing **D**omain **N**ame **S**ystem services, phishing protection, content filtering, cloud security products, and PhishTank. More info: https://www.opendns.com/
Open Group – **R**isk Taxonomy **(O-RT)**	Open Group's taxonomy of risks, version 3.0.1 (2021). "Provides a standard definition and taxonomy for information security risk, as well as information regarding how to use the taxonomy." More info: https://publications.opengroup.org/standards/open-fair-standards/c20b
OpenID Connect	User identification standard building on the user authentication provided by OAuth2. A client verifies the userID and obtains his/her profile. Specified by Microsoft, Google, and others. More info: https://openid.net/specs/openid-connect-core-1_0.html
Openness	See transparency.

TERM	MEANING
OpenPGP	Email cryptosystem that complies with relevant IETF standards. Whereas the original **P**retty **G**ood **P**rivacy incorporated licensed **I**ntellectual **P**roperty, OpenPGP is open-source freeware, unencumbered by licence restrictions. "An open-source implementation of Pretty Good Privacy (PGP), a widely available cryptographic toolkit" *(NZISM)*. See also GPG, S/MIME. More info: https://www.openpgp.org/
OpenPGP Message Format	"An open-source implementation of Pretty Good Privacy, a widely available cryptographic toolkit" *(AusISM)*.
Open relay	Email server that does not properly authenticate email senders, allowing unauthorised parties to send email – typically spam.
Open **S**ecurity **C**ontrols **A**ssessment **L**anguage **(OSCAL)**	NIST-led initiative developing XML, JSON, and YAML machine-readable control catalogues, baselines, system security plans, assessment plans and results, to facilitate automated control assessments, reviews, or audits. More info: https://pages.nist.gov/OSCAL/
Open-source	Software source code that is intentionally disclosed to the public by its owner, whether as a purely benevolent act, to facilitate independent review, or to encourage others to collaborate on or continue the development. See also **F**ree **O**pen-**S**ource **S**oftware, source available. Note: simply releasing or disclosing **I**ntellectual **P**roperty *per se* does not necessarily mean that the owner surrenders all their **I**ntellectual **P**roperty **R**ights unless they explicitly place it into the public domain.
Open Source **S**ecurity **F**oundation **(OpenSSF)**	Community of practice that facilitates collaboration and sharing of good practices and innovative approaches to secure open-source software. More info: https://openssf.org/
Open **S**ource **S**ecurity **T**esting **M**ethodology **M**anual **(OSSTMM)**	200+ pages of free guidance from ISECOM on how to test security. "A methodology to test the operational security of physical locations, human interactions, and all forms of communications such as wireless, wired, analog, and digital." More info: https://www.isecom.org/OSSTMM.3.pdf
Open-source software steward	"A legal person, other than a manufacturer, that has the purpose or objective of systematically providing support on a sustained basis for the development of specific products with digital elements, qualifying as free and open-source software and intended for commercial activities, and that ensures the viability of those products" *(EU CRA)*.
OpenSSH	Popular UNIX client-server application for. More info: https://www.openssh.com/

TERM	MEANING
OpenSSL	Popular open-source software library for secure network communications widely used by Internet servers to provide **S**ecure **S**ockets **L**ayer and **T**ransport **L**ayer **S**ecurity for HTTPS under Apache, and *many* other cryptographic algorithms for encryption, hashing, **P**ublic **K**ey **I**nfrastructure, and key exchange. Maintained and supported by the **O**penSSL **S**oftware **F**oundation. OpenSSL vulnerabilities such as the one exploited in Heartbleed are problematic due to its ubiquity. More info: https://www.openssl.org/
Open **S**upervised **D**evice **P**rotocol **(OSDP)**	Technical standard for connecting proximity card and biometric readers, keypads, *etc.* to physical security systems controlling workers' access through security gates, doors, turnstiles, *etc.* 'Secure Channel' is an optional facility to encrypt OSDP communications between devices, although vulnerabilities have been identified due to implementation and operational flaws.
Open **S**ystems **I**nterconnection **(OSI) reference model, OSI stack**	Conceptual model for datacommunications, notable for defining the seven-layer network stack, an integrated, modular set of conceptual layers (1/physical [base layer], 2/data link, 3/network, 4/transport, 5/session, 6/presentation, and 7/application [top layer]), each providing separate classes of service or function that build on those provided by the lower layers and support those above. Developed by ISO standardisation projects in the 1970s and 80s, becoming ISO/IEC 7498-1 in 1994. "Model that describes the general principles of open systems interconnection and the network architecture resulting from those principles. Note: This model, described in ISO 7498 and CCITT X.200, provides a framework for co-ordinating the development of standards which refer to it" *(ISO/IEC 2382)*. "A standard description or 'reference model' for how messages should be transmitted between any two points in a telecommunication network. Its purpose is to guide product implementers so that their products will consistently work with other products. The reference model defines seven layers of functions that take place at each end of a communication. Although OSI is not always strictly adhered to in terms of keeping related functions together in a well-defined layer, many if not most products involved in telecommunication make an attempt to describe themselves in relation to the OSI model. It is also valuable as a single reference view of communication that furnishes everyone a common ground for education and discussion" *(SANS glossary)*. *Cf.* TCP/IP stack, stack.
OpenVAS	Open-source network security/penetration testing/hacking tool derived from Nessus *before* it became a commercial tool. More info: https://www.openvas.org/

TERM	MEANING
Operating effectiveness	"Evidence that actions & controls operate as intended. This is accomplished by substantive testing of information generated by actions & controls to judge actual results against expected results" *(OCEG GRC Glossary)*. "If a control is operating as designed and the person performing the control possesses the necessary authority and competence to perform the control effectively, the control is considered to be operating effectively" *(ITAF)*.
Operating **S**ystem **(OS)**	Privileged software and/or firmware that operates (directs, monitors, and controls) the hardware of a computer system (sometimes through a hypervisor), providing the operating environment and services through which software applications interact with the hardware. In conjunction with physical security controls, the OS is primarily responsible for securing the system as a whole. Microsoft Windows, MacOS/iOS, Android, and UNIX/Linux are popular examples. "Software that controls the execution of programs and that may provide services such as resource allocation, scheduling, input-output control, and data management. Note: Although operating systems are predominantly software, partial hardware implementations are possible" *(ISO/IEC 2382)*. "A master control program that runs the computer and acts as a scheduler and traffic controller. Notes: The operating system is the first program copied into the computer memory after the computer is turned on; it must reside in memory at all times. It is the software that interfaces between the computer hardware (disk, keyboard, mouse, network, modem and printer) and the application software (word processor, spreadsheet email) which also controls access to the devices, is partially responsible for security components and sets the standards for the application programs that run in it" *(ISACA glossary)*. "System software on enterprise assets that manages computer hardware and software resources, and provides common services for programs. Operating systems are considered a software asset and can be single- and multi-tasking, single- and multiuser, distributed, templated, embedded, real-time, and library" *(CIS Controls)*.
Operation, operations (ops), operational, operating	a. Routine activity within an organisation, particularly those associated with production and core business. b. Discrete activity or step within a process, such as an arithmetic or cryptographic operation. c. Project or initiative or the team responsible as in 'special ops.'
Operational audit	Operational audit. "An audit designed to evaluate the various internal controls, economy and efficiency of a function or department" *(ISACA glossary)*.

TERM	MEANING
Operational control	Operational control. "Deals with the everyday operation of a company or enterprise to ensure that all objectives are achieved" *(ISACA glossary)*.
Operational information	Operational information. "Information that has been contextualized and analysed to provide an understanding of the situation and its possible evolution" *(ISO 22300)*.
Operational **L**evel **A**greement **(OLA)**	"An internal agreement covering the delivery of services that supports the IT organization in its delivery of services" *(ISACA glossary)*. See also **S**ervice **L**evel **A**greement.
Operational resilience	Operational resilience. "The ability of an entity to deliver critical operations through disruptions" *(NZ Financial Markets Authority)*.
Operational risk	All manner of risks associated with an organisation's operations, potentially compromising any of its assets and impacting the business. "The potential for losses caused by inadequate systems or controls, human error or mismanagement, and natural disasters" *(ISACA glossary)*.
Operational **T**echnology **(OT)**	Operational technology, *i.e.* **S**upervisory **C**ontrol **A**nd **D**ata **A**cquisition, **I**ndustrial **C**ontrol **S**ystems, **P**rogrammable **L**ogic **C**ontrollers, and other systems used to operate, manage, monitor, and control the operation of industrial plant and manufacturing operations, as distinct from the **I**nformation **T**echnology used for business and commercial administration (accounting, email, *etc.*). Due to the costs and other impacts when production is disrupted, uptime (availability, resilience, capacity, and performance) is a major concern with OT, plus health and safety and environmental risks. As OT systems and networks are increasingly being connected to the Internet rather than being confined to isolated factory-floor networks, the threats and hence information risks are changing markedly – a particular concern for legacy OT devices using inherently insecure protocols. "Technology for detecting, managing or causing change through the monitoring or control of a physical entity" *(IEC)*. "Combine hardware and software to monitor, control and automate physical processes, particularly in industrial sectors such as energy, manufacturing, water, and transport" *(UK National Cyber Security Strategy 2022)*. See also **I**ndustrial **I**nternet **o**f **T**hings, cyber-physical system, **C**ommunications **T**echnology, **M**obile **T**echnology, **V**irtual **T**echnology, **S**mart **T**echnology.
Operations **Sec**urity **(OPSEC)**	"Systematic and proven process by which potential adversaries can be denied information about capabilities and intentions by identifying, controlling, and protecting generally unclassified evidence of the planning and execution of sensitive activities. The process involves five steps: identification of critical information, analysis of threats, analysis of vulnerabilities, assessment of risks, and application of appropriate countermeasures" *(CNSSI 4009)*. *Cf.* **sec**urity **op**erations.

TERM	MEANING
Operative	Someone who recruits agents to obtain confidential information for them from target organisations. Usually works undercover, *e.g.* posing as a journalist, tourist, or entrepreneur with a seemingly legitimate and innocuous use for the information. Quite spooky though.
Opportunity	Upside of risk, *i.e.* the uncertain possibility of a decision, event, or situation perhaps turning out well, leading to a beneficial outcome or payoff. "Combination of circumstances expected to be favourable to objectives. Notes: An opportunity is a positive situation in which gain is likely and over which one has a fair level of control; An opportunity to one party may pose a threat to another; Taking or not taking an opportunity are both sources of risk" *(ISO 31073).* "An uncertain event that may positively impact meeting objectives" *(ISACA glossary).* "An uncertain future event that may, on balance, have a positive effect on objectives" *(OCEG GRC Glossary).*
Optical **C**haracter **R**ecognition **(OCR)**	"Conversion of images of typed, printed or handwritten text into machine-encoded text" *(ISO/IEC 22989).*
OPSEC	*Abbrev:* **Op**erations **Sec**urity.
Opt-in	Giving someone the option to provide and permit their personal information to be used or communicated for some purpose *only* if they explicitly permit or consent to do so – in other words, the default assumption (in the absence of a valid positive response) is that they do *not* so consent. "Process or type of policy whereby the personally identifiable information (PII) principal is required to take an action to express explicit, prior consent for their PII to be processed for a particular purpose. Note: A different term that is often used with the privacy principle 'consent and choice' is 'opt-out.' It describes a process or type of policy whereby the PII principal is required to take a separate action in order to withhold or withdraw consent, or oppose a specific type of processing. The use of an opt-out policy presumes that the PII controller has the right to process the PII in the intended way. This right can be implied by some action of the PII principal different from consent (*e.g.* placing an order in an online shop)" *(ISO/IEC 29100).* "A declaration or an active motion in which a data subject agrees to particular data processing. Process or type of policy whereby the personally identifiable information (PII) principal is required to take an action to express explicit, prior consent for their PII to be processed for a particular purpose" *(ISACA glossary). Cf.* opt-out.
Opt-out	Giving someone the option to indicate that they *do not* wish their personal information to be used or communicated for some purpose, the default assumption (in the absence of a valid negative response) being that they *do* so permit. "A choice that is made on behalf of a data subject, indicating the subject's desire to no longer receive unsolicited information" *(ISACA glossary). Cf.* opt-in.

TERM	MEANING
Ordinal scale	"From the Stevens Scale of Measurement, a scale that orders and ranks data without establishing a degree of variation between ranks" *(NIST SP 800-55v1).*
Organisation, corporation, business, [commercial] entity, group	Deliberately vague terms for a body of people to some extent structured, directed, aligned, and governed/controlled as one, typically referring to conventional commercial companies or corporations but may also mean partnerships, charities and not-for-profits, (parts of) governments and agencies, groups, clubs, teams, *etc.* "Person or group of people that has its own functions with responsibilities, authorities and relationships to achieve its objectives. Note: the concept of organisation includes but is not limited to sole-trader, company, corporation, firm, enterprise, authority, partnership, charity or institution, or part or combination thereof, whether incorporated or not, public or private" *(ISO/IEC 27000). [Additional note]* "If the organization is part of a larger entity, the term 'organization' refers only to the part of the larger entity that is within the scope of the privacy information management system" *(ISO/IEC 27701).* "The manner in which an enterprise is structured. It can also mean the entity" *(ISACA glossary).* "An entity of any size, complexity, or positioning within an organizational structure" *(NIST SP 800-171).*
Organisational control	In ISO/IEC 27002, a catch-all theme (category) for information security controls that do not fit neatly into the people control, physical control, or technological control themes since they do not concern individual people, physical objects, or technology, respectively, or else they involve more than one of those three themes (*e.g.* policies, access controls, privacy). 'Organisational' emphasises the standard's corporate as opposed to individual or societal contexts, applicability, and perspectives.
Organisational culture	Corporate culture within or characteristic of an organisation. "Collective beliefs, values, attitudes and behaviour of an organization that contribute to the unique social and psychological environment in which it operates" *(ISO 22300).*
Organisation-defined parameter	"The variable part of a security requirement that is instantiated by an organization during the tailoring process by assigning an organization-defined value as part of the requirement" *(NIST SP 800-171).*
Organisational layer, organizational level	"A unit within an organization that is responsible for specific tasks, functions, decisions, actions, and controls and typically referenced in relationship to other layers" (*OCEG GRC Glossary*).
Organisational resilience	Resilience of an organisation. "Ability of an organization to absorb and adapt in a changing environment" *(ISO 22300).*

TERM	MEANING
Organisational unit	Organisational unit. “The part of an organization that is the subject of an appraisal and to which the appraisal results are generalized. An organizational unit deploys one or more processes that have a coherent process context and defined set of process roles and operate within a coherent set of business objectives” *(ISACA glossary)*. “A specific subdivision of an organization that is formed for the purpose of achieving particular objectives” *(OCEG GRC Glossary)*.
Orientation	a. See induction (course or session). b. A person’s preferences, attitudes and beliefs, *e.g.* sexual, national, cultural, or political orientation. c. Three-dimensional position of an object relative to some reference such as a map.
OSCAL	*Abbrev:* **O**pen **S**ecurity **C**ontrols **A**ssessment **L**anguage.
OSDP	*Abbrev:* **O**pen **S**upervised **D**evice **P**rotocol.
OSINT (Open-Source Intelligence), OSIG (Open-Source Intelligence Gathering)	Prior to attacking, hackers, social engineers, and penetration testers can often obtain pertinent information concerning a target from public domain sources, such as web pages, social media messages, and other materials openly and innocently published by the target, plus official records. See also HUMINT, TECHINT, SIGINT, COMINT, IMINT, ELINT.
OSI stack, OSI	See the **O**pen **S**ystems **I**nterconnection reference model.
OSSTMM	*Abbrev:* **O**pen **S**ource **S**ecurity **T**esting **M**ethodology **M**anual.
OT	*Abbrev:* **O**perational **T**echnology.
OTA	*Abbrev:* **O**nline **T**rust **A**lliance.
OTFE	*Abbrev:* **O**n-**T**he-**F**ly **E**ncryption.
OTP	*Abbrev:* **O**ne-**T**ime **P**ad or **O**ne-**T**ime **P**assword, depending on context.
Outage	Computer or information service interruption caused either by a planned activity (such as scheduled maintenance or backup) or an unplanned incident (such as a blackout, **D**istributed **D**enial-**o**f-**S**ervice attack, bug, or equipment/hardware failure).
Outbreak	Rapidly spreading malware incident, analogous to an escalating biological viral or bacterial infection that puts the authorities and medical profession on high alert. See also Warhol worm.

TERM	MEANING
Outlier	Data value that in some way stands out from others in the set. Might be a genuine exceptional value or a measurement anomaly pointing to an error in the process: either way, it probably deserves further attention. "Extreme values that might be errors in measurement and recording or accurate reports of rare events" *(ISACA glossary)*. "An observation that lies an abnormal distance from other values in a random sample from a population" *(NIST SP 800-55v1)*.
Out-of-band	Distinct, alternative, or unconventional communication path, channel, vehicle, or mechanism pre-arranged between the parties that can be used as a secure, trustworthy route, *e.g.* to exchange cryptographic keys, PIN codes, or passwords, or to validate exceptional instructions. Alternatively, a means to maintain or re-establish contact under emergency conditions when the primary in-band communications are down, to coordinate responses to a serious incident or disaster, *e.g.* voice or datacommunications using radio transceivers when cellphones and emails are out of action. "Communication or transmission that occurs outside of a previously established communication method or channel" *(ISO/IEC 27040)*.
Output analyser	"A tool that checks the accuracy of the results produced by a test run. Notes: There are three types of checks that an output analyzer can perform. First, if a standard set of test data and test results exist for a program, the output of a test run after program maintenance can be compared with the set of results that should be produced. Second, as programmers prepare test data and calculate the expected results, these results can be stored in a file, and the output analyzer compares the actual results of a test run with the expected results. Third, the output analyzer can act as a query language; it accepts queries about whether certain relationships exist in the file of output results and reports compliance or noncompliance" *(ISACA glossary)*.
Output control	Control designed to mitigate unacceptable output risks, *e.g.* post-processing checks to identify and flag or block inappropriate unreasonable, exceptional, extreme, crazy, or malicious outputs from **A**rtificial **I**ntelligence systems. See also input control, processing control.
Output risk	Uncertain possibility of issues arising at the output from a process, unit, application, device, system, interface, phase, step, *etc.* leading to incidents, *e.g.* an overheated electronic temperature sensor on an industrial machine might output a negative or zero value, causing a process control system to misinterpret the unexpected data and increase heating still further, crash, or enter an undefined state. See also input risk, processing risk.

TERM	MEANING
Outsider	Someone not within a closed group, team, club, or organisation. Anyone other than the organisation's employees such as third party employees, members of the public, suppliers, and customers. Generally considered less trustworthy than employees or workers, although arguably that is the information security equivalent of xenophobia. *Cf.* insider.
Outsource, outsourcing, outsourcer	Using services provided by another organisation rather than the organisation's own employees and resources, generally for cost reasons although specialist outsourcers *tend* to be more competent and capable as well as efficient. "Make an arrangement where an external organisation performs part of an organisation's function or process. Note: an external organisation is outside the scope of the management system, although the outsourced function or process is within the scope" *(ISO/IEC 27000)*. "Acquisition of services (with or without products) in support of a business function for performing activities using supplier's resources rather than the acquirer's" *(ISO/IEC 27036-1)*. "A formal agreement with a third party to perform IS or other business functions for an enterprise" *(ISACA glossary)*. "Contracting with an independent external provider of internal audit services. Fully outsourcing a function refers to contracting the entire internal audit function, and partially outsourcing (also called 'cosourcing') indicates that only a portion of the services are outsourced" *(IIA GIAS)*.
Outsourced service provider	"A service provider that performs business processes, operations, or controls on behalf of the entity when such business processes, operations, or controls are necessary to achieve the entity's objectives outsourced service providers" *(Trust Services Criteria)*.
Overlay	Physical or notional layer that filters or modifies something. "A specification of security or privacy controls, control enhancements, supplemental guidance, and other supporting information employed during the tailoring process, that is intended to complement (and further refine) security control baselines. The overlay specification may be more stringent or less stringent than the original security control baseline specification and can be applied to multiple information systems" *(NIST SP 800-171)*.

TERM	MEANING
Overload	Situation in which a digital device gets swamped by an excessive amount or rate of arrival of data, pushing it to enter a limited (and perhaps insecure) fallback mode of operation (*e.g.* ignoring low-priority requests), an undefined (and probably insecure) state, or to fail completely, perhaps locking up and becoming unresponsive (blue screen of death or bricked) or shutting down and rebooting. The computing equivalent of information overload. "Hindrance of system operation by placing excess burden on the performance capabilities of a system component" *(SANS glossary)*.
Overpayment fraud	A fraudster plausibly *claims* to have accidentally paid or overpaid the victim, asking them to repay or forward the amount less a percentage for themselves as an inducement. However, when the original payment is subsequently found to have been fraudulent and is retracted or nullified by the bank (perhaps weeks or months later), the victim is left out of pocket.
Over provision	"Technique used by storage elements and storage devices in which a subset of the available media is exposed through the interface. Note: Storage media is used internally and independently by the storage element to improve performance, endurance, or reliability" *(ISO/IEC 27040)*.
Oversight	a. Literally, the capability and act of observing something. Encompasses various forms of supervision and inspection to ensure that important information risk and security management activities, processes, systems, and controls are operating properly, and to identify any anomalies, incidents, or concerns. "The term is used in this document in the following ways: (1) In the context of governance where the term is used to describe the responsibility and requirement to manage, govern, inspect or direct activities to ensure particular outcomes, *e.g.* the oversight of supply contracts. (2) In the physical security context to describe the ability to observe activity (surveillance) and/or read materials which should be protected and shared only under strict guidelines. It enables the systematic observation of places and people by visual, audio, electronic, photographic or other means. Typically this is caused by poor placing of computer screens and desks and proximity to windows, doors, corridors or other means of physical access and overview or oversight. Other physical factors may contribute" *(NZISM)*. b. Forgetfulness, carelessness, neglect, or incompetence, typically leading to errors, omissions, and other security incidents.

TERM	MEANING
OWASP (Open Worldwide Application Security Project)	Nonprofit foundation and global online community supporting the design and development of secure system, web, and Internet of *Things* software. Mission: "To be the global open community that powers secure software through education, tools, and collaboration." Publishes numerous free standards with Creative Commons licensing to encourage widespread adoption of good practices. More info: https://owasp.org/
OWASP **S**ecure **C**oding **P**ractice **Q**uick **R**eference **G**uide **(SCPQRG)**	OWASP's guidance on developing secure software. "This technology agnostic document defines a set of general software security coding practices, in a checklist format, that can be integrated into the software development lifecycle. Implementation of these practices will mitigate most common software vulnerabilities." More info: https://owasp.org/www-project-secure-coding-practices-quick-reference-guide/stable-en/
Owner, ownership, own	Organisation, rôle, or person who literally/legally or notionally owns and feels responsible for something. May also be accountable for its protection and exploitation. Beyond mere possession, ownership of something generally confers legal and social rights and expectations on its owner, *e.g.* the right to protect and control it (determine access to it, its use and exploitation, disclosure, safekeeping, retention, and disposal, *etc.*), to benefit from its value, and to avoid, or prevent it causing, harm. Valuable things tend to be owned (*i.e.* someone normally claims or holds the legal rights to it) but some are shared, social or societal assets in a broader, collective sense. "Entity that legally controls the licensing and user rights and distribution of the object associated with the unique identifier (UID)" *(ISO 22300)*. "An individual or group that holds or possesses the rights of and the responsibilities for an enterprise, entity or asset. Note: Examples include process owners and system owners" *(ISACA glossary)*. See also asset (and liability), control, domain, file, information, infrastructure, network, process, problem (and solution), product, risk, service, security domain, or system owner.

P

TERM	MEANING
PaaS	*Abbrev:* **P**latform-**as**-**a**-**S**ervice.
PABX	*Abbrev:* **P**rivate **A**utomatic **B**ranch e**X**change.
Packet, datagram	Network message consisting of payload data plus a header with addressing/routing and control information used to protect its integrity *in transit*. "Protocol data unit that is routed from source to destination in a packet-switched network. Notes: A packet contains both routing information and data" *(ISACA glossary)*. "A piece of a message transmitted over a packet-switching network. One of the key features of a packet is that it contains the destination address in addition to the data. In IP networks, packets are often called datagrams" *(SANS glossary)*.
Packet analyser	See sniffer. "A tool that captures packets as they travel a network to monitor, intercept and decode data" *(ISACA glossary)*.
Packet filter	First-generation firewalls examined network packets individually, either passing or blocking them according to the packet content considered in isolation. Simply fragmenting unauthorised content across multiple packets was often sufficient to bypass such crude security checks. "Controlling access to a network by analyzing the attributes of the incoming and outgoing packets and either letting them pass or denying them, based on a list of rules" *(ISACA glossary)*. *Cf.* stateful firewall.
Packet-switched network, packet switching	Network architecture and associated protocols and software that break large messages into pieces (packets), transport them from node to node (dynamically switching/diverting individual packets along the most appropriate routes), then reassemble them correctly on receipt. "The process of transmitting messages in convenient pieces that can be reassembled at the destination" *(ISACA glossary)*. "Where individual packets each follow their own paths through the network from one endpoint to another" *(SANS glossary)*.
Packing, packer	Hacker or VXer term for a code obfuscation technique or tool which encodes executable code within a program that is decoded at runtime, thereby making simple static pattern-matching signature detection against the packed file ineffective as an antivirus technique.
Padcrypt	Species of malware.
Padlock	Physical lock where the shackle can be displaced and rotated away from the hull when unlocked with the correct key or lockpicked, *e.g.* using a shim, bolt-cutter, or grinder.
Palmprint	Like a fingerprint, a person's palm has a characteristic pattern that can be used to identify them. A biometric.

TERM	MEANING
PAN	*Abbrev:* **P**rimary **A**ccount **N**umber or **P**ersonal **A**rea **N**etwork, depending on context.
Pandemic	Global epidemic such as COVID19 – one of a class of major incidents with serious repercussions for the entire global economy.
Pan, **T**ilt, **Z**oom **(PTZ)**	Capability of **C**losed **C**ircuit **T**ele**V**ision cameras to be repositioned and refocused in three dimensions to observe subjects of interest within the field of view, either manually by camera operators under remote control or autonomously using smart auto-tracking. Cameras may be programmed to scan areas/zones systematically or move randomly, making it harder for targets (potentially intruders, shoplifters, *etc.*) to determine whether they are being actively tracked at the time (a deterrent control).
PAP	*Abbrev:* **P**assword **A**uthentication **P**rotocol.
Paper wall	See Chinese wall.
Parallel simulation	"Involves an IS auditor writing a program to replicate those application processes that are critical to an audit opinion and using this program to reprocess application system data. Note: The results produced by parallel simulation are compared with the results generated by the application system and any discrepancies are identified" *(ISACA glossary).* See also parallel test, digital twin.
Parallel test, parallel run	Processing essentially the same data through two variants of the same software (*e.g.* the original and updated or replacement versions) allows them to be checked for differences in the outputs as well as assessing factors such as ease of use and performance. Although it takes substantial effort to run them both, systematically compare the results and analyse any unexpected differences, the increase in familiarity and confidence in a new/changed system may make the testing worthwhile, especially if processing integrity issues are identified and resolved. "The process of feeding test data into two systems, the modified system and an alternative system (possibly the original system), and comparing results to demonstrate the consistency and inconsistency between two versions of the application" *(ISACA glossary).*
Parameter, model parameter	Characteristic, *i.e.* information that characterises something. In software, a variable passed to a function or subroutine. "Specific value describing the measurable or theoretical features of the elements of a system" *(ISO 22300).* "Internal variable of a model that affects how it computes its outputs. Note: Examples of parameters include the weights in a neural network and the transition probabilities in a Markov model" *(ISO/IEC 22989).*

TERM	MEANING
Parity	Literally, equivalence. In datacommunications and data storage, a crude, low-cost data integrity control involves simply appending an extra bit to each byte or word such that the numeric sums of all the bits are even (even parity) or odd (odd parity). Later, if the calculated sum does *not* remain even or odd, respectively, it appears that at least one bit must have changed. "A general hardware control that helps to detect data errors when data are read from memory or communicated from one computer to another. Notes: A 1-bit digit (either 0 or 1) is added to a data item to indicate whether the sum of that data item's bit is odd or even. When the parity bit disagrees with the sum of the other bits, the computer reports an error. The probability of a parity check detecting an error is 50 percent" *(ISACA glossary).* See also **C**yclic **R**edundancy **C**heck, checksum.
Parkerian hexad	In 1998, information security guru Donn Parker extended the classic CIA triad with three additional concepts, namely possession/control, authenticity, and utility. While authenticity may be considered an integral part of integrity, the other two aspects are intriguing security objectives worth considering.
Partial-knowledge attack	Attempt to compromise an **A**rtificial **I**ntelligence system, *etc.* by an adversary with some prior knowledge of the target. "Attack carried out by an attacker who has full understanding of the system inputs and outputs, but only a limited understanding of its internal design and operations. Note: This type of attack does not assume knowledge of credentials" *(ISO/IEC 27090 DRAFT).* See also grey box testing. *Cf.* perfect- and zero-knowledge attacks.
Participant	Person, group, or organisation that takes part in an activity, market, *etc.* "Person or organization who performs a function related to an exercise" *(ISO 22300).*
Partitioning	a. Separation of bare metal and host **O**perating **S**ystem resources between guest systems in virtualisation. b. Separation of networks, physical areas, *etc.* into segments or zones with differing risks and controls, an application of the information security principles of classification and access control.
Part-of-speech tagging	"Task of assigning a category (*e.g.* verb, noun, adjective) to a word based on its grammatical properties" *(ISO/IEC 22989).*
PAS 1192 (Publicly Accessible Specification № 1192)	Withdrawn multipart UK standard concerning (in part) the security of information about the architecture and construction of smart buildings and other physical facilities. More info: https://knowledge.bsigroup.com/search?query=pas+1192
Passable	Forged, fake, or counterfeit item that resembles the genuine article closely enough to be accepted as original; hence, it can be passed (handed, given) to the recipient (*e.g.* passable counterfeit banknotes are likely to be accepted by shopkeepers).

TERM	MEANING
Pass card	See access card.
Passive **I**nfra**R**ed **(PIR) detector**	Detection device that identifies the presence of people and other warm-blooded animals or warm bodies (such as motor vehicles) in the detection zone by the infrared radiation they emit. Commonly used to turn on lights when someone enters the area, perhaps covertly triggering **C**losed **C**ircuit **T**ele**V**ision recording and intruder alarms.
Passkey	Digital credential for FIDO **M**ulti**F**actor **A**uthentication using asymmetric cryptography in which a user's private keys are generally stored in a secure subsystem or vault on the user's personal device, such as a smartphone. The user first authenticates to the device using a USB hardware token, biometric, PIN code, or password to unlock the stored private keys, then uses the relevant key to authenticate (logon) to a website or app that has been designed to accept passkeys, having first authenticated the website or app using its public key to reduce the possibility of being phished. For convenience across devices (albeit at some risk), passkeys may also be synchronised and stored in the cloud, while FIDO Security Keys allow recovery of lost passkeys.
Passphrase	Confidential phrase, sentence, saying, lyric, poem, *etc.* that is either used directly as a long and hence strong password, or is used as a prompt to recall one (*e.g.* forming a nonsense password from the initial letters of the words in a memorable song or poem) or to open a password vault. "A sequence of words used for authentication" *(AusISM)*.
Pass The Hash	Hacking technique that exploits vulnerabilities in some authentication mechanisms to accept cached password NTLM hashes presented by the hacker, avoiding the need first to determine the corresponding passwords (*e.g.* by brute force attack on a stolen password file).
Password	Confidential string of characters (ideally *not* a recognisable word or phrase) which can authenticate a person or system as a response to a challenge. A type of credential. Vulnerable to dictionary and brute force attacks, especially if too short or obvious, and to being disclosed inappropriately (*e.g.* due to ignorance, carelessness, social engineering, or coercion). "A protected, generally computer-encrypted string of characters that authenticate a computer user to the computer system" *(ISACA glossary)*. "A sequence of characters used for authentication" *(AusISM)*.
Password **A**uthentication **P**rotocol **(PAP)**	Basic user authentication protocol option within **P**oint-to-**P**oint **P**rotocol passes userIDs and passwords by unencrypted (plaintext) datacommunications from clients to servers for validation. Due to its vulnerability to interception *en route* and replay attacks, PAP is deprecated. Specified in RFC 1334. "A simple, weak authentication mechanism where a user enters the password and it is then sent across the network, usually in the clear" *(SANS glossary)*.

TERM	MEANING
Password complexity	Password complexity. "The use of different character sets, such as lower-case alphabetical characters (a–z), upper-case alphabetical characters (A–Z), numeric characters (0–9) and special characters" *(AusISM).*
Password cracker	See brute-force password attack. "A tool that tests the strength of user passwords by searching for passwords that are easy to guess. It repeatedly tries words from specially crafted dictionaries and often also generates thousands (and in some cases, even millions) of permutations of characters, numbers and symbols" *(ISACA glossary).* "The process of attempting to guess passwords, given the password file information" *(SANS glossary).*
Passwordless authentication	User authentication using credentials other than passwords such as biometrics or security tokens. "Authentication that doesn't involve the use of something users know. Passwordless authentication may be single-factor or multi-factor, with the later often referred to as passwordless multi-factor authentication" *(AusISM).*
Passwordless Multi**F**actor **A**uthentication **(MFA)**	User authentication using multiple factors (credentials) of different kinds other than passwords, *e.g.* biometrics and security tokens. "Multi-factor authentication using something users have that is unlocked by something users know or are. Note, while a memorised secret may be used as part of passwordless multi-factor authentication (*e.g.* to unlock access to a cryptographic private key stored on a device) it is not the primary authentication factor, hence the use of the passwordless terminology" *(AusISM).*
Password-protected	Although this dismissive phrase *implies* the use of strong cryptographic controls, critical details such as password complexity rules and algorithms are rarely specified. In practice, paradoxically, it usually indicates a basic and rather weak form of user authentication, barely better than nothing. "The ability to protect the contents of a file or device from being accessed until the correct password is entered" *(NIST SP 800-101).*
Password sniffing	See sniffing. "Passive wiretapping, usually on a local area network, to gain knowledge of passwords" *(SANS glossary).*
Password synchronisation	Crude way to reduce the burden of having to recall numerous passwords for different systems by setting an identical password on them all, but naturally if the password is compromised at any point, all the systems are at risk of being accessed improperly. Deprecated in favour of more sophisticated controls such as **S**ingle **S**ign **O**n, password vaults, biometrics, and **M**ulti**F**actor **A**uthentication.

TERM	MEANING
Password vault	Trusted program and/or hardware designed to store passwords, cryptographic keys, PIN codes, userIDs, and other credentials or highly confidential pieces of information securely (meaning encrypted using a key derived from the one strong password or passphrase that the user *must* remember), and regurgitate them on demand by the authorised user when logging on to the relevant systems or websites. Good password vaults help the user generate much stronger (*i.e.* longer and more complex) passwords or passphrases than anyone other than a memory freak can manage and store reliably in their heads, limited only by the constraints of the target systems. Bad password vaults may be rogue software, Trojans, or spyware, and may have architectural flaws and bugs creating security vulnerabilities.
Patch, patching	Implementation of one or more piecemeal changes to computer programs, *e.g.* to fix bugs or architectural flaws causing security vulnerabilities. A patch may replace one or more broken parts within executable software or firmware (such as subroutines, functions, or various lines of code) or may replace complete programs within a software package. However, unlike version updates, patches seldom offer additional functionality. Occasionally because of inadequate quality assurance, they may even cause additional problems, requiring further corrections (more patches!) or workarounds (compensating controls). "Fixes to software programming errors and vulnerabilities" *(ISACA glossary)*. "A piece of software designed to remedy security vulnerabilities, or improve the usability or performance of software and ICT equipment" *(AusISM)*. "A small update released by a software manufacturer to fix bugs in existing programs [and] the process of updating software to a different version" *(SANS glossary)*.
Patch cable	"A metallic (usually copper) or fibre optic cable used for routing signals between two components in an enclosed container or rack or between adjacent containers or racks" *(NZISM)*.
Patch management	Process of updating software/firmware promptly when applicable updates are released. "An area of systems management that involves acquiring, testing and installing multiple patches (code changes) to an administered computer system to maintain up-to-date software and often to address security risk. Notes: Patch management tasks include maintaining current knowledge of available patches, deciding what patches are appropriate for particular systems, ensuring that patches are installed properly, testing

TERM	MEANING
	systems after installation and documenting all associated procedures, such as specific configurations required. A number of products are available to automate patch management tasks. Patches are sometimes ineffective and can sometimes cause more problems than they fix. Patch management experts suggest that system administrators take simple steps to avoid problems, such as performing backups and testing patches on noncritical systems prior to installations. Patch management can be viewed as part of change management" *(ISACA glossary)*. "About software security being regularly or automatically patched" *(UK Cyber Security Breaches Survey 2023)*.
Patch panel	"A group of sockets or connectors that allow manual configuration changes, generally by means of connecting cables to the appropriate connector. Cables could be metallic (copper) or fibre optic" *(NZISM)*.
Patent	Legal protection for novel inventions that have been properly registered with the relevant patent authorities. A form of **I**ntellectual **P**roperty **R**ight. Patent laws typically offer protection for 15–30 years depending on the jurisdiction and the type of invention (*e.g.* the US treats design, utility, and plant patents separately). "Protection of research and ideas that led to the development of a new, unique and useful product to prevent the unauthorized duplication of the patented item" *(ISACA glossary)*.
Patent troll	Organisation that assertively threatens legal action as a means to coerce other organisations into paying weighty fees for the right to continue using designs and methods for which it holds the patents or other Intellectual **P**roperty **R**ights. Depending on one's perspective, they are either legitimately exercising their ownership rights, or warty sleaze balls covered in putrid slime.
Path	Actual or figurative route through something, such as a maze. "A sequence of instructions that may be performed in the execution of a computer program" *(ISACA glossary)*.
Path analysis	Path analysis. "Analysis of a computer program (*i.e.,* source code) to identify all possible paths through the program, to detect incomplete paths or discover portions of the program that are not on any path" *(ISACA glossary)*.
Patsy	See target.
Pattern	Some devices with touch screens allow users to authenticate by sliding a finger through a specific sequence of moves to trace a shape, rather than simply tapping the numbers of a PIN code. A weak biometric control.

TERM	MEANING
Payload	a. Malicious function (the harmful 'business end') of malware that performs unauthorised activities such as deleting or modifying files and exfiltrating sensitive/valuable information. "A piece of malicious software that lets an attacker control a compromised computer system. The payload is typically attached to and delivered by an exploit" *(ISACA glossary)*. b. Valuable data content of network packets as distinct from metadata such as source and destination addresses. "The actual application data a packet contains" *(SANS glossary)*.
Paywall	Some commercial information providers restrict access to their **I**ntellectual **P**roperty through the Internet, requiring visitors to register and pay for the information. Visitors seeking the information are generally stonewalled by a user logon/registration screen requiring them to identify and authenticate themselves, although many sites offer sneak previews of the information, enticing visitors to register and pay up for access permission.
PBX	*Abbrev:* **P**rivate **B**ranch e**X**change.
PCAP (Packet Capture)	Family of basic file formats used to record, communicate, and analyse bundles of raw network traffic in tools such as Tcpdump, Wireshark, and Snort.
PCI DSS (Payment Card Industry Data Security Standard)	Cybersecurity standard imposed on card issuers and merchants by the major credit card companies through contractual obligations plus compliance and enforcement actions to limit their liabilities, protect the global credit card infrastructure and brands, and (coincidentally) improve data security, *i.e.* cardholders' privacy and other interests.
PCS	*Abbrev:* **P**rocess **C**ontrol **S**ystem. *Cf.* **P**ersonal **C**omputer**s** (PCs).
PDA (Personal Digital Assistant), palmtop	Handheld computer device, popular in the 1990s before smartphones took off. Although some later models offered WiFi, most could only be physically connected to a PC via a docking cradle, to synchronise their diaries, contact lists, email folders, *etc.* "A handheld computer that serves as a tool for reading and conveying documents, electronic mail, and other electronic media over a communications link, as well as for organizing personal information, such as a name-and-address database, a to-do list, and an appointment calendar" *(NIST SP 800-101)*.
PDB (President's Daily Brief)	US intelligence/security services online briefing to keep the President and close aides informed. Or possibly a policy about regularly changing the President's underwear, who knows?
PDF	*Abbrev:* **P**ortable **D**ocument **F**ormat.
PDoS	*Abbrev:* **P**ermanent **D**enial-**o**f-**S**ervice. See bricking.

TERM	MEANING
Peer [level, unit or layer]	Person, colleague, organisation, group, team, function, department, system, *etc.* having a similar or equivalent status, capability, hierarchical level, *etc.* to another. "Organizational units that are lateral to the organization and often report to or are accountable to the same superior unit" *(OCEG GRC Glossary)*.
Peer review, work product inspection	Critique of a draft report, proposal, paper, *etc.* by a colleague. "Process used by a reviewer to examine the performance of a host, provide feedback on an analysis area and learn lessons that are transferable to its own context. Notes: A peer review can cover multiple analysis areas. The host can replace 'review' with a synonym such as 'assessment,' 'appraisal' or 'analysis' to better describe the activity" *(ISO 22300)*. "The examination of work products performed by similarly skilled personnel during the development of work products to identify defects for removal" *(ISACA glossary)*. "A complete check of the work done involving reviewing all of the analytical work. It does not include re-analysing the items/exhibits" *(FSRCoP)*.
Pegasus	'Military grade' mobile device spyware used for civil and governmental surveillance against various countries and targets, developed by the Israeli cyber intelligence company NSO Group. See also Graphite.
Penetration	See intrusion. "Gaining unauthorized logical access to sensitive data by circumventing a system's protections" *(SANS glossary)*.
Penetration test (pentest), red teaming	Officially authorised/sanctioned/requested and hence legitimate test of an organisation's cybersecurity controls by competent and trustworthy experts (the red team). Primarily intended to detect exploitable vulnerabilities exposed externally (particularly via the Internet), it feeds into risk identification, analysis, and evaluation, a blend of assurance and risk management. The scope of a given pentest may include or exclude checks of network, physical, procedural, and/or other security controls and specific systems, locations, *etc.* "A live test of the effectiveness of security defenses through mimicking the actions of real-life attackers" *(ISACA glossary)*. "Where staff or contractors try to breach the cyber security of an organisation on purpose, in order to show where there might be weaknesses in cyber security" *(UK Cyber Security Breaches Survey 2023)*. "Designed to exercise real-world scenarios in an attempt to achieve a specific goal, such as compromising critical systems or data" *(AusISM)*. "Used to test the external perimeter security of a network or facility" *(SANS glossary)*. See also **T**hreat-**L**ed **P**enetration **T**est.

TERM	MEANING
Pen **R**egister, **T**rap and Trace **(PRTT)**	Originally, an electromechanical device used by the authorities to monitor a phone line, recording on paper the electrical pulses denoting the number when someone makes or receives a call. Although the term is still used, electromechanical plotters have long since been superseded by covert electronic recording devices (which generally store both the addressing information *and* the audio stream) and by direct access to the telephone companies' call routing/charging systems.
PenTest+	CompTIA's qualification for professional penetration testers and red teamers. Covers: engagement management, reconnaissance and enumeration, vulnerability discovery and analysis, attacks and exploits, and post-exploitation and lateral movement. More info: https://www.comptia.org/en-us/certifications/pentest/v3/
People actions & controls	"Human factors, including structure, accountability, education, and enablement used to address risk, reward, and compliance" *(OCEG GRC Glossary)*.
People aspects of business continuity	"Elements associated with the management of people involved in, or affected by, an incident in order to minimize distress, maximize productivity and recovery, and achieve the recovery objectives of the organization's business continuity programme" *(ISO 22300)*.
People at risk	"Individuals in the area who could be affected by an incident" *(ISO 22300)*.
People control	a. Manual, administrative, or management control performed **by** people such as workers. b. Control **of** people, such as the police monitoring and guiding (corralling) crowds of demonstrators. c. One of four 'control themes' in ISO/IEC 27002, defined in the standard as "Controls that concern individual people" *(ISO/IEC 27002)*. Eight types of people control are described, *e.g.* security awareness and security procedures for joiners, movers, and leavers. *Cf.* physical control, technological control, organisational control.
Perfect **F**orward **S**ecrecy **(PFS)**	Architecture of cryptographic datacommunications protocols such as Diffie–Helman, intended to maintain the confidentiality of previously captured communications sessions, *even if* a private key is subsequently compromised, by encrypting sessions with ephemeral session keys derived independently and securely communicated by the original parties (*e.g. using a* **O**ne-**T**ime **P**ad or key loader). "Additional security for security associations in that if one security association is compromised subsequent security associations will not be compromised" *(NZISM)*.

TERM	MEANING
Perfect-knowledge attack	Test simulating insider threats, *i.e.* attacks on a system by an adversary who already knows its internal architecture, cybersecurity arrangements, *etc.*, such as its owners, designers, and administrators. "Attack on a system that assumes no prior knowledge about the internal information of the system under attack. Note: The adversary can use context or historical information to infer model vulnerability. The attacker can probe the system to inform system vulnerabilities" *(ISO/IEC 27090 DRAFT).* See also white box testing. *Cf.* zero-knowledge, partial-knowledge attacks.
Performance	a. Effective speed and efficiency at which a computer system, network, process, team, *etc.* operates, affecting the services delivered. Technology with insufficient capacity for the applied load performs badly, affecting availability (*e.g.* becoming unreliable, partially, or completely failing), and may expose other vulnerabilities when under extreme stress (*e.g.* if controls fail-unsafe). "Measurable result. Notes: performance can relate either to quantitative or qualitative findings. Performance can relate to the management of activities, processes, products (including services), systems or organizations" *(ISO/IEC 27000).* "In IT, the actual implementation or achievement of a process" *(ISACA glossary).* b. Artistic act, such as a plausible scenario played out by a social engineer hoping to fool a victim into falling for their pretext, or a job interview by a candidate hoping to persuade an employer to fall for their charms.
Performance driver	Factor of particular significance to performance. "A measure that is considered the 'driver' of a lag indicator. It can be measured before the outcome is clear and, therefore, is called a 'lead indicator.' Notes: There is an assumed relationship between the two that suggests that improved performance in a leading indicator will drive better performance in the lagging indicator. They are also referred to as key performance indicators (KPIs) and are used to indicate whether goals are likely to be met" *(ISACA glossary).*
Performance evaluation	Process, or the results, of analysing or testing performance, particularly the extent to which objectives are met. "Process to determine measurable results against the set criteria" *(ISO 22300).*

TERM	MEANING
Performance indicator	Measurable performance parameter or characteristic, such as the time taken to complete certain activities, the rate of consumption of resources, the output quality achieved, and the reliability (variation under different loads, operating or environmental conditions). "A set of metrics designed to measure the extent to which performance objectives are being achieved on an on-going basis. Note: Performance indicators can include service level agreements (SLAs), critical success factors (CSFs), customer satisfaction ratings, internal or external benchmarks, industry best practices and international standards" *(ISACA glossary)*. See also **K**ey **P**erformance **I**ndicator.
Performance management	Management of performance. "In IT, the ability to manage any type of measurement, including employee, team, process, operational or financial measurements. The term connotes closed-loop control and regular monitoring of the measurement" *(ISACA glossary)*. "The act of managing processes and resources to pursue reward while addressing risk" *(OCEG GRC Glossary)*.
Performance parameter	See performance indicator. "Measurable criteria used to monitor progress toward quantitative objectives. Collectively, performance parameters provide a metric for determining the success of the business or project" *(ISACA glossary)*.
Performance test	Analysis of the performance achieved by a system, process, team, *etc.* under various loading or environmental conditions. "A test for comparing the system's performance to other equivalent systems using well-defined benchmarks [and] Functional testing to evaluate the compliance of a system or component with specified performance requirements" *(ISACA glossary)*. See also performance evaluation, stress test, down for everyone or just me?
Perimeter	Outermost physical and/or logical/notional boundary around a collection of assets, such as the outer edge of a site, campus, building or facility, or a network boundary partitioning or dividing the organisation's internal network from the Internet and other external networks. Often but not always sharply defined or demarcated, *e.g.* by a fence.
Perimeter network	See **De-M**ilitarised **Z**one.

TERM	MEANING
Peripheral, peripheral device, peripheral equipment	Something supplemental, supporting, or marginal, sitting at or on the edge rather than being central or core. "Device attached to a digital device in order to expand its functionality" *(ISO/IEC 27037)*. "Auxiliary computer hardware equipment used for input, output and data storage. Note: Examples of peripherals include disk drives and printers. [and] Equipment that is directly connected to a computer. A peripheral device can be used to input data, *e.g.,* a keypad, bar code reader, transducer or laboratory test equipment or to output data, *e.g.,* a printer, disk drive, video system, tape drive, valve controller or motor controller" *(ISACA glossary)*.
Peripheral switch	"A device used to share a set of peripherals between multiple computers. For example, a keyboard, video monitor and mouse" *(AusISM)*.
Permission	Authorisation to do something, *e.g.* a data subject may give or withhold their permission for a third party to use their personal information for stated or unstated purposes. A program may or may not have permission to access protected areas of memory. See also access right, privilege.
Permit, consent	a. *[Verb]* To allow, authorise, or fail to prevent. *Cf.* forbid, prohibit. b. *[Noun]* Formal document or credential from an authority confirming that someone has their permission, authorising them to do something, go somewhere, *etc.*
Permit-list	See whitelist.
Permutation	See transposition. "Keeps the same letters but changes the position within a text to scramble the message" *(SANS glossary)*.
Perpetrator, perp	Person who (allegedly or actually) commits a crime, causes or is responsible for causing an incident, *etc.*
Persirai	Species of **I**nternet **o**f ***T**hings* malware in the wild in 2017. Infects particular web cameras, recruiting them to a botnet.
Persistence, persistent	a. Digital forensics term describing the way that data often remain accessible (meaning readable using the appropriate utilities or forensic tools) even after they have been deleted, due to the way they are stored on disk, tape, or **R**andom **A**ccess **M**emory. b. Distinctive characteristic of successful hackers, spies, information security professionals, and business people generally, who refuse to let minor setbacks prevent them from achieving their objectives. c. Mechanisms used by some malware to remain on infected systems, often covertly such that the system *appears* uninfected whereas the malware is simply dormant.

TERM	MEANING
Persistent remote access	Hackers, crackers, and cyber-spooks generally aim to extend their illicit remote access to compromised systems/networks by remaining covert and installing backdoor mechanisms, enabling them to regain control if their primary access mechanisms are blocked (*e.g.* by enhanced network or system security). However, this redundancy also increases their vulnerability to being detected and perhaps traced and prosecuted. It's not just their victims who face information risks!
Personal	a. Concerning an individual person. *Cf.* personnel. b. Something sensitive relating to an individual's privacy.
Personal **A**rea **N**etwork **(PAN)**	*Ad hoc* wireless network used for datacommunications between various smart devices or *things* carried/worn by or in the vicinity (within, say, 10 m) of a person, using protocols such as BluetoothLE. See also **L**ocal **A**rea **N**etwork, **H**ome **A**rea **N**etwork, **M**etropolitan **A**rea **N**etwork, **W**ide **A**rea **N**etwork. *Cf.* **P**rimary **A**ccount **N**umber.
Personal data	Potentially sensitive data relating to or concerning an identifiable individual person. Depending on the context and requirements (such as the acceptable amount of uncertainty, doubt, or risk associated with the identification), several items may be needed (such as the person's full name, date *and* place of birth, or their biometrics) but for some purposes even ambiguous or dubious information may be sufficient … and may create privacy, safety, physical security, information security, or ethical concerns. "Information relating to an identified or identifiable natural person" *(ISACA glossary)*. See also personal information.
Personal data breach	"A breach of security leading to the accidental or unlawful destruction, loss, alteration, unauthorised disclosure of, or access to, personal data transmitted, stored or otherwise processed" *(**G**eneral **D**ata **P**rotection **R**egulation)*. "Any accidental or unlawful destruction, loss, alteration, unauthorized disclosure or access of a subject's data" *(ISACA glossary)*.
Personal firewall	"Those firewalls that are installed and run on individual PCs" *(SANS glossary)*.
Personal **I**dentification **N**umber **(PIN), PIN code, combination**	Weak numeric password or authentication code typically used by digital locks with PIN pads rather than full alphanumeric keyboards. Having just 4 or 6 digits, normally, and very low entropy, PINs alone are highly vulnerable to brute force attacks unless compensating controls (such as security awareness, **M**ulti**F**actor **A**uthentication, throttling, and CCTV recording) are applied. Commonly used to authenticate the holders of security tokens such as chip-n-PIN bank cards and access cards, reducing the risk of someone simply using a found or stolen card to withdraw cash through a bank's **A**utomated **T**eller **M**achine. "A type of password

TERM	MEANING
	(*i.e.,* a secret number assigned to an individual) that, in conjunction with some means of identifying the individual, serves to verify the authenticity of the individual. Note: PINs have been adopted by financial institutions as the primary means of verifying customers in an electronic funds transfer (EFT) system" *(ISACA glossary)*.
Personal information, **P**ersonally **I**dentifiable **I**nformation **(PII)**	Information or data associated with a particular human being that is considered valuable and/or sensitive/confidential, with privacy implications. *Note:* specific terms are explicitly defined in laws and regulations with some significant differences between jurisdictions. Data relating to dead people is classed as personal information in some but not all places, for instance, while certain types or items of personal information (such as sexual orientation) are deemed particularly confidential in some countries (see **P**rotected **H**ealth **I**nformation). "Any information that (a) can be used to establish a link between the information and the natural person to whom such information relates, or (b) is or can be directly or indirectly linked to a natural person. Notes: The 'natural person' in the definition is the PII principal. To determine whether a PII principal is identifiable, account should be taken of all the means which can reasonably be used by the privacy stakeholder holding the data, or by any other party, to establish the link between the set of PII and the natural person; This definition is included to define the term PII as used in this document. A public cloud PII processor is typically not in a position to know explicitly whether information it processes falls into any specified category unless this is made transparent by the cloud service customer" *(ISO/IEC 22989)*. "Any information relating to an identified or identifiable natural person ('data subject'); an identifiable natural person is one who can be identified, directly or indirectly, in particular by reference to an identifier such as a name, an identification number, location data, an online identifier or to one or more factors specific to the physical, physiological, genetic, mental, economic, cultural or social identity of that natural person" *(**G**eneral **D**ata **P**rotection **R**egulation)*. "Information that is or can be about or related to an identifiable individual" *(**T**rust **S**ervices **C**riteria)*. "Information that can be used to distinguish or trace an individual's identity, either alone or when combined with other information that is linked or linkable to a specific individual" *(OMB Circular A-130)*. "A synonym for 'personal data.' [and] Any information that can be used to establish a link between the information and the natural person to whom such information relates or that is or might be directly or indirectly linked to a natural person" *(ISACA glossary)*. See also personal data.

TERM	MEANING
Personal firewall	Firewall application protecting an individual system or device against some network attacks. Typically less sophisticated and capable than a dedicated firewall appliance but can be tightly integrated with the **O**perating **S**ystem. Adds another layer of protection. "A software program that monitors communications between a computer and other computers and blocks communications that are unwanted" *(NIST SP 800-114)*.
Personal **I**nformation **P**rotection and **E**lectronic **D**ocuments **A**ct **(PIPEDA)**	Canadian federal privacy law governs private-sector organisations' collection, use, and disclosure of personal information during commercial activities. Embodies ten fair information principles. Enforced by the **O**ffice of the **P**rivacy **C**ommissioner. More info: https://www.priv.gc.ca/en/privacy-topics/privacy-laws-in-canada/the-personal-information-protection-and-electronic-documents-act-pipeda/
Personally **I**dentifiable **I**nformation **(PII) controller**	"Privacy stakeholder (or privacy stakeholders) that determines the purposes and means for processing personally identifiable information (PII) other than natural persons who use data for personal purposes. Note: A PII controller sometimes instructs others (*e.g.* PII processors) to process PII on its behalf while the responsibility for the processing remains with the PII controller" *(ISO/IEC 29100)*. "A privacy stakeholder (or privacy stakeholders) who determines the purposes and means for processing personally identifiable information (PII) other than natural persons who use data for personal purposes" *(ISACA glossary)*. See also data controller, controller.
Personally **I**dentifiable **I**nformation **(PII) principal**	See data subject. "Natural person to whom the personally identifiable information (PII) relates. Note: The 'natural person' in the definition is the PII principal. To determine whether a PII principal is identifiable, account should be taken of all the means which can reasonably be used by the privacy stakeholder holding the data, or by any other party, to establish the link between the set of PII and the natural person" *(ISO/IEC 27002)*. "The natural person to whom personally identifiable information (PII) relates" *(ISACA glossary)*.
Personally **I**dentifiable **I**nformation **(PII) processor**	See data processor. "Privacy stakeholder that processes personally identifiable information (PII) on behalf of and in accordance with the instructions of a PII controller" *(ISO/IEC 27002)*. "The privacy stakeholder who processes personally identifiable information (PII) on behalf of and in accordance with the instructions of a PII controller" *(ISACA glossary)*.

TERM	MEANING
Personally **O**wned **D**evice **(POD)**	Information and **C**ommunications **T**echnology device such as a laptop, tablet PC, or smartphone that legally belongs to an individual worker rather than the organisation and is used for work purposes (**B**ring **Y**our **O**wn **D**evice). Most PODs are portables but some may be home office desktop PCs, printers, *etc*.
Personnel	Collective noun for an organisation's workers. Earlier name for the **H**uman **R**esources function/department. "Persons doing work under the organization's direction. Note: The concept of personnel includes the organization's members, such as the governing body, top management, employees, temporary staff, contractors and volunteers" *(ISO/IEC 27002). Cf.* personal.
Personnel security	Security and safety arrangements protecting workers. "The discipline of assessing the conduct, integrity, judgment, loyalty, reliability, and stability of individuals for duties and responsibilities requiring trustworthiness" *(NIST SP 800-171).*
PET	*Abbrev:* **P**rivacy-**E**nhancing **T**echnology.
Petya	Unusual species of ransomware that exploits vulnerable systems using EternalBlue, then surreptitiously rewrites the **M**aster **B**oot **R**ecord. Often distributed with Mischa. Although flaws in the cryptosystem implementation substantially weakened this malware, variants were derived such as NotPetya and GoldenEye.
PFS	*Abbrev:* **P**erfect **F**orward **S**ecrecy.
PGP	*Abbrev:* **P**retty **G**ood **P**rivacy.
PHA	*Abbrev:* **P**reliminary **H**azard **A**nalysis or **P**rocess **H**azard **A**nalysis, depending on context.
Pharming	Phishing-like fraud involving the manipulation of **D**omain **N**ame **S**ystem or other network addressing (such as the *hosts* file) to redirect users silently to fake websites that *appear* legitimate. "This is a more sophisticated form of MITM attack. A user's session is redirected to a masquerading website. This can be achieved by corrupting a DNS server on the Internet and pointing a URL to the masquerading website's IP. Almost all users use a URL like www.worldbank.com instead of the real IP (192.86.99.140) of the website. Changing the pointers on a DNS server, the URL can be redirected to send traffic to the IP of the pseudo website. At the pseudo website, transactions can be mimicked and information like login credentials can be gathered. With this the attacker can access the real www.worldbank.com site and conduct transactions using the credentials of a valid user on that website" *(SANS glossary).* See also DNS poisoning.
PHI	*Abbrev:* **P**rotected **H**ealth **I**nformation.

TERM	MEANING
Phishing	Fraud involving a combination of social engineering with technology (such as hyperlinks in plausible emails leading to fake user authentication web pages that resemble the logon screens of legitimate websites used as lures), normally used to harvest victims' credentials (personal information, credit card numbers, passwords, *etc.*) for identity fraud and extortion, or to infect their systems with malware. "Deceptive computer-based means to trick individuals into disclosing sensitive personal information" *(NIST SP 800-114)*. "Fraudulent process of attempting to acquire private or confidential information by masquerading as a trustworthy entity in an electronic communication. Note: Phishing can be accomplished by using social engineering or technical deception" *(ISO/IEC 27032)*. "A type of electronic mail (email) attack that attempts to convince a user that the originator is genuine with the intention of obtaining information for use in social engineering. Notes: For example, phishing attacks may take the form of an attacker masquerading as a lottery organization advising the recipient or the user's bank of a large win; in either case, the intent is to obtain account and personal identification number (PIN) details. Alternative attacks may seek to obtain apparently innocuous business information, which can be used in another form of active attack" *(ISACA glossary)*. "The use of e-mails that appear to originate from a trusted source to trick a user into entering valid credentials at a fake website. Typically the e-mail and the web site looks like they are part of a bank the user is doing business with" *(SANS glossary)*. See also spear phishing, whaling, vishing.
Phishing-**as**-**a**-**S**ervice **(PhaaS)**	Phishing kit provided online as a commercial service.
Phishing kit	Set of web pages and other tools used to perpetrate and manage phishing attacks.
PhishTank	Crowdsourced (community) service run by OpenDNS collates suspected and confirmed phishing **U**niform **R**esource **L**ocators suitable for blackholing.
Photographic **id**entity card **(photo ID)**	Similar to a credit card, an official document displaying a photograph of the authorised holder's face plus other information about their identity and status with the issuing organisation, *e.g.* a driver's licence, gun licence, or access card for a secure area or facility.
Phrack	Popular old-skool magazine by and for the hacking community, sharing information about hacking techniques and exploits. Originally printed and circulated on paper, later online. More info: https://phrack.org/

TERM	MEANING
Phreaker	See cracker. "Those who crack security, most frequently telephone and other communication networks" *(ISACA glossary).*
Physical actions & controls	"Physical safeguards, barriers, or constraints, such as fences, locks, guards, cameras, or other protective mechanisms, used to address risk, reward, and compliance" *(OCEG GRC Glossary).*
Physical capital	"The physical assets of an organization, including manufactured goods, buildings, equipment, and infrastructure" *(OCEG GRC Glossary).*
Physical connection	"A connection between electronic information systems or components implemented using physical means, including through electrical, optical or mechanical interfaces, wires or radio waves" *(EU CRA).*
Physical control, mechanical control	a. Control designed to mitigate unacceptable physical risks, thereby protecting tangible assets such as buildings, equipment, storage media, and people. b. Control involving mechanical elements or devices such as chains, padlocks, doors, gates, and safety interlocks. c. One of four 'control themes' in ISO/IEC 27002, defined in the standard as "Control concerning physical objects" *(ISO/IEC 27002).* Fourteen types of physical control are described. See also people control, technological control, organisational control.
Physical environment	Environs. "Physical hardware parts that make up a network, including cables and routers. The hardware is required for communication and interaction between devices on a network" *(CIS Controls).*
Physical information security	a. That part of physical security concerned with protecting tangible *information* assets such as computer devices plus related equipment, network and power cables, storage media, and workers, thereby helping to protect the intangible and often far more valuable information content. b. Physical controls involving information/digital data, devices, components, or processes, *e.g.* combination locks; **C**losed **C**ircuit **T**ele**V**ision and electronic alarm systems; digital sensors and actuators; card access controls; tamper resistance; security guards; facilities inspection, maintenance, and repair; secure zones, offices, filing cabinets, vaults, and firesafes for backups and archives.
Physical (site) intrusion or penetration	Gaining physical access to 'sites' (facilities, premises, buildings, offices, installations, computer suites, *etc.*) by various means, *e.g.* tailgating; social engineering of receptionists, guards, or other workers; masquerading as a legitimate worker, maintenance staff, visitor, or inspector; draining or breaking-and-entering (burglary or trespass); surveillance using drones, binoculars, or bugs. Generally unauthorised but may be a legitimate part of a penetration test, installation audit, *etc.*

TERM	MEANING
Physical risk	Uncertain possibility of material harm resulting from threats in the physical domain, such as: fire, overheating, smoke, explosion; flood, storm, leak, humidity/dampness, drought, climate change, sea level rise; lightning, static electricity; inadequate or excessive supply voltage, surge, spike, dip, brownout, unreliable power; electronic/equipment failure; corrosion, stress, strain, metal fatigue, zinc whiskers, inadequate specification, engineering, construction or maintenance, poor quality, inappropriate or nonavailability of required materials leading to mechanical failure or collapse, or noncompliance with building codes; cosmic, electromagnetic or ionising radiation; magnetism; earthquake or volcanic eruption; meteor or other falling/moving object; theft, vandalism, sabotage, wanton or accidental damage, collision, mishandling, loss; injury, infection, disease, poison; gradual degradation, mould, decay, entropy; insect or rodent infestation.
Physical security, site security, ...	Protection of physical assets, locations, computer equipment, storage media, people, *etc.* by means of security controls such as locks, chains, walls, barriers, boundaries, perimeters, bollards, security guards, **C**losed **C**ircuit **T**ele**V**ision systems, intruder alarms, heat/smoke detectors and fire alarms, flood/water alarms, **U**ninterruptible **P**ower **S**upply, and armour. Even powered-down computer equipment in storage or *in transit* remains vulnerable to physical incidents such as theft, sabotage, fire, flood, static discharge, extraction of valuable **I**ntellectual **P**roperty (*e.g.* by reverse engineering), accidental damage, and potentially even malicious interference with or replacement/disabling of firmware, embedded processing devices, and various controls.
Physical security system	Integrated suite of physical security controls to mitigate unacceptable physical risks, ideally designed, operated, managed, monitored, and maintained as a complete, coherent, and cost-effective system.
PIA	*Abbrev:* **P**rivacy **I**mpact **A**ssessment.
PIG	*Abbrev:* **P**robability-**I**mpact **G**raphic.
Piggybacking	See tailgating. "1. The act of following an authorized person into a restricted access area. 2. The act of electronically attaching to an authorized telecommunications link to intercept and possibly alter transmissions" *(ISACA glossary).*
PII	*Abbrev:* **P**ersonally **I**dentifiable **I**nformation.
PIMS	*Abbrev:* **P**rivacy **I**nformation **M**anagement **S**ystem.
PIN	*Abbrev:* **P**ersonal **I**dentification **N**umber.

TERM	MEANING
Ping, Packet Internet (or Inter-Network) Groper Packet Inter-Network Groper	Basic network administration utility or function that sends an ICMP echo request to a specified network node, anticipating an ICMP echo reply message in return if the node is accessible via the network, operating normally and has not been configured to ignore pings. Contrived name reflects the classic sonar U-boat sound. The round-trip delay gives an indication of network latency. See also tracert.
PIN mailer	Physical security arrangement to post initial PIN codes to customers in a tamper-evident form that reduces the possibility of them being illicitly viewed, overseen, or copied *en route*, *e.g.* an opaque covering layer through which the PIN is printed by an impact printer located in a physically secure zone.
Ping of death	a. Destroyer's sonar echo from an enemy submarine. b. "An attack that sends an improperly large ICMP echo request packet (a 'ping') with the intent of overflowing the input buffers of the destination machine and causing it to crash" *(SANS glossary)*.
Ping scan	"Looks for machines that are responding to ICMP Echo Requests" *(SANS glossary)*.
Ping sweep	"An attack that sends ICMP echo requests ('pings') to a range of IP addresses, with the goal of finding hosts that can be probed for vulnerabilities" *(SANS glossary)*.
PIN pad	Small keypad used to enter PIN codes. Most lay out the 10 decimal digits 0–9 plus the # and $ or A and B characters in a 3x4 array like a pushbutton telephone.
PIPEDA	*Abbrev:* **P**ersonal **I**nformation **P**rotection and **E**lectronic **D**ocuments **A**ct.
PIPEDREAM	**S**upervisory **C**ontrol **A**nd **D**ata **A**cquisition/**I**ndustrial **C**ontrol **S**ystem/**A**dvanced **P**ersistent **T**hreat targeting Schneider Electric and OMRON Sysmac NEX **P**rogrammable **L**ogic **C**ontrollers, **O**pen **P**latform **C**ommunications **U**nified **A**rchitecture servers, and Windows PCs with ASRock motherboards in 2023.
PIR detector	*Abbrev:* **P**assive **I**nfra**R**ed detector.
Piracy	Making, using, selling, or otherwise distributing illegal copies of copyright material, whether deliberately or not.
Pirate	Someone who commits piracy. May not have a wooden leg, eye-patch, parrot, and/or hook. May never have set sail, yo-ho-ho. Might not enjoy a tot of rum and jaunty sea-shanties, but surely talks like a pirate *every* day.

TERM	MEANING
Pivot, pivot point	Change of direction, pace, focus, or phase during an attack (*e.g.* a hacker moving from passively identifying vulnerable network systems to actively exploiting them), strategy implementation (*e.g.* disposing of a non-core business unit or product line), project, *etc.*
PKCS	*Abbrev:* **P**ublic-**K**ey **C**ryptography **S**tandards.
PKI	*Abbrev:* **P**ublic **K**ey **I**nfrastructure.
Plagiarism, plagiarist, pond scum	Theft of information by copying, using, or disseminating someone else's **I**ntellectual **P**roperty, passing it off as the plagiarist's own work without properly acknowledging, crediting, or attributing it to the legitimate owner, let alone requesting their permission or licence. See also pirate.
Plain English, plain language	Straightforward writing style, designed to be easily understood and readily translated. Uses relatively short, clear sentences. Avoids obscure words, jargon, superfluous text and complex terms (*e.g.* replacing the pseudo-legalese "includes, but is not limited to," with "such as" or "*e.g.*"). However, this ideal is not always feasible, particularly in technical, scientific, and legal texts where precision and lack of ambiguity are paramount and the primary audiences are well educated in the arcane and often archaic language of their fields.
Plaintext, cleartext	Intelligible, readable, and meaningful text, such as this sentence, or other usable forms of information, *e.g.* unencrypted data. "The original, intelligible text, as it was before encipherment, revealed after successful decoding or cryptanalysis" (*A Lexicon of Cryptography, Bletchley Park, 1943*). "Ordinary readable text before being encrypted into ciphertext or after being decrypted" *(SANS glossary)*. "Digital information, such as cleartext, that is intelligible to the reader" *(ISACA glossary)*. *Cf.* ciphertext, encrypted data.
Planned residual risk	"The level of residual risk under planned (or desired) actions & controls" *(OCEG GRC Glossary)*.
Planned (simulated) stress	"Scenarios that use historical, hypothetical, or simulated events to test how forces will be addressed" *(OCEG GRC Glossary)*.

TERM	MEANING
Planning, plan	Process of determining and generally documenting the imperative nature and sequence of activities or steps intended to lead to achievement of identified, desirable objectives. "Part of management focused on setting objectives and specifying necessary operational processes and related resources to fulfil the objectives" *(ISO 22300)*. "<Artificial intelligence> Computational processes that compose a workflow out of a set of actions, aiming at reaching a specified goal. Note: The meaning of the 'planning' used in AI life cycle or AI management standards can be also actions taken by human beings" *(ISO/IEC 22989)*.
Plan of action and milestones	"A document that describes security vulnerabilities in a system and the plans for their rectification" *(AusISM)*.
Plant	a. Industrial equipment or machinery including machine tools, robots, **H**eating, **V**entilating, and **A**ir-**C**onditioning systems, elevators, *etc.* in various buildings. Generally heavy and fixed permanently in place ('planted'), possibly within a specific room (plantroom) frequented by facilities maintenance engineers wearing overalls and carrying oily rags. b. Industrial site or facility where manufacturing takes place, *e.g.* car plant. c. Eukaryotic and photosynthetic organism of the *Plantae* kingdom, *e.g.* a tree.
Plant **V**ariety **R**ight **(PVR)**	Intellectual **P**roperty **R**ight allowing plant breeders to protect their interests in new varieties produced by conventional selective breeding and/or genetic engineering for up to 30 years. Conceptually similar to patents.
Platform	a. Stable foundation on which to build. In the technology context, refers to some sort of computer system or device (such as a PC) prior to being programmed, configured, or customised for a particular purpose. May mean just the hardware (such as a microcontroller) or the hardware plus its **O**perating **S**ystem, various services provided to applications, or something else, depending on context. "The hardware and software that must be present and functioning for an application program to run (perform) as intended. A platform includes, but is not limited to, the operating system or executive software, communication software, microprocessor, network, input/output hardware, any generic software libraries, database management, user interface software, and the like" *(ISACA glossary)*. b. Rhetorical position or opportunity to speak out publicly, perhaps a physical stage complete with lectern and audience.

TERM	MEANING
Platform-as-a-Service (PaaS)	Cloud computing service model providing customers with access to Internet-based virtual systems preloaded with **O**perating **S**ystems and middleware managed by the service provider, on which they can load customer applications. The service provider's responsibilities, including the information security aspects, cover everything *except* the customer applications (*e.g.* the computing platform and services, guest system security configuration and patching). "Offers the capability to deploy onto the cloud infrastructure customer-created or acquired applications that are created using programming languages and tools supported by the provider" *(ISACA glossary)*. "Provides application developers access to all necessary hardware, software, and infrastructure to allow applications to be built, run, and managed. The PaaS infrastructure is typically managed by the cloud service provider" *(NZISM)*. See also **I**nfrastructure-**as**-**a**-**S**ervice, **S**oftware-**as**-**a**-**S**ervice.
Plausible deniability	Situation that allows a culprit to repudiate or deny knowledge of something untoward they have done or been involved in, in such a way that their false denial is credible. Some cryptosystems distribute encrypted data among junk and sections of separately encrypted sacrificial text, allowing the user under pressure to disclose the key needed to decrypt the sacrificial text while feigning ignorance of the remainder which remains encrypted with a different key. *Cf.* non-repudiation.
Playfair system	Encryption algorithm invented in 1854 by Sir Charles Wheatstone and demonstrated to Baron Playfair. A block cypher.
PLC	*Abbrev:* **P**rogrammable **L**ogic **C**ontroller.
Plenum	Pressurised void used as a duct to direct conditioned air into an office, computer room, *etc*. The possibility of smoke and flames spreading rapidly through the plenum emphasises the need for fire safety (*e.g.* 'low smoke' plenum cables, sensitive smoke detectors and interlocks).
PLM	*Abbrev:* **P**robable **L**oss **M**agnitude.
PLS	*Abbrev:* **P**rivacy **L**aw **S**pecialist.
Plug	Cylindrical core of a cylinder lock which can rotate when the correct key is inserted into the keyway.
PlugX	Species of malware used by the Chinese Mustang Panda/Twill Typhoon hacker group from 2014 until 2024, when a vulnerability in the malware, coupled with command and control traffic exchanged with specific **I**nternet **P**rotocol addresses, was used by the **F**ederal **B**ureau of **I**nvestigation to identify infected Windows systems and disable (self-destruct) the malware.

TERM	MEANING
POC	*Abbrev:* **P**oint **O**f **C**ontact, **P**roof-**O**f-**C**oncept, or **P**roof-**O**f-**C**orrectness, depending on context.
POD	*Abbrev:* **P**ersonally **O**wned **D**evice.
Point **O**f **C**ontact **(POC)**	"Defined organizational function or role serving as the coordinator or focal point of information concerning incident management activities. Note: the most obvious PoC is the role to whom the information security event it raised" *(ISO/IEC 27035-1)*. *Cf.* **P**roof-**O**f-**C**oncept, **P**roof-**O**f-**C**orrectness.
Point of encryption	"Location within the Information and Communications Technology (ICT) infrastructure where data are encrypted on its way to storage and, conversely, where data are decrypted when accessed from storage. Note: The point of encryption is only applicable for data at rest" *(ISO/IEC 27040)*.
Point-**O**f-**S**ale **(POS) memory-scraping malware**	Type of Trojan that covertly captures, encrypts, and stores plaintext payment card information from the working memory of infected **P**oint-**O**f-**S**ale retail systems as sales transactions are processed. The encrypted data files may then be sent through the Internet to be exploited by criminals through identity fraud, *etc.* A specific application of memory-scraping malware.
Point-to-**P**oint **P**rotocol **(PPP)**	Data link layer network protocol for datacommunications between directly connected network nodes. Specified in RFC 1661 and others. "A protocol used for transmitting data between two ends of a connection" *(ISACA glossary)*. "A protocol for communication between two computers using a serial interface, typically a personal computer connected by phone line to a server. It packages your computer's TCP/IP packets and forwards them to the server where they can actually be put on the Internet" *(SANS glossary)*.
Point-to-**P**oint **T**unnelling **P**rotocol **(PPTP)**	Obsolete, insecure, and deprecated network protocol used to tunnel **V**irtual **P**rivate **N**etwork traffic through a TCP/IP network. "A protocol used to transmit data securely between two endpoints to create a virtual private network (VPN)" *(ISACA glossary)*. "A protocol (set of communication rules) that allows corporations to extend their own corporate network through private 'tunnels' over the public Internet" *(SANS glossary)*.
Poisoning attack, data poisoning attack	a. Attempt to compromise an **A**rtificial **I**ntelligence/**M**achine **L**earning system by deliberately manipulating the training data, in effect teaching it to be naughty. "Attack where the attacker manipulates data (potentially including parameters) to affect the AI system's behaviour" *(ISO/IEC 27090 DRAFT)*. b. Attempt to harm one or more individuals using toxic substances such as sarin or phosgene.

TERM	MEANING
Policy	a. Formal statement of authority by management defining high-level expectations such as what workers must or must not do under certain circumstances. Clarifies business and/or control objectives through broad statements of intent (axioms or principles). Normally supported by more detailed standards, procedures, and guidelines explaining how the objectives are to be fulfilled, plus security awareness, training, oversight, and conformity/compliance/assurance activities. "Intentions and direction of an organization, as formally expressed by its top management" *(ISO/IEC 27002)*. "A document that communicates required and prohibited activities and behaviors" *(ISACA glossary)*. "A broad articulation of what the organization expects on a particular topic, that describes the 'why' or intent, considers context, sets the tone, and changes infrequently" *(OCEG GRC Glossary)*. "Management or board member statements of what should be done to effect control. Such statements may be documented, explicitly stated in communications, or implied through actions and decisions. Policies serve as the bases for procedures" *(**T**rust **S**ervices **C**riteria)*. b. Technical rule applied by a security device such as a firewall, or service such as **C**loud **A**ccess **S**ecurity **B**roker, defined by management and administrators as part of its configuration. c. Insurance contract defining the coverage and exclusions, insured amounts, terms and conditions, and the premium.
Polyalphabetic	Cryptographic substitution algorithm that draws on substitute characters from more than one alphabet/sequence, frustrating simple frequency analysis.
Polyinstantiation	Replication or duplication of a controlled information asset, such as a cryptographic key or **D**ata**B**ase. "The ability of a database to maintain multiple records with the same key. It is used to prevent inference attacks" *(SANS glossary)*.
Polymorphic, polymorphism	a. Uncorrected DNA or RNA mutations (replication errors) generate variants of a given genotype, some of which may marginally improve the fitness (ability to survive) of living organisms, leading to genetic diversity among the population and, over millennia, the emergence of new species. The same natural process leads to the characteristic variations between individuals exploited by DNA fingerprinting. b. Type of malware which changes its own code to generate variants as it infects successive systems/files, making reliable detection by crude pattern-matching signature identification challenging. "The process by which malicious software changes its underlying code to avoid detection" *(SANS glossary)*.
Polyransom	Highly polymorphic species of ransomware, in the wild in 2015.

TERM	MEANING
Pony	Family of <u>**R**emote **A**ccess **T**rojan</u> <u>malware</u>, <u>in the wild</u> since 2013 when the <u>source code</u> was released. Typically propagated using <u>social engineering</u> as a <u>downloader</u> to deliver further malware.
POODLE (Padding Oracle On Downgrade Legacy Encryption)	Contrived name of a <u>**M**an-**I**n-**T**he-**M**iddle</u> <u>attack</u> on <u>encrypted</u> <u>web</u> connections that <u>forces</u> <u>vulnerable</u> <u>systems</u> to downgrade to <u>**S**ecure **S**ockets **L**ayer</u> 3.0, an insecure <u>deprecated</u> <u>cryptosystem</u>. See also <u>DROWN</u>, <u>Heartbleed</u>.
POP3 (Post Office Protocol version 3)	Third generation of the POP <u>protocol</u> for retrieving <u>email</u> <u>messages</u> from a mail <u>server</u>. By default, POP3 sends <u>users</u>' <u>logon</u> <u>credentials</u> to the mail server in <u>plaintext</u>, making them <u>vulnerable</u> to interception as they transit the <u>network</u> (unless <u>**T**ransport **L**ayer **S**ecurity</u> is used) or while on the <u>client</u> or server <u>systems</u>. <u>Deprecated</u> in favour of <u>**I**nternet **M**essage **A**ccess **P**rotocol</u>. "A standard protocol used to receive electronic mail from a server" *(<u>NIST SP 800-101</u>)*. "An Internet Standard protocol by which a client workstation can dynamically access a mailbox on a server host to retrieve mail messages that the server has received and is holding for the client" *(<u>SANS glossary</u>)*.
Port	Notional point of origin or destination of <u>network</u> <u>traffic</u>, a narrow doorway onto the network. "Endpoint to a connection. Note: In the context of the Internet protocol a port is a logical channel endpoint of a TCP connection or UDP messages. Application protocols which are based on TCP or UDP have typically assigned default port numbers, *e.g.* port 80 for HTTP" *(<u>ISO/IEC 27033-1</u>)*. "A process or application-specific software element serving as a communication endpoint for the transport layer IP protocols (UDP and TCP)" *(<u>ISACA glossary</u>)*. "Nothing more than an integer that uniquely identifies an endpoint of a communication stream. Only one process per machine can listen on the same port number" *(<u>SANS glossary</u>)*.
Portable **D**ocument **F**ormat **(PDF)**	<u>File</u> format originally created by Adobe in 1992 for their Acrobat product, becoming an open <u>standard</u> under ISO 32000. Similar to <u>Java</u>, it is meant to be interpreted in a standardised manner such that content appears much the same on a variety of <u>platforms</u> or <u>devices</u> such as <u>computers</u> and printers. Whereas the early PDF 'password protection' <u>function</u> used the <u>deprecated</u> <u>RC4</u> <u>algorithm</u> for <u>encryption</u>, today's 'strongly encrypted' PDFs using <u>AES</u> are more <u>confidential</u>, *provided* <u>users</u> choose strong <u>passwords</u> and keep them <u>secret</u>!
Portable end-user device	"Transportable, end-user devices that have the capability to wirelessly connect to a network. For the purpose of this document, portable end-user devices can include laptops and mobile devices such as smartphones and tablets, all of which are a subset of enterprise assets" *(<u>CIS Controls</u>)*.

TERM	MEANING
Portable storage device	Portable data storage system (*e.g.* referring to the audio-visual recording capabilities of a smartphone), or subsystem or peripheral device (*e.g.* external disk drive or USB memory stick). "A system component that can be inserted into and removed from a system and that is used to store information or data (*e.g.,* text, video, audio, and/or image data). Such components are typically implemented on magnetic, optical, or solid-state devices (*e.g.,* compact/digital video disks, flash/thumb drives, external solid-state drives, external hard disk drives, flash memory cards/ drives that contain nonvolatile memory)" *(NIST SP 800-171).*
Port scan, port scanning	Systematic process for identifying and characterising open network ports on a computer system. "The act of probing a system to identify open ports" *(ISACA glossary).* "A series of messages sent by someone attempting to break into a computer to learn which computer network services, each associated with a 'well-known' port number, the computer provides. Port scanning, a favorite approach of computer cracker, gives the assailant an idea where to probe for weaknesses. Essentially, a port scan consists of sending a message to each port, one at a time. The kind of response received indicates whether the port is used and can therefore be probed for weakness" *(SANS glossary).*
PoSeidon	Species of **P**oint-**of**-**S**ale memory-scraping malware in the wild in 2016. Had keylogging and other capabilities.
Position of trust, trusted rôle	Privileged rôle, engagement, or assignment requiring a trustworthy person, team, or organisation. "A position that involves duties that require a higher level of assurance than that provided by normal employment screening. In some cases additional screening may be required. Positions of trust can include, but are not limited to, Chief Information Security Officers and their delegates, system administrators and privileged users" *(AusISM).*
Positive feedback	a. Constructive, supportive information passed to the originators of documents, training courses, systems, standards, products, *etc.* b. Connecting the output of an amplifying component, unit, or system directly back to its input can result in exponential increase in level, perhaps leading to a runaway condition and ultimate failure unless constrained or halted by controls. *Cf.* negative feedback.
Positive Vetting, Positively **V**etted **(PV)**	Even more stringent, in-depth, high-assurance, and potentially intrusive form of background checks than ordinary security clearance, typically required for people appointed to highly trusted secret service positions and others with access to highly classified information. May involve polygraph tests and discreet surveillance on the person with similar in-depth checks on their family members, social networks, computer equipment, *etc.*

TERM	MEANING
Possession	a. Asset belonging to a person or organisation. b. Besides the CIA triad, one of the additional security characteristics of information in the Parkerian hexad. "The holding, control, and ability to use information" *(SANS glossary)*.
Possibility	Low but non-zero value of probability. Generally something considered unlikely but conceivable, as opposed to literally impossible or inconceivable. A *remote* possibility is even less likely to occur but it still cannot be totally discounted. A *distinct* possibility is more likely to occur and hence ought to be addressed.
Post Office Protocol version 3	See POP3.
Post-Quantum Cryptography (PQC), quantum-resistant cryptography	Design of cryptographic algorithms that are significantly more resistant than traditional approaches to cryptanalysis involving quantum computers, using techniques such as lattice-based, code-based, hash-based, and multivariate polynomials. Most forms of cryptography in use today (plus encrypted messages and digital signatures currently circulating) will become vulnerable to novel cryptanalytical techniques once quantum computing technology is fully developed. "Cryptographic algorithms that are considered to be secure against a cryptanalytic attack by a quantum computer" *(NZISM)*.
Potential digital evidence	"Information or data, stored or transmitted in binary form, which has not yet been determined, through the process of examination and analysis, to be relevant to the investigation. Note: The process of analysis determines which of the potential digital evidence is digital evidence" *(ISO/IEC 27042)*.
Potential impact	Estimated, predicted, or anticipated adverse effects or consequences if a risk eventuates, *i.e.* a threat acts on an exposed vulnerability. "The loss of confidentiality, integrity, or availability could be expected to have: (i) a limited adverse effect (FIPS Publication 199 low); (ii) a serious adverse effect (FIPS Publication 199 moderate); or (iii) a severe or catastrophic adverse effect (FIPS Publication 199 high) on organizational operations, organizational assets, or individuals" *(NIST SP 800-171)*.
Potentially **U**nwanted **P**rogram **(PUP)**, **P**otentially **U**nwanted **S**oftware **(PUS)**, **P**otentially **U**nwanted **A**pplication **(PUA)**, **greyware**	Software of dubious value, potentially a threat or concern for the person using the computer, such as adware. Antivirus companies use politically correct terms to avoid overtly accusing the authors and distributors of having malicious intent as implied by terms such as malware and spyware, and partly to acknowledge that some users *presumably* find the software worthwhile. "Deceptive software, including malicious and non-malicious software, that exhibit the characteristics of deceptive software" *(ISO/IEC 27032)*.

TERM	MEANING
Power cut	See blackout.
PowerGhost	Species of cryptominer malware, in the wild in 2018. Based on PowerShell scripts.
Power-On Self-Test (POST)	Low-level self-assessment of various critical elements, aspects, or parameters of a device (*e.g.* voltage levels) when power is applied to the circuit. Only if the POST completes successfully does the system proceed to operate normally (*e.g.* executing the boot loader to load and launch the **O**perating **S**ystem, or commencing sensitive cryptographic operations within a **T**rusted **P**latform **M**odule), otherwise processing halts, typically with an alarm (*e.g.* beeps and flashing fault LEDs) signalling a fundamental fault – a fail-safe or fail-secure control.
Power ratio, Signal to Noise Ratio (SNR)	"Measure that compares the level of a desired signal to the level of background noise. Note: It is defined as the ratio of signal power to the noise power" *(ISO/IEC 27033-6)*.
PowerShell	Powerful .NET-based scripting language built-in to the Microsoft Windows **O**perating **S**ystem, intended to automate systems management tasks. Due to flaws in its security architecture, PowerShell may be exploited locally or remotely for malicious purposes, however – built-in malware. See also fileless malware, PowerGhost, Powersploit, **W**indows **M**anagement **I**nstrumentation.
Powersploit	Hacking/penetration testing tool comprised of PowerShell scripts.
Power Worm	Species of ransomware. A bug or flaw in the code corrupted as well as encrypted victims' data, making the information irretrievable even if the ransom was paid.
PPP	*Abbrev:* **P**oint-to-**P**oint **P**rotocol.
PPTP	*Abbrev:* **P**oint-to-**P**oint **T**unnelling **P**rotocol.
PQC	*Abbrev:* **P**ost-**Q**uantum **C**ryptography.
Practitioner	Someone who practices hands-on, a doer who gets on with things and gets stuff done, as opposed to a manager, teacher, or trainer. "As used in this document, a CPA who performs an examination of controls within an entity's system relevant to security, availability, processing integrity, confidentiality, or privacy" *(Trust Services Criteria)*.
PRAGMATIC (Predictive, Relevant, Actionable, Genuine, Meaningful, Accurate, Timely, Independently verifiable, Cost-effective)	Mnemonic for nine valuable characteristics of metrics, providing a rational basis on which to assess, score/evaluate, compare, select/reject, and improve them. More info: https://www.securitymetametrics.com

TERM	MEANING
Pre-action	Type of dry-pipe sprinkler system with two valves in series: the first is opened to flood the system when a fire is detected and the alarm is raised, while the second in each sprinkler head is only opened if there is sufficient heat nearby. Reduces extinguishant damage to unaffected areas.
Preamble	Preface/preliminary statement or sequence preceding the main information content, *e.g.* the short synchronisation and protocol identification pattern (a characteristic series of audio tones) generated by a modem at the start of a datacommunications message to reduce the possibility of the data elements being mis-timed and misinterpreted by a receiving system. "A signal used in network communications to synchronize the transmission timing between two or more systems. Proper timing ensures that all systems are interpreting the start of the information transfer correctly. A preamble defines a specific series of transmission pulses that is understood by communicating systems to mean 'someone is about to transmit data.' This ensures that systems receiving the information correctly interpret when the data transmission starts. The actual pulses used as a preamble vary depending on the network communication technology in use" *(SANS glossary)*.
Pre-audit	See stage 1 audit.
Precision, precise	Sufficiently explicit and definitive description or measurement of something for a given purpose, within the permitted tolerance. An integrity property. "Closeness of agreement between independent test results obtained under prescribed conditions" *(FSRCoP)*. See also accuracy.
Predictability	Reliability with which future behaviours, activities, or decisions can be predicted or forecast, implying sufficient understanding of the situation, parameters, criteria, and/or process. "Property of an AI system that enables reliable assumptions by stakeholders about the output" *(ISO/IEC 22989)*.
Prediction	Forecasting future events or situations. "Primary output of an AI system when provided with input data or information. Notes: Predictions can be followed by additional outputs, such as recommendations, decisions and actions; Prediction does not necessarily refer to predicting something in the future; Predictions can refer to various kinds of data analysis or production applied to new data or historical data (including translating text, creating synthetic images or diagnosing a previous power failure)" *(ISO/IEC 22989)*.

TERM	MEANING
Predictive analytics	Collection and processing of operational data using statistical techniques and **A**rtificial **I**ntelligence/**M**achine **L**earning to forecast and prepare for future events or situations.
Predictive text	Some **I**nformation **T**echnology devices 'guess' and complete words as users type SMS/TXT messages, emails, *etc.* but often make errors (integrity failures) which can be confusing, amusing, and/or embarrassing if not spotted and corrected in time.
Prejudice, prejudicial	Literally, prejudged, *i.e.* someone has prematurely or instinctively formed a firm opinion or position on something before even encountering it for real. See also bias.
Preliminary [or Process] **H**azard **A**nalysis **(PHA) [or evaluation]**	Structured techniques to identify, examine, and evaluate potential health and safety hazards in an industrial process, system, installation, or plant, typically. Performed early in the lifecycle, ideally in the specification and design phase, when risks can be addressed most cost-effectively.
Preparedness	"Activities, programmes, and systems developed and implemented prior to an incident that can be used to support and enhance prevention, protection from, mitigation of, response to and recovery from disruptions, emergencies or disasters" *(ISO 22300)*. See also readiness.
Prescriptive norms	"Customs, rules, or expectations that encourage behavior the group deems positive *(e.g., 'be honest')" (OCEG GRC Glossary)*.
Prescriptive policy	"A policy that states what to do" *(OCEG GRC Glossary)*.
Preservation	Keeping something in good condition, such as securing and protecting the integrity of forensic evidence, *e.g.* by analysing forensic disk image bit-copies made under tightly defined and strictly controlled circumstances (*e.g.* using write-blockers) rather than directly examining the original disks (best evidence). "Process to maintain and safeguard the integrity and/or original condition of the potential digital evidence" *(ISO/IEC 27037)*.
Pre-Shared Key **(PSK)**	Cryptographic protocol and key used, for instance, by WPA and WPA2 to authenticate Wi-Fi devices and initialise/prime the session keys to be used subsequently for encrypted communications.
Pretext, pretexting	Fictitious but plausible scenario, justification, or lie such as that used by a social engineer to persuade or coerce a victim to do their bidding, or a cover story for an act of vandalism, sabotage, or cybertage.

TERM	MEANING
Pretty **G**ood **P**rivacy **(PGP)**	Email cryptosystem created and released for free by Phil Zimmerman in 1991, to the consternation of the US government attempting to restrict the export of strong cryptography. Uses the IDEA encryption algorithm and a distributed trust/reputation architecture that established a distributed 'web of trust' between individuals rather than relying on authoritative **C**ertification **A**uthorities as with a conventional **P**ublic **K**ey **I**nfrastructure. PGP is not guaranteed perfectly secure but is 'pretty good.' Evolved into OpenPGP. "Trademark of Network Associates, Inc., referring to a computer program (and related protocols) that uses cryptography to provide data security for electronic mail and other applications on the Internet" *(SANS glossary)*. See also S/MIME.
Prevent/deter actions & controls	See preventive control. "Actions & controls that decrease the likelihood of an unfavorable event by preventing or deterring it from happening" *(OCEG GRC Glossary)*.
Prevention	Stopping something from occurring. "Measures that enable an organization to avoid, preclude or limit the impact of an undesirable event or potential disruption" *(ISO 22300)*.
Prevention of hazards and threats	"Process, practices, techniques, materials, products, services or resources used to avoid, reduce, or control hazards and threats and their associated risks of any type in order to reduce their potential likelihood or consequences" *(ISO 22300)*.
Preventive action	"Action to eliminate the cause of a potential non-conformity or other undesirable potential situation. Note: There can be more than one cause for a potential nonconformity. Preventive action is taken to prevent occurrence whereas corrective action is taken to prevent recurrence" *(ISO 9000)*.
Preventive control	Control intended to block, slow, or prevent incidents from occurring, normally by reducing vulnerabilities (*e.g.* patching, input validation) but sometimes by reducing threats (*e.g.* deterrent controls). "An internal control that is used to avoid undesirable events, errors and other occurrences that an enterprise has determined could have a negative material effect on a process or end product" *(ISACA glossary)*. *Cf.* detective control, corrective control.
Preventive maintenance	Preventive maintenance – proactive, planned activities to check, adjust, and if necessary align, recalibrate, repair, or replace equipment *before* it experiences significant problems, *e.g.* periodically cleaning accumulated dust from computer equipment and computer room air conditioners is a simple yet effective way to avoid overheating that can lead to unreliable operating, failures, and fires. "Maintenance performed at predetermined intervals or according to prescribed criteria in order to reduce the probability of failure or the degradation of the functioning of a functional unit" *(ISO/IEC 2382)*.

TERM	MEANING
Preventive security	Preventive security. "Planning, preparation, implementation and overseeing of protective security measures which seek to eliminate or reduce risk resulting from a threat" *(ISO 23234)*.
Primary **A**ccount **N**umber **(PAN), account number, credit card number**	Finance industry term for what is commonly known as a credit card number – the ~16-digit identifier normally embossed on a payment card that identifies both the card issuer (the **B**ank **I**dentification **N**umber) *and* the cardholder's account. *Cf.* **P**ersonal **A**rea **N**etwork.
Primary stakeholder	"The person or organization that owns or is accountable for an Asset" *(O-RT)*.
Prime number, prime	Natural number that has no factors other than 1 and itself. The number 7, for instance, is not the product of any other whole or round numbers *except* 1 × 7. "A natural number greater than 1 that can only be divided by 1 and itself" *(ISACA glossary)*.
Primitive, cryptographic primitive, cryptoprimitive	Basic, simple, original, unsophisticated, or fundamental, such as a low-level functional or processing block performing a substitution or transposition step within a cryptographic algorithm. "A fundamental interface, block of code or basic functionality that can be deployed and reused within broader systems or interfaces. Primitives can be combined in various ways to accomplish particular tasks. In cryptosystems, primitives form the building blocks of cryptographic algorithms" *(ISACA glossary)*.
Principal	a. *[Noun]* Leader, chief, head, manager, main person, senior respected authority figure, top dog, boss, ... *e.g.* headmaster, **C**hief **E**xecutive **O**fficer, Prime Minister, President, monarch, ... b. *[Noun]* Money initially invested/deposited or loaned. c. *[Noun]* [Personally Identifiable Information principal] See data subject. d. *[Adjective]* Key, primary, preeminent, most important or significant. *Cf.* principle.
Principal system objective	Key objective of a system (or objective of a key system?). "System objectives that relate to the trust services category or categories addressed by the examination and that could reasonably be expected to influence the relevant decisions of intended users" *(**T**rust **S**ervices **C**riteria)*.
Principle	Fundamental philosophical basis or rationale underpinning various models, practices, approaches, axioms, controls, rules, *etc.* In the context of information security, privacy, and governance, neatly summed up by phrases such as default deny, layered defence, shared responsibility, and least privilege. "A component of a governance system. Principles translate desired behavior into practical guidance for day-to-day management" *(ISACA glossary)*. *Cf.* principal.

TERM	MEANING
Principled performance	"To reliably achieve objectives, address uncertainty, and act with integrity" *(OCEG GRC Glossary)*.
Principles of separation and segregation	"Systems architecture and design incorporating separation and segregation in order to establish trust zones, define security domains and enforce boundaries" *(NZISM)*.
Prioritised activity	Activity that is more important or urgent to the organisation than most. "Activity to which urgency is given in order to avoid unacceptable impacts to the business during a disruption" *(ISO 22300)*.
Priority	Relatively important or urgent compared to other objectives, strategies, concerns, initiatives, matters, *etc.* Usually implies that it takes precedence. "Sequence in which an incident or problem needs to be resolved, based on impact and urgency" *(ENISA RM glossary)*.
Priority call	"Telecommunications made by specific terminals in the event of emergencies which should be handled with priority by restricting public calls. Note: the specific terminals may span different services (VoIP, PSTN, voice, IP data traffic, *etc.*) for wired and wireless networks" *(ISO/IEC 27011)*.
PRISM	SECRET **N**ational **S**ecurity **A**gency electronic mass surveillance program, disclosed by whistleblower Ed Snowden. Exploits legal rights of access to data held by **I**nternet **S**ervice **P**roviders such as Google, Yahoo!, Microsoft, Apple, and Facebook. See also BULLRUN.
Privacy	Under information/data protection laws, privacy may be defined narrowly in relation to a data subject's legal right to control (permit or forbid) the release, disclosure, use, accuracy, and retention of their personal information. In common usage, however, privacy is a broader concept also encompassing freedom of expression, personal choice, personal space, ethics and morality, anonymity, trust, freedom from surveillance and state interference, *etc.* "Freedom from intrusion into the private life or affairs of an individual when that intrusion results from undue or illegal gathering and use of data about that individual" *(ISO/IEC 2382)*. "The right of an individual to trust that others will appropriately and respectfully use, store, share and dispose of his/her associated personal and sensitive information within the context and according to the purposes for which it was collected or derived" *(ISACA glossary)*. See also **G**eneral **D**ata **P**rotection **R**egulation, **D**ata **P**rotection **A**ct, **C**alifornia **C**onsumer **P**rotection **A**ct, **P**ersonal **I**nformation **P**rotection and **E**lectronic **D**ocuments **A**ct, **H**ealth **I**nsurance **P**ortability and **A**ccountability **A**ct, and others around the world. *Reminder:* this hyperglossary is *not* legal advice.

TERM	MEANING
Privacy breach	Incident involving actual or potential unauthorised or inappropriate disclosure, release, or use of personal information, contrary to rules or expectations in laws, regulations, policies, contracts, agreements, or ethics. "Situation where personally identifiable information is processed in violation of one or more relevant privacy safeguarding requirements" *(ISO/IEC 29100)*.
Privacy breech	Underwear designed to conceal one's privates, maybe? More likely a common typo of privacy breach ...
Privacy by default	Requirement of the **G**eneral **D**ata **P**rotection **R**egulation that privacy and security (primarily confidentiality) should be the preferred, automatic state or option in systems, services, and processes handling personal information, *e.g.* the most restrictive privacy settings should apply by default unless a data subject expressly relaxes them. An expression of opt-in. See also privacy by design.
Privacy by design	Requirement of the **G**eneral **D**ata **P**rotection **R**egulation that privacy should be an integral or inherent part of the design of new systems, services, and processes handling personal information. "The integration of privacy into the entire engineering process" *(ISACA glossary)*. See also privacy by default.
Privacy commitment	Commitment regarding privacy. "Declarations made by management regarding the performance of a system processing personal information. Such commitments can be communicated in written agreements, standardized contracts, service level agreements, or published statements (for example, a privacy practices statement). In addition, privacy commitments may be made on many different aspects of the service being provided" *(Trust Services Criteria)*.
Privacy continuous monitoring	"Maintaining ongoing awareness of privacy risks and assessing privacy controls at a frequency sufficient to ensure compliance with applicable privacy requirements and to manage privacy risks" *(OMB Circular A-130)*.
Privacy control	Control designed to mitigate unacceptable privacy risks by protecting personal information. "Measure that treats privacy risks by reducing their likelihood or their consequences. Note: Privacy controls include organizational, physical and technical measures, *e.g.* policies, procedures, guidelines, legal contracts, management practices or organizational structures. Control is also used as a synonym for safeguard or countermeasure" *(ISO/IEC 29100)*. "Measures that treat privacy risk by reducing its likelihood or consequences. Privacy controls include organizational, physical and technical measures, *e.g.,* policies, procedures, guidelines, legal contracts, management practices or organizational structures" *(ISACA glossary)*. "The administrative, technical, and physical safeguards employed within an agency to ensure compliance with applicable privacy requirements and manage privacy risks" *(OMB Circular A-130)*.

TERM	MEANING
Privacy data sharing agreement	"Clauses for privacy protection in a data sharing agreement. Note: A privacy data sharing agreement can involve data transfer, data processing, and sharing of personally identifiable information (PII) between joint PII controllers" *(ISO/IEC TS 27570)*.
Privacy engineering	Privacy engineering. "Within systems engineering, a discipline focused on maximizing the freedom of data subjects from adverse consequence associated with illicit or illegal disclosures or abuse during (or as a result of) processing" *(ISACA glossary)*.
Privacy-**E**nhancing **T**echnology **(PET)**	Tools and techniques to facilitate legitimate exploitation of personal information without unduly compromising privacy, *e.g.* by anonymising data. "Privacy control, consisting of information and communication technology (ICT) measures, products, or services that protect privacy by eliminating or reducing personally identifiable information (PII) or by preventing unnecessary and/or undesired processing of PII, all without losing the functionality of the ICT system. Notes: Examples of PETs include, but are not limited to, anonymization and pseudonymization tools that eliminate, reduce, mask, or de-identify PII or that prevent unnecessary, unauthorized and/or undesirable processing of PII. Masking is the process of obscuring elements of PII" *(ISO/IEC 29100)*.
Privacy impact	Privacy impact. "Anything that has an effect on the privacy of a PII principal and/or group of PII principals. Note: The privacy impact can result from the processing of PII in conformance or in violation of privacy safeguarding requirements" *(ISO/IEC 29134)*. "Anything that has an effect on the privacy of personally identifiable information (PII) owned by a data subject and/or group of data subjects" *(ISACA glossary)*.
Privacy **I**mpact **A**ssessment **(PIA), privacy risk assessment**	Information risk assessment evaluating the possibility of privacy breaches or incidents, emphasising the impacts, *i.e.* potential adverse effects on the data subjects. "Overall process of identifying, analysing, evaluating, consulting, communicating and planning the treatment of potential privacy impacts with regard to the processing of personally identifiable information, framed within an organization's broader risk management framework" *(ISO/IEC 27002)*. "The overall process of identifying, analyzing, evaluating, consulting, communicating and planning the treatment of potential privacy impacts with regard to the processing of personally identifiable information (PII) within the broader risk management framework of an enterprise" *(ISACA glossary)*. See ISO/IEC 29134.
Privacy **I**nformation **M**anagement **S**ystem **(PIMS)**	Management System protecting personal information for privacy reasons. "An information security management system that addresses the protection of privacy potentially affected by the processing of personally identifiable information (PII)" *(ISACA glossary)*. See ISO/IEC 27701.

TERM	MEANING
Privacy Law Specialist (PLS)	IAPP's qualifications for US privacy law specialists. See also CIPP, CIPM. More info: https://iapp.org/pls/
Privacy marking	"Used to indicate that official information has a special handling requirement or a distribution that is restricted to a particular audience" *(NZISM)*.
Privacy notice	Formal disclosure by an organisation of how it intends to use and protect any personal information provided to it. "A notification that provides individuals with information on how their personal data will be processed" *(ISACA glossary)*. "A written communication by entities that collect personal information, to the individuals about whom personal information is collected, about the entity's (a) policies regarding the nature of the information that they will collect and how that information will be used, retained, disclosed, and disposed of or anonymized and (b) commitment to adhere to those policies. A privacy notice also includes information about such matters as the purpose of collecting the information, the choices that individuals have related to their personal information, the security of such information, and how individuals can contact the entity with inquiries, complaints, and disputes related to their personal information. When a user entity collects personal information from individuals, it typically provides a privacy notice to those individuals" *(Trust Services Criteria)*.
Privacy plan	"A formal document that details the privacy controls selected for an information system or environment of operation that are in place or planned for meeting applicable privacy requirements and managing privacy risks, details how the controls have been implemented, and describes the methodologies and metrics that will be used to assess the controls" *(OMB Circular A-130)*.
Privacy policy	Privacy policy. "Overall intention and direction, rules and commitment, as formally expressed by the personally identifiable information (PII) controller related to the processing of PII in a particular setting" *(ISO/IEC 29100)*. "The intention, direction, rules and commitment, as formally expressed by the personally identifiable information (PII) controller, related to the processing of PII in a particular setting. It is a set of shared values governing the privacy protection of PII when processed in information and communication technology systems" *(ISACA glossary)*.
Privacy preference	"Specific choices made by a personally identifiable information (PII) principal about how their PII should be processed for a particular purpose" *(ISO/IEC 29100)*. "Specific choices made by an individual about how their personally identifiable information (PII) should be processed for a particular purpose" *(ISACA glossary)*.

TERM	MEANING
Privacy principle	Privacy principle. "Shared value governing the privacy protection of personally identifiable information (PII) when processed in information and communication technology systems" *(ISO/IEC 29100)*. "A set of shared values governing the privacy protection of personally identifiable information (PII) when processed in information and communication technology systems" *(ISACA glossary)*.
Privacy protection	Privacy protection. "Measures taken to ensure privacy. Note: The measures include data protection and limitations on the gathering, combining, and processing of data about individuals" *(ISO/IEC 2382)*.
Privacy risk	Privacy risk. "Effect of uncertainty on privacy. Notes: Risk is defined as the 'effect of uncertainty on objectives' in ISO Guide 73 [withdrawn]) and ISO 31000. Uncertainty is the state, even partial, of deficiency of information related to, understanding or knowledge of, an event, its consequence, or likelihood" *(ISO/IEC 29100)*. "Any risk of informational harm to data subjects and/or organization(s), including deception, financial injury, health and safety injuries, unwanted intrusion and reputational injuries, where the harm or damage goes beyond economic and tangible losses" *(ISACA glossary)*.
Privacy risk assessment	Privacy risk assessment. "A process used to identify and evaluate privacy-related risk and its potential effects" *(ISACA glossary)*.
Privacy risk map	Heat-map/**P**robability-**I**mpact **G**raphic covering privacy risks, specifically. "Diagram that indicates the level of impact and likelihood of privacy risks identified. Note: The map is typically used to determine the order in which the privacy risks should be treated" *(ISO/IEC 29134)*.
Privacy safeguarding requirement	Objective or obligation to protect privacy, generally involving the use of appropriate controls. "Requirement that an organization takes into account when processing personally identifiable information (PII) with respect to the privacy protection of PII" *(ISO/IEC 29100)*.
Privacy Shield	Privacy arrangements replaced Safe Harbor under which US organisations were permitted to gather and process personal information from Europe *provided* they formally committed to privacy. Whereas this merely involved self-certification, the commitment was binding under US law. It fell short of the **G**eneral **D**ata **P**rotection **R**egulation requirements, however, and was invalidated by a decision of the **E**uropean **U**nion Court of Justice in 2020 to be replaced by the EU-US Data Privacy Framework in 2023.

TERM	MEANING
Privacy stakeholder	Privacy stakeholder. "Natural or legal person, public authority, agency or any other body that can affect, be affected by, or perceive themselves to be affected by a decision or activity related to personally identifiable information (PII) processing" *(ISO/IEC 29100)*.
Private	a. Confidential or sensitive to a person or organisation, something they would rather not be widely known about themselves. Implies them having a reasonable degree of control over their own information. b. "Pertaining to characteristics of language constructs that are not directly available to the user of these language constructs" *(ISO/IEC 2382)*.
Private [Automatic] Branch eXchange (PBX, PABX)	Corporate telephone system.
Private cloud	Cloud services provided exclusively to one or more specific organisations. "An on- or off-premises cloud environment in which a specific enterprise controls all infrastructure resources" *(ISACA glossary)*. See also public cloud, hybrid cloud.
Private key	Confidential member of a public–private key pair in an asymmetric cryptography system or **P**ublic **K**ey **I**nfrastructure. Unlike a shared key or secret key, once generated and allocated, a private key should *never* be divulged to others by its owner. "Key that is intended for decryption for the exclusive use by its owner" *(ISO/IEC 2382)*. "A mathematical key (kept secret by the holder) used to create digital signatures and, depending on the algorithm, decrypt messages or files encrypted for confidentiality with the corresponding public key" *(ISACA glossary)*.
Private network	Private network. "A network and infrastructure owned, managed and controlled by a single entity for its exclusive use. This term includes networks used by private organisations, nongovernment organisations, state owned enterprises, or government department, agencies and ministries. If any part of the transmission path utilises **any** element of a public network, such as telecommunications or data services from a service provider that utilise any component of local, regional or national infrastructure, then the network is defined as a public network" *(NZISM)*.

TERM	MEANING
Private port	See ephemeral port.
Private property	Asset/s belonging to an individual person or organisation. *Cf.* public property. Despite the name, this has more to do with legal ownership rights than privacy.
Private Security Service Provider **(PSSP),** Private Security Company **(PSC)**	"Organization that conducts or contracts security operations and whose business activities include the provision of security services either on its own behalf or on behalf of another. Notes: PSSPs provide services to clients with the aim of ensuring their security and that of others. PSSPs typically work in circumstances where governance is weak or rule of law undermined due to human- or naturally caused events and provide services for which personnel can be required to carry weapons in the performance of their duties in accordance with the terms of their contract. Examples of security services provided by PSSPs include: guarding; close protection; physical protection measures; security awareness and training; risk, security and threat assessment; the provision of protective and defensive measures for individuals' compounds, diplomatic and residential perimeters; escort of transport; and policy analysis. A joint venture is considered part of the organization" *(ISO 22300)*.
Private **V**irtual **L**ocal **A**rea **N**etwork **(PVLAN)**	Virtual Local Area Network that is isolated from others to some extent using traffic encryption. 'To some extent' hints at vulnerabilities in some PVLAN configurations allowing hackers to 'hop' between inadequately isolated PVLANs.
Privilege	Attribute of certain userIDs, applications, functions, *etc.* that allows certain logical access controls to be bypassed in order to execute functions that are normally forbidden to ordinary (non-privileged) users, *e.g.* system-wide data backups need access to copy *all* the files to be backed up, including files that may not belong to the user running the backup utility. "The level of trust with which a system object is imbued" *(ISACA glossary)*.
Privileged **A**ccess [or **A**ccount] **M**anagement **(PAM)**	Given their wide-ranging ability to degrade, disable, or bypass automated controls, managing and controlling access to various privileged userIDs is critical to achieve and maintain adequate system security. PAM comprises the processes, built-in system functions/utilities, and add-on tools to do this. "An access control mechanism that uses a combination of people, processes and technology to safeguard identities with special access or capabilities beyond regular users" *(ISACA glossary)*. "A set of processes and tools for granting, controlling, monitoring, and auditing privileged access" *(NZISM)*. See also **I**dentity and **A**ccess **M**anagement.

TERM	MEANING
Privileged account	UserID for a privileged computer user. "A user account with high levels of access to systems, devices and data. Privileged accounts may, for example, be able to install or remove software, upgrade operating systems, or modify system or application configurations. They may also have access to data that is not normally accessible to standard users" *(NZISM)*. "Includes privileged user accounts and privileged service accounts" *(AusISM)*. "A system account with the authorizations of a privileged user" *(NIST SP 800-171)*.
Privileged operating environments	"[Operating environments] used exclusively for administrative activities" *(AusISM)*.
Privileged instruction	"Instruction that can be executed only in a specific mode" *(ISO/IEC 2382)*.
Privileged user [rôle]	Whereas ordinary nonprivileged user rôles grant minimal rights of access to networks, systems, and data for most users, privileged user rôles confer more powerful access rights that can bypass normal security controls and should therefore only be allocated to highly trustworthy workers with additional procedural and/or technical controls. "Any user account with greater than basic access privileges. Typically, these accounts have elevated or increased privileges with more rights than a standard user account" *(ISACA glossary)*. "A user that is authorized (and, therefore, trusted) to perform security relevant functions that ordinary users are not authorized to perform" *(NIST CSF)*. "A system user who can alter or circumvent system security protections. This can also apply to system users who could have only limited privileges, such as software developers, who can still bypass security precautions. A privileged user can have the capability to modify system configurations, account privileges, audit logs, data files or applications" *(NZISM)*. "A user who can alter or circumvent a system's controls. This can also apply to users who could have only limited privileges, such as software developers, who can still bypass controls. A privileged user can have the capability to modify system configurations, account privileges, event logs and security configurations for applications" *(AusISM)*. "A user who is authorized (and therefore, trusted) to perform security-relevant functions that ordinary users are not authorized to perform" *(NIST SP 800-171)*. See also **R**ôle-**B**ased **A**ccess **C**ontrol.
Privilege escalation	See elevation of privilege.
Proactive actions & controls	"Actions & controls that promote or enable favorable events and prevent or deter unfavorable events" *(OCEG GRC Glossary)*.

TERM	MEANING
Proactive security	See offensive security.
Probability	Mathematical chance of something such as an incident occurring, ranging between zero (meaning there is absolutely no possibility whatsoever, ever) and one (it is absolutely certain: it definitely happens). Whereas probability is precisely defined in mathematics (*e.g.* occurrence within a defined timescale), vague terms such as likelihood, possibility, chance, and luck are used informally in everyday language in reference to uncertainty, unpredictability, often implying the speaker's inability to influence or determine the outcome ('fate'). "Measure of the chance of occurrence expressed as a number from 0 to 1, where 0 is impossibility and 1 is absolute certainty" *(ISO 31073)*. "Extent to which an event is likely to occur" *(ENISA RM glossary)*. "A mathematical-driven measure of the possibility of a specific outcome as a ratio of all possible outcomes" *(ISACA glossary)*.
Probability-**I**mpact **G**raphic **(PIG)**	Two-dimensional graphical representation of risks, reflecting the chances that incidents are anticipated to occur within a finite timescale (typically one or more years) and the anticipated significance or severity of the impacts if they do. Despite normally being a qualitative, subjective, and static representation (not a mathematical graph), a useful means for management to communicate/report, debate, comprehend, and ultimately agree on the relative significance or levels of various risks. Often overlaid on a red-amber-green background, visually emphasising the range, *i.e.* a heatmap.
Probability of **A**ction **(PoA)**	"The probability that a Threat Agent will act against an Asset once contact occurs" *(O-RT)*.
Probable **L**oss **M**agnitude **(PLM)**	One of the risk factors (parameters) in the FAIR method, estimating the impact of incidents affecting the information assets under analysis. See also **C**ontrol **S**trength, **L**oss **E**vent **F**requency, **T**hreat **Cap**ability, **T**hreat **E**vent **F**requency.
Probative data	Proof-related information. "Information that reveals the truth of an allegation" *(NIST SP 800-101)*.
Probe	Metaphorically poke at something to find out about it. Hackers compose specific sequences of carefully crafted packets hoping to reveal the network architecture, **O**perating **S**ystems, application software, and perhaps even software versions installed on target networks. Social engineers use phone calls and emails to probe target organisations for naïve and vulnerable victims. Prison, police, and customs officers sometimes don latex gloves to probe suspects for concealed contraband … "The act of inspecting a network or system to find weak spots" *(ISACA glossary)*.
Probity	Someone's strong sense of ethics, honesty, and trustworthiness. An aspect of personal integrity.

TERM	MEANING
Problem escalation procedure	"The process of escalating a problem from junior to senior support staff and ultimately to higher levels of management. Note: Problem escalation procedure is often used in help desk management when an unresolved problem is escalated up the chain of command until it is solved" *(ISACA glossary)*.
Problem (and solution) owner	Organisation, rôle, or person who owns and is accountable for addressing and ideally solving an identified problem, issue, or concern, taking it to heart. See also asset owner, information owner, risk owner, control owner, system owner.
Procedural control	See manual control.
Procedural knowledge	Competent and experienced person's understanding of a process, perhaps documented in the form of a procedure. "Knowledge which explicitly indicates the steps to be taken in order to solve a problem or to reach a goal" *(ISO/IEC 22989)*.
Procedure	Formal description of a process. Procedures are normally documented to explain processes to those expected to perform them, and are usually formalised through some form of management review, authorisation, endorsement, and/or mandate to ensure their suitability and improve process control, consistency, and conformity. "Specified way to carry out an activity or a process. Notes: Procedures can be documented or not. When a procedure is documented, the term 'written procedure' or 'documented procedure' is frequently used. The document that contains a procedure can be called a 'procedure document'" *(ISO 22300)*. "A document containing a detailed description of the steps necessary to perform specific operations in conformance with applicable standards. Procedures are defined as parts of processes" *(ISACA glossary)*. "A detailed articulation of what the organization expects on a particular topic, that describes the 'how to' or instructions, guides implementation, and is audience-specific" *(OCEG GRC Glossary)*. "A written description of a course of action to be taken to perform a given task" *(ENISA RM glossary)*. See also protocol.
Process, execution, ways	a. Sequence of manual and/or automated activities intended to achieve a specific objective, function, or outcome. May be described in a procedure or protocol. "Predetermined course of events defined by its purpose or by its effect, achieved under given conditions" *(ISO/IEC 2382)*. "Set of interrelated or interacting activities that transforms inputs to deliver a result" *(ISO/IEC 27002)*. "Set of interrelated or interacting activities that uses or transforms inputs to deliver a result. Note: Whether the result of a process is called an output, a product or a service depends on the context of the reference" *(ISO/IEC 42001)*. "Set of activities that have a common goal and last for a limited period of time" *(ISO/IEC 27043)*. "Generally, a collection of activities

TERM	MEANING
	influenced by the enterprise's policies and procedures that takes inputs from a number of sources, (including other processes), manipulates the inputs and produces outputs. Note: Processes have clear business reasons for existing, accountable owners, clear roles and responsibilities around the execution of the process and the means to measure performance" *(ISACA glossary)*. "A series of actions or steps to achieve an objective" *(OCEG GRC Glossary)*. "An organized set of activities which uses resources to transform inputs to outputs" *(ENISA RM glossary)*. b. Particular instance of a program currently running (executing) on a computer.
Process control	a. Control designed to mitigate unacceptable process risks, keeping business processes running properly (smoothly, efficiently, effectively, safely, securely, *etc.*). Implies the need for clear objectives, guardrails, and proactive monitoring, with feedback for smooth, proportional control. May be fully or partially automated using technology, or manual. b. Category of **O**perational **T**echnology equipment and practices monitoring and controlling industrial manufacturing processes, *e.g.* the OT systems integrated within factory production lines for chemical synthesis, fermentation, and mass-produced goods.
Process **C**ontrol **S**ystem **(PCS)**	See **I**ndustrial **C**ontrol **S**ystem. "System that serves to control and monitor the generation, production, transmission, storage and distribution of electric power, gas, oil and heat, including the control of associated supporting processes. Note: Process control systems are often referred to more generally as industrial control systems. In this document, the terms process control system and industrial control system are restricted to technologies and components used in the energy utility industry" *(ISO/IEC 27019)*.
Processing	Sequential and systematic performance of operations. "Any operation or set of operations which is performed on personal data or on sets of personal data, whether or not by automated means, such as collection, recording, organisation, structuring, storage, adaptation or alteration, retrieval, consultation, use, disclosure by transmission, dissemination or otherwise making available, alignment or combination, restriction, erasure or destruction" *(**G**eneral **D**ata **P**rotection **R**egulation)*. "Operation or set of operations performed upon personally identifiable information (PII). Notes: Examples of processing operations of PII include, but are not limited to, the collection, storage, alteration, retrieval, consultation, disclosure, anonymization, pseudonymization, dissemination or otherwise making available, deletion or destruction of PII" *(ISO/IEC 29100)*.

TERM	MEANING
Processing control	Control designed to mitigate unacceptable processing risks, *e.g.* microcode in the **C**entral **P**rocessing **U**nit that traps invalid calls to protected memory locations. See also input control, output control.
Processing risk	Uncertain possibility of issues arising during **D**ata **P**rocessing, *e.g.* programming bugs or flaws, technological glitches or failures, out-of-range values such as buffer overflows, undefined states, conflicts, and delays, or non-arrival of critical items. Can also occur with manual processes, *e.g.* misinterpretation of the information available leading to inappropriate decisions and responses. See also input risk, output risk.
Processor, processing unit, **C**entral **P**rocessing **U**nit **(CPU)**	a. Functional computer subsystem, typically implemented as an **I**ntegrated **C**ircuit, that processes data, *e.g.* Intel i5 **C**entral **P**rocessing **U**nit, microprocessor, graphics processor, cryptographic processor, digital signal processor, quantum processor. "Functional unit that consists of one or more processors and their internal storages [and] in a computer, functional unit that interprets and executes instructions" *(ISO/IEC 2382)*. "Computer hardware that houses the electronic circuits that control/direct all operations of a computer system" *(ISACA glossary)*. b. Organisation handling and manipulating personal information. "A natural or legal person, public authority, agency or other body which processes personal data on behalf of the controller" *(**G**eneral **D**ata **P**rotection **R**egulation)*.
Process owner	Organisation, rôle, or person who owns, is in charge of and is accountable for the results of, a process. Responsibilities (often shared with specialists) may extend to: scoping, definition, and specification of process objectives; process design and documentation (*e.g.* policies, procedures, guidelines, training, and awareness materials); risk, security, change, incident, and Business Continuity Management including dependencies and interfaces/relationships with other processes and owners; resourcing; automation, system, and network administration; and maintenance, metrics, monitoring, assurance, conformity, and benefits realisation. "The person or team responsible for developing, updating or following a process. An organization or project can have multiple owners at different levels of responsibility for: An organization's set of standard processes; Project-specific and project-defined processes" *(ISACA glossary)*. "An individual held accountable and responsible for the workings and improvement of one of the organization's defined processes and its related sub-processes" *(ENISA RM glossary)*.
Process risk	Uncertain possibility of incidents affecting or involving some sort of process such as a manufacturing process. There may be issues concerning the process specification, design, implementation and configuration, documentation, operation, performance, reliability

TERM	MEANING
	and consistency, management, maintenance, or governance. It may be the responsibility of, or allocated to, someone incompetent, lazy, or otherwise inappropriate. There may be compliance or procedural conformity issues. It may be inefficient, ineffective, and inadequate to satisfy the organisation's objectives.
Product	Something produced, the end results of a creative or industrial process, such as goods, services, or **I**ntellectual **P**roperty plus the benefits thereby generated for its suppliers, owners, users, consumers, or others (*e.g.* society). "Any good or service" (*ISO 14050*). "A generic term used to describe software or hardware" *(AusISM)*. "Tangible or intangible goods manufactured or produced by an entity. Throughout this document, the term is used interchangeably with goods" *(**T**rust **S**ervices **C**riteria)*.
Product fraud	Product fraud. "Wrongful or criminal deception that utilizes material goods for financial or personal gain. Notes: Fraud means wrongful or criminal deception intended to result in financial or personal gain that creates social or economic harm. Products include electronic media carried on material goods. Fraud related to digitally transmitted electronic media shall be considered separately" *(ISO 22300)*.
Production **A**cceptance **T**est **(PAT)**	Acceptance test before a new/changed application, system, service, *etc.* is migrated into the production environment, configured, and released for use. Provides assurance that it can be implemented, will function adequately, and can be administered acceptably, without threatening the production environment or impacting its security.
Production data	Digital data and information in other formats involved in the creation, manufacture, or delivery of products. "Data acquired during the operation phase of an AI system, for which a deployed AI system calculates a predicted output or inference" *(ISO/IEC 22989)*.
Production environment, operational environment, live systems	Set or subset of computer systems, networks, devices, data, and the supporting machines, tools, and processes providing information processing services for the organisation. *Cf.* development environment, test environment.
Production file format	Required file format for producing **E**lectronically **S**tored **I**nformation, facilitating its analysis. "Organisation and representation of data and metadata that is presented to a requesting party" *(ISO/IEC 27050-1)*.
Product owner	Product owner. Initially the person or organisation that came up with the design (the intellectual property owner) and eventually the consumer/purchaser/user.

TERM	MEANING
Product with digital elements	"A software or hardware product and its remote data processing solutions, including software or hardware components being placed on the market separately" *(EU CRA)*.
Professional	a. *[Noun]* Competent well-educated person whose occupation, education, qualifications, skills, expertise, and experience are focused in a specialist area. b. *[Adjective]* Competent, knowledgeable, reliable, trustworthy.
Professional competence	Professional competence. "Proven level of ability, often linked to qualifications issued by relevant professional bodies and compliance with their standards and codes of practice" *(ISACA glossary)*.
Professional indemnity insurance, Errors & Omissions (E&O)	Insurance for professionals indemnifying them against claims of incompetence, negligence, *etc.*, typically covering the costs of legal defence and settlements according to the policy terms and conditions.
Professional judgement	"The application of relevant knowledge and experience in making informed decisions about the courses of action that are appropriate in the circumstances of the IS audit and assurance engagement" *(ISACA glossary)*.
Professional scepticism	Capability for critically evaluating the integrity of information, doubting and questioning/challenging its provenance, accuracy, validity, trustworthiness, *etc.* "Questioning and critically assessing the reliability of information" *(IIA GIAS)*. See also fact-checking.
Profile	Set of characteristics used to characterise, understand, and perhaps classify or control something – such as an **I**nformation **T**echnology system user, administrator, fraudster, or hacker.
Profiling	Process of researching, compiling, collating, cross-referencing, and analysing pertinent information to establish a profile. "Any form of automated processing of personal data consisting of the use of personal data to evaluate certain personal aspects relating to a natural person, in particular to analyse or predict aspects concerning that natural person's performance at work, economic situation, health, personal preferences, interests, reliability, behaviour, location or movements" *(**G**eneral **D**ata **P**rotection **R**egulation)*.
Program, programme	a. *[Noun]* Set of structured instructions to be executed by a computer system, device, *thing*, or equipment. b. *[Noun]* Initiative, project, or a set of related activities towards some grand strategic plan or social objective. [Usually spelled 'programme' in British English]. "A structured grouping of interdependent projects that is both necessary and sufficient to achieve a desired business outcome and create value. These projects could include, but are not

TERM	MEANING
	limited to, changes in the nature of the business, business processes and the work performed by people as well as the competencies required to carry out the work, the enabling technology and the organizational structure" *(ISACA glossary)*. c. *[Noun]* Regular segment or show on broadcast television or radio, such as the news at 6. [Also 'programme' to the Brits]. d. *[Verb]* To develop source code or assembler. See software development.
Program library	Controlled folder or **D**ata**B**ase containing executable programs. *Cf.* program source library.
Programmable Read-Only Memory (PROM)	Nonvolatile storage device, an **I**ntegrated **C**ircuit that can be programmed after manufacture. "A chip that can be programmed using a PROM programming device. It can be programmed only once. It cannot be erased and reprogrammed. Each of its bit locations is a fusible link. An unprogrammed PROM has all links closed, establishing a known state of each bit. Programming the chip consists of sending an electrical current of a specified size through each link that is to be changed to the alternate state. This causes the fuse to blow, opening that link" *(ISACA glossary)*. See also **E**rasable **P**rogrammable **R**ead-**O**nly **M**emory.
Programmable **L**ogic **C**ontroller **(PLC)**	Legacy term harping back to the early days of industrial automation using **C**omputer **N**umerically **C**ontrolled milling machines, *etc.* Embeddable **I**ndustrial **C**ontrol **S**ystem subsystem that can be programmed to respond to certain signals from plant with sophisticated sequences of control signals, alarms, alerts, *etc.* PLCs are physically rugged controllers designed for reliable operation in factory floor, outdoor, or other harsh environments. PLC 'programming' evolved from setting internal option switches through using custom connectors, proprietary hardware and software to the use of standardised ports and remote network access, with ever-increasing smarts.
Programmer	See software developer. "Person who designs, writes, or tests programs" *(ISO/IEC 2382)*.
Programming	Writing source code. See software development.
Programming language	Language used to compose program source code. Examples: Fortran, ADA, BASIC, COBOL, Pascal, C++, Java.
Program **S**ource **L**ibrary **(PSL)**	Controlled folder or **D**ata**B**ase containing human-readable source code files. *Cf.* program library.

TERM	MEANING
Program-to-program	Type of balancing control used to ensure integrity of information passed between programs, *e.g.* if one program outputs a data file containing 1,000 records and stores that figure as an additional piece of information, the next program should read the check value and count to confirm receipt of precisely 1,000 data records, otherwise halting further processing, flagging an error, and/or executing an error-handling subroutine.
Project risk	Uncertainty relating to any kind of project, *e.g.* its scope, delivery timescale and quality, costs and benefits. Competent project governance and management involves proactively identifying, analysing, evaluating, and treating the risks in much the same manner as for information or other kinds of risk. "A failed IT project that poses a significant risk to an enterprise, manifesting as lost market share, failure to seize new opportunities or other adverse impacts on customers, shareholders and staff" *(ISACA glossary).*
Promiscuous mode	Datacommunications devices such as Ethernet and Wi-Fi cards routinely ignore passing network packets that are not addressed to their unique network or device addresses, and are not broadcast or multicast packets, discarding them at a low level. When configured in promiscuous mode, however, even packets destined for other devices are passed up the network stack, *e.g.* to a sniffer where any unencrypted content may be read. "Allows the network interface to capture all network traffic irrespective of the hardware device to which the packet is addressed" *(ISACA glossary).* "When a machine reads all packets off the network, regardless of who they are addressed to. This is used by network administrators to diagnose network problems, but also by unsavory characters who are trying to eavesdrop on network traffic (which might contain passwords or other information)" *(SANS glossary).*
Promote/enable actions & controls	"Actions & controls that increase the likelihood of a favorable event by promoting, enabling and incentivizing it to happen" *(OCEG GRC Glossary).*
Pr0n	Leet form of 'porn', *i.e.* pornography, intended to evade crude adult content filters triggered by pornographic terms.
Proof, prove, proven	Demonstrate or verify something so as to dispel or significantly diminish any doubt as to its veracity or truth, *e.g.* by the presentation of objective, sound, and relevant forensic evidence, a rational and logically correct mathematical or scientific theorem, or a proof-of-concept.

TERM	MEANING
Proof-**O**f-**C**oncept **(POC)**	Functional prototype for an innovative system, process, *etc.*, intended to demonstrate convincingly (prove) that it can in fact be produced and operated, and will perform as expected. *Cf.* **P**roof-**O**f-**C**orrectness, **P**oint **O**f **C**ontact.
Proof-**O**f-**C**orrectness **(POC)**	"Proof that results from applying correctness proving" *(ISO/IEC 2382)*. *Cf.* **P**roof-**O**f-**C**oncept, **P**oint **O**f **C**ontact.
Proof of life	Capability of kidnappers to provide information demonstrating, convincingly, that their captive remains alive, thereby removing a key reason for not paying the ransom.
Proof of **S**take **(PoS)**	Blockchain approach used by cryptocurrencies such as Ethereum, in which 'minters' or 'validators' can only add new cryptocoins to the blockchain if they already hold a substantial number of bitcoins, giving them a material stake and hence self-interest in maintaining the integrity of the system. "A type of consensus algorithm by which a cryptocurrency blockchain network aims to achieve distributed consensus. In PoS consensus, the creator of the next block of data is chosen via several combinations of random selection and wealth or age (*i.e.*, the stake) within the blockchain. With PoS, miners can mine or validate block transactions based on amount of cryptocurrency a miner holds. PoS was created as an alternative to PoW, which requires large amounts of energy. PoS gives mining power based on the percentage of cryptocurrency held by a miner. It is seen as less risky in terms of network attacks and security and used only for public blockchains" *(ISACA glossary)*. *Cf.* Proof **o**f **W**ork.
Proof of **W**ork **(PoW)**	Blockchain approach used by cryptocurrencies such as Bitcoin, in which miners have to prove (cryptographically) to the validators that they have expended a *substantial* amount of computational effort (and energy) to mine (create) new cryptocoins, while validation takes minimal effort. "PoW is conducted through miners (participants who keep the blockchain running by providing computing resources) who are competing to solve a cryptographic problem (*i.e.*, hash puzzle). The PoW algorithm is used to confirm transactions and produce new blocks which are added to the chain. With PoW, miners compete against each other to complete transactions on the network and get rewarded. The computational work required to accomplish this is fairly (and usually increasingly) difficult for miners to perform, but easy for the network to verify. As difficulty increases over time, the amount of computational power, and hence, energy consumption, grows. Bitcoin is the first widespread application use of PoW. PoW is applicable to public blockchains" *(ISACA glossary)*. *Cf.* **P**roof **o**f **S**take.

TERM	MEANING
Proofread, proof read	Painstaking review of the 'proof' or 'proof copy' – a final draft version of a book prior to its printing and publication. Issues such as spelling mistakes, grammatical and formatting errors identified and corrected at this stage will not spoil the final product. An integrity control. "A check to ensure a document is properly written and that the English and grammar are acceptable" *(FSRCoP)*.
Propaganda	Biased, inaccurate, false, and/or incomplete information deliberately disclosed/circulated to mislead and influence the intended audience for strategic or political purposes. The content may be purely fictional (*e.g.* fake news) but usually elaborates or exaggerates on a germ of truth giving it credibility. Similar to marketing materials/advertisements, political rhetoric, manipulative teaching, and various forms of washing. A form of social engineering. See also misinformation, disinformation.
Proportional control	Analogue control design such that the strength of its action is proportionate (related) to the 'error', *i.e.* the discrepancy between current and desired levels, *e.g.* the footbrake on a car adjusts the braking effect according to the driver's foot pressure.
Proposition	Asserted explanation, opinion, or conclusion based on analysis of the available evidence, offered for consideration. "A statement that is either true or false and is generated, in part, from the background information but may also depend upon the findings that have been made at the alleged crime scene (or other information obtained before consideration by the expert). In the context of a criminal trial there will most often be a pair of propositions – one representing the prosecution's position, the other representing the defence's position in relation to a particular issue. Propositions shall be mutually exclusive (*i.e.* if one is true then the other must be false) and will often, but not always, be exhaustive (*i.e.* they cover all possibilities within the framework of circumstances of the case)" *(FSRCoP)*.
Proprietary	Commercial information, including highly valuable and sensitive information such as trade secrets, customer lists, and corporate strategies. "That information unique to a company and its ability to compete, such as customer lists, technical data, product costs, and trade secrets" *(SANS glossary)*.
Proscriptive norms	"Customs, rules, or expectations that discourage behavior the group deems negative (*e.g.*, 'do not cheat')" *(OCEG GRC Glossary)*.
Proscriptive policy	"A policy that says what not to do" *(OCEG GRC Glossary)*.
Prospect	"A cause that has the potential to eventually result in benefit" *(OCEG GRC Glossary)*.

TERM	MEANING
Protect, protection, protective	a. Synonymous with secure/security, often used in the sense of benevolent oversight by a parent who looks after and cares about the well-being of a protected asset as if it were their child. "Measures that safeguard and enable an organization to reduce the impact of a potential disruption" *(ISO 22300)*. "Arrangement for restricting access to or use of all, or part, of a computer system" *(ISO/IEC 2382)*. b. Core function within NIST **C**yber **S**ecurity **F**ramework along with identify, detect, respond, and recover. "Develop and implement appropriate safeguards to ensure delivery of critical services. The Protect Function supports the ability to limit or contain the impact of a potential cybersecurity event" *(NIST CSF)*.
PROTECTED area	See controlled area. "An area that has been authorised to process, store or communicate PROTECTED data. Such areas are not necessarily tied to a specific level of security zone" *(AusISM)*.
Protected **H**ealth **I**nformation **(PHI)**	Legally defined US term for sensitive personal information relating to health such as demographics and identity (name, address, date of birth, **S**ocial **S**ecurity **N**umber), medical history (past and present illnesses, medications, treatments, procedures), billing information (health insurance, payment history, claims), and genetic information. It applies to healthcare providers, health plans, and healthcare clearinghouses subject to the **H**ealth **I**nsurance **P**ortability and **A**ccountability **A**ct. See also **E**lectronic **H**ealth **R**ecord.
Protection exception	**O**perating **S**ystem kernel-level preventive control that enforces isolation between executing processes by signalling an exception if a program attempts to access another's memory space – an example of compartmentalisation. "Exception that occurs when a program attempts to access a protected area in a storage device" *(ISO/IEC 2382)*.
Protection mechanism	See control.
Protection **P**rofile **(PP)**	Generic, standardised, documented set of security requirements (a profile) for a class or type of **I**nformation **T**echnology products (*e.g.* firewalls) that are to be formally evaluated and certified under **C**ommon **C**riteria. "A document that stipulates the security functionality that must be included in Common Criteria evaluation to meet a range of defined threats. Protection Profiles also define the activities to be taken to assess the security function of an evaluated product" *(AusISM)*.
Protection racket	Illicit, menacing, and potentially illegal scheme to coerce money out of people or organisations in return for allegedly protecting them against threatened attacks.

TERM	MEANING
Protective marking	Physical and/or digital labelling of information or the storage medium/device to indicate its class (classification level). "A marking that is applied to unclassified or classified information to indicate the security measures and handling requirements that are to be applied to the information to ensure that it is appropriately protected" *(NZISM)*. "An administrative label assigned to data that not only shows the value of the data but also defines the level of protection to be provided" *(AusISM)*.
Protective measure	Protective control (countermeasure). "A measure intended to achieve adequate risk reduction" *(ISACA glossary)*.
Protective security	"Use of measures when managing risk linked to undesirable intentional actions" *(ISO 23234)*.
Protective **S**ecurity **R**equirements **(PSR)**	New Zealand government's policy framework detailing security requirements to protect its people, information, and associated assets. Replaced the earlier NZ Government **P**rotective **S**ecurity **M**anual and Security in Government Sector Manual. "Outlines the Government's expectations for managing personnel, physical and information security" *(NZISM)*.
Protective **S**ecurity **R**equirements **F**ramework **(PSRF)**	"A four-tier hierarchical approach to protective security. Strategic Security Directive (tier one); Core policies, strategic security objectives and the mandatory requirements (tier two); Protocols, standards and best practice requirements (tier three); Agency-specific policies and procedures (tier four)" *(NZISM)*.
Protector	Someone (such as a guardian) or something (such as an effective vaccine) that reduces risks. "A GRC Professional who spends substantial time producing and preserving value and serving as a stabilizing force in their organization" *(OCEG GRC Glossary)*.
Protector mindset	"Traits that strengthen the way that a high-performing Protector makes decisions and appraises problems, solutions, people, and reality. These traits include being: Collaborative, Accountable, Stable, Proactive, Visionary, and Versatile" *(OCEG GRC Glossary)*.
Protector skillset	"Interdisciplinary skills that strengthen the way that a high-performing Protector does their job including the critical disciplines" *(OCEG GRC Glossary)*.
Protocol	Defined and formal process, ordered sequence of activities or ways of doing something, such as authenticating and exchanging symmetric cryptographic keys with a counterparty in a secure manner or using a network, or simply an accepted way of communicating and interacting with others. "Set of rules that determines the behavior of objects in the exchange of messages [and] set of semantic and syntactic rules that determine the behavior of

TERM	MEANING
	entities in the same layer in performing communication functions [and] set of rules that determines the behavior of functional units in achieving communication" *(ISO/IEC 2382)*. "The rules by which a network operates and controls the flow and priority of transmissions" *(ISACA glossary)*. "A formal specification for communicating; an IP address the special set of rules that end points in a telecommunication connection use when they communicate. Protocols exist at several levels in a telecommunication connection" *(SANS glossary)*.
Prototype	Crude and incomplete working model, used to simulate and demonstrate a concept, design, or function, or key parts of it, early in the product/project lifecycle, often before the specifications and plans are finalised. "The process of quickly putting together a working model (a prototype) to test various aspects of a design, illustrate ideas or features and gather early user feedback. Prototyping uses programmed simulation techniques to represent a model of the final system to the user for advisement and critique. The emphasis is on end-user screens and reports. Internal controls are not a priority item since this is only a model" *(ISACA glossary)*. See also proof-of-concept.
Provenance	Assured high-integrity information concerning the source, disposition, and custody of forensic evidence or other information assets, potentially also critical data, software, hardware, and firmware from manufacture to installation if supply chain compromise (*e.g.* substitution of fake and perhaps backdoored components) presents unacceptable risks. Identity, background and qualification checks prior to appointing new recruits to the organisation are, in effect, confirming *their* provenance. "Information that documents the origin or source of Electronically Stored Information, any changes that may have taken place since it was originated, and who has had custody of it since it was originated" *(ISO/IEC 27050-1)*.
Provisioning	Process of establishing (setting up, configuring, preparing) a new user account, server, cloud environment, virtual machine, *etc.* "Allocating resources for cloud computing infrastructure or instance" *(ISACA glossary)*.
Proximity	Closeness in distance, time, form, *etc.* In risk management, potential incidents that are anticipated to occur soon or frequently tend to be emphasised relative to those thought unlikely to occur for some time if at all, but the impacts should also be considered (*e.g.* a 'hundred year flood' or tsunami may seem unlikely but could *devastate* unprepared organisations located in the flood zone should it occur, while climate change is materially increasing the probability).

TERM	MEANING
Proximity card	Physical authentication token that works when placed close to a card reader, such as an access card or NFC payments card.
Proxy	Someone or something that 'stands in for' (represents and acts on behalf of) another to pass their information to a third party, such as the chairman of a meeting voting on behalf of stakeholders who cannot attend (proxy voting), or a network service (application proxy), or network device (proxy server). Requires trust in the proxy from both sides, making it vulnerable to untrustworthy people, compromised devices, coercion, **M**an-**I**n-**T**he-**M**iddle attacks, *etc.*
Proxy server, Internet proxy system	Network server running software that dissembles packets arriving at one network interface to analyse the data content, applies security rules according to the nature of the content, source, destination, protocol, ports, *etc.* and optionally repackages them for onward transmission through other network interfaces. To each of the communicating systems, the server stands in for (proxies) the other, in effect being an authorised and trusted **M**an-**I**n-**T**he-**M**iddle. A type of deep packet inspection firewall. "A server that acts as a gateway between an individual and the internet [and] A server that acts on behalf of a user. Note: Typical proxies accept a connection from a user, make a decision as to whether the user or client IP address is permitted to use the proxy, perhaps perform additional authentication, and complete a connection to a remote destination on behalf of the user" *(ISACA glossary)*. "A server that acts as an intermediary between a workstation user and the Internet so that the enterprise can ensure security, administrative control, and caching service. A proxy server is associated with or part of a gateway server that separates the enterprise network from the outside network and a firewall server that protects the enterprise network from outside intrusion" *(SANS glossary)*.
PRTT	*Abbrev:* **P**en **R**egister, **Tr**ap and **T**race.
Pry	a. To intrude into someone's privacy or physically encroach upon their personal space. b. To physically force open a locked but inadequately secured enclosure, window, door, *etc.* using a tool such as a metal pry bar or jemmy/jimmy, slim jim, shim, or credit card to defeat the locking mechanism.

TERM	MEANING
Pseudonymity, pseudonymisation	Use of a fake/fictitious pseudonym, token, or code word (such as "Witness A") in place of the real name or other identifier of a person. By intention (*e.g.* in conjunction with other information or by guessing) or by mistake, pseudonymisation may potentially be reversed or fail under some circumstances, compromising privacy and perhaps safety or security. "The processing of personal data in such a manner that the personal data can no longer be attributed to a specific data subject without the use of additional information, provided that such additional information is kept separately and is subject to technical and organisational measures to ensure that the personal data are not attributed to an identified or identifiable natural person" ***(General Data Protection Regulation)***. "Process applied to personally identifiable information (PII) which replaces identifying information with an alias. Notes: Pseudonymization can be performed either by PII principals themselves or by PII controllers. Pseudonymization can be used by PII principals to consistently use a resource or service without disclosing their identity to this resource or service (or between services), while still being held accountable for that use. Pseudonymization does not rule out the possibility that there can be (a restricted set of) privacy stakeholders other than the PII controller of the pseudonymized data which are able to determine the PII principal's identity based on the alias and data linked to it" *(ISO/IEC 29100)*. "The processing of personal data in such a manner that the personal data can no longer be attributed to a specific data subject without the use of additional information, provided that such additional information is kept separately and is subject to technical and organizational measures to ensure that the personal data are not attributed to an identified or identifiable natural person" *(ISACA glossary)*. See also anonymisation, tokenisation.
Pseudorandom, pseudo-random	Close *approximation* of true randomness, generated programmatically.
Pseudo**R**andom **N**umber **G**enerator **(PRNG)**	Software algorithms used to generate supposedly random data are only capable of *approximating* true randomness. Given the same inputs and conditions, two identical instances of a PRNG running in parallel will normally generate the same output sequences. Consequently, pseudorandom values used as encryption keys, TCP/IP sequence numbers, *etc.* may conceivably be predicted to some extent, a feature that weakens some cryptosystems but is legitimately exploited by others (*e.g.* in security tokens generating codes that can be validated by the corresponding software but cannot be guessed by an attacker without additional knowledge). See also seed.

TERM	MEANING
Pseudo-random number sequence	Output of a **P**seudo**R**andom **N**umber **G**enerator that has been primed with particular parameters. "Sequence of numbers that has been determined by some defined arithmetic process but is effectively a random number sequence for the purpose for which it is required" *(ISO/IEC 2382).*
PSK	*Abbrev:* **P**re-**S**hared **K**ey.
PSR	*Abbrev:* **P**rotective **S**ecurity **R**equirements.
PSRF	*Abbrev:* **P**rotective **S**ecurity **R**equirements **F**ramework.
Psychological critical incident	"Event or series of events that could cause significant emotional or physical distress, psychological impairment or disturbance in people's usual functioning. Note: Mental health professionals working in this field would normally refer to a 'traumatic event' as a critical psychological incident. The term 'critical psychological incident' is preferred as it implies an incident that may or may not be traumatic to the individual involved. Although there are several definitions of a traumatic event within the psychiatric and scientific world, 'psychological critical incident' provides a more real-world definition" *(ISO 22300).*
Psychological education	"Provision of advice and guidance relating to psychological well-being. Note: It usually includes an overview of common reactions to distressing events in order to normalize them, reduce anxiety, provide simple self-help strategies to facilitate recovery in the first few days, and provide advice on where and when to seek further support" *(ISO 22300).*
Psychological first aid	"Temporary, supportive intervention comparable to the concept of physical first aid. Note: Its goals include stabilizing the crisis situation, reducing emotional distress, providing advice on self-care and psychological education, identifying people who could need professional assistance and referring for further assistance, as necessary" *(ISO 22300).*
Psyops (psychological operations)	Social engineering in a spooky or military context, such as the use of propaganda and other forms of disinformation.
PTZ	*Abbrev:* **P**an, **T**ilt, **Z**oom.
PUA	*Abbrev:* **P**otentially **U**nwanted **A**pplication. See Potentially Unwanted Program.
PUBLIC	Class of information that has been authorised for external publication to select groups or the general public (*e.g.* press releases, marketing materials) or is already in the public domain (*e.g.* newspapers, Internet websites).

TERM	MEANING
Public cloud	Cloud services provided through the Internet on equipment owned by a **C**loud **S**ervice **P**rovider. "A cloud environment in which resources are shared between enterprises and individuals" *(ISACA glossary)*. See also private cloud, hybrid cloud.
Public data	"Data that has been formally authorised for release into the public domain" *(AusISM)*.
Public **D**omain **(PD) software**	Legally defined term for software over which its owner has formally relinquished all **I**ntellectual **P**roperty **R**ights. Anyone can copy, use, modify, and even sell PD software without reference, consideration, or payment to the original intellectual property owner. Also known as freeware. However, IANAL.
Public domain information	"Official information authorised for unlimited public access or circulation, such as agency publications and websites" *(NZISM)*.
Public Interest Disclosure Act 1998	UK law that prohibits an employer from dismissing or victimising a whistleblower, *i.e.* a worker who makes a protected disclosure of information concerning a criminal offence, noncompliance with legal or regulatory obligations, miscarriage of justice, health and safety or environmental danger, or deliberate concealment of such things, to the organisation, a prescribed person/body (*e.g.* an industry regulator), the general public or a lawyer, *etc.* providing legal advice. Broadly similar whistleblower protection laws, regulations, and guidelines apply in several other countries.
Public key	Non-confidential member of a public–private key pair in an asymmetric cryptographic system or **P**ublic **K**ey **I**nfrastructure, normally shared, published, or freely disclosed in some form of digital certificate or text sequence such as a PGP signature block appended to an email or **D**omain **N**ame **S**ystem *txt* records for **S**ender **P**olicy **F**ramework, **D**omain**K**eys **I**dentified **M**ail, and **D**omain-based **M**essage **A**uthentication, **R**eporting, and **C**onformance. "Key that is intended for use by any entity for encrypted communication with the owner of the corresponding private key" *(ISO/IEC 2382)*. "In an asymmetric cryptographic scheme, the key that may be widely published to enable the operation of the scheme" *(ISACA glossary)*. "The publicly-disclosed component of a pair of cryptographic keys used for asymmetric cryptography" *(SANS glossary)*.
Public key cryptography, public key cryptosystem, public key encryption	See asymmetric cryptography. "A cryptosystem that combines a widely distributed public key and a closely held, protected private key. A message that is encrypted by the public key can only be decrypted by the mathematically related counterpart private key. Conversely, only the public key can decrypt data that was encrypted by its corresponding private key. [and] A cryptographic system that uses two keys: a public key, which is known to everyone, and a private or secret key, which is only known to the recipient of the message" *(ISACA glossary)*.

TERM	MEANING
Public-Key Cryptography Standards (PKCS #1 to PKCS #15)	Family of cryptographic protocols published by RSA Security LLC.
Public **K**ey **I**nfrastructure **(PKI)**	Asymmetric cryptographic system as a whole, including the supporting technology infrastructure, services, algorithms, protocols, policies, processes, **C**ertification **A**uthorities, digital certificates, *etc.* "A series of processes and technologies for the association of cryptographic keys with the entity to whom those keys were issued" *(ISACA glossary).* "The framework and services that provide for the generation, production, distribution, control, accounting and destruction of public key certificates. Components include the personnel, policies, processes, server platforms, software, and workstations used for the purpose of administering certificates and public-private key pairs, including the ability to issue, maintain, recover and revoke public key certificates" *(CNSSI 4009).* "Enables users of a basically unsecured public network such as the Internet to securely and privately exchange data and money through the use of a public and a private cryptographic key pair that is obtained and shared through a trusted authority. The public key infrastructure provides for a digital certificate that can identify an individual or an organization and directory services that can store and, when necessary, revoke the certificates" *(SANS glossary). Cf.* web of trust.
Public network, public network infrastructure	Network such as the Internet which is accessible to and used by the public, as opposed to a private one such as a corporate or government network. "Contains components that are outside the control of the user organisation. These components may include telecommunications or data services from a service provider that utilise any component of local, regional or national infrastructure" *(NZISM).* "Network infrastructure that an organisation has no control over, such as the internet" *(AusISM).*
Public property	Communal asset/s owned by the public at large or belonging to nobody in particular. *Cf.* private property.
Public **S**witched **T**elephone **N**etwork **(PSTN)**, **P**ost **O**ffice **[or Plain Old] T**elephone **S**ystem **(POTS)**	"A communications system that sets up a dedicated channel (or circuit) between two points for the duration of the transmission" *(ISACA glossary).* "An historic term describing a public network where voice is communicated using analogue communications. Today almost all communication networks are substantially or entirely digital networks" *(NZISM).* "Public network infrastructure used for voice communications" *(AusISM).*
Public warning	"Notification and alert messages disseminated as an incident response measure to enable responders and people at risk to take safety measures. Note: Public warning can include information to raise public awareness and understanding or to provide advisory or compulsory instructions" *(ISO 22300).*

TERM	MEANING
Public warning system	"Set of protocols, processes and technologies based on the public warning policy to deliver notification and alert messages in a developing emergency situation to people at risk and to first responders" *(ISO 22300)*.
Pulverise	Literally beat to a pulp. "Destruct by grinding media to a powder or dust" *(ISO/IEC 27040)*.
Punycode	Internet host/domain names containing Unicode characters can be represented for **D**omain **N**ame **S**ystem lookups and displayed by browsers using a subset of ASCII containing letters, digits, and hyphens. This allows the use of Internationalised domain names, reducing the risk of users being misdirected to malicious domains containing characters *resembling* but distinct from those in the standard English alphabet.
Purge	Forcibly expel or cleanse. "Sanitize using physical techniques that make recovery infeasible using state of the art laboratory techniques, but which preserves the storage media in a potentially reusable state" *(ISO/IEC 27040)*. See also destroy.
Purple team	Group of people combining the capabilities, methods, and knowledge of both blue and red teams, *e.g.* while a vulnerability is being identified and exploited, the blue teamers learn about it from their red team colleagues and get to work on the security controls necessary to avoid, prevent, or mitigate it. A more collaborative and contemporaneous if constrained version of classical red *vs.* blue team penetration testing. "A cooperative engagement where the red team simulates attacks and exploits while the blue team actively defends against them, allowing for real-time feedback, analysis and evaluation of defensive measures, detection capabilities, incident response processes and overall security controls. The purpose of a purple team is to improve the enterprise's security posture by enhancing communication and collaboration between the red and blue teams" *(ISACA glossary)*. See also black and white teams.
Purpose	Reason, rationale, objective, *etc.* "States who the organization serves, what it does, what it believes, what is stands for, what it hopes to achieve in the near term and long term, and why all of this matters; usually through its Mission, Vision and Values statements" *(OCEG GRC Glossary)*.
Purpose limitation	Privacy principle prohibiting personal information being used for purposes other than any expressly authorised by the data subjects. "A process where data are collected for specified, explicit and legitimate purposes and not further processed in a manner that is incompatible with those purposes" *(ISACA glossary)*.

TERM	MEANING
PUS	*Abbrev:* **P**otentially **U**nwanted **S**oftware. See **P**otentially **U**nwanted **P**rogram.
Pushdo, Cutwail, Pandex	Species of fileless malware – a Trojan downloader botnet in the wild between 2007 and 2019. Distributed spam and other malware.
Push **T**o **T**alk **(PTT), push-to-talk handsets**	Button, key, or digital function that, while pressed (asserted), changes a transceiver temporarily from receive to transmit mode. "Handsets that have a button which must be pressed by the user before audio can be communicated, thus improving offhook audio protection" *(NZISM).*
PVLAN	*Abbrev:* **P**rivate **V**irtual Local **A**rea **N**etwork.
PVR	*Abbrev:* **P**lant **V**ariety **R**ight.
Pwn, pwnage, pwned	Leet references to hackers 'owning' (as in having full control of, not in the legal sense of property ownership) the systems, networks, people, organisations, *etc.* they have compromised and exploited, thereby defeating or making fools of their true owners.
Pyramid scheme, Ponzi scheme, bubble	Form of fraud that employs social engineering techniques to persuade victims to both part with their own money on the promise of eventually making a fortune, and recruit additional victims on the same basis. The only winners of such schemes – if any – are those fraudsters who originate and/or promote them (such as Charles Ponzi in the eponymous scheme) and manage to stay one step ahead of the authorities and their angry victims.

Q

TERM	MEANING
QoS	*Abbrev:* **Q**uality **o**f **S**ervice.
QR code	*Abbrev:* **Q**uick **R**esponse **code**.
QSA	*Abbrev:* **Q**ualified **S**ecurity **A**ssessor.
Qualification, qualify	a. Professional person's knowledge, competence, and suitability for a rôle or position, often certified by an accredited organisation following some form of examination, evaluation, test, or assessment, as evidenced by the award of a credential such as a certificate printed on fancy vellum. b. *Caveat*, concern, or refinement of a statement. c. Counts or is included in a set, type, or category, *e.g.* an apple qualifies as a fruit.
Qualified **S**ecurity **A**ssessor **(QSA)**	Independent professional, certified competent by the PCI Security Standards Council to test or audit (assess and evaluate) organisations handling bank card data against the cybersecurity, privacy, and other requirements (contractual obligations) of PCI DSS. The nature of the assessments (*e.g.* in-depth on-site, remote, or self-assessment) depends the size, complexity, and capacity of the client organisations, affecting the risks and hence assurance needed (and their ability to pay!).
Qualitative	Subjective, based on someone's impressions, beliefs, and emotions rather than rationality and fact. "A description of an examination/analysis that results in findings that cannot be expressed numerically" *(FSRCoP)*. *Cf.* quantitative.
Qualitative risk assessment, qualitative risk analysis	Risk assessment or analysis based on subjective impressions, beliefs, and emotions. "The use of a set of methods, principles, or rules for assessing risk based on nonnumerical categories or levels" *(NIST SP 800-55v1)*. "An approach based on expert opinion, judgment, intuition and experience" *(ISACA glossary)*. *Cf.* quantitative assessment, semi-quantitative assessment.
Quality **A**ssurance **(QA)**	Systematically improving process controls to mitigate the risk of finished products failing **Q**uality **C**ontrol tests. Generally focuses on identifying and stabilising the most variable or wasteful production activities.
Quality **C**ontrol **(QC)**	Wasteful process of testing finished products against specified acceptance criteria and simply rejecting any that substantially fail, or sending them back for rework. "The operational techniques and procedures used to achieve quality requirements" *(ISACA glossary)*. *Cf.* **Q**uality **A**ssurance.

TERM	MEANING
Quality of Service (QoS)	Networking techniques, functions, and protocols allowing time-critical data (such as real-time audio-visual traffic for **V**oice **O**ver **I**nternet **P**rotocol and streaming, or urgent alerts/alarms) to be prioritised or fast-tracked past routine traffic (such as emails and file transfers), particularly when the network becomes congested. Involves managing factors such as allocated bandwidths, latency, packet loss, and jitter. "A process to prioritise network traffic based on availability requirements" *(NZISM)*. "The ability to provide different priorities to different applications, users or data flows, or to guarantee a certain level of performance to a data flow" *(AusISM)*.
Quantitative	Quantified or quantifiable, *i.e.* capable of being measured and expressed as a quantity using established units or a count. "A description of an examination/analysis that results in findings that can be expressed numerically" *(FSRCoP)*. *Cf.* qualitative.
Quantitative risk assessment, quantitative risk analysis	Risk assessment or analysis based on measured, calculated, or mathematically estimated quantities. "The use of a set of methods, principles, or rules for assessing risks based on the use of numbers where the meanings and proportionality of values are maintained inside and outside of the context of the assessment" *(NIST SP 800-55v1)*. "An approach that is based on a calculation of a risk's likelihood and impact using numerical and statistical techniques" *(ISACA glossary)*. *Cf.* qualitative assessment, semi-quantitative assessment.
Quantum computing, quantum technology, quantum	Cutting-edge computer technology based on quantum mechanics. Quantum bits (qubits) appear to have different values simultaneously (a property called superposition) and can appear to be correlated (entanglement). Quantum has significant potential for cryptanalysis and other intensive purposes; hence, it is being actively developed and exploited by the defence, intelligence, pharmaceuticals, and other industries. "Relies on the principles of quantum physics. The advancing understanding and control of what are known as 'quantum effects' such as superposition and entanglement will lead to a new wave of advances that will underpin our economy and society: sensing, data transmission and encryption, timing and computing" *(UK National Cyber Security Strategy 2022)*.
Quantum-safe cryptography	Cryptographic methods, systems, and algorithms specifically designed to resist advanced cryptanalysis using quantum computers.
Quarantine	Safe holding area on a system to which suspected malware is diverted by antivirus software pending further investigation. "To store files containing malware in isolation for future disinfection or examination" *(NIST SP 800-114)*.

TERM	MEANING
Quasar, xRAT	Open-source **R**emote **A**ccess **T**rojan intended for legitimate remote Windows system management and support, now customised for use in **A**dvanced **P**ersistent **T**hreat attacks. Originally named xRAT.
Question answering	Guess! "Task of determining the most appropriate answer to a question provided in natural language. Note: A question can be open-ended or be intended to have a specific answer" *(ISO/IEC 22989)*.
Quick **R**esponse **(QR) code**	Generally, a square monochrome image comprising a two-dimensional pattern of black dots similar in function to a linear barcode. The dots can encode four data types: numbers, alphanumeric characters, binary values, or kanji. High-density QR codes can communicate up to about 4,000 alphanumeric characters (roughly two A4 pages of text) with limited error correction, although most are used for shorter **U**niform **R**esource **L**ocators with strong error correction, allowing smartphones to scan, decode, and pass the URLs directly to the web browser without having to be typed in (and corrected!) manually. See also attagging, baiting.

R

TERM	MEANING
RaaS	*Abbrev:* **R**ansomware-**a**s-**a**-**S**ervice.
Race condition	Design flaw or bug in software applications that, under unusual or abnormal conditions (*e.g.* under heavy processing loads, possibly during an active attack), results in parallel threads becoming incorrectly sequenced, potentially exposing exploitable security vulnerabilities. "Exploits the small window of time between a security control being applied and when the service is used" *(SANS glossary)*.
RACF	*Abbrev:* **R**esource **A**ccess **C**ontrol **F**acility.
RACI	Documentation (table or matrix) formally clarifying who (meaning which rôle, team, department, *etc.*) is **R**esponsible **A**ccountable, **C**onsulted, and **I**nformed about a business decision, process, or activity. A useful way of setting expectations, and determining or designing, documenting, and configuring the associated access rights and procedures. See also RASCI.
RAD	*Abbrev:* **R**apid **A**pplication **D**evelopment.
Radio access network	"Part of a mobile telecommunication system that implements a radio access technology such as WCDMA or LTE to provide access for end-user devices to the core network. Notes: The radio access network resides between the end-user device and the core network. A mobile phone is an example of an end-user device" *(ISO/IEC 27033-6)*.
Radio **F**requency **(RF) device**	"Devices including mobile phones, wireless enabled personal devices and laptops" *(NZISM)*.
Radio **F**requency **(RF) transmitter**	"A device designed to transmit electromagnetic radiation as part of a radio communication system" *(AusISM)*.
Radio network controller	"Network element in a 3G mobile network which controls the base stations, interface to the core network and carries out the radio resource management and mobility management functions of the network" *(ISO/IEC 27033-6)*.
RADIUS	*Abbrev:* **R**emote **A**uthentication **D**ial-**I**n **U**ser **S**ervice.
RAID	*Abbrev:* **R**edundant **A**rray of **I**nexpensive **D**isks (or **D**evices). See disk mirroring.
Rainbow tables	Cryptanalysts' tool to speed up the brute force cracking of passwords on certain systems by pre-compiling and accumulating the hashes for a large number of potential passwords. Generally foiled by salting the hashes on each system, making the rainbow tables too large to generate, store and search.
RAM-scraper	See memory-scraping malware.

TERM	MEANING
Randomness	See entropy. "An important concept, also called entropy, in many cryptographic implementations. It is used to create keys, generate initialization vectors (*i.e.*, random values that seed or initialize an algorithm), generate nonces (*i.e.*, single-use, disposable values) and supply padding (*i.e.*, additional data completing a block of fixed length)" *(ISACA glossary)*.
Random number	"Number selected from a known set of numbers in such a way that each number in the set has the same probability of occurrence" *(ISO/IEC 2382)*. See also pseudo-random, entropy.
Random number sequence	Series of truly random numbers, each one entirely uncorrelated with those either side. "Sequence of numbers each of which cannot be predicted only from a knowledge of its predecessors" *(ISO/IEC 2382)*.
Random sample	Audit sample randomly selected from a population in such a way as to minimise selection bias and thus be representative of the whole (*e.g.* a security awareness survey across all departments). "A method of sampling where each sample has an equal chance of selection in hopes of gathering an unbiased representation" *(NIST SP 800-55v1)*. *Cf.* stratified sample, time series analysis, attribute sample, convenience sample, discovery sample, nonstatistical sample.
Ransom	Coercive and extortionate demands from a criminal adversary who has seized control of valuable assets such as people, systems, or data, *e.g.* in a ransomware attack or kidnapping.
Ransomware, crypto-ransomware, lock-screen ransomware	Malware that (1) restricts access to an organisation's data stored in a network, *e.g.* by encrypting it (crypto-ransomware) and/or to **I**nformation **T**echnology systems within the network, *e.g.* by damaging or replacing essential **O**perating **S**ystem files such as the **M**aster **B**oot **R**ecord (lock-screen ransomware); (2) exfiltrates valuable data; or (3) simply presents a warning message falsely *claiming* to have done (1) and perhaps threatening to do (2) (scareware). The primary intention is to disrupt the victim's operations, threaten data disclosure or further exploitation, and so extort or coerce the victim into paying a ransom. A lucrative, relatively low-risk, and hence popular cybercriminal tool and method. Ransom payments are typically demanded via anonymous services such as Bitcoin. Some crypto-ransomware species can be defeated without paying the ransom using white hat tools (*e.g.* NoMoreRansom.org). "Malware that restricts access to the compromised system until a ransom demand is satisfied" *(ISACA glossary)*. "A type of malicious software designed to block access to a computer system until a sum of money (a ransom) is paid"

TERM	MEANING
	(UK Cyber Security Breaches Survey 2023). "Malicious software that denies the user access to their files, computer or device until a ransom is paid" *(UK National Cyber Security Strategy 2022).* "A type of malware that is a form of extortion. It works by encrypting a victim's hard drive denying them access to key files. The victim must then pay a ransom to decrypt the files and gain access to them again" *(SANS glossary). Cf.* software, middleware, hardware, firmware, wetware, malware, adware, crimeware, scareware, shelfware, spouseware, stalkerware, spyware.
Ransomware-as-a-**S**ervice **(RaaS)**	Just as botnets can be rented on the darknet, so too can ransomware along with the command and control structure, potential victim lists, spamming, money laundering, and other illicit services. A form of **M**alware-**as-a-S**ervice.
Rapid **A**pplication **D**evelopment **(RAD)**	Approach supported by software development tools and methods aimed at speeding up the process of developing applications, typically through frequent small changes (evolutionary) as opposed to infrequent major changes (revolutionary). "A well-defined methodology that enables enterprises to develop strategically important systems faster, while reducing development costs and maintaining quality by using a series of proven application development techniques" *(ISACA glossary).* See also Agile, **C**ontinuous **D**evelopment.
RASCI	Documentation (table or matrix) formally clarifying who (meaning which rôle, team, department, *etc.*) is **R**esponsible **A**ccountable, **S**upporting, **C**onsulted, and **I**nformed about a business decision, process, or activity. A useful way of setting expectations, and determining or designing, documenting, and configuring the associated access rights and procedures. An elaboration on RACI.
RASP	*Abbrev:* **R**untime **A**pplication **S**elf-**P**rotection.
RAT	*Abbrev:* **R**emote **A**dministration **T**ool, **R**emote **A**ccess **T**rojan, or vermin, depending on context – a decidedly ambiguous term.
Ratio scale	"From the Stevens Scale of Measurement, a quantitative measurement scale with a true zero using variables that can be compared to find differences or intervals" *(NIST SP 800-55v1).*
Razor wire	Like barbed wire on steroids, a well-positioned bundle of razor-edged metal ribbon is a strong deterrent to intruders intent on scrambling over a protected fence or wall. A physical security control.
RBAC	*Abbrev:* **R**ule-**B**ased **A**ccess **C**ontrol, **R**ealm-**B**ased **A**ccess **C**ontrol, or **R**ôle-**B**ased **A**ccess **C**ontrol, depending on context.
RBL	*Abbrev:* **R**ealtime **B**lackhole **L**ist.

TERM	MEANING
RC-4 (Rivest **C**ipher № **4)**	Quick and efficient stream cipher used in **S**ecure **S**ockets **L**ayer, SYSKEY, *etc.* Designed by Ron Rivest in 1987. Flaws in the way RC-4 shared keys and nonces are generated/exchanged have seriously weakened common implementations such as WEP. Further cryptographic attacks on RC-4 have since been described, so this algorithm is well past its 'best before' date and hence is deprecated.
RCE	*Abbrev:* **R**emote **C**ode **E**xecution.
RDP	*Abbrev:* **R**emote **D**iagnostic **P**ort.
Reaccreditation	"A procedure by which an authoritative body gives formal recognition, approval and acceptance of the associated residual security risk with the continued operation of a system" *(NZISM).*
Readiness	"Process of being prepared for a digital investigation before an incident has occurred" *(ISO/IEC 27043).* See also preparedness.
Real estate fraud, rental fraud	Type of fraud involving real estate, rental, or similar large transactions, *e.g.* the fraudster poses as an agent or advisor of a property owner (*e.g.* their lawyer, lender, or bank), tricking the buyer/renter into paying into the fraudster's rather than the owner's bank account.
Realm-**B**ased **A**ccess **C**ontrol **(RBAC)**	Access control scheme whereby computer users are granted certain system, application, and/or data access rights according to the domain. *Cf.* **R**ule-**B**ased **A**ccess **C**ontrol, **R**ôle-**B**ased **A**ccess **C**ontrol, and **A**ttribute-**B**ased **A**ccess **C**ontrol.
Real time, real-time, realtime	Contemporaneous, instantaneous, current, live, at the same moment, or without delay as opposed to being recorded and replayed, experienced, recounted, or responded-to later on.
Realtime **B**lackhole **L**ist **(RBL)**	Proactively maintained list of email servers apparently being used by spammers. Used to block emails sent via suspect servers on the basis that they are probably spam. See also blackhole, blacklist.
Real-time **T**ransport **C**ontrol **P**rotocol **(RTCP)**	**V**oice **O**ver **I**nternet **P**rotocol protocol providing feedback on the **Q**uality **of S**ervice and transmission statistics such as packet loss, jitter, and delay, allowing VOIP applications to manage call quality by adapting the transmission rate, codec parameters, *etc.*
Real-time **T**ransport **P**rotocol **(RTP)**	**V**oice **O**ver **I**nternet **P**rotocol transport layer networking protocol for rapid delivery of voice and video content (digital data). Handles the sequencing of packets and timing of the reconstructed data such that sound and video remain sufficiently synchronised. See also **R**eal-time **T**ransport **C**ontrol **P**rotocol, **S**ecure **R**eal **T**ime **P**rotocol. *Cf.* **R**isk **T**reatment **P**lan.
Reasonable	Likely to be accepted by an ordinary person on the basis of rational thought.

TERM	MEANING
Reasonable assurance	Desired or acceptable amount of assurance, deemed sufficient for particular purposes and circumstances (context-dependent). "A level of comfort short of a guarantee, but considered adequate given the costs of the control and the likely benefits achieved" *(ISACA glossary)*. "A special type and level of assurance, provided by external auditors as part of a financial audit or examination, that subject matter conforms to suitable criteria and is free from material error" *(OCEG GRC Glossary)*.
Reasonable **W**orst-**C**ase **S**cenario **(RWCS)**	Subtle, pragmatic moderation of classical worst-case scenario modelling to emphasise credibility and realism over more extreme, outlandish or bizarre possibilities. "A generic representation of a challenging yet plausible manifestation of a risk … the worst case once the high-impact low-likelihood manifestations of a risk have been discounted. It is not a prediction of what will happen, rather an illustration of what we could reasonably expect to arise which is proportionate to use for preparation and planning purposes as a responsible government" *(UK Resilience Lessons Digest 2023)*.
Reasonably foreseeable use	"Use that is not necessarily the intended purpose supplied by the manufacturer in the instructions for use, promotional or sales materials and statements, as well as in the technical documentation, but which is likely to result from reasonably foreseeable human behaviour or technical operations or interactions" *(EU CRA)*.
Reasonably foreseeable misuse	"The use of a product with digital elements in a way that is not in accordance with its intended purpose, but which may result from reasonably foreseeable human behaviour or interaction with other systems" *(EU CRA)*.
Recertification	Renewal of an organisation's conformity certification following a recertification audit.
Recertification audit	More thorough re-examination and evaluation of the organisation's fulfilment of the requirements than the intervening surveillance audits. Essentially a full certification audit but with implicit expectation that the organisation's processes and systems are more mature than when originally certified. Due every 3 years for ISO/IEC 27001.
Recipient	Receiver, the receiving person, organisation, device, *etc.* that actually receives something such as a message, gift, or award. "User or distribution list that may receive a message or to whom a message is addressed [and] user to whom a message is addressed" *(ISO/IEC 2382)*. "A natural or legal person, public authority, agency or another body, to which the personal data are disclosed, whether a third party or not. However, public authorities which may receive personal data in the framework of a particular inquiry in accordance with Union or Member State law shall not be regarded as

TERM	MEANING
	recipients; the processing of those data by those public authorities shall be in compliance with the applicable data protection rules according to the purposes of the processing" *(General Data Protection Regulation)*.
Reciprocity	Mutual understandings, expectations, or obligations. "Mutual agreement among participating organizations to accept each other's security assessments in order to reuse information system resources and/or to accept each other's assessed security posture in order to share information" *(NIST SP 800-39)*.
Reckless	Acting with gay abandon. More severe than mere carelessness or negligence, and yet (normally and apparently) without truly malicious intent to cause harm.
Reclassification	"A change to the security measures afforded to information based on a reassessment of the potential impact of its unauthorised disclosure. The lowering of the security measures for media containing classified information often requires sanitisation or destruction processes to be undertaken prior to a formal decision to lower the security measures protecting the information" *(NZISM)*. "An administrative decision to change the controls used to protect data based on a reassessment of the potential impact of its unauthorised disclosure. The lowering of the controls for media containing sensitive or classified data often requires sanitisation or destruction processes to be undertaken prior to a formal decision to lower the controls protecting the data" *(AusISM)*.
Record	a. *[Verb]* To capture information in a form that is stored for later replay or analysis, such as a log or data file (a recording). b. *[Noun]* Row or entry in a data table, computer file, digital or physical document, *etc.* containing information. "Information created, received and maintained as evidence and as an asset by an organization or person, in pursuit of legal obligations or in the transaction of business. Note: Legal obligations in this context include all legal, statutory, regulatory and contractual requirements" *(ISO/IEC 27002)*. "A collection of related information that is treated as a unit. Separate fields within the record are used for processing of the information" *(ISACA glossary)*. "Document stating results achieved or providing evidence of activities performed" *(ISO 9000)*. "The recordings (automated and/or manual) of evidence of activities performed or results achieved (*e.g.*, forms, reports, test results) that serve as a basis for verifying that the organization and the system are performing as intended. Also used to refer to units of related data fields (*i.e.*, groups of data fields that can be accessed by a program and that contain a complete set of information on particular items)" *(NIST SP 800-171)*.

TERM	MEANING
Reconciliation, reconciling	Investigative process to identify, explore, and determine the reasons for any discrepancies between things that are *supposed* to be identical, *e.g.* differences between the hash values of forensic copies, or differing totals of credit and debit accounts in double-entry bookkeeping.
Reconnaissance	Systematically exploring and amassing useful information about potential targets (such as facilities, systems, and other assets) plus the associated vulnerabilities and security controls, whether to attack or defend them. Can involve Internet research, social media, social engineering, surveillance, malware (*e.g.* spyware), network probes, and/or physical site penetration. "The phase of an attack where an attackers finds new systems, maps out networks, and probes for specific, exploitable vulnerabilities" *(SANS glossary)*.
Recover	Restore normality. A core function (phase) within NIST **C**yber **S**ecurity **F**ramework along with identify, protect, detect, and respond. "Establish a previous or new status of all or part of a system, file, database, or other resource, or of the execution of a program so that required functions can be performed" *(ISO/IEC 2382)*. "Develop and implement appropriate activities to maintain plans for resilience and to restore any capabilities or services that were impaired due to a cybersecurity incident. The Recover Function supports timely recovery to normal operations to reduce the impact from a cybersecurity incident" *(NIST CSF)*.
Recoverability	Ability to recover some semblance of normality following a serious incident, *e.g.* through **D**isaster **R**ecovery. Part of survivability, along with resilience. Highly recoverable organisations have repeatedly demonstrated having the resources, skills, means, and will or determination to bounce back more effectively and efficiently from incidents than most.
Recovery	Restoration of information systems, services, sessions, **D**ata**B**ases, transactions, data, *etc.*, and the dependent business processes, following a significant incident or disaster that interrupted them. Typically a lengthy and stressful process that involves restoring backups onto fresh **I**nformation **T**echnology hardware, testing and authorising their release to users. May involve making security improvements to mitigate the risk of a repeat occurrence. "Restoration of a database, for example by means of backup files and after-images [and] process or the result of recovering [and] process for resolving conflicting or erroneous conditions arising during the transfer of data" *(ISO/IEC 2382)*. "The phase in the incident response plan that ensures that affected systems or services are restored to a condition specified in the service delivery objectives (SDOs) or business continuity plan (BCP)" *(USACA glossary)*. See also resilience, business continuity, **R**ecovery **P**oint **O**bjective.

TERM	MEANING
Recovery actions & controls	"Actions & controls that return the organization to its original state, stable state, or superior state after harm has occurred" *(OCEG GRC Glossary)*.
Recovery **P**oint **O**bjective **(RPO)**	Following a serious incident requiring the invocation of **D**isaster **R**ecovery arrangements, this key parameter/metric defines the point up to which all data should have been recovered (*e.g.* the previous minute, hour, day, week, month, *etc.*), and therefore the maximum tolerable data loss prior to the incident. Has implications for both the business and the backup strategy, *e.g.* the frequency of offsite backups. "Point in time to which data are to be recovered after a disruption has occurred" *(ISO/IEC 27002)*. "Point to which information used by an activity is restored to enable the activity to operate on resumption. Note: Can also be referred to as 'maximum data loss'" *(ISO 22300)*. "The earliest point in time that is acceptable to recover data, determined based on the acceptable data loss in case of a disruption in operations. The RPO effectively quantifies the permissible amount of data loss in case of interruption" *(ISACA glossary)*. See also **R**ecovery **T**ime **O**bjective.
Recovery strategy	Information risk and security management strategy to restore an organisation's failed information services and data from backups following a disaster (*e.g.* a ransomware incident or data centre fire) in order to recover/resume dependent business activities. Complements other aspects of **B**usiness **C**ontinuity **M**anagement such as resilience (*e.g.* cloud computing, cyber resilience, supply chain risk management) and contingency arrangements (*e.g.* a workforce determined and able to cope dynamically with *any* crisis and business interruption insurance), plus the whole gamut of preventive security measures and incident management. Typically involves clarifying requirements (*e.g.* **B**usiness **I**mpact **A**nalysis to explore dependencies and priorities), policies, and key parameters/metrics (*e.g.* **R**ecovery **T**ime **O**bjective), developing suitable plans, implementing the plans (*e.g.* stockpiling essential resources such as backups, spare servers, and trained workers), providing assurance for stakeholders through exercises and tests, and maintaining the arrangements (*e.g.* with strong links to change management). "An approach by an enterprise that will ensure its recovery and continuity in the face of a disaster or other major outage. Notes: Plans and methodologies are determined by the enterprise's strategy. There may be more than one methodology or solution for an enterprise's strategy. Examples of methodologies and solutions include: contracting for a hot site or cold site, building an internal hot site or cold site, identifying an alternate work area, a consortium or reciprocal agreement, contracting for mobile recovery or crate and ship, and many others" *(ISACA glossary)*.

TERM	MEANING
Recovery test	Test of the organisation's recovery arrangements at any level from the overall strategy down to the plans for individual elements such as rebuilding failed servers from scratch. Complements other assurance measures such as **D**isaster **R**ecovery exercises and audits. "A test to check the system's ability to recover after a software or hardware failure" *(ISACA glossary).*
Recovery **T**ime **O**bjective **(RTO)**	Defines the absolute maximum ('worst case') acceptable duration of non-availability of information systems and services due to incidents, which therefore determines the corresponding need for suitable resilience, **D**isaster **R**ecovery, and/or other contingency arrangements. "Period of time within which minimum levels of services and/or products and the supporting systems, applications, or functions are to be recovered after a disruption has occurred" *(ISO/IEC 27002).* "Period of time following an incident within which a product and service or an activity is resumed, or resources are recovered. Note: For products, services and activities, the RTO is less than the time it would take for the adverse impacts that would arise as a result of not providing a product/service or performing an activity to become unacceptable" *(ISO 22300).* "The amount of time allowed for the recovery of a business function or resource after a disaster occurs" *(ISACA glossary).* See also **R**ecovery **P**oint **O**bjective.
Recurrent **N**eural **N**etwork **(RNN)**	"Neural network in which outputs from both the previous layer and the previous processing step are fed into the current layer" *(ISO/IEC 22989).*
Redaction	Process of systematically identifying and then removing, replacing, or concealing sensitive parts of information in a document or data in a computer file or **D**ata**B**ase prior to its publication or disclosure in order to maintain privacy or confidentiality, rather than withholding the entire item. A fail-unsafe control, prone to human errors and technical failures in the redaction process (*e.g.* overlaid opaque blocks may simply be removed), plus various inference attacks (*e.g.* the semantic context and *length* of a redacted word or phrase can be clues).
Redo log	Data file recording the historical sequence of transactional **D**ata**B**ase changes that can be reapplied if necessary following restoration of the system from backups to a breakpoint following a serious incident. "Files maintained by a system, primarily a database management system (DBMS), for the purpose of reapplying changes following an error or outage recovery" *(ISACA glossary).*
Red team	Group tasked by management with compromising one or more targets in emulated attacks on an organisation (or site, system, network, *etc.* thereof) typically involving physical site intrusion, network hacking, **I**nformation **T**echnology systems penetration, and capturing the flags, in order to test, exercise, and hopefully improve both the defensive *and* the offensive capabilities.

TERM	MEANING
	A deadly serious form of penetration testing ... that is also great fun, highly motivational and instructive. "A group of skilled professionals who simulate real-world cyberattacks, security breaches and physical security compromises to evaluate the effectiveness of an enterprise's defenses. The red team identifies vulnerabilities, weaknesses and potential exploits in the enterprise's systems, networks, applications and physical security controls. They often use the same tactics, techniques and procedures as real-world adversaries to provide a realistic testing environment" *(ISACA glossary)*. "A group of people authorized and organised to emulate a potential adversary's attack or exploitation capabilities against an enterprise's security posture. The Red Team's objective is to improve enterprise Information Assurance by demonstrating the impacts of successful attacks and by demonstrating what works for the defenders (*i.e.*, the Blue Team) in an operational environment" *(CNSSI 4009)*. See also blue, purple, black, and white teams.
Redundant, redundancy	Resilience technique in which critical or vital systems, communication paths, network links, rôles, power sources, *etc.* are duplicated and diversified to reduce the risk of point failures disrupting essential information services, jeopardising dependent business processes. Redundancy can be a complex and costly approach with capital, administrative, and even ecological implications, hence the value of a sound strategy coupled with systems security engineering plus **B**usiness **C**ontinuity **M**anagement. Strict change management and assurance controls are also appropriate to ensure redundancy arrangements will function as necessary when invoked. "Existence of a means in addition to the means which would be sufficient for a functional unit to perform a required function or for data to represent information. Examples – The use of duplicate functional components, the addition of parity bits. Note: Redundancy is used primarily to improve reliability or availability" *(ISO/IEC 2382)*. See also diversity.
Redundant **A**rray of **I**nexpensive **D**isks (or **D**evices) **(RAID)**	See disk mirroring.
Reference model	Conceptual framework or generic blueprint used as a comparative model or idealised standard driving maturity. "A defined model describing practices and activities that is used for improving performance or as a benchmark for measuring capability or maturity" *(ISACA glossary)*.
Reference monitor	Privileged access control function in the kernel of an **O**perating **S**ystem that mediates programmatic access to data, devices, memory space, *etc.* in a consistent and verifiable manner. Fundamental basis for system permissions (rights and privileges). "Concept of an abstract machine that enforces Target of Evaluation (TOE) access control policies" *(CNSSI 4009)*. See also access authority.

TERM	MEANING
Referential integrity	Set of integrity controls incorporated into a relational **D**ata**B**ase **M**anagement **S**ystem to help prevent inconsistencies, *e.g.* enforcing links between related tables that disallow deleting or modifying a data value that is used as a key to another table. "Property of a set of relations such that the attribute values of foreign keys are null values or are identical to the values of primary keys of other relations" *(ISO/IEC 2382)*.
Reflection attack	See amplification attack.
Region	Cluster of cloud data centres interconnected by a fast network, geographically and logically separated from other regions by hundreds of miles for resilience against regional disasters.
Regional **O**rganised **C**rime **U**nit **(ROCU)**	Ten specialist police units across England and Wales working to identify, disrupt, and dismantle organised crime including cybercrime, coordinated through the UK NCSC.
Registrar	See **C**ertification **B**ody.
Registration **A**uthority **(RA)**	Trusted organisation within a **P**ublic **K**ey **I**nfrastructure authorised to authenticate those requesting digital certificates, forwarding them to the **C**ertification **A**uthority for issue. "An authority in a network that verifies user requests for a digital certificate and tells the certificate authority (CA) to issue it" *(ISACA glossary)*.
Regression analysis	Statistical method to analyse a set of factors for any with causative as opposed to coincidental correlations. "A statistical technique used to predict the value of a variable based on the relationship between explanatory variables" *(NIST SP 800-55v1)*.
Regression test	Test intended to confirm that a system still meets requirements met by previous versions (*i.e.* it has not regressed). A standardised bank of tests is accumulated using scripts and automation to reduce delays, costs, and inconsistencies. "A testing technique used to retest earlier program abends or logical errors that occurred during the initial testing phase. [and] Rerunning test cases that a program has previously executed correctly to detect errors spawned by changes or corrections made during software development and maintenance" *(ISACA glossary)*. "The use of scripted tests which are used to test software for all possible input [it] should expect. Typically developers will create a set of regression tests that are executed before a new version of a software is released" *(SANS glossary)*.
RegTech	Contraction of **reg**ulatory **tech**nology, particularly the development and exploitation of innovative **I**nformation **T**echnology to satisfy applicable regulatory authorities. See also AgriTech, Biotech, EdTech, FinTech, FoodTech, EcoTech/GreenTech, GovTech, HealthTech, LegalTech, RetailTech, and other tech neologisms.

TERM	MEANING
Regular deletion period	"Maximum time period after which the data objects … of a cluster of personally identifiable information (PII) … should be deleted if used in regular processing in the processes of the PII controller" *(ISO/IEC 27555)*.
Regulation	a. Mandatory rule, typically enshrined in or supported by law. "Rules or laws defined and enforced by an authority to regulate conduct" *(ISACA glossary)*. b. Binding legal mandate imposed across all members of the **E**uropean **U**nion. *Cf.* EU directive, decision, recommendation, or opinion. c. Form of process control using proportional control and feedback to keep a process within safe, sustainable, and productive tolerance limits.
Regulator	Device, organisation or person that regulates.
Reidentification	"Process of associating data in a de-identified dataset with the original data principal. Note: A process that establishes the presence of a particular data principal in a dataset is included in this definition" *(ISO/IEC 20889)*. "The process of discovering the individual to whom deidentified data belong by matching anonymous data with publicly available information or auxiliary data" *(ISACA glossary)*.
Reinforce, reinforcement	Proactive encouragement to fulfil obligations and expectations, *e.g.* by offering some sort of benefit, reward, or bonus (even something as trivial as a 'thank you') to recognise and show appreciation for their compliance. Sadly, an oft-neglected but highly motivational and hence effective compliance mechanism. *Cf.* enforcement.
Reinforcement **L**earning **(RL)**	"Learning of an optimal sequence of actions to maximize a reward through interaction with an environment" *(ISO/IEC 22989)*. "A class of machine-learning algorithms in which the process is not given specific goals to meet but, as it makes decisions, is instead given indications of whether it is doing well or not" *(ISACA glossary)*.
Rekeying, key rotation	a. Cryptographic process of securely replacing an expired session key to continue encrypted datacommunications, *e.g.* using the **I**nternet **K**ey **E**xchange protocol. "The process of changing cryptographic keys. Periodic rekeying limits the amount of data encrypted by a single key" *(ISACA glossary)*. b. Replacing worn pins in a physical lock mechanism, perhaps changing them to accept a different change or master key.
Relationship extraction, relation extraction	"Task of identifying relationships among entities mentioned in a text" *(ISO/IEC 22989)*.

TERM	MEANING
Releasable To data	"Data not to be passed to, or accessed by, foreign nationals beyond those belonging to specific nations which the data has been authorised for release to" *(AusISM)*.
Release management	See version control.
Relevance risk	Uncertainty as to whether information is or will be relevant or pertinent when used – an integrity issue. "The risk that the correct information may not get to the correct recipients at the correct time to allow the correct action to be taken or the correct decisions to be made" *(ISACA glossary)*.
Relevant	On-topic, pertinent, and related to the matter at hand. Forensic evidence must be relevant to the matter at issue to be admissible to the court, preventing one side trying to obscure important details and overwhelm the counterparty or court with an avalanche of irrelevant material.
Relevant and reasoned objection	"An objection to a draft decision as to whether there is an infringement of this Regulation, or whether envisaged action in relation to the controller or processor complies with this Regulation, which clearly demonstrates the significance of the risks posed by the draft decision as regards the fundamental rights and freedoms of data subjects and, where applicable, the free flow of personal data within the Union" *(**G**eneral **D**ata **P**rotection **R**egulation)*.
Relevant audit evidence	Evidence relevant to, and in scope of, a particular audit engagement – a subjective, context-dependent determination. "Audit evidence that pertains to the audit objectives and has a logical relationship to the findings and conclusions it is used to support" *(ISACA glossary)*. See also reliable audit evidence.
Relevant information	Information that is relevant to some purpose or situation. "Relating to controls, tells the evaluator something meaningful about the operation of the underlying controls or control component. Information that directly confirms the operation of controls is most relevant. Information that relates indirectly to the operation of controls can also be relevant, but is less relevant than direct information" *(ISACA glossary)*.
Reliability	Indication or measure of the extent to which something (such as a system, network, person, or control) can be trusted to perform consistently as expected or required, *i.e.* reliably. "Property of consistent intended behaviour and results" *(ISO/IEC 27002)*. *Cf.* liability.
Reliable, reliably	In a trustworthy manner, dependable, expected to perform correctly and achieve desired or specified outcomes every time. "To thoughtfully, consistently, dependably, and transparently do something" *(OCEG GRC Glossary)*.

TERM	MEANING
Reliable audit evidence	Audit evidence that is trustworthy, factual, and essentially undeniable (though it may yet be challenged!). "Audit evidence that, in the IS auditor's opinion, is valid, factual, objective and supportable" *(ISACA glossary)*. See also relevant audit evidence.
Reliable information	Reliable information. "Information that is accurate, verifiable and from an objective source" *(ISACA glossary)*.
Remanence, magnetic remanence	Residual magnetisation, such as the traces of magnetism left behind on disk or tape after data have supposedly been deleted. It may be possible to reconstitute some or all the data using specialist forensic techniques such as electron microscopy. "Magnetic representation of residual information remaining on a magnetic medium after the medium has been cleared" *(CNSSI 4009)*. See also remnants.
Remediate	Apply a remedy intended to mitigate or even eliminate one or more known vulnerabilities, *e.g.* by patching a system, uninstalling vulnerable software, or improving security processes. "Actions taken to mitigate or eliminate a vulnerability after it has been identified and assessed" *(ISACA glossary)*.
Remnants	When a computer process or system exits (stops executing), it can leave behind residual data that may provide forensic evidence or lead to a security incident. Fragments of confidential personal or proprietary data (potentially including passwords, plaintext, and cryptographic keys) may be left in memory or on disk, *e.g.* if a program has not been correctly coded to erase confidential data in its working files when it exits normally, if the program or system crashes or shuts down abnormally leaving the swap file on disk, if a disk controller marks a disk segment containing confidential data unusable, or due to remanence. Controls such as file high-watermarking reduce the risk somewhat. See also memory leakage, remanence.
Remote access	Function allowing users and/or administrators to use and/or administer (monitor and manage, *e.g.* patch) a system, device, or *thing* from a distant location via the Internet, another network, or point-to-point communications link. "Process of accessing network resources from another network, or from a terminal device which is not permanently connected, physically or logically, to the network it is accessing" *(ISO/IEC 27033-1)*. "Access to a system from a location not within the physical control of the system owner" *(NZISM)*. "An authorized user's ability to access a computer or network from anywhere through a network connection" *(ISACA glossary)*. "The ability for an organisation's users to access its non-public computing resources from external locations other than the organisation's facilities" *(NIST SP 800-114)*. "Access to a system that originates from outside an organisation's network and enters the network through a gateway, including over the internet" *(AusISM)*. "Access to an organizational system by a user

TERM	MEANING
	(or a process acting on behalf of a user) communicating through an external network (*e.g.*, the internet). Remote access methods include dial-up, broadband, and wireless" *(NIST SP 800-171)*.
Remote **A**ccess **T**rojan **(RAT)**	Malware that allows hackers remote, privileged access to a compromised system via the Internet. *Cf.* **R**emote **A**dministration **T**ool.
Remote **A**dministration **T**ool **(RAT)**	Software that allows privileged remote access to a system, normally for legitimate system administration purposes. *Cf.* **R**emote **A**ccess **T**rojan.
Remote **A**uthentication **D**ial-**I**n **U**ser **S**ervice **(RADIUS)**	UDP-based network protocol supporting **A**uthentication, **A**uthorisation, and **A**ccounting services. In conjunction with a **N**etwork **A**ccess **S**erver, a RADIUS server determines whether users are authorised to access network resources, and provides usage accounting. "A type of service providing an authentication and accounting system often used for dial-up and remote access security" *(ISACA glossary)*.
Remote **C**ode **E**xecution **(RCE)**	Capability to send instructions (*i.e.* individual commands, scripts, macros, and/or complete programs) to a distant system, normally through a network such as the Internet, and have the system execute them. If the system's security is inadequate, hackers and malware may exploit the function, leading to **R**emote **C**ode [or **C**omputer] **E**xploit.
Remote control	Capability to access, monitor, and control a system, device, vehicle, piece of equipment, *etc.* from afar using a contemporaneous network connection or telecommunications link (*e.g.* a phone line connected to a modem, or a radio control system).
Remote data processing	"Data processing at a distance for which the software is designed and developed by the manufacturer, or under the responsibility of the manufacturer, and the absence of which would prevent the product with digital elements from performing one of its functions" *(EU CRA)*.
Remote device	"Any enterprise asset capable of connecting to a network remotely, usually from public internet. This can include enterprise assets such as end-user devices, network devices, non-computing/Internet of Things (IoT) devices, and servers" *(CIS Controls)*.
Remote **D**iagnostic **P**ort **(RDP)**	Dedicated console port giving privileged access to a device such as a telephone exchange (PABX), system/server, storage subsystem, router, and firewall, intended for authorised technical support, diagnostics, systems management and configuration purposes, whether locally or remotely via a network (such as the Internet) or a dedicated point-to-point link.

TERM	MEANING
Remote File Inclusion (RFI)	Hacking technique used to attack vulnerable web applications with inadequate validation controls by manipulating their client-side scripts to 'include' (call and execute) malicious files from the client. See also Local File Inclusion, SQL injection.
Remote file system	"Enable an application that runs on an enterprise asset to access files stored on a different asset. Remote file systems often make other resources, such as remote noncomputing devices, accessible from an asset. The remote file access takes place using some form of local area network, wide area network, point-to-point link, or other communication mechanism. These file systems are often referred to as network file systems or distributed file systems" *(CIS Controls)*.
Remote maintenance, telemaintenance, online maintenance	Monitoring, configuring, and administering a system from afar via a network or point-to-point datacommunications link. "Maintenance of a functional unit provided through telecommunications with the assistance of, or under the control of, a maintenance facility at a remote location. Note: In this context, telecommunications does not include communication within a local area network on the premises of the functional unit" *(ISO/IEC 2382)*. "Maintenance activities conducted by individuals communicating through an external network (*e.g.*, the internet)" *(NIST SP 800-171)*.
Remote system control	Remote use or administration of a system, typically through the Internet or some other network or point-to-point link (such as radio). "Remotely using a computer at an organisation from a telework computer" *(NIST SP 800-114)*.
Remote Terminal Unit (RTU)	Basic Industrial Control System data collection/control device or unit located in, on, or near the equipment it monitors and controls. Proximity allows monitoring and controlling equipment to be tightly coupled, cutting down on time delays and hysteresis effects, while network connections to Supervisory Control And Data Acquisition and other Operational Technology systems permit remote monitoring and control of tags and multi-unit coordination.
Remote user	"User at a site other than the one at which the network resources being used are located" *(ISO/IEC 27033-1)*.
Remote working	Working while not in a conventional fixed office or similar corporate premises, *e.g.* working from home, on the road, while walking, or at off-site conferences, courses, or meetings.
Removable media	Digital storage device or media that (using the appropriate process) can safely be physically removed from a live computer system without dismantling or crashing the computer or corrupting data, *e.g.* USB memory sticks and flash memory cards, portable hard drives, or CD/DVD disks. "Any type of storage device that can

TERM	MEANING
	be removed from the system while it is running" *(ISACA glossary)*. Storage media that can be easily removed from a system and is designed for removal" *(NZISM)*. "Any type of storage device that can be removed from a computer while the system is running and allows data to be moved from one system to another. Examples of removable media include compact discs (CDs), digital versatile discs (DVDs) and Blu-ray discs, tape backups, as well as diskettes and universal serial bus (USB) drives" *(CIS Controls)*.
Repeatability	Capability to replay an activity in the same manner with the same inputs achieving the same outputs, either precisely identical or substantially equivalent according to circumstances and tolerances. "Property of a process conducted to get the same test results on the same testing environment (same computer, hard drive, mode of operation, *etc.*)" *(ISO/IEC 27037)*. See also reproducibility.
Replay	Display/retransmission and use/exploitation of previously recorded information, *e.g.* showing security guards innocuous CCTV footage of an empty bank vault while a robbery is in progress (as seen on TV). "The ability to copy a message or stream of messages between two parties and replay (retransmit) them to one or more of the parties" *(ISACA glossary)*.
Replay attack	Type of attack on challenge-response authentication processes, electronic business transactions, *etc.* whereby information from legitimate exchanges is recorded, then replayed by an unauthorised party. Normally foiled by replay resistance. "An attack that involves the capture of transmitted authentication or access control information and its subsequent retransmission with the intent of producing an unauthorized effect or gaining unauthorized access" *(CNSSI 4009)*.
Replay resistance	Process integrity controls intended to prevent replay attacks, *e.g.* by including a time-stamp, random sequence number, or nonce in an authentication challenge, coupled with cryptography. Low-level attacks (such as Krack) may succeed by exploiting packet retransmission capabilities. "Protection against the capture of transmitted authentication or access control information and its subsequent retransmission with the intent of producing an unauthorized effect or gaining unauthorized access" *(NIST SP 800-171)*.
Repo	*Abbrev:* code **repo**sitory or **repo**ssession, depending on context.
Representation	"A signed or oral statement issued by management to professionals, where management declares that a current or future fact (*e.g.*, process, system, procedure, policy) is or will be in a certain state, to the best of management's knowledge" *(ISACA glossary)*.

TERM	MEANING
REpresentational **S**tate **T**ransfer **(REST)**	Described as a 'software architectural style,' REST imposes six constraints on the design of loosely coupled client-server network applications ('RESTful' systems) and their **A**pplication **P**rogramming **I**nterfaces to facilitate interoperability across the web.
Representative	Someone or something that represents and can stand in for another. "A natural or legal person established in the Union who, designated by the controller or processor in writing pursuant to Article 27, represents the controller or processor with regard to their respective obligations under this Regulation" *(**G**eneral **D**ata **P**rotection **R**egulation)*.
Reproducibility	Capability to replicate an activity and achieve substantially the same result in a different situation or location such as a different laboratory. "Property of a process to get the same test results on a different testing environment (different computer, hard drive, operator, *etc.*)" *(ISO/IEC 27037)*. See also repeatability.
Repudiation	Credible denial that some activity, decision, transaction, communication, agreement, *etc.* took place at all or as claimed, or that those allegedly involved were indeed involved, *i.e.* plausible deniability. "Denial by one of the entities involved in a communication of having participated in all or part of the communication. Note: In the description of techniques and mechanisms the term 'non-repudiation' is often used to mean that none of the entities involved in a communication can deny its participation in the communication" *(ISO/IEC 2382)*. "A denial by one of the parties to a transaction of participation in all or part of that transaction, or of the content of a communication related to that transaction" *(ISACA glossary)*. *Cf.* non repudiation.
Reputation	Perceptions, opinions, and feelings of third parties concerning a person, organisation, product, *etc.* Both an information asset and an integrity property. Corporate reputations and brands are intimately associated, highly valuable, and yet vulnerable and difficult/costly to influence and protect. Personal reputations can likewise be devastated by scandalous defamation, libel, or slander.
Reputation risk	Risk (uncertain possibility or potential) of an incident (adversely) impacting an organisation's reputation among stakeholders, harming brand value, customer loyalty, investor confidence/trust, *etc.* "The current and prospective effect on earnings and capital arising from negative public opinion. Notes: Reputation risk affects a bank's ability to establish new relationships or services, or to continue servicing existing relationships. It may expose the bank to litigation, financial loss or a decline in its customer base. A bank's reputation can be damaged by Internet banking services that are executed poorly or otherwise alienate customers and the public.

TERM	MEANING
	An Internet bank has a greater reputation risk as compared to a traditional brick-and-mortar bank, because it is easier for its customers to leave for a different bank and since it cannot discuss any problems in person with the customer" (ISACA glossary).
Requirement	Something that is desired, wanted, expected, or demanded. Ideally developed by a formal requirements analysis process involving thorough and competent needs analysis, then explicitly and formally specified and documented for clarity, review, and approval/authorisation before being used. Can be categorised as functional or nonfunctional. "Essential condition that a system has to satisfy" *(ISO/IEC 2382)*. "Need or expectation that is stated, generally implied or obligatory. Notes: 'Generally implied' means that it is custom or common practice for the organisation and interested parties that the need or expectation under consideration is implied. A specified requirement is one that is stated, for example in documented information" *(ISO/IEC 27000)*. "1. A condition or capability needed by a user to solve a problem or achieve an objective. 2. A condition or capability that must be met or possessed by a system or system component to satisfy a contract, standard, specification or other formally imposed document. 3. A documented representation of a condition or capability as in definition 1 or 2" *(ISACA glossary)*.
Requirements analysis	Systematic, formal process of developing and analysing requirements to understand both the explicit statements ('the letter of the law') and (by 'reading between the lines') any implicit/unstated aspects such as the associated rationale, assurance arrangements, and risks. An important part of formulating, planning, and checking the organisation's response or solution, particularly if the requirements are strong, strict, ambiguous, difficult, or costly to satisfy (*e.g.* complex legal or regulatory compliance obligations). "Systematic investigation of user requirements to arrive at a definition of a system" *(ISO/IEC 2382)*.
Residual data	Data marked for deletion, perhaps even deleted, that is potentially fully or partially recoverable from the storage medium using forensic techniques. "Data left in a data medium after deletion of a file or a portion of a file. Note: Residual data remain recoverable until clearing of the data medium has taken place" *(ISO/IEC 2382)*. See also sanitisation, remnants, remanence.
Residual effect	"The effect of uncertainty in the presence of actions & controls" *(OCEG GRC Glossary)*.

TERM	MEANING
Residual risk, retained risk, net risk, controlled risk	Risk that remains despite any and all risk treatments applied, *e.g.* the possibility that security controls might fail in service, unrecognised/unresolved vulnerabilities might be exploited, new threats might emerge, and unanticipated impacts may occur. Errors and omissions in the risk analysis process are always possible, along with black swan events; hence, some amount of residual risk is *inevitable* no matter how much effort is expended on the risk management process, emphasising the value of contingency planning. "Risk remaining after risk treatment. Notes: Residual risk can contain unidentified risk. Residual risks can also contain retained risk" *(ISO/IEC 27005)*. "The remaining risk after management has implemented a risk response" *(ISACA glossary)*. "Portion of risk remaining after security measures have been applied" *(CNSSI 4009)*. "The risk remaining after management takes action to reduce the impact and likelihood of an adverse event, including control activities in responding to a risk (Institute of Internal Auditors)" *(NZISM)*. "The level of risk in the presence of actions & controls" *(OCEG GRC Glossary)*. "The portion of inherent risk that remains after management actions are implemented" *(IIA GIAS)*.
Residue	Leftovers, *e.g.* the skin oils that leave behind characteristic fingerprints on touched surfaces and wear marks on PIN pads, or the feint magnetism that remains when a magnetic disk is inadequately sanitised of data. See also residual risk, residual data, remnants, remanence.
Resilience, resilient, antifragile	Robustness, stability, dependability. The ability for systems, networks, services, processes, people, functions, departments, business units, business operations, organisations, business relationships, and even entire nations to continue operating more-or-less unaffected by security incidents, thereby ensuring availability and hence business continuity. Can involve a wide range of techniques such as competent security design, hardening, multiple redundant or mirrored facilities with automated or manual failover, fault tolerance and 'over-engineering' (=engineering!), the minimisation of and special protective arrangements for **S**ingle **P**oints **o**f **F**ailure, contractual obligation and liabilities, training and support for critical workers, and various assurance controls. "Ability of a system to recover operational condition quickly following an incident" *(ISO/IEC 22989)*. "Adaptive capacity of an organization in a complex and changing environment" *(ISO 31073)*. "Ability of an organization to resist being affected by disruptions" *(ISO/IEC 27031)*. "Capability of a system to maintain its functions and structure in the face of internal and external

TERM	MEANING
	change, and to degrade gracefully when this is necessary" *(ISO/IEC TS 5723)*. "Ability of a cloud service to recover operational condition quickly after a fault occurs" *(ISO/IEC 19086-1)*. "Ability to absorb and adapt in a changing environment. Note: In the context of urban resilience the ability to absorb and adapt to a changing environment is determined by the collective capacity to anticipate, prepare and respond to threats and opportunities by each individual component of an urban system" *(ISO 22300)*. "The ability of a system or network to resist failure or to recover quickly from any disruption, usually with minimal recognizable effect" *(ISACA glossary)*. "Evidence that the organization can withstand or recover quickly from difficult conditions and even become stronger after stress" *(OCEG GRC Glossary)*. "The ability to prepare for and adapt to changing conditions and withstand and recover rapidly from disruption. Resilience includes the ability to withstand and recover from deliberate attacks, accidents, or naturally occurring threats or incidents" *(OMB Circular A-130)*. See also **F**ailure **M**odes and **E**ffects **A**nalysis. *Cf.* recovery.
Resistance strength	"The strength of a Control as compared to the probable level of force (as embodied by the time, resources, and technological capability; measured as a percentile) that a Threat Agent is capable of applying against an Asset" *(O-RT)*.
Resource	Organisational, societal, human, informational, technological, physical, or financial asset. "All assets (including plant and equipment), people, skills, technology, premises, and supplies and information (whether electronic or not) that an organization has to have available to use, when needed, in order to operate and meet its objective" *(ISO 22300)*. "Any enterprise asset that can help the organization achieve its objectives" *(ISACA glossary)*.
Resource **A**ccess **C**ontrol Facility **(RACF)**	Mainframe user access control and auditing application for IBM z/OS and z/VM **O**perating **S**ystems. See also ACF2.
Resource **P**ublic **K**ey Infrastructure **(RPKI), resource certification**	**P**ublic **K**ey **I**nfrastructure used to protect **B**order **G**ateway Protocol.
Respond	a. React positively, proactively, and appropriately to a stimulus, event, trigger, situation, *etc.* rather than remaining unresponsive ('asleep at the wheel'), perhaps leading to a disaster. "Information sent that is responding to some stimulus" *(SANS glossary)*. b. Core function (phase) of NIST's **C**yber **S**ecurity **F**ramework, along with identify, protect, detect, and recover. "Develop and implement appropriate activities to take action regarding a detected cybersecurity incident. The Respond Function supports the ability to contain the impact of a potential cybersecurity incident" *(NIST CSF)*.

TERM	MEANING
Response plan	"Documented collection of procedures and information that is developed, compiled and maintained in preparedness for use in an incident" *(ISO 22300)*.
Response programme	"Plan, processes, and resources to perform the activities and services necessary to preserve and protect life, property, operations and critical assets. Note: Response steps generally include incident recognition, notification, assessment, declaration, plan execution, communications, and resources management" *(ISO 22300)*.
Response team	"Group of individuals responsible for developing, executing, rehearsing, and maintaining the response plan, including the processes and procedures" *(ISO 22300)*.
Responsibility	Obligation on, or expectation of, an individual person or organisation, *e.g.* to ensure that an asset is properly protected (a duty of care) and legitimately exploited. In contrast to accountability, responsibility *can* be, and often is, delegated or passed from one person, function, team, company, *etc.* to another, but the originator remains personally accountable for their decision to delegate and hence retains a stake in the outcome.
Responsible disclosure	For genuine, appropriate, ethical reasons, voluntarily informing a system owner, manager, organisation, *etc.* about a vulnerability of some sort that the informer believes they should be aware of. See also bug bounty.
Responsive actions & controls	"Actions & controls that aim to accelerate or compound the benefit of favorable events, and correct and recover from the harm of unfavorable events" *(OCEG GRC Glossary)*.
REST	*Abbrev:* **RE**presentational **S**tate **T**ransfer.
Restoration	"Level of recovery of data, ICT systems and business operations to the normal state after a disruption with a minimal loss, if any" *(ISO/IEC 27031 DRAFT)*.
Restore point	Through the system protection function, Microsoft Windows systems automatically backup their system settings (critical **O**perating **S**ystem files, programs, and registry settings) weekly by default, and manually at any time, to the *System Volume Information* hidden system folder on the root drive. Provided a backup is available and not corrupted, overwritten or lost, the user can restore it in order to revert subsequent changes and hopefully correct problems created by, for instance, a failed software installation, malware infection, or some types of user error (principally configuration errors).

TERM	MEANING
Restricted key [system]	Physical key with an unusual proprietary (often trademarked or patented) profile/design, intended to prevent locksmiths not authorised and supplied with masters (blanks) by the manufacturer from cutting new keys, and to prevent authorised locksmiths from providing keys without authorisation and authentication of customer representatives (*e.g.* for a prison). A form of copy-protection.
Restriction of processing	"The marking of stored personal data with the aim of limiting their processing in the future" *(General Data Protection Regulation).*
RetailTech	Contraction of **retail tech**nology, particularly the development and exploitation of innovative **I**nformation **T**echnology within the retail sector. See also AgriTech, Biotech, EdTech, FinTech, FoodTech, GovTech, EcoTech/GreenTech, HealthTech, LegalTech, RegTech, and other tech neologisms.
Retbleed	See Spectre.
Retention	Holding back, continuing to store and failing to destroy information, potentially beyond the period or purpose for which it was originally collected or created. Increases the risk of inappropriate/unauthorised disclosure/theft. According to some privacy/information protection laws, personal information must not be retained indefinitely but must be securely destroyed, unless specific exemptions apply. "A phase of the data life cycle that pertains to how long an entity stores information for future use or reference" *(Trust Services Criteria).* See also archive.
Retention period	Minimum length of time for which valuable information is supposed or required to be retained and made available for authorised and legitimate purposes, for business reasons. The actual duration may, due to incidents, negligence, or other reasons, be shorter (potentially a compliance exception) but is usually longer. "Length of time for which data on a data medium is to be preserved" *(ISO/IEC 2382).* "Time period within which the data objects ... of the cluster of personally identifiable information (PII) ... is required to be available in the PII controller's organization because of the functional use or legal retention obligations. Note: A specific cluster of PII typically has the same retention period" *(ISO/IEC 27555).*
Retraining	Training again, in the forlorn hope that, this time around, students learn something useful by retaining a more substantial part of the imparted knowledge. "Updating a trained model by training with different training data" *(ISO/IEC 22989).*

TERM	MEANING
Return **O**n **I**nvestment **(ROI)**	Estimate of the anticipated future value of an investment over a given period (the expected productive life of the investment), having subtracted the costs associated with the investment itself. *Cf.* **R**isk **O**f **I**ncarceration.
Return **O**n **S**ecurity **I**nvestment **(ROSI)**	Simply the **R**eturn **O**n **I**nvestment where the investment is intended to improve security, reduce risk and so reduce the probability and/or impact of incidents, or improve assurance, relative to not investing. The return can only be estimated since it is virtually impossible to know exactly how much the probability and/or impact have been reduced or to quantify the value of improved assurance, but tracking the appropriate metrics can help.
Return-**O**riented **P**rogramming **(ROP)**	Family of hacking/malware techniques in which execution of a legitimate program is surreptitiously diverted to malicious code "gadgets" by manipulating return calls held in the stack, exploiting **C**entral **P**rocessing **U**nit design flaws that fail to prevent such manipulation.
Revenge porn[ography]	Posting of revealing/embarrassing/explicit personal photographs, videos, *etc.* of a former lover or sex partner on the Internet as a spiteful, callous, and potentially illegal attack on the victim's privacy or as a means of coercion/blackmail.
Reverse engineering	Working out the internals of a device, program, malware, system, process, *etc.* through painstaking analysis without access to its original design, source code, documentation, *etc.* Generally performed without the owner's permission and/or knowledge, *e.g.* to steal **I**ntellectual **P**roperty, identify exploitable vulnerabilities in software or cryptographic processes, to understand how malware operates or to hack. "The process of deconstructing and interpreting an electronic device or data format without prior access to the creator's specification or design" *(FSRCoP)*. "Acquiring sensitive data by disassembling and analyzing the design of a system component" *(SANS glossary)*.
Review	Literally, to view again. Encompasses various checks that are generally informal and hence does not usually offer the same level of assurance as, say, an audit. "Activity undertaken to determine the suitability, adequacy and effectiveness of the subject matter to achieve established objectives. Note: Review can be applied to a risk management framework, risk management process, risk or risk control" *(ISO 31073)*. "A re-assessment or re-evaluation of any of the following: (a) Findings from an examination/analysis. (b) Evaluation/interpretation of findings from an examination. (c) Contract requirements (includes MoU, SLA *etc.*). (d) Process" *(FSRCoP)*.

TERM	MEANING
Review object	Item, issue, risk, system, control, process, organisation, function, department, building, person, relationship, entity, *etc.* within the scope of a review, hence subject to inspection, possibly but not necessarily the main focus. "Specific item being reviewed" *(ISO/IEC 27000)*.
Review objective	Aim or purpose of a review. "Statement describing what is to be achieved as a result of a review" *(ISO/IEC 27000)*.
Review visit	"Participation by reviewers in peer review activities at the host location(s). Note: Review visit activities include presentations, individual interviews, focus groups, site visits, and the observation of live and table-top exercises" *(ISO 22300)*.
Reviewer	Person, group, function, or organisation that reviews. "Entity that provides feedback as part of a peer review with expert knowledge and experience in the analysis area. Note: The entity may be an organization, partnership, community, city, region, country or other body" *(ISO 22300)*.
REvil	Hacker/malware/cybercriminal gang active in 2022.
Revision management	See version control.
Reward, performance	"A measure of the positive, favorable effect of uncertainty on objectives" *(OCEG GRC Glossary)*.
Right	a. Correct, proper, appropriate, *etc.* b. Something that a person ororganisation is reasonably and perhaps legally permitted or allowed to do or expect if they so choose. See also access right, permission, privilege.
Right to be forgotten, right to erasure	Controversial right to have certain types of damaging or embarrassing personal information about oneself erased from the web including search engines, plus cached and archived copies. Partly supported by privacy and human rights laws. Intended to nullify revenge porn and other embarrassing disclosures of a personal nature, such as old police reports concerning minor incidents and false/unproven accusations. The right is tricky to define, administer, and facilitate in practice, especially given the global and decentralised nature of the Internet (making it hard to put the genie back in the bottle), plus there are concerns about the right being misused for unethical/inappropriate reasons including political motivations, propaganda, and fraud.
Rights holder	"Legal entity either holding or authorised to use one or more intellectual property rights" *(ISO 22300)*.

TERM	MEANING
Risk	In general, uncertainty relating to a particular context, scenario, situation, circumstance, asset, threat, vulnerability, impact, outcome, consequence, *etc.* Expressed mathematically, precisely/absolutely, and objectively as a probability value or range less than 1 (meaning absolute certainty), or subjectively in imprecise, vague, and relative terms such as doubt, ambiguity, potential, possibility, or likelihood. Can be reduced to some extent by risk analysis and mitigation through controls as part of risk management, but in practice there is inevitably some residual risk, leading to concerns, fears, indecision, reluctance to commit, *etc.* In relation to information, the predicted or projected frequency and magnitude of future loss if a threat were to exploit an exposed vulnerability, causing adverse business, personal, social, environmental or other impacts. Expressed either in relative terms, implying degrees or levels of risk, or as absolute values over a defined period, preferably with specified tolerances or margins for error given the uncertainties. Information security controls seldom eliminate information risks; hence, other risk treatments (such as accepting residual risks) are also appropriate. "Possibility that a particular threat will exploit a particular vulnerability of a data processing system" *(ISO/IEC 2382)*. "Effect of uncertainty. Notes: An effect is a deviation from the expected — positive or negative. Uncertainty is the state, even partial, of deficiency of information related to, understanding or knowledge of, an event, its consequence, or likelihood. Risk is often characterized by reference to potential events ... and consequences ... or a combination of these. Risk is often expressed in terms of a combination of the consequences of an event (including changes in circumstances) and the associated likelihood ... of occurrence" *(ISO/IEC 42001)*. "A measure of the negative, unfavorable effect of uncertainty on objectives" *(OCEG GRC Glossary)*. "Combination of the probability of occurrence of harm and the severity of that harm" *(ISO/IEC Guide 51)*. "The combination of the likelihood of an event and its impact" *(ISACA glossary)*. "A measure of the extent to which an entity is threatened by a potential circumstance or event, and typically a function of: (i) the adverse impacts that would arise if the circumstance or event occurs; and (ii) the likelihood of occurrence" *(NIST CSF)*. "The possibility that an event will occur and adversely affect the achievement of objectives" *(**T**rust **S**ervices **C**riteria)*. "The positive or negative effect of uncertainty on objectives" *(IIA GIAS)*. "The product of the level of threat with the level of vulnerability. It establishes the likelihood of a successful attack" *(SANS glossary)*.

TERM	MEANING
Risk acceptance	Management or personal decision to live with rather than mitigate, share, or avoid a risk. A form of risk treatment. Ideally such a decision should be made explicitly (consciously and deliberately) by a well-informed, competent, and responsible person who truly appreciates the implications but, in practice, risks are often accepted implicitly (without thinking) and/or without being recognised and fully understood, which itself constitutes a further risk. "Managerial decision to accept a certain degree of risk, usually for technical or cost reasons" *(ISO/IEC 2382)*. "Informed decision to take a particular risk. Notes: Risk acceptance can occur without risk treatment or during the process of risk treatment; Accepted risks are subject to monitoring and review" *(ISO/IEC 27005)*. "A decision to accept a risk, made according to the risk appetite and risk tolerance set by senior management, where the enterprise can assume the risk and absorb any losses" *(ISACA glossary)*. "The appropriate risk response when the identified risk is within the organizational risk tolerance" *(NIST SP 800-39)*.
Risk aggregation	Association or linking of risks relevant to the subject of analysis. Although risks may be acceptable when considered individually (*e.g.* blackouts and data centre fires, each mitigated by controls), the cumulative effects with dependencies and common or compounding factors (*e.g.* power failure disabling data centre sprinklers, and fires disabling power systems) may be unacceptable. "Combination of a number of risks into one risk to develop a more complete understanding of the overall risk" *(ISO 31073)*. "The process of integrating risk assessments at a corporate level to obtain a complete view of the overall risk for the enterprise" *(ISACA glossary)*.
Risk-agnostic	General-purpose/non-specific control. "Describes the ability of a capability, process or response to address 'common' impacts of risks (*i.e.* those impacts that occur across multiple scenarios). For example, major fires, terrorist incidents and flooding are all likely to produce mass casualties; developing capabilities to handle mass casualties is, therefore, a risk-agnostic approach" *(UK Resilience Lessons Digest 2023)*.
Risk analysis	In-depth analytical, investigative, or modelling part of risk assessment, a core part of risk management. "Systematic method of identifying the assets of a data processing system, the threats to those assets, and the vulnerability of the system to those threats" *(ISO/IEC 2382)*. "Process to comprehend the nature of risk and to determine the level of risk. Notes: Risk analysis provides the basis for risk evaluation and decisions about risk treatment. Risk analysis includes risk estimation" *(ISO/IEC 27005)*. "1. A process by which the frequency and magnitude of IT risk scenarios are estimated. 2. The initial steps of risk management: analyzing the value of assets to the business, identifying threats to those assets and

TERM	MEANING
	evaluating how vulnerable each asset is to those threats. Note: Risk analysis often involves an evaluation of the probable frequency of a particular event, as well as the probable impact of that event" *(ISACA glossary)*. "Examination of information to identify the risk to an information system" *(CNSSI 4009)*.
Risk appetite	Expresses senior management's willingness or desire for the organisation to take (accept) a specified quantity, volume, or level of risk, provided that (in their opinion) the likelihood of achieving business objectives and hence anticipated business benefits make it advantageous to do so. Implies a mature, forward-thinking business-focused strategic outlook. Often expressed quite subtly, *e.g.* "We must consolidate to protect our core business" or conversely "We are pursuing innovative opportunities to expand the business." "Amount and type of risk that an organization is willing to pursue or retain" *(ISO/IEC 27005)*. "The amount of risk, on a broad level, that an entity is willing to accept in pursuit of its mission" *(ISACA glossary)*. "The level and type of risk the organization is WILLING to address given the level and type of reward it pursues" *(OCEG GRC Glossary)*. "The types and amount of risk that an organization is willing to accept in the pursuit of its strategies and objectives" *(IIA GIAS)*. "The types and amount of risk, on a board level, an organization is willing to accept in pursuit of value" *(COSO)*. *Cf.* risk tolerance.
Risk articulation	Important part of the rôle of information risk and security management professionals involves describing and explaining relevant risks and related items in terms that not only make sense to the audiences, but inspire or motivate them to make appropriate decisions and act accordingly – going beyond mere awareness.
Risk assessment	Structured, formal process for systematically examining and assessing information security threats, vulnerabilities, and impacts relating to a given system, process, activity, or situation, prior to determining whether additional controls or other forms of risk treatment might be necessary. "Overall process of risk identification, risk analysis and risk evaluation" *(ISO/IEC 27005)*. "A process used to identify and evaluate risk and its potential effects. Notes: Risk assessments are used to identify those items or areas that present the highest risk, vulnerability or exposure to the enterprise for inclusion in the IS annual audit plan. Risk assessments are also used to manage the project delivery and project benefit risk" *(ISACA glossary)*. "The process of identifying, prioritizing, and estimating risks. This includes determining the extent to which adverse circumstances or events could impact an enterprise. Uses the results of threat and vulnerability assessments to identify risk to organisational operations and evaluates those risks in terms of likelihood of occurrence and impacts if they occur. The product of a risk assessment is a list of estimated potential impacts

TERM	MEANING
	and unmitigated vulnerabilities. Risk assessment is part of risk management and is conducted throughout the Risk Management Framework (RMF)" *(CNSSI 4009)*. "The process of identifying risks to organizational operations (including mission, functions, image, reputation), organizational assets, individuals, other organizations, and the Nation, resulting from the operation of a system" *(NIST SP 800-171)*. "A scientific and technologically based process consisting of three steps, risk identification, risk analysis and risk evaluation" *(ENISA RM glossary)*. "A structured and auditable process of identifying potentially significant events, assessing their likelihood and impacts, and then combining these to provide an overall assessment of risk, as a basis for further decisions and action" *(UK Resilience Lessons Digest 2023)*. "The identification and analysis of risks relevant to the achievement of an organization's objectives. The significance of risks is typically assessed in terms of impact and likelihood" *(IIA GIAS)*. "The process by which risks are identified and the impact of those risks determined" *(SANS glossary)*. See also risk analysis.
Risk attitude	Combination of risk perception and risk appetite with risk treatment. "Organization's approach to assess and eventually pursue, retain, take or turn away from risk" *(ISO 31073)*.
Risk averse, risk aversion	Low risk appetite, a general reluctance to accept risks. "Attitude to turn away from risk" *(ISO 31073)*. "Avoiding risk even if this leads to the loss of opportunity. For example, using a (more expensive) phone call vs. sending an e-mail in order to avoid risks associated with e-mail may be considered 'Risk Averse'" *(SANS glossary)*.
Risk avoidance	Form of risk treatment. Rather than mitigating unacceptable risks using controls or sharing them with third parties, it is sometimes more appropriate not to enter into risky situations in the first place (*e.g.* not deploying a risky new **I**nformation **T**echnology system or not entering into a risky relationship with a dubious partner) or to pull out (*e.g.* prematurely halting a risky business venture). "Informed decision not to be involved in, or to withdraw from, an activity in order not to be exposed to a particular risk. Note: Risk avoidance can be based on the result of risk evaluation and/or legal and regulatory obligations" *(ISO 31073)*. "The process for systematically avoiding risk, constituting one approach to managing risk" *(ISACA glossary)*.
Risk awareness program	See security awareness. "A program that creates an understanding of risk, risk factors and the various types of risk that an enterprise faces" *(ISACA glossary)*.

TERM	MEANING
Risk capacity	See risk appetite. "The objective magnitude or amount of loss that an enterprise can tolerate without risking its continued existence" *(ISACA glossary)*. "The MAXIMUM cumulative level and type of risk that the organization can address. Anything over the risk capacity may affect the organization's survival" *(OCEG GRC Glossary)*.
Risk catalogue	See risk register.
Risk communication	"Exchange or sharing of information about risk between the decision maker and other interested parties. Note: The information can relate to the existence, nature, form, probability, severity, acceptability, treatment or other aspects of risk" *(ISO 22300)*. "Set of continual and iterative processes that an organization conducts to provide, share or obtain information, and to engage in dialogue with interested parties regarding the management of risk. Notes: The information can relate to the existence, nature, form, likelihood, significance, evaluation, acceptance and treatment of risk; Consultation is a two-way process of informed communication between an organization and its interested parties on an issue prior to making a decision or determining a direction on that issue. Consultation is: a process which impacts on a decision through influence rather than power; an input to decision making, not joint decision making" *(ISO/IEC 27005)*.
Risk control	See risk treatment. "Measure that maintains and/or modifies risk. Notes: Risk controls include, but are not limited to, any process, policy, device, practice, or other conditions and/or actions which maintain and/or modify risk; Risk controls do not always exert the intended or assumed modifying effect" *(ISO 31073)*.
Risk [and] **control matrix**	Table relating risks to the associated mitigating controls. "A tool that facilitates the performance of internal auditing. It typically links business objectives, risks, control processes, and key information to support the internal audit process" *(IIA GIAS)*.
Risk criteria	Ranges or boundary conditions used to classify, characterise and determine priorities and options for treating identified risks. "Terms of reference against which the significance of a risk is evaluated. Notes: Risk criteria are based on organizational objectives, and external and internal context. Risk criteria can be derived from standards, laws, policies and other requirements" *(ISO 31073)*.
Risk culture	Shared, general or typical attitudes towards risk-taking among a social group or culture. A highly subjective comparative, dynamic, and context-dependent assessment. "An organization's shared values and beliefs that govern attitudes toward risk-taking, care and integrity, and determine how openly risk and losses are reported and discussed" *(ISACA glossary)*.

TERM	MEANING
Risk DataBase	See risk register.
Risk description	Statement succinctly explaining or characterising a risk in terms that make sense to the intended audience/s, *e.g.* the business scenario, technical situation, or general circumstances in which, due to various causative factors, the risk may materialise, causing an incident with consequences. Given uncertainties about the exact nature, timing, *etc.*, the description may be merely a representative/evocative illustration of a cluster of similar risks or types of incident. "Structured statement of risk usually containing four elements: sources, events, causes and consequences" *(ISO Guide 73)*.
Risk driver	See risk factor. "Factor that has a major influence on risk" *(ISO 31073)*.
Risk estimation	Risk concerns probabilities not certainties; hence, it can only ever be *estimated* with degrees of confidence ranging between *near* certainty and sheer finger-in-the-air wild-arse guesswork.
Risk evaluation	Determining the significance of identified risks. "Process of comparing the results of risk analysis with risk criteria to determine whether the risk and/or its significance is acceptable or tolerable. Note: Risk evaluation assists in the decision about risk treatment" *(ISO/IEC 27005)*.
Risk factor	Factor, parameter, or characteristic relevant to or affecting risk, *e.g.* a threat, vulnerability, exposure, impact, control, treatment, severity, likelihood, decision quality, dynamics, trend, environment, … "A condition that can influence the frequency, the magnitude and ultimately the business impact of IT-related risk scenarios" *(ISACA glossary)*. "The individual components that determine risk, including Loss Event Frequency, Loss Magnitude, Threat Event Frequency, *etc.*" *(O-RT)*.
Risk financing	Contingency arrangements to fund the possible financial losses arising from failed investments, *e.g.* from reserves. "Form of risk treatment involving contingent arrangements for the provision of funds to meet or modify the financial consequences should they occur" *(ISO 31073)*.
Risk governance	Risk governance. "Provides the transparency, responsibility, and accountability that enables managers to effectively manage risk" *(NIST IR 8286C)*.
Risk identification	Initial recognition, appreciation or acknowledgement, and documentation or characterisation of the potential existence of a risk perhaps worth assessing. "Process of finding, recognizing and describing risks. Notes: Risk identification involves the identification of risk sources, events, their causes and their potential consequences; Risk identification can involve historical data, theoretical analysis, informed and expert opinions, and interested parties' needs" *(ISO/IEC 27005)*. "The process for determining and documenting the risk an enterprise faces" *(ISACA glossary)*.

TERM	MEANING
Risk indicator	Information that flags or demonstrates a risk (*e.g.* an adverse audit report, a security survey) or a change (*e.g.* the increasing/decreasing prevalence or significance of various risk factors) potentially worth addressing. "A metric capable of showing that the enterprise may realize a risk" *(ISACA glossary)*.
Risk inventory	See risk register.
Risk landscape	See risk profile and risk universe.
Risk lifecycle, risk cycle	Lifecycle/sequence of risk management activities that take place before, during, and after an incident. "A conceptual model that breaks the management of a risk down into stages at which different preparatory actions can be taken. The UK government is using six stages: anticipation, assessment, prevention, preparation, response and recovery" *(UK Resilience Lessons Digest 2023)*.
Risk list	See risk register.
Risk management	a. Ongoing process for identifying, assessing, evaluating, and addressing risks using appropriate risk treatments. "Coordinated activities to direct and control an organization with regard to risk" *(ISO 31073)*. "The process of managing risks to organizational operations (including mission, functions, image, or reputation), organizational assets, individuals, other organizations, or the nation resulting from the operation or use of an information system, and includes: (1) the conduct of a risk assessment; (2) the implementation of a risk mitigation strategy; (3) employment of techniques and procedures for the continuous monitoring of the security state of the information system; and (4) documenting the overall risk management program" *(CNSSI 4009)*. "The process of identifying, assessing, and responding to risk" *(NIST CSF)*. "The act of managing processes and resources to address risk while pursuing reward" *(OCEG GRC Glossary)*. "The process, distinct from risk assessment, of weighing policy alternatives in consultation with interested parties, considering risk assessment and other legitimate factors, and selecting appropriate prevention and control options" *(ENISA RM glossary)*. "All activities and structures directed towards the effective assessment and management of risks and their potential adverse impacts" *(UK Resilience Lessons Digest 2023)*. "A process to identify, assess, manage, and control potential events or situations to provide reasonable assurance regarding the achievement of the organization's objectives" *(IIA GIAS)*. "One of the governance objectives. Entails recognizing risk; assessing the impact and likelihood of that risk; and developing strategies, such as avoiding the risk, reducing the negative effect of the risk and/or transferring the risk, to manage it within the context of the enterprise's risk appetite" *(ISACA glossary)*. b. Specialist corporate department/function responsible for leading and promoting good practices in the management of financial and other forms of risk.

TERM	MEANING
Risk management audit	Audit of the risk management process. "Systematic, independent and documented process for obtaining evidence and evaluating it objectively in order to determine the extent to which the risk management framework, or any selected part of it, is adequate and effective" *(ISO 31073)*.
Risk **M**anagement **F**ramework **(RMF)**	"A structured approach used to oversee and manage risk for an enterprise" *(CNSSI 4009)*.
Risk management plan	Plan laying out how management intends to implement, monitor, and maintain the organisation's risk management policies, strategies, processes, *etc.* "Statement of the overall intentions and direction of an organization related to risk management" *(ISO Guide 73)*.
Risk management policy	Principles/axioms and directives (rules) expressed by managers concerning the management of risk. "Statement of the overall intentions and direction of an organization related to risk management" *(ISO Guide 73)*.
Risk management process	Process of risk management. "Systematic application of management policies, procedures and practices to the activities of communicating, consulting, establishing the context, and identifying, analysing, evaluating, treating, monitoring and reviewing risk" *(ISO/IEC 27005)*.
Risk map, risk chart	"A (graphic) tool for ranking and displaying risk by defined ranges for frequency and magnitude" *(ISACA glossary)*.
Risk matrix, risk table	Table relating estimated probability of occurrence against estimated impact or severity of various risks or types of incident. See also risk map, heatmap.
Risk mitigation	Mitigating (reducing or limiting) the probability (likelihood) of occurrence and/or the impact (adverse consequences) of one or more unacceptable risks, generally using controls although sometimes it is better to share or avoid them. "Lessening or minimizing of the adverse impacts of a hazardous event" *(ISO 22300)*. "The management of risk through the use of countermeasures and controls" *(ISACA glossary)*. "Prioritizing, evaluating, and implementing the appropriate risk-reducing controls/countermeasures recommended from the risk management process" *(CNSSI 4009)*.
Risk monitoring	"Maintaining ongoing awareness of an organization's risk environment, risk management program, and associated activities to support risk decisions" *(NIST SP 800-39)*.

TERM	MEANING
Risk multiplier	The confluence or coincident occurrence of disparate risks can have a multiplying or compounding effect, *e.g.* a widespread situation or incident that stresses the regional, national, or international socio-economic system (such as a pandemic or trade war) can increase the probability and/or impact of risks such as ransomware infections, hacks, or cybertage destabilising and perhaps disrupting an organisation's supply chains (affecting its suppliers, partners, *and* customers).
Risk **O**f **I**ncarceration **(ROI)**	Leet term for the possibility of a lawbreaker (such as a hacker or fraudster) being caught and imprisoned. *Cf.* **R**eturn **O**n **I**nvestment.
Risk owner	Organisation, rôle, or person who notionally 'owns' and may be held to account if a risk eventuates, causing unacceptable impacts, on the basis that they patently failed to ensure it was adequately treated, *e.g.* mitigated with controls. As the explicit or implicit owner of residual risk, they also have an interest in the incident management and business continuity arrangements. "Person or entity with the accountability and authority to manage a risk" *(ISO/IEC 27005)*. "The person in whom the organization has invested the authority and accountability for making risk-based decisions and who owns the loss associated with a realized risk scenario. Note: The risk owner may not be responsible for the implementation of risk treatment" *(ISACA glossary)*.
Risk perception	Awareness, appreciation and understanding of risk. "Interested party's view on risk. Note: Risk perception reflects the interested party's needs, issues, knowledge, beliefs and values" *(ISO 31073)*.
Risk portfolio view	"1. A method to identify interdependencies and interconnections among risk, as well as the effect of risk responses on multiple types of risk. 2. A method to estimate the aggregate impact of multiple types of risk (*e.g.*, cascading and coincidental threat types or scenarios, or risk concentration or correlation across silos) and the potential effect of risk response across multiple types of risk" *(ISACA glossary)*.
Risk profile, risk landscape, risk surface	Conceptual three-dimensional view (profile) of the organisation's risks relative to each other. In practice, most risks are difficult to quantify, many change dynamically, and it is tough to compare markedly different kinds of risk; hence, this is a subjective perspective. A security metric. "Description of any set of risks. Note: The set of risks can contain those that relate to the whole organization, part of the organization, or as otherwise defined" *(ISO Guide 73)*. See also security landscape, risk universe, attack surface, heatmap.
Risk rating matrix	See risk matrix. "A table showing the likelihood and potential impact of events or situations, in order to ascertain and visualise risks" *(UK Resilience Lessons Digest 2023)*.

TERM	MEANING
Risk reduction	See risk mitigation. "Actions taken to lessen the probability or negative consequences, or both, associated with a risk" *(ISO 22300)*. "The implementation of controls or countermeasures to reduce the likelihood or impact of a risk to a level within the organization's risk tolerance" *(ISACA glossary)*.
Risk register, risk inventory, risk catalogue, risk list, risk log, risk DataBase, ...	Essentially a list, table or **D**ata**B**ase of identified risks, normally with additional details resulting from some form of risk analysis giving users the ability to sort or prioritise the list on criteria such as impact, likelihood, current status, risk type, assets affected, and risk owners. The scope of the register may include all risks to the organisation, all significant or key risks (howsoever determined and specified), or one or more subsets or categories of risk such as information risks, compliance risks, market and product risks, health and safety risks, financial risks, currency risks, and strategic risks. "Record of information about identified risks. Note: Compilation for all risks identified, analysed and evaluated in the risk assessment process, including information on the risk register includes information on likelihood, consequences, treatments and risk owners" *(ISO 22300)*. "A list of risk scenarios that have been identified, analyzed and prioritized" *(ISACA glossary)*.
Risk reporting	Provision of pertinent information concerning risk. "Form of communication intended to inform particular internal or external interested party by providing information regarding the current state of risk and its management" *(ISO 31073)*.
Risk response	See risk treatment. "Accepting, avoiding, mitigating, sharing, or transferring risk to organizational operations (*i.e.*, mission, functions, image, or reputation), organizational assets, individuals, other organizations, or the Nation" *(NIST SP 800-39)*. "Any combination of risk avoidance, risk acceptance, risk sharing or transfer, or risk mitigation that leads to a situation in which as much future residual risk (*i.e.*, current risk with the risk response defined and implemented) as possible (usually depending on budgets available) falls within risk appetite limits" *(ISACA glossary)*. "Accepting, avoiding, mitigating, sharing, or transferring risk to agency operations, agency assets, individuals, other organizations, or the Nation" *(OMB Circular A-130)*. "The decision to accept, avoid, reduce, or share a risk" *(**T**rust **S**ervices **C**riteria)*.
Risk response measure	"A specific action taken to respond to an identified risk" *(NIST SP 800-39)*.

TERM	MEANING
Risk retention	See risk acceptance. "Temporary acceptance of the potential benefit of gain, or burden of loss, from a particular risk. Notes: Retention can be restricted to a certain period of time; The level of risk retained can depend on risk criteria" *(ISO/IEC 27005)*. "Acceptance of the potential benefit of gain, or burden of loss, from a particular risk. Note: Risk retention includes the acceptance of residual risks. The level of risk retained can depend on risk criteria" *(ISO Guide 73)*.
Risk scenario	Hypothetical situation used for risk analysis, security awareness and training, planning and preparation purposes, in which one or more threats materialise, exploiting exposed vulnerabilities causing incidents. "Sequence or combination of events leading from the initial cause to the unwanted consequence" *(ISO/IEC 27005)*. "A tangible and assessable representation of risk. Note: One of the key information items needed to identify, analyze and respond to risk" *(ISACA glossary)*.
Risk scope	The scope of a risk. "The selection of items included in the risk activities, based on understanding the full risk universe and then down-selecting to the specific part of the enterprise to which the risk activities will be applied" *(ISACA glossary)*.
Risk sharing, risk transfer	Treating risk by passing a substantial proportion to a third party, such as an insurer, stakeholder, customer, business partner, auditor, standards body, regulator, or authority. To an extent, the third party accepts and indemnifies the directly impacted organisation against the consequences of incidents, in some cases accepting defined liabilities. "Form of risk treatment involving the agreed distribution of risk with other parties. Notes: Legal or regulatory requirements can limit, prohibit or mandate risk sharing. Risk sharing can be carried out through insurance or other forms of contract. The extent to which risk is distributed can depend on the reliability and clarity of the sharing arrangements. Risk transfer is a form of risk sharing" *(ISO/IEC 27005)*.
RISKS List, RISKS Digest, RISKS Forum	Since August 1985, the "ACM Committee on Computers and Public Policy – Forum on Risks to the Public in Computers and Related Systems," chaired by Peter G. Neumann, has produced a regular newsletter concerning risks, incidents, controls, security, privacy, safety, *etc.* involving computers.
Risk source	Origin or cause of an incident. "Element which alone or in combination has the potential to give rise to risk. Notes: A risk source can be one of these three types: human; environmental; technical. A human risk source type can be intentional or unintentional" *(ISO/IEC 27005)*. "Element which alone or in combination has the intrinsic potential to give rise to risk. Note: A risk source can be tangible or intangible" *(ISO Guide 73)*. See also threat agent.

TERM	MEANING
Risk target	"The level and type of risk the organization EXPECTS to address given the level and type of reward it pursues" *(OCEG GRC Glossary)*.
Risk taxonomy	Categorisation or grouping together of risks of similar types, natures, significance, scopes, *etc.* Can help ensure that all relevant risks are considered on a comparable basis, but can lead to a confusing picture (*e.g.* a serious risk to the financial system may be classified as business, financial, technological, Information Technology, data, system, cybersecurity, serious, or some other kind of risk). "A scheme for classifying sources and categories of risk that provides a common language for discussing and communicating risk to stakeholders" *(ISACA glossary)*.
Risk tolerance	Relates to the mathematical concept of a range defined by tolerance limits or bounds within which the values (of risk in this case) are deemed acceptable. A way to define criteria for treating risks. Often confused or conflated with risk appetite as in the amount of risk deemed tolerable by management. "The acceptable level of variation that management is willing to allow for any particular risk as the enterprise pursues its objectives [and] Risk that is within a tolerable or acceptable range, based on management's appetite" *(ISACA glossary)*. "Organization's or interested party's readiness to bear the residual risk in order to achieve its objectives. Note: Risk tolerance can be influenced by legal or regulatory requirements" *(ISO 31073)*. "The level and type of risk the organization is UNWILLING to exceed given the level and type of reward it pursues" *(OCEG GRC Glossary)*. "Acceptable variations in performance related to achieving objectives" *(IIA GIAS)*.
Risk transfer	See risk sharing. "The process of assigning risk to another enterprise, usually through the purchase of an insurance policy or by outsourcing the service" *(ISACA glossary)*.
Risk treatment	Method to deal with (*i.e.* mitigate, share, avoid, or accept) one or more identified risks. "Process to modify risk. Notes: Risk treatment can involve: avoiding the risk by deciding not to start or continue with the activity that gives rise to the risk; taking or increasing risk in order to pursue an opportunity; removing the risk source; changing the likelihood; changing the consequences; sharing the risk with another party or parties (including contracts and risk financing); and retaining the risk by informed decision; Information security risk treatment does not include 'taking or increasing risk in order to pursue an opportunity' but the organization can have this option for general risk management. Risk treatments that deal with negative consequences are sometimes referred to as 'risk mitigation,' 'risk elimination,' 'risk prevention' and 'risk reduction.' Risk treatment can create new risks or modify existing risks" *(ISO/IEC 27005)*. "Measures to reduce the likelihood of an emergency occurring from a given risk, and/or implement measures to mitigate the impacts of that emergency should arise" *(UK Resilience Lessons Digest 2023)*.

TERM	MEANING
Risk **T**reatment **P**lan **(RTP)**	Formally documented approach to address identified risks by resourcing, designing/selecting, implementing, and monitoring and maintaining suitable risk treatments within an ISO/IEC 27001 **I**nformation **S**ecurity **M**anagement **S**ystem. Can be an implementation project plan, security improvement strategy, or something more creative (the standard is not prescriptive). *Cf.* **R**eal-time **T**ransport **P**rotocol.
Risk universe, risk landscape	High-level broad perspective on *all* kinds of risks facing the organisation, that being the full scope of Enterprise Risk Management. "An enterprise's overall conception of risk, which encompasses the overall risk environment, defines the areas that risk management activities will address and provides a structure for information and technology (I&T)-related risk management" *(ISACA glossary).*
RL	*Abbrev:* **R**einforcement **L**earning.
RMF	*Abbrev:* **R**isk **M**anagement **F**ramework.
RNN	*Abbrev:* **R**ecurrent **N**eural **N**etwork.
Robot	Robotic electromechanical device, mechanism, or machine that senses its environment, taking decisions and acting to some extent autonomously (according to its programming) to perform various designated tasks. Derived from a Czech word for 'slavery.' "Automation system with actuators that performs intended tasks in the physical world, by means of sensing its environment and a software control system. Notes: A robot includes the control system and interface of a control system; The classification of a robot as industrial robot or service robot is done according to its intended application; In order to properly perform its tasks, a robot makes use of different kinds of sensors to confirm its current state and perceive the elements composing the environment in which it operates" *(ISO/IEC 22989).*
Robotics	Engineering discipline concerning the design, development, use, and control of robots. "Science and practice of designing, manufacturing and applying robots" *(ISO/IEC 22989).* "The design, development, and operation of autonomous or semiautonomous machines capable of performing tasks in the physical world" *(ISACA glossary).*
Robustness	Form of resilience characterised by the inherent strength of a system, network, service, process, lock, wall, barrier, organisation, team, person, *etc.,* rendering it invulnerable to incidents that would damage or cause weaker ones to fail or falter. Conceptually and practically different to the capability to failover, failsafe or recover, robust systems, *etc.* are less likely to fail and need to be restored to service: they simply carry on working reliably, albeit perhaps with reduced performance and/or functionality (fallback). "Ability of a system to

TERM	MEANING
	maintain its level of performance under any circumstances" *(ISO/IEC 22989)*. "Ability of a system to resist virtual or physical, internal or external attacks. Note: Particularly, the ability to resist attempted imitation, copy, intrusion or bypassing" *(ISO 22300)*. "The degree to which a software system or component can function correctly in the presence of invalid inputs or stressful environmental conditions" *(ISACA glossary)*. "Information Assurance entity to operate correctly and reliably across a wide range of operational conditions, and to fail gracefully outside of that operational range" *(CNSSI 4009)*.
ROCU	*Abbrev:* **R**egional **O**rganised **C**rime **U**nit.
Rogue	Someone or something at the boundaries of social acceptability in some way, pushing or exceeding the limits, often unauthorised and potentially or actually malicious (*e.g.* rogue devices or *things* that somehow manage to connect to a network). Potentially 'lovable,' to a limited extent. More likely a vagrant, scoundrel, and outcast.
Rogue address	Disinformation about the location of a resource, such as an **I**nternet **P**rotocol address pointing to a malicious domain, web page, or file, surreptitiously substituted for the legitimate address in a **D**omain **N**ame **S**ystem poisoning attack.
Rogue software	Free or cheap software that is advertised and appears to be legitimate, often security-related (*e.g.* antivirus programs, anti-spyware software, and password vaults), but is itself a Trojan, spyware, or other malware. See also **P**otentially **U**nwanted **P**rogram.
Rogue system	Unauthorised computer system or *thing* connected illicitly to the network, perhaps a **P**ersonally **O**wned **D**evice not approved for **B**ring **Y**our **O**wn **D**evice, or a system installed by a spy to monitor or intercept network traffic, perhaps to launch hacking attacks on authorised network systems.
Rogue wireless access point	Unauthorised Wi-Fi access point connected to a network, typically installed at work by well-meaning but naïve workers who fail to appreciate the additional information risks created by the wireless coverage, perhaps not even realising that wired routers and other devices may also have wireless capabilities. "An unauthorised Wireless Access Point operating outside of the control of an agency" *(NZISM)*.
ROI, RoI	*Abbrev:* **R**eturn **O**n **I**nvestment or **R**isk **O**f **I**ncarceration, depending on context.
Rôle, role	Main function or purpose of a worker or person interacting with a system or performing a process. Rôles and job descriptions generally change less often than the people who perform them, and hence require less maintenance than the individuals' names when used in procedures.

TERM	MEANING
Rôle-**B**ased **A**ccess **C**ontrol (RBAC)	Access control scheme whereby users are granted certain system, application, and/or data access rights according to the particular rôles they are required to perform for the organisation and the access policy for the information assets. Typically implemented through some combination of group and individual access rights, *e.g.* using ACLs. "Access control based on user roles (*i.e.*, a collection of access authorizations a user receives based on an explicit or implicit assumption of a given role). Role permissions may be inherited through a role hierarchy and typically reflect the permissions needed to perform defined functions within an organisation. A given role may apply to a single individual or to several individuals" *(CNSSI 4009)*. "Model employs pre-defined roles that carry a specific set of privileges associated with them and to which subjects are assigned" *(NZISM)*. "Assigns users to roles based on their organizational functions and determines authorization based on those rôles" *(SANS glossary)*. *Cf.* **R**ule-**B**ased **A**ccess **C**ontrol, **R**ealm-**B**ased Access **C**ontrol, and **A**ttribute-**B**ased **A**ccess **C**ontrol.
ROOT, root	a. Default userID for the fully privileged system administrator on UNIX systems, usually written in shouty CAPITALS. "Name of the administrator account in Unix systems" *(SANS glossary)*. b. Fundamental basis or lowest level of something, such as the folder structure on a disk, the chain of digital certificates in a **P**ublic **K**ey **I**nfrastructure, of trust, or of problem causes. *Cf.* route.
Root cause	Fundamental issues, reasons, or failures that could have and perhaps did lead to, or failed to prevent, or might yet cause, an incident. Failing to identify and deal with the root causes (plural!) is a common reason for recurring incidents, but even if they are identified, some root causes can be difficult to remedy, so tend to persist. "The underlying source of a defect or problem" *(ISACA glossary)*. "Core issue or underlying reason for the difference between the criteria and the condition of an activity under review" *(IIA GIAS)*.
Root cause analysis	Systematic and thorough determination and examination of root causes. "A process of diagnosis to establish the origins of events that can be used for learning from consequences, typically from errors and problems" *(ISACA glossary)*. "A principle-based, systems approach for the identification of underlying causes associated with a particular set of risks" *(NIST SP 800-39)*.
Root certificate	Self-signed digital certificate belonging to a **C**ertification **A**uthority, used to sign certificates issued by the CA.

TERM	MEANING
Root of **T**rust **(RoT)**	Secure computing relies on the trustworthiness of the **D**ata **P**rocessing and storage equipment, down to the level of the **I**ntegrated **C**ircuits and firmware. Designing truly secure systems involves attention to technical details such as the **P**ower-**O**n **S**elf-Test and boot sequence, **T**rusted **P**latform **M**odules, JTAG ports, anti-tampering, and other physical security controls.
Rooting	a. Process of gaining unauthorised ROOT (fully privileged) access to an **I**nformation **T**echnology system, normally by hacking it or installing a rootkit. b. Vulgar term for sexual intercourse. *Cf.* routing.
Rootkit	Hacker toolset typically containing malware such as Trojans used to take and retain full control of a compromised computer system. Often includes hacked variants of normal **O**perating **S**ystem or utility programs with backdoors and other covert functions to conceal the compromise and persist. May be surreptitiously installed at any stage of the **S**oftware or **S**ystem **D**evelopment **L**ife**C**ycle, including during manufacture (perhaps inserted by the authorities or spooks for national security reasons). Usually hidden deep in the system kernel, device drivers, firmware, or microcode, and may actively evade detection (*e.g.* by manipulating the system calls and functions used for folder/file listings), hence very hard to identify and eradicate. "A software suite designed to aid an intruder in gaining unauthorized administrative access to a computer system" *(ISACA glossary)*. "A collection of tools (programs) that a hacker uses to mask intrusion and obtain administrator-level access to a computer or computer network" *(SANS glossary)*. See also bootkit.
ROP	*Abbrev:* **R**eturn-**O**riented **P**rogramming.
ROSI	*Abbrev:* **R**eturn **O**n **S**ecurity **I**nvestment.
RoT	*Abbrev:* **R**oot **o**f **T**rust. *Cf.* rot (gradual degradation).
ROT13	Trivial, extremely weak substitution function that simply 'rotates' each character in the plaintext 13 positions through the letters of the normal English alphabet arranged in a circle. Since there are 26 letters in the alphabet, ROT13 has the equally trivial advantage of being reversible simply by repeating the same process. Barely adequate for naughty kids to conceal rude words from their elders.

TERM	MEANING
Round	a. Cycle. Most cryptographic algorithms repeat steps such as transposition and substitution several times in a specific sequence: each run through the sequence is called a round. b. Approximation process to reduce the precision of a number, typically for convenience. According to the mathematical function chosen for the purpose, numbers may be rounded up (increased to the next higher round or whole number), rounded down (reduced to the next lower round or whole number), or rounded off (moved up or down to the nearest round or whole number, possibly with a rule to handle a middle value consistently).
Route	See communication path.
Router, routing	Network device that forwards traffic towards its destination via appropriate paths through a network. Using protocols such as **B**order **G**ateway **P**rotocol, a router builds, shares, and maintains its internal routing tables with pertinent details of paths (*e.g.* the number of hops through intermediate routers, and transit time/delay) and their status (up and stable, unstable or down). "Functional unit that establishes a path through one or more computer networks. Note: In computer networks conforming to the OSI model, a router operates at the network layer" *(ISO/IEC 2382)*. "Network device that is used to establish and control the flow of data between different networks by selecting paths or routes based upon routing protocol mechanisms and algorithms. Notes: The networks can themselves be based on different protocols. The routing information is kept in a routing table" *(ISO/IEC 27033-1)*. "A networking device that can send (route) data packets from one local area network (LAN) or wide area network (WAN) to another, based on addressing at the network layer (Layer 3) in the open systems interconnection (OSI) model. Notes: Networks connected by routers can use different or similar networking protocols. Routers usually are capable of filtering packets based on parameters such as source addresses, destination addresses, protocols and network applications (ports)" *(ISACA glossary)*.
Rowhammer	Exploit that flips bits in memory directly using electrical properties of high-density memory chips: if particular areas (rows) of RAM are repeatedly accessed (hammered) by malware, physically adjacent memory bits may be flipped due to leakage currents in the silicon, even if those bits are in supposedly protected memory that cannot be accessed through applications or by conventional malware. The flipped bits, in turn, may affect system security, *e.g.* granting additional privileges, permissions, or rights.

TERM	MEANING
Royalty	Fee payable by licensees to licensors in return for the opportunity to use or exploit the licensors' **I**ntellectual **P**roperty according to the terms of copyright, trademarks, patents or other rights, restrictions, licences, agreements, and contracts.
RPA	*Abbrev:* **R**obotic **P**rocess **A**utomation.
RPO	*Abbrev:* **R**ecovery **P**oint **O**bjective.
RSA	Asymmetric cryptographic algorithm described in 1977 by Ron **R**ivest, Adi **S**hamir, and Leonard **A**dleman. Provided sufficiently long keys are used (at least 1024 bits, preferably 2048 or 4096) and there are no design, implementation, process, or protocol flaws, RSA-based systems are currently considered sufficiently secure for general use, although the **N**ational **S**ecurity **A**gency's involvement may be of concern in high-security situations. "A public key cryptosystem developed by R. Rivest, A. Shamir and L. Adleman used for both encryption and digital signatures. Notes: The RSA has two different keys, the public encryption key and the secret decryption key. The strength of the RSA depends on the difficulty of the prime number factorization. For applications with high-level security, the number of the decryption key bits should be greater than 512" *(ISACA glossary)*. See also FREAK.
RTCP	*Abbrev:* **R**eal-time **T**ransport **C**ontrol **P**rotocol.
RTO	*Abbrev:* **R**ecovery **T**ime **O**bjective.
RTP	*Abbrev:* **R**isk **T**reatment **P**lan or **R**ealtime **T**ransport **P**rotocol, depending on context.
RTU	*Abbrev:* **R**emote Terminal **U**nit.
Rubber hose cryptanalysis	Alludes to the use of coercion, violence, or torture to pressure someone into disclosing cryptographic keys. A very physical form of brute force attack.
Rule	Constraint on acceptable, permitted, authorised activity in a specific situation or context, whether formally defined and documented or not. "Accepted principle or instruction that states the organization's expectations on what is required to be done, what is allowed or not allowed. Note: Rules can be formally expressed in topic-specific policies and in other types of documents" *(ISO/IEC 27002)*.

TERM	MEANING
Rule-**B**ased **A**ccess **C**ontrol **(RBAC)**	Access control scheme implemented by the reference monitor applying access control rules reflecting the combination of access permission for the subjects attempting access, and access constraints or restrictions associated with the objects being accessed. *Cf.* **R**ôle-**B**ased **A**ccess **C**ontrol, **A**ttribute-**B**ased **A**ccess **C**ontrol, and **R**ealm-**B**ased **A**ccess **C**ontrol.
Ruleset	Coherent suite of rules, *e.g.* security rules on a firewall or server defining permissible and forbidden network protocols/ports, access rights, event logging, *etc.* "A table of instructions used by a controlled interface to determine what data is allowable and how the data is handled between interconnected systems" *(CNSSI 4009).*
Rule**S**et-**B**ased **A**ccess **C**ontrol **(RSBAC)**	Open-source Linux security framework offers strong **R**ôle-**B**ased **A**ccess **C**ontrol. "Targets actions based on rules for entities operating on objects" *(SANS glossary).*
Run-to-run, run-to-run total	Type of balancing control used to ensure integrity of information saved between executions of a particular program, *e.g.* the sequential number of the last bank transaction processed on the previous run of a batch process is recorded and checked when the next run starts, ensuring that no transactions have been missed or inserted between runs. "Aggregate numbers that provide evidence that a program processed all input data and that it processed the data correctly" *(ISACA glossary).* See also batch control.
Runtime **A**pplication **S**elf-**P**rotection **(RASP)**	Security-related instrumentation of application programs, such that they monitor themselves for exceptions or conditions indicating security issues, logging alerts, or triggering alarms and perhaps responding proactively if hacked, *etc.* See also **S**tatic **A**pplication **S**ecurity **T**esting, **I**nteractive **A**pplication **S**ecurity **T**esting.
Rust	Programming language with valuable integrity features, such as being 'memory-safe' (the compiler ensures that executables enforce strict controls over access to memory locations).
RWCS	*Abbrev:* **R**easonable **W**orst-**C**ase **S**cenario.
Ryuk	Hacker/malware/cybercriminal gang active in 2022. Distributed ransomware through Emotet botnets, targeting medium to large organisations such as municipalities, with *substantial* ransom demands ($5.3m in the case of the City of New Bedford).

S

TERM	MEANING
SaaS	*Abbrev:* **S**oftware-**a**s-**a**-**S**ervice.
Sabotage	Deliberate, wilful, and unauthorised damage, devaluation or destruction of assets such as information, physical facilities, machinery/equipment, business processes, commercial prospects, reputation, and brand. See also cybertage, Luddite, arson.
Saboteur	Person who commits sabotage. See also cyberteur.
SAE	*Abbrev:* **S**imultaneous **A**uthentication of **E**quals.
Safe	a. *[Noun]* Physically and/or logically secure space designed to reduce the risk of unauthorised access, removal or damage to stored assets, *e.g.* firesafe, key locker, vault, password vault, **T**rusted **Pl**atform **M**odule, and **H**ardware **S**ecurity **M**odule. b. *[Adjective]* See safety.
Safeguard	See control. "A practice, procedure or mechanism that reduces risk" *(ISACA glossary).*
Safe Harbor	US privacy laws are so different from the information protection laws in Europe and elsewhere that many non-US organisations may be legally forbidden from sending personal information to the US without additional information security. The Safe Harbor scheme was introduced as a way for US organisations to assert or self-certify their compliance voluntarily. Widely discredited and distrusted due to poor design, limited compliance, and especially the obvious conflicts of interest, the scheme finally collapsed in 2015 when ruled invalid by the European Court of Justice. Replaced by Privacy Shield the following year.
Safety	Protected against dangers (especially physical hazards or threats) giving little possibility of harm, injury, or death. "Freedom from risk which is not tolerable" (*ISO/IEC Guide 51*). "A condition of protection from harm. The two key domains of safety are workplace environment and functional safety" *(ISACA glossary).* "The need to ensure that the people involved with the company, including employees, customers, and visitors, are protected from harm" *(SANS glossary).* See also health and safety, security.
Safety-critical, safety critical	See vital. Class of information asset, system, process, or control that is essential to the safety of individuals, particularly in respect of its integrity. An information security incident could therefore have grave impacts, *e.g.* injury or death; hence, control systems should be designed to fail-safe. *Cf.* tier 1, 2, or 3, business-critical.
Safety integrity level	System/process/assurance integrity metric relating to safety.

TERM	MEANING
Safety system	System of one or more devices, processes, controls, *etc.* intended to protect safety. "System and component that are required to ensure safety" *(ISO/IEC 27019)*.
Salami fraud, salami technique	Fraud in which the fraudster steals small amounts of money through lots of separate transactions (like thin slices of salami), each individual theft being so insignificant as to escape the victim's notice or concern while accumulating a tidy sum for the fraudster. If a discrepancy even comes to their attention, a victim will typically assume the deficit or debit is simply a consequence of legitimate rounding or measuring errors, whereas it may be deliberate, unethical, illegitimate, and perhaps illegal. "A method of computer fraud involving a computer code that instructs the computer to slice off small amounts of money from authorized transactions and reroute these amounts to the perpetrator's account" *(ISACA glossary)*.
Sality	Species of malware in the wild since 2010, forming large botnets in 2015.
Salt, salting	Technique for including a unique string or sequence specific to the system when hashing passwords, *etc.*, such that the hash values for identical passwords, *etc.* differ across systems. Unless the salt is also compromised along with the hash file, salting frustrates attacks using rainbow tables. "Random data string added to the start or the end of a hash to strengthen its resistance to attack. Typically used in the generation of a password hash or checksums" *(NZISM)*.
Salt Typhoon	Allegedly a Chinese state-sponsored (spooky) hacker group responsible for several serious cyber incidents since 2019. Compromised large mature organisations including telecommunications carriers and federal networks in the US, plus smartphones used by politicians and government officials. One of a number of similarly sophisticated and subversive groups (*e.g.* Volt Typhoon and Flax Typhoon) threatening critical national infrastructure.
SAM	*Abbrev:* **S**ecurity **A**ccounts **M**anager.
Samas, SamSam	Species of ransomware in the wild in 2019.
SAML	*Abbrev:* **S**ecurity **A**ssertion **M**arkup **L**anguage.
Sample, sampling	a. Subset of individual subjects or data points selected for analysis, in the belief that they are sufficiently representative or characteristic of the entire population or dataset. "The process of taking samples of something for the purpose of analysis" *(NIST SP 800-55v1)*. b. "Atomic data element processed in quantities by a machine learning algorithm or an AI system" (*ISO/IEC 22989*).

TERM	MEANING
Sampling risk	Uncertainty relating to the choice of sampling technique/method and its execution, *e.g.* whether the sampling process and sample size adequately and accurately reflect the population or might in some way be biased or skewed. "The probability that an IT auditor has reached an incorrect conclusion because an audit sample, rather than the entire population, was tested. Note: While sampling risk can be reduced to an acceptably low level by using an appropriate sample size and selection method, it can never be eliminated" *(ISACA glossary)*.
SAN	*Abbrev:* **S**torage **A**rea **N**etwork.
Sandbox, jail, walled garden	System partition and other security controls intended to prevent applications from accessing unauthorised resources, particularly privileged **O**perating **S**ystem function calls and address spaces beyond the restricted range. Used for security testing, malware detection and analysis, *etc*. Typically implemented as a virtual machine emulating a specific OS. Analogous to keeping the kids occupied in a play-pen: fine so long as they don't escape and go nuts with the crayons. "Using an isolated environment for testing purposes" *(ISACA glossary)*. See also jailbreak.
Sanitisation	Process or act of sanitising. "Process or method to sanitize" *(ISO/IEC 27040)*. "Actions taken to render data written on media unrecoverable by ordinary and — for some forms of sanitization — extraordinary means. A process to remove information from media such that data recovery is not possible, including the removal of all classified labels, markings, and activity logs" *(NIST SP 800-171)*.
Sanitise	Securely overwrite, delete, or destroy sensitive data such as personal information, passwords, and encryption keys from storage media such that the information cannot later be recovered or restored, even by thorough forensic means. Theoretically unnecessary with strongly encrypted data but in practice safer than relying indefinitely on the strength of the encryption and confidentiality of the key. "Removing sensitive information from a document to reduce its sensitivity" *(ISO/IEC 2382)*. "Process to remove information from media such that data recovery is not possible at a given level of effort. Note: Clear, purge, and destruct are actions that can be taken to sanitize storage media" *(ISO/IEC 27040 and ISO/IEC 27050-1)*. "The process of making potentially harmful data safe through the use of data removal, replacement, encoding or escaping of the characters" *(SCP QRG)*. See also zero-fill, secure destruction, shredding, redaction.

TERM	MEANING
Sanity test	a. See smoke test. b. Checks to determine whether a person or **A**rtificial **I**ntelligence system is losing, or has lost, his/her/its marbles, and has a screw loose. Is there any hope of a return to rationality and sensible decisions, or are there bats in the belfry? One sandwich short of a picnic maybe, away with the fairies, more nuts than an autumnal squirrel, lost the plot or plain bonkers? Are the lights on but no one is home? Crazy as a box of frogs? These are all euphemisms for someone who inhabits a parallel reality, believes alternative facts in a post-truth world, a knucklehead who keeps on doing the same things while expecting different results.
SANS Glossary of Cyber Security Terms	Glossary by SANS succinctly defines ~500 cybersecurity, **I**nformation **T**echnology, and networking terms. More info: https://www.sans.org/security-resources/glossary-of-terms/
SANS Institute	US-centric global training provider for cybersecurity professionals, offering an extensive range of well-regarded courses and GIAC qualifications, plus white papers, summits, email newsletters, and topical alerts. Founded by Alan Paller in 1989. More info: https://www.sans.org/
SANS Internet **S**torm **C**enter **(SANS ISC)**	Part of the SANS Technology Institute responsible for collating cybersecurity information streaming from DShield, a globally distributed network of intrusion detection sensors and firewall logs, analysing it and disseminating Internet threat intelligence. More info: https://isc.sans.edu/
SANS Technology Institute	SANS college for cybersecurity undergraduates and graduates. More info: https://www.sans.edu/
SAR	Abbrev: **S**ecurity **A**ssurance **R**equirement or **S**ubject **A**ccess **R**equest (see **D**ata **S**ubject **A**ccess **R**equest), depending on context.
SAS 70	*Abbrev:* **S**tatement on **A**uditing **S**tandards № **70**.
SASE	*Abbrev:* **S**ecure **A**ccess **S**ervice **E**dge.
SAST	*Abbrev:* **S**tatic **A**pplication **S**ecurity **T**esting.
SBC	*Abbrev:* **S**ession **B**order **C**ontroller.
SBoM, SBOM	*Abbrev:* **S**oftware **B**ill **of** **M**aterials.
SBU	*Abbrev:* **S**ensitive **B**ut **U**nclassified.

TERM	MEANING
SCA	*Abbrev:* **S**oftware **C**omposition **A**nalysis.
SCADA	*Abbrev:* **S**upervisory **C**ontrol **A**nd **D**ata **Ac**quisition.
Scalability, scaling, elasticity	Highly automated capability to alter the capacity and performance of a system dynamically in response to, or in expectation of, changes in demand, loading, or priorities, typically by changing the number of allocated/assigned resources (*e.g.* cloud servers, virtual clusters, **C**entral **P**rocessing **U**nits, or network paths) to maintain a reasonably consistent performance.
Scale	Reference points for the absolute or relative measurement of parameters such as quantity, size, volume, risk, severity, and disaster. "Ordered set of values, continuous or discrete, or a set of categories to which the attribute is mapped. Note: the type of scale depends on the nature of the relationship between values on the scale. Four types of scale are commonly defined: nominal – the measurement values are categorical; ordinal – the measurement values are rankings; interval – the measurement values have equal distances corresponding to equal quantities of the attribute; ratio – the measurement values have equal distances corresponding to equal quantities of the attribute, where the value of zero corresponds to none of the attribute. These are just examples of the types of scale" *(ISO/IEC/IEEE 15939)*.
Scam	Relatively basic/simple form of fraud committed by a scammer that normally (but not always) causes minor impacts on each individual victim but may lead on to more substantial incidents. Can be significant in aggregate since most scams are 'a numbers game.' See also scareware.
Scammer	Low-life fraudster who commits a scam. Whereas career criminals and fraudsters are sometimes portrayed as cheeky chappies and lovable rogues, scammers are the lowest-of-the-low, marginalised and despised by everybody *including* their peers (since they take 'untrustworthy' to new depths) and even, on occasions, themselves. Entirely selfish and mean-spirited, they have absolutely no compunction about preying on the vulnerable, young, elderly, sick, charitable, naïve, and intellectually challenged, let alone fine upstanding members of society. They would *literally* sell their own grandmothers if only they could find a buyer dumb enough to fall for their spiel and trust that they would ever deliver on a deal. When caught (for they are not, as a breed, the most significant bits in a byte), they invariably plead poverty and desperation as if that somehow explains and excuses their bare-faced total disregard for the accepted social norms and reasonable expectation of any civilised society. Incarceration and lethal injections are too humane for them. "Off with their goolies" we say!

TERM	MEANING
SCAP	*Abbrev:* **S**ecurity **C**ontent **A**utomation **P**rotocol.
Scapy	Low-level network management/penetration testing/hacking tool for capturing, manipulating, and transmitting packets.
Scareware	Malware intended to scare and perhaps extort the user. One example claims that the system has been flagged by the **F**ederal **B**ureau of **I**nvestigation due to illegal content, so the user must pay a fine to avoid being prosecuted (they seem a bit confused about the process!). Another is simply an online advertisement for security software of dubious value, emulating a pop-up warning message. More malicious forms include bluff ransomware. See also ransomware, adware, crimeware, spouseware, stalkerware, spyware.
Scattered Spider, Scatter Swine, UNC3944, Octo Tempest, Roasted 0ktopus, Storm-0875, Starfraud, Muddled Libra	Hacker/social engineering group active since 2022, believed to have targeted multiple industry sectors (including telecommunications service providers to facilitate SIM-swap attacks) and used DragonForce ransomware in 2025. Native English speakers, possibly UK/US-based.
Scavenge	Systematically trawl through data storage media for potentially valuable information, perhaps including remnants and metadata. "Search, without authorization, through residual data to acquire sensitive information" *(ISO/IEC 2382)*. "Searching through object residue to acquire data" *(CNSSI 4009)*. "Searching through data residue in a system to gain unauthorized knowledge of sensitive data" *(SANS glossary)*. See also dumpster-diving.
SCCM	*Abbrev:* **S**upply **C**hain **C**ontinuity **M**anagement.
Scenario	Hypothetical situation. "Pre-planned storyline that drives an exercise, as well as the stimuli used to achieve exercise project performance objectives" *(ISO 22300)*.
Scheduled maintenance	See preventive maintenance. "Preventive maintenance carried out in accordance with an established time schedule. Note: The time schedule is set according to the elapsed time, the operating time, or the number of uses" *(ISO/IEC 2382)*.
SCF	*Abbrev:* **S**ecure **C**ontrols **F**ramework.
SCF Architect	SCF's advanced qualification for professionals with the knowledge and skills to design cybersecurity and data protection programs based on the Secure Controls Framework. More info: https://securecontrolsframework.com/content/syllabus/scf-architect.pdf

TERM	MEANING
SCF Assessor	SCF's qualification for professionals capable of assessing conformity with the SCF Conformity Assessment Program. More info: https://securecontrolsframework.com/content/syllabus/scf-assessor.pdf
SCF Conformity **A**ssessment **P**rogram **(SCF CAP)**	SCF scheme to assess and certify organisations' conformity with applicable statutory, regulatory, and contractual obligations mandating cybersecurity and privacy controls. More info: https://securecontrolsframework.com/content/cap/scf-cap-bok.pdf
SCF Practitioner	SCF's entry-level qualification for professionals with the basic knowledge and skills to implement and maintain cybersecurity and data protection controls. More info: https://securecontrolsframework.com/content/syllabus/scf-practitioner.pdf
SCI	*Abbrev:* **S**ensitive **C**ompartmented **I**nformation.
SCIF	*Abbrev:* **S**ensitive **C**ompartmented **I**nformation **F**acility.
Scope	Relevant and generally defined area of concern, involvement, and application. "The boundaries, limitations, and extent where the GRC Capability Model is applied. The scope is often expressed in terms of organizational unit, geographic area, or functional department" *(OCEG GRC Glossary)*.
Scope of exercise	"Magnitude, resources and extent that reflects the needs and objectives" *(ISO 22300)*.
Scorched earth	Term with military origins referring to the methodical destruction of assets that might benefit adversaries (*e.g.* using flamethrowers and explosives) when retreating from hostile territory. As happened in the Sony hack, hackers, fraudsters, *etc.* sometimes attempt to cover their tracks by destroying any remaining digital evidence of their activities (such as hacking tools, log files, and audit trails), most likely causing collateral damage through destruction or corruption of business data and systems causing **D**enial-**o**f-**S**ervice, a disruptive information security incident.
SCP QRG	*Abbrev:* OWASP **S**ecurity **C**oding **P**ractices **Q**uick **R**eference **G**uide.
Screen burn	See image persistence.
Screened subnet	See **D**e-**M**ilitarised **Z**one.
Screwdriving	Hacking teledildonics.

TERM	MEANING
Script, scripting	a. Software programming language such as Bash, JavaScript, PHP, Perl, Ruby, Python, **D**IGITAL **C**ommand **L**anguage, PowerShell, and **V**isual **B**asic for **A**pplications. Instructions (lines of code) are generally interpreted individually when the application runs, rather than being compiled. Useful for automating routine system administration tasks. See also macro. b. Playbook, *e.g.* instructions for installing, configuring, and administering a system, performing a certain type of test, or committing or responding to a social engineering or other type of attack. "Story of the exercise as it develops, which allows directing staff to understand how events should develop during exercise play as the various elements of the master events list are introduced. Note: The script is often written as a narrative of simulated events" *(ISO 22300)*.
Script kiddie, skid	Pejorative term for a relatively unsophisticated, unskilled, or novice hacker or wannabe who simply uses scripts, tools, or malware created by more highly skilled, capable, and competent hackers, without necessarily understanding them fully.
SCRM	*Abbrev:* **S**upply **C**hain **R**isk **M**anagement.
SCuBA	*Abbrev:* **S**ecure **Cl**oud **B**usiness **A**pplications.
SD-WAN (Software-Defined Wide Area Network)	Private **W**ide **A**rea **N**etwork service that tunnels through various available connections such as fibre and 4G/5G cellular. See also **S**ecure **A**ccess **S**ervice **E**dge.
SDDC	Abbrev: **S**oftware-**D**efined **D**ata **C**entre.
SDLC	*Abbrev:* **S**oftware **D**evelopment **L**ife**C**ycle.
SDN	Abbrev: **S**oftware-**D**efined **N**etwork.
Search	Forensic process to find or extract useful, relevant information from forensic evidence. "Use of various methods for identifying and finding Electronically Stored Information that meets criteria for potential relevance, privilege, or other attributes that may be of interest. Notes: The actual process of searching can take many forms (*e.g.,* keyword, fuzzy, Boolean, phonic, synonym, *etc.* searches). The content considered a match for a particular search may not be an exact match to the criteria" *(ISO/IEC 27050-1)*.

TERM	MEANING
Search **E**ngine **O**ptimisation **(SEO) scam**	Fraud claiming to promote victims' organisations through online directories and search engines using methods that are largely ineffective or short-lived in practice. Typically involves social engineering techniques such as misrepresentation, pretexting, and coercion.
Secondary stakeholder	"Individuals or organizations that may be affected by events that occur to Assets outside of their control. For example, consumers are Secondary Stakeholders in a scenario where their personal private information may be inappropriately disclosed or stolen" *(O-RT)*.
Seconded foreign national	"A representative of a foreign government on exchange or long-term posting to an agency" *(NZISM)*.
Second line [of defence or accountability]	In the three lines model, the second line provides expert assistance on risk management to the first line, and in turn is overseen and audited by the third line. "Individuals and teams that establish performance, risk, and compliance programs for the First Line. The Second Line provides oversight through frameworks, standards, policies, tools, and techniques to support performance, risk, and compliance management. The Second Line often manages its own portfolio of objectives and associated performance, risk, and compliance. The Second Line may provide limited assurance over First Line activities" *(OCEG GRC Glossary)*.
Secret, secrecy	Extraordinarily confidential, extremely sensitive, and/or business-critical information that *must* therefore be strongly protected against unauthorised or inappropriate access. Examples include an organisation's strategies, plans, Board minutes, system security information (*e.g.* passwords, keys, firewall rules), extremely valuable trade secrets, and other **I**ntellectual **P**roperty. "Data and/or knowledge that are protected against disclosure to unauthorised entities" *(ISO 22300)*.
SECRET	Commonplace classification label (often CAPITALISED for emphasis) for highly confidential information that must remain secret. Applies to a significant amount of governmental and military/defence information. While the intention is reasonably self-evident, the label, definition, and associated controls are organisation- and context-specific. "Information, the unauthorized disclosure of which reasonably could be expected to cause serious damage to the national security that the original classification authority is able to identify or describe" *(Executive Order 13526)*. *Cf.* CONFIDENTIAL and TOP SECRET.
SECRET area	"An area that has been authorised to process, store or communicate SECRET data. Such areas are not necessarily tied to a specific level of security zone" *(AusISM)*.

TERM	MEANING
Secret code	Basic type of covert communications code explicitly intended to be understood easily by the intended recipient/s (*e.g.* can often be decoded manually without the need for computer technology) but unintelligible (not so readily decoded) if intercepted by third parties. May be physically concealed (*e.g.* written in 'secret ink,' tattooed under the hairline of a messenger), use simple substitution (*e.g.* ROT13, code book), or rely on obscurity (*e.g.* slang, Navajo code-talkers, passwords). Generally weak and vulnerable to cryptanalysis, *e.g.* "Attack at dawn!" might be represented or signalled by the seemingly innocuous mention of, say, "native daffodils" at some point in an otherwise legitimate news broadcast, web page, press release, blog posting, tweet, or private advertisement in the personal columns of a national newspaper. *Cf.* encode, encryption, steganography, war chalking.
Secret **I**ntelligence **S**ervice **(SIS), MI6** (**M**ilitary **I**ntelligence branch **6)**	UK's foreign intelligence agency. Originally the spooky sixth branch of the Directorate for Military Intelligence, part of the War Office in the first World War that was not officially acknowledged by the British government until the 1980's. See also MI5. *Cf.* US **S**pecial **I**ntelligence **S**ervice. More info: https://www.sis.gov.uk/
Secret key	Key used for both encryption and decryption in symmetric cryptography; hence, keeping it confidential Is crucial to prevent unauthorised access to the plaintext, while its integrity and availability are crucial for authorised purposes. "Key that is intended for use by a limited number of correspondents for encryption and decryption" *(ISO/IEC 2382)*. *Cf.* private key.
Secure	See security. "State of being free from danger or threat where procedures are followed or after taking appropriate measures" *(ISO 22300)*.
Secure **A**ccess **S**ervice **E**dge **(SASE)**	Commercial bundle of secure networking capabilities such as SD-WAN, SWG/NGFW, **C**loud **A**ccess **S**ecurity **B**roker, and **Z**ero **T**rust **N**etwork **A**ccess.
Secure area	Zone with strong physical security arrangements. "An area that has been certified to physical security requirements as either a Secure Area; a Partially Secure Area; or an Intruder Resistant Area to allow for the processing of classified information" *(NZISM)*.
Secure boot	**U**nified **E**xtensible **F**irmware **I**nterface anti-malware feature uses a **T**rusted **P**latform **M**odule (ideally) to authenticate the bootloader before allowing it to execute.

TERM	MEANING
Secure-by-default	Security engineering principle or objective that a system should have a specified level of security when initially installed or if reset to factory defaults. "A software development principle whereby products and services are configured for maximum security by default" *(AusISM)*. See also failsafe. *Cf.* secure-by-design.
Secure-by-design	Security engineering principle or objective to design a system in such a way as to prevent it falling below a specified minimal/baseline level of security under *all* foreseeable circumstances. "A software development principle whereby security is designed into every stage of a product or service's development" *(AusISM)*. "Software, hardware and systems that have been designed from the ground up to be secure" *(UK National Cyber Security Strategy 2022)*. See also failsafe. *Cf.* secure-by-default.
Secure **C**loud **B**usiness Applications **(SCuBA)**	US **C**ybersecurity and **I**nfrastructure **S**ecurity **A**gency project offering guidance on cloud security, including a **T**echnical **R**eference **A**rchitecture and **e**xtensible **V**isibility **R**eference **F**ramework. More info: https://www.cisa.gov/resources-tools/services/secure-cloud-business-applications-scuba-project
Secure **C**ontrols **F**ramework **(SCF)**	Freely available comprehensive cross-mapping (a large spreadsheet) of more than a thousand controls recommended or required by about 180 security and privacy frameworks published by ISO/IEC, CIS, COSO, CSA, NIST, various governments, and more. See also **C**ommon **C**ontrols **H**ub. More info: https://securecontrolsframework.com/
Secured space	"An area certified to the physical security requirements for a Security Zone Two to Security Zone Five area, as defined in the Attorney-General's Department's Protective Security Policy Framework, Entity facilities policy, to allow for the processing or storage of sensitive or classified data" *(AusISM)*.
Secure destruction, secure erasure	Permanent, irreversible, and complete destruction of information (*e.g.* by sanitisation, degaussing, and/or physical destruction of the storage media by shredding and burning, or by strongly encrypting data and destroying the key) such that it cannot subsequently be retrieved, recovered, or recreated from remnants, even using forensic analysis. Extends basic erasure, increasing assurance and information security. See also zero-fill.
Secure **E**lectronic **T**ransaction **(SET)**	Datacommunications security protocol designed by VISA to protect online transactions involving credit cards. Superseded by 3-D Secure. "A standard that ensures credit card and associated payment order information travel safely and securely between the various involved parties on the Internet" *(ISACA glossary)*. "A protocol developed for credit card transactions in which all parties (customers, merchant, and bank) are authenticated using digital signatures, encryption protects the message and provides integrity, and provides end-to-end security for credit card transactions online" *(SANS glossary)*.

TERM	MEANING
Secure **E**ncrypted **V**irtualisation **(SEV)**	AMD's implementation of a **T**rusted **E**xecution **E**nvironment – a chip-level hardware cryptosystem designed to prevent data leakage between virtual machines and the hypervisor. Can encrypt the **C**entral **P**rocessing **U**nit registers when a virtual machine is swapped out for another, and protect the integrity of a virtual machine's RAM.
Secure **M**ultipurpose **I**nternet **M**ail **E**xtension **(S/MIME)**	Public key cryptosystem used to encrypt and/or to digitally sign and authenticate emails. In contrast to PGP's web of trust approach, S/MIME is a conventional **P**ublic **K**ey **I**nfrastructure with X.509 digital certificates formally issued and controlled by trustworthy **C**ertification **A**uthorities. Certificates may be revoked and listed on a **C**ertificate **R**evocation **L**ist. "A protocol which allows the encryption and signing of email messages" *(AusISM)*. "Cryptographic security services for electronic messaging applications: authentication, message integrity and nonrepudiation of origin (using digital signatures); and privacy and data security (using encryption) to provide a consistent way to send and receive MIME data (RFC 2311)" *(ISACA glossary)*.
Secure multi-tenancy	"Type of multi-tenancy that employs security controls to explicitly guard against data breaches and provides validation of these controls for proper governance. Notes: Secure multi-tenancy exists when the risk profile of an individual tenant is no greater than it would be in a dedicated, single-tenant environment. In very secure environments even the identity of the tenants is kept secret" *(ISO/IEC 27040)*.
Secure **R**eal-time **T**ransport **P**rotocol **(SRTP)**	Security extension to **R**eal-time **T**ransport **P**rotocol providing data encryption, authentication, and replay prevention for **V**oice **O**ver **I**nternet **P**rotocol calls.
Secure **S**hell **(SSH)**	Cryptosystem involving a cryptographic network protocol commonly used for remote access to privileged accounts on UNIX-based systems for systems administration purposes. SSH1 has known flaws and is therefore deprecated in favour of SSH2. "Network protocol that uses cryptography to secure communication, remote command line login and remote command execution between two networked computers" *(ISACA glossary)*. "A network protocol that can be used to securely log into a remote workstation, executing commands on a remote workstation and securely transfer file(s)" *(NZISM)*. "A network protocol that can be used to securely log into, execute commands on, and transfer files between remote workstations and servers" *(AusISM)*. "A program to log into another computer over a network, to execute commands in a remote machine, and to move files from one machine to another" *(SANS glossary)*.

TERM	MEANING
Secure **S**ockets **L**ayer **(SSL)**	Protocol used to protect HTTPS web traffic between web servers and web browsers (clients). Uses RC-4. Vulnerable to cryptographic attacks, hence deprecated in favour of **T**ransport **L**ayer **S**ecurity. "A protocol used to transmit private documents through the Internet. Note: The SSL protocol uses a private key to encrypt the data to be transferred through the SSL connection" *(ISACA glossary)*. "A protocol developed by Netscape for transmitting private documents via the Internet. SSL works by using a public key to encrypt data that's transferred over the SSL connection" *(SANS glossary)*.
Secure **S**oftware **D**evelopment **F**ramework **(SSDF)**	NIST's secure software development practices supporting SP 800-218 with guidance from the **B**usiness **S**oftware **A**lliance, **O**pen **W**orldwide **A**pplication **S**ecurity **P**roject, **S**oftware **A**ssurance **F**ramework for **E**xcellence in **Code**, and others.
Secure **T**elephone **I**dentity **R**evisited **(STIR)**	Protocol use by telecommunications carriers to authenticate the caller ID on a call, preventing caller ID spoofing. See also **S**ignature-based **H**andling of **A**sserted information using to**KEN**s.
Secure **T**erminal **E**quipment **(STE)**	Device such as a telephone designed to communicate government/military classified information, incorporating security features such as a verifiable unique and un-spoofable identifier, RFI shielding, tamper resistance, and data encryption.
Secure **W**eb **G**ateway **(SWG)**	Protocol-aware firewall controlling web traffic by applying the organisation's access rules at the application layer (top of the OSI stack). See also **N**ext-**G**eneration **F**ire**W**all.
Security, secure	State in which assets are adequately protected to prevent, resist, or survive incidents. A relative measure since perfect or absolute security is literally unattainable in any real world situation: even assets protected by strong controls remain vulnerable to extreme, novel, or currently unappreciated/unrecognised threats that happen to negate, overwhelm, bypass, or undermine the controls, and to control failures. "State of relative freedom from threat or harm caused by deliberate, unwanted, hostile or malicious acts" *(ISO 19650-5)*. "Resistance to intentional, unauthorized act(s) designed to cause harm or damage to a system" *(ISO/IEC 23643)*. "A condition that results from the establishment and maintenance of protective measures that enable an organization to perform its mission or critical functions despite risks posed by threats to its use of systems. Protective measures may involve a combination of deterrence, avoidance, prevention, detection, recovery, and correction that should form part of the organization's risk management approach" *(NIST SP 800-171)*. See also information security.

TERM	MEANING
Security **A**cceptance **T**est **(SAT)**	Acceptance test by competent specialists concerning the cybersecurity aspects of a new/changed application, system, cloud service, network, *etc*., hoping to gain assurance that the information risks are within the corporate risk appetite. Checks conformity with security-related policies, requirements, *etc*., correct operation of security administration and other security functions, and evaluates the information risks, including vulnerabilities and applicable security, privacy, and safety controls plus potential impacts on the existing infrastructure, organisation, business, *etc*., both during and following implementation. See also security audit.
Security **A**ccounts **M**anager **(SAM)**	**O**perating **S**ystem security **D**ata**B**ase on Windows systems containing information such as userIDs and hashed passwords
Security **Admin**istration [or **Admin**istrator] **(SecAdmin), administrative security**	a. Commonplace name for the trusted corporate information security function and professionals typically responsible for administering userIDs, passwords, access to **I**nformation **T**echnology systems, applications, *etc*. As such, they have privileged access to systems and other assets and, in the absence of effective governance and security controls such as training, security monitoring and logging, and competent oversight, could easily grant themselves or third parties unauthorised or inappropriate access, perhaps being coerced by social engineering. "The person responsible for implementing, monitoring and enforcing security rules established and authorized by management" *(ISACA glossary)*. b. Manual activities or processes performed by workers supporting or providing physical and/or information security and cybersecurity controls, systems, alerts, alarms, logs, *etc*. Generally documented in procedures, supported and enabled by technology, and reinforced by controls such as awareness, training, and management oversight. "Administrative measures for computer security. Note: These measures may be operational and accountability procedures, procedures of investigating breaches in security, and reviewing audit trails" *(ISO/IEC 2382)*.
Security alarm	Security alarm – an alarm system triggered by a breach of physical security, such as an intruder on the premises, or a logical alarm warning of a cybersecurity breach.
Security architecture	Architecture concerning or relating to various aspects of security.
Security aspect	"Characteristic, element, or property that reduces the risk of unintentionally-, intentionally- and naturally-caused crises and disasters that disrupt and have consequences on the products and services, operation, critical assets and continuity of an organization and its interested parties" *(ISO 22300)*.

TERM	MEANING
Security Assertion Markup Language (SAML)	XML standard for web Single Sign On, used to exchange authentication and authorisation data between identity providers and service providers. "A protocol consisting of XML-based request and response message formats for exchanging security information, expressed in the form of assertions about subjects, between online business partners" *(CNSSI 4009)*.
Security assessment	Process of assessing protective arrangements (security controls) addressing security risks. "An activity undertaken to assess controls for a system and its environment to determine if they have been implemented correctly and are operating as intended" *(AusISM)*.
Security assessment report	Results of assessing protective arrangements. "A document that describes that outcomes of a security assessment and contributes to the development of a plan of action and milestones" *(sic, AusISM)*.
Security Association (SA)	Set of parameters for network security protocols such as IPsec or Transport Layer Security, negotiated between network devices to secure their datacommunications, *e.g.* particular cryptographic algorithms, modes, and key lifetimes. "A collection of connection-specific parameters containing information about a one-way connection within IPSec that is required for each protocol used" *(NZISM)*. "A collection of connection-specific parameters used for IPsec connections" *(AusISM)*.
Security association lifetime	"The duration for which security association information is valid" *(NZISM)*.
Security Assurance Requirement (SAR)	Formal descriptions of the testing and other assurance controls (such as version control) taken to ensure that certified Information Technology products truly satisfy their security requirements under Common Criteria.
Security audit	Audit of security by competent, independent specialists. "Independent review and examination of data processing system records and activities to test for adequacy of system controls, to ensure compliance with established security policy and operational procedures, to detect breaches in security, and to recommend any indicated changes in control, security policy, and procedures" *(ISO/IEC 2382)*.
Security awareness	General appreciation by workers of their rôles in the process of securing the organisation's information assets, *e.g.* through compliance with policies, laws, and other security obligations and responsibilities. A workforce that is vigilant and alert for, aware of, and responds appropriately to, information risks (threats, vulnerabilities, near misses, events, incidents, and disasters) is a valuable general-purpose internal control. "The extent to which every member of an enterprise and every other individual who

TERM	MEANING
	potentially has access to the enterprise's information understand: Security and the levels of security appropriate to the enterprise; The importance of security and consequences of a lack of security; Their individual responsibilities regarding security (and act accordingly)" *(ISACA glossary)*. See also education, training, security culture, risk articulation, situational awareness.
Security awareness initiative [or campaign, project, session, event, topic, focal point, target, …]	Discrete package of communications, materials, interactions, presentations, courses, exercises, challenges, games, *etc.* focused on raising awareness of a particular information risk and security-related topic, audience, aspect, policy, *etc.* within the context of the security awareness programme. A 'corporate security conference' might be an opportunity to inform and align specialists and managers, perhaps involving supply chain partners, other stakeholders, and invited speakers. "A predefined, organized number of actions aimed at improving the security awareness of a special target audience about a specific security problem. Each security awareness program consists of several security awareness campaigns" *(ISACA glossary)*.
Security awareness manager [or leader, administrator, coordinator, specialist, advocate, evangelist, trainer, guru, …]	Rôle or person responsible for planning, leading, managing, and often delivering the security awareness programme, ideally with the proactive support and assistance of senior and general management, other specialists, and various corporate functions. "The individuals responsible for creating and maintaining the security awareness program and coordinating the different campaigns and efforts of the various groups involved in the program. They are also responsible for ensuring that all materials are prepared, advocates/trainers are trained, campaigns are scheduled, events are publicized and the program as a whole moves forward" *(ISACA glossary)*.
Security awareness programme [or initiative …]	Overall plan for the activities and resources needed to deliver the security awareness strategy. Typically involves a combination of continuous, periodic and sporadic activities (*e.g.* an intranet site offering policies, procedures, guidelines, newsletters, briefings, advisories, alerts, metrics, and courses; regular security awareness initiatives covering a series of topics; and *ad hoc* awareness activities in response to particular risks and opportunities). "A clearly and formally defined plan, structured approach and set of related activities and procedures with the objective of realizing and maintaining a security-aware culture. Notes: This definition clearly states that the goal is to realize and maintain a security-aware culture, *i.e.,* attaining and sustaining security awareness at all times. This implies that a security awareness program is not a one-time effort but a continuous process" *(ISACA glossary)*.

TERM	MEANING
Security awareness strategy	The organisation's overall approach to security awareness, with defined business objectives, suitable governance arrangements, and adequate resources. Complements related business strategies (*e.g.* for technology, information management, risk management, security, **H**uman **R**esources, compliance, safety, business continuity).
Security by obscurity	Cheap but fragile form of security control that simply relies on attackers not knowing or discovering the existence of an information asset or vulnerability. Fails-insecure, for obvious reasons. An ironic, oxymoronic term.
Security clearance, security cleared	Formal background check, normally performed on people appointed to trusted military or government service, defence organisations, audit and security professionals, *etc.* "Process of verifying the trustworthiness of people who will have access to security sensitive information" *(ISO 22300)*. See also positive vetting.
Security **C**ommittee **(SC), security forum**	Governing body for physical and information security. Oversees and directs all security activities across the organisation at the strategic level. Operates under the delegated authority of executive management, liaising as necessary with the **C**hief **I**nformation **S**ecurity **O**fficer, **I**nformation **S**ecurity **M**anager, Local Security Committees, Internal Audit, Risk Management, Legal/Compliance functions, *etc.* "Responsible for information security governance within the enterprise. Notes: A security forum can be part of an existing management body. Because information security is a business responsibility shared by all members of the executive management team, the forum needs to involve executives from all significant parts of the enterprise. Typically, a security forum has the following tasks and responsibilities: Defining a security strategy in line with the business strategy; Identifying security requirements; Establishing a security policy; Creating an overall security program or plan; Approving major initiatives to enhance information security; Reviewing and monitoring information security incidents; Monitoring significant changes in the exposure of information assets to major threats" *(ISACA glossary)*.
Security Construction and Equipment Committee	"An Australian Government interdepartmental committee responsible for the evaluation and endorsement of security equipment and services. The committee is chaired by the Australian Security Intelligence Organisation" *(AusISM)*.
Security **C**ontent **A**utomation **P**rotocol **(SCAP)**	Collection of open standards to automate vulnerability assessment and conformity evaluation. More info: https://csrc.nist.gov/projects/security-content-automation-protocol

TERM	MEANING
Security control	Control designed to mitigate unacceptable security risks, thereby achieving and maintaining adequate security. "An action that mitigates a potential vulnerability and helps ensure that the software behaves only in the expected manner" *(SCP QRG)*. "The safeguards or countermeasures prescribed for an information system or an organization to protect the confidentiality, integrity, and availability of the system and its information" *(OMB Circular A-130)*. See also information security control.
Security control assessment	Security control assessment. "The testing or evaluation of security controls to determine the extent to which the controls are implemented correctly, operating as intended, and producing the desired outcome with respect to meeting the security requirements for an information system or organization" *(OMB Circular A-130)*.
Security control baseline	Security control baseline. "The set of minimum security controls defined for a low-impact, moderate-impact, or high-impact information system" *(OMB Circular A-130)*.
Security culture	Security-related attitudes, beliefs, and practices (culture) generally shared, espoused, and exhibited collectively by members of a social group, such as their security awareness; acceptance of, respect for, and conformity with security and privacy rules defined in policies; and willingness to report incidents. The way people naturally think and generally behave in risky situations, even when they believe they are not being overseen, monitored, or logged.
Security declaration	"Documented commitment by a business partner, which specifies security measures implemented by that business partner, including, at a minimum, how goods and physical instruments of international trade are safeguarded, associated information is protected and security measures are demonstrated and verified. Note: It will be used by the organization in the supply chain to evaluate the adequacy of security measures related to the security of goods" *(ISO 22300)*.
Security documentation	Security documentation, *i.e.* written materials concerning security, primarily administrative information (*e.g.* policies, procedures, plans, strategies, awareness and training content) and records (*e.g.* security logs, reports on incident and audits, completed forms, and emails) generated for and by security activities. "An organisation's cyber security strategy; system-specific security documentation; and any supporting diagrams, plans, policies, processes, procedures and registers" *(AusISM)*.

TERM	MEANING
Security domain	Security domain, *i.e.* an area or group of assets facing similar risks and hence with similar security requirements, an example of classification. "Set of assets and resources subject to a common security policy" *(ISO/IEC 27033-1)*. "A system or collection of systems operating under a security policy that defines the classification and releasability of the information processed within the domain. It can be defined by a classification, a community of interest or releasability within a certain classification. This term is NOT synonymous with Trust Zone" *(NZISM)*. "A domain that implements a security policy and is administered by a single authority" *(NIST SP 800-171)*. See also zone, domain.
Security domain (cloud)	"A group of trust zones operating under a common set of security requirements and policies" *(NZISM)*.
Security domain owner	Owner of a security domain. "The individual responsible for the secure configuration of the security domain throughout its life-cycle, including all connections to/from the domain" *(NZISM)*.
Security engineering	Application of professional engineering practices and rigour to the field of information security. "An interdisciplinary approach and means to enable the realization of secure systems. It focuses on defining customer needs, security protection requirements, and required functionality early in the systems development life cycle, documenting requirements, and then proceeding with design, synthesis, and system validation while considering the complete problem" *(CNSSI 4009)*.
Security environment	Context for security, particularly the external context enveloping the organisation.
Security event	a. Security event. "An occurrence, arising from actual or attempted unauthorized access or use by internal or external parties, that impairs or could impair the availability, integrity, or confidentiality of information or systems, result in unauthorized disclosure or theft of information or other assets, or cause damage to systems" *(**T**rust **S**ervices **C**riteria)*. b. Security awareness activity such as a quiz or seminar.
S**ecurity** E**vent** M**anagement** **(SEM)**	Applications/systems for centralised storage and real-time analysis of cybersecurity events, alerts, and alarms logged by disparate networked systems (*e.g.* correlating potentially related events generated by multiple systems such as physical and network access control systems). See also **S**ecurity **I**nformation **M**anagement, **S**ecurity **I**nformation and **E**vent **M**anagement.

TERM	MEANING
Security function	Protective function, department, team, or unit responsible for organisational, national, information, physical, site/facility, personal, system, network, or some other form of security, depending on context. "The hardware, software, or firmware of the system responsible for enforcing the system security policy and supporting the isolation of code and data on which the protection is based" *(NIST SP 800-171)*.
Security **F**unctional **R**equirement **(SFR)**	Standardised suite of formal descriptions for security functions such as access control and authentication, under **C**ommon **C**riteria.
Security gateway	See firewall and gateway. "Point of connection between networks, or between subgroups within networks, or between software applications within different security domains intended to protect a network according to a given security policy" *(ISO/IEC 27033-1)*.
Security glass	Whereas ordinary glass panes are quite easily smashed, windows made with glass containing an embedded grid of strengthening wires, toughened or laminated 'safety' and 'bullet-proof' glass, extra thick 'plate' glass, or sealed double-glazing units, are stronger and hence more intruder-resistant *provided* the frames, hinges, locks, and surrounding walls are also sufficiently strong to resist violent physical attacks.
Security guard	Trusted physical security specialist, typically responsible for physical patrols of the premises, manning checkpoints and various emergency responses, operating **C**losed **C**ircuit **T**ele**V**ision surveillance, *etc.* Generally has ready access to assets throughout the facilities especially when patrolling unaccompanied outside normal working hours, using master keys and/or access-all-areas passes. Often a contractor employed by a specialist physical security company.
Security IDentity [or IDentifier]	Security **ID**entity – a unique key value assigned by an **I**nformation **T**echnology system to individual users, user groups, *etc.* primarily for access control purposes.
Security implementation standard, corporate security standard	Standard laying out a reasonably detailed specification or description of configuration parameters, processes, and/or activities and other controls deemed necessary to implement and achieve compliance with an organisation's information security policy. "Document specifying authorized ways for realizing security" *(ISO/IEC 27000)*.

TERM	**MEANING**
Security incident	Incident involving compromise, loss, or insufficiency of some aspect of security, *e.g.* physical/site security, personnel security/safety, information security, cybersecurity, network security, system security, national/state security, supply chain security, security compliance/conformity. "Any act or circumstance that produces a consequence" *(ISO 22300)*. "A series of unexpected events that involves an attack or series of attacks (compromise and/or breach of security) at one or more sites. A security incident typically includes an estimation of its level of impact. A limited number of impact levels are defined and, for each, the specific actions required and the people who need to be notified are identified" *(ISACA glossary)*. "A security event that requires action on the part of an entity in order to protect information assets and resources" *(Trust Services Criteria)*.
Security **I**ncident **R**esponse **T**eam **(SIRT)**	Crack team of competent professionals, fully trained, tooled up to the hilt, willing and ready to drop everything, responding cooly and calmly yet promptly to a security incident anywhere at barely a moment's notice, saving the world 24×7, like Batman on speed – well, maybe: the reality is a little more modest. "Cross-functional team responsible for addressing security incidents" *(ISACA glossary)*. See also **I**ncident **R**esponse **T**eam.
Security **I**nformation and **E**vent **M**anagement **(SIEM)**	Application/system to aggregate and analyse network security alerts, alarms, and logs from disparate systems in order to identify events and incidents of concern. Combines **S**ecurity **I**nformation **M**anagement with **S**ecurity **E**vent **M**anagement. See also **U**ser **B**ehaviour **A**nalytics, **N**etwork **T**raffic **A**nalysis, **I**ntrusion **D**etection **S**ystem/**I**ntrusion **P**revention **S**ystem.
Security **I**nformation **M**anagement **(SIM)**	Application/system to aggregate, store, and analyse security logs from disparate networked systems, allowing the identification of trends and other relatively long-term indicators of information security incidents. See also **S**ecurity **E**vent **M**anagement, **S**ecurity **I**nformation and **E**vent **M**anagement.
Security intelligence	Security intelligence. "Intelligence that helps Government agencies identify, understand and mitigate security threats" *(NZSTE)*.
Security landscape	Notional, visual, three-dimensional representation of the organisation's overall or information security situation, where peaks or high points may indicate strengths while dips or valleys represent weaknesses. A figurative security metric. See also attack surface, risk profile, risk universe, heatmap.
Security level	See security metric.

TERM	MEANING
Security log, security-related log file, security record	Security log. Most **I**nformation **T**echnology systems, applications and security appliances, and some devices, generate records of events (such as successful access to the system or card access-controlled door) and incidents (such as failed access attempts) that are stored in logs, as well as triggering alarms and alerts in specific situations (such as when log settings or other security parameters are changed, or when multiple events occur together). Security logs are a critical source of evidence supporting subsequent forensic analysis of security-relevant situations, provided they are adequately secured against unauthorised access, tampering, falsification, manipulation, corruption, deletion, overwriting, or wholesale replacement by the perpetrators or anyone else. Security logs should be retained for as long as is necessary to complete the review and analysis, or according to legal and/or business requirements typically identified in a policy. See also audit trail.
Security markings	Printed, written, or stamped markings (such as SECRET) visibly applied to storage media, **I**nformation **T**echnology systems, *etc.* to indicate their classification. "Human-readable indicators applied to a document, storage media, or hardware component to designate security classification, categorization, and/or handling restrictions applicable to the information contained therein. For intelligence information, these could include compartment and sub-compartment indicators and handling restrictions" *(CNSSI 4009)*.
Security management	Security management. "Coordinated activities to direct and control an organization with regard to security and resilience" *(ISO 22300)*. "The process of establishing and maintaining security for a computer or network system. Notes: The stages of the process of security management include prevention of security problems, detection of intrusions and investigation of intrusions and resolution. In network management, the stages comprise controlling access to the network and resources, finding intrusions, identifying entry points for intruders and repairing or otherwise closing those avenues of access" *(ISACA glossary)*.
Security management objective	Security management objective. "Specific outcome or achievement required of security in order to meet the security management policy. Note: It is essential that such outcomes are linked either directly or indirectly to providing the products, supply or services delivered by the total business to its customers or end users" *(ISO 22300)*.

TERM	MEANING
Security management policy	Security governance – the suite of corporate arrangements, policies, priorities, controls, and activities laid out by senior management to direct, manage, monitor, and maintain risk, security, compliance, resilience, *etc*. "Overall intentions and direction of an organization, related to the security and the framework for the control of security-related processes and activities that are derived from and consistent with its policy and regulatory requirements" *(ISO 22300)*.
Security management programme	"Process by which a security management objective is achieved" *(ISO 22300)*.
Security management target	"Specific level of performance required to achieve a security management objective" *(ISO 22300)*.
Security measure	a. Security metric (measurement). b. Security control (countermeasure).
Security metric, security level	Measurement of some aspect or parameter of security. "A standard of measurement used in management of security-related activities" *(ISACA glossary)*.
Security model	Conceptual framework, simulation, or emulation of (some aspect, type, or part of) security, perhaps a digital twin of a complex system to explore its vulnerabilities. "An engineering model informed by policies that specify how a system will enforce security" *(ISACA glossary)*.
Security Monkey	Simian Army tool that scans cloud systems for known vulnerabilities and issues such as expired **S**ecure **S**ockets **L**ayer/**T**ransport **L**ayer **S**ecurity and **D**igital **R**ights **M**anagement digital certificates. Extends Conformity Monkey.
Security objective	Security objective, the intended outcome, progress, result, or status to be achieved as a result of risk mitigation.
Security Operations (SecOps)	Team, function, department, unit, or rôle responsible for, or the set of activities involved in, operating (administering, configuring, monitoring, managing) an organisation's cybersecurity and/or physical security controls, *e.g.* initiating and coordinating the response to alerts and alarms from network devices. Integrates routine operations in the **I**nformation **T**echnology and information security domains. "Activity and function related to the protection of people, and tangible and intangible assets. Note: Security operations can require the carrying and operating a weapon in the performance of their duties. The concept includes the International Code of Conduct (ICoC) definition of security services: guarding and protection of people and objects, such as convoys, facilities, designated sites, property or other places (whether armed or unarmed) or any other activity for which the personnel of companies are required to carry or operate a weapon in the performance of their duties" *(ISO 22300)*.

TERM	MEANING
Security **O**perations **C**entre **(SOC)**	Corporate function responsible for security operations. *Cf.* **S**ystem **o**n **C**hip.
Security operations management	Management of the **Sec**urity **Op**erations function. "Coordinated activities to direct and control an organization with regard to security operations. Note: Direction and control with regard to security operations management generally includes establishment of the policy, planning and objectives directing operational processes and continual improvement" *(ISO 22300).*
Security operations objective	Objective of the **Sec**urity **Op**erations function. "Objective sought, or aimed for, related to security operations. Notes: Security operations objectives are generally based on the organization's security operations policy. Security operations objectives are generally specified for relevant functions and levels in the organization" *(ISO 22300).*
Security operations personnel	**Sec**urity **Op**erations professionals. "People working on behalf of an organization who are engaged directly or indirectly in security operations" *(ISO 22300).*
Security operations policy	Policy concerning **Sec**urity **Op**erations. "Overall intentions and direction of an organization related to security operations as formally expressed by top management. Notes: Generally, the security operations policy is consistent with the overall policy of the organization and provides a framework for the setting of security operations objectives. Security operations management principles presented in [ISO 22300] can form a basis for the establishment of a security operations policy consistent with the principles and obligations outlined in the International Code of Conduct (ICoC) and the Montreux Document" *(ISO 22300).*
Security operations programme	Programme of work planned for the **Sec**urity **Op**erations function. "Ongoing management and governance process supported by top management and resourced to ensure that the necessary steps are taken to coordinate the efforts to achieve the objectives of the security operations management system" *(ISO 22300).*
Security **O**rchestration, **A**nalytics and **R**esponse **(SOAR)**	Advanced form of **S**ecurity **I**nformation and **E**vent **M**anagement making still greater use of automation to react more rapidly to network security alerts, alarms, situations, events, or incidents.
Security perimeter	Literal or notional scope and trust boundary of a security domain. "The boundary that defines the area of security concern and security policy coverage" *(ISACA glossary).*
Security personnel	Workers in security-related rôles, such as security guards. "People in an organization in the supply chain who have been assigned security related duties. Note: These people can be employees of the organization" *(ISO 22300).*

TERM	MEANING
Security plan	Plan to develop and improve various aspect/s of security, in support of the security strategy. "Planned arrangements for ensuring that security is adequately managed. Note: It is designed to ensure the application of measures that protect the organization from a security incident. The plan can be incorporated into other operational plans" *(ISO 22300)*.
Security policy	Corporate or national policy covering one or more aspects of security. "Plan or course of action adopted for providing computer security" *(ISO/IEC 2382)*. "A high-level document representing an enterprise's information security philosophy and commitment" *(ISACA glossary)*. "A set of rules and practices that specify or regulate how a system or organization provides security services to protect sensitive and critical system resources" *(SANS glossary)*.
Security posture	Projected or apparent security status, stance, or strength of an organisation, *i.e.* how secure it believes or claims itself to be. Part of its brand and reputation with a deterrent effect and value, especially if the posture truly reflects reality. "The level of security risk to which a system is exposed. A system with a strong security posture is exposed to a low level of security risk while a system with a weak security posture is exposed to a high level of security risk" *(AusISM)*.
Security procedure	Description of a security process. "The formal documentation of operational steps and processes that specify how security goals and objectives established in the security policy and standards are to be achieved" *(ISACA glossary)*.
Security programme [or program]	a. Strategy/approach, governance structure, and/or plan/schedule for the organisation's security-related activities, both ongoing and forthcoming. Note: usually spelled 'programme' in British English. b. Security-related application, *e.g.* antivirus. Note: usually spelled 'program' by the Brits.
Security program rating	Metric for a security programme.
Security protection	See control. "Measures against threats that are intended to compensate for a computer's security weaknesses" *(NIST SP 800-114)*.
Security requirement	Requirement for or relating to security. "A requirement levied on a system or an organization that is derived from applicable laws, Executive Orders, directives, regulations, policies, standards, procedures, or mission/business needs to ensure the confidentiality, integrity, and availability of information that is being processed, stored, or transmitted" *(NIST SP 800-171)*. "A set of design and functional requirements that help ensure the software is built and deployed in a secure manner" *(SCP QRG)*.

TERM	MEANING
Security researcher	See hacker. Black or grey hat hackers with dubious pedigrees and unclear or nefarious motivations often *claim* to be white hat 'security researchers' but unless they have been explicitly commissioned and authorised to test security by the owners of the affected networks, systems, devices, applications, *etc.*, their efforts are generally unwelcome, unethical, and may well be illegal. Genuine, legitimate security researchers include authorised system, application and penetration testers, and computer scientists.
Security resilience	a. Resilience of the information risk and security management function, *i.e.* its ability to keep the business on top of information risks, handle routine security events and incidents competently, and establish and maintain the capability to cope with disasters. b. Resilience in general or just of the corporate security arrangements or function/s. "The ability to prepare for and adapt to changing conditions and withstand and recover rapidly from security disruptions, including cybersecurity. Resilience includes the capability to withstand and recover from deliberate attack, accidents or naturally occurring threats, vulnerabilities or other security events" *(ISACA glossary)*.
Security review and evaluation	Review and evaluation of the organisation's security arrangements against requirements specified in security strategies, policies and initiatives, compliance obligations, and good practices, plus general business objectives and expectations such as efficient and cost-effective performance. Such areas are typically covered by high-level security metrics, suggesting aspects worthy of greater or lesser attention, improvement, and assurance. "The coverage or inclusion of security needs, constraints, efforts and activities in a continuous manner over time throughout the life cycle of a solution or when triggered by a security event. These reviews and evaluations focus on identifying and addressing, and when possible, preventing the most critical and urgent security issues first. Security events, trends, potential threats and disruptions can also trigger reviews or evaluations" *(ISACA glossary)*.
Security risk	The uncertain possibility of security incidents such as invasion by hostile forces. "Any event that could result in the compromise, loss of integrity or unavailability of data or resources, or deliberate harm to people measured in terms of its likelihood and consequences" *(AusISM)*. See also information risk and information security risk.

TERM	MEANING
Security risk appetite	Management's willingness, preparedness, or desire to accept (take) some security-related risks. "Statements that communicate the expectations of an organisation's senior management about their security risk tolerance. These criteria help an organisation identify security risks, prepare appropriate treatments and provide a benchmark against which the success of mitigations can be measured" *(AusISM)*.
Security risk management	See information risk and security management. "The process of identifying, assessing and taking steps to reduce security risks to an acceptable level" *(AusISM)*.
Security risk management plan	See **R**isk **T**reatment **P**lan. "A plan that identifies the risks and appropriate risk treatments including controls needed to meet agency policy" *(NZISM)*.
Security screw, one-way screw	Tough, tamper-resistant fixture with a specially shaped head making it easy to insert and tighten but hard to loosen and remove. Some designs are removable using a special tool but most (including bolts with hexagonal heads that shear off at a certain torque once they are in tight, leaving just a plain, embedded surface) are meant to be permanently installed. Used to fix security grills, frames, locks, *etc*. firmly in place.
Security-sensitive information, security-sensitive material	"Information or material, produced by or incorporated into the supply chain security process, that contains information about the security processes, shipments or government directives that would not be readily available to the public and would be useful to someone wishing to initiate a security incident" *(ISO 22300)*.
Security service	Security service or function.
Security software	Applications supporting security administration and automation of: network and system security monitoring; information risk, incident, business continuity, and safety management; plus security utilities such as antivirus, intrusion detection, and security log analysis. "Software used to administer security, which usually includes authentication of users, access granting according to predefined rules, monitoring and reporting functions" *(ISACA glossary)*.
Security standard	Formally documented good practices for security, either internally sourced (supporting corporate security policies) or external/public/international (*e.g.* ISO/IEC 27002, NIST **C**yber**S**ecurity **F**ramework). "Practices, directives, guidelines, principles or baselines that state the required work and focus areas of current relevance and concern and are a translation of issues already mentioned in the security policy" *(ISACA glossary)*.

TERM	MEANING
Security strategy	Strategy for security.
Security strength	Metric quantifying the capability and resilience of a security control, system, *etc.* to prevent, resist, or withstand attack, failure, breach, compromise, *etc.* "Number associated with the amount of work that is required to break a cryptographic algorithm or system" *(ISO/IEC 27040).*
Security **T**arget **(ST)**	Under **C**ommon **C**riteria, a set of specific security requirements for an **I**nformation **T**echnology product associated with a specific implementation as opposed to the generic **P**rotection **P**rofile. "An artefact of Common Criteria evaluations. It contains the information security requirements of an identified target of evaluation and specifies the functional and assurance security measures offered by that target of evaluation to meet the stated requirements" *(NZISM).* "An artefact of Common Criteria evaluations that specifies conformance claims, threats and assumptions, security objectives, and security requirements for an evaluated product" *(AusISM).*
Security test	Test of the security protecting, provided by, or relating to one or more computer systems, subsystems, devices, units, interfaces, networks, **D**ata**B**ases, functions, processes, controls, services, suppliers, models, assumptions/beliefs, governance and management arrangements, documentation, rôles, responsibilities, accountabilities, architectures, policies, strategies, tactics, plans, changes, issues/concerns, incidents, performance, capacity, resilience, recovery, response, compliance, conformity, *etc.* against the requirements specifications, designs, and/or applicable standards and reasonable ethical expectations to gain assurance regarding the associated risks and, where relevant, drive improvements. The nature, extent, and depth of testing, and hence the assurance provided, range from a small, almost incidental part of unit, integration, system, and self-assessments in low-risk situations, up to major in-depth assessments, penetration tests, or audits by teams of independent, competent, experienced, and highly skilled specialists for those that are business-, mission-, or safety-critical. "Assurance that the modified or new system includes appropriate controls and does not introduce any security holes that might compromise other systems or misuses of the system or its information" *(ISACA glossary).* See also regression test, load test, acceptance test.
Security threat	See threat. "Any circumstance or event with the potential to adversely impact organizational operations including mission, functions, assets, personnel, processes, systems or brand reputation through unauthorized access, destruction, disclosure, modification of information or denial of service" *(ISACA glossary).*

TERM	MEANING
Security threat scenario	"Means by which a potential security incident can occur" *(ISO 22300).*
Security token	a. Security token – a hardware device for user authentication that generates credentials, *e.g.* a smartcard or key fob containing a cryptographic processor and display that generates and presents a sequence of **O**ne-**T**ime **P**asswords. b. "Digital assets or tokens created to represent a quantity of a specified investment, including rights to ownership, payment of a specific sum under a contract, entitlement to future profits, *etc.*" *(ISACA glossary).*
Security update	Security-related change such as a software patch addressing a known vulnerability, revised system security configuration, implementation of a new security policy or control, or additional threat intelligence.
Security utility function	Function of a security utility, such as an antivirus application.
Security vulnerability	See vulnerability. "A weakness in a system's security requirements, design, implementation or operation that could be accidentally triggered or intentionally exploited and result in a violation of the system's security policy" *(AusISM).*
SecurityX, CASP+	CompTIA's expert-level qualification for cybersecurity architects and engineers. Covers: security architecture; **G**overnance, **R**isk, and **C**ompliance; security operations; and security engineering and cryptography. Formerly called CASP+. More info: https://www.comptia.org/certifications/comptia-advanced-security-practitioner
Security zone boundary	Perimeter of a zone where internal meets external.
Seed	Confidential random or pseudorandom number used to initialise or prime a **P**seudo**R**andom **N**umber **G**enerator, determining the start point in the sequence of pseudorandom numbers generated.
[Network] Segmentation, segment	Logical separation or partitioning of a network into distinct subnetworks, zones, or layers with differing trust levels, typically monitoring traffic and controlling access between segments at any points of contact, *e.g.* using firewalls. "A logical grouping of the separate components of a network or system for design, control, installation, security and management purposes. This may occur where similarities of function, control and management exist or will be of advantage" *(NZISM).*
Segregation	See separation. "May be achieved by isolation, enforcing separation of key elements of a virtual system, removing network connectivity to the relevant device or applying access controls to prevent or limit access" *(NZISM).*

TERM	MEANING
Segregation of duties	See division of responsibilities. "A basic internal control that prevents or detects errors and irregularities by assigning the responsibility for initiating and recording transactions and the custody of assets to separate individuals. Note: Segregation/separation of duties is commonly used in large IT organizations so that no single person is in a position to introduce fraudulent or malicious code without detection" *(ISACA glossary)*.
SEH	*Abbrev:* **S**tructured **E**xception **H**andling.
Self-assessment, self-check, self-test	Low-cost low-assurance review, assessment, analysis, check, or test by a person, organisation, device, *etc.* of their own performance, capability, functionality, competence, *etc.* Much like 'marking your own homework,' patently lacking in independence, hence liable to bias and subjectivity, but a useful form of motivation to improve that, if necessary, may be validated by further checks on a sample basis to ensure sufficient integrity. See also Dunning–Kruger effect, **P**ower-**O**n **S**elf-**T**est.
S**elf-A**ssessment **Q**uestionnaire **(SAQ)**	a. Process for an organisation processing less than six million credit card transactions per year to review and attest to its conformity with the privacy and cybersecurity requirements of PCI-DSS, without necessarily requiring the costly services of a **Q**ualified **S**ecurity **A**ssessor. b. Documentation concerning any structured review conducted by the reviewed organisation itself rather than by some other party (such as an auditor).
Self-defence	"Protection of one's person or property against some injury attempted by another" *(ISO 22300)*.
Self-signed certificate	Digital certificate both signed and encrypted with the same private key.
Self-test	See self-assessment.
SEM	*Abbrev:* **S**ecurity **E**vent **M**anagement.
Semantic computing	"Field of computing that aims to identify the meanings of computational content and user intentions and to express them in a machine-processable form" *(ISO/IEC 22989)*.
Semi-quantitative assessment	Blend of both quantification and qualitative assessments, leading typically to a subjective/imprecise indication (*e.g.* 'extreme risk') or relative ranking (*e.g.* 'maturity level 4 of 5') rather than generating a measured value or range. "The use of a set of methods, principles, or rules for assessing risk based on bins, scales, or representative numbers whose values and meanings are not maintained in other contexts" *(NIST SP 800-55v1)*.
Semi-supervised machine learning	"Machine learning that makes use of both labelled and unlabelled data during training" *(ISO/IEC 22989)*. *Cf.* supervised machine learning, unsupervised machine learning.

TERM	MEANING
Sender **P**olicy **F**ramework **(SPF)**	Cryptographic email authentication protocol intended to trap spoofed emails sent from mail servers not authorised to send email from a given domain. Domain owners publish their SPF public keys as *txt* records through **D**omain **N**ame **S**ystem. See also **D**omain**K**eys **I**dentified **M**ail, **D**omain-based **M**essage **A**uthentication, **R**eporting and **C**onformance.
Senior management	Executive management plus (in some contexts) the Board of Directors. "The person or persons who provide the policy and overall guidance for the process but do not typically provide the direct day-to-day monitoring and controlling of the process. A senior manager has authority to direct the allocation or reallocation of resources in support of organizational process improvement effectiveness. A senior manager can be any manager who satisfies this description, including the CEO of the organization" *(ISACA glossary)*. "The chief executive officer or equivalent organizational leader and senior management team" *(**T**rust **S**ervices **C**riteria)*. "The highest level of executive management of an organization that is ultimately accountable to the board for executing the organization's strategic decisions, typically a group of persons that includes the chief executive officer or head of the organization" *(IIA GIAS)*. *Cf.* top management.
Sensing function	Purpose of a sensor.
Sensitive	a. See confidential and private. b. Delicate, perceptive, having heightened senses, 'touchy.'
Sensitive attribute	See sensitive information. "A human attribute that may be given special consideration for legal, ethical, social or personal reasons" *(ISACA glossary)*.
Sensitive **B**ut **U**nclassified **(SBU)**	Deprecated US government term, officially superseded by **C**ontrolled **U**nclassified **I**nformation.
Sensitive **C**ompartmented **I**nformation **(SCI)**	Essentially, SECRET information.
Sensitive **C**ompartmented **I**nformation **F**acility **(SCIF)**	Vault specifically designed to isolate and contain SECRET information. Strongly constructed facility with embedded electromagnetic barriers (Faraday cages), sound insulation, and strong physical access controls with strict procedures.
Sensitive data	Confidential, private, and/or valuable data. "Data that would cause limited damage to the national interest, an organisation or an individual if compromised" *(AusISM)*.

TERM	MEANING
Sensitive information	Confidential and/or valuable information considered to be at especially high risk of unauthorised and inappropriate disclosure or modification, *e.g.* proprietary or personal information. "Information that, as determined by a competent authority, must be protected because its disclosure, modification, destruction, or loss will cause perceivable damage to someone or something" *(ISO/IEC 2382)*. "Information that needs to be protected from unavailability, unauthorized access, modification or public disclosure because of potential adverse effects on an individual, organization, national security or public safety" *(ISO/IEC 27002)*. "Information that is protected from public disclosure only because it would have an adverse effect on an organization, national security or public safety" *(ISO 22300)*.
Sensitive information storage or transmission	"A set of controls that help ensure the software handles the sending, receiving and storing of information in a secure manner" *(SCP QRG)*.
Sensitive personal information [or Personally Identifiable Information **(PII) or personal data]**	Category of sensitive personal information deemed particularly confidential for some reason, *e.g.* if it would cause acute embarrassment or prejudicial treatment if disclosed inappropriately, *e.g.* a person's sexual, medical, cultural, religious, or other attributes, preferences, history, or orientation. Legally defined in some privacy laws. "Category of personally identifiable information (PII), either whose nature is sensitive, such as those that relate to the PII principal's most intimate sphere, or that can have a significant impact on the PII principal. Note: In some jurisdictions or in specific contexts, sensitive PII is defined in reference to the nature of the PII and can consist of PII revealing the racial origin, political opinions or religious or other beliefs, personal data on health, sex life or criminal convictions, as well as other PII that can be defined as sensitive" *(ISO/IEC 29100)*.
Sensitivity	Subjective assessment of the degree to which something is sensitive. "Measure of importance assigned to information by the information owner to denote its need for protection" *(ISO/IEC 2382)*. "A measure of the impact that improper disclosure of information may have on an enterprise" *(ISACA glossary)*.
Sensor	Device or component that senses, detects, or measures something. "A device or component that gathers information critical to an IoT application and converts it to data" *(ISACA glossary)*.
Sentience, sentient	Capability to experience emotions and subjective sensations (such as joy, pain, pleasure, and guilt), to be self-aware and feel a part of (and to some extent committed to further the interests of) one's surroundings, family, community, organisation, nation, ethnic group, team, *etc. Cf.* intelligence.

TERM	MEANING
Sentiment analysis	"Task of computationally identifying and categorizing opinions expressed in a piece of text, speech or image, to determine a range of feeling such as from positive to negative. Note: Examples of sentiments include approval, disapproval, positive toward, negative toward, agreement and disagreement" *(ISO/IEC 22989)*. "The process of automatically determining the emotional tone, such as positive, negative, or neutral, expressed in a piece of text (*e.g.*, opinions, reviews, social media posts) using natural language processing (NLP) and machine learning (ML) models trained on labeled data" *(ISACA glossary)*.
Separation, segregation, segmentation	Keeping incompatible things apart using logical and/or physical and administrative controls. "Includes partitioning and physically dividing systems and networks into smaller components. Separation should be applied as a design and control principle to networks where agencies have physical control over devices and components, such as in-office Wi-Fi systems, MFD's, desktops, laptops and other system or user devices [and] Architectural, design and management strategies to limit the effect and impact of network intrusions and system attacks and exploits. They will improve the ability to detect, and also improve the speed and effectiveness of any response to such events" *(NZISM)*.
Separation of duties	See division of responsibilities. "Dividing responsibility for sensitive information so that an individual acting alone can compromise the security of only a limited portion of a data processing system" *(ISO/IEC 2382)*. "The principle of splitting privileges among multiple individuals or systems" *(SANS glossary)*.
Sequence check	Context-dependent determination of whether things are in the correct or anticipated order. "Verification that the control number follows sequentially and any control numbers out of sequence are rejected or noted in an exception report for further research. Note: Can be alpha or numeric and usually utilizes a key field" *(ISACA glossary)*.
Sequential authentication	"When authentication data is requested on successive pages rather than being requested all at once on a single page" *(SCP QRG)*.
Server, computer server, email server, file server, application server, web server	Networked computer system providing information services such as email, websites, applications, and file management. "In a computer network, functional unit that provides services to workstations, to personal computers or to other functional units [and] functional unit that provides shared services to workstations or to other functional units over a data network" *(ISO/IEC 2382)*. "1. A computer dedicated to servicing requests for resources from other computers on a network. Servers typically run network operating systems. 2. A computer that provides services to another computer (the client) [and] A high-speed computer in a network shared by multiple users that holds the programs and

TERM	MEANING
	data shared by all users" *(ISACA glossary)*. "A computer used to run programs that provide services to multiple users. For example, a file server, email server or database server" *(NZISM)*. "A computer that provides services to users or other systems. For example, a file server, email server or database server" *(AusISM)*. "A device or system that provides resources, data, services, or programs to other devices on either a local area network or wide area network. Servers can provide resources and use them from another system at the same time. Examples include web servers, application servers, mail servers, and file servers" *(CIS Controls)*. "A system entity that provides a service in response to requests from other system entities called clients" *(SANS glossary)*.
Server **M**essage **B**lock **(SMB)**	Microsoft client-server file-, printer-, and port-sharing protocol. The original SMB v1, developed with IBM in the 1980s and released in 1996, is deprecated due to having numerous significant security vulnerabilities that can be exploited by hackers and malware to infect and spread through vulnerable organisations' internal networks. Later versions such as the current SMB v3.1.1 are more secure, incorporating user authentication, encryption, and digital signatures for instance. See also **C**ommon **I**nternet **F**ile **S**ystem, SMBGhost.
Service	Package of related business activities performed and delivered by a worker, agent, application, system, or organisation to another, such as information, **I**nformation **T**echnology, development, support, cloud, infrastructure, network, platform, software, email, file, financial, emergency, transportation, retail, government, money-laundering, malware, ransomware, assurance, audit, or security services. "Capability of a given layer and the layers below it that is provided to the entities of the next higher layer. Note: The service of a given layer is provided at the boundary between this layer and the next higher layer" *(ISO/IEC 2382)*. "An activity that provides a promised exchange of value between a service provider and customer, product or work product. Services do not always produce tangible or storable products; in such instances, the service itself is the deliverable" *(ISACA glossary)*. "Refers to a software functionality or a set of software functionalities, such as the retrieval of specified information or the execution of a set of operations. Services provide a mechanism to enable access to one or more capabilities, where the access is provided using a prescribed interface and based on the identity of the requestor per the enterprise's usage policies" *(CIS Controls)*.
Service account	Non-interactive userID reserved for automated information services, applications, and scheduled administrative activities such as backups. Often privileged. "A dedicated account with

TERM	MEANING
	escalated privileges used for running applications and other processes. Service accounts may also be created just to own data and configuration files. They are not intended to be used by people, except for performing administrative operations" *(CIS Controls)*. "User accounts that are used to perform automated tasks without manual intervention, such as machine to machine communications. Service accounts will typically be configured to disallow interactive logins" *(AusISM)*.
Service bureau	Business/facility providing standardised information services in volume, *e.g.* a high street print shop, commercial data centre, or **C**loud **S**ervice **P**rovider. "A computer facility that provides data processing services to clients on a continual basis" *(ISACA glossary)*.
Service desk	See help desk. "The point of contact within the IT organization for users of IT services" *(ISACA glossary)*.
Service **L**evel **A**greement **(SLA)**	Lays out requirements for services to be provided by internal or external service providers to users/customers, covering key aspects such as information security, reliability, and quality, plus the management arrangements such as performance evaluation and metrics, reporting, incident handling, and liabilities or consequences if requirements are unsatisfied. May be supported by **O**perational **L**evel **A**greements for subsidiary/related services necessary to deliver what the customer actually needs (*e.g.* cloud services typically require data centre facilities, computing, storage, networking, *and* telecommunications services). "An agreement, preferably documented, between a service provider and the customer(s)/ user(s) that defines minimum performance targets for a service and how they will be measured" *(ISACA glossary)*.
Service mark	Similar to a trademark but for a commercial service rather than goods, giving it distinctive branding. A form of **I**ntellectual **P**roperty, sometimes denoted by ℠.
Service-**O**riented **A**rchitecture **(SOA)**	Software engineering approach that weaves discrete information services or microservices together into a coherent application design. Information processing, business, security, and other services may be provided by custom-written functions and subroutines within the program plus generic, reusable network services accessed through **A**pplication **P**rogramming **I**nterfaces. "A cloud-based library of proven, functional software applets that can be connected together to become a useful online application" *(ISACA glossary)*.
Service owner	Organisation, rôle, or person designated as the owner of an information service, or a business service (*e.g.* Customer Services). Responsible and generally accountable for its design, operation, and legitimate exploitation, optimising the value obtained.

TERM	MEANING
Service provider	Organisation, person, server, *etc.* providing a service. "Abstract representation of all the entities that provide a service to peer service users" *(ISO/IEC 2382)*. "An organization supplying services to one or more (internal or external) customers" *(ISACA glossary)*. "A supplier (such as a service organization) engaged to provide services to the entity. Service providers include outsourced service providers as well as suppliers that provide services not associated with business functions, such as janitorial, legal, and audit services" *(**T**rust **S**ervices **C**riteria)*.
Service **S**et **Id**entifier **(SSID)**	Name for a Wi-Fi network service set (group of communicating devices), usually broadcast periodically by access points. "A name assigned to a wireless AP" *(NIST SP 800-114)*. "A 32-character unique identifier attached to the header of packets sent over a wireless local area network (WLAN) that acts as a password when a mobile device tries to connect to the base station subsystem (BSS). Notes: The SSID differentiates one WLAN from another, so all access points and all devices attempting to connect to a specific WLAN must use the same SSID. A device will not be permitted to join the BSS unless it can provide the unique SSID. Because an SSID can be sniffed in plaintext from a packet, it does not supply any security to the network. An SSID is also referred to as a network name because it is a name that identifies a wireless network" *(ISACA glossary)*.
Session	a. Interactive period or connection, *e.g.* from an **I**nformation **T**echnology user's logon or initial access to a computer system, application, network, or service until their logoff, timeout, or final access. "A virtual connection between two hosts by which network traffic is passed" *(SANS glossary)*. b. A boozy evening sharing war stories at a security conference.
Session **B**order **C**ontroller **(SBC)**	"Security features for Voice-over IP (VoIP) traffic similar to that provided by firewalls. Note: SBCs can be configured to filter specific VoIP protocols, monitor for denial-of-service (DOS) attacks and provide network address and protocol translation features" *(ISACA glossary)*. "A device (physical or virtual) used in IP networks to control and manage the signalling and media streams of real-time UC and VoIP connections. It includes establishing, controlling, and terminating calls, interactive media communications or other VoIP connections. SBCs enable VoIP traffic to navigate gateways and firewalls and ensure interoperability between different SIP implementations. Careful selection of SBCs will provide such functionality as prevention of toll fraud, resistance to denial of service attacks and resistance to eavesdropping" *(NZISM)*.
Session hijack	See **M**an-**I**n-**T**he-**M**iddle. "Take over a session that someone else has established" *(SANS glossary)*.

TERM	MEANING
Session **I**nitiation **P**rotocol **(SIP)**	Application layer network signalling protocol to establish, change, and terminate **V**oice **O**ver **I**nternet **P**rotocol sessions for voice and video calls, with call forwarding, on-hold, and call transfer functions.
Session key	Key used for symmetric encryption of traffic between two parties within single session. May be changed after a defined period or a certain number of messages have been exchanged. The initial key for the first session may be generated and shared offline (*e.g.* on a **One-Time Pad** or key loader) or exchanged securely between the parties using asymmetric cryptography. Subsequent session keys may be generated, encrypted with the current session key, and passed to the counterparty, or the key establishment process might restart from scratch (rekeying). "In the context of symmetric encryption, a key that is temporary or is used for a relatively short period of time. Usually, a session key is used for a defined period of communication between two computers, such as for the duration of a single connection or transaction set, or the key is used in an application that protects relatively large amounts of data and, therefore, needs to be re-keyed frequently" *(SANS glossary)*.
Session management	Session management. "A set of controls that help ensure web applications handle http sessions in a secure manner" *(SCP QRG)*.
SET	*Abbrev:* **S**ecure **E**lectronic **T**ransaction.
Setpoint, set-point, set point	Desired or optimal value configured for a controlled parameter, such as a temperature of 4°C for the thermostat in a refrigerator. The actual measured value varies around the setpoint in practice due to the time taken for the control to act, *e.g.* after starting and running the compressor, it takes a while to chill the fridge including the temperature sensor (forming a hysteresis loop). Various business, security, and compliance objectives are also, in a sense, setpoints with their own measurement and control tolerances for practical reasons.
SEV	*Abbrev:* **S**ecure **E**ncrypted **V**irtualisation.
Severity	Quantification, measure, or relative assessment of the significance, scale, importance, criticality, or vitality of something. "Estimation of the magnitude of potential impacts on the privacy of a PII principal" *(ISO/IEC 29134)*.
Sexting	Portmanteau of 'sex' and 'texting' involving explicit text messages or other supposedly private person-to-person communication between friends or lovers. Once sent, messages may be forwarded or disclosed by the recipient and/or by anyone who intercepts the communications or has control of the devices, and perhaps used for sextortion.

TERM	MEANING
Sextortion	Neologism concerning threatening to disclose highly personal and private, often sexual, information about someone (such as explicit selfies – photographs of someone taken by them – or sexting or captured webcam footage) as a means of coercing them into doing something (*e.g.* pay a ransom) to avoid embarrassment and shame. See also revenge porn.
SFR	*Abbrev:* **S**ecurity **F**unctional **R**equirement.
SGX (Software Guard eXtension)	**C**entral **P**rocessing **U**nit instruction-set security extension designed to isolate trusted from untrusted code as it executes, introduced by Intel with the Skylake microarchitecture. Intended to prevent exploitation by malware, even subverted kernel functions in **O**perating **S**ystems.
SHA-1 (Secure Hash Algorithm № 1)	One of a set of hash algorithms developed by the **N**ational **S**ecurity **A**gency in 1995. Generates a 160-bit hash. Due to known cryptographic vulnerabilities and successful cryptanalytic attacks demonstrated in 2017 and 2019, SHA1 is deprecated in favour of stronger algorithms such as SHA-2 but lingers in some digital signatures, **S**ecure **S**ockets **L**ayer, PGP, SSH, and S/MIME. "A one way cryptographic hash function" *(SANS glossary)*. See also MD5.
SHA-2 (Secure Hash Algorithm № 2)	Set of six related cryptographic hash algorithms developed by the **N**ational **S**ecurity **A**gency, generating hashes with bit lengths evident from their names (*i.e.* SHA-224, SHA-256, SHA-384, and SHA-512). Believed strong enough for all current applications, with SHA-3 available when vulnerabilities are discovered and disclosed.
SHA-3 (Secure Hash Algorithm № 3)	Further generation of cryptographic hash and extendable output algorithms approved by NIST in the FIPS PUB 202 standard in 2015. Based on Keccack, a sponge function. Anticipated to supersede MD5, SHA-1, and SHA-2. More info: https://nvlpubs.nist.gov/nistpubs/fips/nist.fips.202.pdf
Shadow Brokers	Hacker group allegedly associated with Russian intelligence.
ShadowHammer	Malware incident in 2018/2019 which initially compromised ASUS servers, infecting motherboard software and firmware updates distributed through the ASUS Live Update mechanism. The updates were digitally signed using genuine ASUSTek Computer Inc. digital certificates, hence *appeared* legitimate. The malware targeted devices with specific MAC addresses on their network adapters, suggesting a cyber-spooky purpose. The attack was linked to the BARIUM group.
Shadow IT	Unofficial, informal, and weakly governed computer-literate workers outside **I**nformation **T**echnology **D**epartment using IT equipment (*e.g.* **B**ring **Y**our **O**wn **D**evice) and services (*e.g.* cloud computing) with little if any IT Department involvement.

TERM	MEANING
	Although non-IT workers are embedded in the business, they *may* not be aware of and/or conform to corporate IT strategies, policies, standards, guidelines, procedures, protocols, good practices, or comply with applicable laws/regulations. Implies a threat to IT Department's political power and management control. "The use of systems, services, hardware or software on an enterprise network or within an enterprise's infrastructure without proper vetting and approval from the IT or cybersecurity department" *(ISACA glossary)*.
Shadow password file	Early networked computers saved user authentication credentials in a plaintext 'password file' that was patently vulnerable to theft and exploitation by hackers. That highly insecure approach was soon replaced by saving password hash values, except they too were vulnerable to brute force attacks. Soon, passwords or hashes were encrypted into the 'shadow password file' with additional security controls to prevent intrepid hackers intercepting, misusing, or compromising system functions to decrypt them or bypass user authentication altogether. "A system file in which encryption user password are stored so that they aren't available to people who try to break into the system" *(SANS glossary)*.
Shadow regulations	Organisations sometimes acquiesce to unofficial requests from the authorities, *e.g.* to disclose sensitive information or take offline material previously published online, without being legally compelled to do so. Presumably they simply agree with the intent, are persuaded on ethical grounds, or are coerced through 'agreements,' 'codes of conduct', *etc.*
Shamoon	Species of malware used to attack Saudi Aramco in 2012, with variants still in the wild as of 2019. Incorporated a dropper and wiper.
SHARE design option	"To outsource, joint ventures, partnerships, buy insurance, or use other financial instruments to address the opportunity, obstacle, or obligation" *(OCEG GRC Glossary)*.
Shared facility	"Where an organisation's facility resides within a larger facility that is shared with one or more different organisations" *(AusISM)*.
Shared key, shared secret	Cryptographic key for both encryption and decryption that is *meant* to be available only to authorised users of a symmetric cryptosystem and no others. Also known as a secret key. *Cf.* private key.
Shared responsibility	Information security principle that we are both collectively and individually responsible for maintaining adequate security to protect information assets. *Cf.* accountability.

TERM	MEANING
Shared responsibility model	"The responsibility for the selection, implementation, management and maintenance of controls in public cloud services is shared between provider and consumer. Where the responsibilities lie depends on the provider, and the service and deployment models" *(NZISM)*. "A framework that describes the management and operational responsibilities between different parties for a system. Where responsibilities relating to specific controls are shared between multiple parties, enough detail is documented to provide clear demarcation between the parties" *(AusISM)*.
Shelfware	Documents such as policies and procedures that are 'collecting dust on the shelf', *i.e.* disregarded, neglected, and forgotten, rather than being actively used and complied with. *Cf.* software, hardware, firmware, wetware, malware, ransomware, adware, crimeware, scareware, spouseware, stalkerware, spyware.
Shellcode	Malware that covertly opens a command interpreter (the 'shell') to call powerful low-level system commands.
Shellshock, Bashdoor	Festering cluster of bugs in the Bash shell/command interpreter, some of which trivially permit hackers or malware root access to vulnerable UNIX systems. Nasty. Responsible disclosure of the vulnerability by its discoverer and ready availability of patches towards the end of 2014 did not prevent Shellshock being widely exploited because of patching delays caused by tardiness and incompetence.
Shell site	See cold site.
Shelter in place	"Action to move people to predetermined areas inside the building/site in order to protect them from external dangers during an incident. Note: This may be referred to as 'invacuation.' [Alternatively to] Remain or take immediate refuge in a protected location relevant to the risk" *(ISO 22300)*.
Shift left	The earlier in the product development process that information risk is addressed, the less likely that products will end up with inadequate information security. The term reflects the conventional left-to-right overall time sequence of process flow diagrams, and involves early involvement of functions or people (such as security testers and documenters).
Shill bid	Auction bid made by the seller of an item (directly or through an accomplice) to drive up the hammer price. A form of fraud.
Shim	Thin strip of metal used to trip the catch or catches holding the shackle and hence force open a locked padlock without the correct key or combination.

TERM	MEANING
Shock	Sudden dramatic event, electric discharge, or the life-threatening symptoms associated with low blood pressure arising from severe trauma. "Uncertain, abrupt or long-onset event, that has potential to impact upon the purpose or objectives of an urban system" *(ISO 22300)*.
Shodan	Search engine for Internet-connected devices (*things*), popular with hackers and cybersecurity professionals. Characterises devices by their responses to various queries and network packets. More info: https://www.shodan.io/
ShopAdmin	Hacker term for an exploit that enables unauthorised access to the privileged administrative/management functions of Internet shopping/eCommerce sites.
Short **M**essaging **S**ervice **(SMS)**, Te**XT** messaging **(TXT)**	Cellular network service originally designed to facilitate the exchange of brief (<161 character) text messages and greetings between people. Subsequently extended (**M**ultimedia **M**essaging **S**ervice) to cater for lengthier messages with icons, attached images, *etc.*, and automated machine-to-machine data communications (such as smart meter readings). "A cellular network facility that allows users to send and receive text messages of up to 160 alphanumeric characters on their handset" *(NIST SP 800-101)*.
Shoulder surfing	Literally or figuratively looking over someone's shoulder as they use a portable digital device, PIN pad, *etc.*, watching them enter passwords/PIN codes, *etc.* and snooping at the screen. A physical security and social engineering threat, especially in public places.
Shred, shredding	Physical destruction of paperwork (or other storage media) in order to destroy or permanently withhold the information content. Cross-cut 'confetti' shredders are somewhat more effective than strip-cut shredders since the fragments are smaller and more difficult to piece back together (even using automated image analysis and reconstruction techniques) but shredding followed by incineration of the waste is advisable or required for highly confidential or SECRET information. "Destruct by cutting or tearing media into small particles" *(ISO/IEC 27040)*.
Shrink-wrapped	Packaging **C**ommercial **O**ff-**T**he-**S**helf software in transparent plastic film through which the marketing blurb and copyright notice or licence agreement may be read prior to purchasing, and is deemed to have been accepted if the user merely opens the package.
SID	*Abbrev:* **S**ecurity **ID**entifier.
Side channel	a. Cryptanalytic attack that exploits some peripheral characteristic, side-effect, or unintentional feature of a cryptosystem, such as observing fluctuations in the power consumption or electromagnetic radiation when performing different types of cryptographic function and thereby

TERM	MEANING
	deducing useful knowledge about, for instance, the number of rounds or the length of the key. *Cf.* covert channel. b. Class of exploits that take advantage of unanticipated, abnormal, and/or insecure communications channels or mechanisms to bypass controls over the usual channels and mechanisms, *e.g.* Spectre.
Sideloading	Installing unofficial (unauthorised, unapproved, and potentially malicious) software on a jailbroken device, outside the sandbox as it were.
SIEM	*Abbrev:* **S**ecurity **I**nformation and **E**vent **M**anagement.
SIGINT (Signals **Int**elligence**)**	Military practice of gleaning intelligence through surveillance on [primarily] foreign communications (COMINT) and other signals (ELINT) which potentially includes analogue and digital communications, wired or wireless networks, and point-to-point links, data and voice radio transmitters, radar, beacons, steganography, cryptanalysis, **T**raffic **A**nalysis, *etc*. See also TECHINT, OSINT, COMINT, IMINT, ELINT.
Signature	a. Characteristic way that a person writes their own name, providing a means to authenticate them (*i.e.* a biometric). b. Set of characteristics that uniquely identify a species of malware, a system, or a device. "A distinct pattern in network traffic that can be identified to a specific tool or exploit" *(SANS glossary)*. See also digital signature.
Signature-based **H**andling of **A**sserted information using to**KEN**s **(SHAKEN)**	Contrived name for a framework determining how telecommunications carriers exchange and deal with missing or invalid **S**ecure **T**elephone **I**dentity **R**evisited-authenticated caller ID information.
Significance, significant	Importance, relevance, priority, substantiveness, value, *gravitas*, *etc*. Usually expressed subjectively (*e.g.* relative to others) but objective criteria (such as the lowest financial value deemed material to the organisation) may be defined. "The relative importance of a matter within the context in which it is being considered, including quantitative and qualitative factors, such as magnitude, nature, relevance, and impact. Professional judgment assists internal auditors when evaluating the significance of matters within the context of the relevant objectives" *(IIA GIAS)*.
Significant cybersecurity risk	Significant cybersecurity risk. "A cybersecurity risk which, based on its technical characteristics, can be assumed to have a high likelihood of an incident that could lead to a severe negative impact, including by causing considerable material or non-material loss or disruption" *(EU CRA)*.

TERM	MEANING
Significant cyber threat	Significant cyber threat. "A cyber threat which, based on its technical characteristics, can be assumed to have the potential to have a severe impact on the network and information systems of an entity or the users of the entity's services by causing considerable material or non-material damage" *(NIS2)*.
Significant deficiency	Significant vulnerability. "A deficiency or a combination of deficiencies, in internal control, that is less severe than a material weakness, yet important enough to merit attention by those responsible for oversight. Notes: A material weakness is a significant deficiency or a combination of significant deficiencies that results in more than a remote likelihood of an undesirable event(s) not being prevented or detected" *(ISACA glossary)*.
Significant information asset	Information asset or a related group/set of information assets of material value to the owner. Significance may be defined formally in a policy or standard, typically in terms of its financial or strategic value to the organisation, or may be left to the owners' discretion.
Sign-on procedure	See logon. "The procedure performed by a user to gain access to an application or operating system. Note: If the users are properly identified and authenticated by the system's security, they will be able to access the software" *(ISACA glossary)*.
Silent alarm	Covert alarm that, when triggered manually or automatically by some event or exception, is not obvious to those in the immediate vicinity or directly involved but quietly alerts remote guards, managers, authorities, *etc.* Duress alarms and tell-tales are specific examples.
Silent cyber risk	See non-affirmative cyber risk.
Silk Road, Silk Road 2.0	Online black markets where the tools (including malware and related services) and proceeds of crime (fullz, illegal drugs, and more) were traded anonymously through the Tor network for Bitcoins. The original Silk Road was active from 2011 until being shut down by the **F**ederal **B**ureau of **I**nvestigation in 2013. It was resurrected as Silk Road 2.0 and lasted another year before again being shut down by the authorities.
SIM	*Abbrev:* **S**ecurity **I**nformation **M**anagement or **S**ubscriber **I**dentity **M**odule, depending on context.
SIM card	*Abbrev:* **S**ubscriber **I**dentity **M**odule card.
Simian Army	Collection of open-source **A**mazon **W**eb **S**ervices cloud tools developed by Netflix to test the reliability, cybersecurity, and resilience of the AWS infrastructure it depends upon. See chaos engineering, Chaos Monkey, Latency Monkey, Conformity Monkey, Security Monkey.

TERM	MEANING
Simple **M**ail **T**ransfer **P**rotocol **(SMTP)**	Protocol used to deliver emails to a mail server. "The standard electronic mail (email) protocol on the Internet" *(ISACA glossary)*. See also **I**nternet **M**essage **A**ccess **P**rotocol, **P**ost **O**ffice **P**rotocol.
Simple **N**etwork **M**anagement **P**rotocol **(SNMP)**	Popular application-layer datacommunications protocol suite for network management, *i.e.* remotely monitoring and administering network devices. Versions 2 and especially 3 of SNMP offer improved security with stronger authentication and encryption. "The protocol governing network management and the monitoring of network devices and their functions. A set of protocols for managing complex networks" *(SANS glossary)*. *Cf.* **I**nternet **C**ontrol **M**essage **P**rotocol.
Simple Object Access Protocol	Now known as SOAP.
Simplocker	Species of Android ransomware. Demanded ransom payments in Ukrainian hryvnias, *hinting* at the malware's origin.
SIM swap [fraud, attack]	Fraudsters socially engineer the mobile phone companies into transferring a target's cellphone number to the IMSI held on a **S**ubscriber **I**dentity **M**odule card in their possession, then use it to hijack the victim's email, banking, and other online services by diverting two-factor authentication SMS/TXT messages typically used to reset forgotten password/s or authenticate/approve transactions.
Simulate, simulation	Model or reproduce something in order to predict and learn about its characteristics. "Use of a data processing system to represent selected behavioral characteristics of a physical or abstract system. Example: The representation of air streams around airfoils at various velocities, temperatures, and air pressures" *(ISO/IEC 2382)*. *Cf.* emulate/emulation.
Simultaneous **A**uthentication of **E**quals **(SAE), Dragonfly**	Flawed cryptographic protocol used in WPA3 to authenticate Wi-Fi devices to each other, prior to establishing encrypted communications between them.
Single **P**oint **o**f **F**ailure **(SPoF)**	Essential component or link between components whose failure would interrupt (*i.e.* impact the availability of) dependent services, processes, customers, *etc.* Eliminating SPoFs where possible through redundancy, along with reinforcing unavoidable SPoFs through solid engineering practices, are valuable forms of resilience. "Element or component of a system, a path in a system, or a system that, if it fails, the whole system or an array of systems are unable to perform their primary functions. Note: A single point of failure is often considered a design flaw associated with a critical element" *(ISO/IEC 27040)*. "A resource whose loss will result in the loss of service or production" *(ISACA glossary)*. See also **F**ailure **M**odes and **E**ffects **A**nalysis.

TERM	MEANING
Single **S**ign **O**n **(SSO)**	Software that manages a suite of diverse passwords unique to multiple systems. Unlike crude password synchronisation schemes, the compromise of a password for a single target system being managed through a well-designed SSO system or application should not give access to other target systems since they each have unique passwords. However, compromising the SSO system itself may still facilitate unauthorised access to *all* the subsidiary systems; hence, security remains paramount for the SSO system. "A single point authentication system used by multiple systems and applications" *(ISACA glossary)*. See also password vault.
Sinister	Dark, underhand, deceptive, surreptitious, foreboding, and usually malicious behaviour, *e.g.* coercive, threatening, or menacing. Derived from the Latin word for left, referring to a Roman soldier's discreet use of, say, a dagger held in the left hand *in addition* to the obvious sword in his right hand, or perhaps the tactical advantage that a left-handed swordsman might have when fighting at tight quarters, *e.g.* in a spiral staircase.
Sinkhole	See bit-bucket.
SIP	*Abbrev:* **S**ession **I**nitiation **P**rotocol.
SIPRnet	*Abbrev:* **S**ecret **I**nternet **P**rotocol **R**outer **net**work. US **D**epartment **of D**efense network for classified information up to SECRET. Authorisation to connect is required from **S**IPRnet **C**onnection **A**pproval **O**ffice within **D**efense **I**nformation **S**ystems **A**gency. See also NIPRnet.
SIS	*Abbrev:* **S**ecret **I**ntelligence **S**ervice (UK MI6) or **S**pecial **I**ntelligence **S**ervice (US).
Situational awareness	Heightened appreciation of the risks inherent in a given context, particularly significant threats to a person's safety in a particular locality (*e.g.* a dark city alleyway) and time of day (*e.g.* at night). "The ability to identify, process and comprehend the critical elements of information through a cyber threat intelligence process that provides a level of understanding that is relevant to act upon to mitigate the impact of a potentially harmful event" *(Bank for International Settlements and International Organization of Securities Commissions Guidance on cyber resilience for financial market infrastructures)*. See also vigilance, security awareness. More info: https://www.bis.org/cpmi/publ/d146.pdf
S/KEY	Unix/Linux **O**ne-**T**ime **P**assword system, trademarked by Telcordia Technologies. "A security mechanism that uses a cryptographic hash function to generate a sequence of 64-bit, one-time passwords for remote user login. The client generates a one-time password by applying the MD4 cryptographic hash function multiple times to the user's secret key. For each successive authentication of the user, the number of hash applications is reduced by one" *(SANS glossary)*.

TERM	MEANING
Skill	Ability to do something particularly well – more than merely competently, perhaps expertly. "Ability to perform a task or activity with a specific intended outcome acquired through education, training, experience or other means … An example of a skill is the ability to identify and classify the risks associated with a project" *(ISO/IEC TS 17027)*.
Skill gap	"The difference between the current skill level and the target skill level" *(OCEG GRC Glossary)*.
Skipjack	Deprecated symmetric encryption algorithm (a block cipher with an 80-bit key), presumably invented by someone working for the **N**ational **S**ecurity **A**gency or seized by them. Originally classified SECRET and incorporated in the Clipper chip but subsequently opened to public scrutiny. Deliberately weakened by NSA to facilitate cryptanalysis (a backdoor).
SLA	*Abbrev:* **S**ervice **L**evel **A**greement.
Slack space	Gap between the full extent of a file (up to the end-of-file marker) and the remaining disk space allocated for the file (including any further sectors in a cluster), which may contain residual data (remnants) from files that previously occupied the area before being moved/deleted but not securely erased. Slack space can also exist in working memory, depending on the **O**perating **S**ystem. See also unallocated space.
Slander, slanderous	Transitory and generally unrecorded form of defamation, *e.g.* a spoken statement or gesture, perhaps falsely accusing someone of something untoward and inappropriate. *Cf.* libel.
Sleeper	Deep cover mole who remains under cover for an extended period (years) in the target organisation/group/culture in order to establish the (ill-founded) trust of his/her colleagues and ascend to a position of power and authority from which he/she may be 'awoken' to commit an act of espionage, sabotage, or betrayal. An extreme example of social engineering.
Slim Jim	Original trademarked brand name of a tool designed to defeat car door locks by physically manipulating the lock actuation rods inside the door. Subsequently became a generic term for similar/copycat tools (genericide).
SMART (criteria)	Five generic factors to consider when formulating, specifying, or selecting goals, objectives, metrics, *etc*. "Specific, measurable, attainable, realistic and timely, generally used to describe appropriately set goals" *(ISACA glossary)*. "Criteria used to design/set Objectives to work with Indicators; to be specific, measurable, achievable (yet aspirational), relevant, and time-bound" *(OCEG GRC Glossary)*. See also PRAGMATIC.

TERM	MEANING
Smart-	Generic prefix normally referring to something electronic having an embedded processor, ranging from basic (dumb) devices to highly advanced *things* (*e.g.* autonomous military drones and cyberweapons) using **A**rtificial **I**ntelligence (**S**mart **T**echnology).
Smart appliance	Smart device such as a refrigerator or oven, and home entertainment system, typically found in smart homes.
Smart building	Building, home, or other facilities containing integrated computer systems and networks for monitoring, control, security, *etc.*
Smart button	Smart switch *thing* used to trigger a programmed action elsewhere via the network.
Smartcard, smart card	Credit card-sized device or token usually containing a cryptographic processor plus gold-flashed contact pads and/or short-range wireless networking capabilities. "A small electronic device that contains electronic memory and possibly an embedded integrated circuit. Note: Smart cards can be used for a number of purposes including the storage of digital certificates or digital cash, or they can be used as a token to authenticate users" *(ISACA glossary)*. "An electronic badge that includes a magnetic strip or chip that can record and replay a set key" *(SANS glossary)*.
Smart contract	"Software (computer code) that automatically executes transactions and/or enforces agreements based on the fulfillment of the terms of the agreement by leveraging decentralized ledger technology that uses public validation to ensure correct and reliable performance according to agreed rules" *(ISACA glossary)*.
Smart device	Device with an embedded **S**mart **T**echnology processor, usually also network-capable making it a *thing*. Some dumb devices can be smartened-up using add-on smart interfaces, ranging from remotely switchable power plugs up to quite sophisticated automation involving both monitoring/measurement and control.
Smart grid	Electricity grids have long been used by the power companies to pass low-rate data and commands to their remote substations, switchgear, *etc.* through the power cables. Modern networking technologies, communicating either over the power lines themselves or by some other medium (normally radio, *e.g.* mesh networks), allow greater bandwidths so power companies can extend the reach of their power control into consumer premises, particularly industrial plants, for metering and demand management (*e.g.* shedding non-critical loads such as household and office air conditioners if peak demands or limited supplies threaten to overload the grid). "Electric power system that utilizes information exchange and control technologies, distributed computing and associated sensors and actuators. Note: Smart grid technologies

TERM	MEANING
	are used for purposes such as: integrating the behaviour and actions of the network users and other stakeholders; efficiently delivering sustainable, economic and secure electricity supplies" *(ISO/IEC 27019)*.
Smart home	Residential property that uses home automation, typically involving a **H**ome **A**rea **N**etwork connecting *things* (**S**mart **T**echnologies) monitoring and controlling lights, locks, thermostats, white goods, entertainment, and security systems.
Smart hub	Smart hub interconnects a **H**ome **A**rea **N**etwork to the Internet. While smart home devices and *things* typically use mesh network topologies, a smart hub can provide a focal point for monitoring, management (such as device configuration and patching), and control (*e.g.* a Wi-Fi curfew or prohibition of unsavoury or dangerous domains).
Smart lock	*Thing* that locks a door and can be commanded to open through the network, for instance when the owner's smartphone is detected in the vicinity, or when hacked.
Smart meter	Electricity meter that can be remotely interrogated (for meter readings) and perhaps commanded (*e.g.* switching between charging bands or dis/connecting services), typically through a mesh network. Within a smart home or business, the smart meter may communicate wirelessly with *things* such as smart appliances, typically monitoring and perhaps controlling them for power demand management purposes, raising information security and privacy concerns.
Smartphone	Modern cellphones (cellular telephones) have sophisticated processing capabilities – they are in fact miniature networked computers and cryptographic systems. With powerful processors running multitasking **O**perating **S**ystems such as IOS and Android, solid-state storage, high-resolution touch screens, access to multiple networks, and other technically advanced capabilities such as **G**lobal **P**ositioning **S**ystem, they can run a wide variety of applications … as well as being nifty portable telephones, Internet terminals, and surveillance devices.
Smart plug, smart socket	Power plug or socket *thing* that can be commanded to switch connected equipment on or off through the network, at predefined times, when it gets dark/cold, or when someone is in the room, *etc*.
Smart **T**echnology **(ST)**	**A**rtificial **I**ntelligence concepts, techniques, tools, and approaches involved in smart systems. See also **C**ommunications **T**echnology, **I**nformation **T**echnology, **O**perational **T**echnology, **M**obile **T**echnology, **V**irtual **T**echnology.

TERM	MEANING
Smart thermostat, smart HVAC controller	Controller *thing* monitoring the ambient temperature, humidity, or other parameters relative to setpoints or other criteria, signalling or commanding **H**eating, **V**entilating, and **A**ir-**C**onditioning equipment to operate as appropriate.
Smart worker	More than simply an employee who dresses to impress, achieving this well-informed, highly motivated and alert state among workers is an interim goal of security awareness, training, and educational programs, marking a significant step on the way towards building a security culture that reduces information risks.
SMB	*Abbrev:* **S**erver **M**essage **B**lock or **S**mall- to **M**edium-sized **B**usiness, depending on context.
SMBGhost	Remote code-execution vulnerability in the **S**erver **M**essage **B**lock v3.1.1 protocol.
SME	*Abbrev:* **S**ubject **M**atter **E**xpert (see expert) or **S**mall- to **M**edium-sized **E**nterprise, depending on context.
S/MIME	*Abbrev:* **S**ecure/**M**ultipurpose **I**nternet **M**ail **E**xtensions.
Smoke detector	Device that detects smoke particles in the air, triggering an alert or alarm for the presence of fire. Common types use either an infrared light beam or a small radioactive source for detection – the latter type is more sensitive when new but loses its sensitivity gradually as the source decays and should be replaced every few years. Fire safety experts may advise the use of *both* types, with periodic maintenance and testing.
Smoke test, sanity test	Crude pass/fail test to confirm that a new, modified, or repaired device, system, application, *etc.* will not (figuratively or literally!) release the smoke and expire or 'go nuts' when powered up or executed for the first time, and hence is stable enough for further testing.
SMS, TXT, SMS/TXT	*Abbrev:* **S**imple **M**essaging **S**ervice/**T**e**XT** messaging.
SMTP	*Abbrev:* **S**imple **M**ail **T**ransfer **P**rotocol.
Smurf attack	This early Internet **D**istributed **D**enial-**O**f-**S**ervice technique simply involved spoofing the **I**nternet **P**rotocol address of a target system in ICMP echo request (ping) messages sent to the broadcast addresses for numerous systems which duly sent their ICMP echo replies to the target, potentially overloading it. A type of amplification attack. "Works by spoofing the target address and sending a ping to the broadcast address for a remote network, which results in a large amount of ping replies being sent to the target" *(SANS glossary)*.

TERM	MEANING
SNAFU (Status/Situation Normal: All Fouled Up)	Acronym popular in the US Marine Corp in the second World War. The original version was cruder than 'all fouled up.' Generally refers to incidents arising from errors, mistakes, and accidents.
Snake	Species or family of modular, stealthy **O**perational **T**echnology ransomware allegedly used by FSB for espionage purposes in more than 50 countries in 2023. Evolved over 20 years from Uroburos malware. A very short (128-bit) Diffie–Hellman prime enabled Western state cryptanalysts to reverse-engineer it.
Snake oil	Virtually worthless liquid medicine *allegedly* derived from snakes with magical cure-all properties, sold by charlatans to vulnerable/naïve/desperate customers in the 18th and 19th Centuries. Mobile snake oil salesmen used hard-sell social engineering techniques to fleece customers of their money, moving rapidly on to the next town before victims realised they had been duped. A classic fraud. As with today's homeopathy, any medical effect is probably psychosomatic – the placebo effect.
Sniffer, sniffing, packet analyser, packet analysis	Using networking software or dedicated hardware (such as a network analyser) to passively monitor passing network traffic, *e.g.* using Tcpdump with an Ethernet card in promiscuous mode to capture **P**assword **A**uthentication **P**rotocol messages containing plaintext passwords. "Device or software used to capture information flowing in networks" *(ISO/IEC 27033-1)*. "The act of capturing network packets, including those not necessarily destined for the computer running the sniffing software [and] Programs or hardware that monitor Internet traffic in real time [and] The process by which data traversing a network are captured or monitored" *(ISACA glossary)*. "A synonym for 'passive wiretapping' [and] A tool that monitors network traffic as it [is] received in a network interface" *(SANS glossary)*.
Snitch	See whistleblower.
Snitchline	See whistleblower's hotline.
SNMP	*Abbrev:* **S**imple **N**etwork **M**anagement **P**rotocol.
Snoop, snooper, snooping	Generally a low-grade, crude, amateurish, or inept form of spying such as voyeurism, but sometimes refers to high-grade surveillance by the authorities. Either way, it suggests something illicit, unethical, and somewhat sinister.
Snoopers' charter	See **I**nvestigatory **P**owers **A**ct.
Snort	Open-source software for a **N**etwork **I**ntrusion **D**etection **S**ystem, available in free and commercial versions. With the appropriate rules in place, Snort can detect, alert, and in some cases respond to *thousands* of different network attacks/hacks, worms, *etc.*

TERM	MEANING
Snowshoe spamming	Small-scale spamming, deliberately designed to 'leave a small footprint 'and thereby evade the automated checks that normally catch and quickly block mass spamming. Analogous to spear phishing, it typically involves spamming a relatively small group of targets with carefully crafted custom messages less likely to be flagged as spam.
SOA, SoA	*Abbrev:* **S**ervice-**O**riented **A**rchitecture or **S**tatement **o**f **A**pplicability, depending on context.
SOAP	Datacommunications protocol for applications to exchange XML-formatted structured information over a network. SOAP is transport-independent but commonly uses **H**yper**T**ext **T**ransfer **P**rotocol. Originally known as **S**imple **O**bject **A**ccess **P**rotocol. "A platform-independent formatted protocol based on extensible markup language (XML) enabling applications to communicate with each other over the Internet. Notes: Use of SOAP may provide a significant security risk to web application operations because use of SOAP piggybacks onto a web-based document object model and is transmitted via HyperText Transfer Protocol (HTTP) (port 80) to penetrate server firewalls, which are usually configured to accept port 80 and port 21 File Transfer Protocol (FTP) requests. Web-based document models define how objects on a web page are associated with each other and how they can be manipulated while being sent from a server to a client browser. SOAP typically relies on XML for presentation formatting and also adds appropriate HTTP-based headers to send it. SOAP forms the foundation layer of the web services stack, providing a basic messaging framework on which more abstract layers can build. There are several different types of messaging patterns in SOAP, but by far the most common is the Remote Procedure Call (RPC) pattern in which one network node (the client) sends a request message to another node (the server), and the server immediately sends a response message to the client" *(ISACA glossary)*.
SOAR	*Abbrev:* **S**ecurity **O**rchestration, **A**nalysis and **R**esponse.
SOC, SoC	*Abbrev:* **S**ecurity **O**perations **C**entre, **S**ystem **on** **C**hip, or **S**ystem and **O**rganization **C**ontrol (see SOC 1, SOC 2, SOC 3), depending on context.
SOC 1 (System and Organization Control report № 1)	Report on an outsourced/**C**loud **S**ervice **P**rovider giving information and opinion about its controls relevant to financial reporting, specifically. Provided by **C**ertified **P**ublic **A**ccountants accredited by the **A**merican **I**nstitute of **C**ertified **P**ublic **A**ccountants. Superseded SAS 70. Requirements are defined in SSAE 18.

TERM	MEANING
SOC 2 (System and Organization Control report № 2)	Prescriptive cybersecurity controls assurance standard for outsourced/**C**loud **S**ervice **P**roviders from the **A**merican **I**nstitute of **C**ertified **P**ublic **A**ccountants. Concerns controls *other* than those relating to financial reporting, across up to five **T**rust **S**ervice **C**riteria: security (general controls over access, *etc.*, included in all SOC 2 reports) plus availability, processing integrity, confidentiality, and privacy (each included only if applicable). May identify reliance on subcontractors' and customers' controls to achieve the required security. A SOC 2 Type 1 report concerns the organisation's conformity with the requirements at a single point in time, a snapshot of the controls in place. A SOC 2 Type 2 report extends the timeline, assessing the operation of the controls over at least three months. Requirements are defined in SSAE 18, SSAE 20, and SSAE 21.
SOC 2 engagement	SOC 2 engagement. "An examination engagement to report on the fairness of the presentation of management's description of the service organization's system, the suitability of the design of the controls included in the description, and, in a type 2 engagement, the operating effectiveness of those controls. This engagement is performed in accordance with the attestation standards and AICPA Guide SOC 2® Reporting on an Examination of Controls at a Service Organization: Relevant to Security, Availability, Processing Integrity, Confidentiality, or Privacy" *(**T**rust **S**ervices **C**riteria)*.
SOC 3 (System and Organization Control report № 3)	Non-sensitive *summary* of a SOC 2 report, intended for public release (*e.g.* through a service provider's website).
SOC 3 engagement	SOC 3 engagement. "An examination engagement to report on the suitability of design and the operating effectiveness of an entity's controls over a system relevant to one or more of the trust services categories" *(**T**rust **S**ervices **C**riteria)*.
SOC for Cybersecurity examination	"An examination engagement to report on whether (a) management's description of the entity's cybersecurity risk management program is presented in accordance with the description criteria and (b) the controls within that program were effective to achieve the entity's cybersecurity objectives based on the control criteria. A SOC for Cybersecurity examination is performed in accordance with the attestation standards and AICPA Guide Reporting on an Entity's Cybersecurity Risk Management Program and Controls" *(**T**rust **S**ervices **C**riteria)*.

TERM	MEANING
SOC for Supply Chain examination	"An examination engagement to report on whether (a) the description of the entity's system is presented in accordance with the description criteria and (b) the controls stated in the description, which are necessary to provide reasonable assurance that the entity achieved its principal system objectives, were effective based on the applicable trust services criteria. Such an examination is based on guidance contained in AICPA Guide SOC for Supply Chain: Reporting on an Examination of Controls Relevant to Security, Availability, Processing Integrity, Confidentiality, or Privacy in a Production, Manufacturing, or Distribution System" *(Trust Services Criteria)*.
Social contract	Refers to unwritten understandings, ethical expectations, and commitments or undertakings between the parties, *e.g.* between employees and employers, business partners, suppliers and customers, or politicians and the electorate.
Social engineering, social hacking, cognitive hacking	Hacking/scamming/fraud techniques involving the manipulation of people through a combination of deception (such as pretexting, masquerading, misinformation, and narratives) and persuasive, coercive, or assertive behaviour (such as 'bravado' and manipulative psychological tricks), typically leading to them revealing or permitting unauthorised access to sensitive information. "A general term for attackers trying to trick people into revealing sensitive information or performing certain actions, such as downloading and executing files that appear to be benign but are actually malicious" *(NIST SP 800-114)*. "An attack based on deceiving users or administrators at the target site into revealing confidential or sensitive information" *(ISACA glossary)*. "Involves manipulation of specific individuals to extract important information, such as passwords or personal data, from an organisation, for example, through impersonation" *(UK Cyber Security Breaches Survey 2023)*. "Refers to a broad range of malicious activities accomplished through human interactions on various platforms, such as email or phone. It relies on psychological manipulation to trick users into making security mistakes or giving away sensitive information" *(CIS Controls)*. "A euphemism for non-technical or low-technology means – such as lies, impersonation, tricks, bribes, blackmail, and threats – used to attack information systems" *(SANS glossary)*.
Social identity, social ID	Social media applications and functions (such as those allowing visitors to comment on news items, blogs, *etc.* or review products) often invite users to identify and authenticate themselves using their Facebook, Twitter, Google, or LinkedIn accounts (their 'social identities' or 'socials'), provided the users are willing for those social media sites to disclose selected personal information to the social media apps and functions. This **S**ingle **S**ign **O**n approach avoids users having to register separately in each case but raises privacy concerns.

TERM	MEANING
Social insecurity	Neologism refers to information security and privacy risks, controls, and incidents directly involving human factors and affecting people, including insecurity, social engineering, scams, frauds, social media, social networking, social proofing, blended attacks, phishing, spear phishing, pretexting, coercion, spoofing, and masquerading.
Social media	Interactive websites and applications (such as Facebook, Tumblr, LinkedIn, Twitter, Blogger, Myspace, YouTube, blogs, and discussion forums) that facilitate social networking and personal interaction, both benign and malicious.
Social network	Community of people, organisations, *etc.* with common interests, connected by personal interactions and mutual contacts through social media, messaging, email, *etc.* We tend to drop our guards in relaxed social situations, typically trusting people and often revealing information and accepting things at face value, increasing our vulnerability to social engineering. Conversely, when needed, friends and acquaintances can provide valuable guidance and support.
Social proofing, group affirmation, group-think	People in tight-knit social groups tend to believe in, trust, and respect similar things. Therefore, if a friend (or someone who has stolen a friend's ID) recommends a link or an application, naïve users are inclined to load it without necessarily considering the risks of malware, fraud, *etc.* Misunderstandings, misinterpretations, misinformation, and disinformation can 'infect' (spread through) a social network, particularly if members are not adept at critical thinking.
Social protection	"Preventing, managing and overcoming situations that adversely affect people's well-being. Note: It consists of policies and programmes designed to reduce poverty and vulnerability by promoting efficient labour markets, diminishing people's exposure to risks, and enhancing their capacity to manage economic and social risks, such as unemployment, exclusion, sickness, disability and old age" *(ISO 22300)*.
Sockpuppet	Fake online identity, used by social engineers to deceive and manipulate targets.
Sodinokibi, REvil	Family of ransomware in the wild in 2019 and 2020. Responsible for the Travelex incident. Encrypts certain file types on a Windows system, then demands a ransom payment to decrypt them, with an escalating charge if the victim delays. Can also exfiltrate data. The code bears similarities to the GandCrab malware.
SOE	*Abbrev:* **S**tandard **O**perating **E**nvironment.

TERM	MEANING
Soft computing	"Field of computing that is tolerant of and exploits imprecision, uncertainty and partial truth to make problem-solving more tractable and robust. Note: Soft computing encompasses various techniques such as fuzzy logic, machine learning and probabilistic reasoning" *(ISO/IEC 22989)*.
Soft error, transient error	"Error that occurs sporadically and that may not appear on successive attempts to read data" *(ISO/IEC 2382)*.
Softphone	See **V**oice **O**ver **I**nternet **P**rotocol. "A software application that allows a workstation to act as a VoIP phone, using either a built-in or an externally connected microphone and speaker" *(NZISM)*. "An application that allows a workstation to act as a phone using a built-in or externally-connected microphone and speaker" *(AusISM)*.
Software	One or more computer programs. "All or part of the programs, procedures, rules, and associated documentation of an information processing system. Note: Software is an intellectual creation that is independent of the medium on which it is recorded" *(ISO/IEC 2382)*. "Programs, procedures, rules and any associated documentation pertaining to the operation of a system. It contrasts with hardware" *(ISACA glossary)*. "An element of a system including, but not limited to, an application or operating system" *(AusISM)*. "The part of an electronic information system which consists of computer code" *(EU CRA)*. "Computer programs (which are stored in and executed by computer hardware) and associated data (which also is stored in the hardware) that may be dynamically written or modified during execution" *(SANS glossary)*. *Cf.* hardware, firmware, middleware, data, wetware, malware, ransomware, adware, crimeware, scareware, shelfware, spouseware, stalkerware, spyware.
Software-**as**-**a**-**S**ervice **(SaaS)**	Cloud computing services model providing customers with access to Internet-based applications. The **C**loud **S**ervice **P**rovider's responsibilities, including the information security aspects, cover almost the entire service provision on the server/s up to the network port. "Offers the capability to use the provider's applications running on cloud infrastructure. The applications are accessible from various client devices through a thin client interface, such as a web browser (*e.g.,* web-based email)" *(ISACA glossary)*. "A software distribution model in which a cloud provider hosts applications and makes them available to end users over the internet" *(UK Cyber Security Breaches Survey 2023)*. See also **I**nfrastructure-**as**-**a**-**S**ervice, **P**latform-**as**-**a**-**S**ervice.
Software asset	Software asset. "Also referred to as software in this document, these are the programs and other operating information used within an enterprise asset. Software assets include operating systems and applications" *(CIS Controls)*.

TERM	MEANING
Software **B**ill **o**f **M**aterials **(SBoM, SBOM)**	Compilation of comprehensive, up-to-data information about the: tools; software subunits, libraries and functions; services; hardware; and firmware, that go into developing software. If any of the processes (*e.g.* assembling **P**rinted **C**ircuit **B**oards) or components is substantially compromised (*e.g.* by exploiting a zero-day vulnerability in a ubiquitous product such as Log4j), dependent products are untrustworthy. SBoM allows them, and the associated information risks, to be more readily identified. "Inventory of software components, sub-components and dependencies with associated information" *(ISO/IEC 27036-3)*. "A formal record containing details and supply chain relationships of components included in the software elements of a product with digital elements" *(EU CRA)*. See also **S**oftware **C**omposition **A**nalysis.
Software component	Software component. "An element of a system, including but not limited to, a database, operating system, network or Web application" *(NZISM)*.
Software **C**omposition **A**nalysis **(SCA)**	Painstaking process of systematically identifying open-source or proprietary modules, libraries, functions, *etc.* within or called by application programs, facilitating licence and vulnerability management. See also **S**oftware **B**ill **o**f **M**aterials.
Software-**D**efined **D**ata **C**entre **(SDDC)**, **V**irtual **D**ata **C**entre **(VDC)**	Assembly of virtual computers and services in the cloud using hardware platforms owned either by the organisation or by third parties. Has all the advantages *and* disadvantages of cloud architectures.
Software-**D**efined **N**etwork **(SDN)**	Virtual networking in which virtualisation software provides an abstraction layer mediating between real or virtual systems, applications, and storage, and real networks.
Software developer, software engineer, programmer	Individual, team, or organisation creating/modifying software by writing/amending program source code. Often but not necessarily a competent, qualified, and experienced professional (*e.g.* citizen programmer).
Software development [process], programming	Process of creating or modifying software by writing/amending program source code. Some consider similar but simpler activities such as developing scripts and spreadsheet macros, loading model files and parameters into **C**omputer **N**umerically **C**ontrolled machine tools, and crafting **A**rtificial **I**ntelligence/**L**arge **L**anguage **M**odel prompts, to be programming. Technically speaking, even writing this hyperglossary qualifies as programming since, when processed by various software programs, the document data file determines what we read. "The process by which user needs are translated into a software product. The process involves translating user needs into software requirements, transforming the software requirements into design, implementing the design in code, testing

TERM	MEANING
	the code and sometimes installing and reviewing the software for operational activities. Note that these activities may overlap or be performed iteratively" *(ISACA glossary)*. See also **N**euro-**L**inguistic **P**rogramming and **N**atural **L**anguage **P**rogramming.
Software **D**evelopment **L**ife**C**ycle **(SDLC), system development lifecycle, system lifecycle**	Entire cradle-to-grave sequence (lifecycle) or process through which a software application or system is conceived, specified, developed, tested, implemented, operated, managed, maintained, and eventually retired or withdrawn from service.
Software documentation	All or part of the documentation relating to software including software-based information/cloud services, *e.g.* requirement specifications, marketing collateral; licences and contracts; architectural designs and **D**ata **F**low **D**iagrams; source code listings and comments; test cases, findings/results, and reports; installation, configuration, user and technical support manuals; on-screen informational, error, warning, alert, and alarm messages. "Human-readable technical data or information, including computer listings and printouts, that describe or specify design features or other details, explain capabilities, or provide operating instructions to help users obtain desired results from a software system. [and] Technical data or information, including computer listings and printouts in human-readable form, that describe or specify the design or details, explain the capabilities or provide operating instructions for using the software to obtain desired results from a software system. Types of software documentation include: Project planning documents, *i.e.,* software development plans and software verification and validation (V&V) plans; Software requirements and design specifications; Test documentation; Customer-deliverable documentation; Program source code; Representation of software solutions implemented in firmware; Reports, *e.g.,* review, audit and project status; Data, *i.e.,* defect detection and test; It contrasts with software item" *(ISACA glossary)*.
Software engineer	See software developer.
Software engineering, systems engineering	Formal, structured, systematic, rigorous, and professional approach to software system/product development, using engineering principles and disciplines, *e.g.* investing in the analysis necessary to prepare detailed and comprehensive design specifications truly reflecting stakeholders' goals and objectives, before moving too far ahead. "Systematic application of scientific and technological knowledge, methods, and experience to the design, implementation, testing, and documentation of software to optimize its production, support, and quality" *(ISO/IEC 2382)*. "The application of a systematic, disciplined, quantifiable approach to the development, operation and maintenance of software, *i.e.,* the application of engineering to software" *(ISACA glossary)*. See also systems security engineering.

TERM	MEANING
Software piracy	Software piracy. "Unauthorized use, copying, or distribution of software products" *(ISO/IEC 2382)*.
Software reliability	Indicator of the extent to which software can be relied upon (trusted) to perform according to its formal specifications, normally as demonstrated by several types of testing and analysis. Reliability, availability, resilience, capacity, performance, assurance, and other requirements relate to the impacts of software/system failure, and have significant implications for the software engineering, architecture, and build quality. Even *if* the specifications are accurate and comprehensive, reliability actually achieved in practice, however, varies with complex dynamic operational factors such as: the maturity and stability of the processing platform and any required system or network services; software configuration, loading, usage, management, and maintenance (*e.g.* changes); competition for scarce resources; the possibility of multiple failure modes and recovery approaches; and the nature of threats experienced. "1. The probability that software will not cause the failure of a system for a specified time under specified conditions. The probability is a function of the inputs to and use of the system in the software. The inputs to the system determine whether existing faults, if any, are encountered. 2. The ability of a program to perform its required functions accurately and reproducibly under stated conditions for a specified period of time" *(ISACA glossary)*.
Solar flare	Eruption of intensely energetic particles from the sun that can bombard the Earth, affecting the Earth's magnetosphere and ionosphere, possibly unsettling electrical power grids plus wired and wireless communications and damaging delicate electronics, particularly on orbiting satellites (such as those providing **G**lobal **P**ositioning **S**ystem) and high-altitude aircraft. The frequency and intensity of flares, and hence the threat, correlate with the number of sunspots which peaks every 11 years or so, most recently in 2025.
SolarWinds, Sunburst	American software company's 'Orion' remote-access network monitoring software was hacked by Cozy Bear/APT29, a unit of the Russian foreign intelligence service (SVR) in 2020. A **S**erver **M**essage **B**lock exploit enabled the malware to spread laterally following initial infection. Subsequently, the company unknowingly distributed malware to 18,000 customers including 9 US federal agencies and hundreds of US companies that were specifically targeted, including FireEye, a US cybersecurity company. A classic example of a supply chain cyberattack.
Solid-state drive	"Non-volatile media that uses flash memory media to retain its information when power is removed" *(NZISM)*. "Non-volatile media that uses non-volatile flash memory media to retain its data when power is removed and, unlike non-volatile magnetic media, contains no moving parts" *(AusISM)*.

TERM	MEANING
Solution	a. Solute dissolved in solvent. b. The literal or philosophical answer to a problem such as 1 + 1 = ? or how to achieve happiness and contentment. c. The customer outcome and value implied by a commercial product's glossy advertisements, coupled with the supplier's brands and reputation. "A product, product component, service, service system, service system component or delivered or acquired product or service including relevant safety or security components" *(ISACA glossary)*.
Sony hack	Major information security incident at the end of 2014 affecting Sony Pictures Entertainment. Malicious hackers allegedly working for the North Vietnamese government compromised Sony's corporate network, stealing a large quantity of sensitive proprietary and personal information over several months which they then used to extort Sony by disclosing some (creating a media storm) and threatening to disclose more embarrassing and damaging content. Presumably in an effort to cover their tracks (scorched earth), the hackers also unleashed a network worm that displayed a scary graphic and threatening messages on desktop PC screens, destroyed data, and took critical Information Technology systems out of service for months, massively disrupting Sony's business activities and causing serious commercial, legal, and brand impacts.
SOP	*Abbrev:* **S**tandard **O**perating **P**rocedure.
Soraya	Species of memory-scraping malware.
Source	Whistleblower, spy, informant, defector, *etc.* who discreetly discloses sensitive information or facilitates its acquisition by an intelligence agency (HUMINT) or a technological equivalent (TECHINT).
Source available	Some software owners are willing to disclose their source code to specific third parties, usually in confidence (*e.g.* after entering into a nondisclosure agreement), in order for them to be able to check the design, functionality, quality, supportability, security, *etc.*
Source code	Lines in a human-readable computer programming language comprising a program for a software application, function, system, utility, *etc.* A type of code. Source code is compiled or interpreted into the low-level machine code instructions understood by the **C**entral **P**rocessing **U**nit. "Code expressed in a form suitable for input to an assembler, compiler, or other translator" *(ISO/IEC 2382)*. "Computer instructions and data definitions documented in a form suitable for input to an assembler, compiler or other translator" *(ISACA glossary)*. "Character or bit pattern that is assigned a particular meaning to express a computer program in a programming language. Notes: Source codes are instructions and data definitions expressed

TERM	MEANING
	in a form suitable for input to an assembler, compiler, or other translator. Coding is the process of expressing logic and data from design specifications or descriptions into a programming language. A programming language is a language used to express computer programs" *(IEC 62628)*. See also assembly language.
Source code escrow	Escrow of program source code, enabling it to be released to users/customers, *etc.* under specific conditions, *e.g.* if the developer dies, the team breaks up, the company ceases trading or for some other reason is unwilling or unable to continue supporting and maintaining the software.
SP 800 series	See NIST SP 800 series.
Spaghetti code	a. Convoluted, tangled, messy, unstructured, incoherent, opaque, and hence virtually unmaintainable source code more likely than most to contain design flaws and programming bugs. "Program source code written without a coherent structure. It implies the excessive use of GOTO instructions and contrasts with structured programming" *(ISACA glossary)*. b. Deliberately obfuscated malware, security, or other software, intended to resist reverse engineering, protect Intellectual Property and commercial interests (*e.g.* costly support contracts), and/or conceal nefarious functions such as backdoors or fraud. c. Software written by Italian developers.
Spam, Unsolicited Bulk Email (UBE)	Advertisements pumped out by some low-life scammer or naïve/overzealous/unethical marketer taking advantage of the negligible costs of emails and contact lists. "Unsolicited emails, which can carry malicious contents and/or scam messages. Note: While the most widely recognized form of spam is e-mail spam, the term is applied to similar abuses in other media: instant messaging spam, Usenet newsgroup spam, Web search engine spam, spam in blogs, wiki spam, mobile phone messaging spam, Internet forum spam and junk fax transmissions" *(ISO/IEC 27032)*. "Computer-generated messages sent as unsolicited advertising" *(ISACA glossary)*. "Electronic junk mail or junk newsgroup postings" *(SANS glossary)*. Note: SPAM in capitals shouts the trademarked name of a pink spiced ham product made infamous by a 1970's Monty Python sketch. See also SPIM.
Spam bomb	See email bomb.
Spambot	Robotic program that systematically harvests email addresses from the web and/or sends spam. Typically, part of a botnet.
Spamtrap	Honeypot system designed to improve anti-spam controls by luring, monitoring, logging, capturing, analysing, and/or characterising spam messages.

TERM	MEANING
Speak Up	Species of malware (a backdoor Trojan) in the wild in 2019. Installed a cryptominer on Linux systems.
Spear phishing	Narrowly targeted phishing attack that uses information about or of direct interest to specific target individuals as a pretext to establish contact and false credibility with them, thereby increasing the scammers' chances of success. "An attack designed to entice specific individuals or groups to reveal important information. Social engineering techniques are used to masquerade as a trusted party to obtain important information, such as passwords from the victim" *(ISACA glossary)*.
Special **A**ccess **P**rogram **(SAP)**	"Sensitive acquisition, intelligence, or operations and support program, that imposes need-to-know and access controls beyond those normally provided for access to confidential, secret, or top secret information" *(DoD dictionary)*.
Special audit, special investigation, forensic audit	Narrowly scoped audit investigating a significant and specific concern, suspicion, or credible report of impropriety. Exceptional, not part of the routine audit schedule. Discretion and rapidity are often necessary, particularly if there has been an allegation of fraud, embezzlement, collusion, or other illegality, in order to gather and secure forensic evidence that might otherwise be concealed, destroyed, or spoiled.
Special collection	**C**entral **I**ntelligence **A**gency term for surveillance that would require a warrant if performed within the US for law enforcement … but not when performed overseas, nor if it would be permitted domestically for other purposes (such as counterterrorism or national defence) or for testing/training, nor if conducted by other agencies (such as the **F**ederal **B**ureau of **I**nvestigation or Five Eyes) at the CIA's request, perhaps using information and tools (*i.e.* surveillance capabilities and tradecraft) furnished by the CIA. This level of access is indeed 'special,' as in exceptional. See also basic collection, standard collection.
Special **I**ntelligence **S**ervice **(SIS)**	Covert counterintelligence unit of the **F**ederal **B**ureau of **I**nvestigation, mostly hunting Nazi spies in South America during World War II. Subsumed into the **C**entral **I**ntelligence **A**gency. *Cf.* UK **S**ecret **I**ntelligence **S**ervice.
Special investigation	See special audit.
Species	By analogy to living organisms, malware is rapidly 'evolving.' Several distinct 'families' of malware are known, containing one or more 'species' often with multiple 'variants' or 'mutants' – *millions* of them in the case of highly polymorphic or heavily obfuscated types.

TERM	MEANING
Specification	Precise, detailed description of requirements. "Detailed formulation, in document form, which provides a definitive description of a system for the purpose of developing or validating the system" *(ISO/IEC 2382)*.
Spectre, Meltdown, Chipzilla, Foreshadow, Fallout, Retbleed	Design flaws in some **C**entral **P**rocessing **U**nit chips relating to pre-emptive execution allows malicious user-mode programs to read and perhaps modify memory supposedly reserved for trusted functions, thereby negating a fundamental low-level security control critical to protecting the **O**perating **S**ystem. Although OSs can be patched as a workaround (at the cost of slower execution), malware probably exists to exploit unpatched systems. See also ZombieLoad.
Speech recognition, **S**peech-**T**o-**T**ext **(STT)**	"Conversion, by a functional unit, of a speech signal to a representation of the content of the speech" *(ISO/IEC 22989)*.
Speech synthesis, **T**ext-**T**o-**S**peech **(TTS)**	"Generation of artificial speech" *(ISO/IEC 22989)*.
SPF	*Abbrev:* **S**ender **P**olicy **F**ramework.
Spike	Momentary/transient peak in the supply voltage, typically caused by switching heavy inductive loads such as large motors on the same circuit, or a lightning strike on or near the power cables and electrical/electronic devices. May overload and cause unreliability or premature failure of sensitive electronics having inadequate voltage regulation or protection such as **M**etal **O**xide **V**aristors. See also surge, dip, brownout, blackout, **E**lectro**M**agnetic **P**ulse.
Spikes	Physical security control consisting of upward-pointing sharpened strong steel rods or similar, normally firmly fixed to the top of a wall or fence or implanted in the ground (sometimes on hinged plates allowing vehicles to pass safely in one direction) to deter or prevent intrusion.
[Data] Spill	Incident involving the unauthorised accidental leak or deliberate transmission or exfiltration of classified information to a system, network, or some other recipient classified to a lower level, perhaps unclassified.
SPIM (SPam via IM)	Spam sent over **I**nstant **M**essaging, a term allegedly created by the marketing departments of certain antivirus/anti-spam companies desperate to sell their services to naïve IM users.
Split key	"A cryptographic key that is divided into two or more separate data items that individually convey no knowledge of the whole key that results from combining the items" *(SANS glossary)*.

TERM	MEANING
Split knowledge	Application of the principle of division of responsibility whereby critical information (such as a trade secret, PIN code, or cryptographic key) is deliberately divided among multiple people, systems, *etc.* who are required to keep their parts confidential so that that none of them alone holds the complete picture. "A security technique in which two or more entities separately hold data items that individually convey no knowledge of the information that results from combining the items. This is a condition under which two or more entities separately have key components that individually convey no knowledge of the plaintext key that will be produced when the key components are combined in the cryptographic module" *(ISACA glossary)*. "1. Separation of data or information into two or more parts, each part constantly kept under control of separate authorized individuals or teams so that no one individual or team will know the whole data. 2. A process by which a cryptographic key is split into multiple key components, individually sharing no knowledge of the original key, which can be subsequently input into, or output from, a cryptographic module by separate entities and combined to recreate the original cryptographic key" *(CNSSI 4009)*.
Split tunnelling	Capability to pass specific network traffic through a **V**irtual **P**rivate **N**etwork tunnel for security reasons, while allowing other/general traffic to traverse the network directly but insecurely, typically for network performance and efficiency reasons. "The process of allowing a remote user or device to establish a non-remote connection with a system and simultaneously communicate via some other connection to a resource in an external network. This method of network access enables a user to access remote devices, and simultaneously, access uncontrolled networks" *(NZISM)*. "Functionality that allows personnel to access both public network infrastructure and a Virtual Private Network connection at the same time, such as an organisation's system and the internet" *(AusISM)*. See also VPN split tunnelling
Sploit	Leet/hacker slang for exploit.
Splunk	Commercial application for analysing logs.
SPoF	*Abbrev:* **S**ingle **P**oint **o**f **F**ailure.
SPOKE	Obsolete and deprecated US **S**pecial **I**ntelligence **S**ervice term for COMINT. See also UMBRA, MORAY.
Spoliation	Deliberate (malicious) or accidental (benign) spoilage (*i.e.* destruction, discrediting, or otherwise devaluing) of forensic evidence. "Act of making or allowing a change to Electronically Stored Information where there is a requirement to keep it intact. Note: Spoliation can take the form of ESI destruction, corruption, or alteration of the ESI or associated metadata as well as rendering

TERM	MEANING
	ESI unavailable (*e.g.*, due to encryption with no access to the decryption key, loss of media, under the control of a third party, *etc.*)" *(ISO/IEC 27050-1)*. "Act of making or allowing change(s) to the potential digital evidence that diminishes its evidential value" *(ISO/IEC 27037)*.
Sponge function	Family of cryptographic algorithms that can generate an arbitrary length output string from an arbitrary length input string, using defined internal states, transformation, and padding. Has applications in hashing, stream ciphers, and pseudorandom number generation.
Spoof, spoofing	Deliberate faking or falsification of identity information in systems, networks, or protocols that lack adequate authentication controls, *e.g.* email addresses, caller ID numbers, IP and MAC addresses. Typically used to conceal the perpetrator's true identity, bypass simplistic identity-based access controls, socially engineer a target, commit fraud or hack. "Take action intended to deceive a user, an observer (such as an eavesdropper), or a resource" *(ISO/IEC 2382)*. "Impersonating a legitimate resource or user" *(ISO/IEC 27033-1)*. "The act of faking the sending address of a transmission in order to gain illegal entry into a secure system" *(ISACA glossary)*. "Attempt by an unauthorized entity to gain access to a system by posing as an authorized user" *(SANS glossary)*. See also masquerade.
Spook, spooky	Deliberately vague, tongue-in-cheek yet somewhat sinister reference to someone who appears to be part of the intelligence community, *i.e.* a spy, agent, intelligence operative, source, collector, *etc.* working for or on behalf of one or more government agencies. See also cyber spook.
Spouseware	Neologism for spyware used by one partner in a personal relationship to spy on (typically track and monitor) another, having exploited opportunities to infect the partner's Information Technology systems. See also malware, ransomware, adware, crimeware, scareware, stalkerware.
Spora	Species of ransomware in the wild since 2017.
Spread spectrum	Radio communications technique involving the transmission of (usually covert) messages across a range of frequencies simultaneously, reducing the possibility of an unauthorised interceptor identifying the transmission and ascertaining the information content, and accidental or deliberate interference (jamming) corrupting the information. "Telecommunications techniques in which a signal is transmitted in a bandwidth considerably greater than the frequency content of the original information. Frequency-hopping, direct sequence spreading, time scrambling, and combinations of these techniques are forms of spread spectrum" *(CNSSI 4009)*.

TERM	MEANING
Spy	Secret agent working undercover to gather intelligence, usually for commercial (industrial or economic espionage) or national security purposes. See also spook.
Spying, espionage, counterintelligence	Covertly selecting, collecting, and analysing intelligence, typically for commercial and/or national security/military purposes but sometimes for personal reasons, *e.g.* to sell to an information broker or to exploit through social engineering, fraud, hacking, blackmail, *etc.*
Spyware	Category of malware used to spy on victims through their **I**nformation **T**echnology devices, *e.g.* covertly sending information about the programs executed, websites visited, or data submitted, to a remote system or hacker. May involve surreptitious access to the microphone, camera, and/or keyboard. "Deceptive software, that collects private or confidential information from a computer user. Note: Information can include matters such as websites most frequently visited or more sensitive information such as passwords" *(ISO/IEC 27032)*. "Software whose purpose is to monitor a computer user's actions (*e.g.,* websites visited) and report these actions to a third party without the informed consent of that machine's owner or legitimate user" *(ISACA glossary)*. See also spouseware, stalkerware.
SQL injection **(SQLi)**	Versatile, effective, and hence very common means of hacking vulnerable **D**ata**B**ase applications involving the entry of malicious SQL commands through interfaces that were naïvely anticipated by the system owners, designers, and developers only to pass legitimate, benign data, not program instructions and privileged DB commands. A form of code injection. "A type of input validation attack specific to database-driven applications where SQL code is inserted into application queries to manipulate the database" *(SANS glossary)*.
SRTP	*Abbrev:* **S**ecure **R**eal-time **T**ransport **P**rotocol.
SSAE 16 (Statements on Standards for Attestation Engagements № 16)	**A**merican **I**nstitute of **C**ertified **P**ublic **A**ccountants**'** standard "Reporting on Controls at a Service Organization," released in 2010. Superseded by SSAE 18.
SSAE 18 (Statements on Standards for Attestation Engagements № 18)	**A**merican **I**nstitute of **C**ertified **P**ublic **A**ccountants**'** standard "Attestation Standards: Clarification and Recodification" specifies SOC 1 and SOC 2 audit reports and attestations concerning an outsourced/**C**loud **S**ervice **P**rovider's financial and non-financial controls, respectively.
SSAE 20 (Statement on Standards for Attestation Engagements № 20)	**A**merican **I**nstitute of **C**ertified **P**ublic **A**ccountants**'** standard "Amendments to the description of the concept of materiality" slightly amends the wording of SSAE 18.

TERM	MEANING
SSAE 21 (Statement on Standards for Attestation Engagements № 21)	American Institute of Certified Public Accountants' standard "Direct Examination Engagements" substantially amends the wording of SSAE 18.
SSCP	*Abbrev:* **S**ystems **S**ecurity **C**ertified **P**ractitioner.
SSDF	*Abbrev:* **S**ecure **S**oftware **D**evelopment **F**ramework.
SSH	*Abbrev:* **S**ecure **SH**ell.
SSH-agent	Application that holds private keys for SSH-based authentication in memory, responding to authentication requests on behalf of the user without exposing the keys to the client applications directly. "A programme storing private keys used for public key authentication thus enabling an automated or script-based Secure Shell session" *(NZISM)*.
SSID	*Abbrev:* **S**ervice **S**et **ID**entifier.
SSL	*Abbrev:* **S**ecure **S**ockets **L**ayer.
SSO	*Abbrev:* **S**ingle **S**ign **O**n or **S**ystem **S**ecurity **O**fficer, depending on context.
SSVC	*Abbrev:* **S**takeholder-**S**pecific **V**ulnerability **C**ategorisation.
ST	*Abbrev:* **S**ecurity **T**arget.
Stack	Small areas of memory, managed by the **O**perating **S**ystem, containing code, pointers, and variables sequentially placed on and retrieved from the stack by programs. See also heap, network stack.
Stack overflow, stack smashing	Class of software vulnerability similar to buffer overflow in which programs exceed the allocated bounds of the stack (*e.g.* due to excessively numerous or large variables having been saved to the stack), leading to the unauthorised execution of code inserted by a hacker or malware. "The technique of using a buffer overflow to trick a computer into executing arbitrary code" *(SANS glossary)*. See also heap overflow.
Staff, team member	"Junior-level personnel who typically do not manage others" *(OCEG GRC Glossary)*. *Cf.* worker.
Stage 1 audit, pre-audit	Relatively brief and high-level preliminary assessment of an organisation's readiness for the stage 2 audit due a month or two later. A chance for the auditor/s to meet their main auditee/s and prepare both themselves and the client for the formalities ahead.
Stage 2 audit	Formal main part of a certification audit.

TERM	MEANING
Stagefright	Exploit for old unpatched versions of Android, arising from a buffer overflow bug in an **O**perating **S**ystem library used to process video files. A malware-infected video message sent to a vulnerable mobile device may be preprocessed and compromise the device on receipt, before the user even has the chance to open, check, or delete it.
Stakeholder	Person or organisation with a stake – a material interest – in something, such as the owners, managers, workers, suppliers, customers, partners/associates, or regulators of an organisation, investment, infrastructure, information, *etc.* "Any individual, group, or organization that can affect, be affected by or perceive itself to be affected by a decision or activity" *(ISO/IEC 22989)*. "Individual or organization with interest in an asset in the supplier relationship. Note: For the purpose of this International Standard, an asset is information associated with products and services" *(ISO/IEC 27036-1)*. "Anyone who has a responsibility for, an expectation of or some other interest in an enterprise" *(ISACA glossary)*. "A self-legitimizing person, group, or other entity with a direct or indirect stake in the organization's actions because of actual or perceived impact" *(OCEG GRC Glossary)*. "Parties that are affected by the entity, such as shareholders, the communities in which an entity operates, employees, customers, and suppliers" *(**T**rust **S**ervices **C**riteria)*. "A party with a direct or indirect interest in an organization's activities and outcomes. Stakeholders may include the board, management, employees, customers, vendors, shareholders, regulatory agencies, financial institutions, external auditors, the public, and others" *(IIA GIAS)*.
Stakeholder expectation (or want or need)	"A general term that refers to what a stakeholder requests, wants, or expects from the organization" *(OCEG GRC Glossary)*.
Stakeholder-**S**pecific **V**ulnerability **C**ategorisation **(SSVC)**	Approach created by **C**arnegie **M**ellon **U**niversity's renowned **S**oftware **E**ngineering **I**nstitute uses decision trees to rank/prioritise vulnerabilities. *Cf.* **C**ommon **V**ulnerability **S**coring **S**ystem.
Stalkerware, creepware	Neologism for surreptitious and creepy mobile device spyware potentially used by stalkers to spy on, track, monitor, and harass their marks/targets/victims. See also malware, ransomware, adware, crimeware, scareware, spouseware.
STAMP/STPA/CAST (Systems-Theoretic Accident Model and Processes/ Systems-Theoretic Process Analysis/Causal Analysis based on Stamp)	Analytical approach developed by Nancy Leveson of MIT to engineer safer systems, plus accompanying processes for analysing the causes of accidents. Has potential in information security.

TERM	MEANING
Stampado	Species of ransomware offering basic functions. Was readily available on the Darknet.
Standard	a. Conventional, default, normal, not fancy, or exceptional. Widely acknowledged, respected, accepted, and used. Commonplace. b. Documented, formal specification, or description of something conventional. May be published and publicly available or internal/proprietary to an organisation. "A mandatory requirement, code of practice or specification approved by a recognized external standards organization, such as the International Organization for Standardization (ISO)" *(ISACA glossary)*. See also security standard, security implementation standard.
Standard collection	**C**entral **I**ntelligence **A**gency term for surveillance obtained neither by basic collection (**O**pen-**S**ource **Int**elligence) nor by special collection, such as "requesting another government agency to provide their records about a United States person, asking a current CIA asset about the activities of a United States person living in a foreign country, or asking a foreign government for information about the same person" *(CIA Updated Executive Order 12333 Attorney General Guidelines)*.
Standard deletion period	"Unified deletion periods for the personally identifiable information PII controller. Note: A standard deletion period is a deletion period used for several clusters of PII to standardize several deletion periods lying close to one another" *(ISO/IEC 27555)*.
Standard **O**perating **E**nvironment **(SOE)**	"A standardised build of an operating system and associated software that is deployed on multiple devices. A SOE can be applied to servers, workstations, laptops and mobile devices" *(NZISM)*. "Instructions for following a defined set of activities in a specific manner. For example, an approved data transfer process" *(AusISM)*.
Standard **O**perating **P**rocedure **(SOP)**	See procedure. "Written procedures that prescribe and describe the steps to be taken in normal and defined conditions and that are necessary to ensure control of production and processes" *(ISACA glossary)*. "Instructions for the operation of a system and complying with security requirements" *(NZISM)*. "A written procedure that describes how certain examination or test activities are carried out in a given forensic unit" *(FSRCoP)*.
Standard user account	Normal userID lacking the powerful privileges needed for system administration, hence lower risk if compromised. "A user account with limited privileges that will be used for general tasks such as reading email and surfing the web" *(NIST SP 800-114)*.

TERM	MEANING
Standing data, static data	Reference items or fields that are static and unchanging (*e.g.* bank account numbers) relative to volatile or dynamic user data (*e.g.* current account balances). "Permanent reference data used in transaction processing. Note: These data are changed infrequently, *e.g.,* a product price file or a name and address file" *(ISACA glossary)*.
STAR (Security, Trust and Assurance Registry)	**C**loud **S**ecurity **A**lliance scheme for information security attestation and certification of **C**loud **S**ervice **P**roviders, with several variants. The trust-based basic level 1 involves low-risk organisations simply self-assessing and (optionally) formally asserting that they fulfil the requirements of both ISO/IEC 27001 and the **C**loud **C**ontrols **M**atrix, with no independent assessments necessary. Level 2 requires periodic independent conformity assessments (audits) and certification by accredited assessors in conjunction with conformity to other standards such as SOC 2 or ISO/IEC 27001.
State data	"When data or parameters are used, by the application or server, to emulate a persistent connection or track a client's status across a multi-request process or transaction" *(SCP QRG)*.
Stateful firewall, stateful [packet] inspection, dynamic packet filtering	In contrast to simple packet filters, second-generation firewalls analyse packets in context and maintain internal state tables for the TCP/IP connections, *e.g.* reconstructing fragmented packets before scrutinising the content or identifying spoofed responses lacking the corresponding requests. "A firewall architecture that tracks each connection traversing all interfaces of the firewall and makes sure they are valid" *(ISACA glossary)*. "A firewall architecture that works at the network layer. Unlike static packet filtering, which examines a packet based on the information in its header, stateful inspection examines not just the header information but also the contents of the packet up through the application layer in order to determine more about the packet than just information about its source and destination" *(SANS glossary)*. *Cf.* deep packet inspection.
Statement	See instruction.
Statement **o**f **A**pplicability **(SoA)**	List or matrix identifying information security controls needed to satisfy relevant control objectives, *i.e.* those that address (mitigate) information risks of concern to the organisation. Essentially a completeness check, confirming that all 90+ generic controls from ISO/IEC 27001 Annex A, have been duly considered and not ignorantly neglected by management. "Documented statement describing the control objectives and controls that are relevant and applicable to the organization's ISMS" *(ISO/IEC TR 27019)*. "Documentation of all necessary controls and justification for the inclusion or exclusion of such controls" *(ISO/IEC 27701 DRAFT 2nd edition)*. "Documentation of all necessary controls and justification for inclusion or exclusion of controls. Notes: Organizations may not

TERM	MEANING
	require all controls listed in Annex A or may even exceed the list in Annex A with additional controls established by the organization itself. All identified risks shall be documented by the organization according to the requirements of this document. All identified risks and the risk management measures (controls) established to address them shall be reflected in the statement of applicability" *(ISO/IEC 42001)*.
Statement on Auditing Standards № 70 – Service Organisations (SAS 70)	Deprecated US financial services audit standard, superseded by SSAE 18 and SOC reports. See also ISAE 3402.
Static Application Security Testing (SAST)	Automated testing of application program source code for flaws and bugs that create security vulnerabilities. See also **D**ynamic **A**pplication **S**ecurity **T**esting, **I**nteractive **A**pplication **S**ecurity **T**esting, linting.
Static data	See standing data.
Static electricity	Electrostatic charging and discharging of insulating materials by very high voltages, normally induced by the frictional movement of surfaces past each other. Static discharges can damage semiconductor junctions in electrostatically sensitive electronic devices, causing them to fail immediately … or at some future point. A lightning storm is a dramatic demonstration of the immense power of static discharges.
Static Kitten	Group of elite hackers/cyber-spooks apparently employed, backed, or tolerated by the Iranian government, active in 2023.
Static testing	See **S**tatic **A**pplication **S**ecurity **T**esting.
STE	*Abbrev:* **S**ecure **T**erminal **E**quipment.
Stealth virus	Cryptic virus that attempts to conceal its presence on the system, typically by intercepting and manipulating folder/disk access requests. When for instance an unskilled user or a crude antivirus program searches the disk, the virus dynamically removes or changes program names, file names, *etc.* in the information provided/presented by the **O**perating **S**ystem. More sophisticated methods are widely used by more advanced malware, including **A**dvanced **P**ersistent **T**hreats. "Stealthing is a term that refers to approaches used by malicious code to conceal its presence on the infected system" *(SANS glossary)*.
Steganalysis	"The process of detecting and defeating the use of steganography" *(SANS glossary)*.

TERM	MEANING
Steganography, stego, steg	Hiding information 'in plain sight,' *e.g.* by cryptographically manipulating the least significant data bits of certain pixels in a graphic image causing changes that are virtually invisible to the human eye but can be identified by a program that checks the same pixel values. Commonly used to watermark and assert ownership of and copyright on digital content, or to pass covert messages despite surveillance. "The art, science, and practice of communicating in a way that hides the existence of the communication" *(CNSSI 4009)*. "The art and science of communicating in a way that hides the existence of the communication. For example, a child pornography image can be hidden inside another graphic image file, audio file, or other file format" *(NIST SP 800-101)*. "Methods of hiding the existence of a message or other data. This is different than cryptography, which hides the meaning of a message but does not hide the message itself. An example of a steganographic method is 'invisible' ink" *(SANS glossary)*.
STELLARWIND	One of several secret US surveillance programs.
Stepping stone	See foothold.
Stingray	Family of commercial surveillance devices capable of spoofing cellular phone base stations, enabling the police, **F**ederal **B**ureau of **I**nvestigation, *etc.* to conduct **M**an-**I**n-**T**he-**M**iddle attacks in order to intercept voice calls and SMS/TXT messages, capture metadata, *etc.* from cellphones within range, *sometimes* with valid court orders or warrants. See also IMSI-catcher.
STIR/SHAKEN	*Abbrev:* **S**ecure **T**elephone **I**dentity **R**evisited/**S**ignature-based **H**andling of **A**sserted information using to**KEN**s.
STIX (Structured Threat Information eXpression)	Structured, flexible, extensible language for sharing unclassified threat information in machine- and human-readable form for purposes such as security awareness and real-time network defence and threat analysis. See also TAXII, CybOX, ATT&CK, CRITS.
Stoned	One of the earliest boot-sector viruses, allegedly written by students at the University of Wellington, New Zealand in 1987. It displayed the message "Your PC is now Stoned!" on some infected systems. Copycat variants followed, displaying different messages.
Storage	Medium or mechanism for retaining information. "Device, function, or service supporting data entry and retrieval" *(ISO/IEC 27040)*.
Storage **A**rea **N**etwork **(SAN)**	"Network whose primary purpose is the transfer of data between computer systems and storage devices and among storage devices. Note: A SAN consists of a communication infrastructure, which provides physical connections, and a management layer, which organises the connections, storage devices, and computer systems so that data transfer is secure and robust" *(ISO/IEC 27040)*. "A variation of a local area network (LAN) that is dedicated

TERM	MEANING
	for the express purpose of connecting storage devices to servers and other computing devices. Note: SANs centralize the process for the storage and administration of data" *(ISACA glossary)*.
Storage device	Hardware designed to store stuff, such as a cardboard box, tank, wardrobe, cupboard, filing cabinet, brain, or computer disk. "Any storage element or aggregation of storage elements, designed and built primarily for the purpose of data storage and delivery" *(ISO/IEC 27040)*. "A unit into which data or programs can be placed, retained and retrieved" *(ISACA glossary)*.
Storage ecosystem	"Complex system of interdependent components that work together to enable storage services and capabilities. Note: The components often include storage devices, storage elements, storage networks, storage management, and other Information and Communications Technology (ICT) infrastructure" *(ISO/IEC 27040)*.
Storage element	"Component that is used to build storage devices and which contributes to data storage and delivery. Note: Common examples of a storage element include a disk or tape drive" *(ISO/IEC 27040)*.
Storage limitation	"The [privacy] principle that personal data must be kept in a form that permits identification of data subjects for no longer than is necessary for the purposes for which the personal data are processed" *(ISACA glossary)*.
Storage medium, storage media, media [plural]	Physical substrate/s on which information can be recorded and retained, *e.g.* computer disks, magnetic tapes, papers, brass nameplates, cave walls, or stone tablets. "Material on which Electronically Stored Information or digital data are or can be recorded" *(ISO/IEC 27040)*.
Storage security	"Application of physical, technical, and administrative controls to protect storage systems and infrastructure as well as the data stored within them. Notes: Storage security is focused on protecting data (and its storage infrastructure) against unauthorized disclosure, modification, or destruction while assuring its availability to authorized users. These controls may be preventive, detective, corrective, deterrent, recovery, or compensatory in nature" *(ISO/IEC 27040)*.
Store	Keep, stash, accumulate, squirrel-away for a rainy day. "Record data on volatile storage or non-volatile storage" *(ISO/IEC 27040)*.
Stored procedure	In some **D**ata**B**ase **M**anagement **S**ystems, subroutines or functions for manipulating data can be stored in data tables, blurring the distinction between data and code.
Strategic objective, strategic goal	Key objective forming part of a strategy. "Long-term objectives typically at higher levels of the organization" *(OCEG GRC Glossary)*.

TERM	MEANING
Strategic planning	"The process of deciding on the enterprise's objectives, changes in these objectives, and the policies to govern their acquisition and use" *(ISACA glossary).*
Strategic risk	Business risk with strategic (significant) implications. Major incidents are likely to impact the organisation's achievement of strategic objectives, and might even be existential. "The risk associated with the future business plans and strategies of an enterprise" *(ISACA glossary).*
Strategy, strategic	Declarative description of one or more grand objectives.
Stratified sample, strata	Audit sample selected from different subsets (strata) of the whole population in order to analyse, compare, and contrast them, *e.g.* surveying the security awareness of managers, general workers, and **I**nformation **T**echnology professionals separately to determine whether different communication techniques or content might be appropriate. "The process of segmenting a population across levels of some factors to minimize variability within those segments" *(NIST SP 800-55v1).* "Sampling technique used to divide the units into homogeneous groups (strata) and draw a simple random sample from each group" *(ISACA glossary). Cf.* random sample, systematic stratified sample, time series analysis, attribute sample, convenience sample, discovery sample.
Stream cipher	Type of cryptographic algorithm that rapidly encrypts each character, byte, or bit as it flows through the process by combining (typically XORing) it with a character, byte, or bit from a parallel pseudorandom keystream. Examples: RC4, AES-CTR, Salsa20, ChaCha20. "Works by encryption a message a single bit, byte, or computer word at a time" *(SANS glossary). Cf.* block cipher.
Stress	Perceived or physical tension. "Chronic and ongoing dynamic pressure originated within an urban system, with the potential for cumulative impacts on the ability and capacity of the system to achieve its objectives" *(ISO 22300).* "A significant magnitude of force applied to the organization" *(OCEG GRC Glossary).* See also distress, stress test.
Stresser, booter	Commercial Internet traffic load-testing services, rentable for minutes or hours at a time, ostensibly for legitimate performance and capacity stress-testing of websites by their owners but in reality mostly used by black hats for **D**istributed **D**enial-**o**f-**S**ervice attacks, extortion, and hacking of third parties. Typically use [[Reflection]] reflection attacks[[#Reflection]] to amplify TCP or UDP traffic.

TERM	MEANING
Stress test, marginal test, marginal check	Simulation, under safe conditions, of a challenging condition or situation to determine and gain assurance re how a system, application, device, network, team, process, *etc.* will behave under stress. "Test in which certain operating conditions are varied about their rated values in order to detect or to locate potential faults" *(ISO/IEC 2382)*. "Testing to evaluate a system or component at or beyond the limits of its specified requirements. Synonymous with testing, boundary value" *(ISACA glossary)*. See also capacity test, load test, smoke test, unit test, integration test, system test, security test, usability test, acceptance test.
Stretch value	"A value that is unlikely to be achieved, but still possible" *(OCEG GRC Glossary)*.
STRIDE	Application security threat assessment method used by Microsoft to evaluate the potential for: **S**poofing identities, **T**ampering with data, **R**epudiation, **I**nformation disclosure, **D**enial-of-Service and **E**levation of privileges … plus other threats or risks.
Strong authentication	Relatively high-integrity, trustworthy form of authentication involving cryptography. "Authentication by means of cryptographically derived multi-factor credentials" *(ISO 22600-1)*. "Authentication procedure using a minimum of two independent (from the security point of view) authentication mechanisms, with at least one of them being dynamic" *(ISO 12812-1)*.
Strontium	State-sponsored Russian-speaking hacking/malware group behind the SolarWinds incident, among others.
Structured **E**xception **H**andling **(SEH)**	Windows security technique to control the way various events are dealt with during the execution of programs, in an attempt to trap and gracefully resolve issues arising from flaws and bugs, whether accidentally or deliberately caused, such as divide-by-zero errors, program crashes, buffer overflows, malware, and hacks. SEH is *supposed* to ensure that designated error-handling or process-termination code cannot be bypassed, *e.g.* by redirection at run time.
Structured test	Scripted and often automated test following a preplanned sequence or pattern designed to test and hopefully confirm the correct operation of a system, or specific parts of it, in a particular way, *e.g.* a regression test. *Cf.* unstructured test.
STT	*Abbrev:* **S**peech-**T**o-**T**ext. See speech recognition.

TERM	MEANING
Student, learner	Person who attends classes or other learning/training opportunities. "Individual who learns" *(OCEG GRC Glossary)*.
Stuxnet	**A**dvanced **P**ersistent **T**hreat malware used by the US and Israeli governments to attack and damage Natanz, a supposedly highly secure but patently vulnerable Iranian nuclear fuel processing facility in 2010. The malware escaped the intended target and spread globally, giving an unintended public demonstration of advanced cyberwar capabilities. Developed by the **N**ational **S**ecurity **A**gency's **T**ailored **A**ccess **O**perations unit.
Stylometry, stylometric analysis	Neologism about identifying originators of artistic works by analysing linguistic cues and writing styles, brushwork techniques, chord sequences, *etc.*, typically to spot fakes, forgeries, and plagiarism, or attribute the true authors of unattributed works.
Subject access request	"Request by data subject to receive a copy of personal data that an enterprise processes, to understand the purpose of said processing, or to understand and/or delimit how the data may be shared by the enterprise" *(ISACA glossary)*.
Subjective, subjectivity	Interpretation of information subject to an individual's unique perspective, understanding, opinion, and emotional feelings. May be biased, prejudiced, at odds or in accordance with the facts. Something 'highly subjective' bears little if any relation to objective reality and is likely to differ substantially between people.
Subject matter	"The specific information subject to an IS auditor's report and related procedures, which can include things such as the design or operation of internal controls and compliance with privacy practices or standards or specified laws and regulations (area of activity)" *(ISACA glossary)*. "Identifiable statements, conditions, events, or activities for which there is evidence" *(OCEG GRC Glossary)*.
Subject **M**atter **E**xpert **(SME)**	See expert.
Sub-master key	Physical key that can only open a subset of master-keyed locks, such as all the locks on a particular floor, possibly just one (a change key).
Subordinate [level, unit, layer, worker]	Something or someone of lower status, significance, or priority than its superior or master. "Organizational units that are accountable to the organization in scope" *(OCEG GRC Glossary)*.
Subpoena	Legally binding order for someone to appear in person before, or provide evidence to, a court (usually). Relevant and potentially incriminating emails, memoranda, **D**ata**B**ase records, and other notes or files are commonly demanded in commercial disputes and compliance cases.

TERM	MEANING
Subscriber Identity Module (SIM), SIM card	Tamper-resistant smart card containing the unique identification numbers (particularly the IMSI) used to associate (identify and authenticate) a cellular service subscriber (customer) with the physical device (such as a smartphone, laptop, or smart meter) they are using. Also stores other data such as the emergency services phone number for the issuing country, some phone book entries, preferred mobile networks when roaming internationally, text messages, and dialled phone numbers. The cryptographic **I**ntegrated **C**ircuit chip is electrically connected to the host device via 14 standard-sized gold-plated contact pads housed in different sizes of plastic carrier (standard, micro, or nano SIMs). "A smart card chip specialized for use in GSM equipment" *(NIST SP 800-101)*. See also UICC, **G**lobal **S**ystem for **M**obile communications, **U**niversal **M**obile **T**elecommunications **S**ervice. *Cf.* **S**ecurity **I**nformation **M**anagement.
Subsequent event	Something that happens afterwards. "Events or transactions that occur after the specified period addressed by the description but prior to the date of the practitioner's report; such events or transactions could have a significant effect on the evaluation of whether the description is presented in accordance with the description criteria or whether controls were effective to provide reasonable assurance that the entity's principal system objectives were achieved based on the applicable trust services criteria" *(**T**rust **S**ervices **C**riteria)*.
Substantial modification	Significant change to something, such as fitting a jet turbine to a tractor. "A change to the product with digital elements following its placing on the market, which affects the compliance of the product with digital elements with the essential cybersecurity requirements set out in Part I of Annex I or which results in a modification to the intended purpose for which the product with digital elements has been assessed" *(EU CRA)*.
Substantive testing	Verifying the integrity of accounting records by audit testing, *e.g.* stocktake to confirm the existence and status of a representative sample of the assets recorded in inventories, and examining calculations and methods for potentially significant errors in recorded transactions. "Obtaining audit evidence on the completeness, accuracy or existence of activities or transactions during the audit period" *(ISACA glossary)*.
Substitution	Cryptographic process in which characters or bytes in the plaintext are replaced by different characters/bytes in the ciphertext using a simple rule (*e.g.* 'Use the next letter in the alphabet,' Caesar's cipher) or a more complex scheme (*e.g.* Vigenére's cipher). "Encryption that replaces bit strings or character strings with other bit strings or character strings. Note: The resulting ciphertext is called substitution cipher" *(ISO/IEC 2382)*.

TERM	MEANING
Subsymbolic AI	"AI based on techniques and models that use an implicit encoding of information, that can be derived from experience or raw data. Note: Compared to symbolic AI. Whereas symbolic AI produces declarative outputs, subsymbolic AI is based on statistical approaches and produces outputs with a given probability of error" *(ISO/IEC 22989)*. See also symbolic AI.
Subterfuge	Deceptive and often covert activities conducted under the pretence of something innocuous and/or legitimate. A form of social engineering. May be malicious or benign according to situations, motives, and perspectives. See also camouflage, fakery.
Subversive	a. *[Adjective]* Refers to activities intending to subvert (undermine, bypass, or negate) controls, constraints, requirements, or expectations. b. *[Noun]* Person who commits subterfuge.
Succession planning	Planning that paves the way for workers currently performing critical rôles in the organisation to be replaced by someone sufficiently knowledgeable and competent, typically a deputy or understudy in training for the rôle, for business continuity purposes in due course, in the event of incapacity, illness or death, retirement, promotion, demotion, resignation, termination of contract, reassignment, information overload, exhaustion, *etc.* A valuable resilience control.
Sufficient evidence	"The measure of the quantity of audit evidence; supports all material questions to the audit objective and scope" *(ISACA glossary)*.
Sufficient information	"Information is sufficient when evaluators have gathered enough of it to form a reasonable conclusion. For information to be sufficient, however, it must first be suitable" *(ISACA glossary)*.
Suitable criteria	"Benchmarks used to evaluate subject matter that yield consistent and meaningful results" *(OCEG GRC Glossary)*.
Suitable information	"Relevant (*i.e.*, fit for its intended purpose), reliable (*i.e.*, accurate, verifiable and from an objective source) and timely (*i.e.*, produced and used in an appropriate time frame) information" *(ISACA glossary)*.
Sunburst	See SolarWinds.
Superior [level, unit, layer, person …]	a. Something or someone of a higher status in a hierarchy giving them a degree of authority and control over subordinates. "Organizational units to which the organization in scope is accountable" *(OCEG GRC Glossary)*. b. Better or higher, as applied to lakes and mothers.

TERM	MEANING
Supervise, supervision, supervisor, supervisory	To direct, control, and/or oversee someone or something, such as a worker or system performing important tasks. Supervisors are generally experienced, competent, and trusted, effectively junior or blue-collar managers.
Supervised machine learning	"Machine learning that makes only use of labelled data during training" *(ISO/IEC 22989)*. *Cf.* semi-supervised machine learning, unsupervised machine learning.
Supervisory authority	"An independent public authority which is established by a Member State pursuant to Article 51" *(General Data Protection Regulation)*.
Supervisory authority concerned	"A supervisory authority which is concerned by the processing of personal data because: (a) the controller or processor is established on the territory of the Member State of that supervisory authority; (b) data subjects residing in the Member State of that supervisory authority are substantially affected or likely to be substantially affected by the processing; or (c) a complaint has been lodged with that supervisory authority" *(General Data Protection Regulation)*.
Supervisory control	See management control.
Supervisory **C**ontrol **A**nd **D**ata **A**cquisition **(SCADA)**	Control system that monitors and responds in real time to the state of industrial plant and machinery (such as machine tools, conveyor belts, pumps, electrical systems, and elevators) through the associated **I**ndustrial **C**ontrol **S**ystems. 'Supervisory' reflects the way that modern **O**perational **T**echnology devices on industrial plant (including **I**ndustrial **I**nternet **o**f *Things* things) are largely autonomous, reacting to local conditions without real-time remote control. SCADA typically directs, oversees, and coordinates the distributed devices, *e.g.* showing operators what is going on through a mimic panel, logging operational parameters/metrics, updating tags on the distributed devices, and raising alerts or alarms when appropriate. It may intervene remotely to exert control under certain conditions, *e.g.* to shut down a malfunctioning or suspect device, particularly if that is necessary to ensure safety. "Process control system generally used to control dispersed assets using centralized data acquisition and supervisory controls" *(ISO/IEC 27019)*. "Systems used to control and monitor industrial and manufacturing processes and utility facilities" *(ISACA glossary)*. See also **I**ndustrial **A**utomation and **C**ontrol **S**ystems.
Superzap	Privileged IBM mainframe program allows the user to override logical access controls that would otherwise prevent their access to executable programs, in order to apply binary patches. Exemplifies the powerful rights that system administrators have or can potentially obtain, emphasising the need for them to be both competent and trustworthy.

TERM	MEANING
Supplier, contractor, producer, seller, vendor	Commercial source of <u>products</u>. "Organization or an individual that enters into agreement with the acquirer for the supply of a product or service. Note 1: Other terms commonly used for supplier are contractor, producer, seller, or vendor. Note 2: The acquirer and the supplier can be part of the same organization. Note 3: Types of suppliers include those organizations that permit agreement negotiation with an acquirer and those that do not permit negotiation with agreements, *e.g.* end-user license agreements, terms of use, or open source products copyright or intellectual property releases" *(<u>ISO/IEC 27036-1</u>)*. "An entity having an agreement with an acquirer to design, develop, manufacture, maintain, modify, deliver or supply solutions under terms of an agreement. Examples include individuals, partnerships, companies, corporations, and associations" *(<u>ISACA glossary</u>)*. "Organisations, such as application developers, ICT equipment manufacturers and service providers, that provide products and services. Suppliers can also include other organisations involved in distribution channels" *(<u>AusISM</u>)*.
Supplier relationship	Ongoing <u>business</u> arrangement between a <u>supplier</u> and customer involving the exchange of <u>information</u> pertinent to the <u>products</u> supplied. "Agreement or agreements between acquirers and suppliers to conduct business, deliver products or services, and realize business benefit" *(<u>ISO/IEC 27036-1</u>)*.
Supply chain, supply network, supply mesh, supply web	<u>Production</u> and delivery of commercial <u>products</u> normally involves several <u>suppliers</u> sequentially adding value to the raw materials, often but not necessarily in a linear sequence. Due to the many-to-many commercial relationships, '<u>network</u>,' '<u>web</u>,' or 'mesh' is more descriptive of the <u>complexities</u> than 'chain.' "Set of organizations with linked set of resources and processes, each of which acts as an acquirer, supplier, or both to form successive supplier relationships established upon placement of a purchase order, agreement, or other formal sourcing agreement. Note 1: A supply chain can include vendors, manufacturing facilities, logistics providers, distribution centres, distributors, wholesalers, and other organizations involved in the manufacturing, processing, design and development, and handling and delivery of the products, or service providers involved in the operation, management, and delivery of the services. Note 2: The supply chain view is relative to the position of the acquirer" *(<u>ISO/IEC 27036-1</u>)*. "Two-way relationship of organizations, people, processes, logistics, information, technology and resources engaged in activities and creating value from the sourcing of materials through the delivery of products or services. Note: The supply chain may include vendors, subcontractors, manufacturing facilities, logistics providers, internal distribution centres, distributors, wholesalers and other entities that lead to the end user" *(<u>ISO 22300</u>)*. "A linked set of resources and processes between multiple

TERM	MEANING
	tiers of developers that begins with the sourcing of products and services and extends through the design, development, manufacturing, processing, handling, and delivery of products and services to the acquirer" *(OMB Circular A-130)*.
Supply chain compromise or attack	a. Some sort of incident or attack disrupting the supply of products (*i.e.* goods such as computer chips, or services such as cloud computing) from upstream suppliers to downstream customers. b. Attack ultimately targeting one or more customers of one or more compromised suppliers, exploiting the trusted commercial relationships. c. Compromise of one or more products at some indeterminate upstream point in the supply chain (*e.g.* surreptitious substitution or sabotage of security-relevant hardware components, subunits or subsystems, firmware, software, or shared library functions, deliberate insertion or non-removal of flaws and bugs, infection with malware, or coercion of workers during product manufacture, logistics, storage, installation, or maintenance) causing a cascade of downstream risk for all dependent customers and users.
Supply **C**hain **C**ontinuity **M**anagement **(SCCM)**	"Application of business continuity management to a supply chain. Notes: Business continuity management should be applied to all the tiers of an organization's supply chain. In practice, an organization usually would only apply it to the first tier of their suppliers and influence critical suppliers to apply SCCM to their suppliers" *(ISO 22300)*.
Supply-chain **L**evels for **S**oftware **A**rtifacts **(SLSA, salsa)**	OpenSSF's software supply chain security framework with incremental guidelines enabling software developers to improve security and software consumers to make trust-based decisions. Supports NIST's **S**ecure **S**oftware **D**evelopment **F**ramework. More info: https://slsa.dev/
Supply chain risk	Uncertainty regarding or arising from supply chains. "Risks that arise from the loss of confidentiality, integrity, or availability of information or information systems and reflect the potential adverse impacts to organizational operations (including mission, functions, image, or reputation), organizational assets, individuals, other organizations, and the Nation" *(OMB Circular A-130)*.
Supply **C**hain **R**isk **M**anagement **(SCRM)**	Management of risks throughout a supply chain, potentially going further than both **T**hird **P**arty **R**isk **M**anagement and **V**endor **R**isk **M**anagement by covering subcontractors, partners, *etc.* "The process of identifying, assessing, and mitigating the risks associated with the global and distributed nature of information and communications technology product and service supply chains" *(OMB Circular A-130)*.

TERM	MEANING
Support process	Typically, an administrative process or activity. "Process that supports core processes by providing and managing necessary resources without delivering direct customer value" *(ISO/IEC 27022)*. See also business process, core process, management process.
Support **V**ector **M**achine **(SVM)**	"Machine learning algorithm that finds decision boundaries with maximal margins. Note: Support vectors are sets of data points that define the positioning of the decision boundaries (hyper-planes)" *(ISO/IEC 22989)*.
Surge	Excessive supply voltage lasting more than just a few micro- or milliseconds. May blow fuses or damage electronics having inadequate voltage regulation. See also spike, dip, brownout.
Surge protector, surge suppressor	Relatively cheap, low-quality substitute for properly engineered power regulation and protection techniques, often consisting of nothing more than an **M**etal **O**xide **V**aristor across the power supply. "Filters out electrical surges and spikes" *(ISACA glossary)*.
Surrogation	Whereas metrics are usually intended to help improve things for the benefit of all stakeholders, individuals sometimes find ways to game the system by intentionally manipulating or misrepresenting the metric itself to give the *appearance* of improvement, rather than truly improving the object of measurement – particularly if they stand to benefit individually, *e.g.* through enhanced reputations, bonuses, or promotions. Surrogation may also be unintentional, where misunderstandings, biases, or poor metrics definitions and measurement processes lead to inappropriate decisions and changes. 'Managing strictly by the numbers' can be a risky approach if the numbers are not sufficiently representative of and correlated with performance.
Surveillance	a. Process of covertly observing, snooping, or spying on someone's activities, whether literally watching them, surreptitiously monitoring and perhaps recording their activities and movements, or tapping in to their network/online and/or telephone communications, *e.g.* using spyware. See also mass surveillance and workplace surveillance. b. Overt and legitimate (above-board) process of observing, assessing, and evaluating something – a form of oversight, *e.g.* surveillance audit.
Surveillance audit, interim audit	Periodic re-evaluation of an organisation's conformity with the obligations and expectations of laws/regulations, standards, and contracts such as ISO/IEC 27001. Typically conducted near the first and second anniversary of a certification audit.

TERM	MEANING
Survivability	Capability to survive serious and potentially existential incidents or disasters, not necessarily unscathed but still operating to some extent.
Susceptibility	Vulnerability or inability to avoid being successfully attacked.
Suspense file	See hold file. "A computer file used to maintain information (transactions, payments or other events) until the proper disposition of that information can be determined. Notes: Once the proper disposition of the item is determined, it should be removed from the suspense file and processed in accordance with the proper procedures for that particular transaction. Two examples of items that may be included in a suspense file are receipt of a payment from a source that is not readily identified or data that do not yet have an identified match during migration to a new application" *(ISACA glossary)*.
Suspicion, suspicious	Something that strikes an alert and security-aware person as unusual and causes concern as a potential information security matter, such as a stranger in a controlled area, information assets unexpectedly going missing, or the belief that confidential information may have been disclosed inappropriately. While some suspicious events may turn out to be entirely innocuous or benign, some may be near-misses, events, or incidents worth reporting to management or the Help Desk.
Sustainability	Since few information risks are short-term, it is generally necessary for the corresponding information security controls to persist, operating effectively for considerable periods (years or decades). Sustainable controls are self-perpetuating, justifying their continued operation because of the risk mitigation value they generate, provided the stakeholders appreciate that as a result of appropriate metrics and information about threats and incidents.
SVM	*Abbrev:* **S**upport **V**ector **M**achine.
Swap	Mutual exchange A ⇄ B, *e.g.* when pages or segments of data are swapped back-and-forth between fast primary memory (RAM) for processing and relatively slow secondary (disk) storage, or in social engineering scams such as bait-and-switch and SIM swap.
SWG	*Abbrev:* **S**ecure **W**eb **G**ateway.
Swiss cheese model	Conceptual model in which, under unfortunate circumstances, imperfections (holes) in overlapping but imperfect layers of control (cheese slices) may align, allowing safety hazards, dangers or threats to penetrate multilayered defences and so harm or compromise a vulnerable resource.

TERM	MEANING
Switch	a. *[Noun]* Local Area Network device providing interconnections with basic network traffic management and routing capabilities at layers 2 (data link) or 3 (network) of the OSI stack. "Device which provides connectivity between networked devices by means of internal switching mechanisms, with the switching technology typically implemented at layer 2 or layer 3 of the OSI reference model" *(ISO/IEC 27033-1)*. "A data link layer device that enables local area network (LAN) segments to be created and interconnected, giving the added benefit of reducing collision domains in Ethernet-based networks" *(ISACA glossary)*. Cf. hub. b. *[Noun]* Electromechanical or purely electronic device to open or close an electrical connection – a binary choice. c. *[Verb]* To swap items, generally surreptitiously, *e.g.* bait-and-switch.
Symbolic AI	"AI based on techniques and models that manipulate symbols and structures according to explicitly defined rules to obtain inferences. Notes: Compared to subsymbolic AI, symbolic AI produces declarative outputs, whereas subsymbolic AI is based on statistical approaches and produces outputs with a given probability of error" *(ISO/IEC 22989)*. See also subsymbolic AI.
Symmetric cryptography, symmetric cryptographic system, symmetric cipher	Cryptosystem in which an identical or trivially related key is used for both encryption and decryption. Clearly the key must be kept secret from anyone not authorised to encrypt or decrypt the information, and must be sufficiently long and complex to resist brute force attacks or simple guesses. "Cryptography in which the same key is used for encryption and decryption" *(ISO/IEC 2382)*. "An algorithm that encrypts data using a single key. In symmetric cryptographic algorithms, a single key is used for encipherment (encrypting) and decipherment (decrypting)" *(ISACA glossary)*. "A branch of cryptography involving algorithms that use the same key for two different steps of the algorithm (such as encryption and decryption, or signature creation and signature verification). Symmetric cryptography is sometimes called 'secret-key cryptography' (versus public-key cryptography) because the entities that share the key" *(SANS glossary)*. *Cf.* asymmetric cryptography.
Synchronous transmission	Type of digital datacommunications protocol or modulation method in which each character of a message is transmitted with precise timing that is matched accurately by the receiving system. With no need for start and stop bits surrounding each character, this is a more efficient process that relies on stable clocks at both ends, possibly with a special (re)synchronisation sequence at various points in the transmission. "Block-at-a-time data transmission" *(ISACA glossary)*. *Cf.* asynchronous transmission.

TERM	MEANING
SYN flood	"A denial of service attack that sends a host more TCP SYN packets (request to synchronize sequence numbers, used when opening a connection) than the protocol implementation can handle" *(SANS glossary)*.
SYNful Knock	Persistent exploit against Cisco routers involving the installation (using a privileged userID) of a hacked version of the **O**perating **S**ystem (malware) with a C^2 capability allowing the router to be remotely controlled through HTTP and custom TCP packets.
Sysinternals	Microsoft's suite of Windows system, network, and security management tools. Useful to diagnose problems with performance, slow booting, spyware, *etc.* Originally open-source thanks to the generosity of its original author but no longer, having been absorbed by Redmond like a whale consumes a plankton.
SYSKEY	Windows function optionally encrypts stored password hashes to frustrate brute force and rainbow table attacks in the event a hacker successfully obtains the **S**ecurity **A**ccounts **M**anager (called the 'Windows Account Database' by SYSKEY.exe). The RC-4 encryption key is normally stored in the registry but Windows can be configured to demand that it is typed in or provided on removable media as a password at startup in order to continue booting. Fake 'Microsoft support' phone scammers sometimes socially engineer this configuration change in order to lock victims out of their own computers and so coerce them into paying a ransom, unless they simply revert the change by loading a previous restore point or registry backup ... assuming they have one and it hasn't been deleted or corrupted by the scammers.
Syslog	*De facto* technical standard for system and application logging, primarily on UNIX systems. "The system logging facility for Unix systems" *(SANS glossary)*.
System	Elements, components, subsystems, *etc.* working together in harmony to achieve objectives. Usually, in the technology context, refers to a *computer* system, *i.e.* hardware platform plus the associated firmware and software forming a discrete functional unit. Otherwise, an integrated suite of related items and processes, such as a **M**anagement **S**ystem or **O**perating **S**ystem, or an even broader holistic assemblage including the associated people, processes, physical environment, business, social context, *etc.* "Combination of interacting elements organized to achieve one or more stated purposes" *(ISO/IEC/IEEE 21840)*. "A related set of IT equipment and software used for the processing, storage or communication of information and the governance framework in which it operates" *(NZISM)*. "Combination of interacting elements organised to achieve one or more stated purposes. Notes: A system

TERM	MEANING
	can be considered as a product or as the services it provides. In practice, the interpretation of its meaning is frequently clarified by the use of an associative noun, *e.g.* aircraft system. Alternatively, the word 'system' can be substituted simply by a context-dependent synonym, *e.g.* aircraft, though this can then obscure a system principles perspective" *(ISO/IEC 27036-1)*. "A generic term covering the operating systems, web server, application frameworks and related infrastructure" *(SCP QRG)*. "Refers to the infrastructure, software, people, processes, and data that are designed, implemented, and operated to work together to achieve one or more specific business objectives (for example, delivery of services or production of goods) in accordance with management-specified requirements" *(**T**rust **S**ervices **C**riteria)*. "An interconnected set of information resources under the same direct management control which shares common functionality. A system normally includes hardware, software, information, data, applications, communications, and people. A system can be, for example, a local area network (LAN) including smart terminals that supports a branch office, an agency-wide backbone, a communications network, a departmental data processing center including its operating system and utilities, a tactical radio network, or a shared information processing service organization (IPSO)" *(OMB Circular A-130)*. See also device, **V**irtual **M**achine, host, node, server.
System analysis, systems analysis	System analysis – an in-depth, systematic examination for design, troubleshooting, or improvement purposes, of the processes, machines, tools, applications, resources, *etc.* (including the information security aspects) needed to produce a specified product. "Systematic investigation of a real or planned system to determine the information requirements and processes of the system and how these relate to each other and to any other system" *(ISO/IEC 2382)*. "A systematic investigation of a real or planned system to determine its functions and how they relate to each other and any other system" *(ISACA glossary)*.
Systematic	Methodical, step-by-step, structured, considered, logical, *etc.*, as if determined by a system.
Systematic stratified sample	Periodic/regular audit sample, *e.g.* pick out every eleventh security alert, invoice, or expenses claim for more detailed analysis. "A method of sampling where samples are taken at a regular interval" *(NIST SP 800-55v1)*. *Cf.* random sample, time series analysis, attribute sample, convenience sample, discovery sample.
System audit	See technology audit.

TERM	MEANING
System boundary	The notional edge or outer limits of the scope where a system meets non-system or another system. "The specific aspects of an entity's infrastructure, software, people, procedures, and data necessary to perform a function (such as producing, manufacturing, or distributing a product) or provide a service. When systems for multiple functions or services share aspects, infrastructure, software, people, procedures, and data, the systems will overlap but the boundaries of each system will differ" *(Trust Services Criteria)*.
System call	A call by an application (user space) program for an **O**perating **S**ystem (kernel) function or resource. The trusted and privileged kernel mediates such calls, applying low-level security rules built in to the OS and computer platform. See also hypercall.
System classification	System classification. "The highest classification of information for which the system is approved to store or process" *(NZISM)*. "The classification of a system is the highest classification of data which the system is authorised to store, process or communicate" *(AusISM)*.
System component	Component, unit, or subunit of a system. "Refers to the individual elements of a system. System components can be classified into the following five categories: infrastructure, software, people, processes, and data" *(Trust Services Criteria)*. "A discrete identifiable information technology asset that represents a building block of a system and may include hardware, software, and firmware" *(NIST SP 800-171)*.
System configuration management	"A set of controls that help ensure the infrastructure components supporting the software are deployed securely" *(SCP QRG)*.
System development audit, software project audit …	Audit, assessment, analysis, or review providing assurance to stakeholders regarding a project or initiative developing a new or updated information system, application, service, *etc*. Depending on the agreed scope, may investigate and evaluate aspects such as: project governance and management (*e.g.* business case/rationale, oversight and direction, progress against plan, resourcing, stakeholder engagement, development and project management policies and methods plus conformity), project risk management (*e.g.* priorities, contingency arrangements, change management, rescoping and replanning, documentation), and application/system risk management (*e.g.* analysis and specification of security control requirements, compliance, security testing). See also application development, acquisition, implementation, maintenance reviews.

TERM	MEANING
System **D**evelopment **L**ifeCycle **(SDLC)**	See Software Development LifeCycle. "The phases deployed in the development or acquisition of a software system. Notes: SDLC is an approach used to plan, design, develop, test and implement an application system or major modification to an application system. Typical phases of SDLC include the feasibility study, requirements study, requirements definition, detailed design, programming, testing, installation and postimplementation review but not the service delivery or benefits realization activities" *(ISACA glossary)*.
System design	a. The architectural design of a system, showing how various units work together and what each unit does. b. The process of designing a system. "A process of defining the hardware and software architecture, components, modules, interfaces and data for a system to satisfy specified requirements" *(ISACA glossary)*.
System event	Event affecting or involving a system. "An occurrence that could lead to the loss of, or disruption to, operations, services, or functions and could result in an entity's failure to achieve its system objectives. Such an occurrence may arise from actual or attempted unauthorized access or use by internal or external parties and (a) impair (or potentially impair) the availability, integrity, or confidentiality of information or systems; (b) result in unauthorized disclosure or theft of information or other assets or the destruction or corruption of data; or (c) cause damage to systems. Such occurrences also may arise from the failure of the system to process data as designed or from the loss, corruption, or destruction of data used by the system" *(Trust Services Criteria)*.
System for **C**ross-domain **I**dentity **M**anagement **(SCIM)**	Protocol to automate the provisioning, de-provisioning and synchronisation of userIDs, groups, and access rights. Defines a consistent schema and RESTful Application Programming Interface for creating, reading, updating, and deleting identity resources, allowing different systems to exchange identity data in a standardised manner. "An application-level protocol for provisioning and managing identity data specified through SCIM schemas. A SCIM server provides a set of resources, the allowable contents of which are defined by a set of schema URIs and a resource type. SCIM's schema is not a document-centric one. Instead, SCIM's support of schema is attribute based, where each attribute may have different type, mutability, cardinality, or returnability" *(NZISM)*.
System files	Primarily software comprising a computer's Operating System but can include the associated device drivers, boot loaders, configuration files, startup and logon scripts, and even applications in some contexts, but not usually the data files.
Systemic	Pertaining to a system. *Cf.* systematic.

TERM	MEANING
System incident, systemic incident	Incident affecting or involving a system. "A system event that requires action on the part of entity management to prevent or reduce the impact of a system event on the entity's achievement of its system objectives" *(Trust Services Criteria)*.
System integrity	System integrity. "Quality of a data processing system fulfilling its operational purpose while both preventing unauthorized users from making modifications to or use of resources and preventing authorized users from making improper modifications to or improper use of resources" *(ISO/IEC 2382)*.
System lifecycle, system life cycle	See **S**oftware **D**evelopment **L**ife**C**ycle. "Course of developmental changes through which a system passes from its conception to the termination of its use" *(ISO/IEC 2382)*. "The course of developmental changes through which a system passes from its conception to the termination of its use, *e.g.*, the phases and activities associated with the analysis, acquisition, design, development, test, integration, operation, maintenance and modification of a system" *(ISACA glossary)*.
System objective	Requirement, goal, or intended purpose for a system – what it is meant to achieve. "The entity's objectives, established by entity management, that are embodied in the product commitments it makes to customers, including producing or manufacturing a product that meets product performance specifications and other production, manufacturing, or distribution specifications. The system objectives also include the requirements established for the functioning of the system to meet production, manufacturing, or distribution commitments" *(Trust Services Criteria)*.
System on **C**hip **(SoC)**	**I**ntegrated **C**ircuit containing multiple logical units (*e.g.* **C**entral **P**rocessing **U**nit, memory and input/output functions such as analogue to digital converters and networking) within the same chip of silicon, manufactured as one physical unit rather than being assembled from separate chipsets on a **P**rinted **C**ircuit **B**oard. See also microcontroller. *Cf.* **S**ecurity **O**perations **C**entre.
System owner	Organisation, rôle, or person who notionally or literally owns and is responsible for a computer or other system. They are generally expected to protect it against unacceptable risks and legitimately exploit it to optimise and release its value. "The person responsible for the information resource" *(NZISM)*. "The executive responsible for a system" *(AusISM)*. See also asset owner, information owner, risk owner, control owner, process owner, problem owner.

TERM	MEANING
System requirement	Something required *of* a system (what it is meant to do) or the requirement *for* a system. "Specifications regarding how the system should function to (a) meet the entity's commitments to customers and others (such as customers' customers); (*b*) meet the entity's commitments to suppliers and business partners; (c) comply with relevant laws and regulations and guidelines of industry groups, such as business or trade associations; and (d) achieve other entity objectives that are relevant to the trust services category or categories addressed by the description. Requirements are often specified in the entity's system policies and procedures, system design documentation, contracts with customers, and government regulations. System requirements may result from the entity's commitments relating to security, availability, processing integrity, confidentiality, or privacy. For example, a commitment to programmatically enforce segregation of duties between data entry and data approval creates system requirements regarding user access administration" *(Trust Services Criteria)*. *Cf.* system objective.
Systems analysis	Process of analysing all aspects of a business process or activity, focusing on the information flows and processing in order to design automation or technological approaches that would achieve its objectives more efficiently and effectively. "The systems development phase in which systems specifications and conceptual designs are developed based on end-user needs and requirements" *(ISACA glossary)*.
Systems engineering	The engineering of systems – particularly computer systems and software but the approach extends to the wider systems of which computers are just a part, *e.g.* it includes the administrative processes and administrators. "An interdisciplinary approach governing the technical and managerial effort required to transform a set of customer needs, expectations and constraints into solutions and to support solutions throughout their life cycle" *(ISACA glossary)*.
System **S**ecurity **O**fficer **(SSO)**	"A person responsible for enforcement or administration of the security policy that applies to the system" *(SANS glossary)*. See also Information **S**ystem **S**ecurity **O**fficer.
System security plan	Output/result of a planning activity concerning the information security arrangements for an **I**nformation **T**echnology system. "A document that describes a system and its associated controls" *(AusISM)*. "A formal document that provides an overview of the security requirements for an information system and describes the security controls in place or planned for meeting those requirements" *(NZISM)*. "A document that describes how an organization meets or plans to meet the security requirements for a system. In particular, the system security plan describes the system boundary, the environment in which the system operates, how the security requirements are satisfied, and the relationships with or connections to other systems" *(NIST SP 800-171)*.

TERM	MEANING
System service	Service provided by a system. "A capability provided by a system that facilitates information processing, storage, or transmission" *(NIST SP 800-171)*.
System software	See **O**perating **S**ystem. "1. Application-independent software that supports the running of application software. 2. Software designed to facilitate the operation and maintenance of a computer system and its associated programs, *e.g.*, operating systems, assemblers and utilities. This contrasts with application software" *(ISACA glossary)*.
System-specific control	"A security or privacy control for an information system that is implemented at the system level and is not inherited by any other information system" *(OMB Circular A-130)*.
System-specific policy	"A policy written for a specific system or device" *(SANS glossary)*.
System-specific security documentation	"A system's system security plan, incident response plan, continuous monitoring plan, security assessment report, and plan of action and milestones" *(AusISM)*.
Systems **S**ecurity **C**ertified **P**ractitioner **(SSCP)**	ISC2's junior-level qualification for cybersecurity professionals with at least a year's work experience. Covers: security concepts and practices; access controls; risk identification, monitoring, and analysis; incident response and recovery; cryptography; network and communications security; and systems and application security. More info: https://www.isc2.org/certifications/sscp
Systems security engineering	Rational, formal, and systematic process for specifying and designing coherent sets of information security, safety, privacy, and/or business continuity controls for computer systems, mitigating unacceptable information risks. A specialism within systems engineering. "A specialty engineering discipline of systems engineering. It applies scientific, mathematical, engineering, and measurement concepts, principles, and methods to deliver, consistent with defined constraints and necessary trade-offs, a trustworthy asset protection capability that satisfies stakeholder requirements; is seamlessly integrated into the delivered system; and presents residual risk that is deemed acceptable and manageable to stakeholders" *(OMB Circular A-130)*.
System test	Test to gain assurance of a complete system's conformity with and satisfaction of the specifications, expectations, or requirements. "Testing conducted on a complete, integrated system to evaluate the system's compliance with its specified requirements. Notes: System test procedures are typically performed by the system maintenance staff in their development library. [and] The process of testing an integrated hardware and software system to verify that the system meets its specified requirements. Such testing may be conducted in the development environment and the target environment" *(ISACA glossary)*. See also unit test, integration test, smoke test, load test, stress test, security test, penetration test, acceptance test, regression test.

TERM	MEANING
System time	"Time generated by the system clock and used by the operating system, not the time computed by the operating system" *(ISO/IEC 27037)*.
System user	See user. "A general user or a privileged user of a system" *(NZISM)*. "An individual or (system) process acting on behalf of an individual that is authorized to access a system" *(NIST SP 800-171)*.

T

TERM	MEANING
TA	*Abbrev:* **T**raffic **A**nalysis.
Tabletop exercise	Pragmatic process of simulating or emulating some sort of incident, emergency scenario, crisis, or process to practice, evaluate, and prove/improve the activities plus the associated documentation (strategies, policies, procedures, and guidelines) and decisions. Often conducted by a team physically sharing a conference room, huddled around the table, but can also take place online or in a hybrid or entirely virtual environment. See also desk check.
Tacit knowledge, know-how	Expertise and understanding picked up intuitively through experience. A valuable form of **I**ntellectual **P**roperty/intangible information.
Tactics**, T**echniques and **P**rocedures **(TTPs)**	Methods and tools, *e.g.* those used by hackers and spooks to compromise their victims.
Tag	a. **S**upervisory **C**ontrol **A**nd **D**ata **A**cquisition/**I**ndustrial **C**ontrol **S**ystems/**O**perational **T**echnology term for a data setpoint, upper/lower limit, and rate, *e.g.* the braking pressure requested at any instant by a car's brake controller. Tag processing can be quite sophisticated, *e.g.* the extent to which the brakes operate may depend on a combination of factors such as the *rate of change* of speed required, the vehicle's momentum, the dynamic action of regenerative braking, and wheel traction, as well as the driver's pressure on the pedal. See also hysteresis. b. Physical or electronic label.
Tailgating, piggybacking	Gaining unauthorised physical access to a site, building, *etc.* by slipping through an access-controlled door, gate, car-park barrier, turnstile, *etc.* at the same time as an authorised person is authenticated and enters. May involve social engineering or masquerading. A simple yet effective technique to get inside areas that lack adequate physical and procedural security controls without having the requisite permission.
Tailored **A**ccess **O**perations **(TAO)**	**N**ational **S**ecurity **A**gency's elite hacking unit.
Tailoring	"The process by which security control baselines are modified by identifying and designating common controls; applying scoping considerations; selecting compensating controls; assigning specific values to agency-defined control parameters; supplementing baselines with additional controls or control enhancements; and providing additional specification information for control implementation. The tailoring process may also be applied to privacy controls" *(OMB Circular A-130).*
TAILS	*Abbrev:* **T**he **A**mnesic **I**ncognito **L**ive **S**ystem.

TERM	MEANING
Tamper evident	Physical control that aims to make it evident or obvious that someone has been tampering with something, such as the uniquely identified tamper-resistant seal on a forensic evidence bag or the grossly distorted facial features of someone who has overindulged on Botox.
Tampering, tamper	"Act of deliberately making or allowing change(s) to digital evidence (*i.e.* intended or purposeful spoliation)" *(ISO/IEC 27037)*. "To deliberately alter a system's logic, data, or control information to cause the system to perform unauthorized functions or services" *(SANS glossary)*.
Tamper resistant, tamper proof	Physical access controls are often important to prevent other security mechanisms from being breached, bypassed, or otherwise compromised by attackers with sufficient physical access to the systems or devices concerned. Since no control is absolutely effective, however, 'tamper resistance' is more accurate than 'tamper proofing.' See also tamper evident.
Tangible	From the Latin verb *tangere* (to touch), literally something 'touchable', *i.e.* having a physical or material presence. Sometimes used metaphorically, *e.g.* regardless of their physicality, so-called tangible assets can be counted and valued much more readily and accurately than intangibles, *e.g.* because they have a definite market value. *Cf.* intangible.
Tangible asset, tangible resource	Tangible asset. "Any assets that have physical form" *(ISACA glossary)*. "Resources that refer to physical assets, such as land, buildings, and equipment" *(OCEG GRC Glossary)*.
TAO	*Abbrev:* **T**ailored **A**ccess **O**perations.
Tap	Monitor traffic on a network or datacommunications link, generally covertly, *i.e.* without the knowledge or consent of those communicating. Used also for legitimate technical administration, *e.g.* to diagnose the reasons for connection failures or poor performance. "Wiring devices that may be inserted into communication links for use with analysis probes, local area network (LAN) analyzers and intrusion detection security systems" *(ISACA glossary)*.
Target, mark, patsy	a. Vulnerable person, organisation, system, network, program, **D**ata**B**ase, *etc.* singled out for a deliberate attack such as a hack, malware infection, or fraud. Implies that they are identified and aimed at specifically, although indiscriminate attacks, threats, or incidents may also lead to compromise. "Detailed performance requirement, applicable to the organization or parts thereof, that arises from the objectives, and that needs to be set and met in order to achieve those objectives" *(ISO 22300)*. "Person or asset selected as the aim of an attack" *(ISACA glossary)*. See also victim. b. Aiming point, ideal value, or sweet spot for a metric. "An expected or planned value for an indicator" *(OCEG GRC Glossary)*.

TERM	MEANING
TargetCompany, Xollam, Mallox, Fargo …	Family of ransomware in the wild in 2021. Variants mostly exploit vulnerable Microsoft SQL **D**ata**B**ase servers.
Target data	"Information subject to a given process, typically including most or all information on a piece of storage media" *(ISO/IEC 27040)*.
Target of **E**valuation **(TOE)**	**I**nformation and **C**ommunications **T**echnology product, system, or component whose security is evaluated under a certification scheme such as **C**ommon **C**riteria. "The functions of a product subject to evaluation under the Common Criteria" *(NZISM)*.
Target skill level	"The desired level of skill a person, or 'typical' person in a group, is expected to possess" *(OCEG GRC Glossary)*.
Tarpit	System specifically designed to delay network worms and probes using TCP/IP timeouts, malformed responses, multiple retransmissions, *etc.*, either in the hope that attackers will go after easier targets or giving analysts time to examine their activities and perhaps respond. Often combined with honeynets.
Task	a. *[Noun]* Discrete unit of work to be performed, a step in the process leading towards an objective. "<Artificial intelligence> Action required to achieve a specific goal. Notes: Actions can be physical or cognitive. For instance, computing or creation of predictions, translations, synthetic data or artefacts or navigating through a physical space; Examples of tasks include classification, regression, ranking, clustering and dimensionality reduction" *(ISO/IEC 22989)*. b. *[Verb]* To assign a work responsibility to someone or something (such as a robot), often holding them accountable for achieving the anticipated results (or lack thereof!).
TAXII (Trusted Automated eXchange of Indicator Information)	Protocol for services and messages for sharing unclassified threat information in machine-readable form for cybersecurity situational awareness, real-time network defence and threat analysis. See also STIX, CybOX, ATT&CK, CRITS.
TCap	*Abbrev:* **T**hreat **Cap**ability.
TCB	*Abbrev:* **T**rusted **C**omputing **B**ase.
TCP	*Abbrev:* **T**ransmission **C**ontrol **P**rotocol.
Tcpdump	Network analysis tool, the source of the Libpcap/WinPcap packet capture library used by nmap and others. "A network monitoring and data acquisition tool that performs filter translation, packet acquisition and packet display" *(ISACA glossary)*. "A freeware protocol analyzer for Unix that can monitor network traffic on a wire" *(SANS glossary)*.

TERM	MEANING
TCP fingerprinting	Hacking technique intended to Identify network system types according to their responses to carefully crafted **T**ransmission **C**ontrol **P**rotocol messages, assuming they are not configured deliberately to spoof responses to throw them off the scent. "The [use] of odd packet header combinations to determine a remote operating system" *(SANS glossary)*.
TCP/IP, TCP/IP stack	Suite of standardised protocols (such as **T**ransmission **C**ontrol **P**rotocol, **I**nternet **P**rotocol, **U**ser **D**atagram **P**rotocol, **D**omain **N**ame **S**ystem) and services in a 5-layer network stack. "Provides the basis for the Internet, a set of communication protocols that encompass media access, packet transport, session communication, file transfer, electronic mail (email), terminal emulation, remote file access and network management" *(ISACA glossary)*. "A synonym for 'Internet Protocol Suite;' in which the Transmission Control Protocol and the Internet Protocol are important parts. TCP/IP is the basic communication language or protocol of the Internet. It can also be used as a communications protocol in a private network (either an Intranet or an Extranet)" *(SANS glossary)*. *Cf.* OSI stack, stack.
TCP Wrapper	"A software package which can be used to restrict access to certain network services based on the source of the connection; a simple tool to monitor and control incoming network traffic" *(SANS glossary)*.
TDD	*Abbrev:* **T**est-**D**riven **D**evelopment.
TEA	*Abbrev:* **T**ETRA **E**ncryption **A**lgorithm.
Team	People in a group, unit, or function collaborating productively to achieve shared objectives. "The smallest organizational unit. Teams may be part of a department or maybe cross-functional. Teams may be permanent or temporary" *(OCEG GRC Glossary)*.
TECHINT (Technical Intelligence)	Use of technological sources or means to acquire intelligence. See also HUMINT, SIGINT, OSINT, COMINT, IMINT, ELINT, EMSEC.
Technical	Relating to technique. Implies extensive, accurate, in-depth knowledge or information relating specifically to a particular method, subject, field, craft, or specialism. *Cf.* technological.
Technical architecture	Technical design for an information system consisting of one or more computers, applications, networks, and services, *e.g.* how components such as the microprocessor, memory, WiFi subunit, and actuator mechanism interact in a smart lock. See also technology architecture.
Technical area	Technical subject, field, craft, or specialism. "Area characterized by commonalities of processes relevant to a specific type of management system and its intended results" *(ISO/IEC 17021-1)*.

TERM	MEANING
Technical control	Complex control, difficult for non-experts to understand. See technological or technology control.
Technical debt	Cynically alludes to insufficient past investment to maintain and update technologies, leading to legacy IT.
Technical expert (texpert)	Technical expert. "Person who provides specific knowledge or expertise to the audit team. Note: Specific knowledge or expertise is that which relates to the organization, the process or activity to be audited" *(ISO/IEC 17021-1)*.
Technical **R**eport **(TR)**	Report on a technical topic with expert input. ISO describes its TRs as "data of a different kind from that which is normally published as an International Standard ([*e.g.*] data obtained from a survey, ... on work in other international organizations or data on the 'state of the art') ... entirely informative in nature" *(ISO/IEC Directives, part 1)*. Unlike full international standards, ISO TRs are not subject to formal review after a few years. *Cf.* **T**echnical **S**pecification.
Technical reporting, factual reporting	"The reporting of findings based solely on the technical competence of the individual. No inferences/explanations (opinion) are drawn from the findings. An example would be where a digital forensics practitioner has used a specified software tool to extract data from a mobile phone. A factual report explains what the practitioner has done and the findings, such as a list of the files of a certain type that were retrieved. It offers no opinion on how the files came to be on the device or whether any of their content is relevant to a fact in issue in the case" *(FSRCoP)*.
Technical security measure	See cybersecurity.
Technical **S**pecification **(TS)**	Specification on a technical subject. ISO TSs are for "When the subject in question is still under development or where for any other reason there is the future but not immediate possibility of an agreement to publish an International Standard. A Technical Specification may contain normative provisions. No technical changes are allowed on approved draft Technical Specifications." In other words, if there has been insufficient consensus among members to complete and approve a full international standard on an evolving topic, a TS may suffice, for now. TSs are to be formally reviewed within 3 years of their publication, ideally reaching consensus for release as an international standard. *Cf.* **T**echnical **R**eport.
Technical [security] standard	Standard documenting the configuration parameters recommended or required for a particular technology platform or situation. Interprets generic control requirements from information security policies for the specific context.

TERM	MEANING
Technical support	Function providing technical guidance, expertise, and assistance on technology matters.
Technical **S**urveillance **C**ounter**M**easures **(TSCM)**	Bug-detection and related techniques to identify and perhaps nullify or subvert covert transmitters and recorders, *e.g.* by transmitting pulsed RF signals and monitoring for tiny 'reflections' radiated by semiconductor junctions in bugs secreted within a supposedly secure zone. "The process of surveying facilitates to detect the presence of technical surveillance devices and to identify technical security weaknesses that could aid in the conduct of a technical penetration of the surveyed facility" *(NZISM)*.
Technological	Relating to technology. *Cf.* technical.
Technological control, technology control, tech control	a. Administrative control designed to mitigate unacceptable technological risks *e.g.* strategies, policies, and processes for procuring computer systems and information services only if they incorporate the requisite security, privacy, and safety controls. b. Control involving the use of technology and automation, *e.g.* cryptographic authentication. See also cybersecurity, automated control. c. One of four 'control themes' in ISO/IEC 27002, defined in the standard as "Controls that concern technology" *(ISO/IEC 27002)*. Thirty-four types of technological control are described, *e.g.* **D**ata **L**eakage **P**revention, logging, information backup, and change management. See also people control, physical control, organisational control.
Technological risk	Uncertain possibility of incidents involving **I**nformation **T**echnology, **O**perational **T**echnology, **C**ommunications **T**echnology, **M**obile **T**echnology, **V**irtual **T**echnology, or **S**mart **T**echnology. See cyber risk.
Technology (tech)	Scientific knowledge and practice applied through engineering, *e.g.* **I**nformation **T**echnology, **O**perational **T**echnology, **C**ommunications **T**echnology, **M**obile **T**echnology, **V**irtual **T**echnology, or **S**mart **T**echnology.
Technology actions & controls	"Hardware and software systems used to address risk, reward, and compliance" *(OCEG GRC Glossary)*.
Technology architecture (tech architecture)	Design for the technologies supplying various information services, *e.g.* the **I**nformation **T**echnology running a company's Finance System, the **V**irtual **T**echnology behind **H**uman **R**esources' cloud services and the **O**perational **T**echnology keeping Production rolling smoothly. Stitches together the individual technical architectures, services, and information flows at the department, business unit, organisation, or enterprise level if not beyond, *e.g.* cloud services shared with supply chain partners.

TERM	MEANING
Technology audit (tech audit), IT audit, ICT audit, computer audit, Information Systems audit (IS audit), systems audit, network audit …	Type of audit, or name of the business function, providing management and other stakeholders with assurance concerning various technologies such as **I**nformation **T**echnology, **O**perational **T**echnology, **C**ommunications **T**echnology, **M**obile **T**echnology, **V**irtual **T**echnology, and **S**mart **T**echnology. According to the scope and objectives, tech audits may involve competent, independent review of technology-related: governance arrangements, oversight, management structures, rôles and responsibilities, accountabilities, reporting lines; systems, networks, applications, middleware; cloud computing; information risks and information security; social engineering, fraud, hacking, malware; access rights, **P**ublic **K**ey **I**nfrastructure, cryptography, key management; backups and archives; privacy; safety; strategies plus plans and arrangements for their execution and management; projects and initiatives; architecture and design; information management, asset management, **I**ntellectual **P**roperty **R**ights, licence management, contract management; hardware, firmware, software, systems or product development; DevSecOps and secure development practices, secure coding, **C**ontinuous **I**ntegration/**C**ontinuous **D**elivery pipeline security and implementation, **A**pplication **P**rogramming **I**nterface security, embedded systems and third-party integrations; policies, procedures, and other documentation, plus security awareness and training; conformity and compliance, exceptions and exemptions; incident management, resilience, and business continuity; operation, management, maintenance, monitoring; methods, tools, and techniques; investment returns, efficiency, cost-effectiveness, metrics; culture, ethics, tone at the top; internal and external supply chain relationships; tech asset lifecycle management; emerging technologies such as **A**rtificial **I**ntelligence/**M**achine **L**earning, generative AI, **A**rtificial **G**eneral **I**ntelligence, **I**nternet **o**f *Things*, quantum computing, *etc*.
Technology capital	"Hardware, software, and related technological resources that an organization may use to achieve its objectives" *(OCEG GRC Glossary)*.
Technology control	See technological control.
TEE	*Abbrev:* **T**rusted **E**xecution **E**nvironment.
TEF	*Abbrev:* **T**hreat **E**vent **F**requency.
Telecommunications, telecoms	Transmission and reception of audio-visual communications over a distance by analogue or digital means. "Electronic communication by special devices over distances or around devices that preclude direct interpersonal exchange" *(ISACA glossary)*. *Cf.* data communications.
Telecommunications applications	"Applications such as Voice over IP (VoIP) that are consumed by end-users and built upon the network based services" *(ISO/IEC 27011)*.

TERM	MEANING
Telecommunications business	Telecommunications business. "Business to provide telecommunications services in order to meet the demand of others" *(ISO/IEC 27011)*.
Telecommunications equipment room	Controlled area housing a substantial quantity of telecommunications devices. "A secure location or room within a general building where equipment for providing telecommunications businesses are sited" *(ISO/IEC 27011)*.
Telecommunications facility	Telecommunications facility. "Machines, equipment, wire and cables, physical buildings or other electrical facilities for the operation of telecommunications" *(ISO/IEC 27011)*.
Telecommunications organisation	Telecommunications organisation. "Business entities who provide telecommunications services in order to meet the demand of others" *(ISO/IEC 27011)*.
Telecommunications record	Metadata relating to telecommunications, such as a telephone call log. "Information concerning the parties in a communication excluding the contents of the communication, and the time, and the duration of the communication that took place" *(ISO/IEC 27011)*.
Telecommunications service	Telecommunications service. "Communications using telecommunications facilities, or any other means of providing communications either between telecommunications service users or telecommunications service customers" *(ISO/IEC 27011)*.
Telecommunications service customer	"Person or organization who enters into a contract with telecommunications organizations to be offered telecommunications services by them" *(ISO/IEC 27011)*.
Telecommunications service user	"Person or organization who utilizes telecommunications services" *(ISO/IEC 27011)*.
Teledildonics	Neologism meaning smart networked sex toy *things*. See also screwdriving.
Telemetry	Streaming data concerning the operation of a system, important parameters used to monitor, manage, and secure it remotely. "The automatic measurement and transmission of data collected from remote sources. Such data is often used within systems to measure the use, performance and health of one or more functions or devices that make up the system" *(AusISM)*.
Telephone	"A device that converts between sound waves and electronic signals that can be communicated over a distance" *(NZISM)*. "A device that is used for point-to-point communication over a distance. This includes digital and IP telephony" *(AusISM)*. Gosh.
Telephone system	"A system designed primarily for the transmission of voice traffic" *(NZISM)*.

TERM	MEANING
Telework	"The ability for an organization's employees, contractors, business partners, vendors, and other users to perform work from locations other than the organization's facilities" *(NIST SP 800-114)*.
Tell-tale	In the same way that school children sometimes 'tell tales' on each other, claiming that their peers have behaved badly or broken the rules, tell-tales can be built in to systems and processes to flag information security situations, inconsistencies, incidents, to management or other authorities, typically by raising some form of alert or more often a silent alarm. An offensive security practice.
Telnet	Basic datacommunications application and protocol to connect remote client terminals to servers over a TCP/IP network. Telnet traffic is plaintext and vulnerable to interception, hence deprecated in favour of **S**ecure**SH**ell. "Network protocol used to enable remote access to a server computer. Note: Commands typed are run on the remote server" *(ISACA glossary)*. "A TCP-based, application-layer, Internet Standard protocol for remote login from one host to another" *(SANS glossary)*.
TEMPEST	Shielding, filtering, and related approaches designed to prevent electronic equipment (particularly **I**nformation **T**echnology systems) radiating ('emanating') signals that may prove useful to an adversary. Square-wave signals in digital computers, point-of-sale card readers, **H**ardware **S**ecurity **M**odules, *etc.* generate high-frequency signals and harmonics that are radiated from inadequately shielded wiring as radio waves that may be monitored covertly on a receiver, thus enabling confidential data to be determined (a side-channel attack). "A name referring to the investigation, study, and control of compromising emanations from telecommunications and automated information systems equipment" *(CNSSI 4009)*. "A short name referring to investigations and studies of compromising emanations" *(NZISM)*. See also EMSEC.
TEMPEST rated IT equipment	"IT equipment that has been specifically designed to minimise TEMPEST emanations" *(NZISM)*.
Tempora	SECRET UK mass surveillance program, disclosed by whistleblower Ed Snowden, tapping into hundreds of fibre-optic communications cables through the services of 'intercept partners' (Internet and telecommunications service providers). See also Edgehill, BULLRUN.
Terminate and **S**tay **R**esident **(TSR)**	**D**isk **O**perating **S**ystem program that *appears* to terminate but continues processing in the background, waiting for specific interrupts. Overcomes the DOS mono-threading limitation. Early viruses were often TSR programs, as were various utilities (later known as services in Windows) and suspended user programs that could be reactivated rapidly (*e.g.* Sidekick).

TERM	MEANING
Terminal	a. Dumb network workstation, with barely enough processing capability to display or print data received from a server. Also known as a slim client. "A device, usually equipped with a CRT display and keyboard, used to send and receive information to and from a computer via a communication channel" *(ISACA glossary)*. b. Point of connection for wires. c. Final, the end. It is no more.
Terminal facilities	"Telecommunications facilities which are to be connected to one end of telecommunications circuit facilities and part of which is to be installed on the same premises (including the areas regarded as the same premises) or in the same building where any other part thereof is also to be installed" *(ISO/IEC 27011)*.
Termite	Ransomware gang responsible for compromising Australian in vitro fertilisation company Genea in 2025, exfiltrating 940 Gb of data including sensitive medical information.
Terrorism	One or more deliberate attacks on a population, nation, or race by violent extremists or anarchists intent on causing maximum media coverage, terrifying, *etc.*, generally by killing and injuring people but sometimes by other means such as sabotaging the **C**ritical **N**ational **I**nfrastructure, safety-critical computer networks and/or systems to inflict physical or economic damage, disruption, and chaos (note: these are not mutually exclusive goals).
Teslacrypt	Species of ransomware voluntarily terminated by its originators when they released the 'master key' in 2016, having presumably made their fortunes and retired, or been coerced by the authorities or competitors.
Test, testing, tester	Assurance process to check and hopefully confirm (to some level of certainty or proof) that a system, or some part of it (such as a security function or control), meets the specified requirements prior to it being accepted, authorised, and released for use in production, otherwise feeding information about failures and improvement opportunities back into the development process. A wide variety of testing approaches, scopes, purposes, techniques, tools, and terms are in use, reflecting innovation and the importance of this activity. "Unique and particular type of exercise, which incorporates an expectation of a pass or fail element within the aim or objectives of the exercise being planned. Note: The terms 'test' and 'testing' are not the same as 'exercise' and 'exercising'" *(ISO 22300)*. "An activity in which a system or component is executed under specified conditions, the results are observed or recorded and an evaluation is made of some aspect of the system or component" *(ISACA glossary)*. "The determination of one or more characteristics according to a procedure and,

TERM	MEANING
	although typically quantitative, it can be qualitative (*e.g.* a presumptive test with a colour change)" *(FSRCoP)*. See also structured and unstructured test; black, grey, and white box test; unit test, smoke test, usability test, stress test, system test, regression test, security test, acceptance test, self-test, penetration test (among others), oh, and audit. And qualification. And fact-check.
Test case	Business or technical scenario with the associated test data, used to test or exercise a system or some part of it. May be based on an actual situation or one created expressly for the purpose, *e.g.* simulating an obscure hack or an unusual combination of circumstances. Essentially an experiment or trial with a predicted or desired outcome. "Documentation specifying inputs, predicted results and a set of execution conditions for a test item" *(ISACA glossary)*. Innovative court case exploring the meaning and ramifications of a particular law in order to set a legal precedent. It tests the particular understanding and interpretation of the statute, *e.g.* an ambiguous clause or apparent conflict.
Test data, evaluation data	Digital data, ideally generated entirely artificially for testing a system, process, product, function, device, *etc.* against the specified requirements for security, privacy, resilience, performance, capacity, *etc.* That implies deep knowledge of the data structures, values, ranges, and relationships, requiring competent systems analysis. More often, however, test data are sampled and modified from production data raising confidentiality, integrity, privacy, and other concerns. "Data used to assess the performance of a final model. Note: Test data is disjoint from training data and validation data" *(ISO/IEC 22989)*. "Simulated transactions that can be used to test processing logic, computations and controls actually programmed in computer applications. Individual programs or an entire system can be tested" *(ISACA glossary)*.
Test design	"Documentation specifying the details of the test approach for a software feature or combination of software features and identifying the associated tests" *(ISACA glossary)*.
Test documentation	Documentation concerning the scoping, objectives, planning, execution, results/findings, analysis, and eventual outcome/conclusion of testing. "Documentation describing plans for, or results of, the testing of a system or component. Types include test case specification, test incident report, test log, test plan, test procedure and test report" *(ISACA glossary)*.

TERM	MEANING
Test-Driven Development (TDD), test-first development	Software development method that involves preparing test criteria, test cases, *etc.* from the system specifications at the earliest opportunity, possibly *during* the specification phase as an integral activity. Software is then developed and if necessary modified explicitly to pass the tests, thereby satisfying the specified requirements. The method is critically dependent on, and hence should improve, the quality (accuracy, comprehensiveness, appropriateness, integrity) of the specifications and analysis, but may struggle with changes that emerge *during* the development process (*e.g.* additional control requirements to resist newly recognised threats).
Test environment	Set of computer systems, networks, devices, data, and supporting tools and processes used for testing and gaining assurance on developed software. Ideally isolated from both development and production environments using separate hardware or virtual systems to strengthen change control and reduce risks, particularly to production services and data. See also sandbox.
Test harness, automated test framework	Combination of a test execution engine (software to automate the testing process) and a repository of test scripts (details of the tests to be conducted plus the associated test data), used for regression testing of software.
Test procedure	"A formal document developed from a test plan that presents detailed instructions for the setup, operation and evaluation of the results for each defined test" *(ISACA glossary)*.
TETRA **E**ncryption **A**lgorithm **(TEA)**	Set of four proprietary cryptographic algorithms (TEA1 through TEA4) specified and licenced by the **E**uropean **T**elecommunications **S**tandards **I**nstitute for use in TETRA (**Te**rrestrial **Tr**unked **Ra**dio) systems. These are stream ciphers, used to encrypt and decrypt digital messages streaming through a TETRA network. TEA1 is known (through reverse engineering and cryptanalysis) to use just 32 bits selected from an 80-bit key, a fundamental flaw and a classic illustration of the weakness of security by obscurity.
THC Hydra, Hydra	Brute force network authentication attack tool from **T**he **H**acker's **C**hoice, a hacker group. Can perform dictionary attacks on more than 50 protocols. More info: https://www.thc.org/
The **A**mnesic **I**ncognito **L**ive **S**ystem **(TAILS)**	Linux-based open-source portable **O**perating **S**ystem and applications designed to leave behind no forensic evidence of user activity on the computer and to conceal online activities. Used by hackers, spies, spooks, activists, investigative journalists, and others attempting to ensure their anonymity.

TERM	MEANING
TheHarvester	Google application ostensibly designed to support the target research initial phase of penetration testing, or as a means to check how much information about one's organisation is publicly accessible on the web through search engines, social media, *etc*. An example of dual-use technology that can be used for both offensive and defensive purposes. More info: https://code.google.com/archive/p/theharvester/
The Internet Worm	See Morris Worm.
Thermal runaway	Exothermic (heat-generating, energy-releasing) processes or reactions that become even more exothermic at higher temperatures can become uncontrollable, leading to smoke, fire, and meltdown incidents. A destructive form of positive feedback. Physical damage, overloading, or short circuits in lithium-ion batteries, for instance, can be significant risks for **M**obile **T**echnologies such as in **E**lectric **V**ehicles and portable electronics. Likewise control failures, accidents, or cyber incidents affecting chemical plants, oil refineries, **B**attery **E**nergy **S**torage **S**ystems, nuclear power stations, *etc*.
Thing*, Internet of *Things* device, system, equipment *etc	Networkable smart device, *e.g.* **B**uilding **M**anagement **S**ystem, **H**eating, **V**entilating, and **A**ir-**C**onditioning system, alarm system, lighting controller or lightbulb, home entertainment system, door lock, garage door opener, refrigerator, vending machine, baby monitor, meter, vehicle, smartphone, laptop, smart sensor (*e.g.* fitness monitor), pacemaker, or some other such gizmo (including processors embedded within or attached to dumb equipment) that is, or could become, part of the **Internet of *Things***. Often but not necessarily cheap, small, and low-powered, with limited **D**ata **P**rocessing capabilities and storage capacity. Vulnerable to design flaws and bugs, hacking, and malware, including ransomware and physical threats.
Third line [of defence or accountability]	In the three lines model, the third line provides assurance through audit and oversight of the second-line experts advising the first line on risk management. In World War I, the third line trenches were for reserves, while the second line supported brave troops in the front (first) line, sent over the top into no man's land. "Individuals and teams that specialize in and provide a high level of assurance on activities performed by the First Line and Second Line. The Third Line may include internal audit, external audit or outside experts who are sufficiently objective and competent" *(OCEG GRC Glossary)*.

TERM	MEANING
Third party, third-party, member of the extended enterprise	Independent person or external organisation not directly employed or owned by the organisation itself (the first party). "A natural or legal person, public authority, agency or body other than the data subject, controller, processor and persons who, under the direct authority of the controller or processor, are authorised to process personal data" *(**G**eneral **D**ata **P**rotection **R**egulation)*. "Privacy stakeholder other than the personally identifiable information (PII) principal, the PII controller and the PII processor, and the natural persons who are authorized to process the data under the direct authority of the PII controller or the PII processor" *(ISO/IEC 29100)*. "A partner that conducts substantial actions & controls on behalf of the organization" *(OCEG GRC Glossary)*. "An individual or organization other than the entity and its employees. Third parties may be customers, suppliers, business partners, or others" *(**T**rust **S**ervices **C**riteria)*. See also external party.
Third **P**arty **R**isk **M**anagement **(TPRM)**	Techniques to identify, assess, evaluate, address, and gain assurance regarding supply chain risks relating to business relationships with third parties (not necessarily suppliers, as with **V**endor **R**isk **M**anagement).
Threat	Person, organisation, situation, or event (whether deliberate or accidental, targeted, or generic in nature) that is hazardous or dangerous, capable of acting on an exposed vulnerability to cause or trigger an information security incident. An essential element of risk. "Potential violation of computer security" *(ISO/IEC 2382)*. "Potential cause of an unwanted incident, which can result in harm to a system or organization" *(ISO/IEC 27000)*. "Potential cause of an unwanted incident, which could result in harm to individuals, assets, a system or organization, the environment or the community" *(ISO 22300)*. "Potential cause of an unwanted incident, which can result in harm to a system, individual or organization" *(ISO/IEC 27032)*. "Potential source of danger, harm, or other undesirable outcome. Notes: A threat is a negative situation in which loss is likely and over which one has relatively little control; A threat to one party may pose an opportunity to another" *(ISO 31073)*. "Potential, deliberate action that can cause harm to an asset. Note: A threat is always related to a threat actor, which can be an individual or an organization" *(ISO 23234)*. "Anything (*e.g.*, object, substance, human) that is capable of acting against an asset in a manner that can result in harm" *(ISACA glossary)*. "Any circumstance or event with the potential to adversely impact organizational operations (including mission, functions, image, or reputation), organizational assets, individuals, other organizations, or the Nation through an information system via unauthorized access, destruction, disclosure, modification of information, and/or denial of service" *(CNSSI 4009)*. "Anything that is capable of acting

TERM	MEANING
	in a manner resulting in harm to an Asset and/or organization; for example, acts of God (weather, geological events, *etc.*), malicious actors, errors, failures" *(O-RT)*. "Malicious risks such as acts of terrorism, hostile state activity and cyber-crime. Contrast with hazard" *(UK Resilience Lessons Digest 2023)*. "A potential for violation of security, which exists when there is a circumstance, capability, action, or event that could breach security and cause harm" *(SANS glossary)*. See also risk source.
Threat actor, threat agent	Normally the person responsible for, or capable of, deliberately causing an information security incident *e.g.* a fraudster, hacker, or cyberteur. May be an organisation enabling, supporting, sponsoring, or commissioning such attacks (*e.g.* competitor, adversary, or sworn enemy) or their agent/s, perhaps acting independently. Conceivably could also be a natural event or situation such as an accident, flood, or climate change, or an authority enforcing compliance obligations. "Methods and things used to exploit a vulnerability. Note: Examples include determination, capability, motive and resources" *(ISACA glossary)*. "Any agent (*e.g.*, object, substance, human) that is capable of acting against an Asset in a manner that can result in harm" *(O-RT)*. "Any entity which may have a negative impact on the system. This may be a malicious user who wants to compromise the system's security controls; however, it could also be an accidental misuse of the system or a more physical threat like fire or flood" *(SCP QRG)*. See also risk source.
Threat analysis	Analysis (rational examination, investigation, or study) of one or more threats. "Process of identifying, qualifying and quantifying the potential cause of an unwanted incident, which could result in harm to individuals, assets, a system or organization, the environment or the community" *(ISO 22300)*. "An evaluation of the type, scope and nature of events or actions that can result in adverse consequences, identification of the threats that exist against enterprise assets. Note: The threat analysis usually defines the level of threat and the likelihood of it materializing" *(ISACA glossary)*. *Cf.* threat assessment, risk analysis, risk assessment.
Threat assessment	Cursory examination of one or more threats. "The identification of types of threats that an organization might be exposed to" *(SANS glossary)*.

TERM	MEANING
Threat **cap**ability **(TCap)**	One of the risk parameters in the FAIR method estimating the ability of a threat agent to compromise the information asset/s under analysis. "The probable level of force (as embodied by the time, resources, and technological capability) that a Threat Agent is capable of applying against an Asset" *(O-RT)*. See also **C**ontrol **S**trength, **P**robable **L**oss **M**agnitude, **L**oss **E**vent **F**requency, **T**hreat **E**vent **F**requency.
Threat community	"A subset of the overall Threat Agent population that shares key characteristics" *(O-RT)*.
Threat event	See attack. "Any event during which a threat element/actor acts against an asset in a manner that has the potential to directly result in harm" *(ISACA glossary)*. "Occurs when a Threat Agent acts against an Asset" *(O-RT)*.
Threat **E**vent **F**requency **(TEF)**	One of the risk factors in FAIR estimates the probability of a threat agent coming into contact with and acting upon the information asset/s under analysis. It alludes to the assets being exposed to threat agents. "The probable frequency, within a given timeframe, that a Threat Agent will act against an Asset" *(O-RT)*. See also **C**ontrol **S**trength, **P**robable **L**oss **M**agnitude, **L**oss **E**vent **F**requency, **T**hreat **Cap**ability.
Threat intelligence (threat intel), cyber threat intelligence	Actionable intelligence about actual, emerging, or potential threats to an organisation's information and technologies, and hence its business. There are strategic (*e.g.* novel types of attacks and attackers), tactical (*e.g.* attack vectors), and operational (*e.g.* **I**ndicators **o**f **C**ompromise used to identify successful attacks, and guidance on how to address attacks in progress) aspects to this. Strictly speaking, 'vulnerability intelligence' is a distinct consideration although in practice it may be treated as part of threat intel. "Information an organization uses to understand the threats that have, will, or are currently targeting the organization. This information is used to prepare, identify, and prevent security and cybersecurity threats looking to take advantage of valuable resources" *(ISACA glossary)*. "Where an organisation may employ a staff member or contractor, or purchase a product to collate information and advice around all the cyber security risks the organisation faces" *(UK Cyber Security Breaches Survey 2023)*. "Information that has been aggregated, transformed, analysed, interpreted or enriched to provide the necessary context for decision-making and to enable relevant and sufficient understanding in order to mitigate the impact of an ICT-related incident or of a cyber threat, including the technical details of a cyber-attack, those responsible for the attack and their modus operandi and motivation" *(DORA)*. See also threat model.

TERM	MEANING
Threat **I**ntelligence **P**latform **(TIP)**	System, software, or service to automate the collection, analysis, communication, and use of threat intelligence.
Threat-**L**ed **P**enetration **T**est **(TLPT)**	Form of penetration testing involving attack techniques being actively used by determined and competent adversaries to compromise victims (according to research and knowledge of the field, *i.e.* threat intelligence), as opposed to more theoretical or academic techniques. "A framework that mimics the tactics, techniques and procedures of real-life threat actors perceived as posing a genuine cyber threat, that delivers a controlled, bespoke, intelligence-led (red team) test of the financial entity's critical live production systems" *(DORA)*.
Threat model	Conceptual construct, scenario, system, or service fed by threat intelligence, used to simulate and explore attack vectors exploiting exposed vulnerabilities, potentially leading to incidents unless blocked or mitigated by controls. "Used to describe a given threat and the harm it could to do a system if it has a vulnerability" *(SANS glossary)*.
Threat tree	Top-down graphical representation generated by successively deconstructing threats, risks, hazards, or undesirable outcomes to expose the contributory factors, elements, or root causes, such as potential attacks. See also **F**ailure **M**odes and **E**ffects **A**nalysis.
Threat vector	See attack vector. "The path or route used by the adversary to gain access to the target" *(ISACA glossary)*. "The method a threat uses to get to the target" *(SANS glossary)*.
Three lines [of defence] model	Conceptual governance/management control model that divides risk management and assurance responsibilities across several organisational functions. Originally formulated in the 2000s, then adopted by The **I**nstitute of **I**nternal **A**uditors in 2013, and now popular globally. OCEG extended the classical model by two further levels, becoming the **L**ines **o**f **A**ccountability model. See also first, second, third, fourth, and fifth line.
Threshold	Boundary condition that, when reached or passed, triggers decisions and actions, *e.g.* if an unfolding situation has become so serious as to constitute an incident (passing a significance threshold relating to, say, its anticipated adverse impact on important business activities), management may decide to initiate the relevant incident response process. Some thresholds are objectively determined according to the measured values or trends in certain parameters (*e.g.* "An office temperature of 37 Celsius"), while others are at least partially subjective (*e.g.* "Too hot to continue working"). Either type may have defined tolerance levels for practical reasons (*e.g.* "An office temperature of 37 ± 2 degrees Celsius").

TERM	MEANING
Throttling	Rate-limiting technical security controls designed to reduce the risk of repeated attacks such as brute force guessing of PIN codes and passwords or **A**rtificial **I**ntelligence model exfiltration. Once triggered by exceeding a defined threshold, further interactions, guesses, queries, *etc.* from the user are ignored even if they are correct. The user may or may not be informed about this, and details of the associated security events are generally sent to the security logging, alarming, or alerting subsystems.
TIA	*Abbrev:* **T**ransfer **I**mpact **A**ssessment.
Tier 1, 2, or 3	Classification labels relating to the availability requirements or business-criticality of business processes and the supporting information systems. Tier 1 is normally the most critical class.
Time-based **O**ne-**T**ime **P**assword **(TOTP)**	**M**ulti**F**actor **A**uthentication scheme involves proving possession of a shared secret using a SHA-2 based cryptographic challenge and response specific to a point in time (a **O**ne-**T**ime **P**assword), preventing later replay. Specified in RFC 6238. More info: https://datatracker.ietf.org/doc/html/rfc6238
Time bomb	Type of logic bomb or explosive weapon designed to detonate at a specific time or after a particular delay. "Resident computer program that triggers an unauthorized act at a predefined time" *(CNSSI 4009)*.
Timeout	Function that automatically suspends and password-locks, or terminates, a computer session after a specified period (normally several minutes) without user activity. Reduces the risk of someone taking advantage of a system from which the legitimate user has walked away without having screen-locked or logged off (naughty naughty).
Timescale	The period during which an event/incident (such as a fraud) or activity (such as a project) occurs. "The expected or planned time frame to achieve an objective or meet a target" *(OCEG GRC Glossary)*.
Time series analysis	Analysis of audit samples selected at particular times, *e.g.* testing recoverability of one backup per month. "The analysis of an ordered sequence of values of a variable at equally spaced time intervals" *(NIST SP 800-55v1)*. *Cf.* random sample, stratified sample, attribute sample, convenience sample, discovery sample.
Timestamp	"Time variant parameter which denotes a point in time with respect to a common time reference" *(ISO/IEC 11770-1)*.
Timing	"A measure that estimates when an event or impact might occur" *(OCEG GRC Glossary)*.

TERM	MEANING
Tinba (Tiny banker)	Species of bank Trojan in the wild in 2016. Manipulated the lure bank's logon page using HTML injection, capturing customers' credentials and presenting them with an error message while sending the credentials to a command and control node for subsequent exploitation.
Tiny fragment attack	"With many IP implementations it is possible to impose an unusually small fragment size on outgoing packets. If the fragment size is made small enough to force some of a TCP packet's TCP header fields into the second fragment, filter rules that specify patterns for those fields will not match. If the filtering implementation does not enforce a minimum fragment size, a disallowed packet might be passed because it didn't hit a match in the filter. STD 5, RFC 791 states: Every Internet module must be able to forward a datagram of 68 octets without further fragmentation. This is because an Internet header may be up to 60 octets, and the minimum fragment is 8 octets" *(SANS glossary).*
TIP	*Abbrev:* **T**hreat **I**ntelligence **P**latform.
TISAX (Trusted Information Security Assessment eXchange)	Conformity certification and assurance scheme for supply chain information security within the automotive industry, assessing companies against security control requirements specified in the **I**nformation **S**ecurity **A**ssessment, then sharing the assessment results in confidence among members of the scheme. "An assessment and exchange mechanism for the information security of enterprises [that] allows recognition of assessment results among the participants." More info: https://enx.com/en-us/tisax/
TLP	*Abbrev:* **T**raffic **L**ight **P**rotocol.
TLPT	*Abbrev:* **T**hreat-**L**ed **P**enetration **T**est.
TLS	*Abbrev:* **T**ransport **L**ayer **S**ecurity.
TOCTOU (Time Of Check, Time Of Use)	Type of hack that changes or switches something (such as a file) *after* it has been checked and authorised or granted permission for access, but *before* subsequent steps in the program or process including the actual access. Similar to a race condition. An example involves smugglers exploiting the pre-clearance and consequent enhanced trustworthiness of frequent travellers, using them as (presumably unwitting) mules to carry contraband across borders. Bait-and-switch is another form.
TOE	*Abbrev:* **T**arget **O**f **E**valuation.

TERM	MEANING
Token	Something that represents or stands in for something else, such as a security token (physically authenticates the user) or a fictitious value in a file (see tokenisation). "1. In security systems, a physical device that is used to authenticate a user, typically in addition to a username and password; in programming languages, a single element of the language. 2. In natural language processing (NLP), a unit of data representing individual words, subwords, or characters typically used as input for models" *(ISACA glossary)*. See also honeytoken, authenticator.
Token-based access control	"Associates a list of objects and their privileges with each user. (The opposite of list based.)" *(SANS glossary)*.
Tokenisation	a. Process of systematically replacing names, labels, *etc.* that identify specific individuals with fictitious, generic, or randomly generated tokens, tags, code words, alphanumeric identifiers, *etc.,* usually for privacy reasons such as pseudonymity. b. [In **N**atural **L**anguage **P**rocessing] "The process of breaking down text or data into smaller units" *(ISACA glossary)*.
Tolerance, tolerable error, margin for error	Willingness to allow, accept, expect, or forgive variation, imprecision, or error, 'within reason' (implying insignificance). "The maximum error in the population that professionals are willing to accept and still conclude that the test objective has been achieved For substantive tests, tolerable error is related to professionals' judgment about materiality. In compliance tests, it is the maximum rate of deviation from a prescribed control procedure that the professionals are willing to accept" *(ISACA glossary)*. "A range for an indicator that defines an acceptable, though not preferred, level of variation around a target the organization is willing and able to address" *(OCEG GRC Glossary)*. See also risk tolerance.
Topic-specific policy	Corporate policy concerning a particular information security subject, such as cryptography or access control. "Intentions and direction on a specific subject or topic, as formally expressed by the appropriate level of management" *(ISO/IEC 27002)*.
Top management, top-level management	See executive management. "Person or group of people who directs and controls an organisation at the highest level. Notes: top management has the power to delegate authority and provide resources within the organization. If the scope of the management system covers only part of an organization then top management refers to those who direct and control that part of the organization" *(ISO/IEC 27000)*. "The highest level of management in the enterprise, responsible for direction and control of the enterprise as a whole (such as director, general manager, partner, chief officer and executive manager)" *(ISACA glossary)*. *Cf.* senior management.

TERM	MEANING
TOP SECRET	Commonplace classification label (often CAPITALISED for emphasis) for information even more confidential than SECRET. TOP SECRET information may be further classified according to its nature and distribution, often on nationalistic/xenophobic lines, *e.g.* 'NOFORN' (no foreign nationals) or 'NZ eyes only.' While the intention is reasonably self-evident, the label, definition, and associated controls are organisation- and context-specific. "Information, the unauthorized disclosure of which reasonably could be expected to cause exceptionally grave damage to the national security that the original classification authority is able to identify or describe" *(Executive Order 13526)*. *Cf.* CONFIDENTIAL, SECRET, ULTRA.
TOP SECRET area	"Any area certified to operate at TOP SECRET, containing TOP SECRET servers, workstations or associated network infrastructure" *(NZISM)*. "An area that has been authorised to process, store or communicate TOP SECRET data. Such areas are not necessarily tied to a specific level of security zone" *(AusISM)*.
Tor (The onion router)	Internet communications application and associated global network. Tor traffic passes through thousands of Tor relays, using multiple layers of encryption to reduce (but not eliminate) the risk of interception, monitoring, surveillance, and **T**raffic **A**nalysis, and so protect users' privacy. A mix network.
Torrentlocker	Species of ransomware.
Tort	Legal term for a civil – as opposed to criminal – wrong. The tort victim or plaintiff in a civil court case may seek compensation for the damages they have suffered from, and/or court orders (injunctions) concerning, the defendant (tortfeasor).
Total performance	"A model of balanced performance that includes effectiveness (soundness), efficiency (leanness), responsiveness (agility), and resiliency (antifragility)" *(OCEG GRC Glossary)*.
TOTP	*Abbrev:* **T**ime-based **O**ne-**T**ime **P**assword.
TPM	*Abbrev:* **T**rusted **P**latform **M**odule.
TPRM	*Abbrev:* **T**hird **P**arty **R**isk **M**anagement.
TR	*Abbrev:* **T**echnical **R**eport.

TERM	MEANING
Traceability	Ability to link a person, event, incident, transaction, product, system component, *etc.* unambiguously back to its origin, source, or cause, *e.g.* telephone callers can be traced using a pen register; audit trails and change logs may implicate or exonerate someone in relation to an information security incidents; and vulnerable software libraries, *etc.* can be identified with an effective **S**oftware **B**ill **o**f **M**aterials. "Property that allows the tracking of the activity of an identity, process, or an element throughout the supply chain" *(ISO/IEC 27036-3)*. "1. The degree to which a relationship can be established between two or more products of the development process, especially products having a predecessor-successor or master-subordinate relationship to one another, *e.g.*, the degree to which the requirements and design of a given software component match. 2. The degree to which each element in a software development product establishes its reason for existing, *e.g.*, the degree to which each element in a bubble chart references the requirement that it satisfies" *(ISACA glossary)*.
Tracert, trace route	Network administration utility to trace and measure (time) the route from the local system to a given remote device through intermediate nodes using a sequence of **I**nternet **C**ontrol **M**essage **P**rotocol pings or **U**ser **D**atagram **P**rotocol messages with increasing **T**ime **T**o **L**ive counters, starting at 1, to query each intermediate host individually. "A tool [that] maps the route a packet takes from the local machine to a remote destination" *(SANS glossary)*.
Track, tracking, tracing	Path or sequence followed by someone or something. a. Accumulating potentially sensitive information about assets through covert observation (snooping), monitoring, and surveillance of their online activities, physical movements, interactions/associations with others, *etc.* May involve the use of discreet tracking technologies such as bugs and spyware on smartphones, and small **G**lobal **P**ositioning **S**ervice-enabled geolocation systems in/attached to vehicles, packages, or valuables. May be performed by agents such as the police, private investigators, and spies for criminal or terrorist profiling, crime detection, *etc.*, or by third-parties such as the providers of professional services such as analytics for targeted advertising and other purposes – whether illicit or legitimate. Can lead to privacy breaches, identity fraud, and targeting of individuals, *e.g.* kidnapping. Can help track down lost or stolen smartphones, vehicles, briefcases and suitcases, money bags, keys, pets, children, Alzheimer's sufferers, *etc.* b. Monitoring a parameter or metric over time, determining trends and anomalies by analysis.

TERM	MEANING
Tradecraft	Valuable skills and spooky techniques for spying or performing similar clandestine or indeed overt activities. Cunning tricks-of-the-trade accumulated and, in some cases, invented or actively developed by experienced professionals and talented amateurs (lockpicking, for instance). Information risk management, penetration testing, and auditing methods are, in effect, forms of tradecraft.
Trademark, trade mark	Legal protection for words/phrases, images, designs, and other characteristics distinctive of branded products. An **I**ntellectual **P**roperty **R**ight, often designated by ® if formally registered with the authorities or ™ if claimed in common law. "A sound, color, logo, saying or other distinctive symbol closely associated with a certain product or company" *(ISACA glossary)*. See also service mark.
Trade secret	Confidential information asset such as proprietary knowledge owned by an organisation which gives it competitive advantage so long as it remains unknown and/or unexploited by competitors, *e.g.* an invention may be both valuable and vulnerable to **I**ntellectual **P**roperty theft through industrial or economic espionage.
Traffic	The flow of messages, packets, chatter, vehicles, or products (including arms, drugs, and people trafficking) through a computer or social network or communications path, infrastructure, or supply chain.
Traffic **A**nalysis **(TA)**	Use of metadata relating to communications to derive potentially sensitive and/or valuable information. Even if communications between two or more parties are strongly encrypted so that the pure information *content* of the exchanges themselves remains confidential, an observer may glean, deduce, or infer useful information from the nature and volume of the traffic flows. The mere fact that communication appears to be occurring at all may be incriminating in some circumstances, *e.g.* if the particular counterparties (identified by their phone numbers, names, email addresses, *etc.*), or the timing of traffic indicates what might be going on (*e.g.* secretive negotiations between business partners, financiers, and other advisors prior to a merger or deal, or criminals conspiring). "Inference of information from observation of traffic flow. Note: Example: Analysis of the presence, absence, amount, direction, and frequency of traffic" *(ISO/IEC 2382)*. "Gaining knowledge of information by inference from observable characteristics of a data flow, even if the information is not directly available (*e.g.*, when the data is encrypted). These characteristics include the identities and locations of the source(s) and destination(s) of the flow, and the flow's presence, amount, frequency, and duration of occurrence" *(CNSSI 4009)*. See also **N**etwork **T**raffic **A**nalysis.

TERM	MEANING
Traffic flow filter	"A device that has been configured to automatically filter and control the form of network data" *(NZISM)*.
Traffic **L**ight **P**rotocol **(TLP)**	Classification scheme specified by US-CERT for security information potentially of national importance, with four traffic-light colours: **TLP:RED** (not to be disclosed), **TLP:AMBER** (limited disclosure permitted within the recipient organisation), **TLP:GREEN** (limited disclosure permitted within the information security community), and **TLP:WHITE** (freely disclosable, distribution unrestricted). In some jurisdictions, **TLP:CLEAR** is the unrestricted label. More info: https://www.us-cert.gov/tlp
Traffic padding	Control against **T**raffic **A**nalysis involves generating and blending in fake communications traffic (essentially, noise), making it harder for adversaries to identify genuine information flows. Note: this is distinct from the *message* padding needed to form fixed-length network packets. "Countermeasure that generates spurious data in transmission media to make traffic analysis or decryption more difficult" *(ISO/IEC 2382)*. "Generation of mock communications or data units to disguise the amount of real data units being sent" *(CNSSI 4009)*. See also chaff, flare, mix network.
Tragedy of the commons	While everyone may benefit collectively from pooling resources and participating in shared activities, cheats may seize the opportunity to profit at the expense of others, *e.g.* by exploiting **I**ntellectual **P**roperty without considering or compensating its owners (piracy) or flagrantly using, mining, refining, selling, and burning fossil fuels without mitigating the associated environmental harm.
Trained model	Model who knows how to smile alluringly at the camera, walk, and pivot elegantly on the podium, that sort of thing. "Result of model training" *(ISO/IEC 22989)*.
Training, model training	Educational activity in which human students or **M**achine **L**earning models are instructed in some depth, for instance how to perform particular activities or tasks such as administering user access rights or distinguishing malicious from benign network traffic. "Activities designed to facilitate the learning and development of knowledge, skills and abilities, and to improve the performance of specific tasks or roles" *(ISO 22300)*. "Process to determine or to improve the parameters of a machine learning model, based on a machine learning algorithm, by using training data" *(ISO/IEC 22989)*. "The process of determining the ideal parameters comprising a model" *(ISACA glossary)*. *Cf.* security awareness.

TERM	MEANING
Training data	Information or data used for training. "Data used to train a machine learning model" *(ISO/IEC 22989)*.
Transaction	a. Commercial/business deal or trade, *e.g.* purchasing a product. b. Group of closely related processing operations, *e.g.* updating a bank account or ledger to record a debit, updating another account or ledger to record a credit of the same value, then simultaneously committing both changes to the finance system's **D**ata**B**ase. "Business events or information grouped together because they have a single or similar purpose. Note: Typically, a transaction is applied to a calculation or event that then results in the updating of a holding or master file. [and] 1. A command, message or input record that explicitly or implicitly calls for a processing action, such as updating a file. 2. An exchange between an end user and an interactive system. 3. In a database management system, a unit of processing activity that accomplishes a specific purpose, such as a retrieval, an update, a modification or a deletion of one or more data elements of a storage structure" *(ISACA glossary)*.
Transmission **C**ontrol **P**rotocol **(TCP)**	Connection-oriented transport layer networking protocol that provides reliable, ordered, and error-checked data delivery between devices. A key part of the TCP/IP suite of protocols. Before data are exchanged, the systems connect at a basic **I**nternet **P**rotocol level to negotiate and agree the datacommunications protocols and parameters they will use through a short sequence of transmissions and acknowledgements. "A connection-based Internet protocol that supports reliable data transfer connections. Notes: Packet data are verified using checksums and retransmitted if they are missing or corrupted. The application plays no part in validating the transfer" *(ISACA glossary)*. "A set of rules (protocol) used along with the Internet Protocol to send data in the form of message units between computers over the Internet. While IP takes care of handling the actual delivery of the data, TCP takes care of keeping track of the individual units of data (called packets) that a message is divided into for efficient routing through the Internet. Whereas the IP protocol deals only with packets, TCP enables two hosts to establish a connection and exchange streams of data. TCP guarantees delivery of data and also guarantees that packets will be delivered in the same order in which they were sent" *(SANS glossary)*. *Cf.* **U**ser **D**atagram **P**rotocol.
Tranquillity	a. Information security principle that an object's classification level must not change while it is being processed, except for privileged, strictly controlled functions relating to the classification process itself. b. Sense of calm, quiet reflection, unwinding, a happy place for stress relief.

TERM	MEANING
Transcription check	"A check to ensure that any data transferred between any records and/or systems has been transferred correctly" *(FSRCoP)*.
Transfer cross-domain solution	"A system that facilitates the transfer of data, in one or multiple directions (low to high or high to low), between different security domains" *(AusISM)*.
Transfer design option	"A special case of a sharing design option where an attempt is made to give close to 100% of consequence to another party such as an insurance company" *(OCEG GRC Glossary)*.
Transfer gateway	"Facilitates the secure transfer of information, in one or multiple directions (*i.e.* low to high or high to low), between different security domains" *(NZISM)*.
Transfer **I**mpact **A**ssessment **(TIA)**	Formal process potentially required under the **G**eneral **D**ata **P**rotection **R**egulation to ensure that personal data will be adequately protected if it is sent out of the **E**uropean **U**nion, *e.g. passed through a transfer tool to be processed by* cloud applications hosted in countries whose privacy practices are not deemed adequate by the European Commission. Supplementary privacy controls such as pseudonymisation may be appropriate.
Transfer tool	Mechanism (*e.g. binding* contractual clauses) designed to facilitate the secure transfer of personal data to countries whose privacy practices fall short of requirements under the **G**eneral **D**ata **P**rotection **R**egulation according to the European Commission.
Transformation	Notable step-change or discontinuity, *e.g.* from ciphertext to plaintext, or pupa to butterfly. "The conversion of one state or format into another state or format" *(NIST SP 800-55v1)*.
Transition	Moving between states, modes, phases, or activities, *e.g.* from the previous to a new version of a standard, procedure, system, or protocol. May be a sharply defined point in time (a step-change) or more gradually (evolutionary change). May be proactively managed and directed/driven, or may occur naturally.
Transition audit	Recertification audit confirming that the organisation has successfully adopted and achieved conformity to a new version of a standard such as ISO/IEC 27001.
Transitive trust	In many situations, if our trusted colleague, business partner, computer system, *etc.* trusts a third party, we also implicitly trust the third party to some extent. In effect, trust is capable of transiting or spanning multiple relationships, albeit weakening with distance, *e.g.* placing trust in an organisation's ISO/IEC 27001 certificate implies trusting the **C**ertification **B**ody that issued it, and *vice versa*. Likewise with **P**ublic **K**ey **I**nfrastructures, where root certificates from two or more PKIs may be cross-certified to enable interoperability.

TERM	MEANING
Transmission system	"Transmission grid for the transport of electrical energy using a high voltage or ultra-high voltage grid or a gas transmission network for the transport of natural gas using a high-pressure pipeline network" *(ISO/IEC 27019)*.
Transparency, openness	Information security governance, management, privacy, and integrity principle to be open and honest, freely disclosing ownership, risks, controls, incidents, *etc.* under appropriate circumstances. Strongly associated with trust. "Property of a system or process to imply openness and accountability" *(ISO/IEC 27036-3)*. "<Organization> Property of an organization that appropriate activities and decisions are communicated to relevant stakeholders in a comprehensive, accessible and understandable manner. Note: Inappropriate communication of activities and decisions can violate security, privacy or confidentiality requirements. <System> Property of a system that appropriate information about the system is made available to relevant stakeholders. Notes: Appropriate information for system transparency can include aspects such as features, performance, limitations, components, procedures, measures, design goals, design choices and assumptions, data sources and labelling protocols; Inappropriate disclosure of some aspects of a system can violate security, privacy or confidentiality requirements" *(ISO/IEC 22989)*. "Open, comprehensive, accessible, clear and understandable presentation of information" *(ISO 16759)*. "Refers to an enterprise's openness about its activities and is based on the following concepts: How the mechanism functions is clear to those who are affected by or want to challenge governance decisions; A common vocabulary has been established; Relevant information is readily available. Note: Transparency and stakeholder trust are directly related; the more transparency in the governance process, the more confidence in the governance" *(ISACA glossary)*.
Transport **L**ayer **S**ecurity **(TLS)**	Cryptographic protocol using X.509 digital certificates for authentication and secure exchange of session keys used for symmetric encryption, *e.g.* of data flowing between a browser and a web server, or for **L**ightweight **D**irectory **A**ccess **P**rotocol, **I**nternet **M**essaging **A**ccess **P**rotocol, and FTP traffic. Replaced the insecure and hence deprecated **S**ecure **S**ockets **L**ayer in 1999, although several exploitable vulnerabilities in TLS have since been discovered (*e.g.* Heartbleed, DROWN). "A cryptographic protocol that provides secure communications, endpoint security and privacy on the Internet" *(ISACA glossary)*. "A protocol that ensures privacy between communicating applications and their users on the Internet. When a server and client communicate, TLS ensures that no third party may eavesdrop or tamper with any message. TLS is the successor to the Secure Sockets Layer" *(SANS glossary)*.

TERM	MEANING
Transport mode	IPsec can encrypt and/or authenticate just the payload of an IP packet, providing confidentiality, data, and communications integrity when sent over a trusted network. "An IPSec mode that provides a secure connection between two endpoints by encapsulating an IP payload" *(NZISM)*. See also tunnel mode.
Transposition, permutation	Cryptographic process for re-sequencing and hence scrambling characters or bits from the plaintext to create the ciphertext, often systematically such that the process can later be reversed using the same key. A trivial example might involve writing the plaintext into a grid structure column-wise left-to-right, then reading off the ciphertext row-wise top-to-bottom, reversing the process for decryption. Modern cryptographic algorithms make the transposition process *far* more complex and convoluted. *Cf.* substitution.
Trap and trace	See pen register.
Trapdoor	a. Physical security mechanism (the door) that permits/encourages someone to enter into a confined area (the trap) but then closes behind them to resist/prevent their escape. Sometimes used as a single-person portal to regulate ingress and egress for a highly secure facility such as a data centre, bank vault, or fancy jeweller. b. In cryptography, a function that is easy to compute *if* you know the key/s, *e.g.* encrypting a sensitive message, otherwise *extremely* hard (computationally intensive), *e.g.* decrypting the ciphertext *without* the key/s. In other words, it goes one way. See also backdoor. c. Covert capability in some programs, allowing access to hidden functions for coding and debugging, or for nefarious/spooky purposes (see backdoor). "Hidden software or hardware mechanism, usually created for testing and troubleshooting, that may be used to circumvent computer security" *(ISO/IEC 2382)*. "Unauthorized electronic exit, or doorway, out of an authorized computer program into a set of malicious instructions or programs" *(ISACA glossary)*.
Treason	Serious act of betrayal that threatens to cause, or causes, material harm to the state, the crown, or a similar authority or ruler, or that aides, or attempts to aide, an enemy of the state. An insider threat.
Trembler	Motion-detection device (such as a magnetic reed switch and magnetic steel ball, a blob of mercury in a glass vial with wire contact points, or an inertial sensor) attached to or embedded within an object such as a server, door, window, safe, media transporter or vehicle, that is triggered by vibration, shock, or tumbling, perhaps indicating unauthorised removal or penetration.

TERM	MEANING
Trespass	Unauthorised physical entry into private property, zone, or area, or assaulting or interfering with property belonging to another person. Whether a trespasser acts accidentally or maliciously affects the level of risk to the victim and has legal ramifications for the trespasser, while the victim's negligence (*e.g.* in not clearly designating the area private) may also affect the outcome in court.
Triada	Species of malware that infected Android smartphones, in the wild in 2018. Exploited a privilege elevation vulnerability, allowing it and other malware to take control of infected devices.
Triage	Term borrowed from the emergency medical practice of quickly evaluating an influx of patients to distinguish and focus limited resources on those who can probably be saved from those who stand little if any chance of survival. Information security is seldom literally a life-or-death matter but similar difficult decisions must be made, often rapidly and with limited, low-quality information, following serious incidents and disasters. Establishing the capability to perform triage is part of **B**usiness **C**ontinuity **M**anagement and contingency planning.
Trickbot	Hacker/cybercriminal gang and a species of malware in the wild in 2022.
Trigger	Action, situation, or condition that initiates, prompts, or causes something to occur. "Event that causes the system to initiate a response. Note: Also known as triggering event" *(ISO/IEC 27031).*
Triple **D**ata **E**ncryption **S**tandard **(3DES)**	Cryptographic algorithm which repeats DES three times in succession using two (ABA, AAB, or ABB) or three (ABC) different keys. Specified in FIPS PUB 46-3. Vulnerable to brute force attacks and hence deprecated in favour of **A**dvanced **E**ncryption **S**tandard. "A block cipher created from the Data Encryption Standard (DES) cipher by using it three times. 3DES was broken in 2016" *(ISACA glossary).* "A block cipher, based on DES, that transforms each 64-bit plaintext block by applying the Data Encryption Algorithm three successive times, using either two or three different keys, for an effective key length of 112 or 168 bits" *(SANS glossary).*
Triton, Trisis	Species of malware in the wild in 2017–2019 that targeted Triconex plant control systems (**O**perational **T**echnology), raising safety and **C**ritical **N**ational **I**nfrastructure concerns.
Trojan horse, Trojan	Malware program that appears to the user simply to be genuinely useful and benign, but in fact contains hidden malicious functions, typically allowing remote control of the system by hackers, or installing keyloggers to steal personal information, passwords, PIN codes, credit card numbers, or online banking credentials (*e.g.* Man-In-The-Browser). "Apparently harmless program containing malicious logic that allows the unauthorized collection,

TERM **MEANING**

falsification, or destruction of data" *(ISO/IEC 2382)*. "A computer program that appears to have a useful function, but also has a hidden and potentially malicious function that evades security mechanisms, sometimes by exploiting legitimate authorizations of a system entity that invokes the program" *(CNSSI 4009)*. "Malware that appears to perform a desirable function for the user but that mislead the user of its true intent" *(ISO/IEC 27032)*. "Purposefully hidden malicious or damaging code within an authorized computer program" *(ISACA glossary)*. "A computer program that appears to have a useful function, but also has a hidden and potentially malicious function that evades security mechanisms, sometimes by exploiting legitimate authorizations of a system entity that invokes the program" *(SANS glossary)*.

Troll, trolling Intentionally provoking others online to elicit strong emotional reactions or disrupt conversations, typically by repeatedly and flagrantly posting inflammatory content, spreading misinformation and off-topic content, or mounting *ad hominem* attacks.

True value "Value that characterizes a quantity perfectly defined in the conditions which exist when that quantity is considered. The true value of a quantity is an ideal concept and, in general, cannot be known exactly" *(FSRCoP)*.

Trust, trolling Relatively weak but commonplace information security control in which supposedly trustworthy people, systems, programs, functions, organisations, *etc.* are expected, anticipated, or to various extents required to behave with integrity, predictably, appropriately, responsibly, honestly, ethically, transparently, and in the trusting party's best interests. Trust usually takes time to be established and yet can be decimated in an instant by an incident; hence, contingency arrangements and/or other controls (such as compliance checks and predefined liabilities) are generally advisable, where possible. "Relationship between two entities and/or elements, consisting of a set of activities and a security policy in which element *x* trusts element *y* if and only if *x* has confidence that y will behave in a well-defined way (with respect to the activities) that does not violate the given security policy" *(ISO/IEC 27036-1)*. "Determine which permissions and what actions other systems or users can perform on remote machines" *(SANS glossary)*. *Cf.* trustworthy, untrusted.

Trust boundary Trust boundary. "The interface between two or more Trust Zones" *(NZISM)*. "Typically … the components of the system under your direct control. All connections and data from systems outside of your direct control, including all clients and systems managed by other parties, should be consider untrusted and be validated at the boundary, before allowing further system interaction" *(SCP QRG)*.

TERM	MEANING
Trust centre	Web page, showcase, dashboard, or portal typically outlining in general terms the organisation's information security and privacy arrangements (such as its security certifications, governance, policies, and cybersecurity controls) for current and prospective business partners, customers, *etc.* Intended to reduce the need for supply chain security questionnaires, reviews, and audits, presuming that the information provided is sufficiently accurate and complete, and the organisation is trustworthy. May offer additional, more sensitive information for selected third parties and corporate users.
Trusted computer system	"Data processing system that provides sufficient computer security to allow for concurrent access to data by users with different access rights and to data with different security classification and security categories" *(ISO/IEC 2382).*
Trusted **C**omputing **B**ase **(TCB)**	Relatively secure and trustworthy low-level computing subsystem typically comprising hardware, software, and firmware specifically designed to perform certain privileged security activities, with the integrity necessary to secure the system as a whole. May be formally designed and mathematically proven secure for high assurance.
Trusted download	Special process for exporting information from a highly classified, lowly classified, or unclassified system, in an approved simple data format (*e.g.* plain ASCII, HTML, JPG, BMP, or GIF rather than MS Office or other complex file types) that can be and in fact is inspected for any inappropriate content before being authorised for release.
Trusted **E**xecution **E**nvironment **(TEE)**	**I**nformation **T**echnology systems, cryptosystems, devices, communication paths, *etc.* protected within a notional design boundary or situation, sharing a comparable level of information security and hence trustworthiness.
Trusted information communication entity	Trustworthy organisation or individual with whom even sensitive information relating to information security, risks, threats, vulnerabilities, *etc.* can be shared. "Autonomous organisation supporting information exchange within an information sharing community" *(ISO/IEC 27000).*
Trusted **P**latform **M**odule **(TPM)**	Type of **H**ardware **S**ecurity **M**odule incorporated into recent PCs, providing safe storage for cryptographic keys and functions such as random number generation, key storage, and authentication in an embedded subsystem built around a tamper-resistant TPM chip. A unique private RSA key, burned into the chip during manufacturing, allows the TPM to be authenticated by systems or programs that need this level of trust (*e.g.* for whole disk encryption or DRM). However, researchers claim to have overcome the tamper-resistance physical security features of some TPM chips, while the **N**ational **S**ecurity **A**gency's involvement with RSA indicates the distinct possibility that TPM security may have been *deliberately* weakened, raising doubts about the value of this physical security control.

TERM	MEANING
Trusted port	Low-numbered network port. "Ports below number 1024 usually allowed to be opened by the root user" *(SANS glossary)*.
Trusted rôle	Privileged rôle, position/job, engagement, or assignment requiring and depending on the trustworthiness and integrity of a person, team, or organisation.
Trusted source	"A person or system formally identified as being capable of reliably producing information meeting defined parameters, such as a maximum data classification and reliably reviewing information produced by others to confirm compliance with defined parameters" *(NZISM)*.
Trusted **T**hird **P**arty **(TTP)**	Organisation or individual that is trusted by others, and may therefore act as a mutually acceptable intermediary between them, *e.g.* to hold and transfer valuables such as cryptographic keys or money (escrow) or to audit one party and report the overall findings to the others without necessarily disclosing confidential details (*e.g.* **C**ertification **B**ody).
Trust service	Digital signature service ensuring integrity (such as identification, authentication, and nonrepudiation) for electronic and online transactions, contracts, *etc.* "An electronic service normally provided for remuneration which consists of: (a) the creation, verification, and validation of electronic signatures, electronic seals or electronic time stamps, electronic registered delivery services and certificates related to those services, or (b) the creation, verification and validation of certificates for website authentication; or (c) the preservation of electronic signatures, seals or certificates related to those services" *(EU regulation 910/2014)*. "A set of professional attestation and advisory services based on a core set of criteria related to security, availability, processing integrity, confidentiality, or privacy" *(**T**rust **S**ervices **C**riteria)*.
Trust **S**ervices **C**riteria **(TSC)**	"TSP Section 100 – 2017 Trust Services Criteria for Security, Availability, Processing Integrity, Confidentiality, and Privacy – Includes March 2020 updates" document from the **A**ssurance **S**ervices **E**xecutive **C**ommittee of the **A**ssociation of **I**nternational **C**ertified **P**rofessional **A**ccountants, founded by the **A**merican **I**nstitute of **C**ertified **P**ublic **A**ccountants, "for use in attestation or consulting engagements to evaluate and report on controls over the security, availability, processing integrity, confidentiality, or privacy of information and systems (a) across an entire entity; (b) at a subsidiary, division, or operating unit level; (c) within a function relevant to the entity's operational, reporting, or compliance objectives; or (d) for a particular type of information used by the entity." Defines five categories of controls against which organisations' compliance can be audited for their SOC 2

TERM	MEANING
	reports: security, availability, confidentiality, processing integrity, and privacy. More info: https://www.aicpa-cima.com/resources/download/2017-trust-services-criteria-with-revised-points-of-focus-2022
Trustworthy, trustworthiness	Measure of the extent to which someone or something is truly worthy of being trusted. An integrity property. Snake oil salesmen, spooks, and *some* politicians score low on this scale. "Ability to meet stakeholders' expectations in a verifiable way. Notes: Depending on the context or sector, and also on the specific product or service, data, technology and process used, different characteristics apply and need verification to ensure stakeholders' expectations are met. Characteristics of trustworthiness include, for instance, accountability, accuracy, authenticity, availability, controllability, integrity, privacy, quality, reliability, resilience, robustness, safety, security, transparency and usability. Trustworthiness is an attribute that can be applied to services, products, technology, data and information as well as to organizations. Verifiability includes measurability and demonstrability by means of objective evidence" *(ISO/IEC TS 5723)*. "The attribute of a person or enterprise that provides confidence to others of the qualifications, capabilities, and reliability of that entity to perform specific tasks and fulfill assigned responsibilities" *(CNSSI 4009)*. *Cf.* untrustworthy.
Trustworthy information system	"An information system that is believed to be capable of operating within defined levels of risk despite the environmental disruptions, human errors, structural failures, and purposeful attacks that are expected to occur in its environment of operation" *(OMB Circular A-130)*.
Trust zone	"A logical construct encompassing an area with a high degree of trust between the data, users, providers and the systems. It may include a number of capabilities such as secure boot, codesigning, trusted execution and Digital Rights Management (DRM). This term is NOT synonymous with Security Domain" *(NZISM)*.
Trust zone (cloud)	"In the public cloud environment, trust zones represent combinations of public cloud services (made up of user, system, and data object combinations) that are authorised to interact with each other and are protected by a common set of security capabilities" *(NZISM)*.
TS	*Abbrev:* **T**echnical **S**pecification.
TSCM	*Abbrev:* **T**echnical **S**urveillance **C**ounter**M**easures.

TERM	MEANING
TSR	*Abbrev:* **T**erminate and **S**tay **R**esident.
TTP	*Abbrev:* **T**rusted **T**hird **P**arty or **T**actics, **T**echniques, and **P**rocedures, depending on context.
TTS	*Abbrev:* **T**ext-**T**o-**S**peech. See speech synthesis.
TUNA	*Abbrev:* **T**urbulent, **U**ncertain, **N**ovel, and **A**mbiguous.
Tunnel	Relatively secure, trustworthy path through an insecure or untrusted communication path and network such as a **V**irtual **P**rivate **N**etwork. "Data path between networked devices which is established across an existing network infrastructure. Note: Tunnels can be established using techniques such as protocol encapsulation, label switching, or virtual circuits" *(ISO/IEC 27033-1)*. "Used to protect traffic between different networks when traffic must travel through intermediate or untrusted networks. Tunnel mode encapsulates the entire IP packet with an AH or ESP header and an additional IP header" *(ISACA glossary)*. "A communication channel created in a computer network by encapsulating a communication protocol's data packets in (on top of) a second protocol that normally would be carried above, or at the same layer as, the first one. Most often, a tunnel is a logical point-to-point link – *i.e.*, an OSI layer 2 connection – created by encapsulating the layer 2 protocol in a transport protocol (such as TCP), in a network or inter-network layer protocol (such as IP), or in another link layer protocol. Tunneling can move data between computers that use a protocol not supported by the network connecting them" *(SANS glossary)*.
Tunnelling	Creation, provision, or use of a tunnel. "Technology enabling one network to send its data via another network's connections. Tunneling works by encapsulating a network protocol within packets carried by the second network" *(CNSSI 4009)*.
Tunnel mode	IPsec can encrypt and/or authenticate an entire original IP packet (header and payload) and encapsulate it within a new IP packet, providing confidentiality, data, and communications integrity when sent over an untrusted network such as the Internet. "An IPSec mode that provides a secure connection between two endpoints by encapsulating an entire IP packet. The entire packet is encrypted and authenticated" *(NZISM)*. See also transport mode.
Turbulent, **U**ncertain, **N**ovel and **A**mbiguous **(TUNA)**	Alludes to the challenges involved in dealing with today's difficult and potentially hostile times. See also **V**olatile, **U**ncertain, **C**omplex, and **A**mbiguous.

TERM	MEANING
Two-Factor Authentication (2FA)	Simplest form of **M**ulti**F**actor **A**uthentication, *e.g.* requiring a password plus the current value displayed on a security token or a biometric to authenticate the claimed identity of a computer user. "The use of two independent mechanisms for authentication (*e.g.*, requiring both a smart card and a password), typically the combination of something you know, are or have" *(ISACA glossary)*. "An electronic authentication method in which a user is granted access to a network or application only after successfully presenting two or more pieces of evidence to an authentication mechanism (*e.g.* a password and a one-time passcode)" *(UK Cyber Security Breaches Survey 2023)*. "An authentication process that requires the user to produce two distinct types of credentials. Typically this is based on something they have (*e.g.*, smartcard) and something they know (*e.g.*, a pin). Other implementations may use the third type of credential based on something you are (*e.g.*, biometric readers)" *(SCP QRG)*.
TXT (TeXT) messaging	See **S**hort **M**essaging **S**ervice.
Type I error	See false acceptance.
Type II error	See false rejection.
Typex machine	Electromechanical typewriter-style rotor-based cryptographic machine, modelled on the pre-WWII Enigma, used by the UK government from 1937 until the late 1960s.
Typo, typoo	Typing or keyboard error, a common cause of information security incidents that are usually relatively minor but in rare cases can be extremely serious, costly, life-threatening even.
Typosquatter, typosquatting	Someone who registers a lookalike domain name remarkably similar to a legitimate website (*e.g.* bank.net instead of bank.com) intending to deceive website visitors who make typos when typing the intended **U**niform **R**esource **L**ocator or click phishing links, into believing that they are interacting with the genuine website. May be part of social engineering, identity fraud, drive-by downloads, and other frauds/scams, malware infection, *etc.* May infringe trademarks. May involve **D**omain **N**ame **S**ystem redirection to frustrate attempts to shut down the fakes. See also cybersquatting.

U

TERM	MEANING
UAT	*Abbrev:* **U**ser **A**cceptance **T**est.
UAV	*Abbrev:* **U**nmanned **A**utonomous **V**ehicle. See drone.
UBA	*Abbrev:* **U**ser **B**ehaviour **A**nalytics.
UBE	*Abbrev:* **U**nsolicited **B**ulk **E**mail. See spam.
Ubiquitous computing (ubicomp)	See **I**nternet **o**f ***T**hings*.
UC	*Abbrev:* **U**nified **C**ommunications.
UCF	*Abbrev:* **U**nified **C**ompliance **F**ramework.
UDP	*Abbrev:* **U**ser **D**atagram **P**rotocol.
UEBA	*Abbrev:* **U**ser **E**ntity **B**ehaviour **A**nalytics.
UEFI	*Abbrev:* **U**nified **E**xtensible **F**irmware **I**nterface.
UICC	*Abbrev:* **U**niversal **I**ntegrated **C**ircuit **C**ard.
UK Cyber Security Breaches Survey 2023	UK government **D**epartment for **S**cience, **I**nnovation and **T**echnology report on "a research study for UK cyber resilience, aligning with the National Cyber Strategy ... to inform government policy on cyber security." The survey took place from the end of 2022 into 2023 and the multipart report was published remarkably quickly in April 2023. More info: https://www.gov.uk/government/statistics/cyber-security-breaches-survey-2023
UK National **C**yber **S**ecurity **S**trategy 2022 **(UKNCSS)**	UK government's National Cyber Security Strategy. More info: https://www.gov.uk/government/publications/national-cyber-strategy-2022/national-cyber-security-strategy-2022
UK Resilience **L**essons **D**igest 2023 **(UKRLD)**	"Part of the government's commitment to strengthening whole-society resilience. It sits at the heart of a programme of work at the Cabinet Office Emergency Planning College (EPC) to synthesise lessons learned of all major exercises and emergencies." More info: https://tinyurl.com/UKRLD
ULTRA	UK classification level *above* TOP SECRET for military intelligence whose very existence would be strenuously and plausibly denied, since that would indicate the presence of, and hence threaten, effective espionage capabilities and compromised sources, putting the targets on guard. Intelligence gathered through cryptanalysis of radio intercepts at Bletchley Park during WWII was classified ULTRA, sustaining the enemy's unwarranted trust in Enigma and other flawed cryptographic devices and practices. While the intention is reasonably self-evident, the label, definition, and associated controls are organisation- and context-specific. *Cf.* CONFIDENTIAL, SECRET, TOP SECRET.

TERM	MEANING
UMBRA	Obsolete and deprecated US Special Intelligence Service term for COMINT more sensitive than MORAY and SPOKE.
UMTS	*Abbrev:* Universal Mobile Telecommunications System.
Unallocated space	"Area on digital media, including primary memory, which has not been allocated by the operating system, and which is available for the storage of data, including metadata" *(ISO/IEC 27037)*. See also slack space.
Unauthorised	Lacking the requisite authority, rights, or permission. Not permitted, accepted, or agreed by management as being in the best interests of the organisation or other stakeholders, and therefore implicitly or explicitly forbidden, prohibited, or restricted. *Cf.* authorised.
Unauthorised access	Access that is unauthorised – either expressly forbidden, or perhaps unspecified. "Access to information or system components that (a) has not been approved by a person designated to do so by management and (b) compromises segregation of duties, confidentiality commitments, or otherwise increases risks to the information or system components beyond the levels approved by management (that is, access is inappropriate)" *(Trust Services Criteria)*.
Unaware	Naïve, ignorant, blasé, and hence vulnerable, particularly but not only to social engineering. Lack of awareness is a factor in many incidents including accidents, gradual, slow-acting threats such as climate change, and attacks involving stealth, deception, and subterfuge (*e.g.* fraud). Workers who do not know about or fail to appreciate their obligations and expectations under various laws, policies, and rules are obviously less likely to comply. More subtly, it can be difficult to hold those who can legitimately *claim* or *feign* ignorance to account for failings.
Unbiased	Balanced, equitable, fair, objective, reasonable, and lacking in prejudice or favour towards or away from one party, view, position, *etc. Cf.* biased.
Uncertainty, uncertain	Doubted, doubtful, lacking in confidence, assurance, or surety, unpredictable, risky. "State, even partial, of deficiency of information related to understanding or knowledge. Notes: In some cases, uncertainty can be related to the organization's context as well as to its objectives; Uncertainty is the root source of risk, namely any kind of 'deficiency of information' that matters in relation to objectives (and objectives, in turn, relate to all relevant interested parties' needs and expectations" *(ISO 31073)*. "The difficulty of predicting an outcome due to limited knowledge of all components" *(ISACA glossary)*. "A state of being unsure about something due to incomplete knowledge or underlying randomness making it difficult to understand with complete confidence" *(OCEG GRC Glossary)*.

TERM	MEANING
Uncertainty of measurement	Risk of measurement errors. "The estimation of the uncertainty of measurement is a Codes and accreditation requirement and is based upon the principle that all measurements are subject to uncertainty and that a value is incomplete without a statement of accuracy. Sources of uncertainty can include unrepresentative samples, rounding errors, approximations and inadequate knowledge of the effect of external factors" *(FSRCoP)*.
UNC4191	One of several groups of elite hackers/cyber-spooks apparently of Chinese origin, active in 2023.
Unclassified	Paradoxical term for information, systems, networks, *etc.* that *have*, in fact, been classified but at the lowest level, requiring few if any protective controls. Alternatively, it *may* mean that they have not (yet) been assessed and classified, with markedly different implications.
UNCLASSIFIED information	"Information that is assessed as not requiring a classification" *(NZISM)*.
UNCLASSIFIED systems	"Systems that process, store or communicate information produced by the New Zealand Government that does not require a classification" *(NZISM)*.
Undercover	Covert, surreptitious, discreet, camouflaged.
Unethical	Behaviour which is not ethical and hence generally considered inappropriate, distasteful, or undesirable if not totally unacceptable and possibly even illegal. The willingness to disregard social norms and constraints on behaviour sets liars, cheats, spies, hackers, fraudsters, criminals, and other reprobates apart from the general population, and is itself a threat to unaware victims. At the same time, different social groups have their own unique ethics, codes, and sense of what is right or wrong, *e.g.* hacking is deemed acceptable (cool or revered in fact) within the hacker community, whereas cracking is generally frowned upon and despised (regardless of what may happen in private).
Unified **C**ommunications **(UC)**	Integrated approach to managing various communications services within an organisation, streamlining real-time and asynchronous channels to improve efficiency and productivity. Typically combines voice calls, video conferencing, instant messaging, email, and file sharing with a centralised management system, enabling seamless switching between different modes of communication and productive collaboration across devices and locations. "The integration of real-time and near real time communication and interaction services in an organisation or agency. Unified Communications (UC) may integrate several communication systems including unified messaging, collaboration, and interaction systems; real-time and near real-time communications; and transactional applications" *(NZISM)*.

TERM	MEANING
Unified **C**ompliance **F**ramework **(UCF)**	Commercial information service provides clients with consolidated compliance information drawn from about a thousand current 'authority documents' (standards, laws/regulations, guidelines, *etc.*) concerning information security, privacy, cybersecurity, *etc.* More info: https://www.unifiedcompliance.com/home
Unified **E**xtensible **F**irmware **I**nterface **(UEFI)**	Standardised interface between a computer's firmware (from initial power-up, accessing and controlling the underlying hardware) and the **O**perating **S**ystem which takes over to boot and run the system. Supports secure boot and much bigger disks than the original BIOS.
Unified **S**ervice **M**anagement **(USM)**	"A universal methodical approach for service management. The USM method provides a standardized management system for a service organization of any size, in any line of business, to manage its people, its processes, its technology, and its services, based on an explicit service management architecture" *(USM Wiki).* More info: https://usmwiki.com/
Uninterruptible **P**ower **S**upply **(UPS)**	Resilient auxiliary power supply connected to batteries and/or an electrical power generator intended to maintain power to attached computer equipment, *etc.* if the incoming main power source should fail. A contingency and business continuity control. Paradoxically, inadequately specified, designed, manufactured, tested, and managed UPSs are a major *cause* of power problems and unplanned outages, making this a relatively fragile fail-unsafe control unless professionally engineered, proven, monitored, and maintained. "A type of power supply that provides short-term backup power from batteries to a computer system when the electrical power fails or drops to an unacceptable voltage level" *(ISACA glossary).*
Unit	Individual thing, item, person, *etc.*, generally a small, discrete part of something bigger, *e.g.* a block, byte, function, team, or subsystem. "1. A separately testable element specified in the design of a computer software element. 2. A logically separable part of a computer program" *(ISACA glossary).* See also unit of measure, component.
Unit 8200, Central Collection Unit of the Intelligence Corps, **I**sraeli **S**IGINT **N**ational **U**nit **(ISNU)**	Military intelligence corps, allegedly the largest unit of the **I**sraelis **D**efence **F**orces with several thousand cyber-spooks. Originally a SIGINT function; it now conducts both offensive and defensive cybersecurity operations, *i.e.* cyberwar plus support for Israeli government departments and businesses.
Unit of measure, measurement unit	Defined standardised reference unit, quantity, or amount against which things can be compared and hence measured or quantified, *e.g.* gram, metre, second. "Particular quantity, defined and adopted by convention, with which other quantities of the same kind are compared in order to express their magnitude relative to that quantity" *(ISO/IEC/IEEE 15939).*

TERM	MEANING
Unit test	Assurance test against the specifications and design for the functionality, capacity, *etc*. of a unit (a discrete software or hardware module, section, component, device, function, capability, *etc*.) in isolation, prior to its incorporation into the complete program or system. "Test of individual programs or modules in order to ensure that there are no analysis or programming errors" *(ISO/IEC 2382)*. "1. A testing technique used to test program logic within a particular program or module. Notes: The purpose of the test is to ensure that the internal operation of the program performs according to specification. It uses a set of test cases that focus on the control structure of the procedural design. 2. Testing of individual hardware or software units" *(ISACA glossary)*. See also integration test, system test, regression test, incremental test, penetration test, load test, stress test, security test, acceptance test.
Universal **I**ntegrated **C**ircuit **C**ard **(UICC)**	Extended smartphone **S**ubscriber **I**dentity **M**odule card with additional storage for contact lists, *etc*., supplementing the device's built-in storage in a portable format. "An integrated circuit card that securely stores the international mobile subscriber identity (IMSI) and the related cryptographic key used to identify and authenticate subscribers on mobile devices. A UICC may be referred to as a: SIM, USIM, RUIM or CSIM, and is used interchangeably with those terms" *(NIST SP 800-101)*.
Universal **M**obile **T**elecommunications **S**ystem **(UMTS)**	Deprecated third-generation (3G) cellular network standards. "A third-generation (3G) mobile phone technology standardized by the 3GPP as the successor to GSM" *(NIST SP 800-101)*.
Universal **P**lug and **P**lay **(UPnP)**	Suite of protocols by which various devices, *things*, and peripherals 'announce' (broadcast) their presence and capabilities on a network, allowing other devices to 'discover' and utilise them ... and perhaps exploit known vulnerabilities in them. A triumph of convenience over security.
Universal **S**erial **B**us **(USB)**	Standardised serial data interface and connectors for computer peripherals such as keyboards, displays, headsets, webcams, memory sticks, and biometric authentication devices, and for data transfer and power supply to charge smartphones and other devices. The maximum datacommunications rates have increased from 1.5/12 Mbps (USB version 1.1 in 1998) to 80 Gbps (USB 4.2 in 2019), allowing external portable disk drives to perform similarly to internal fixed hard drives. Three main variants – USB A, B, and C – have different connectors, capacity, and performance. "A hardware interface for low-speed peripherals such as the keyboard, mouse, joystick, scanner, printer, and telephony devices" *(NIST SP 800-101)*. "An external bus standard that provides capabilities to transfer data at a rate of 12 Mbps. Note: A USB port can connect to up to 127 peripheral devices" *(ISACA glossary)*.

TERM	MEANING
Unlinkable	Items of information relating to a single source (such as personal information on a data subject) that cannot be readily correlated or associated with that source. Generally achieved through information security and privacy controls such as anonymisation. "A condition of privacy-relevant data that cannot be linked (*i.e.*, related) across domains" *(ISACA glossary)*.
Unmanaged [device]	Systems and *things* within the corporate **I**nformation **T**echnology environment that are not managed by the organisation, hence depend on their users/owners securing them adequately, *i.e.* security configurations, prompt patching, antivirus software running and updated, backups taken, *etc.* (which is unlikely).
Unmanned **A**utonomous **V**ehicle **(UAV)**	See drone.
Unpatched software	Software that, for some reason, has not been updated with all the relevant and available patches due to ineffective patch management. May exhibit known and potentially exploitable vulnerabilities in addition to any that are currently unrecognised or for which patches are not yet available. The information risks are complex, relating to: (a) the nature of the vulnerabilities themselves; (b) the extent, duration, and visibility of their exposure; (c) the associated threats (*e.g.* hackers and malware); (d) the potential impacts if compromised; and (e) the presence and effectiveness of any compensating controls (*e.g.* firewalls and other access controls, antivirus, network and host security monitoring with alerts, alarms, and vigilant **I**nformation **T**echnology staff, incident response processes, and business continuity arrangements). At a higher level, if an organisation has accumulated much unpatched software, that *suggests* a serious systematic governance issue with weak cybersecurity, asset, change or risk management, missing/ineffective vulnerability assessment, and/or inadequate investment and resourcing in this area.
Unprivileged accounts	UserIDs for ordinary, regular, normal, everyday computer users. "Include unprivileged user accounts and unprivileged service accounts" *(AusISM)*.
Unprivileged operating environments	"[Environments] used for non-administrative activities, such as reading emails and browsing the web" *(AusISM)*.
Unprotected share	"In Windows terminology, a 'share' is a mechanism that allows a user to connect to file systems and printers on other systems. An 'unprotected share' is one that allows anyone to connect to it" *(SANS glossary)*.
Unsecure	Inadequately protected and hence vulnerable. *Cf.* insecure.

TERM	MEANING
Unsecure area	Zone with as-yet-unchecked physical security that should be *presumed* insecure. "An area that has not been certified to physical security requirements to allow for the processing of classified information" *(NZISM).*
Unsecured space	"An area [having] not been certified to the physical security requirements for a Security Zone Two to Security Zone Five area, as defined in the Attorney-General's Department's Protective Security Policy Framework, Entity facilities policy, to allow for the processing or storage of sensitive or classified data" *(AusISM).*
Unstructured test, *ad hoc* test	Informal, unplanned, unscripted, and largely or entirely manual test depending on a competent tester's capabilities and interests to exercise and explore a system for flaws and bugs, dynamically reacting to the situation, *e.g.* following through on glitches or unexpected responses to find failure modes and exploit vulnerabilities such as a penetration test emulating a hack. May use automated test tools (such as Chaos Monkey). *Cf.* structured test.
Unsupervised machine learning	"Machine learning that makes only use of unlabelled data during training" *(sic, ISO/IEC 22989). Cf.* supervised machine learning, semi-supervised machine learning.
Untrusted	Person, organisation, system, network, control, *etc.* that is presently not trusted having either been deemed untrustworthy and inherently risky (such as the Internet) by another, or just not yet adequately authenticated, secured, and assured.
Untrustworthy	Person, organisation, system, network, control, *etc.* that cannot or should not ('does not deserve to') be trusted, or that lacks sufficient credibility or is for some reason considered unsuitable or too risky to be trusted by another.
Upatre	Downloader/backdoor Trojan used to spread GameOver Zeus, Locky, and other malware since 2013.
Update	Change, revise, improve, or modernise something, bringing it up-to-date. Often required by the supplier to continue providing technical support such as security patches. *Cf.* upgrade.
Upgrade	Change or replace something (such as a computer or control) to offer better functionality, performance, security, *etc. Cf.* update.
UPnP	*Abbrev:* **U**niversal **P**lug **and P**lay.
UPS	*Abbrev:* **U**ninterruptible **P**ower **S**upply.

TERM	MEANING
Upstream	Previous activities in a time sequence, such as the production and delivery of a business's input supplies of raw materials, commodities, or constituent products, or prior stages in a lifecycle. "Handling processes and movements of products and services that occur before an entity in the supply chain takes custody of the products and responsibility for information and communication technology (ICT) services" *(ISO/IEC 27036-1)*. *Cf.* downstream.
Usability	Suitability, utility, and value of something for its intended purpose. "Extent to which a system product or service can be used by specified users to achieve specified goals with effectiveness, efficiency and satisfaction in a specified context of use. Notes: The 'specified' users, goals and context of use refer to the particular combination of users, goals and context of use for which usability is being considered. The word 'usability' is also used as a qualifier to refer to the design knowledge, competencies, activities and design attributes that contribute to usability, such as usability expertise, usability professional, usability engineering, usability method, usability evaluation, usability heuristic" *(ISO 9241-11)*. "The ease with which a user can learn to operate, prepare inputs for and interpret outputs of a system or component" *(ISACA glossary)*.
Usability test	Test of the ease with which an application program, system, device, *thing*, service, process, *etc.* can be used by, and satisfy the needs of, its intended users. Typically concerns relevant aspects of the user interface such as interactive responsiveness, intuitive controls and outputs, and accessibility. Addresses rhetorical questions such as "Is the system usable in its current state? Where are the pain points? What needs to be improved, first?" "Tests designed to evaluate the machine/user interface. Determines if the communication devices are designed in a manner so that the information displayed is understandable, enabling the operator to correctly interact with the system" *(ISACA glossary)*.
USB	*Abbrev:* **U**niversal **S**erial **B**us.
USBKill	When triggered, this nasty little device resembling an innocuous USB memory stick generates high-voltage bursts, injecting them through the data lines of a USB, Ethernet, VGA, HDMI, or DisplayPort port into a vulnerable **I**nformation **T**echnology system, instantly damaging it. Conceivably of use to damage old computer equipment before disposal or to evaluate its resilience to electrostatic discharge, but much more likely a malicious weapon. See also USB Rubber Ducky.

TERM	MEANING
USB memory stick, thumb drive, flash drive, pen drive …	Small, portable, USB-connected, high-capacity (up to 1 Tb) data storage device containing flash memory that retains its contents for about a decade, even when unplugged. Associated threats include malware and malicious hardware, data exfiltration or theft, keylogging, social engineering, physical damage or loss, and counterfeiting.
USB Rubber Ducky	USB memory stick emulates a keyboard to inject scripted commands or code into a computer, and a disk device to store exfiltrated data – conceivably for legitimate system administration purposes but more likely mischief, malware, and data exfiltration.
Use case	Representative or typical scenario in which a system, application, function, *etc.* is used productively.
User, end-user	Person who uses computer systems, networks, information, *etc.* Nothing to do with abuse of narcotics, in this context. "Interested party with access to the organization's information systems" *(ISO/IEC 27002)*. "Person or organization who utilizes information processing facilities or systems, *e.g.* employee, contractor or third party user" *(ISO/IEC 27011)*. "Any person, organization or functional unit that uses the services of an information processing system [and] 1. A person, device, program or computer system that uses an information system for the purpose of data processing in information exchange. 2. A person whose occupation requires the use of an information system but does not require any knowledge of computers or computer programming" *(ISACA glossary)*. "An individual that is authorised to access a system" *(AusISM)*. "A person, organization entity, or automated process that accesses a system, whether authorized to do so or not" *(SANS glossary)*.
User **A**cceptance **T**est **(UAT), C**ustomer **A**cceptance **T**est **(CAT), user test**	Acceptance test of a new/changed system, service, product, *etc.* by or on behalf of the intended users/customers confirming (providing assurance) that their requirements are sufficiently satisfied to migrate it into production and commence using it, settle the supplier's invoice, *etc.* Theoretically, UAT simply checks conformity with the documented functional requirements, but in practice the documentation often falls well short of the actual requirements (especially if various types of 'system documentation' are not even be specified as requirements), so the scope of testing tends to be broadened to include nonfunctional requirements, such as information security, resilience, and recoverability, including contingency and fallback arrangements in case of problems with the implementation process – a particularly risky part of the lifecycle: as well as the product, the organisation is also about to accept the residual risks. See also unit test, system test, regression test, incremental test, performance test.

TERM	MEANING
User account	Account for a computer user – see userID. "An identity created for a person in a computer or computing system. For the purpose of this document, user accounts refer to 'standard' or 'interactive' user accounts with limited privileges and are used for general tasks such as reading email and surfing the web. User accounts with escalated privileges are covered under administrator accounts" *(CIS Controls)*. "Includes privileged user accounts and unprivileged user accounts" *(AusISM)*.
User **B**ehaviour **A**nalytics **(UBA)**, **U**ser **E**ntity **B**ehaviour **A**nalytics **(UEBA)**	Cluster of techniques to identify anomalous and potentially concerning activities by users of networks and systems. "The process of monitoring an account for abnormal activity and atypical usage to identify patterns (heuristics) that highlight user activity trends. UEBA can act as a proactive access control mechanism by identifying threat indicators, alerting on malicious behavior earlier and improving threat intelligence" *(ISACA glossary)*. See also **S**ecurity **I**nformation and **E**vent **M**anagement, **N**etwork **T**raffic **A**nalysis, **I**ntrusion **D**etection **S**ystem/**I**ntrusion **P**revention **S**ystem, **C**ontinuous **A**daptive **R**isk and **T**rust **A**ssessment.
User contingency plan	See **B**usiness **C**ontinuity **P**lan "The alternative methods of continuing business operations if IT systems are unavailable" *(SANS glossary)*.
User **D**atagram **P**rotocol **(UDP)**	Connectionless/broadcast transport layer networking protocol, normally used to send data packets over a TCP/IP network where communications speed and efficiency are more important than reliable delivery in the correct sequence of all the packets sent, *e.g.* streaming real time audio/visual content such as **V**oice **O**ver **I**nternet **P**rotocol. "A connectionless Internet protocol that is designed for network efficiency and speed at the expense of reliability" *(ISACA glossary)*. "A communications protocol that, like TCP, runs on top of IP networks. Unlike TCP/IP, UDP/IP provides very few error recovery services, offering instead a direct way to send and receive datagrams over an IP network. It's used primarily for broadcasting messages over a network. UDP uses the Internet Protocol to get a datagram from one computer to another but does not divide a message into packets (datagrams) and reassemble it at the other end. Specifically, UDP doesn't provide sequencing of the packets that the data arrives in" *(SANS glossary)*.
User endpoint device	Worker's **I**nformation **T**echnology equipment such as a desktop or portable PC, tablet, or smartphone. "Endpoint device used by users to access information processing services. Note: User endpoint device can refer to desktop computers, laptops, smart phones, tablets, thin clients, *etc*" *(ISO/IEC 27002)*.

TERM	MEANING
UserID (User IDentifier or IDentity or IDentification), username, login, login name, account	Unique label used to identify a user and their activities on a computer system so that they may be assigned appropriate user rôles, logical access rights and permissions, and be linked to their system activities recorded in system accounts, log files, audit trails, *etc.* Asserted and normally authenticated during the logon process. "Character string or pattern that is used by a data processing system to identify a user" *(ISO/IEC 2382).*
User mode	An unprivileged and hence relatively low-risk processing context for ordinary applications that do not need privileges. "A mode used for the execution of normal system activities" *(ISACA glossary). Cf.* kernel mode.
User profile, account	Collection of data relating to an individual computer user, such as their userID, given or first and family names, location, rôle, and access rights. "Description of a user, typically used for access control [and] pattern of a user's activity that can be used to detect changes in the activity" *(ISO/IEC 2382).*
User profiling	"Activity to retrieve a set of attributes used by the system that are unique to a specific user/user group" *(ISO/IEC 27562).*
User rôle	Logical access rights are standardised by defining and assigning the minimal rights necessary for computer users in certain positions within the organisation to perform their associated rôles or functions. See also privileged user rôle.
User test	See **U**ser **A**cceptance **T**est.
USM	*Abbrev:* **U**nified **S**ervice **M**anagement.
Usufruct	Legal right to use and benefit from another's property temporarily (as opposed to permanent transferal of property ownership), such as the owner voluntarily granting someone else a licence to exploit their **I**ntellectual **P**roperty in return for a consideration, typically a licence fee, subscription, or one-off charge.

V

TERM	MEANING
Valid, validity	a. True, accurate, complete, authentic, *etc.,* and within applicable specifications, limits, or constraints. b. Weighty or significant, having a sound, logical, and acceptable basis in law, fact, *etc.*, hence potentially or presumably true.
Validation	Assurance process plus associated mechanisms and controls to check and hopefully confirm that something (such as data entered by a person or generated by a computer) is valid. "Confirmation, through the provision of objective proof, that the requirements for a specific intended use or application have been fulfilled" *(ISO/IEC 27004).* "The process of establishing documented evidence that provides a high degree of assurance that a specific process will consistently produce a product meeting its predetermined specifications and quality attributes" *(ISACA glossary).* "Confirmation, through the provision of objective evidence, that the requirements for a specific intended use or application have been fulfilled. Note: A system is able to accomplish its intended use, goals and objectives (*i.e.* meet stakeholder requirements) in the intended operational environment. The right system was built" *(ISO/IEC/IEEE 15288).* "Confirmation (through the provision of strong, sound, objective evidence) that requirements for a specific intended use or application have been fulfilled (*e.g.*, a trustworthy credential has been presented, or data or information has been formatted in accordance with a defined set of rules, or a specific process has demonstrated that an entity under consideration meets, in all respects, its defined attributes or requirements)" *(CNSSI 4009).* "Confirmation (through the provision of strong, sound, objective evidence) that requirements for a specific intended use or application have been fulfilled" *(AusISM).* "The process of providing objective evidence that a method, process or device is fit for the specific purpose intended" *(FSRCoP).* See also verification, authentication.
Validation data, development data	Data about or resulting from validation. "Data used to compare the performance of different candidate models. Notes: Validation data is disjoint from test data and generally also from training data. However, in cases where there is insufficient data for a three-way training, validation and test set split, the data is divided into only two sets – a test set and a training or validation set. Cross-validation or bootstrapping are common methods for then generating separate training and validation sets from the training or validation set; Validation data can be used to tune hyperparameters or to validate some algorithmic choices, up to the effect of including a given rule in an expert system" *(ISO/IEC 22989).*
Validation test	See **U**ser **A**cceptance **T**est. "Test to determine whether an implemented system fulfils its specified requirements" *(ISO/IEC 2382).*

TERM	MEANING
Value	a. Data point or item. b. Belief. "Beliefs an organization adheres to and the standards that it seeks to observe" *(ISO 22300)*. "Fundamental beliefs, principles, and ideals than an organization, group, or individual demonstrates and adheres to when making decisions and acting" *(OCEG GRC Glossary)*. c. Intrinsic or realisable worth. "The relative worth or importance of an investment for an enterprise, as perceived by its key stakeholders, expressed as total life cycle benefits net of related costs, adjusted for risk and (in the case of financial value) the time value of money" *(ISACA glossary)*.
Vandal, vandalism	Someone who commits mindless acts of relatively minor malicious damage. Named after an itinerant Germanic tribe, originally from Scandinavia, who sacked and looted Rome in 455 AD. Whereas modern-day vandalism normally involves physical acts such as spray painting graffiti, it sometimes involves electronic attacks such as hacking, website defacement, email bombing, and cybertage.
VAPT	*Abbrev:* **V**ulnerability **A**nd **P**enetration **T**esting.
Vault	a. Large physically strong safe, such as a cave or a heavily fortified and protected storage room within a facility such as a bank, often underground. b. Virtual safe, *e.g.* a password vault. "A secure environment to store critical data that is isolated from production and backup storage environments to limit exposure to cyberthreats" *(ISACA glossary)*.
VCS	*Abbrev:* **V**ersion **C**ontrol **S**ystem.
VDC	*Abbrev:* **V**irtual **D**ata **C**entre. See **S**oftware-**D**efined **D**ata **C**entre.
VEC	*Abbrev:* **V**endor **E**mail **C**ompromise.
Velocity	Speed, *i.e.* distance travelled in a defined time period. "A measure that estimates how quickly an event or impact might occur" *(OCEG GRC Glossary)*.
Vendor	See supplier. "An individual or business (and its employees) that is engaged to provide goods or services to the entity. Depending on the services provided (for example, if the vendor operates certain controls on behalf of the entity that are necessary to achieve the entity's objectives), it also might be a service provider" *(**T**rust **S**ervices **C**riteria)*.

TERM	MEANING
Vendor **E**mail **C**ompromise **(VEC)**	Variant of **B**usiness **E**mail **C**ompromise in which the fraudsters masquerade as vendor (supplier) representatives rather than managers to trick customer Procurement or Finance professionals into changing payment details, thereby diverting funds intended for the supplier. The fraudsters may initially compromise the supplier using phishing, malware, *etc.*, gathering intelligence about their customers, contacts, invoicing arrangements and frequency (*e.g.* regular payments), *etc.* to identify the most lucrative target/s and make their frauds more credible.
Vendor **R**isk **M**anagement **(VRM)**	Process of managing upstream supply chain risks involving commercial suppliers. See also **T**hird **P**arty **R**isk **M**anagement, **S**upply **C**hain **R**isk **M**anagement.
Verification, verify, verifiable	Assurance process (with associated controls) to check and hopefully confirm the integrity and/or authenticity of something. "Comparing an activity, a process, or a product with the corresponding requirements or specifications. Examples: Comparing a specification with a security policy model or comparing object code with source code" *(ISO/IEC 2382)*. "Confirmation, through the provision of objective evidence, that specified requirements have been fulfilled. Note: Verification only provides assurance that a product conforms to its specification" *(ISO/IEC 27041)*. "Confirmation, through the provision of objective evidence, that specified requirements have been fulfilled. Note: this could also be called compliance testing" *(ISO 9000)*. "Confirmation, through the provision of objective evidence, that specified requirements have been fulfilled. Note: Verification is a set of activities that compares a system or system element against the required characteristics. This includes, but is not limited to, specified requirements, design description and the system itself. The system was built right" *(ISO/IEC/IEEE 15288)*. "Can be checked for correctness by a person or tool" *(ISO/IEC/IEEE 15289)*. "Confirmation, through the provision of objective evidence, that specified requirements have been fulfilled (*e.g.*, an entity's requirements have been correctly defined, or an entity's attributes have been correctly presented; or a procedure or function performs as intended and leads to the expected outcome)" *(CNSSI 4009)*. "Confirmation, through the provision of objective evidence, that specified requirements have been fulfilled" *(AusISM)*. "Confirmation, through the assessment of existing objective evidence or through experiment that a method is fit (or remains fit) for the specific purpose intended. The forensic unit must demonstrate the reliability of the procedure in-house against any documented performance characteristics of that procedure" *(FSRCoP)*. See also validation, authentication.

TERM	MEANING
Verification function	Verification function. "Function which is used to verify that two sets of data are identical. Notes: No two non-identical data sets should produce an identical match from a verification function. Verification functions are commonly implemented using hash functions such as MD5, SHA1, *etc.*, but other methods may be used" *(ISO/IEC 27037)*. "Checks that data is entered correctly" *(ISACA glossary)*.
Verification test	See system test. "Test of a system to prove that it meets all its specified requirements at a particular stage of its development" *(ISO/IEC 2382)*.
VERIS (Vocabulary for Event Recording and Incident Sharing)	Verizon's long-running annual **D**ata **B**reach **I**nvestigations **R**eport has standardised its use of key terms and metrics relating to incidents, to reduce ambiguity and improve consistency. VERIS is a structured data format for victims or analysts to describe incidents and (optionally) share information with third parties, such as Verizon, anonymously and responsibly. More info: https://veris-framework.org/
Vernam cypher	Theoretically unbreakable encryption algorithm invented in 1917 by Joseph Mauborgne and Gilbert Vernam. See also **O**ne-**T**ime **P**ad.
Version control, revision control, release management	Part of change control and configuration management concerning the control of software, firmware, hardware, and documentation updates including minor and major releases and patches. A well-engineered process involves allocating unique identifiers for each new version, traceability of the changes, various checks (including security tests) along the way, and some form of release authorisation (sign-off). "A practice that identifies the correct versions of work products and ensures they are available for use or for restoring to a previous version. It also includes the establishment and maintenance of baselines and the identification of changes to baselines to obtain previous baselines" *(ISACA glossary)*.
Version **C**ontrol **S**ystem **(VCS)**	System providing version control, such as a code **repo**sitory.
Victim	Person or organisation actually harmed by an incident, whether deliberate (*i.e.* an attack) or accidental in nature. May have been a target, but could also have been an innocent bystander (collateral damage) or business partner (consequential damage).
Victimise, victimisation	Singling someone or something out and perhaps attacking them, making them a victim.

TERM	MEANING
Vigenére's cipher	Polyalphabetic encryption protocol named after the 16th Century French cryptographer, Blaise de Vigenére, despite having been described by Giovan Battista Bellaso 3 decades earlier. Adds entropy to Caesar's cipher by substituting successive letters of the plaintext from not one but a *sequence* of offset alphabets, each one offset according to the key.
Vigilance	Alert and cognisant of the surroundings or situation, wary of potential threats. Encouraging workers to be vigilant for current threats is a key objective of security awareness, along with guidance on how to react.
Vigilante worm	Malware (such as BrickerBot and Wifatch) created and released into the wild ostensibly as an automated tool to address widespread cybersecurity issues (*e.g.* warning of, or even patching, currently unpatched vulnerabilities). Can create more problems than it solves, hence a risky as well as unethical and potentially illegal approach.
Violation	Security incident or infringement involving the failure to uphold one or more rights, *e.g.* a person's right to privacy, often *implying* the use of coercion, violence, aggression, or victimisation.
VIPS	*Abbrev:* **V**oice **I**ntrusion **P**revention **S**ystem.
Virtual environment	See **V**irtual **M**achine. "Simulates hardware to allow a software environment to run without the need to use a lot of actual hardware. Virtualized environments are used to make a small number of resources act as many with plenty of processing, memory, storage, and network capacity. Virtualization is a fundamental technology that allows cloud computing to work" *(CIS Controls)*.
Virtualisation, virtual network, virtual storage, virtual application, virtual system ...	Emulation of the bare metal using **V**irtual **T**echnology in such a way that each guest system *appears* to have complete, independent access to and control of (selected elements of) the underlying computer platform, whereas in fact it is being shared with other virtual systems. Mediated by the hypervisor. As well as **O**perating **S**ystems, networks, data storage, and applications can also be virtualised. "Pertaining to a functional unit that appears to be real, but whose functions are accomplished by other means" *(ISO/IEC 2382)*. "The process of adding a guest application and data onto a virtual server, recognizing that the guest application will ultimately be removed from the physical server" *(ISACA glossary)*. "The software simulation of the components of an information system and may include the simulation of hardware, operating systems, applications, infrastructure and storage" *(NZISM)*. "Simulation of a hardware platform, operating system, application, storage device or network resource" *(AusISM)*. See also **V**irtual **M**achine, **v**irtual **L**ocal **A**rea **N**etwork, emulation, digital twin.

TERM	MEANING
virtual **L**ocal **A**rea **N**etwork **(vLAN)**	Virtualised Local Area Network domain overlaid on, yet logically distinct from, the physical LAN/s, typically used to transport network administration or voice and video traffic securely, separately from user data. "Independent network created from a logical point of view within a physical network" *(ISO/IEC 27033-1)*. "Logical segmentation of a LAN into different broadcast domains. Notes: A VLAN is set up by configuring ports on a switch so devices attached to these ports may communicate as if they were attached to the same physical network segment even though the devices are located on different LAN segments. A VLAN is based on logical rather than physical connections" *(ISACA glossary)*. "Network devices and other ICT equipment grouped logically based on resources, security or business requirements instead of their physical location" *(AusISM)*. See also Private **vLAN**.
Virtual **M**achine **(VM), virtual system**	Software emulation of a guest system within a host computer using **V**irtual **T**echnology. "Virtual data processing system that appears to be at the exclusive disposal of a particular user, but whose functions are accomplished by sharing the resources of a real data processing system" *(ISO/IEC 2382)*. "Complete environment that supports the execution of guest software. Note: A virtual machine is a full encapsulation of the virtual hardware, virtual disks, and the metadata associated with it. Virtual machines allow multiplexing of the underlying physical machine through a software later called a hypervisor" *(ISO/IEC 27017)*. "An emulation of a computing environment or operating system separate from the host computing system" *(ISACA glossary)*.
Virtual **M**achine **M**onitor **(VMM)**	See hypervisor.
Virtual **P**rivate **N**etwork **(VPN)**	Application of cryptography to create a relatively secure, trustworthy data tunnel between **I**nformation **T**echnology systems through an insecure or untrustworthy network (such as the Internet) or path (such as a dial-up modem connection). "A secure private network that uses the public telecommunications infrastructure to transmit data. Notes: In contrast to a much more expensive system of owned or leased lines that can only be used by one enterprise, VPNs are used by enterprises for both extranets and wide areas of intranets. Using encryption and authentication, a VPN encrypts all data that passes between two Internet points, maintaining privacy and security" *(ISACA glossary)*. "The tunnelling of a network's traffic through another network, separating the VPN traffic from the underlying network. A VPN can encrypt traffic if necessary" *(NZISM)*. "A tunnel that connects the teleworker's computer to the organization's network" *(NIST SP 800-114)*. "Encrypted network connections, allowing remote users to securely access an organisation's services" *(UK Cyber Security Breaches Survey 2023)*.

TERM	MEANING
	"A network that maintains privacy through a tunnelling protocol and security procedures. Virtual Private Networks may use encryption to protect network traffic" *(AusISM)*. "A restricted-use, logical (*i.e.*, artificial or simulated) computer network that is constructed from the system resources of a relatively public, physical (*i.e.*, real) network (such as the Internet), often by using encryption (located at hosts or gateways), and often by tunneling links of the virtual network across the real network. For example, if a corporation has LANs at several different sites, each connected to the Internet by a firewall, the corporation could create a VPN by (a) using encrypted tunnels to connect from firewall to firewall across the Internet and (b) not allowing any other traffic through the firewalls. A VPN is generally less expensive to build and operate than a dedicated real network, because the virtual network shares the cost of system resources with other users of the real network" *(SANS glossary)*.
Virtual system	See **V**irtual **M**achine.
Virtual **T**echnology **(VT)**	Technical concepts, techniques, tools, approaches, and technologies involved in virtualisation. See also **I**nformation **T**echnology, **C**ommunications **T**echnology, **O**perational **T**echnology, **M**obile **T**echnology, **S**mart **T**echnology.
Virus	a. Strictly speaking, the type of malware that replicates by attaching itself to other programs, but colloquially refers to malware in general. Usually contains a payload that performs unauthorised functions such as displaying messages, and deleting or modifying files. "Program that propagates itself by modifying other programs to include a possibly changed copy of itself and that is executed when the infected program is invoked. Note: A virus often causes damage or annoyance and may be triggered by some event such as the occurrence of a predetermined date" *(ISO/IEC 2382)*. "A piece of code that can replicate itself and spread from one computer to another. It requires intervention or execution to replicate and/or cause damage" *(ISACA glossary)*. "A hidden, self-replicating section of computer software, usually malicious logic, that propagates by infecting – *i.e.*, inserting a copy of itself into and becoming part of – another program. A virus cannot run by itself; it requires that its host program be run to make the virus active" *(SANS glossary)*. b. Subcellular parasite consisting of little more than a protein coat and a strand of DNA or RNA. Some viruses carry barely enough genetic information to encode multiple copies of themselves that the host cell faithfully assembles and accumulates until it bursts, thus releasing the virus to infect (attack) other vulnerable cells. Others (such as COVID) encode additional proteins that cause symptoms of infection such as sneezing and coughing, spreading themselves further afield.

TERM	MEANING
Virus hoax, hoax	Chain letter spreading a false virus warning. A form of social engineering. Hoaxes can cause alarm and waste time but are generally benign rather than malicious.
Virus signature, virus signature file	Identifying characteristics of a computer virus or other malware. "Unique bit string that is common to each copy of a particular virus and that may be used by a scanning program to detect the presence of the virus" *(ISO/IEC 2382)*. "The file of virus patterns that are compared to existing files to determine whether they are infected with a virus or worm" *(ISACA glossary)*.
VirusTotal	Online service that freely scans potentially infected file samples uploaded by concerned users against a sizeable panel of antivirus applications (virus scanners). Prone to both false negatives and false positives, particularly with obscure software, novel malware, and low-quality antivirus apps. See also hybrid analysis. More info: https://www.virustotal.com/gui/home/upload
Vishing (VoIP phishing, Voice phishing)	Phishing-type attack using **V**oice **O**ver **I**nternet **P**rotocol to spoof caller identities, misleading victims while concealing the true origin of the scam. May involve deepfaked voices of famous or familiar people (such as relatives or managers). "Voice phishing done to acquire private or confidential information by masquerading as a trustworthy entity. Note: Vishing can be conducted by voice email, VoIP (voice over IP), or landline or cellular telephone" *(ISO/IEC 27032)*. "Phishing attacks that involve the use of voice calls, using either conventional phone systems or Voice over Internet [Protocol] (VoIP) systems" *(SANS glossary)*.
Visibility	Extent to which something is exposed and hence can be seen (literally) or perceived and noticed (figuratively) by others. "Property of a system or process that enables system elements and processes to be documented and available for monitoring and inspection" *(ISO/IEC 27036-1)*.
Vision	Sight or hallucination. "An objective that describes what the organization aspires to be and why it matters" *(OCEG GRC Glossary)*.
Vital	Essential to sustain life, *i.e.* safety-critical. *Cf.* critical.
vLAN	*Abbrev:* **V**irtual **L**ocal **A**rea **N**etwork.
VM	*Abbrev:* **V**irtual **M**achine.
VMM	*Abbrev:* **V**irtual **M**achine **M**onitor – see hypervisor.

TERM	MEANING
Voice firewall	"A physical discontinuity in a voice network that monitors, alerts and controls inbound and outbound voice network activity based on user-defined call admission control (CAC) policies, voice application layer security threats or unauthorized service use violations" *(SANS glossary)*.
Voice **I**ntrusion **P**revention **S**ystem **(VIPS)**	"A security management system for voice networks which monitors voice traffic for multiple calling patterns or attack/abuse signatures to proactively detect and prevent toll fraud, Denial of Service, telecom attacks, service abuse, and other anomalous activity" *(SANS glossary)*.
Voice Over Internet Protocol (VoIP, VOIP), IP telephony, Internet telephony, broadband phone	Networking protocols and applications to pass digital data such as telephone calls and multimedia content over a TCP/IP network such as the Internet. **I**nternet **P**rotocols such as H.323, **S**ession **I**nitiation **P**rotocol, **R**eal-time **T**ransport **P**rotocol plus **S**ecure **R**eal-time **T**ransport **P**rotocol, and **R**eal-time **T**ransport **C**ontrol **P**rotocol are used to initiate sessions (calls), pass data, manage link quality, and secure the data streams. "A technology that makes it possible to have a voice conversation over the Internet or any dedicated Internet Protocol (IP) network instead of over dedicated voice transmission lines" *(ISACA glossary)*.
Void	a. Enclosed space in a building, such as a plenum or cable duct. In the movies, if not in real life, voids allow intruders to crawl covertly between rooms without even getting dirty. b. Invalid, cancelled (as in null and void).
VoIP, VOIP	*Abbrev:* **V**oice **o**ver **I**nternet **P**rotocol.
Volatile	"A property that refers to the susceptibility of a system and its parts to experience rapid, significant and often unpredictable changes" *(OCEG GRC Glossary)*.
Volatile data	Ephemeral data that normally exist only temporarily or fleetingly unless captured and stored, such as the content of a device's working memory (DRAM), or session keys. "Data that is especially prone to change and can be easily modified. Note: Change can be switching off the power or passing through a magnetic field. Volatile data also includes data that changes as the system state changes. Examples include data stored in RAM and dynamic IP addresses" *(ISO/IEC 27037)*. "Data that changes frequently and can be lost when the system power is shut down" *(ISACA glossary)*.
Volatile media	a. Propensity of sensationalist journalists to create a fuss over nothing in order to foment outrage and increase ratings. b. See volatile storage. "A type of media, such as RAM, which gradually loses its information when power is removed" *(NZISM)*.

TERM	MEANING
Volatile storage, volatile memory	a. Type of data storage that gradually 'forgets' once disconnected from the power supply such as the decades-old delay-line, **C**athode **R**ay **T**ube/phosphor display and magnetic core memory technologies, and today's **D**ynamic **R**andom **A**ccess **M**emory chips. Data normally persist inside RAM chips for a period after a computer is powered down, especially if they are deep-frozen, and may therefore be recoverable using specialist forensic techniques. b. "Storage that fails to retain its contents after power is removed" *(ISO/IEC 27040)*. "Memory that loses its content when power is turned off or lost" *(NIST SP 800-101)*.
Volatile, **U**ncertain, **C**omplex and **A**mbiguous **(VUCA)**	Acronym coined by the US Army War College, alluding to the challenges involved in dealing with difficult and potentially hostile situations. "A reality that an organization must face that is volatile, uncertain, complex, and ambiguous" *(OCEG GRC Glossary)*. See also **T**urbulent, **U**ncertain, **N**ovel, and **A**mbiguous.
Volt Typhoon	Chinese state-sponsored hacker group, accused by several Western governments of 'pre-positioning' in preparation for cybertage against **C**ritical **N**ational **I**nfrastructures in connection with their claims to Taiwan, rather than the usual espionage and theft of **I**ntellectual **P**roperty. See also Salt Typhoon.
Volume test	a. See capacity stress test. "Testing designed to challenge the ability of a system to manage the maximum amount of data over a period of time. This type of testing also evaluates the ability of a system to handle overload situations in an orderly fashion" *(ISACA glossary)*. b. Rock group sound engineer's daunting task of turning all knobs to 11 to 'see what happens.'
Voluntary behaviours	"Intentional human actions informed by beliefs and values and governed by free will and discipline" *(OCEG GRC Glossary)*.
Voluntary boundary	"Obligations an organization chooses to address because of voluntary decisions (*e.g.*, contracts, agreements and values)" *(OCEG GRC Glossary)*.
Voyeur, voyeurism	Someone who surreptitiously and inappropriately watches or snoops on others without their permission. A breach of privacy, unethical and potentially an illegal form of surveillance.
VPN	*Abbrev:* **V**irtual **P**rivate **N**etwork.
VPN split tunnelling	**V**irtual **P**rivate **N**etwork split tunnelling. "Functionality that allows personnel to access both a public network and a VPN connection at the same time, such as an agency system and the Internet" *(NZISM)*.

TERM	MEANING
VRM	*Abbrev:* **V**endor **R**isk **M**anagement.
VUCA	*Abbrev:* **V**olatile, **U**ncertain, **C**omplex, and **A**mbiguous.
Vulnerability, vuln, vulnerable, susceptibility, susceptible, prone	Inherent/latent, potentially exploitable weakness within an information asset, system, process, organisation, *etc. Note:* sometimes understood to include weak or missing information security controls, a related but distinct concern that only constitutes a risk *if* the controls are relevant and necessary; hence, their omission or failure would expose inherent weaknesses to threats potentially causing impacts of concern. "Weakness or flaw in a data processing system. Note: If a vulnerability corresponds to a threat, a risk exists" *(ISO/IEC 2382)*. "Weakness of an asset or control that can be exploited by one or more threats" *(ISO/IEC 27000)*. "Weakness of an asset or control that can be exploited so that an event with a negative consequence occurs" *(ISO/IEC 27005)*. "Intrinsic properties of something resulting in susceptibility to a risk source that can lead to an event with a consequence" *(ISO 31073)*. "Lack of resilience against an undesirable intentional action or inability to recover a new stable condition of an asset" *(ISO 23234)*. "A weakness in the design, implementation, operation or internal control of a process that could expose the system to adverse threats from threat events" *(ISACA glossary)*. "A security weakness in a computer" *(NIST SP 800-114)*. "The probability that a Threat Event will become a Loss Event; probability that Threat Capability is greater than Resistance Strength. (Synonym: Susceptibility)" *(O-RT)*. "A weakness that makes the system susceptible to attack or damage" *(SCP QRG)*. "Bugs in software programs that have the potential to be exploited by attackers" *(UK National Cyber Security Strategy 2022)*. "A weakness, susceptibility or flaw of an asset, system, process or control that can be exploited" *(DORA)*. "A weakness, susceptibility or flaw of a product with digital elements that can be exploited by a cyber threat" *(EU CRA)*.
Vulnerability analysis	Vulnerability analysis. "Process of identifying and quantifying something that creates susceptibility to a source of risk that can lead to a consequence" *(ISO 22300)*. "A process of identifying and classifying vulnerabilities" *(ISACA glossary)*. See also vulnerability assessment.
Vulnerability **A**nd **P**enetration **T**esting **(VAPT)**	Pretentious name for plain ol' penetration testing that *may* involve additional testing for security vulnerabilities other than the usual network and application security issues. Or not.

TERM	MEANING
Vulnerability assessment	Systematic analysis of vulnerabilities within computer systems, networks, applications, devices, processes, facilities, organisations, *etc.* According to the perceived risk level and resourcing, can range from a cursory check for unpatched software using a vulnerability scanner, to an in-depth security design review, perhaps even a wide-ranging analysis of potential weak points and gaps in the defences for an entire supply chain, industry, or nation. May involve self-assessment, penetration testing, and auditing. Daunting, maybe, but not as scary as only discovering significant vulnerabilities through serious incidents. "Process of identifying and quantifying vulnerabilities" *(ISO 22300)*. "Can consist of a documentation-based review of a system's design, an in-depth hands-on assessment or automated scanning with software tools. In each case, the goal is to identify as many security vulnerabilities as possible" *(AusISM)*.
Vulnerability management	Proactive management (identification, analysis, evaluation, mitigation, and monitoring) of vulnerabilities – a critical part of information risk and security management.
Vulnerability reporting service	"A mechanism through which an organisation can be alerted to security flaws before they are exploited by attackers" *(UK National Cyber Security Strategy 2022)*.
Vulnerability scanner	Software tool/service to scan networked systems for known vulnerabilities – primarily unpatched or misconfigured **O**perating **S**ystems and applications. "An automated process to proactively identify security weaknesses in a network or individual system" *(ISACA glossary)*.
VXer	Leet term for 'virus writer,' a black hat programmer who creates new species of malware or variants/mutants. See also hacker, cracker.

W

TERM	MEANING
w3af	Penetration testing/hacking tool to find and exploit vulnerabilities in web applications.
Wabbit	See fork bomb.
WAD	*Abbrev:* **W**orks **A**s **D**esigned. *Cf.* BAD.
WAF	*Abbrev:* **W**eb **A**pplication **F**irewall.
Waiver	See exemption. "The formal acknowledgement that a particular compliance requirement of the NZISM cannot currently be met and that a waiver is granted by the Accreditation Authority on the basis that full compliance with the NZISM is achieved or compensating controls are implemented within a time specified by the Accreditation Authority. Waivers are valid in the short term only and full accreditation cannot be granted until all conditions of the waiver have been met" *(NZISM)*.
Waivers and exceptions	"A waiver means that some alternative controls or conditions are implemented. An exception means that the requirement need not be followed. An exception is NOT the same as a waiver" *(NZISM)*. See waiver, exception, exemption.
Walled garden	See sandbox.
WANK worm	Malware that infected DEC VMS systems on the early Internet in 1989, displaying hacktivist politically motivated anti-war messages under the banner **W**ORMS **A**GAINST **N**UCLEAR **K**ILLERS. Reportedly created by an Australian hacker group including Julian Assange.
Wannabe	Disparaging term for someone who wants-to-be something (such as a leet hacker) but falls short. See also script kiddie.
WannaCry (WannaCryptor)	Species of ransomware still in the wild in 2020, *years* after it was first spotted. A worm based on EternalBlue, exploited a known Windows vulnerability, spreading via **S**erver **M**essage **B**lock. A global outbreak caused life-threatening and business disruptive incidents in 2017.
WAP	*Abbrev:* **W**ireless **A**ccess **P**oint or **W**ireless **A**pplication **P**rotocol, depending on context.
Wapiti	Hacking/penetration testing tool that automates a range of exploits against HTML web pages and websites.
Wapomi, Simfect	Species of malware (described as a virus with Trojan and worm-like features) that established a massive botnet in 2015.

TERM	MEANING
War chalking	Wireless hackers in some cities allegedly used to physically mark the locations of vulnerable/accessible wireless networks with chalk symbols designating the types of network and their security parameters. Vanishingly rare in practice, largely confined to the fertile imaginations of technology news reporters of the last millennium. "Marking areas, usually on sidewalks with chalk, that receive wireless signals that can be accessed" *(SANS glossary)*.
Ward	Obstruction in the keyway of a physical lock, designed to prevent the insertion of the wrong types of key, or lock picks or screwdrivers/levers/torque wrenches, *etc.*
War dialling, war dialler	Old-school hacking or penetration testing technique involving automatically calling phone numbers within certain number ranges using hacking software and one or more modems in an attempt to locate vulnerable modems, FAX machines, voicemail systems, **R**emote **D**iagnostic **P**orts, *etc.* Originally seen in the 1983 film War Games, hence the name (it is not literal). "Software packages that sequentially dial telephone numbers, recording any numbers that answer" *(ISACA glossary)*. "A computer program that automatically dials a series of telephone numbers to find lines connected to computer systems, and catalogs those numbers so that a cracker can try to break into the systems" *(SANS glossary)*.
War driving	Wireless hackers sometimes identify and record information on wireless networks automatically while driving along using mobile **I**nformation **T**echnology equipment. "The process of traveling around looking for wireless access point signals that can be used to get network access" *(SANS glossary)*.
Warez	Leet spelling of 'wares' referring to pirated and cracked (unprotected and illicit) copies of commercial software.
Warhol worm	Network worm that spreads in a flash throughout the entire vulnerable population of systems on the Internet, gaining its 'fifteen minutes of fame.' SQL Slammer was a classic example back in 2002, achieving notoriety by reportedly infecting ~90% of vulnerable systems across the early Internet within just ten minutes of its release.
War flying	Some enterprising wireless hackers allegedly collect information on vulnerable wireless networks using private planes, remote-controlled aircraft or drones to traverse wide or inaccessible areas.

TERM	MEANING
Warm site	Secondary (fallback) location with an Information Technology facility that can be brought fully into operation typically within a few days of a disaster affecting the main site. Falls between cold site and hot site on a notional scale, but exactly where it falls is a matter of conjecture unless specified. "A site that is similar to a hot site but not fully equipped with all of the necessary hardware needed for recovery" *(ISACA glossary).* "Backup site which typically contains the data links and preconfigured equipment necessary to rapidly start operations, but does not contain live data. Thus commencing operations at a warm site will (at a minimum) require the restoration of current data" *(CNSSI 4009).*
Warrant canary	Public statement confirming that an organisation is *not* subject to a **N**ational **S**ecurity **L**etter. If the **F**ederal **B**ureau of **I**nvestigation serves an NSL, it may also (under specified conditions) forbid the organisation from disclosing that fact directly but cannot legally prevent the organisation from withdrawing its warrant canary, thereby signalling the fact indirectly. A civil rights passive-aggressive response to the perceived lack of control/oversight and intrusive/oppressive nature of certain US government agencies.
War room	See **E**mergency **O**perations **C**entre.
War walking	Like war driving but performed on foot using portable **I**nformation **T**echnology equipment. War jogging, war cycling, war hopping, war crawling, war slithering … you get the idea – these are all frivolous terms derived from and paying homage to war dialling.
-Washing	Refers to exaggerated, inaccurate, misleading, or fraudulent marketing and promotional claims, such as greenwashing (claiming to be more ecologically sound or sustainable than is truly the case) or AI-washing (falsely claiming to be using advanced **A**rtificial **I**ntelligence technologies). Such claims may be insinuated or implied rather than explicit, and can be hard to substantiate or refute, yet may be significant elements of an organisation's brand. Reminiscent of 'brainwashing', *i.e.* using psychological manipulation and propaganda for coercion and control of the population.
Waste from **E**lectrical and **E**lectronic **E**quipment **(WEEE)**	See e-waste. "Electrical and electronic equipment contains a complex mix of materials, components and substances, many which can be poisonous, carcinogenic or toxic in particulate or dust form. Destruction and disposal of WEEE needs to be managed carefully to avoid the potential of serious health risk or environmental hazard" *(NZISM).*

TERM	MEANING
Waterfall software development method, waterfall development, waterfall model, traditional development	Sequential software development method in which requirements analysis (including information security risk analysis) precedes design and development, leading on to testing then implementation. As the software 'cascades' through the process, any poor decisions or other issues experienced early on can accumulate adverse consequences downstream – a risk with this approach. "A procedure-focused development cycle with formal sign-off at the completion of each level [and] A model of the software development process in which the constituent activities, typically a concept phase, requirements phase, design phase, implementation phase, test phase, installation and checkout phase, and operation and maintenance, are performed in that order, possibly with overlap but with little or no iteration. It contrasts with incremental development, rapid prototyping and spiral model" *(ISACA glossary)*. *Cf.* iterative software development.
Watering hole attack, waterhole technique	Hacking method that uses social engineering to entice victims to an interesting website where their systems are compromised through drive-by downloads, Trojans, or other exploits. "Technique inciting people to access a website that specifically contains (lots of) malware" *(ISO/IEC 27032)*.
Weak key	Mathematical constraints in some cryptographic algorithms make it inadvisable to use specific key values. "Key that interacts with some aspect of a particular cipher's definition in such a way that it weakens the security strength of the cipher" *(ISO/IEC 27040)*.
Wear levelling	"A technique used in flash memory that is used to prolong the life of the media. Data can be written to and erased from an address on flash memory a finite number of times. The wear levelling algorithm helps to distribute writes evenly across each memory block, thereby decreasing the wear on the media and increasing its lifetime. The algorithm ensures that updated or new data is written to the first available free block with the least number of writes. This creates free blocks that previously contained data" *(NZISM)*. "A technique used in non-volatile flash memory media to prolong the life of the media. As data can be written to and erased from memory blocks a finite number of times, wear-levelling helps to distribute writes evenly across each memory block, thereby decreasing wear and increasing its lifetime" *(AusISM)*.
Wearable	Portable smart device such as a small computer or *thing* that is literally worn about the person, *e.g.* smart watch, smart glasses.

TERM	MEANING
Web, World Wide Web **(WWW)**	Global system of interlinked documents, applications, and other information services/resources, each identified by **U**niform **R**esource **L**ocators and provided through the Internet. Uses **H**yper**T**ext **T**ransfer **P**rotocol and many other protocols. Invented by Tim Berners-Lee at CERN in 1989. "Universe of network-accessible information and services" *(ISO 19101-1).*
Web **A**pplication **F**irewall **(WAF)**	Firewall designed to protect a web application, *e.g.* by monitoring network traffic for suspicious activities and filtering out/blocking malicious attacks such as Cross-Site Scripting and SQL injection. Close integration with a specific app means a smart WAF can be context-aware, reacting intelligently to suspicious situations and data flows that may appear innocuous to conventional multi-purpose network firewalls, *e.g.* triggering the app to impose additional authentication controls or tighten transaction limits under certain conditions. "A buffer used between a web application and the Internet to mitigate cyberattacks" *(ISACA glossary).*
Web bug	Tracking hyperlink within a web page that refers the user's browser to a particular file, typically an unnoticeable single-pixel image or an innocuous image such as this copyright symbol: © When the user's browser reads the page, interprets the HTML code, and retrieves the file, the web server records the network access by the user's **I**nternet **P**rotocol address in its log, potentially compromising the user's privacy. Normally used for relatively benign marketing purposes, occasionally to indicate and trace **I**ntellectual **P**roperty theft. "Malicious code, invisible to a user, placed on Web sites in such a way that it allows third parties to track use of Web servers and collect information about the user, including IP address, host name, browser type and version, operating system name and version, and Web browser cookie" *(CNSSI 4009).*
Web-inject malware	See drive-by download and code injection.
Web of trust	Distributed authentication approach relies on transitive trust between individual people forming a social mesh, rather than trusted authorities. Used by PGP and others. "The trust that naturally evolves as a user starts to trust other's signatures, and the signatures that they trust" *(SANS glossary). Cf.* **P**ublic **K**ey **I**nfrastructure.
Web server	"A software process that runs on a host computer connected to the Internet to respond to HTTP requests for documents from client web browsers" *(SANS glossary).*

TERM	MEANING
Website	Collection of web pages hosted on a web server, referenced and accessed through the Internet or locally on a corporate intranet using a web browser. Identified by unique **U**niform **R**esource **L**ocators, domain names, *etc*. Web pages can consist of text, images, multimedia content, and code, *e.g.* HTML, JavaScript. "One or more web pages that may originate at one or more web server computers. Note: A person can view the pages of a web site in any order, as he/she would read a magazine" *(ISACA glossary)*.
Website defacement	Vandalistic hacker/cracker attack on a web server, altering or replacing the website's content typically to demonstrate the hacker's prowess, to infect website visitors' systems with malware, to make some ideological or political statement (hacktivism), or to discredit/embarrass and thus harm the website's real owner (cybertage).
Web storage	See cloud storage.
WEEE	*Abbrev:* **W**aste from **E**lectrical and **E**lectronic **E**quipment.
WEP	*Abbrev:* **W**ired **E**quivalent **P**rotocol.
Wetware	People, or more specifically our brains. Alludes to the fact that we human beings are about 60% water, and some of us are 'wet behind the ears', *i.e.* naïve, gullible, and hence vulnerable. *Cf.* hardware, software, middleware, firmware, malware, ransomware, adware, crimeware, scareware, shelfware, spouseware, stalkerware, spyware.
Whaling	Refers to the use of phishing, spear phishing, and other social engineering, fraud, or scamming techniques to coerce 'big fish' such as corporate financial controllers and executives, *e.g.* sending an email that *appears* to come from the CEO instructing the Head of Finance to authorise a large wire transfer for a secretive special project.
Whistleblower, snitch	Informant who privately discloses, reports, or calls out a breach of ethics, security, policy, law, *etc.* to management, an auditor, an authority, *etc.* triggering the process of evidence gathering and investigation and, if appropriate, calling the perpetrator and/or participants to account for their actions or inactions. Those making certain disclosures in the public interest *may* qualify for legal protection and even financial rewards in some countries.

TERM	MEANING
Whistleblower's hotline, ethics hotline, snitchline	Confidential service for whistleblowers to disclose, report, or call out their knowledge or suspicions about improprieties such as coercion, fraud, bribery, corruption, and malpractice by various mechanisms, in order for them to be formally and independently investigated. Anonymity, coupled with discreet investigation by competent and trustworthy investigators, reduces the possibility of identification and reprisals or retribution against whistleblowers, but inevitably the residual risks for whistleblowers are substantial; hence, explicit policies are important.
White box testing, clear box testing, glass box testing, transparent box testing ...	Testing approach in which the testers are given information about the internal design of an application, system, device, or whatever under test, allowing more specific and thorough evaluation and emulating attacks by knowledgeable insiders. "A method of testing software that tests internal structures or workings of an application, as opposed to its functionality (*i.e.,* black box testing)" *(NIST SP 800-192). Cf.* black box testing, grey box testing.
White-collar crime	Generic term for fraud, theft, tax evasion, insider dealing, blackmail, counterfeiting, and other crimes typically committed by office workers or professionals.
White hat	Benign, ethical hacker, or information security professional. *Cf.* black hat, grey hat.
Whitelist, permit-list, allow list	Explicit list of **U**niform **R**esource **L**ocators, programs, email senders, *etc.* that is considered benign or (to some extent) trusted and hence to which access is permitted, while access is denied to unlisted items by default (hence fail-secure). "A set of inclusive accepted items that confirm the item being analysed is acceptable. It is the opposite of a blacklist which confirms that items are not acceptable" *(NZISM).* "A list of email senders known to be benign, such as a user's coworkers, friends, and family" *(NIST SP 800-114). Cf.* blacklist.
White team	"1. The group responsible for refereeing an engagement between a Red Team of mock attackers and a Blue Team of actual defenders of their enterprise's use of information systems. In an exercise, the White Team acts as the judges, enforces the rules of the exercise, observes the exercise, scores teams, resolves any problems that may arise, handles all requests for information or questions, and ensures that the competition runs fairly and does not cause operational problems for the defender's mission. The White Team helps to establish the rules of engagement, the metrics for assessing results and the procedures for providing operational security for the engagement. The White Team normally has responsibility for deriving lessons-learned, conducting the post engagement assessment, and promulgating results. 2. Can also refer to a small group of people who have prior knowledge of unannounced Red Team activities.

TERM	MEANING
	The White Team acts as observers during the Red Team activity and ensures the scope of testing does not exceed a predefined threshold" *(CNSSI 4009)*. See also blue, red, black, and purple teams.
Wibree	See **B**luetooth **L**ow **E**nergy.
Wide **A**rea **N**etwork **(WAN)**	Digital network connecting geographically dispersed systems. "A computer network connecting multiple offices or buildings over a larger area" *(ISACA glossary)*. See also **L**ocal **A**rea **N**etwork, **P**ersonal **A**rea **N**etwork, **M**etropolitan **A**rea **N**etwork, **S**torage **A**rea **N**etwork.
Wifatch	Vigilante worm that infects insecure Linux-based *things* such as network routers, then patches them and joins them to a botnet. Exploits basic vulnerabilities such as default Telnet passwords.
Wi-Fi	*Abbrev:* **Wi**reless **Fi**delity. "Wi-Fi" is a registered trademark.
Wi-Fi Access Point	See **A**ccess **P**oint.
Wi-Fi ad hoc network, wireless ad hoc network	"Decentralized wireless network which does not rely on a pre-existing infrastructure. Note: Examples of pre-existing infrastructure are routers in wired networks or access points in managed (infrastructure) wireless networks" *(ISO/IEC 27033-6)*.
Wi-Fi curfew	Parents time-limiting youngsters' access to the Internet through home Wi-Fi. May be combined with family policies, security awareness, parental oversight, monitoring, and prohibition of inappropriate Internet domains, content, and services (*e.g.* social media). May be actively undermined, bypassed, or evaded by smart kids (or their peers).
Wi-Fi **P**rotected **A**ccess **(WPA)**	Flawed and short-lived second-generation Wi-Fi cryptosystem, broken by wireless hackers just as WEP had been. Deprecated in favour of WPA2. "A class of security protocols used to secure wireless (Wi-Fi) computer networks" *(ISACA glossary)*. "Protocols designed to replace WEP. They refer to components of the 802.11i security standard" *(NZISM)*. "A protocol designed for communicating data over wireless networks" *(AusISM)*.
Wi-Fi **P**rotected **A**ccess № **2** **(WPA2)**	Third-generation Wi-Fi cryptosystem specified in IEEE 802.11i standard, replacing WPA. Allows the use of **A**dvanced **E**ncryption **S**tandard for strong encryption *provided* the cryptographic key (or the passphrase used to generate the key) is strong, confidential to the intended parties to the session key exchange, and cannot be substituted with a chosen key, *e.g.* by wireless hackers using Krack against vulnerable Android systems. Oops. "A wireless security protocol that supports 802.11i encryption standards to provide greater security. This protocol uses Advanced Encryption Standards (AES) and Temporal Key Integrity Protocol (TKIP) for stronger encryption" *(ISACA glossary)*. "A protocol designed to replace the Wi-Fi Protected Access protocol for communicating data over wireless networks" *(AusISM)*. See also WEP, WPA3.

TERM	MEANING
Wi-Fi **P**rotected **A**ccess № **3** **(WPA3)**	Fourth-generation Wi-Fi cryptosystem introduced by the Wi-Fi Alliance in 2018. Uses **S**imultaneous **A**uthentication of **E**quals to overcome the offline/asynchronous password brute force vulnerability in WPA2, and **O**pportunistic **W**ireless **E**ncryption to encrypt Wi-Fi connections automatically. Designed to make it easy to connect mobile devices including *things* to Wi-Fi networks, securely, *e.g.* by scanning a **Q**uick **R**esponse code displayed in a café or library. "A wireless security protocol released in mid-2018 that improves on WPA2 by eliminating the preshared key (PSK), which is susceptible to dictionary attacks" *(ISACA glossary)*. "A protocol designed to replace the WPA2 protocol for communicating data over wireless networks" *(AusISM)*. See also WEP, WPA.
Window bars	a. Strong steel bars permanently fitted across a window or opening to reduce the risk of physical intrusion. For extra strength, may be welded to a steel frame firmly attached to the wall with security screws. A physical security mechanism. b. Seattle watering holes where Microsofties hang out of an evening?
Windows Defender	Microsoft's antivirus software, built in to recent versions of Windows.
Windows Defender ATP (Advanced **T**hreat **P**rotection**)**	Cloud-based system for malware prevention, incident detection, automated investigation, and incident response. Part of Windows 10 Enterprise. Subsequently renamed Microsoft Defender for Endpoint, perhaps to avoid confusion with **A**dvanced **P**ersistent **T**hreat.
Windows **M**anagement **I**nstrumentation **(WMI)**	Integral part of the Windows **O**perating **S**ystem, provides system management capabilities such as Windows updates. Due to flaws in its security architecture, WMI may be exploited for malicious purposes, however, *i.e.* built-in malware. See also Powershell.
Windump	The Windows version of Tcpdump. "A freeware tool for Windows that is a protocol analyzer that can monitor network traffic on a wire" *(SANS glossary)*.
Wipe	See clear.
Wiper	Destructive type of malware that deliberately wipes data from infected systems, possibly for extortion (*i.e.* ransomware), cybertage, or cyberterrorism, or to destroy forensic evidence. May be part of multifunctional malware. Examples: NotPetya and Shamoon. See also logic bomb.

TERM	MEANING
Wired **E**quivalent **P**rotocol **(WEP)**	Flawed and deprecated first-generation cryptosystem hastily incorporated into early IEEE 802.11 Wi-Fi wireless networking equipment but soon broken by wireless hackers. Was designed to emulate the limited/basic security typically available on wired networks. Used RC-4 for encryption. Vulnerabilities in the way shared keys are generated render WEP only marginally better than no encryption at all; hence, it is deprecated in favour of better cryptosystems such as WPA2 or WPA3. "A scheme that is part of the IEEE 802.11 wireless networking standard to secure IEEE 802.11 wireless networks (also known as Wi-Fi networks). Notes: Because a wireless network broadcasts messages using radio, it is particularly susceptible to eavesdropping. WEP was intended to provide comparable confidentiality to a traditional wired network (in particular, it does not protect network users from each other), hence the name. Cryptoanalysts identified several serious weaknesses, and WEP was superseded by Wi-Fi Protected Access (WPA) in 2003 and then by the full IEEE 802.11i standard (also known as WPA2) in 2004. Despite the weaknesses, WEP provides a level of security that can deter casual snooping" *(ISACA glossary)*. "A security protocol, specified in the IEEE 802.11 standard, that is designed to provide a WLAN with a level of security and privacy comparable to what is usually expected of a wired LAN. WEP is no longer considered a viable encryption mechanism due to known weaknesses" *(NIST SP 800-48)*. "A deprecated 802.11 security standard" *(NZISM)*. "A security protocol for wireless local area networks defined in the standard IEEE 802.11b" *(SANS glossary)*.
Wireless **A**ccess **P**oint **(WAP)**	See **Access Point**. "A device which enables communications between wireless clients. It is typically also the device which connects wired and wireless networks" *(AusISM)*.
Wireless **A**pplication **P**rotocol **(WAP)**	"A standard that defines the way in which Internet communications and other advanced services are provided on wireless mobile devices" *(NIST SP 800-101)*. "A specification for a set of communication protocols to standardize the way that wireless devices, such as cellular telephones and radio transceivers, can be used for Internet access, including e-mail, the World Wide Web, newsgroups, and Internet Relay Chat" *(SANS glossary)*.
Wireless communications	"The transmission of data over a communications path using electromagnetic waves rather than a wired medium" *(NZISM)*.

TERM	MEANING
Wireless Fidelity (Wi-Fi, WiFi, wifi)	Extensive suite of short-range radio networking standards (IEEE 802.11), used by wireless Local Area Networks. "Wireless local area networking technology that allows electronic devices to network, mainly using the 2.5 GHz and 5 GHz radio bands. Note: 'Wi-Fi' is a trademark of the Wi-Fi Alliance. 'Wi-Fi' is generally used as a synonym for 'WLAN' since most modern WLANs are based on these standards" *(ISO/IEC 27033-6)*.
Wireless hacker, wHacker	Hacker who exploits security vulnerabilities in wireless networks.
Wireless Local Area Network (wLAN, WLAN), wireless network	Local Area Network using UHF/microwave radio transceivers to connect in-range wireless-capable devices. "A wireless communication network that serves several users within a specified limited geographic area" *(ISACA glossary)*. "A network based upon the 802.11 set of standards" *(NZISM)*.
Wireless networking	Communications Technologies using radio frequency datacommunications transmissions and protocols such as WiFi and Bluetooth. While most are designed for short-range communications, mid-range radio-based (such as cellphone) and long-range short-wave or satellite systems also qualify as wireless networks.
WireLurker	Trojan exploiting Apple macOS and iOS devices, whether jailbroken or not. The infection spread in 2014 via unofficial app stores, evading the official Apple app store's anti-malware controls.
Wireshark, Ethereal	Open-source network monitoring, packet capture, and analysis application. Understands *hundreds* of networking protocols. An example of dual-use technology, popular with black, grey, and white hats.
Wiretap	Covert surveillance device physically attached to a phone line or network cable, or configuration settings on the systems, which enables phone calls and network traffic on the line to be secretly replicated on another line or port, hence monitored and/or recorded. Generally installed by the phone company as demanded by a court order to capture forensic evidence for criminal investigations. Sometimes installed by hackers to snoop on the spooks. "Surreptitious access to some part of a data circuit to obtain, modify, or insert data" *(ISO/IEC 2382)*. "The practice of eavesdropping on information being transmitted over telecommunications links" *(ISACA glossary)*. "Monitoring and recording data that is flowing between two points in a communication system" *(SANS glossary)*. See also pen register.
Wisdom	Extremely valuable form of tacit information borne of experience, knowledge, understanding, and insight. Generally held and espoused by respected elders of a community.

TERM	MEANING
Wizard Spiders	Hacker/malware/cybercriminal gang active in 2022.
wLAN	*Abbrev:* **w**ireless **L**ocal **A**rea **N**etwork.
WMI	*Abbrev:* **W**indows **M**anagement **I**nstrumentation.
Word	Processing unit or block of digital data typically consisting of 16, 32, or 64 bits (*i.e.* 2, 4, or 8 × 8-bit bytes).
Workaround	See compensating control. "A sequence of actions the user should take to avoid a problem or system limitation until the computer program is changed. They may include manual procedures used in conjunction with the computer system" *(ISACA glossary)*.
Worker	Permanent or temporary employee of theorganisation (whether a member of staff or a manager), or someone self-employed or employed by a third party such as a consultant, contractor, business associate, or student intern acting in a similar capacity to employees, *i.e.* working on behalf of, and to a large extent directed and controlled by, the organisation. Generally excludes visitors, *e.g.* job interviewees, supplier representatives, spouses. Often an unappreciated and undervalued information asset but potentially also a liability, *e.g.* due to their ineptitude, carelessness, greed, and self-interest, or ill-health. "Person performing work or work-related activities that are under the control of the organization. Notes: Persons perform work or work-related activities under various arrangements, paid or unpaid, such as regularly or temporarily, intermittently or seasonally, casually or on a part-time basis. Workers include top management, managerial and non-managerial persons. The work or work-related activities performed under the control of the organization may be performed by workers employed by the organization, workers of external providers, contractors, individuals, agency workers, and by other persons to the extent the organization shares control over their work or work-related activities, according to the context of the organization" *(ISO 45001)*.
Workforce	Workers, collectively, or staff or employees in particular (context-dependent). "Anyone engaged in the delivery of the organization's objectives, including direct employees, agency staff, contractors and volunteers" *(ISO 22300)*. "The collection of individuals the organization employs" *(OCEG GRC Glossary)*.
Workplace surveillance	Overt or covert security monitoring and oversight of workplaces and workers (*e.g.* by CCTV, guard inspections, or stop-and-search bag checks) to detect and gather (additional) evidence of wrongdoing, safety concerns (*e.g.* no lone working), intruders, *etc.* Raises ethical, privacy, trust, civil liberty, cultural, legal compliance, and policy conformity concerns but may be a necessary, appropriate, justifiable, and legitimate *part* of risk mitigation with management authorisation plus various internal controls, governance constraints, rules, and processes.

TERM	MEANING
Workstation	"A stand-alone or networked single-user computer" *(NZISM)*.
Worm	Form of malware consisting of mobile code that exploits network connections to spread itself between systems and often performs unauthorised functions such as sending unsavoury emails or spam, and **D**enial-**o**f-**S**ervice attacks (including unintentional attacks due to overwhelming networks/systems). Unlike a virus, a worm is self-contained and does not need to hitch a ride on other programs. Unlike a Trojan, it does not appear to be a useful program and does not mislead humans into executing it. Unlike a Helminth or the miscreant who codes and releases a worm, it is not literally a slimy parasite. "Self-contained program that can propagate itself through data processing systems or computer networks. Note: Worms are often designed to use up available resources such as storage space or processing time" *(ISO/IEC 2382)*. "A programmed network attack in which a self-replicating program does not attach itself to programs but rather spreads independently of users' action" *(ISACA glossary)*. "A computer program that can run independently, can propagate a complete working version of itself onto other hosts on a network, and may consume computer resources destructively" *(SANS glossary)*.
WORM drive	*Abbrev:* **W**rite **O**nce **R**ead **M**any drive.
Worst-case scenario	Notional scenario, situation, or model representing the worst possible potentially disastrous outcome from an event or combination of events constituting a serious information security incident. Often developed to help people understand and address the challenges of **B**usiness **C**ontinuity **M**anagement albeit at the risk of constraining plans to versions of the specific situations discussed, ignoring other scenarios and black swan events. See also contingency planning, **R**easonable **W**orst-**C**ase **S**cenario.
WPA	*Abbrev:* **Wi-Fi P**rotected **A**ccess.
WPA2	*Abbrev:* **Wi-Fi P**rotected **A**ccess № **2**.
WPA3	*Abbrev:* **Wi-Fi P**rotected **A**ccess № **3**.
Write-blocker	Hardware device that physically prevents data changes being made on an attached storage device by blocking write, update, or delete access while permitting read access. Typically required to avoid spoliation of forensic evidence, or to prevent malware transmission and data exfiltration via USB devices. "A device that allows investigators to examine media while preventing data writes from occurring on the subject media" *(NIST SP 800-101)*. "A device that allows the acquisition of information on a drive without creating the possibility of accidentally damaging the drive" *(ISACA glossary)*.

TERM	MEANING
Write Once Read Many (WORM) drive	Data storage device or medium that can only be written-to once or, more accurately, new data can only be *appended* to any already present. In theory, if not in practice, data are immutable, *i.e.* stored permanently and cannot be modified, overwritten, or deleted short of physical destruction.
Write protection	Some storage media and devices have physical slots, tabs or sliders, or software/driver controls, that can either permit changes to the data content or prevent write access. Being trivial to reset or disregard, these typically provide weak protection at best – more user convenience than security control really. "Hardware or software methods of preventing data from being written to a disk or other medium" *(NIST SP 800-101)*. "The use of hardware or software to prevent data from being overwritten or deleted" *(ISACA glossary)*.

X

TERM	MEANING
X.509 (2019)	ITU standard "Information technology – Open Systems Interconnection – The Directory: Public-key and attribute certificate frameworks" defines digital certificates used for secure web browsing, digital signatures, *etc.* Having somehow verified the claimed identity of a certificate requester, a **C**ertification **A**uthority generates, digitally signs and issues a certificate, binding (associating) the requester's public key to their identity as stated on the certificate. In use, web browsers, email applications, *etc.* can confirm the certificate's authenticity by validating the digital signature using the CA's public key. More info: https://www.itu.int/rec/T-REC-X.509/en
X.1056 (2009)	ITU standard "Security incident management guidelines for telecommunications organisations" recommends how to manage information security incidents affecting telecommunications organisations, or indeed telecoms functions/departments/units/teams within any organisation. More info: https://www.itu.int/rec/T-REC-X.1056/en
X.1500 (2011)	See CYBEX. More info: https://www.itu.int/rec/T-REC-X.1500/en
X11 forwarding	"X11, also known as the X Window System, is a basic method of video display used in a variety of operating systems. X11 forwarding allows the video display from one network node to be shown on another node" *(NZISM).*
Xafecopy	Species of Trojan malware that exploited Android systems in 2017.
XAI	*Abbrev:* **E**x**plainable** **A**rtificial **I**ntelligence.
XDR	*Abbrev:* e**X**tended **D**etection and **R**esponse.
Xkey**s**core **(XKS)**	TOP SECRET US surveillance system disclosed by whistleblower Ed Snowden. Intercepts from spy stations around the globe can be searched using **N**ational **S**ecurity **A**gency **D**ata**B**ases, making it like 'Google for spooks.'
XML e**X**ternal **E**ntities **(XXE)**	External files, *etc.* referenced within XML documents, may be interpreted by insecurely designed or configured XML applications, leading to the disclosure of sensitive information, command execution, *etc.* An XML-specific form of injection flaw.
Xorist	Species of ransomware in the wild in 2016.
XSRF	*Abbrev:* **Cross-S**ite **R**equest **F**orgery.
XSS	*Abbrev:* **Cross-S**ite **S**cripting.
XXE	*Abbrev:* **X**ML e**X**ternal **E**ntities.

Y

TERM	MEANING
YiSpecter	Species of malware exploiting Apple devices running iOS prior to version 8.4.

Z

TERM	MEANING
Z-wave	See ZigBee. "A protocol that operates in the Part 15 unlicensed industrial, scientific and medical (ISM) band (approximately 900 MHz, depending on the location), giving it excellent barrier penetration and low power utilization. Z-Wave is similar to LoRa. It was originally developed by Zensys in 1999 for system on a chip (SoC) applications" *(ISACA glossary)*.
Zero-day, 0-day, O-day, oh-day	Originally referred to pirated software that was available on the black market *before* the legitimate original had officially been released. Became a term for exploits against software security vulnerabilities that have not yet been recognised as such by the software authors, and hence for which security patches are not yet available. The term continues to evolve and is reinterpreted so often that nobody but the writer knows for sure *what* it means any more, except that it spells *trouble*. "The day a new vulnerability is made known. In some cases, a 'zero day' exploit is referred to an exploit for which no patch is available yet. ('day one' – day at which the patch is made available)" *(SANS glossary)*. See also lifespan.
Zero-day attack, zero-day exploit, zero-hour, day zero	Zero-day attack. "A vulnerability that is exploited before the software creator/vendor is aware of its existence. It may also refer to known flaws that do not have an available patch" *(ISACA glossary)*. "A computer threat that tries to exploit computer application vulnerabilities that are unknown to others or undisclosed to the software developer. Zero-day exploits (actual code that can use a security hole to carry out an attack) are used or shared by attackers before the software developer knows about the vulnerability. [and] A computer threat that tries to exploit computer application vulnerabilities that are unknown to others or undisclosed to the software developer. Zero-day exploits (actual code that can use a security hole to carry out an attack) are used or shared by attackers before the software developer knows about the vulnerability" *(SANS glossary)*.
Zero-fill, zeroise	Process to delete a cryptographic key or other highly confidential data from a system, whether on disk or in RAM, by overwriting it with zeroes or pseudorandom bits in order to render the original information permanently irretrievable.
Zero-knowledge attack	Attempt to compromise an **A**rtificial **I**ntelligence system, *etc.* by an adversary with no prior knowledge of its internal architecture, cybersecurity arrangements, *etc.* although these may be determined during the process. "Attack on a system that assumes no prior knowledge about the internal information of the system under attack. Note: The adversary can use context or historical information to infer model vulnerability. The attacker can probe the system to inform system vulnerabilities" *(ISO/IEC 27090 DRAFT)*. See also black box testing. *Cf.* perfect-knowledge, partial-knowledge attacks.

TERM	MEANING
Zero-**K**nowledge **P**roof **(ZKP)**	Cryptographic protocol through which a prover confirms their knowledge/possession of sensitive information (such as a password) *without* disclosing the secret itself, nor any part of it, to the verifier. "A critical aspect of cryptography, a method by which one party (Party A) is able to prove to another party (Party B) that Party A is aware of the value of a specific variable without conveying any additional information about that variable other than that they know its value" *(ISACA glossary)*. See also challenge-response, nonce.
Zero trust, zero trust network, zero trust architecture, zero trust model	Cybersecurity concept or architecture founded on the premise that **I**nformation **T**echnology systems and networks are inherently untrustworthy and must therefore be proactively secured, continuously evaluating and dynamically responding to the evolving external and internal/insider threats for assurance. Even supposedly well-secured internal/private **L**ocal **A**rea **N**etworks cannot be *entirely* trusted; hence, information assets (regardless of their location) need controls such as continuous validation of userIDs and monitoring of network activities, **M**ulti**F**actor **A**uthentication, least privilege, micro-segmentation, and strong access controls such as encrypted communications to minimise the possibility of unauthorised/inappropriate access, hacks, malware, *etc*. "A security model based on microsegmentation and the continuous validation of digital interactions to address the threat of lateral movement within a network. [and] A security model anchored in the assumption of breach, which means that anything outside or inside the network cannot be trusted and anyone who tries to access the network needs to be verified in advance" (*ISACA glossary*). "A security concept based around the idea that systems and users should not be given access to any information without verification, even when they are connected to internal networks" *(NZISM)*. See also **S**ecure **A**ccess **S**ervice **E**dge.
Zero **T**rust **N**etwork **A**ccess **(ZTNA)**	Secure networking services form an integral part of the zero trust approach.
ZeuS, Zeus, Zbot	Crimeware kit, a multifunctional Trojan that generates Windows malware. Discovered in 2007, source code disclosed on the Internet in 2011, with variants still in the wild in 2019. Used by keylogging bank Trojans, CryptoLocker, *etc*. Spread by drive-by downloads, phishing attacks, and infectious email attachments.
ZigBee, Z-wave	Low-rate short-range low-power wireless networking protocols used by some smart devices and *things* to form *ad hoc* **L**ocal **A**rea **N**etworks, **H**ome **A**rea **N**etworks, or **P**ersonal **A**rea **N**etworks. Along with Bluetooth, BluetoothLE, Wi-Fi, and others, there is strong commercial competition involving incompatible technology standards and **I**ntellectual **P**roperties. "An IEEE 802.15.4 personal area network (PAN) protocol developed in 1998 that aims to provide moderate throughput and reliable connectivity via a mesh topology (similar to Z-Wave)" *(ISACA glossary)*.

TERM	MEANING
Zinc whiskers	Through mechanical abrasion, microscopic crystalline zinc fibres can form slowly from the galvanised plating on typical computer room floor and ceiling tiles. When spread by mass air flow, they may cause short circuits (perhaps being instantly vapourised) and unreliable operation in electronic equipment in similar fashion to other air-borne conductive contaminants such as soot and moisture.
Zip bomb	Malware that decompresses a massive file, consuming system resources until the system crawls to a halt and maybe crashes. A crude type of logic bomb.
ZKP	*Abbrev:* **Z**ero-**K**nowledge **P**roof.
Zombie, zombie computer	See bot. "A computer connected to the Internet that has been compromised by a hacker, a computer virus, or a trojan horse. Generally, a compromised machine is only one of many in a botnet, and will be used to perform malicious tasks of one sort or another under remote direction. Most owners of zombie computers are unaware that their system is being used in this way. Because the owner tends to be unaware, these computers are metaphorically compared to zombies" *(SANS glossary)*.
ZombieLoad, ZombieLoad 2	Exploits capable of compromising some Intel **C**entral **P**rocessing **U**nits. Design flaws deep in the CPU hardware can allow rogue processes (malware) to access information belonging to other processes held transiently in internal buffers, despite higher-level firmware and software controls meant to prevent precisely that. Firmware and software patches can mitigate these attacks by disabling hyperthreading and improving buffer flushing, but a CPU hardware redesign is necessary to fix the underlying vulnerabilities without the functionality and performance impacts caused by workarounds. See also Spectre.
Zone	Defined physical area or logical grouping within which a common physical or logical security baseline applies. Perimeter controls such as firewalls, walls, and doors usually isolate or separate different zones. High-security zones, such as the keep in a castle, the data centre, or **L**ocal **A**rea **N**etwork in a commercial organisation or a cryptographic system, deserve to be protected more strongly against unauthorised access than the surrounding areas. Zoning is akin to classification in that things within a given zone are treated similarly, although their individual information risks and security requirements may vary somewhat. See also domain, security domain.
Zoo	Malware collection typically maintained by security researchers and antivirus companies, as well as by VXers, hackers, and crackers.
ZTNA	*Abbrev:* **Z**ero **T**rust **N**etwork **A**ccess.